GREENE
ON
GREENS &
GRAINS

GREENE ON GREENS & GRAINS

BERT GREENE

Two Volumes in One:

Greene on Greens
&
The Grains Cookbook

ILLUSTRATIONS BY NORMAN GREEN

NEW YORK

This edition published by arrangement with
Workman Publishing Company

Published by
Tess Press an imprint of Black Dog & Leventhal Publishers, Inc.
151 West 19th Street
New York, NY 10011

ISBN: 1-57912-132-2

Manufactured in the United States of America

Library of Congress Cataloging-in-Publication Data

Greene, Bert, 1923-
     Greene on greens & grains/ [Bert Greene].
            p.cm.
     Includes index.
     ISBN   1-57912-132-2
1. Cookery (Vegetables) 2. Cookery (Cereals) I. Title.
TX801.G72423 2000
641.6'5–dc21   00-027318

DEDICATION

This book is for my late parents, Paula and Sam Greene, both of whom would, I suspect, have been
proud to lend their names to this title.

More pertinently, it is also for my sister, Myra, the true-bluest of the Greenes. A very small measure of
appreciation for a lifetime of friendship that would be hard to match, in or out of the family.

Publisher's Thanks

To Phillip S. Schulz for his generous help in getting The Grains Cookbook
from manuscript to book.

CONTENTS

A GARLAND OF GREENE

*T*his book is actually a love letter to the thirty or so vegetables, green and otherwise, that I prize most in all the world.

More than a recipe collection, it is a garland of Greene's gossip, garden advice, culinary trivia, and shopping wisdom, well tossed with, I hope, a measure of stove-top logic. In fact, it contains all the savvy that I have managed to acquire over several decades of cooking vegetables without foregoing the pleasures of either meat or fish. For while I dearly love vegetables, I am certainly no vegetarian.

Like most of a generation born between the years of boom and crash, I grew up in something of a gastronomic vacuum. Ours was strictly a meat-and-potatoes household. Vegetables came to the table as a matter of course, but mostly as spongy counterfeits of nature: served up straight from the can or else swimming in pools of water. To me, consuming these greens was a penance rather than a pleasure and I ate all garden produce grudgingly, never for a moment convinced that a dreaded forkful of canned spinach would provide me with the requirements of pep, punch, and pluck that Popeye and my elders predicted it would.

Today, from the vantage point of long distance, I have decided that prior to World War II, most cooks in America must have either nurtured grave suspicions about the bacteria inherent in fresh vegetables or just downright hated them. Why else would they have punished the produce with such assiduous overcooking? I realize there were, even then, a few vitamin zealots around who ate their vegetables nearly raw. But by and large, that slim cadre was considered to be part of the lunatic fringe—

adjudged almost as quirky as folks who dunked their bodies in the surf in January or (heaven forfend) slept in the nude!

As a tad in the kitchen, I was instructed that cauliflower was to be boiled for one hour, and string beans, broccoli, asparagus, and cabbage not less than half that duration. They were never drained from the kettle until the cooking liquid had turned as green as Tintex dye, while the poor veggie was a heck of a lot paler—not to mention devitaminized—in the process.

I cannot rightly recollect when I learned to cook a vegetable properly, that is to say with respect for its inalienable bite. But I suspect the conversion took place between the summer I planted my first grown-up vegetable garden in the late 1950s and the opening of The Store in Amagansett half a dozen years later. As innovators of what is now called "carry-out cuisine," my partners and I realized early on that what made a cooked-vegetable salad irresistible was its crunch. What caused the crunch was very abbreviated cooking time plus the freshest of ingredients. Working close to the cornucopia of produce that the South Fork of Long Island offers all summer long made it easy to prepare vegetables well—and we did! Almost twenty years later, nothing in the kitchen elicits a more immediate response from this cook than a still life of fresh, crisp greenery. And I cannot wait to get my hands on those glittering spoils as they tumble from a garden basket (or a shopping bag, for that matter) to turn them into a soup, casserole, soufflé, bread, relish, and yes, even a cake or sorbet on occasion.

For a long, long while I wanted to write down a grand accumulation of recipes for the vegetables I love. Every one of them appears in this book—accompanied by tales of my vegetable connections (some thorny as artichokes, others silky as nubile zucchini). They are highly personal memoirs, and inspired, I must admit, by the maxim of yet another vegetable lover, Popeye, who summed up his philosophy in one pithy sentence: "I yam what I yam!" Me too.

With that out of the way, have a big helping of Greene on greens.

ARTICHOKES

Sublime from Leaf to Heart

Artichokes are actually thistle-like stalks nipped in the bud, but sweeter by far with a dab of hollandaise than any purple posies picked in my backyard.

Savants claim that the word "artichoke" itself is a culinary hybrid. The true moniker for this thorny bite of green stuff is said to be cooked up from two Middle English words: *hortus* and *chokt*, literally meaning "a garden strangler." And from the smattering of knowledge that I have picked up about the cultivation of artichokes, there is considerable substance to that description. For the roots of the globe artichoke (*Cynara scolymus*) grow like weeds in the right climate and must be restrained from taking over a garden by some very assiduous surgery.

To tell the truth, I have never attempted to grow an artichoke. They grew wild on a mountainside in Eze (overlooking the Mediterranean) where I lived for a happy autumn, and just attempting to pick them for dinner left my hands bloody and my pot empty; they are well-rooted plants and very prickly into the bargain.

The artichoke, like the oyster, is a food that makes an indelible impression on the untried tongue. Ask me when and where I lost my gastronomic virginity and I will read you chapter and verse. It was on March 15, 1946. I remember that date precisely, because the dinner at which I consumed my first artichoke took place six months to the day after the Japanese forces surrendered in the Pacific and World War II came to an end.

The meal was a postponed celebration, given by a well-known writer and his wife in whose company I had observed the original event on a beach at Provincetown. As bells rang out the news and U.S. Coast Guard cutters sent trajectories of orange flares into the summer sky, victory was celebrated, as appropriately as possible in wartime Massachusetts, with warm domestic champagne and even warmer tears. But a valedictory feast, it was agreed, should not be undertaken until the smoke of armistice had truly cleared.

Perhaps the memorable occasion of that delayed celebration still stands out with such clarity because peace seemed a good deal more tenuous that night than it had in September. The Russians, formerly our allies, had in six months' time become our virtual enemies and the world appeared, if anything, less tranquil and more unsettled than ever before.

The meal took place in an elegant dining room high above Central Park. There were perhaps a dozen guests at the table, but I was the youngest by far (barely out of my teens) and little used to the ministrations of uniformed waiters who quietly served and removed plates at the barest summons of the hostess' bell.

What stands out in my memory, almost forty years later, is my utter trepidation at the approach of each successive dish. Though I had been instructed by my parents that a diner begins his meal with the first (farthest) fork on the left and proceeds inward, no memory of this injunction guided my etiquette that day. Instead I sat transfixed at my place, waiting an eternity, it seemed, until my

table partners ended their conversation and attacked the first course: *artichokes!*

As the correct utensil for eating an artichoke is the fingers, the shock was mesmerizing. Served my portion with a small bowl of warm hollandaise, I could not perceive (even at close scrutiny) what joy was to be obtained by sloshing a leaf in the liquid and then apparently only wetting one's tongue with it. However, that experience, once tried, altered my culinary perceptions forever.

I must have praised that first course extravagantly, for the table partner on my right raised an eyebrow. Pushing her untouched artichoke in my direction, she exchanged plates so discreetly that neither our hostess nor any other guest was aware of the transaction. But I could not resist a question. Why?

She smiled sweetly at the empty plate before her. "I was born in Castroville," she said. "It's a small town in Northern California that some people call the artichoke capital of the world. My father grew nothing but artichokes on his farm and I ate them every day of my life until I got out of there."

My table companion was a very attractive blond and despite her forthrightness was so soft-spoken no one else heard a word. "I'd rather eat a rattlesnake than an artichoke," she murmured. "And come to think of it, I have!"

Nothing she said cooled my ardor, for I finished her portion as well. I do not remember another dish of the meal. But the first sublimely nutty flavor of that leaf I will not forget until my last breath is taken.

Vegetable Roots

The Greeks had a rather uncomplimentary word for artichokes. Noting a similarity between the plant's petals and a canine's incisor, they dubbed the green *kinara kyon*, or "the tooth of a dog." Greeks boiled their artichokes in a mix-

A rtichokes have certainly had their detractors. Supporters, too. Pliny the Elder declared them "the most monstrous production of the earth." However, Catherine de Medici, who introduced this vegetable to France in the sixteenth century, so doted on them that she often fainted from overconsumption.

ture of wine and water and sometimes drank the brew as a restorative after a night on the town—presaging the notion of "hair of the dog" as well! The Romans altered the spelling after they inherited the artichoke as part of their victory spoils at Magnesia in 190 B.C. Insisting that the vegetable was misnamed, they rechristened it *cinara*, "ashes," in honor of its gray-green appearance. To compound the error they also roasted artichokes on open fires, like potatoes, peeling off the outer leaves when they were completely charred and consuming only the smoky hearts. No wonder artichokes went out of style for the next ten centuries!

At the end of the Middle Ages, according to food historian John Evelyn, the artichoke did have a slight revival, but not as a food. One ancient cookbook describes its usage plainly: "If when the pithe and pare be taken away, the roote bee boiled in wine and dronken, it is good against the ranke smell of armeholes."

What to Look For

W hen selecting an artichoke, look for the brightest, greenest globes you can find. Avoid specimens obviously past their prime, with mottled leaves or shriveled cones that are splayed open. The sweetest artichokes usually have compact heads and bottom leaves that break off with a decided snap between a shopper's thumb and forefinger. Winter is a critical period for artichokes and an unseasonal frost may cause the outer leaves to bronze. These artichokes are known as "Winter Kist" varieties and their outward appearance has nothing to do with their tender hearts, although it does tend to discourage a chef somewhat. Small (baby) artichokes, usually found in summer, are harvested before the prickly choke matures and are sweet and succulent enough to be served raw or barely blanched. Large globes are the best choice for serious artichoke eaters since they have ideal cavities for stuffing.

Artichokes have the special virtue of being rather low in calories. One medium-size cooked artichoke, weighing about ½ pound, usually totals between 10 and 50 calories, depending on its freshness. (Young artichokes have the lowest calorie count.) In addition, artichokes are chock-full of calcium, phosphorus, potassium, and *sodium*. So if you're trying to cut down on salt, you might want to eliminate it altogether in these recipes.

Preparation

F or weeks after that fateful dinner I ate artichokes in some form or other at almost every meal. One slight obstacle sullied my passion for this unusual vegetable, however. No one had ever told me how to properly cook an artichoke. More to the point, I had no clue whatsoever that the purplish-yellow fuzz at the base of the inner leaves had to be removed before an artichoke was considered tableworthy. Consequently my dinner guests (with all those artichokes there *had* to be guests, you know) usually coughed or gagged through my entire repertoire, bravely spitting out bits of fiber as they murmured, "*Delicious*, Bert!"

What took me so long to learn I will pass on to you first thing. Some cooks prefer to remove the choke after an artichoke is cooked, but I find that scraping it beforehand lessens any possible damage to the artichoke's delectable heart.

1. Using a sharp knife, trim off the stem so the artichoke rests firmly on its bottom and does not topple over.

2. Using a serrated knife, cut 1 inch off the top of the artichoke. Rub the cut surfaces with half a lemon to prevent discoloration.

3. Pull off any small or coarse leaves at the base. Using a kitchen shears or scissors, trim the sharp pointed tips off the remaining leaves.

4. Hold the trimmed artichoke under cold running water until the leaves separate. Using your fingers, gently pull out the purple-tipped prickly leaves in the center of the artichoke. Then, using a small teaspoon, scrape out the hairy choke. Sprinkle the exposed artichoke bottom with a little lemon juice and press the cone of leaves closed. *Voilà*—the artichoke is ready for the saucepan.

My favored way to cook an artichoke is to poach it in simmering water, but many enthusiasts steam them, in either a steamer or a colander placed over simmering water. Cooking time varies with the size and freshness of the artichoke at hand, but my rule of thumb is about 15 to 20 minutes. You know that an artichoke is done when the leaves pull off easily and the heart is tender when pricked with a knife. (Never use aluminum, iron, or carbon steel to cut or poke an artichoke. These base metals blacken the vegetable's surface and, even worse, leave an unpleasant metallic taste.)

POACHED ARTICHOKES

A classic way to prepare artichokes, followed by two unrivaled accompaniments.

4 medium artichokes, trimmed, chokes
   removed
Juice of 1 lemon
1½ tablespoons red wine vinegar
10 peppercorns, tied in a cheesecloth bag
½ teaspoon salt

1. Place the artichokes, tips up, in a large saucepan. Add cold water to cover, then the remaining ingredients. Heat to boiling; reduce the heat. Simmer, covered, until tender, 15 to 20 minutes.

2. Remove the artichokes and drain them upside-down in a colander. If you are serving them warm, reheat in a warm oven, loosely covered with aluminum foil. If serving them cold, chill, covered, several hours in the refrigerator.

3. Serve with Mayonnaise or Fail-

Safe Hollandaise sauce (see pages 408–409), or one of the sauces below.
   Serves 4.

Cold Anchovy Sauce

*H*ere is a variation on the classic mayonnaise sauce for artichokes.

1 egg yolk
1½ teaspoons Dijon mustard
1½ teaspoons anchovy paste
Juice of ½ lemon
1½ cups oil (use 1 cup vegetable and ½
   cup olive)
1 teaspoon red wine vinegar

Whisk the egg yolk with the mustard, anchovy paste, and lemon juice in a medium bowl until smooth. Slowly beat in the oil, a few drops at a time, until incorporated. Stir in the vinegar.

Makes about 1½ cups.

Cobbled Crab Dressing

A somewhat richer accessory to a cold artichoke felicitously combines mayonnaise with sour cream and cooked crab.

2 teaspoons minced shallots
½ cup cooked crabmeat
1 cup Mayonnaise (see page 408)
½ cup sour cream
1 teaspoon lime juice
Dash of hot pepper sauce
⅓ cup chopped fresh dill
Salt and freshly ground black pepper

Combine the shallots, crabmeat, mayonnaise, sour cream, lime juice, and hot pepper sauce in a large bowl. Mix well. Add the fresh dill, and salt and pepper to taste. Chill thoroughly before serving.

Makes about 1½ cups.

ARTICHOKE AND COLD MEAT SALAD

A culinary invention (not quite a chef's salad) was composed in my own kitchen recently. It combines artichoke hearts with raw mushrooms, slivers of cheese, and any leftover meat in the refrigerator.

1 package (9 ounces) frozen artichoke
    hearts
¼ pound mushrooms, sliced (about 1 cup)
¼ pound Monterey jack cheese, cut into
    thin strips 1½ inches long (about ½
    cup)
6 to 7 ounces leftover roast beef, ham,
    chicken, turkey, or tongue, cut into
    strips (about 1 cup)
1 large scallion, bulb and green top,
    minced
1 small clove garlic, minced
¼ teaspoon salt
1 teaspoon Dijon mustard
Juice of ½ lime
⅓ cup olive oil
1 tablespoon sour cream
1 teaspoon red wine vinegar
Salt and freshly ground black pepper

1. Cook the artichoke hearts in boiling salted water until tender, 5 to 8 minutes. Drain. Cool.

2. Combine the artichokes with the mushrooms, cheese, meat, and scallion in a large bowl.

3. Mash the garlic with the ¼ teaspoon salt in a small bowl. Stir in the remaining ingredients. Pour this dressing over the salad and toss well. Add salt and pepper to taste. Serve at room temperature or slightly chilled.

Serves 4.

ALICE B. TOKLAS' ARTICHOKE PUREE

Ms. Toklas served this cold, but I prefer it hot.

4 medium artichokes, trimmed
1 lemon, halved
4 tablespoons (½ stick) unsalted butter
4 cups Chicken Stock (see page 410)
1½ cups water
2 medium potatoes, peeled, thickly sliced
Salt and freshly ground black pepper

1. Wash the artichokes well, and cut each one in quarters vertically. Remove the chokes, rubbing all cut edges with half the lemon.

2. Melt the butter in a medium saucepan over low heat. Add the artichoke quarters; toss well to coat each piece with butter. Add the chicken stock and water. Heat to boiling; reduce the heat. Simmer, covered, 25 minutes.

3. Add the potatoes to the saucepan. Cook, covered, about 20 minutes longer, until the potatoes are tender. With a slotted spoon, remove the artichokes to one bowl and the pieces of potato to another. Strain and reserve the cooking liquid.

4. Using a spoon, scrape all edible parts from each artichoke, including the edible part of each leaf. Add this to the potatoes.

5. Place half the artichoke-potato mixture in a blender or processor; add half the reserved liquid. Purée until smooth. Transfer to a saucepan. Repeat with the remaining artichokes, potatoes, and liquid.

6. Stir the juice from the remaining half lemon into the purée. Cook over low heat, stirring occasionally, until warmed through. Season with salt and pepper to taste.

Serves 6.

CAJUN ARTICHOKES AND SPINACH

In the Cajun country of Louisiana, the artichoke takes an unusual partner, spinach, and an even more exotic seasoning, anise liqueur.

2 pounds spinach, washed, trimmed
1 package (9 ounces) frozen artichoke
    hearts
4 slices bacon
1 small onion, finely chopped
1 tablespoon all-purpose flour
1 clove garlic, minced
3 whole scallions, bulbs and green tops,
    finely chopped
½ cup heavy or whipping cream
Dash of hot pepper sauce
Salt and freshly ground black pepper

2 teaspoons Pernod or other anise-base
    liqueur
2 tablespoons unsalted butter
¼ cup fine fresh bread crumbs

1. Preheat the oven to 400°F. Cook the spinach in boiling salted water until just barely tender, about 2 minutes. Drain thoroughly; roughly chop.

2. Cook the artichoke hearts in boiling salted water for 5 minutes. Drain.

3. Sauté the bacon in a large heavy

skillet until crisp. Drain on paper towels. Crumble and reserve.

4. Pour off all but 1 tablespoon bacon fat from the skillet. Stir in the onion and flour, and cook, stirring constantly, over low heat for 3 minutes. Add the garlic and scallions. Stir in the cream. Cook until the mixture is slightly thickened, about 5 minutes.

5. Add the spinach, artichoke hearts, and bacon to the skillet. Toss well. Add the hot pepper sauce, salt and pepper to taste, and the Pernod. Transfer the mixture to a buttered baking dish.

6. Melt the butter in a small skillet over medium heat. Stir in the bread crumbs. Cook, stirring constantly, until golden. Spoon over the vegetables. Bake until golden brown and bubbly, about 20 minutes.

Serves 6.

ARTICHOKE AND POTATO CASSEROLE

In Spain potatoes, artichokes, and black olives appear in myriad local dishes. The best, a kind of variation on *patatas pobres* ("poor man's potatoes"), finds them baked together in a casserole.

1 package (9 ounces) frozen artichoke
   hearts
3 tablespoons unsalted butter
2 tablespoons olive oil
1 medium onion, thinly sliced
3 medium potatoes, peeled, thinly sliced
1 clove garlic, bruised
½ cup sliced black olives
Salt and freshly ground black pepper
½ cup freshly grated Parmesan cheese

1. Preheat the oven to 400°F. Cook the artichoke hearts in boiling salted water for 5 minutes. Drain, and cut into thin slices.

2. Heat 1 tablespoon of the butter with the olive oil in a large heavy skillet over medium heat. Sauté the onion slices until golden; reduce the heat.

3. Add the potatoes to the skillet and toss to coat them well. Toss in the artichoke hearts; remove from the heat.

4. Rub a large 2-inch-deep ovenproof baking dish with the bruised garlic. Spread the vegetable mixture over the bottom of the dish. Lay the olive slices over the mixture. Sprinkle with salt and pepper to taste. Dot the top with the remaining 2 tablespoons butter.

5. Bake 15 minutes. Remove from the oven, stir well, and continue to bake until the potatoes are tender, about 15 minutes longer. Sprinkle the top with cheese and bake until golden, an additional 5 to 10 minutes. Let stand a few minutes before serving.

Serves 6.

In Italy, where the artichoke is known as *carciofo*, old women at the market stalls usually rub two together before they make a selection for their shopping bags. If the artichokes make a proper little squeak on contact, they are deemed fresh. If they are *muto* (silent), the ladies simply pass them by.

CARCIOFI ALLA GIUDEA
(Fried Baby Artichokes)

*T*he most famous of all Italian artichoke recipes was discovered in Rome's Jewish ghetto about a hundred years ago. I prefer it when the dish is made with tiny baby artichokes in late summer; but it is equally delicious year round with any size globes, particularly when paired with broiled meats or other vegetable dishes.

12 baby artichokes, or 4 medium
1 lemon, halved
Vegetable oil for frying
4 cloves garlic
Salt

1. If using baby artichokes, cut off the stems, rubbing cut surfaces with lemon. If using larger artichokes, trim off the stems and pull off the tough outer leaves, leaving only the pale interior ones. Remove the chokes, and rub all cut surfaces with lemon.

2. Place the artichokes, one at a time, upside-down on a flat surface. Push down on each artichoke to slightly flat-ten the tops.

3. Pour oil into a heavy saucepan to a depth of about 1 inch. Heat the oil and add the garlic. When the oil is very hot, add the artichokes, tops down. Using a small lid, press down on the artichokes to flatten the tops. Cook, pressing constantly, until golden, 8 to 10 minutes. Turn the artichokes over and continue to cook until tender, 3 to 4 minutes longer. Baby artichokes will take slightly less time. Drain on paper towels. Sprinkle with salt to taste.

Serves 4.

BRAISED ARTICHOKES WITH PEAS

*P*eas and artichokes braised together is an old Sicilian peasant dish. They cook it for hours, but I do not.

1 package (9 ounces) frozen artichoke hearts
3 tablespoons unsalted butter
2 tablespoons olive oil
1 small onion, finely chopped
1 small clove garlic, minced
½ cup chopped Black Forest ham or ¼ cup
  chopped prosciutto
½ cup Chicken Stock (see page 410)
Pinch of sugar
2 cups shelled fresh peas, or 1 package (10
  ounces) frozen

Salt and freshly ground black pepper
2 tablespoons minced fresh parsley

1. Cook the artichoke hearts in boiling salted water for 5 minutes. Drain.

2. Heat the butter with the oil in a large heavy skillet over medium-low heat. Stir in the onion and cook 2 minutes. Add the garlic; cook 2 minutes longer. Add the ham and artichoke hearts. Toss to coat well with the butter. Add the chicken stock and sugar. Simmer, covered, 10 minutes. Stir in the peas. Simmer, covered, 5 minutes longer.

3. Raise the heat slightly and remove the cover. Continue to cook, tossing occasionally, until the vegetables are tender and most of the liquid has evaporated. Add salt and pepper to taste. Sprinkle with parsley.

Serves 4.

ARTICHOKE RISOTTO

An unusual vegetable dish from Portugal pairs artichoke hearts, tomatoes, and rice in a sensuous meld of flavorings.

1 package (9 ounces) frozen artichoke hearts
3 tablespoons unsalted butter
2 tablespoons olive oil
1 small onion, finely chopped
1 small clove garlic, minced
2 teaspoons chopped fresh basil, or ½
*   teaspoon dried*
1 large tomato, peeled, seeded, chopped
2 cups hot Chicken Stock (see page 410)
1 cup long-grain rice
½ teaspoon salt
¼ teaspoon freshly ground black pepper
Chopped fresh parsley
Freshly grated Parmesan cheese

1. Cook the artichoke hearts in boiling salted water for 5 minutes. Drain.

2. Heat 1 tablespoon of the butter with the olive oil in a small saucepan over medium-low heat. Stir in the onion; cook 2 minutes. Stir in the garlic, basil, tomato, and ½ cup of the chicken stock.

Heat to boiling; reduce the heat. Simmer, uncovered, 10 minutes. Remove from the heat.

3. Heat the remaining 2 tablespoons butter in a heavy 4-quart pot or Dutch oven over medium-low heat. Stir in the rice and cook, stirring constantly, until the rice is transparent. Stir in the tomato mixture, 1 cup of the chicken stock, and the salt and pepper. Heat to boiling; reduce the heat. Simmer, covered, 10 minutes.

4. Stir the artichoke hearts and remaining ½ cup chicken stock into the rice mixture. Continue to cook, covered, until the rice is tender, about 8 minutes longer. If the rice seems too wet, raise the heat slightly and cook uncovered until the liquid is absorbed. Sprinkle with parsley; pass the Parmesan cheese.

Serves 6.

ARTICHOKE PASTA

This pale pasta (perhaps the most delicate ever nibbled) can be used to make lasagne, fettuccine, or any pasta shape desired. It was invented by my friend Jan Weimer. Serve with heavy cream that you have reduced slightly and freshly grated Parmesan cheese, Creamy Tomato Sauce (see page 375), or simply mushrooms sautéed in browned butter.

1 large artichoke, trimmed
½ lemon
2 tablespoons unsalted butter
1 cup Chicken Stock (see page 410)
2 cups all-purpose flour
½ teaspoon salt
2 eggs, lightly beaten

1. Wash the artichoke well. Cut into quarters vertically. Remove the choke, rubbing all cut surfaces with lemon.

2. Melt the butter in a small saucepan over low heat. Add the artichoke pieces; toss well to coat with butter. Add the chicken stock. Heat to boiling; reduce the heat. Simmer, covered, 40 minutes. Drain thoroughly.

3. Using a spoon, scrape all edible parts from the artichoke, including the edible part of each leaf.

4. Place the artichoke pulp, 1¾ cups of the flour, and the salt in the container of a food processor fitted with a steel blade. Purée until the mixture is smooth. With the motor running, add the eggs and process until the mixture begins to form a soft dough.

5. Transfer the dough to a lightly floured board. Knead by hand for 10 minutes, working in more flour as needed to make a smooth dough. Let stand, covered, 20 minutes; then roll to desired shape by hand or with a pasta machine.

Makes about ¾ pound.

HEARTY ARTICHOKE TART

Martha Washington's favorite recipe was said to be a "Harty Choke Pie." The following tart is based on that invention—and crammed with cheese, ham, and artichokes.

Short Crust Pastry (see page 412)
3 medium artichokes*
1 lemon, halved
1 tablespoon red wine vinegar
5 peppercorns, tied in a cheesecloth bag
½ teaspoon salt
Juice of ½ lemon
1 tablespoon unsalted butter
1 shallot, minced
½ cup finely diced cooked ham
2 teaspoons Madeira
¼ cup freshly grated Parmesan cheese
¼ pound Fontina cheese, diced
¼ pound mozzarella cheese, diced
½ cup heavy or whipping cream
Salt and freshly ground black pepper

1. Make the Short Crust Pastry and set aside.

2. Preheat the oven to 375°F. Cut the stems from the artichokes, rubbing cut surfaces with half a lemon. Pull off the tough outer leaves, leaving only the pale interior ones. Cut the artichokes in half vertically and then in thirds vertically. Remove the chokes. Rub cut surfaces with lemon.

3. Place the artichoke pieces in a medium saucepan with cold water to cover. Add the vinegar, peppercorns, salt, and lemon juice. Heat to boiling; reduce the heat. Simmer, covered, until tender, about 10 minutes. Drain.

4. Melt the butter in a small skillet. Add the shallot and sauté it lightly. Stir in the ham and Madeira. Cook over medium heat until the ham is lightly browned and all liquid has evaporated. Cool.

5. Line a buttered 10-inch loose-bottom tart pan with the pastry. Trim.

Sprinkle the ham over the bottom of the crust, and arrange the artichokes over the ham. Add the cheeses, then pour the cream over the top. Sprinkle with salt and pepper to taste. Bake until golden, about 40 minutes. Let stand 10 minutes before serving.

Serves 6.

*Frozen artichoke hearts may be substituted for fresh. Use one 9-ounce package cooked in ¼ cup boiling salted water until tender, about 5 minutes.

CARCIOFI RIPIENI
(Artichokes Stuffed with Sausage)

*T*his superlative recipe (stuffed artichokes crammed with savory herbs and bits of sausage) was a gift from an Italian acquaintance. Serve it as an appetizer, or as a luncheon dish with buttered pasta on the side.

4 large artichokes, trimmed, chokes removed
4 sweet Italian sausages
1 teaspoon vegetable oil
1 cup fresh bread crumbs
1 clove garlic, minced
3 tablespoons minced fresh parsley
Pinch of dried oregano
Pinch of dried thyme
2 eggs, lightly beaten
¼ cup milk
Salt and freshly ground black pepper
1 can (8 ounces) imported plum tomatoes, drained
1½ tablespoons olive oil
Boiling water
2 whole cloves garlic
2 teaspoons unsalted butter

1. Prepare the artichokes for cooking, but do not press the leaves back together.

2. Remove the sausages from their casing. Rub a heavy skillet with 1 teaspoon oil. Place the skillet over medium heat; add the sausage, breaking up the lumps with a fork. Continue to cook, stirring constantly, until lightly browned. Drain on paper towels, and transfer to a large bowl.

3. Add the bread crumbs, minced garlic, 2 tablespoons of the minced parsley, the oregano, thyme, eggs, and milk to the sausage. Mix thoroughly. Season with salt and pepper to taste.

4. Divide the filling into four equal portions. Stuff the artichokes with filling, starting with the centers, then stuffing between the leaves, pushing the stuffing down as it is added. Press the artichokes closed and tie them around the centers with string.

5. Mash the tomatoes with a fork, and spoon some over the top of each artichoke.

6. Place the artichokes in a large saucepan. Add the oil to the pan with enough boiling water to come 1 inch up the sides of artichokes. Add the whole garlic cloves to the pan. Return to boiling; reduce the heat. Simmer, covered, until tender, 30 to 35 minutes.

7. Remove the artichokes from the liquid. Drain them briefly and transfer to a serving platter. Remove the strings. Dot each artichoke with ½ teaspoon butter and sprinkle with the remaining parsley.

Serves 4.

ITALIAN OMELET WITH ARTICHOKE AND CRAB

*T*his excellent Italian *frittata* (open-faced omelet) combines artichoke hearts and crab in a velvety amalgam that is both irresistible and expeditious. Cooking time: 15 minutes.

3 medium artichokes*
1 lemon, halved
1 tablespoon red wine vinegar
5 peppercorns, tied in a cheesecloth bag
½ teaspoon salt
Juice of ½ lemon
4 tablespoons (½ stick) unsalted butter
1 teaspoon olive oil
1 small onion, chopped
1 clove garlic, minced
½ red bell pepper, seeded, chopped
½ cup cooked crabmeat
3 tablespoons chopped fresh parsley
5 eggs
2 tablespoons freshly grated Parmesan cheese

1. Cut the stems from the artichokes, rubbing cut surfaces with half a lemon. Pull off the tough outer leaves, leaving only the pale interior ones. Cut the artichokes in half vertically and then in thirds vertically. Remove the chokes. Rub cut surfaces with lemon.

2. Place the artichoke pieces in a medium saucepan with cold water to cover. Add the vinegar, peppercorns, salt, and lemon juice. Heat to boiling; reduce the heat. Simmer, covered, until tender, about 10 minutes. Drain.

3. Heat 2 tablespoons of the butter with the oil in a 10-inch cast-iron skillet. Stir in the onion; cook 2 minutes. Stir in the garlic and red pepper; cook, uncovered, 8 minutes longer. Add the drained artichoke hearts and the crabmeat and parsley. Toss well. Remove from the heat.

4. Beat the eggs in a large bowl until light. Stir in the artichoke-crab mixture.

5. Preheat the broiling unit. Wipe out the skillet and heat the remaining 2 tablespoons butter over medium heat. When the foam subsides, pour in the egg mixture, spreading it evenly in the skillet. Immediately reduce the heat to low. Cook, uncovered, without stirring for 12 minutes. Sprinkle the top with the cheese and place the skillet under the broiler to lightly brown the top, about 1 minute.

Serves 4 to 6.

*Frozen artichoke hearts may be substituted. Use one 9-ounce package cooked in ¼ cup boiling salted water until tender, about 5 minutes.

ARTICHOKE SOUFFLE

*I*n France, *artichaut* was once a derogatory term for a "loose woman"; most probably because artichokes were considered to have aphrodisiac powers. The following is a lovely prescription for an artichoke soufflé that stimulates no other organ than the tongue.

Creamy Tomato Sauce (see page 375)
2 large artichokes, trimmed
1 lemon, halved
6 tablespoons (¾ stick) plus 1 teaspoon
   unsalted butter
1½ cups Chicken Stock (see page 410)
2 tablespoons freshly grated Parmesan
   cheese
1 shallot, minced
3 tablespoons all-purpose flour
¾ cup milk, hot
4 egg yolks
Pinch of cayenne pepper
⅛ teaspoon freshly grated nutmeg
Salt and freshly ground black pepper
6 egg whites

1. Make Creamy Tomato Sauce. Keep warm.

2. Wash the artichokes well. Cut each artichoke into six pieces vertically. Remove the chokes, rubbing all cut surfaces with lemon.

3. Melt 3 tablespoons of the butter in a medium saucepan over low heat. Add the artichoke pieces; toss well to coat each piece with butter. Add the chicken stock. Heat to boiling; reduce the heat. Simmer, covered, 40 minutes. Drain, reserving the stock.

4. Using a spoon, scrape all edible parts from each artichoke, including the edible part of each leaf. Place this in the container of a food processor or blender with ⅓ cup of the reserved stock. Purée until smooth. Reserve.

5. Preheat the oven to 400°F. Rub a 2-quart soufflé dish with 1 teaspoon butter. Sprinkle with 1 tablespoon of the cheese. Set aside.

6. Melt the remaining 3 tablespoons butter in a medium saucepan over low heat. Stir in the shallot; cook 5 minutes. Stir in the flour, blending it well to form a thick paste. Cook, stirring constantly, 2 minutes. Whisk in the milk all at once. Beat the mixture until smooth and very thick. Remove from the heat.

7. Add the egg yolks, one at a time, beating thoroughly after each addition. Add the cayenne pepper, nutmeg, and salt and pepper to taste. Combine in a bowl with the puréed artichokes.

8. Beat the egg whites until stiff but not dry. Fold them into the artichoke mixture. Pour into the prepared soufflé dish.

9. Place the soufflé in the middle of the oven and bake for 15 minutes. Reduce the heat to 375°F and continue to bake until the soufflé is set and golden brown, about 15 minutes longer. The soufflé is done when a cake tester inserted in the center comes out fairly clean. Serve immediately with Creamy Tomato Sauce.

Serves 6.

ARTICHOKES CROISETTE
(Cold Poached Eggs and Artichokes)

*T*his recipe works for lunch, brunch, or supper. At the heart of the matter is a poached egg, blanketed with a peppery Mediterranean sauce called *rouille*. I inherited the dish from Raymond Sokolov who says it may be served warm or cold, but I prefer the latter version. Try it both ways!

Sauce Rouille (recipe follows)
4 large artichokes
2 lemons, halved
1 tablespoon plus 1 teaspoon red wine
    vinegar
5 peppercorns, tied in a cheesecloth bag
½ teaspoon salt
4 eggs
1 tablespoon minced fresh parsley

1. Make Sauce Rouille. Chill.

2. Cut the stems from the artichokes, rubbing the cut surfaces with half a lemon. Pull off and discard all the leaves and remove the chokes. Trim the edges of the artichoke bottoms with a sharp knife, again rubbing all cut surfaces with lemon. As they are prepared, place the bottoms in a bowl of cold water to which you have added the juice of ½ lemon.

3. Place the artichoke bottoms in a medium saucepan with fresh cold water to cover. Add the juice of ½ lemon, 1 tablespoon vinegar, the peppercorns, and the salt. Heat to boiling; reduce the heat. Simmer, covered, until tender, 15 to 20 minutes. Drain. Chill.

4. Break each egg into an individual small bowl. Fill a medium saucepan with water; add 1 teaspoon vinegar. Heat to boiling; reduce the heat so that the water barely simmers. Slip the eggs into the water, one at a time. Poach until the whites are firm. Remove them with a slotted spoon, drain well, and transfer to small individual bowls. Cool. Chill, covered, until ready to serve.

5. To serve: Arrange the artichoke bottoms on individual serving plates. Drain off any accumulated water from the cold poached eggs, and slide an egg onto each artichoke bottom. Top each egg with 2 tablespoons Sauce Rouille. Sprinkle each with parsley. Pass the remaining sauce.

Serves 4.

Sauce Rouille

¾ cup Chicken Stock, approximately (see
    page 410)
1 small potato, peeled, diced
¼ cup seeded, chopped red bell pepper
1 large clove garlic, chopped
1 teaspoon crushed dried hot red peppers
3 to 4 tablespoons olive oil
Salt and freshly ground black pepper

1. Place the chicken stock and the potato in a small saucepan. Heat to boiling; reduce the heat. Simmer, uncovered, over medium-low heat 10 minutes. Add the bell pepper; simmer 5 minutes longer, adding more chicken stock if necessary. The potato and pepper should be just barely covered.

2. Transfer the mixture to a blender container (there should be slightly less than ¼ cup cooking liquid), and add the garlic and crushed peppers. Purée until smooth. Transfer to a small bowl and beat in the oil, a drop at a time, until the mixture is smooth. Cool. Chill, covered, until ready to serve.

3. Just before serving, stir the sauce well and season with salt and pepper to taste.

Makes about 1 cup.

ASPARAGUS

The Harbinger of Spring

For the past ten years I have lived in companionable tranquility with a beautiful redhead named Dinah, whose only real character flaw is an uncontrollable urge for asparagus.

As a matter of fact, Dinah is so affixed on the flavor and crunch of this supple green that she has been known to leap headlong into a sink in April (prime asparagus season, of course) in order to pry a stalk or two from under a flowing tap of cold water. And this extremely fastidious apricot-colored cat is one female who really hates getting her hair wet.

I have been permitted to share Dinah's good graces for the better part of a decade. No small honor, for this feline is extremely choosy about the company she keeps. She loathes dogs; cats are not exactly her dish of tea either. All other quadrupeds (like rabbits, squirrels, and mice) she dismisses with an icy stare and a resolute flick of her tail. Antipathy to the animal kingdom would seem to imply a greater degree of affection for the human race. Not so. Dinah will tolerate the admiration of a few votaries she knows well but, by and large, like the legendary Garbo, *she wants to be alone!*

At a recent party I gave, Dinah disappeared promptly when the first guest arrived at eight and did not surface again until two in the morning (with bursting kidneys) after the last celebrant departed.

However, it is of Dinah's appetite, not her lack of social amenity, that I speak. A delicate, small-boned creature weighing less than eight pounds, she has little interest in nourishment generally and none whatsoever in commercial pet food. What she likes best are bay scallops (sautéed in butter, white wine, and garlic, if you please) and the aforementioned asparagus. Dinah's predilection for the last-named victual is so overwhelming she will even face an alien dinner party if she knows a few asparagus stalks are to be on the menu.

On one notable occasion when I planned to open a meal with a course of this tender vegetable upholstered in mustardy hollandaise, I made a grave error. Busy in the kitchen with the other components of the dinner, I allowed a pound and a half of asparagus (fully peeled and blanched) to rest on the dining room table. When I eventually brought out plates for the asparagus, I discovered that my elegant cat had bitten the green tip from every single spear with the precision of a surgeon's scalpel.

As dinner was less than a half hour off, there was not even time for punishment to fit the crime. Instead the remains were whisked into a blender to become a cool jade soup.

Like the rugged individualist she is, Dinah refused a spoonful when it was proffered her. But she purred all evening long nonetheless!

Vegetable Roots

*E*gyptians were eating wild asparagus no bigger than a child's forefinger before the second pyramid was constructed at Gizeh, but the delicate stalks firmly resisted all efforts at cultivation along the Nile. It took Roman ingenuity to perform that agrarian miracle several centuries later.

The ancients doted on the flavor of this vernal vegetable. The Greek word *aspharagos* means "as long as one's throat," a label, the pundits tell us, that was conferred on the slender spears because overeager diners often consumed

them whole—in one fell swoop—at mealtimes. Soused with dressing, one hopes!

What to Look For

*A*sparagus is a harbinger of spring.

Or at least it was, before advanced agricultural technology and supersonic transport systems stuck their collective thumbs in the garden. Today fresh green asparagus may be found in metropolitan greengroceries across the country from January to July—with varying levels of flavor and price!

France is home of the famous white asparagus. However, despite the delicacy of this remarkable spear, I must confess that I cling to the American varieties I was raised on, namely the smooth-crowned Mary Washington, and the early-blooming Paradise which, in the words of Alice B. Toklas, "should be no thicker than a darning needle when it is picked!"

To a prejudiced palate like mine, the only true asparagus is marketed from early April, when the southwestern yield is harvested, until late June, when the bumper crops from the Northeast hit the vegetable stands.

When I purchase asparagus for a springtime orgy, I look for spears with straight stalks, uniform green color, and compact, pointed tips. The freshest asparagus will be crisp to the fingernail and usually no thicker than a fat crayon. Buy only the stalks with a scant inch of woody white fiber at the base, since that portion is trimmed off in the kitchen.

This nutritious vegetable is not only super-rich in vitamin A but equally endowed with vitamins B_1, B_2, and C. Asparagus is also a dieter's dream food: less than 35 calories per cup, cooked.

Preparation

*C*ooked asparagus may be served, hot or cold, as a vegetable first course or as an adjunct to the meal itself. French chefs have been known to substitute it for a salad course in a pinch, but you eschew *that* practice please! Asparagus is too distinctively flavored to cleanse the palate.

I never wash asparagus until after it is peeled, contrary to the advice you may have read elsewhere. Peeling is a necessity (unless the asparagus is pencil-slim and super-fresh) because the tough outer flesh is hard to digest. Before peeling, break off and discard the bottom of each stalk at the point where it snaps off most easily. I never slice off the bottoms because, as with cut flowers, water enters more freely if the stalk is roughly torn.

Peel the asparagus stalks with a vegetable peeler, removing the scales and stringy skin, but stop at least an inch from the tips. Wash the peeled stalks in a large basin of cold water before they are to be cooked.

I always blanch asparagus, uncovered, in a large flat saucepan or deep skillet half filled with boiling salted water. My technique is to place the stalks loosely in the pan, allow the water to return to the boil, reduce the heat, and simmer 3 to 5 minutes or until just barely tender. Do not overcook! When the asparagus is cooked, place the pan under cold running water until the stalks are cool to the touch. Drain on paper towels before using.

To steam asparagus, place the spears upright, loose or tied in bunches of six to ten, in a deep pot or in the bottom of a double boiler. Add boiling water to a depth of 1 inch, plus salt if desired. Cover with a lid or with the inverted top of the double boiler. Cook over medium heat approximately 10 minutes. By this method, the tougher ends cook in water while the tender tips cook in steam.

A serving note: Most of these asparagus recipes are based on a serving of ½ pound per person. However, if you are serving more than one vegetable with dinner, ⅓ pound probably will suffice.

COLD ASPARAGUS IN MUSTARD CREAM

*T*he following was passed along to me by Ethelyn Maruccia, chef and co-owner of a charming—but no longer extant—Greenwich Village eatery appropriately named The Heavenly Host. Ms. Maruccia's mustard cream is a culinary treasure.

2 pounds asparagus, trimmed, peeled
3 egg yolks
2 tablespoons lemon juice
¼ cup Dijon mustard
½ cup olive oil
Salt and freshly ground black pepper
Chopped fresh parsley

1. Blanch the asparagus and drain it on paper towels. Arrange the asparagus in a shallow serving dish, cover, and chill thoroughly.

2. Meanwhile, in the large bowl of an electric mixer, beat the egg yolks with the lemon juice and mustard for 4 minutes. On low speed, slowly beat in the oil. The mixture will have the consistency of a thin mayonnaise. Add salt and pepper to taste. Chill thoroughly.

3. To serve: Spoon some of the sauce over the asparagus and sprinkle with parsley. Pass the remaining sauce.

Serves 4.

CLASSIC COLD ASPARAGUS VINAIGRETTE

*T*o my tongue, nothing anoints a cold spear of asparagus more felicitously than the combined flavors of lemon and mustard. The first such rendering is for a dish I would nominate as the classic chilled appetizer: Asparagus Vinaigrette.

2 pounds asparagus, trimmed, peeled
1 small shallot, minced
1 small clove garlic, crushed
½ teaspoon coarse (kosher) salt
1½ teaspoons Dijon mustard
Juice of ½ lemon
¾ cup vegetable or olive oil
2 teaspoons red wine vinegar
½ teaspoon freshly ground black pepper
1 hard-cooked egg, yolk and white minced
    separately
¼ cup chopped fresh parsley

1. Blanch the asparagus and drain it on paper towels. Arrange the spears in a shallow serving dish and sprinkle with the minced shallot.

2. Place the garlic and salt in a small bowl, and mash them together with the back of a spoon until the mixture forms a paste. Stir in the mustard and lemon juice. Whisk in the oil, vinegar, and pepper. Spoon this dressing over the asparagus.

3. Garnish the asparagus with alternating bands of chopped egg white, parsley, and egg yolk. Chill thoroughly before serving.

Serves 4.

ASPARAGUS AND SPINACH SOUP

*A*s a kid raised on pale seas of canned asparagus soup, I find it a decided treat to dip a spoon into the genuine article. The following devise is for such a purée: a melding of green asparagus and even greener spinach leaves steeped in golden chicken stock. Although not the soup I hastily concocted after Dinah made her raid, it is one you certainly should consider when the stalks are plentiful. I always serve it hot, but friends tell me it is equally tonic chilled.

1 pound asparagus, trimmed, peeled
3 cups Chicken Stock (see page 410)
1 cup chopped fresh spinach leaves, washed
2 tablespoons unsalted butter
10 whole scallions, bulbs and green tops,
    roughly chopped
Pinch of ground cloves
3 tablespoons cornstarch
1 cup heavy or whipping cream

Salt and freshly ground black pepper
Sour cream (optional)

1. Place the asparagus in a medium saucepan and cover with the chicken stock. Heat to boiling over high heat; reduce the heat. Simmer, covered, 3 minutes. Remove the asparagus from the broth and set aside. Add the spinach to the saucepan and cook 3 minutes. Drain; reserve the broth.

2. Cut the tips off the asparagus; reserve. Chop the stems into 1-inch pieces; reserve.

3. Melt the butter in a medium saucepan over low heat. Add the scallions; cook until wilted. Stir in the cloves, cooked spinach, and asparagus stems. Cook, covered, over low heat for 10 minutes. Remove the cover; add the reserved broth.

4. Place the cornstarch in a small bowl. Slowly beat in the cream until the mixture is smooth. Stir this into the vegetable mixture in the saucepan. Heat to boiling; remove from the heat.

5. Cool the mixture slightly and purée it in a blender or processor in two batches (being careful: hot liquid will expand). Return the purée to the saucepan and reheat over low heat. Season with salt and pepper to taste; stir in the asparagus tips. Serve garnished with dabs of sour cream if desired.

Serves 6 to 8.

ASPARAGUS AND SHRIMP SALAD

*T*here is something curiously refreshing about the fearless pairing of two strong flavors in a single pot. Asparagus and shrimp, both ingredients with independent spheres of influence on the taste buds, marry most happily in the following spring-into-summer salad—a dish that my mother would have called "good for what ails you!"

1½ pounds asparagus, trimmed, peeled
½ cup water
1 slice lemon
1 sprig parsley
5 peppercorns
½ teaspoon salt
16 to 20 small shrimp
½ cup Mayonnaise (see page 408)
½ cup sour cream
½ teaspoon lemon juice
¼ teaspoon dry mustard
½ teaspoon prepared horseradish (optional)
1 tablespoon gin
Salt and freshly ground black pepper
Lettuce leaves

1. Blanch the asparagus and drain it on paper towels. Cut off the tips; cut the stems diagonally into 2-inch pieces. Place tips and stem pieces in a large bowl and set aside.

2. Combine the water, lemon slice, parsley, peppercorns, and salt in a medium saucepan. Heat to boiling; reduce the heat. Add the shrimp and simmer, uncovered, until they turn pink, about 4 minutes. Drain; cool slightly, then shell and devein the shrimp and add them to the asparagus.

3. Combine the mayonnaise with the sour cream in a medium bowl. Beat in the lemon juice, mustard, horseradish, gin, and salt and pepper to taste. Spoon this dressing over the asparagus and shrimp, and toss well. Serve on lettuce leaves, at room temperature or slightly chilled.

Serves 4.

FRENCH-FRIED ASPARAGUS

One of the quickest (and most unusual) ways to prepare asparagus is to french-fry it. Time: 3 minutes flat.

1 egg
½ cup milk
Dash of hot pepper sauce
⅛ teaspoon freshly grated nutmeg
1 teaspoon beef bouillon powder
½ teaspoon salt
¼ teaspoon freshly ground black pepper
½ cup all-purpose flour
⅔ cup fresh bread crumbs
1 ½ pounds asparagus, trimmed, peeled
Vegetable oil for frying

1. Beat the egg with the milk in a medium-size shallow dish. Add the hot pepper sauce, nutmeg, bouillon powder, salt, and pepper. Mix thoroughly.
2. Place the flour and the bread crumbs in separate shallow dishes. Roll each spear of asparagus first in the flour; shake off any excess. Then dip the asparagus into the egg-milk mixture, coating it well, and finally roll it in the bread crumbs.
3. Pour oil into a large heavy skillet to a depth of 1 inch. Heat it until hot but not smoking. Add the asparagus in one layer, in two or more batches as necessary. Cook over medium-high heat until golden, about 3 minutes. Drain each batch on paper towels and keep warm while frying the remaining asparagus.
Serves 4.

ASPARAGUS RISOTTO

Asparagus may be low in calories, but do not delude yourself about the thinning potential of the next dish; borrowed practically intact from a Venetian trattoria, it is clearly meant for overindulgers only!

½ pound asparagus, trimmed (unpeeled)
3 ½ tablespoons unsalted butter
2 large shallots, minced
Salt and freshly ground black pepper
¼ cup dry white wine
1 cup Italian rice (I prefer Arborio)
2 ½ to 3 cups Chicken Stock, simmering
　(see page 410)
⅓ cup freshly grated Parmesan cheese
2 tablespoons chopped fresh parsley

1. Cut the tips from the asparagus; reserve. Chop the stems into ½-inch pieces; set aside.
2. Melt 2½ tablespoons of the butter in a large heavy skillet, and sauté the shallots in it until golden, about 5 minutes. Add the asparagus stems; sprinkle with salt and pepper to taste. Cook 1 minute. Stir in the wine and cook, stirring constantly, until almost all the liquid has evaporated.
3. Stir the rice into the skillet and add 1 cup of the chicken stock. Stir once. Cook, uncovered, over medium-low heat without stirring until the stock is absorbed, about 10 minutes. Reduce

the heat if the liquid absorbs at a faster rate.

4. Pour 1 more cup of the stock over the rice. Cook without stirring 10 minutes longer.

5. Stir the reserved asparagus tips into the rice. Add ½ cup of the stock and cook until the liquid is absorbed and the rice is tender, about 8 more minutes. (If rice is not tender at this point, add some more stock. If rice is too wet, raise the heat slightly until liquid is absorbed.) Stir in the cheese, sprinkle with parsley, and serve immediately.

Serves 4 to 6.

Asparagus was a springtime staple of the Roman diet almost two thousand years ago. Even then, chefs knew better than to overcook it. Food snoops tell us that whenever Emperor Augustus wished to terminate some unpleasant business at hand, he would proclaim: "Let it be done quicker than you would cook an asparagus!"

ASPARAGUS A LA PARMIGIANA

*T*his classic from Emilia Romagna (in northern Italy) is served in Italy as an *antipasto*: before the true business of the meal begins. At my table it makes a dandy accompaniment to roast meat or fowl.

2 pounds asparagus, trimmed, peeled
4 tablespoons (½ stick) unsalted butter,
* melted*
Salt and freshly ground black pepper
½ cup freshly grated Parmesan cheese

1. Preheat the oven to 400°F. Blanch the asparagus and drain it on paper towels. Arrange the asparagus in a shallow ovenproof serving dish.

2. Pour the melted butter over the asparagus. Sprinkle with salt and pepper to taste. Spoon the cheese evenly over the top. Bake until lightly browned, about 20 minutes.

Serves 4.

MARGI SMITH'S ASPARAGUS A LA HOLSTEIN
(Asparagus with Fried Egg and Lemon)

*M*argi Smith, a good friend who is also an intrepid cook, told me about a dish she invented one night after returning home late from the office and discovering only half a bunch of asparagus, some eggs, capers, and a hunk of Parmigiano Reggiano cheese in the refrigerator. It sounded good, so I memorized her formula verbatim. Margi Smith's "fast food" is now one of my favorite light meals during the vernal equinox.

1 pound asparagus, trimmed, peeled
1½ to 2 tablespoons unsalted butter
2 eggs
1 teaspoon lemon juice
½ teaspoon red wine vinegar
2 teaspoons capers
Freshly ground black pepper
1 tablespoon freshly grated Parmesan cheese

1. Preheat the oven to 200°F. Cook the asparagus in boiling salted water, or steam until just tender. Place drained asparagus in a shallow serving dish and keep it warm in the oven. (Asparagus may be blanched ahead of time and reheated in a warm oven, if desired.)

2. Melt ½ to 1 tablespoon of the butter in a medium-size skillet and fry the eggs sunny side up. Place the eggs over the asparagus and return the dish to the oven.

3. Add the remaining 1 tablespoon butter to the skillet and stir in the lemon juice, vinegar, and capers. Cook over medium heat until slightly thickened. Spoon the sauce over the eggs and sprinkle with pepper to taste and the Parmesan cheese. Serve immediately.

Serves 2.

BEDDED ASPARAGUS

1½ to 2 pounds asparagus, trimmed, peeled
4 strips bacon
2 tablespoons unsalted butter
1 small clove garlic, minced
1 shallot, minced
2 hard-cooked eggs, finely chopped
1 cup watercress leaves
1 tablespoon red wine vinegar
Salt and freshly ground black pepper

1. Preheat the oven to 250°F. Cook the asparagus in boiling salted water, or steam, until just tender. Place drained asparagus in a baking dish, and keep it warm in the oven. (Asparagus may be blanched ahead of time and reheated in a warm oven, if desired.)

2. Sauté the bacon strips in a large heavy skillet until crisp. Drain on paper towels, crumble, and reserve.

3. Pour off all but 1 tablespoon bacon drippings from the skillet. Add the butter. Sauté the garlic and shallot over medium-low heat until golden. Stir in the eggs and toss in the watercress. Cook until the watercress is just wilted. Sprinkle with the vinegar, and add salt and pepper to taste.

4. To serve, spread the watercress-egg mixture over the bottom of a serving dish. Lay the asparagus over the top, and sprinkle with the crumbled bacon.

Serves 4.

ASPARAGUS IN MINT CREAM

*T*his dish, plus the two that follow—Asparagus in Whipped Cream and Asparagus Meringue—are all delicate side dishes that make excellent partners to fish and fowl alike; or they can stand alone as a separate course.

2 pounds asparagus, trimmed, peeled
4 sprigs fresh mint
1 sprig fresh tarragon, chopped
1 sprig parsley, chopped
2 shallots, chopped
3 tablespoons dry white wine
3 tablespoons white wine vinegar
¼ cup heavy or whipping cream
1 egg yolk, lightly beaten
¾ cup (1½ sticks) unsalted butter, frozen

1. Preheat the oven to 250°F. Cook the asparagus in boiling salted water, or steam, until just tender. Place the drained asparagus in a shallow serving dish, and keep it warm in the oven. (Asparagus may be blanched ahead of time and reheated in a warm oven, if desired.)

2. Remove the mint leaves from their stems; reserve the stems. Finely chop the leaves; reserve.

3. Combine the mint stems with the tarragon, parsley, shallots, white wine, and vinegar in a small saucepan. Heat to boiling; reduce the heat. Simmer, uncovered, until reduced to 2 tablespoons. Stir in the cream. Return to the boil and again reduce to about 2 tablespoons.

4. Strain the herbed mixture into the top of a double boiler. Beat in the egg yolk. Place over simmering water. Cut the butter into 12 pieces. Using a small wire whisk, beat the butter into the mixture, one piece at a time, stirring well after each addition. When thick, stir in the reserved mint leaves; pour over the asparagus.

Serves 4.

ALICE B. TOKLAS' ASPARAGUS IN WHIPPED CREAM

1½ to 2 pounds asparagus, trimmed, peeled
4 tablespoons (½ stick) unsalted butter
1 cup heavy or whipping cream
½ teaspoon salt
¼ teaspoon freshly ground black pepper

1. Preheat the oven to 250°F. Cook the asparagus in boiling salted water, or steam, until just tender. Place the drained asparagus in a shallow serving dish, and keep it warm in the oven. (Asparagus may be blanched ahead of time and reheated in a warm oven, if desired.)

2. In a small saucepan, melt the butter with ¼ cup heavy cream over low heat. Stir, and pour over the asparagus; return the asparagus to the oven.

3. Beat the remaining ¾ cup cream with the salt and pepper until stiff. Spoon over the hot asparagus. Serve immediately.

Serves 4.

Asparagus is one of a select bunch of garden greens that man has always seemed to invest with aphrodisiac powers. In nineteenth-century France, for instance, convention decreed that a bridegroom's prenuptial dinner contain at least three courses of warm asparagus... Make of that what you will!

ASPARAGUS MERINGUE

2 pounds asparagus, trimmed, peeled
¾ cup Mayonnaise (see page 408)
¼ cup sour cream
1½ teaspoons Dijon mustard
1 teaspoon lemon juice
1½ tablespoons minced chives or scallion
    tops
4 egg whites
½ teaspoon salt
¼ teaspoon ground white pepper
Pinch of sugar

1. Preheat the oven to 250°F. Cook the asparagus in boiling salted water, or steam, until just tender. Place the drained asparagus in a shallow oven-proof serving dish, and keep it warm in the oven. (Asparagus may be blanched ahead of time and reheated in a warm oven, if desired.)

2. Combine the mayonnaise, sour cream, mustard, lemon juice, and chives in a medium bowl. Mix well.

3. In another bowl, beat the egg whites with the salt and white pepper until soft peaks form. Sprinkle with sugar; beat until stiff. Fold the egg whites into the mayonnaise mixture, and spread evenly over the top of the asparagus. Place the asparagus under the broiler until the top is slightly browned, about 3 minutes.

4. To serve, use a thin spatula to break through the meringue and gently lift out both a piece of meringue and several asparagus spears. Spoon any remaining sauce over the individual portions.

Serves 4.

ASPARAGUS AND SHRIMP PIE

Asparagus' cognomen in early English evolved to a rather neat semi-description: "sparrow's grass." This in turn was altered to "sperage" and eventually "grass" alone, a fact that may account for an ancient British recipe (much written about but undetailed as to ingredients) for a "grass and prawn pie." My stimulated imagination produced the unauthentic rendering that follows.

Short Crust Pastry (see page 412)
¾ pound asparagus, trimmed, peeled
1 tablespoon unsalted butter
1 shallot, minced
1 tablespoon Madeira
½ pound shrimp, shelled, deveined, cut in
    half crosswise
2 eggs
1 cup heavy or whipping cream
½ cup coarsely grated Jarlsberg cheese
Dash of hot pepper sauce

⅛ teaspoon freshly grated nutmeg
Salt and freshly ground black pepper
1 tablespoon freshly grated Parmesan
    cheese

1. Make the Short Crust Pastry.
2. Preheat the oven to 375°F. Line a 9-inch loose-bottom tart pan with the pastry. Trim. Line the pastry with aluminum foil weighted down with uncooked rice or dried beans. Bake 10 minutes.

Remove the foil and rice or beans. Prick the bottom of the crust with a fork to allow steam to escape. Bake 3 minutes longer. Cool on a wire rack.

3. Blanch the asparagus and drain it on paper towels.

4. Melt the butter in a medium skillet, and sauté the shallot over medium-low heat until golden, about 5 minutes. Stir in the Madeira and shrimp. Toss 1 minute. Spoon the mixture evenly over the bottom of the prepared crust.

5. Beat the eggs with the cream in a medium-size bowl. Add the Jarlsberg cheese, hot pepper sauce, nutmeg, and salt and pepper to taste. Mix well, and pour over the shrimp. Place the asparagus spears on top in a spoke pattern with the tips facing outward (trim the stalks to fit if necessary). Sprinkle with Parmesan cheese. Bake 30 minutes.

Serves 6 to 8.

CRAVATTA
(Asparagus Ties)

*T*he next asparagus invention springs from Italy. These slim packages of ham wrapped around asparagus and cheese make a perfect lunch, brunch, or supper—just add a loaf of crusty bread and a bottle of dry white wine.

16 medium asparagus spears, trimmed, peeled
½ teaspoon unsalted butter
1 large shallot, minced
1 teaspoon Dijon mustard
2 tablespoons heavy or whipping cream
½ teaspoon lemon juice
½ pound thinly sliced boiled ham (8 slices)
3 tablespoons freshly grated Parmesan cheese
½ pound Fontina cheese, coarsely grated
Freshly ground black pepper

1. Preheat the oven to 400°F. Blanch the asparagus and drain it on paper towels.

2. Melt the butter in a small skillet over medium-low heat. Add the minced shallot and sauté until lightly browned. Remove from the heat. Stir in the mustard, cream, and lemon juice, and blend well.

3. Spread a small amount of the shallot-mustard mixture over each slice of ham. Sprinkle each piece with Parmesan cheese. Divide the Fontina cheese into two portions, and sprinkle one portion evenly over the ham slices.

4. Place two asparagus spears in the center of each ham slice. Fold the ham over the asparagus, and arrange the packages in a lightly greased ovenproof serving dish, seam side down. Sprinkle the remaining Fontina cheese over the top, and add a grating of pepper. Bake until lightly browned and bubbly, 15 to 20 minutes.

Serves 4.

AVOCADOS

A Fruit in Vegetable's Clothing

The avocado was decidedly not a staple of the average American diet when I was growing up. On the East Coast, these leathery-skinned objects were known to consumers as "alligator pears" and were regarded with only a shade less suspicion than might have been accorded the actual reptiles if they had been discovered nesting on a greengrocer's shelf. In that dim culinary time, such comestibles were judged indigestible or, worse yet, immoral, and the middle class gave them a wide berth.

Luckier than most, I was born to high-spirited parents who enjoyed good things and good times. Prior to the Depression our family would go "on the town," as my parents called our weekend outings to Manhattan restaurants. I was something of a finicky eater in those days, but despite that, these outings pleased me as much as my parents. The glitter of crystal, the gleam of silver, and the deferential mien of waiters in tuxedos offered a glimpse of an adult life I longed to inherit.

My parents always ate conventional dishes like shrimp, fruit cocktail, steak, or roast beef for dinner. But not me. Possessed of insatiable fascination for the exotic, I would order items from the à la carte side of the menu: inevitably fare that whetted my imagination if not necessarily my appetite.

Whenever I chose one of these untried dishes, my mother's eyebrows always raised perceptibly. This expression, which my sister Myra called *Mama's famous look,* implied "You will be sorry you ordered that!" Mama's famous look never stopped me from selecting snails or frogs' legs, but it also never made swallowing these mistakes any easier. One entree I did not even consider ordering was the avocado—for the menu price automatically inhibited even my inquiring taste buds. Luckily time and tide made it more accessible.

Years later when I was a grown man with a substantial position (and an expanded palate), I took my mother to a well-known restaurant in Manhattan. It was French and expensive, situated in the parlor floor of an East Side brownstone long since demolished for a skyscraper. My mother, I knew, was impressed with the surroundings despite her natural reservation about my extravagance. Seated on a banquette across from her, I opened the impressive bill of fare and perused the lefthand side.

"The avocado vinaigrette is particularly good here, Mother."

My parent did not reply to the suggestion but her eyebrows flared wildly. "People do not change" was an opinion she stated often.

"Listen! I've had it before. It's delicious."

I don't think she believed me, but despite her misgiving she allowed me to order two portions. In truth, her dubious expression did not alter until she had tasted the avocado twice.

"You're right," she announced, licking her spoon. "It's not bad at all."

The rest of the dinner was delicious but nothing obviously compared with the appetizer. "You know," my mother shook her head thoughtfully over her coffee cup, "I can't get over that avocado. What I've been missing all these years!"

I never inherited my mother's way with an eyebrow so there would have been little point in elevating mine. Besides, I knew from experience . . . it was love at first bite!

Vegetable Roots

*T*he avocado is an anomaly, a fruit that has been consumed as a vegetable for centuries. Archaeologists digging in the pre-Incan city of Chan Chan, Peru, unearthed a cache of avocado pits along with jars of grain and corn, indicating that it was a diet staple prior to 900 A.D.

Hernando Cortez was probably the first European to ever chomp an avocado in the New World. Happily this conquistador never ventured very far afield without an aide to record his peregrinations, be they combative or gastronomic. The Spanish historian Gonzalo Fernandez Oviedo y Valdes, noting the memorable culinary proceedings for posterity, also gave the first directions for eating a fresh avocado.

> In the center of the greenish-gold oval is a seed resembling a peeled chestnut that must be removed and thrown away because it is both bitter and exceedingly hard to chew. Between this and the tough rind of the skin however is a paste that the Indians consume with great relish. Soft as butter in texture, it is of a very good taste.

Oviedo also observed that the Aztecs ate their avocados directly from the shell, scraping the pulp with their front teeth. Cortez took his with a silver spoon, adding a pinch of salt from time to time because he found the flavor somewhat bland. (That smooth flavor, of course, is what makes the avocado a perfect foil for the accompaniments soon to follow).

What to Look For

*T*he avocado (*Persea americana*) is distantly related to the laurel and shares a common heritage with other nondeciduous evergreens. Over the past hundred years, avocados have migrated from their original home in Mexico to such southerly outposts as Hawaii, Australia, Africa, and Israel and north to California and Florida, where avocado growing has become a major industry.

The most familiar avocado on supermarket shelves in winter is the silky Fuerte, encased in a glossy green rind flecked with gold. The summer avocado is a rough-pebbled globe with much darker skin, known as Hass. Whatever their outer packaging, both have the same creamy texture and subtle nutlike flavor.

The wise buyer purchases an avocado just before it is fully ripe, as the fruit at maturity has a relatively short shelf-life. To test for ripeness, cradle an avocado in the palm of your hand and squeeze it lightly. If fully developed, it will be soft to the touch and will yield to pressure. An underdeveloped one will be quite firm and resistant. Some canny cooks hurry the ripening process by storing avocados in brown paper sacks or wrapping them in layers of tissue paper or foil. This forces the maturation process by concentrating the natural carbon dioxide that the fruit exudes.

I simply store an avocado in a warm, dry place (like an earthenware bowl) until it is obviously ready for slicing. Once ripe, an avocado may be held for a day or so in the refrigerator, but never frozen.

An avocado should be sliced lengthwise, using a sharp stainless-steel knife, and twisted gently to separate the halves. The large center pit is easily removed with the tip of the knife. To prevent darkening, rub the cut surfaces with plenty of fresh lime or lemon juice. I follow the Mexican injunction and always replace the seed when storing a cut half for any length of time; it seems to keep the flesh firmer and greener.

When avocados are served warm, make sure they do not overcook, which will turn the flesh somewhat bitter.

The avocado, which is often thought of as a rich food, produces no serum cholesterol whatsoever and maintains a relatively high protein content despite its immoderate appetite appeal. An average avocado half contains a mere 136 calories, and at least 8 essential vitamins and 5 vital minerals.

Preparation

For many, the classic way to serve an avocado is merely to brush the cut surface with lime or lemon juice and sprinkle with salt and pepper. But that is surely the super-purist approach. Speaking for myself, I would choose an avocado well soused with oil, vinegar, and a mite of chopped onion. And, of course, any of the inspirations that follow.

A *word of advice to chary consumers*: The avocado ripens best in its own sweet time. According to those Californians (and Floridians) lucky enough to own trees, the fruit is ready to be eaten only when it falls to the ground. Commercial growers pick avocados when they are underripe so the fruit will season on its way to a greengrocer's shelf. An avocado

The avocado pit you're about to toss out may be persuaded to grow into a handsome and hardy houseplant—and with some extra cultivation perhaps, to a full-grown tree.

John Canaday, art and food critic and author of *The Artful Avocado*, is the past master of avocado green-thumbery. He advises that the pit be washed and dried first, then stuck with three or four strong toothpicks to hold it suspended, broad side down, in an ordinary glass filled with tepid (not hot) water.

Keep the seed out of direct sunlight, and it will split and send forth a sprout and roots in about two to six weeks. When it does, plant it, and pray!

that is firm to the touch but appears brownish or discolored inside is the result of refrigerator burn (or too long in cold storage) and, according to the Avo-cado Information Bureau, should be promptly returned to the seller. For serious queries write: Avocado Information, P.O. Box 19159-MT, Irvine, CA 92713.

AVOCADOS VINAIGRETTE NEW ORLEANS STYLE

1 hard-cooked egg, chopped
1 teaspoon chopped chives or scallion tops
1 teaspoon chopped fresh basil, or ¼
    teaspoon dried
1 teaspoon chopped fresh parsley
1 tablespoon red wine vinegar
¼ cup olive oil
2 slices Milano or Genoa salami, cut into
    thin 1-inch-long strips
2 avocados
Juice of 1 lemon
Freshly ground black pepper

1. Combine the egg, chives, basil, parsley, vinegar, oil, and salami in a small bowl. Toss well.

2. Cut the avocados in half lengthwise, and remove the pits. Sprinkle with lemon juice.

3. Fill each avocado half with the salami-egg mixture. Sprinkle with pepper to taste. Chill well before serving.

Serves 4.

GUACAMOLE

*T*his wondrous hors d'oeuvre, often referred to by food snobs as "the avocado's finest hour," comes from Mexico, where there are as many versions as there are dialects. One rule, however, is unvarying: this dish requires a ripe, mashable avocado, which is seasoned with salt, lime juice, and judicious doses of hot green chile peppers and chopped fresh coriander. The rest is up to the cook's imagination and tolerance for incendiarism.

My favorite guacamole recipe, authentic as a gringo appetite will allow, comes from San Antonio, Texas. With it, have a *damnyankee* warning: A hot pepper's fire is contained in its seeds and pale interior spines. To temper a pepper's pungency, remove both with a sharp knife, but do not touch your face or any other sensitive area of skin until you wash your hands first!

2 tablespoons minced yellow onion
1 small hot green pepper, seeded, minced
4 sprigs fresh coriander leaves (also known
    as cilantro or Chinese parsley), finely
    chopped

¼ teaspoon salt
2 medium avocados
¼ cup chopped, seeded tomatoes
2 tablespoons finely chopped red onion
1 tablespoon lemon or lime juice

1. Combine the yellow onion, hot green pepper, half the coriander, and the salt in a small bowl or mortar. Mash until a smooth paste is formed. Set aside.

2. Cut the avocados in half lengthwise; remove the pits and reserve them. Scoop out the flesh of the avocados and mash in a medium bowl until smooth. Add the reserved onion paste. Mix thoroughly. Stir in the tomatoes, red onion, and the remaining coriander. Press the reserved pits into the mixture. Sprinkle with lemon or lime juice. Cover; refrigerate.

3. Just before serving, remove the pits and stir thoroughly. Serve with corn chips, corn tortillas, or flour tortillas.

Makes about 2 cups.

JODY GILLIS' SWEET AND SOUR AVOCADOS

One of the best uses for the "lawyer's pear" is as an appetizer prior to dinner. This recipe for a somewhat radical version comes to me from the treasury of my good cooking friend, Jody Gillis of Santee, California. Jody declares shamelessly, "This dish is so sure fire that when I serve it, I wait for the spoons to hit the lips so the *mmmm's* can begin!"

8 strips bacon
8 tablespoons (1 stick) unsalted butter
¼ cup sugar
¼ cup ketchup
¼ cup red wine vinegar
1 tablespoon soy sauce
3 avocados
Juice of 1 lemon

1. Sauté the bacon strips in a heavy skillet until crisp. Drain on paper towels, crumble, and reserve.

2. Melt the butter in a small saucepan, and add the sugar, ketchup, vinegar, and soy sauce, stirring over low heat until the sugar dissolves. Keep warm.

3. Cut the avocados in half lengthwise. Remove the pits and sprinkle with the lemon juice.

4. Divide the crumbled bacon into six portions and place some in each avocado cavity. Spoon the warm sauce evenly over the avocados. Serve immediately.

Serves 6.

AVOCADO GRATINE

1 shallot, minced
1 tablespoon minced fresh parsley
3 tablespoons freshly grated Parmesan
  cheese
2 tablespoons olive oil

1 avocado
Juice of 1 lime
Salt and freshly ground black pepper
Lime wedges

1. Preheat the broiling unit. Combine the shallot, parsley, cheese, and oil in a small bowl. Mix well.

2. Just before serving, cut the avocado in half lengthwise; peel carefully, and remove the pit. Sprinkle well all over with the lime juice.

3. Place the avocado halves on a heatproof dish. Spoon the cheese mixture evenly over the tops and into the cavities. Sprinkle with salt and pepper to taste. Place under the broiler until golden, about 4 minutes. Serve with lime wedges.

Serves 2.

AVOCADO GAZPACHO

*H*ere is a wholly unclassic version of this cold Andalusian soup.

1 cucumber, peeled, seeded, chopped
2 cloves garlic, quartered
2 shallots, quartered
1 green bell pepper, seeded, roughly
  chopped
1 cup torn lettuce
1 tablespoon plus 1 teaspoon chopped fresh
  dill
1 tablespoon red wine vinegar
1 cup Chicken Stock (see page 410)
1 avocado
Juice of ½ lemon
2 tablespoons vodka
Salt and ground white pepper

1. Place the cucumber, garlic, shallots, green pepper, lettuce, 1 tablespoon dill, vinegar, and chicken stock (in that order) in the container of a blender or food processor. Blend until smooth.

2. Cut the avocado in half lengthwise. Peel, and remove the pit. Roughly chop half the avocado and add it to the mixture in the blender or processor. Blend until smooth. Transfer to a medium bowl.

3. Finely chop the remaining avocado and sprinkle with the lemon juice. Stir this into the gazpacho; add the vodka, and salt and white pepper to taste. Stir gently, and chill thoroughly before serving. Garnish with the remaining chopped dill.

Serves 4.

HOT AVOCADO SALAD

4 strips bacon
1 green or red bell pepper, seeded, cut into
  strips
½ small hot green pepper, seeded, minced
  (see Guacamole headnote, page 37)
1 small yellow onion, finely chopped

1 avocado
Juice of 1 lemon
3 tablespoons red wine vinegar
1 small red onion, thinly sliced
Salt and freshly ground black pepper

1. Sauté the bacon strips in a large skillet over medium heat until crisp. Drain on paper towels, crumble, and reserve.

2. Pour off all but 2 tablespoons bacon drippings from the skillet. Add both peppers and the yellow onion. Cook over medium heat, stirring occasionally, until the onions are golden, about 5 minutes. Reduce the heat to low. Cook, covered, until the peppers are tender, 5 minutes. Remove from the heat; set aside.

3. Cut the avocado in half lengthwise. Peel, and remove the pit. Cut each half into ¼-inch-thick slices crosswise, and sprinkle with the lemon juice.

4. Toss the avocado slices into the onion-pepper mixture. Sprinkle with the vinegar. Toss in the red onion slices and the crumbled bacon. Add salt and pepper to taste.

Serves 2 to 4.

COLD POACHED FISH WITH AVOCADO MAYONNAISE

Avocado mayonnaise is also a perfect partner for raw vegetables or as a fillip for jellied consommés or salads. Be my guest!

Cold Poached Fish:

2½ cups water
½ cup dry white wine
1 small onion stuck with 1 clove
½ rib celery with leaves
1 small bay leaf
½ lemon
6 peppercorns
½ teaspoon salt
1½ to 2 pounds small, firm-fleshed fish
    filets (such as sole, lemon sole, or
    flounder), or ¾-inch-thick salmon
    steaks

Avocado Mayonnaise:

1 cup Mayonnaise (see page 408)
Juice and finely grated peel of 1 large lime
1 avocado
Salt and ground white pepper

1. To poach the fish: Combine all the ingredients except the fish in an enamel skillet or fish poacher. Heat to boiling; reduce the heat. Simmer, uncovered, 5 minutes. Add the fish, a few pieces at a time. Poach gently, uncovered, until the fish flakes easily when pierced with a fork—about 4 minutes for filets, 8 minutes for salmon. Remove the fish from the pan with a spatula and transfer it to a serving platter. Refrigerate, covered, at least 1 hour.

2. To make the Avocado Mayonnaise: Place the mayonnaise and lime juice in the container of a blender or processor. Cut the avocado in half lengthwise; remove the pit. Scoop out the flesh and add it to the blender. Purée until smooth. Transfer the mayonnaise to a bowl, add salt and white pepper to taste, and refrigerate, covered, 1 hour.

3. To serve: Drain off any liquid that has accumulated around the fish. Spoon 2 to 3 tablespoons of avocado mayonnaise over each piece of fish, and sprinkle with the grated lime peel. Pass the remaining mayonnaise.

Serves 4 to 6.

AVOCADO AND SPINACH

1 avocado
Juice of 1 lime
2 tablespoons unsalted butter
1 small onion, finely chopped
10 ounces fresh spinach, washed, trimmed,
    roughly chopped
1 teaspoon bouillon powder
Dash of hot pepper sauce
Salt and freshly ground black pepper

1. Cut the avocado in half lengthwise. Peel, and remove the pit. Cut each half into a fine dice. Sprinkle with the lime juice, cover, and reserve.

2. Melt the butter in a large heavy skillet over medium-low heat. Stir in the onion; cook 3 minutes.

3. Add the spinach with just the water that clings to the leaves. Sprinkle the bouillon over the leaves. Cook, covered, until the spinach wilts, about 3 minutes.

4. Stir the diced avocado into the spinach mixture. Add the hot pepper sauce, and salt and pepper to taste.

Serves 4.

AVOCADO AND SHRIMP VELVET

According to Diana Kennedy, my sibyl on the subject of Mexican cuisine, the leaves of the avocado tree add a delicate but unmistakable anise flavor to a dish if they are toasted and sprinkled on prior to serving. In the following silken blending of avocado and shrimp, a splash of anise-flavored spirits makes a tasty substitute.

One-Cup Hollandaise (recipe follows)
1 avocado
Juice of 1 lemon
2 tablespoons unsalted butter
Whole scallion, bulb and green top, finely
    chopped
1 tablespoon chopped fresh tarragon, or ½
    teaspoon dried
16 large shrimp, shelled, deveined, split
    down the backs
¼ cup Pernod, or other anise-based
    liqueur, warmed
Chopped fresh parsley

1. Make the One-Cup Hollandaise. Keep warm, stirring occasionally, over hot water.

2. Cut the avocado in half lengthwise. Peel, and remove the pit. Cut each half into ¼-inch slices crosswise. Sprinkle the slices with the lemon juice, cover, and reserve.

3. Melt the butter in a large heavy skillet over medium heat. Stir in the scallion; cook 1 minute. Add the tarragon and shrimp. Toss until the shrimp turn pink, 3 to 4 minutes. Toss in the avocado slices. Reduce the heat to low. Add the warmed Pernod. Being very careful, set the Pernod aflame. Shake the pan until the flames subside.

4. Transfer the shrimp mixture to a serving dish. Spoon the hollandaise sauce over the top. Sprinkle with parsley. Toss at the table before serving.

Serves 4.

One-Cup Hollandaise

*T*o make the cook's lot somewhat easier, the essential ingredients of Fail-Safe Hollandaise have been amended here to produce a single cup.

2 egg yolks
2 teaspoons lemon juice
½ teaspoon Dijon mustard
8 tablespoons (1 stick) unsalted butter, frozen
Dash of hot pepper sauce
Pinch of ground white pepper
Salt

1. Beat the egg yolks with the lemon juice in the top of a double boiler. Place over the simmering water; stir in the mustard.

2. Cut the butter into eight pieces. Using a small wire whisk, beat the butter into the egg yolk mixture, one piece at a time, stirring well after each addition. Stir in the hot pepper sauce, white pepper, and salt to taste.

Makes about 1 cup.

*A*vocado comes from the Aztecs' *ahuacatl*, roughly translated as "green testicles." The Spanish conquistadors, obviously of a somewhat priggish nature, censored that cognomen. They phonetically translated the word as *abogado*, which means "lawyer." Time eventually altered that to *aguacate*, but the damage was done. Both the French and the Germans compounded the misconception. France's *poire d'avocat* and Germany's *advokatbirne* have the same meaning: "lawyer's pears."

CURRIED CHICKEN WITH AVOCADO

*I*nstead of mixing and matching it with astringent flavor contrasts, the French most often cloak the sensual avocado in even more luxuriant upholsteries—to wit: a purely Francophile translation of a curry dish. Serve it for supper, lunch or brunch. Chutney and condiments are optional.

4 tablespoons (½ stick) unsalted butter
1 onion, chopped
1 clove garlic, chopped
1 small apple, peeled, cored, chopped
2 to 3 tablespoons curry powder
⅛ teaspoon ground turmeric
3 tablespoons all-purpose flour
1½ cups Chicken Stock (see page 410)
1 cup heavy or whipping cream
2 cups cooked boned chicken
⅛ teaspoon hot pepper sauce
½ teaspoon salt
2 tablespoons lemon juice

1 avocado
Hot Steamed Rice (see page 412)

1. Melt the butter in a medium saucepan over medium-low heat. Stir in the onion; cook 3 minutes. Stir in the garlic, apple, curry powder, turmeric, and flour. Mix well. Cook over low heat, stirring constantly, 2 minutes. Stir in the chicken stock and cream. Heat to boiling; reduce the heat. Simmer gently, uncovered, 15 minutes. Remove from the heat.

2. Place half the curry mixture in a blender or processor. Purée until smooth (carefully, as hot liquid will expand). Transfer to a medium saucepan. Purée the remaining curry mixture and add it to the saucepan.

3. Place the puréed curry mixture over low heat. Stir in the chicken, hot pepper sauce, salt, and 1 tablespoon of the lemon juice. Cook, uncovered, until warmed through, about 10 minutes.

4. Cut the avocado in half lengthwise; peel, and remove the pit. Cut each half into ¼-inch-thick slices crosswise. Sprinkle with the remaining 1 tablespoon lemon juice.

5. Gently stir the avocado slices into the curry. Heat until just warmed through, about 4 minutes. Do not allow to boil. Serve over rice.

Serves 4.

BRAZILIAN AVOCADO CREAM

*T*his dish, *crema aguascate*, might be considered a dessert, but in Brazil (whence it comes) it is most often consumed for breakfast, with a pot of strong black coffee on the side.

1 avocado
Juice of 2 limes
¼ cup light rum or coconut Amaretto
¼ teaspoon vanilla extract
½ cup plus 2 tablespoons confectioners'
*   sugar*
1 cup heavy or whipping cream
2 teaspoons finely slivered lime peel

1. Cut the avocado in half lengthwise; remove the pit. Scoop out the flesh from the avocado and place it in the container of a food processor or blender.

Add the lime juice, light rum or coconut Amaretto, vanilla, and ½ cup confectioners' sugar. Purée until smooth. Transfer to a large bowl.

2. In a medium bowl, beat the cream with the remaining confectioners' sugar until stiff. Fold the whipped cream into the avocado mixture. Transfer to a serving bowl and sprinkle with slivered lime peel. Chill thoroughly before serving.

Serves 4 to 6.

BEETS
Robust and Red Blooded

To paraphrase Charles Dickens, the very best meals of my life have always been consumed in the very worst of times.

I grew up in the dark, drear days of the thirties, when necessity smothered invention at our kitchen table. If beets were cheap (and they usually were), we ate beets for better or worse, meal after meal—without complaint, knowing that my mother would change the menu as soon as the corner market altered its current "marked-down" merchandise.

My parent was a fierce shopper who saw the battle for her family's survival in terms of pennies, not dollars. Unfortunately I had no such stout heart and a bad sense of arithmetic into the bargain. So I dreaded being elected as her accomplice on market rounds, a ritual that was embarked upon every Saturday evening when she returned from work.

Paula Greene was a born trader, a gift she inherited from her mother. My grandmother, who was a superb cook, could have achieved detective status on a police force if she'd put her mind to it. That woman could spot a thumb on a butcher's scale at fifty yards and had the kind of shrewd, appraising eye that would turn larcenous shopkeepers ashen whenever she appeared at their counters. Long before she pried open a bin of stale coffee or sniffed into a moldy pickle barrel, her deportment implied the righteous mistrust of a consumerist Carrie Nation.

On the rare occasions when they shopped together, my mother and grandmother would make any small businessman quail. In tandem they would chastise a greengrocer about his puny tomatoes (or strawberries) as if he had planted the crop himself; and then laugh when they heard the price. Laugh, I might add, with such a resounding lack of mirth that the poor man usually lowered the cost immediately to put an end to his harassment.

Like seasoned horse traders they would converge upon some article of grocery (a chine of beef or a bushel of beets) and poke, pinch, and tug at the comestible for so long and with such obvious contempt that the outraged seller would finally snatch it from their reach in order to keep it whole. Only then, when the poor man had been hectored and harangued beyond belief, would my grandmother discreetly lower her eyelids and sigh. "I don't really need this. It's not the quality of merchandise I buy. Actually I had something else in mind when I came into the store. But I feel bad taking up so much of your time." Then, looking the purveyor straight in the eye, her voice would drop an octave. "How much?"

Whatever she was quoted would be dismissed out of hand, and the eventual price would be negotiated like a peace treaty, with much bowing, bending, and breaking away on both parts before my grandmother handed her daughter the commodious black leather pocketbook she carried at all times.

"Pauline. Pay the man," she would finally command, always managing at the last moment to secure exactly the cut of beef or quality of beet she had wanted for her stockpot in the first place.

The shopkeeper's reward for the terrible ordeal of having my mother and grandmother in his store was the hasty retreat the pair made once a purchase was finally realized.

My reward was somewhat more residual. It came from the amalgam of maligned ingredients—the contested beets and beef—into a revivifying bowl of steaming borscht.

Consuming passion alone kept me steadfast, then and now!

Vegetable Roots

The garden-variety beet is a vegetable with a fairly florid past. Columella, the early Roman agriculturist, noted in the first century A.D. that "this curious plant owes its name, *Beta Vulgaris*, to a physical resemblance to the second letter of the alphabet." That beets grow in clumps is an indisputable fact, but I have rarely uncovered a pair that was impacted end-over-end in my garden. So take that information like the beet itself—with a grain of salt.

Early diners prized beets for the wrong reasons, it seems to me, choosing to consume only the red-veined outer leaves in salads and relegating what Pliny referred to as "the crimson nether parts" to pharmacists, surgeons, and soothsayers. In fact, this habit of picking the leaves created a swollen and juicy root, which was to provide future tables with one of the tenderest comestibles that grows. But it took close to a millennium before some trencherman had the good sense to consume a plateful drenched with butter and a jot of lemon juice.

What to Look For

Beets are a year-round vegetable in most parts of the country, but they are undeniably at their best (read tenderest) when picked fresh any time between late June and early October.

Beet shoppers should look out for smooth, spherical orbs with dark red (unmarred) skins and crisp green (never yellowing) leaves. Beet tops, parenthetically, are a good source of potassium and calcium, besides husbanding 7,400 milligrams of vitamin A per cup.

Preparation

*F*or all their earthly connections, beets require only a scant scrub-up (in cold water) before entry into a saucepan. I use a small nailbrush to remove the loose particles of dirt but am exceedingly careful not to break the skin—which bleeds into the cooking liquid if a beet is bruised. Likewise never, never peel a beet prior to cooking, and leave a good inch or so at the stem and root ends to preserve the vegetable's rosy hue.

There is more than one way to cook a beet, but boiling is the most common method. I also fancy the Italian way of oven-steaming them in aluminum foil, a technique I acquired from Marcella Hazan, cooking teacher and author par excellence, in Bologna several years ago—but more of that anon. The generally accepted practice for boiling beets is to place them in a large heavy-duty saucepan filled with unsalted cold water. Bring the water slowly to a boil and simmer, uncovered, until the beets are barely tender, about 35 to 40 minutes. Then plunge the cooked beets under cold running water to retard the cooking and drain them well before peeling.

Beet tops are best wilted. Cook them quickly in a skillet or sauté pan without any liquid other than the water in which they have been washed. Mature beet tops are too tough for such gentle cookery. Boil large, fibrous leaves in salted water for a few minutes to remove any bitterness.

The classic way to prepare beets (in my prejudiced opinion) was limned in a yellowing cookbook written a hundred years ago. This fragile relic was recently sent to me by the writer's great-great-grandson, who felt I could put his forebear's culinary legacy to good use. The "receipt" for *Grandma Clemon's Beets* reads:

> Cut cooked beets fine. Then make sauce as follows: a little sugar, a little vinegar and a little butter. If you like add a few tablespoons of cream to thicken.

All my best beet recipes are variations on that theme.

FINNISH POLAR BEAR'S EYE

*I*t was in a southern climate that beets first grew and found their way into cultivated gardens, but they certainly thrive best in less temperate zones. Red beets are a much-prized staple in Russian and Scandinavian kitchens all winter long. As a matter of fact, one of the best beet dishes in my lexicon comes from Denmark, where it is most unceremoniously dubbed "The Finnish Polar Bear's Eye."

I must add that no Finn I have ever met has acknowledged knowing or having tasted this savory treat. Who cares? The dish is a must as a warm-weather luncheon dish or a year-round hangover cure, depending upon your physical condition. The original prescription appeared in a long-out-of-print tome, Dagmar Freuchen's *Cookbook of the Seven Seas.*

1 large beet (about ½ pound), trimmed
2 medium potatoes
*8 anchovy filets, chopped, with the oil from
    a 2-ounce can*

1 medium onion, diced
4 unbroken egg yolks
Freshly ground black pepper

1. Place the beet in a saucepan; cover with cold unsalted water. Heat slowly to boiling; reduce the heat. Simmer, uncovered, until barely tender, about 35 minutes. Drain under cold water. Remove the skin, dice, and reserve.

2. Meanwhile, cook the potatoes, uncovered, in boiling salted water until barely tender, about 20 minutes. Drain; let stand 5 minutes. Peel and dice.

3. While the potatoes are still warm, combine them with the diced beet, the anchovy filets and oil, and the onion. Toss lightly.

4. To serve, divide the beet mixture into four portions and place each on a separate plate. With the back of a spoon, make a small indentation in each portion. Slide an egg yolk into each little "well" and sprinkle it with pepper. Each person mixes the egg yolk into the beets at the table before eating.

Serves 4.

COLD PINK BORSCHT

*T*o my prejudiced tongue another truly classic beet formula (definitely on a par with the aforementioned Grandma Clemon's) is a very unclassic bowl of borscht.

This version, a shocking pink pottage, is a variation on my mother and grandmother's perennial summer cooler. Both ladies would scoff at the addition of cucumbers and (God forbid) garlic, but that gives this rendering its essential savor in my opinion.

They both served borscht in the best American-Jewish tradition: chilled for hours and hours in a refrigerator and then diluted to lukewarm neutrality by the addition of steaming boiled potatoes at the table. I, however, would never consider an adjunct weightier than chopped chives and parsley in my icy soup bowl!

1 pound beets, trimmed
2 medium cucumbers, peeled, seeded
1 clove garlic, chopped
1 cup milk
16 ounces sour cream
Salt and freshly ground black pepper
Chopped chives or scallion tops
Chopped fresh parsley

1. Place the beets in a saucepan and cover with cold unsalted water. Heat slowly to boiling; reduce the heat and cover. Simmer, uncovered, until barely tender, about 35 minutes. Drain under cold water. Remove the skins and chop the beets fine; reserve.

2. Finely chop 1 cucumber; reserve.

3. Roughly chop the remaining cucumber and place it in the container of a blender or food processor. Add the garlic and milk. Process until smooth.

4. Combine the puréed cucumber mixture with the sour cream in a large bowl. Whisk until smooth. Add the chopped beets and cucumber and add salt and pepper to taste. Chill well before serving garnished with chives and parsley.

Serves 4 to 6.

HOT RED KIEV BORSCHT

*T*he following prescription was acquired in the Ukraine, where the morning borscht is flavored with ham and sausage. Contrary to my prior injunction, you will observe that this calls for peeled raw beets to be grated directly into the stockpot. The reason is simple: rather than being washed away, the beets' color literally hues the brew!

2¾ quarts chicken broth (see page 414)
1 pound leftover cooked ham
2 tablespoons unsalted butter
1 tablespoon oil
1 large onion, finely chopped
1 large clove garlic, minced
1 large carrot, peeled, finely chopped
1 turnip, peeled, finely chopped
1 parsnip, peeled, finely chopped
2 large tomatoes, seeded, chopped
1 pound beets, peeled, roughly grated
(about 2½ cups)
1 small cabbage (about 1 pound), shredded
1 pound potatoes, peeled, diced
½ teaspoon freshly ground black pepper
⅛ teaspoon ground ginger
2 tablespoons red wine vinegar
1 pound Kielbasa (Polish sausage), sliced
Salt
1 tablespoon chopped fresh parsley

1. Place the chicken broth and the ham in a large heavy pot. Heat to boiling; reduce the heat. Simmer, uncovered, 25 minutes. Remove the ham and allow it to cool. Reserve the broth. Shred the ham and set aside.

2. Heat the butter with the oil in another large heavy pot over medium-low heat. Add the onion; cook 2 minutes. Add the garlic; cook 1 minute longer. Stir in the carrot, turnip, parsnip, tomatoes, and grated beets. Add 2½ cups of the reserved chicken broth. Heat to boiling; reduce the heat. Simmer, covered, 25 minutes.

3. Add the remaining chicken broth to the vegetable mixture. Add the reserved ham, the cabbage and potatoes. Cook, partially covered, 30 minutes.

4. Stir in the pepper, ginger, and vinegar. Continue to cook, covered, over low heat for 1 hour. (Recipe may be prepared in advance to this point, cooled, and refrigerated until ready to serve. The flavor will improve as it stands.)

5. To serve, reheat the soup if it was made in advance, and add the sliced sausage. Simmer, partially covered, 15 minutes. Add salt to taste, and more vinegar if needed. Sprinkle with chopped parsley.

Serves 8 to 10.

PERSIAN BEETS

*O*ne of the most felicitous salads I can name is this one comprised of peeled baby beets anointed with a sauce of heavy sour cream and fresh mint leaves.

1½ pounds small beets, trimmed
2 shallots, minced
1 cup plain yogurt
¼ cup heavy or whipping cream
1 tablespoon strong Chicken Stock,
    reduced from ⅓ cup (see page 410), or
    1 teaspoon bouillon powder
Salt
¼ cup fresh mint leaves

1. Place the beets in a saucepan; cover with cold unsalted water. Heat slowly to boiling; reduce the heat. Sim-mer, uncovered, until barely tender, about 25 minutes. Drain under cold water. Remove the skins but leave whole.

2. Pat the beets dry with paper towels and place them in a serving dish. Sprinkle with the shallots.

3. Beat the yogurt with the cream in a medium bowl. Beat in the stock or bouillon powder until smooth, adding salt to taste. Spoon the sauce over the beets and decorate with mint leaves.

Serves 4.

OVEN-STEAMED BEETS

*E*arlier I alluded to the Italian way of oven-steaming beets. This is a must for any vitamin-conscious cook, and the technique is *molto bonario* (very easy). I learned it from Marcella Hazan during a week of her remarkable kitchen wizardry in Bologna, and I never deviate from it a jot.

1. Wash and trim the fresh beets, and wrap each one tightly in aluminum foil. Place them on a rack in a preheated 350°F oven and steam them in their own juices until they sizzle and are tender-crisp, about 1½ hours.

2. Remove the foil, allow the beets to stand until they can be handled, and then proceed with any recipe at hand.

Careful! It's easy to burn your hands when removing the foil, so watch it!

MARCELLA HAZAN'S BAKED BEETS AND ONIONS

*A*fter steaming, start dreaming. This makes a simple but heavenly dish.

4 large beets (about 2 pounds), trimmed
1 large Bermuda onion with skin
1½ tablespoons red wine vinegar
½ teaspoon balsamic vinegar (optional; see
    Notes on Ingredients, page 417)
½ teaspoon salt

⅓ cup olive oil

1. Preheat the oven to 350°F. Wrap each beet tightly in aluminum foil.

2. Cut a ⅛-inch-deep X into the root end of the onion. Place the onion

and the beets in a shallow baking pan and bake until barely tender, 1 to 1¼ hours. (To test, pierce the onion and each beet with a wooden skewer.) Remove the foil from the beets; let stand 20 minutes.

3. Remove the skins from the beets and cut into ⅓-inch-wide julienne strips. Peel the onion and cut crosswise into ¼-inch-thick slices, then cut the slices in half. Combine the beets and onions in a medium-size bowl.

4. Combine the vinegars, salt, and oil in a small bowl. Mix well. Pour the dressing over the beets and onion. Let stand at room temperature for 3 hours before serving.

Serves 6.

TANGY MINTED BEETS

In my garden, beets grow in a sunny tract that is otherwise overrun with headstrong mint. The connection is my design. Long ago I discovered that leaf miners (insects that devastate garden greens) abhor the scent of mint and avoid that patch like the plague.

My tender beets are therefore unsullied, and as a reward I season them with lots of fresh mint.

1½ pounds beets, trimmed
2 tablespoons unsalted butter
1 shallot, minced
⅓ cup apple jelly
2 tablespoons chopped fresh mint
2 teaspoons lemon juice
Salt and freshly ground black pepper

1. Place the beets in a saucepan; cover with cold unsalted water. Heat slowly to boiling; reduce the heat. Simmer, uncovered, until barely tender, about 35 minutes. Drain under cold water. Remove the skins and cut the beets into slices; reserve.

2. Melt the butter in a large skillet over medium-low heat. Stir in the shallot; cook 4 minutes. Stir in the beets, apple jelly, mint, and lemon juice. Cook until warmed through. Add salt and pepper to taste.

Serves 4.

BEETS IN HORSERADISH CREAM

1½ pounds beets, trimmed
2 tablespoons unsalted butter
4 slices Canadian bacon, diced
½ cup heavy or whipping cream
2 tablespoons prepared horseradish
3 tablespoons chopped fresh dill
Salt and freshly ground black pepper

1. Place the beets in a saucepan; cover with cold unsalted water. Heat slowly to boiling; reduce the heat. Simmer, uncovered, until barely tender, about 35 minutes. Drain under cold water. Remove the skins and chop the beets; reserve.

2. Melt the butter in a large skillet over medium heat. Sauté the bacon until light brown, about 3 minutes. Stir in the beets, cream, horseradish, and 2 tablespoons of the dill. Reduce the heat to low, and cook 6 minutes. Add salt and pepper to taste and sprinkle with the remaining 1 tablespoon dill.

Serves 4.

BEETS IN MUSTARD SAUCE

1½ pounds beets, trimmed
3 tablespoons unsalted butter
¼ cup minced shallots
1 tablespoon all-purpose flour
½ cup strong Chicken Stock (see page 410)
3 tablespoons Dijon mustard
¼ cup heavy or whipping cream
Salt and freshly ground black pepper
Chopped fresh parsley

1. Place the beets in a saucepan and cover with cold unsalted water. Heat slowly to boiling; reduce the heat. Simmer, uncovered, until barely tender, about 35 minutes. Drain under cold water. Remove the skins and cut into slices; reserve.

2. Melt the butter in a large skillet over medium-low heat. Add the shallots; cook 4 minutes. Stir in the flour and cook, stirring constantly, 2 minutes. Whisk in the stock, then add the mustard and heavy cream. Cook until slightly thickened.

3. Add the beets to the sauce. Cook, stirring often, until warmed through. Add salt and pepper to taste and garnish with chopped parsley.

Serves 4.

GINGERED BEETS

*H*ere's another tasty partnership: beets with a spiking of ginger.

1½ pounds small beets, trimmed
⅓ cup seedless raisins
2 tablespoons unsalted butter
1½ teaspoons minced fresh ginger root
1 tablespoon sugar
1 teaspoon red wine vinegar
1 teaspoon finely slivered lime peel

1. Place the beets in a saucepan; cover with cold unsalted water. Heat slowly to boiling; reduce the heat. Simmer, uncovered, until barely tender, about 25 minutes.

2. Remove just enough beet liquid to cover the raisins in a small bowl. Let them stand 10 minutes. Meanwhile, drain the beets under cold water. Remove the skins and cut the beets into slices; reserve. Drain the raisins; reserve.

3. Melt the butter in a large skillet over medium-low heat. Stir in the ginger; cook 5 minutes. Add the reserved beets and raisins, the sugar, and the vinegar. Cook until warmed through; sprinkle with the lime peel.

Serves 4.

ORANGE-SCENTED BEETS

*B*eets are fairly hardy in the kitchen, holding their own with any number of otherwise overwhelming flavors. Take, for instance, the next prescription.

1½ pounds small beets, trimmed
2 tablespoons unsalted butter
1 small onion, finely chopped
3 tablespoons sugar
1 tablespoon red wine vinegar
Grated peel of 1 medium orange
Grated peel of 1 small lemon
Juice of 1 medium orange
Pinch of ground cinnamon
Salt and freshly ground black pepper
Chopped fresh parsley

1. Place the beets in a saucepan; cover with cold unsalted water. Heat slowly to boiling; reduce the heat. Simmer, uncovered, until barely tender, about 25 minutes. Drain under cold water. Remove the skins and cut the beets into slices; reserve.

2. Melt the butter in a large skillet over medium heat. Add the onion; cook until golden. Add the sugar, vinegar, orange and lemon peel, orange juice, and the cinnamon. Stir in the beets. Cook, stirring often, 10 minutes. Add salt and pepper to taste, and garnish with chopped parsley.

Serves 4.

IRMA WEHAUSEN'S PICKLED BEETS

*W*hen I was a youngster, the same grandmother who made the pink borscht seriously insisted that a small plateful of her pickled beets taken along with meat and vegetables at dinner would ward off "heartache." (She meant heartburn.) Malaprops aside, my grandmother's nostrums were not to be sneezed at: she made a very *tonic* peck of pickled beets, and who knows what magic went into the formula?

A most unlikely successor to my Jewish grandmother is a spare and dignified Lutheran churchgoer from Golden, Colorado, who gave me her own prescription some while back. Mrs. Wehausen's beets may not inhibit heartache, exactly—but they sure taste good enough to give it a whirl.

10 medium beets (about 3 pounds),
    trimmed
2 cups sugar
2 cups distilled white vinegar
2 teaspoons whole mixed pickling spices
1 medium onion, thinly sliced

1. Place the beets in a saucepan; cover with cold unsalted water. Heat slowly to boiling; reduce the heat. Simmer, uncovered, until barely tender, about 35 minutes. Drain under cold water. Remove the skins and cut into ⅛-inch-thick slices. (You should have about 6 cups.)

2. Combine 2 cups water, the sugar, vinegar, and pickling spices in a large saucepan. Heat to boiling; add the sliced beets. Return to boiling, reduce the heat, and simmer 10 minutes.

3. With a slotted spoon, transfer the beets to a large mixing bowl. Add the sliced onion and toss well.

4. Return the syrup in the saucepan to boiling; simmer until slightly reduced, about 4 minutes.

5. Place the beet-onion mixture in sterilized jars. Pour enough hot syrup into each jar to cover the beets. Seal, and let stand unrefrigerated at least one week. Chill well before serving.

Makes about 4 pints.

F or all its history of culinary restraint, the beet is a most decisive flavor-enhancer to many essentially nonbeet recipes.

For instance: a small beet added to a pan of stewing apples will produce a sweetly roseate sauce; and a mite of grated raw beet (never more than a tablespoon) will give a boost to any lackluster meat loaf, particularly if one amends the drippings with a spoon of heavy cream later.

SOUFFLE ROSE
(Beet Soufflé)

A confession.

In case you hadn't noticed, my American cooking hand is sometimes at war with a European hankering for high-blown nomenclature. Take the next recipe as a case in point: a soufflé with not a drop of *rose* in its architecture; just beets, eggs, and the usual high hopes.

3 tablespoons unsalted butter
1 tablespoon fresh fine bread crumbs
1¼ pounds beets, trimmed, tops reserved
1 teaspoon sugar
3 tablespoons all-purpose flour
1 cup hot milk
⅛ teaspoon freshly grated nutmeg
¼ teaspoon salt
⅛ teaspoon freshly ground black pepper
4 egg yolks
¾ cup grated Swiss cheese
5 egg whites
2 teaspoons cornstarch
¾ cup Beef Stock (see page 409)
3 tablespoons heavy or whipping cream

1. Rub a 1½-quart soufflé dish with 1 teaspoon of the butter. Sprinkle with bread crumbs; set aside.

2. Place the beets in a saucepan; cover with cold unsalted water. Heat slowly to boiling; reduce the heat. Simmer, uncovered, until barely tender, about 35 minutes. Drain under cold water. Remove the skins and roughly grate the beets; reserve.

3. Preheat the oven to 375°F.

4. Remove the veins from the beet tops. Cook the tops for 5 minutes in boiling water to which you have added 1 teaspoon sugar. Drain under cold water. Press lightly to remove excess liquid. Chop and reserve.

5. Melt 2 tablespoons of the butter in a medium saucepan over medium-low heat. Stir in the flour. Cook, stirring constantly, 2 minutes. Whisk in the hot milk all at once. Beat until smooth; continue to cook until very thick. Add the nutmeg, salt and pepper. Remove from the heat and beat in the egg yolks, one at a time, beating well after each addition. Transfer the mixture to a bowl. Stir in the grated beets and cheese.

6. Beat the egg whites until stiff but not dry. Fold them into the beet mixture and spoon into the prepared soufflé dish. Bake until puffed and firm, about 30 minutes.

7. Meanwhile, melt the remaining 2 teaspoons butter in a medium saucepan over medium-low heat. Stir in the cornstarch until smooth. Whisk in the beef stock. Heat to boiling; add the reserved beet tops and the cream. Reduce the heat and simmer until slightly thickened. Taste and add more salt and pepper if needed, and serve the sauce with the soufflé.

Serves 4 to 6.

RED FLANNEL HASH

T his recipe is so old-fashioned it hurts. But out of a wealth I have encountered, this is the *most* definitive version, and it's the beet's finest hour. Or maybe the second finest, after the aforementioned borscht!

½ pound beets, trimmed
2 medium potatoes, peeled
3 cups cubed cooked corned beef
2 carrots, peeled, finely chopped
1 small green pepper, seeded, finely chopped
1 large onion, finely chopped
1 small clove garlic, minced
3 tablespoons chopped fresh parsley
2½ tablespoons unsalted butter
1 teaspoon Worcestershire sauce
1 teaspoon hot pepper sauce, or to taste
¼ cup tomato juice, approximately
Salt and freshly ground black pepper
4 to 6 poached eggs

1. Place the beets in a saucepan; cover with cold unsalted water. Heat slowly to boiling; reduce the heat. Simmer, uncovered, until barely tender, about 35 minutes. Drain under cold water. Remove the skins, cube, and place in a large bowl.

2. Cook the potatoes in boiling salted water for 10 minutes. Drain. Cool slightly, cut into cubes, and add to the beets.

3. To the beets and potatoes add the corned beef, carrots, green pepper, onion, garlic, and parsley. Mix well.

4. Melt the butter in a 10-inch ovenproof skillet over medium heat. Press the corned beef mixture into the skillet. Cook, uncovered, 6 minutes. Stir in the Worcestershire sauce, hot pepper sauce, tomato juice, and salt and pepper to taste. Cook over medium-low heat, without stirring, 30 minutes.

5. While the corned beef mixture is cooking, preheat the oven to 350°F.

6. Using two large spatulas, turn the mixture over in the skillet (or flip it over into a second skillet). Place the skillet in the oven and bake until the potatoes are tender and the top is browned, about 30 minutes. Add more tomato juice if the mixture seems too dry. Serve topped with poached eggs.

Serves 4 to 6.

BROCCOLI
The Five Fingers of Jupiter

My maternal grandfather was the eldest of five brothers and a paternal type to boot. So it is not surprising that after he emigrated to America he felt compelled to send for his siblings, one by one.

Each successive "greenhorn" brother lived under my grandfather's roof—some for months, others for years—remaining in the familial nest until his patriarchal kinsman had deemed him sufficiently Americanized to fly. And long after these men had advanced to maturity (married and sired progeny of their own) their brother's opinion was inevitably sought on any business matter that concerned their well-being. No one went into business (nor out of it into bankruptcy) without his counsel. And his word, once pronounced, was considered law—except once.

Grandfather's youngest brother, Max, was twenty-five years his junior and of a very different stripe. Sent to this country as a boy (to escape conscription in the Russian army), he was obviously no trailblazer for he remained in my grandparents' home until he was past fifty. Unlike the headstrong brothers who had preceded him, the last arrival never seemed to hunger for independence. He lived most of his life in a bleak room above my grandmother's kitchen, at the top of a steep and exceedingly dark back staircase.

Max's room was like a commercial lodger's, so devoid of belongings or personal stamp it had no smell other than cleansing powder. Besides being anonymous, Max's room was also separated from the body of the house by a hallway bathroom that peremptorily locked him out of the mainstream of the family's life.

Almost a son in age to my grandmother, Max was seemingly unable to elicit from her any form of emotional response other than aloofness. Unquestionably she took pains to see he was well fed and cared for, but nothing else. And though a lifetime has passed, I can still remember how cold her soft eyes would become whenever she spoke to him. Mr grandmother had lost her first born (and only male) child shortly before Max came into her life and while no one in the family ever hinted at any Freudian connection, it seems evident that her public distaste for one stemmed from a private grief about the other.

I never knew my great-uncle when he was young, of course, but he was rumored to have had quite an eye for the ladies. Despite the gossip, Max was hardly a bachelor one might have mistaken for a romantic figure. He had a bad squint for one thing and a hoarse, laryngitic voice for another, plus a touch of deafness. Nor, to put it bluntly, was he much of a *bon vivant*; his thrift was so well marked in the family that my father always referred to him as "your mother's skinflint relative."

Max's single splurge in life was his unexpected courtship of a not-quite-divorced lady. The object of my uncle's affection was a red-haired, boisterous, and extremely well-endowed woman from Cleveland who had come, with a distant cousin of the family, to celebrate Passover in my grandparents' house.

Seder, the holiday dinner at which Jews commemorate the flight of their ancestors, is usually a fairly solemn affair, but not in our family. Both my father and uncles were irreligious types whose attitude inevitably turned the holiday into an unbridled orgy of my grandmother's cooking.

The Ohio guests were rather florid women, speaking in flat accents and laughing louder than necessary at family jokes that were made ritually, year after year. My cousin's friend, who was prettier, laughed loudest and her large bosom shook when she did.

"That lady needs a corset" was my grandmother's only comment after her Passover guest departed. Max did not respond; he had not taken his eyes off her the whole evening.

Family accounts were cloudy (particularly when one was an adolescent whose morals had to be protected at all costs) but from overheard conversations it became increasingly clear that my uncle's passion was full-fledged. And fulfilled.

Less than a month after Passover, Uncle Max made a trip to the Midwest, ostensibly on business. When he returned, he announced to my grandfather that he intended to marry the red-haired Clevelander as soon as she could obtain a divorce.

Prior to World War II, this type of behavior was not common except perhaps in Hollywood—and that was a far cry from Queens. My grandfather heartily disapproved of the match, but my uncle defied him. In due time, leaving his good graces *and* his home, he married the lady in question.

My grandparents were conspicuously absent from the wedding, though to be fair, it was held in Cleveland. My grandmother professed delight to be rid of her brother-in-law, but with a shade of foreboding: "She's too young for him and she dyes her hair. She only married him for one thing—his money. Mark my words, she'll leave him in a year's time," she warned direly, "and he'll want to come back here." That none of her prognostications came about nettled her considerably more than if they had.

To mend the family rift, after Max and his wife returned and established a home of their own, his wife prepared a long and elaborate dinner to which she invited the entire family. There was much admiration of her china and silver (assembled from the prior marriage), but my grandmother was neither swayed by these artifacts nor mollified by her evident cooking talents. I can still recall her comments on the ride home. My mother, to lighten the mood—for it was funereal, professed mild surprise that her new "aunt" cooked with such apparent proficiency.

"You call that cooking?" my grandmother expostulated with some rancor. "He'll be dead in a year's time . . . mark my words." She shook her head gravely. "Never, never trust a woman who would turn a perfectly respectable vegetable like broccoli into a *casserole* with cheese!"

And that was her last word on the subject.

Vegetable Roots

*B*roccoli is a legacy we inherited from the Romans. Caesar and all the rest of his crowd loved that leggy green (*Brassica oleracea italica*) with such a passion that it was served up twice and sometimes even three times during a meal— apparently always to the diner's delight although the method of its cookery never varied. Roman chefs simply boiled broccoli "before bruising it" in the manner that Apicius prescribed: "with a mixture of cumin and coriander seeds, chopped onion plus a few drops of oil and sun-made wine."

Drusus, the eldest son of the Emperor Tiberius, was so addicted to this recipe that the poor fellow ate nothing but broccoli for a month. According to Pliny the Elder, Drusus gave up broccoli only when his urine turned bright green, and he was severely upbraided by his father for "living precariously." Let all manic broccoli lovers profit by his example.

The word *broccoli* is a corruption of the Latin *bracchium*, which means a strong arm or branch; Roman farmers referred to this vegetable as "the five green fingers of Jupiter."

What to Look For

*U*nfortunately most broccoli comes prepackaged these days, but wise shoppers will seek out a supermarket shelf where it is kept cool. You will recognize a fresh bunch by its tight blue-green flowerets and firm stalks. Woody stems and open-cored branches should be avoided; they're hard to chew. Likewise pass by any yellowing or limp buds—always a dead giveaway of an overlong shelf-life. Strong-smelling broccoli will be even stronger-flavored when it is cooked. Skip it, please.

A good method for storing broccoli in the refrigerator comes from Janeen Sarlin, a green-thumbed cooking friend. After breaking the stalks roughly and removing the green leaves, she places the stems of an entire bunch in a 1- to 2-quart pitcher or wide-mouthed jar filled with ice water and covers it with a loose plastic bag. The broccoli stays fresh and tight as a bunch of jonquils for a week.

Preparation

*B*roccoli is easy to grow and equally easy to prepare. The trick is to cook it quickly, so that each stalk retains a measure of "bite" at the knuckle.

The classic preparation is to blanch (or steam) broccoli quickly in a small amount of boiling salted water in a covered saucepan, never longer than 4 to 5 minutes for a fork-tender floweret and a slightly more resilient stem. If you steam, allow an additional 5 or so minutes.

Different cooks have differing opinions on the steps prior to the pot. One sure-fire way to guarantee that broccoli tops and bottoms cook evenly is to peel the stalks with a vegetable parer, exactly as you would asparagus. Some kitchen pundits claim that a prefatory 30-minute soaking in cold water with a teaspoon each of sugar and salt will ensure a perfect, crisp branch. Others insist that an X incised in the base of every stem before it hits the boiling water does the trick for them. I eschew all such excess groundwork because my kitchen space and time are both severely limited. More to the point, I can never tell the difference once it's on the fork.

FLAMMIFERO

*T*his most tempting cold hors d'oeuvre comes from Rome and uses broccoli *stalks* only. The raw stalks are whittled to the size of kitchen matches. Hence the moniker: it means "matches." Reserve the flowerets for another recipe.

3 or 4 large, thick broccoli stalks (1½ to 2 pounds)
2 small ripe tomatoes, peeled, seeded, chopped
1 small clove garlic, mashed
¼ teaspoon coarse (kosher) salt
2 teaspoons lemon juice
1 teaspoon red wine vinegar
¼ cup olive oil
3 tablespoons freshly grated Parmesan cheese
Freshly ground black pepper

1. Peel the broccoli stalks and cut them into thin julienne strips, about 2 inches long. Place the strips in a bowl and add the tomatoes. Set aside.

2. Mash the garlic with the salt in a small bowl until a paste is formed. Beat in the lemon juice, vinegar, and oil. Pour the dressing over the broccoli. Add the cheese and pepper to taste. Toss well. Chill at least 1 hour before serving.

Serves 4 to 6.

BROCCOLI HOT POT

*B*roccoli is an excellent base for soups as it has a remarkable affinity for those things dear to any tureen: chicken broth, potatoes, leeks, and garlic too! My favored broccoli soup prescription actually has a double life. It comes to the table first as a rough-and-tumble hot chowder; then the leftovers make a second appearance, as a pale viridian Broccoli Vichyssoise.

1 pound broccoli
2 leeks
1 tablespoon unsalted butter
1 clove garlic, minced
⅛ teaspoon crushed dried hot red peppers

3 medium potatoes, peeled, diced
3½ cups chicken broth (see page 414)
¼ teaspoon freshly grated nutmeg
Salt and freshly ground black pepper

1. Cut the broccoli tops into flowerets and set them aside.

2. Cut off the top 3 inches of the stems, peel them, and cut them into thin strips, about 1½ inches long. Set them aside.

3. Trim the leeks, leaving about 2 inches of green ends. Wash the leeks thoroughly under cold running water to remove all sand. Pat dry on paper towels. Chop, and set aside.

4. Melt the butter in a large saucepan over medium-low heat. Add the chopped leeks. Cook, stirring occasionally, 4 minutes. Add the garlic and crushed red pepper; cook 3 minutes longer.

5. Add the broccoli flowerets, broccoli stems, and potatoes to the saucepan. Toss lightly. Add the chicken broth and heat to boiling; reduce the heat. Simmer the soup, uncovered, until the broccoli and potatoes are tender, about 25 minutes. Season with the nutmeg, and salt and pepper to taste.

Serves 4 to 6.

BROCCOLI VICHYSSOISE

A long while back, Craig Claiborne started a campaign to instruct Americans how *vichyssoise* should be pronounced. For the record, it's not *veeshy-swah*, but *veeshee-swahze*! The campaign never got very far, but the soup has endured on restaurant menus around the world for almost fifty years. My version, based on the Broccoli Hot Pot above, merely blends the soup (warm) with cream and milk. If you are using leftover soup, just add equal amounts of cream and milk until you come up with a velvety texture. Chill it well before serving.

1 whole recipe Broccoli Hot Pot (see above)
2 cups heavy or whipping cream
2 cups milk, approximately
Salt and freshly ground black pepper
3 tablespoons finely chopped raw broccoli flowerets

1. Make the Broccoli Hot Pot and allow it to cool slightly.

2. Purée the soup in a blender or processor (carefully: warm liquid will expand). Transfer it to a large bowl and add the cream and enough milk for a smooth consistency. Season to taste. Chill thoroughly before serving garnished with chopped broccoli.

Serves 8 or more.

BROCCOLI VALENCIENNE

Two of my best broccoli recipes are summer dividends that may be eaten all year round. Salads (or first courses if you insist), they are amended with the flavors of orange or tomato. The first is a residual of a trip to Spain; the second—Tomato Broccoli—springs full-blown from my catering days at The Store in Amagansett.

1½ to 2 pounds broccoli
2 large shallots, minced
1 small red onion, thinly sliced
1 teaspoon finely slivered orange peel
1 teaspoon Dijon mustard
3 tablespoons tarragon vinegar
1 tablespoon dry sherry
¾ cup olive oil
Salt and freshly ground black pepper
¼ cup toasted slivered almonds

1. Cut the broccoli tops into flowerets. Cut off the top 3 inches of the stems, peel them, and cut into thin strips, about 1½ inches long. Cook flowerets and stems, covered, in 3 inches boiling salted water until just barely tender, 4 to 5 minutes. Rinse under cold running water. Drain.

2. Transfer the drained broccoli to a large bowl. Add the shallots, onion, and orange peel. Toss lightly.

3. Combine the mustard with the vinegar, sherry, and oil in a medium bowl. Pour the dressing over the broccoli

T hough broccoli became popular in America in the mid-twentieth century, it arrived here a heck of a long time before that. Most food snoops credit Thomas Jefferson with the distinction of bringing broccoli seeds from Italy to his bountiful gardens at Monticello.

Jefferson's broccoli plants flourished, but the green was never a popular dish at his table. Having done some research on Jeffersonian cuisine lately, I suspect it was because his kitchen staff overcooked it! And as T.J. liked vegetables to have a bite . . . he overlooked it!

and season with salt and pepper to taste. Chill thoroughly before serving sprinkled with almonds.

Serves 4 to 6.

TOMATO BROCCOLI

1½ pounds broccoli
2 tablespoons unsalted butter
1 tablespoon vegetable oil
1 medium onion, chopped
1 clove garlic, minced
2 medium tomatoes, chopped
1 teaspoon sugar
1 teaspoon fresh basil, or ½ teaspoon dried
1 teaspoon fresh oregano, or ½ teaspoon dried
½ cup Mayonnaise (see page 408)
Salt and freshly ground black pepper
Halved cherry tomatoes (optional)

1. Cut the broccoli tops into flowerets. Cut off the top 3 inches of the stems,

peel them, and cut them into thin strips, about 1½ inches long. Cook flowerets and stems, covered, in 3 inches boiling salted water until just barely tender, 4 to 5 minutes. Rinse under cold water. Drain, and set aside.

2. Heat the butter with the oil in a medium saucepan over medium-low heat. Add the onion; cook 2 minutes. Add the garlic; cook 2 minutes longer. Stir in the tomatoes; sprinkle with the sugar, basil, and oregano. Simmer, uncovered, over medium heat until soft, about 15 minutes. Cool slightly.

3. Transfer the tomato mixture to

the container of a food processor or blender. Process until smooth. In a large bowl, combine the tomato purée with the mayonnaise. Add the broccoli; mix thoroughly. Add salt and pepper to taste. Chill thoroughly before serving garnished with cherry tomato halves.

Serves 4.

BLEU BROCCOLI WITH WALNUTS

An alliance of broccoli sauced with bleu cheese and walnuts that may soon become a classic.

1½ pounds broccoli
¼ pound creamy bleu cheese
¼ cup heavy or whipping cream
2 teaspoons unsalted butter
1 small clove garlic, minced
½ cup roughly chopped walnuts
¼ teaspoon freshly ground black pepper

1. Cut the broccoli tops into flowerets. Cut off the top 3 inches of the stems, peel them, and cut them into thin strips, about 1½ inches long. Cook flowerets and stems, covered, in 3 inches boiling salted water until just barely tender, 4 to 5 minutes. Drain.

2. Mash the bleu cheese with the cream in a small bowl until fairly smooth. Set aside.

3. Melt the butter in a medium-size saucepan over medium heat. Add the garlic and walnuts. Cook, stirring constantly, until lightly browned.

4. Add the broccoli to the walnuts. Add the cheese mixture and pepper. Toss until just warmed through.

Serves 4.

PAPPA D'BROCCOLE

The name of this Venetian dish translates literally as broccoli porridge. But if you would feel better calling it a purée, be my guest.

1½ pounds broccoli
3 tablespoons unsalted butter
2 shallots, chopped
1¼ cups beef broth (see page 414)
⅓ cup chopped sliced prosciutto
½ cup heavy or whipping cream

1. Cut the broccoli tops into flowerets and set them aside.

2. Cut off the top 3 inches of the stems, peel them, and cut them into thin strips, about 1½ inches long. Set them aside.

3. Melt the butter in a medium saucepan over medium-low heat. Add the shallots; cook 2 minutes. Add the broccoli stems and beef broth. Cook, covered, until tender, about 10 minutes.

4. Add the broccoli flowerets, raise

the heat, and cook, uncovered, until almost all liquid has evaporated. Add the prosciutto and continue to cook until all the liquid has evaporated, about 3 minutes. Stir in the cream; cook 3 minutes longer.

5. Transfer the broccoli mixture to a blender or food processor, and process until smooth but not mushy. Reheat slightly before serving.

Serves 4.

CHEVRE'D BROCCOLI

A second broccoli-cum-cheese presentation. This time the vegetable is bedded in a snowy blanket of goat cheese and herbs.

1½ pounds broccoli
2 tablespoons unsalted butter
1 tablespoon olive oil
2 shallots, minced
1 clove garlic, minced
¼ cup Chicken Stock (see page 410)
⅔ cup crumbled chèvre (goat cheese)
1 teaspoon chopped chives
1 teaspoon chopped fresh basil, or ½
*   teaspoon dried*
½ teaspoon chopped fresh tarragon, or a
*   pinch of dried*
1 teaspoon chopped fresh parsley
Salt and freshly ground black pepper

1. Cut the broccoli tops into flowerets. Cut off about 3 inches of the stems, peel them, and cut them into thin strips, about 1½ inches long. Set both aside.

2. Heat the butter with the oil in a medium saucepan over medium-low heat. Add the shallots; cook 2 minutes. Add the garlic; cook 1 minute longer. Add the broccoli flowerets and stems and toss to coat each piece. Add the chicken stock. Cover, and cook until just barely tender, 4 to 5 minutes.

3. Raise the heat slightly and cook, uncovered, until all but 1 tablespoon liquid has evaporated. (Do not leave more than that in the pan.) Toss in the

chèvre and continue to cook, tossing constantly, until the cheese melts and forms a sauce. Sprinkle with the herbs and add salt and pepper to taste.

Serves 4.

Until the late 1920s virtually no one in America had ever heard of broccoli, let alone tasted it—with the exception of Italian immigrants like our neighbors the Pitellas. I can still recall their garden because it was so unlike everyone else's neatly manicured plot of greenery on the street. No zinnia, gladiolus, or blue flag iris flourished in the sun trap behind their house. Instead, the Pitellas staked tomatoes, peppers, eggplant, and zucchini. Basil bordered their rows and broccoli grew like a weed betwixt the bamboo tethers. It was a windfall of flavors, a veritable *verdura Siciliano*, on the vine. Yet no Greene could be persuaded to try a forkful. Why? Fear of the unknown, I guess. There is a moral here: live and learn—to love broccoli!

BROCCOLI FRITTATA, PARMA STYLE

*T*his is the very best Italian frittata I have ever sampled.

5 tablespoons unsalted butter
1 tablespoon olive oil
1 medium onion, chopped
1 clove garlic, minced
½ cup cooked chopped ham or Canadian
    bacon
2 cups small broccoli flowerets (from about
    1¼ pounds broccoli)
20 strands cooked spaghetti, roughly
    chopped (leftover is fine)
6 eggs
½ cup freshly grated Parmesan cheese
½ teaspoon crushed dried hot red pepper

1. Heat 3 tablespoons of the butter with the oil in a heavy 10-inch skillet over medium heat. Sauté the onion until golden. Add the garlic and ham; cook 3 minutes. Stir in the broccoli flowerets and spaghetti; toss until well coated with the mixture. Remove from the heat.

2. Beat the eggs in a large bowl until light. Add the broccoli mixture and all but 2 tablespoons of the Parmesan cheese.

3. Melt 1 tablespoon of the butter in the same skillet over medium heat. Pour in the broccoli-egg mixture. Immediately reduce the heat to low; cook, without stirring, 20 minutes.

4. Using a long spatula, carefully loosen the edges of the frittata and run the spatula underneath to loosen the bottom. Place a shallow plate over the skillet and quickly invert the frittata onto it.

5. Melt the remaining 1 tablespoon butter in the same skillet over medium-low heat. Carefully slide the frittata back into the pan. Sprinkle it with the crushed pepper and the remaining Parmesan cheese. Cook 5 minutes longer. Serve from the pan, in wedges—hot, cold, or at room temperature.

Serves 4 to 6.

BROCCOLI MOUSSELINE

*I*n Italy broccoli is sometimes called the "poor man's asparagus," because the ideal rendering for one is so much like the other. Hollandaise sauce is indubitably asparagus' finest upholstery, and you won't go wrong with a spoonful of it on broccoli either. But, in my opinion at least, the rougher texture of the latter green benefits from a silkier and somewhat lightened dressing on occasion. Hence broccoli sluiced with mousseline sauce: hollandaise plus unsweetened whipped cream.

1½ to 2 pounds broccoli
2 egg yolks
2 tablespoons lemon juice
1½ teaspoons Dijon mustard
8 tablespoons (1 stick) unsalted butter,
    frozen

Dash of hot pepper sauce
Pinch of ground white pepper
Salt
¼ cup heavy or whipping cream

1. Pull apart the large stems of the broccoli bunch. Cut off the bottoms of the stems, leaving about 3½ inches. Peel the stems, and split the large ones in half lengthwise. Cook the broccoli, covered, in 3 inches of boiling salted water until just barely tender, 4 to 5 minutes. Drain. Transfer to a serving platter and keep warm.

2. Beat the egg yolks with the lemon juice in the top of a double boiler. Place it over boiling water, being careful that the bottom of the pan does not touch the water. Stir in the mustard.

3. Divide the butter into eight pieces. Using a fork, stir the butter into the egg yolk mixture, one piece at a time. Stir well after each addition. Stir in the hot pepper sauce, white pepper, and salt to taste. Remove from the heat.

4. Beat the cream until stiff and fold it into the egg yolk mixture. Spoon the sauce over the broccoli.

Serves 4 to 6.

BROCCOLI AND PASTA TIMBALE

Despite my grandmother's pox on the subject, this is the best broccoli casserole formula I have ever encountered. If my forebear were alive, her riposte would be: "Casserole, schmasserole. If it tastes good—that's all that matters!"

1½ pounds broccoli
7 tablespoons unsalted butter
2 tablespoons olive oil
1 shallot, minced
½ cup chopped cooked ham
4 tablespoons all-purpose flour
1 cup hot Chicken Stock (see page 410)
1 cup heavy or whipping cream
¼ teaspoon freshly grated nutmeg
1 tablespoon lemon juice
Dash of hot pepper sauce
1 pound rigatoni (stem pasta) or fusilli
    (corkscrew pasta)
1 cup ricotta cheese
½ cup freshly grated Parmesan cheese
½ cup cubed Fontina cheese (cut in ¼-inch
    cubes)
Chopped fresh parsley

1. Cut the broccoli tops into flowerets. Cut off the top 3 inches of the stems, peel them, and cut them into strips, about 1½ inches long. Set both aside.

2. Heat 2 tablespoons of the butter with the oil in a large skillet over medium-low heat. Add the shallot; cook 3 minutes. Add the broccoli flowerets and stems and the ham. Cook, covered, until the broccoli is tender, about 10 minutes. Raise the heat and cook, uncovered, until all moisture has evaporated. Set aside.

3. Melt the remaining 5 tablespoons butter in a medium skillet over low heat. Beat in the flour. Cook, stirring constantly, 2 minutes. Beat in the hot chicken stock all at once. Beat in the cream. Heat to boiling; reduce the heat. Simmer until very thick. Add nutmeg, lemon juice, and hot pepper sauce. Set aside.

4. Meanwhile, cook the pasta in boiling salted water until just barely tender (al dente), about 10 to 12 minutes. Drain.

5. Transfer the pasta to a large bowl. Add the sauce, the ricotta cheese, and the Parmesan cheese. Mix thoroughly.

6. Preheat the oven to 400°F.

7. Butter a 2-quart soufflé dish. Place one third of the pasta mixture in the dish. Add half the broccoli mixture and half the Fontina cheese, pressing down lightly. Add another one third of the pasta, then the remaining broccoli and Fontina cheese. Finish with the remaining pasta.

8. Place in the oven and bake 25 minutes. Let stand for 8 minutes, then run a knife around the edges of the dish. Cover with a serving platter. Gently invert to unmold. Sprinkle with parsley.

Serves 6.

BROCCOLI PESTO

*B*roccoli is one of the vitamin-high Brassicas (4,500 units vitamin A, 481 milligrams potassium, and 158 milligrams calcium per stalk). It is also happily low in calories (a scant 40 per cupful). This fortuitous happenstance gives a chef some license. Witness the following broccoli pesto sauce to drench over yards and yards of buttered pasta.

2 cups small broccoli flowerets (from about 1½ pounds broccoli)
½ cup coarsely chopped fresh basil leaves
2 large cloves garlic, roughly chopped
¼ cup pine nuts
½ teaspoon coarse (kosher) salt
¼ teaspoon freshly ground black pepper
1 cup olive oil
½ cup freshly grated Parmesan cheese

Place the broccoli in the container of a food processor or blender. Add the basil, garlic, pine nuts, salt, pepper, and oil. Process until smooth. Transfer to a bowl and stir in the cheese. To serve, toss into warm buttered pasta.

Note: Pesto can be kept refrigerated in a tightly covered jar for a week. It may also be frozen, but then it is best not to stir in the cheese until after defrosting.

Makes about 2½ cups, 8 to 10 servings.

BRUSSELS SPROUTS

Belgium's Best Known Ambassadors

Coming from a time unblessed (or unblemished) by modern horticultural technology, I clearly remember when vegetables tasted and looked as Mother Nature intended: flavorful without a doubt, but cosmetically for the birds!

My childhood was spent scrupulously avoiding almost every green gift of the garden that came to the table—not out of dislike but out of panic. For the greenest were inevitably tainted with plant borers, rust, and Lord knows what other form of agricultural scourge.

Skipping the "nightly greens" wasn't easy. My mother, who had once contemplated going to medical school, was not a squeamish person. More pertinently, she did not condone that weakness in either her spouse or her offspring. Her appetite was never dampened by a pinch of sand in the spinach or, worse yet, the discovery of some parboiled alien in the Brussels sprouts, so she could never understand our hue and cry over these indignities. She even had an umbrella maxim to cover any such contingency: "You have to eat a peck of dirt in this life," she would announce airily, pushing any offending object aside on her dinner plate.

She was probably right, but all the earthly contaminations wilted my enthusiasm for second helpings. And I felt victimized by all manner of headed greens for years to come.

Bouts with Brussels sprouts were most painful because I dearly admired the sight of those rosebud cabbages blooming on a single stalk in my grandmother's garden. I also prized the way she cooked them: tossed in brown butter and adorned with chopped nuts or bread crumbs. But then I had spent hours at that good housekeeper's kitchen sink, watching as she scrupulously parted each tiny leaf to make absolutely sure no offending insect ever entered a skillet.

My mother tried that too. But, poor lady, her flesh was weak when it came to what I now recognize as arduous precooking preparation. After unfurling and picking over the first dozen sprouts, she would usually dump the rest into boiling water and let nature take its course.

I will never forget the sensation of utter helplessness when I uncovered a curled denizen of the garden in the center of a partially consumed sprout at our dinner table.

"A worm," I shrieked, throwing my utensils to the floor and kicking my heels. For it was actually *half* a worm I had found. And no amount of supplication or the promise of chocolate cake later could assuage the offense to my wounded sensibilities.

"You let me eat a worm!" I accused.

My mother was sanguine on the subject. "Listen," she said, "I'm sorry. But what happened to you was just part of the balance of nature. Worms have to eat and survive like everybody else, don't they?"

She got no argument from me. Worms' territorial rights were inviolate from that moment on. I simply never ate another Brussels sprout for a decade. Perhaps two.

I also cheered the invention of DDT, which demonstrates how a warped appetite can affect one's sense of survival. But later on, when I had become a gardener myself, I recanted—especially when I read the fine print on the insecticide bottles. And anyway, the cabbage caterpillar is one of the loveliest butterflies in the garden.

Vegetable Roots

Romans called these tender buttons *bullata gemmifera* (diamond-makers) because consumption was rumored to enhance a diner's mental agility. However, Mark Antony is said to have chewed sprouts for days before the battle of Actium—so take that hearsay with a grain of salt.

What was true about these minicabbages during antiquity was their rareness. Roman chefs imported them from the seacoasts of western Europe, where they grew wild. Because the cabbage formed a "head," early surgeons assumed sprouts were a natural cure for "drunkenness and the head-ache proceeding from the same," according to Pliny the Elder.

No one knows for certain how or when the Brussels sprout first came to Brussels, but most certainly it is a vegetable that flourishes best in Belgium's particularly rich and loamy soil.

Sprouts have been a source of Flemish national pride for over eight centuries now, gracing palace tablerie and rough peasant boards alike; most often paired with smoky sausages or tender cuts of pink ham. But not until 1820 was the Brussels sprout officially recognized by the king of Belgium's seedsmen as that country's official green.

What to Look For

In Belgium and elsewhere, Brussels sprouts are grown as a fall crop; aficionados claim they are at their best after the first snow falls, for curiously a touch of frost is reputed to sweeten a sprout's flavor.

Shoppers are well advised to search

Anyone who has ever seen a crop of Brussels sprouts in full bloom will understand the kitchen gardener's ambivalence about harvesting them. Like vertical corsages, *Brassica oleracea gemmifera* grow in tight green rosettes on a single stalk that towers over every other leaf vegetable in its immediate vicinity. The furled globes (jammed together on a thick stem) are crowned, moreover, by a full-blown cabbage rose, so top-heavy it appears to dwarf the green treasures in its shadow. But have no fear, Brussels sprouts grow sweeter in the shade!

out the smallest and tightest buds they can find. Garden-fresh sprouts are inevitably crisp to the fingernail and bright green to the eye. Pass by any loose-leafed varieties; Brussels sprouts, like rosebuds, tend to open up after a hiatus on the refrigerator shelf. Likewise avoid yellowing (or rusted) leaves because that is a dead giveaway that the sprout is well past its prime—and usually too strong-tasting to mate with other seasonings.

In Belgium they consider it *déclassé* to serve up a Brussels sprout that is bigger than a child's fingernail. I once watched a large and obviously self-indulgent gentleman consume a whole plateful at one sitting, using nothing but his fingers plus a vast napkin stretched across his chest to catch the overflow. Gastronome or glutton? I cannot say, but he certainly must have had a smattering of nutrition. A cup of cooked Brussels sprouts contains a whopping 810 units of vitamin A, 423 milligrams of potassium, and 112 milligrams of phosphorus with healthy jots of thiamine, riboflavin and

ascorbic acid for good measure. Brussels sprouts make choice diet food too, containing a scant 55 calories to every dozen average-size buds. The child's fingernail variety (if ever you could find them) not only taste like velvet but contain less than 2 calories apiece. So bring on the oil and vinegar!

Brussels sprouts are usually packaged in 10-ounce cartons, which yield approximately four servings. Most diners will find that amount sufficient; but for heartier appetites cooks should use their own judgment.

Preparation

*T*he classic way with a Brussels sprout, prior to any other kitchen dress-up, is to either blanch or parboil it, covered, in a large heavy saucepan—preferably one of nonreactive metal such as enameled cast iron or stainless steel. Always pull off any loose outer leaves and trim the stems to a bare minimum. But take care not to slice the stems so close that the sprouts disintegrate in the cooking process. A tiny X cut in the base of each sprout with a sharp knife will hasten the cooking considerably.

To boil sprouts, place them in lightly salted boiling water and cook, covered, for about 12 to 15 minutes, depending upon their size—until they may be easily pierced with a fork. I usually allow 1 cup of boiling water to 1 cup of Brussels sprouts. When they are done, plunge the sprouts under cold running water to retard the cooking. Then proceed with the recipe at hand.

To steam them, place the trimmed sprouts in a steamer tray (or a colander) over a minimum amount of boiling water. Take care that the steamer does not actually touch the water. Cover, and steam until the sprouts are tender-crisp (or *al dente*, as the Italians say), about 10 to 15 minutes. Do not overcook!

BRUSSELS SPROUTS A LA GRECQUE

One of the most enticing openers I know is a melding of Brussels sprouts with herbs and oil, Greek style. This recipe is the brainchild of Roseanne Schlussel, who makes an infinite number of airplane trips between Birmingham, Michigan, and New York City yearly, but never without an interesting recipe tucked up her sleeve.

1 cup water
½ cup olive oil
¼ cup lemon juice
Bouquet garni: 2 parsley sprigs, 1 bay leaf,
*   2 tarragon sprigs, 6 peppercorns, and*
*   ½ teaspoon celery seed, tied in a small*
*   cheesecloth bag*
1 pound Brussels sprouts, trimmed, an X
*   cut in each stem end*
1 teaspoon red wine vinegar
1 teaspoon finely slivered lemon peel
Salt and freshly ground black pepper
1 tablespoon chopped fresh parsley

1. Combine the water, olive oil, lemon juice, and bouquet garni in a medium saucepan. Heat to boiling; reduce the heat. Simmer, uncovered, 10 minutes.

2. Add the Brussels sprouts to the saucepan; return to boiling. Continue to cook, uncovered, until the sprouts are barely tender, about 10 minutes. Remove from the heat; let the sprouts cool in the liquid. Discard the bouquet garni.

3. Transfer the sprouts with their liquid to a serving bowl. Add the vinegar, lemon peel, and salt and pepper to taste. Toss well; chill thoroughly. Serve garnished with parsley.

Serves 4 to 6.

BRUSSELS SPROUTS IN PECAN BUTTER

Another classic rendition of Brussels sprouts is to combine them with crunchy chestnuts—this is the way they are usually eaten in the British Isles. However, my American tongue has a preference for a somewhat more flavorsome nut: pecans.

1 pound Brussels sprouts, trimmed, an X
*   cut in each stem end*
3 tablespoons unsalted butter
¼ cup roughly chopped pecans
Freshly ground black pepper

1. Cook the Brussels sprouts, covered, in boiling salted water until tender, about 10 minutes. Drain. Transfer the sprouts to a shallow serving dish and keep warm.

2. Heat the butter in a small saucepan until it begins to turn brown. Add the chopped pecans; toss until they are lightly browned, but do not allow them to burn. Pour the pecans over the Brussels sprouts and sprinkle with pepper to taste.

Serves 4 to 6.

CLASSIC CREAMED BRUSSELS SPROUTS

*P*robably the most generally accepted upholstery for a Brussels sprout is a mite of butter and a pinch of bread crumbs. My own preference runs to more velvety alliances. For instance, consider this version of creamed Brussels sprouts, which I found scribbled in pencil on the margin of a yellowing recipe book (circa 1918) by an unknown but obviously knowing cook.

1 pound Brussels sprouts, trimmed, an X
  cut in each stem end
1½ cups milk
1 tablespoon unsalted butter
⅓ cup heavy or whipping cream
Salt and freshly ground black pepper

1. Cook the Brussels sprouts in boiling salted water for 10 minutes. Drain.

2. In a medium saucepan slowly heat the milk to boiling; do not scorch. Stir in the Brussels sprouts. Simmer, uncovered, over medium-low heat until almost all the milk has evaporated, about 30 minutes.

3. Add the butter and cream to the Brussels sprouts. Continue to cook until warmed through, 4 to 5 minutes. Add salt and pepper to taste.

Serves 4 to 6.

MARY BALL'S SPROUT AND FENNEL CHOWDER

A dozen years ago I spent an autumn on a steep and rocky mountainside in Provence where my neighbors were a retired British Navy commander and his wife. As "resident colonials" they kept track of all new arrivals and regularly issued invitations to share a meal and/or the *London Times*.

The Commander's wife was an excellent cook. One of her memorable creations was a stockpot union of very Anglo-Saxon sprouts with a bulb of equally Gallic fennel. The result is no mere soup, I think you'll agree.

4 tablespoons (½ stick) unsalted butter
1 medium onion, chopped
1 small clove garlic, minced
10 ounces Brussels sprouts, trimmed, sliced
  lengthwise
1 small fennel bulb, trimmed, chopped
  (about 2 cups)
1 teaspoon anise seed, crushed
3 cups chicken broth (see page 414)

Salt and freshly ground black pepper
4 to 6 slices toasted French bread
4 to 6 teaspoons freshly grated Parmesan
  cheese

1. Melt the butter in a large saucepan over medium-low heat. Add the onion; cook 2 minutes. Stir in the garlic and sauté until golden, 4 to 5 minutes.

Add the Brussels sprouts, fennel, and anise seed. Cook, covered, 15 minutes.

2. Add the chicken broth to the saucepan. Heat to boiling; reduce the heat. Simmer, covered, 30 minutes. Add salt and pepper to taste.

3. To serve: Preheat the broiler. La-dle the soup into individual heatproof serving bowls. Float a piece of toast in each bowl. Sprinkle each toast with 1 teaspoon cheese and heat under the broiler until golden.

Serves 4 to 6.

BRUSSELS SPROUTS SOUFFLE

Many good cooks rebel at the notion of converting the eminently chewable sprout into a semiliquefied pool of green ooze. You name it: *purée, mousse,* or even, God save us, *sorbet.* I too applaud the notion of this vegetable as an honest-to-goodness viand rather than a nouvelle cuisine adjunct, but I must confess that my favored sprout formula is a soufflé so airy it almost floats out of the oven on its own steam. If not actually an art form, this may be Brussels sprouts' finest hour.

Unsalted butter
1 tablespoon freshly grated Parmesan
*   cheese*
8 to 10 ounces Brussels sprouts, trimmed
1 medium potato, peeled, cubed
½ cup heavy or whipping cream
3 egg yolks
⅛ teaspoon freshly grated nutmeg
Dash of hot pepper sauce
Salt and freshly ground black pepper
4 egg whites

1. Butter a 1-quart soufflé dish and sprinkle the grated cheese over the bottom and sides. Set aside in a cool place.

2. Cook the Brussels sprouts with the potato, uncovered, in boiling salted water for 15 minutes; drain.

3. Preheat the oven to 400°F.

4. Place half the Brussels sprouts and potato in the container of a food processor or blender. Add ¼ cup cream and process until smooth. Transfer to a medium saucepan and repeat with the remaining sprouts, potato, and cream. Add the second batch to the saucepan.

5. Heat the puréed mixture to boiling; remove from the heat and let stand 1 minute. Beat in the egg yolks, one at a time, beating thoroughly after each addition. Add the nutmeg, hot pepper sauce, and salt and pepper to taste.

6. Beat the egg whites until stiff; fold them into the puréed mixture. Pour the mixture into the prepared soufflé dish. Place the dish in the oven and immediately reduce the heat to 375°F. Bake until puffed up and golden, 30 to 35 minutes.

Serves 6.

Brussels sprouts come with a clutch of odd monikers in other languages. Though the French dub them *chou de Bruxelles* (literally the cabbage of Brussels), Germans disguise them into another plant entirely: *Rosenkohl* (cabbage roses). Italians for some unfathomable reason know them as *cavolina de Brusselle* (the little horses of Brussels).

BLAZING BRUSSELS SPROUTS AND GINGERED SHRIMP

One cuisine that my addled brain could not possibly think of adapting the Brussels sprout to is the Chinese. But curiously, one of the signal dishes in my sprouts repertoire was appropriated from Szechuan cuisine. A fiery compound of shrimp, peppers, ginger, and sprouts, this dish may be whipped up (in a wok) in minutes. But the memory stays a good bit longer on the tongue.

10 ounces Brussels sprouts, trimmed, an X
   cut into each stem end
¼ cup peanut or vegetable oil
8 whole scallions, bulbs and green tops
   chopped separately
2 cloves garlic, minced
1½ tablespoons minced fresh ginger root
1 pound shrimp, shelled, deveined
1 teaspoon crushed dried hot red peppers
2 tablespoons chili sauce
1 teaspoon ground mild chiles or chili
   powder
2 tablespoons sesame oil
2 tablespoons dry sherry
2 tablespoons water
Cooked rice

1. Cook the Brussels sprouts, uncovered, in boiling salted water for 8 minutes. Rinse under cold running water; drain. Cut into ¼-inch-thick slices crosswise; reserve.

2. Heat the oil in a wok or large skillet over medium heat until hot but not smoking. Add the chopped scallion bulbs; cook 1 minute. Stir in the garlic and ginger. Cook until golden, about 3 minutes. Add the shrimp and hot peppers. Cook, tossing constantly, until the shrimp turn pink, 3 to 4 minutes.

3. Combine the chili sauce, ground chiles, sesame oil, sherry, and water in a small bowl. Stir this into the shrimp mixture and cook 1 minute. Add the Brussels sprouts; continue to cook, stirring constantly, until warmed through. Add the chopped scallion tops. Serve over rice.

Serves 4 or 5.

CABBAGE

You Never Have to Ask "What's Cooking"

Raised in what I choose to recollect as simpler times, almost any memory I have of a holiday is indelibly associated with good things to eat.

Thanksgiving, for instance, was never so much a time of benediction in my family as it was an occasion of absolutely unreined feasting. And though the house was filled with an aggregate of odd relatives who spoke in unfamiliar (Midwestern) accents and often wore rather startling clothes, it was the gaudier assemblage of dishes prepared in the kitchen that truly bedazzled me.

To be utterly candid, my parents were curiously matched celebrants. What my mother loved best were all the accoutrements of entertaining. Gleaming silver, snowy damask, and rose-rimmed Limoges (with reassuring bands of eighteen-karat gold on every plate) heartened her far more than the idea of wining and dining the myriad guests who yearly invaded her home. My father, on quite the other hand, preferred the people to the panoply. He simply demanded bounteous and inexhaustible provisions to feed them all.

Even though the wintry economic weather of the 1930s inhibited my father's largess a trifle, the Depression never totally blighted his generous impulses toward company, particularly at the dinner table. In Sam Greene's judgment, holidays were meant to be observed with masses of food and an open liquor cabinet. Indeed these commemorative meals, boasting a prodigious number of courses, went on so long that my mother would take pity on the hired girl in the kitchen and send her home long before dessert and coffee were served. As a consequence my mother would usually wash the dishes herself past midnight (cursing all the while) as my father, the hospitable host, snored in his bed.

If my parent's nature was generous, his tastebuds were frugal as can be. Also, his teeth were faulty and the only foods he actually enjoyed were either boiled, stewed, or fricasseed, so turkey never pleased him in the least. On one occasion, I remember my mother prior to the holiday meal, poring over the kitchen bible she summoned up for culinary ammunition (Fannie Farmer) as her husband ticked off the reasons why the big bird be excluded that year.

"Turkey takes so much time to chew." he complained. "The only thing I ever give thanks for is that I've finally swallowed it!"

My mother kept her temper under control during his diatribe. "Okay," she said at last, "what do you want instead? Duck? Chicken? There's a recipe here for squab under glass."

"No, no, Paulie dear." My father knew how to pointedly ignore her sarcasm. "What I would like for Thanksgiving is something *really* different."

"Like what *really*?"

My father winked before he answered her. "Like corned beef and cabbage."

My mother's reaction is unprintable. But it was a significant riposte.

Oddly enough, his request was duly honored but what transpired between the principals to occasion its happening I cannot tell you. I do know that I will never forget that meal as long as I live. Fully four months prior to Saint Patrick's Day, our house was virtually awash with the eye-stinging perfume of salt beef bubbling away on the stove. And though chrysanthemums were crammed into every vase my mother could muster to counter the scent, cabbage alone was the Greenes' Thanksgiving bouquet.

Vegetable Roots

Historians who have sifted the evidence of man's first serious attempts at cookery conclude it may very well have been a green head of *Brassica oleracea capitata* that occasioned the invention of the cooking pot. When the Paleolithic tongue demanded surcease from an exclusive diet of scorch, pragmatic firetenders fashioned small flat vessels on which to cook meat over live coals rather than tossing it into the fire itself—thus changing the concept of sustenance into something akin to pleasure for the very first time.

With formal cookery came other changes in tribal habits. Meal-taking became a communal ritual, and grasses and grains eventually were added to the meat to stretch it to feed the entire family. Wild cabbage required a larger vessel to fit its ample proportions—and the first cooking pot came into being.

Or so it is bruited about by archeological types.

As I mentioned elsewhere, Brussels sprouts, broccoli, cauliflower—kale and kohlrabi too—are all kissing cousins, descendants of this *true* cabbage. And though it is hard to find a distinct family resemblance, all offshoots of the initial *Brassica* plant do share at least one common characteristic: a strong and unmistakable aroma that is emitted during protracted bouts of cooking. But even that drawback has obviously not diminished the ardor of deep-dyed cabbage lovers from Dublin to Djakarta.

Actually, cabbage has held its own as

Early cabbages grew straight up rather than in the round. The plant's Latin name was *caulia*, which means stem, or more precisely, a very thick stalk. From that etymological evidence one must presume that all inaugural cabbages resembled the Chinese bok choy in shape—if not in subtle flavoring, since *caulia* was a term of slight disparagement among the Romans, implying rudeness!

No one seems to know for sure when cabbages headed up. However, when Caesar invaded Britain, he brought spherical cabbages along as K-rations, and they are noted in his diaries as *capitalae*, "with heads," so evolution or agronomy must have had something to do with its mutation. Fast!

a food staple in Europe and northern Africa for over four thousand years. Until the beginning of the twentieth century, most agronomists assumed that this green-leafed vegetable was native to western soil. However, during the Boxer Rebellion in China, scrolls from 1000 B.C. were uncovered which detail the prescription of white cabbage as the only cure for barrenness in males of advanced age. The Egyptians raised altars to it, and Greeks (and Romans too) believed that cabbage infallibly cured every disease from paralysis to pleurisy. From my own experience, I will tell you that sauerkraut (pickled cabbage) taken in sensible doses prior to a night of heavy drinking will go pretty far to alleviate the *angst* inherent in most hangovers!

What to Look For

The English word "cabbage" is a corruption of the old French word *caboche*, which means "head." Shoppers are advised to take the word to heart. Look for only the headiest (firm, smooth, and tightly circumscribed) oval on your greengrocer's shelf and it will usually be the most flavorsome on the fork.

At the tip of Long Island (where I reside from time to time), hardy cabbage lovers are encouraged to pick their own during the last autumnal blooming before Thanksgiving, when these greens are at their best. A touch of late November chill gives cabbage an extra measure of sweetness, it seems; so the cognoscenti always wait till the air is so bone-chilling that one's hand freezes on contact with the frosty leaf!

Cabbage is really low in calories: a shade under 15 per cupful (and that goes for green, white, and Savoy varieties as well). Red cabbage, slightly sweeter, is slightly higher: 20 calories per cup.

Cabbage is high in potassium (163 milligrams in the average portion), and high in water as well (92 percent per cup), which makes enriching it no hardship—even for a serious dieter.

Preparation

Unlike most of the vegetables in this book, there is no one classic method for preparing cabbage. To my tongue at least, it is equally tonic whether blanched, braised, baked, or even stir-fried.

For years cabbage was considered "immigrant fare" and was usually boiled till it was as limp as the contents of a washing machine. To compound the injury it was then served forth in a puddle of water—which may provide some clue to the dearth of cabbage aficionados prior to World War II.

When I cook cabbage, I always discard the tough outer leaves and quarter the head. Then I core it by cutting out the hard center portions at the base. Cabbage is best when shredded into ¼-inch-wide strips with a long, sharp vegetable knife, so the pieces will be long and slightly chewy. For my money, processor-chopped cabbage inevitably has too fine a texture and tends to become rather mushy after cooking; so I chop it by hand.

Blanch cabbage by cooking it in a large heavy-duty saucepan (not aluminum as it alters the flavor) with enough boiling salted water to cover. Boil the cabbage, uncovered, for no longer than 5 to 8 minutes; you want it to be *al dente*. After it has boiled, plunge the cut cabbage under cold running water to retard the cooking process. Then season and reheat it as you desire afterward.

SPICY CABBAGE HOT POT WITH PORK

*H*eaded cabbages have been a source of much myth and more mystery in the garden from the very beginning. Babies were said to be found under enveloping cabbage leaves as far back as the third century B.C. And even today, sensible Scots will send their young daughters, blindfolded, out into the cabbage patches on All Hallows Eve. According to lore, they will be able to foretell the nature of their future spouse's physique by the hardiness of the cabbages they stumble upon (if the poor girls do not break their necks doing so). The best part of that ritual is that after the high jinks among the potagerie everyone retires to the kitchen for a hearty meal of (what else?) cabbage soup!

2 pounds pork chops or meaty pork bones, trimmed of excess fat
2 tablespoons minced salt pork
1 medium onion, chopped
2 large shallots, minced
1 large clove garlic, minced
2 pounds green cabbage, trimmed, shredded
6 cups strong Chicken Stock (see page 410)
4 cups water
1½ tablespoons red wine vinegar
⅛ teaspoon ground allspice
⅛ teaspoon ground mace
¼ teaspoon chopped fresh thyme, or a pinch of dried
1 teaspoon salt
¼ teaspoon freshly ground black pepper

For the meatballs:

½ pound ground pork
½ cup fresh bread crumbs
1 egg, lightly beaten
¼ cup milk

1 shallot, minced
½ teaspoon salt
⅛ teaspoon freshly ground black pepper
Pinch of freshly grated nutmeg
2 tablespoons unsalted butter

1. Place the pork chops or bones in a large pot. Cover with cold water; heat to boiling. Remove from the heat and place the pot with chops or bones under cold running water until the water in the pot runs clear. Wipe out the pot; reserve the chops or bones.

2. Sauté the salt pork in the pot over medium-low heat until lightly browned. Add the onion; cook 2 minutes. Add the shallots and garlic; cook 3 minutes. Stir in the cabbage, tossing to coat it well. Add the chicken broth and water. Heat to boiling; reduce the heat. Cook, covered, over medium-low heat for 1½ hours.

3. Add the pork chops or bones to the soup. Continue to cook, covered, another 45 minutes. Add the vinegar, allspice, mace, thyme, salt, and pepper. Remove from the heat and let stand at least 4 hours, or refrigerate overnight.

4. Before serving, combine all the ingredients for the pork meatballs through the nutmeg. Mix thoroughly and form into small meatballs. Melt the butter in a large heavy skillet over medium heat and sauté the meatballs, about a third at a time, until golden brown.

5. Bring the soup to boiling; remove the chops or bones. Shred the meat from the chops and add it to the soup along with the meatballs. Cook, covered, 25 minutes before serving.

Serves 8.

MARY SURINA'S YUGOSLAVIAN SLAW

I have been collecting cole slaw recipes since I was old enough to shred a cabbage and spare a thumb. Out of several hundred renderings, good sense bids me narrow down the list to the quartet that follows.

My dear friend Mary Surina—who adds luster to San Pedro, California, each time she goes near a stove—sent me the first slaw (amended with potatoes, oil, and garlic) with a caveat. "Bert," she wrote, "some people love this dish...and some don't!" Count me among the lucky lovers.

1 large potato, peeled, cubed
1 clove garlic, minced
1 teaspoon salt
2½ tablespoons white wine vinegar
⅓ cup olive oil
1½ to 2 pounds green cabbage, trimmed, shredded
Freshly ground black pepper

1. Cook the potato in boiling salted water until tender, about 15 minutes.

2. Meanwhile, with the back of a spoon, mash the garlic in a small bowl with the salt until a paste is formed. Beat in the vinegar and oil.

3. Place the cabbage in a large bowl. Drain the potato and immediately mash the hot potato into the cabbage. The cabbage will wilt slightly. Add the dressing, toss well, and season with pepper to taste. Serve immediately.

Serves 4 to 6.

GERMANTOWN SLAW

*T*his slaw recipe is from a wondrously well-fed section of America (roughly northeast of Cincinnati, Ohio), where the countryside is still lush and largely devoid of tract housing and the creamy cole slaw is often incomparable. Why shouldn't it be good? The Mennonites brought the secret with them!

1½ to 2 pounds green cabbage, trimmed,
shredded
1 medium red onion, halved, thinly sliced
1 carrot, peeled, diced
½ green pepper, cored, seeded, finely
chopped
1 tablespoon unsalted butter
1 cup cooked ham, cut into strips
1 cup Mayonnaise (see page 408)
½ cup sour cream
2 tablespoons red wine vinegar
1½ tablespoons Dijon mustard
½ teaspoon caraway seeds
Salt and freshly ground black pepper
1 small tomato, seeded, cubed
¾ cup white Cheddar cheese, cut into
strips
1½ tablespoons chopped fresh parsley

G ermans call cabbage *kohl.*
Early Britons dubbed it *cole.* Long
before some Francophile English
dandy translated *caboche* to cabbage, Saxons had persuaded Angles
that there was pleasure in partaking
of the chewy noggin raw: hence *cole
slaw.* Which actually means "cabbage sliced."

When I was a kid I always
spelled it *cold* slaw, which seemed
logical as it was my favorite chilled
dish after ice cream!

1. Combine the cabbage, onion, carrot, and green pepper in a large bowl.

2. Melt the butter in a small skillet
over medium-low heat. Sauté the ham
until lightly browned. Transfer the ham,
using a slotted spoon, to the vegetable
mixture in the bowl.

3. Combine the mayonnaise with
the sour cream in a medium bowl. Beat
in the vinegar, mustard, caraway seeds,
and any ham drippings. Pour this over
the cabbage mixture. Mix thoroughly.
Add salt and pepper to taste. Add the
tomato and cheese, toss lightly, and
sprinkle with the parsley. Serve at room
temperature.

Serves 6 to 8.

DONALD SACKS' GINGER-DILL SLAW

M ore geographic slaw. Across the street from the august and protean Dean &
DeLuca in New York City's SoHo, there is a tidy little food shop dubbed simply
Donald Sacks. Mr. Sacks is an amiable young man who is a kitchen wizard into the
bargain. His store sells all manner of good comestibles "to go," with a particular
emphasis on green salads, to wit: one of the greenest! The interesting facet of this
vaguely Oriental slaw is the mild pickling process, which removes a good bit of the
acidity of the raw cabbage and onion.

1½ pounds green cabbage, trimmed,
shredded
3 tablespoons coarse (kosher) salt
4 medium red onions, thinly sliced
2-inch piece ginger root, peeled, minced

¾ cup lemon juice
⅓ cup olive oil
1 tablespoon fennel seeds, crushed
¼ teaspoon freshly ground black pepper
1½ cups minced fresh dill

1. Toss the cabbage with 2 tablespoons of the salt in a large bowl; let stand 4 hours. Cover with cold water; let stand 1 hour longer.

2. Meanwhile, combine the onions with the remaining 1 tablespoon salt in a medium bowl; let stand 1 hour. Cover with cold water; let stand 1 hour longer.

3. Rinse the cabbage and the onions separately with cold running water. Drain thoroughly and squeeze dry. Combine the cabbage and the onions in a large bowl.

4. Press the ginger root in a fine-mesh sieve over a small bowl to extract all the juice. Discard the pulp. Whisk the lemon juice, oil, fennel, and pepper into the ginger juice. Pour the dressing over the cabbage mixture; toss well. Add the fresh dill; toss once more. Serve well chilled.

Serves 6 to 8.

SLAW BERNOISE

Berne is a city on the dewlaps of the Jura mountains, which separate Switzerland from France. This local dish combines the best of both sides of the border: good French cabbage and great Swiss Emmenthal cheese.

1½ to 2 pounds green cabbage, trimmed, shredded
1 cup finely chopped celery
¼ pound Emmenthal cheese, cut into strips (1 cup)
1 small clove garlic, minced
4 anchovy filets
1 teaspoon Dijon mustard
1 tablespoon lemon juice
1½ teaspoons white wine vinegar
⅓ cup olive oil
Freshly ground black pepper
2 hard-cooked eggs, quartered

1. Combine the cabbage, celery, and cheese in a large bowl.

2. Mash the garlic with the anchovies in a small bowl until smooth. Stir in the mustard, lemon juice, vinegar, and oil. Pour the sauce over the vegetables and cheese. Mix well. Add pepper to taste. Serve well chilled, garnished with quartered hard-cooked eggs.

Serves 4 to 6.

AMISH SWEET AND SOUR CABBAGE

2½ to 3 pounds green cabbage, trimmed, shredded
½ cup Chicken Stock (see page 410)
1 egg yolk
¼ cup sugar
¼ cup red wine vinegar
2 tablespoons unsalted butter, cut into bits
1 teaspoon Dijon mustard
½ cup heavy or whipping cream
¼ cup chopped fresh dill
Salt and freshly ground black pepper

1. Place the cabbage with the stock in a medium saucepan. Heat to boiling; reduce the heat. Cook, covered, over medium-low heat until the cabbage is

tender, about 8 minutes. Drain; keep warm.

2. Meanwhile, combine the egg yolk with the sugar and vinegar in a small heavy saucepan. Cook, stirring constantly, over low heat until the mixture begins to thicken. Do not boil. Stir in the butter, bit by bit. Add the mustard, cream, and dill.

3. Combine the cabbage with the sauce. Add salt and pepper to taste.

Serves 6 to 8.

VENETIAN VERZE SOFEGAE
(Smothered Cabbage)

*T*he following cabbage devise from Venice is a gift from a good cooking companion, Anna Teresa Callen, who also happens to be one of the best teachers of Italian cuisine around. Anna Teresa lives on the same street as me, albeit on the sunnier side. Though our stoves are separated by at least fifty others on the block, I swear I can recognize the good scent of her Abruzzi cooking whenever the wind is right.

3 tablespoons minced pancetta (Italian
    bacon), fatty prosciutto, or thick bacon
1 clove garlic
Pinch of rosemary
1 tablespoon olive oil
2½ pounds green cabbage, trimmed,
    shredded
½ cup Chicken Stock (see page 410) or
    white wine

1. Chop the pancetta with the garlic and rosemary until well minced. This mixture is known as *battuto* in Italy.

2. Heat the oil in a medium saucepan over medum heat. Add the *battuto*. Cook, stirring constantly, until the mixture begins to sizzle. Stir in the cabbage, tossing to coat it well. Cook, covered, over low heat for 1 hour, adding the stock or wine a little at a time.

Serves 6.

FRENCH CHOU CHOU
(Dilled Creamy Cabbage)

*O*ne of cabbage's staunchest herbal allies is fresh dill. In this classic cabbage rendering, and also Amish Sweet and Sour, page 79, dill plays a prominent role. Each dish is a peasant bequest: obviously the root of all great cabbage cabala.

1½ to 2 pounds green cabbage, trimmed,
    finely shredded
4 tablespoons (½ stick) unsalted butter
4 slices Canadian bacon, cut into thin
    strips
1 teaspoon Dijon mustard
3 tablespoons cognac

1 large onion, finely chopped
1 small package (3 ounces) cream cheese
1 tablespoon heavy or whipping cream
3 tablespoons chopped fresh dill
Pinch of ground cloves
Salt and freshly ground black pepper

1. Cook the cabbage in boiling salted water 5 minutes; drain.

2. Melt 1 tablespoon of the butter in a small saucepan. Add the Canadian bacon and cook over medium-high heat until the strips begin to brown. Reduce the heat to low, stir in the mustard and cognac, and cook 3 minutes. Remove from the heat.

3. Melt the remaining 3 tablespoons butter in a large saucepan. Add the onion and cook over medium-low heat 3 minutes. Stir in the cream cheese and heavy cream. Cook until the cheese melts. Stir in the cabbage, tossing well to coat each piece. Cook 4 minutes. Add the Canadian bacon with the pan juices; continue to cook, tossing frequently, until the cabbage is tender, about 5 minutes longer. Add dill, cloves, and salt and pepper to taste.

Serves 4 to 6.

CABBAGE PANCAKES

*H*ere is the ultimate cabbage dish. If you say it is fit for a king, I will argue. That's a low estimate.

1¼ pounds green cabbage, trimmed, shredded
2 eggs
1 egg yolk
½ cup milk
1 cup all-purpose flour
3 tablespoons unsalted butter, melted
½ teaspoon salt
1½ tablespoons chopped chives or scallion tops
2 to 3 tablespoons unsalted butter

1. Cook the cabbage, uncovered, in boiling salted water for 5 minutes. Rinse under cold running water until cool; drain, pressing out all liquid with your hands. Place the cabbage in a large bowl.

2. Combine the eggs, egg yolk, milk, flour, melted butter, and salt (in that order) in a blender container. Blend until smooth. Combine this mixture with the cabbage in the bowl; stir in the chives or scallions.

3. Melt 1 tablespoon of the butter in a large heavy skillet over medium heat. Spoon the batter, 1 large tablespoon for each pancake, into the skillet. Cook three or four at a time until golden on both sides. Keep warm in a low oven while frying the remaining batter, adding more butter to the skillet as needed.

Serves 4 to 6.

CORNED BEEF AND CABBAGE IN HORSERADISH CREAM

*M*y mother's formula for a cabbage-cum-corned-beef boiled dinner (taught her by my Jewish grandmother) always required the meat to be sliced into rosy quadrangles in the kitchen and served with crisp-cooked carrot sticks and chopped, barely cooked cabbage—which was prepared in a separate pan with a good lump of butter and a *schmecken* of the cooking juices "to ease the pain," as my grandmother said.

The dish, served mostly in mid-March (but on the last Thursday in November on at least one occasion), was inevitably sauced with a snowy alliance of cream, mustard, and freshly grated horseradish—though why I will never know, since my mother's mother had been born into a strictly kosher household in Poland. Obviously she became a freethinker early on. And an even freer cook.

1 corned brisket of beef, about 4 pounds
1 large carrot, peeled, halved
1 white turnip, peeled, halved
1 parsnip, peeled, halved
1 large onion
4 whole cloves
2 tablespoons red wine vinegar
2 sprigs parsley
1 large bay leaf
1 clove garlic
10 whole peppercorns
1 teaspoon mustard seed
Wilted Cabbage (recipe follows)
6 large carrots, peeled, cut into julienne
  strips
Horseradish Cream (recipe follows)
2 tablespoons chopped fresh dill
2 tablespoons chopped fresh parsley

1. Place the corned beef in a heavy 5-quart pot. Add the ingredients through the mustard seed. Add enough water to cover by 2 inches. Heat to boiling, removing scum as it rises to the top; then reduce the heat to low. Simmer, partially covered, skimming the surface occasionally, until the meat is tender when pierced with a fork, about 3½ hours. Add more water if necessary during the cooking. Remove the beef when tender and place it on a serving dish. Keep it, covered, in the oven on low heat.

2. Remove 1½ cups liquid from the pot. Strain, and reserve. Leave the remaining liquid in the pot.

3. Make the Wilted Cabbage.

4. While the cabbage is cooking, tie the julienned carrots in a cheesecloth bag. Heat the remaining liquid in the pot to boiling. Add the carrots and cook,

uncovered, until just tender, about 10 minutes. Remove the carrots, undo the cheesecloth bag, and arrange the carrots around the corned beef. Return the serving dish, covered, to the oven.

5. When the cabbage is done, place it in an ovenproof serving dish and keep it warm in the oven.

6. Make the Horseradish Cream. Remove the serving dishes from the oven and spoon some of the horseradish sauce over the meat. Sprinkle the meat and carrots with dill and parsley. Serve with Wilted Cabbage and mashed potatoes. Pass the remaining sauce.

Serves 8.

Wilted Cabbage

4 tablespoons (½ stick) unsalted butter
1 large shallot, chopped
2 large tomatoes, peeled, seeded, chopped
2½ pounds green cabbage, trimmed,
  coarsely chopped
½ cup reserved corned-beef liquid
Salt and freshly ground black pepper

Melt the butter in a medium saucepan over medium-low heat. Add the shallot; cook 2 minutes. Add the tomatoes; cook 3 minutes. Add the cabbage and reserved corned-beef liquid, tossing to coat the cabbage well. Cook, partially covered, stirring occasionally, until the cabbage is tender, about 10 minutes. Add salt and pepper to taste.

Serves 6 to 8.

Horseradish Cream

1 tablespoon unsalted butter
2 tablespoons all-purpose flour
1 cup reserved corned-beef liquid
2 tablespoons freshly grated horseradish, or
    1½ tablespoons prepared horseradish
1½ tablespoons Dijon mustard
¼ cup sour cream
¼ cup heavy or whipping cream
1 teaspoon lemon juice

1. Melt the butter in a small saucepan over medium-low heat. Whisk in the flour. Cook, stirring constantly, 2 minutes. Whisk in the corned-beef liquid, stirring until smooth. Add the horseradish and mustard. Cook 2 minutes.

2. Remove the sauce from the heat and beat in the sour cream and heavy cream. Stir in the lemon juice. Return it to low heat until warmed through, but do not boil.

Makes about 1½ cups.

CHOU FARCI

Here is stuffed cabbage of a somewhat homelier stripe, in the form of a recipe that came to me via the owner-chef of a boardinghouse I stayed at in Holland a dozen years ago. The lady and I communicated in fractured Franco-Dutch, which is the way I acquired her savory recipe. What puts the savor in a plate of *chou farci*? A mystery ingredient sprinkled on the green envelopes of cabbage just before they gently poach: namely, a little whiff of gin.

2 cups leftover cooked pork, chopped
¼ pound sliced boiled ham, chopped
    (about 1 cup)
1½ cups cooked rice
1 small onion, finely chopped
1 clove garlic, finely minced
1 tablespoon finely chopped fresh dill
⅛ teaspoon ground allspice
⅛ teaspoon freshly grated nutmeg
¼ teaspoon hot pepper sauce
2 eggs, lightly beaten
Salt and freshly ground black pepper
1½ to 2 pounds green cabbage, leaves
    separated
2 cups Chicken Stock (see page 410)
1 tablespoon dry gin
2 teaspoons unsalted butter, softened
2 teaspoons all-purpose flour
1½ teaspoons Dijon mustard
1 egg yolk
¼ cup heavy or whipping cream
Dill sprigs

1. Combine all the ingredients through the 2 eggs in a large bowl. Mix well. Add salt and pepper to taste, and set aside.

2. Cook the cabbage leaves in boiling salted water until slightly wilted, about 1 minute. Drain.

3. Place ⅓ to ½ cup filling on each leaf (depending on the size of the leaf) and roll up the leaf, tucking the edges under. Place the rolls in a skillet or heavy saucepan large enough to hold them all in one layer. Add the chicken stock; sprinkle with the gin. Heat to boiling; reduce the heat. Simmer, covered, until tender, about 30 minutes. Remove the cabbage rolls with a slotted spoon. Keep warm, covered, in a low oven.

4. Meanwhile, raise the heat under the cooking liquid and allow it to boil for 3 minutes; reduce the heat to low.

5. Mash the butter with the flour until smooth. Stir this into the cooking liquid. Add the mustard; cook until slightly thickened.

6. Combine the egg yolk with the cream in a small bowl. Whisk this into the sauce. Cook until warmed through, but do not boil. Spoon the sauce over the cabbage and top each roll with a sprig of fresh dill.

Serves 6.

JEFFERSONIAN BAKED CHARTREUSE

One of the most notable fans of *Brassica oleracea capitata* was Thomas Jefferson, who campaigned for this vegetable's acceptance by his fellow Americans his entire food-loving life.

In his incredible gardens at Monticello, Jefferson raised over twenty-two different varieties of cabbage, imported from seedsmen and agronomists all over the world. One of Jefferson's prides was Savoy cabbage: "the wrinkled jade green head with a surface like crackled faience." He brought the seeds back from a trip to Italy and crossbred the plants until they became hardy enough to withstand the coldest Virginia winter. One of the most startling recipes in his voluminous collection was for a monumental loaf called a *Chartreuse*: Savoy cabbage filled with layers of chopped ham and potatoes, carrots, turnips, mushrooms, and veal. A stuffed cabbage like no other before or after! I dread to think how long it took to assemble in Jefferson's time. A processor makes the work load considerably lighter today!

3 pounds firm Savoy cabbage
4 medium potatoes, peeled, quartered
6 tablespoons (¾ stick) unsalted butter
½ cup heavy or whipping cream
2 small onions, finely chopped
¾ pound ground cooked ham
⅛ teaspoon ground mace
1 clove garlic, minced
½ pound mushrooms, minced
Pinch of ground cloves
½ pound ground veal
1 egg, lightly beaten
¼ cup fresh bread crumbs
Pinch of dried thyme
½ teaspoon salt
¼ teaspoon freshly ground black pepper
½ pound carrots, peeled, minced
¼ cup chopped fresh dill
1 teaspoon finely grated lemon peel
½ pound turnips, peeled, minced
1 stalk celery, minced
¼ cup chopped fresh parsley
2 tablespoons minced red bell pepper
⅔ cup dry white wine
1 quart chicken broth (see page 414)
1½ tablespoons all-purpose flour
½ teaspoon Dijon mustard
Dash of hot pepper sauce
1 teaspoon lemon juice

1. Using a sharp knife, slice off the stem end of the cabbage and remove the core. Cook the cabbage, uncovered, in a large pot of boiling salted water 10 minutes, turning once. Drain; cool thoroughly. Separate the cabbage leaves and pat them dry. Reserve.

2. Cook the potatoes in boiling salted water until tender, about 20 minutes. Drain. Mash the potatoes with 1 tablespoon of the butter and ¼ cup of the cream. Cool slightly and combine with 1 chopped onion, the ground ham, and the mace. Mix well; reserve.

3. Melt 2 tablespoons of the butter in a large skillet over medium heat. Add the remaining onion; cook 1 minute. Add the garlic and mushrooms. Cook, stirring constantly, until browned. Remove from the heat and transfer to a bowl. Cool slightly and combine with the cloves, veal, egg, bread crumbs, thyme, salt, and pepper. Mix well; reserve.

4. Combine the carrots, dill, and lemon peel in a bowl. Mix well; reserve.

5. Combine the turnips, celery, parsley, and red pepper in another bowl. Mix well; reserve.

6. To assemble the Chartreuse, lay out a large linen napkin or towel on a flat surface. Arrange the largest cabbage leaves in the center, slightly overlapping with the stems pointing outward, in a circular pattern. (This should look as if the cabbage had been opened upside down.) Spoon half the ham mixture over the leaves. Place the next layer of leaves (overlapping and centered) on top. Spoon half the carrot mixture over the leaves. Continue layering (always stems outward) with half the veal and mushroom filling, and finally, half the turnip filling. Repeat the process in the same order until leaves and fillings are used up. (Stems may be removed on innermost layers of cabbage for easier assembly.) End with the turnip filling. Place 1 tablespoon of the butter in the center of the last layer. Gather the edges of the napkin and pull the corners up and together, returning the cabbage to its original shape. Tie securely with kitchen string.

7. Preheat the oven to 350°F. Place the cabbage in a large ovenproof pot, tied side up. Pour the wine and chicken broth around the cabbage. Heat to boiling. Cover, and cook in the oven for 1¾ hours.

8. Remove the pot from the oven. Carefully move the cabbage to a plate, reserving the cooking liquid. Untie the napkin, place a large shallow ovenproof serving dish over the top, and quickly, but carefully, invert. Remove the napkin. Cook the cabbage in the oven for another 10 minutes.

9. Meanwhile, melt the remaining 2 tablespoons butter in a medium saucepan over medium-low heat. Add the flour. Cook, stirring constantly, 2 minutes. Whisk in 2 cups stock from the pot, the mustard, hot pepper sauce, lemon juice, and the remaining ¼ cup cream. Cook until slightly thickened.

10. To serve, spoon some of the sauce over the cabbage and cut the cabbage into pie-shaped wedges. Pass the remaining sauce.

Serves 8 to 10.

RED CABBAGE ALSATIAN-STYLE

*T*his makes a fine one-dish supper with a plate of tiny boiled potatoes on the side. The recipe came to me on a stained fragment of brown paper after I supplicated long and hard for it after a hearty dinner. It was scribbled in a mixture of French and

German, but as you will see when you have made the dish, nothing whatsoever was lost in the translation!

Incidentally, don't worry that an unlucky dinner guest may chance upon one of the four garlic cloves. The garlic disappears after three hours of cooking and tossing.

4 tablespoons (½ stick) unsalted butter
4 cloves garlic
2½ pounds red cabbage, trimmed, shredded
1 pound smoked pork butt (or smoked shoulder), cut into 1-inch cubes
½ cup dry white wine
½ cup strong Chicken Stock (see page 410), or 1½ cups chicken broth (see page 414) reduced to ½ cup
1 medium onion stuck with 2 whole cloves
Salt and freshly ground black pepper

1. Preheat the oven to 250°F. Melt the butter in a Dutch oven over medium-low heat. Add the garlic; cook 3 minutes. Remove from the heat.

2. Place the cabbage and smoked pork in layers in the Dutch oven. Pour in the wine and the chicken stock. Place the onion in the center, cover, and bake 1 hour.

3. Remove from the oven and toss the mixture. Bake, covered, 1½ hours longer.

4. Raise the oven heat to 350°F. Remove the cover and cook 30 minutes longer. Discard the onion and cloves. Add salt and pepper to taste.

Serves 4 to 6.

CARROTS

Worth Their Weight in Gold

When my grandmother died, the glories of her kitchen expired with her. But her garden, no less glorious, survived for almost seventeen years because my grandfather doggedly took over the task of its cultivation. It was not an easy chore for an old man with a bad leg and no apparent horticultural skills, but clearly he undertook the enterprise as a memorial to his wife.

When she was alive, my indomitable grandmother would have rejected the honor out of hand. To her mind there was a sharp division between the labors permissible to a homemaker and those to a breadwinner. And she would have no more allowed her husband to thin a flower bed than she would have permitted his presence at her stove. Anything to do with house or garden was exclusively her bailiwick and all interlopers were dispatched without ceremony.

But then my grandmother's agricultural act was a hard one to follow. She was blessed with a thumb of pure jade plus a natural instinct for generating life. Any alien cutting that she surreptitiously snipped from a botanical garden or forest woodland immediately took root in her backyard. Even more astonishing, these fragile shoots—wild blue lupine or lady's slipper orchids—did not merely bloom, they grew to awesome proportions, ministered by her constant nagging and massive doses of vitamins, most of which were the detritus of her cooking pots, which she carefully strained before spading into the soil.

"You see what I am doing here, mister?" I recall her quizzing me when I was perhaps eight or nine years old and involved in planning my very first garden.

"This—" indicating the saucepan she held aloft, "—is the water in which last night's vegetables cooked. See how I sprinkle a little on the gladiolas, dahlias, even tulips—the bulbs that need help to send up new shoots. Not roots." She shook her head to emphasize the point. "Soup stock or fish broth is what makes a root grow strong. And as a special treat, maybe a little meat juice once in a while. But be sure to skim off every bit of the fat first. I want you to remember that a slob in the kitchen can be a murderer in the garden!"

Did I heed her advice? My very first vegetable garden was a flag of thick moss behind our garage. The only living thing that ever flourished there was an unpruned and utterly inviolate wild rose bush—a shrub that, like the great god Shiva, sent out a strong-armed threat of new brambles every spring.

In my initial garden, inspired by our Italian neighbors behind the hedge, I planted every glowing packet of vegetable seeds that Burpee and friends provided at our local Woolworth's counter. And though my grandmother duly enjoined me that "crowded gardens are inferior gardens," my enthusiasm for planting knew no bounds. Leaf lettuce, celery, corn, and peppers bisected rows of peas, cucumbers, cabbage, runner beans, and watermelon, with carrots forming a natural border around it all.

I need not have constructed the elaborately staked markers of seed envelopes to identify each seedling. Aside from a feathery line of carrot tops no other trace of green ever appeared in that dark tract. And no matter how many pints of metallic-smelling vegetable juices (accrued from my mother's nightly supply of canned goods) were sluiced on the ground, my only harvest was a clutch of tiny orange fingers poking up—like Mother Nature's reproach for greed.

It might have been worse. The carrots were tasty and plentiful besides. As soon as one was picked, another took its place in the earthly assembly line, seemingly overnight.

After we had dined on produce from my garden for some while, however, my father rebelled.

"This mouthful makes the fortieth carrot I have chewed this week," he declared righteously, laying down his fork and knife. "And enough is enough. What I suggest—request, actually—is that our young gardener here leave the spoils he's still got coming up in the backyard to those who are *needier*."

He paused dramatically for the idea to sink in before winking broadly. "Like rabbits!"

Usually I had some ready answer to my father's jibes, but not that night. Frankly I was so tired of eating carrots myself that I acquiesced at once. With a thin smile.

Of course what neither father nor son realized at that moment was that carrots are a biennial crop. Both Greenes and rabbits dined on those "golden assets" again the following summer. But in moderation. Decidedly in moderation, for I had started planting flowers by then. And compared to a zinnia a carrot is only a carrot, after all. Unless of course it turns out to be a stalk of Queen Anne's lace!

Vegetable Roots

Daucus carota sativa, the benign confederate to stew and pot roast for hundreds of years, has a host of quite unruly relatives beyond the garden gate. Known as the Umbelliferae, this botanical assemblage—whose ranks include anise, caraway, celery, chervil, fennel, parsley, and parsnip as well as Queen Anne's lace—has the odd distinction of being dubbed a "kitchen mafia" in certain culinary circles, for these strong flavors are known to take over and territorialize the contents of a saucepan!

Queen Anne's lace is obviously the most delicate member of this tribe. In the Balkans, where the plant is cultivated, it is referred to as the "white carrot." American farmers are a bit less generous. They call it "cow's currency," for a herd of cattle has been known to charge through barbed wire for a tasty nibble when the umbels are in bloom.

On the opposite side of the family, carrot's most uncordial relative is the poison hemlock. Now we are talking mafia for real, for this umbellale has a more potent after-dinner effect than all the others put together. It knocks you dead!

Earliest carrot consumption is traced to the hill people of Afghanistan, who were sun-worshipers and believed that eating orange or yellow-colored foods instilled a sense of righteousness.

Greeks and Romans prized this vegetable for somewhat earthier reasons. Sequestered in the Trojan Horse, Athenian foot soldiers subsisted exclusively on a diet of raw carrots, to bind their bowels. On quite the other hand, invad-

As a kid whose first reading material consisted of the *Mother West Wind Stories*, followed in short order by *Peter Rabbit* and the works of Beatrix Potter, I developed early on a solid affection for all the members of his long-eared, cotton-tailed breed.

But not in my garden.

At Amagansett, Long Island, where I have harvested a gilded share of carrots from time to time, the crop may be just a tad sweeter than any other I have known, for the soil is sandy loam and runs deep besides. It certainly produces what I deem "the carrot-lover's carrot"! Why else would a crop of otherwise circumspect rabbits gather daily from May to midsummer to check the growth of my seedlings? These not-so-dumb bunnies sense that something really special is coming up, I can tell you!

Amagansett rabbits are carrot cognoscenti. They even know the difference between a Nantes Half Long, which appears in early spring, and a Coreless Amsterdam, which comes to harvest late every summer. And they await the growth of the latter with the same degree of discrimination that local girl-watchers mark the arrival of a well-filled bikini on the beach.

In the past, I have waged (mild) wars on the rabbit population, using rubber snakes and fences to discourage their attentions. But nothing proved effective in the final analysis. Nowadays we share the yield. I consume whatever the rabbits conspicuously do *not*.

Weeding carrots is probably the most serendipitous experience a gardener can have.

In a well-calculated *potager*, the plants must be thinned so they are far enough apart for healthy growth: a laborious chore, but the gardener can revive his flagging spirit with a little nourishment at the source.

A carrot picked straight from the soil cannot be consumed without a fast brush of any residual loam, but that's what shirttails are for. No matter what time of day the carrot is picked, the temperature will be the same: warm at the skin from its earthly bed but chill as the night wind at the heart, a taste sensation unequaled by any other fresh-dug thing in the universe—up to and including the truffle of Perigord!

ing Roman legions fed their captive females carrots (cooked into a broth) to unloose their stringent morals.

From its obvious erotic design came the carrot's sexual reputation, I suppose. Caligula is purported to have once fed the entire Roman Senate a banquet composed solely of carrot dishes, in one form or another, just to observe these high-minded gentlemen "fornicating like beasts of the field." No account of the proceedings exists but I'll warrant it was more of an ordeal than an orgy for the guests. Since carrots contain more sugar than any other vegetable except the sugar beet, an all-carrot menu could bring on a mass attack of hyperglycemia rather than lust!

Long after the myth of the carrot's aphrodisiac powers waned, physicians in the Middle Ages still prescribed them as an antidote for every imaginable affliction, from syphilis to dog bite. No one ever ate a carrot for pleasure, it seems, until the middle of the Renaissance.

The Dutch actually grew carrots in profusion, having inherited the seeds as a residual of the Saracen invasion centuries earlier. But no Dutchman gave the carrot room on his dinner plate. The lowland dairy farmers reserved the entire crop for their native Holstein cows, which produced the richest, yellowest butter in all of Europe as a consequence.

It was actually a Dutch or Flemish nobleman (history is cloudy on the pedigree) who brought the carrot into our Anglo-Saxon diet. A deputy to the English court, making overtures to Elizabeth I, he presented the queen with two gifts: a tub of native butter and a wreath of tender carrots emblazoned with diamonds, to wear in her hair.

Having better sense than the emissary, good Queen Bess removed the diamonds and sent carrots and butter together to the royal kitchen. And that's how the classic side dish, buttered carrots, entered the menu!

What to Look For

Carrots may be seasonal in a garden but they certainly are permanent residents on greengrocers' shelves these days.

I tend to buy carrots in bunches with their tops intact, because the sprightliness of the greens is always a giveaway of the vegetable's freshness. It is tough for a consumer to judge just how long a topless, plastic-sealed carrot has been around, although there are clues. Old carrots are usually cracked or brittle and send out a rash of tiny white roots. So stay clear of those!

Of late, I have been increasingly aware of the emphasis on "miniature carrots" in supermarkets. The uniform size and pale color of these packaged bantams implies that they have been picked at the prime of garden freshness, so the buyer is expected to pay more for the privilege of adding them to a stew. However, these pale young carrots are decidedly deficient in carotene, the deep rich coloring agent that the human body converts into vitamin A. So my advice is to pass them by. To give the next carrot dish a lighter complexion, use deeply colored carrots and add cream!

Carrots have a curious chemistry. Though they contain more natural sugar than any other vegetable aside from the sugar beet, the calories in a whole average-size carrot amount to less than a package of sugarless gum, about 30. Carrots are also an incredibly high source of vitamin A (7,930 units each) and contain high levels of potassium, calcium, and phosphorus.

Preparation

The classic preparation for any fresh carrot is to peel it first, using a swivel-bladed vegetable peeler that lightly removes the skin. Then, depending upon the recipe, slice, dice, julienne, shred—or leave it whole!

I never peel baby carrots because the tender skin has a particularly appealing sweet flavor, and it is vitamin-high into the bargain, but that option is up to you.

Likewise, out of a purely personal crotchet, I hardly ever steam or boil a carrot until soft, as my mother always did. Instead I blanch them in water, broth, vegetable juices, or a mixture of water and butter, allowing just enough liquid to cover, and cook them over moderate heat, uncovered, until they reach a stage that French chefs call *à point*: barely tender to the fork. I often cook carrots in advance, cool them immediately under cold running water, and reheat them again in a little more butter just before I serve them.

The technique for cooking a carrot à la Greene varies with each one of my recipes, but a small dose of general carrot-cookery wisdom would not be amiss here. To wit: the optimum cooking time for a *sliced* or *diced* carrot is usually 8 minutes flat. Unless of course the slices are on the thick side; then merely increase the cooking time according to your own good judgment. But remember, please: a perfectly prepared carrot is never mushy! *Julienne-cut* carrots (once again depending upon the size of the strips) should cook firm-tender in less time; about 4 minutes. When a recipe calls for *shredded* carrots I actually don't cook them at all, preferring to merely toss them in melted butter over high heat for a few seconds until they warm through. *Whole* carrots, despite whatever other advice you have heard on the subject, are best cooked over low heat in a small amount of liquid in a partially covered saucepan. My timetable? Approximately 20 minutes—but garden-fresh produce will take less.

ELYSIAN BISQUE

*T*his singularly thick and satisfying soup comes from Holland. Its Dutch title translates as "soup of supreme bliss."

5 strips bacon, chopped
1 pound carrots, peeled, chopped
6 whole scallions, bulbs and green tops, chopped
10 mushrooms, chopped (about 1 cup)
3 ribs celery with leaves, chopped (about 1 cup)
1 teaspoon fresh thyme, or ¼ teaspoon dried
1 small bay leaf, crumbled
4 cups chicken broth (see page 414)
1 cup water
1 cup light cream or half-and-half
Salt and freshly ground black pepper

1. Sauté the bacon in a medium saucepan over medium heat until crisp. Stir in the carrots, scallions, mushrooms, and celery. Cook uncovered, 5 minutes.

2. Add the thyme, bay leaf, chicken broth, and water to the saucepan. Heat to boiling; reduce the heat. Simmer, covered, 50 minutes. Remove from the heat and allow to cool slightly.

3. Place the soup in the container of a food processor or blender. Process until smooth, being very careful as hot liquid will expand. Return it to the saucepan and reheat slowly, adding the cream and salt and pepper to taste.

Serves 6.

COLD CARROTS VICHY

*T*his slaw is a brand-new version of an old (and justly honored) salad I used to make when I ran The Store in Amagansett for a golden decade.

1 pound carrots, peeled, shredded
4 whole scallions, bulbs and green tops
  minced separately
½ cup minced cooked ham
½ cup Mayonnaise (see page 408)
¼ cup sour cream
¼ cup Chinese duck sauce
½ teaspoon Dijon mustard
Salt and freshly ground black pepper

1. Combine the shredded carrots, minced scallion bulbs, and the ham in a large bowl. Mix well.

2. Beat the mayonnaise with the sour cream in a small bowl until smooth. Beat in the duck sauce and mustard. Pour the sauce over the carrot mixture, toss well, and add salt and pepper to taste. Serve at room temperature or chilled, sprinkled with the minced scallion tops.

Serves 6.

MARILYN HARRIS' BAKED CARROTS AU NATUREL

*B*efore the Second World War, most Americans sliced their carrots the size of poker chips but then perversely boiled them in quarts and quarts of water until the slender rounds acquired the shape and texture of damp powder puffs.

The tide had to turn of course, if only for the sake of vitiated vitamins, and it did in the early 1960s. Since then, mostly in the guise of health food, one is often served carrots so undercooked that cutting them with a fork can cause irremediable damage to heirloom silver.

One of the happiest compromises, a tender yet nutritive carrot dish, follows. I acquired the recipe from Marilyn Harris, director of the cooking school at Pogue's in Cincinnati.

1 pound carrots, peeled
2 tablespoons unsalted butter
Salt and freshly ground black pepper
1 tablespoon chopped fresh parsley

1. Preheat the oven to 325°F. Cut the carrots into strips 2 inches long and ¼ inch thick.

2. Place the butter in a 1½-quart earthenware baking dish or casserole with a cover. Heat the dish in the oven until the butter melts. Then add the carrots, tossing to coat them with the butter. Sprinkle with salt and pepper to taste. Bake, covered, for 1¼ hours. Sprinkle with the parsley before serving.

Serves 6.

ELIZABETHAN BRAISED AND GLAZED CARROTS

To my mind the classic carrot rendition is ultimately the simplest—in this case merely tossed with butter plus an amendment of honey. Since Queen Elizabeth I of England was responsible for the carrot's initial popularity, can one pay greater homage than to name it in her honor?

2 tablespoons unsalted butter
1 shallot, minced
1 pound carrots, peeled, sliced into rounds
½ cup Chicken Stock (see page 410)
1½ tablespoons honey
⅛ teaspoon freshly grated nutmeg
1 tablespoon chopped fresh parsley

1. Melt the butter in a medium saucepan over medium-low heat. Add the shallot; cook 1 minute. Stir in the sliced carrots and the chicken stock. Cook, covered, stirring occasionally, until just tender, about 12 to 15 minutes.

2. Add the honey and nutmeg. Raise the heat slightly, and cook, uncovered, stirring constantly, until the liquid becomes syrupy. Remove from the heat; toss in the chopped parsley.

Serves 4.

PLUM-CRAZY CARROTS

Yet another carrot classic, this one of Polish-Jewish ancestry and said to date back at least 300 years, is a vegetable and fruit amalgam known as *tsimmes.*

A good *tsimmes,* which was meant to be eaten on the sabbath or at a special holiday meal, usually required a full day's cooking time and often depended upon a multitude of odd ingredients (like sweet potatoes, pineapple, apricots, even a cut of brisket on occasion) to flavor the pot. But the mainstays of this dish were always carrots and dried prunes.

Over the years, the word *tsimmes* has acquired a totally different second meaning in Yiddish. These days it generally connotes "an awful fuss."

I offer up my own totally inauthentic rendition of a *tsimmes,* concocted of tender orange carrots and seasonal purple plums. I call it "plum-crazy carrots" and hope that no one feels called upon to make a *tsimmes* about that, please!

1 pound carrots, peeled
2½ tablespoons unsalted butter
2 teaspoons sugar
½ cup chopped pitted fresh blue plums
1 teaspoon finely slivered orange peel
1½ teaspoons brandy
Salt and freshly ground black pepper
Chopped fresh parsley

1. Cut the carrots into strips 3 inches long and about ¼ inch thick. Cook in boiling salted water until just barely tender, about 4 minutes. Rinse under cold running water; drain.

2. Melt 2 tablespoons of the butter in a medium skillet over medium heat. Add the carrots; sprinkle with the sugar.

Cook, tossing gently, until the carrots begin to caramelize.

3. Add the plums and orange peel to the carrots. Cook over medium-low heat until the plums give off their juice and are almost tender, about 5 minutes. Stir in the brandy and remaining ½ table-spoon butter. Raise the heat slightly and cook, tossing gently, until most of the liquid has evaporated. Season with salt and pepper to taste. Serve sprinkled with chopped parsley.

Serves 4.

AMISH CARROT DUMPLINGS

This is a dish of thrifty Pennsylvania Dutch antecedents; it really makes a carrot stretch, and it solves the problem of using up those leftover potatoes!

1 ¼ cups cold mashed potatoes
1 large carrot, peeled, finely grated
1 small white onion, grated
2 eggs
½ cup finely grated Swiss cheese
⅛ teaspoon freshly grated nutmeg
½ teaspoon salt
¼ teaspoon ground white pepper
1 ½ cups all-purpose flour, approximately
2 tablespoons unsalted butter
2 tablespoons freshly grated Parmesan
*   cheese (optional)*

1. Combine all the ingredients through the pepper in a large bowl; mix thoroughly. Work in the flour with your hands, starting with 1 cup and adding more until a soft dough is formed. Refrigerate, covered, 1 hour.

2. Roll the dough on a well-floured pastry board into ropes about ½ inch thick. Cut each rope into individual dumplings about 1 inch long. Press each end with the tines of a fork. Cook, about ten at a time, in a large pot of boiling salted water just until they float to the surface, about 1 minute or less. Remove with a slotted spoon and drain lightly on paper towels. Transfer to a well-buttered shallow baking dish, and reserve. Continue until all dumplings are cooked. Let them stand, covered, at room temperature until ready to heat.

3. Preheat the oven to 325° F. Dot the dumplings with butter and cook them in the oven until warmed through, 15 to 20 minutes. Sprinkle with Parmesan cheese before serving, if you like.

Serves 6.

PENNSYLVANIA DUTCH BARBECUED CARROTS

This most unusual dish is a souvenir of an absolutely overwhelming feast (half sweets, half sours) enjoyed in the Amish country more years ago than I care to say. The "stickin' sauce," incidentally, will do equal justice to any rib, wing or leg of your choice. The Pennsylvania Dutch, however, splash it on carrots.

1 pound carrots (approximately equal in
    size), peeled
1 cup Amish Stickin' Sauce (recipe follows)
1 tablespoon chopped fresh parsley

1. Preheat the oven to 350°F. Place the whole carrots in an ovenproof baking dish or casserole. Spoon the sauce over the carrots and toss well.

2. Bake the carrots, covered, 45 minutes. Remove the cover and continue to bake, turning and basting frequently, until crisp and tender, about 45 minutes longer. Sprinkle with the parsley before serving.

Serves 4 to 6.

Amish Stickin' Sauce

2 tablespoons unsalted butter
1 onion, finely chopped
2 cloves garlic, minced
Juice of 1 orange
1 tablespoon raisins
2 tablespoons cider vinegar
2 tablespoons vegetable oil
Grated peel of 1 orange
1 cup molasses
1 cup ketchup
2 teaspoons chili powder
Pinch of ground cloves
1 teaspoon prepared mustard
1 teaspoon Worcestershire sauce
2 teaspoons crushed dried hot red peppers
½ teaspoon salt

1. Melt the butter in a medium saucepan over medium-low heat. Add the onion and garlic. Cook 5 minutes; do not brown.

2. Meanwhile, combine the orange juice with the raisins, vinegar, and oil in the container of a food processor or blender. Process until smooth. Add this mixture, along with the remaining ingredients, to the saucepan. Heat to boiling; reduce the heat. Simmer, uncovered, 15 minutes.

Makes about 3 cups.

CARROT VELVET

*T*o my mind, the tonic thing about such a good-tasting but relatively low-calorie vegetable is that one may enrich it unsparingly, without a speck of guilt.

3½ cups chicken broth (see page 414)
1 pound carrots, peeled, cut in half
3 tablespoons unsalted butter
3 tablespoons all-purpose flour
½ cup heavy or whipping cream
⅛ teaspoon ground allspice
⅛ teaspoon freshly grated nutmeg
Dash of hot pepper sauce
Salt and freshly ground black pepper
¼ cup fresh bread crumbs
2 tablespoons minced fresh parsley
1 tablespoon freshly grated Parmesan
    cheese

1. Preheat the oven to 350°F. Place the chicken broth in a medium saucepan and bring it to the boil. Add the carrots and reduce the heat. Simmer, uncovered, until the carrots are very soft, about 25 minutes. Drain the carrots, reserving the cooking liquid. Mash the carrots until smooth. Set aside.

2. Melt 2 tablespoons of the butter in a medium saucepan over medium-low heat. Stir in the flour. Cook, stirring constantly, 2 minutes. Whisk in 1 cup of the reserved cooking liquid. Heat to boiling; reduce the heat. Add the cream, allspice, nutmeg, hot pepper sauce, and salt and pepper to taste. Remove from the heat and combine with the mashed carrots. Spoon into a lightly greased shallow baking dish.

3. Melt the remaining 1 tablespoon butter in a small skillet over medium

heat. Stir in the bread crumbs and cook until they are golden. Remove from the heat and stir in the minced parsley. Spread the bread crumbs evenly over the carrots. Sprinkle with the Parmesan cheese. Bake until bubbly, about 15 minutes.

Serves 4 to 6.

SAUSAGE AND CARROT PIE

*T*his recipe is a Georgian dividend—from America, not Russia. It is for a luncheon pie, meant to be eaten lukewarm. The formula is over 100 years old and never altered a whit in all that time.

1 recipe Short Crust Pastry (see page 412)
2 tablespoons unsalted butter
1 teaspoon minced shallot
½ pound carrots, peeled, grated
¼ cup Chicken Stock (see page 410)
¼ teaspoon ground mace
¼ teaspoon salt
½ pound mild Italian sausages, sliced
1¼ cups heavy or whipping cream
1 egg
1 egg yolk

1. Make the Short Crust Pastry.

2. Preheat the oven to 400°F. Roll out the pastry on a lightly floured board. Line a buttered 10-inch loose-bottom tart pan with the pastry and trim the edges. Line the pastry with aluminum foil; weight with rice or beans. Bake 10 minutes. Remove the foil and beans; bake 5 minutes longer. Cool on a wire rack. Reduce the oven heat to 375°F.

3. Melt the butter in a large skillet over medium heat. Add the shallot; cook until golden. Stir in the carrots, chicken stock, mace, and salt. Cook until the carrots are tender, about 8 minutes. Raise the heat slightly and continue to

cook, tossing and stirring, until all liquid has evaporated. Transfer the carrots to a medium bowl and set aside.

4. In the same skillet, sauté the sliced sausages over medium heat until golden brown on both sides. Drain on paper towels.

5. Spoon the carrots evenly over the bottom of the prepared pastry. Arrange the sausage slices on top.

6. Beat the cream with the egg and egg yolk in a medium bowl and pour it over the sausages. Place the tart pan on a foil-lined baking sheet and bake until the pie is puffed and golden, about 30 minutes. Let it stand at least 10 minutes before serving.

Serves 6 to 8.

FINNISH MEATBALLS

Despite (or because of) the carrot's evanescent flavor, its presence may be hard to pinpoint in a dish. For instance in this Scandinavian dish, obviously a first cousin to the Swedish meatball but lighter and more aureate.

1½ pounds ground veal
2 medium carrots, peeled, finely grated
1 egg, lightly beaten
½ cup fresh bread crumbs
¼ teaspoon freshly grated nutmeg
1 cardamom seed, crushed
½ teaspoon salt
⅛ teaspoon freshly ground black pepper
1 medium onion, quartered
½ cup chicken broth (see page 414)
3 tablespoons unsalted butter,
    approximately
1 tablespoon vegetable oil
1½ cups heavy or whipping cream
½ cup sour cream
⅓ cup chopped fresh dill

1. Combine all the ingredients through the pepper in a large bowl.
2. Place the onion with the chicken broth in the container of a food processor or blender. Process until smooth. Add this to the meat mixture, blend thoroughly, and form into small meatballs.
3. Heat 2 tablespoons of the butter with the oil in a heavy skillet over medium heat. Sauté the meatballs, about ten at a time, until golden on all sides. Transfer to a medium saucepan and keep warm. Add more butter as needed to sauté the remaining meatballs.
4. Place the saucepan over medium-low heat. Add the heavy cream and the sour cream to the meatballs. Simmer gently, uncovered, 20 minutes. Stir in the dill just before serving. Serve with rice, buttered noodles, or boiled potatoes.
Serves 4 to 6.

CARROT-RICE PUDDING

The following nostrum is one that is solid gold, yet lighter than air. A pudding that is definitely *no* dessert.

½ pound carrots, peeled, roughly chopped
1 cup strong Chicken Stock (see page 410)
½ cup heavy or whipping cream
1 tablespoon unsalted butter
2 tablespoons all-purpose flour
½ cup hot milk
Pinch of cayenne pepper
⅛ teaspoon freshly grated nutmeg
Salt and freshly ground black pepper
2 cups cooked rice

1. Preheat the oven to 375°F. Place the carrots with the stock in a medium saucepan. Heat to boiling; reduce the heat. Simmer, uncovered, until the carrots are very tender, about 12 to 15 minutes. Drain, reserving the stock.
2. Place the cooked carrots in the container of a food processor or blender. Add the cream and process until smooth. Reserve.

3. Melt the butter in a medium saucepan over medium-low heat. Stir in the flour. Cook, stirring constantly, 2 minutes. Whisk in the reserved stock and the hot milk. Heat to boiling; reduce the heat. Simmer until thickened, about 5 minutes. Add the cayenne pepper, nut-meg, and salt and pepper to taste. Remove from the heat; stir in the puréed carrots and the rice. Transfer the mixture to a buttered baking dish and bake 15 minutes.

Serves 6 to 8.

CARROT-VANILLA TART

*U*nfortunately there is no splendid carrot dish of my grandmother's repertoire left to end this memoir of her gorgeously green garden. So you will have to make do with one of my own inventions instead. It is a sweet custard tart of sufficient brilliance to make her proud of her old kitchen acolyte.

1 recipe Orange-Crust Pastry (see page 412)
¼ pound carrots (about 4 medium), peeled, cubed
4 eggs
1 cup sugar
¼ cup orange juice
2 tablespoons vanilla
1 cup heavy or whipping cream
4 tablespoons (½ stick) butter, melted

1. Preheat the oven to 400°F. Roll out the pastry on a lightly floured board. Line a buttered 10-inch loose-bottom tart pan with the pastry and trim the edges. Line the pastry with aluminum foil; weight with rice or beans. Bake 10 minutes. Remove the foil and beans. Bake 5 minutes longer. Cool on a wire rack. Reduce the oven heat to 350°F.

2. Cook the carrots in boiling water to cover until they are very tender, about 20 minutes. Drain. Place the carrots in the container of a food processor and process, using the on/off switch, until smooth.

3. Beat the eggs with the sugar in a large bowl until light and lemon colored. Add the puréed carrots, the orange juice, vanilla, cream, and melted butter. Pour into the prebaked shell and bake 40 minutes. Reduce the heat to 325°F and bake until firm, about 10 minutes longer.

Serves 6 to 8.

CAULIFLOWER
The Cabbage with the College Education

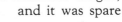

Twenty-five years ago, I became an exurbanite in earnest—without design, however.

There was certainly overpopulation in the area of Manhattan where I lived, and even then the signs of air pollution were unmistakable to anyone with working sinuses. But those were *not* the factors that drove me from city to hinterland. No, it was a deeper need that caused my initial foray to the virtual end of Long Island: love of sea, sand, and most important of all, seclusion.

The place I chose for my retreat would be judged a most unlikely territory for any hermit today, as it is technically part of the very tony Hamptons scene. But a quarter-century ago, Amagansett was so far out of the social swim

that it might have been mistaken for East Lynne.

It was a place that real estate agents of stature automatically bypassed when they showed summer rental houses to prospective tenants because the right people did not stop there. I obviously appeared so insubstantial, both socially and financially, that it was the *only* area I was offered.

The small house I eventually rented was known as "the Ely place" (always pronounced *eely* by some odd quirk of the Bonacker tongue) and it was spare and sparse. But to my eye it was a castle. Set back from the beach road, it faced little other than miles of ocean and a remarkable stretch of sand dunes and gorse where ripe blackberries and beach plums grew in abundance. I settled in this place to rusticate and write a play. Those berries and plums proved too narcotic to resist, however, so I spent half my days gathering them and the rest over a hot stove, sweating the spoils into gleaming jars of jam. How could I not? My private fruit reserve was just across the way, on a tract of overgrown land owned by the federal government that had once been the site of a vital Coast Guard operation housing five hundred young men in regimental whites.

By the late 1950s, the station and barracks had long since been abandoned. A faded sign still proclaimed the property to be "off limits" to civilians but no one in the vicinity took that admonition very seriously. For the blackberry and beach plum would surely have stained the white sand purple and red by summer's end, if willing hands had not come to the rescue and picked them!

At the termination of the first summer's lease, I knew the taste of the wildest berry (not to mention the anodyne of salt in the air) had had an irrevocable effect on my well-being. And shortly thereafter I bought a home of my own in Amagansett.

In those days, like most fellow Hamptonites, I locked the door and turned off the gas and electricity in late fall and did not return to my home in the country again until the following spring.

When I made my vernal reappearance, the signal that the territory had not irremediably altered in my absence was the rash of hand-lettered placards along the highway; signs, crudely crayoned, on farm stands, pickup trucks, and oil-cloth-covered tables along the road announcing: *Strawberries, Pick Your Own, 25¢ a Quart.*

That always meant summer was not far off.

Time does not stand still. Like it or no, a quarter-century wreaks irreparable changes in any landscape. The Coast Guard buildings, for instance, have been razed long since. Blackberry and beach plum likewise vanished, stripped bare by teenage vandals some years back. And rather than the scent of salt in the air these days one smells only high-octane gasoline, for the streets of Amagansett are clogged with trendy summer visitors, most in expensive foreign cars. No canines wander across the dunes any longer, for a town ruling insists that dogs be kept on leashes at all times. Even the once-deserted beaches require an official permit before a resident is allowed to dip his bottom into the sea.

Today, when the signs proclaim *Strawberries, Pick Your Own,* I blush somewhat deeper than the color of the fruit itself at the prices asked. And in summer, I do what all sensible householders have done since the sack of Rome. I rent my home to the invaders and go away!

When I return again in late September, the vital signs are still those hand-lettered placards along the road. But the legend that gives hope in autumn reads somewhat differently: *Cauliflower, 3 Heads for $1.*

I take heart then.

Not only because this greenstuff is the best grown anywhere along the Eastern seaboard (it is, it is) but also because the presence of those jade and white vegetables in the fields is a sure sign that summer is finally over. The earth and the slightly frigid sea are mine again. Without a beach permit.

Vegetable Roots

Cauliflower has been around for a good long time. Brought to Europe when the Moorish armies invaded Spain, this homely plant was promptly dubbed

From time to time in my hot pursuit of vegetable lore, I dip into some fairly esoteric tomes.

A *Wyf's Bok of Gardyning*, written in 1709, is a good case in point. Consider the following note: "Witches say coleflores eaten reguler by a childeless wyfe alwayes resulten praenansy." The witch's logic, in this case, undoubtedly arose from observation of the cauliflower plant in the garden, which grows to conspicuous proportions, discreetly hidden from any prying eye—a model judged worthy of emulation in the early eighteenth century.

cavoli a fiore (the cabbage that blooms like a flower), and initially its virtues were assumed to be ornamental rather than edible. Indeed, food sleuths tell us that a small, perfect cauliflower was often pressed into the décolletage of an unmarried Spanish maiden to call attention to her natural endowments.

Mark Twain once said, "Cauliflower is just a cabbage with a college education!" He wasn't very far from the mark. Originally known as wild winter cabbage, *Brassica oleracea botrytis* in its purest (uncultivated) state is a tall-growing green flower stalk, slightly on the fibrous side and better loved by goats than gastronomes. Its evolution into one of the staples of the world took place long, long before the birth of Christ, but the changeover was due to man's ingenuity rather than Mother Nature's diligence.

The great snowy head of succulent buds nesting in a wreath of green leaves was the handiwork of an early gardener (most probably a Babylonian) who first cultivated the plant for his dinner table in the Tigris-Euphrates Valley. The technique he used to shape the plant is much the same as the cauliflower growers of eastern Long Island employ two thousand years later.

Shortly after a cauliflower seed is sown in late summer, a stemless green whorl resembling a young cabbage appears. The farmer watches its growth scrupulously, waiting for precisely the right moment to interrupt its cycle. When a small round rosette of green forms in the center of the plant, he gathers the outer leaves and draws them together like a loose pouch. The leaves continue to grow larger while the nourished bud at the heart of the leafy tent increases in size. By harvest time an immense head has formed, tender because it was sheltered from the sun's evaporating rays and pure white because it literally blossomed under wraps.

What to Look For

Use your nose when purchasing cauliflower, in or out of its rightful growing season. Over-the-hill heads of cauliflower smell strong as the dickens and taste worse cooked. A good rule of thumb for freshness is a faint cabbage scent; a reasonably white curd, not turning brown at the leafy ruff; and a texture that retains a measure of crispness after it has been scraped with a fingernail. Avoid excessively crumbly cauliflower in any season: it has usually remained in the field too long after being cut for harvest.

Perhaps the fact that most Long Island cauliflower is permitted to tarry on the vine until the local farmers deem it ready for sale at the roadside accounts for its high proportion of nutritive riches. In addition to the usual complement of *Brassica* vitamin endowments (80 units of vitamin A, 90 milligrams of vitamin C, 339 milligrams of potassium, and 64 grams of phosphorus per cup), the winter vegetable maintains exceedingly high levels of folic acid, prime source of vitamin B in the diet. Since the lack of folic acid is known to cause anemia, this local cauliflower is sometimes described by waggish members of the community as "a roadside vitamin B shot."

Preparation

Cauliflower may be a vegetable for all seasons, but the appropriate method for its cookery varies with those times of the year when it is at its absolutely freshest.

For instance, I do very little preculinary tampering with any head that I pick up from a roadside stand or greengrocer in the fall or winter. I merely cook the cauliflower whole (after it has been trimmed and the core removed) in the largest pot I own—one that can contain at least 3 quarts of water. The simplest way to prepare a whole cauliflower for the pot is to remove the tough outer leaves first, then hollow out the core using a sharp knife. This allows a head to cook evenly. The amount of cooking time depends upon the weight and size of the head, but 8 to 12 minutes usually suffices for blanching. Always cook cauliflower head-down and uncovered.

Once I deem the head to be tender (by poking it with the tip of a sharp knife), I plunge it under cold running water in a colander to retard the cooking. When it is completely cooled I take the recipe from there.

Some culinary savants advise the addition of salt to the boiling water (1 teaspoon salt per quart of water is the rule of thumb), but frankly I do not. I prefer to add salt later when it neither tenderizes nor alters the vegetable's sweetness.

Another crotchet: I never break up a cauliflower into flowerets before I blanch it, as I discovered some while back that a whole cauliflower is more easily divided into segments after it is cooked because then it never disintegrates or crumbles. For flowerets I merely trim the cooked cauliflower with a paring knife to the size that suits my preference.

Less than fresh (cold storage) cauliflower is perfectly acceptable but it demands more attention, for this cold-weather vegetable develops a somewhat stronger flavor as it is stored, even under optimum root-cellar conditions. I always soak out-of-season cauliflower in a bath of cold water for at least half an hour prior to cooking to remove any excessive acidity. Some cooks add a jot of fresh milk or lemon juice to the boiling water to whiten the head as it cooks. I never do, preferring to add a teaspoon or so of white wine vinegar to the cooking water. That's a trick I learned a while back in Italy, and it seems to both bleach and sweeten the head at the same time.

CRÈME DU BARRY
(Cream of Cauliflower Soup)

Cauliflower soup has been a personal favorite since childhood; my grandmother served it whenever she surmised that a member of her family looked "under the weather." It is a creamy caloric concoction that I always knew as "white soup" until I learned better.

This emollient—most often served warm but quite tonic cold, thinned with milk—is said to be the invention of that French expert in matters both sensual and savory, Madame Du Barry, who started out as a farm girl named Marie-Jeanne Bécu and ended up as the great and good friend of Louis XV, the last king of France to die a natural death.

The lady may have lost her head over royalty but she retained a sense of delight in simple pleasures (at the table certainly). Just see for yourself.

1½ pounds cauliflower, leaves trimmed,
*   core removed*
1 small carrot, peeled, sliced
3 cups chicken broth (see page 414)
⅓ cup unconverted long-grain rice
2 cups milk
1 tablespoon lemon juice
¼ teaspoon freshly grated nutmeg
¼ teaspoon cayenne pepper
½ cup heavy or whipping cream
Salt
Chopped fresh chives or scallion tops

1. Cook the cauliflower in at least 3 quarts of boiling water for 2 minutes. Drain. Cut or break the cauliflower into flowerets. (If using out-of-season cauliflower, soak in cold water for 30 minutes prior to cooking and add 1½ teaspoons white wine vinegar to the cooking water.)

2. Place the cauliflower in a medium saucepan. Add the carrot and the chicken broth. Heat to boiling. Stir in the rice and reduce the heat. Simmer, uncovered, 30 minutes.

3. Place half the cauliflower mixture into the container of a processor or blender with 1 cup of the milk. Process until smooth being very careful, as hot liquid will expand. Transfer the mixture to a medium saucepan. Repeat the process with the remaining cauliflower mixture and milk. Add this to the saucepan. Add the lemon juice, nutmeg, cayenne pepper, cream, and salt to taste. Place over medium-low heat until warmed through. Do not boil. Serve garnished with chives or scallion tops. (Soup may be served cold, thinned with milk after chilling.)

Serves 6.

CAULIFLOWER AND SHRIMP IN A BLANKET OF MAYONNAISE

My most favored cauliflower rendering at the moment (my tastes do change) is a decidedly summer salad in which the pale blanched flowerets are tossed with bright pink shrimp in a snowy mayonnaise.

1½ pounds cauliflower, leaves trimmed,
*   core removed*
¾ cup dry vermouth
6 whole peppercorns
3 sprigs fresh parsley, plus 1 tablespoon
*   finely chopped*
Pinch of thyme
1 small bay leaf
1 shallot, roughly chopped, plus 2

*   tablespoons minced*
1 whole clove garlic
1 pound raw shrimp
1 cup Mayonnaise (see page 408)
½ cup sour cream
1 tablespoon minced fresh basil
2 teaspoons Dijon mustard
Salt and freshly ground black pepper

1. Cook the cauliflower in at least 3 quarts of boiling water until barely tender, about 10 minutes. Drain. Cut or break the cauliflower into flowerets. Chill. (If using out-of-season cauliflower, soak in cold water for 30 minutes prior to cooking and add 1½ teaspoons white wine vinegar to the cooking water.)

2. Combine the vermouth, peppercorns, sprigs of parsley, thyme, bay leaf, roughly chopped shallot, and garlic in a medium saucepan. Heat to boiling; reduce the heat. Add the shrimp and cook, tossing gently, until the shrimp turn pink, 4 to 5 minutes. Remove the shrimp from the liquid. Strain the cooking liquid and reserve it. When cooled, shell and devein the shrimp and chill them.

3. Beat the mayonnaise with the sour cream in a large bowl until smooth. Beat in the minced shallots, basil, and mustard. Thin the mixture with about ¼ cup of the reserved shrimp broth. Add the cauliflower and shrimp. Toss well; add salt and pepper to taste. Garnish with the finely chopped parsley.

Serves 6.

CARNABEET
(Sephardic Cauliflower)

Carnabeet is a spicy vegetable stew. It is long-cooked over low heat, yet the ingredients retain a remarkable degree of bite and crunch because the vegetables are placed in the pot raw, with only a splash of liquid. It is part of the culinary repertoire of Sephardic cooks, those descendants of the Semitic peoples who settled in Spain, Portugal, Greece, Turkey, North Africa, and in fact most of the countries that form the lush Mediterranean basin. Theirs was a cuisine quite unlike what many uninitiated diners think of as Jewish food, which is usually an amalgam of Russian and Polish cookery that has been altered by a sea change on its way to the New World.

My version of Carnabeet has altered over the years with the kitchen ingredients I have had at hand. Orthodox Jews, of course, will omit the butter, but ecumenical food lovers will want to add it to bring out the flavor.

1½ pounds cauliflower, leaves trimmed,
   core removed
1½ tablespoons vegetable oil
1 small onion, finely chopped
1 rib celery, minced
1 large tomato, seeded, chopped
¼ pound string beans, trimmed
Juice of ½ lemon
⅓ cup strong Chicken Stock,
   approximately (see page 410)
Salt and freshly ground black pepper
2 tablespoons unsalted butter (optional)

1. Cook the cauliflower in at least 3 quarts of boiling water for 2 minutes. Drain. Cut or break the cauliflower into flowerets. (If using out-of-season cauliflower, soak in cold water for 30 minutes prior to cooking and add 1½ teaspoons white wine vinegar to the cooking water.)

2. Heat the oil in a medium saucepan over medium-low heat. Add the onion; cook 3 minutes. Add the celery, tomato, string beans, cauliflower, lemon

juice, and chicken stock. Cook, covered, until tender, about 30 minutes. Add more chicken stock if the mixture dries out. Add salt and pepper to taste. Toss in the butter just before serving, if desired.

Serves 4.

WHITE-ON-WHITE PUREE
(Cauliflower and Turnip Purée)

*T*here are cauliflower purées and white turnip purées ad infinitum. However, none has the upright character or decided savor of the following partnership.

1 to 1¼ pounds cauliflower, leaves
* trimmed, core removed*
4 tablespoons (½ stick) unsalted butter
½ pound white turnips, peeled, chopped
1 slice lemon
1 small bay leaf
¼ cup heavy or whipping cream
Pinch of ground cloves
Salt and ground white pepper
Dash of hot pepper sauce
1 tablespoon chopped fresh parsley

1. Cook the cauliflower in at least 3 quarts of boiling water until very tender, about 10 minutes. Drain. Break the cauliflower into flowerets. (If using out-of-season cauliflower, soak in cold water for 30 minutes prior to cooking and add 1½ teaspoons white wine vinegar to the cooking water.)

2. Melt 2 tablespoons of the butter in a medium skillet over medium-low heat. Add the turnips; toss to coat them with the butter. Add the lemon slice and bay leaf. Cook, covered, until the turnips are tender, about 12 minutes. Discard the lemon and bay leaf.

3. Place the cauliflower in the container of a food processor. Process until smooth, then transfer the cauliflower to the top of a double boiler. Add the turnips to the processor container and process until smooth. Add them to the cauliflower purée. Stir in the cream, cloves, salt and pepper to taste, and the hot pepper sauce. Reheat over simmering water. Stir in the remaining 2 tablespoons butter and sprinkle with parsley.

Serves 4.

AUSTRO-HUNGARIAN GREEN-TOPPED CAULIFLOWER

*T*his most exquisite combination of cauliflower and bright green peas is a bequest from Austria-Hungary. I first encountered this dish toward the close of World War II in the cooking repertoire of an ex-countess of Hapsburg lineage (or so she claimed), who lived in a tiny suite of rooms at the glossy Sherry-Netherland Hotel with her ten-year-old daughter and an old family servant, while waiting for her husband (the Count) to be mustered out of the RAF in London.

Her recipe was a zealously guarded secret, and I never tried to pry it from her. Instead, I have reconstructed it with a recipe given to me by another enchanting Eastern European lady, Marina Polvay. This version is freely adapted from her book, *All Along the Danube*.

1½- to 2-pound head of cauliflower, leaves
    trimmed, core removed
5 tablespoons unsalted butter
3 whole scallions, bulbs and green tops,
    minced
1 package (10 ounces) frozen peas, thawed
Pinch of sugar
1 tablespoon chopped fresh parsley
½ cup heavy or whipping cream

1. Preheat the oven to 275°F. Cook the cauliflower in at least 3 quarts of boiling water until just tender, 10 to 12 minutes. Drain. (If using out-of-season cauliflower, soak in cold water for 30 minutes prior to cooking and add 1½ teaspoons white wine vinegar to the cooking water.)

2. Meanwhile, melt 3 tablespoons of the butter.

3. Place the whole cauliflower in a deep serving dish. Pour the melted butter over and keep it warm in the oven.

4. Melt the remaining 2 tablespoons butter in a medium skillet over medium-low heat. Stir in the scallions; cook until soft, about 5 minutes. Stir in the peas; sprinkle with sugar. Cook 4 minutes. Add the parsley and cream. Transfer the pea mixture to the container of a food processor or blender. Process until smooth. Reheat in a medium saucepan; do not boil. Spoon over the cauliflower and serve.

Serves 4 to 6.

GRATIN OF CAULIFLOWER WITH GINGERED CRUMBS

1½ pounds cauliflower, leaves trimmed,
    core removed
3 tablespoons unsalted butter
2 tablespoons all-purpose flour
1 cup light cream or half-and-half
1 teaspoon lemon juice
¼ teaspoon freshly grated nutmeg
Dash of hot pepper sauce
¼ cup grated Swiss cheese
¼ cup fresh bread crumbs
⅛ teaspoon ground ginger
2 tablespoons freshly grated Parmesan
    cheese

1. Preheat the oven to 350°F. Cook the cauliflower in at least 3 quarts of boiling water until just tender, 10 to 12 minutes. Rinse under cold running water. Drain. Cut or break the cauliflower into flowerets. (If using out-of-season cauliflower, soak in cold water for 30 minutes prior to cooking and add 1½ teaspoons white wine vinegar to the cooking water.) Set aside.

2. Melt 2 tablespoons of the butter in a medium saucepan over medium-low heat. Stir in the flour. Cook, stirring constantly, 2 minutes. Whisk in the cream. Raise the heat slightly; cook until thick. Add the lemon juice, nutmeg, hot pepper sauce, and cheese. Remove from the heat and set aside.

3. Place the cauliflower in a well-buttered 1½- to 2-quart soufflé dish or casserole. Spoon the cheese sauce over the top.

4. Melt the remaining 1 tablespoon butter in a small skillet over medium heat. Stir in the bread crumbs and ginger. Cook, stirring constantly, until golden. Spoon the crumbs over the cauliflower and sprinkle with the Parmesan cheese. Bake in the oven until bubbly, 15 to 20 minutes. Let stand 5 minutes before serving.

Serves 4.

BAKED CAULIFLOWER CREAM

*T*o my mind, the most classic versions of pale baked cauliflower (acquired from the kitchens of France, Italy, and Austria) are usually enriched with even paler emollients: cream, sweet butter, or cheese—sometimes all three. As I was raised on cauliflower that was mashed like potatoes, I still retain a childlike affection for the crushed-velvet texture on my tongue. In remembrance of that delectable amalgam, here is the simplest creamed cauliflower dish in my repertoire. It is a splendid adjunct to roasted or broiled meat and may be prepared well in advance of dinner, refrigerated, and then reheated for a scant half hour in a 350°F oven prior to its appearance at the table.

1½ pounds cauliflower, leaves trimmed,
core removed
3 tablespoons unsalted butter
1 chicken bouillon cube, crushed
1 medium onion, roughly chopped
1 small clove garlic, chopped
1 cup sour cream
Salt and freshly ground black pepper
Chopped fresh parsley

1. Preheat the oven to 350°F. Cook the cauliflower in at least 3 quarts of boiling water until very tender, 12 to 15 minutes. Drain. Cut or break the cauliflower into flowerets. (If using out-of-season cauliflower, soak in cold water for 30 minutes prior to cooking and add 1½ teaspoons white wine vinegar to the cooking water.)

2. Melt 1 tablespoon of the butter in a medium skillet over medium-low heat. Stir in the bouillon and onion. Cook 1 minute. Add the garlic; cook 4 minutes longer. Remove from the heat.

3. Place the sour cream in the container of a food processor. Add the onion mixture and the cauliflower. Add the remaining 2 tablespoons of butter bit by bit. Process until smooth; the mixture should be the texture of mashed potatoes. Add salt and pepper to taste.

4. Spoon the cauliflower mixture into a lightly buttered 1-quart baking dish. Bake 15 minutes. Garnish with parsley.

Serves 4 to 6.

HEADED CAULIFLOWER

No food writer confers the title "classic" on a recipe without inviting vituperative dissent from the world's culinary arbiters. My tastes (if you haven't noticed already) are all eclectic and I offer no apologies for them. But I do believe, however, that one could not possibly list archetypal cauliflower renditions without including the simplest version I have ever sampled, to wit: the following head, blanched, well buttered, then well cheesed and baked till that upholstery turns a deep golden hue.

1½- to 2-pound head of cauliflower, leaves
    trimmed, core removed
4 tablespoons (½ stick) unsalted butter,
    melted
½ cup grated Gruyère or Jarlsberg cheese
⅔ cup freshly grated Parmesan cheese
Freshly ground black pepper

1. Preheat the oven to 400°F. Cook the cauliflower in at least 3 quarts of boiling water until just tender, 10 to 12 minutes. Rinse under cold running water. Drain. (If using out-of-season cauliflower, soak in cold water for 30 minutes prior to cooking and add 1½ teaspoons white wine vinegar to the cooking water.)

2. Very gently pry apart the cauliflower flowerets, but do not detach them from the head. Place the melted butter in a bowl large enough to hold the cauliflower. Place the cauliflower upside-down in the butter. Let it stand 10 minutes.

3. Turn the cauliflower upright and place on a sheet of waxed paper; pour any leftover butter over it. Pat the Gruyère cheese between the flowerets. Dust the whole head with the Parmesan. Sprinkle generously with pepper. Transfer the head to a shallow baking dish and bake 15 minutes. Place under a broiler to brown the top if desired.

Serves 4 to 6.

VENETIAN CAULIFLOWER AND RICE CASSEROLE

This prescription of cauliflower layered over rice with a gilded *besciamella* sauce is unique to the watery landscape of Venice and the provinces of the Po Valley nearby, where Italy's short-grained rice is harvested.

The recipe is a slightly amended version of one in a book I admire enormously and cook from with regularity: *The Cuisine of Venice & Surrounding Northern Regions* by Hedy Giusti-Lanham and Andrea Dodi.

1½ pounds cauliflower, leaves trimmed,
    core removed
1 cup Italian rice (I prefer Arborio)
6 tablespoons (¾ stick) unsalted butter
1 shallot, minced
¼ cup finely chopped fresh parsley
2 tablespoons all-purpose flour
1 cup chicken broth (see page 414)
⅛ teaspoon freshly grated nutmeg
Salt and freshly ground black pepper
½ cup freshly grated Parmesan cheese

1. Preheat the oven to 400°F. Cook the cauliflower in at least 3 quarts of boiling water until just tender, 10 to 12 minutes. Remove, reserving the cooking liquid, and rinse in a colander under cold running water. Drain. Cut or break the cauliflower into flowerets. (If using out-of-season cauliflower, soak in cold water for 30 minutes prior to cooking and add 1½ teaspoons white wine vinegar to the cooking water.) Set aside.

2. Return the cooking water to the boil. Add the rice, stir once, and cook, uncovered, until just tender, about 12 minutes. Drain, and set aside.

3. Melt 2 tablespoons of the butter in a medium skillet over medium heat. Add the shallot; cook until golden. Stir in the drained rice and 2 more tablespoons of the butter. Stir in the parsley; remove from the heat and set aside.

4. Melt the remaining 2 tablespoons butter in a medium saucepan over medium-low heat. Stir in the flour. Cook, stirring constantly, 2 minutes. Whisk in the chicken broth and cook until thick. Add the nutmeg and salt and pepper to taste. Remove from the heat.

5. Spoon one third of the rice over the bottom of a buttered 2-quart soufflé or deep baking dish. Drizzle with one third of the sauce. Add one third of the cheese and then half the cauliflower. Repeat the layers twice, ending with the cheese. Bake in the oven until bubbly, about 20 minutes. Let stand 5 minutes before serving.

Serves 6.

PARMA-STYLE FRIED CAULIFLOWER

Cauliflower is a truly international vegetable that takes a distinct coloration in each native landscape, and more important, from the natural ingredients of each region where it is prepared.

This batter-fried cauliflower comes from Parma, in the northern bootstrap of Italy. Offhand I cannot think of anything more succulent than those gleaming flowerets forked out of pots of sizzling lard as a ravenous diner waits, salivating, at the prospect of his tongue's immolation.

The secret (no secret at all) is Parmesan cheese in the batter.

1½ to 2 pounds cauliflower, leaves
    trimmed, core removed
½ cup water
1 teaspoon lemon juice
Dash of hot pepper sauce
6 tablespoons all-purpose flour

6 tablespoons freshly grated Parmesan
    cheese
1 egg, lightly beaten
1 teaspoon finely grated lemon peel
Vegetable oil for frying
Salt

1. Cook the cauliflower in at least 3 quarts of boiling water until just tender, 10 to 12 minutes. Rinse under cold running water. Drain. Cut or break the cauliflower into small flowerets. (If using out-of-season cauliflower, soak in cold water for 30 minutes prior to cooking and add 1½ teaspoons white wine vinegar to the cooking water.)

2. Combine the water, lemon juice, and hot pepper sauce in a medium bowl. Beat in the flour until smooth. Beat in the cheese, egg, and lemon peel.

3. Heat 2 inches of oil in a medium saucepan until almost smoking. Dip the flowerets into the batter and then fry them, about six at a time, until golden, about 4 to 5 minutes. (Oil should be hot enough that cauliflower will turn dark gold in this time.) Drain on paper towels and keep warm in a low oven while frying the remaining cauliflower. Before serving, sprinkle on salt to taste.

Serves 4 to 6.

CAULIFLOWER AND HAM GRATIN

Gratin is a corruption of the middle-French verb *grater*, which means "to scrape." My best scrapings on the subject include this, which is of French descent, from an old cookbook I found in Burgundy.

1½ to 2 pounds cauliflower, leaves
    trimmed, core removed
3 tablespoons unsalted butter
1 large shallot, minced
½ pound cooked ham, finely chopped
1 tablespoon Madeira
2 tablespoons all-purpose flour
1 cup hot Chicken Stock (see page 410)
¼ teaspoon freshly grated nutmeg
Salt and freshly ground black pepper
⅔ cup grated Jarlsberg cheese

1. Preheat the oven to 350°F. Cook the cauliflower in at least 3 quarts of boiling water until just tender, 10 to 12 minutes. Rinse under cold running water. Drain. Cut or break the cauliflower into flowerets. (If using out-of-season cauliflower, soak in cold water for 30 minutes prior to cooking and add 1½ teaspoons white wine vinegar to the cooking water.) Set aside.

2. Melt 1 tablespoon of the butter in a medium skillet over medium heat. Add the shallot; cook 1 minute. Add the ham; cook until lightly browned. Sprinkle with the Madeira. Cook, stirring constantly, until all liquid has evaporated. Remove from the heat and set aside.

3. Melt the remaining 2 tablespoons butter in a medium saucepan over medium-low heat. Stir in the flour. Cook, stirring constantly, 2 minutes. Whisk in the hot stock. Cook until thick. Add the nutmeg, and salt and pepper to taste.

4. Place half the cauliflower in a well-buttered 2-quart soufflé dish or casserole. Spoon the ham mixture evenly over the top. Spoon half the sauce over that, and sprinkle with half the cheese. Repeat the layers of cauliflower, sauce, and cheese. Bake in the oven until bubbly, 15 to 20 minutes. Let stand 5 minutes before serving.

Serves 4 to 6.

CAULIFLOWER AND CHEESE WAFFLES

What follows is a recent cauliflower invention: a waffle composed of leftover cauliflower, cheese, eggs, flour, and the usual waffle adjuncts. This dish is ideal for a fast pick-up supper, unexpected luncheon guests, or even a cocktail party nibble in a pinch, when the olive and almond supply is low. Amend the waffle with any topping you desire (creamed chicken, mushrooms, chipped beef) or, here, a splash of shocking-pink tomato sauce.

¾ cup cooked cauliflower, roughly chopped
1 egg
1 cup milk
¼ cup heavy or whipping cream
¾ cup all-purpose flour, sifted
1 teaspoon baking powder
2 tablespoons unsalted butter, melted
½ cup grated mild Cheddar cheese
2 tablespoons freshly grated Parmesan
    cheese
1 egg white
Creamy Tomato Sauce (see page 375)

1. Place the cauliflower, egg, milk, and cream in the container of a food processor or blender. Process until smooth. Transfer to a medium bowl.

2. Sift the flour with the baking powder. Stir the flour into the cauliflower mixture. Beat until smooth. Add the melted butter and both kinds of cheese.

3. Beat the egg white until stiff. Fold it into the batter. Cook the waffles on a preheated waffle iron according to the manufacturer's directions. Keep the waffles warm on a rack in a low oven while you make the remaining ones. Serve with Creamy Tomato Sauce.

Makes 6 or 7 large waffles.

Note: This batter may be used for pancakes as well.

The French call cauliflower *chou fleur* (cabbage blossom); Germans dub it *Blumenkohl* (blooming cabbage); Italian chefs compromise on *cavolfiore* (cabbage flower).

CELERY AND CELERY ROOT

A Popular Stalk with an Up-and-Coming Root

I never met the celebrated French writer Colette, but she influenced my life as much as anyone I have ever known.

It was in the early 1950s when I first discovered her, during a long summer's bout with the flu. The doctor had prescribed absolute bed rest to combat the fever—so there was nothing to do but read, and I even did that fitfully. Of all the books I skimmed during those torpid days and sleepless nights only Colette's managed to hold my attention. I resolved to write her immediately after I recovered. But good intentions do not often mix with natural timidity and habitual inanition, so I allowed the impulse to pass. When Colette died (at eighty-two) some while after, I deeply regretted that I had not made contact. But our lives did converge (as obviously they were meant to) despite the omission.

A decade later I adapted some stories about her childhood into a theater piece that was performed at The Poetry Center and became the basis for a television play starring Colleen Dewhurst. That my work received praise (and money) gave me considerable gratification, but the fact that it also pleased Maurice Goudeket (Colette's widower) compounded the joy.

"You alone have captured my wife's voice," he wired me from Paris after he had read the script. That compliment became the basis of one of the most satisfying friendships I have ever had. Maurice Goudeket and I became close friends despite the obvious barriers of geography and time. He had been seventeen years younger than Colette and knew how to bridge the differences in our ages with infinite good grace. A tall, extremely elegant man even in his late sixties, Goudeket never chided me for not finishing a play about Colette on which I had fleetingly embarked. Instead he bid me do whatever I really wanted in life. "But Bert...sink your teeth into something real!"

Together we would sit for hours in the afternoon at a table in an empty restaurant overlooking Central Park. Despite the waiter's baleful glances at the clock, Maurice remained completely unperturbed, drinking pot after pot of herbal tea (his choice) and speaking endlessly of his wife's zest for life.

Though I knew much about her already, he filled in all the blanks. Colette's way of making contact in life was utterly sensory. Not content to merely admire a wild plant or herb, she had to sniff and taste it as well. When she entered an unfamiliar garden, he reported, she would kick off her shoes and walk barefoot—crumpling leaves on her tongue and chewing random stalks (even of poisonous berries and deadly toadstools) because, in his words: "She simply had to know every single thing there was to know about life. *Everything!*" When Colette left a garden it was never the same. Nor was she. Her nose would be dusted with more pollen than powder, her hair a wild disarray of twigs and thorns, and her voice breathless with excitement at all she had just discovered. At the end of her life, too!

Colette had a reputation for a voracious appetite. When I asked him once what foods she liked best, her husband laughed out loud.

"Oh my God. That woman loved to sink her teeth into things of substance; crisp roots, ash-roasted potatoes, and chestnuts. Peasant breads with crust so rough it would bruise a normal diner's upper lip. But never hers...."

"I will tell you a story of my wife's appetite," he said. "When she had to have her photograph taken with the members of the French Academy for the first time, she went on a rare diet to lose five pounds. For a week she ate nothing but celery. Celery with water. Celery with salt and pepper. But only celery for seven days. Never once complaining even when I was served my normal meals. Later, after she had lost the weight, she confided that one day she had cheated. There had been a small red caterpillar at the heart of a celery stalk, but she was so hungry for meat, she ate it too!" Maurice sighed, "That was Colette."

To someone who had once consumed half a worm, the story made her seem more monumental than ever!

Colette has influenced my life in many ways: her love of rustic things, provincial dishes, and homely furnishings, her love of flowers—all I adopted long, long ago. And I have one more inheritance from this incredible woman: one of her very own paperweights. Maurice gave it to me after our second meeting and it was the basis for my own, not inconsiderable, collection of these baubles. But though I have several dozen on my table always, I never mistake the one that once belonged to Colette with any other. A clear, graceful globe, it holds a crystal bouquet of pale yellow whorls and glass buds; quite perfect but for an infinitesimal flaw of color at the center. Red, like a scarlet surprise in a stalk of celery.

Vegetable Roots

I must admit I treasure celery—in every form except stuffed—almost as much as the Greeks, who awarded great green bunches as prizes to victorious athletes after their games were done. Why not? Celery is composed of 95 percent water, and tastes a heck of a lot better than Gatorade!

Celery is one of those tried and true denizens of the garden whose present discreet mien bears scant resemblance to the wild life it once led, before cultivators brought it into the fold. The original renegade stalk still blossoms in salt marshes along the coastline of southern France. Bees love its tiny white flowers and in fact gave the plant its Latin name, *Apium graveolens*, which means "heavy with bees." All other mammals (man and beast alike) cut a wide swath wherever the wild celery grows, for its bitter flavor marks a lethal dose in every rib.

Wild celery stems from the *Umbelliferae* clan, the same family tree, in fact, that links a parsnip to a carrot to a parsley sprig. But there the resemblance ends. For celery in its wildest guise is a stubby, tough, fibrous weed that holds no possibilities whatsoever for any stockpot.

From wild celery early horticulturists bred two separate and distinct strains of vegetables that have proven the test of palatability for almost four thousand years. *Apium graveolens dulce* (sweet only in comparison with its bitter forebear) is the crunchy green stalk that is every dieter's staff of life. *Apium graveolens rapaceum* (so dubbed because it must be literally ripped from the garden by force) is a bulbous white root that is the indispensable ingredient in one of the world's classiest hors d'oeuvres, *céleri rémoulade*.

Food historians claim that both celery and celery root were developed by the gardeners of the king of Persia around the year 2000 B.C. Cyrus the First was reputedly a vegetarian, and a finicky eater besides. Out of dietary doldrums, he commanded a crew of royal gardeners to come up with something different for his supper. Celery filled the gap—if one can believe the backstairs scuttlebutt after all these years!

One fact about celery may be verified, however: a bunch of this leafy green was sent as a wedding gift to the Empress of China during the T'ang dynasty— which bespeaks a measure of the Persians' high regard for its savor.

It is hard to believe when one brushes past stacks of packaged celery on a supermarket shelf that this leafy stalk was ever so prized, or so rare.

The ancient Egyptians, Greeks, and Romans considered celery a gift from the gods, quite capable of regenerating the human body and mind. Egyptian physicians divided celery's medicinal properties sexually: the strong stalks that grew upward from the ground were judged to be a cure for all masculine dysfunctions from bed-wetting to impotence, while the hairy, tuberous root that swelled beneath the earth's surface was prescribed for female disorders.

Even today in Crete newly married couples are pelted with either celery seeds or barley as they leave the church. Never both. It is claimed that the seed of celery ensures fertility and barley promises a full larder. And obviously both take equal concentration to acquire.

In Rome a stalk of celery was thought to be a cure for both constipation and hangover. Apicius lists at least two sure-fire remedies for the first ailment and a word of advice for the second: overimbibers are counseled "to wear a wreath of celery 'round the brow to ease the pain."

My own hangover cure seems frankly a jot more effective. The prescription? One large Bloody Mary, well laced with vodka and seasoned generously with lemon juice and Tabasco sauce, served up in a goblet so cold that one's fingers freeze to the surface when it is held aloft. And, oh yes, as anesthetic: a celery stalk in the glass.

Celery

What to Look For

There are celeryphiles and celeryphobes, but even the most unenthusiastic cannot deny this vegetable its due as a pot-flavoring and enhancer of other comestibles.

Celery was once an autumn vegetable, but these days shoppers will find it in plenteous supply year round. Unfortunately the more toothsome stalks (like snowy "White Ice" and self-blanching "Golden") are not a common sight at most greengrocers' except as packaged celery hearts, because the paler varieties have an abbreviated shelf life.

Pascal (the green-ribbed, full-branched, tender-leafed) celery is the hands-down favorite in American households because it is always super-crisp—with a pleasantly astringent flavor that makes it a favored between-meal snack.

Celery shoppers should look for tight heads with compact outer stalks. Never buy browned or cracked bunches of celery; the discoloration is a dead giveaway that the vegetable is less than fresh.

Packaged celery is supposedly prewashed. But, as with garden celery, I always rinse it under cold running water when I get it home. Heeding the advice of the English naturalist John Evelyn, who wrote about celery in 1699:

> For its high and grateful Taste it is ever plac'd in the middle of the Grand Sallet, at our Great Mens Tables, and Praetor Feasts, as the Grace of the whole Board. But *Caution* is to be given of a small red *worm*, often lurking in these stalks.

Happily for dieters, stalk celery is extremely low in calories. A portion averages less than 20 calories per cupful, yet is relatively high in minerals (409 milligrams of potassium) and vitamin A (320 units in each 1 cup serving).

Preparation

Since the dawn of time (or at least dating back to Cyrus the First of Persia), the classic way to consume a stalk of celery has been raw, preferably chilled and stripped of its fibrous strings.

Cooked celery is another kettle of greens entirely. To my captious palate, the only classic method of celery cookery is braising. That is to say, cooking the stalks, covered, with a small amount of liquid until they are barely fork tender.

Though I must confess I rarely bother except when I'm using the celery raw, many culinary savants peel celery prior to cooking it, claiming that it makes the vegetable easier to chew. It's a simple trick. Here's how to do it: With a sharp knife make a small incision at the wide end of a celery stalk without actually cutting through it. Gently loosen the fibers and pull them down the outer layer of the flesh to the narrow end.

Celery Root

Celery root (celeriac) is one vegetable that enjoys enormous popularity at European dinner tables but only the mildest form of approbation over here. The reason, I suspect, is that while this vegetable's flavor is extraordinary, its appearance on a vegetable stand is positively awesome.

Celery root has had other notable drawbacks: it is difficult to peel and to slice. However, rotary-type vegetable peelers and food processors now eliminate those objections.

There are three important reasons for the uninitiated to try celery root immediately: the texture (crisp and rooty even when cooked), the flavor (like superconcentrated celery), and the calories (practically nonexistent—less than 20 in a cupful).

Preparation

Celery root is one vegetable I opt *not* to eat raw. Instead sometimes I boil it unpeeled and then peel and slice it after it has cooled. Or I peel it first, then boil it either whole or in slices.

I most often parboil celery root (to tenderize the tuberous flesh) prior to further cookery. A whole peeled celery root, depending upon its size, takes about 20 to 30 minutes to cook until crisp-tender. Peeled sliced celery root (cut into ¼-inch-thick strips) takes considerably less time, about 8 minutes. Unseasonal celery root (the kind found in late spring and summer) cooks in a shorter time.

The alternative method for cooking celery root (when crunch is not a prerequisite) is to boil it whole, unpeeled, for 40 to 45 minutes. When it is sufficiently tender, remove the root from the saucepan; allow it to cool, peel and slice it, and proceed with the recipe at hand.

CELERY SLAW

No matter where your celery is grown, snip a stalk or two for the most tonic salad you will ever toss.

1 small bunch celery, trimmed
¼ pound mushrooms, sliced
¼ pound Monterey jack cheese, chopped
½ cup olive oil
1 small clove garlic, crushed
3 tablespoons red wine vinegar
¼ teaspoon freshly ground black pepper
Salt
4 strips crisp-fried bacon, crumbled

1. Cut the celery into very thin strips, about 1 inch long; or cut it into paper-thin slices crosswise. Place the celery in a large bowl with the mushrooms and cheese.

2. Combine the olive oil with the garlic, vinegar, and pepper in a small bowl. Pour this dressing over the celery mixture and toss well. Cover and let it stand in a cool place for 1 hour.

3. Add salt to taste, transfer to a serving dish, and sprinkle with the crumbled bacon.

Serves 4 to 6.

COOL, COLLECTED CELERY

*I*n my book, boiling celery is an utter desecration! My mother did it all the time, and I grew up with the notion that all cooked celery was supposed to taste like wet laundry. It is *not*. A prolonged stay in a pan of boiling water may tenderize a bunch of celery on occasion, but it also depletes its natural flavor beyond redemption. For the same reason I do not recommend steaming celery. Even in sophisticated electric steamers, the process takes so long that the nutrients vaporize in the steam, and anyway, steamed celery is uniformly flat-tasting and watery.

My favorite way to cook celery (after braising) is to poach it in broth, with the cooking liquid kept well below the boiling point. This is a version of a small culinary masterpiece offered up by my good friend M. F. K. Fisher in her book *With Bold Knife and Fork*, where it appeared under the imposing title "Celery Victor-Solari-Veneto." After a little adjusting, my amendment carries a far less formal cognomen.

1 large, thick bunch of celery
3½ cups chicken broth, approximately (see page 414)
Simple Vinaigrette Sauce (recipe follows)
1 hard-cooked egg, yolk and white chopped separately
4 anchovy filets
Approximately 8 canned pimiento strips
¼ cup chopped fresh parsley
Freshly ground black pepper

1. Trim the celery of tough outer ribs and trim the top of leaves, leaving the bunch of celery about 8 inches long. Pare the bottom of the celery with a vegetable peeler but do not cut it off. Slice the bunch into 4 quarters lengthwise.

2. Place the celery sections in a large shallow saucepan. Add just enough chicken broth to cover. Heat to boiling; reduce the heat. Cover and cook, barely simmering, until tender, about 25 minutes. Let the celery cool in the broth.

3. Drain the cooled celery and arrange it in a shallow serving dish.

4. Make the Simple Vinaigrette Sauce; pour it over the celery. Chill, turning the celery several times.

5. When well chilled, garnish the celery with alternating bands of chopped egg white, chopped egg yolk, anchovy filets, pimiento strips, and parsley. Season with fresh pepper to taste.

Serves 4.

Simple Vinaigrette Sauce

1 small clove garlic, crushed
½ teaspoon coarse (kosher) salt
1 teaspoon Dijon mustard
Juice of ½ lemon
½ cup olive oil
2 teaspoons red wine vinegar
½ teaspoon freshly ground black pepper

Mash the garlic and the salt together in a small bowl with the back of a spoon. Stir in the mustard and lemon juice. Whisk in the oil, vinegar, and pepper.

Makes about ½ cup.

BOOZY CELERY

*T*his and the recipe that follows—Butter-Crumbed Celery—call for celery stalks that may be peeled or left *au naturel* at your discretion. Both are braise-first, bake-later devises, with cheese as their common topping, but otherwise as unalike as day and night. The first is cloaked in a brandied cream. The second is dusted with fennel seeds and bread crumbs. Each makes an admirable adjunct to a simple dinner where the main course is either broiled or grilled—*sans* sauce.

1 large, thick bunch of celery
½ cup Chicken Stock (see page 410)
½ cup white wine or dry vermouth
1 clove garlic, unpeeled
3 tablespoons unsalted butter
3 tablespoons all-purpose flour
¼ cup heavy or whipping cream
Salt and ground white pepper
1 tablespoon brandy
2 tablespoons freshly grated Parmesan cheese

1. Trim the celery of tough outer ribs and trim the top of the leaves, leaving the bunch of celery about 8 inches long. Pare the bottom of the celery with a vegetable peeler but do not cut it off. Slice the bunch into 4 quarters lengthwise.

2. Place the celery sections in a large shallow saucepan. Add the chicken stock, wine, and garlic. Heat to boiling; reduce the heat. Cook, covered, over medium-low heat until the celery is just tender, about 25 minutes.

3. Meanwhile, preheat the oven to 400°F. Remove the cooked celery from the saucepan with a slotted spoon, reserving the cooking liquid, and transfer it to a shallow baking dish. Set it aside. Discard the garlic.

4. Melt the butter in a medium saucepan over medium-low heat. Stir in the flour. Cook, stirring constantly, 2 minutes. Whisk in 1 cup of the reserved cooking liquid and the cream. Cook until very thick, 3 to 4 minutes. Add salt and pepper to taste. Stir in the brandy.

5. Spoon the sauce over the celery and sprinkle with the cheese. Bake until hot and bubbly, about 15 minutes.
Serves 4.

BUTTER-CRUMBED CELERY

1 large, thick bunch of celery
3 tablespoons unsalted butter
½ cup Chicken Stock (see page 410)
1 tablespoon plus 1 teaspoon Pernod
1 small clove garlic, bruised
½ teaspoon fennel seeds
½ teaspoon salt
¼ teaspoon freshly ground black pepper
½ cup fresh bread crumbs

1. Cut the celery crosswise into ½-inch slices. Combine the celery with 1 tablespoon of the butter, the chicken stock, and 1 tablespoon of the Pernod in a medium saucepan. Heat to boiling; reduce the heat. Cook, covered, over medium-low heat until the celery is crisp-tender, 15 to 20 minutes. Drain.

2. Meanwhile, preheat the oven to

350°F. Rub a shallow baking dish with the bruised garlic. Add the celery and sprinkle it with the fennel seeds, salt, and pepper.

3. Melt the remaining 2 tablespoons butter in a small skillet over medium heat. Stir in the bread crumbs and sauté until golden. Spoon the crumbs over the celery and sprinkle with the remaining 1 teaspoon Pernod. Bake, uncovered, until the celery is tender, about 30 to 35 minutes.

Serves 4.

BRAISED CELERY IN BASIL LEAVES

This recipe is a souvenir from a stay near Nice, where not only celery but also garlic, anchovies, olive oil, and basil are in aromatic profusion year round.

1 large, thick bunch of celery
2 tablespoons unsalted butter
1 tablespoon olive oil
1 onion, finely chopped
1 clove garlic, minced
1 teaspoon anchovy paste
¼ teaspoon chopped fresh thyme, or a
*   pinch of dried*
½ cup loosely packed fresh basil leaves,
*   chopped*
¼ cup dry white wine
¼ cup strong Chicken Stock (see page 410)
Chopped fresh parsley
Freshly ground black pepper

1. Trim the celery of tough outer ribs and trim the top of leaves, leaving the bunch of celery about 8 inches long. Pare the bottom of the celery with a vegetable peeler but do not cut it off. Slice the bunch into 4 quarters lengthwise. Set aside.

2. Heat the butter with the oil in a large shallow saucepan over medium-low heat. Add the onion; cook 1 minute. Add the garlic; cook 2 minutes longer. Do not brown. Stir in the anchovy paste and thyme. Add the celery sections and turn them several times to coat them with the butter mixture. Add the basil, wine, and chicken stock. Heat to boiling; reduce the heat. Cook, covered, over very low heat until just tender, about 25 minutes.

3. Remove the celery to a shallow serving dish and keep warm. Raise the heat under the saucepan and boil the juices until thick and syrupy. Pour the pan juices over the celery and sprinkle with parsley and fresh pepper.

Serves 4.

Celery is *chin-t'sai* in China, *sedano* in Italy, *céleri* in France, *selle-rio* in Germany, and *apio* in Spain—which brings us to the matter of bees.

Celery's flower is a small, compact blossom, creamy in color and shaped like the bell of a lily of the valley. The blooms appear in summer and have a scent that obviously drives the drones wild, for (if you will forgive the pun) they make a beeline to the celery patch like clockwork every August.

CELERY SOUFFLE

My last culinary thought on celery, before attacking its awesome root, is a pale leaf-green soufflé that has been known to inspire diners (even a few celeryphobes). It may be worth noting (before you discover it for yourself) that the celery for the base is boiled—an exception makes all rules unruly.

3 large ribs of celery, chopped
1 inner heart of celery with leaves, chopped
2 baking potatoes, peeled, cut into 1-inch
    cubes
2 tablespoons strong Chicken Stock (see
    page 410)
⅓ cup heavy or whipping cream
2 ounces creamy bleu cheese
1 tablespoon unsalted butter
2 egg yolks
Salt and freshly ground black pepper
3 egg whites
1 tablespoon fine fresh bread crumbs

1. Cook the chopped celery, celery heart, and potatoes in boiling salted water until tender, about 20 minutes. Drain.

2. Preheat the oven to 425°F. Place the celery-potato mixture into the container of a food processor (or in batches in a blender). Add the chicken stock, cream, bleu cheese, and butter. Process until smooth but not mushy.

3. Transfer the mixture to a large bowl. Beat in the egg yolks, one at a time. Beat in salt and pepper to taste.

4. Beat the egg whites until stiff but not dry. Fold them into the soufflé mixture.

5. Lightly grease a 1½-quart soufflé dish. Sprinkle it with the bread crumbs. Add the soufflé mixture and place it in the oven. Immediately reduce the heat to 375°F. Bake until fairly firm and dark golden, 35 to 40 minutes. The flavor improves as it cools.

Serves 6.

BROWNSTONE SOUP
(Beef and Celery Soup)

A hearty turn-of-the-century recipe from New York, this soup is composed of both stalk and root and cooked with beef to form a rich and aromatic one-dish meal.

1 tablespoon olive oil
1 to 1¼ pounds flank or skirt steak,
    trimmed of fat
1 tablespoon unsalted butter
1 large onion, finely chopped
1 clove garlic, minced
2 medium carrots, finely chopped

3 large ribs celery, finely chopped (about
    1½ cups)
3 cups beef broth (see page 414)
3 cups water
1 tablespoon chopped fresh parsley, plus
    extra for garnish

½ teaspoon chopped fresh thyme, or ¼
    teaspoon dried
1 small celery root (about ½ pound),
    trimmed, peeled, cut into thin strips
    about 1 inch long
Salt and freshly ground black pepper

1. Heat the oil in a large pot or Dutch oven over medium heat. Brown the meat well on both sides. Remove the meat to a plate and discard the cooking fat.

2. Melt the butter in the same pot over medium heat. Add the onion; cook 1 minute. Add the garlic; cook until lightly browned, about 5 minutes. Add the carrots and celery. Cook over medium-low heat 5 minutes. Stir in the beef broth, scraping the sides and bottom of the pot. Return the meat to the pot and add the water. Heat to boiling, removing the scum as it rises to the surface. Reduce the heat and add the 1 tablespoon parsley and the thyme. Cook, covered, over medium-low heat for 1 hour.

3. Add the strips of celery root to the soup. Continue to cook until the meat and celery root are tender, about 30 minutes. Remove from the heat. Allow to cool.

4. Remove the meat from the soup and separate it into chunks with two forks. Return the meat to soup and refrigerate ovenight.

5. Remove any accumulated fat from the surface of the soup and then reheat it over medium-low heat. Add salt and pepper to taste and sprinkle with parsley.

Serves 4 to 6.

CELERY ROOT AND GREEN BEAN SALAD

Celery root makes a sterling stand-in for a potato on occasion, as in this nearly-Niçoise formula. I wanted to dub it "Celery Root Masquerading as Salade Niçoise" until a lack of anchovies in the prescription dictated otherwise.

1 medium celery root (about 1½ pounds)
3 tablespoons dry white wine or dry
    vermouth
¼ pound thin young string beans, trimmed
1 clove garlic, bruised
2 shallots, minced
½ teaspoon coarse (kosher) salt
1½ tablespoons Dijon mustard
2 tablespoons lemon juice
1 tablespoon white wine vinegar
⅓ cup olive oil
¼ teaspoon chopped fresh thyme, or a
    pinch of dried
1 teaspoon chopped fresh basil, or ½
    teaspoon dried

¼ cup chopped fresh parsley
Salt and freshly ground black pepper
1½ tablespoons slivered black olives

1. Trim and peel the celery root. Cut it into strips about ¼ inch wide, ¼ inch thick, and 1 inch long. Cook in boiling salted water 5 minutes. Rinse under cold running water, drain, and pat dry with paper towels. Place the celery root in a bowl and sprinkle it with the wine.

2. Cook the string beans in boiling salted water until crisp-tender, about 3 minutes. Rinse under cold running water. Drain.

3. Rub a large serving bowl with the bruised garlic. Add the celery root, beans, and shallots. Toss.

4. Crush the garlic and combine it with the salt in a small bowl. Mash until a smooth paste is formed. Stir in the mustard, lemon juice, and vinegar. Beat in the oil. Pour this dressing over the vegetables and add the thyme, basil, and 3 tablespoons of the parsley. Add the salt and pepper to taste. Lightly toss in the olives and sprinkle with the remaining 1 tablespoon parsley. Serve well chilled or at room temperature.

Serves 4 to 6.

CELERY ROOT ABLUSH

*T*here are many wonderful celery root dishes, but the classic rendition is one that a well-seasoned traveler will have encountered on hors d'oeuvre trolleys and at buffet tables all over the western world: *céleri-rave rémoulade*, which means celery root in sharp mustard sauce. My version of this international treasure is, I am afraid, slightly unclassical, since it is not so sharp as it is shocking pink—tinged with the merest dab of rosy tomato.

1 celery root (1¼ to 1½ pounds)
⅓ cup lemon juice
1 egg yolk
2 teaspoons Dijon mustard
1½ teaspoons tomato paste
1 tablespoon red wine vinegar
¼ cup olive oil
½ cup vegetable oil
Salt and freshly ground black pepper
1 tablespoon chopped fresh basil, or ½
    teaspoon dried basil chopped with 1
    tablespoon fresh parsley

1. Trim and peel the celery root. Cut it into very fine julienne strips about 1 inch long. You should have 3½ to 4 cups. As you cut them, place the strips in a large bowl of ice water to which you have added 3 tablespoons of the lemon juice, to prevent discoloring.

2. Beat the egg yolk with the mustard and the tomato paste in a medium bowl until smooth. Slowly beat in the vinegar and both oils. When smooth and thick, beat in the remaining 3 tablespoons lemon juice, and add salt and pepper to taste.

3. Drain the celery root and pat it dry. Combine it with the dressing and marinate the salad, covered, at least 2 hours in the refrigerator. Sprinkle with the basil before serving.

Serves 6.

CREAMED-AGAIN CELERY ROOT

*W*ith such scant calories, it hardly seems amiss to suggest enriching the basic ingredient a jot—with cream and butter in this case. For a change, serve it with a slice of rosy beef in lieu of potatoes.

1 celery root (1 to 1¼ pounds)
3 tablespoons lemon juice
1 tablespoon unsalted butter
1 shallot, minced
2 cups chicken broth (see page 414)
¼ cup heavy or whipping cream
1 egg yolk, lightly beaten
Salt and freshly ground black pepper
Chopped fresh parsley

1. Trim and peel the celery root. Cut it into fine julienne strips about 1 inch long. As you cut them, place the strips in a large bowl of ice water to which you have added the lemon juice, to prevent discoloring.

2. Melt the butter in a large saucepan over medium-low heat. Add the shallot; cook until lightly browned, about 5 minutes. Drain the celery root and add it to the saucepan. Toss the celery root well to coat it with the butter. Add the chicken broth. Heat to boiling; reduce the heat. Simmer, uncovered, until tender, 10 to 15 minutes.

3. Drain the celery root, reserving the broth. Transfer the celery root to a serving dish and keep it warm in a low oven.

4. Return the cooking liquid to the saucepan. Heat to boiling; boil until reduced to ½ cup. Stir in the cream. Return to boiling; remove from the heat.

5. Gradually mix 2 tablespoons of the hot liquid with the egg yolk. Slowly whisk the egg yolk mixture into the remaining hot liquid. Place it over low heat and cook, stirring constantly, until

A ccording to gardening lore (often highly erroneous) the first stalk of celery grew in America a scant sixteen years after the Declaration of Independence was signed. The seedlings, sent for by Thomas Jefferson's gardeners, were meant to grace the herbary at Monticello. However, the plants waned in the torpid Virginia climate, and celery lovers had to go without.

A Dutch immigrant who came to Kalamazoo, Michigan, with a sack of celery seed in his duffel is responsible for celery's full flowering in the U.S. In 1874 the first celery plant was harvested—and a hundred years later it was the third largest agricultural industry in the country (after potatoes and tomatoes).

According to Elizabeth Gordon in *Mother Earth's Children*:

> Said the Endive: I was born in
>   France,
> But travel when I get the chance.
> Said the Celery: I travel too,
> But my real home's in Kalamazoo.

thickened. Do not allow it to boil. Add salt and pepper to taste. Spoon the sauce over the celery root and sprinkle with parsley.

Serves 4.

SUPER-CRISPY ROAST CHICKEN WITH CELERY ROOT DRESSING

O ne of my favorite dispositions for a hunk of celery root is to install it inside a chicken. It matters not a whit whether you supplicate a greengrocer for *céleri-rave* (in France), *Knollensellerie* (in Germany), or *apio-nabo* (in Spain)—the pertinent thing is to stuff your very next bird with it!

By the way, this technique of dredging an uncooked fowl with a mixture of buttery crumbs and brandy is old as the hills and eminently worthy of revival, as it produces the most crunchy top crust, without any basting whatsoever.

1 large celery root (about 1 ¾ pounds)
12 tablespoons (1 ½ sticks) unsalted butter,
  softened
1 large shallot, minced
½ cup plus 2 tablespoons heavy or
  whipping cream
1 tablespoon lemon juice
⅛ teaspoon freshly grated nutmeg
¼ teaspoon freshly ground black pepper
Dash of hot pepper sauce
3 tablespoons chopped fresh parsley
Salt
5½- to 6-pound roasting chicken, interior
  cavity rinsed and patted dry
1 clove garlic, crushed
½ cup plus 2 tablespoons fresh bread
  crumbs
2 teaspoons brandy
1 cup Chicken Stock (see page 410)
2 tablespoons all-purpose flour
Freshly ground black pepper

1. Preheat the oven to 425°F. Trim and peel the celery root. Cut it into strips about ¼ inch wide, ¼ inch thick, and 1 inch long. You should have 4½ to 5 cups. Cook in boiling salted water for 2 minutes. Rinse under cold running water and drain. Place the celery root in a large mixing bowl.

2. Melt 2 tablespoons of the butter in a small skillet over medium-low heat. Add the shallot and cook until tender, about 5 minutes. Add this to the celery root.

3. Place ½ cup of the heavy cream in a small saucepan. Slowly heat to boiling; reduce the heat. Simmer until reduced to ¼ cup, about 8 minutes. Add this to the celery root, along with the lemon juice, nutmeg, pepper, hot pepper sauce, parsley, and salt to taste. Mix well.

4. Spoon the celery root mixture into the cavity of the roasting chicken.

Sew securely and truss. Pat the chicken dry with paper towels. Place it on a rack in a roasting pan.

5. Mash the garlic with 8 tablespoons of the softened butter. Beat in the bread crumbs until smooth. Slowly beat in the brandy. Spread the butter mixture evenly over the top and sides of the chicken. (Make sure chicken is well coated.)

6. Place the chicken in the oven. Roast 15 minutes. Reduce the heat to 350°F and continue to roast until done, about 2 hours. (Juices will run clear when thigh is pricked with a fork.) Thirty minutes before the chicken is done, add the chicken stock to the juices in the roasting pan.

7. When the chicken is done, transfer it to a platter and let it stand 15 minutes. Remove the trussing strings. Strain the pan juices.

8. Melt the remaining 2 tablespoons butter in a medium saucepan over medium-low heat. Stir in the flour. Cook, stirring constantly, 2 minutes. Whisk in the pan juices and remaining 2 tablespoons cream. Cook until slightly thickened. Add salt and pepper to taste. Serve with the chicken.

Serves 6.

CELERY ROOT AND WILD MUSHROOM HASH

*B*ecause it is both smooth in flavor and crisp to the tooth, celery root makes an admirable partner to spicier and softer-textured viands. Consider, for instance, the following lunch (or brunch) hash of shiitake mushrooms, Black Forest ham, and celery root. Obviously a *ménage à trois* made in heaven!

1 small celery root (½ to ¾ pound)
2½ tablespoons unsalted butter
2 tablespoons vegetable oil
1 shallot, finely minced
1 clove garlic, minced
4 ounces shiitake mushrooms (stems removed), cut into ½-inch-wide strips (see Note)
4 ounces Black Forest or smoked ham, cut into ½-inch strips
1 tablespoon lemon juice
Salt and freshly ground black pepper
Chopped fresh parsley

1. Trim and peel the celery root. Cut it into strips about ¼ inch wide and 1 inch long. You should have about 1½ cups. Cook in boiling salted water until just barely tender, 5 to 10 minutes. Drain.

2. Heat 1 tablespoon of the butter with 1 tablespoon of the oil in a large skillet over medium-low heat. Add the shallot; cook 1 minute. Add the garlic; cook 4 minutes.

3. Add the remaining 1½ tablespoons butter and remaining 1 tablespoon oil to the pan. Stir in the mushrooms and cook, tossing frequently, over medium heat until lightly browned. Add the ham and celery root. Continue to cook, tossing frequently, until tender, about 5 minutes. Add the lemon juice and salt and pepper to taste. Sprinkle with parsley.

Serves 4.

Note: See Notes on Ingredients, page 416, for information on shiitake mushrooms.

CORN

The Sooner It's Cooked the Better It Tastes

Gastronomes have different notions of paradise than do mortal men, it seems. The grandest treat for a deep-dyed epicure, I have been reasonably assured, is dining *al fresco* on a freshly dug truffle in Perigord or slurping malossol caviar from a just-caught sterlet along the Volga. My own likes are a darn sight more pedestrian, although the same optimum state of freshness certainly applies. Greene's dream meal? Half a dozen ears of sweet summer corn (preferably picked before sundown) from a cornfield in Iowa. If the geography seems a tad imprecise, I will confess that I have only minimal first-hand knowledge of the Great Plains. I simply chose that terri-

tory because it is obviously the "in place" to sample lots and lots of corn—something I have done before, albeit not in Iowa—and therein lies a tale, of course.

I left home to be completely on my own when I was twenty-two. Many things conspired to arrange my independence. The war ended; my father died unexpectedly; and after a cursory period of mourning, my mother remarried. "For security reasons only," she announced, to ward off any infelicitous hint of romance that might be construed by this rash action. Though she was still exceedingly attractive at forty-eight, my parent seemed openly offended at any sexual implication inherent in her second union. That my stepfather (and her choice for matrimony) turned out to be wildly eccentric seemed beside the point in her view. He was a former suitor who had not only pined after her for thirty years but also managed to accrue some solid assets with which to press his suit.

When my mother announced her plans to marry, I moved. Actually I had been paying rent on an apartment for some time, but put off taking occupancy when my father became ill. No conventional studio, my first home was once the ballroom of a grand mansion off upper Fifth Avenue. From a carved stone balustrade I could even see a stretch of Central Park. Aside from that, and its vast size, this apartment had very few virtues. There was no kitchen or closet, and the bathroom was a mahogany cave equipped with turn-of-the-century fixtures. However, I was young and adventurous, the rent was reasonable, and the building had a private elevator. True, it accommodated only two persons at a time, but it certainly added a touch of class to my bachelor existence.

When I settled into my first apartment I had no furniture whatsoever. In time I acquired a large bed and a bookcase. I had planned to add more household goods before I entertained but natural gregariousness and a new girlfriend, Norma, changed my plans. Norma had recently arrived in New York as well (from a small town in New England), and she lived in a hotel for women where males were forbidden above the lobby floor. Of necessity much of our courtship took place in my quarters.

Norma did not cook. I did, of course, but had nowhere to do it. In the end we spent most of our time like picnickers, roasting our dinner over a log fire in one of the most opulent marble fireplaces ever carved.

Our romance had one other setback. Norma was a vegetarian. We grilled an awful lot of corn (and potatoes) between kisses and I will never forget the flavor of a single singed kernel, though in time my tastebuds rebelled at the diet and I also gained twenty pounds. I enrolled Norma in the best cooking school I knew at the time: Dione Lucas Cordon Bleu, where she shortly gave up her vegetarian principles, and me too, for she married a more aggressive fellow that she met in class. All of which sounds *corny* but is absolutely true!

Norma never heard of it, but there is a tart New England adage that puts down the cooking instructions for corn very concisely. "You may stroll to the garden to cut the corn but you had darn well better run back to the kitchen to cook it!"

That is no exaggeration. As soon as a corn's cob is cut, natural sugar in the kernel's fiber starts to convert to starch. Consequently, the longer the cut corn sits, the mealier each bite will be!

Vegetable Roots

Corn—on the cob and off—antedated Columbus's discovery of America by three thousand years at least—some hint even longer. The first Indian corn, maize (*Zea mays*), was the chief staple of the Mayan, Aztec, and Incan diets. Corn's origin is traced so far back in Indian history, in fact, that it may date from the very first appearance of man in the western world—when he ate grass seeds to survive.

Food sleuths assert that these precious food seeds, planted along the way of his migration to warmer climes, crossbred; and the result was early corn. Other historians cast a cold eye on that theory, however, insisting that maize, rather than being a wild hybrid, was developed through centuries of cultivation—plus nature's unerring sense of selectivity, of course. Whatever its origin, corn had developed into a tall proud plant long before the first Mayan began to carve his history in stone.

To the early Indian tribes, nature was the only true god. They prayed for fertile fields and strong sons to work them, so it is not surprising that a corn stalk (tall, erect, and capable of reproducing itself *ad infinitum*) was revered as their supreme deity.

Chieftains who considered a maize stalk divine also believed that every kernel off its cob possessed some minor jot of divinity as well. Two or three corn kernels felicitously placed under a brave's marriage blanket was insurance that only strong, worthy (male) offspring would issue from that union.

All Indians held festivals of thanksgiving for a good corn harvest, some of which became bloodbaths of gratitude, since human sacrifices were deemed the ultimate thank-you for a bumper crop. If there was a mite less fervor over corn in the hearts of the early colonists to North America, put it down to dogged puritanism. The first Pilgrims would surely have starved had it not been for the maize they obtained from the local Indians before they had time to plant their own crops.

When the white man added Indian corn to his diet, he added many Indian ways of preparing it too. Hoecake, corn fritters, succotash, and cornbread were all native bequests.

There was one Indian dispensation, however, that early colonists obdurately refused to sample. Dubbed "a soupe," it was a tonic the braves asserted would cure any illness from childbed fever to snakebite. Indians prepared this brew with new corn, boiling ears and husks together for a very long time, then leaving the infusion in the pot for weeks, "until the juices remaining turned soursweet and bubbled extensively without the aid of a flame."

The settlers temperately forswore even a drop of this "soupe" because, in the words of Young Spelman, a Virginia homesteader, "Lesse than one pynt consumed causet wild flyinging of arms and legs amng the svges." Worse yet, "wringinge the air with wilde sounds till the spell of this choudier wears off." Corn soup seems a considerably tamer indulgence nowadays. And come to think of it, so does bourbon!

The meal at which the first sweet corn is brought steaming to the table in late July is still a tribal rite for most diners. And the rush of fingers snatching at the ears—ready and willing to be burnt scarlet, it seems, in order to experience the first sensual split of pure gold on the tongue—is a ceremony any Indian would clearly understand.

What to Look For

Corn lovers who do not grow their own should shop early and store the ears (unshucked) in a cold refrigerator until dinner.

When I shop for corn, I look for very grassy green husks with the exposed silk no darker than deep amber in color. A fresh-picked ear of corn will feel gently silken to the thumb, with a slight dampness apparent in the husk.

If your greengrocer has a tolerance for such undertakings, try to peel back the silk to make sure the rows are filled with even, plump kernels. They ought to show a slight ooze when pricked with a fingernail.

The tip-off for old corn is always the stem. After too long a stay on a shelf, the end invariably rusts. So pass those ears by for your next pot of boiling water.

Corn is an uncommonly healthful food—loaded with vitamins (580 units of vitamin A per cupful) and relatively low in calories (a scant 70 for the same amount). Corn also has a large quantity of potassium, phosphorus, and calcium in every ear. Best of all, a single corncob contains less than a trace of salt.

Preparation

Over the years I have developed a wealth of corn wisdom and some very practical advice for its quick cookery. I always bake or roast the ears, depending upon which is more convenient. In my opinion, fresh corn is absolutely at its best when stripped of silk, lightly buttered, then briefly dipped into cold water and rewrapped in the original husks or an ample covering of aluminum foil and then baked or roasted. Twenty minutes in a 350°F oven will usually produce a moist, juicy row of kernels, but more time may be required over an open fire.

Shaker cooks, whose culinary skills I dearly admire, place ears of husked and desilked corn in a large pot of cold water seasoned with the barest pinch of sugar (never salt because it toughens the tender fibers) until the water boils. At that point they cover it and cook it one minute more or as long as it takes to say the Lord's Prayer *fast*. Then they drain and serve the ears as quickly as they can with lots of sweet butter, salt, and pepper on the side.

Another felicitous style of corn cookery comes from Mississippi by way of Evan Jones in his well-versed history, *American Food*. This technique, recommended for less-than-garden-fresh ears and only slightly amended at my New York stovetop, calls for a half-dozen ears of husked and desilked corn to be immersed in a boiling potful of milk and water (one quart each) in which a quarter-pound of sweet butter has been melted. The corn cooks very briefly—5 minutes on my range. What is so special about this method is that the corn tastes as if it had been picked in the garden minutes before. Better yet, each ear is so sweetly succulent that I skip the additional butter entirely. And if, like me, you feel guilty tossing those cooking juices down the drain, simply strain and store the liquid in a covered container in your refrigerator. A cupful will make a head start in most creamed sauces or soups—or sweeten a pan of cornbread in a pinch.

A word or two is probably in order here about "grated corn." There are any number of corn strippers or graters on the market (several in my kitchen cabinet too), but all one needs to be able to scrape corn kernels successfully is a sharp, firm-bladed knife.

To cut kernels, as for Clam and Corn Chowder, stand an ear of corn upright on a plate and carefully slice beneath the rows in a steady downward motion.

To grate kernels, as for the Spicy Texas Corncake, cut off the kernels at about half their depth and then, with the back of the blade, scrape off what is left on the cob, mixing the cut pulp and "milk" with the kernels.

Corn (which rises to heaven as it grows) was believed by Europeans to have otherworldly powers ever since Columbus brought the first samples back to Spain from the Caribbean in 1496.

Early Spanish churchmen, for instance, assumed that the ingestion of raw kernels would cure souls possessed by the devil. Poor martyrs suspected of unearthly connections were often force-fed with a mixture of corn and water (like the geese of Strasbourg) and made to sit naked in the hot sun until the swollen compound either purged them of their sins or they burst. If it sounds terrible, consider the alternative antidote: trial by fire!

MAIS-NOIX
(Corn Nuts)

Old (that is to say, mature) corn has its place in the kitchen from time to time. One of the most addictive cocktail nibbles I know is much dependent upon the texture and bland flavor of aged corn. This is *mais-noix*, a peppery street food that is sold in brown paper sacks on the avenues of Port-au-Prince.

When I visited Haiti for the first time a dozen years ago, my traveling companion was horrified whenever I indulged in the less-than-hygienic snacks the various vendors offered, predicting dire maladies as a consequence of each sampling.

I lived to tell the tale, however, and now happily pass the spoils on to you.

Vegetable oil
1 clove garlic, crushed
1 cup corn kernels (from 2 large mature ears)
1 cup salted dry-roasted peanuts
1 tablespoon mild chili powder or ground fresh sweet chiles

Lightly rub a large cast-iron skillet with oil. Then rub with paper towels. Place the skillet over medium-high heat and add the garlic and corn kernels. Toss, scraping the bottom with a metal spatula, for about 30 seconds. Stir in the peanuts and sprinkle with the chili powder. Toss, continuing to scrape the bottom of the pan, 3 minutes. Transfer to a bowl and serve immediately. (The corn kernels will moisten the peanuts if the mixture sits too long.)

Makes about 2 cups.

TALL-GRASS CORN RELISH

This is one recipe I can never make in sufficient quantity. No matter how many gleaming gilded jars I put up in August, my cupboard is always bare in January. The original formula came from Iowa (where else?) and was rumored to have once taken a blue ribbon at that state's stately fair. Pedigree or no, it is certainly prime piccalilli!

5 cups corn kernels (from 10 large ears)
5 cups finely shredded cabbage
3 cups chopped onions
2½ cups seeded chopped red bell pepper (about 3 medium)
1 cup seeded chopped green bell pepper (about 1 large)
1 quart cider vinegar
1½ cups packed dark brown sugar
¼ cup dry mustard
2 tablespoons salt
1 tablespoon celery seeds

1. Combine all the ingredients in a large heavy pot. Slowly heat to boiling; reduce the heat. Simmer, uncovered, stirring occasionally, 1 hour.

2. Using a slotted spoon, pack the vegetables into sterilized pint jars, leaving 1 inch at the top. Add the hot syrup to each jar to cover. Seal. Process in a hot water bath for 15 minutes.

Makes 5 to 6 pints.

CLAM AND CORN CHOWDER

*T*he early Americans' first original use of corn is rumored to have taken place in a tureen, when the sweet vegetable became a thickener for nourishing chowders. One of the most felicitous reproductions of a Plymouth Rock soup, this was acquired in Truro, at the almost-end of Cape Cod. A velvety mélange of fresh clams, sweet cream, and even fresher, sweeter corn off the cob, it is definitely more than a mere pottage. It is practically poetry.

1½ to 2 quarts clams or quahogs
1½ cups water (or 1 cup clam juice and ½ cup water)
8 tablespoons (1 stick) unsalted butter, at room temperature
2 sprigs parsley, plus chopped parsley for garnish
1 bay leaf
1 small onion stuck with 1 whole clove
4 thick slices bacon, diced
1 large onion, minced
1 large clove garlic, minced
1 rib celery, finely chopped
½ green bell pepper, seeded, minced
6 potatoes, peeled, diced, parboiled 3 minutes
2 cups milk, scalded (just below the boiling point)
2 tablespoons all-purpose flour
2 cups heavy or whipping cream
Dash of hot pepper sauce
Dash of Worcestershire sauce
¼ teaspoon chopped fresh thyme, or a pinch of dried
Salt and freshly ground black pepper
1½ to 2 cups fresh corn kernels (from 3 or 4 large ears)

1. Scrub the clams well and place them in a large pot with the water, 2 tablespoons of the butter, 2 sprigs parsley, the bay leaf, and the onion stuck with a clove. Cover and bring to a boil over high heat. Reduce the heat; simmer 5 minutes. Remove the clams, reserving the liquid, and remove them from their shells; if large, cut them in half. (The clams will be open far enough to pry the shell open with a knife if necessary. Discard any clams that do not open.) Set the clams aside. Strain the liquid and keep it warm.

2. Cook the bacon in 1 quart boiling water for 5 minutes. Drain; pat dry with paper towels. Then fry the bacon in a medium skillet until crisp and golden brown. Drain on paper towels.

3. Remove all but 1 tablespoon bacon fat from the skillet and add 2 tablespoons of the butter. Cook the minced onion over medium heat 1 minute. Add the garlic, celery, and green pepper. Cook 5 minutes.

4. Transfer the onion mixture to a large pot. Add the sautéed bacon, the potatoes, and the milk. Heat to boiling; add the reserved clam liquid.

5. Mix 3 tablespoons of the butter with the flour in a small bowl until smooth. Stir this into the soup. Add the cream and return the soup to boiling; reduce the heat. Simmer 5 minutes. Add the hot pepper sauce, Worcestershire, thyme, and salt and pepper to taste. Stir in the corn. Cook until the chowder is slightly thickened, 5 to 10 minutes. Add the clams and warm through. Stir in the remaining 1 tablespoon butter and sprinkle with parsley.

Serves 6 to 8.

DAUFUSKIE QUILT

*T*he next recipe hails from Daufuskie Island, in the Gullah country of South Carolina—a rural archipelago that one must rent a launch to visit, almost entirely peopled by blacks who have lived and farmed the land there for centuries.

The following dish, as stylized in its own way as the patchwork quilts the "old-timey" island women are famous for, is called *"a lef'over sla."*

I must admit I never acquired a recipe for this salad—Daufuskians are notoriously shy of strangers. But I think my rendering is a fair enough duplication.

2 large ears corn
1½ cups chopped cooked chicken
1 small zucchini, thinly sliced
1 small red tomato, halved and sliced
½ green bell pepper, seeded, finely chopped
2 tablespoons minced red onion
1 clove garlic, crushed
½ teaspoon salt
2 tablespoons red wine vinegar
3 tablespoons olive oil
2 tablespoons chopped fresh parsley
1 tablespoon chopped fresh basil, or ½
    teaspoon dried
¼ teaspoon chopped fresh thyme, or a
    pinch of dried

¼ teaspoon cumin seeds (comino), crushed,
    or a pinch of ground cumin

1. Cook the ears of corn in boiling water for 3 minutes. Rinse under cold running water; drain. Cut the kernels from the cobs and combine in a large bowl with the chicken, zucchini, tomato, pepper, and onion. Toss lightly.

2. Mash the garlic with the salt in a small bowl to form a paste. Beat in the vinegar, oil, and herbs. Pour this dressing over the salad and toss well. Serve well chilled or at room temperature.

Serves 4.

AMAGANSETT CORN SALAD

*L*ong Island is no slouch as corn-growing territory. This dish is my own invention, a residual of my years as co-proprietor of The Store in Amagansett. Bored with making the same salads day after day, I borrowed a notion from the Shinnecock Indians down the road and put the local harvest to use in a salad bowl.

6 large ears corn
1 large green bell pepper, seeded, minced
1 red onion, finely chopped
2 shallots, sliced thin
4 whole scallions, bulbs and green tops
    chopped separately
1 large tomato, seeded, cut into ½-inch
    cubes

¼ cup sour cream
½ cup Mayonnaise (see page 408)
¼ cup strong beef broth (see page 414)
2 tablespoons red wine vinegar
Salt and freshly ground black pepper
Approximately 5 pimiento strips

1. Cook the ears of corn in boiling water for 3 minutes. Rinse under cold running water; drain. Cut the kernels from the cobs and combine them in a large bowl with the pepper, onion, shallots, scallion bulbs, and tomato. Toss lightly.

2. Beat the sour cream with the mayonnaise in a medium bowl. Beat in the broth and vinegar. Pour this dressing over the salad and toss well. Add salt and pepper to taste, and decorate with chopped scallion tops and pimiento strips. Chill well before serving.

Serves 6.

DOROTHY SHANK'S AMISH CORN FRITTERS

I grew up on corn fritters.

They were most often deep-fried and devised by my mother out of the ingredients always found in her kitchen: canned creamed corn, flour, eggs, and a spike of baking soda. I must admit I loved them dearly though they were greasy as the dickens and probably as lethal to one's digestive system as a depth charge. That childhood fritter, however, has absolutely nothing in common with the incredibly airy griddle-sautéed cakes limned below. These fritters virtually melt on the tongue. The recipe came my way by one of those supreme happenstances I generally call "fate."

I was being interviewed on the radio in Niagara Falls a few years ago. The station was a small local outlet and the interviewer was a motherly lady who had obviously faced a thousand authors across the microphone in her time. It was a hot, sultry day and the studio's air conditioning had unpredictably gone awry. The interview began fitfully, she fanning herself with a sheaf of papers and I gulping cold water as the red light that indicated "on the air" flickered ominously. The temperature was probably close to a hundred degrees in the glass booth, but for some reason the show went well. Before either of us knew it we had talked ourselves dry (if not precisely cool), praising the pleasures of American cooking.

At some point during a recorded commercial my interviewer turned to me. "Do you like Amish food?" she asked.

When I assured her I did, she smiled and handed me a small memorandum pad. "I was sure you did," she said happily. "I am of Pennsylvania Dutch stock myself—and heat or no heat, we all love to talk about food in that part of the world. Have you got a pencil? I want to give you a present to remember me by. It's a very special recipe for corn fritters—one that's been in my family for generations. So write fast!"

I did. But it was an easy formula to log—composed of six ingredients and only three sentences of instruction.

Take my word for it: in the end length has nothing to do with magnificence. These are simply the best corn fritters you will ever eat!

4 large ears corn
2 eggs, separated
2 tablespoons all-purpose flour

1 tablespoon sugar
Salt and freshly ground black pepper
Unsalted butter

1. Cut the corn kernels from 2 ears of corn and place them in a medium bowl. With the back of the knife, scrape the cobs over the bowl to extract the juices. Grate the corn from the remaining ears, as described on page 129. Add the grated kernels with their pulp and juice to the whole kernels in the bowl. The mixture will resemble scrambled eggs.

2. Beat the egg yolks in a large bowl until light. Beat in the flour, sugar, and salt and pepper to taste. Stir in the corn.

3. Beat the egg whites in a large bowl until stiff. Fold them into the corn mixture.

4. Heat a heavy skillet or griddle over medium heat and grease it lightly with butter. Drop the batter by small spoonfuls onto the hot griddle and cook until golden, about 30 seconds per side. Transfer the cooked fritters to a lightly buttered serving platter and keep them warm in a low oven while cooking the remaining fritters.

Serves 4.

SPICY TEXAS CORNCAKE

Corn and its natural offspring, cornmeal, are the underpinnings of the Southwestern diet. Where would Tex-Mex cookery be without *masa harina*? Obviously *sans* corn tortillas for starters. My most treasured corn-and-cornmeal prescription (and I have a few at hand) comes from the acknowledged first lady of Tex-Mex cookery, Anne Lindsay Greer, author of *Cuisine of the American Southwest*: a red-hot corncake, meant to be eaten as a brunch, lunch, or picnic adjunct. It is also the single most perfect accompaniment to an egg that I know.

3 large ears corn
1 pound Spanish sausages (chorizos), chopped
1 onion, finely chopped
3 tablespoons unsalted butter, softened
3 eggs
1 cup sour cream
1 can (7 ounces) Mexican "Home Style" or "Green Chile" salsa (available in most supermarket specialty food sections)
1 poblano chile, roasted, peeled, seeded, minced (see Note)
1¼ cups very fine yellow cornmeal
½ cup all-purpose flour
1 teaspoon baking soda
1 teaspoon baking powder
1 teaspoon sugar
½ teaspoon salt
1 cup milk
8 ounces Monterey jack cheese, grated

1. Preheat the oven to 350°F. Grate the corn kernels as described on page 129. Set aside.

2. Sauté the chopped chorizos in a large heavy skillet over medium-low heat until they are lightly browned and all grease has exuded. With a slotted spoon, transfer the sausages to a dish and set aside.

3. Pour off all but 1 tablespoon fat from the skillet. Sauté the onion until lightly browned. Set aside.

4. Beat the butter with the eggs in a large mixing bowl until smooth. Beat in the sour cream. Add the onion, *salsa*, and minced poblano chile.

5. Combine the cornmeal, flour, baking soda, baking powder, sugar, and salt in another bowl. Add this to the sour cream mixture. Stir in the milk with a wooden spoon. Stir in the cheese, corn, and sausages.

6. Butter a round baking dish, about 12 inches across and 2 inches deep. Pour the batter into the dish. Bake in the oven until golden, about 45 minutes. Let stand 5 minutes before serving.

Serves 8 to 10.

Note: To roast a poblano chile, hold the chile with a roasting fork over a gas flame. Turn the chile until it is blackened all over. Or place the chile under a broiler until crisp on all sides. Carefully wrap the chile in paper towels and place it in a small paper bag. Let it stand to cool. The peel will easily rub off.

POLENTA PLUS

Corn recipes abound in every cuisine under the sun. This one is a traditional cornmeal porridge of Italian descent. Polenta is served up as a meal in itself or as an accompaniment to meats, depending upon the eater's pocketbook. My version, I must confess, is untraditionally crammed with corn kernels, hence the "plus."

2 large ears corn
2½ cups milk
1 cup chicken broth (see page 414)
1 cup yellow cornmeal
¾ teaspoon salt
1½ tablespoons unsalted butter, melted
1½ tablespoons freshly grated Parmesan
*   cheese*

1. Using a sharp knife, grate the corn kernels from the cobs as described on page 129. Set aside.

2. Heat the milk and chicken broth slowly to boiling in a medium saucepan over medium-low heat. (Do not allow to scorch.) Slowly beat in the cornmeal with a wire whisk. Continue to beat until the mixture is smooth and thick. Remove from the heat and stir in the salt and reserved corn. Immediately pour the mixture into a lightly greased shallow 1½-quart baking dish. Place the dish on a rack and keep it, uncovered, in a cool place for at least 1 hour.

3. Before serving, preheat the oven to 375°F. Brush the top of the polenta with the melted butter and sprinkle it with the cheese. Bake 15 minutes. Let stand 10 minutes before serving.

Serves 6.

SOUR-CREAMED CORN

For the record: my idea of the classic way to serve corn is *on the cob* without any embellishment other than a pat of butter and a shaking of salt! Even freshly ground pepper seems a distraction if the corn is good. But there are other less purist renditions. Consider, for instance, the following alignment of barely sautéed corn kernels, scallions, butter, and a dab of sour cream. To be baldly alliterative, it is a dish that is one of corn's consummate collaborations.

4 large ears corn
2 tablespoons unsalted butter
3 whole scallions, bulbs and green tops,
    chopped
¼ cup sour cream
Dash of hot pepper sauce
Salt and freshly ground black pepper
Chopped fresh parsley

1. Cut the corn kernels from the ears and place them in a bowl. You should have about 2 cups. With the back of the knife, scrape the cobs over the bowl to extract the juices.

2. Melt the butter in a large heavy skillet over medium-low heat. Add the scallions; cook 1 minute. Stir in the corn; cook until barely tender, 4 to 5 minutes. Add the sour cream and hot pepper sauce. Cook until warmed through; do not allow to boil. Add salt and pepper to taste and sprinkle with parsley.

Serves 4.

LOUISIANA MAQUECHOUX
(Sautéed Corn with Vegetables)

Corn, like tomatoes and peppers, is a totally native American vegetable that shows up with stunning frequency in all of our varied culinary geography.

This example stems from the bayou country of Louisiana. A side dish, it is variously known as *"mock shoe," "mark show,"* and *"maquechoux,"* depending upon which strand of the Archafalaya River you travel. The latter spelling means "false cabbage" in the Cajun tongue, but that's not much help because the dish has no relation to any cabbage (or corn) concoction consumed anywhere else in the world. It's a purely local dispensation—and in Louisiana always accompanies turkey to the table at Thanksgiving.

6 ears fresh corn
2 slices bacon
6 whole scallions, bulbs and green tops
    chopped separately
1 red bell pepper, seeded, chopped
2 ripe tomatoes, seeded, chopped
½ teaspoon sugar
¼ teaspoon fresh thyme, or a pinch of
    dried
1 teaspoon chopped fresh basil, or ¼
    teaspoon dried
½ cup heavy or whipping cream
Salt and freshly ground black pepper

1. Cut the kernels from 2 ears of corn and place them in a medium bowl. Grate the remaining cobs as described on page 129. Add grated corn, pulp, and juice to the kernels in the bowl. Set aside.

2. Sauté the bacon in a large heavy skillet until crisp. Remove the bacon; drain on paper towels. Cook the chopped scallion bulbs with the red pepper in the bacon drippings until soft, about 5 minutes. Add the tomatoes, sugar, thyme, and basil. Cook, uncovered, over medium heat 5 minutes. Add the corn and cream; cook, stirring constantly, until the corn is tender and the mixture is creamy, about 10 minutes. Add salt and pepper to taste. Sprinkle with the scallion tops; crumble the reserved bacon over the top.

Serves 6.

HOT CORN FLAN

*T*he next corn endowment is for a silken vegetable custard—the issue of a mixed marriage between red-hot Texas seasonings and nouvelle cuisine! My father, a man whose wife always cut the corn off a cob to spare his tender gums, would have loved it. It's a corn dish that goes down easy.

1 tablespoon unsalted butter
2 tablespoons minced onion
3 tablespoons minced seeded green bell
    pepper
3 tablespoons minced canned mild green
    chiles
1 to 2 tablespoons minced canned hot
    jalapeño peppers (depending on taste)
1½ cups corn kernels (from 3 large ears)
1½ tablespoons all-purpose flour
½ cup milk
3 eggs
1 cup heavy or whipping cream
1 teaspoon salt
⅛ teaspoon freshly ground black pepper
¼ teaspoon freshly ground nutmeg
Pinch of ground allspice
2 cups grated Monterey jack cheese (about
    6 ounces)

1. Preheat the oven to 350°F. Melt the butter in a large skillet over medium-low heat. Add the onion and green bell pepper. Cook 5 minutes. Raise the heat to medium and add the canned chiles, the jalapeño peppers, and 1 cup of the corn kernels. Cook, uncovered, stirring often, 10 minutes. Remove from the heat.

2. Place the remaining ½ cup corn kernels into the container of a blender. Add the flour and milk and blend until smooth.

3. Beat the eggs in a large bowl until light. To the eggs beat in the corn mixture from the blender, the cream, salt, pepper, nutmeg, and allspice. Stir in the corn-pepper mixture and cheese. Pour into a 1½-quart shallow soufflé dish. Place the dish in a roasting pan. Add boiling water to the pan to reach halfway up the sides of the dish. Place the pan in the oven and cook until the mixture is firm, about 1 hour. Let stand 15 minutes before serving. This may also be served chilled.

Serves 6 to 8.

CORN CREPES WITH TWO FILLINGS

*I*n 1515, Thomas Tusser, a British nature-lover, made the following observation on corn's cultivation:

> Sensible seedsmen never sow peas'n corn nor any plant which matures high above the ground—'cept under a rising (waxing) moon.
>
> While rooted stuffs like p'tatoes, parsnips and such are set out during the moon's dark (waning) periods. This is so the moon's light will draw up those seeds which need light and keep safe till they mature, those which need the cover of warm earth.

With that sage advice in mind, I always plant corn when the moon is no larger than a lemon rind and have not had cause to regret the instance yet.

In the kitchen I am somewhat more unorthodox. A while back I invented a corn pancake (crepe if you will) that also waxes and wanes depending upon its filling.

In the first instance, this delicate cover is filled with an amalgam of creamy corn kernels and ham and is rolled conventionally. It makes a refreshing luncheon or supper treat. In the second variation, the thin pancakes are folded into (forgive the pun, please) tiny cornucopias dabbed with creamy corn and whipped egg mixture that makes each turnover rise like a mini soufflé in the oven.

For the Crepes

2 eggs
1 cup milk
½ cup corn kernels (from 1 large ear)
¾ cup all-purpose flour
2 tablespoons vegetable oil
¼ teaspoon salt
¼ teaspoon freshly ground black pepper
⅛ teaspoon ground mace

1. Place the eggs, milk, and corn kernels in the container of a blender and blend until smooth. Add the flour, oil, salt, pepper, and mace. Blend 2 minutes. Scrape down the sides and blend 1 minute longer. Refrigerate, covered, at least 2 hours.

2. Remove the batter from the refrigerator. Line a plate with two sheets of paper towels and set it aside.

3. Lightly rub a crepe or small omelet pan (preferably with a nonstick surface) with a buttered or oiled cloth. Place the pan over medium heat until it is very hot. Remove the pan from the heat and pour about 3 tablespoons of the batter into the center of the pan. Quickly tilt the pan in all directions to cover the bottom evenly, then return the pan to the heat and cook until the edges of the crepe are brown, about 1 minute. Lightly loosen the edges with a spatula. (These crepes are especially tender and limp, so you'll need a flexible spatula to free the edges before inverting.) Holding the towel-lined plate in one hand, quickly invert the pan over the plate with the other hand, so the crepe drops onto the paper towels. Lightly oil the pan once more and continue this process until all the batter is used, placing a double layer of paper towels over each finished crepe.

Makes 12 to 14 7-inch crepes.

Corn and Ham Filling

12 to 14 7-inch crepes
3 tablespoons unsalted butter
1 whole scallion, bulb and green top, minced
2 tablespoons seeded minced red bell pepper
2 tablespoons seeded minced green bell pepper
½ cup diced cooked ham
1 cup corn kernels (from 2 large ears)
2 tablespoons all-purpose flour
¾ cup Chicken Stock (see page 410)
½ cup heavy or whipping cream
Pinch of freshly grated nutmeg
Salt and freshly ground black pepper

1. Preheat the oven to 350°F.

2. Melt 1 tablespoon of the butter in a medium skillet over medium-low heat. Add the scallion, both peppers, and ham. Cook 5 minutes. Add the corn; toss well. Remove from the heat.

3. Melt the remaining 2 tablespoons butter in a small saucepan. Stir in the flour. Cook over medium-low heat, stirring constantly, 2 minutes. Whisk in the stock and cream; cook until thick. Season with the nutmeg, and salt and pepper to taste. Stir half the cream mixture into the corn mixture.

4. Invert the crepe stack onto another plate so that all cooked sides are down. Carefully remove the top layers of paper towels. Spoon about 1 tablespoon of the corn filling down the side of the crepe and roll up. Place the crepes on a lightly greased baking dish. When all the crepes are prepared, drizzle the remaining sauce over the top. Bake for 10 minutes before serving.

Makes 12 to 14 filled crepes.

Corn Soufflé Filling

12 to 14 7-inch crepes
1 tablespoon unsalted butter
2 tablespoons all-purpose flour
1 cup milk
2 egg yolks
½ teaspoon salt
¼ teaspoon freshly ground black pepper
Pinch of freshly grated nutmeg
Dash of hot pepper sauce
2 cups corn kernels (from 4 large ears)
3 egg whites

1. Preheat the oven to 350°F.
2. Melt the butter in a medium saucepan over medium-low heat. Stir in the flour; cook, stirring constantly, 2 minutes. Whisk in the milk; cook until thickened, 2 to 3 minutes. Remove from the heat. Beat in the egg yolks, one at a time, beating thoroughly after each addition. Return to low heat, stirring constantly, 1 minute. Do not allow to boil. Add the salt, pepper, nutmeg, and hot pepper sauce. Remove from the heat and stir in the corn.

3. Beat the egg whites until stiff. Fold them into the soufflé base.

4. Invert the crepe stack onto another plate so that all cooked sides are down. Carefully remove the top layers of paper towels. Spoon about 3 level tablespoons of soufflé mixture onto the lower left-hand quarter of each crepe. Gently fold the crepe in half over the soufflé mixture, then fold it in half once more. Place the crepes on a lightly greased baking dish. When all the crepes are prepared, bake until the soufflé centers are cooked and well puffed, 8 to 10 minutes. Serve immediately.

Makes 12 to 14 filled crepes.

NEW MEXICO CORN TART

*T*he Hopi Indians predict weather by the size of a corn row. If the stalks are tall and the leaves grow tight, a hard winter is on the way and they harvest early to prepare for its rigors. If the leaves are full and the ears are heavy, they do not cut the first corn until the full (pumpkin) moon rises in late September or October.

While not exactly a dessert, this Hopi tart makes an excellent breakfast item when topped with a slosh of maple syrup and a dab of sour cream.

8 tablespoons (1 stick) plus 1 teaspoon
    unsalted butter, softened
¼ cup ground pumpkin seeds ("pepitas";
    available in health-food stores)
6 medium ears corn
½ cup heavy or whipping cream
½ cup sugar
3 eggs, separated
1 teaspoon baking powder
⅛ teaspoon ground cinnamon
¼ teaspoon salt
⅛ teaspoon freshly ground black pepper
3 tablespoons dark rum

    1. Preheat the oven to 350°F. Rub a round baking dish, 10 inches across and about 2 inches deep, with 1 teaspoon of the butter. Sprinkle with 2 teaspoons of the ground pumpkin seeds. Set aside.

    2. Cut the corn kernels from the ears and place them in a bowl. With the back of the knife, scrape the cobs over the bowl to extract the juices. Place half the corn kernels in the container of a blender or food processor. Add the cream and process until fairly smooth. Combine with the corn in the bowl. Reserve.

    3. Beat the 8 tablespoons butter with the sugar in a large bowl until light and fluffy. Beat in the egg yolks, one at a time, beating well after each addition. Beat in the baking powder, cinnamon, salt, pepper, and rum. Stir in the corn mixture and the remaining ground pumpkin seeds. Mix well.

    4. Beat the egg whites in a large bowl until stiff; fold them into the corn mixture. Pour the mixture into the prepared baking dish. Bake until golden brown and slightly puffed, about 35 minutes. Let stand 10 minutes before serving.

    Serves 6 to 8.

CUCUMBERS
The Basis for Success

"Cool as a cucumber" is an expression to which I have never properly related, because most of my experiences with those green gherkins took place in kitchens that were literally hot as hell!

I am thinking specifically of the airless back room of The Store in Amagansett where I toiled for ten summers under a pair of transom windows that could not be opened wider than two inches. In 1966 a misguided workman installed the windows' hinges behind a stainless-steel stove hood, and while The Store's fortunes waxed more than they waned during the next decade, renovation always seemed such a staggering prospect (emotionally as well as financially) that it seemed easier to sweat.

As I said earlier, I came to the town of Amagansett to escape a hectic urban pace. The Store's existence was conceived to prolong my stay near the calming sea, year round. But from the moment this take-out food establishment opened, I knew my serendipitous days were numbered. Almost from the first day the parade of automobiles parked outside caused traffic burdens for miles.

Not just a local success, the venture I co-founded shortly became a national institution. From all over came the rich, the famous, and the hungry through its saffron-colored screen door, eager to partake of the homemade foods prepared daily. It was a period of my life that I tend to think of as "Cucumber Time," because dilled cucumbers, with or without sour cream, were in a salad whose presence was daily made manifest in a chalked scrawl on the blackboard. And I can rarely remember leftovers returning to the kitchen at closing time. Admirers of The Store cucumbers were dogged in their devotion. We must have prepared tons of it every summer and I can remember a notable occasion in midwinter when the wife of a famous TV talk-show host made the hundred-mile trek from Manhattan to Amagansett just to have this dish on the table for her husband's birthday.

What made the cucumbers so memorable? According to my ex-partner, Denis Vaughan, it was the thinness of each slice. Denis was always given to hyperbole, but he claimed that if a cucumber was properly cut for a cucumber salad, one should be able to read the editorials in the *New York Times* through any given slice. Not through my wedges, however. The cutting of these gossamer concentric circles took hours and were the bane of my cooking life at The Store. Very often, I would throw in the towel (or paring knife) before a bowl was even half-filled because the task was not only arduous, it was indigestible as well—at least to a kitchen worker who sampled as he worked. And I always maintained there had to be a better way to do the job.

In the early 1970s I discovered it. On a holiday in France, I observed a curious object that was used for slicing vegetables in most every kitchen I visited. Called a *mandoline*, it was rather like a lethal cross between a miniature slide and a guillotine. Made of wood, this small troughed object was fitted with an adjustable razor-sharp blade and drop slot. The first French housewife I observed using it held a cucumber in the palm of her hand and by dexterously moving it up and down, shaved cucumbers thin enough to read the classified advertisements in *Le Monde*...in seconds! Needless to say, I returned to America with two *mandolines* stashed away in my luggage for The Store's

kitchen. There, I regret to say, both hung on the wall collecting dust (like decorative objects) ever after.

No. That is not wholly accurate. One of the *mandolines was* used to cut a cucumber once...by me, as a matter of fact. But after a trial run, the sight of my hand dripping blood on the kitchen floor was so unnerving it discouraged all other takers. We continued to cut our cucumbers as before—and I for one shut up about it!

Vegetable Roots

Most diners tend to think of the cucumber as a raw food or salad ingredient. That, I suspect, is purely a biblical inheritance. The Old Testament tells us that Moses' one regret after the Red Sea parted and his people made their exit from Egypt was that he had neglected to bring a peck of cucumber seeds into the desert. Israelites (and Egyptians too) ate this cylindrical green at every meal, usually dipped into bowls of salted water, for it was believed that the ingestion of three raw *Cucumis* daily protected the human body from the bite of deadly insects and vipers.

Any man with a hoe who has ever staked and poled a cucumber patch will give a nod of credence to that superstition. The area of any garden where cucumbers grow is decidedly off-limits to the red-blooded mosquito and gnat. And I've noticed that garter snakes make detours to avoid that territory as well.

The cucumber, a member of the gourd family, *Cucurbitaceae*, is the distant relative of a host of other vegeteria like pumpkin, squash, melon, and chayote. Like its garden cousins, the cucumber is a native of the region of Pakistan where the overflowing Indus River makes the land muddy and fertile and the warm wind off the Sulaiman mountains blows the tiny seedlets for thousands of miles every spring.

Green-thumbed archeologists tell us

Roman addiction to the cucumber was so marked, according to Pliny, that the Emperor Tiberius consumed at least ten a day, year round. The Romans stole the cucumber from the Greeks after a defeat in the wars with King Pyrrhus of Epirus. The Macedonians (under Alexander the Great's helm) in turn appropriated cucumber plants from the Persian troop ships as spoils of the battle of Granicus. The Persians had filched the cucumber as seed from the Medes, who most probably brought this curiously shaped object back to the Babylonian gardens as a souvenir of some Indian expedition.

The first serious appraisal of cucumbers in Europe occurred in France during the reign of Pepin the Wise at the end of the eighth century. According to his gardener's record books, Pepin ordered that *con-combres* be planted in triple rows surrounding his vineyards, to protect the precious grapes from bolls, borers, and cutworms. It took another fifty years before his son finally ate a cucumber for sheer pleasure. It must have tickled his fancy, for Charlemagne decreed at once that the cucumber was a favorite "fruit." He ate them only as dessert, in sweet tarts and custards. Later Frenchmen were also tempted to gild the lily, but good sense turned the cucumber custard from sweet to savory in the nick of time.

that traces of cucumber spore have been unearthed in spirit caves as far off as Burma and Thailand, indicating that thousands of years before formal agriculture existed, this gourd was offered up as appeasement to the gods by the early Asians.

The original Indian species (still found wild from Kumai to Sikkim) had a smooth brownish skin and extremely bitter flesh. Time and tide turned the shell prickly green and the flavor sweeter. Ancient Greeks considered the cucumber so ambrosial that they mixed the pulp with honey and snow, and only dished it up on important occasions (like victory celebrations and royal weddings). The Romans, who prided themselves on their exotic diet, served cucumbers every day of the week when they were in season. But they flavored them so imprudently (with splashes of fish sauces, vinegar and pinches of herbs) that it is doubtful a deep-dyed cucumber-lover would recognize the source from the sauce.

What to Look For

I must declare that I am so long in the tooth, I can perfectly call to mind the days before cucumbers were spray-waxed to give them an extra spate of shelf-life. In that dim past, cucumber eaters ate them skins and all. Today I would not advise such rash consumption, unless you are lucky enough to have a farm stand in the immediate vicinity.

The only unwaxed cucumbers I come upon in urban areas these days (and then only in summer and early fall) are the "kirbies" I use for home pickling. These jade-hued baby gherkins will not add stature to a salad bowl but they make fine eating all the same, since the tiny seeds are tender and easy to digest.

I usually look for a hard cucumber when I shop. Deep viridian is the shade that assures a fairly recent stint on a vine. Skip any large cucumbers that are yellowing, as that is a dead giveaway of a longish stay in the vegetable bin. Likewise cucumbers that are pulpy or pitted to the touch. Soft cucumbers are a residual of an early frost or an over-refrigerated transport truck. Pass 'em by, please!

Cucumber is one vegetable dieters

may consume with a clear conscience. The average size (7-inch variety) tallies at less than 10 calories and is comprised mostly of water. The vitamin content (70 units of vitamin A) vanishes once the peel is removed.

Preparation

My prescription for detoxifying a raw cucumber's bitterness was borrowed intact from the matriarch of a large Swedish family who lived next door to us when I was growing up. Mrs. Johnson's formula was very simple. So is mine.

First, trim the ends from the cucumber. Then carefully peel the outer skin, taking care not to bruise the flesh. The form your raw ingredient takes (either sliced, quartered, or even left whole) is up to you. Merely place the cucumber in an earthenware bowl and add a pinch of salt, a dash of vinegar and a jot of sugar. Allow it to stand for half an hour. That's all. Salt draws out the excess water while vinegar and sugar sweeten the flesh and make it taste more "cucumbery."

The same procedure never hurts a cucumber that is to be cooked. The removal of water is almost critical in any sautéed, stir-fried, or baked cucumber dish since warming inevitably releases the vegetable's juices and can result in a dreadfully waterlogged mess if the cook does not look sharp.

I prefer cooked cucumbers on the *al dente* side—with a measure of resilience to the tooth. Sautéing cut-up cucumbers will usually take about 5 minutes over medium heat. Baked whole cucumbers will take considerably longer: anywhere from 30 to 50 minutes depending upon your addiction to crunch.

Whenever I cook a cucumber I generally seed it first. This job is not as mettlesome as it may appear. After peeling a cucumber, simply halve it lengthwise. Then, using a sharp spoon (like a grapefruit cutter), scoop out all the seeds and any watery flesh that clings to the inside edge. What you will have left is a cucumber "bark" not unlike a slender green canoe—which may be filled, sliced, or cut into chunks.

POUNGIOU
(Cucumber Yogurt Cheese)

Greek farmers today still eat the cucumber just as their great-great-great-grandfathers did—combined with yogurt and herbs into a tangy cheese that is a staple everywhere from the Aegean Sea to the Gulf of Messina. The official name of this dish is *yaourti tou pouggiou,* "yogurt of the pocket," but I never found it in Greece. The estimable Craig Claiborne was my source. Since it is a relatively low-caloried concoction, I serve Poungiou as a diet-minded hors d'oeuvre with lots of fresh vegetables alongside, or spoon a dab over a ripe tomato for lunch.

1 pound unflavored yogurt
2 cucumbers (each about 7 inches long), peeled, seeded, finely chopped
1 tablespoon white wine vinegar
½ teaspoon salt
⅛ teaspoon sugar

1 small clove garlic, minced
2 tablespoons chopped fresh dill
1 tablespoon olive oil
2 teaspoons tarragon vinegar
Salt and ground white pepper

1. Line a colander with cheesecloth. Spoon the yogurt into the cheesecloth; drain. Bring up the edges of the cheesecloth and tie them with a long piece of string. Hang the yogurt in the refrigerator, letting it drip into a bowl, for 24 hours, draining the bowl as necessary.

2. Combine the cucumbers with the wine vinegar, salt, and sugar. Toss well; let stand 1 hour. Drain, pressing out all liquid with your hands.

3. Remove the yogurt "cheese" from the refrigerator and scrape it into a bowl. Add the cucumbers, garlic, dill, olive oil, and tarragon vinegar. Beat until smooth. Add salt and white pepper to taste.

Makes about ¾ cup. Serves 4 as a first course.

CUCUMBER RISOTTO

*F*rom the time of its disappearance as a staple of the salad bowl after the sack of Rome until its introduction as a flavoring for the exotic fare conceived during the Renaissance, the *cetriuolo* was frankly in limbo.

Thought to be an unmentionable apothecary ingredient not spoken of in polite society, the cucumber's chief attribute was reputedly aphrodisiac. No one knows how it was disabused of that florid reputation, but let us give thanks that it was.

Better yet, let's add a gramercy for the nameless kitchen worker who first combined a measure of cucumber (chopped) with a saucepan of Italian rice. The result is quite a different renaissance but no less tonic, I assure you.

2 tablespoons unsalted butter
2 shallots, finely chopped
1 small clove garlic, minced
½ cup Italian rice (I use Arborio)
Pinch of crushed dried hot red peppers
2 cucumbers (each about 7 inches long),
    peeled, seeded, diced
1¾ cups hot chicken broth, approximately
    (see page 414)
Salt and freshly ground black pepper
Chopped fresh dill

1. Melt 1 tablespoon of the butter in a heavy skillet over medium-low heat. Add the shallots; cook 2 minutes. Add the garlic; cook 1 minute. Stir in the rice, hot peppers, and cucumbers. Mix well.

2. Pour ¾ cup of the hot broth over the rice, and without stirring, let the rice absorb it. This should take about 15 minutes. Reduce the heat to low if the rice is cooking too fast.

3. Stir the rice to mix thoroughly. Pour ½ cup of the remaining hot broth over the rice and again, without stirring, let the rice absorb it, about 15 minutes.

4. Stir the rice once more and pour the remaining ½ cup broth over it. Cook until the rice is creamy and just tender but not mushy, about 10 minutes. (If the rice is not tender when all the liquid has been absorbed, add more broth. The rice should have a bite. If it is too wet when fully cooked, raise the heat slightly. The entire cooking of the rice should take at least 40 minutes.) Stir in the remaining 1 tablespoon butter; add salt and pepper to taste and sprinkle with dill.

Serves 4 as an appetizer.

M.F.K. FISHER'S CUCUMBER SHRIMP SOUP

*T*he cucumber soup of my dreams is one I have swiped from my good friend M.F.K. Fisher. This pottage is a fireless bit of Slavic cookery that Mary Frances claims is "no flimflam." She mixes hers in a pitcher, which takes up less space in the refrigerator than a tureen, and chills it overnight, stirring only when she remembers. I am more compulsive and make it in the morning, so I can stir it every couple of hours.

The secret of this soup is *ease*. The original Fisher formula calls for a can of peeled shrimp, but I am too far gone a gastronome to concur. In my version, the shrimp are freshly poached, then peeled. We do agree on the seasoning, however: it must be yellow (not Dijon) mustard—the mild kind that slathers a stadium hot dog.

1 cup water
½ cup dry white wine
2 parsley sprigs
2 lemon slices
½ pound raw shrimp
1 large cucumber (about 8 inches long),
*   peeled, seeded, chopped*
2 tablespoons prepared mustard
1 quart buttermilk
Salt and ground white pepper

1. Combine the water and wine in a heavy (non-aluminum) 10-inch saucepan. Add the parsley sprigs and lemon slices. Heat to boiling; boil until reduced to ½ cup, about 8 minutes. Add the shrimp and cook until pink, about 1½ minutes per side. Remove the shrimp and allow to cool. Strain and cool the cooking liquid.

2. Peel and devein the shrimp. Cut each in half lengthwise, and then cut into ½-inch pieces. Combine the shrimp with the cucumber in a large bowl. Stir in the reserved cooking liquid and the mustard. Mix well; stir in the buttermilk. Cover and chill at least 6 hours. Add salt and white pepper to taste before serving.

Serves 6 to 8.

CUCUMBER AND BAY SCALLOP SLAW

*C*olumbus planted and harvested the first cucumbers sown in the New World, on Hispaniola in 1494. He must have had a remarkably green thumb for it was a bumper crop, and cucumber cultivation spread rapidly to North America.

Hernando de Soto noted cucumber vines growing in profusion in Florida a scant fifty years later, and Jacques Cartier logged row upon row of cucumber plants tended by Iroquois tribesmen in Montreal in 1545.

Although universal in appeal, in the matter of size however, New and Old World cucumber fanciers decidedly do not agree. Americans prefer their cucumbers on the plump and stubby side, never longer than seven or eight inches. Continental cucumbers are usually grown twice that size. When you are cucumber shopping for this delicate salad, however, pass by any that are longer than a man's hand.

2 cups water (see Note)
¾ cup dry white wine
½ lemon
2 parsley sprigs
4 whole peppercorns
1¼ pounds bay scallops
2 cucumbers, each 6 to 7 inches long
3 tablespoons tarragon vinegar
½ teaspoon salt
⅛ teaspoon sugar
½ red bell pepper, seeded, chopped
2 teaspoons finely slivered fresh ginger root
2 teaspoons finely chopped chives or
    scallion tops
½ teaspoon crushed dried hot red peppers
3 tablespoons lemon juice
1 tablespoon soy sauce
1½ tablespoons olive oil
Salt and freshly ground black pepper
1 tablespoon chopped fresh parsley
Lettuce leaves

1. Combine the water, wine, lemon half, parsley sprigs, and peppercorns in a medium (non-aluminum) saucepan. Heat to boiling; reduce the heat. Simmer 10 minutes. Add the scallops; cook, uncovered, until just tender, 4 or 5 minutes. (Test by cutting a scallop open with

a knife.) Drain, and cool the scallops; chill 1 hour.

2. Meanwhile, peel the cucumbers. Cut them in half lengthwise and scoop out the seeds with a spoon. Cut each piece across into thin slices. Place the cucumbers in a bowl with 2 tablespoons of the vinegar, the salt, and the sugar. Let stand 30 minutes. Drain, and chill for 30 minutes.

3. Drain the cucumbers once more if necessary. Combine them with the scallops in a medium bowl. Add the bell pepper, ginger root, chives, and crushed peppers. Toss.

4. Combine the lemon juice, soy sauce, remaining 1 tablespoon vinegar, and olive oil in a small bowl. Pour this dressing over the cucumber-scallop mixture. Toss well and add salt and pepper to taste. Transfer to a serving dish and sprinkle with the chopped parsley. Serve on lettuce leaves.

Serves 4.

Note: 2¼ cups Fish Stock (see page 410) may be substituted for the first five ingredients.

COOL AND CREAMY CUCUMBER SALAD

What I deem the classic method for preparing cold cucumbers is a residual of my long tenure at The Store in Amagansett, an establishment that produced at least a thousand gallons of dill-flecked cucumber salad, to the local gentry's delight, every summer for a decade.

The following devise is the salad that helped make The Store memorable.

2 cucumbers, each about 7 inches long
½ teaspoon salt
2½ tablespoons cider vinegar
1 teaspoon sugar
1 cup sour cream
1 small shallot, minced
½ teaspoon celery seed
1 tablespoon chopped chives
¼ cup chopped fresh dill
Salt and freshly ground black pepper

1. Peel the cucumbers. Cut into thin slices and place them in a large bowl. Sprinkle the cucumber with ½ teaspoon salt, ½ tablespoon vinegar, and ¼ teaspoon sugar. Gently toss. Let stand 30 minutes. Drain, gently pressing out liquid with the back of a spoon. Pat dry with paper towels.

2. Meanwhile, place the sour cream in a medium bowl and whisk until light. Whisk in the shallot, the remaining 2 tablespoons vinegar, the remaining ¾ teaspoon sugar, the celery seed, chives, and salt to taste.

3. Layer one third of the cucumber slices in the bottom of a small shallow serving dish. Spoon one third of the sour cream mixture over the top. Sprinkle with one third of the dill. Continue to layer until all ingredients are used up. Sprinkle the top with pepper to taste. Chill well.

Serves 4.

COOL CUCUMBER SPAGHETTI

*T*he Store cucumbers were prepared two ways: with and without sour cream. This calorie-reduced version has been amended, somewhat, by time and my inability to leave a recipe alone. Instead of being sliced, the green cucumber flesh is finely shredded (with a steel zester) into thin pasta-like strands.

4 cucumbers, each about 7-inches long
⅓ cup plus 1 tablespoon red wine vinegar
½ teaspoon salt
2 teaspoons sugar
1 large shallot, minced
2 tablespoons water
¼ teaspoon freshly ground black pepper
3 tablespoons chopped fresh dill

1. Peel the cucumbers, then scrape the flesh with a vegetable zester lengthwise to form long spaghetti-like strands. Place the strands in a colander; sprinkle them with 1 tablespoon vinegar, the salt, and ½ teaspoon sugar. Let stand 30 minutes.

2. Shake the colander to remove any excess liquid. Do not squeeze the cucumber strands. Transfer them to a bowl and add the shallot.

3. Combine the remaining ⅓ cup vinegar, 1½ teaspoons sugar, and the water. Pour the dressing over the cucumbers; add the pepper and 2 tablespoons dill. Toss lightly with two forks. Refrigerate, covered, 30 minutes. Sprinkle with the remaining 1 tablespoon dill.

Serves 4.

JACK CARNEY'S OUT-OF-THIS-WORLD OUTHOUSE PICKLES

*T*he greatest use for a cucumber is indubitably the pickle, and I have tried lots of impeccable pickle recipes in my time. But this one is special: a bread-and-butter chip with a spicy flavor and, even more important, quintessential crunch.

The prescription is a gift from Jack Carney, Missouri's leading citizen (aside from the governor, of course). Definitely the state's loudest voice, Jack is a talk-show host on a three-hour daily marathon on station KMOX in St. Louis.

Carney conservatively describes his pickles as "simply the greatest in the world." So who am I to disagree? Their firm, inimitable bite is dependent upon a mineral that was once a necessity for every privy user: hydrated lime. Urbanites need not despair, however. This product is sold in hardware stores everywhere—even in Greenwich Village.

3½ pounds small pickling (kirby)
   cucumbers
1 cup hydrated lime
1 gallon water
1 quart cider vinegar (5% acid content)
4 cups sugar
½ teaspoon salt
½ teaspoon celery seed
½ teaspoon pickling spices
½ teaspoon whole cloves
1 3-inch stick cinnamon

1. Cut the cucumbers, unpeeled, crosswise into ¼-inch-thick slices. Place them in a large crock or heavy enameled pot.

2. Combine the lime and water and pour it over the cucumber slices. Let stand, covered, 24 hours.

3. Rinse the cucumbers at least 8 times under cold running water. Return the cucumber slices to a clean pot. Cover with cold water; let stand, uncovered, 3 hours. Drain. Place the cucumbers in a large pot.

4. Combine the vinegar, sugar, and salt in a large saucepan. Tie the celery seed, spices, cloves, and cinnamon stick in a cheesecloth bag and add this to the pan. Heat to boiling; pour over the cucumbers. Cool, then cover and let stand 24 hours.

5. The next day, drain the cucumbers, transferring the liquid to a saucepan. Heat the liquid to boiling; reduce the heat. Gently simmer (do not boil), uncovered, 35 minutes. Remove the bag of spices. Place the pickles with the juices in sterilized jars while hot. Seal.

Makes about 6 pints.

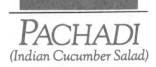

PACHADI
(Indian Cucumber Salad)

*T*he Indian salad known as *pachadi* is said to soothe the enflamed tongue whenever the curry seasoners run amok along the Ganges.

Pachadi is a mix of chopped vegetables and cucumbers sluiced with vinegar and yogurt to taste. This dish is a happy adjunct to a quickly organized summer picnic (or a beach cookout) when cold meat or an unadorned grilled fish is to be the meal's mainstay.

2 cucumbers, each about 7 inches long
1 tablespoon white wine vinegar
1 teaspoon salt
⅛ teaspoon sugar
1 small red onion, halved, thinly sliced
1 cup sliced red radishes (8 to 10 large radishes)
1 ripe tomato, seeded, chopped
2 small green chile peppers, seeded, minced (see Guacamole headnote, page 37)
½ cup black Greek olives, pitted, sliced
¾ cup unflavored yogurt
2 tablespoons sour cream
Salt and freshly ground black pepper
2 tablespoons chopped fresh mint

1. Peel the cucumbers. Cut each cucumber into quarters lengthwise and scoop out the seeds with a spoon. Cut each piece across into thin slices. Place the slices in a large bowl and sprinkle with the vinegar, salt, and sugar. Toss well. Let stand 30 minutes. Drain, gently pressing out the liquid with the back of a spoon.

2. Place the cucumber slices in a medium bowl. Add the onion, radishes, tomato, chile peppers, and olives. Toss. Stir in the yogurt and sour cream. (Add more sour cream if needed to bind the mixture.) Add salt and pepper to taste just before serving; sprinkle with the mint.

Serves 6.

CUCUMBER RIGADON

*T*his is a Burgundian devise called a *rigadon*, in this instance tempered with sweet cream cheese and flavored with a remarkable fresh green garden herb known as burnet. Why burnet? Because it is a leaf that curiously makes every cucumber taste more cucumbery!

Burnet is easy to grow from seed in a window box or garden. But if you have none at hand, simply skip it.

2 cucumbers, each about 7 inches long
1 tablespoon red wine vinegar
1 teaspoon salt
⅛ teaspoon sugar
1 tablespoon unsalted butter
2 shallots, minced
1 cup milk
3 ounces cream cheese, cubed
4 eggs
1½ tablespoons all-purpose flour
½ cup heavy or whipping cream
½ teaspoon minced fresh burnet (optional)

½ teaspoon chopped fresh dill
Freshly ground black pepper

1. Peel the cucumbers. Cut each in half lengthwise and scoop out the seeds with a spoon. Roughly grate the cucumbers and place them in a large bowl. Sprinkle with the vinegar, salt, and sugar. Let stand 30 minutes.

2. Meanwhile, preheat the oven to 350°F. Melt the butter in a medium saucepan over medium-low heat. Add the shallots and cook until soft but not browned, about 5 minutes. Add the milk and cream cheese; stir until the cheese melts. Remove from the heat.

3. Beat 1 egg with the flour in a large bowl until smooth. Beat in the remaining eggs, heavy cream, milk-cream cheese mixture, burnet, and dill. Strain the cucumbers, pressing out all liquid with your hands. Add them to the egg mixture. Add pepper to taste.

4. Pour the mixture into a 1- to 1½-quart shallow soufflé dish. Place the dish in a roasting pan. Add enough boiling water to the pan to reach halfway up the sides of the dish. Place the pan in the oven and cook until the custard is set, about 1 hour. Let stand 10 minutes before serving.

Serves 6.

BAKED POTATO-STUFFED CUCUMBERS

A variation on the *Backgurcken* described on page 153-154.

2 cucumbers (each about 7 inches long), peeled, halved lengthwise, seeded
2 teaspoons red wine vinegar
1½ cups cold mashed cooked potatoes
1 small egg, beaten
½ teaspoon salt
¼ teaspoon freshly ground black pepper
¼ teaspoon freshly grated nutmeg
1 rounded tablespoon toasted pine nuts, finely chopped
2 tablespoons chopped fresh parsley
1 tablespoon unsalted butter
2 teaspoons minced fresh chives or scallion tops

1. Preheat the oven to 350°F. Cook the cucumber halves in boiling salted water to which you have added the vinegar, 3 minutes. Drain. Place them, hollow side down, on paper towels.

2. Place the potatoes in a large bowl. Add the egg, salt, pepper, nutmeg, pine nuts, and parsley. Mix thoroughly. Fill the cucumber halves with the potato mixture.

3. Rub a shallow baking dish with 1 teaspoon of the butter. Place the cucumbers in the dish. Press the chives into the tops and dot the cucumbers with the remaining butter. Bake 45 minutes.

Serves 4.

BAKED CUCUMBERS IN BASIL CREAM

*T*he following recipe (of French origin) is a minor vegetable classic in my opinion. Cucumbers are baked first, then tossed in a delicate upholstery of reduced cream and fresh green basil. Nothing else!

4 cucumbers, each about 7 inches long
1½ tablespoons red wine vinegar
1 teaspoon salt
¼ teaspoon sugar
2 tablespoons unsalted butter, melted
1 whole scallion, bulb and green top, finely
    chopped
¼ teaspoon freshly ground black pepper
1 cup heavy or whipping cream
½ cup plus 2 teaspoons chopped fresh basil
Salt and freshly ground black pepper

1. Peel the cucumbers. Cut each in half lengthwise. Scoop out the seeds with a spoon. Cut the cucumbers into ¼-inch-thick strips lengthwise; cut the strips into 2-inch pieces. Place the cucumber strips in a large bowl; sprinkle them with the vinegar, salt, and sugar. Toss; let stand at least 30 minutes. Drain and pat dry on paper towels.

2. Preheat the oven to 375°F. Place the cucumber strips in a shallow baking dish. Add the melted butter, scallion, and pepper. Toss well. Bake, stirring occasionally, until just tender, about 45 minutes. (Cucumbers will color slightly but not burn. Reduce the heat to 350°F if they start to turn brown.)

3. Meanwhile, heat the cream to boiling in a small saucepan. Stir in ½ cup of the basil; reduce the heat. Simmer until the cream has reduced to half, about 10 minutes.

4. Pour the cream sauce over the baked cucumbers. Add salt and pepper to taste and sprinkle with the remaining basil.

Serves 4.

BASQUE CUCUMBERS

*T*his recipe is a most unusual pairing of the prime ingredients of the Basque locale: oranges, onions, bacon, and *pepinos, certiamente.*

3 cucumbers, each about 7 inches long
3 tablespoons red wine vinegar
½ teaspoon salt
½ plus ⅛ teaspoon sugar
3 strips bacon
1 medium red onion, chopped
Juice of 1 small orange or tangerine
Salt and freshly ground black pepper
1 small orange or tangerine, peeled, seeded,
    cut into thin slices

1. Peel the cucumbers. Cut each cucumber in half crosswise. Scoop the seeds from each piece with a thin knife or a grapefruit spoon. Cut each hollowed-out cucumber into ¼-inch-thick rounds. Place the cucumber slices in a large bowl and sprinkle with 1 tablespoon of the vinegar, the salt, and ⅛ teaspoon of the sugar. Let stand 30 minutes. Drain; pat dry on paper towels.

2. Sauté the bacon in large heavy skillet until crisp. Remove the bacon and drain it on paper towels.

3. Pour off all but 2 tablespoons of the bacon drippings. Sauté the cucumber slices in the pan over medium heat until they just begin to wilt, 3 or 4 minutes. Add the onion; sprinkle with the remaining 2 tablespoons vinegar, ½ teaspoon sugar, and the orange juice. Continue to cook, tossing gently, until all liquid has evaporated. Add salt and pepper to taste. Remove from the heat and stir in the orange slices.

Serves 4.

BROILED TILEFISH WITH GREEN-AND-GOLD SAUCE

The English word for cucumber at one time was *cowcumber*. As the early British naturalist Nicholas Culpepper informs us: "The green tumors grow fullest and fairest when planted upon fields that were once fields of pasturage, enriched by a dominion of cowes dropyngs."

One of the more felicitous sauces in my kitchen repertoire is an English import known as "Green and Gold." I whip up a batch as either upholstery or underpinning for plain-Jane dinners where the entrée is either poached or broiled. Being a British devise, the sauce did come with a culinary caveat. "Always serve a dab over a fillet of fish and under a slice of meat." You take it from there.

4 filets of tile fish (about ½ pound each), skinned
1½ tablespoons olive oil
1 teaspoon red wine vinegar
1 tablespoon finely minced chives
1 teaspoon finely grated lemon peel
1 teaspoon salt
½ teaspoon freshly ground black pepper
1 tablespoon unsalted butter
1 large shallot, minced
1 cucumber (about 7 inches long), peeled, seeded, finely chopped
1 sprig fresh thyme, finely chopped, or a pinch of dried
2 teaspoons lemon juice
⅓ cup sour cream
Salt and freshly ground black pepper

1. Pat the fish dry with paper towels. Combine the oil, vinegar, chives, lemon peel, salt and pepper in a bowl. Spread this mixture over both sides of the fish filets. Let stand at least 30 minutes. (Or longer, covered, in the refrigerator.) Place the fish filets on a broiler tray.

2. Melt the butter in a small saucepan over medium heat. Sauté the shallot until golden.

3. While the shallot is cooking, put the filets under the broiler, to broil about 4 minutes per side.

4. When the shallot is cooked, reduce the heat to medium-low and add the cucumber and thyme. Cook, stirring constantly, 2 minutes. Add the lemon juice and sour cream. Cook over low heat 5 minutes. Do not allow to boil. Add salt and pepper to taste and spoon over the broiled fish.

Serves 4.

BAKED CHICKEN-AND-HAM-CRAMMED CUCUMBERS

If one must lay blame for the cucumber blackout from Rome to Renaissance, put the debit to the account of Attila the Hun. That wild fellow seems to have had extremely limited tastebuds and even more abbreviated sensibilities. But in all fairness one must give his thundering horde a mite of gratitude since one way or another a cucumber seed must have made its way back to the fatherland in time. How else can one explain the next German-inspired prescription: *Backgurcken* (baked cucumbers).

2 cucumbers, each about 7 inches long
Juice of ½ lemon
1 teaspoon salt
1 tablespoon plus 2 teaspoons unsalted butter
1 shallot, minced
1¼ cups finely chopped cooked chicken
3 tablespoons finely chopped Black Forest ham or prosciutto
1 tablespoon finely chopped toasted almonds
2 tablespoons fine fresh bread crumbs
¼ teaspoon chopped fresh thyme, or ⅛ teaspoon dried
¼ teaspoon freshly ground black pepper
¾ cup chicken broth, approximately (see page 414)
¼ cup heavy or whipping cream
2 teaspoons all-purpose flour
1 teaspoon Madeira
Salt and freshly ground black pepper
Chopped fresh parsley

1. Peel the cucumbers. Cut each cucumber in half lengthwise and scoop out the seeds with a spoon. Sprinkle the scooped-out cucumbers with the lemon juice and ½ teaspoon of the salt. Place them, hollow sides down, on paper towels. Let stand 30 minutes.

2. Preheat the oven to 350°F. Melt 1 tablespoon of the butter in a small skillet over medium-low heat. Add the shallot; cook until soft but not browned, about 5 minutes.

3. Transfer the shallot with its butter to a medium bowl. Add the chicken, Black Forest ham, almonds, bread crumbs, thyme, remaining ½ teaspoon salt, and the pepper. Mix thoroughly. Add 3 tablespoons of the broth and 3 tablespoons of the cream to moisten. Mix thoroughly. Add more broth if needed for the mixture to hold together.

4. Brush the salt off the cucumber halves and fill them with the meat mixture. Place the stuffed cucumber halves in a Dutch oven just large enough to hold them snugly. Add enough chicken stock to reach halfway up the sides of the cucumbers. Heat the liquid around the cucumbers to boiling and then transfer the pot, uncovered, to the oven and bake until just tender, about 45 minutes.

5. Remove the pot from the oven. Carefully transfer the cucumbers to a shallow baking dish and keep them warm in a low oven. Strain the cooking juices.

6. Melt the 2 teaspoons of butter in a small saucepan over medium-low heat. Stir in the flour. Cook, stirring constantly, 2 minutes. Whisk in the cooking juices. Heat to boiling; reduce the heat. Cook until slightly thickened. Stir in the remaining 1 tablespoon cream and the Madeira. Add salt and pepper to taste. Spoon the sauce over the cucumbers and sprinkle with parsley.

Serves 2 to 4.

EGGPLANT
The One Perfect Health Food

I painted a picture of a purple eggplant long before I ever contemplated cooking one! But then, the artist's *palette* preceded the trencherman's *palate* as the focus of my existence.

As a child I drew constantly. Any scrap of paper I could unearth around the house became a vehicle for my compulsive drawing—which, I realize now, usually consisted of bad line-for-line copies of the baroque Nell Brinkley illustrations that appeared in the Hearst newspaper our family doted upon in the twenties and thirties.

I suspect my parents considered my interest in art questionable to say the least. My father, I knew, held the profession of painter only a small step above the rank of gigolo, or even worse. My mother was somewhat more sanguine in the matter. After realizing that a ban on my artistic animus was impossible to monitor, she eventually framed the best results for her living room, claiming that the talent was probably inherited from her side of the family, since her father was a designer in the fur trade, after all.

I drew night and day, no matter what inhibitory sanctions were placed upon me, for pencil and brush were my only release from a world of painful shyness and introspection.

By the time I was in my last year of grade school, my mother was convinced that I "had the stuff" to study art. In the late 1930s, however, art classes (in high school at least) were joyless exercises. Rather than releasing creative energies, most courses seemed to stunt or downright diminish them. Outfitting the neophyte student for the narrow job market were classes in perspective and mechanical drawing, architectural rendering and block lettering—all studies that required the use of a compass, triangle, and French curve, tools unsuited to the inept hands of a free spirit like me.

When I was fifteen I was summoned to the office of the principal, a command that filled me with trepidation.

"Greene," he said. Never looking up to acknowledge me, he stared hard at my record card as he spoke. "Several of your teachers feel you show a true aptitude for the graphic arts. Now, there is a highly regarded academy [the august Academy of Fine Arts] in New York City that holds a yearly competition for scholarship students. And you...." He coughed discreetly. "Your name has been selected to enter as this school's representative. Of course, you are not obliged to do this, you understand, but it reflects significant honor on this school in passing...." I know he talked on, but I had stopped listening several sentences before. Frankly, I could not believe it. That I had been selected—picked out—over a host of other highly proficient (and, I felt, vastly more talented) classmates was the first real indication of public endorsement I had ever experienced. I liked the emotion enormously. I still do!

The competition for an "actual" art scholarship was the most vivid experience of my young life. What I remember most of this terrible, wonderful ordeal was not the gray stone mansion where it took place, nor the trial by charcoal that came later—but rather the utterly adult lack of condescension to the dozen or so students who had come to compete. I felt more secure on that day than I ever had in the past—even when I discovered I would be faced with the paralyzing prospect of a life-study model who would pose in the nude!

I cannot truly remember the quality of the nude studies I sketched. But the still life—a brace of shiny purple eggplant beside a bowl of green and red peppers, papery onions, and pale gold-flecked zucchini squash—I will never forget as long as I live, for it was a highly impressionistic rendering and unlike any high-school performance I had given prior to that day.

More to the point, I discovered as our paintings were being collected that the entire contents of the composition had been acquired with a dual purpose in mind. Those vegetables were to be the basis of the proctor's dinner later that evening. Though I had never heard of the dish, we competitors had literally painted a ratatouille on the hoof!

I was accepted for the scholarship and studied at the Academy for the next two years, until I went away to college. The people I met there were totally unlike any I had ever known. The ideas exchanged openly about art, politics, dance, theater—and yes, even food—altered my perceptions.

Regretfully I must admit I no longer draw, unless I happen to be in some utterly foreign place. Photography being an alien and terrifying form of expression, I generally sketch the local color instead. At home, my hand is too busy stirring some pot in the kitchen or tapping at my typewriter to miss the vagrant brush or pen. If that seems sad, take my word that it is not, for when I discovered that I could speak, write, and successfully articulate my feelings, I no longer felt the need!

Vegetable Roots

On canvas or in a casserole, the eggplant today is one of the world's most cherished ingredients. But because its appearance was startling to say the least, primitive man eschewed eggplant as an edible entirely.

The Chinese first speculated upon its

possibility as table fare in the third century A.D. It was noted, erroneously, as "stalk of the lotus" in *Erhya*, a dictionary of ancient Chinese terms compiled by the philosopher, Kuo P'u, who formally dubbed it *ch'ieh*—which is the same name Chinese cooks use today, seventeen centuries after the fact.

It took another 300 years for anyone to actually taste an eggplant at the end of his chopstick, however. Chinese diners regarded this victual with the same sense of trepidation that anyone (other than a deep-dyed gastronome) accords rattlesnake or blowfish; the vegetable possessed a reputation for high toxicity in unskilled hands. In the sixth century, in fact, the name *ch'ieh* was officially amended to *ch'ieh-pʐu*, which means "medicine" or "poison."

It's not such a stretch of the imagination. Eggplant formally belongs to the Solanaceae, or nightshade, family, which, though it has connections to tomato, potato, and pimiento, also has stronger ties to belladonna, horse nettle, and tobacco—none exactly a source of life-giving nourishment!

The first eggplant grown in China was small, pendant-shaped, and very delicate—presenting a fragile, pearly-hued appearance that many associated with bird's eggs.

Unfortunately, the earliest Occidental to sample one went mad after the first bite. This unlucky diner was an Indian traveler so smitten with the eggplant's appearance that he ate it raw and promptly had a fit. Or more probably a case of acute gastritis.

Sorry for him, but worse luck for the eggplant, as the calamity added yet another blemish to an already spotted reputation. Long, long after the vegetable's migration to the Levant (where it grew larger) and the western Mediterranean (where it developed a deep lustrous color), eggplant was still known as *mala insana*, which means "a bad egg" or "a mad apple," depending upon the latitude of one's Latin! And to this very day the Italian name *melanzana* is a direct descendant of that original slur.

In the late seventeenth century, when Linnaeus, the Swedish naturalist (and codifier of everything that grows in and out of a garden) listed eggplant in his voluminous dossier, he compounded the injury. Designating the vegetable as "a fruited edible" he still called it *Solanum insanum*. But Scandinavian good sense and his own strict conscience must have chafed at the cognomen. Eggplant by that late date was fairly common and exhibited no evidence whatsoever of turning a diner dotty, so Linnaeus renamed it. Compromising (and fracturing the meaning somewhat), he tagged the plant *Solanum melongens*, which means "soothing mad fruit"!

A staple the world was obviously ready for.

What to Look For

*E*ggplant is one vegetable never out of season, for it seems to bloom anywhere the sun shines and is virtually always available at greengrocers'. Summer, however, brings my favorite crop to the shelf: the small, early variety not much larger than Seckel pears. Equally sweet too!

These mauve-skinned miniatures—sometimes called Italian or Oriental eggplant, since they are inevitably found in those ethnic markets—have many stovetop virtues aside from their blushing hue. Fewer seeds keep them from turning bitter in a skillet for one thing, and thin skins sharply reduce their cooking time for another. No matter what size eggplant you choose, however, make certain to select only spherically shaped globes with firm, taut exteriors and a uniform glossy color. My first cooking teacher (after my grandmother) was the redoubtable Dione Lucas, who claimed somewhat airily that over-the-hill eggplant betrayed its age precisely in the same manner as over-the-hill debutantes: slack skin and slightly puckered posteriors!

It is a good idea for a consumer to press any eggplant of questionable vintage with a judicious thumb. If the slight pressure causes a minor blemish, pass that debutante by, for it obviously sat on the vine too long and will be discolored below the surface. Prime eggplant has a certain weight: a globe should feel substantial to the palm. Lightweight eggplant invariably indicates pulpy or pitted flesh. Likewise, skip an eggplant with a scarred or bruised surface. That is a sure sign of decay in the garden or out. A green cap and stem, if it is truly green, is an emblem of freshness.

In the 1980s, eggplant seems to be enjoying a new vogue among vegetable buyers who choose it for its designer color rather than its flavor. A new summer garden strain, snowy in appearance, is being marketed as "Easter Eggplant," and another pale golden hybrid is on the vine ready to climb, even as we sauté.

No matter what hue eggplant you elect, know that it is a perfect food for dieters: a half cup tabbed at a mere 25 calories. And while relatively low in vitamins, eggplant is extremely mineral-rich and heavy with the amino acids that control essential proteins in the body. Every slice of cooked eggplant affords a diner with megadoses of potassium, phosphorus, calcium, and magnesium.

Preparation

*E*ven avid eggplant growers (like me) are somewhat ambivalent about its kitchen preparation, however. For instance, some cooks never peel the skin; others always do. I play it by ear. If the vegetable is small and appears to be tender (fairly thin-skinned), I skip the amenity entirely. But if the eggplant is large and likely to be fibrous, I zap it with my rotary blade.

Salting eggplant is another matter of mild dissent. I inevitably salt this vegetable prior to cooking. Not only does salt extract the bitterness inherent in most eggplant, I have discovered after myriad bouts of eggplant cookery that a well-salted (drained and dried) slice will absorb fully a third less oil or butter in a skillet than a similar unsalted portion. The result? A healthier and eminently more digestible dish; and somewhat less costly in the final analysis as well. A prudent salting also rids eggplant of its excessive moisture.

My method is routine. I sprinkle coarse salt uniformly on all cut slices and then place them in a colander to drain for at least 30 minutes. Later, I pat the slices free of excessive salt between several layers of paper towels.

Other than salting, another way to avoid bitterness in an eggplant dish is to blanch it first. Boiling the raw vegetable slightly (one minute maximum) flushes away any excessive acidity.

MELITZANOSALATA
(Greek Eggplant Salad)

*O*ne eggplant endowment, a cool but tangy salad or first course from Greece, gives the vegetable an entirely unexpected flavor as it is roasted over an open flame first. The recipe came my way from a bright and wildly enthusiastic teacher of her Hellenic kitchen heritage, the estimable Athena Forogolu.

1 medium eggplant (about ¾ pound)
1 large tomato, peeled, seeded, chopped
1 green bell pepper, seeded, finely chopped
1 small onion, grated
1 large clove garlic, crushed
½ teaspoon salt
¼ teaspoon freshly ground black pepper
3 tablespoons red wine vinegar
¼ cup olive oil
Sliced black olives
Chopped fresh parsley

1. Roast the eggplant over a gas flame (or under a broiler) until the skin has blackened and is crisp. Cool.

2. Rub the skin off the eggplant with damp paper towels. Chop the eggplant pulp.

3. Place the eggplant in a bowl and add the tomato, pepper, onion, and garlic.

4. Combine the salt, pepper, vinegar, and oil in a small bowl. Pour this dressing over the vegetables. Toss well. Garnish with olive slices and parsley. Serve well chilled.

Serves 2 to 4.

EGGPLANT AND RED PEPPER POTHER

Delectable as it is, eggplant is habitually bypassed in a soup kettle, for it turns sallow as it cooks—but never when stirred up with a florid pair of tomatoes and a rubescent red pepper, thank goodness!

My next offering, a velvety chowder of British antecedents and pale rosy hue, is unaccountably known as a "pother." Unaccountable (to me) because Webster and friends define that noun as synonymous with "plague," "turmoil," and like emotional disturbances! Nothing could be further from the fact of this pacific brew. Obviously a pother of a different color!

1 large eggplant (about 1½ pounds),
    peeled, cubed
Salt
1 red bell pepper
1 hot red or green chile pepper (see
    Guacamole headnote, page 37)
3 tablespoons unsalted butter
1 teaspoon olive oil
1 medium onion, roughly chopped
2 large cloves garlic, chopped
1 medium potato, peeled, cubed
2 medium tomatoes, peeled, seeded,
    chopped
4 cups chicken broth (see page 414)
Salt and freshly ground black pepper

1. Place the eggplant cubes in a colander. Sprinkle with salt; let stand 30 minutes. Brush the eggplant with paper towels to remove the salt; pat dry.

2. Meanwhile, roast the bell and chile peppers over a gas flame until the skins blacken and are crisp (or place them under a broiler). Carefully wrap them in paper towels, place them in a plastic bag, and let them cool 5 minutes. Rub the skins off with paper towels. Seed and devein. Roughly chop.

3. Heat the butter with the oil in a large heavy saucepan over medium-low heat. Add the onion; cook 1 minute. Add the garlic; cook 3 minutes longer. Add the potato and eggplant, tossing well to coat with the onion mixture. Stir in the peppers and tomatoes; cook 10 minutes. Add the chicken broth. Heat to boiling; reduce the heat. Simmer, uncovered, 30 minutes.

4. Cool the soup for about 15 minutes and then blend it, in batches, in a blender or food processor until smooth.

Be careful, as hot liquid will expand. Reheat slightly over medium-low heat before serving. Add salt and pepper to taste. Serve soup warm but not hot.

Serves 6 to 8.

FRIED EGGPLANT SALAD

*T*his is one of the eggplant's finest recipes, and certainly its most egalitarian rendering: it all takes place in one skillet.

1 large, or 2 small, eggplant (about 1½ pounds)
Salt
½ cup olive oil, approximately
1 medium onion, halved, thinly sliced
1 large clove garlic, minced
Juice of 2 lemons
Salt and freshly ground black pepper
Chopped fresh parsley
Lemon wedges

1. Cut the stem from the eggplant and slice it in half lengthwise. Cut each half into ¼-inch-thick slices. Place the slices in a colander, sprinkle them with salt, and let stand 30 minutes. Brush the eggplant with paper towels to remove the salt; pat dry.

2. Heat 2 tablespoons of the oil in a large heavy skillet over medium heat until hot but not smoking. Add enough eggplant slices to cover the bottom. Sprinkle lightly with more oil, and sauté

until golden brown on both sides. Drain on paper towels. Continue to sauté the eggplant slices, adding more oil as needed.

3. Pour off all but 2 teaspoons oil from the skillet. Add the onion; cook over medium-low heat 1 minute. Add the garlic; cook until lightly browned, about 5 minutes.

4. Place one fourth of the eggplant in the bottom of a deep, narrow serving bowl. Sprinkle with the juice of ½ lemon. Sprinkle with salt and pepper to taste. Top with one fourth of the onion mixture. Continue to layer, squeezing lemon juice over each successive layer of eggplant, until all ingredients are used up. End with the onion mixture. Chill well. Serve garnished with parsley and lemon wedges.

Serves 4 as an appetizer.

EGGPLANT AU GRATIN

*T*he following dish is French in origin and like most vegetable offerings from France tastes both earthy and ethereal at the same time. No mean trick—whether the chief ingredient is an eggplant or an egg!

1 medium eggplant (about 1 pound),
    peeled, cut into 1-inch-thick strips
    about 2 inches long
6 tablespoons (¾ stick) unsalted butter
2 shallots, minced
½ pound mushrooms, sliced
Juice of ½ lemon
1 teaspoon olive oil
1½ tablespoons all-purpose flour
⅓ cup milk
½ cup heavy or whipping cream
¼ teaspoon freshly grated nutmeg
Dash of hot pepper sauce
1 egg, lightly beaten
1 teaspoon minced fresh chives
2 tablespoons minced fresh parsley
Salt and freshly ground black pepper
2 tablespoons fine fresh bread crumbs
1 tablespoon freshly grated Parmesan
    cheese

1. Cook the eggplant in boiling salted water until tender, 5 to 8 minutes. Drain well, pressing out all liquid with the back of a wooden spoon. Reserve.

2. Melt 2 tablespoons of the butter in a large heavy skillet over medium heat. Stir in the shallots; cook 1 minute. Add the mushrooms and cook, stirring constantly, until lightly browned, about 4 minutes. Sprinkle with lemon juice and continue to cook until all moisture has evaporated. Transfer to a large bowl.

3. Heat 1 tablespoon of the butter with the oil in the same skillet. Add the eggplant strips and sauté over high heat until lightly browned, about 5 minutes. Transfer to the bowl containing the mushroom mixture.

4. Preheat the oven to 375°F. Melt 1½ tablespoons of the butter in a medium saucepan over medium-low heat. Stir in the flour. Cook, stirring constantly, 2 minutes. Whisk in the milk and cream. Heat to boiling; reduce the heat. Cook until thick, about 3 minutes. Add the nutmeg and hot pepper sauce. Stir this into the mushroom-eggplant mixture. Add the egg, chives, parsley, and salt and pepper to taste. Transfer to a shallow baking dish.

5. Melt the remaining 1½ tablespoons butter in a small sauté pan over medium heat. Stir in the bread crumbs; cook until golden. Spoon the crumbs over the eggplant mixture and sprinkle with the cheese. Bake 15 minutes, then place under the broiler to lightly brown the top.

Serves 4.

EGGPLANT ROLLATINI

The following recipe is an Italian-American devise, the gift of a friend who refuses credit for her handiwork since she claims it changes every time she prepares it. Not my rendition . . . nor yours, either, I'll warrant!

1 large eggplant (about 1½ pounds)
Salt
2 eggs, lightly beaten
¾ cup fresh bread crumbs, approximately
4 tablespoons (½ stick) unsalted butter
¼ cup olive oil
1 medium onion, finely chopped
1 clove garlic, minced

½ pound mild Italian sausages, removed
    from casings, broken up
1½ cups Basic or Creamy Tomato Sauce
    (see pages 374 and 375)
⅓ pound mozzarella cheese, chopped
Freshly ground black pepper
3 tablespoons freshly grated Parmesan
    cheese

1. Cut off the stem, then peel the eggplant and cut it lengthwise into ¼-inch-thick slices. Place the slices in a colander, sprinkle with salt, and let stand 30 minutes. Brush the eggplant with paper towels to remove the salt; pat dry.

2. Place the beaten eggs in a shallow bowl. Place the bread crumbs in another shallow bowl.

3. Preheat the oven to 350°F. Melt 2 tablespoons of the butter in 2 tablespoons of the oil in a large heavy skillet over medium heat. Dip each eggplant slice into the beaten egg, then roll it in bread crumbs, and sauté the slices, a few at a time, until golden on both sides. Add more butter and oil as needed. Drain the eggplant on paper towels.

4. Discard the grease and wipe the skillet with paper towels. Heat 1 tablespoon of the butter in the skillet over medium-low heat. Add the onion; cook 1 minute. Stir in the garlic and sausage. Cook over medium heat, breaking up the lumps with a fork, until lightly browned.

5. Spoon about 2 teaspoons of the tomato sauce over each eggplant slice. Sprinkle with the mozzarella cheese and the sausage mixture. Roll each slice (the short way) and place them in a lightly buttered shallow baking dish. Spoon the remaining sauce over the top. Sprinkle with pepper to taste and the Parmesan cheese. Bake 30 minutes.

Serves 4.

MOUSSAKA SOUFFLE

Seven egg whites and a little imagination create a transubstantiation of the great Greek classic dish.

2 medium eggplants (about 2 pounds)
Salt
Olive oil
7½ tablespoons unsalted butter
⅓ cup freshly grated Parmesan cheese
2 large shallots, minced
1 large clove garlic, minced
1¼ cups finely chopped cooked lamb
¼ pound mushrooms, chopped
¼ teaspoon chopped fresh thyme, or
⅛ teaspoon dried
¼ teaspoon chopped fresh rosemary, or
⅛ teaspoon dried
½ teaspoon salt
¼ teaspoon freshly ground black pepper
5 tablespoons all-purpose flour
1½ cups milk, hot
½ cup heavy or whipping cream
¼ teaspoon freshly grated nutmeg
⅛ teaspoon cayenne pepper

6 egg yolks
¼ cup grated Jarlsberg or Gruyère cheese
7 egg whites
Creamy Tomato Sauce (see page 375)

1. Cut the stems from the eggplants and slice each in half lengthwise. Cut lengthwise slashes into the eggplant pulp, but do not pierce the skin. Place the eggplant in a colander skin-side down. Sprinkle with salt; let stand 30 minutes. Brush the eggplant with paper towels to remove the salt; pat dry.

2. Preheat the oven to 350°F. Lightly brush the top of the eggplant halves with oil. Place the eggplant in a shallow baking dish or roasting pan. Add ½ inch of water to the pan. Bake until tender, about 30 minutes. Remove the eggplant and drain upside down on paper towels

until cool enough to handle.

3. When cool, trim ¼ inch off the bottom end of each eggplant. Loosen the pulp from the skin with a spoon and pull the pulp away from the skin. Scrape the skins to remove all the pulp. Reserve the skins. Chop the pulp and divide it into two equal parts. Set aside.

4. Rub a 2-quart soufflé dish with ½ tablespoon of the butter. Sprinkle it with 1 tablespoon of the Parmesan cheese. Cut the eggplant skins in half lengthwise. Rub the outside of each piece with butter (about 1 tablespoon). Trim the skins to fit evenly along the sides of the dish. Place any leftover pieces, buttered side down, on the bottom. Press the skins into the side of the dish. Set aside in a cool place.

5. Raise the oven heat to 400°F. Melt 1½ tablespoons of the butter in a large heavy skillet over medium-low heat. Add the shallots; cook 1 minute. Add the garlic; cook 1 minute longer. Raise the heat to medium and stir in the lamb. Cook, stirring constantly, until the meat is heated through. Transfer to a medium bowl.

6. Heat 1 tablespoon of the butter with 1 teaspoon oil in the same skillet over high heat. Add the mushrooms; cook, stirring constantly, until golden. Add the mushrooms to the lamb mixture along with the thyme, rosemary, salt, pepper, and half the chopped eggplant. Mix thoroughly; set aside.

7. To make the base, melt the remaining 3½ tablespoons butter in a medium saucepan over medium-low heat. Stir in the flour. Cook, stirring constantly, 2 minutes. Whisk in the hot milk and the cream. Raise the heat slightly and cook, stirring constantly, until thick, about 3 minutes. Remove from the heat and add the nutmeg, cayenne pepper, and salt and pepper to taste. Stir ½ cup of the base into the eggplant-lamb mixture.

8. Beat the egg yolks, one at a time, into the remaining base. Return it to low heat and cook, stirring constantly, until very thick. Do not allow it to boil. Transfer to a medium-size bowl and cool slightly. Stir in the remaining chopped eggplant, ¼ cup of the Parmesan cheese, and the Jarlsberg cheese.

9. Beat the egg whites until stiff but not dry. Gently fold them into the base.

10. Spoon slightly more than half the eggplant-lamb mixture into the prepared soufflé dish. Spoon half the base over it, then sprinkle with the remaining eggplant-lamb mixture. Top with the remaining base and sprinkle with the remaining Parmesan cheese. Place in the oven and immediately turn down the heat to 375° F. Bake 55 minutes. Let stand a few minutes before serving. Cut into wedges and pass the Creamy Tomato Sauce on the side.

Serves 6.

GOLDEN EGGPLANT CROQUETTES

*E*ggplant is a vegetable of such protean possibilities that it is very often dubbed the one perfect health food! When I was younger (and so was the vegetarian movement), adherents of meatless meals routinely offered up some mashed or hashed version of eggplant masquerading as "not-for-real veal cutlet" or "mock filet mignon" on their menus. The curious thing about these culinary counterfeits is that, while never precisely on target in either texture or taste, the dishes were not half bad—basically because eggplant is so mutable. For further evidence, note these delicate golden croquettes.

1 medium eggplant (about ¾ to 1 pound),
    peeled, cubed
1 medium tomato, peeled, seeded, chopped
1 whole scallion, bulb and green top, finely
    chopped
1 clove garlic, minced
½ cup chopped fresh parsley
2 tablespoons chopped fresh basil, or
    1 teaspoon dried
¾ teaspoon salt
⅛ teaspoon freshly ground black pepper
⅛ teaspoon freshly grated nutmeg
1 egg, lightly beaten
2 tablespoons freshly grated Parmesan
    cheese
½ teaspoon baking powder
½ cup fresh bread crumbs
Oil for frying

1. Cook the eggplant in boiling salted water until tender, 5 to 8 minutes. Drain well, pressing out all liquid with the back of a wooden spoon.

2. Transfer the eggplant to the container of a blender or food processor. Add the tomato and blend until smooth.

3. Transfer the puréed eggplant-tomato mixture to a medium-size bowl. Add the remaining ingredients, except the oil. Mix thoroughly.

4. Heat 2 inches of oil in a heavy skillet over medium-high heat. Form the eggplant mixture into croquettes, about 1 heaping tablespoon at a time, and drop into the hot oil. Cook until very well browned on both sides, 4 to 5 minutes. Drain on paper towels and keep warm while frying the remaining croquettes.
Serves 4.

SHAKLE-MESHI
(Baked Eggplant Boats)

*I*n Middle Eastern countries, some form of eggplant is consumed at all the important meals that mark a man's life: the birth celebration, wedding, and funeral supper. One dish of Jordanian derivation seems highly appropriate for each of the foregoing transitional feeds, since the eggplant in question is trimmed to a boat shape before it is cooked. Actually it's one of the most delectable forms of "Bon Voyage" on record.

1 large eggplant (about 1½ pounds)
Salt
Olive oil
1 tablespoon unsalted butter
1 medium onion, finely chopped
1 clove garlic, minced
2 tablespoons chopped pine nuts
½ pound ground raw lamb
½ teaspoon ground allspice
⅛ teaspoon ground cinnamon

1 tablespoon minced fresh parsley plus
    additional chopped for garnish
Salt and freshly ground black pepper
1 can (14 ounces) plum tomatoes, drained,
    crushed

1. Cut the stem from the eggplant, then peel it. Cut the eggplant into four equal quarters lengthwise. Carefully cut a pocket in the top of each piece and gently push the pieces open so that they resemble small boats. Sprinkle with salt and place in a colander; let stand 30 minutes. Brush the eggplant with paper towels to remove the salt; pat dry.

 2. Rub each eggplant quarter lightly with oil. Place them on a baking sheet; bake 30 minutes.

 3. Preheat the oven to 350°F. Melt the butter in a large heavy skillet over medium-low heat. Add the onion; cook 1 minute. Add the garlic and pine nuts; cook until lightly browned, about 4 min-

utes. Add the lamb. Cook over medium heat, chopping the meat up with a fork, until the lamb is lightly browned all over. Add the allspice, cinnamon, 1 tablespoon minced parsley, and salt and pepper to taste. Carefully spoon this mixture into the baked eggplant boats.

 4. Place the filled eggplant boats in a shallow baking dish and spoon some of the crushed tomatoes over each boat. Bake 45 minutes. Sprinkle with chopped parsley before serving.

 Serves 4.

RATATOUILLE AND SHRIMP PIE

*R*atatouille is a dish I never savored until I lived in France. For, while I had sampled various recipes on home ground, I never knew what all the shouting was about until I finally managed to sample a forkful in the landscape of its origin. Perhaps, as it is claimed, the hot Midi sun gently ripening each ingredient is responsible for the dish's preeminence, but the stirring arm of the Provençal cook deserves some kudos as well. I once saw a Mediterranean housewife nurse a baby, pluck a chicken, and polish her kitchen floor (with rags tied round her shoes), while she also managed to throw a handful of fresh herbs into her ratatouille pot as it simmered on the stove because the smell did not sufficiently "arouse" her practiced nose. Only when she and her baby had sneezed twice did she deem it ready for the night's dinner!

 What follows is not her devise, but indulge in it anyhow. An unexpected version of ratatouille, it nestles between layers of buttery pastry—with fresh shrimp blushing bright pink in the heart of all that largess of eggplant and tomato.

Old-Fashioned Lard and Vinegar Crust
 (recipe follows)
1 large eggplant (about 1½ pounds)
Salt
½ cup olive oil, approximately
2 small zucchini (about 1 pound),
 trimmed, sliced
1 tablespoon unsalted butter
1 large onion, halved, thinly sliced
2 large cloves garlic, minced
1 large green pepper, seeded, thinly sliced
2 medium tomatoes, peeled, cut into
 ½-inch-thick wedges

½ teaspoon salt
¼ teaspoon freshly ground black pepper
⅓ pound shrimp, shelled, deveined, halved
¼ cup chopped fresh parsley
2 cups grated Fontina cheese
½ cup freshly grated Parmesan cheese
1 egg yolk
2 teaspoons water

 1. Make the Old-Fashioned Lard and Vinegar Crust.

 2. Trim the eggplant and halve it lengthwise. Cut into ¼-inch-thick slices, place them in a colander, and sprinkle with salt. Let stand 30 minutes. Brush the eggplant with paper towels to remove the salt; pat dry.

3. Heat 2 tablespoons of the oil in a heavy skillet over medium heat. Sauté the eggplant slices, a few pieces at a time, until golden on both sides. Add more oil as needed. Drain the slices on paper towels, then transfer to a bowl. In 2 teaspoons oil in the same pan, sauté the zucchini over high heat, tossing constantly, until golden. Reduce heat and cook until soft, about 8 minutes. Drain, and add to the eggplant in the bowl.

4. Wipe out the skillet and melt the butter over medium heat. Add the onion

and cook 1 minute. Add the garlic and pepper. Cook, covered, 5 minutes. Stir in the tomatoes, salt, and pepper. Raise the heat and cook, uncovered, until all liquid has evaporated. Stir in the shrimp; cook 1 minute. Add the parsley and the eggplant and zucchini. Mix well.

5. Preheat the oven to 425°F. Roll out half the dough and line a lightly buttered 10-inch glass or ceramic quiche dish with it. Spoon one third of the ratatouille mixture over the bottom of the crust. Sprinkle with one third of each cheese. Continue to layer until all the ingredients are used up, ending with the Parmesan cheese. Roll out the remaining dough, place it over the top, and trim and flute the edges. Cut a slit in the top to allow the steam to escape. Beat the egg yolk with the water; brush over the crust. Bake 10 minutes; reduce the heat to 375°F. Bake 30 minutes longer. Let stand 10 minutes before serving. Serves 6.

White eggplants were known as "Italian Mad Apples" for centuries. When the color deepened to a ripe purple, however, eggplant's bad name took on an even less virtuous hue. In England in the sixteenth century, eggplants were referred to as "Apples of Sodom." And most diners of any sensibility at all passed them by, no matter what prandial joy seemed inherent in any seedy slice.

Most diners . . . but not all! Enough solid trencherfolk of confirmed taste still indulged in the pleasures that this exotic berry had to offer to cause John Gerard, the pious naturalist who lived in the seventeenth century, to rail against its consumption publicly.

"I wish English men to content themselves with meats and sauce of our owne country," he declared, "than with fruit eaten with apparent perill; for doubtless these Raging Apples have a mischevious qualitie, the use whereof is utterly to be forsaken."

Old-Fashioned Lard and Vinegar Crust

2 cups plus 2 teaspoons all-purpose flour
2 teaspoons sugar
1 teaspoon salt
¾ cup lard
1 egg, beaten
1½ teaspoons red wine vinegar
2 tablespoons cold water

Sift 2 cups of the flour with the sugar and salt into a large bowl. Cut in the lard. Blend with a pastry blender until the mixture is the texture of coarse crumbs. Combine the egg, vinegar, and water in a small bowl. Using a fork, cut the liquid into the flour mixture to form a soft dough. (Do not overwork.) Sprinkle with the remaining 2 teaspoons flour. Chill for 1 hour before using.

Makes enough dough for a 9- to 10-inch double-crust pie.

MIDI-POCHE
(Eggplant Bake)

*H*undreds of delectable eggplant dishes have crossed my lips since I have cooked for a living, but the few that remain vividly imprinted on my tastebuds are those I first tasted in the kitchens of Provence. In that area of France, eggplant is a fixed staple at most meals, largely because it grows with such profusion in those clement airs. Frugal housewives there pick the newly sprouted globes before they even have time to purple up. "Less seeds," they claim, "produce sweeter marriages with other vegetables in the pot!" Old wives' tales or no, these ladies know their eggplant to a fare-thee-well. And this is the eggplant's classic rendition. It is a simply wonderful offering—fried first and baked later in a blanket of spicy tomato sauce—served up at least once a week for dinner, supper, and sometimes next morning's breakfast as well.

When pressed for the name of this dish, one cook shrugged at the absurd notion of calling it anything at all. But a wise old chef I met in Nice, who also gave me the general details of its prescription, described it as a *midi-poche*. Literally translated it means a *noon pocket*, which, to my mind at least, implies the optimum time and means of transportation of its ingredients from garden to stove.

2 small eggplants (about ¾ pound), sliced
2 tablespoons lemon juice
1 tablespoon plus ½ teaspoon salt
4 tablespoons (½ stick) unsalted butter
2 tablespoons olive oil
1 shallot, minced
1 small onion, finely chopped
1 clove garlic, minced
3 cups chopped, seeded tomatoes (about 2
*   pounds)*
Pinch of sugar
½ teaspoon chopped fresh thyme, or a
*   pinch of dried*
1 tablespoon minced fresh basil, or 1½
*   teaspoons dried*
1 teaspoon crushed allspice
¼ cup all-purpose flour
1 cup cooked rice
¼ cup freshly grated Parmesan cheese

1. Preheat the oven to 350°F. Place the sliced eggplant in a colander. Sprinkle it with the lemon juice and 1 tablespoon salt; let stand 30 minutes.

2. Meanwhile, heat 2 tablespoons of the butter with 1 tablespoon of the oil in a medium saucepan over medium heat.

Add the shallot and onion; cook 2 minutes. Stir in the garlic; cook 1 minute longer. Add the tomatoes; sprinkle with sugar. Add the thyme, basil, allspice, and ½ teaspoon salt. Cook, uncovered, over medium-low heat 20 minutes. Set aside.

3. Brush the eggplant with paper towels to remove the salt; pat dry. Dust the eggplant slices lightly with the flour. Heat the remaining butter and oil in a heavy skillet and sauté the eggplant over medium heat until golden on both sides. Drain on paper towels.

4. Spoon one fourth of the tomato sauce over the bottom of an ovenproof baking dish or casserole. Layer half the eggplant over the sauce. Sprinkle the eggplant with half the rice and then spoon half the remaining tomato sauce over the rice. Top with half the grated cheese. Repeat the layers of eggplant, rice, tomato sauce, and cheese. Bake until bubbly, about 15 to 20 minutes. Serve hot or at room temperature.

Serves 4.

LONI KUHN'S BAKED STUFFED EGGPLANT

*T*he next eggplant recipe, while not precisely Italian, is a bequest from Italy-loving Loni Kuhn. A notable American cook and founder of Kuhn's Cook's Tours, one of the first (and best) cooking schools in San Francisco, Loni is one of those wonderful warmhearted, fun-loving, fast-talking women who cook as naturally as they breathe. I have watched her stir a pot, talk on the telephone, and compose a grocery list—and the dish was delectable despite (or because of) the extracurricular kitchen activity. Have one of Loni's best prescriptions. It works equally well for a one-track-minded chef, I promise you.

2 medium eggplants (about ¾ pound each)
¼ cup olive oil
1 large onion, finely chopped
2 large cloves garlic, minced
½ cup drained, seeded canned plum
 tomatoes
2 teaspoons chopped fresh oregano, or
 ½ teaspoon dried
¼ cup chopped fresh parsley
¼ teaspoon crushed dried hot red peppers
1½ tablespoons chopped anchovy filets
½ cup cooked rice
⅓ cup plus 1 tablespoon ricotta cheese
½ cup grated mozzarella cheese
2 tablespoons toasted pine nuts
Salt and freshly ground black pepper
2 tablespoons unsalted butter
½ cup fresh bread crumbs
2 tablespoons freshly grated Parmesan
 cheese

1. Cut the stems from the eggplants and slice each in half lengthwise. Scoop out the flesh with a spoon or grapefruit knife, leaving a shell about ¼ inch thick. Chop the scooped-out flesh.

2. Heat the oil in a large heavy skillet over medium heat. Add the onion; cook 1 minute. Stir in the garlic and chopped eggplant. Reduce the heat to medium-low. Cook the eggplant, tossing constantly, until tender, about 4 minutes. Add the tomatoes, oregano, and parsley.

Cook 5 minutes longer. Remove from the heat; cool.

3. Preheat the oven to 350°F. Place the cooled eggplant mixture in a medium bowl. Add the hot peppers, anchovies, rice, both cheeses, and pine nuts. Mix thoroughly. Add salt and pepper to taste. Fill each eggplant half with this mixture.

4. Melt the butter in a small skillet over medium heat. Stir in the bread crumbs. Cook, stirring constantly, until golden, about 2 minutes. Spoon some crumbs over each stuffed eggplant and sprinkle with the Parmesan cheese. Place the eggplants in a shallow baking dish and add ½ inch of water to the dish. Bake 45 minutes.

Serves 4.

EGGPLANT AND SHRIMP SOUFFLE

1 medium eggplant (about ¾ pound)
4 tablespoons (½ stick) unsalted butter
1 tablespoon grated Jarlsberg or Swiss
    cheese
3 tablespoons all-purpose flour
1½ cups milk, hot
⅓ cup heavy or whipping cream
1 tablespoon cornstarch
1½ tablespoons water
½ teaspoon salt
¼ teaspoon freshly ground black pepper
Pinch of cayenne pepper
⅛ teaspoon freshly grated nutmeg
4 eggs, separated
⅓ cup freshly grated Parmesan cheese
⅓ cup grated Jarlsberg or Gruyère cheese
1 large shallot, minced
1 clove garlic, minced
¼ teaspoon chopped fresh thyme, or a
    pinch of dried
¼ pound raw shrimp, shelled, deveined,
    chopped
1½ tablespoons Dijon mustard
Basic or Creamy Tomato Sauce
    (see pages 374 and 375)

1. Preheat the oven to 400°F. Wrap the eggplant in aluminum foil; bake 40 minutes. Cool; then cut in half and scrape out the pulp. Reserve the pulp.

2. Grease a 1½- to 2-quart soufflé dish with ½ tablespoon of the butter; sprinkle with the Jarlsberg cheese. Chill.

3. Melt 2½ tablespoons of the butter in a saucepan. Stir in the flour; cook, stirring constantly, 2 minutes. Whisk in the milk and half the cream; cook 3 minutes. Combine the cornstarch with the water and stir it into the mixture. Cook until thick. Add the salt, pepper, cayenne pepper, and nutmeg. Remove from the heat. Add the egg yolks, one at a time, beating well after each addition. Stir in the cheeses. This is your soufflé

base. Set aside.

4. Melt the remaining butter in a medium skillet. Add the shallot; cook 1 minute. Add the garlic, thyme, and reserved eggplant. Cook, covered, over medium heat, 3 minutes. Stir in the shrimp; cook, covered, 3 minutes longer. Stir in the remaining cream and the mustard. Spoon into the prepared soufflé dish.

5. Beat the egg whites until stiff but not dry, gently fold them into the soufflé base, and pour it over the eggplant. Bake until puffed up and golden, about 40 minutes. Serve with homemade tomato sauce.

Serves 4 to 6.

Greeks call eggplant *melitzano*, an offshoot of the mad Italian apple tree, obviously. In India, this fruit was originally known as *brinjal*; which in time became corrupted to *batinjan* by the Arabians, who acquired a taste for eggplant that was practically deleterious—they ate it at every meal. When the eggplant-loving Arabians invaded Spain, *batinjan* plants went along, to become *berenjena*. Germans call the stuff *Eirfrucht* (egg fruit), while the British stick with the French tag, *aubergine*.

FENNEL

Licorice Flavored and Crunchy, to Boot

As I have said before, my tiny maternal grandmother, Minna Cohn, was an absolutely towering figure at the stove. Yet if you ask me flat out what single dish I associate with her masterful talents, the answer will come as a surprise. For what I remember best (and most lovingly) of all her carefully orchestrated meals is the way they inevitably began: with raw fennel!

A platter of that greenish vegetable, simply trimmed and quartered, was unflaggingly sent to the table—a salt shaker its sole accompaniment—to assuage any vagrant hunger pains before the serious business of dining began.

I cannot know, a century after the fact, how a Polish country girl from a modest farm on the fringes of Warsaw acquired a taste for this exotic Mediterranean stalk. But it was decidedly one of her favored vegetables.

Being a licorice-lover from the time I learned to properly chew, the flavor of this spiky bulb (redolent of Black Crows, gum-drop tar-babies and all the other assorted whips, ropes, and braids that regularly dyed my tongue the color of a full-blooded chow's) became my favorite too.

"Fin-nook" is what my grandmother always called Florence fennel.

"How's your fin-nook today, Joe?" she would demand of the Italian vegetable peddler, whose horse-drawn wagon (literally a pyramid of gleaming produce), she thought nothing of rending asunder to find the single verdant head that gratified her innate sensibilities. "Show me what you got in the way of fin-nook."

"Nice *finocchio*," he would very gently correct her. "You'll like it missus. Very fresh picked."

Truthfully they both knew that my grandmother never liked what she was offered initially, but the interchange never varied. The object she ended up with always seemed to be one that was embedded in the very foundation of his stockpile and had to be extracted with much tugging, and a period of careful reassembly afterward.

Joe started his day before dawn, selecting vegetables and fruit at the old Hunts Point Market in Long Island City, and spent the next twelve or fourteen hours crisscrossing the borough of Queens selling them. Ringing a rope of bells stretched across the front of his horse-drawn wagon, to announce his presence on the tree-lined streets, he never left the bailiwick until his entire supply was depleted.

At my grandmother's stop, he invariably fed his horse (an ignoble gray mare who wore a faded but beribboned straw hat), because she could easily chomp down a bag of oats in the time it took my forebear to make her purchase.

Sometimes Joe would even unwrap his own lunch as well, while my grandmother prowled around the perimeters of his cart, searching for the perfect fennel stalk (rosiest tomato or crispest asparagus by turns) to meet her demanding specifications.

When she found it, she would turn suddenly generous, calling to my maiden Aunt Frances (in the kitchen) to bring out a glass of grape juice and water to help Joe digest his meal on the run.

She was, as you may gather, no easy customer—either in or out of the kitchen! But on later reflection it seems that big family holiday dinners brought out her true iron fist. If a monumental arrangement of the bespoke fennel plus radishes and black olives, prepared by my aunt, displeased her over-captious eye, she would demolish it with an impervious thumb, and then watch critically as it was reconstructed to her exacting standard. Though almost four decades have passed since she died, I can still recall watching her run to the kitchen between courses—while others at her festive table dined happily—to supervise the next awesome round of food.

Approaching the stove, she would don a voluminous apron, toss some meat on a platter, empty a skillet of its perfectly cooked *à point* vegetables, sprinkle a handful of chopped parsley over all, and then, like a proficient strip-tease artist, remove the apron, allowing it to fall to the floor with a shake of her hips as she made her way back into the dining room again, the precious dish held aloft.

I never taste a slice of fresh-cut fennel without the image of that wonderful (impossible) woman returning. I discovered some while back that there is no living up to her precedent, so I no longer try...merely pass the fennel in her honor, instead.

Vegetable Roots

*F*oeniculum vulgare is a stalk that has been scrunched and munched for millennia. Inhabitants of Mohenjo-Daro (4,000 years before the birth of Christ) believed that knowledge, in the form of fire, was transmitted by the gods to humanity in the lacy branches of fennel. Accordingly, the roots, seeds, and even delicate fronds of this plant were seared and roasted until they turned to fine ash, and the powder used to season most of the foods Mohenjo-Darians consumed. One cannot speculate on the degree of knowledge it brought them, but the flavor obviously tempered their lackluster rations a mite.

Another member of the slightly promiscuous parsley clan, the Umbelliferae (which numbers over 2700 variant species), fennel is somewhat distantly related to all herbs that store essential oils in their seeds—like anise, caraway, coriander, cumin, and dill—as well as being pertinently connected (in a gardening sense) to its carrot, parsnip, and celery-root cousins. But fennel, I must aver, has a taste and odor entirely its own that makes it popular.

What to Look For

*T*o set the record straight, the name fennel covers both the herb and the vegetable. The former is a tall, highly aromatic, but absolutely uncontrollable wayside vagrant—not unlike its cousin-once-removed, Queen Anne's lace. This yellowish umbel flourishes in every warm-tempered quarter of the globe. I myself have tried to weed it from a Provençal garden (impossible) and years later watched with hypnotic fascination as it sprouted from (and eventually ripped apart) some very solid cable car tracks in San Francisco.

Garden fennel is another dish of greens entirely. Not dissimilar to the herb in either appearance or flavor, it is a smaller plant that must be tended carefully to make it "head."

Try to buy fennel with the stalks intact, because it will have more flavor. Test for freshness by lightly pressing the flesh with your thumb. Fresh bulbs will resist the pressure and be on the firm side; skip any that are pulpy or soft.

Fennel is practically a weightless food. A half-pound (raw) totals 56 calories and is high in potassium (784 milligrams) and super-high in vitamin A (7000 units). More importantly for weight-watchers, a large stalk contains at least 94 percent water.

Preparation

*T*here are several accepted methods for cooking a fennel bulb, but only one proper way to prepare it, in my opinion. The optimum procedure is to wash, dry, and trim the stalks so that the bulb itself forms a neat package that may easily be sliced or quartered. (Save any green fronds or thin stalks to enrich a stockpot or garnish a bowl of vegetables at another time.) I usually pare the root end of fennel with a rotary peeler to remove the tough, fibrous portions before I carve it up. Any dry, discolored, or pulpy outer stalks should be removed as well.

Fennel may be blanched (or steamed) first, then sautéed, baked, or fried according to your taste. But to my mind, the classic method for its cookery (like celery) is braising. That is, cooking the slices, covered, on top of the range or in the oven, with a smallish amount of liquid until the fennel is tender and its surface can be easily pierced with a sharp knife or a fork.

FRAGRANT FENNEL SOUP

*B*ecause it has been around for so long, fennel is the subject of the best and most curious folklore. Its ingestion has, for instance, been variously credited with restoring sight to the blind, turning the barren fertile, and adding grit to fainthearted soldiers in battle.

A chew or two is also reputed to be a foolproof appetite depressant for dieters. Actually, consuming a little fennel always makes me want to eat more. Speaking of which, here is my recipe for a particularly aromatic and ambrosial brew. It makes me hungry just to write about it.

1 small to medium head fennel (about
    ½ pound)
2 tablespoons unsalted butter
2 tablespoons vegetable oil
1 large onion, sliced
1 clove garlic, crushed
1 medium potato, peeled, cubed
2 medium tomatoes, peeled, seeded,
    roughly chopped
Bouquet garni: 1 sprig parsley, 1 bay leaf,
    pinch of dried thyme, and pinch of
    dried savory tied in a cheesecloth bag
3 cups chicken broth (see page 414)
2 tablespoons Pernod
1 egg yolk
¼ cup heavy or whipping cream
Salt and ground white pepper

1. Trim the stems from the fennel and peel the bottom. Chop the fronds and reserve. Roughly chop the bulb.

2. Melt the butter in the oil in a medium saucepan over medium-low heat. Add the onion; cook 1 minute.

Add the garlic; cook 1 minute longer. Stir in the fennel and the potato. Cook 5 minutes.

3. Add the tomatoes, bouquet garni, and chicken broth to the soup. Heat to boiling; reduce the heat. Cook, covered, over low heat until the fennel is very soft, about 30 minutes. Discard the bouquet garni.

4. Cool the mixture slightly and then purée it (in batches) in a food processor or blender, taking care as hot liquid will expand. Transfer the purée to a clean saucepan. Stir in the Pernod over medium-low heat.

5. Beat the egg yolk with the cream and slowly stir it into the soup. Warm the soup through, but do not allow it to boil. Season with salt and white pepper to taste. Sprinkle with the chopped fennel fronds.

Serves 4 to 6.

FENNEL AND CHICKEN SALAD

More fennel and fowl. A fragrantly crunchy dish which parenthetically would not be harmed a jot by the substitution of leftover Thanksgiving turkey in lieu of an everyday pullet.

2 medium heads fennel (about 1¼ pounds)
2 cups chopped cooked chicken or turkey
1 large shallot, minced
1 cup Mayonnaise (see page 408)
½ teaspoon Dijon mustard
2 tablespoons Pernod
Salt and freshly ground black pepper

1. Trim the stems from the fennel and peel the bottoms. Chop the fronds so you have about 1 tablespoon; reserve. Chop the bulbs and combine with the chicken and shallot in a medium bowl.

2. Beat the mayonnaise with the mustard and Pernod in a large bowl until smooth. Add the fennel and chicken mixture. Mix well. Add salt and pepper to taste and sprinkle with the chopped fennel fronds.

Serves 4 or 5.

SICILIAN COLD BRAISED FENNEL

Since Italians favor fennel in their daily diet, another of my classic braisings (not so curiously) stems from that quarter. It is a Sicilian dish: a first course or salad accompaniment, traditionally served cold. *Molto bene.*

1 large or 2 medium heads fennel (about
    1 ¼ pounds)
2 tablespoons unsalted butter
3 tablespoons olive oil
1 medium onion, finely chopped
1 clove garlic, minced
½ teaspoon salt
½ teaspoon freshly ground black pepper
1 ½ teaspoons anise seeds
2 cups chicken broth (see page 414)
½ teaspoon finely grated orange peel
2 tablespoons lemon juice

1. Trim the stems from the fennel and peel the bottoms. Chop the fronds and reserve. Cut each bulb in half from top to bottom. Slice each half lengthwise into four sections.

2. Heat the butter with the oil in a medium saucepan over medium-low heat. Add the onion; cook 1 minute. Add the garlic; cook 1 minute longer. Stir in the fennel, salt, pepper, and anise seeds. Cook, uncovered, 10 minutes, shaking the pan occasionally.

3. Add the chicken broth and orange peel. Cook, covered, over low heat until tender, about 20 minutes. With a slotted spoon, transfer the fennel to a serving dish.

4. Heat the cooking liquid in the saucepan to boiling. Boil until reduced to about ½ cup. Cool slightly and add the lemon juice. Pour this over fennel, cool, and chill for at least 3 hours before serving, sprinkled with chopped fennel fronds.

Serves 4.

BAKED FENNEL WITH CHEESE

No other partner complements a stalk of fennel with more eloquence, in my opinion, than cheese. Not any cheese, but definitely Parmesan and Gruyère. Check out this recipe and the one for Cheese-Fried Fennel, which follows.

1 large or 2 medium heads fennel (about
    1 ¼ pounds)
4 tablespoons (½ stick) unsalted butter
1 small onion, chopped
1 medium carrot, diced
1 ½ cups chicken broth (see page 414)
3 tablespoons all-purpose flour
¼ cup heavy or whipping cream

3 minced fresh rosemary leaves, or a pinch
    of dried
Salt and freshly ground black pepper
½ cup grated Gruyère cheese
3 tablespoons freshly grated Parmesan
    cheese

1. Preheat the oven to 300° F. Trim

the stems from the fennel and peel the bottoms. Cut the bulbs into ½-inch-thick slices.

2. Melt 1 tablespoon of the butter in a medium saucepan over medium-low heat. Add the onion; cook 3 minutes. Stir in the carrot and sliced fennel. Toss to coat with the butter mixture. Add the chicken broth. Heat to boiling; reduce the heat. Simmer, covered, over medium-low heat until tender, about 15 minutes. Drain, reserving the broth.

3. Transfer the vegetables to a lightly greased shallow baking dish. Keep warm in the oven.

4. Meanwhile, melt the remaining butter in a small saucepan over medium-low heat. Stir in the flour. Cook, stirring constantly, 2 minutes. Whisk in the reserved broth and the cream. Cook until thick, about 3 minutes. Add the rosemary, and salt and pepper to taste. Spoon the sauce over the vegetables in the oven.

In Italy, where fennel is practically a table staple, Italians eat it raw with just a sluice of olive oil and sometimes lemon—and it always tastes absolutely marvelous. I once noticed that Italian housewives only buy fennel when the bulbs are fat as baby rabbits and the tops are deep green and shrubby. They usually break off the smaller stalks and chew the fronds as they make their shopping rounds. You may do the same with utter impunity, since fennel is very, very low in calories.

5. Combine the two cheeses and sprinkle them over the fennel mixture. Place the dish under a broiling unit until the cheese melts and is golden.

Serves 4.

CHEESE-FRIED FENNEL

2 large heads fennel (1½ to 2 pounds)
½ cup all-purpose flour
½ teaspoon salt
2 large eggs
2 tablespoons water
⅔ cup freshly grated Parmesan cheese
⅔ cup fresh bread crumbs
Vegetable oil for frying

1. Trim the stems from the fennel and peel the bottoms. Cut the bulbs lengthwise into ½-inch-wide pieces. Cook in boiling salted water until just tender, about 8 minutes. Drain. Cool slightly and pat dry on paper towels.

2. Combine the flour and salt on a plate. Beat the eggs with the water in a shallow bowl. Combine the Parmesan cheese with the bread crumbs on another plate.

3. Heat about 2 inches of oil in a large saucepan until hot. Roll the fennel pieces lightly in the flour, then dip in the egg mixture, and then roll in the cheese mixture. Fry in hot oil until golden, about 6 minutes. Drain on paper towels. Keep warm in a low oven while frying the remaining pieces.

Serves 6.

GOODWIVES' BRAISED FENNEL

My paradigm example of fennel-braising comes from the South of France. It is a recipe that I reconstructed with a good deal of difficulty because the donor always gave me outrageously misleading clues as to its "secret" ingredient.

A neighbor and friend, who was (as the French say) "a lady of a certain age," drank as she cooked; and it was her penchant for a mid-morning *pastis* (a thimbleful of Pernod in a tumbler of water) that made me realize what made her dish so potently "lickerish" in flavor. She would splash the saucepan with the contents of her glass when she thought no one was watching!

I have been reasonably well informed that the classic French name for such a mixture of cooked fennel, onions, and tomatoes would be *Fenouil Braisé à la Bonne Femme*. But I much prefer the Americanization.

1 large or 2 medium heads fennel (about
*   1¼ pounds)*
2 tablespoons unsalted butter
1 medium onion, finely chopped
2 medium tomatoes, seeded, chopped
Pinch of dried thyme
¼ cup strong beef broth (see page 414)
1½ teaspoons Pernod, Ricard or other
*   anise-based liqueur*
Salt and freshly ground black pepper

1. Trim the stems from the fennel and peel the bottoms. Chop the fronds and reserve. Chop the bulb and cook it in boiling salted water 2 minutes. Drain.

2. Melt the butter in a medium saucepan over medium-low heat. Add the onion; cook until lightly golden, about 5 minutes. Add the tomatoes, thyme, beef broth and drained chopped fennel. Cook, covered, over low heat until tender, about 25 minutes.

3. Remove the cover from the saucepan and cook until any excess liquid has evaporated. Add the Pernod, raise the heat slightly, and cook 2 minutes. Add salt and pepper to taste and sprinkle with the chopped fennel fronds.

Serves 4.

MARLENE LEVINSON'S POACHED FENNEL AND PARSLEY

The next fennel recipe is pacific enough to bridge the most troubled familial water. It is an endowment from yet another excellent San Franciscan cook, Marlene Levinson. I met this bright and mettlesome lady some years ago when I was teaching my very first cooking class in California. The class was held in a home in the hills of Sonoma, during the heaviest rainfall to hit northern California in a decade. The kitchen was filled with damp but extremely enthusiastic food lovers from the community, along with a contingent of hardy professionals who had ventured north of the Golden Gate Bridge through the torrent to check out "the man who invented ziti salad." Or so I was told later.

Marlene was one of the hardiest checker-outers. An instant friendship ensued over a bowl of cioppino and one of the residuals of that fraternity is the splendid offering below.

2 medium heads fennel (about 1¼ pounds)
2 cups chopped fresh parsley
4 tablespoons (½ stick) unsalted butter
1 small onion, finely chopped
½ cup heavy or whipping cream
⅛ teaspoon freshly grated nutmeg
Salt and freshly ground black pepper

1. Trim the stems from the fennel and peel the bottoms. Discard any tough outer stems. Separate the bulb into pieces. Cut the large ones in half lengthwise. Chop the fronds and reserve.

2. Place the fennel pieces with the parsley in a medium saucepan. Cover with water. Heat to boiling; boil until tender, 8 to 10 minutes. Drain through a wire sieve.

3. Melt the butter in a large skillet over medium-low heat. Add the onion; cook 5 minutes. Add the cream; cook until fairly thick, about 5 minutes. Toss in the fennel and parsley. Cook until warmed through. Add the nutmeg, and salt and pepper to taste. Sprinkle with the chopped fennel fronds.

Serves 4.

FENNEL PUREE

*F*ennel's low calorie count makes it an ideal confederate to high-carbohydrate food like potatoes. Two of the very best fennel prescriptions in this log are brightened up with a mite of that snowy tuber.

The first, below, a velvety purée, is yet another *douceur* from the fennel-loving French, while the second—Home-Fried Fennel and Potato Hash, which follows—is as American as a dish can get: a vegetable hash, circa 1900.

2 medium heads fennel (about 1¼ pounds)
2 ribs celery, chopped
2 medium potatoes, peeled, cut into 1-inch cubes
2 to 3 tablespoons strong Chicken Stock (see page 410)
1½ tablespoons unsalted butter
1½ tablespoons Pernod
⅓ cup heavy or whipping cream
Salt and freshly ground black pepper
Chopped fresh parsley

1. Trim the stems from the fennel and peel the bottoms. Chop the fennel bulbs and the fronds and place them in a medium saucepan, along with the celery and potatoes. Add cold water to cover. Heat to boiling; reduce the heat. Simmer, uncovered, until just tender, about 20 minutes. Drain.

2. Place the vegetables in the container of a food processor. Add the chicken stock; process until smooth.

3. Transfer the puréed vegetables to the top of a double boiler. Stir in the butter, Pernod, and cream. Cook, stirring occasionally, over simmering water until warmed through. Add salt and pepper to taste. Transfer to a serving bowl and sprinkle with parsley.

Serves 4 to 5.

HOME-FRIED FENNEL AND POTATO HASH

1 small to medium head fennel (about
   ½ pound)
2 medium potatoes
2 strips bacon
1 tablespoon unsalted butter
1 small onion, chopped
1 clove garlic, minced
1½ teaspoons fennel seeds
Salt and freshly ground black pepper

1. Trim the stems from the fennel and peel the bottoms. Chop the fronds; reserve.

2. Cook the fennel bulbs with the potatoes in boiling salted water, 12 minutes. Drain and allow to cool. Chop the bulbs and the potatoes, separately, into about 1-inch pieces.

3. Fry the bacon in a large skillet over medium heat until crisp. Drain on paper towels. Add the butter to the skillet. Add the onion; cook 1 minute. Add the garlic; cook 1 minute longer. Add a layer of potatoes to the skillet. Add a layer of fennel pieces. Sprinkle with fennel seeds and salt and pepper to taste. Continue to layer until all the vegetables are used up. End with either potatoes or fennel. Cook over medium heat until the bottom is nicely browned. Turn over in one piece with a large spatula (or flip over into another skillet). Reduce the heat and continue to cook until the vegetables are soft, about 10 minutes.

4. Crumble the reserved bacon and sprinkle it over the fennel-potato mixture. Sprinkle with the chopped fennel fronds.

Serves 4.

FENNEL-STUFFED ROAST TURKEY

One of the stalk's most agreeable appearances takes place within the breast of a capacious bird. Combined with rice, onion, and sausage, it makes a dressing one may truly give thanks for on the last Thursday in November.

Fennel Dressing (recipe follows)
1 fresh turkey (18 to 20 pounds)
2 large cloves garlic, 1 bruised
Salt and freshly ground black pepper
3 strips bacon
⅓ cup dry white wine
1 quart water
1 onion
1 stalk celery, broken
3 sprigs parsley, plus additional for garnish
¼ teaspoon salt
4 peppercorns
1½ tablespoons unsalted butter
1½ tablespoons all-purpose flour
¼ cup heavy or whipping cream

1. Make the Fennel Dressing.

2. Preheat the oven to 325°F. Remove the giblets from the turkey; reserve the giblets, except the liver, for the gravy. You may wish to reserve the liver for another purpose. First wipe the turkey inside and out with a damp cloth, then rub it well, inside and out, with the bruised garlic, salt, and pepper. Stuff the cavity with the dressing, and truss. Place the turkey on a rack in a roasting pan, laying the bacon strips across the breast. Cut a piece of cheesecloth large enough to fit over the turkey. Soak the cheesecloth in the wine and place it over the turkey. Pour any remaining wine over the turkey and roast 30 minutes.

3. Meanwhile, combine the giblets (*not* the liver), water, onion, celery, the remaining garlic clove, 3 sprigs parsley, ¼ teaspoon salt, and the peppercorns in a large saucepan. Heat to boiling, then reduce the heat. Simmer, uncovered, until the liquid is reduced to 2 cups. Strain the giblet stock.

4. Baste the turkey with the giblet stock. Roast, basting with stock every 30 minutes, until the legs move freely and juices run clear when the inner thigh is pierced with a fork, about 5½ to 6 hours total. During the last half hour of roast-

ing, remove the cheesecloth by first wetting the turkey with basting juices. It should lift off easily. Raise the oven heat to 375°F to crisp the skin. Transfer to a carving board; let stand 15 minutes.

5. Meanwhile, strain the turkey drippings, degreasing if necessary. Melt the butter in a medium saucepan over medium-low heat. Whisk in the flour. Cook, stirring constantly, 2 minutes. Whisk in the drippings and cream; simmer 5 minutes. Taste and adjust seasonings. Garnish the turkey with the remaining parsley sprigs. Serve with the gravy and fennel dressing.

Serves 8 to 10 (with leftovers).

Fennel Dressing

1 head fennel (about 1 pound)
1 pound sweet Italian sausage, roughly chopped
1 medium onion, chopped
2 tablespoons fennel seeds
2 cups cooked rice
1 teaspoon salt
½ teaspoon freshly ground black pepper
⅛ teaspoon hot pepper sauce

1. Trim the stems from the fennel and peel the bottoms. Cut the bottoms into ½-inch cubes and place them in a large bowl. Chop the fronds and add them to the cubes in the bowl.

2. Place the sausage in a large heavy skillet and sauté over medium heat until lightly browned and rendered of grease. Using a slotted spoon, transfer the sausage to the bowl with the fennel.

3. Remove all but 2 tablespoons grease from the skillet. Add the onion and fennel seeds. Cook, stirring constantly, over medium heat for 3 minutes. Add the onion mixture to the fennel-sausage mixture along with the rice, salt, pepper, and hot pepper sauce. Mix.

Makes enough dressing for an 18- to 20-pound turkey.

W hen my grandmother spoke of fennel, invariably she called it "fin-nook." Because her command of English was faulty, she would often intersperse a sentence with liberal sprinklings of Yiddish, a language I never understood except by sense meaning. So I was often confused by what I thought she said. The word "fin-nook" for instance, always sounded remarkably like the Yiddish expression *genug* (gen-nook) that emphatically means "enough."

So I grew up—at least until early puberty—believing that all family arguments or heated discussions always ended with a call for *fennel* by my grandmother. Which curiously never arrived!

FENNEL-POACHED FLOUNDER AND SHRIMP

In France, fennel is unalterably associated with fish. One of the most felicitous dishes to be found in a Mediterranean kitchen is *loup de mer au fenouil*, which is a kind of small sea bass that is grilled and flamed over dried fennel leaves and stalks until the skin is so redolent it perfumes your tongue. I must admit, however, that I have *never* been able to successfully duplicate its wonders on a barbecue pit (or broiler) on home shores. So here is an arresting alternative, also French: a poached fennel, shrimp, and flounder dish that converts the actual poaching liquid (plus cream) into an unusually fragrant blanket for the filets.

1 medium head fennel (about ½ pound)
6 large filets of flounder or sole
Juice of 1½ lemons
18 cooked shrimp, shelled, deveined
½ bottle dry white wine, approximately
1 small onion stuck with 2 cloves
1 slice lemon
Bouquet garni: 1 sprig parsley, 1 bay leaf,
*   and a pinch of dried thyme tied in a*
*   cheesecloth bag*
3 tablespoons unsalted butter
1 cup heavy or whipping cream
⅛ teaspoon fennel seeds
Salt and freshly ground black pepper
2 egg yolks, lightly beaten

1. Trim the stems from the fennel and peel the bottom. Chop the fennel fronds and reserve. Cook the bulb in boiling salted water until tender, about 20 minutes. Drain, cool slightly, and chop fine.

2. Cut the flounder filets in half crosswise. Arrange them on a plate and sprinkle them with the juice of 1 lemon. Spread a small amount of finely chopped fennel over each piece. Place a cooked shrimp on each. Roll up the filets and place them seam-side down in a large heavy saucepan. Pour in wine to half the depth of the filets. Add the onion, lemon slice, and bouquet garni. Use 1½ teaspoons butter to heavily butter a piece of wax paper. Cover the pan with it. Cook over low heat until the fish flakes easily when pierced with a fork, about 5 minutes. Remove the filets with a slotted spoon to an ovenproof serving dish and keep warm.

3. Preheat the oven broiling unit. Heat the cooking liquid in the saucepan to boiling; boil until reduced by half. Strain the cooking liquid into a medium saucepan and add the juice of ½ lemon, the cream, the remaining butter, and fennel seeds. Heat to boiling; remove from the heat. Add salt and pepper to taste. Stir ¼ cup of the sauce into the egg yolks; slowly beat this mixture back into the sauce. Return to low heat, stirring constantly, until thick. Do not allow to boil.

4. Drain any liquid that has accumulated around the fish filets. Pour the sauce over the filets. Place them under the preheated broiler until lightly browned, 1 to 2 minutes. Garnish with the remaining shrimp and reserved fennel fronds.

Serves 6.

HUNGARIAN FENNEL BREAD

*F*rom the Mediterranean area (but from a Hungarian chef), this sensuous white bread is seasoned with a purée of cooked fennel, feathery fronds, and a hailstorm of seeds for good measure.

2 small heads fennel (about 1 pound)
1 small potato, peeled, grated
1 cup Chicken Stock (see page 410)
1 teaspoon salt
1 tablespoon fennel seeds
1 package dry yeast
¼ cup lukewarm water
1 teaspoon sugar
4 cups all-purpose flour, approximately
1 teaspoon unsalted butter, plus 1½
    tablespoons melted

1. Trim the stems from the fennel and peel the bottoms. Chop the fennel fronds and reserve. Chop the bulbs and place them in a medium saucepan, along with the potato. Add the chicken stock. Heat to boiling; reduce the heat. Simmer, covered, until tender, about 15 minutes. Drain, reserving ¼ cup of the cooking liquid.

2. Place the vegetables in the container of a food processor or blender.

Add the reserved cooking liquid and process until smooth. Transfer to a large bowl. Stir in 1 tablespoon of the chopped fennel fronds, the salt, and the fennel seeds.

3. Combine the yeast with the water and sugar in a small bowl. Let it stand (proof) 10 minutes, then stir it into the fennel purée. Add enough flour to make a fairly stiff dough, about 3 cups.

4. Transfer the dough to a lightly floured board and add the remaining 1 cup flour, kneading for about 10 minutes. Use the 1 teaspoon butter to butter a large bowl. Place the dough in the bowl, turning it to coat it with butter. Cover, and let rise until doubled in volume, about 1½ hours.

5. Punch down the dough; knead briefly. Form it into a loaf and place it in a buttered 9-inch bread pan. Cover with a floured cloth; let stand 1 hour.

6. Preheat the oven to 375°F. With a sharp knife, cut a slash down the center of the risen dough. Brush the top well with the melted butter. Place a roasting pan containing 1 inch of water on the bottom of the oven. Place the bread on a rack in the top third of the oven. Bake until golden brown and hollow-sounding when tapped with your finger, about 45 minutes. Cool on a rack for 10 minutes. Gently loosen the bread from the pan and unmold. Cool completely on the rack. Makes 1 loaf.

*F*ennel is known as *fenouil* in France, *Fenchel* in Germany, *finocchio* in Italy, and *hinojo* in Spain. The ancient Greeks, however, called it *marathon*, after the verb "to grow thin," and ate it mainly as a diet food. Socrates advised a stalk of fennel and a glass of water as the only cure for a night of culinary excess. I haven't a Greek bone in my body, but I couldn't be in more agreement if I had.

GREENS

The Edible Bouquet

From the reminiscences that stitch this book together a reader might assume that my strongest attachments were reserved for my mother's side of the family, but that is not wholly accurate.

My mother's relatives were certainly closest in proximity—but never quite closest in my heart. It was the Greene descendants who lived miles away—none closer than upper Manhattan and most more distant, in such diverse geography as Passaic, Boston, and Baltimore—for whom that honor was reserved. My father's sisters and their offspring were warm, good-natured people who frankly adored him, and their affection extended to his wife and children too.

Who could help but love this family? Loud, boisterous, and utterly unstinting in their generosity, they turned our infrequent visits into gala holidays. Banquets of usually denied delicatessen foods overloaded the table: steaming frankfurters, glistening porringers of potato salad, pickles, and slabs of rye bread so heavily buttered that a slice usually buckled in the middle before it reached one's lips. These comestibles inevitably led to a mild case of indigestion on the way home, but who cared? From these sporadic get-togethers I managed to glean an image of my father's early life.

If family tales can be believed, my paternal grandmother was a mail-order bride. A very religious girl, speaking nary a word of English, on the advice of a marriage broker she crossed the ocean to wed an itinerant New York blacksmith. Her husband spoke not a word of Russian, and very little Yiddish either. How they communicated is sheer speculation, but somehow this couple managed to produce a dozen children despite the language barrier.

Progeny aside, their union was not a happy one. There were many separations and reconciliations. My grandfather, Michael Greene, was Americanized and not overly religious. He plied his trade—shoeing horses and mending pots and pans in a covered wagon that took him far from New York's lower East Side; clear across the Great Divide, in fact. According to his middle daughter (my aunt Rae, who lived in Boston) he was never home for longer than a month at a time in his entire married life. "Because," she claimed, "the man could abide neither his wife's piety nor her constant accusations."

Grandfather Greene died before he was forty-five, leaving his widow with a houseful of growing children and the nagging rumors of a dozen others born outside the state line.

My grandmother survived him by thirty years. Her children went to work early to support her, but she was never mollified for she strongly disapproved of all of their secular lifestyles. Her youngest son, my father, chose to live in his free-thinking older sister's household when he was barely an adolescent. When he married a young girl whose family was also irreligious, his mother's worst fears were confirmed. She made up for her children's defection with prayer. Resisting any creature comforts pressed upon her, she spent the rest of her life in dark ghetto synagogues. Never having learned to speak English, she mistrusted the world outside the tenements and held in cold contempt all the gaiety and love of life that her children embraced.

My mother was sanguine on the subject of her mother-in-law.

"She was a driven person," she said on more than one occasion. "All she did was pray. She gave any money her children sent her to the poor because she couldn't enjoy it." In point of fact, she expired on her way to a synagogue (where she collected prayer books for Friday night service), with over a thousand dollars in her pocketbook.

I have never seen a photograph of my grandmother Bessie Greene, for it was against her religious principles to permit such an act of vanity, but I am named to honor her memory—so that gives us a common denominator. Her children (my father and aunts) were loving siblings. But, to me at least, the fact that they never spoke of their mother when they gathered as a family meant that her pleasureless life was always manifest—like a pain one has learned to ignore.

My father used to light a candle on the anniversary of his mother's death, but claimed not to be able to remember anything remarkable about her. "She did as well and no better than anyone in her circumstances," he would reply to my questioning. Meaning, I knew, a life of self-denial and little joy. When I asked about the dishes she prepared, he shrugged. "Green soup. She made lots of that."

"Green. What made it green?"

"Beats me. In those days we were so poor we couldn't afford chicken but once a week. My mother used to collect free vegetable tops from markets all over the neighborhood. With a little bit of meat, she made those leaves into a kind of soup-stew." My father shook his head at the recollection. "But y'know, it wasn't half bad."

From my Russian grandmother's pot to her American grandchild's spoon there must be quite a connection, for I do much the same thing. Buying greens at a fancy greengrocer's is of little importance in the final analysis: it's the Greene tradition that counts!

Vegetable Roots

What I call "greens" is a varied crop of leaves, all bearing the same color—some mild, some bitter, some crisp, some crumpled. These plants (all highly nutritious and incredibly tasty) usually act as partners in a saucepan in my kitchen. But in some instances they show up in the salad bowl as well. They are: arugula, chard, collards, dandelion greens, mustard greens, romaine, sorrel, turnip greens, and watercress.

ARUGULA (sometimes known as rocket-salad, ruculo or tiro) is a Cruciferal. The ancients considered that eating it brought good luck.

CHARD, on the other hand, is a beettop that went wild in the garden. This leaf grew outside when its root (*Beta vulgaris*) shriveled in the cold Swiss soil. The name is a total erratum; early vegetable lovers mistook its splendid foliage for that of the thistlelike cardoon (or *chardon*). They called it Swiss chard and so have greengrocers ever since.

COLLARD is a corruption of the earlier handle *colewort*. It is a member of the cabbage family, but somehow lighter to the tongue and distinctly less weighty in the alimentary canal. Romans and Greeks attributed great therapeutic powers to its consumption. Julius Caesar in fact is rumored to have eaten a plateful after a heavy banquet (much as one would slurp Bromo-Seltzer) to ward off indigestion.

The DANDELION is nothing but a garden desperado gone straight—and tall too! Cousin of the sunflower, marigold, and zinnia (the Compositae tribe), it tastes remarkably better than all three—particularly after a dressing-down with oil and vinegar!

MUSTARD GREENS have a long history. Another member of the populous *Brassicas*, it was growing wild in Asia Minor in the first century, and peoples of the Indus valley ate their barley seasoned with its shoots. Mustard can be found growing wild in the vacant lots of New York City today.

ROMAINE (at times tagged Cos lettuce) is named for the way its long cupped leaves resembled Roman table spoons. Actually romaine was a prandial refinement that Caesar borrowed from the Greeks. Indeed, a persistent rumor in food circles has it that Socrates quaffed his lethal dose of hemlock from just such a "spoon" of fresh romaine.

SORREL is another dish of tea entirely. A pot herb (of the *Rumex* genus and distantly related to buckwheat), sorrel grew wild in Eurasia for centuries without a smidgen of it ever seasoning a pot. For years it was considered a poison because of its slightly astringent flavor. But while its flavor may have been off-putting to humans, sorrel seeds have always been extremely popular with migratory birds. Indeed some food snoops claim that this hardy perennial spread to Europe and the New World on the wing. Henry Cabot, the British explorer, was said to have had a pet bird who doted on sorrel. In most of the world sorrel goes by the pejorative name of sour grass, which is a misnomer; it is merely piquant!

TURNIP GREENS are the curly tops of the garden-variety turnip plant. When the leaves are snipped in May, a fatter, more flavorsome turnip is harvested in July. Of less gastronomic note but equally tonic, the green leaf of this vegetable is said to "awaken slumbering desire in even the most quiescent spouse"—at least according to John Milton's diaries. It must have had some therapeutic effect, for turnip foliage was brewed into potions, restoratives, and pick-me-ups from the sixteenth to the nineteenth century with varying reports of its good pharmacy. Even today in the deep South, a cup of turnip green "pot likker" is still reputed to be the best cure for hangover ever invented.

WATERCRESS can scarcely be dubbed a "garden green" since it requires a babbling brook or a small stream close by to feed its thirsty roots. Watercress thrives best in the shade, a fact that has given it something of a bad name in the past. There was a theory (held by all Puritan diners) that since this plant was grown in the darkness it was a living example of deviltry, "and no consumer of its leaves would profit with good health lest it was mingled with foodstuffs harvested in pure sunlight." Which may explain in part why a stalk of watercress hardly ever arrives on a salad plate without a leaf of lettuce nearby!

What to Look For

Greens have a high water content, so they wilt easily. And once faded they are hard to revive. Search out the bunches at your greengrocer's that have the freshest, greenest leaves. Don't buy yellow or discolored greens; they're a waste of money. I store greens unwashed in the refrigerator, lightly wrapped in damp paper towels inside a plastic bag that has been punctured to allow an even air supply. That way I generally manage to hold greens, with an occasional change of toweling, for up to a week's time.

The green per se is no heavy indulgence. Most are low in the calorie depart-

I f I were to rate greens by "bite," I would start with the mildest: chard, collard, dandelion, and romaine. Arugula, sorrel, and watercress are semi-mild in my opinion, while mustard and turnip greens are the sharpest in flavor. You should experiment with combinations to discover the taste you like best.

ment: a mere 10 calories in a heaping cupful of watercress; less than 65 in a whole one-pound bunch of dandelion and mustard greens. And most are high in potassium (465 milligrams per cupful for turnip, mustard, arugula and watercress) and calcium (125 milligrams in the same quantity). Unfortunately most greens are high in sodium, so low-salt-dieters are advised to consult nutrition charts before going hog-wild in the kitchen. Some greens (like chard, collards, mustard, arugula, and dandelion) contain whopping amounts of vitamin A (7,830 units per cupful).

Preparation

My view of greens may be influenced by my stint in the South, when I was going to college. Even today, those who live below the Mason-Dixon Line dote on these leaves, slow-cooked in a copious potful of broth or bouillon that is well seasoned with a ham hock or a chunk of fatty bacon and some onions. And I must confess to a predilection for a "mess" of them whenever I am in that geography. However, at my own stove I tend to braise greens in somewhat more abbreviated cooking time, with equally felicitous results.

First I wash the greens well on both sides; hidden dirt often clings to the undersides of the leaves. I believe in three separate washings for all such gardenry, plus a longish stint in the colander to drain them well after the final bath. Then I braise the greens in a covered saucepan with a small amount of liquid plus a jot of butter (or bacon drippings) until the leaves are wilted but not mushy—about 10 to 15 minutes depending upon the toughness of the greens.

Greens may also be blanched first and reheated later. Blanch greens by placing the chopped vegetables in a pot of boiling salted water for a minute or two. Rinse them in a colander under cold running water to retard the cooking. Then drain well, gently pressing out any excess liquid with the back of a spoon. Blanched greens may be prepared early on in the day and then reheated just before serving. Reheat in butter or bacon drippings, tossing them well to warm thoroughly, and season with salt, pepper, and a sluice of vinegar or lemon juice.

Steam greens by placing the chopped vegetables in a steamer basket or colander over a small amount of boiling water for approximately 6 to 10 minutes. Toss gently with a fork and cook a minute or two longer if you prefer them softer (I do not). Be apprised, however, that steaming greens will sometimes intensify the bitter undertaste in the stronger-flavored varieties.

I never cook watercress in advance, as these leaves wilt considerably over heat. Likewise romaine, which is technically a lettuce and will exude moisture, should be cooked over higher heat to dry it. Lettuce is a nice braising partner with sturdier greens (like chard or collards) but will not stand up as well in the pan. Try adding it to greens after half the cooking time has elapsed.

For the record, 2 pounds of large-leafed greens (like chard or collards) will yield 1 pound stemmed chopped leaves. Most raw packed greens will yield approximately one-quarter the amount when long-cooked, more when lightly braised or wilted. A good rule of thumb is to allow ½ cup of cooked greens per serving.

CHARD SHCHAV

I feel certain that my grandmother Greene would have approved of this soup. It is derived from a classic Russian-Polish cold dish named *shchav* or *schav*. The word comes from a local Polish name for sorrel leaves (*szczaw*), of which most such soups are composed. There is rumored to be a *shchav* recipe for every *shtetl* (Jewish community) that existed in both Poland and Russia at the turn of the century. Mine, however, you will never find recorded among them, for I made it up out of whole cloth a while back. It actually is no *shchav* at all in the generic sense, since the main ingredient in this soup is Swiss chard, not sorrel. Chard makes a very tonic difference to the contents of the soup ladle, for it is both sweeter and blander.

2 pounds Swiss chard
6 whole scallions, bulbs and green tops, chopped
2 quarts Vegetable Stock (see page 411)
4 eggs, lightly beaten

1 pint sour cream
¼ cup lemon juice
⅛ teaspoon hot pepper sauce
Salt and ground white pepper

1. Trim the chard, discarding the stems. Finely chop the leaves.

2. Combine the chard, scallions, and vegetable stock in a medium saucepan. Heat to boiling; reduce the heat. Simmer, uncovered, 12 minutes. Transfer to a heatproof bowl and allow to cool for 10 minutes.

3. Beat the eggs with the sour cream in a medium bowl until smooth. Slowly add the mixture to the chard. Stir in the lemon juice, hot pepper sauce, and salt and white pepper to taste. Serve warm or well chilled.

Serves 6 to 8.

CLARA LESS' ZUPA SZCZAFU
(Polish Sorrel Soup)

*T*hough it is sorrel-based and stems from Poland, this is no *shchav*. My late grandmother would never have allowed a drop to pass her lips, as in the ingredients list there are not only chicken soup and sour cream but salt pork as well. But it comes without any apology, for it is simply one of the best soups I have ever consumed! The prescription is a bequest from a good friend and treasured confidante, Clara B. Less of Dearborn, Michigan.

1 pound fresh sorrel
¼ pound salt pork, finely chopped
1 large onion, finely chopped
2 tablespoons all-purpose flour
2 medium potatoes, peeled, diced
2 cups chicken broth (see page 414)
1 cup water
1 cup sour cream, at room temperature
Salt and freshly ground black pepper
Chopped fresh parsley

1. Trim the sorrel, discarding the stems. Chop the leaves and set aside.

2. Sauté the salt pork in a medium saucepan over medium heat until golden and crisp, about 10 minutes. Stir in the onion; cook until lightly browned, about 5 minutes.

3. Reduce the heat to low and whisk in the flour. Cook, stirring constantly, 2 minutes. Stir in the potatoes, chicken broth, water, and sorrel. Heat to boiling; reduce the heat. Cook, uncovered, over medium-low heat until the potatoes are tender, about 30 minutes.

4. Remove the soup from the heat and slowly stir in the sour cream. Return it to low heat and cook (do not allow to boil) until warmed through. Add salt and pepper to taste and sprinkle with parsley.

Serves 4 to 6.

*G*reens go by odd appellations in other tongues, some untranslatable. The French call them *légumes verts*, while the Germans dub them *grüne Gemüse*. Italians lump all vegetables together as *verdura*, and though it's a tad imprecise, so do the Spanish. The Swedish call them *grönsaker*, which covers a multitude of garden goods as well.

RED AND GREEN SALAD WITH MELON VINAIGRETTE

*T*he dressing for my mixed red and green salad is a recent invention: a mixture of sweet and sour made with lime juice, mustard, and surprisingly, a sweet melon liqueur. A simply stunning palliation for the green bounty.

4 or 5 heads mache, or corn salad,
  separated into leaves (about ¼ pound)
2 bunches watercress, leaves only
2 small heads bibb lettuce, leaves separated
3 small radicchio (Italian red lettuce) or
  red-tipped lettuce, leaves separated
4 heads Belgian endive
3 tablespoons green basil leaves
2 tablespoons torn geranium blossoms

For the melon vinaigrette:

1 small clove garlic
½ teaspoon coarse (kosher) salt
¼ teaspoon Dijon mustard
Juice of 1 lime
1 tablespoon melon liqueur
½ to ¾ cup olive oil

1. Wash all the various leaves well, and pat them dry. Make a pile of green lettuce and watercress leaves in a salad bowl. Surround it with the red lettuce leaves. Cut the endives into quarters lengthwise, then into long thin strips, and place them around the edge of the bowl, interspersed with the basil leaves. Sprinkle the top with the geranium blossoms.

2. To make the melon vinaigrette: Mash the garlic with the salt in a small bowl. Stir in the mustard, lime juice, and liqueur. Whisk in the oil. Toss the salad with the dressing at the table.

Serves 6 to 8.

GREEN QUILLS

*A*fter whipping up many of the dishes in this chapter, I often find myself with a refrigerator residual that gets me down, namely bags and bags of Swiss chard stems. The plan is always to use these vitamin-high end products in a soup or vegetable stock, but in truth I usually toss them out to make room for new comestibles before I get around to that chore. To make use of this accumulation of raw ingredients I devised the following dish. It's simple, eminently satisfying as a side dish, and most important of all, an economic boon for the cook!

3 tablespoons unsalted butter
2 shallots, minced
1 clove garlic, minced
1 pound Swiss chard stems (from
  approximately 2 pounds Swiss chard),
  cut into pieces 2 inches long and ½
  inch wide

½ cup chicken broth (see page 414)
3 tablespoons chopped fresh parsley
Salt and freshly ground black pepper

1. Melt the butter in a large skillet over medium-low heat. Stir in the shallots; cook 1 minute. Stir in the garlic;

cook 1 minute longer. Add the chard stems, tossing well to coat with the mixture. Stir in the broth. Cook, covered, until tender, about 15 minutes.

2. Remove the cover and raise the heat. Stir in the parsley. Cook over medium heat, tossing constantly, until all excess liquid has evaporated. Add salt and pepper to taste.

Serves 4.

WILTED DANDELIONS AND POTATOES

M y grandmother used to make a dandelion liqueur (not a wine) from time to time when I was a small child. I thought it tasted perfectly horrible. But I thought cognac tasted horrible too! Tastes change but my feelings about the dandelion endure. To this day, I like them best in a pot!

1 pound dandelion greens
3 medium potatoes, peeled, cut into 1½-inch cubes
½ cup Beef Stock (see page 409)
1 tablespoon unsalted butter
½ cup chopped smoked ham (I prefer Black Forest)
1 tablespoon lemon juice
Salt and freshly ground black pepper

1. Trim the dandelion greens and discard the stems. Roughly chop the leaves. Set aside.

2. Place the potatoes with the beef stock and butter in a medium saucepan. Heat to boiling; reduce the heat. Cook, covered, over medium-low heat until the potatoes are not quite tender, 12 to 15 minutes.

3. Stir the dandelion greens into the potatoes. Stir in the ham. Cook, covered, 5 minutes.

4. Remove the cover and stir in the lemon juice. Cook until any excess liquid has evaporated. Add salt and pepper to taste.

Serves 4 to 6.

BRIE ROMAINE

T his next bequest comes from a greens-loving young American chef, Paul Henskens, who has been known for brilliant derring-do at the range. Pencil his name on your list of rising cooking stars. Henskens' dish is a first course or possibly a luncheon dish of brie cheese baked in a leafy green for only minutes. Diet food? I seriously doubt it, but delectable without a doubt.

6 large romaine lettuce leaves
¾ pound firm Brie cheese, from a 7-inch
    Brie
4 tablespoons (½ stick) unsalted butter
3 tablespoons sliced blanched almonds
Quartered cherry tomatoes (optional)

1. Preheat the oven to 450°F. Drop the romaine leaves into boiling salted water and cook until wilted, 45 to 60 seconds. Drain, and pat dry with paper towels. Remove the tough center ribs.

2. Cut the cheese into six equal wedges, each about 3½ inches long. Wrap each wedge in a leaf of romaine. Place them on an ovenproof serving dish and dot with the butter. Sprinkle with the almonds. Bake until the cheese starts to melt, about 5 minutes. Serve immediately, garnished with cherry tomatoes if you like.

Serves 6.

GREENS AND CORNMEAL DUMPLINGS

In the American South, greens are more than a dining prerogative; they are a way of life. Have my version of a classic "Alabama-Tennessee-Georgia-Mississippi" rendering, though I must warn the purists that it is somewhat less long-cooked than it would be in any of those territories. To make up for that lack, I amended it with a Virginia legacy, heavenly cornmeal dumplings. What follows is one *very* filling and fabulous dish. I inevitably make up a batch when I have a larder of leftover greens of varying hues and flavors in the fridge. But you use your own good green judgment in the selection.

1¼ pounds Swiss chard or collard greens
¾ pound mixed greens—mustard, arugula,
    and watercress
2 tablespoons unsalted butter
1 large onion, chopped
½ pound cooked ham, cut into large bite-
    size pieces
½ cup chicken broth (see page 414)
½ cup cake flour
½ cup yellow cornmeal
1½ teaspoons baking powder
½ teaspoon salt
1 egg, lightly beaten
⅓ cup milk
1 tablespoon lemon juice
Dash of hot pepper sauce
Chopped fresh parsley

1. Trim the leaves from the chard or collards; chop and reserve. Cut the stems into ½-inch-long pieces; reserve.

2. Trim the leaves from the mustard greens, arugula, and watercress; reserve.

3. Melt the butter in a large heavy skillet over medium-low heat. Stir in the onion; cook 2 minutes. Stir in the ham; cook 4 minutes. Stir in the chard or collard stems and the broth. Cook, covered, 10 minutes. Add the remaining greens; cook, covered, 10 minutes longer.

4. Meanwhile, sift the flour with the cornmeal, baking powder, and salt into a medium bowl. Beat in the egg and milk with a wooden spoon until smooth.

5. Stir the lemon juice and hot pepper sauce into the greens. Drop the cornmeal batter by the tablespoonful over the greens. Cook, covered, until firm, about 18 minutes. Sprinkle with parsley.

Serves 4.

WILTED SUMMER GREENS

My classic way with greens is biblically inspired. The *Pantropheon* tells us that the way the ancient Hebrews ate the fresh leaves that grew in their gardens was "seasoned lightly with herbs and spice and pot roasted till they lay down about a Pascal lamb."

My method is to braise the greens of course, but that roast lamb is not a bad notion as the greens' dinner partner. I make this side dish when the garden (or the greengrocer) has a wide variety of leaves to mix and match in the pot. But it is really a dish for all seasons, despite the summery moniker.

4 tablespoons (½ stick) unsalted butter
1 large onion, minced
1 large clove garlic, minced
2 medium tomatoes, peeled, seeded, roughly chopped
½ cup chopped fresh basil
¼ teaspoon ground ginger
4 to 5 cups (2 to 3 pounds) trimmed, roughly chopped mixed greens, such as chard, collards, turnip, blanched mustard, dandelions, arugula, sorrel
Salt and freshly ground black pepper

Melt the butter in a large saucepan over medium-low heat. Stir in the onion; cook 1 minute. Stir in the garlic; cook until golden, about 5 minutes. Add the tomatoes, basil, and ginger. Cook, uncovered, stirring occasionally, until slightly thickened, about 5 minutes. Stir in the greens and cook, covered, until wilted, 3 to 4 minutes. Add salt and pepper to taste. Serve hot or at room temperature.

Serves 4.

DANDELION GREENS WITH PROSCIUTTO

I first tasted a dandelion leaf when I was thirty and instantly regretted my (till then) misspent appetite, for this is one green that is wondrously trenchant to the tongue. And while I have never joined the forces of those dandelion lovers who hunt the waysides of expressways and thruways with scissors in hand, I do scout the greenest markets (in season) to keep my saucepans and salad bowl amply supplied. Like all greens, dandelion's tangy flavor marries well with the smoky taste of ham, bacon, and the like. For evidence, try this melding of wilted greens and Italian prosciutto. Incidentally, the word "dandelion" is a corruption of the French *dent de lion* ("lion's tooth"), referring to the plant's prominently incised leaves. It's not an odd association, truly, for this green is exceedingly toothsome.

1 to 1¼ pounds dandelion greens
2 tablespoons unsalted butter
1 medium onion, chopped

1 clove garlic, minced
2 tablespoons finely chopped prosciutto
Freshly ground black pepper

1. Wash the dandelions well. Tear the leaves from the stems. Chop the stems.

2. Melt the butter in a large skillet over medium-low heat. Add the onion; cook 1 minute. Stir in the garlic; cook until golden, about 5 minutes. Stir in the prosciutto and dandelion stems. Cook, covered, 4 minutes.

3. Add the dandelion leaves to the skillet. Cook, covered, until the leaves start to wilt, about 30 seconds. Remove the cover and raise the heat to medium. Cook, tossing constantly, until the leaves are tender, about 2 minutes. Add pepper to taste.

Serves 4.

To the gardener, dandelions are something less than splendor in the grass because no matter how hard one weeds them out, they return with a vengeance the following spring. In earlier times, the dandelion was used almost exclusively for medicinal purposes, and American folklore is crammed with notations for its use for malaises as disparate as ptomaine poisoning and water on the knee. Indeed, the dandelion (and its green leaf) was considered so eminently therapeutic that the *United States Pharmacopoeia* listed it as nostrum from 1831 to 1926.

GREEN TIMBALE
(Swiss Chard or Collard Green Custard)

Chard is beet-related, collards are cabbage-connected, and both have seasoned dishes for a millennium. Each is a hardy grower and will withstand a hot summer or a moist one and still remain unruffled in the vegetable patch. In the following prescription for a lofty vegetable custard, an expedient cook might substitute either with a handier green on occasion. Like what? Well, kale or spinach would do—for they are greens too!

4 tablespoons (½ stick) unsalted butter
1 large onion, finely chopped
1 pound Swiss chard or collard greens,
    stems and leaves chopped separately
    (about 2 cups leaves, 1½ cups stems)
¼ cup milk
½ cup heavy or whipping cream
½ teaspoon salt
¼ teaspoon freshly ground black pepper
⅔ cup fresh bread crumbs
½ cup grated Jarlsberg cheese
5 eggs, lightly beaten

1. Melt 1 tablespoon of the butter in a large skillet over medium-low heat. Add the onion; cook 2 minutes. Stir in the chard or collard stems; cook, covered, until tender, about 15 minutes. Stir in the chard or collard leaves; cook, covered, until tender, about 3 minutes. Raise the heat to medium-high and remove the cover. Cook, tossing constantly, until all liquid has evaporated. Transfer to a large bowl and set aside to cool.

2. Preheat the oven to 325°F. Melt the remaining 3 tablespoons of the but-

ter and add it along with all the remaining ingredients to the greens mixture in the bowl. Mix well and pour into a buttered 1½-quart soufflé dish. Place the dish in a roasting pan. Pour boiling water in the pan to half the depth of the soufflé dish. Bake until a knife inserted in the center comes out clean, 45 minutes to 1 hour. Remove the dish from the pan; let it stand 10 minutes.

3. Run a sharp knife around the edges of the soufflé dish and very carefully invert it onto a shallow serving platter.

Serves 6.

GREENE'S SOUFFLE

*T*he "bite" that greens can display on the tongue is very noticeable in the next recipe, which combines a spicy variety with the tang of creamy goat cheese. I choose watercress or arugula leaves because those greens are tender enough to mix raw with the other ingredients. And since both watercress and arugula are usually found in salads, their appearance in a soufflé is eminently refreshing.

¼ pound goat cheese
4 egg yolks
½ cup ricotta cheese
1 cup watercress or arugula leaves
Salt
Pinch of cayenne pepper
7 egg whites

1. Preheat the oven to 425°F. Mash the goat cheese with the yolks in a mixing bowl until smooth. Beat in the ricotta cheese. Stir in the watercress or arugula. Add salt to taste and the cayenne pepper.

2. Beat the egg whites until stiff but not dry. Fold them into the mixture. Pour into a lightly buttered 1½- to 2-quart soufflé dish. Bake until puffed, 25 to 30 minutes. Serve immediately.

Serves 4 to 6.

DANDELION FRITTELLA

*T*hese greens have always inspired a plethora of lawn-to-stovetop cooking. Here's another: an Italian green quasi-pancake or fritter. Need I add that the little golden "fritterings" are best when the dandelions are fresh and picked at the peak of their seasonal perfection? Romaine lettuce will work well if dandelion is out of season.

1 pound dandelion greens
Coarse (kosher) salt
1 medium onion, minced
1 tablespoon chopped fresh basil
1 tablespoon chopped fresh parsley
½ teaspoon beef bouillon powder

¼ cup freshly grated Parmesan cheese
3 eggs, lightly beaten
1 cup fresh bread crumbs
Salt and freshly ground black pepper
2 tablespoons unsalted butter
Vegetable oil

1. Trim the dandelions, discarding the stems.

2. Place the dandelion leaves in a colander and sprinkle them well with coarse salt. Let stand 1 hour. Rinse under cold running water; drain. Squeeze the leaves dry in a towel. Chop fine.

3. Place the chopped leaves in a medium bowl. Stir in the onion, basil, parsley, bouillon powder, cheese, eggs, bread crumbs, and salt and pepper to taste.

Beat with a wooden spoon until mixed.

4. Melt the butter in a 9-inch skillet over medium heat. Add enough oil so that there is ¼ inch of shortening in the pan. Using 1 generous tablespoon of the mixture for each fritter, fry the frittelle a few at a time until deep golden, about 3 minutes per side. Drain on paper towels. Keep warm in a low oven while frying the remaining ones.

Serves 4.

POACHED GREEN SAUSAGE

*T*he next "greens-and" devise is a dish that is made in Provence, France, with regularity whenever there is a fresh crop of green leaves showing in the kitchen garden. Needless to say, in that precinct there is always some leftover meat in the kitchen. These sausages are skinless of course but freeze remarkably well after the light poaching period. Chard or collard greens (the mild ones in my spectrum) meld best with all the provincial flavorings.

1½ cups chopped Swiss chard or collard leaves (from about 1 pound)
1½ tablespoons unsalted butter
3 large shallots, minced
½ pound lean ground round of beef, raw
6 ounces sweet Italian sausages, removed from casings
1½ cups ground cooked beef (from pot roast)
2 cloves garlic, crushed
1 teaspoon salt
¼ teaspoon freshly ground black pepper
¼ teaspoon ground allspice
¼ teaspoon ground mace
¼ teaspoon oregano
¼ teaspoon hot pepper sauce
3 tablespoons Madeira
½ cup freshly grated Parmesan cheese
2 eggs, lightly beaten
½ cup all-purpose flour, approximately
1 cup homemade Basic or Creamy Tomato Sauce (see pages 374 and 375)

1. Cook the greens in boiling water until tender, about 1 minute. Rinse under cold running water and drain, pressing out all liquid with the back of a spoon. Place in a large bowl.

2. Melt the butter in a small skillet over medium-low heat. Add the shallots; cook until tender, about 5 minutes. Transfer the shallots to the bowl with the greens, and add all the ingredients through the eggs. Mix well. Form into sausage shapes, about 2 inches long.

3. Preheat the oven to 375°F. Roll the sausages lightly in the flour. Poach, about six at a time, in boiling salted water until firm, about 30 seconds. Remove with a slotted spoon, drain lightly on paper towels, and transfer to a well-buttered shallow baking dish. When all are poached, spoon the tomato sauce over them and bake for 20 minutes.

Serves 6.

CRUSTLESS GREENS PIE

*F*or centuries, greens were more beloved by peasants than by princes. With good reason too, for the populace most often used what was closest at hand for their dinner table. One such devise is a great personal favorite. I found it in Eze, but I suspect its genesis is closer to the Italian border. It is a crustless pie made up of all the greens, onions, peppers, and zucchini a farm wife can carry from a garden in her apron. No cousin to either quiche or pizza, it could substitute admirably for each without a second thought. And more to the point, perhaps, it is the quintessential one-dish vegetarian meal.

1½ pounds Swiss chard
½ pound arugula
¾ pound dandelion greens
3 tablespoons unsalted butter
1 tablespoon olive oil
1 onion, finely chopped
2 cloves garlic, minced
½ small yellow pepper, seeded, finely chopped (about ½ cup)
2 small zucchini (about ½ pound), grated
⅓ cup chopped fresh basil
¼ cup chopped fresh parsley
½ teaspoon salt
¼ teaspoon freshly ground black pepper
3 extra-large eggs, lightly beaten
¼ cup freshly grated Parmesan cheese
¼ cup grated Jarlsberg cheese
¼ cup fresh bread crumbs

1. Trim the chard, arugula, and dandelion greens. Discard the stems and chop the leaves.

2. Preheat the oven to 375°F. Heat 1 tablespoon of the butter with the oil in a medium saucepan. Add the onion; cook 1 minute. Add the garlic; cook 1 minute longer. Stir in the pepper, chard, arugula, dandelions, zucchini, basil, parsley, salt, and pepper. Cook, covered, over medium heat until very tender, about 15 minutes. Remove the cover and cook, stirring frequently, until all liquid has evaporated, about 25 minutes. Transfer to a large mixing bowl.

3. Beat the eggs into the greens and pour the mixture into a buttered 9-inch glass or ceramic quiche pan. Sprinkle with the Parmesan and Jarlsberg cheeses.

4. Melt the remaining 2 tablespoons butter in a small skillet over medium heat. Stir in the bread crumbs and sauté until golden. Spoon them over the pie. Bake 25 minutes. Let stand at least 10 minutes before serving.

Serves 6.

GREENS-STUFFED PORK CHOPS

*A*n unusual green and meat partnership follows. It is a dish I first tasted in the South: pork crammed with wilted and vinegar-seasoned greens. It is a match made in heaven for a deep-dyed pork chop lover like me. The mix of greens is fairly arbitrary; use whatever is freshest in your market.

1 pound Swiss chard or ¾ pound collard,
    turnip, or dandelion greens
4 tablespoons (½ stick) unsalted butter
1 small onion, finely chopped
1 clove garlic, minced
¼ cup heavy or whipping cream
2 tablespoons red wine vinegar
1¼ cup stale bread cubes
Salt and freshly ground black pepper
4 double pork chops with pockets for
    stuffing
1 cup dry white wine
2 teaspoons cornstarch
2 teaspoons water
Chopped fresh parsley

1. Trim the chard or other greens and discard the stems. Chop the leaves; you should have about 1 cup.

2. Preheat the oven to 350°F. Melt 3 tablespoons of the butter in a medium saucepan over medium heat. Add the onion; cook 1 minute. Add the garlic; cook 2 minutes. Stir in the chard or other greens and cook, covered, tossing occasionally, over medium-low heat until tender, about 15 minutes. Remove the cover; stir in the cream and vinegar. Cook until thickened, about 5 minutes. Stir in the bread cubes, and salt and pepper to taste. Mix well. Remove from the heat.

3. Stuff the pork chop pockets with the greens mixture. Close the pockets with wooden toothpicks.

4. Melt the remaining 1 tablespoon butter in a Dutch oven over medium heat. Sauté the pork chops until well browned on both sides. Pour the wine over the chops. Bake, covered, turning once, 1 hour.

5. Remove the chops to a platter and keep warm. Mix the cornstarch with the water in a small bowl until smooth. Stir the cornstarch into the cooking juices. Heat to boiling; reduce the heat. Cook until slightly thickened. Spoon over the pork chops. Sprinkle with parsley.

Serves 4.

BUTTERFLIED FLANK STEAK WITH GREENS

My father always preferred his greens cooked with meat, so the flavor of one would enhance the other. I obviously inherited his taste for all such greenly combinations, as you will observe from the recipe that follows: a rolled flank steak, filled with a compound of greens and ground veal, pot-roasted on top of the stove. It is a very satisfying dinner entrée hot and also makes the best cold dinner-party fare I know.

½ pound Swiss chard or collard greens
½ pound arugula
3½ tablespoons unsalted butter
3 onions: 1 large, finely chopped, and 2
    medium, sliced
1 pound ground veal
2 eggs, lightly beaten
1 tablespoon chopped fresh parsley, plus
    extra for garnish

¾ teaspoon chopped fresh thyme, or ⅛
    teaspoon dried
Salt and freshly ground black pepper
1½- to 2-pound flank steak, butterflied
1 carrot, peeled, chopped
½ cup Beef Stock (see page 409)
½ cup red wine
½ teaspoon tomato paste

1. Trim the chard or collard greens and the arugula, discarding the stems. Chop the leaves.

2. Melt 1 tablespoon of the butter in a large skillet over medium-low heat. Add the chopped onion; cook until soft, about 8 minutes. Stir in the chard or collard greens and the arugula. Cook, covered, until soft, about 15 minutes. Raise the heat and remove the cover. Cook, tossing constantly, until all the liquid has evaporated. Transfer to a mixing bowl and allow to cool.

3. Mix the veal with the greens. Add the eggs, the 1 tablespoon parsley, the thyme, and salt and pepper to taste. Mix well.

4. Spread the veal mixture over the flank steak and roll it up. Use household string to tie the meat in various places, to keep it from unrolling.

5. Melt 1 tablespoon of the butter in a large Dutch oven over medium heat. Sauté the tied meat roll on all sides until well browned. Place the sliced onions and the carrot around the meat and stir them slightly. Add the beef stock and wine. Heat to boiling; reduce the heat. Cook, covered, over medium-low heat until tender, about 1¼ hours.

6. Remove the meat to a serving platter and keep it warm. Strain the meat juices into a small saucepan. Stir in the tomato paste, and cook over medium

Greens often show up in my salad bowl as a nightly digestive. I eat salad like a trencherman but always *after* a meat course—and usually in place of dessert. These days, I often tear up the most unusual varieties of lettuce (and/or greens) that I can find for tossing—notably corn salad (which the French export under the name *mache*, but which my friends in the Midwest always called lamb's lettuce) or radicchio (red Italian lettuce), which seems to be everywhere I look on the greengrocers' shelves these days. But any combination of bitter and mild leaves will do. Ever since I lived in the South of France, I have come to like the flavor of tangy geranium blossoms torn into my salad too. If you are not a daring soul, you can skip that amenity. But be assured, this is not just some cookbook writer's crotchet: the tiny scarlet or pink petals give a salad a very special tang.

heat until slightly thickened. Stir in the remaining 1½ tablespoons butter. Spoon some sauce over the meat and sprinkle with parsley. Pass the remaining sauce.

Serves 6 to 8.

WATERCRESS AND MUSHROOM CREPES

My favorite indulgence at the moment is a watercress-and-mushroom crepe much reduced in flour and milk from conventional crepes and absolutely smashing for the alteration.

This crepe (which may be made in advance and frozen, then thawed and filled before reheating) makes a very winning dish for lunch, brunch, or supper.

For the crepes:

2 tablespoons unsalted butter
1 medium shallot, chopped
½ cup sliced mushrooms (about 7 small
    mushrooms)
1 egg
¾ cup milk
2 tablespoons water
¼ cup watercress leaves
2 tablespoons vegetable oil
⅓ cup all-purpose flour
¼ teaspoon salt
¼ teaspoon freshly ground black pepper
Pinch of ground allspice

For the filling:

1 cup sour cream, plus extra for garnish
1 tablespoon lemon juice
1 cup sliced mushrooms
½ cup watercress leaves
Salt and freshly ground black pepper
6 slices bacon, fried crisp and crumbled

1. To make the crepe batter: Melt the butter in a small skillet over medium-high heat. Add the shallot and mushrooms. Cook, tossing the mixture constantly, until the mushrooms are deep golden. Cool slightly. Place the egg, milk, water, watercress, and mushroom mixture in the container of a blender. Blend until smooth. Add the oil, flour, salt, pepper, and allspice. Blend at high speed, 2 minutes. Scrape down the sides and blend 1 minute longer. Let stand 15 minutes.

2. To make the crepes: Place the crepe mixture in a bowl. Line a plate with two sheets of paper towels and set it aside. Lightly rub a crepe or omelet pan (preferably with a nonstick surface) with a buttered cloth. Place the pan over medium heat until hot. Remove the pan from the heat and pour about 3 tablespoons of the batter into the center of the pan. Quickly tilt the pan in all directions to coat the bottom evenly. Return the pan to the heat and cook until the edges of the crepe are brown, about 1 minute. Turn the crepe with your fingers; cook the second side 15 seconds. Flip out onto the paper-towel-lined plate. Cover the crepe with another paper towel. Lightly grease the pan once more and continue the process until all the batter is used up, placing paper towels between the finished crepes.

3. To make the filling: Beat the sour cream with the lemon juice until light. Add the mushrooms, watercress leaves, salt and pepper to taste, and the crumbled bacon. Mix well.

4. Spoon about 1 tablespoon of the mixture down one side of each crepe and roll it up. Place the rolled crepes in a lightly buttered shallow baking dish.

5. Before serving, heat the crepes in a preheated 350°F oven for 10 minutes. Place a dab of sour cream on top of each.

Makes about 12 crepes.

WATERCRESS AND GOAT CHEESE SCRAMBLE

6 eggs
¼ cup heavy or whipping cream
2 tablespoons unsalted butter
2 ounces goat cheese, crumbled or chopped

½ cup watercress leaves
Salt and freshly ground black pepper
Hot cooked spaghetti (optional)

1. Beat the eggs with the cream.

2. Melt the butter in a large heavy skillet over low heat. Pour in the eggs and cook, uncovered, whisking frequently, until they are velvety, about 25 minutes. (Eggs can be removed from the heat to hold, or to keep from cooking too quickly.) Stir in the cheese and watercress. Add salt and pepper to taste. Serve immediately over spaghetti or as a brunch dish.

Serves 2 or 3.

WATERCRESS-PINEAPPLE SNOW

Watercress' finest hour (in my prejudiced opinion) is also its chilliest. The devise is something the French call a sorbet, but in my lexicon it's a *snow*. Have my favorite all-year blizzard—green of course!

1½ cups sugar
1 cup water
¼ cup watercress leaves, plus extra for
    garnish
Pulp of 2 large or 3 small limes, seeds
    removed
2½ cups chopped fresh pineapple (about 1
    medium pineapple)

1. Combine the sugar with the water in a medium saucepan over medium heat. Stir to dissolve the sugar. Remove from the heat and allow to cool.

2. Combine the watercress, lime pulp, and pineapple in the container of a food processor or blender. Purée until smooth. Combine with the cooled sugar syrup.

3. Pour the mixture into the canister of an ice cream maker and proceed according to manufacturer's directions.

4. To serve, spoon the sorbet into dessert glass dishes and garnish each with a watercress leaf.

Makes about 1½ quarts.

KALE

A Survivor of the Dinosaur Age

Before her marriage to my father, my mother had been trained as a concert pianist. Highly praised after her first recital, she was denied the opportunity of pursuing a musical career or even accompanying other performers in concert (if they were male) by her strict father—something she never entirely forgave him for, even when she was middle-aged. She claimed it showed a lack of confidence in her ability, but in all candor, I suspect my grandfather's misgivings had more to do with his eldest daughter's passionate nature than with her talent at the keyboard.

"Play for pleasure," he reputedly counseled, "or teach if you must." Being a dutiful girl she did the latter until she

married, but never with the pleasure or patience needed to become an inspired instructor. Yet when our family finances faltered, my mother turned to her piano.

With a small accumulation of savings and the halfhearted support of her sister Muriel, who had studied the violin, she rented the top floor above our local movie theater. There she installed a very large mirror, a ballet barre, and a rented piano. Then she had a sign painted, which announced in bold script: *Home of the Paula School of Arts & Crafts.*

How artistic this school truly was, I cannot verify, but it certainly appeared to be a crafty venture. Instruction took place in a large "studio" that overlooked the lights of the theater marquee.

The ground floor of the building was shared by an open-air vegetable market and a Greek luncheonette, and the way in was often strewn with green vegetables (frozen in bushel baskets) that would be bought up cheaply by the Greek, who converted them into all manner of spicy soups and stews. My memory of the Paula School of Arts & Crafts is still, in fact, indelibly printed with the scent of those aromas *and* the sound of endless music exercises.

My mother and my aunt gave private lessons in the studio's front rooms, which faced a major thoroughfare with a trolley line that offered up a counterpoint of clanging bells during each student's crucial trill and cadenza. My aunt's friend, an artist named Kay Quinn, was persuaded to instruct classes in portraiture, clay sculpture, and *nature morte* (as my mother referred to still-life painting) in a small bleak room at the rear where the required north light was almost completely obscured by a looming elevated structure.

Besides teaching desultory piano students, my mother also instructed a few culture seekers in Voice and Elocution and provided accompaniment for the dance classes (Ballet, Eurythmics, and Modern Tap) presided over by a birdlike Frenchwoman, Mademoiselle Ginsburg (pronounced Gans-bourg), who always dressed in a severe black leotard and ballet slippers and demonstrated every *plié, jeté,* and *entrechat* with a cigarette dangling from her lips.

I do not know where my mother acquired this foreign adjunct to her faculty but they never maintained a very amicable business relationship—the dance mistress mistrusted the school's fiscal surety and insisted on being paid in cash daily. After every class, in fact.

I came to know Mademoiselle G (as she was addressed by the school body) when I was importuned to attend the Saturday morning "Beginners Ballet Class." This offer of dancing lessons had been made by my mother not so much to add poise to my sluggard comportment as to flesh out the scanty student enrollment. But that cut no ice with Mademoiselle. And being a "shill" neither protected me from her sarcasm nor her cigarette ashes, which fell in constant flurries as she forced me to repeat the dreaded first, second, third, fourth, and fifth dance positions over and over again for hours. The repetitions were asked of me not to improve my elevation, but as an object lesson to all the other maladroit in the class. I only appeared for several weeks of dance instruction before my involvement was summarily interrupted—whether as a result of Mademoiselle G's jeremiads or my own diffidence, I will never know.

It was of little matter, in the final analysis, as the children's class was disbanded, for want of takers, soon after, and agile artist Kay Quinn, who had been waiting in the wings—metaphorically—observing Mademoiselle's measured movements, took over all other dance classes shortly thereafter.

Eventually lack of students and funds sent my mother to other forms of employment, but there was some residual for us all in the blighted enterprise: I learned to know (and in time, cook) the wintery blue-green leaves of a vegetable that was regularly displayed in the market located downstairs from my mother's school. If you are thinking that arctic leaf was *kale,* you are absolutely correct!

If the discovery of kale as something good to eat is a remnant of my mother's Depression-era venture into the arts, some of the ways I learned to prepare it are no less indebted to that enterprise. After a period over the picture palace, the Paula School of Arts & Crafts moved from the noisy Junction Boulevard movie house to the Greene residence. That was when I first found myself pressed into domestic service: preparing our family's nightly dinner in the kitchen, while Aunt Muriel fiddled and my mother pounded the ivories.

I was a frightfully excessive child-chef, and only strongly scented dishes seemed to enflame my culinary sensibilities. When I cooked kale, for instance, it was spiced with garlic and curry powders, plus oregano to give it sufficient savor to meet my demanding tastebuds. The dish passed muster, I guess; everyone but my less-than-stoic father consumed it with apparent grace. But the house reeked for days afterward.

Not willing to kill the goose that had laid the golden eggs, so to speak, my mother said nothing about my incautious seasoning. She merely lit incense and sprayed the light bulbs with cologne before a class began.

Her sister, my feisty Aunt Muriel, was not so sanguine, however. "Listen, kiddo," she rebuked me sharply the morning after one of my headier undertakings at the stove, "you have to learn to cook with judgment—so it doesn't smell like an opium den crossed with a hash-house in here! Otherwise we lose this ball game altogether!"

Mindful of the value of a dollar, I learned to cook with more discretion. That the music-and-dancing academy bit the dust was probably a foregone conclusion. The residual of its existence was my burgeoning recipe collection.

Vegetable Roots

Kale (or *Brassica oleracea acephala*, formally) is sometimes known as a cabbage that will not grow up, but that is hardly an apt description, for this plant with neither head nor heart—which grows resolutely flat in every season—is actually a worthy survivor. Some scientists claim that a wild grass not unlike this one covered the earth billions of years

Kale's moniker in other languages is highly descriptive, to say the least. French call it *chou frisé* ("curly cabbage"), while Germans tag it *Krauskohl* ("crispy cabbage") and Italians know it as *cavolo arricciato* ("curled cabbage"). The Spanish *col rizada* ("cabbage waves") is no less graphic. But leave it to the sensible Dutch to come up with the perfect cognomen. Knowing a good bucolic viand when they grew it, Netherlanders christened kale *boerenkool* ("farm cabbage").

In the British isles, kale is considered to be a plant with mystical powers. For example, the Irish say fairies ride kale stalks in the dark of the moon. When an Irish farmer finds the curly leaves in disarray at sunup, it means his crops will all flourish and grow tall.

My own experience growing kale has been less positive, however. When I find the leaves splayed horizontally in my vegetable patch, it most often augurs an invasion of aphids on the underside of every stalk. Go fight legends, as my mother would say!

ago, transplanted to dry ground from the sea where it had once flourished. Leaf impressions discovered in the remains of eluvial ooze where dinosaurs once lumbered are in fact almost line-for-line copies of the same vegetable I batter-fry or chop into a skillet whenever the yearning for honest winter greens assails my tongue.

I usually choose to dine on kale in its true season, which begins in late November and barely lasts until March. The ancient Egyptians had a shorter growing season and believed that the lack of this green in their diet was a punishment from the gods. Serious wine-bibbers considered kale a prophylactic against hangovers; when the stalks withered, headaches flourished, including the pharaoh's, it appears. In Akhenaton's tomb, the sarcophagus was paved with kale leaves carved of jade so they would never shrivel.

What to Look For

Do yourself a favor when you shop for kale: buy it fresh! Frozen kale has an anonymous texture that makes it interchangeable with kelp or khas-khas and has a taste as flavorsome as antic hay.

Kale is a winter vegetable, which means that farmers by and large do not harvest it until after the first (killing) frost—which seems to intensify its flavor. As kale is mostly water anyway (and does not store particularly well once it is cut), sensible gardeners usually leave it in the ground until the first snowfall as well. Look for dark bluish-green bunches with a jot of curl to the stalk ends. Skip yellowed leaves or any foliage that appears wilted or shopworn. Kale that sits overlong on a greengrocer's shelf de-

velops a bite that has nothing in common with succor.

Inordinately high in vitamin A (over 9,000 units per cup), kale is also a veritable windfall of calcium (206 grams) and potassium (243 milligrams), which helps to build strong bones and enrich the blood supply.

Preparation

As kale is basically a peasant food with no pretension to *haute cuisine*, its optimum classic rendering is a homely braising—covered with only a minimal amount of liquid.

Not actually as harsh-tasting as some of the greens already discussed, kale does not require an obligatory blanching prior to cooking, in my opinion. Wash it well, however. I usually separate the leaves first and soak them in tepid water for about ten minutes before moving on to any advance preparation. This helps to remove the loose soil that often accumulates in the folds. After bathing the leaves I rinse them under cold running water, then simply remove the tough center ribs before I start the cooking.

DANISH KALE SOUP

My favored soup dispensation comes from Denmark. More than a menu starter, this hearty quaff is actually a meal unto itself, as each jade bowlful is enriched with a perfect poached egg at the heart. Serve it with salad, cheese, bread, wine, and a roaring fire if possible.

2 tablespoons unsalted butter
1 onion, minced
1 clove garlic, minced
⅛ teaspoon ground cinnamon
¾ pound kale, stems removed, finely
    chopped
4 cups strong Beef Stock (see page 409)
4 eggs

1 teaspoon red wine vinegar
Salt and freshly ground black pepper
Chopped chives or scallion tops

1. Melt the butter in a large saucepan over medium-low heat. Add the onion; cook 5 minutes. Do not brown. Add the garlic; cook 2 minutes longer.

2. Stir the cinnamon into the onion mixture. Add the kale, tossing to coat it well. Add the stock. Heat to boiling; reduce the heat. Simmer, covered, 20 minutes.

3. Break each egg into an individual small bowl. Fill a medium-size skillet with water; add the vinegar. Heat to boiling; reduce the heat so the water barely simmers. Poach the eggs, two at a time. Remove with a slotted spoon and place in individual serving bowls. Spoon the hot soup over the eggs. Sprinkle with salt and pepper to taste and chopped chives. Serve immediately.

Serves 4.

KALE SLAW

*T*hese next two kale devises—this one raw and crunchy, the other, Batter-Fried Kale, crispy golden—are both long on taste, short on smell.

3 strips bacon
1 pound young, tender kale, stems
*   removed, leaves chopped*
½ small cabbage, shredded (1 to 1½ cups)
1 small red onion, sliced thin
1 medium tomato, seeded, cubed
½ green bell pepper, seeded, finely chopped
½ red bell pepper, seeded, finely chopped
1 cup Mayonnaise (see page 408)
½ cup sour cream
1 teaspoon Dijon mustard
½ teaspoon curry powder
2 tablespoons milk
1 tablespoon white wine vinegar
Salt and freshly ground black pepper
2 tablespoons chopped fresh parsley

1. Sauté the bacon in a medium skillet until crisp. Drain on paper towels. Crumble and reserve. Reserve the bacon drippings.

2. Combine the kale with the cabbage, red onion, tomato, green pepper, and red pepper in a large bowl. Lightly toss.

3. Combine the mayonnaise with the sour cream in a medium bowl. Beat in the reserved bacon drippings, the mustard, curry powder, milk, vinegar, and salt and pepper to taste. Pour the dressing over the salad. Toss until well mixed. Sprinkle with the reserved bacon and the chopped parsley. Serve at room temperature.

Serves 4 to 6.

BATTER-FRIED KALE

½ cup all-purpose flour
1 teaspoon dry English mustard
½ teaspoon freshly grated nutmeg
¼ teaspoon salt
2 eggs, separated
1 teaspoon Dijon mustard

½ cup beer
1 pound young, tender kale, stems trimmed
*   but leaves left intact*
Vegetable oil for frying
Salt

1. Combine the flour, dry mustard, nutmeg, and salt in a medium bowl. Combine the egg yolks, Dijon mustard, and beer in another bowl. Whisk the egg mixture into the flour mixture until smooth. Refrigerate, covered, 8 hours.

2. Wash the kale well and pat it dry with paper towels.

3. Beat the egg whites until stiff; fold them into the chilled batter.

4. Heat 2 inches of oil in a heavy saucepan until hot but not smoking. Dip the kale leaves into the batter. Shake off excess batter, and fry, a few at a time, until golden on both sides. Drain on paper towels. Sprinkle with salt to taste, and serve immediately; or reheat in a preheated 400°F oven for 5 minutes.

Serves 4 to 6.

KALE PUDD'

Scotland is a place where kale flourishes in prophesy as well as pot!

It is a favored pastime of marriageable maidens in the Highlands to strip the leaves from kale as we would from a daisy, calling out the name of every eligible male in town as each leaf is tossed into a casserole. The name assigned to the very last leaf is reputedly the spouse-to-be!

Scottish lassies may alter the prognostication, however—by simply refusing to eat the dish concocted of those leaves. If a girl skipped the following Scottish baked pudding out of such high-handedness, she would certainly not have my sympathy. For it is *verra verra* special!

¾ pound kale, stems removed
½ cup Chicken or Beef Stock (see page 410 or 409)
½ cup water
2 tablespoons unsalted butter
3 tablespoons all-purpose flour
1 cup milk, hot
½ cup heavy or whipping cream, hot
Dash of hot pepper sauce
Pinch of ground allspice
¼ teaspoon freshly grated nutmeg
¼ teaspoon freshly ground black pepper
Salt
2 cups cooked rice
½ cup cubed white cheese (I like mozzarella)
2 tablespoons freshly grated Parmesan cheese

1. Preheat the oven to 350°F. Combine the kale with the stock and water in a medium saucepan. Heat to boiling; reduce the heat. Simmer, covered, until tender, about 15 minutes. Drain, reserving the cooking liquid.

2. Transfer the drained kale to the container of a food processor or blender. Add ¼ cup of the cooking liquid; process until smooth. Reserve.

3. Melt the butter in a medium saucepan over low heat. Stir in the flour. Cook, stirring constantly, 2 minutes. Whisk in the milk and cream. Raise the heat slightly and cook until thick, about 5 minutes. Add the hot pepper sauce, allspice, nutmeg, pepper, and salt to taste. Stir in the puréed kale.

4. Transfer the mixture to a large bowl. Add the rice and white cheese, and mix well. Transfer to a buttered baking dish and sprinkle with the Parmesan cheese. Bake until bubbly, about 20 minutes.

Serves 4 to 6.

COUNTY KERRY KALE

The Irish donation to my collection of kale recipes may appear, at first glance, no different from the Farm-Style braising ahead. But it is. While the vegetable is sautéed in bacon drippings first and seasoned with vinegar later, the Irish potato that joins the green gives a very different flavor to the dish. It is a confederation every denizen of Eire may be rightfully proud to claim, but I picked up the recipe from a Dubliner.

6 strips bacon
2 tablespoons unsalted butter
1 clove garlic, minced
¼ cup Chicken Stock (see page 410)
1 pound kale, stems removed, roughly
    chopped
3 medium potatoes, peeled, diced
1 tablespoon red wine vinegar
Salt and freshly ground black pepper
Chopped fresh parsley

1. Sauté the bacon in a large saucepan until crisp. Drain on paper towels. Crumble and reserve.

2. Remove all but 1 tablespoon bacon drippings from the saucepan. Add the butter and garlic. Cook over medium-low heat until golden, about 3 minutes. Add the stock and kale. Heat to boiling; reduce the heat. Cook, covered, 5 minutes. Stir in the potatoes. Cook, uncovered, stirring occasionally, until the potatoes are tender and almost all the liquid has evaporated, about 15 minutes. Sprinkle with the vinegar and add salt and pepper to taste. Sprinkle with the crumbled bacon and chopped parsley.

Serves 4 to 6.

KALE FRIBBLE

I have decided to add a second offering to my classic nominations. A version of baked kale at its very best, this is one dish I truly pine for whenever the green is out of season—which is practically half the year. Some might consider the following mixture of chopped kale, cream, and cheese in a shell of buttery crumbs a "crustless pie." But not I. The recipe was given to me by a British cook who announced, "It's a fribble but delicious anyway!" According to Webster and friends, a fribble seems to be a lightweight affair—so I let the name stand, unaltered.

2½ pounds kale, stems removed
4½ tablespoons unsalted butter
2½ tablespoons all-purpose flour
1 cup Chicken Stock, hot (see page 410)
½ cup grated Gruyère or Jarlsberg cheese
½ teaspoon salt
½ teaspoon freshly ground black pepper
¼ teaspoon freshly grated nutmeg

Dash of hot pepper sauce
½ cup fresh bread crumbs

1. Preheat the oven to 425°F. Cook the kale, covered, in boiling salted water until very tender, about 15 minutes. Rinse under cold running water; drain, pressing out all liquid with the back of a spoon. Chop fine.

2. Melt 2½ tablespoons of the butter in a medium saucepan over low heat. Stir in the flour. Cook, stirring constantly, 2 minutes. Whisk in the hot chicken stock. Cook until very thick, about 2 minutes. Add ¼ cup of the cheese, the salt, pepper, nutmeg, and hot pepper sauce. Stir in the kale. Transfer to a buttered shallow baking dish.

3. Melt the remaining 2 tablespoons butter in a small skillet over medium heat. Stir in the bread crumbs. Cook, stirring constantly, until golden. Spoon over the kale mixture. Sprinkle with the remaining ¼ cup cheese. Bake until bubbly, 15 to 20 minutes.

Serves 6 to 8.

FARM-STYLE BRAISED KALE

My prototypical kale recipe is borrowed from a farm kitchen. Not just one, however, for I have uncovered the very same recipe performance with ever so slight variations at homespun stoves everywhere from Caen to Kansas City. And inevitably dined well on each offering.

Serve this dish hot off the stove with any main dish you have up your sleeve and gather the hurrahs with confidence!

2 strips bacon
1 tablespoon unsalted butter
1 small onion, finely chopped
1 pound kale, stems removed, roughly chopped
Salt and freshly ground black pepper
Pinch of ground allspice
1 tablespoon red wine vinegar
1 lemon, sliced thin

1. Sauté the bacon strips in a large skillet until crisp. Drain on paper towels. Crumble and reserve.

2. Add the butter to the bacon drippings in the skillet. Cook the onion over medium-low heat until golden, about 5 minutes.

3. Meanwhile, rinse the kale in cold water.

4. Add the kale to the skillet, with just the water that clings to the leaves. Cook, covered, stirring occasionally, until tender, 15 to 20 minutes. Add salt and pepper to taste, the allspice, and the vinegar. Sprinkle with the reserved bacon and garnish with lemon slices.

Serves 4.

TURKISH MEATBALLS WITH KALE AND BARLEY

Turks have a saying about kale that roughly translates as "Every leaf you chew adds another branch to the tree of your life!" To make the point greener, Turkish housewives serve kale in a multitude of different ways with stunning regularity—often three times a day.

Here's the best version I know. It is nutritious as the dickens; it is also wonderful into the bargain.

½ cup barley
1½ pounds ground raw lamb
1 onion, minced
3 tablespoons finely chopped parsley
½ cup fresh bread crumbs
1 egg, lightly beaten
1½ cups chicken broth, approximately
    (see page 414)
Pinch of ground allspice
⅛ teaspoon freshly grated nutmeg
¾ teaspoon salt
¼ teaspoon freshly ground black pepper
2 teaspoons olive oil
1 tablespoon unsalted butter
¾ pound kale, stems removed, roughly
    chopped
2 cloves garlic, crushed
1 teaspoon ground coriander
1 cup sour cream

1. Cook the barley in a large pot of boiling salted water, partially covered, until tender, about 20 minutes. Drain; reserve.

2. Meanwhile, combine the ground lamb with the onion, parsley, bread crumbs, egg, ½ cup of the chicken broth, the allspice, nutmeg, ½ teaspoon of the salt, and the pepper in a large bowl. Mix well. Form into small meatballs.

3. Rub a heavy skillet with 1 teaspoon of the oil. Sauté the meatballs, a few at a time, over medium-high heat, until lightly browned on all sides. Set aside.

4. Melt the butter in a large pot or Dutch oven over medium-low heat. Add the kale and ½ cup of the chicken broth. Simmer, covered, 20 minutes.

5. Mash the garlic with the coriander and the remaining ¼ teaspoon salt until a paste is formed. Heat the remaining 1 teaspoon oil in a small skillet over medium heat. Add the garlic mixture and sauté until golden, about 3 minutes.

6. Stir the garlic mixture into the kale. Add the barley, meatballs, and remaining ½ cup chicken broth. Mix well, being careful not to damage the meatballs. Simmer, covered, 30 minutes, adding more chicken broth if the mixture seems too dry. (This dish may be made in advance to this point and reheated.)

7. Just before serving, stir the sour cream into the meatball mixture. Cook until warmed through; do not allow to boil.

Serves 6.

NETHERLANDERS' BAKED KALE

*T*his dish makes an eminently serviceable meatless main course. If you wish to serve it as an adjunct to a full-course meal, eliminate the butter sauce and simply use drippings or gravy in its place. The flavor increases as it bakes, so do not be tempted toward overseasoning.

For the sauce:

8 tablespoons (1 stick) unsalted butter
1 shallot, minced
½ teaspoon minced fresh tarragon, or
*   ¼ teaspoon dried*
Pinch of dried thyme
1 teaspoon tarragon vinegar

For the kale:

1 pound kale, stems removed
4 medium potatoes, peeled, cubed
4 tablespoons (½ stick) unsalted butter
1 cup heavy or whipping cream
3 egg yolks, lightly beaten
1½ cups grated Edam cheese
⅛ teaspoon freshly grated nutmeg
¼ teaspoon ground white pepper
Salt
4 egg whites

1. To make the herbed butter sauce: Melt the 8 tablespoons butter in a small heavy saucepan over very low heat. Add the shallot, tarragon, and thyme. Cook, uncovered, stirring occasionally, 1 hour. Do not allow the butter to brown.

2. Meanwhile, preheat the oven to 400°F. Cook the kale, covered, in boiling salted water until very tender, about 15 minutes. Drain well. Chop fine.

3. Cook the potatoes in boiling salted water until tender, about 15 minutes. Drain. Rice or mash the potatoes until smooth. Stir in the 4 tablespoons butter and the cream. Beat in the egg yolks, chopped kale, 1¼ cups of the cheese, the nutmeg, pepper, and salt to taste.

4. Beat the egg whites until stiff but not dry. Fold them into the potato-kale mixture.

5. Lightly butter a 2-quart soufflé dish. Sprinkle the bottom and sides with the remaining ¼ cup cheese. Spoon the potato-kale mixture into the dish. Bake 30 minutes.

6. Just before serving, stir the vinegar into the herbed butter sauce. It is traditional to have each person make a well in their potatoes to hold the butter sauce, which is passed on the side.

Serves 6 to 8.

KOHLRABI
Its Ugliness Is Only Skin Deep

Back when I was young, the term "Public Enemy" was in common usage around the nation—at our house as well, but for a somewhat more personal reason.

True, it was an era when Bonnie and Clyde, Dillinger and Capone made headlines daily, and movies like *Scarface* or radio shows like *Gang Busters* held most of the U.S. in thrall. But the public enemy list I logged had nothing to do with run-of-the-mill gangsters. It was instead a hand-scrawled sheet, thumb-tacked to our kitchen cupboard (by me), that listed all the vegetables I hated and absolutely refused to ever eat!

If my action seems like strong stuff, it was not. Because when push came to shove, I usually consumed whatever was placed before me, just like every other American kid during the Depression. I was just a tad more vocal about my prejudices.

My list of enemy vegetables was long and labored. It changed with the seasons and the somewhat lacklustre seasonings in our kitchen. But one name inevitably led all the rest. *Kohlrabi!* For reasons not exclusively based on taste.

When I was young, scholarship was not my strong point. I read haltingly. My handwriting was illegible. More to the point, I could neither add, subtract, multiply, or (Oh God!) face a fraction without the use of every outside appendage I possessed.

Athletics were no better, and forget my manual skills entirely! It took two terms of weekly "shop" classes for me to construct a very rudimentary birdhouse.

A hapless if not hopeless student, I did have one small aptitude, however: spelling. My mother claimed I inherited this gift from her. As a young girl she had been an accomplished winner of spelling contests and never lost her zeal for the ABC's. Her favorite litanies "*i before e unless after c*" and "*it always takes four s's to possess*" are still the very maxims I dredge up when in doubt at the typewriter today.

My mother's pride at knowing how to spell was infectious, and I would often study the dictionary for hours, trying to uncover really big words (of four or five syllables at the very least) that would stump her. I never succeeded. But the training and my pleasure in these words (though often mispronounced) managed to impress one of my teachers, who determined that I would make an eminently worthy team captain at the fourth grade spelling bee.

This contest, if won, usually led to an interschool, then a borough-wide tournament that in turn presaged a city, state, and (with any luck at all) national handicap. I knew well—from the rotogravure section of the Sunday newspapers—the image of a small serious child (hair slicked down and bandbox-neat) standing on tiptoe to receive a solid gold medal plus a kiss from Eleanor Roosevelt. The new spelling champion of the United States. And I dearly coveted that hour of glory.

I studied for weeks before the event, drilled by my mother. *Ostensible, science, languish,* and even *rendezvous* were all words I could unfurl at the tongue's end—long before the day of the fateful meet arrived.

Where did all this confluence of verbiage end? In disaster, I regret to say. For while he lasted through rounds of jaw-breakers like *carousel* and *homogenized* and *piety,* Greene the speller was felled in the very last round by *kohlrabi,* the

green. It was one word I had never come across in my nightly perusal of Webster, and I assumed that since it tasted not unlike cauliflower, it was probably spelled the same way.

"C–A–U–L–R . . ." I began, and went down to defeat in ignominy.

Kohlrabi entered my public enemy list that very night and stayed there, if not forever, far too long.

Obviously I was the loser in more ways than one. It's a delicious vegetable.

Vegetable Roots

Not just another pretty face in the garden, kohlrabi is one of the least-consumed vegetables that grow, because its appearance is frankly so off-putting to most cooks.

Yet another *Brassica* cousin, this member of the cabbage tribe is long on stem and short on stern, with rather formidable bulbs that rise like pale green tennis balls just above the earth's surface. The plant is topped with a network of spiky dark leaves that are extremely tender on the fork when newly sprouted, and will, in a pinch, perform admirably as a stand-in for some of the more rugged greens already limned in this book.

Grace notes about kohlrabi's antecedents are rather sketchy. The name itself is Teutonic in origin and literally means "a cabbage turnip," which may be technically correct but more than a tad imprecise if one is describing the flavor. The eclectic Alice B. Toklas once particularized kohlrabi's taste as "having the pungency of a high-born radish bred to a low-brow cucumber." That's somewhat closer to the mark.

Rumor has it that kohlrabi came to Western Europe from Asia along with Attila the Hun. Its earliest notation in manuscripts (as wild head cabbage) dates back to the fourth century, when that barbarian was making the first of his "cultural missions" abroad. Attila was repulsed half a century later, but kohl-

If the kohlrabi we dine on has a decidedly German name, so does the vegetable that "cabbage-turnip" lovers conspicuously consume in the rest of the world, for it is almost always a literal translation: *chou rave* in France; *col rabáno* in Spain; *cavolo rapa* in Italy; *kohlrabee* in Russia; *kaalrabi* in Denmark, and *couve rábano* in Portugal.

Greeks, however, give it a slightly different tag. As they consider this wild cabbage to be a vegetable that "sprang from the sweat of Jupiter," they dub it *agrio lahano*, which in its classic sense means "wild heat."

rabi stayed on to flavor the stew pots of the Holy Roman Empire. But not Charlemagne's. He fed "caulo-rapa" exclusively to grazing cows because his court physicians asserted that digestion of this "wintry root" turned fighting men bovine. No mention is made of its effect on the cows.

The initial botanical record of kohlrabi's other therapeutic properties (compiled by Matthiolus in 1554) states that "immeasurable amounts" taken as part of the diet will cure dropsy, arrest rising wind, and retard temporary deafness as well. There is, of course, no mention in his pharmacy of just what would constitute an "immeasurable amount."

For what it is worth, Doctor Greene's advice is more specific: keep your kohlrabi out of the medicine chest. Its health-giving attributes are decidedly more pronounced in a saucepan!

What to Look For

Kohlrabi is harvested in home gardens from mid to late summer but never makes its appearance on greengrocers' shelves till the tan is on the pumpkin and frost covers everything else. Look for relatively small, well-rounded, uniform globes when you shop, though in all honesty I must tell you that a standard-size kohlrabi is hard to find. Pass on any that are larger than three inches in diameter, however, as they have obviously stayed in the garden patch too long and will be slightly "woody" in texture if not woebegone in taste. Likewise avoid cracked or split kohlrabi. The leaves of this vegetable are generally a clue to its tenderness. Choose the foliage of brightest hue and crispest character if there is an option.

I judge a pound of raw kohlrabi (with leaves) to yield approximately twelve ounces cooked—about two to three generous servings.

A highly nutritive green, kohlrabi is a dieter's dream dish since it contains a scant 29 calories per ⅔ cup. This vegetable is also sky-high in potassium (372 milligrams) and, like other *Brassicas*, filled with healthy jolts of calcium (42 milligrams), magnesium (37 milligrams) and phosphorus (51 milligrams). Not as vitamin-enriched, kohlrabi still contains a healthy dose of ascorbic acid (66 milligrams) per 100 grams.

Preparation

Many reputable authorities declare that this vegetable should be cooked first and peeled later (because the more flavorsome flesh is closest to the skin.) I do not agree for a multitude of reasons. Frankly it is a nuisance to peel hot vegetables, and as kohlrabi is a particularly dense root, it does not cook evenly. If a recipe calls for the cooked kohlrabi to be diced or cut into julienne strips, I discover that while the center may indeed be firm, the outer portion is often disconcertingly mushy and soft. As a consequence, I inevitably attack this vegetable with a rotary blade prior to its cookery.

Peeling a kohlrabi can be tricky. It is best to trim off the green stems with a sharp knife first. Make sure to remove all veins as you peel the skin, as there is nothing more unpleasant than discovering a hint of this fibrous matter in a finished dish. A well-peeled, uncooked kohlrabi is almost white.

KALARABELEVES
(Hungarian Kohlrabi Soup)

According to my best source of Hungarian information (the quick-witted, bright-eyed, and super-sensuously-tongued George Lang), "the secret of good Hungarian string instrumentalists is that they have a well-developed *sound sense* just as Hungarian housewives and cooks are either born with or develop a keen *soup sense.*"

In Hungary, according to George, thickened soups are with limited logic called either "white soup" or "brown soup." The following rendering (though not Lang's) is what one might safely adjudge to be a tawny (tangy) compromise.

2 strips bacon, chopped
2½ tablespoons unsalted butter
1 large onion, halved, sliced
1 clove garlic, chopped
2 large ribs celery, chopped
1 large carrot, chopped
1 tablespoon chopped fresh parsley
3½ cups chicken broth (see page 414)
1 large chicken (3½ to 4 pounds), cut into
  serving pieces
1 cup water
1 pound kohlrabi with leaves (2 to 3 bulbs)
1 tablespoon all-purpose flour
1½ tablespoons lemon juice
Salt and freshly ground black pepper

1. Sauté the bacon in a medium-size saucepan over medium heat until crisp. Add 1 tablespoon of the butter and the sliced onion; cook 1 minute. Add the garlic, celery, carrot, and parsley. Cook, covered, 5 minutes. Add 1 cup of the chicken broth and continue to cook, covered, until the vegetables are tender, about 10 minutes.

2. Transfer the mixture to the container of a blender or food processor. Process until smooth (being careful: hot liquid will expand). Strain the mixture into a large saucepan. Heat to boiling.

Add the remaining chicken broth, the chicken pieces, and the water. Return to boiling; reduce the heat. Simmer, covered, skimming the surface occasionally to remove fat, until the chicken is tender, about 50 minutes.

3. Meanwhile, trim, peel, and dice the kohlrabi bulbs. Wash the leaves and cook them in boiling water 1 minute. Rinse the leaves under cold running water, drain, and chop. Set aside.

4. Remove the chicken from the soup. Add the diced kohlrabi bulbs to the soup. Cook, uncovered, until the kohlrabi is tender, about 15 minutes.

5. Meanwhile, remove the meat from the chicken; keep warm.

6. Melt the remaining 1½ tablespoons butter in a medium saucepan. Stir in the flour. Cook, stirring constantly, 2 minutes. Whisk in 1 cup hot soup. Stir this mixture back into the soup; cook until slightly thickened, about 10 minutes. Add the cooked chicken and the chopped kohlrabi leaves; cook 5 minutes. Add the lemon juice, and salt and pepper to taste.

Serves 6 to 8.

KOHLRABI AND CARROT SLAW

Add carrots, peppers, and onions to kohlrabi for a crunchy salad, then add up the vitamins, and count your culinary blessings.

1¼ pounds kohlrabi, trimmed, peeled,
    shredded
2 large carrots, shredded
½ red bell pepper, seeded, diced
½ cup chopped whole scallions, bulbs and
    green tops
1 teaspoon chopped fresh dill
1 egg
⅓ cup olive oil
⅓ cup tarragon wine vinegar
⅓ cup sour cream
1 teaspoon ground mild chiles
½ teaspoon ground cumin

½ teaspoon salt
¼ teaspoon freshly ground black pepper

1. Combine the kohlrabi, carrots, bell pepper, scallions, and dill in a large bowl. Toss lightly.

2. Beat the egg in a medium bowl. Slowly add the oil, vinegar, sour cream, chiles, cumin, salt, and pepper. Pour this dressing over the vegetables and toss well. Refrigerate, covered, for 2 hours before serving.

Serves 4 to 6.

KOHLRABI BENNE SALAD

Farmers in the South first planted kohlrabi as a rotation crop with cotton—not for sale, but as "vittles" for the slave quarters in the hard-pressed Southern winter. One remnant of the black cooks' inventions still remains. It is a North Carolina formula: a salad of raw kohlrabi pickled in vinegar, onion, and ginger and seasoned with benne (sesame) seeds to bring the diner good luck.

2 large kohlrabi bulbs (about 2½ pounds),
    trimmed, peeled
2 small white onions, sliced thin
½ cup tarragon wine vinegar
¼ cup sugar
2 teaspoons benne (sesame) seeds
½ teaspoon minced fresh ginger root
½ teaspoon crushed dried hot red peppers
1 teaspoon salt
½ teaspoon freshly ground black pepper

1. Cut the kohlrabi bulbs into strips about ¼ inch thick and 2 inches long. Cook them in boiling salted water for 1 minute. Rinse under cold running water

and drain. Transfer the kohlrabi to a bowl, add the onions, and toss lightly.

2. Combine the vinegar and sugar in a small bowl. Add the benne (sesame) seeds, ginger root, hot peppers, salt, and pepper. Pour this dressing over the kohlrabi and onions and toss well. Chill, covered, for 2 hours before serving.

Serves 4 to 6.

WARM KOHLRABI AND SMOKED SAUSAGE SALAD

One place kohlrabi is popular is in the provincial kitchens of France. Devotees of *haute* and *nouvelle cuisine* usually give it a wide berth, but less rarefied appetites seem to dote on its astringency, particularly in winter when other pickings are slim.

The best *chou rave* I ever tasted in France grew in Alsace-Lorraine, not far from the German border, where kohlrabi first took root in Europe. A dish I am extremely fond of owes its genesis to that locale. It is borrowed almost intact from the French dish known as *pommes de terre à l'huile avec saucisse* (sliced potatoes in oil and vinegar dressing with smoked sausage). Kohlrabi does not exactly take the place of a potato, mind you, but it makes an arresting proxy. Less than half the calories too!

6 medium kohlrabi bulbs (about 2 ½
  pounds), trimmed, peeled
3 tablespoons dry vermouth
2 tablespoons red wine vinegar
2 teaspoons Dijon mustard
¼ teaspoon salt
⅓ cup olive oil
2 tablespoons unsalted butter
1 pound smoked sausage (I use a soft beef
  variety), sliced about 1 inch thick, on
  the diagonal
2 whole scallions, bulbs and green tops,
  trimmed, chopped
1 tablespoon chopped fresh parsley

1. Cook the peeled kohlrabi bulbs in boiling salted water, uncovered, until tender, about 40 minutes. Drain.

2. Meanwhile, in a small bowl, combine the vermouth, vinegar, mustard, salt, and oil. Set aside.

3. Melt the butter in a large skillet over medium-low heat. Sauté the sausage slices until golden brown on all sides, about 8 minutes. If the slices are excessively fatty, drain on paper towels.

4. Meanwhile, cut the kohlrabi into ¼-inch-thick slices and place them in a medium bowl. Whisk the vermouth dressing and pour it over the kohlrabi. Add the sliced sausage and scallions. Toss lightly and serve sprinkled with fresh parsley.

Serves 4 to 6.

KOHLRABI IN AVGOLEMONO SAUCE

The next rendering, Greek of course, is a toss of cooked kohlrabi roots and leaves together in a golden lemon sauce.

4 medium kohlrabi (about 2 pounds) with
  leaves
2 cups chicken broth (see page 414)
1 tablespoon unsalted butter
1 tablespoon all-purpose flour

2 eggs
Juice of 2 ½ lemons
Salt and ground white pepper

1. Trim and peel the kohlrabi bulbs.

Reserve the leaves. Cut each bulb into ¼-inch-thick slices. Place the slices in a medium saucepan, add the chicken broth, and heat to boiling; reduce the heat. Simmer, covered, until tender, about 20 minutes. Drain, reserving 1 cup of the cooking liquid. Keep the kohlrabi slices warm.

2. Trim the leaves of any tough stems. (You should have about 1 cup of leaves.) Cook the leaves in boiling salted water, uncovered, until very tender, about 10 minutes. Drain, pressing out the liquid with the back of a spoon. Chop the leaves.

3. Melt the butter in a medium saucepan over medium-low heat. Stir in the flour. Cook, stirring constantly, 2 minutes. Whisk in the reserved cooking liquid. Cook 2 minutes.

4. Beat the eggs in a small bowl. Slowly beat ½ cup of the hot sauce into the eggs. Beat this mixture back into the sauce. Add the lemon juice. Cook, stirring constantly, over low heat until

I n the garden, kohlrabi grows a foot tall. Twice as wide too, if the tender blossoms are dutifully pinched back before the growing season. Mine never are. Not just because I like the flowers (these creamy yellow petals are particularly graceful), but for an ulterior motive as well: fragrant kohlrabi blooms discourage more garden pests than a pint of malathion!

thickened, about 10 minutes. Do not boil. Add the chopped kohlrabi leaves, and salt and white pepper to taste. Spoon the sauce over the kohlrabi slices.

Serves 4.

Note: The sauce for the kohlrabi can be held for at least 30 minutes in the top of a double boiler over hot water.

BRAISED KOHLRABI WITH TARRAGON

*T*he ultimate rendering of kohlrabi would appear to depend entirely on the taste buds of the diner. To my mind, however, its most classic rendering is a fast braise (in a covered pot) with only the most elemental seasonings as its amendment—in the following case, a sluice of strong chicken stock and a sprinkling of tarragon leaves, which seem to enhance the kohlrabi's quintessential crunch.

1½ to 2 pounds kohlrabi, trimmed, peeled
2 tablespoons unsalted butter
¼ cup strong Chicken Stock (see page 410)
1 teaspoon fresh tarragon, minced
Salt and freshly ground black pepper
Chopped fresh parsley

1. Cut the peeled kohlrabi bulbs into strips about 3 inches long and ¼ inch thick.

2. Melt the butter in a large heavy skillet over medium-low heat. Add the kohlrabi strips, tossing well to coat them. Add the stock and tarragon. Cook, covered, until just tender, about 15 minutes. Remove the cover and raise the heat slightly. Cook until golden. Add salt and pepper to taste. Sprinkle with parsley before serving.

Serves 4 to 6.

KOHLRABI MORVANDELLE

T his is kohlrabi's finest hour—standing in for potatoes again, this time in a sea of cream. I'd rather eat this dish than win a spelling bee, any day!

3 tablespoons unsalted butter
1 small onion, minced
1 small clove garlic, minced
¼ cup chopped cooked ham
1 tablespoon chopped fresh parsley
2 eggs
3 tablespoons heavy or whipping cream
½ cup grated Jarlsberg cheese
1½ to 2 pounds kohlrabi, trimmed, peeled,
  coarsely grated
Salt and freshly ground black pepper

1. Preheat the oven to 375°F. Melt 1 tablespoon of the butter in a small skillet over medium-low heat. Add the onion; cook 1 minute. Stir in the garlic and ham, raise the heat slightly, and cook 2 minutes. Remove from the heat. Stir in the parsley.

2. Beat the eggs with the cream in a medium bowl until light. Stir in the ham-onion mixture and the grated cheese.

3. Squeeze all liquid out of the grated kohlrabi with your hands. Add the kohlrabi to the ham-cheese mixture. Add salt and pepper to taste.

4. Place the remaining 2 tablespoons butter in a shallow ovenproof baking dish and heat it in the oven until the butter foams. Spoon the kohlrabi mixture into the dish. Bake 25 minutes.

Serves 4.

COMFORTED KOHLRABI

A less established kohlrabi prototype is my own invention. It is a style of creamed vegetable cookery, I must add, that is rapidly becoming a classic in its own right since the briefly blanched ingredient cooks in seasoned cream alone, just until the sauce thickens and turns velvety. No flour added, no stirring necessary, and only one pot to wash up afterward! I call this technique "comforting."

6 small kohlrabi bulbs (1½ to 2 pounds),
  trimmed, peeled
2 tablespoons unsalted butter
1 cup heavy or whipping cream
1½ tablespoons lemon juice
Dash of hot pepper sauce
Salt and freshly ground black pepper
1½ tablespoons chopped fresh dill

1. Cut the peeled kohlrabi bulbs into ⅛-inch-thick slices. Cook in boiling salted water, 5 minutes. Drain.

2. Melt the butter in a large skillet over medium-low heat. Add the kohlrabi slices, tossing well to coat with butter. Add the cream. Heat to boiling; reduce the heat. Simmer, uncovered, until the kohlrabi is tender and the cream is thick, about 10 minutes.

3. Stir in the lemon juice, hot pepper sauce, and salt and pepper to taste. Sprinkle with the fresh dill.

Serves 4 to 6.

KOHLRABI BAKE

Of Magyar extraction, this is a reworking of one of Marina Polvay's prescriptions pairing kohlrabi with ham in a paradigm casserole.

2 pounds kohlrabi, trimmed, peeled
4 tablespoons (½ stick) unsalted butter
Salt and freshly ground black pepper
½ to ¾ pound cooked ham, cut into 1-inch
strips
¼ cup chopped fresh parsley
2 tablespoons all-purpose flour
1½ cups heavy or whipping cream
⅛ teaspoon freshly grated nutmeg
4 egg yolks

1. Preheat the oven to 350°F. Cut the kohlrabi bulbs into ⅛-inch-thick slices.

2. Melt the butter in a large saucepan. Toss in the kohlrabi slices. Cook, covered, over medium-low heat, tossing occasionally, about 15 minutes.

3. With a slotted spoon transfer one third of the kohlrabi to a 1½- to 2-quart baking dish. Sprinkle with salt and pepper to taste. Add half the ham. Sprinkle with half the parsley. Continue to layer, finishing with a layer of kohlrabi. Reserve the pan liquids.

4. Add the flour to the cooking juices in the saucepan and whisk until smooth. Cook over medium-low heat, stirring constantly, 2 minutes. Add the cream. Continue to cook until slightly thickened, about 3 minutes. Add the nutmeg, and salt and pepper to taste.

5. Beat the egg yolks in a small bowl. Add ½ cup of the hot sauce. Stir this mixture back into the sauce. Pour the sauce over the kohlrabi and bake until bubbly, about 30 minutes. Let stand 5 minutes before serving.

Serves 4 to 6.

VEAL-STUFFED KOHLRABI

This Germanic dish is stuffed first and then stewed—a pouch of kohlrabi crammed to the hilt with subtly herbed ground veal.

8 medium kohlrabi bulbs (of equal size if
possible), trimmed, peeled
2 tablespoons unsalted butter
1 small onion, minced
1 small clove garlic, minced
¾ pound ground veal
1 egg, lightly beaten
½ teaspoon chopped fresh tarragon, or a
pinch of dried
1 teaspoon chopped fresh parsley plus
additional for garnish

½ cup fresh bread crumbs
¼ cup heavy or whipping cream
½ teaspoon salt
¼ teaspoon freshly ground black pepper
1½ cups chicken broth (see page 414)
2 tablespoons all-purpose flour

1. Slice the bottoms off the kohlrabi bulbs so they will stand upright. With a small spoon scoop out the centers, leaving a shell about ¼-inch thick. Finely

chop enough scooped-out kohlrabi to make ¼ cup. (Reserve remaining centers for salads or stock.)

2. Cook the prepared kohlrabi bulbs in boiling salted water until almost tender, about 20 minutes. Drain. Preheat the oven to 350°F.

3. Melt 1 tablespoon of the butter in a small skillet over medium-low heat. Add the onion and the reserved kohlrabi; cook 6 minutes. Add the garlic and raise the heat slightly; cook about 5 minutes more.

4. Place the veal in a medium bowl. Add the onion mixture, egg, tarragon, 1 teaspoon parsley, bread crumbs, cream, salt, and pepper. Mix thoroughly.

5. Fill the prepared kohlrabi bulbs with the meat mixture. Place them snugly in a baking dish or Dutch oven. Pour the broth around, not over, the kohlrabi. Cover, and bake 30 minutes.

6. Transfer the kohlrabi bulbs to a shallow platter and keep warm. Reserve the cooking juices. Melt the remaining 1 tablespoon butter in a medium saucepan over medium-low heat. Stir in the flour. Cook, stirring constantly, 2 minutes. Whisk in the cooking juices. Heat to boiling; cook until slightly thickened, about 5 minutes. Spoon the sauce over the kohlrabi and sprinkle with the remaining chopped parsley.

Serves 4.

KOHLRABI GOUGERE

I crossed kohlrabi off my public enemy list years ago when I discovered how compatible this vegetable could be when paired with other viands of equally strong flavors. The next recipe proves the root's versatility more eloquently than any prose. A Burgundian loaf (perfect for lunch or hors d'oeuvres), it is seasoned with kohlrabi plus a smattering of prosciutto and Swiss cheese.

7 tablespoons unsalted butter
¾ pound kohlrabi, trimmed, peeled, diced
  (about 1¼ cups)
1 cup milk, scalded
1 teaspoon salt
⅛ teaspoon freshly ground black pepper
1 cup all-purpose flour, sifted
4 eggs
¾ cup diced Swiss or Jarlsberg cheese
¼ cup chopped prosciutto
1 teaspoon chopped fresh chives or scallion
  tops
1 tablespoon cold milk

1. Melt 3 tablespoons of the butter in a medium skillet over medium-low heat. Stir in the diced kohlrabi, tossing well to coat it with butter. Cook, covered, until tender, about 10 minutes.

2. Strain the scalded milk into a large saucepan; add the remaining 4 tablespoons butter, the salt, and the pepper. Heat to boiling; reduce the heat. Add the flour all at once. Cook over low heat, beating briskly with a wooden spoon, until the mixture forms a ball and cleans the sides of the pan.

3. Remove the pan from the heat. Beat in the eggs, one at a time, with a wooden spoon, making sure that each egg is well blended into the mixture. When the mixture is shiny and smooth, stir in slightly more than ½ cup of the cheese, the kohlrabi, prosciutto, and chives. Cool.

4. Preheat the oven to 375°F. Using a stick of butter, trace or loosely draw a

7-inch circle on a baking sheet. Divide the dough in half. From the first half of the dough, shape rounds with a large serving spoon and arrange them on the circle, using a rubber spatula to scrape the dough from the spoon. Smooth the tops of the rounds with the back of a spoon to connect them into a ring. With a teaspoon, shape smaller rounds from the second half of the dough, and arrange them on top of the ring. (Dough should resemble a bumpy coffee ring.)

5. Brush the dough with the cold milk and sprinkle the remaining cheese over the top. Bake until the gougère is puffed and golden brown, 45 to 50 minutes. Cut into wedges to serve.

Serve 6 to 8.

Note: Gougère can be prepared in advance, formed into a ring, and frozen uncooked. Before serving, bake it in a preheated 350°F oven until done, about 1 hour and 10 minutes.

OKRA
There's More to It Than Gumbo

I was printed by the flavor of okra early. And though it was a vegetable alien to most Northern households at the time, I came to know it through expedience rather than choice. I can date my first bite to a period during the Depression when the demise of my mother's "dancing school" (as my father always called the Paula School of Arts & Crafts) sent that intrepid lady out to work to keep our family finances alive.

My mother's term of employment was long and varied, but the single trauma for me was not the matter of an absent parent or coming home from school to an empty house. Truly, I never minded being alone. But I actively dreaded the idea of eating a cold lunch.

As soon as I developed sufficient manual skills to properly use a can opener, I banished all the packages of cold cuts and the icy cartons of potato salad that my mother had left in our refrigerator for my noonday meal—and heated a bowl of soup instead.

Being a compulsive type even as a small boy, I would go to the corner grocer's long shelf of tinned soups and select a new flavor daily, until I had worked my way through the entire Campbell's *oeuvre*.

In retrospect most of those soups—aside from some miscalculations, like sludgy Mock Turtle or blistering Pepper Pot—were highly edible. Waiting for the liquid to bubble up in the pan, I would scrupulously study the serving instructions on the back of each can, though more out of affection for the kewpie-doll cooks (in chef's hats and aprons) on the label than any culinary wisdom they imparted.

How does all this relate to okra? Circuitously.

You see, my favorite Campbell's offering was Chicken Gumbo. I adored that soup so much and consumed it so often that I sometimes depleted our grocer's entire stock in a mere week's time. I realized, as I sipped each delectable spoonful, that the ingredient that gave the gumbo its elusive savor was the spoke-shaped flecks of green that floated on the surface like miniature life preservers. Okra.

I would like to be able to report that I promptly learned to make an okra-thickened chicken gumbo from scratch, but that would be a lie. It took nearly forty years until I successfully duplicated that wondrous dish—after I had been instructed in the homely art by a generous Cajun cook in southwestern Louisiana. But my tastebuds had been primed for it practically from the day my mother first went off to work.

Vegetable Roots

In the Deep South, slender green okra is sometimes referred to as "slave fruit" without a mite of disparagement. For this vegetable came to the New World out of Africa along with the first black Americans. The earliest records in the Carolina House of Burgesses (dated 1627) list sales of *nkruman* seed (the original Tshi name; it is a Gold Coast word) to arriving English colonists at twelve shillings per twelve-pound sack. Which apparently was a bargain no settler could resist, since okra crops flourished like wildflowers thereafter.

It's not as offhand a simile as one would imagine. While most vegetables we grow are relatively closely connected (potato being cousin to tomato and eggplant, and cabbage not only father to sprout but titular head of the entire Brassica family as well), okra stands

alone. For this viand is technically not a vegetable at all but the edible pod of the mallow, *Hibiscus esculentus*.

The blossom of *Hibiscus esculentus* (which precedes the pod) is exceedingly showy. Pale yellow at dawn, this flower turns golden as the sun rises, its petals flaring wider and wider until it reveals a slash of crimson at the heart—usually at the moment the sun sets. For this reason, ancient Arab physicians called okra pods "sun vessels." They believed the ripening seeds contained therapeutic properties that, once consumed, floated through a man's body forever. This notion, shared by many primitive peoples, caused okra to be highly prized in their diet.

There are even tales of bloody *ngombo* (an Angolan word for okra) raids in the folklore of Angola. Lootings would occur periodically when one tribe, covetous of another's thriving *ngombo* crop, would make "sharp-knife" raids in the dark of the moon to lay hands on their neighbor's fields, often killing any man, woman, or child who offered resistance.

The taking of this okra probably caused them little joy, however. According to old gardener's lore, no mallow can be rudely plucked from the ground without leaving a stigma of retribution on the hands of the plunderer. Just touching the green leaves, in fact, will cause a scarlet rash that takes days and sometimes even weeks of calamine lotion to palliate. Wise pickers therefore wear long sleeves and a pair of stout gloves before entering an okra patch!

What to Look For

Okra is a vegetable that comes with a caveat. Although I would never consider using a pod that was not fresh, frozen okra is a possibility in a gumbo or a long-steeped stew where texture is not of prime importance. But do not, even for a moment, consider the idea of substituting frozen for fresh in a dish where crispness is a major prerequisite.

At the greengrocer's, the brightest, sprightliest pods are usually the ones that came to market last, so search them out. Smaller pods are most often tenderer and worth the nuisance of sifting through the pile. Test a pod for elasticity; the crunchiest will bend slightly without oozing. Old pods that darken or are spotty should be passed by.

Dieters may consume okra with utter impunity as there are less than 36 calories in every handful, figuring 10 pods per hand. This vegetable is likewise high in amino acids and minerals—the same handful scoring a rousing 520 units of vitamin A and over 249 milligrams of potassium. This applies to okra that is barely blanched or raw. The health quotient (though not the calories) lessen as the pods are cooked—which is the best reason in the world for eating it practically off the vine.

Preparation

*F*or centuries okra has had more detractors than admirers in the kitchen, largely because of the way it was traditionally served up. Okra changes as it is cooked. From being extremely crisp and firm-textured in its raw state, it becomes thick, gooey, and almost mucilaginous after a long stint in a saucepan. This viscous quality is the result of a high sugar-carbohydrate content, which releases a thickening agent when heated. It took a strong stirring arm plus a litany of handed-down family recipes to turn *ngombo* into the dish with which it has become synonymous: Southern Gumbo. But truly there is more than one way to cook up a mess of okra.

My method is to cook okra as little as possible. I leave the pod practically uncut, simply shaving off the tip of the stem as it enters the pot. The tenderest okra is never more than 2 inches long and is as thin as a child's pinky. More mature pods (2½ to 3 inches in length) may require a jot more surgery at the tip and even the complete removal of a tough stem, but never, never cut into the body of the pod unless it is to be sliced into rounds.

This unorthodox way of preparing okra is its most classic rendition, to my mind at least: merely blanch the okra whole for less than a minute (no matter what its size), plunge it into icy cold water to retard the cooking, and then reheat it briefly in a warm oven before it is to be served.

Never cook okra in an iron, copper, or brass utensil. The metal will turn the pod a grayish hue which, while harmless enough, may occasion a qualm in the finicky. I always use glass or enamel-over-cast-iron pots for okra.

SNAPPY PICKLED OKRA

*T*he crunchiest pickle ever to cross my lips—truly!

½ pound tender young okra, stems lightly
   trimmed
2 hot green peppers (see Guacamole
   headnote, page 37)
2 cloves garlic

2 cups distilled white vinegar
¼ cup water
¼ cup salt
1 teaspoon celery seed
1 teaspoon mustard seed

1. Wash the okra and pack it into two sterilized pint jars. Add 1 hot pepper and 1 clove garlic to each jar.

2. Combine the remaining ingredients in a medium saucepan. Heat to boiling; remove from the heat. Pour this over the okra in the jars. Seal. Let stand 2 weeks, turning occasionally. Chill well before serving.

Makes 2 pints.

OPTIMIST'S SALAD
(Okra and Tomato Salad)

This okra and tomato salad is reputed to cure a hangover! I believe it, but then I am a confirmed optimist.

¼ cup olive oil
1 tablespoon red wine vinegar
1 tablespoon lemon juice
½ teaspoon salt
¼ teaspoon freshly ground black pepper
1 small clove garlic
1 tablespoon sour cream
¼ pound tender young okra, stems lightly trimmed, cut in half lengthwise
1 large ripe tomato, cut into ½-inch-thick wedges
Lettuce leaves
Chopped fresh parsley

1. Combine the oil, vinegar, lemon juice, salt, pepper, and garlic in a small jar. Seal the jar and shake well. Let it stand 30 minutes. Remove the garlic clove. Add the sour cream. Seal and shake well again.

2. Place the okra halves and tomato wedges in a medium bowl. Pour the dressing over, mix gently, and let stand 15 minutes.

3. Line a small salad bowl with lettuce leaves. Spoon the tomato and okra mixture into the center; sprinkle with parsley.

Serves 2 or 3.

OKRA WITH RUMMED MUSTARD SAUCE

This *al dente* rendition is crisp as the dickens, and eminently receptive to its unctuous sauce.

1½ pounds okra, stems lightly trimmed
2 egg yolks
2 teaspoons Dijon mustard
2 teaspoons lemon juice
¼ teaspoon finely grated lemon peel

1 tablespoon dark rum
8 tablespoons (1 stick) unsalted butter, frozen, cut into 8 pieces
Salt and ground white pepper

1. Cook the okra in boiling salted water 45 seconds; drain. Keep warm in a low oven. (If blanching in advance of cooking time, rinse the blanched okra under cold running water until cool, and then drain. Reheat in a 350°F oven for 8 to 10 minutes.)

2. Combine the egg yolks, mustard, lemon juice, lemon peel, and rum in the top of a double boiler. Place over simmering water and stir constantly until slightly thickened. Add the frozen butter, one piece at a time, until the sauce is smooth and thick. (If the sauce should curdle, beat in a few drops of boiling water until it is smooth again.) Add salt

Unlike the Southern blacks, who depended on okra as a staple, the Arabs deemed it a rare delicacy and prepared it only for special occasions like weddings and baptisms. The Arab name for okra, *uëhka*, means "a gift."

and white pepper to taste. Spoon the sauce over the okra.

Serves 4.

LIMPING SUSAN
(Okra with Bacon and Rice)

"Limping Susan" came my way from Jean Hewitt, a brilliant editor and good friend. Jean's "Sue" (a slightly backwoodsy version of risotto) is slightly different from the one I dug up in Savannah, but she pointed me in the right direction.

4 thick strips bacon, diced
½ pound okra, cut into ½-inch-thick
    rounds
1 cup long-grain rice
1 tablespoon chopped fresh basil, or 1½
    teaspoons dried
2 cups Beef Stock (see page 409)
⅛ teaspoon hot pepper sauce
Salt and freshly ground black pepper

    Sauté the diced bacon in a medium saucepan over medium heat until crisp. Stir in the okra; cook 1 minute. Stir in the rice, basil, stock, hot pepper sauce, and salt and pepper to taste. Heat to boiling; reduce the heat. Cook, covered, over medium-low heat until the rice is tender, about 25 minutes. Remove the cover and continue to cook until the mixture is fairly dry.

Serves 4 to 6.

MEDITERRANEAN STEWED OKRA WITH TOMATOES

There are probably as many recipes for stewed tomatoes and okra in the South as there are spatterware enamel skillets in which the dish is traditionally made. Most versions are thick, anonymous in hue, and frankly less than felicitous to my Northern tongue. The genesis of okra cooked with tomato, however, is old as the hills. Paula Wolfert, in *Couscous and Other Good Food From Morocco*, reports that in Tetuan, cooks who make okra and tomato *tagines* and do not wish the sauce to be inordinately thick, string the pods together with a needle and thread. The okra "necklace" is poached in the sauce but lifted up every time the tomatoes need stirring. The okra cooks yet remains ornamental in the dish. I haven't the patience or the threading-eye for such hijinks myself, so I borrow my okra-tomato stew from the good housewives of Provence. They cook the tomatoes with olives and garlic early in the day, and later toss the okra into the pot, for only as long as it takes a bottle of wine to breathe—10 minutes in my kitchen!

1 pound okra, stems lightly trimmed
½ cup red wine vinegar
2 tablespoons salt
½ cup olive oil
2 medium onions, coarsely chopped
2 cloves garlic, minced
2 large tomatoes, peeled, seeded, chopped
1 can (14 ounces) imported Italian plum
    tomatoes
Pinch of sugar
2 tablespoons chopped fresh basil, or 2
    teaspoons dried
Pinch of thyme
¼ cup sliced Greek or Italian olives
2 anchovy filets, chopped
1 tablespoon unsalted butter
Freshly ground black pepper

1. Combine the okra, vinegar, and salt in a medium bowl. Let stand 30 minutes. Rinse under cold running water; drain.

2. Heat the oil in a medium saucepan over medium heat. Add the onions; cook 1 minute. Add the garlic; cook until golden, about 3 minutes. Add the fresh and canned tomatoes, sugar, basil, thyme, olives, and anchovies. Cook, uncovered, over medium-low heat until thick, about 40 minutes. Add the butter, okra, and pepper to taste. Cook 10 minutes longer.

Serves 4 to 6.

"OLE MISS" OKRA FRITTERS

I have a friend in Jackson, Mississippi, who sends me long missives and short homey recipes from time to time. I have promised never to divulge this donor's identity as she has a considerable reputation in another field. However, I am permitted to pass on her recipes to the grateful world.

½ cup all-purpose flour
1 teaspoon dry mustard
½ teaspoon freshly grated nutmeg
¼ teaspoon salt
2 eggs, separated
1 teaspoon Dijon mustard
½ cup beer

¼ cup chopped fresh basil, or 1 tablespoon
    dried chopped with 3 tablespoons fresh
    parsley
Vegetable oil for frying
1 pound tender young okra, stems lightly
    trimmed
Salt

1. Combine the flour with the dry mustard, nutmeg, and ¼ teaspoon salt in a small bowl.

2. Combine the egg yolks with the Dijon mustard and beer. Add this to the flour mixture and whisk until smooth. Refrigerate, covered, 8 hours.

3. Stir the chopped basil into the batter. Beat the egg whites until stiff but not dry; fold them into the batter.

4. Heat 2 inches of oil in a large heavy saucepan until hot but not smoking.

5. Dip the okra into the batter, letting the excess batter run off. Fry the okra in the hot oil, about ten pieces at a time, until golden, about 4 minutes. Drain on paper towels. Sprinkle with salt to taste. Keep warm in a low oven while frying the remaining okra.

Serves 4 to 6.

BAMIYA
(Stewed Okra and Apricots)

*T*he first record of okra as an ingredient in a formal recipe was made by Abul-Abbas el Nebáti, a Spanish Moor from Seville, in the thirteenth century. An eminent botanist (and obviously a food lover), he first tasted this vegetable in a stew in Egypt in 1216 and noted in his diary that its qualities seemed eminently medicinal, "but reviving to the body without being repulsive to the tongue." Which is more than could be said for most other health foods of his day!

In his notes, Abul-Abbas calls okra *bamiyah*, which is curiously akin to *bamiya*, the tag for this vegetable in Armenian. It also happens to be the name for an utterly beatific ragout of stewed okra and apricots—Armenian as well.

1 tablespoon unsalted butter
1 medium onion, halved, sliced
¾ cup Beef Stock (see page 409)
2 tablespoons tomato paste
Juice of ½ lemon
¼ teaspoon ground allspice
½ pound okra, stems lightly trimmed
8 dried apricots, halved
Salt and freshly ground black pepper
Chopped fresh parsley

Melt the butter in a medium saucepan over medium heat. Add the onion; sauté until golden, about 4 minutes. Add the stock, tomato paste, lemon juice, and allspice. Mix thoroughly. Stir in the okra. Arrange the apricots over the top. Heat to boiling; reduce the heat. Simmer, covered, over medium-low heat for 45 minutes. Add salt and pepper to taste, and sprinkle with chopped parsley. Serve over rice or barley.

Serves 4.

CROSS CREEK SHRIMP AND OKRA

*O*ne of my favorite cookbooks was written by a woman who claimed never to measure an ingredient—Marjorie Kinnan Rawlings, denizen of Cross Creek, Florida, where she wrote both her Pulitzer Prize–winning novel *The Yearling* and *South Moon Under.* Mrs. Rawlings's last book, *Cross Creek Cookery*, was the genesis of the following okra and shrimp fry, a dish I urge you to pair with an equally Southern dish, a hominy pudding called Awendaw Bread, which you will find in the chapter on Peppers.

4 tablespoons (½ stick) unsalted butter
2 whole scallions, bulbs and green tops,
    chopped
1 clove garlic, minced
1 pound raw shrimp, shelled, deveined
½ pound okra, cut into ½-inch-thick
    rounds
Salt and freshly ground black pepper

1. Melt 2 tablespoons of the butter in a large heavy skillet over medium-low heat. Add the scallions; cook until slightly wilted, about 3 minutes. Add the garlic; cook 2 minutes longer.

2. Add the remaining 2 tablespoons butter to the skillet. Add the shrimp and cook, tossing constantly, 3 minutes. Add the okra and cook, tossing constantly, 3 minutes longer. Add salt and pepper to taste.

Serves 4.

ROUMANIAN SHEPHERD'S SUMMER STEW

After first flowering in tropical Africa, okra became transplanted to the Arab countries, where it flourished. The Arabs, who were great wanderers, added it to the pack of other exotic vegeteria, like eggplant, peppers, and cucumbers, that they traded with the rest of the world. Consequently okra grew wherever the European sun was brightest. A nice example of its transmigration is the gift that follows. A Roumanian dish, it has a name that translates into *Shepherd's Summer Stew.*

¼ cup all-purpose flour
½ teaspoon salt
¼ teaspoon freshly ground black pepper
2 pounds boneless lamb, cut into 1-inch
    cubes
3 tablespoons unsalted butter,
    approximately
3 tablespoons vegetable oil, approximately
1 large onion, finely chopped
1 clove garlic, minced
3 large tomatoes, peeled, seeded, chopped
2 teaspoons dark brown sugar
½ cup dry white wine
1 cup Chicken Stock (see page 410)
¾ pound tender young okra
2 tablespoons Scotch whisky or cognac
Chopped fresh parsley

1. Preheat the oven to 350°F. Combine the flour with the salt and pepper in a shallow bowl. Roll the meat in the flour mixture, shaking off any excess. Reserve the excess flour mixture.

2. Heat 2 tablespoons of the butter with 2 tablespoons of the oil in a Dutch oven over medium heat. Sauté the meat, a few pieces at a time, until well browned on all sides. Transfer each batch to a plate as you continue to sauté. Add more butter and oil as needed.

3. Add the onion to the Dutch oven. Cook over medium-low heat, 1 minute. Add the garlic; cook 3 minutes. Return the meat to the Dutch oven and sprinkle with 1 teaspoon of the remaining flour mixture. Stir in the tomatoes; sprinkle with the brown sugar. Add the wine and chicken stock. Heat to boiling. Transfer to the oven and cook, covered, 1 hour.

4. Remove the stew from the oven and stir in the okra and whisky or cognac. Place the Dutch oven over medium heat and simmer, stirring constantly, 3 minutes. Sprinkle with parsley, and serve with rice or boiled potatoes.

Serves 6.

SEAFOOD AND OKRA GUMBO

Seafood gumbo is a fairly free-form dish. Flavor it with whatever catch of the day is at hand (or affordable to the pocket). Okra gives it territorial authority.

¼ cup vegetable oil
¼ cup all-purpose flour
5 tablespoons unsalted butter
2 large onions, chopped
1 pound okra, coarsely chopped
3 large tomatoes, peeled, seeded, chopped
2 large green bell peppers, seeded, chopped
3 large cloves garlic, minced
1 pound raw shrimp, shelled, deveined
1 quart Fish Stock (see page 410)
1 quart water
2 tablespoons crushed dried hot red peppers
1½ teaspoons salt
2 bay leaves
2 teaspoons Worcestershire sauce
1 teaspoon ground allspice
¼ teaspoon dried thyme
1 pound red fish or red snapper, cut into
    pieces
1 pound cleaned crabmeat
16 small oysters, shucked
Freshly ground black pepper
4 cups Hot Steamed Rice (see page 412)
Filé powder (see Note)
Hot pepper sauce

1. Whisk the oil with the flour in a large heavy skillet (preferably cast iron) until smooth. Cook, stirring frequently, over medium-low heat until the roux turns a dark mahogany brown, about 1 hour. Do not allow it to burn. Set aside.

2. Melt 3 tablespoons of the butter

Gumbo is my favorite okra soup—but it is hardly a soup at all in most diner's lexicons, as it is actually a meal in a soup plate.

The dish is best, I think, when prepared in the manner of the Cajun country folk of southwest Louisiana, where the Acadiens stir the flour for the roux an hour or longer, until it is deemed sufficiently colored to marry the other ingredients in the pot.

In this part of the world, gumbo is composed of any ingredients a cook may have on hand. What gives a gumbo its gumption, however, is the African ingredient (okra) that thickens the pottage, and the Choctaw seasoning (filé powder) that gives it dimension. The last-named ingredient is a mixture of dried, crushed sassafras that imparts a truly distinctive bite (faintly like the tang of pine needles) to the finished dish. No Cajun ever adds filé powder to the cooking pot, however, as it turns stringy as it cooks.

in a large heavy pot over medium-low heat. Add the onions; cook 3 minutes. Stir in the okra; cook 3 minutes. Stir in the tomatoes, and cook, uncovered, 30 minutes.

3. Meanwhile, melt the remaining 2 tablespoons butter in a large skillet. Add the peppers and garlic; cook 5 minutes. Stir in the shrimp and continue to cook, tossing constantly, until the shrimp turn pink, about 3 minutes.

4. Transfer the shrimp mixture to the pot containing the tomato mixture. Stir in the roux. Add the fish stock, water, hot red peppers, salt, bay leaves, Worcestershire sauce, allspice, and thyme. Heat to boiling; reduce the heat. Cook, covered, over medium-low heat for 1½ hours. Remove the bay leaves.

5. Add the fish, crabmeat, and oysters to the gumbo. Return to boiling; reduce the heat. Cook over medium-low heat, 15 minutes. Add pepper to taste.

True gumbophiles share an idiosyncrasy. They never combine okra and filé powder in the same pot, claiming the two make one superfluous thickening agent. Nonpurists I encountered in the environs of New Iberia and Abbeville do add a pinch of the greenish powder to their soup bowls even when okra is part of the dish, but say it goes for "seasonin'" only.

Serve in shallow soup bowls. Pass the rice, filé powder, and hot pepper sauce.
Serves 8.

Note: A little filé powder goes a long way for most folks, so if you have never had filé before, I suggest you start with just a sprinkle and go from there.

OKRA, SAUSAGE AND GAME-HEN GUMBO

In Cajun country, the hens in the following dish are often wild game bagged in the field. Mine are Cornish, from the supermarket, bagged at the checkout counter.

2 Cornish hens (about 2½ pounds total weight), cut into serving pieces
1½ teaspoons salt
¼ teaspoon freshly ground black pepper
3 tablespoons unsalted butter
2 tablespoons vegetable oil
3 tablespoons all-purpose flour
¾ pound okra, coarsely chopped
2 medium onions, finely chopped
1 small green pepper, seeded, finely chopped
1 medium rib celery, finely chopped
2 cloves garlic, minced

1 quart Chicken Stock (see page 410)
1 cup water
1 teaspoon cayenne pepper
1 pound smoked sausage, cut into ¾-inch-thick slices
3 cups Hot Steamed Rice (see page 412)
Filé powder (see Note, above)

1. Sprinkle the Cornish hen pieces with ½ teaspoon of the salt and the pepper.

2. Heat 2 tablespoons of the butter with 1 tablespoon of the oil in a large

heavy pot over medium heat. Sauté the hen pieces until golden brown on both sides, about 15 minutes. Transfer to a plate.

3. Add the remaining 1 tablespoon butter to the pot. Whisk in the flour. Cook, stirring frequently, over medium-low heat until the roux turns a dark mahogany brown, about 1 hour. Do not allow it to burn.

4. Meanwhile, heat the remaining 1 tablespoon oil in a medium skillet over medium-low heat. Add the okra, onions, green pepper, celery, and garlic. Cook, stirring occasionally, 25 minutes.

5. Stir the okra mixture into the roux (after it has cooked for an hour). Add the chicken stock, water, remaining 1 teaspoon salt, and cayenne pepper. Heat to boiling; reduce the heat. Stir in the Cornish hen pieces, along with any juices. Cook, covered, over medium-low heat for 1 hour. Stir in the sausage. Cook, covered, 40 minutes longer, skimming any fat that rises to the surface. Serve in shallow soup bowls, and pass the rice and the filé powder.

Serves 6.

CHICKEN, HAM, AND OKRA GUMBO

¼ cup plus 1 tablespoon vegetable oil
¼ cup all-purpose flour
1 large chicken (3½ to 4 pounds), cut into 12 pieces
Salt and freshly ground black pepper
4 tablespoons (½ stick) unsalted butter
1 ¼-pound ham steak, cut into strips ¼ inch wide and about 2½ inches long
2 medium onions, chopped
2 cloves garlic, minced
2 ribs celery, chopped
1 green pepper, seeded, chopped
2 cups peeled, seeded, chopped tomatoes (about 3 medium)
6 cups Chicken Stock (see page 410)
1 tablespoon Worcestershire sauce
1 bay leaf
½ teaspoon chopped fresh thyme, or ¼ teaspoon dried
¼ teaspoon dried oregano
¼ teaspoon ground allspice
⅛ teaspoon ground cloves
¾ pound okra, trimmed, cut into ½-inch rounds (about 2 cups)
2 scallion tops, chopped
2 tablespoons chopped fresh parsley
3 cups Hot Steamed Rice (see page 412)
Filé powder (see Note, Seafood and Okra Gumbo)

1. Whisk the ¼ cup oil with the flour in a large heavy skillet (preferably cast iron) until smooth. Cook, stirring frequently, over medium-low heat until the roux turns a dark mahogany brown, about 1 hour. Do not allow it to burn. Set aside.

Roux is the backbone of Cajun cookery. A properly made, long-stirred roux becomes dark in color and deep in taste. Its rich, earthy flavor melds a rather highly seasoned cuisine; and according to Louisiana cooks it tickles the tastebuds, makes food easier to digest, and for some mysterious reason inhibits spoilage, important in a hot climate.

2. Sprinkle the chicken with salt and pepper to taste.

3. Heat 2 tablespoons of the butter with the remaining 1 tablespoon oil in a large heavy pot over medium heat. Sauté the chicken pieces, about half at a time, until dark golden, 8 to 10 minutes per side. Transfer to a plate.

4. Remove all but 1 tablespoon fat from the pot. Sauté the ham strips over medium-high heat until lightly browned, about 4 minutes. Transfer them to the plate with the chicken, along with any juices.

5. Melt the remaining 2 tablespoons butter in the pot over medium-low heat. Add the onions; cook 3 minutes. Add the garlic; cook 1 minute. Add the celery, green pepper, and tomatoes. Cook 5 minutes. Stir in the roux; mix well. Add the chicken stock, Worcestershire sauce, bay leaf, thyme, oregano, allspice, and cloves. Heat to boiling and stir in the sautéed chicken and ham, including any accumulated juices. Return the gumbo to boiling; reduce the heat. Cook, covered, over medium-low heat for 1 hour. Add the okra and cook, uncovered, 30 minutes longer. Discard the bay leaf. Sprinkle with the scallion tops and parsley. Serve in shallow soup bowls, and pass the rice and filé powder.

Serves 6.

ONIONS AND LEEKS

Finally—Superstar Status

When I was barely twenty-five, I moved to Greenwich Village, ostensibly to write the great American novel. Geography was incidental to economics in my change of address: In the late 1940s, this area of New York was the very cheapest place for a struggling artist to live, and a scant forty dollars per month afforded me half the capacious top floor of a very old wooden building that had once been a thriving livery stable.

It was then (and is now) a remarkably decrepit building. In those days it housed a crew of somewhat raffish tenants, most of whom like myself were young and envisioned a future in "the arts." But what was unique about this dwelling was not its current inhabitants' aspirations, but rather its former occupants' effloresence. Every time it rained, the entire edifice reeked of horses!

My neighbor from the front half of the top floor was Helen. Recently shed of a husband, this pretty young woman announced her intention to quit a dreary job and audition for the Actors Studio, one morning when we met at the mailbox. It was surprising news, yet not as wholly capricious as it sounded. I knew she had come to New York from a small town some years before with dreams of becoming an actress. More pertinently, there was an aura about her that caused absolute strangers to stop and stare whenever she walked down a street. But it was not star quality that attracted me to Helen. On the contrary, it was her cooking ability.

Born on a farm, this girl was an absolute whiz at the stove. After she confessed her theatrical ambitions, I would often find myself knocking at Helen's door at dinner time to discuss her upcoming audition. Together we would eat first, then read plays together the whole evening, searching for a scene that would display her talents to the fullest. After a week of exemplary dining, we came upon one. It was a brief love scene from a highly romantic drama called "Lilliom," in which the part of unworldly Julie complemented Helen's lissome good looks.

The leading man in the scene was a carnival barker, a handsome rogue no woman could resist. It was a hard part to fill. All of Helen's actor friends were either "engaged" or frankly unwilling to commit the amount of time she demanded to polish her performance. As a consequence she and I (as stand-in) would rehearse the scene together, night after night.

One evening after we had both memorized the lines, Helen turned to me and broke her concentration.

"You know...you *were* Lilliom just now," she said. "No other actor could play that part better. Why don't you do the audition with me?"

I had known this would happen, even as I demurred and deprecated, for though I was certainly not the physical type of this dashing *macho* man, I had begun to sense his presence between the lines, and had dredged up almost alien feelings to fit the specifications.

What I remember most of those endless rehearsal sessions is the weather. In late spring it rained incessantly, and the former stable smelled so strongly of horses that one could hardly breathe. As we practiced the scene (with windows wide open to the storm), Helen would sauté huge pans of onions to dispel the equine aroma. But to my consternation, I often would find myself thinking more of food (and what dish Helen would whip up from those slow-frying onions) than the infatuation Lilliom was supposed to feel for the young girl beside him. After our rehearsals ended, we would consume onions in every conceivable guise that resourceful Helen could invent (tarts, soup, croquettes), with a ravenous kind of gluttony.

The onions (and Helen too) kept me in a state of emotional and digestive turmoil. For little by little, and not entirely against my will, I began to see the audition as *my* entrance into the world of the theater, not Helen's. I was so certain that the Actors Studio would choose me instead (as the chunkier Brando, Dean, or Newman) that I began to devise ways to make amends to Helen for the bypass. I need not have bothered.

On the day of our audition, my feet turned to clay. The lines I had rehearsed for a month fled from my tongue; instead of speaking, I choked, losing all sense of Lilliom (as well as the scene) in the throes of a paralyzing attack of stage fright. Helen, on quite the other hand, was a vision. She bloomed under the footlights, and was so assured that she rose at the scene's end and walked across the stage with a grace I could never have imagined she possessed. I watched her transfixed, knowing full well that our onion-eating days were over.

Of course she was accepted at the Studio. I went back to ignominy—and my novel, which was almost as bad. Realizing that the stage was decidedly not my metier was a hard pill to swallow. As for Helen, our paths which had become so inexplicably entwined came apart like a raveled string. We never ate together again for she never had the time. Some while afterward she moved, and the only memory of our nightly sessions (when I dreamed of a life on the stage) are random scraps of paper: recipes, all onion dishes too!

Vegetable Roots

In every other chapter of this book, from artichokes to zucchini, the onion acts as an architectural underpinning or seasoning to make other vegetables more flavorsome. Not here. Now the onion stands alone.

In spite of its strong flavor and frankly tear-making complexion, the onion is probably the noblest vegetable that grows. The name itself bears testament to the high esteem in which the plant was held by earlier civilizations. *Onion* stems from the Latin *unus*, which means "one" and was conferred on that single-bulbed stalk because its spherical shape was equated with a symbol of the universe. The fact that it sprouted from the same family tree as the sacred lily (*Allium*) invested the onion with its official touch of reverence, perhaps, but thousands of years before the first Christian celebrated Easter, early man had anointed his body as well as his cookpots with onion juices. Hardly for its aromatic incense: the scent of onions kept his predators at bay!

Onion history goes farther back in time than most food chroniclers care to delve. It's a very pungent subject. In Central Asia, where anthropologists place the site of its first cultivation, the onion (and its siblings: garlic, leek, chive, and shallot) was invested with absolute divinity. Where an onion bloomed, a temple was erected. Where an onion withered, the land was considered fallow and not even beasts of the field were permitted to graze. Yet, though they tended onions assiduously, no resident seems to have ever chomped or sautéed a slice. For in the Eastern view, the golden fruit with its myriad

---

The onion has provoked many snippets of *pro* and tatters of *con* in its time.

In his seventeenth-century *Herbal* John Gerard, for instance, noted: "The juice of an onion annointed upon a bald head in the sun bringeth the haire again very speedily." However, the same gentleman was less than praiseful about its culinary bequests. "Though it be boyled, the onion causeth head ache, hurteth the eyes and make a man dim-sighted and . . . dull!"

George Washington, no slouch at pronouncements himself, never heard Gerard's theory, for a hundred years after Gerard he wrote in his journals: "The onion is the most favored food that grows!" And he vowed that he would eat one any way that it was prepared, "even cored, baked and stuffed with mincemeat like an apple!"—then and now a curious conceit at best.

Robert Louis Stevenson, obviously another *Allium*-lover, called the globe onion "the poetic soul of a capacious salad bowl."

layered skins was regarded as a symbol of eternity, a globe to be held close to the heart when invoking a solemn oath, perhaps, but far too celestial for mere human consumption.

The ancient Egyptians transplanted the same preconceptions about the onion along with the green seedlings they planted on the banks of the Nile. Egyptian high priests considered the onion to be sacred, like the lotus, a dispensation from Ra, the sun god. Instead of eating onions or using them to season their barley, these holy fellows wore them. Entwining ropes of onions like phylacteries around their naked bodies, they said their daily prayers. They most probably were weeping as well, for the onions that bloom on Egyptian soil have always been particularly thin-skinned!

Happily this custom was short-lived. By the time the great pyramid was under construction in Gizeh, the onion had achieved a place at the Egyptian table. It is often bruited about (among onion lovers of course) that the workmen who performed the arduous task of building the pyramids would never have had the energy to lift the first stone if nutritious onions had not been part of their daily fare. In fact, onions were so firmly entrenched in the Egyptians' culture that the one regret voiced by the Israelites leaving for the Promised Land, once the Red Sea had precipitously closed behind them, was the absence of onion in their desert diet. Then God performed yet another miracle. After a hundred days, chives were said to be found blossoming in Canaan.

According to Herodotus, Greek males preparing for the Olympic races were advised to consume one onion the size of a fist upon arising and one onion the size of a thumb before retiring, "to lighten the balance of the blood." Roman physicians must have concurred with that nostrum. In Caesar's time, athletes were fed a breakfast of nothing

Though onion and leek are close garden relatives, their names have decidedly varying antecedents. Leek is a corruption of *loch*, a word Romans used to describe any medicine that could be licked to cure a sore throat. Nero (who sang as well as or better than he fiddled) had a partiality to keeping a leek in his mouth, the way other males chomp cigars—to add timbre to his vocal chords. Eventually Roman *loch* became early English *leác* and German *lauch*. Leek in French is *poireau*, however, which like the Italian *porro* and the Spanish *puerro* means "pear-shaped." Which may be an oblique reference to Nero's golden tenor. Who knows?

Onion's cognomen, on quite the other hand, translates into some numerical configuration. French dub it *oignon*, a derivation of *unum*, which means "first." German *Zweibel* is "more than once," obviously referring to the onion's two-season stay in the ground before it blooms. Italian *cipolla* and Spanish *cebolla* are less concise. Some etymologists claim they mean "singularity" or "uniqueness" whereas others insist they refer to "blessings."

but onions before they entered any competitive games. A hundred years later, during Nero's reign, gladiators were massaged with the juice of onions before entering the arena of the Forum, to keep their bodies firm and in passing to deplete the lions' appetite somewhat.

In the Middle Ages, ingestion of a raw onion was deemed "the only sure cure for dog or adder bites—besides being helpful to the bladder and a curative for the stings of certain venomous worms." Later still, in the Shaker colonies of America in the early nineteenth century, onions were adjudged to cure heart disease, diabetes, falling hair, and rheumatism. The patient with any or all of those diseases was merely spooned an extract of roasted onions daily to ensure complete recovery.

Americans have always loved onions. Some food historians claim they are even indigenous to this continent, as traces of wild garlic and *ramps* (a strong clumping chive) have been found in shards of the earliest Indian cooking artifacts. Be that as it may, the yellow onion positively entered American saucepans courtesy of the *Mayflower* contingent at Plymouth Rock. According to colonists' diaries, onion seeds were planted as soon as the Pilgrim fathers could clear the land. But sad to say, no harvested onion made it to the first Thanksgiving. For onions are notorious slowpokes in the garden!

What to Look For

*T*he onion is a year-round vegetable, one of the handful that grows with equal felicity in northern and southern climates. When buying onions, I look for orbs with papery dry skins and no scent whatsoever. A strong-smelling onion is usually bruised beneath its bland exterior. In supermarkets, I search out flat white Bermudas and dusky gold Spanish giants that are firm to the touch, or red-purple Italian onions that are slightly supple to the palm. Always avoid onions that have begun to sprout or that are wet-skinned: that is a sure sign they are on their way to spoilage.

I store my onions in a wire egg basket so they receive the benefit of air circulation, which keeps them compact. However, a basket lined with paper towels in the refrigerator will do equally well.

The one onion available year round is the *yellow* or *golden globe* variety known by its dry and tawny skin. A yellow onion varies in size depending upon its grower. It may weigh in at an ounce or a pound. Size has little to do with its flavor, however, which while pungent raw is extremely palliative in all cooking alliances. *White* or *pearl* onions are smaller, firmer, and sweeter. These may be successfully substituted in recipes calling for medium yellow onions but since their size is so dainty (one truly makes a mouthful), they are most often served up whole in stews or casseroles. *Baby pearls* are the tiniest pick of the white crop and usually end up in a cocktail glass, converting a dry martini into a drier Gibson. *Spanish* onions are not from Spain at all. Though they originated in Europe, these large brown or yellow spheres have been one of the prime southwestern vegetable crops for the past fifty years. Spanish onions require a bit of culinary concern. Reputedly the mildest onion of all, they often have a bitter undertaste when raw that must be ameliorated by slow cooking and judicious seasoning. *Bermuda* onions, which truly do come from Bermuda, are ivory-colored, flat-topped and

*B*eing a biennial, onion plants require two years' growth. During the first summer, however, when the scallions bloom, an onion field is at its prettiest. By mid-June, each bears a ruff of tiny white flowers that eventually becomes round as a small peach. These blossoms are known as puffballs, for the wind demolishes them like puffs of smoke.

In Ireland there is a superstition that the Little People (the leprechauns) choose the farmhouse with the largest puffballs for their summer revels. As a reward for leaving his scallions intact, the farmer's chickens are made to lay twice as many eggs the rest of the year.

sweet as can be. Consider a wedge on your next hamburger or on a slice of freshly baked, lavishly buttered bread! Bermudas have a brief shelf life. April to June are the months to buy them most economically. *Red Italian* onions, also grown in the U.S., are mildest of all. This is a sweet onion variety that takes kindly to salad greens and vegetables in creamy dressings. Unfortunately, red onions are seasonal as well. Look for them in spring and summer—and buy them on a rope you can hang. Air retards their spoilage considerably.

A word or two about SCALLIONS, sometimes called green onions. Onions are slow bloomers, so farmers plant more seeds than they actually require. When these seeds germinate (usually in late spring or early summer) and the base of the onion stalks are no larger than a child's forefinger, they are dug up, then pulled and bunched. These green onions are known as scallions.

The name is a bastardization of *ascalonia caepa*, which means onion of Ascalon, where, according to food lorists, chives first bloomed in Canaan.

The scallions you purchase should be unscarred (and clean of soil at the root ends) and possessed of long sturdy green stems that will not collapse in a refrigerator crisper for at least a week's time. I store scallions, wiped well, in lightly moistened paper towels inside plastic bags.

SHALLOTS (somewhat sweeter than the mildest onion) have a tenuous shelf life. It is a good idea to buy them in small quantities and store them in some cool, dry place. Many cooks keep shallots wrapped loosely in paper towels on the lowest shelf of the refrigerator. As a heavy user, I keep mine in a wire basket where fresh air can freely circulate about them. Shallots keep for about 3 weeks at a normal kitchen temperature.

CHIVES are usually sold in clay pots from early spring to late fall. To keep chives thriving it is a good idea to transplant the clump to a larger pot after several weeks of snipping. A good light window will keep a pot of chives lively for a year with a little prudent removal of the withered stems from time to time.

The LEEK (*Allium porrum*) has no bulb like the onion's and no slender shoot like the scallion's, but only a tall thick stalk of shaded green layerings closely wrapped one over the other.

The base and the white part of the leaves are the parts of the leek that are eaten, and no onion, not even the delicate purple shallot, has a comparable flavor.

The best leeks to buy are never more than 1½ to 2 inches in diameter. Slender leeks cook quickly, while larger leeks become tougher and more pronounced in flavor over extended periods on the stove. A fat leek is fine for soup but less than felicitous in a vinaigrette or a wine-basted casserole. I usually trim a leek lengthwise, never allowing more than 2 inches of green to remain above the white base.

Onions, and leeks too, are superhealthful, totally therapeutic vegetables that provide an immeasurable quantity of minerals and acids for the body's daily requirements. An average onion (only 38 calories) contains over 157 milligrams of potassium and 36 milligrams of bone-building phosphorus. Yellow varieties of onion are endowed with high jots of vitamin D as well. Leeks are equally low in calories; three or four large stems contain a scant 52, plus 347 milligrams of potassium. Leeks are also rich in calcium (52 milligrams) and phosphorus (50 milligrams), and each individual stalk is further blessed with 40 units of vitamin A into the bargain.

Preparation

During my cooking lifetime I have been offered many sure-fire methods for peeling and slicing onions. Holding a crust of dry bread between the teeth is a noteworthy scheme; it is supposed to absorb the onion's acid spray. But what happens is that I get hungry and eat the crunchy morsel before the first batch of onions is even halved. So the deluge of tears comes. A different trick calls for the onion to be peeled and sliced under running water. The hydrogen in water reputedly washes out a measure of the onion's oils so that any mincing that follows may be accomplished with a clear cool eye. I tried that too; and almost amputated a finger for my effort and wailed like a banshee, though whether from the loss of blood or the redolent onion I am still uncertain.

I must confess I peel onions wearing my reading glasses, which seem to protect the tear ducts a bit. If you have better vision, a scuba-diver's mask will work just as well, but try answering the doorbell in that getup—even in Greenwich Village! The best method for peeling an onion is to cut a shallow slice from each end, place it on a firm surface, and then quickly slit and remove the skin. To slice, I halve peeled onions vertically from tip to root without absolutely penetrating the root end, which holds the onion in place as I turn it around and slice it horizontally as well. The root attachments are always severed in the final mincing that follows. But to my mind "roughly chopped" means exactly that; I leave well enough alone.

Before attempting to skin a passel of tiny white onions for a stewpot, I first drop them into a saucepan of boiling water for approximately half a minute; then immediately plunge them under cold running water. While not cooking long enough to blanch the onions, the hot water bath certainly loosens their skins so they may be easily removed without damage to the snowy underlayers. Use the sharpest vegetable knife you can muster to peel them, and always cut a shallow X at the root end of each onion to ensure even cooking.

Washing leeks can be sheer hell. But persist and you will be amply rewarded, for the end result is decidedly worth the bother. I fill a sink half full of lukewarm water first and plunge the stalks in until a healthy collection of grit is washed out. Then I empty the water, fan out the leaves with my fingers, and hold the stalks under cold running water as long as I possibly can. I have a friend who washes leeks in her dishwasher (on the rinse cycle) three times before holding them under cold running water, but even after all that one can never be sure all sand is removed until a grain hits your tongue at the dinner table.

PICKLED ONIONS AND FISH

My grandmother always made a dish of pickled onions and fish whenever one of her brood developed a case of quinsy or croup. She swore that "once the onion smell got through the kids' stuffed noses, throats opened like magic!"

No such bona fide cure is claimed for the next recipe. A pickled onion and fish dish of another color, it is the handiwork of Ray deNardo, chef of the prestigious Pear Tree Restaurant in Rumson, New Jersey. His hors d'oeuvre, while utterly delectable, is guaranteed to open nothing but taste buds. But that's saying a lot.

2 pounds boned, cut-up fish: salmon,
    swordfish, and lemon sole or halibut, in
    equal parts
2 cups red or white Burgundy
2 cups red or white wine vinegar
1 cup vegetable oil
1 small carrot, cut into thin julienne strips
1 cucumber, peeled, seeded, sliced thin
2 large red onions, halved, sliced thin
1/4 cup chopped fresh dill (fresh is a
    prerequisite here)
2 bay leaves
1 tablespoon whole black peppercorns
1 tablespoon green peppercorns

1 teaspoon fresh thyme, or 1/2 teaspoon
    dried
Salt

1. Combine all the ingredients in a large crock or glass jar. Refrigerate, tightly covered, for at least three days. (This dish can be held for about 1 week.)

2. Before serving, let the crock stand at room temperature for 30 minutes, as the oil will have congealed. Remove the bay leaves and toss lightly before serving. Serves 10 to 12.

KAREN CHEWNING'S REMARKABLE ONION SOUP

One of the best—if least traditional—onion soups I have ever slurped requires a scant four onions. But I warn you: they must be very, very finely sliced.

This wonderful pottage is a bequest from a smashingly attractive young lady named Karen Chewning, whom I was lucky enough to meet when I gave some cooking classes at elegant Sea Pines Island in South Carolina a while back. Luckier than most, I was also invited to dine at the Chewning home afterward and permitted to guess at the components of Karen's unusual brew. Like other admirers of this velvety concoction, I failed of course. But Karen's handsome husband, George, insisted she pass along her culinary secret. This privy information describes a priceless soup. George Chewning reputedly proposed marriage after the first sip.

2 tablespoons unsalted butter, plus
    1 tablespoon melted
4 medium yellow onions, peeled, sliced thin
1 tablespoon all-purpose flour
4 cups beef broth (see page 414)
1 beef bouillon cube
1/4 cup boiled milk
1/2 cup sour cream
1/2 cup grated mozzarella cheese
Salt and freshly ground black pepper
4 thin slices dry French bread

1. Melt the 2 tablespoons butter in a medium saucepan over medium heat. Add the onions; cook until golden,

about 5 minutes. Reduce the heat.

2. Sprinkle the onions with the flour. Cook, stirring constantly, over low heat for 2 minutes. Stir in the beef broth and bouillon cube. Heat to boiling, stirring constantly with a wooden spoon; reduce the heat. Simmer, uncovered, 20 minutes. Stir in the boiled milk.

3. Preheat the broiling unit. Combine the sour cream with 1/2 cup of the soup mixture. Stir this mixture back into the soup. Add 1/4 cup of the grated cheese. Cook, stirring constantly, over low heat until the cheese melts. Do not allow the soup to boil. Add salt and pepper to taste.

4. Pour the soup into an ovenproof serving dish. Place the sliced bread on the top. Sprinkle the bread with the remaining ¼ cup grated cheese and the melted butter. Place under the broiler until golden, about 1 minute.

Serves 4.

CHILLED TANGERINE AND ONION SLAW

*T*he onion and orange are longtime culinary confederates. Tangerines, however, give the salad a bright new tang!

8 tangerines, well chilled
1 medium red onion, thinly sliced, rings
*   separated*
Peel of 1 lemon, finely slivered
1 clove garlic, minced
½ teaspoon coarse (kosher) salt
1 teaspoon Dijon mustard
Juice of 1 lemon
½ cup olive oil
Juice of 1 orange (about ¼ cup)
Freshly ground black pepper
1 teaspoon chopped fresh tarragon
1 bunch watercress, leaves only

1. Peel the tangerines. Using a sharp knife, remove the pith and slice off the inner edges to remove any seeds. Place the sections in a serving dish. (You should have about 3 cups.) Place the onion slices over the tangerine slices. Sprinkle with the lemon peel.

2. In a medium bowl mash the garlic with the salt, using the back of a spoon. Stir in the mustard and lemon juice. Very slowly whisk in the oil. The mixture will be quite thick. Thin with the orange juice. Pour this dressing over the tangerine-onion mixture. Sprinkle with pepper to taste. Chill until ready to serve.

3. Just before serving, sprinkle the top of the salad with the chopped tarragon and garnish with watercress leaves. Toss the salad at the table.

Serves 4 to 6.

ONION MARMALADE

*I*ndubitably one of the great inventions to come out of the kitchen of Michel Guérard, this rich, dark conserve was originally meant to enrich the somewhat bland fare of his Cuisine Minceur regimen.

With a deep bow to the master plus a mite of literary license, I have adapted his formula into an equally intense marmalade that while far too heady for any slice of toast will produce a roast of unbelievable savor. Try a dab or two on a raw steak prior to the barbecue pit, or a hamburger before it hits the skillet, for true culinary derring-do. A speck of onion marmalade will also do wonders for unbuttered vegetables or a baked potato. And it stores well—up to six months in a sterilized jar in the fridge.

8 tablespoons (1 stick) unsalted butter
2 pounds yellow or white onions, halved,
    sliced ½ inch thick
1 teaspoon salt
½ teaspoon freshly ground black pepper
⅔ cup sugar
2 tablespoons dry sherry
2 tablespoons red wine vinegar
1 cup red wine
¼ cup honey
½ cup chopped dried pitted prunes

1. Melt the butter in a large skillet over medium heat until bubbly. Stir in the onion slices, tossing well to coat them with the butter. Sprinkle with the salt and pepper; reduce the heat to low. Cook, covered, 30 minutes.

2. Remove the cover from the skillet, add the remaining ingredients, and cook, uncovered, over medium heat until very dark in color and thickened, about 2 hours. Take care, as the marmalade will burn easily toward the end of the cooking time. Reduce the heat if it is cooking too fast. Cool and store, tightly covered, in the refrigerator.

Makes about 2 pints.

ONION PROSCIUTTO BREAD

*F*or the following onion and prosciutto bread, put all the hybrids out of your mind. Only red Italian onions give the loaf its definitive bite.

1 package dry yeast
¼ teaspoon sugar
1⅔ cups warm water
3½ cups all-purpose flour
2 teaspoons salt
2 tablespoons olive oil
1 large red onion (about ½ pound), finely
    chopped
1 clove garlic, minced
¼ pound thinly sliced prosciutto, chopped
Cornmeal
1 egg yolk
2 teaspoons water

1. In a medium-size bowl, dissolve the yeast and sugar in ⅓ cup of the water. Whisk in 2 tablespoons of the flour and let the mixture stand until bubbly, about 10 minutes.

2. Add the remaining water to the yeast mixture. Stir in the salt, and enough flour to make a soft dough, about 3 cups. Turn the dough onto a well-floured surface; let it rest 3 minutes. Knead the dough until it is smooth and elastic, adding more flour if needed, about 10 minutes. Let it rest 3 minutes. Knead 1 minute longer and transfer to a lightly greased bowl. Cover and let rise until tripled in volume, about 2½ hours.

3. Meanwhile, heat the oil in a large skillet over medium-low heat. Add the red onion; cook 1 minute. Add the garlic; cook 3 minutes. Stir in the prosciutto; set aside.

4. Turn the dough out onto a lightly floured board; punch it down and roll it out into a circle about ½-inch thick. Spread the onion-prosciutto mixture over the dough. Fold the left third over the center; cover with the right third. Fold the top third over the center; cover with the bottom third. Turn the dough over and place it in a greased bowl. Cover and let it rise 1 hour.

5. Turn the dough out onto a floured board; let it rest 3 minutes. Knead briefly, roll out, and repeat the folding steps listed above. Place the dough on a baking sheet sprinkled with cornmeal. Form a long loaf. Cover the dough with a flour-rubbed towel and let it rise until doubled in volume, about 1 hour.

6. Preheat the oven to 400°F. Make three slashes across the top of the bread. Combine the egg yolk and 2 teaspoons water; brush this over the loaf. Place a roasting pan half-filled with water in the bottom of the oven. Place the bread, still on the baking sheet, in the top third of

Chopping onions in a food processor can be a tricky business if you are not particularly adept with the on-off switch. Overprocessing turns even a crisp onion mushy, so a measure of care should be exercised. Frankly I do not think it is worth the bother of a cleanup operation to chop a single onion in a food processor. Large batches should be done in relays—with a word of caution. Always quarter the onions prior to processing!

the oven. Bake 30 minutes. Remove the pan of water from the oven; continue to bake 25 minutes longer.

Makes 1 large loaf.

GOLDEN ONION LOAF CAKE

One of the onion dishes I give thanks for is solely American. Known as Onion Loaf, but no bread at all, this is a collection of batter-dipped onion rings loosely crammed into an oblong wire basket and fried till golden.

My version (sans basket and French-fryer) is a trifle simplistic. The onions are fried first, baked later; then turned out like a cake, which in turn is cut into thick crusty wedges. Different—but not a jot less addictive, I promise.

Beer Batter (recipe follows)
2 large Bermuda onions (about 2 pounds)
Vegetable oil for frying
1¼ cups grated Monterey jack cheese,
    regular or with jalapeño peppers
Salt and freshly ground black pepper

1. Make the Beer Batter.

2. Cut the onions into ¼-inch-thick slices. Place the sliced onions in a large bowl, cover with ice water, and let stand 30 minutes.

3. Heat 2 inches of oil in a large heavy saucepan until hot but not smoking. Drain the onions, divide into rings, and lightly pat them dry.

4. Dip the onions into the batter, shaking off any excess. Fry them in the hot oil, about four or five at a time, until golden brown. Drain on paper towels.

5. Preheat the oven to 400°F. Generously butter an 8- or 9-inch springform pan. Line the sides with onion rings. Place one third of the remaining onion rings over the bottom. Sprinkle with ½ cup of the grated cheese. Add another layer of onion rings and sprinkle with ½ cup of the cheese. Top with the remaining onion rings and sprinkle with the remaining ¼ cup cheese. Bake 15 minutes.

6. To remove from the springform pan, first run a knife around the edges. Remove the sides of the pan, then gently flip the onion loaf over onto a serving platter. Carefully remove the bottom of the pan. Sprinkle with salt and pepper to taste.

Serves 6 to 8.

Beer Batter

1 cup all-purpose flour
2 teaspoons dry mustard
1 teaspoon freshly grated nutmeg
½ teaspoon salt
4 eggs, separated
2 teaspoons Dijon mustard
1 cup beer

Sydney Smith was a nineteenth-century English clergyman and poetaster. Have his "Recipe for Salad Dressing":

> Let onion atoms dwell within the bowl
> And scarce suspected, animate the whole.

1. Combine the flour with the dry mustard, nutmeg, and salt in a medium bowl.

2. Combine the egg yolks with the Dijon mustard and beer. Add this to the flour mixture and stir until smooth. Refrigerate, covered, 8 hours.

3. Just before using the batter, beat the egg whites until stiff; fold them into the batter.

Makes about 3½ cups.

GREEN-CRESTED ONIONS

Another baked onion partnership, this one clearly demonstrating the incredible savor an onion adds in combination with creamy mounds of green spinach blended with potatoes. I serve this as an adjunct to turkey on Thanksgiving.

4 large yellow onions
½ cup chopped fresh spinach leaves, washed
2 medium potatoes
2 tablespoons unsalted butter, softened
¼ cup heavy or whipping cream
¼ teaspoon freshly grated nutmeg
Salt and ground white pepper
2 tablespoons freshly grated Parmesan cheese

1. Peel the onions and cut an X in the root end of each one. Cook the

onions in boiling salted water for 8 minutes; drain. When cool enough to handle, slice off the onion tops, and with your fingers carefully remove the insides, leaving a double layer of onion to be filled. (Reserve leftover onions for use at another time.)

2. Cook the spinach in boiling salted water until tender, about 3 minutes. Drain, pressing out all liquid with the back of a wooden spoon. Set aside.

3. Preheat the oven to 400°F. Peel

the potatoes; cut them into eighths. Cook the potatoes in boiling salted water until tender, about 18 minutes. Drain, and mash or rice until smooth. Beat in the butter, cream, nutmeg, and spinach. Mix well; add salt and white pepper to taste. (Add more cream if the mixture

seems too heavy.) Spoon the potato mixture into the onion shells, mounding the filling high. Place the onions in an ovenproof baking dish; sprinkle them with the cheese. Bake until the tops are lightly browned, about 20 minutes.

Serves 4.

BAKED GLAZED ONIONS

My favored method for cooking onions is simply to bake them in a glaze of very down-to-earth ingredients (honey, mustard, paprika, and vinegar), a confluence that produces a crunchy orb that is neither sweet nor sour yet perfectly suited to any other dish, be it fish, fowl, or fine red meat.

4 medium yellow onions, peeled
1 tablespoon unsalted butter, softened
¼ cup honey
2 teaspoons Dijon mustard
1 tablespoon red wine vinegar
½ teaspoon ground paprika
Pinch of ground cloves
½ teaspoon salt
⅛ teaspoon freshly ground black pepper
¼ cup water

1. Preheat the oven to 350°F. With a sharp knife, score the top of each onion about ½ inch deep. Using your fingers,

slightly open each onion.

2. Combine the butter, honey, mustard, and vinegar in a small bowl. Whisk until smooth. Add the paprika, cloves, salt, and pepper and mix well.

3. Place the onions in an ovenproof dish so that they fit fairly snugly. Pour the water around the onions. Spoon about 2 teaspoons of the glaze over each onion. Bake for 1 hour, basting with the remaining sauce every 10 minutes.

Serves 4.

BAKED WHITE ONIONS

One of my best baked onion confederations, this would make a splendid adjunct to any meal. It combines white onions with crescents of fresh, aromatic *shiitake* (Golden Oak) mushrooms.

¾ pound medium white onions, unpeeled
1½ tablespoons unsalted butter
¼ pound shiitake mushroom caps, sliced
¼ cup olive oil
2 cloves garlic, minced

1½ teaspoons finely chopped fresh parsley
Salt and freshly ground black pepper

1. Preheat the oven to 300°F. Place the onions in a medium saucepan and cover with cold water. Heat to boiling; reduce the heat. Simmer, uncovered, 12 minutes. Drain, and allow to cool slightly. Peel the onions and place them, whole, in a lightly buttered baking dish.

2. Melt the butter in a medium skillet over medium heat. Add the sliced mushrooms and sauté until lightly browned.

3. Add the mushrooms to the onions in the baking dish. Sprinkle with the olive oil, garlic, parsley, and salt and pepper to taste. Bake, covered, until tender, about 1 hour. Remove the cover during the last 20 minutes of baking if necessary to reduce the juices.

Serves 4 to 6.

PRASSA
(Leeks)

*T*he first leek recipe is a Jewish bequest. It stems from a small but fascinating recipe book, *The Sephardic Cooks,* compiled and published by Congregation OR VeShalom Sisterhood, in Atlanta, Georgia. It's a slim volume, but eminently collectible.

2 tablespoons olive oil
6 leeks, trimmed of green tops, washed, cut
    into 1-inch pieces
1 large onion, chopped
1 clove garlic, minced
1 can (14 ounces) plum tomatoes, drained
1 cup chicken broth (see page 414)
½ teaspoon salt
1 teaspoon sugar
Juice of 1 lemon
1 medium potato, peeled, cubed
1 tablespoon chopped fresh basil or parsley

1. Heat the oil in a medium saucepan over medium-low heat. Add the leeks and onion. Cook, stirring constantly, 4 minutes. Add the garlic; cook 2 minutes longer.

2. Add the tomatoes to the onion mixture. Stir in the chicken broth, salt, sugar, and lemon juice. Simmer, covered, 40 minutes.

3. Add the potato to the vegetable mixture. Continue to cook, covered, until the potato is tender, about 20 minutes longer. If the mixture seems too wet, remove the cover, raise the heat, and cook until thickened. Sprinkle with the basil or parsley before serving.

Serves 4 to 6.

POIREAUX NICOISE
(Stewed Leeks and Tomatoes)

*T*he next devise, leeks stewed in olive oil with tomatoes, is frankly a borrowing from the estimable Elizabeth David's *Provincial French Cooking*. But I must admit I have been fiddling and fussing with this recipe for so long, I don't think Mrs. David would care to own up to it any longer.

¼ cup olive oil
2 pounds leeks, trimmed of green tops,
    washed (about 6 to 8 leeks)
½ teaspoon salt
¼ teaspoon cayenne pepper
2 medium tomatoes, peeled, seeded, chopped
2 cloves garlic, minced
¼ teaspoon ground allspice
1 tablespoon chopped fresh basil
Juice of ½ lemon
2 tablespoons chopped fresh parsley

1. Heat the oil in a large heavy skillet over medium heat. Add the leeks in one layer. As the oil starts to bubble, turn the leeks over. Sprinkle with the salt and cayenne pepper. Cook for 1 minute; reduce the heat to medium-low. Cook, covered, until the leeks are tender, 12 to 15 minutes.

2. Transfer the leeks to a serving dish. Keep warm.

3. Add the tomatoes to the skillet and cook over high heat 1 minute. Add the garlic, allspice, and basil. Cook 1

Leeks are long garden survivors. Seeds of this plant were carried to Britain by Roman invaders as an indispensable medicinal safeguard against the inclement dampness and rainwashed air. The herb must have worked. For though the Romans eventually decamped, most of them survived, and the leeks flourished like daisies on British soil. To this very day, every proper Welshman wears a leek in his hat on Saint David's Day to commemorate its unwonted arrival.

minute longer. Add the lemon juice and 1 tablespoon of the parsley. Stir to mix, and spoon over the leeks. Sprinkle with the remaining parsley. Serve hot or cold.

Serves 4 to 6.

DRUNKEN LEEKS IN RED WINE

This heavenly first course is a Francophile offering: green leek stalks soused with butter, garlic, and good red wine, baked, and eaten either hot or cold as you wish. My choice? Room temperature.

3 tablespoons unsalted butter
6 to 8 small leeks, trimmed of green tops,
    washed
1 large clove garlic
¼ teaspoon salt
½ cup red wine
1 teaspoon red wine vinegar
Freshly ground black pepper
2 tablespoons chopped fresh parsley

1. Melt the butter in a large heavy skillet over medium heat. Add the leeks and garlic. Cook 3 minutes. Turn the

leeks over and sprinkle with the salt and red wine. Cook, covered, 10 minutes. Remove the cover and cook until the leeks are tender, about 5 minutes longer. Discard the garlic. Transfer the leeks to a serving dish and keep warm.

2. Add the vinegar to the sauce in the skillet. Mix well, and pour over the leeks. Sprinkle with pepper to taste and the chopped parsley.

Serves 4.

LEEKS VINAIGRETTE A LA LUCAS

As learned years ago from an expert—Dione Lucas, who certainly knew her onions.

1 quart water
½ cup dry white wine
½ lemon
2 whole cloves
½ teaspoon salt
10 whole peppercorns
2 sprigs parsley
10 to 12 small leeks, trimmed of green
     tops, washed
1 small clove garlic, minced
½ teaspoon coarse (kosher) salt
4 teaspoons Dijon mustard
1 teaspoon lemon juice
3 tablespoons red wine vinegar
½ cup olive oil
¼ cup vegetable oil
Chopped chives

1. Combine the ingredients through the parsley in a large saucepan. Heat to boiling; reduce the heat. Simmer 5 minutes. Add the leeks; return to boiling; reduce the heat. Simmer, covered, until tender, about 10 minutes. Drain the leeks and transfer them to a shallow serving dish.

2. In a medium bowl mash the garlic with the coarse salt, using the back of a spoon. Stir in the mustard, lemon juice, and vinegar. Whisk in both oils. Pour the dressing over the leeks. Serve chilled or at room temperature, sprinkled with chopped chives.

Serves 4 to 6.

FRITTERRA

My favorite scallion chomp (after raw) is the following tender-hearted patty, Israeli in heritage. It was a gift from a taxi driver, who related it in pieces—each time we stopped for a light.

12 whole scallions, bulbs and green tops
2 eggs, lightly beaten
¼ teaspoon freshly grated nutmeg
½ teaspoon salt
Freshly ground black pepper
¼ cup fresh bread crumbs
1½ cups cold mashed potatoes
1 tablespoon olive oil
2 tablespoons vegetable oil

1. Wash and trim the scallions, leaving about 2 inches of green stems. Cook in boiling water until tender, about 5 minutes. Drain and chop.

2. Place the scallions in a medium-size bowl. Add the eggs, nutmeg, salt, pepper to taste, bread crumbs, and mashed potatoes. Mix well.

3. Heat the oils in a large skillet until hot but not smoking. Shape the onion-potato mixture into patties, using 2 rounded tablespoons of the mixture for each patty. Sauté, about six at a time, until golden brown on both sides, 2 or 3 minutes per side. Keep warm while sautéing the remaining patties.

Serves 4.

KERRY CHICKEN WITH SCALLIONS

3½-pound chicken, cut into 10 pieces
1 clove garlic, bruised
½ cup all-purpose flour
½ teaspoon salt
¼ teaspoon freshly ground black pepper
⅛ teaspoon ground allspice
4 tablespoons (½ stick) unsalted butter
1 tablespoon vegetable oil
¼ cup chopped scallions, bulbs and green
tops
¼ cup dry white wine
1½ cups Chicken Stock (see page 410)
16 scallions, trimmed, leaving 1½ inches
green tops
1 egg yolk
½ cup heavy or whipping cream
Pinch of ground cloves
Salt and freshly ground black pepper
¼ cup chopped fresh parsley

1. Rub the chicken pieces well with the bruised garlic. Discard the garlic. Combine the flour, salt, pepper, and allspice in a medium paper bag. Add the chicken pieces. Shake well to coat; reserve the excess flour.

2. Heat 3 tablespoons of the butter with the oil in a 12-inch heavy skillet over medium heat. Sauté the chicken pieces until deep golden on all sides, about 12 minutes. Transfer to a Dutch oven.

3. Remove all but 1 tablespoon grease from the skillet. Add the remaining 1 tablespoon butter and the chopped scallions. Cook over medium-low heat 2 minutes. Stir in 2 tablespoons of the reserved flour mixture; cook over low heat, stirring constantly, 2 minutes. Whisk in the wine and chicken stock. Heat to boiling; pour over the chicken in the Dutch oven.

4. Heat the mixture in the Dutch oven to boiling; reduce the heat. Cook, covered, over medium-low heat 15 minutes. Add the whole scallions, sticking the bulbs down into the stock. Cook, covered, until the chicken is tender, about 10 minutes. The scallions should still be slightly crunchy.

5. Transfer the chicken pieces to a serving dish and arrange the scallions around the chicken. Keep warm. Meanwhile, strain the sauce if desired. Heat to boiling. Boil until slightly thickened, about 5 minutes. Remove from the heat.

6. Combine the egg yolk with the cream in a small bowl. Slowly stir it into the hot sauce. Return the sauce to medium-low heat; cook 2 minutes. Do not allow it to boil. Add the cloves, and salt and pepper to taste. Pour the sauce over the chicken and sprinkle with the chopped parsley.

Serves 4.

All of the onion kith and kin that grow in a garden—Spanish Golds, Pearl Whites, Italian Reds, slender scallions—have a common denominator. Each is an amazing stimulator, able to invigorate even an anesthetized tongue. Why, you ask? Sheer biological impulse. Because the onion, like the hot pepper, is possessed of astringent oils which irritate the membranes of the mouth, forcing the taste buds to react positively to flavor. More important perhaps, it is also capable of carrying that flavor to the seat of all taste, the wondrous sensual barometer known as the nose.

FLAMICHE
(Onion and Cheese Tart)

*T*his Alsatian tart is tender-crusted, meltingly rich, and onion-bedezined beyond description. The name means "spark," and it will excite even a tired appetite.

Short Crust Pastry (see page 412)
2 tablespoons unsalted butter
2 tablespoons olive oil
¾ pound yellow onions, finely chopped
¾ pound white onions, finely chopped
1 teaspoon sugar
2 cloves garlic, minced
⅛ teaspoon ground cloves
1 tablespoon all-purpose flour
Salt and freshly ground black pepper
3 eggs
½ cup heavy or whipping cream
4 ounces Roquefort cheese, crumbled (about ½ cup)
2 tablespoons freshly grated Parmesan cheese

1. Preheat the oven to 400°F. Roll out the pastry and line a 9-inch pie plate. Trim and flute the edges. Line the pastry with aluminum foil; weight with rice or beans. Bake 10 minutes. Remove the foil and rice or beans; bake 5 minutes longer. Cool. Reduce the oven heat to 375°F.

2. Heat 1 tablespoon of the butter with the oil in a large skillet over medium-low heat. Stir in both the onions; cook, stirring frequently, until the onions lose their color, about 8 minutes. Sprinkle with the sugar. Add the garlic and cloves. Cook, uncovered, over low heat, stirring occasionally, until the onions are tender, about 40 minutes. Stir in the flour and add salt and pepper to taste. Remove from the heat.

3. Beat the eggs with the cream in a large bowl. Slowly add the onion mixture. Add the Roquefort cheese. Pour this mixture into the prepared pastry shell. Sprinkle the top with the Parmesan cheese. Dot with the remaining ta-blespoon of butter cut into bits. Bake until golden, about 30 minutes. Allow to stand 5 minutes before serving.

Serves 6 to 8.

*T*o the roll of yellow onions, there probably should be an amendment to include some succulent new hybrids that have recently hit the American marketplace—notably the Vidalias ·from Georgia, the Walla Wallas from Oregon, and the Mauis from Hawaii.

All of these relatively new onions have in common a remarkable sweetness to the tongue and a low acid threshold that will *not* bring tears to the eye. However, each bears an uncomfortably high price tag that is sure to bring a howl to most shoppers' lips. Why? Because of demand and no supply. All these hybrids require a nine-month growing cycle that culminates in a very abbreviated harvest, which in turn means little or no shelf life.

The reason for the new onions' popularity is indubitably their flavor, which stems from an extremely loamy soil that is low in sulphur in the first two instances and high in volcanic ash in the third. Onion cognoscenti who will insist on a bite no matter what the tariff can take heart: Mail-order sources are listed in the Notes on Ingredients at the back of the book.

LEEK CUSTARD

*T*he next is an Alpine offering. And why not—since no people on earth make a custard dish better than the Swiss. Particularly when the foamy eggs and cream are commingled round nubbins of pink ham and green leek. Consume it for lunch, supper, or picnic fare. It chills to perfection.

4 large leeks, trimmed of green tops,
   washed
2 teaspoons unsalted butter
1 shallot, minced
¼ cup diced cooked ham
1 tablespoon Madeira
1 cup heavy or whipping cream
2 eggs
Salt and freshly ground black pepper
⅓ cup grated Jarlsberg cheese
2 tablespoons freshly grated Parmesan
   cheese
⅛ teaspoon freshly grated nutmeg

1. Preheat the oven to 350°F. Cook the leeks in boiling salted water until very tender, about 15 minutes. Drain; cut in half lengthwise; reserve.

2. Melt the butter in a small skillet over medium-low heat. Add the shallot and ham; cook 3 minutes. Stir in the Madeira; cook, stirring constantly, until all liquid has evaporated. Remove from the heat.

3. Lightly grease a 2-inch-deep baking dish, about 1¼ quarts in capacity. Layer the leeks in the bottom. Spoon the ham mixture between the leeks.

4. Beat the cream with the eggs in a large bowl until smooth. Add salt and pepper to taste, the Jarlsberg, 1 tablespoon of the Parmesan, and the nutmeg. Pour this over the leek mixture. Sprinkle the remaining 1 tablespoon Parmesan over the top. Bake until puffed and golden, about 30 minutes.

Serves 4.

PARSNIPS

A Chequered Career

Curiously, I have spent both the early and the late summers of my life in houses by the sea, watching parsnips grow.

The first was a small bungalow my parents owned on the South Shore of Long Island. It was a trim shingle cottage, shaded front and back by screened porches and set, without a foundation, in a row of absolutely uniform dwellings on a treeless, unpaved street. Slatted wooden footpaths were the only sidewalks.

In those days only Long Beach's main avenues were hard-topped. Streets were dusty arteries that began at the railway station and ended abruptly at either the Atlantic Ocean or the Sound, depending upon which side of the tracks you lived on.

The oceanside we inhabited was the territory most residents chose to swim in during the day and to promenade along most of the night, for it was the site of Long Beach's legendary boardwalk. What I remember most clearly from the months spent "at the shore" are the remarkable attractions that wooden thoroughfare offered. There were hotels, theaters, swimming pools, Turkish and Russian bathhouses, penny arcades, plus popcorn and hot dog vendors at every crosswalk. My favorite enterprise of all was the salt water taffy factory.

My father spent only weekends at the

shore, so the hard work of running this second household was inherited by my mother. And she detested it.

"Too much sun," she would complain. "Too much rain," she would rail. "And sand underfoot no matter the weather. Get me out of here before I go nuts."

My father brought visitors to cheer her up, but was hardly thanked for his efforts. "If I wanted to run a boarding house, I'd put a sign in the window!"

My mother's parents and her unmarried sisters were frequent sojourners at our summer quarters. But the air of *pater familias* did nothing to mollify my mother's discontent. Indeed her parents' presence, and her younger sister Sally's constant stream of suitors, only seemed to worsen her temper. When my grandmother took over most of the kitchen chores and her sisters "straightened" the house, she acted as if her housewifely abilities were a subject of censure. And the air of strife in our bungalow was manifest as the film of salt, outside. I will never forget my mother's mute irritation one summer when her garden-loving mother and sister (my Aunt Frances), challenged by the unused sun trap behind our back porch, planted rows of seedlings in the sandy soil.

She observed their action with raised eyebrows but no comment, and scrupulously avoided watering this garden once they left for home. "It's simply not worth bothering about" was her rationale. "My mother has a green thumb so she thinks anything she puts in the ground will grow. But not in *this* desert."

Despite her tacit dismissal, at summer's end some of the vegetables they planted had actually managed to survive the gritty soil. They were woody and overgrown, but my thrifty parent managed to pick a clump of ivory parsnips from the bed. She cooked them for our supper—swallowing, with grim asperity, more than her actual share, as I recall.

The story has a coda.

Thirty-odd years later, my mother and I shared another meal of beach-grown parsnips. This supper took place in my first rented house in Amagansett, also on Long Island's South Shore but practically at its outermost point.

It was end of summer and the friends with whom I had shared the tenancy of this dwelling had all decamped for autumnal pursuits. My mother surveyed the quarters critically, for she never had liked houses by the sea. This one, the antithesis of a bungalow, was gray clapboard, a turn-of-the-century farmhouse with a trellised porch covered with climbing morning glories and runner beans.

My mother inspected the old-fashioned kitchen and the remnants of my first vegetable garden on the table with some amused tolerance. "You really inherited my mother's thumb," she said as she pushed a pale cooked parsnip to the edge of her plate. "More than that. You got her whole *gesheft*."

In Yiddish that word literally means "a store." Figuratively it implies a treasury, however, and that was quite a compliment coming from my mother. But I was not permitted to bask in the glow of her observation for very long.

"Unfortunately," she continued, "you don't know a hill of beans about parsnips. Look!" She made a circle of her thumb and forefinger. "You don't pick them when they get bigger than this. No. You leave them in the ground till the following spring when they either soften up—or you feed 'em to horses!" My mother smiled. "Now that's a piece of advice you inherited from me. Remember it!"

I remember.

Vegetable Roots

*P*arsnips grew wild in the northern, windswept territories of Eastern Europe for thousands of years. Food pundits assert they would be there still if some mettlesome Visigoth raiding party had not brought them to Rome to season their spearheads: wild parsnip roots are exceedingly lethal.

The barbarians were repulsed without a contest, but their ammunition apparently took root and was cultivated, the sandy banks of the Tiber providing an ideal setting.

Cultivated parsnips are a mild lot, so sweet that nursing mothers in the Middle Ages weaned their babies by giving them this root to suck. Wild parsnips (then and now) are lethal bulbs that even intrepid weed-eaters like cows avoid.

The word "parsnip" itself is an appropriation, albeit a horticultural one. Early Roman farmers furrowed their vegetable fields with a long tapering tool known as a *pastinum* that made deep, even holes in the ground for easy planting. Because the equally tapering parsnip resembled that tool, they dubbed it a *pastinaca*.

That cognomen remained unaltered for almost five hundred years, until the fifteenth century when a loyal English farmer demonstrating his support of Henry VIII's break with the Church of Rome altered the Latin names of all the vegetables that grew in his garden. *Pastinaca* became *pastinepe*, which in time was corrupted to *pasnepe*. Some early Virginia housewife, who obviously could not spell, is credited with the name's final evolution. Among the Roanoke Colony farm records is a listing: "Two mere bushels parnips picked. Half a hundred other snips left in the ground to winter." Taxonomists, scientists unswayed by political and religious feelings, have retained *Pastinaca sativa* for the official label.

The parsnip has had a chequered career at the dining room table. When they were first consumed in Rome, the aristocracy alone dined on them—usually as a sweetmeat, preserved in honey or grated with fruits and frothed up into little cakes.

In the Middle Ages, parsnips began to be eaten by the masses as well, but not for dessert. All extant *moyen age* recipes couple parsnips with salted cod, pickled eel, or smoked herring.

From the Renaissance to the late eighteenth century, the parsnip decidedly moved to the center of the table. Before the potato entered the European diet (courtesy of Sir Walter Raleigh), this vegetable was considered the only fitting accompaniment to the roasted birds, sides of beef, broiled swans, and other fanciful dishes that made groaning boards groan. When the potato arrived, the little p's popularity in the Old World waned a jot—but the unsinkable root acquired twice as many admirers among the colonists in the New one!

In Virginia and Massachusetts (the two earliest outposts in America) there is overwhelming evidence of parsnip popularity; this vegetable came to the table as wine, whipped into puddings, baked into bread, mashed into casseroles, and even fried with fish. There is even an actual recording of a parsnip wedding cake (composed of dried parsnip flour) that was served in Jamestown, unfortunately *sans* recipe.

What to Look For

The reason why parsnips flourished near the beach is quite simple: the burrowing taproot of this vegetable likes a loose and sandy soil for *lebensraum*. And little other attention. When I have mulched and fertilized them to a fare-thee-well, the pickings are inevitably slimmer and a lot less tasty.

Like their cousin the carrot, parsnips are slow bloomers. When they do appear, the young shoots are extremely delicate and lacy, much affected by changes of weather. The wise noncoastal agrarian often plants radishes in the same vegetable furrow since those more vigorous shoots, pushing upward with almost gravitational force, loosen the soil and provide the frailer parsnip with a healthy head start. Of course by the time the parsnips are sufficiently hardy to fend for themselves, the radishes have long since hit the road, or more precisely, the alimentary canal.

A truly ripe parsnip takes a growing season of almost six months to mature, never developing to the required size (4 inches long and 1½ to 2 inches in diameter) until late September or October.

To compensate for their slow growth, parsnips are exceedingly hardy and will overwinter in most climates underground. I have a friend in Vermont who digs them up from under a blanket of snow whenever the irresistible urge for a parsnip comes upon him—most often around St. Patrick's Day, for this sweet root turns the alliance of mere corned beef and cabbage into a celestial culinary confederation (see page 82).

When parsnip shopping—even for those that come in plastic wrappers—keep a weather eye out for smooth roots and plump, shaded members that are free of nicks or deep pits. Pass on any bags of disproportionate sizes as well, for they are difficult to time in cookery. Likewise skip "waxed" parsnips or any produce with shriveled roots or, perish the thought, soft, flabby skins.

Besides flavor, parsnips have an added virtue for our daily meals: they are literally diet food. An 8-ounce cupful, or half a large cooked parsnip, contains a scant 76 calories. The same amount, however, provides over 50 units of vitamin A plus 541 milligrams of potassium and 16 milligrams of vitamin C, as well as healthy increments of phosphorus and iron.

Preparation

My first precept about cooking parsnips is to choose only those of equal size for your pot. Surprisingly, the best are not easily found at greengrocers', unless one has the time to sift through the pile and match the root ends. I must confess I usually buy mine at a supermarket, choosing the prepackaged, plastic-wrapped variety that are graded as to size. My preference in a parsnip is a short, squat root, which has less core and more flesh.

To prepare parsnips for cooking, merely wash off any residual dirt and peel them. Although many recipe manuals advise cooking parsnips whole before they are peeled, I do not. The vegetable is much easier to handle raw. In most of the recipes that follow, the parsnips are peeled, parboiled, and then cooked or sauced. Steamed parsnips, however, are always left unpeeled, as the skins slip off easily once they cool.

I have discovered that halving (or quartering in the case of super-size roots) will allow the parsnip's central core to cook to the perfect degree of tenderness and save time into the bargain. I never cook a halved parsnip longer than 5 to 8 minutes. A whole parsnip, on the other hand, may take anywhere from 12 to 15 minutes until it is tender.

Really monster parsnips (the kind that have stayed in the ground for almost a year's time) may require removal of the core with a sharp knife after precooking. Large cores will become tender but the texture is always slightly woody. Use your judgment and your tongue—taste it first.

PIKE'S PEAK SOUFFLE

One of the most unusual guises a parsnip has ever taken is indubitably the following dish: a pale ivory soufflé, the title resurrected from a menu found in Colorado's Central City and the dish reconstructed in my small apartment kitchen in New York. On my honor, it will hit your tongue like a steaming blizzard.

3 tablespoons plus 1 teaspoon unsalted
   butter
1 pound medium parsnips, peeled,
   quartered
1 small onion, minced
3 tablespoons all-purpose flour
1 cup milk, boiling
4 egg yolks
¼ teaspoon cayenne pepper
½ teaspoon salt
½ teaspoon ground mace
¼ teaspoon freshly ground black pepper
3 tablespoons dark rum
6 egg whites

1. Preheat the oven to 400°F. Lightly butter a 1½-quart soufflé dish with the 1 teaspoon butter. Set aside.

2. Cook the parsnips in boiling salted water until very tender, about 8 minutes; drain. Remove the cores.

3. Chop the cored parsnips and transfer them to the container of a food processor. Process until smooth. (You should have about 1¼ cups.) Set aside.

4. Melt the remaining 3 tablespoons butter in a large heavy saucepan over medium-low heat. Add the onion and cook, stirring occasionally, until tender, about 5 minutes. Do not allow it to brown. Stir in the flour. Cook, stirring constantly, 2 minutes. Whisk in the milk. Return to boiling; boil 1 minute. Remove from the heat. The mixture will be quite thick.

5. Beat the egg yolks, one at a time, into the soufflé base. Add the cayenne pepper, salt, mace, black pepper, and rum. Stir in the puréed parsnips.

6. In a medium bowl, beat the egg whites until stiff but not dry. Stir one quarter of the egg whites into the parsnip mixture. Fold in the remaining egg whites. Spoon the mixture into the prepared soufflé dish.

7. Place the soufflé in the oven and immediately reduce the heat to 375°F. Bake until puffed and golden, about 30 minutes.

Serves 4 to 6.

PALE FRIED PARSNIPS

To my mind, the classic rendering of a parsnip always takes place in a skillet. One such felicitous fry that I have loved since I was a young kid is a reconstruction of a recipe described in Laura Ingalls Wilder's *Little House on the Prairie*. According to the author, no Christmas dinner was ever official without this dish on hand.

1 pound medium parsnips, peeled, halved
    lengthwise
2 tablespoons unsalted butter
2 tablespoons dark brown sugar
2 tablespoons red wine vinegar
Salt and freshly ground black pepper
Chopped fresh parsley

1. Cook the parsnips in boiling salted water until just tender, about 5 to 8 minutes. Drain. Cut each parsnip lengthwise into ¼-inch-thick slices.

2. Melt the butter in a large skillet over medium heat. Add the parsnips; cook until lightly browned, about 4 minutes. Sprinkle with the brown sugar. Turn the parsnips over; continue to cook until very tender, about 4 minutes longer.

3. Transfer the parsnips to a serving platter. Sprinkle with the vinegar, salt and pepper to taste, and chopped fresh parsley.

Serves 4.

UNPARALLELED PARSNIP CREAM

*P*arsnips have a wonderful fragrance that has endeared them to man's palate for centuries. In no rendering of this vegetable is that elusive scent more manifest than in a soup bowl. Consider inclusion of a whole parsnip in any chicken, beef, or vegetable chowder in your kitchen repertoire. It will add body to each brew.

Or merely try your hand at the following pale creamy eminence. Actually, this recipe is a variation of a classic vichyssoise, unclassically seasoned and spiced to make it seem newly minted. It is the handiwork of a brilliant young chef, Felipe Rojas-Lombardi of The Ballroom restaurant in New York City.

1½ tablespoons unsalted butter
1 large onion, chopped
1 small leek, white part only, washed,
    chopped
1 small green chile pepper (see Guacamole
    headnote, page 37), or canned jalapeño,
    seeded, chopped
½ teaspoon sugar
½ teaspoon minced fresh ginger root
⅛ teaspoon ground turmeric
⅛ teaspoon freshly grated nutmeg
1 pound parsnips, peeled, chopped
1 medium potato, peeled, chopped
3 cups chicken broth (see page 414)
4 cups water
Salt and ground white pepper
⅓ cup sour cream
Chopped fresh parsley

1. Melt the butter in a large saucepan over medium-low heat. Add the on-

*P*arsnip has a very flexible moniker. The original Latin was translated into French as *panais*. Hidebound Italians still call it by a generic tag, *pastinaca*, while the Spanish dub it with an entirely improbable sound, *chirivia*, and a most logical meaning: a "dug-up"! The Germans, who probably brought the parsnip to Rome in the first place, are a tad ambivalent about its sobriquet: they call it *Pastinak, Pastinake,* or *Pastinakwurzel*, depending upon their geography.

ion, leek, chile pepper, sugar, ginger root, turmeric, and nutmeg. Cook, stirring constantly, 5 minutes. Add the parsnips and potato; cook, stirring occasionally, 5 minutes.

2. Add the chicken broth and water to the vegetable mixture. Heat to boiling; reduce the heat. Simmer, uncovered, until the vegetables are tender, about 20 minutes. Add salt and white pepper to taste. Cool.

3. Purée the soup, in batches, in a food processor or blender. To serve the soup hot: reheat over medium-low heat without boiling, and serve with a dab of sour cream in each bowl, sprinkled with parsley. To serve the soup cold: chill well, and just before serving stir in the sour cream, then sprinkle with parsley.

Serves 6 to 8.

PARSNIPS IN MELTING MUSTARD SAUCE

*T*his dish is a purely personal invention. The parsnips are sluiced with mustard, honey, and bourbon. Definitely worth writing home about!

1 pound medium parsnips, peeled, halved lengthwise
3 tablespoons unsalted butter
2 tablespoons Dijon mustard
1 teaspoon honey
3 tablespoons bourbon
Salt and freshly ground black pepper
Chopped fresh parsley

1. Preheat the oven to 375°F. Cook the parsnips in boiling salted water until just tender, about 5 to 8 minutes. Drain. Cut each parsnip lengthwise into ¼-inch-thick slices. Place them in a but-tered shallow baking dish in a single layer. Bake 10 minutes.

2. Melt the butter in a small saucepan over low heat. Slowly add the mustard, honey, and bourbon. Cook 5 minutes. Brush this sauce evenly over the baked parsnips. Sprinkle with salt and pepper to taste. Place the parsnips under a preheated broiler to lightly brown, about 1 minute, before serving sprinkled with parsley.

Serves 4.

PARSNIPS IN GINGERY CREAM

*F*rom the American South, a dish of sautéed parsnips cloaked in a delicately gingered warm sour cream—perfect with fried chicken or ham.

1 pound parsnips, peeled
1 tablespoon unsalted butter
½ cup sour cream

Pinch of ground mace
1 teaspoon roughly chopped candied ginger
Salt and freshly ground black pepper

1. Cook the parsnips in boiling salted water until barely tender, about 10 minutes. Drain. Cut into ¼-inch-thick rounds.

2. Melt the butter in a large skillet over medium heat. Add the parsnips. Sauté until lightly browned, about 4 minutes. Reduce the heat to low.

3. Slowly stir the sour cream into the parsnips. Add the mace and cook until warmed through. Do not allow to boil. Add the candied ginger, and salt and pepper to taste.

Serves 4.

LULLWORTH CROQUETTES

*T*o mix a metaphor totally, parsnips are decidedly not everyone's cup of tea! The French, for instance, will not touch this vegetable with a ten-foot *cuillère*. They may slip one into pot au feu but would never consider the prospect of attacking one with a knife or fork.

The English have better sense. They add parsnips to all manner of stews. On occasion they even stir them into fritters and croquettes as well. *Par example* the next devise, from Devonshire.

1½ pounds parsnips, peeled, quartered
1 teaspoon salt
2 tablespoons dark brown sugar
2 eggs, lightly beaten
1½ teaspoons finely slivered orange peel
¼ teaspoon freshly grated nutmeg
¼ cup all-purpose flour
2 tablespoons unsalted butter

1. Cook the parsnips in boiling salted water until very tender, about 10 minutes. Drain and mash.

2. In a medium-size bowl combine the mashed parsnips with the salt, sugar, eggs, orange peel, and nutmeg. Shape into small patties and roll them in the flour.

3. Melt the butter in a large skillet over medium heat. Sauté the parsnip croquettes until golden on both sides, about 2 minutes per side. Keep warm in a low oven until ready to serve.

Serves 4 to 6.

APPLE 'N' PARSNIP SAUCE

A sensational variation on applesauce. Serve it with roast pork or duckling for a real tastemaker. Or put it out on Thanksgiving in lieu of cranberries.

1 pound medium parsnips, peeled,
  quartered
Salt
1 pound tart green apples (about 3
  medium), peeled, cored, sliced

1 cup apple juice or cider
½ cup packed dark brown sugar
1 tablespoon slivered orange peel
3 tablespoons apple brandy or apple
  schnapps

1. Cook the parsnips in boiling salted water until barely tender, about 5 minutes. Drain. Remove the cores and roughly chop the parsnips.

2. Combine the parsnips, apples, apple juice, and brown sugar in a medium saucepan. Slowly heat to boiling; reduce the heat. Cook, uncovered, over medium heat until the apples and parsnips are soft, about 15 minutes. Remove from the heat.

3. Lightly mash the parsnips and apples in the saucepan. Stir in the slivered orange peel and apple brandy or apple schnapps. Allow to cool.

Makes about 2½ cups.

OLD-FASHIONED PARSNIP MARMALADE

*T*his recipe has its heritage in the Midwest. Its period: the early nineteenth century, when winters were hard, fruit was scarce, and farmers' children were sweet-toothed.

1 pound parsnips, peeled, grated (about
*   3½ cups)*
Finely slivered peel of 1 lemon
Juice of 1 lemon
Finely slivered peel of 3 small oranges
Pulp and juice of 3 small oranges
2 cups sugar
Pinch of ground cinnamon
¼ cup orange liqueur

Combine all the ingredients except the liqueur in a medium saucepan. Slowly heat to boiling, then reduce the heat. Simmer, uncovered, stirring occasionally, 25 minutes. Stir in the orange liqueur and cook 5 minutes longer. Pour into sterilized jars and seal. Process in a hot water bath for 12 minutes.

Makes 3 cups.

CARAMEL CHICKEN WITH PARSNIPS

*H*ave the following dish of glistening golden chicken sautéed with parsnips. It is the closest thing I know to sublimity at the dinner table.

1 teaspoon ground cinnamon
1 teaspoon salt
¼ teaspoon freshly ground black pepper
1 large chicken (about 3½ to 4 pounds),
*   cut into 10 pieces*
2 tablespoons unsalted butter
1 tablespoon vegetable oil

1 pound medium parsnips, peeled, halved
*   lengthwise*
¼ cup sugar
¼ cup water
2 tablespoons tarragon wine vinegar
2 tablespoons chopped fresh parsley

1. Preheat the oven to 325°F. Combine the cinnamon, salt and pepper in a small bowl. Rub the mixture into the chicken pieces.

2. Heat the butter with the oil in a large skillet over medium heat. Sauté the chicken pieces until golden brown on both sides, about 15 minutes. Transfer the chicken to a shallow baking dish, reserving the drippings in the skillet. Place the chicken in the oven.

3. Cook the parsnips in boiling salted water for 5 minutes. Drain, and cut them lengthwise into ¼-inch-thick slices. Cut each slice into pieces about 3 inches long and 1 inch wide.

4. Heat 3 tablespoons of the reserved drippings in the skillet used for sautéing the chicken. Add the parsnips; cook over medium-low heat until tender, 12 to 15 minutes. Place the parsnips around the chicken and return to the oven.

5. Lightly wipe out the skillet and add the sugar. Heat, stirring constantly, over medium heat until the sugar melts and begins to caramelize. Carefully stir in the water and vinegar. Stir until smooth. Spoon this sauce over the chicken and parsnips and bake 10 minutes longer. Serve sprinkled with parsley. Serves 4.

PURITAN PIE

A parsnip conceit that marries the old-fashioned American marmalade and a wondrous, strictly Viennese linzer torte. The issue should probably be dubbed a *Pastinakwurzel* torte, but I prefer to think of it as . . . Puritan Pie. I am no purist but since I use the processor to make almond paste for this recipe, I advise its use for the other steps as well.

For the Pastry:

6¾ ounces blanched almonds
1½ cups all-purpose flour
¾ cup sugar
Finely grated peel of 2 lemons
¼ teaspoon ground cinnamon
½ teaspoon ground allspice
8 tablespoons (1 stick) unsalted butter, cut into bits
3 egg yolks
2 teaspoons water, approximately

For the Almond Paste:

5 ounces blanched almonds
½ cup sugar
1 egg, lightly beaten

For the Final Assembly:

1¾ cups Old-Fashioned Parsnip
    Marmalade (see preceding recipe)

1 egg yolk
2 teaspoons water

1. To make the pastry: Place the almonds in the container of a food processor fitted with a steel blade. Process until finely ground. Add the flour, sugar, lemon peel, cinnamon, and allspice. Process briefly. Add the butter and process until well mixed. Add the egg yolks and water. Process until a soft dough is formed, adding more water if needed. Scoop out the dough onto a lightly floured board. Knead briefly.

2. Remove slightly more than half the dough. Place the smaller half, wrapped, in the freezer. Line a 10-inch loose-bottom tart pan with the remaining dough, pressing the dough over the sides and bottom with your fingers.

3. Preheat the oven to 375°F. Wipe out the processor container; put back the steel blade. To make the almond paste: combine the almonds and sugar in the container of the processor. Process until finely ground. Add the beaten egg, and process until a smooth paste is formed. Carefully spread the paste over the bottom of the prepared tart pan.

4. Spoon the Old-Fashioned Parsnip Marmalade over the almond paste in the shell.

5. Remove the chilled dough from the freezer. Roll it out between layers of waxed paper until thin. Remove the top layer of waxed paper. With scissors, cut the dough into strips about 1 inch wide, cutting right through the bottom paper with the scissors. Pick up the strips, one at a time, and flip them over onto the top of the tart to form a lattice pattern. Carefully pull off the waxed paper. Press the edges into the shell.

6. Combine the egg yolk with the water in a small bowl. Brush this over the pastry. Bake 10 minutes. Reduce the heat to 350°F and bake 20 minutes longer. Cool on a wire rack. Remove the outside ring from the pan before the pie has completely cooled.

Serves 8 to 10.

PEAS

From Marble Size to Petits Pois

My older sister, Myra, brought culture into my life after my parents gave up trying. A worldly type even as an adolescent, she permitted me to join her (whether as acolyte or accomplice I am not certain) in the sophisticated pursuit of grace and style. Most of our education was acquired from the movies we attended three or four times a week; our role models were the movie stars, whose elegant manners and modish dress we attempted to emulate whenever our parents were out of earshot.

When I was still very young, we would play elaborate games of "let's pretend," sometimes imagining that the airy upstairs bedroom we shared was the cabin of a luxury zeppelin gliding across the Atlantic or the suite of a chic European hotel, where breakfast served on trays (prepared earlier by my sister) would be consumed sybaritically in bed on Sunday mornings.

Myra also kept a collection of scrapbooks stocked with pictures of elegant homes and all manner of tony furnishings, which she clipped from a pile of magazines on my mother's subscription list. With shears in hand, Myra would study a color photo thoughtfully before she decided whether or not to paste it into her "Dream House" book. Her favored color scheme in those days was "old rose and pearl gray," so any advertisement of a household object (be it limousine or lingerie case) in either shade would instantly be removed to her bulging file. When I asked her once why she collected such a multitude, her answer was vague, if optimistic.

"One never knows when Dame Fortune will smile," said Myra. "I may need lots and lots of options."

As the Depression grew ever more pronounced in our lives, she banished the mundane present with prospects of a rosier future. She knew that one day we would both be dining on lamb chops in frilled white paper millinery and *petits pois* along with our vintage champagne.

My sister's sole food fixation was tiny green peas—the littler the better. Even during the depths of the Depression, whenever she assisted my mother on shopping expeditions, a can always ended up in the family grocery bag, usually bearing the legend *Product of France*.

For my own part I was never particularly impressed with these underdeveloped legumes. They were too soft and olive drab to satisfy either my tongue or my eye. But Myra doted on them. And *petits pois* (as she always referred to them) inevitably became a part of all celebratory meals. I recall her favorite birthday dish well. It was creamed chicken studded with those tiny greenish seed pearls, served up in brittle and unfailingly soggy-bottomed patty shells.

Myra considered that meal to be the height of prandial elegance, and once spent the better part of a Saturday morning showing me how to consume the contents of a patty shell without causing a hailstorm of pastry at a table setting. It was a valuable lesson, like all of my sister's cultural bequests.

I haven't tasted creamed chicken and peas (with or without patty shells) in years, but if my sister made the request I would gratefully whip up a batch tomorrow.

Vegetable Roots

A truly wild pea is almost impossible to find these days, although *Pisum sativum* has been part of man's diet since the Bronze Age, when sticks and stones were his only tablerie. Traces of early peas have in fact been carbon-dated in the prehistoric lake dwellings at Herzogenbuchsee, Switzerland: roughly 9,750 years before the birth of Christ. A record for any vegetable that is still consumed with a measure of relish!

The peas favored by cavemen, however, were far from the kind that migratory birds (or even Birdseye) would opt for today. The earliest peas were as large as marbles and probably as tasty. Archeologists believe they were always roasted and peeled (like chestnuts) before they were deemed fit for a tribe's digestion. Uncultivated peas grew in bogs and rambled rather than climbed, which made picking them a considerable chore for the lady of the cave. But they must have been worth the trouble because in time they were planted and tended as crops.

From Switzerland to India is decidedly no short hop, but pea seeds migrated there and flowered in the cool climate of Himachal Pradesh. However,

In 1602 the Mayflower Colony log book records that peas planted by Captain Bartholomew Gosnold bloomed and bore fruit on the island of Cuttyhunk. Soon peas flourished and were tossed into skillets with every other ingredient that was harvested on the island: beans, barley, sweet potatoes, and corn.

the cultivated peas that were eaten in India and later in Greece and Rome were inevitably dried and involved lengthy cooking.

For centuries a tender pea, straight from its green pod, was regarded to be a near-lethal pellet and was dried to cure it of its "noxious and stomach-destroying canker." Farmers in Rome often left green peas on the vine in their fields to kill foraging rabbits, who, having better sense than the agrarians, flourished instead.

The standard dish of dried peas that Apicius describes as a household staple was cooked for hours until it became a thick gruel, then splashed with a mite of oil and vinegar and eaten for breakfast. If it brings to mind *pease porridge* rumored to stay in the pot until nine days old, it is no coincidence. That recipe stuck to the ribs of western Europe in one form or another for over 500 years.

It took a Frenchman, of course, a gardener named Michaux, to convince the world that green peas were not only edible but, more pertinently, delectable. In the sixteenth century he developed a hybrid pod that climbed on trellises and grew sweeter and tenderer with each foot of elevation. These legumes, at first known as *miches* (small lumps) in honor of their grower, eventually received a more generic tag, *vert pois* (green or garden peas), and became the rage of

France. In one of her letters, dated 1696, Madame de Maintenon warmed to the subject of the pea at the court of Louis XIV: "The impatience to eat them, the pleasure of having eaten them, the joy of eating them again, are the three questions that have occupied our princes for the last four days!"

A sharp observer of the pea's effect on court life, she also wrote: "There are ladies here, who having supped with the King and supped well, retire to the privacy of their chambers; there to feast in secret on dishes of petits pois." She concluded, *"C'est une mode et une fureur!"* (This is both a fashion and a madness!) Pea-preoccupation to say the least, and it never abated until the French Revolution, when the vegetable entered the diet of the proletariat with no less partiality.

What to Look For

As a pea fancier, I am highly prejudiced on the subject of what is offered for sale these days. The most tender—and that implies a desirable jot of moisture under the skin—must be grown in a backyard or window box, I regret to say. The varieties I opt for in seed catalogues (in order of preference) are "Laxton's Progress," "Little Marvels," and "Dwarf Telephones," with "Mammoth Melting Sugars" the runner-up.

Shopping for a passel of peas at the greengrocer's or on a supermarket shelf, I pick whatever seems perkiest. One should try to buy pods that will snap rather than bend under slight pressure from the thumb; likewise those with the brightest color. One can tell the old-timers: they are usually frayed at the edges or bedraggled-looking.

Like most vegetables, raw peas are somewhat higher in nutrients than cooked. Three quarters of a cup of blanched shelled peas represents about 84 calories with an extremely high ratio of amino acids and minerals; notably 316 milligrams of potassium, 27 units of vitamin C, and a whopping 640 units of vitamin A. So eat them with surety. They are making you healthy and satisfied at one and the same time.

Preparation

Unlike my sister, Myra, I judge a pea to be prime *only* when it is served up near-raw. My grandmother, who never ate between meals, was so addicted to the flavor of fresh-from-the-pod peas that she could never shell a handful without popping at least one out of every four into her mouth "for energy!"

Peas, like corn, are rich in natural sugar which turns to starch within hours after picking, so wise gardeners usually cook them minutes after they are harvested. Without the lucky option of a pea patch at your back door, try blanching them first and reheating them later. My technique is to drop the peas into boiling salted water for a scant minute— less if they are particularly small. Without waiting for the water to return to the boil, I immediately plunge them under cold running water. Once cool, I drain and store them for later use. To my mind, steaming peas is slightly dispiriting since the color fades appreciably. If you admire a bright-eyed pea as much as I do, pass on that cooking technique.

I must admit in all candor, however, that when peas are either over the hill or overpriced, I make do with the commercially frozen kind. I look for the variety that are labeled "Baby Peas," but never boil them first as the directions on the package suggest. Instead I merely defrost and use them thawed in the same manner I would a batch of blanched—with no appreciable loss of taste though the texture is a far cry from fresh.

GREEN AND GOLD CREAM OF PEA SOUP TOKLAS

Although Alice Toklas spent much of her life cooking on French soil, this dish is characteristically American in style, as the peas in it are neither puréed nor mashed but allowed to float gently on its surface like polka dots.

One caveat: This soup most definitely depends upon a good strong chicken stock for its base. Canned broth will produce an anemic approximation of its goodness.

1 tablespoon unsalted butter, plus 4
    tablespoons (½ stick), cut into bits
1 tablespoon olive oil
½ cup ¼-inch bread cubes
3 cups Chicken Stock (see page 410)
1 small onion, peeled
1 small clove garlic, peeled
1 sprig parsley
1 pound fresh peas, shelled (about 1 cup),
    blanched 1 minute, or ½ (10-ounce)
    package frozen peas, thawed

1 extra large egg yolk
3 tablespoons heavy or whipping cream

1. Heat the 1 tablespoon butter with the oil in a medium skillet over medium-high heat. Add the bread cubes; sauté until golden, about 4 minutes. These are now croutons. Drain on paper towels; reserve.

2. Heat the stock to boiling in a medium saucepan. Tie the onion, garlic, and parsley in a cheesecloth bag. Add this to the stock; reduce the heat. Simmer, uncovered, over medium-low heat 15 minutes. Add the peas; cook 2 minutes longer. Remove the soup from the heat and discard the cheesecloth bag.

3. Dot the surface of the soup with the butter bits. Allow the butter to melt over the surface of the soup without stirring.

4. Beat the egg yolk with the cream in a serving bowl or tureen. Pour the soup over the yolk-cream mixture. Serve immediately with croutons.

Serves 4.

Newly Minted Peas

*T*his is a cold salad devised of fresh peas and fresh mint in a creamy golden dressing. I first made it years ago at The Store in Amagansett, but it always tastes newly minted.

½ cup Mayonnaise (see page 408)
¼ cup sour cream
1 small onion, minced
¼ cup coarsely chopped fresh mint
¼ teaspoon Dijon mustard
3 pounds fresh peas, shelled, blanched
*   1 minute*
Salt and freshly ground black pepper
Pimiento strips

Combine the mayonnaise with the sour cream in a medium bowl. Add the onion, mint, and mustard. Stir in the peas, and season with salt and pepper to taste. Transfer to a serving dish and garnish with pimiento strips. Serve chilled.

Serves 4 to 6.

Peas and Knepp

*T*he German word for pea is *Erbse*, which according to some keen etymologist friends is a corruption of an earlier Saxon noun, *erbe*, which means an inheritance. The pea is a bequest wherever it is found in my book, but in the following instance it makes a particularly felicitous gift. In this formula, highly prized by the Pennsylvania Dutch, short golden swirls of dough poach as the bright green peas cook.

4 tablespoons (½ stick) unsalted butter
6 tablespoons all-purpose flour
¼ teaspoon salt
Pinch of cayenne pepper
⅛ teaspoon freshly grated nutmeg
½ teaspoon chopped chives

¼ cup water
½ cup chicken broth (see page 414)
2 pounds fresh peas, shelled (about 2 cups),
*   blanched 1 minute, or 1 package (10*
*   ounces) frozen peas, thawed*

1. Combine 2 tablespoons of the butter with the flour in a small bowl. Mix well. With a wooden spoon, work in the salt, cayenne pepper, nutmeg, chives, and water. Beat until thick and smooth. Set aside.

2. Heat the remaining 2 tablespoons butter with the chicken broth in a medium skillet. When it starts to boil, add the peas; cook 1 minute. Reduce the heat.

3. Add the dumpling mixture (knepp) by teaspoonfuls. Cook, covered, over medium-low heat, until the knepp are firm, about 6 minutes.

Serves 4.

SAUTEED PEAS WITH WALNUTS

While peas did not cause the French Revolution (pearls did), they most certainly brought an end to the reign of King John of England. He, poor addictive soul, was reputedly so affixed on the flavor of these green goods that he died from an attack of overindulgence at dinner—after consuming seven bowls of peas!

You be more circumspect with the following pea sauté livened by the addition of toasted walnuts and honey.

1 tablespoon unsalted butter
1 large shallot, minced
¼ cup Chicken Stock (see page 410)
2 teaspoons honey
2 pounds fresh peas, shelled (about 2 cups),
    blanched 1 minute, or 1 package (10
    ounces) frozen peas, thawed
⅛ to ¼ teaspoon hot pepper sauce
    (depending on taste)
Salt and freshly ground black pepper
½ cup roughly chopped walnuts, toasted in
    a 400°F oven for 5 to 8 minutes

Melt the butter in a large skillet over medium-low heat. Add the shallot; cook 3 minutes. Add the chicken stock and honey. Raise the heat to medium-high; stir in the peas. Cook, stirring constantly, until the liquid has evaporated and the peas are tender, about 3 minutes. Add hot pepper sauce, salt, and pepper to taste. Stir in the walnuts.

Serves 4.

WILTED PEAS AND LETTUCE

For the classic alignment of peas and lettuce, which the French have made into a national side dish, I choose a purely American version. Its kitchen architect was no less than the estimable Thomas Jefferson. This devise is from his daughter Martha's kitchen notebook and is not much altered from the original, written in a mercurial downhill scrawl, now in the Jefferson collection at the University of Virginia.

1½ cups Chicken Stock (see page 410)
1¼ pounds fresh young peas, shelled
1 cup heavy or whipping cream
1 cup torn lettuce (bibb, Boston, or
     romaine)
2 tablespoons finely chopped chives or
     scallion tops
Salt and freshly ground black pepper

1. Heat the chicken stock to boiling in a medium saucepan. Add the peas, cook 1 minute, and drain. (Reserve the stock to use at another time.)

2. Heat the cream to boiling in a medium skillet; reduce the heat. Simmer until the cream has reduced to half, about 12 minutes. Stir in the peas and lettuce. Toss until the lettuce is just wilted, about 3 minutes. Add the chives and the salt and pepper to taste.

Serves 4.

GREEN AND GOLD SPOONBREAD

A rendering of the pea in its greenest and most original form: as spoonbread. This is a culinary invention for which I can take no credit, for it is solely the bright work of my collaborator, co-worker, and closest friend, Phillip Stephen Schulz. Phillip's fine hand is in evidence on every page of this book, but this is one of his finest gifts.

2 pounds fresh peas, shelled (about 2 cups),
     blanched 1 minute, or 1 package (10
     ounces) frozen peas, thawed
¼ cup heavy or whipping cream
2 cups light cream or half-and-half
4 tablespoons (½ stick) unsalted butter
1 tablespoon honey
1 cup white cornmeal
4 eggs, separated
1 teaspoon baking powder
⅛ teaspoon hot pepper sauce
Salt and freshly ground black pepper

1. Preheat the oven to 375°F. Place the peas in the container of a food processor and add the heavy cream. Process, using the on/off switch, until finely chopped but not mushy. Set aside.

2. Combine the light cream, butter, and honey in a medium saucepan. Cook over low heat, without boiling, until the butter melts. Stir in the cornmeal. Continue to cook, stirring constantly and without boiling, until thick, about 4 minutes. Transfer to a large bowl.

3. Beat the egg yolks, one at a time, into the cornmeal mixture. Beat in the processed peas, baking powder, hot pepper sauce, and salt and pepper to taste.

4. Beat the egg whites until stiff but not dry, and fold them into the spoonbread mixture. Pour into a buttered 2-quart soufflé dish. Bake until puffed and golden, about 35 minutes.

Serves 6 to 8.

A pea crop set down by the colonists of Jamestown, Virginia, was so abundant that Captain John Smith wrote in his diaries in 1614: "Pease dry everywhere for nxt winter's fodder but stille the green seedkins are so bounteous we eat of them at evry meale in some forme or t'other. Namely on porridges, in pigeon pots and over puddings too!"

MUSTARDY PEAS WITH HAM

*P*eas aligned with snippets of frizzled ham.

2 tablespoons unsalted butter
1 small onion, finely chopped
½ cup chopped cooked ham
¼ cup dry white wine
1 teaspoon Dijon mustard
¼ cup chicken broth (see page 414)
2 pounds fresh peas, shelled (about 2 cups),
     blanched 1 minute, or 1 package (10
     ounces) frozen peas, thawed
1 teaspoon finely slivered orange peel
Salt and freshly ground black pepper

1. Melt the butter in a large skillet over medium-low heat. Add the onion; cook 1 minute. Stir in the ham; raise the heat slightly. Cook until the ham is lightly browned, about 2 minutes. Add the wine and cook over medium heat, stirring constantly, until the liquid is syrupy, about 5 minutes.

2. Stir the mustard into the ham mixture. Add the broth and peas. Cook, stirring constantly, until the liquid has evaporated and the peas are tender, about 3 minutes. Add the orange peel and salt and pepper to taste.

Serves 4.

CLOAKED CHICKEN AND PEAS IN CREAM

A Virginia recipe, this aromatic casserole pairs homegrown peas with fowl in a minty cream gravy—tasty enough to cause even my sister to forswear any other version of creamed chicken. Though, I never asked her up till now.

¼ cup all-purpose flour
½ teaspoon salt
¼ teaspoon freshly ground black pepper
1 chicken, cut into serving pieces
3 tablespoons unsalted butter
1 tablespoon vegetable oil
¼ cup chicken broth (see page 414)
2 pounds fresh peas, shelled (about 2 cups),
     blanched 1 minute, or 1 package (10
     ounces) frozen peas, thawed
½ cup heavy or whipping cream
1 egg yolk
¼ teaspoon ground white pepper
Pinch of cayenne pepper

2 tablespoons chopped fresh mint
Salt
1 tablespoon cognac
Chopped fresh parsley

1. Preheat the oven to 325°F. Combine the flour, salt, and pepper in a paper bag. Add the chicken pieces; shake well to coat with the flour.

2. Heat the butter with the oil in a large heavy skillet over medium heat. Sauté the chicken pieces until golden brown on all sides, about 12 minutes. Transfer the chicken to a shallow baking dish. Bake 30 minutes.

3. Remove all but 1 tablespoon fat from the skillet. Add the chicken broth; heat to boiling. Stir in the peas; cook 2 minutes. Remove from the heat.

4. Combine the cream with the egg yolk in a small bowl. Slowly stir this into the peas. Place over low heat; cook until slightly thickened, about 5 minutes. Do not allow to boil. Add the white pepper, cayenne pepper, mint, and salt to taste. Stir in the cognac. Pour this sauce over the chicken; sprinkle with parsley.

Serves 4.

FETTUCCINE CON FETTI

Keep a store of Pea-Green Pasta in the freezer, and with only some pink smoked ham bits, purple shallots, and red pepper flakes in a blanket of cream, you will have an incredibly festive party dish. Best of all, it takes less than fifteen minutes to prepare. I timed it!

5 tablespoons unsalted butter
2 shallots, minced
¾ cup finely chopped smoked ham
1 cup heavy or whipping cream
¼ teaspoon hot pepper sauce
1 teaspoon lemon juice
Salt and freshly ground black pepper
1 pound homemade Pea-Green Pasta
    (recipe follows), cut into fettuccine
    noodles
Freshly grated Parmesan cheese

1. Melt 2 tablespoons of the butter in a medium saucepan over medium heat. Add the shallots; cook 1 minute. Stir in the ham; cook 3 minutes longer. Add the cream, hot pepper sauce, and lemon juice. Heat to boiling; reduce the heat. Simmer until slightly thickened, about 5 minutes. Add salt and pepper to taste.

2. Meanwhile, cook the pasta in boiling salted water until just tender, about 2 minutes, longer if frozen. Drain, and wipe out the pot the pasta was cooked in. Add the remaining 3 tablespoons butter and place over low heat. Return the pasta to the pot. Toss well.

Pour the ham-cream mixture over the pasta. Toss lightly and serve with Parmesan cheese.

Serves 4 to 6.

Pea-Green Pasta

A light green pea-dappled pasta also devised by *confrère* Schulz.

½ cup shelled peas (about ½ pound fresh
    unshelled peas)
¼ cup water (for processing peas)
2 cups all-purpose flour, approximately
1 egg, lightly beaten
1 tablespoon vegetable oil

1. Cook the peas in boiling salted water until very tender—about 5 minutes for frozen peas, longer for fresh. Drain.

2. Place the peas in the container of a blender or processor. Add ¼ cup water. Blend until smooth. (You will end up with tiny flecks of peas, but don't worry about that. If you use a processor, keep

scraping down the sides until the mixture is fairly smooth.)

3. Place the flour in a large bowl. Make a well in the center. Add the beaten egg, the oil, and the puréed pea mixture. Using a fork or your fingers, incorporate the mixture into the flour until a fairly stiff dough is formed. Scoop the mixture out onto a lightly floured board. Knead, keeping the board lightly floured, for 10 minutes. Allow the dough to rest, covered, 30 minutes.

4. Roll the pasta dough out by hand or by machine until 1/16 inch thick. Cut into desired shape.

Makes about 1 pound.

Note: Because of the fresh vegetable ingredient, it is not a good idea to dry the pasta. It can be frozen successfully, however.

FETTUCCINE DUE VERDI

A toss of pea pasta with smoked salmon, vodka, butter, and more peas of course. This dish may be whipped up in a mere ten minutes!

4 tablespoons (½ stick) unsalted butter
2 whole scallions, bulbs and green tops, minced
½ pound smoked salmon, cut into strips
⅓ cup vodka
½ pound fresh peas, shelled (about ½ cup), blanched 1 minute, or 1 package (10 ounces) frozen peas, thawed
Salt and freshly ground black pepper
1 pound Pea-Green Pasta (see page 271), cut into fettuccine noodles
Chopped fresh parsley

1. Melt 2 tablespoons of the butter in a large skillet over medium-low heat. Add the scallions and salmon. Cook, tossing gently, 4 minutes. Add the vodka and peas; cook 2 minutes. Add salt and pepper to taste.

2. Meanwhile, cook the pasta in boiling salted water until just tender, about 2 minutes, longer if frozen. Drain, and toss with the remaining 2 tablespoons butter. Combine the pasta with the salmon-pea mixture and sprinkle with parsley.

Serves 4 to 6.

GREEN PEA PASTA SOUFFLE

The final pea creation is my own bright idea, presented with a deep bow to two ladies I am extremely fond of, Jo Bettoja and Anna Maria Cornetto. Jo is an American from Georgia; Anna Maria stems from Rome. Together they run a remarkable school for cooks near the Fontana di Trevi, called *Lo Scaldavivande*, which means "the covered dish." They had the original notion of a pasta soufflé. With a little luck, Greene turned it upside down and coincidentally green.

5 tablespoons unsalted butter

1 cup plus 3 tablespoons freshly grated
　　Parmesan cheese

1 clove garlic, minced

2 tablespoons all-purpose flour

1⅓ cups milk, boiling

4 egg yolks

¼ pound fresh fettuccine noodles (Pea-
　　Green Pasta, page 271, may be used)

1 cup plus 3 tablespoons grated Jarlsberg
　　or Gruyère cheese

½ cup finely chopped cooked ham

2 teaspoons chopped fresh basil, or ½
　　teaspoon dried

1 pound fresh peas, shelled (about 1 cup),
　　blanched 1 minute, or half a 10-ounce
　　package frozen peas, thawed

6 egg whites

1. Preheat the oven to 400°F. Rub a 1½-quart soufflé dish with 1 tablespoon of the butter; sprinkle it with 3 tablespoons of the Parmesan cheese. Set aside in a cool place.

2. Melt the remaining 4 tablespoons butter in a medium saucepan over medium-low heat. Add the garlic; cook 1 minute. Stir in the flour. Cook, stirring constantly, 2 minutes. Whisk in the milk. Heat to boiling; boil until thick and smooth, about 1 minute. Remove from the heat. Beat in the egg yolks, one at a time. Set aside.

3. Cook the fettuccine noodles in boiling salted water for 2 minutes, longer if frozen. Rinse under cold running wa-

Though cultivated in India, non-dried peas were first eaten by the early Chinese who called them dō or dōū, depending upon the season of their flowering.

That is a far cry (phonetically) from the Latin *pisum* or the Anglo-Saxon *pisu*, which eventually became *pois* in French and *pease* in English. The abbreviation took place (or so it is reported) on our native shores. Two were *pease* but one was a pea.

Pea translations are a mite abstract. The Spanish *guisante* means health-making. *Pisello* ("pea" in Italy), on the other hand, means "little tiny seed."

ter; drain. Add the noodles to the soufflé base. Stir in the remaining 1 cup Parmesan cheese, the Jarlsberg cheese, ham, basil, and peas. Mix well.

4. Beat the egg whites until stiff but not dry. Stir one fourth of the egg whites into the soufflé mixture. Fold in the remaining whites. Pour into the prepared soufflé dish, place it in the oven, and immediately reduce the heat to 375°F. Bake until puffed and golden, about 45 minutes.

Serves 6.

PEPPERS

Another of Columbus' Discoveries

In December of the year I turned sixteen (and was already well over six feet in height), my father secured temporary employment for me for the holidays. Through one of his cronies at the Democratic Club, I was offered a job at the post office for the princely sum of two and half dollars an hour: incredible pay for an unskilled worker when average salaries were less than thirty-five a week.

It was, needless to say, not an opportunity to be dismissed lightly. Still, I was reluctant.

"What will I have to do?" I asked my father charily.

"Clerking. Sorting mail. Selling stamps . . . whatever they ask you to do!"

"Not carrying the mail, Sam!" my mother interjected, her voice rising tremulously.

"Of course not," my father replied. "I told them he's just a kid!"

Next morning, in the freezing cold and when it was still dark outside, I reported to the post office to begin my tenure. At the cavernous entry I was inspected briefly by a white-haired deputy, given a badge, and handed a bulging leather bag.

"I thought I was supposed to have an inside job," I protested weakly.

"That's work for women and cripples only," said the veteran with a curl of his lip. "You're a big, strapping fella. You can handle it!"

My father's injunction as I left home still rang in my ears. "Don't give 'em any guff," he had said. "There's fifty other guys waitin' for the job."

So I agreed to carry the mail.

In those dim days, there were no carts to share the heavy burden of Christmas packages and endless brightly colored envelopes. Instead the load was slung across your shoulder like an ammunition belt.

In the unheated mail truck that took me and the other raw recruits to our assigned territories, we were advised of our rights and responsibilities as government employees, albeit temporary ones.

"No smoking on the job. No loafing. No secret meetings with friends. And what is more, no coffee break or lunch until the bag is completely empty."

Along with our back-breaking freight, we were supplied huge sets of master keys on rings, maybe a hundred icy metal stipes that clanged at the hip as one walked to announce an arrival more overwrought than Marley's ghost.

As we temporary mail carriers started on our appointed rounds, another young red-faced "temp" examined my key ring.

"Jeez." He whistled. "So they gave you *the stuffed peppers!*"

"Stuffed peppers?" I brightened instantly. It was barely eight o'clock in the morning but my stomach was rumbling.

"That's what they call the big housing development in Woodside. There are three and four tenants in every apartment, so you have to read the names on each box carefully or else you mix up the mail. It's a helluva place, dark in the halls and stray dogs in the courtyard."

I was slightly afraid of dogs. But hungry enough to pursue this subject further. "Do a lot of people *make* stuffed peppers there?" I asked him, innocently.

"A lot of people *are* the stuffed peppers."

I did not arrive at the housing project until almost noon. With chapped hands and frost-bitten ears I had pounded the pavements of Queens, squeezing large envelopes into narrow slots and pressing down packages in order to slip them under doorways. Still my leather bag bulged ominously. I had to go to the bathroom, but was so imtimidated by my role as a surrogate member of the postal system, I did not dare. My bladder was held tight by sheer willpower by the time I reached the large, looming brick edifices. As predicted, the hallways were dim and the names on the mailboxes barely discernible. Instead of the warm homey aroma of braised meat nestling in peppers, the vestibules smelled of insecticide and cat urine. Worse yet, every building in this vast complex had its own set of keys that needed to be extricated from the big ring I carried, and the boxes unlocked before the mail could be sorted.

I had completed a scant third of the delivery when from behind me a huge vulpine creature appeared. It was the largest dog I had ever seen, with a black tongue and reddish eyes that betrayed it was part Chow. Its remaining pedigree was anyone's guess, but it was not a friendly canine. Instantly it lunged for my pants leg, snarling and shaking its head.

"Good boy. Down!" I quaked as it came closer, all the while stuffing letters into the open mailboxes wholesale, with no regard for matching up correct names or addresses. The dog was openly snapping by this time and I tossed letters into slots like confetti.

As soon as I left that building, I found a corner mailbox and shamelessly emptied the contents of my bag into it.

Then I went home, never to return to the P.O.

One good thing came out of this misadventure. I got the flu and my father never berated me for defection in the line of duty. After I recovered, I looked up a recipe for stuffed peppers and learned to make them—very, very well. But see for yourself.

Vegetable Roots

It may give a diner pause, as he is about to swallow a mouthful of green pepper, stuffed or otherwise, to learn that this aromatic vegetable was discovered in America by Columbus.

Some deep-dyed pepper lovers, who are to be sure a tad prejudiced in their behalf, adjudge the former act on a par with his more celebrated uncovering. For the *Capsicum frustescens* is a flavoring few kitchen practitioners can do without.

To set the pepper story straight, the captain of the *Santa Maria*, *Nina*, and *Pinta* observed sweet green and red peppers growing on the vine almost immediately after his convoy landed in the West Indies in 1492. Since his commission from the queen of Spain had been to find a more efficacious route to the Indies in order to corner the spice market, Columbus knew he was on to something big.

What his eye noticed his nose and tongue confirmed. Once Columbus had sampled cooked peppers in dishes that the local Indians hospitably offered his crew, he had the hold of one entire ship stocked with this produce for a return voyage to Spain. Though he had actually been seeking the berries of *Piper nigrum*, the spicy seasoning we crush in our pepper grinders, Columbus, with his fine Italian palate, knew Europeans would flip over his tangy cargo. And they did.

Peppers made Columbus a hero. The vegetable was instantly named "Spanish Pepper" and reports of its culinary wonders spread all over the continent—even to England. In 1493 a British courier to the king wrote that Columbus had brought back to Isabella "a pepper more pungent than any fruit from the Caucasus." Pepper plants were at once cultivated in royal Spanish gardens and a brisk trade in the vegetable was shortly in operation. More important (to me at least), the green and red bell pepper entered the world's cooking pots!

What to Look For

All vegetable peppers, sweet and hot alike, are members of the *Capsicum* family tree. The sweets are often referred to as "bells" by virtue of their shape. The hots are known as chile peppers or *chiles* and grow in a multitude of sizes and shapes, from long and skinny to conical and round, with varying degrees of heat. Red bell peppers are no hotter than greens, merely riper.

What makes a chile pepper hot is the amount of sheer warmth (known as capsaicin) lodged within its innocent-looking seeds and pale interior spines. Remove both with a sharp knife and you considerably defuse a hot pepper's pungency. But I am not speaking of peppers as seasoners here, only as vegetables; and they are uniformly mild.

Bell peppers turn a tad sweeter as they redden. They also require more care on the vine, so consumers inevitably pay an increment for ripeness. However, many deep green bells, jade Cubanelles, light yellow-green Italians, and even bright yellow banana varieties have exactly the right degree of "bite" to give a dish its desired stimulating flavor.

When pepper shopping, scout for firm globes that are bright in color. Anemic-shaded skin indicates that a bell tolled too early for this pepper; it was picked before it had a chance to ripen and develop flavor.

Dehydrated peppers are the wallflowers of the patch: they were picked after their prime. You can usually tell a less than juicy pepper by its feel; lacking water content, they are less weighty than they appear.

Peppers store well in the refrigerator. I keep mine a week or longer in a ventilated plastic bag, away from excessive moisture. However, red (riper) peppers will not have the same degree of shelf-life. Use them sooner.

Pepper is a healthy indulgence for your diet. One large bell pepper (either green or red) tallies less than 22 calories. Better yet, this glistening harbinger of good living is high in amino acids with a relatively good jot of minerals as well. Each average globe contains 213 milligrams of potassium and is rich in vitamin A (420 units) and vitamin C (120 units).

Preparation

*T*here are no hard and fast rules on pepper cookery. They are delicious raw, fried, roasted, or blanched first and then sautéed or braised, depending upon the recipe at hand. Charring a raw pepper over a gas flame (or close up to a broiler unit) until the skin blisters and blackens gives a peeled pepper still another totally different taste and texture. Positive pepper-lovers will try each method with (forgive the pun) relish!

BURRO ROSSO

*O*ne of my best friends, in or out of a kitchen, is Cornelius O'Donnell. Neal is a slightly cherubic charmer, whose form and face you are bound to recognize from his cookbook, billed simply as *Cooking with Cornelius*. I for one have cooked with this man—and he's unbeatable. More pertinently, Neal is one of the most generous and good-natured cooking teachers in the business. His bequest to this collection is called *Burro Rosso* (Red Butter). It is a sauce he teaches his students to splash over curly pasta or use as a basting sauce for roast chicken or pork. Coming from Neal, it is pure and wonderful. Coming from Bert, it is less pure (I added a red pepper for extra bite) but just as wonderful. Even Cornelius agrees.

1 small red bell pepper
2 cloves garlic
¼ cup heavy or whipping cream
8 tablespoons (1 stick) unsalted butter
2 tablespoons tomato paste
½ teaspoon chopped fresh sage, or
  ¼ teaspoon dried, crumbled

1 teaspoon ground paprika (preferably
  Hungarian)
Salt
⅓ cup freshly grated Parmesan cheese
½ pound cooked spiral-shaped pasta

1. Roast the bell pepper over a gas flame, turning until charred all over (or place under a broiler until charred). Carefully wrap the pepper in paper towels and place it in a plastic bag. Let it stand until cool. Rub the charred skin from the pepper with paper towels. Core the pepper; roughly chop.

2. Place the pepper, garlic, and cream in the container of a food processor or blender. Process until smooth.

3. Melt the butter in a medium saucepan over medium-low heat. Whisk in the tomato paste and the pepper-garlic purée. Add the sage, paprika, and salt to taste. Cook, without boiling, until hot. Stir in the cheese and hot cooked pasta. Serve immediately.

Serves 4 as a first course.

POTTED PEPPER CHOWDER

*T*he best soup in my pepper repertoire is *not* Pepper Pot. That is a pottage dependent upon tripe as well as peppers, and frankly more work than it is worth in my opinion. And I will take my lumps gladly when the Pepper Pot lovers (all from Philadelphia, if rumormongers are to be believed) send their letters of protest.

Until then, have this next brew. It's a breeze to make, peppery but still a beatitude in the soup spoon!

2 large potatoes, peeled, cubed
4 tablespoons (½ stick) unsalted butter
1 medium onion, finely chopped
1 clove garlic, minced
1 cup cubed cooked ham
½ cup chopped celery
1 medium green bell pepper, seeded,
  chopped
1 medium red bell pepper, seeded, chopped
¼ teaspoon crushed dried hot red peppers
1 can (4 ounces) jalapeño peppers, finely
  chopped
1 quart milk
1½ teaspoons salt
12 allspice berries, crushed, or ½ teaspoon
  ground
¼ teaspoon cumin seeds (comino)
¼ cup chopped fresh parsley
1 teaspoon chopped chives or scallion tops

1. Cover the potatoes with cold water in a medium saucepan. Heat to boiling; drain.

2. Melt 3 tablespoons of the butter in a large heavy saucepan over medium-low heat. Add the onion; cook 1 minute. Add the garlic; cook 1 minute longer. Stir in the ham, celery, green pepper, red pepper, dried red peppers, and jalapeño peppers. Cook, stirring constantly, 3 minutes.

3. Stir the potatoes into the pepper mixture. Add the milk. Slowly heat, stirring constantly, to boiling; reduce the heat. Add the salt, allspice, and cumin seeds. Cook, stirring occasionally, until the potatoes are very tender and the soup is slightly thickened, about 30 minutes. Stir in the remaining 1 tablespoon butter, and sprinkle with the parsley and chives.

Serves 6.

HOT TUNA AND PEPPER SALAD

This is a provincial recipe, easy to do and economical besides. Also great to eat. A salad, but a hot one!

2 tablespoons olive oil
1 small shallot, minced
1 clove garlic, minced
1 red bell pepper, seeded, cut into thin
    strips
1 green bell pepper, seeded, cut into thin
    strips
3 anchovy filets, chopped
1 can (7 ounces) tuna, drained
½ teaspoon crushed dried hot red peppers
Salt

1. Heat the oil in a large skillet over medium heat. Add the shallot; cook 1 minute. Add the garlic, both bell peppers, and the chopped anchovies. Reduce the heat to medium-low. Cook, covered, 5 minutes.

2. Add the tuna and dried red peppers to the mixture in the skillet. Cook, stirring constantly, until the peppers are just barely tender, about 4 minutes. Add salt to taste. Serve as a warm salad or over cooked spaghetti.

Serves 2 or 3.

COLD LAMB AND PEPPER SALAD

Add peppers to a salad dish next time the vinaigrette is dark and mustardy. The one below, composed of leftover roast lamb and roasted peppers, can be served cool or at room temperature. In this instance, the peppers are baked (blanched first to give them a measure of tenderness) rather than charred.

4 green bell peppers
4 red bell peppers
¼ cup chopped shallots
1½ to 2 cups cold cooked lamb, cut into
    strips
2 tablespoons Dijon mustard
2 tablespoons red wine vinegar
2 teaspoons soy sauce
⅓ to ½ cup olive oil
Salt and freshly ground black pepper
¼ cup chopped fresh parsley

1. Preheat the oven to 350°F. Cook the peppers in boiling salted water 1 minute; drain. Place the peppers on a foil-lined baking sheet. Bake until they are lightly browned and the skins peel off easily, about 50 minutes.

2. Cool the peppers slightly; peel, core and seed them. Cut the peppers into thin strips, and combine them with the shallots and lamb in a large bowl.

3. Combine the mustard, vinegar, and soy sauce in a medium bowl. Slowly beat in the oil, a few drops at a time. Add salt and pepper to taste. Pour this dressing over the lamb and pepper mixture. Sprinkle with the parsley. Serve chilled or at room temperature.

Serves 4.

BARBECUED SWEET PEPPERS

One of the most original pepper notions I know is a relish (or condiment, you name it) of charred, scraped peppers in a spicy Texas-inspired emollient. Select thick, firm-skinned peppers for this. Otherwise you will find yourself with more sauce than substance.

4 green bell peppers
4 red bell peppers
1 recipe Dynamite Barbecue Sauce

1. Roast the peppers over a gas flame, turning until charred all over (or place under a broiler until charred). Carefully wrap the peppers in paper towels and place them in plastic bags. Let them stand until cool. Rub the charred skin from the pepper with paper towels.

2. Meanwhile, make the Dynamite Barbecue Sauce.

3. Core and seed the peppers; cut them into 2-inch-long strips, about ¼ inch wide. Place the pepper strips in sterilized pint jars (about 1¼ cups peppers per jar). Fill each jar with sauce (¾ to 1 cup sauce per jar). Seal.

Makes about 2½ pints.

Dynamite Barbecue Sauce

1 tablespoon vegetable oil
3 small onions, finely chopped
2 cloves garlic, minced
1¼ cups ketchup
¼ cup Worcestershire sauce
3 tablespoons A-1 steak sauce
1½ tablespoons dark brown sugar
6 tablespoons water
⅛ teaspoon hot pepper sauce

Heat the oil in a medium saucepan over medium-low heat. Add the onions; cook 1 minute. Add the garlic; cook 4 minutes. Add the remaining ingredients. Heat to boiling, reduce the heat, and simmer, uncovered, 20 minutes.

Makes about 3 cups.

RED PEPPER CHEESE BREAD

The red bell pepper's sweet alliance in meat and vegetable dishes is not particularly surprising. However, its appearance in the three totally unalike breads that follow is a good deal less predictable. No coincidence, each is indescribably good. Peppery too!

1 large red bell pepper
1 package dry yeast
1¼ cups lukewarm water
1 teaspoon light brown sugar
2 teaspoons salt
⅛ teaspoon cayenne pepper
1 teaspoon crushed dried hot red peppers
1 teaspoon sesame seeds

1 teaspoon fennel seeds
1 teaspoon anise seeds
½ cup lukewarm milk
1½ cups stone-ground whole-wheat flour
1 cup grated Monterey jack cheese
3 cups all-purpose flour, approximately
1 tablespoon unsalted butter, melted

1. Roast the bell pepper over a gas flame, turning, until charred all over (or place under a broiler until charred). Carefully wrap the pepper in paper towels and place it in a plastic bag. Let it stand until cool. Rub the charred skin from the pepper with paper towels. Core and seed the pepper; chop fine.

2. Place the yeast in a large bowl and sprinkle it with ¼ cup of the water. Let stand a few minutes to soften; then stir in the sugar, salt, cayenne pepper, dried red peppers, chopped bell pepper, sesame seeds, fennel seeds, anise seeds, and milk. Stir in the whole-wheat flour, alternating with the remaining 1 cup water. Beat in the grated cheese.

3. Slowly beat in 2 cups of the all-purpose flour with a heavy wooden spoon. Transfer the dough to a lightly floured board. Knead the dough for 15 minutes, incorporating the remaining 1 cup all-purpose flour. Add more flour as needed. When the dough is elastic, let it stand 5 minutes.

4. Divide the dough in half; roll each half into long French- or Italian-style loaves. Place the dough in French bread pans. Cover with a flour-rubbed tea towel. Let stand until doubled in volume, 1½ to 2 hours.

5. Preheat the oven to 400°F. Gently slash the top of each loaf lengthwise with

In my garden years ago, I observed a fascinating aspect of the pepper's adaptive nature. When its vines are filled with tiny green fruit (usually in midsummer), a pepper bush will unpredictably drop its blossoms, leaving a faint trail of delicate petals on the ground to confound an anxious gardener, who will spray and spade it to absolutely no avail. Only when the bush turns so feeble its yield is plucked out of desperation, will the plant come back to life again. Once its heavy load is harvested, a pepper bush will even sprout blossoms again and allow the growing cycle to continue.

The moral of this earthly sensibility? Peppers are an example of good economy in the garden.

a sharp knife. Brush the tops with the melted butter. Place a roasting pan half-filled with water in the bottom of the oven. Place the bread in the top third; bake 12 minutes. Reduce the heat to 325°F and continue to bake 35 minutes longer. Cool on racks.

Makes 2 loaves.

RUTH SUGAR BERESH'S SWEET RED PEPPER CORNBREAD

The next bread 'n' pepper confederation is a sweet one. It came to me from a student in a cooking class in Michigan a while back. A wonderful dish, it arrived with the following pedigree:

"I prepare this with our Thanksgiving dinner. I don't know its actual origin but the source I received it from said her source said that her sources said that . . . *it's old!*"

I hope you enjoy this, for it is most unusual.

2 medium red bell peppers
1½ cups cornmeal
½ cup all-purpose flour
2 tablespoons sugar
1 teaspoon baking powder
1 teaspoon baking soda
1 teaspoon salt
2 eggs, lightly beaten
1 cup buttermilk
2 cups sweetened condensed milk
3 tablespoons unsalted butter, melted

1. Preheat the oven to 400°F. Cook the peppers in boiling salted water for 1 minute. Drain. Core, seed, and finely chop.

2. Sift the dry ingredients together into a large bowl. Combine the eggs, buttermilk, and 1 cup of the condensed milk in another bowl. Stir the liquid into the dry ingredients. Stir in the chopped peppers and melted butter.

3. Pour the mixture into a lightly buttered 9-by-13-inch cake pan (or any 8-cup casserole about 2 inches deep). Drizzle the remaining condensed milk over the top of the batter, taking care not to allow the milk to build up in the corners. Do not tip the pan. Bake until set and golden brown, 25 to 30 minutes.

Serves 10.

AWENDAW BREAD

*T*he last pepper bread association comes from the Gullah people, who live along the windswept Atlantic coastline of South Carolina. Awendaw (pronounced ow! endow) is part of the black grandmotherly tradition of dropping everything and baking a batter bread when someone unexpectedly stops in around dinnertime. It is made of grits, cornmeal, and peppers mainly—all the other ingredients are improvised depending upon "what's in the icebox!" Or so I was told.

4 tablespoons (½ stick) unsalted butter
½ red bell pepper, cut into thin strips
    about 1 inch long
½ green bell pepper, cut into thin strips
    about 1 inch long
1 small hot green pepper, seeded, minced
    (see Guacamole headnote, page 37)
2 cups milk
2 cups water
1 teaspoon salt
1 cup hominy grits
1½ cups milk, boiling
½ cup cornmeal
2 eggs, lightly beaten
1 cup grated Monterey jack cheese with
    jalapeño peppers

1. Preheat the oven to 375°F. Melt 2 tablespoons of the butter in a small skillet over medium-low heat. Stir in the bell

peppers and the hot pepper. Toss well to coat the pieces with butter. Cook, covered, until tender, about 8 minutes. Remove from the heat.

2. Combine the 2 cups milk with the water in a medium saucepan. Heat to boiling; reduce the heat. Stir in the salt and hominy grits. Cook, stirring constantly, over low heat until very thick, about 8 minutes. Stir in the remaining 2 tablespoons butter.

3. Transfer the grits mixture to a large bowl. Slowly stir in the 1½ cups boiling milk, the cornmeal, beaten eggs, and cheese. Pour into a well-buttered 2-quart soufflé dish or casserole. Bake until firm and golden brown, 45 to 50 minutes.

Serves 6 to 8.

MISS TOKLAS' BRAISED STUFFED PEPPERS

Stuffing a pepper is my favorite way to cook this vegetable. This classic version is yet another borrowing, only slightly altered, from the kitchen mentor I never met, Alice B. Toklas. I keep her slim cookbook always within hand's reach on the shelf and her yellowed obituary inside the volume as a bookmark. She would, I know, approve of the notion enormously.

*2 bell peppers, preferably 1 red and
   1 yellow
4 tablespoons (½ stick) unsalted butter
¼ cup chopped mushrooms
1 cup lean ground veal (about ½ pound)
½ cup ground cooked ham
1 egg yolk, lightly beaten
1 tablespoon chopped fresh basil, or
   1 teaspoon dried
1 tablespoon chopped fresh parsley
1 tablespoon dry white wine
Juice of ½ lemon
1½ tablespoons freshly grated Parmesan
   cheese
¼ teaspoon ground cumin
⅛ teaspoon crushed saffron
Salt and freshly ground black pepper
½ cup chicken broth (see page 414)
2 medium tomatoes, peeled, seeded,
   chopped
Chopped fresh parsley*

1. Cut the peppers in half lengthwise; remove the core and seeds. Cook in boiling salted water 2 minutes; drain and pat dry.

2. Melt 1 tablespoon of the butter in a medium skillet over medium heat. Add the mushrooms; sauté until golden, about 4 minutes. Remove from the heat.

3. Place the veal and ham in a large bowl. Mix lightly. Add the mushrooms, egg yolk, basil, parsley, wine, lemon juice, Parmesan cheese, cumin, saffron, and salt and pepper to taste. Mix well.

4. Fill the blanched pepper halves with the meat filling.

5. Melt the remaining 3 tablespoons butter in a medium saucepan over medium-low heat. Add the peppers, filled side up. Pour the chicken broth around the peppers. Sprinkle the tomatoes over and around the peppers. Heat the sauce to boiling; reduce the heat. Simmer, covered, over medium heat 20 minutes. Transfer the peppers to a serving platter with a slotted spoon and keep warm. Raise the heat under the saucepan and boil the liquid until slightly thickened, about 4 minutes. Pour this over the peppers and sprinkle with chopped parsley.

Serves 2 to 4.

The French, somewhat more sophisticated about food than we, adjust pepper's name topically. What comes out of a shaker may be *poivre*, but what is sautéed with onion and garlic is inevitably *pimenton doux*. In Germany a pepper is a sweet pepper always (*Ziegenpfeffer*), while in Italy it is a little or diminutive one (*peperone*) whether it is hot or not. The Spanish dub all sweet peppers *pimiento*, which is such a good idea the British and Americans borrowed it—but only for cooked sweet peppers in little jars.

TAMALE-PIE STUFFED PEPPERS

*T*he second stuffed pepper amalgam is my invention—a swipe of one of my best recipes (for Southwestern Tamale Pie) crammed into green pepper shells rather than a pie plate. The change of venue makes for even more flavor and twice the bite.

3 tablespoons cornmeal
¼ cup cold water
½ cup plus 1 tablespoon boiling water
1 tablespoon unsalted butter
¼ pound sausage meat
¾ cup finely chopped onion
1 large clove garlic, minced
1 tablespoon chili powder
⅛ teaspoon ground cumin
½ pound ground beef
⅛ teaspoon hot pepper sauce
¼ cup finely chopped celery
1 ½ teaspoons seeded, minced hot green
   peppers (see Guacamole headnote,
   page 37)
1 large tomato, peeled, seeded, chopped
1 ear fresh corn
Salt
4 green bell peppers
5 pitted black olives, sliced
¼ cup grated Monterey jack cheese
⅓ cup grated mild Cheddar cheese

1. Gradually stir the cornmeal into the cold water in a small bowl. Stir this mixture into the boiling water in a small saucepan. Heat, stirring constantly, to boiling; reduce the heat to medium-low. Stir in the butter. Cook, covered, stirring occasionally, 35 minutes. Remove from the heat.

2. While the cornmeal is cooking, sauté the sausage meat in a large heavy skillet over medium heat, breaking up the lumps with a fork, until it begins to lose its pink color. Add the onion and garlic; cook 5 minutes. Stir in the chili powder and cumin. Add the ground beef and continue to cook, breaking up the lumps with a fork, until the beef loses its color, about 5 minutes. Add the hot pepper sauce, celery, and hot green pepper. Cook 5 minutes. Stir in the tomato; cook 5 minutes longer.

3. With a sharp knife, cut the corn kernels off the cob, slicing about halfway through the kernels. Using the back of the knife, scrape the cob to remove the remaining kernel bits and milky residue. Add the corn to the tomato-meat mixture. Cook 10 minutes longer. Add salt to taste; remove from the heat.

4. Preheat the oven to 350°F. Cook the peppers in boiling salted water 2 minutes. Trim off the tops with a sharp knife. Core, and remove the seeds.

5. Fill each pepper with the meat mixture, packing it down firmly with the back of a spoon. Leave about ½ inch of space at the top of each pepper. Cover the top of each pepper with olive slices. Sprinkle with Monterey jack and cheddar cheese. Spread a thin layer of the cornmeal mixture over the top, using about 2 teaspoons per pepper. Place the peppers in a baking dish. Bake 50 minutes. Let stand 5 minutes before serving.
Serves 2 to 4.

PEPPERED MEAT LOAF

See how wondrously a little bit of peppers stretch (and give style to) a lowly dish like meat loaf. Because of its coloration, this loaf will nicely grace a buffet.

1¼ pounds lean beef, ground
½ pound veal shoulder, ground
¼ pound pork shoulder, ground
1 medium onion, finely chopped
2 small shallots, minced
¼ cup minced green bell pepper
¼ cup minced red bell pepper
1 can (10 ounces) mixed tomatoes and
    jalapeño peppers, roughly chopped
1 teaspoon chopped fresh basil, or ½
    teaspoon dried
1 teaspoon chopped fresh parsley
⅛ teaspoon thyme
½ teaspoon salt
½ teaspoon freshly ground black pepper
1 egg, lightly beaten
½ cup fresh bread crumbs

2 teaspoons Dijon mustard
2 teaspoons chili sauce
1 teaspoon chili powder

1. Preheat the oven to 375°F. Place the three ground meats in a large bowl and mix thoroughly. Add the remaining ingredients through the bread crumbs and again mix thoroughly. Form into a loaf in a shallow baking dish.

2. Combine the mustard, chili sauce, and chili powder in a small bowl. Mix well and spread over the meat loaf. Bake 15 minutes. Reduce the heat to 350°F and bake 1 hour longer.

Serves 6 to 8.

SMOKED TONGUE WITH RED PEPPER SAUCE

In this instance, blazing red pepper is the basis of a crimson sauce to amend a slice of smoked tongue. Even if you have always shunned this meat, this is a dish you will not care to miss.

4 pounds smoked tongue
1 large carrot, peeled, halved
1 white turnip, peeled, halved
1 parsnip, peeled, halved
1 large onion, unpeeled, halved
4 whole cloves
2 tablespoons red wine vinegar
2 sprigs fresh parsley
1 large bay leaf
1 clove garlic

1 teaspoon mustard seeds
2 red bell peppers
2 tablespoons unsalted butter
2 tablespoons all-purpose flour
2 tablespoons prepared horseradish
1 teaspoon Dijon mustard
¼ cup heavy or whipping cream

1. Place the tongue in a 5-quart pot or Dutch oven. Add the carrot through the mustard seeds, plus enough water to cover the meat by two inches. Heat to boiling; reduce the heat. Cook, partially covered, over medium-low heat 45 minutes per pound, or about 3 hours.

2. Half an hour before the meat is done, add the bell peppers to the pot. Simmer, covered, 20 minutes, then remove them from the broth. Peel, core, seed, and roughly chop the peppers.

3. Place the peppers in the container of a food processor or blender. Add ¼ cup of the meat liquid. Process until smooth.

4. Melt the butter in a medium saucepan over medium-low heat. Stir in the flour. Cook, stirring constantly, 2 minutes. Whisk in 1¼ cups of the meat liquid and the puréed peppers. Heat to boiling; reduce the heat. Stir in the horseradish and Dijon mustard; continue to cook until the mixture is slightly thickened, about 5 minutes. Stir in the cream. Cook another 2 minutes.

5. Remove the tongue from the cooking liquid. Remove the skin, and slice on the diagonal. Spoon some of the sauce over the meat. Pass the remaining sauce on the side.

Serves 6 to 8.

ALL-AMERICAN PEPPER JAMBALAYA

*F*irst tasted by Columbus in the Caribbean, peppers were simmered and stewed by the Indians over low fires until they became so thick that a handful could be lifted out of the barely steaming pot with two fingers, blown upon, and then swallowed without burning hand or mouth! This kind of dish was known as *abalay*.

Without any evidence to support the theory except a good nose for a story, I suggest that when pepper *abalay* was seasoned with *jambon*, the cured ham that French colonists brought to Louisiana, and stirred up by the strong slave arms that sprinkled African scallions and herbs into the pot as well, the dish suffered a name change—to *jambalaya*.

You don't agree? Well, I said it was only my notion.

The dish that inspired the reverie is something closer to gospel, however, leastwise among jambalaya aficionados. It is a mixture of ham, shrimp, apricots, and (bless them all) five separate and distinct varieties of pepper.

½ cup chopped dried apricots
⅓ cup apricot brandy
3 tablespoons unsalted butter
1 tablespoon vegetable oil
1 cup thinly sliced whole scallions, bulbs
    and green tops
1 clove garlic, minced
¾ cup ¼-inch-wide strips of cooked ham
1 large green bell pepper, cut lengthwise
    into ⅛-inch-wide strips
1 large red bell pepper, cut lengthwise into
    ⅛-inch-wide strips

1 pound raw shrimp, shelled, deveined
1 tablespoon lemon juice
1 tablespoon soy sauce
2 teaspoons cornstarch
⅛ teaspoon crushed dried hot red peppers
1½ tablespoons chili powder
⅓ cup roughly chopped pimiento
¼ cup slivered almonds, toasted
Hot Steamed Rice (see page 412)

1. Combine the apricots and apricot brandy in a small bowl; let stand, covered, at least 15 minutes.

2. Heat the butter with the oil in a large heavy skillet over medium heat. Add the scallions; cook 1 minute. Add the garlic, ham, and the green pepper and red pepper strips. Cook, stirring constantly, until the peppers are almost tender, about 5 minutes. Stir in the shrimp; cook, stirring constantly, 3 minutes. Add the apricot mixture; cook 3 minutes longer.

3. Combine the lemon juice, soy sauce, cornstarch, and dried red pepper in a small bowl. Stir this into the shrimp-pepper mixture. Add the chili powder and pimiento. Continue to stir until the chili powder is well incorporated and the mixture is slightly thickened, about 4 minutes. Sprinkle with the toasted almonds. Serve over rice.

Serves 4.

POTATOES

Apples of Love

I have dwelled long on my love for the Atlantic shore. But how I moved from an early infatuation with suburban Long Beach to a more mature passion for countrified Amagansett is worth a speck more sandy amplification.

The emotional distance, you see, was traveled with a stopover: Fire Island.

Much has been written of this curiously raffish resort and the denizens of sun-and-fun seekers who invade its isolated ten-mile boundaries every summer. But no one's view of the place is quite like my own, for I was an unassessed homeowner there one fateful summer—living on a semi-deserted dune. A strip of beach property that had been occupied (illegally) by squatters for years before me, my home was known simply as "The Dump."

Actually the place where I summered was not a garbage disposal area at all but more of a landfill constructed of the island's detritus in order to preserve the natural character of the dunes. But "The Dump" is what residents called it, and its mountainous confines held a veritable treasure trove of goodies: abandoned jeeps lurked there along with sun-dried bricks, deck chairs, refrigerators, and Thonet rockers, plus piles of lumber and pipe, mostly the remains of over fifty island households blown thither by a devastating hurricane in 1938.

I came upon this sequestered beach during a Sunday excursion to Fire Island with some acquaintances who claimed to be house-hunting. The time was the mid-1950s. They had a car. I didn't drive and so literally came along for the ride. Then as now, one parked vehicles in a black-topped lot across the water from Fire Island, for no cars other than beach-buggy taxis are permitted on its shores. A ferry is the only way in or out.

As I recall, we looked at dreary houses for sale without any real incentive or enthusiasm until the real estate agent left, and then we ventured out of the rabbit warren of cedar shingle cottages. Trudging in the sand past sleek modern houses on the far perimeter of the town, we discovered an utterly deserted stretch of dune and beach (albeit flanked by the bespoke "dump") that was so inviting not one of us could resist tearing off our clothes and swimming in the surf, naked as water babies. Later, drying in the warm sun, we resolved to come back to this place and "camp out" the following weekend. Or at least I did.

Fire Island and that incredible baptism in its wild surf forced me to buy my first automobile. It was a postwar Chevy convertible, precisely the color of beach sand, and cost one hundred dollars, third-hand. A car owner but unable to drive, I persuaded first one friend then another to chauffeur the camping trips. Once a driver was established at the helm, however, the old coupe was so crammed with passengers and assorted gear that it rarely exceeded forty miles per hour on the highway.

We would leave Manhattan at dawn on Saturday mornings to avoid beach traffic. No breakfast was ever taken prior to the ride. Not even a cup of coffee was consumed until we had arrived at our point of destination: a supermarket near the ferry where we shopped like demons for the weekend. Since there is little for sale on the island itself, all comestibles must be hauled and tugged by hand. Our initial meal (after we arrived on land and rented a jeep and driver to convey us to "The Dump") was always the same: Danish pastries oozing butter and washed down with Bloody Marys. The first of many odd repasts to come.

Members of the camping team expanded and altered during the course of the summer. More friends and more cars were invited, and the "commune at the dump," as we were known to anxious householders nearby, often harbored as many as a dozen adults plus one small child and two dogs per weekend.

It was the most carefree summer of my life, though we never stopped working from the moment of arrival until the hired beach buggy appeared to carry its weary band back to the boat on Sunday night. After spending the first night out-of-doors in makeshift sleeping bags, we built a house (of sorts) to protect our motley crew from the elements. It was made of found lumber and fitted with a heavy-duty clear plastic roof and walls. Like a glass house it shimmered in the sunlight and could be seen for miles along the surf. More important, this shelter withstood all manner of seasonal catastrophes (like windstorms and wasps) and remained intact even after a troop of hiking boys impounded it for a midweek hostel. Though to be truthful, the walls, much ventilated by cigarette burns, did have to be replaced the following week.

Besides sleeping quarters, we also

built a long trestle table and benches for dining, an ice house, a latrine (well secluded in a bluff of dwarf pine), *and* a pit where we barbecued and cooked. This outdoor stove was actually a deep-dug trench, lined with rocks and covered with a steel grate under a hinged Volkswagen trunk lid (yet another prize resurrected from our dump), where potatoes roasted nightly for dinner.

Fire Island potatoes were usually barbecued, slow-cooked over embers and sluiced with tomatoey glop that turned the skins to bronze and fissured them like Chinese gongs. No potato anywhere has ever tasted so good. A small lifetime has passed but I can still recall the cries of ravenous diners in bathing suits (returning from a fourth or fifth dip in the surf), demanding that the potatoes be served before the moon rose.

At summer's end, I traded in my old jalopy for a newer-model Chevy and eventually pressed eastward to Long Island. All I brought from Fire Island to Amagansett were memories—and a great potato recipe.

Vegetable Roots

Over a beach fire or in a boiling pan of water, what a wonder is the potato!

Eaten by mankind for subsistence for almost three thousand years, the starchy appendage of the *Solanum tuberosum* has been under fire by its detractors almost as long as it has been over fire as a source of nourishment. In the fifteenth century, the Pope denounced this "apple of love" as the "root of man's licentious and depraved moral behavior," and righteous churchgoers were warned to avoid its aphrodisiac taint for their very salvation. One hundred years after, *pommes de terre* were still in jeopardy. Believed to be the cause of leprosy, potatoes were burned in great Burgundian conflagrations ignited by order of the crown to protect the citizenry from "its base addiction and

craving." According to one report, the bonfires served only to whet appetites, for the scent of potatoes roasting proved utterly irresistible to the peasants. Snatching them from the burning embers, many ate them on the spot, blackened skins and all. Lived to tell the tale, too.

The potato, like the pepper and the tomato, is native to the Americas. It grew and was eaten (mostly raw) in Peru as far back as 3000 B.C. The cooked potato was brought to European kitchens courtesy of the Spanish explorer Gonzalo Jiménez de Quesada, whose scouting parties discovered a strain of small potatoes blooming under crowns of brilliant blue flowers, sixteen thousand feet up in the Andes. Being somewhat short-rationed and cold (besides faint from the high altitude), these resourceful fellows dug up the plum-size tubers of these blue blossoms to stoke their campfires. Anyone who has ever sniffed the perfume of a potato roasting in the wild will understand at once why they not only sampled the burnt offerings but became positive aficionados after the first steamy bite.

Potatoes came to Spain on the next boat.

Within fifty years this tender-hearted vegetable had achieved such a toehold in European larders that (detractors aside) it was adjudged to be a prime necessity for the colonists in the New World. And by reverse logic, the potato crossed the Atlantic to be planted on its native soil once again.

Another distant relative of deadly nightshade, the potato is its least virulent cousin. Neither a fruit nor a root, it is a portion of the underground stem of the plant. According to potato farmers at the eastern end of Long Island, a potato "peeps" (or is ready for the plucking) only when the earth has been at a base temperature of 55 degrees or more for at least one month's time. Potatoes may take a long time to ripen but they grow sweeter and more toothsome every day spent undercover. Ancient Incas believed they flourished best when fertilized with human blood and held gory sports on potato fields to guarantee a hearty crop, but spring rain usually does just as well in my part of the country!

What to Look For

Shoppers might be advised that there are over 400 varieties of potatoes grown at the moment, but ask for any one of 396 at your supermarket and you will be met with a rude comment or, even worse, a vacant stare. Most greengrocers codify the potato by geography alone: Maine, Long Island, California, and Idaho. Wholesalers are not much better, classifying them as round whites, round reds, russets, and long whites with no amend. If you wish to know the difference between a Red Pontiac Chippewa, Norgold Russet, and a Mohawk, you'll have to dip into a seed catalogue, I expect.

Farmers know potatoes by their growing cycles. New potatoes are fresh-dug. Old potatoes have lingered longer in the ground and as a consequence have grown starchier for their hiatus. New (low-starch) potatoes have firm textures and thin skins and are your best bet for boiling, roasting, casserole dishes, and potato salad. Old (high-starch) potatoes are mealier and more substantial—prime nominees for the french-fryer, the skillet, and the baking rack.

In the supermarket, choose weighty potatoes that are firm, relatively clean—if that is possible—and smooth to the touch. Avoid a tuber that is sprouting, for that indicates a long stay on the shelf. Likewise pass on any potato that is bruised, soft, or patched with green. A pale, mottled-green potato is not merely underripe—it is bitter, containing a high proportion of solanine, a mildly toxic

Though the Irish are generally credited as being Europe's prime potato eaters, the Germans got there first. *Ein Neu Kochbuch (A New Cookbuch)*, compiled and printed on Gutenberg's press in 1581, contains the first annotated German recipes; and there are a dozen potato dishes listed among them. One, surprisingly enough, is a very tasty baked tart. A hundred years after its publication, however, no more potatoes were being eaten than before. Those that were, were consumed mainly by noblemen who imported them from France or the Lowlands. Frederick Wilhelm, sensing that the potato could prove a windfall for his country's laggard economy (and feed the peasantry into the bargain), issued what is sometimes referred to as "The Brandenberg Potato Paper." An edict, it ordered Prussian farmers to plant potatoes or risk the pain of having their ears (and noses) cut off! Will it come as a shock to discover that the potato shortly became a staple in the German diet? Frederick was soon after dubbed "Frederick the Great," and great potato dishes proliferated all along the Rhine—and westward, in time, as well.

substance that will (in large doses) cause skin irritations.

I store potatoes in a ventilated cabinet, or on the lowest shelf in the refrigerator. Cool air retards spoilage; warm, confined, moist environments (like plastic bags) increase it.

Contrary to specious rumor, the potato is not fattening in the least. Butter and cream *are*, however, but let's skip that for the moment. A naked medium-size baked potato is tabbed at less than 100 calories, and boiling will reduce the calories to a scant 80. As you may have surmised (if you have ever grated a potato for a potato pancake), the reason they are low in calories is that potatoes are mostly water: 77 to 80 percent of their total composition, in fact. In terms of dry weight, a potato consists of an average of 66 percent starch, 9 percent protein, and 4 percent sugars, with about 0.5 percent assorted potassium, phosphorus, fats, vitamins, and random minerals. High in vitamin B (including niacin, thiamine, riboflavin, and pyridoxine), the potato is really good for you—as well as being good to eat.

Preparation

In my opinion, nothing beats a new potato boiled tender and served up neat—with salt and pepper on the side and butter as a caloric elective. Whether you cook a potato peeled or unpeeled is up to personal preference. However, what you choose to boil is not. Low-starch or waxy new varieties are to my mind the most felicitous choices for boiling, particularly if you plan to mash the potatoes. Avoid using baking potatoes; they tend to remain lumpy no matter how long one flails at them, and old high-starch potatoes turn gluey and thick. I always boil potatoes uncovered, in cold water, salting the water only after it has boiled. Cooking times vary with potato sizes but the average spud will take approximately 20 to 25 minutes, after the water has come to the boil, to become fork-tender.

The optimum mashed potato is put through a ricer, then beaten hard with a wooden spoon as the butter and cream are added. My generous rule of thumb: 1 to 1½ tablespoons butter per cupful of potatoes, plus 2 to 4 tablespoons of heavy cream, depending upon the texture you prefer. I like mine to drift heavy

on the plate (Illinois-blizzard style)!

No baking potato is ever foil-wrapped in my oven, as this steams rather than bakes the contents. But I very often grease the skins with a smidgen of vegetable oil, as I admire a chewy exterior. In a baked potato, I skip any amendment other than unsalted butter—but sour cream, chives, crumbled bacon, and a splash of red wine vinegar all make very acceptable gildings of this lily.

I rarely fry a potato these days, because I am watching my waistline assiduously. That is a shame because a good French fry is as hard to find as a slice of homemade apple pie. The optimum method for frying potatoes requires either an electric deep-fat fryer or a large pot that will comfortably hold a metal strainer. The size of a fried potato is important: first, I slice mine lengthwise, never thicker than ¼ inch. These slices are then cut into ¼-inch-wide strips. It is a good idea to soak the cut potatoes in ice water for at least an hour prior to frying, and then drain them thoroughly on paper towels before placing them in the pot. I fry potatoes in hot (375°F) Crisco in two stages. First, I fry them for 2 to 3 minutes until lightly golden but not crisp, then drain them on brown paper (or in a paper bag) until they cool. Before serving, I refry the potatoes for 2 to 3 minutes until all the moisture in the potato evaporates. The fries will be *really* crisp. While they drain on paper towels or more brown paper, I get busy with the salt and pepper, and serve them up immediately.

Fried-potato buffs insist that a minimal amount of meat fat (lard, suet, bacon, etc.) when added to the hot grease will produce a sublimely flavored shoestring. I do not disagree, but never reserve that grease to use a second time, as the flavor intensifies as it cools.

CRIMPED POTATO SKINS

When I was a kid, I would watch dumbfounded at the table as my father carefully removed the snowy contents of a baked potato. He would always butter and mash the stuffing, then push the crunchy (and infinitely more delectable) potato skins to the side of his plate. I expect he meant them for the garbage pail but they never got that far, thanks to my sister's and my own watchful eye. Much affixed on the crackling texture of buttered skins, we would ask his permission to spear the detritus once his napkin was laid upon the table.

These days my potato skins are toasted and broiled, a trick I learned from the kitchen wisdom of James Beard. They make a great hors d'oeuvre, if you have the self-control to husband a batch after you have made those Heavenly Mashed Potatoes.

4 medium baking potatoes
Vegetable oil
3 tablespoons unsalted butter
Salt and freshly ground black pepper

1. Preheat the oven to 375°F. Prick the potatoes with a fork, and lightly rub them with oil. Bake the potatoes on a rack until tender, about 1 hour. Allow them to cool slightly.
2. Cut the potatoes in half length-wise and scoop out the interiors. (Reserve the interiors for hash, or use for Heavenly Mashed Potatoes.) With scissors, cut the skins lengthwise into strips. Rub the skins well with the butter, and sprinkle with salt and pepper to taste. Place them under a preheated broiling unit until crisp on both sides.

Serves 2 or 3.

SOPA DE APATZINGAN
(Potato and Cantaloupe Soup)

I have two favored potato soup nominations, neither of which is vichyssoise. Not out of animus—merely overexposure, for I made that velvety brew twice a day for ten summers of my life when I ran The Store in Amagansett and now cannot face a spoonful.

This cold potato soup comes from Mexico. It is a fabled confederation of cooked potato and raw melon fused in a blender—brought to my attention by the doyenne of Latin American cuisine, Diana Kennedy.

1 pound potatoes, peeled, cubed
2 cups cubed cantaloupe (about 1 medium melon)
2 cups milk
4 tablespoons (½ stick) unsalted butter
Juice of 1 large lime

4 egg yolks
Salt and freshly ground black pepper
Ground cinnamon
1 cup unsweetened whipped cream

1. Cook the potatoes in boiling

salted water until tender, 15 to 20 minutes. Drain.

2. Place the potatoes and cantaloupe in the container of a food processor. Add 1 cup of the milk and process until smooth.

3. Melt the butter in a large saucepan over medium-low heat. Add the puréed potato mixture and remaining 1 cup milk. Stir in the lime juice. Cook over low heat 5 minutes.

4. Beat the egg yolks until light and lemon-colored. Stir the egg yolks into the soup. Remove the soup from the heat. Add salt and pepper to taste. Cool.

5. Chill the soup for at least 4 hours. Serve in individual soup bowls, sprinkled with cinnamon. Add a dab of whipped cream to each bowl.

Serves 6.

PO' POTTAGE
(Potato-Ham Soup)

*T*his hot soup stems from the potato fields of Tennessee. It is a farmer's supper (only slightly enriched in my kitchen) and still one of the best one-dish meals around.

2 tablespoons unsalted butter
1 medium onion, chopped
1 small clove garlic, minced
⅓ cup diced cooked ham
2 ribs celery, finely chopped (about ½ cup)
⅛ teaspoon dried thyme
1 small bay leaf
2 medium baking potatoes (about ¾
  pound), peeled, cubed
3 cups chicken broth (see page 414)
Salt and freshly ground black pepper
¼ cup chopped fresh parsley
2 tablespoons sour cream

1. Melt the butter in a medium saucepan over medium heat. Add the onion; cook 1 minute. Add the garlic and ham; cook until lightly browned, about 5 minutes. Reduce the heat. Add the celery, thyme and bay leaf; cook, covered, over medium-low heat for 5 minutes.

2. Remove the cover and add the potatoes; toss well. Add the chicken broth. Heat to boiling; reduce the heat. Simmer, uncovered, until the potatoes are tender, about 20 minutes. Add salt and pepper to taste.

3. Remove the soup from the heat; stir in the parsley. Combine the sour cream with ½ cup of the soup in a small bowl. Whisk this mixture back into the soup. Serve immediately.

Serves 2 as a main course, 4 as a first course.

FRENCH PROVINCIAL POTATO SALAD

*D*edicated potato salad fanciers are a very special breed—prejudiced about mayonnaise versus oil and vinegar, or hot opposed to cool, and (more importantly) what or what not to slice up as the main ingredient.

Speaking for the French and not myself, they always opt for a mealy (high-starch) tuber like a White Rose or Mohawk, which often goes by the generic family tag Idaho though in fact they are merely deep-dug denizens of any ashy western soil.

Other potato salad heads of my acquaintance hold equally strong opinions about round reds (medium starch) in their salads. Pontiacs, La Sodas, La Rouges, and McClures are all red-skinned members I have chewed with equal relish.

In the final analysis, the only criteria for a potato salad potato are its crispness and flavor. Try your favorite tuber (if you have one) in either of the next two alliances.

This version is a full century old. It springs from France—Provence to be exact, where there are as many potato salad variations as there are garlic buds.

8 medium potatoes
1 large clove garlic, bruised
⅓ cup dry white wine
½ cup plus 1 tablespoon olive oil
1 tablespoon white wine vinegar
2 thick slices stale French bread
1 tablespoon unsalted butter
2 large shallots, minced
3 tablespoons chopped fresh parsley
Salt and freshly ground black pepper

1. Cook the potatoes in boiling salted water until just tender, about 18 minutes. (Centers should not be thoroughly cooked.) Drain. Cool, peel, and cut into ¼-inch-thick slices.

2. Rub a large bowl with the garlic.

(Do not discard the garlic.) Add the potatoes; sprinkle with the wine, ½ cup oil, and vinegar. Toss gently. Let stand, covered, 1 hour.

3. Meanwhile, rub the French bread on both sides with the garlic. Cut the bread into croutons. Heat the remaining 1 tablespoon oil and the butter in a medium skillet over medium-high heat. Add the croutons. Sauté, stirring constantly, until golden. Drain on paper towels; reserve.

4. Add the shallots, parsley, and salt and pepper to taste to the potato salad. Fold in the croutons just before serving.
Serves 6.

SPECK'S FAMED POTATO SALAD

Another nifty potato salad, this one is of German descent. Only *half* a century old, it springs from a vanished restaurant, Speck's, once a St. Louis hostelry of deserved repute. The formulation for this salad (yellowing with age) was copied and sent by a loyal friend from that admirable precinct along the broad Mississippi. Ricky Duhart amended the copy with three brief words: "Old but good."

That says it all.

3 pounds potatoes
¼ cup finely chopped bacon
1 small onion, finely chopped
2 tablespoons all-purpose flour
1 teaspoon salt
4 teaspoons sugar
¼ teaspoon freshly ground black pepper

⅔ cup cider vinegar
⅓ cup water
½ teaspoon celery seed
3 tablespoons chopped fresh parsley
1 egg white, lightly beaten (optional)

1. Cook the potatoes in boiling

salted water until just tender, about 18 minutes. Centers should be slightly firm. Drain, peel, and slice thin. Place in a large bowl.

2. Sauté the bacon in a large heavy skillet over medium heat until crisp. Add the onion; cook 1 minute. Stir in the flour, salt, sugar, and pepper. Cook, stirring constantly, 1 minute. Add the vinegar and water. Cook, stirring frequently, 10 minutes. Pour over the potatoes.

3. Sprinkle the potato mixture with the celery seed and parsley. Toss gently until thoroughly mixed. If you are using it, pour the egg white over the top. Serve while still warm.

Serves 6 to 8.

Potatoes have names in other lands that are as diverse as the ways in which they are cooked at home. If, for instance, you are forking into a *patata*, it's either Spain or Italy; a *peruna*, Finland; a *papa*, Colombia; and a *pomme de terre*, France. Roumanians dub their potatoes *cartofi*, the Russians and Germans call them *Kartoffel*, and the Czechs tag them *brambors*—all of which may prove a bit unsettling to a traveling potato lover.

NEW POTATOES IN LEMON

This recipe is a gift from Elaine Light, a gracious and extraordinarily good cook, author of *The New Gourmets and Groundhogs*, which is published in Punxsutawney, Pennsylvania—where the groundhog and Elaine are both to be found.

1¼ pounds small new potatoes, red or
   white
6 tablespoons (¾ stick) unsalted butter
1 teaspoon grated lemon peel
1½ teaspoons lemon juice
1 tablespoon minced chives
Salt and freshly ground black pepper

1. Cook the potatoes in boiling salted water until tender, 10 to 12 minutes. Drain. Allow to cool slightly, then remove the skins with your fingers or a sharp knife.

2. Melt the butter in a large heavy skillet over medium-low heat. Stir in the lemon peel, lemon juice, and chives. Add the potatoes; roll until well coated with the mixture. Sprinkle with salt and pepper to taste.

Serves 4.

NEW POTATOES IN MUSTARD

Number two new-potato recipe is a dispensation from San Francisco—from friend Marlene Levinson, in fact.

1 ¼ *pounds small new potatoes, red or white*
4 *tablespoons (½ stick) unsalted butter*
1 ½ *tablespoons Dijon mustard*
⅓ *cup chopped fresh parsley*
1 *teaspoon chopped fresh chervil, or ½ teaspoon dried*
Salt and freshly ground black pepper

1. Cook the potatoes in boiling salted water until tender, 10 to 12 minutes. Drain. Allow to cool slightly, then remove the skins with your fingers or a sharp knife.

2. Melt the butter in a large heavy skillet over medium-low heat. Stir in the mustard, parsley, and chervil. Add the potatoes; roll until well coated with the mixture. Sprinkle with salt and pepper to taste.

Serves 4.

NEW POTATOES IN WHITE WINE

Number three is a slightly less conventional mating: the tuber is poached in good white wine. From Cincinnati's Marilyn Harris.

1 ¼ *pounds small new potatoes, red or white*
4 *tablespoons (½ stick) unsalted butter*
⅔ *cup dry white wine*
Salt and freshly ground black pepper
3 *tablespoons chopped fresh parsley*
1 *tablespoon chopped fresh dill*

1. Cut away a small strip of peel around each potato with a vegetable peeler. The potatoes should look candy-striped. Cook the potatoes in boiling salted water until barely tender, 8 to 10 minutes. Drain.

2. Melt 2 tablespoons of the butter in a large skillet over medium heat. Add the potatoes and roll them in the skillet until a light crust forms, but do not let them brown. Add the wine; raise the heat and cook, stirring constantly, until the wine is reduced and the sauce is fairly thick, about 5 minutes. Sprinkle with salt and pepper to taste, the parsley and the dill. Stir gently to coat the potatoes with the herbs.

Serves 4.

NEW POTATOES SLICED IN TARRAGON CREAM

Number four is the end of all that potato name-dropping. I invented it myself.

2 *tablespoons unsalted butter*
1 *large shallot, minced*
½ *teaspoon chopped fresh tarragon, or ¼ teaspoon dried*

½ *pound new potatoes, red or white, sliced ⅛ inch thick*
1 *cup heavy or whipping cream*
Salt and freshly ground black pepper

1. Melt the butter in a large heavy skillet over medium-low heat. Add the shallot; cook 2 minutes. Add the tarragon and potatoes. Toss to coat the potatoes with butter.

2. Pour the cream over the potatoes. Heat to boiling; reduce the heat. Simmer, stirring occasionally, until just tender, 18 to 20 minutes. Add salt and pepper to taste.

Serves 4.

ALSATIAN POTATO TART

This recipe is a residual of my stay in France in the early 1970s. A devise of obviously mixed heritage (part French, part German), it is one culinary instance in which potatoes dabbed with bacon and frothed in egg do not a breakfast make. Serve it instead with roast chicken or turkey!

3 strips bacon
¼ cup heavy or whipping cream
2 eggs, at room temperature
3 tablespoons finely grated onion
2 tablespoons all-purpose flour
1 teaspoon salt
¼ teaspoon freshly ground black pepper
2 allspice berries, crushed, or a pinch
   ground
6 medium potatoes

1. Preheat the oven to 400°F. Sauté the bacon in a 9- or 10-inch cast-iron skillet until crisp. Drain on paper towels, crumble, and reserve. Reserve the bacon drippings in the skillet.

2. Beat the cream with the eggs until light. Stir in the onion, flour, salt, pepper, and allspice. (If possible, use dried, crushed berries. They are more potent.)

3. Peel the potatoes and grate them directly into the cream-egg mixture. Mix well. Stir in the reserved bacon.

4. Place the bacon skillet with its drippings in the oven for 5 minutes. Swirl the drippings over the bottom and sides of the skillet, then pour the potato mixture into the hot skillet. Bake until puffed and lightly browned, 30 to 35 minutes. Cut into wedges to serve.

Serves 6 to 8.

POTATO PUNTS

A year ago, I stumbled onto yet another tonic use for the potato skin: as a hangover cure. Or perhaps a preventive; you be the judge. I am not at all certain of the efficacy of potato therapy, but this medicine is inspired stuff. The dish was created as a late-night snack at a New York restaurant called Simon's. Instead of a plate of crunchy skins with a drink, this hostelry serves up the shell as a slender skiff, packed with a precious cargo of sautéed, herbed potato balls. A wonderful idea for your very next steak!

2 large baking potatoes
Vegetable oil
4 teaspoons unsalted butter
Dried rosemary
Salt and freshly ground black pepper

1. Preheat the oven to 375°F. Prick the potatoes with a fork, and lightly rub them with oil. Bake the potatoes on a rack until tender, about 1¼ hours. Let cool for 30 minutes.

2. Cut the potatoes in half lengthwise and scoop out the interiors with a melon scoop. Set aside.

3. Heat ½ inch of vegetable oil in a medium skillet until hot but not smoking. Fry the potato skins until crisp on all sides. Rub each interior with 1 teaspoon of the butter and sprinkle with rosemary to taste.

4. Add the potato balls to the hot oil. Fry until crisp and golden. Drain quickly on paper towels. Fill each potato boat with potato balls, sprinkle with salt and pepper to taste, and serve immediately.

Serves 4.

Potatoes have had their share of roasting, mainly at the hands of church fathers.

Ever since the Pope's pronouncement about these brown orbs' erotic potential, Catholic priests in Rome sprinkle holy water on potato patches, religiously, at the close of Lent.

In Scotland, the Presbyterian clergy in 1770 declared the potato unsafe to eat—not for moral reasons, but simply because it was one food *not* mentioned in the Bible.

A hundred years later, an American minister in Boston cited the potato as the start of moral decay among city dwellers. Far from being an aphrodisiac, Reverend Richard Sewell declared that potato cookery led to wantonness in housewives because it required far too little kitchen preparation and left hands idle!

CRUNCHY BAKED POTATOES

Another baked potato of remarkable savor is roasted in salt and darn little else. The formula was sent me by a friend, Janet Cook Wilmoth, an American writer who lives in England. Janet and I became pen pals some while back and became recipe exchangers shortly afterward. Her spuds are very special—but they're not a good choice for those on low-sodium diets.

4 medium baking potatoes
Vegetable oil
Salt

Preheat the oven to 425°F. Pierce each potato with a fork. Pour about 1½ tablespoons oil in your hands and rub each potato thoroughly. Pour an equal amount of salt (or more if desired) into your hands. Rub into each potato. Place the potatoes on a rack and roast them in the oven until tender and crisp, about 45 minutes. (Reduce the heat if the potatoes begin to get too dark.)

Serves 4.

BARBECUED BAKED POTATOES

*T*he potato cookery that requires the least possible amount of energy is roasting. My favorite version (brought back from Fire Island) is splashed with barbecue sauce as it bakes. Use whatever sluice pleases you most, but one will not go wrong with the spicy stuff teamed with barbecued peppers in the previous chapter.

4 medium baking potatoes
½ cup Dynamite Barbecue Sauce (see page 280)

Preheat the oven to 350°F. Lightly prick the surface of the potatoes with a fork and place them on a roasting rack set in an oven pan. Brush each potato with barbecue sauce. Bake in the oven 1¼ hours, basting and turning the potatoes every 10 minutes.

Serves 4.

TATER 'N' TOMATER PIE

*G*lowing orange as a Texas sunrise, this recipe was passed on to me by a rawboned lady who sat through three of my cooking demonstrations at a department store in San Antonio. As the lights at Foley's winked a closing notice, she pressed the formula for this dish in my palm. "It's good. It has no name. It's old and it's made outta unpeeled taters and tomaters."

4 tablespoons (½ stick) unsalted butter
1 medium onion, finely chopped
1 clove garlic, minced
2 medium tomatoes, seeded, roughly chopped
½ teaspoon thyme
1½ teaspoons chopped fresh basil, or ½ teaspoon dried
¼ teaspoon sugar
1 beef bouillon cube, mashed
2 large baking potatoes, unpeeled, cut into ⅛-inch-thick slices
Salt and freshly ground black pepper
Chopped fresh parsley

1. Preheat the oven to 350°F. Melt 2 tablespoons of the butter in a large oven-proof skillet over medium heat. Add the onion; cook 1 minute. Add the garlic; cook 1 minute. Add the tomatoes, thyme, basil, sugar, and bouillon cube. Cook, uncovered, over medium heat, stirring occasionally, until thickened, about 20 minutes. Transfer the mixture to a bowl.

2. Melt 1 tablespoon of the butter in the same skillet over medium heat. Spread one third of the sauce over the bottom of the skillet. Add one third of the potato slices. Repeat the layers twice, ending with the potato slices, and dot with the remaining 1 tablespoon butter. Bake 30 minutes.

3. Run a knife around the edges of the potato pie and loosen the bottom with a spatula. Invert onto a serving platter. Sprinkle with salt and pepper to taste and chopped fresh parsley. Cut into wedges to serve.

Serves 4.

HEAVENLY MASHED POTATOES

My classic mashed potato franchise is unorthodox to be sure, since the potato is not boiled but baked first, then scooped out of its shell, creamed, seasoned, and buttered last of all. However, it is a treasure of a recipe—a slightly amended version of one my friend Miss Toklas invented.

2 pounds baking potatoes
Vegetable oil
1 teaspoon salt
¼ teaspoon freshly ground black pepper
¼ teaspoon freshly grated nutmeg
12 tablespoons (1½ sticks) unsalted butter,
   softened, plus 2 tablespoons melted
4 egg yolks
½ cup whipped cream

1. Preheat the oven to 350°F. Prick the potatoes with a fork and rub them lightly with oil. Bake them, on a rack, until tender, about 1 hour. Cut the potatoes in half lengthwise and scoop out the interiors. Reserve the skins for Crimped Potato Skins (see page 293), if desired. Rice the potatoes or mash them through a strainer.

2. Place the potatoes in a large bowl. Add the salt, pepper, nutmeg, and softened butter. Beat until smooth. Beat in the egg yolks, one at a time, beating thoroughly after each addition. Stir in the whipped cream.

3. Transfer the mixture to a baking dish. Bake 15 minutes. Drizzle the melted butter over the top, raise the heat to 450°F, and bake 5 minutes longer.

Serves 6.

KAREN'S MASHED POTATO ROLLS

Let's let the potato fatten us up, pleasurably. My choice of decadence? The sticky bun! This is the best version and a half you will ever sample, upon my honor. The donor is a food writer for the San Antonio *Express-News*, Karen Haram. Karen forfeited this treasured family recipe for mashed potato rolls with variations when she heard me bemoaning the loss of homey good things to eat. Her formula is old as the hills—from the Midwest, as was Karen originally—but it suffers no alteration whatsoever in either the dry airs of the Lone Star or the damp ones of the Empire State. Save up the calorie allowance for this one!

1 cup milk
½ cup sugar
2 teaspoons salt
1 package dry yeast
2 large eggs, lightly beaten
1 cup mashed potatoes

5½ cups all-purpose flour, approximately
8 tablespoons (1 stick) unsalted butter,
   melted

1. Scald the milk; cool it to lukewarm and pour it into a large bowl.

2. Add the sugar and salt to the lukewarm milk and stir well. Then, stir in the yeast; let stand 2 minutes. Beat in the eggs, mashed potatoes, and 1½ cups of the flour. Do not overbeat; some lumps will remain. Let stand until bubbly, about 5 minutes.

3. Add the melted butter to the flour-yeast mixture. Stir in the remaining flour, 1 cup at a time, until smooth and not sticky. Transfer to a floured board and knead 2 minutes, adding more flour if necessary.

4. Place the dough in a well-buttered large bowl. Turn the dough to coat it

Although Jiménez de Quesada brought potatoes from Peru to Spain, it was Sir Francis Drake who hustled them to England. The last of a longish line of Elizabethan explorers, Drake's reputation was based as much on his amatory pursuits as his naval intelligence. When he came upon the bespoke potato blooming in the Andes and heard of its prandial wonders, Drake simply took a shipload home as a souvenir for the Queen.

On the way back, however, a rampant case of scurvy broke out aboard ship. Against Drake's injunction, the captain-at-arms fed the crew the Queen's potatoes, raw, which saved their lives. How he knew that valuable vitamin C lay beneath the potato's umber cover is anyone's guess.

Queen Elizabeth received a single potato plant as booty. But the story has a bitter end. The Queen's cook, unaccustomed to foreign ingredients, threw all the potatoes away and served Her Majesty the green leaves instead.

The Queen was *not* amused.

with butter. Cover the dough and let it rise until tripled in volume, about 2 hours. Proceed with the variations that follow.

Karen's Parker House Rolls

1 recipe Mashed Potato Rolls
Flour for dusting
3 tablespoons unsalted butter, plus 2
    tablespoons melted

1. To make Parker House–type rolls, pull off pieces of dough slightly larger than a Ping-Pong ball. Flatten each with your hands. Then, using a floured knife, make a crease down the middle of each. Lightly butter one half and fold it over, pressing the edges securely with your fingers. Place the rolls, seam side up, about 1 inch apart on a greased baking sheet. Brush with melted butter. Cover loosely and let rise 40 minutes.

2. Preheat the oven to 400°F. Bake the rolls until lightly browned, about 15 to 18 minutes.

Makes 18 rolls.

Karen's Caramel Rolls

1 recipe Mashed Potato Rolls
½ cup granulated sugar
2½ teaspoons ground cinnamon
8 tablespoons (1 stick) unsalted butter,
    softened
1 cup firmly packed dark brown sugar
1 cup heavy or whipping cream

1. Divide the risen mashed potato dough in half. Roll each half into a rectangle, ¼ inch thick.

2. Combine the granulated sugar with the cinnamon and softened butter. Beat until smooth and spread over each rectangle. Roll up like a jelly roll and slice into 1-inch pieces. You should get nine pieces per roll.

3. Combine the brown sugar with

the heavy cream. Pour into two buttered 8-inch-square cake pans. Place the rolls, flat-side down, on top of the sugar mixture, nine rolls in each pan. Cover and let rise until doubled in volume, about 1 hour.

4. Preheat the oven to 350°F. Bake the rolls until golden brown, 25 to 30 minutes. When done, cover with a serving platter and invert. Remove the pan after 1 minute, allowing the caramel to run down over the rolls.

Makes 18 rolls.

Karen's Butter Pecan Rolls

1 recipe Mashed Potato Rolls
8 tablespoons (1 stick) unsalted butter,
 melted, plus 12 tablespoons (1½ sticks)
2½ cups firmly packed dark brown sugar
2 teaspoons ground cinnamon
1½ cups chopped pecans

1. Divide the risen mashed potato dough in half. Roll each half into a rectangle, ¼ inch thick.

2. Brush each rectangle with the melted butter. Combine ½ cup of the brown sugar with the cinnamon and sprinkle this over the dough. Roll up like a jelly roll and slice into 1-inch pieces. You should get nine pieces per roll.

3. Melt the 12 tablespoons butter with the remaining 2 cups brown sugar over medium heat. Divide the mixture between two buttered 8-inch-square cake pans. Sprinkle the nuts evenly over the sugar mixture. Place the rolls, flat side down, on top of the nuts, nine rolls in each pan. Cover and let rise until doubled in volume, about 1 hour.

4. Preheat the oven to 350°F. Bake the rolls until golden brown, 25 to 30 minutes. When done, cover with a serving platter and invert. Remove the pan after 1 minute, allowing the caramel to run down over rolls.

Makes 18 rolls.

MYRA'S POTATO LATKES

*L*et me state at once that I am very much in favor of these weighty ovals. I was raised on *latkes* that were not only light but greaseless and highly digestible, which is not a common occurrence in every Jewish-American home. The lightness was due to a speck of baking powder; the lack of grease related to a minimum of shortening (always Crisco) in the pan; and the digestibility was reinforced by quick cookery.

The recipe came from my grandmother, who passed it on to my mother, who passed it on to my sister. I could never get the hang of the darn things. My sister grates her potatoes by hand, using the finest blade. Quite by accident I grated them roughly once and had to process them afterward. The trick worked, so I recommend it to all but hard-nosed latke makers.

In our house the potato pancake was always served with a rich meaty gravy, plus applesauce on the side. Never, never with sour cream!

1½ pounds baking potatoes
Juice of 1 lemon
1 small onion, finely grated
1 large egg, lightly beaten
2 tablespoons all-purpose flour

2 teaspoons baking powder
Salt and freshly ground black pepper
Crisco shortening
Mechana (recipe follows)
Applesauce

1. Preheat the oven to 250°F. Peel the potatoes and roughly grate them into a large bowl of cold water to which you have added the lemon juice. Let stand 30 minutes.

2. After the potatoes have soaked in the water, drain them and squeeze them dry with your hands. Place the potatoes in the container of a food processor. Process, using the on/off switch, until fairly smooth but not wet. Transfer to a large bowl. Add the onion, egg, flour, baking powder, and salt and pepper to taste. Stir until smooth.

3. Place a large cast-iron skillet over medium heat. Film the bottom of the skillet with the shortening. Using about 1 large tablespoon for each, add four latkes to the skillet. Cook until golden brown and puffed, about 1 minute. Turn over and brown the other side. Place on a rack and keep warm in the oven while sautéing the remaining latkes. Film the bottom of the skillet after each batch.

Serve with *mechana* and applesauce.
Serves 4.

Mechana
(Meat Sauce)

1 large yellow onion, thinly sliced
4 pounds beef brisket
1 to 3 bay leaves (optional)
1½ cups beef broth (see page 414)

1. Preheat the oven to 350°F. Place the onions over the bottom of a large Dutch oven. Add the beef, and the bay leaves if desired. Cook, covered, in the oven for 1 hour.

2. Continue to cook, adding beef broth to the pot as needed, until the meat is very tender and shreds easily, about 2½ hours longer. Lightly shred the meat into its cooking juices before serving.
Serves 6 to 8.

SPINACH

The Chinese Flower

If I were faced with the onerous chore of selecting a last meal on earth, one of the dishes would have to include spinach. I'd choose a salad of tender greens with a healthy tinge of grit between the leaves to remind me of the transitory retribution mortality imposes. But, come to think of it, I have already consumed that repast. Memorably.

The meal was taken at the Broadmoor Hotel in Colorado Springs, in the shadow of Pike's Peak, and it was a belated birthday celebration I would just as lief have skipped. My host and tour guide to Colorado was Phillip Schulz, a young man raised in that rustic state who has since become my collaborator, advisor, and truest friend in and out of the kitchen. On this occasion, after a month of successful, if wearying, cooking

classes in Denver and parts west, we were playing hookey. Phillip proposed a day off "to see the mountains" before we flew on to Chicago to resume teaching, and I agreed with alacrity.

Our sortie began early because a Schulz family gathering was planned to honor the prodigal son at his parents' home later that evening. I knew those fabulous dinners well, having had the good luck to be included among the clan on more than one occasion and would not have missed it for the world. That I almost did is the sand in this spinach story, for the Broadmoor's bowlful was flawless.

Like a Victorian castle preserved in amber, this old hotel nestles among tall aspen trees and taller mountains scarred with ski trails. We had come there via a superhighway dotted with tract homes and shopping centers, and the alteration of the virgin landscape was dispiriting to both of us. Phillip had done a stint of army duty at Fort Carson nearby and knew every conceivable route back to his parents' home in Golden, so when he proposed a return through the Cheyenne Mountain pass and Cripple Creek, I jumped at the opportunity. The names alone were a whiff of the Old West I had come here expressly to inhale. The moment I agreed, Phillip seemed a tad reluctant.

"It *is* a longer way back of course," he announced soberly, settling into the driver's seat of our rented car. "And the mountain roads can be dangerous."

"On a day like this?"

It was mid-October but so warm we had both divested ourselves of our jackets after lunch. Phillip scanned the mountainside with a native's eye. "It doesn't seem likely. But there is a touch of snow along the ridges."

"Phillip! Let's go."

We did, and with pleasure for the first few miles, for the road up Cheyenne Mountain was relatively untraveled and the twisting single lane of macadam that took us high above the town made driving easy. Then, quite abruptly, the pavement ended—or more specifically, became a dirt road that in time turned to icy mud as we traveled higher, past the timberline. Worse than the loss of road was the absence of sunlight; what had been a golden day minutes before became gray, patchy fog, and the light snow observed from below was now a treacherous embankment that made the car swerve precipitously as we inched along.

"How far is it to Cripple Creek?" I asked charily after a terrible quarter-hour of silence.

"I don't know. Twenty or thirty miles. Think we should go back?"

The question was rhetorical, for clearly there was no way. We drove at a virtual snail's pace now, taking each new twisting curve with bated breath. The road had diminished to a trail barely wider than the car and we hugged the cliff side so tightly that loose rocks and snow often covered the windshield. The alternative was a sheer glacial descent of perhaps two thousand feet.

"Phillip! What happens if another car comes along this road?"

He looked straight ahead before answering, his fingers never leaving the wheel. "Technically, the car going uphill has the right of way. If we are on a downside, we would have to drive in reverse until we reached a stretch that's passable. But I will tell you right now, I have no intention of testing the principle. If one comes, we simply abandon ship!"

"Then what?"

"I don't know. Hike, or hitch a ride!"

Thankfully none came, but the drive was an endless torment nevertheless. After several hours of hairpin turns, I pressed my friend for a judgment on how much farther we would have to travel. It was the only time he ever lost his composure, for Phillip Schulz is a most proficient driver.

"How the hell do I know? I can't remember. I was younger when I did this last. I was probably drunk too! If you can't face it, go to sleep."

I tried, but without much success. So to calm my nerves, I worked on thinking about pleasanter things. It had grown dark in the car and at one point I must have been murmuring, for my friend turned to me and asked, "Are you saying your prayers?"

"No. Recipes. How do you think spinach salad would taste with bits of bacon and a warm goat cheese dressing?"

"Good. But then, anything would," said Schulz the pragmatist. "I'm hungry."

Truthfully, so was I. And with that

heartening life sign intact, we eventually crossed the mountain—but not until I had had the time to work on a few more culinary notions, my most calming topic of thought!

We arrived for dinner late and unkempt, but starving and glad to be alive. I wish I could report that we ate spinach in some guise but we did not; it was roast pork and absolutely mouth-watering. In the Schulz family, no meal is ever begun without a grace. Never was a benediction spoken with more fervor or gratitude than by the mountain climbers that night. And the last meal on earth was postponed once more.

Vegetable Roots

*T*he ancient Medes prescribed twelve washings for every leaf of spinach that went into a pot—eleven of which (in water) were meant to free the vegetable of its dark, earthly associations. The twelfth (in human tears) was supposed to season it with God's wisdom.

Tears probably came easily after all that laundering; it will come as no real shock to discover that few Medes ever consumed a forkful!

A late bloomer, *Spinacia oleracea* was originally noted growing wild near the desert lands of Dasht-e-Kavir and was transplanted to Persian gardens, where it was cultivated mainly to satisfy the appetites of much-prized Persian cats. The absence of a proper Sanskrit name for this vegetable suggests that the first seeds were planted well after the death of Christ. In Persia, spinach was (and still is) known as *isfānākh*, which means a green hand.

From Persia fingers of that hand traveled east to China in the sixth century. Whether Chinese cats appreciated its peppery flavor is not recorded, but spinach certainly made its way into the population's soup bowls, as "Persian herbs."

The Chinese raised spinach extensively along the outer fringes of their rice fields, where the soil is sandiest; and in time they transported the green to India and Nepal as well, where it bore the designation "China flower."

The invading Moors introduced spinach to Spain in the twelfth century—along with beheadings, circumcisions, and several other cultural gratuities. Only spinach took root. Within a hundred years this therapeutic leaf was known all over Western Europe as *spanacha*, or Spanish greens.

Some say Columbus brought spinach to the New World. Others claim it was part of the *Mayflower* cargo. True or false, it matters not a whit for this vegetable was resolutely unpopular with settlers and natives alike. An early Pilgrim child's prayer invokes the Good Lord's protection from fire, famine, flood, and *unclean foreign leaves*; read, sandy spinach. And it took another five hundred years (along with the invention of spin-dry vegetable laundering machines) to convince American kids that a random portion of green on a plate does not necessarily indicate a deposit of grit between the molars!

What to Look For

I must confess I am something of a Tartar when I buy spinach, always poking about the packages on the supermarket shelf to uncover the freshest bundle. Less than prime spinach develops an acrid, unpalatable taste, so it is wise to sniff as well as scrutinize the produce you plan to purchase. Freshly picked spinach has a fine green earthy scent; sour cabbage-smelling leaves mean the stuff is definitely over the hill.

Fresh (unpacked) leaf spinach is a shopper's best buy. Prepackaged bunches tend to yield a high proportion of stems, not to mention bruised leaves, under their plastic covers; these bruised leaves must be removed prior to refrigerating or they will rot the rest. Fresh spinach, on the other hand, is sandy; so you pays your money and takes your choice in the matter!

When I buy fresh spinach, I search for the crispest, greenest leaf. When plastic is the option, the bundle should retain a measure of spring when it is pinched. Avoid all spinach, in or out of a wrapper, that is yellowing, moldy, or wet.

As a kid I believed (doubtless out of devotion to Popeye) that regular dinner doses of spinach built muscles of cast iron or maybe even steel. There is indeed some basis for that assumption, since spinach is famous for its iron content. Unfortunately the iron in spinach is not in a readily assimilated form, so weight lifting is still the answer for the muscle-bound. However, do not get me wrong. A single cup of cooked spinach is exceptionally rich in vitamins (14,580 units of A alone), and contains 583 milligrams of potassium and 167 grams of calcium to boot. The best spinach news of all is the calorie count: less than 15 calories in a cup of raw spinach and a scant 40 in a cup of cooked.

Preparation

As recently as fifty years ago, cookbooks dictated seven washings for all leaf spinach prior to cooking. I usually settle for a longish stint under a running faucet while I remove the fibrous stems—even when the content of my colander is plastic-packaged spinach. Newly picked leaves take a good deal longer. After an initial shower under the tap, I place garden spinach in a basin of cool water for fifteen minutes; then I change the water and keep changing it until no trace of sand is left in the bottom of the bowl.

Cooking spinach is a somewhat more personal matter. On occasion I wilt it briefly in boiling water (no longer than five minutes) and then plunge it under cold running water to retard the cooking; then I drain it well before proceeding with my recipe. At other times I will add the (cleaned, chopped) raw spinach directly to the dish I am making. However, my basic cooking approach—recommended for general use—is what I call pot-steaming. I place the cleaned spinach in a heavy-duty (non-aluminum) saucepan with a tight-fitting lid. I add no water other than the drops that cling to the leaves after rinsing, and cook the spinach over low heat. Time? About five minutes per pound, or until the leaves crumple and soften. Then I drain the spinach thoroughly in a colander (saving any juices for my soup-stock collection) and proceed with the recipe.

It might be a good idea to note in passing that 2 to 3 pounds of fresh spinach yields 2 cups of cooked, and ½ cup cooked spinach is the average amount most diners will usually consume.

BRUMMAGEMS
(Spinach Rolls)

In my formula for Viennese vegetable rolls, the filling is homemade tomato purée and diced mushrooms, and the roll (100 percent spinach) is anointed with oil and vinegar. It makes a fine first course, salad dish, or hors d'oeuvre, garnished with a slice of the reddest onion you can find.

1 tablespoon olive oil, plus extra to taste
1 onion, finely chopped
2 cloves garlic, minced
3 pounds ripe tomatoes, peeled, seeded,
     diced
Sprig of marjoram, chopped, or a pinch of
     dried
Pinch of ground allspice
Salt and freshly ground black pepper
⅓ pound mushrooms, finely chopped
10 ounces fresh spinach, washed, stems
     trimmed
Red wine vinegar
½ red onion, sliced very thin

1. Heat the oil in a large saucepan over medium-low heat. Add the onion; cook 1 minute. Add the garlic; cook 4 minutes. Stir in the tomatoes, the marjoram, and allspice. Heat to boiling; reduce the heat. Simmer, uncovered, stirring frequently, until the sauce is as thick as a paste, about 1 hour. Season to taste with salt and pepper. Set aside.

2. Cook the mushrooms in a medium skillet over medium heat (without oil or butter) until all liquid has evaporated, stirring occasionally. Set aside.

3. Preheat the oven to 350°F. Cook the spinach in boiling salted water until just wilted, about 30 seconds. Drain immediately under cold running water. Unfold the leaves and pat them dry with paper towels.

4. On a work surface, place 3 or 4 spinach leaves, overlapping, to form a crepe shape, about 4 inches across. Spread with 2 tablespoons of the tomato mixture and 1 tablespoon of the mushrooms. Roll up and place on a lightly greased baking sheet. Continue until all ingredients are used up. Bake for 15 minutes.

5. Cool and refrigerate, covered, overnight. Sprinkle with vinegar and oil to taste before serving. Garnish with red onion slices.

Makes about 12.

SLOW-BAKED SPINACH TART

This borrowing from M.F.K. Fisher is a heavenly cracker-wafer-toast fabrication. A most unusual canape or accompaniment to cold or hot dishes, it is a recipe well worth notching on your culinary belt. But you must make sure to bake it for the required time: four hours! It may look done before that time, Mrs. Fisher cautions, but it is not!

10-ounce package frozen spinach, or 10
     ounces fresh, washed, stems trimmed,
     cooked until tender
½ cup spinach liquid (see step 1)
1 medium onion, roughly chopped
1 clove garlic
2 large ribs celery, chopped
⅓ cup roughly chopped fresh parsley
8 to 10 fresh basil leaves
2 sprigs fresh thyme, or ¼ teaspoon dried

¾ cup olive oil
2 eggs
1 cup grated Jarlsberg cheese
Salt and freshly ground black pepper
⅛ teaspoon freshly grated nutmeg
1 cup fresh bread crumbs
¼ cup freshly grated Parmesan cheese

1. Thaw the spinach over a strainer if using frozen; reserve ½ cup of the liquid. If using fresh, press the liquid from the cooked spinach to get ½ cup. Add water if necessary.

2. Preheat the oven to 275°F. In the container of a blender or food processor, combine the spinach with the juice, onion, garlic, celery, parsley, basil, thyme, and ½ cup of the oil. Blend until smooth. Add the eggs; blend 30 seconds longer. Transfer to a bowl and stir in the Jarlsberg cheese. Add salt and pepper to taste and the nutmeg. Spread this mixture evenly over the bottom of a lightly oiled 10-by-15-inch baking sheet. Sprinkle the top with the bread crumbs and Parmesan cheese. Drizzle the remaining oil over the top. Bake until dry and crisp, about 4 hours. Serve hot or cold, sliced into squares. (The spinach squares can be stored in an airtight container or in the freezer.)

Makes 2½ to 3 dozen.

POTAGE VERT
(Spinach and Vegetable Soup)

*F*rench workers and farmers enjoy a *bonne soupe* as their midday meal; the contents change with the topography and local produce. I have eaten cabbage soups in Alsace Lorraine and bean versions in Burgundy, always with a goodly measure of green vegetables in proportion to the other weighty endowments in the pot. The following *bonne soupe* comes from the Alpes-Maritimes, where the spinach grows thick as poppies—maybe thicker. The dish (bright green with uncooked spinach) is a perfect way to begin a winter's dinner or—more likely—serves excellently as a meal in itself. To the local formula for a *bonne soupe* I have added another French amendment: my friend Julia Child's dipping sauce for the chicken and beef that turns any *soupe* super.

1 tablespoon unsalted butter
1 teaspoon vegetable oil
2 to 2½ pounds beef chuck roast
1 beef bone (leftover bones are fine)
2 onions, finely chopped
1 clove garlic, minced
2 large carrots, chopped
1 stalk celery with leaves, chopped
2 leeks, well cleaned, trimmed, sliced
2½-pound chicken
4 parsley sprigs, tied together with string
5 cups chicken broth (see page 414)
3 cups water
1 tomato, peeled, seeded, chopped
2 tablespoons lemon juice
½ cup broken thin spaghetti
8 to 10 ounces fresh spinach, washed, stems trimmed, shredded

Salt and freshly ground black pepper
Sauce de Sorges (recipe follows)

1. Heat the butter with the oil in a large heavy pot or Dutch oven over medium heat. Add the beef and beef bone. Sauté until browned; remove from the pot and set aside.

2. Add the onions to the pot; cook 1 minute. Add the garlic, carrots, celery, and leeks; cook 5 minutes. Add the chicken, browned beef and bone, parsley sprigs, chicken broth, and water. Heat to boiling, skimming the surface as necessary; reduce the heat. Simmer, covered, 1 hour. Remove the chicken when tender; set aside and cover with aluminum foil. Continue to cook the soup until the

beef is tender, about 1 hour longer.

3. Remove the beef, bone, and parsley from the soup. Set aside.

4. Add the tomato and lemon juice to the soup; simmer, uncovered, 10 minutes. Add the spaghetti. Continue to cook until the spaghetti is tender, about 12 minutes longer.

5. Meanwhile, cut the beef into slices; remove the meat from the beef bone; and remove the meat from the chicken, discarding the skin and bones.

6. When the spaghetti is tender, add the beef, chicken, and spinach to the soup. Cook 5 minutes longer. Add salt and pepper to taste. Serve with Sauce de Sorges.

Serves 6 to 8 as a main course.

Sauce de Sorges
(Herbal Mayonnaise)

1 egg
1 teaspoon Dijon mustard
Pinch of salt
1 tablespoon white wine vinegar
¾ cup olive or vegetable oil
1 tablespoon heavy or whipping cream
2 small shallots, minced
2 teaspoons capers
2 to 3 tablespoons chopped fresh dill

1. Boil the egg for 3 minutes. Shell the egg, and carefully scoop the soft yolk into a small bowl. Chop the white and set it aside.

The spinach plant is a rather aggressive member of the goosefoot family, whose other members include Swiss chard and beets. Spinach grows on spines which resemble a webbed biped—or at least they did to some unnamed naturalist's eye. Out of that association the veg's moniker might have been "goose-green," and in fact the British called it that for a time in the twelfth century to show their distaste for the rash of Frenchifications that had entered their language. Somewhat later they relented and allowed the Francophile *épinard* to become the Anglo-Saxon *spynoches*, which in time was trimmed to mere spinach—which is a blessing for a man who makes his grocery list on his shirt cuff.

Armenians call spinach *spanax*. Germans dub it *Spinat*. But it's really best abbreviated: *spnch!*

2. To the egg yolk, add the mustard, salt, and vinegar. Slowly beat in the oil, then thin with the cream. The sauce should be the texture of a thin mayonnaise. Stir in the egg white, shallots, capers, and dill.

Makes about 1 cup.

WARM GOAT CHEESE AND SPINACH SALAD

On any occasion, a spinach salad is the better for a thorough washing of the greens first. Though its invention is definitely a result of that treacherous trip through Colorado's mountains, this dish also owes a debt to the green cuisine of my Californian friend, Wolfgang Puck, owner and chef at the restaurant Spago.

½ pound fresh goat cheese (chèvre)
¾ cup olive oil
1 teaspoon chopped fresh thyme, or
     ⅛ teaspoon dried
1 pound fresh spinach
1 teaspoon Dijon mustard
1 teaspoon chopped fresh tarragon, or
     ¼ teaspoon dried
1 tablespoon hazelnut liqueur
2 teaspoons tarragon vinegar
1 egg yolk
¼ teaspoon salt
Freshly ground black pepper
3 strips crisp-fried bacon, crumbled

1. Cut the goat cheese into eight equal pieces. Place them in a shallow bowl, and drizzle with ¼ cup of the oil. Sprinkle with the thyme. Cover, and refrigerate overnight.

2. Remove the goat cheese from the refrigerator 1 hour before serving.

3. Trim the stems from the spinach, wash the leaves well, and tear them into bite-size pieces. With paper towels, gently squeeze out the excess liquid. Place the spinach in a large bowl.

4. In a medium bowl, whisk the mustard with the tarragon, liqueur, vinegar, egg yolk, and salt. Slowly whisk in the remaining ½ cup oil. Add pepper to taste. Pour this dressing over the salad and toss well.

5. Place 2 tablespoons of the oil marinade from the cheese in a large heavy skillet over medium heat. When hot but not smoking, add the cheese pieces, lifting them out of the remaining marinade with a slotted spoon. Sauté 30 seconds per side. Add the cheese to the salad, and sprinkle with the bacon.

Serves 4.

SPINACH WITH SESAME SEED DRESSING

One diet food I dearly dote upon is a spinach salad. Everyone knows the bacon, egg, and Parmesan cheese version, but few are acquainted with an equally brilliant spinach salad that is a Japanese invention: spinach cooked and then sluiced with soy sauce and sesame seeds. The recipe is one given to me by Elizabeth Andoh, author of *At Home with Japanese Cooking*. It's terrific.

1 pound fresh spinach, washed, stems
     trimmed
3 tablespoons sesame seeds
2 tablespoons superfine sugar
2½ tablespoons soy sauce

1. Cook the spinach leaves in boiling water until just wilted, about 30 seconds. Rinse under cold running water, drain well, and chop coarsely.

2. Heat a large heavy skillet over medium-high heat. Add the sesame seeds and cook, shaking the pan constantly, until they are lightly browned. Transfer the seeds to a small bowl or mortar and crush them with a heavy wooden spoon or pestle until finely ground. Add the sugar and continue to grind. Stir in the soy sauce.

3. Toss the spinach with the dressing in a serving bowl. Serve chilled or at room temperature.

Serves 2 to 4.

FOUR-DAY SPINACH

*T*his spinach out-take is of Russian descent, and a number worthy of some czar's kitchen. It is a curious but fabled rendition: spinach that is seasoned with only butter and vodka and cooked, then set aside, then enriched and cooked again, over a period of ninety-six hours. The recipe is from Phillip Schulz's excellently spirited cookbook, *Vodka 'n Vittles.*

*2 pounds fresh spinach, washed, stems
    trimmed*
1 cup (2 sticks) unsalted butter
5 teaspoons vodka
2 teaspoons lemon juice
⅛ teaspoon freshly grated nutmeg
Salt and freshly ground black pepper

1. Heat 4 quarts of salted water to boiling. Turn off the heat and stir in the spinach. Let it stand 2 minutes, then rinse under cold running water and drain. Gently squeeze the spinach to remove excess liquid. Roughly chop.

2. Melt 4 tablespoons of the butter in a medium saucepan over low heat. Add the spinach. Cook, stirring constantly, until all the butter has been absorbed into the spinach and the spinach is warmed through. Sprinkle with 1 teaspoon of the vodka. Transfer the spinach to a bowl and allow it to cool. Cover, and chill 24 hours.

3. The next day, heat the spinach in another 4 tablespoons of the butter. Cook, stirring constantly, until all the butter has been absorbed and the spinach is warmed through. Sprinkle with another 1 teaspoon of the vodka. Transfer to a bowl, cool, cover, and chill 24 hours.

4. Repeat this process again on the third day.

5. On the fourth day, repeat the process once more. When the spinach is warmed through, add the remaining 2 teaspoons vodka, the lemon juice, nutmeg, and salt and pepper to taste. Serve immediately.

Serves 4.

SPINACH AND COCONUT MORUGA

*O*ne of the most unusual spinach devises in my file stems from the Caribbean island of Trinidad, where it is most often served up with hard-cooked eggs after a long church service. Not a lunch or dinner dish, it might be considered something between a snack and a repast. At my table it accompanies broiled chicken or a grilled chop.

One point worth noting: in the recipe I acquired, coconut milk was the sole liquid. Since fresh coconuts often are hard to come by outside of an island paradise, I modified the ingredients and made a "milk" all my own. It's delicious and a jot more practical.

1 can (3½ ounces) sweetened coconut
·1 cup milk
3 tablespoons unsalted butter
¼ teaspoon crushed dried hot red peppers
¼ teaspoon salt
⅓ cup chopped macadamia nuts
10 ounces fresh spinach, washed, stems
    trimmed, roughly chopped

1. Combine the coconut with the milk in the container of a blender or processor. Blend until fairly smooth. Strain the coconut into a small bowl. Skim the surface of the milk, reserving ½ cup milk.

2. Melt 2 tablespoons of the butter in a small skillet over medium heat. Stir in the peppers, salt, and macadamia nuts. Cook, stirring constantly, until the nuts are lightly browned, about 4 minutes. Stir in the strained coconut. Continue to cook, stirring constantly, 3 minutes. Remove from the heat.

3. Melt the remaining 1 tablespoon butter in a medium saucepan over medium heat. Add the spinach and reserved ½ cup coconut milk. Cook, tossing constantly, until the spinach is wilted, about 5 minutes. Raise the heat slightly and continue to cook until almost all liquid has evaporated. Stir in the coconut–macadamia nut mixture.

Serves 4.

GNOCCHI TICINESE

*T*his version of gnocchi stems from the Swiss Italian Alps—the canton of Ticino, to be exact. It is a province far to the north of Milan, where cheese making is the way of life. Not surprising to discover, then, that there gnocchi are a mixture of nothing but spinach and ricotta cheese. An unbelievably delicate devise, this recipe was passed on to me by a wonderfully talented writer and cook from Elmira, New York: Mary Cassetti.

10 ounces fresh spinach, washed, trimmed
    of stems
1 pound ricotta cheese
1 large egg, beaten
¼ teaspoon freshly grated nutmeg
¾ cup grated Jarlsberg cheese
¼ cup freshly grated Romano cheese
½ cup all-purpose flour
1 cup heavy or whipping cream
¼ cup freshly grated Parmesan cheese

1. Cook the spinach in boiling water for 4 minutes. Drain, and gently squeeze out the excess liquid. Place the spinach in the container of a food processor and add the ricotta cheese. Process 10 seconds. Add the egg, nutmeg, Jarlsberg cheese, Romano cheese, and flour. Process until mixed.

2. With floured hands form the dough into small balls or ovals and place them on a plate. Cover, and chill for 24 hours.

3. The next day, drop the gnocchi, about 6 at a time, into boiling salted water until they rise to the top. Remove with a slotted spoon and drain lightly on paper towels. Transfer to a well-buttered baking dish. When all the gnocchi are done, reheat in a 300°F oven for 12 minutes.

4. Meanwhile, heat the cream to boiling in a small saucepan. Simmer until thickened, about 5 minutes. Pour the cream over the gnocchi and sprinkle with the Parmesan cheese.

Serves 8.

GNOCCHI SPINACIO

(Spinach Dumplings)

*I*n Italy dishes that are dappled green with spinach are usually dubbed Florentine this or Florentine that on menus. I never knew why until I drove to this Renaissance city on the Arno and saw the mountainsides nearby covered with a delicate plant, which I took to be myrtle but was actually spinach. *Spinacio* grows like a weed in Florence in the springtime.

Naturally enough the vegetable is shipped to other areas of the boot and flavors varied Italian dishes. These Roman *gnocchi* are potato dumplings fused with spinach. Each forkful is as light as a cloud.

6 ounces fresh spinach, washed, trimmed
  of stems, chopped
2 eggs
½ cup all-purpose flour
1¼ cups cold cooked mashed potatoes
¼ teaspoon freshly grated nutmeg
½ teaspoon salt
3 tablespoons freshly grated Parmesan
  cheese
Ground white pepper

1. Place the spinach with just the water that clings to the leaves in a medium saucepan. Cover, and cook over medium-low heat until very tender, about 10 minutes. Remove from the heat, drain, gently squeeze out the excess liquid, and cool.

2. Beat the eggs in a large bowl until light. Beat in the spinach, flour, mashed potatoes, nutmeg, salt, and Parmesan cheese. Mix thoroughly. Add white pepper to taste.

3. Scoop up the dough with a spoon, 1 tablespoon at a time, and drop into boiling salted water. Do no more than 6 gnocchi at one time. Let simmer until firm, about 1½ minutes. Remove with a slotted spoon and drain lightly on paper towels. Transfer to a well-buttered baking dish. When all the gnocchi are done, reheat in a 300°F oven for about 12 minutes. Serve with extra Parmesan cheese if desired.

Serves 4.

GREEN CREAMED RICE

*T*o my mind, the classic spinach rendering is always enveloped in cream and delicately scented with nutmeg. My favorite such alliance is also fortified with cooked rice. The originator is a good cook named Gail Firestone, though I doubt she would now recognize her creation. Things have a way of changing at my stove.

⅔ cup long-grain rice
1 pound fresh spinach, washed, stems
  trimmed
¼ teaspoon crushed dried hot red peppers
1 cup hot milk
4 tablespoons (½ stick) unsalted butter

2 tablespoons all-purpose flour
½ cup heavy or whipping cream
1 teaspoon honey
⅛ teaspoon freshly grated nutmeg
Salt and freshly ground black pepper

1. Add the rice to a large pot of boiling salted water; stir once while the water returns to boiling. Simmer over medium heat until the rice is just tender, about 12 minutes. Drain in a colander. Place the colander over simmering water and cover with a layer of paper towels. Let the rice steam for 15 minutes or longer.

2. Place the spinach with just the water that clings to the leaves in a large skillet. Sprinkle with the crushed red peppers. Cover, and cook over medium-low heat until the spinach is wilted, about 5 minutes. Place the spinach in the container of a blender or food proc-

essor; add ¼ cup of the milk. Blend until smooth. Set aside.

3. Melt 2 tablespoons of the butter in a medium saucepan over medium-low heat. Stir in the flour. Cook, stirring constantly, 2 minutes. Whisk in the remaining ¾ cup milk and the cream. Add the honey and nutmeg. Heat to boiling; reduce the heat. Simmer until slightly thickened, about 5 minutes. Add the spinach; cook 3 minutes.

4. Combine the spinach mixture with the cooked rice. Mix well. Add salt and pepper to taste, and cut in the remaining 2 tablespoons butter.

Serves 4.

SANTA FE SPINACH AND BEAN BAKE

*B*ecause of its Mideastern heritage, spinach is largely aligned to exotic dishes and dark, long-cooked brews. However, it is an ingredient that has adapted itself to other environments. Here, for example, is a "Tex-Mex" casserole of beans and peppers out of Sante Fe.

½ pound dried pinto beans
3 strips bacon, chopped
1 large onion, finely chopped
1 clove garlic, minced
1 small hot red pepper, seeded, deveined, minced (see Guacamole headnote, page 37)
10 ounces fresh spinach, washed, stems trimmed, chopped
2 tablespoons mild ground chiles
1 teaspoon salt
¼ pound Monterey jack cheese with jalapeño peppers
¼ cup beef broth (see page 414)

1. Cook the beans in boiling salted water until tender, 1½ to 2 hours. Drain.

2. Preheat the oven to 400°F. Sauté the bacon in a medium skillet over medium heat until crisp. Add the onion;

cook 1 minute. Add the garlic and hot pepper; cook 3 minutes. Stir in the spinach and continue to cook, stirring constantly, until the spinach is wilted, about 5 minutes. Stir in the ground chiles, salt, the cooked beans, cheese, and beef broth. Pour into a baking dish. Bake 20 minutes.

Serves 6.

LONG ISLAND BANK ROLL

*T*his is a recent creation of mine: spinach-and-shrimp-stuffed fish filets, named in memory of palmy days at The Store in Amagansett.

1 cup clam juice
1 cup dry white wine
1 slice lemon
1 teaspoon fennel seeds, tied in a
    cheesecloth bag
6 raw shrimp, shelled and deveined
1 cup roughly chopped fresh spinach,
    washed and trimmed first
2 shallots, minced
1 tablespoon chopped fresh basil, or 1
    teaspoon dried
4 flounder filets, about ¼ pound each
1 tablespoon unsalted butter
1 medium cucumber, peeled, seeded, finely
    chopped
1 sprig fresh thyme, chopped, or a pinch of
    dried
2 teaspoons lemon juice
⅓ cup sour cream
Salt and freshly ground black pepper

1. Heat the clam juice, wine, lemon slice, and fennel seeds to boiling in a heavy enameled skillet; reduce the heat. Simmer 5 minutes.

2. Chop 2 of the shrimp and place them in a medium-size bowl. Add the spinach, half of the minced shallots, and the basil. Mix well and spread over the fish filets. Roll the filets up lengthwise. Place the filets in the skillet and poach, covered, in the liquid for 3 minutes. Turn the fish over and add the whole shrimp to the pan. Cook, uncovered, until the fish flakes easily and the shrimp are pink, about 4 minutes. Transfer the fish to a serving platter and keep warm in a low oven. Reserve the shrimp.

3. Melt the butter in a small saucepan over medium-low heat. Add the remaining minced shallot; cook 2 minutes. Add all the remaining ingredients; cook without boiling for 4 minutes. Spoon this sauce over the fish and decorate with the whole shrimp.

Serves 2 to 4.

SPINACH-AND-RICE-STUFFED CHICKEN

3- to 3½-pound roasting chicken
Salt and freshly ground black pepper
2 tablespoons unsalted butter, plus 1
    tablespoon softened
1 shallot, minced
2 tablespoons all-purpose flour
½ cup hot chicken broth (see page 414)
½ cup heavy or whipping cream

½ cup chopped cooked ham
1 cup cooked rice
10 ounces fresh spinach, washed, stems
    trimmed, chopped
½ teaspoon freshly grated nutmeg
1 teaspoon lemon juice
1 clove garlic, bruised

1. Preheat the oven to 375°F. Rinse the chicken and pat it dry with paper towels. Sprinkle the chicken inside and out with salt and pepper to taste.

2. Melt the 2 tablespoons butter in a medium saucepan over medium-low heat. Add the shallot; cook 3 minutes. Add the flour; cook, stirring constantly, 2 minutes. Whisk in the broth and cream. Heat the mixture to boiling, stirring constantly until very thick. Remove from the heat and stir in the ham, rice, spinach, nutmeg, and lemon juice. Mix thoroughly.

3. Stuff the chicken with the spinach-rice mixture. Sew up the cavity securely so the stuffing will not leak out. Truss.

4. Rub the chicken with the garlic and softened butter. Roast on a rack for 20 minutes. Reduce the heat to 350°F and continue to roast, basting occasionally with pan juices, until juices run yellow when pricked with a fork, about 1 hour longer.

Serves 2 to 4.

ISFANAKH FATIRA
(Spinach Pancake)

Speaking, as I was, of things Mideastern—here's the real thing: a wondrous pale green spinach-and-egg pancake. Neither *frittata*, *piperade*, nor *crêpe*, it is a reminder of all three on the tongue. I serve it for brunch sluiced with sour cream; Persians choose yogurt, so you be the judge. It is easy as the dickens to make and (unlike its Arabic forebears) permits a slice of bacon alongside.

4 tablespoons (½ stick) unsalted butter
4 scallions, bulbs and green tops, chopped
¼ cup chopped fresh parsley
½ pound spinach, washed, trimmed of
  stems, chopped
3 eggs
Salt and freshly ground black pepper
Sour cream or yogurt

1. Melt 3 tablespoons of the butter in a medium skillet over medium-low heat. Add the scallions and chopped parsley. Cook, stirring constantly, 2 minutes. Add the spinach and cook, covered, until the spinach starts to wilt, about 5 minutes. Remove the cover and continue to cook, stirring occasionally, 20 minutes.

2. Beat the eggs in a large bowl until light. Beat in the spinach mixture. Add salt and pepper to taste.

3. Melt the remaining 1 tablespoon butter in a 10-inch heavy skillet over medium heat. Pour in the spinach mixture. Cook, covered, 10 minutes.

4. Loosen the edges of the pancake with a spatula and turn it out onto a serving platter. Serve with sour cream or yogurt.

Serves 2 to 4.

SQUASH
A True American Original

Neither my mother nor my father was an animal lover, which probably explains why both my sister and I are.

To be fair, Father was something of a pushover for puppies, and from time to time he would manage to sneak some small furry orphan into our home. Unerringly not housebroken, this stray creature would be allowed a limited tenancy (the back steps or the cellar) until my mother declared it had gotten under foot too often. Then it would disappear, either under its own steam or by way of my mother's "open door" policy.

Her attitude toward animals not in her possession was exceedingly tolerant. She loved our four-footed friends, or so she claimed, but felt that enforced domesticity was a burden that robbed an animal of its right to pursue happiness where and with whom it chose.

"Animals should be free!" Mother would discourse airily. What she really meant was that humans should be freed of the obligation of caring for them.

When I became an adult and collected first a cat, then a dog and eventually two more in quick succession, my mother professed amazement.

"I never knew you were such a Saint Francis," she remarked pointedly after a car ride with my menagerie. "You certainly never showed any such inclination when you were a kid!"

Mother had a short memory. Mine is longer.

I recall a snub-nosed terrier pup that was a gift from my father when he felt such responsibility would be character-building for his son. My mother dismissed that theory as cant.

"You can't learn anything from a nervous dog," she announced at breakfast one morning, "and that dog is *neurasthenic*. It cried all night long! I say when he gets to know us better, he'll bark all day as well!"

She was right. Fluffy yelped constantly. To keep his high-pitched cries out of my mother's earshot, I attached him to a long rope which gave him access to our yard but kept him tethered to the cellar doorknob, away from the areas of the house where my mother held her bridge games or played the piano.

Neurotic or no, Fluffy hated the restraint and neither his barking nor his crying diminished. One afternoon when I returned from school, the rope was still attached to the doorknob but Fluffy was decidedly *not* at the opposite end.

When I rushed inside to inform my mother he had gotten loose, she was utterly insentient.

"The dog did not seem to be happy here," she explained. "So I gave him a test and loosened the rope. If Fluffy hung

around, we'd have known he wanted to be with us. Right?"

The first family dog I can remember was called Tootsie. She was a poodle with bad breath and a mane of dun- to rust-colored ringlets that obscured her vision considerably. Tootsie was not lovable: she too barked a good deal, and she pushed her face into one's lap at awkward moments, but I loved her dearly.

Tootsie's end was tragic. Allowed to roam loose (by my mother, of course) she was hit by a passing vehicle not far from our house. Discretion led my family to shield me from this scene of carnage but I made my way there despite them.

Tootsie had been so flattened by the impact that a policeman was forced to shoot her—as I watched. It was my first encounter with the inevitable and horrifying. I returned home in hysterics, screaming, "Squashed. Tootsie was squashed!"

My mother, who had been sitting at the kitchen table composing a grocery list for dinner, attended to my grief solicitously, drying my tears between each new outburst as I screamed, "Squashed! She was squashed!"

My mother's patience must have been tried by these ear-splitting wails, for she rose at last and went back to the table.

"Now, that's enough," she stated with finality. "Tootsie may have been squashed on earth but she is whole again in heaven. And there is absolutely nothing else we can do for her."

Her tone silenced me at last and I watched through reddened eyes as she picked up her grocery list again, penciling in an addition to her inventory.

I could read the word upside down: squash. My mother was a lady who made fast word associations, you see.

Vegetable Roots

*T*he word *squash* is actually a "cut down," abbreviated by the Pilgrims who had a difficult time with the tongue-twisting Indian name for this gourd. The Narragansetts called it *askutasquash*, the Iroquois, *isquoutersquash* and the Algonquins, *askoot*. All of which have precisely the same meaning: "something that is eaten raw." Curiously, it was the first dish the Indians taught the settlers how to cook!

Squash is decidedly a native American food, and an old one to boot. Stems, rinds, and seeds found in the Ocampo Caves in Mexico's Tamaulipas mountains date this gourd's appearance in a local pot to about 3000 B.C. Ancient Indian peoples called squash "the apple of God," since its seeds were believed to increase fertility when planted in close proximity. Braves with large squash crops inevitably produced large families, which in turn led to larger crops.

The earliest American colonists obviously had small knowledge of squash's potential fruitfulness for they never cultivated the plant at all, considering its size "uncivilized to contemplate." Evidently they did not appreciate the vegetable's flavor either, as few recipes for its preparation (aside from "pompion pie") survive. However, a dubious beauty tip does: the following advice from a bride's book written by Elisabeth Skinner in Roanoke, Virginia, dated 1611.

> The seeds [of certain squash] pounded with meale and their own sweet iuyces...doth beautifie the face, for it taketh away freckles and al spottes...if the place be well rubbed with it—in the sonne's light.

All squash are Cucurbitaceae but there are two distinct branches to the family tree. *Cucurbita pepo* (yellow crookneck and straightneck, patty pan, zucchini, and pumpkin too) are known as summer squash, though in point of fact most supermarkets carry these varieties year round. *Cucurbita maxima* (acorn, butternut, chayote, Hubbard, spaghetti squash, and turban) are winter squash. They too are available much of the year.

Summer Squash

What to Look For

Summer squash have different names and assorted shapes, but when you come right down to it, most are very similar in flavor and may be used interchangeably in a recipe without any noticeable alteration to the finished dish. Zucchini, a stand-out summer variety, has its own chapter in this book, but you might want to check those recipes, too, for further interchanges.

Among *yellow squash*, there are two familiar types: crookneck and straightneck. The pear-shaped crookneck has a long furled throat and creamy yellow pulp. Straightneck is somewhat plumper and grainier in texture, with whiter pulp. When buying either, look for the smallest and firmest available. Fresh yellow squash bruises easily. A sure way to judge its state of vitality is to scrape the surface with a fingernail. If there is resistance, pass it by. *Patty pan*, also known as cymling, is a disk-shaped squash with a pretty scalloped edge. Patty pan are best picked young and no wider in circumference than an English muffin. Look for this variety to be a light apple-green shade; patty pans whiten as they mature, so a chalky-looking one will usually have a pulpy interior, not to mention a decided lack of flavor.

Preparation

Summer squash requires very little kitchen "prep" prior to the stove. I never peel a yellow squash because I always bring home the tiniest I can find and they don't require it. I never wash them either. Unless a squash is really dirty, a fast wipe with a dampened paper towel will usually suffice. Farm-picked squash may require a sluice of cold water but do *not* presoak this vegetable please; too much liquid breaks down the cell structure. I hardly ever salt a summer squash before I cook it. Salting releases a measure of the vegetable's excessive moisture and some cooks claim that this facilitates even cooking, but unfortunately it also wilts the flesh in the process, turning crisp slices sodden in no time at all. There is one exception to my no-salt rule. When I shred squash I find that a very light salting (plus a stint in the colander) will shorten the cooking time. I never blanch or parboil summer squash, as it is watery to begin with. I most often braise or sauté this vegetable in its own juices with only a pat of butter or a speck of bacon drippings to temper the saucepan. Quick cooking over moderately high heat just prior to serving dispels the excess liquid nicely. With few exceptions, the aim in cooking summer squash is to achieve a crisp *al dente* texture. At least when Greene is at the stove.

Pumpkin

What to Look For

*P*umpkin, although botanically listed as summer squash, is available only in the fall. Since it has a texture and physiognomy in common with winter squash, I tend to think of it as a "pre-winter" variety.

Although it has something of an abbreviated season in the marketplace, pumpkin lasts much, much longer than one would suspect, particularly if the globe is unsullied and the storage temperature low enough. Pumpkin pundits claim this squash will stay best on a bed of straw or hung in a mesh bag to allow air to freely circulate about its girth. Do not take that as gospel, however. I have

had a pumpkin sitting in the cool hallway of my house for the past five months, without any sign of wear or tear yet.

Preparation

*T*he biggest problem with pumpkin is getting at the tender flesh inside. The prospect of carving and cooking a pumpkin is so overwhelming that most kitchen practitioners reach for a can instead of a carving knife. But don't!

The easiest way to cut up a pumpkin (according to my friend Sandra Silfven of the *Detroit News*) is to pretend it's an orange. First, Sandy sets a pumpkin on its side on a cutting board and slices straight across the stem end. Then she cuts straight across the bottom end too, so the darn thing will sit upright. Following the curve of the globe, she slides her knife under the skin and pares it from top to bottom before cutting it in half and scooping out the strings (and saving the seeds for roasting later). Once she has a peeled pumpkin, she steams, boils, or bakes it until the flesh is tender.

For pumpkin purée my trick is a jot less surgical. After cutting the unpeeled pumpkin in half and scraping out the seeds and strings, I place the halves in a buttered pan, shell sides up, and simply bake it in a 325°F oven. The baking time depends upon a pumpkin's size of course, but an hour usually will do the trick. When it is done the pumpkin shell begins to fall in and the pulp is very tender. After it cools, I scrape out the pulp and process or blend it until it is very smooth. For the record: a medium-size pumpkin (2 to 2½ pounds) will yield enough pulp for one pie (1½ cups).

Winter Squash

*W*inter squash, to many Americans, is an unknown quantity. While hundreds of varieties are grown, most never make their way beyond the farm stand or specialty greengrocer because chary product managers at supermarkets give shelf space only to those with proven track records at the check-out counter.

The winter squash's common denominator is a rough-silk texture within—after it is cooked—and a hard protective shell without. Unlike their summer counterparts, winter squash have very separate and distinct flavors. And while a cooked acorn squash might conceivably stand in for pumpkin in a pie shell at Thanksgiving dinner, there would be a discernible difference on the tongue.

What to Look For

*W*hen buying winter squash, large size is never a deterrent; in the matter of the gigantic Hubbard squash, bulk indicates a long stay on the vine and the squash will inevitably be sweeter for it.

Happily for the consumer, winter varieties like green *acorn* squash, tan *butternut* squash, and gaily striped *turban* squash all *keep*. That is to say, any one may be stored in a cool dry area for months or even a year without fear of spoilage. Sharp-eyed shoppers will look for winter squash that are smooth to the touch and brightly complexioned. A deep exterior shade (even when the skin is naturally mottled) is usually an indication that the interior flesh will be dry and sweet. *Spaghetti* squash is the sole exception to this rule: the sweetest of those are always a very pale yellow. Winter squash should be weighty. A light acorn squash will not be more tender, merely dehydrated. So go for the heavy-weights every time!

Preparation

*E*ssentially I cook winter squash three basic ways: I bake it, braise it, or boil it (sometimes stuffing it as well). Baked halved squash is rather a plus for the cook as it goes straight from the oven to the table, eliminating the problem of serving dishes. It's good besides! I halve squash either lengthwise or at the midriff depending upon its size, and scoop out any stringy fiber and seeds. Squash seeds (like pumpkin seeds) should be saved. They are really quite tasty seasoned and/or salted and dry-roasted in a low oven for several hours.

If I am serving baked acorn squash, I slice a small section from the rounded bottom so it will sit felicitously in my baking pan. Seasoning is optional, but butter is a necessity to an acorn squash. I place mine in a pan and add an inch of water to keep the vegetable moist. Then I bake it, cut side up of course, in a pre-heated 350°F oven for about 45 minutes to an hour.

The one *Cucurbita maxima* I always boil is spaghetti squash. This hybrid is a relative newcomer to the kitchen. A so-called winter squash (it actually blooms from early October to mid-December), spaghetti squash came originally from Italy. It was hybridized in Japan but then developed in America during the past century and grows best in a semi-dry climate. This squash has a hard shell and considerable girth; the average size is between two and three pounds. Its football shape makes it appear to be more of a candidate for the Super Bowl than the serving dish, but nothing could be further from the truth.

The special virtue of spaghetti squash is its delectable fleshy interior. When boiled (30 to 45 minutes depending upon its size), halved, and seeded, the squash unravels into an enormous quantity of pasta-like strands that are the exact circumference and translucent shade of *capelli d'angelo* (angel-hair noodles) but a hundred times less caloric on a fork end.

However, spaghetti squash is *not* pasta. Strong tomato sauce or garlic overwhelms its tenuous flavor.

NATIVE AMERICAN BOUILLABAISSE
(Summer Squash and Seafood Soup)

According to food historians, one of the first foods that the Narragansett Indians shared with the Pilgrims of Plymouth Rock was a chowder composed of seafood and squash. However, those starchy folk (as narrow in their dining habits as in their morals) refused to sample a spoonful. After the Indians left, they fed the soup to their pigs, dubbing it "the meanest of God's blessings."

My version of the pottage comes with a brand-new name and an age-old benediction: "Praise the Lord for he is good and his mercy endureth forever."

1/4 cup olive oil
1 leek, trimmed, washed, chopped
2 whole scallions, bulbs and green tops, trimmed, chopped
2 cloves garlic, minced
2 ribs celery, finely chopped
1 small green bell pepper, finely chopped
1 1/4 pounds summer squash, trimmed, grated
1 teaspoon chopped fresh thyme, or 1/4 teaspoon dried
1/4 cup chopped fresh basil, or 2 tablespoons dried (chop with the parsley)
1/4 cup chopped fresh parsley
1 teaspoon fennel seeds
Pinch of saffron
6 cups Fish Stock (see page 410)
Salt and freshly ground black pepper
1 1/2 pounds mussels
1/4 teaspoon cornstarch
1 large red snapper, cleaned
1 pound flounder filets
1/2 pound bay scallops
1 pound shrimp, shelled, deveined (use shells in stock)
Aioli (recipe follows)

1. Heat the oil in a large heavy saucepan over medium-low heat. Add the leek and scallions; cook 2 minutes. Add the garlic, celery, and green pepper. Cook, uncovered, 5 minutes. Stir in the squash, thyme, basil, parsley, fennel seeds, saffron, and fish stock. Heat to boiling; reduce the heat. Simmer, uncov-

ered, 30 minutes. Add salt and pepper to taste.

2. Meanwhile, scrub the mussels and place them in a large pot of cold water with the cornstarch (this will cause the mussels to effectively clean themselves). Let stand 15 minutes, then wash under cold running water and set aside. Cut the snapper into 1-inch-wide pieces. Cut the flounder into pieces.

3. Add all the seafood to the bouillabaisse. Cook, covered, until the fish flakes and the mussels are open, 5 to 8 minutes.

4. To serve: spoon some of the soup liquid into serving bowls; add seafood to each bowl. Add about 1 teaspoon aioli to each bowl as well, and pass the remaining aioli.

Serves 6.

Aioli
(Garlic Mayonnaise)

1 slice stale homemade white bread, or 2 slices French bread, 1/2 inch thick
3 tablespoons milk
6 cloves garlic, crushed
1 egg yolk, at room temperature
1/4 teaspoon salt
1 cup vegetable oil
1/2 cup olive oil
3 tablespoons boiling water
2 to 3 tablespoons lemon juice

1. Trim the crusts from the bread and break the bread into pieces in a small bowl. Add the milk; let stand 10 minutes. Place the milk-soaked bread in the corner of a clean tea towel and squeeze it dry. Transfer the bread to a large bowl.

2. Add the garlic to the bread and pound them together with the back of a heavy spoon or a pestle until very smooth. Pound in the egg yolk and salt.

3. Whisk in the oils, a drop at a time, until the mixture thickens; then slowly whisk in the remaining oil, 3 tablespoons at a time, until smooth. Whisk in the boiling water, and lemon juice to taste. Refrigerate, tightly covered, until ready to use.

Makes 2 cups.

T he American Indians of colonial times lived on a fairly spartan diet—squash, beans, and corn—which they supplemented in summer with berries and greens and in winter with wild fowl or fish. Unfortunately the winged and finned denizens were not always eaten fresh, so the Indians developed worms from the change of diet. As a worm expellant, they chewed squash seeds. And while there is only folklore and hearsay to document the cure, the high degree of potassium and ascorbic acid in a summer squash might just have done the trick!

KATE'S PAN-FRIED SUMMER SQUASH

Kate's pan-fried squash is a dispensation from Nathalie Dupree's Southern kitchen. Kate Almand is her factotum wherever Nathalie teaches—and in her own right one of the best down-home cooks below the Mason-Dixon line. Or above it for that matter. Kate's summer squash, despite my earlier injunction about fast cookery, is "sweated" in a skillet for over half an hour. But remarkable for every second on the fire.

1½ pounds yellow summer squash,
*   trimmed, sliced*
1 cup chicken broth (see page 414)
1 medium onion, thinly sliced
½ teaspoon salt
¼ teaspoon freshly ground black pepper
3 tablespoons fatback or fatty bacon
*   drippings*
3 tablespoons unsalted butter

1. Combine the squash, chicken broth, onion, salt, and pepper in a large skillet. Heat to boiling; reduce the heat to medium. Cook, uncovered, stirring frequently, until all liquid has evaporated, about 10 minutes.

2. Add the fatback or bacon drippings and the butter to the squash. Cook, uncovered, stirring occasionally, over low heat, 30 minutes longer.

Serves 4 to 6.

SUMMER SQUASH IN TARRAGON CREAM

Summer squash is what I deem a mutable vegetable. Pair it with a stronger flavor and rather than losing its own identity, it becomes fortified (and enriched) by the alliance.

3 tablespoons unsalted butter
1 large shallot, minced
1 pound summer squash, trimmed, sliced
⅔ cup heavy or whipping cream
1 teaspoon chopped fresh tarragon
Salt and freshly ground black pepper
Chopped fresh parsley

Melt the butter in a large heavy skillet over medium-low heat. Add the shallot; cook 1 minute. Add the squash and cook, uncovered, tossing constantly, 3 minutes. Add the cream. Heat to boiling; reduce the heat. Simmer over medium heat, 5 minutes. Stir in the tarragon; cook 5 minutes longer. Add salt and pepper to taste and sprinkle with the parsley.

Serves 4.

MUCVER
(Turkish Squash Cakes)

From the Pilgrims on, summer squash has had its detractors. When this vegetable crossed the Atlantic to England in the late seventeenth century it was known as "harrow marrow," for only cattle would eat it. The French were no better; when the famed geese of Strasbourg choked on summer squash seeds, they gave the entire vegetable a bad name, calling it *malmain* ("bad hand").

Only the Turks consumed summer squash with any relish. They reputedly acquired a taste for it when a ship bound for Russia with a cargo of fodder in the hold sank in the harbor at Constantinople. All hands were lost but the squash floated across the isthmus and took root. Fact or fiction is utterly beside the point: squash certainly became part of the Middle Eastern diet shortly afterward. For further evidence, try these delicate squash and cheese fritters.

½ pound crookneck squash (about 2 small), trimmed, grated
2 tablespoons crumbled feta cheese
2 tablespoons ricotta cheese
2 tablespoons finely chopped fresh dill
2 tablespoons finely chopped fresh mint
1 tablespoon finely chopped fresh parsley
¼ teaspoon salt, plus extra to taste
⅛ teaspoon freshly ground black pepper
1 egg, lightly beaten
½ cup all-purpose flour
Oil for frying

1. Combine the squash, cheeses, dill, mint, parsley, salt, and pepper in a bowl. Add the egg and flour; mix thoroughly.

2. Heat ¾ inch of oil in a heavy skillet until hot but not smoking. Drop rounded tablespoons of the mixture, a few at a time, into the oil. Fry until golden, about 2 minutes per side. Drain on paper towels. Sprinkle with salt to taste before serving.

Makes 8 to 10; serves 4.

SQUASH AND SAUSAGE RATATOUILLE

*T*hough summer squash is as American as you can get, my classic rendering for this vegetable is totally European. It is a devise for a provincial *ratatouille* minus the traditional ingredients and the slow cooking process. Unorthodox? Unchauvinistic? Certainly. Delectable? You bet. Serve it with a good crusty loaf to soak up the juices.

2 tablespoons olive oil
1 small onion, chopped
1 clove garlic, minced
¾ pound sweet Italian sausage, sliced into
  ⅛-inch-thick rounds
1 pound yellow summer squash, trimmed,
  sliced into ⅛-inch-thick rounds
1 medium green Italian frying pepper,
  seeded, cut into thin rounds
1 tablespoon red wine vinegar
Salt and freshly ground black pepper

1. Heat the oil in a large heavy skillet over medium-low heat. Add the onion; cook 1 minute. Add the garlic; cook 4 minutes longer. Stir in the sausage slices. Cook, stirring frequently, until well browned, about 12 minutes. Using a slotted spoon, transfer the mixture to a plate.

2. Pour off all but 3 tablespoons fat from the skillet. (If there is not enough fat, add butter to compensate.) Add the squash and Italian pepper. Cook, tossing frequently, until tender, about 10 minutes.

3. Return the sausage mixture to the skillet, stirring well. Cook, covered, over medium-high heat for 5 minutes. Remove the cover and sprinkle the mixture with the vinegar. Cook, uncovered, stirring constantly, 3 minutes longer. Add salt and pepper to taste.

Serves 4.

MARILYN HARRIS' SUMMER SQUASH CASSEROLE

*A*nother summer squash endowment (baked) is a gift from a great Midwestern kitchen, Marilyn Harris's to be specific. This wonderful cook teams the ingredient with cream, white wine, and cheese. The result is a delight!

4½ tablespoons unsalted butter
1 small onion, finely chopped
1 pound summer squash, trimmed, sliced
      ⅛ inch thick
½ cup grated Monterey jack cheese
1 egg, lightly beaten
½ cup sour cream
2 tablespoons dry white wine or vermouth
½ teaspoon salt
½ teaspoon sugar
Dash hot pepper sauce
½ cup fresh bread crumbs
1 tablespoon chopped fresh parsley

1. Preheat the oven to 350°F. Melt 1 tablespoon of the butter in a large skillet over medium-low heat. Add the onion; cook until tender, about 5 minutes. Transfer to a bowl.

2. Add 2 tablespoons of the butter to the pan over medium heat. Stir in the squash. Cook, tossing frequently, until all moisture has evaporated and the squash is tender, about 10 minutes. Transfer to the container of a food processor and process, using the on/off switch, until fairly smooth.

3. Transfer the puréed squash to a large mixing bowl. Add the cheese, egg, sour cream, wine, salt, sugar, hot pepper sauce, and sautéed onions. Mix well. Pour into a buttered baking dish.

4. Melt the remaining 1½ tablespoons butter in a small skillet over medium-high heat. Stir in the bread crumbs; sauté until golden, about 2 minutes. Sprinkle the crumbs over the squash mixture. Bake until lightly golden, about 30 minutes. Sprinkle with the parsley before serving.

Serves 4.

SWEET SUMMER SQUASH BUNDT

Summer squash has a multitude of kitchen uses but to my mind its finest guise is undubitably the sweetest. Take, for example, the bundt below. Golden in color and texture, this elegant cake is the best thing to hit a tea tray (or brunch table) in years. Serve it all year round—with the amendment of sweetened whipped cream at your own discretion.

For the cake:

¼ pound yellow summer squash, trimmed,
      grated (about 1 cup)
1 teaspoon finely slivered orange peel
½ cup chopped dried dates
½ cup chopped pecans
2 cups plus 1 tablespoon all-purpose flour
1 teaspoon baking powder
1 teaspoon baking soda
¼ teaspoon salt
3 eggs
1 teaspoon vanilla extract
1¼ cups granulated sugar
1 cup sour cream

For the glaze:

2 tablespoons orange juice
2 tablespoons lemon juice
2 tablespoons superfine sugar

For the icing:

1 cup confectioners' sugar
1 teaspoon ground cinnamon
2 tablespoons orange juice
1 teaspoon heavy or whipping cream

1. Preheat the oven to 350°F. Combine the squash, orange peel, dates, and pecans in a small bowl. Toss thoroughly with the 1 tablespoon flour. Set aside.

2. Sift the remaining flour with the baking powder, baking soda, and salt. Set aside.

3. Beat the eggs in a large bowl until frothy. Add the vanilla and granulated sugar; beat until light and lemony. Beat in the sour cream. Add the sifted ingredients and beat until smooth. Add the squash mixture and mix well.

4. Pour the batter into a lightly buttered and floured 1½- to 2-quart bundt cake pan. Bake until a toothpick inserted in the center comes out clean, about 1 hour. Cool on a rack for 10 minutes. Unmold. Prick the top and sides of the cake with a toothpick.

5. Meanwhile, make the glaze: Combine the orange juice, lemon juice, and superfine sugar in a small bowl. Spoon this over the cake, allowing it to soak in until the cake is moist but not wet. Cool completely.

6. Before serving, make the icing: Combine all the ingredients in a small bowl. Beat until smooth, and drizzle over the cake.

Serves 8 to 10.

PUMPKIN ROLLS

*P*umpkin rolls are the best dinner companions I know. This recipe comes from New Hampshire, from a Methodist church bulletin printed around the turn of the century, when most everything in America still had natural savor.

1½ teaspoons dry yeast
1 teaspoon granulated sugar
¼ cup lukewarm water
3 cups all-purpose flour, approximately
3½ tablespoons unsalted butter
2 tablespoons light brown sugar
¼ teaspoon salt
1 cup puréed cooked pumpkin
    (see page 322)
1 egg, lightly beaten
¼ cup maple syrup
¼ teaspoon ground cinnamon
1 cup stone-ground whole-wheat flour

1. Combine the yeast, granulated sugar, and water in a large bowl; let stand 5 minutes. Stir in ½ cup of the all-purpose flour. Cover, and let rise for 1 hour.

2. Melt 2 tablespoons of the butter and pour it in a medium bowl. Beat in the brown sugar, salt, pumpkin, egg, maple syrup, and cinnamon. Add this mixture to the risen roll base. Beat until smooth. Add the whole-wheat flour and enough all-purpose flour, about 2½ cups, to make a firm dough. Knead it briefly in the bowl. Cover, and let rise for 2 hours.

3. Punch the dough down and transfer it to a floured board. Knead briefly and roll out until about ½ inch thick. Cut into 1-inch circles. Place them on flour-rubbed baking sheets, cover with flour-rubbed tea towels, and let rise for 1 hour.

4. Preheat the oven to 425°F. Melt the remaining 1½ tablespoons butter and brush the rolls with it. Bake 15 minutes.

Makes about 2 dozen rolls.

PUMPKIN PROSCIUTTO GNOCCHI

1 cup puréed cooked pumpkin
   (see page 322)
1 egg, lightly beaten
¼ cup freshly grated Parmesan cheese, plus
   extra for garnish (optional)
¾ cup finely chopped prosciutto (or any
   smoked ham)
1¾ cups all-purpose flour
¼ teaspoon freshly grated nutmeg
¼ teaspoon salt

1. Whisk the pumpkin with the egg in a large mixing bowl. Stir in the cheese and prosciutto. Slowly stir in the flour and beat with a wooden spoon until fairly elastic, about 4 minutes. Add the nutmeg and salt; beat 1 minute longer.

2. Using two demitasse spoons, form small ovals of dough and drop them into a large pot of boiling salted water. When the gnocchi rise to the surface, remove them with a slotted spoon and drain them lightly on paper towels. Transfer to a buttered baking dish. Continue until all batter is used up.

3. Before serving, reheat for 15 minutes in a 350°F oven. Serve with more Parmesan cheese on the side if desired.
Serves 4.

POT-ROASTED BEEF WITH PUMPKIN

In the pumpkin recipe department, consider a wholly untraditional burnished pot roast enriched with amber chunks of this squash in lieu of potatoes. It's not a new idea. A seventeenth-century Oneida recipe specified that pumpkin "be boiled with meat till it achieves the consistency of potato soup." This is not that formula, however—this is better!

2½- to 3-pound boneless chuck roast
1 large clove garlic, bruised
2 tablespoons unsalted butter
1½ teaspoons vegetable oil
1 medium onion, finely chopped
3 peeled carrots, 1 chopped and 2
   quartered
1 small tomato, peeled, seeded, chopped
½ teaspoon chopped fresh thyme, or a
   pinch of dried
1 teaspoon chopped fresh basil, or ¼
   teaspoon dried
1 teaspoon chopped fresh parsley, plus
   extra for garnish
1½ cups strong beef broth (see page 414)

4 small potatoes, peeled, halved
1 pound fresh pumpkin, peeled, cut into
   1½-inch cubes

1. Preheat the oven to 350°F. Rub the roast well with the bruised garlic. Mince the garlic and reserve.

2. Heat 1 tablespoon of the butter with half the oil in a large heavy skillet over medium heat. Brown the meat on all sides. Transfer to a Dutch oven.

3. Add the remaining butter and oil to the skillet. Add the onion; cook 1 minute. Add the reserved garlic and the chopped carrot and tomato. Cook 3 min-

utes. Sprinkle with the thyme, basil, and parsley. Stir in the beef broth. Heat to boiling, scraping the sides and bottom of the pan with a wooden spoon. Pour over the meat. Bake, covered, until the meat is not quite tender, about 2½ hours. Add the potatoes, quartered carrots, and pumpkin. Continue to cook, covered, until the vegetables and meat are very tender, about 45 minutes longer. Sprinkle with parsley.

Serves 4 to 6.

PUMPKIN MOUSSE

Simply a pale orange blizzard trying to pass itself off as a pumpkin mousse. Calorie counters beware: there is rum and ruination in every spoonful.

3 eggs, separated
⅓ cup granulated sugar
1½ tablespoons cornstarch
¼ teaspoon vanilla extract
¾ cup milk, scalded
2 tablespoons golden rum
1 cup puréed cooked pumpkin
  (see page 322)
⅛ teaspoon ground cinnamon
⅛ teaspoon ground cloves
⅛ teaspoon freshly grated nutmeg
⅛ teaspoon ground ginger
¼ cup orange juice
1 tablespoon unflavored gelatin
2 cups heavy or whipping cream
3 tablespoons confectioners' sugar
Slivered candied ginger

1. Beat the egg yolks in a medium bowl until light. Slowly beat in the granulated sugar. Whisk in the cornstarch and vanilla until smooth. Whisk in the scalded milk. Transfer to the top of a double boiler and cook, stirring constantly, over boiling water until thick enough to coat a wooden spoon, about 10 minutes. Remove from the heat; stir in the rum. Cool, then stir in the puréed pumpkin and spices.

2. Combine the orange juice with the gelatin in a small bowl. Let stand 5 minutes. Place the bowl over hot water and stir until the gelatin dissolves. Cool.

3. Combine the custard and gelatin mixtures in a medium bowl. Place the bowl in a larger bowl filled halfway with ice. Stir the custard with a wooden spoon until the mixture begins to thicken.

4. Beat 1 cup of the cream with 2 tablespoons of the confectioners' sugar until thick. Fold into the pumpkin mixture.

5. Beat the egg whites until stiff but not dry. Fold them into the mixture and pour it into a 6-cup soufflé dish or serving bowl. Refrigerate, covered, at least 6 hours or overnight.

6. About 1 hour before serving, beat the remaining 1 cup cream with the remaining 1 tablespoon confectioners' sugar. Fill a pastry bag with the whipped cream and pipe a decorative pattern over the mousse. Garnish with slivered candied ginger.

Serves 8.

PUMPKIN FRUITCAKE

*T*his pumpkin fruitcake is designed for those who eschew fruitcake in any form. It is tender, nutty, and only vaguely scented with rum and spice. Parenthetically, it keeps wonderfully well—if you can keep your hands off it. I cannot!

1 cup seedless raisins
¼ cup plus 3 tablespoons dark rum
1 cup pitted dates, roughly chopped
3½ cups all-purpose flour
1 cup (2 sticks) unsalted butter, softened
3 cups granulated sugar
4 eggs
1 cup puréed cooked pumpkin
   (see page 322)
1 teaspoon ground cinnamon
1 teaspoon ground ginger
1 teaspoon baking powder
½ teaspoon salt
1 teaspoon baking soda
1¼ cups buttermilk
1 cup walnuts, chopped, lightly toasted
Finely slivered peel of 1 orange
Finely slivered peel of 1 lemon
½ cup orange juice
Confectioners' sugar

1. Place the raisins in a bowl and add the ¼ cup rum. Cover and let stand several hours or overnight.

2. Preheat the oven to 325°F. Butter and flour a 9-cup bundt or tube pan. Set it aside. Sprinkle the dates with 1 tablespoon of the flour. Set that aside.

3. Beat the butter in the large bowl of an electric mixer until light. Slowly beat in 2 cups of the granulated sugar. Add the eggs, one at a time, beating thoroughly after each addition. Beat in the pumpkin, cinnamon, and ginger.

4. Sift the remaining flour with the baking powder and salt. Combine the baking soda and buttermilk. Using a wooden spoon, stir the flour mixture into the pumpkin mixture in three parts, alternating with thirds of the buttermilk mixture. Stir in the reserved raisins and rum. Stir in the dates, walnuts, orange peel, and lemon peel. Spoon the batter into the prepared cake pan. Bake until a toothpick inserted in the center comes out clean, about 1¼ hours. Cool on a rack for 10 minutes. Unmold.

5. Meanwhile, combine the remaining 1 cup granulated sugar with the remaining 3 tablespoons rum and the orange juice. Brush this over the cake until it is moist but not wet. Sprinkle with confectioners' sugar before serving.

Serves 8 to 10.

THE ULTIMATE PUMPKIN PIE

I do not think lovers of that American treasure, pumpkin pie, would forgive its omission here. The recipe is the best I have ever tasted in forty-eight states (never made it to Alaska or Hawaii), and that's a strong statement. It is borrowed from my earlier book, *Bert Greene's Kitchen Bouquets,* with no apology whatsoever.

Short Crust Pastry for a 10-inch pie (see
  page 412)
1½ cups puréed cooked pumpkin
  (see page 322)
3 tablespoons unsalted butter, melted
½ cup sugar
¼ cup maple syrup
1 teaspoon ground cinnamon
½ teaspoon freshly grated nutmeg
¼ teaspoon ground cloves
3 eggs, separated
½ cup milk
¼ cup heavy or whipping cream
Sweetened whipped cream

1. Make the pie pastry. Roll it out
and line a 10-inch pie plate. Trim and
flute the edges.

2. Preheat the oven to 350°F. Combine all the ingredients except the egg
whites and sweetened whipped cream.
Mix thoroughly.

3. Beat the egg whites until stiff but
not dry. Fold them into the pie mixture.
Pour the mixture into the pie shell and
bake until a toothpick inserted in the

The name *pumpkin* was bestowed on that grand and glorious
globe by a misguided scholar in the
late seventeenth century. Actually
the moniker was an amalgam lifted
from the Indian word *pompom*
(which means round) and the classic
Greek *sikuous pepon* (which indicates
a weighty proportion). Early colonists called pumpkins by many
names—pompions, pommions,
pumpions—and in the case of Captain John Smith, never spelt the
word the same way twice, so a formal appellation obviously helped.

center comes out clean, about 50 minutes. Cool. Serve with sweetened
whipped cream.
Serves 8.

ACORN SQUASH FLAN

This squash flan is *not* a dessert. Though it is delicately caramelized, the taste is
decidedly vegetable! Serve it as a first course or as a prime luncheon dish with cold
meat and a salad.

1 medium acorn squash
½ cup sugar
¼ teaspoon ground cinnamon
2 tablespoons unsalted butter, melted
½ teaspoon ground ginger
¼ teaspoon freshly grated nutmeg
⅛ teaspoon ground cloves
⅛ teaspoon crushed dried hot red pepper
½ teaspoon salt
1½ cups milk

1 cup heavy or whipping cream
3 eggs
3 egg yolks
1 tablespoon brandy

1. Preheat the oven to 350°F. Cut
the squash in half lengthwise; scoop out
the seeds. Place the squash, cut sides
down, on a lightly buttered baking
sheet. Bake in the oven until very tender,

about 45 minutes. Cool, then scoop out the pulp.

2. Place a 1-quart soufflé dish in the oven for 5 to 6 minutes to warm.

3. Meanwhile, heat the sugar with the cinnamon in a small saucepan over high heat until the sugar starts to melt. Continue to cook, stirring constantly, until the sugar has melted and the caramel turns a deep golden color. Remove the soufflé dish from the oven and carefully pour the caramel into the dish, turning the dish to coat the bottom and sides. Invert the soufflé dish on a buttered sheet of foil (to prevent drippings from hardening on any work surfaces). Let stand.

4. Place the squash pulp in the container of a food processor or blender. Add the melted butter, ginger, nutmeg, cloves, red pepper, and salt. Process until smooth.

5. Meanwhile, combine the milk and cream in a saucepan and place over medium-low heat until hot. Do not allow to boil.

6. Beat the eggs with the egg yolks in a large bowl. Beat in the puréed squash mixture. Slowly stir in the hot milk and cream. Add the brandy.

7. Pour the custard mixture into the prepared soufflé dish and place the dish in a roasting pan. Pour boiling water into the pan to come halfway up the side of the soufflé dish. Bake until a knife inserted in the center comes out clean, about 1 hour. Remove the dish from the pan and let it stand 10 minutes.

8. Run a sharp knife around the edge of the soufflé dish and very carefully invert it onto a shallow serving platter. Serve the flan warm or well chilled.

Serves 8.

CURRIED WINTER SQUASH BISQUE

*T*he most silken winter squash soup I know is a delicate blending of curried butternut squash combined with winter's best plum tomatoes, onions, garlic, and a mite of ham. A soup for all seasons, perhaps this brew is best of all in late winter when the supper table is set early. Consume yours with bread, cheese, and salad as the only other courses, for this soup is filling.

2 tablespoons unsalted butter
6 whole scallions, bulbs and green tops, finely chopped
1 clove garlic, minced
1 small green pepper, seeded, finely chopped
¼ cup chopped fresh parsley, plus extra for garnish
2 teaspoons chopped fresh basil, or 1 teaspoon dried
2-pound butternut squash, peeled, seeded, cubed (see Note)

1 ham bone, or ½-pound chunk of smoked ham
1 can (14 ounces) plum tomatoes
4 cups chicken broth (see page 414)
½ teaspoon ground allspice
¼ teaspoon ground mace
Pinch of freshly grated nutmeg
2 teaspoons curry powder
Salt and freshly ground black pepper

1. Melt the butter in a large saucepan over medium-low heat. Add the scallions; cook 2 minutes. Add the garlic, green pepper, ¼ cup chopped parsley, and basil. Cook, stirring occasionally, 5 minutes.

2. Add the squash to the saucepan. Toss to coat it with the scallion mixture. Add the ham bone or meat, tomatoes, broth, allspice, mace, and nutmeg. Heat to boiling; reduce the heat. Simmer, covered, until the squash is very tender, about 1 hour. Remove the ham bone. (If ham meat was used, remove and save for use at another time.)

3. Purée the soup in batches in a blender, being careful as hot liquid will expand. Transfer it to another large saucepan and stir in the curry powder. Heat to boiling; reduce the heat. Simmer 10 minutes, stirring frequently. Add salt and pepper to taste and sprinkle with parsley.

Serves 6 to 8.

Note: You may use an acorn squash for this recipe. If you do, bake it cut-side down, on a lightly buttered baking dish, in a 350°F oven for 45 minutes. Skip the water bath.

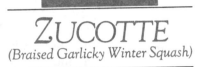

ZUCOTTE
(Braised Garlicky Winter Squash)

*T*o braise winter squash it must be peeled first, then uniformly sliced or diced to ensure even cooking. I always braise squash in the Italian manner—in a covered saucepan with a small amount of butter, white wine, or chicken broth as flavoring. In the following instance, another Italian notion, the butter is literally loaded with garlic—and the dish is breathtaking!

3 tablespoons unsalted butter
2 tablespoons white wine
10 cloves garlic, peeled
1¼ pounds butternut or other winter
  squash, peeled, seeded, diced
Salt and freshly ground black pepper
3 tablespoons chopped fresh parsley

1. Melt 1 tablespoon of the butter in a large heavy skillet over low heat. Add the wine and garlic. Cook, covered, stirring occasionally, 20 minutes. The garlic will brown slightly but should not burn.

2. Mash the garlic with a fork. Stir in the remaining 2 tablespoons butter and the squash. Toss thoroughly to coat. Cook, covered, stirring occasionally, until the squash is tender, about 20 minutes. Add salt and pepper to taste and sprinkle with the parsley.

Serves 4.

*S*ummer and winter squash may bear the same family name but they have practically nothing else in common. Not flavor, not texture, not even nutrition! Summer squash is diet food: low in sodium and calories and high in vitamins C, A, and niacin. Winter squash is comfort food: higher in calories and lower in vitamin C, though it does contain over 8,600 milligrams of vitamin A per cupful and is a prime source of riboflavin and iron to boot. Luckily there's room for both—in the garden and at the stove.

CRANBERRIED SQUASH PUREE

*T*he classic winter squash recipe in my collection is also rather untraditional: a purée of acorn squash combined with other chill-factor ingredients like red wine, fresh cranberries, and zippy spices. The result is a most elegant and different side dish. But try it for yourself.

2 medium acorn squash
4 teaspoons unsalted butter, plus 2
   tablespoons softened
1 cup water
2 tablespoons dark brown sugar
2 tablespoons red wine
⅛ teaspoon ground allspice
¼ cup fresh cranberries, rinsed, finely
   chopped
Salt and freshly ground black pepper

1. Preheat the oven to 400°F. Cut each squash in half; scrape out the seeds. Place the squash in a shallow roasting pan, cut side up. Place 1 teaspoon of the butter in each cavity. Pour the water around the squash, and bake until tender, about 1 hour.

2. Remove the squash from the oven; cool slightly. Scrape out the cooked flesh and process it in the container of a food processor or blender until smooth. Transfer it to the top of a double boiler.

3. Add the brown sugar, red wine, softened butter, and allspice ·to the puréed squash. Cook over boiling water 5 minutes. Add the cranberries; cook 10 minutes longer. Add salt and pepper to taste.

Serves 4 to 6.

SPAGHETTI SQUASH TETRAZZINI

*S*paghetti squash's finest culinary hour may be at hand—the vegetable's presence in a plate of fabled Chicken Tetrazzini has to be some kind of milestone!

1 medium spaghetti squash (about 2½
   pounds)
1 clove garlic
1 small onion stuck with a clove
3 sprigs parsley
Pinch of dried basil
1½ cups chicken broth (see page 414)
1 whole chicken breast, skinned, boned,
   halved
4 tablespoons (½ stick) unsalted butter
2 tablespoons minced shallots or scallion
   bulbs
1 cup sliced mushrooms

2 tablespoons all-purpose flour
¾ cup heavy or whipping cream
2 teaspoons dry vermouth
¼ teaspoon freshly grated nutmeg
Dash of hot pepper sauce
1 teaspoon lemon juice
Salt and freshly ground black pepper
¼ cup freshly grated Parmesan cheese

1. Place the whole squash in a large pot; cover with cold water. Heat to boiling; reduce the heat. Simmer, covered, until fork-tender, turning once, about 45 minutes. Drain and allow to cool slightly. Cut the squash in half lengthwise. Scrape out the seeds with a fork. Scrape the remaining squash with the fork, carefully separating the vegetable into pasta-like strands. Set the strands aside.

2. Meanwhile, preheat the oven to 375°F. Combine the garlic, onion with clove, parsley, basil, and chicken broth in a large skillet. Heat to boiling; reduce the heat. Add the pieces of chicken breast; cook, covered, until tender, about 4 minutes per side. Remove the chicken to a plate. Reduce the broth to 1 cup; strain. Cut the chicken into strips and reserve.

3. Melt 2 tablespoons of the butter in a skillet over medium-low heat. Add the shallots or scallions; cook 3 minutes. Add the mushrooms; cook over medium heat until golden. Set aside.

4. Melt the remaining 2 tablespoons butter in a large saucepan over low heat. Stir in the flour; cook, stirring constantly, 2 minutes. Stir in the cream, vermouth, nutmeg, hot pepper sauce, lemon juice, and salt and pepper to taste. Cook until thick, about 4 minutes. Stir in the chicken, squash, and mushrooms. Transfer to a buttered baking dish. Sprinkle with the cheese. Bake until golden and bubbly, about 20 minutes.

Serves 4.

SPAGHETTI SQUASH PRIMAVERA

"Spaghetti squash is best served with a light and delicate pasta sauce," according to James Beard. To second the master's notion, I came up with several exceedingly delicate variations. Consider the following velvety upholstery for starters.

1 medium spaghetti squash (about 2½ pounds)
1 cup heavy or whipping cream
5 tablespoons unsalted butter
1 shallot, minced
¼ cup minced cooked ham
1 carrot, minced
1 tablespoon Madeira
Dash of hot pepper sauce
Pinch of freshly grated nutmeg
⅓ cup lightly blanched peas
Salt and freshly ground black pepper
3 tablespoons freshly grated Parmesan cheese, plus extra for serving

1. Place the whole squash in a large pot; cover with cold water. Heat to boiling; reduce the heat. Simmer, covered, until fork-tender, turning once, about 45 minutes. Drain and allow to cool slightly. Cut the squash in half lengthwise. Scrape out the seeds with a fork. Scrape the remaining squash with the fork, carefully separating the vegetables into pasta-like strands. Set the strands aside.

2. In a small saucepan heat the cream to boiling; reduce the heat. Simmer until reduced by half. Stir in 4 tablespoons of the butter; remove from the heat.

3. Melt the remaining 1 tablespoon butter in a large saucepan over medium-low heat. Add the shallot, ham, and carrot. Cook 3 minutes. Raise the heat slightly and add the Madeira. Cook until most of the liquid has evaporated.

4. Stir the reduced cream mixture into the vegetable mixture over low heat. Add the hot pepper sauce, nutmeg, peas, and salt and pepper to taste. Toss in the cooked spaghetti squash. Toss over low heat until warmed through. Stir in 3 tablespoons Parmesan cheese. Pass more cheese on the side.

Serves 4.

SQUASH BOATS

In pre-Columbian times, the cave dwellers in the Tamaulipas mountains used dried winter squash shells for carrying water and goat's milk. Three thousand years later this vegetable still takes well to odd culinary cargo. To be specific, consider the one-dish meal below. Any meaty squash will do as a boat, but the delicately flavored varieties are most compatible: consider acorn, turban, buttercup, or even green chayote. Butternut squash is perfect from the standpoint of flavor, but be forewarned: the skin is thin and the cavity small, so it must be carefully enlarged prior to stuffing.

2 medium winter squash
5½ tablespoons unsalted butter
1 small onion, minced
1 clove garlic, minced
½ cup chopped cooked ham
1 tablespoon bourbon
1 small tomato, peeled, seeded, chopped
1 whole scallion, bulb and green top, finely
*   chopped*
½ cup diced cooked chicken
2 tablespoons all-purpose flour
½ cup hot chicken broth (see page 414)
3 tablespoons heavy or whipping cream
½ teaspoon ground allspice
Dash of hot pepper sauce
2 tablespoons chopped fresh parsley
Salt and freshly ground black pepper
¼ cup dry bread crumbs

1. Preheat the oven to 350°F. Cut the squash in half lengthwise and scoop out the seeds. Place the squash shell side up in a lightly buttered baking dish. Bake until tender, about 45 minutes to 1 hour, depending on the squash you use. Remove from the oven. Cool, then scoop out the pulp, leaving about ½ inch of pulp inside the shells. Chop the scooped-out pulp and reserve. Place the shells on a lightly buttered ovenproof serving dish.

2. Reduce the oven temperature to 325°F. Melt 2 tablespoons of the butter in a large skillet over medium-low heat. Add the onion; cook 1 minute. Add the garlic; cook 4 minutes longer. Stir in the ham, bourbon, tomato, scallion, chicken, and reserved pulp. Cook 1 minute. Remove from the heat and set aside.

3. Melt 2 more tablespoons of butter in a small saucepan; whisk in the flour. Cook, stirring constantly, until the mixture is golden, about 15 minutes. Whisk in the broth and cream. Heat to boiling; cook until very thick, about 3 minutes. Add the cream mixture to the chicken and ham mixture. Add the allspice, hot pepper sauce, parsley, and salt and pepper to taste, and stuff the shells.

4. Melt the remaining 1½ tablespoons butter in a small skillet. Sauté the bread crumbs over medium heat until golden, about 4 minutes. Spoon them over the squash. Bake 25 minutes.

Serves 4.

WINTER SQUASH CREME BRULEE

An aureate *crème brulée* compounded of winter squash and more deviltry than a deep-dyed Puritan could shake a stick at—and crusted to the nines with burnt sugar.

3 cups heavy or whipping cream
½ cup granulated sugar
6 egg yolks
⅓ cup puréed cooked winter squash
¼ teaspoon ground cinnamon
⅛ teaspoon ground ginger
Pinch of ground cloves
1 tablespoon dark rum
⅓ cup packed light brown sugar

1. Preheat the oven to 325°F. Heat the cream and granulated sugar in the top of a double boiler over hot water until the sugar has dissolved. Remove from the heat.

2. Beat the egg yolks in a medium bowl until light. Add the squash, cinnamon, ginger, and cloves. Whisk in the hot cream mixture. Stir in the rum.

3. Pour the squash mixture into a 1½-quart soufflé dish. Place the dish in a roasting pan and add boiling water to the pan to come halfway up the sides of the dish. Bake until the center is fairly firm, about 1½ hours. Remove from the water and allow to cool. Refrigerate overnight.

4. About 15 minutes before serving, preheat the broiling unit. Sprinkle the brown sugar over the custard. Place the dish in a pan and surround it with ice cubes. Heat it under the broiler, gently shaking the pan, until the sugar melts. Serve immediately.

Serves 6 to 8.

STRING BEANS

With No More Strings Attached

W hen I was a youngster, one of the unalloyed joys of my life was being sent to spend the afternoon at my father's place of business. Or better yet, to sit in the back of his grubby automobile amid the assorted nippers, wrenches, pliers, and coils of shiny wire while he visited "The Job" to inspect the status of the houses he had under construction.

There among the skeletal wooden dwellings I would play solitary games while my father checked the naked uprights with tape measure and spirit level before he allowed his men to lay the thick ropes of insulated cable in place. My father's job sites were almost always treeless, muddy quarries where cement foundations surrounded blank holes smelling of sewage and other earthly entrails, and whose yawning darkness was terrifying.

But if I skinned an elbow or cut a finger, I always knew that one of the burly fellows in my father's employ would bandage the spot with a handkerchief that I would be bidden to spit into first. My favorite among these helpers was a red-haired fellow named Herman who always gave me a stick of chewing gum or a cough drop as an anodyne. "Does it hurt bad, Stringbean?" he would ask. I always shook my head, no. Even if it did I would never have admitted the suffering, for I liked being thought a stoic. I also liked being called "Stringbean."

I received that appellation when I was about seven or eight years old and started to grow tall, almost overnight. My father's secretary, a tall blond young woman who used to let me draw on the triplicate pages of billheads while she typed envelopes, started that nickname.

"You grew so tall over the summer," she announced when I returned from my first year at summer camp, "I can't tell you apart from a stringbean!"

"I'm tougher," I replied.

"No," said Ruth. "You're just fresher!" But the name stuck.

As I said before, I loved to spend the afternoon at my father's business. Aside from the permissiveness of easy-going Ruth there was so much to see and smell there. I can still summon up the crackling hiss of copper wire as it was unwound and the faintly dangerous scent of live electric current in the air.

As my father's finances fluctuated from bad to worse during the Depression, he would attempt to cut back on his monthly overhead. First one man, then another (all good companions of mine), was laid off. Good-hearted Ruth was forced to look for another job, and finally the shop itself was shuttered, the contents auctioned to satisfy creditors.

My father's business went on, however, albeit spiritlessly. My mother claimed that he ran it out of his hat. Indeed, the brim of the soiled gray fedora he wore was always crammed with business cards and folded bits of paper, where other men fancied feathers or Tyrolean brushes.

Once when I was in my last year at grammar school, I accompanied my father to "The Job" once again. The marshy landscape had not altered a whit and the frame underpinnings of architecture were still raw and sere. This time, almost an adolescent, I no longer played along the sidings nor allowed my knees and wrists to be scraped. I sat in the car alone, reading a book.

After my father had been gone for what seemed hours but was probably fifteen minutes, I heard a knock on the car window and immediately recognized my old friend, Herman.

"Is that really you, Stringbean?" he asked through the glass. "You got so big I almost didn't recognize you."

"I am over five feet, seven inches tall," I said eagerly. "I'll show you." And clambering out of the car, I stood against the hood so he could observe my increased height.

"You really grew up." Herman whistled, wiping his hands on his overalls. "All around. Can't rightly call you Stringbean any more." He laughed. "Broad bean'd be a better name now."

It was true of course. I had become increasingly chunky with each added inch of height. But I hated to have the matter aired in public. By the time I had returned to the car and rolled up the window, I resolved never to go to my father's job again. And I do not think I ever did.

Sic transit glorious stringbeans.

Vegetable Roots

*D*espite my pique at having outgrown its sobriquet, the green bean (stringless or otherwise) is a vegetable that has never suffered alienation of my affections. A plateful appears at my dinner table at least three or four times a week. For to my mind, nothing in the garden (or on the greengrocer's shelf) can be prepared as easily and yet remain so eminently toothsome.

Phaseolus vulgaris was another bequest to European kitchens from the New World, where they grew wild. It is hard to believe, but the green bean was originally brought back to Spain by the conquistadors as a flowering plant, not as a food. Adjudged too intractable for civilized tongues (or teeth), bean pods were grown only ornamentally. These red-to-pink blossoms known as *pincel* ("paintbrush") glorified Spanish gardens for over half a century and would be there still if not for a happy accident. According to vegetable lore, a bunch of green pods fell into a pot of soup one day. Since it was too close to dinner to start the dish anew, the soup was served up without amend and pronounced *"perfecto!"* Who the enterprising cook was is anyone's guess, but let bean lovers everywhere give thanks for the culinary stratagem.

Once the Spanish cooked string beans, the rest of Europe followed suit. As they were easy to grow and simpler to harvest, beans shortly became a kitchen staple, eaten fresh in summer and dried during the rest of the year. In France, where they prized a stew of meat and vegetables known as a *hericoq*, beans were added to the dish and consumed with such apparent relish that the single legume soon replaced all other ingredients. When the bean took over the stew, it appropriated its name as well. Frenchmen have called beans *haricots* ever since, making the distinction between dried and fresh by dubbing the latter *haricot vert*, "green bean." String beans are now grown the world over. There are a hundred varieties in seed catalogues, but to give the Gallic original its due, none is tenderer, more delicately flavored, or thinner (often no wider than a darning needle) than the *haricot vert*. To honor it, cooks everywhere slice less svelte string beans vertically and call them "Frenched."

Though string beans have been consumed in the Americas for thousands of years, they have been raised commercially in the U.S. only since 1836. The very first string bean crop was harvested by an enterprising truck farmer outside Utica, New York, who reportedly mortgaged his family home to import the seeds from France. Ten years later, they

say, he was so filthy rich that he moved his family to the Riviera. One thing is certain, however: his initial product made good. In the latter half of the nineteenth century string beans were so fashionable that they were marketed by vegetable distributors as "The Ninth Wonder of the World." Eventually lawyers for P. T. Barnum, who had coined the phrase, threatened legal action and the legend was amended to read: "The Wonder of the World [and in smaller type] of Food!"

Despite all the flim-flam, the string bean was truly popular, and it never lost favor at the dining table. A couple of decades ago the string bean (though stringless since 1894) was ranked the fifth-best-liked vegetable in America. And while it came in well after the potato and the pea, it still outdistanced the cucumber!

What to Look For

String beans come to the table year round these days. However, we pay for the privilege of out-of-season consumption with largely lackluster produce. I can remember the days prior to World War II when the only string beans eaten between September and June sprang from a formidable Del Monte can; and one literally went crazy for fresh by spring. Women who gardened (like my grandmother) would mark off the days on a calendar, waiting for the bean runners to send out sufficient pods for the first meal of the year. Young diners (like me) were always instructed to make a wish before sampling the first slender pod. In our family we often ate new string beans slightly before they were deemed pickable according to the Burpee catalogue—but who cared? Starved for the taste of fresh, we simply could not wait a day longer.

At the supermarket, look for packages of string beans of evenly matched lengths; they will cook more uniformly. If a greengrocer allows you to select your own, try for beans that are unblemished, relatively crisp, and endowed with small seeds. Fresher beans have slightly fuzzier skins. I do not recommend the practice, but my mother always snapped a bean in half to ascertain how long it had been in circulation. Fresh beans will snap with dispatch and reveal a generous spurt of juice at the seam. Buy them immediately. Avoid limp, soggy-looking pods or any that appear to be swollen with seeds. Those beans stayed on the vine too long!

If the label "string bean" is merely a vestigial cognomen these days, since most beans are stringless, it still conjures up a nice thin image for me. No surprise, I guess, since the green bean is composed of 92 percent water and there are less than 30 calories in a cooked cupful. The bean is at its optimum state when fresh— literally loaded with potassium (180 milligrams), calcium (63 milligrams), and phosphorus (46 milligrams) in every eight ounces. Plus a whopping shot of vitamin A (680 units) per 125-gram serving, which averages out to a scant cup.

Preparation

If I am lucky enough to acquire produce that is freshly picked (and luckier still, pencil slim), I leave the beans whole.

Mature, thick-waisted beans I usually run through a small hand-held device known variously as a "Beanex" or a "Krisk Bean Stringer & Slicer," which will halve even a huge pod admirably.

My sole crotchet in the matter of cooking string beans is to blanch them first and then reheat them later.

To blanch string beans: Bring a large pot of salted water to a rolling boil. My rule of thumb for salt is light these days: a scant half teaspoon per quart of water. But I do go heavy on the water because the more water you use, the faster it will return to the boil once the beans are added. I always cook beans uncovered and boil them only long enough to ensure a crisp-tender texture, about 1½ to 2 minutes after the water returns to the boil. If you like your string beans more tender, add a minute or two to the cooking time. Drain the cooked beans in a colander and rinse under cold running water until they are cool. The icy bath not only guarantees a bright green color, it retards the cooking process as well. When the beans are cool to the touch, drain them dry and either proceed with the recipe at hand or refrigerate. Chilled beans may be stored in an airtight plastic bag and held in the refrigerator up to 24 hours.

MARY SURINA'S BEAN AND BARLEY SOUP

One of the heartiest soups I know is compounded of two kinds of beans, dried and green, as well as a multitude of old-fashioned ingredients like a ham hock, spareribs, and barley. This might intimidate the untried soup maker, but dismiss that notion at once. The soup is easy to make and all its components can be found at any supermarket. I know, I bought them there! This stick-to-the-ribs pottage is of Yugoslavian extraction by way of San Pedro, California. It was given to me by my friend Mary Surina, who is without challenge one of the finest cooks in San Pedro.

8 ounces dried pinto beans
1 pound spareribs, trimmed of fat, cut into
   2-inch sections
1 tablespoon unsalted butter
1 onion, chopped
2 cloves garlic, minced
2 carrots, finely chopped
2 ribs celery, finely chopped
1 ham hock (about 1 pound)
1 quart chicken broth (see page 414)
2 quarts vegetable broth or water
   (see page 414)
1 cup barley
½ pound string beans, trimmed, cut
   French-style, halved
Salt and freshly ground black pepper
1 tablespoon chopped fresh parsley

1. Cover the pinto beans with water in a large pot. Heat to boiling; boil 2 minutes. Remove from the heat and let stand, covered, 1 hour. Drain.

2. Preheat the oven to 350°F. Cover the spareribs with cold water in a large pot. Heat to boiling; drain immediately under cold running water until cool. Pat dry with paper towels.

3. Melt the butter in a 5-quart Dutch oven over medium-low heat. Stir in the onion; cook 1 minute. Add the garlic, carrots, and celery. Cook 4 minutes. Add the pinto beans, spareribs, ham hock, chicken broth, and 1 quart of the vegetable broth or water. Heat to boiling; remove from the heat. Cook, covered, in the oven for 1 hour.

4. Remove the Dutch oven and stir in the remaining 1 quart vegetable broth or water. Stir in the barley and string beans. Return the soup to the oven and continue to bake, covered, until barley is tender, about 1 hour longer.

5. Remove the soup from the oven. Remove the spareribs and ham hock. Cut the meat off the bones and return the meat to the soup. Add salt and pepper to taste. Serve sprinkled with the parsley.

Serves 6 to 8.

VAGUELY CHINESE STRING BEAN SALAD

*T*his is the handiwork of Donald Sacks, who runs a charming food shop in New York. Donald has one caveat about his slaw: the beans must be crunchy or all is lost.

1 pound tender young string beans,
   trimmed
1½-inch piece fresh ginger root, minced
¼ cup vegetable oil
1½ tablespoons sherry vinegar
¼ teaspoon sesame oil
¼ teaspoon coarse (kosher) salt
Pinch of sugar
⅛ teaspoon ground white pepper
1½ to 2 tablespoons toasted sesame seeds

1. Cook the beans in boiling salted water until crisp-tender, about 1½ to 2 minutes. Rinse under cold running water; drain. Cover, and chill 1 hour.

2. Press the ginger root in a fine-mesh sieve over a large bowl to extract the juice; discard the pulp. Whisk in the vegetable oil, vinegar, sesame oil, coarse salt, sugar, and white pepper. Add the beans; toss to coat them with the dressing. Cover, and chill 4 hours, tossing every hour.

3. Just before serving, sprinkle with the sesame seeds.

Serves 4.

ROMAN GREEN BEANS WITH FONTINA CHEESE

My favorite time to eat string beans is in summer. Besides being at their tenderest when in season, nothing makes a more spectacular salad. For further evidence, see this dispensation from Efrem Funghi Calingaert and Jacquelyn Days Serwer, from their excellent book *Pasta and Rice, Italian Style*. A mix of green beans with Fontina cheese, it is atypical *antipasto* but devilishly good eating.

1 pound string beans, trimmed
½ pound Fontina cheese, cut into strips
about 3 inches long and ¼ inch wide
1 clove garlic, minced
½ teaspoon Dijon mustard
¼ cup lemon juice
½ cup olive oil
Salt and freshly ground black pepper

1. Cook the beans in boiling salted water until crisp-tender, about 1½ to 2 minutes. Rinse under cold running water; drain. Combine with the cheese in a large bowl.

2. Mash the garlic with the mustard in a small bowl. Stir in the lemon juice. Slowly whisk in the oil. Pour this dressing over the beans and cheese. Toss well and add salt and pepper to taste. Serve at room temperature or slightly chilled.

Serves 4.

HOT WAX BEAN CHEF'S SALAD

Another unusual wax bean rendering, this is a warm salad that combines the pods with strips of chicken, ham, and herbs in a delicate mustardy vinaigrette. Yes . . . you read it right, warm! And wonderful too. Serve it for lunch or dinner with a good loaf of crusty bread.

For the mustard vinaigrette:

2 tablespoons Dijon mustard
1 tablespoon red wine vinegar
1 tablespoon lemon juice
6 tablespoons olive oil
1 tablespoon vodka

For the salad:

½ pound wax beans, trimmed, cut French-style
1 small red bell pepper, seeded, cut into thin strips
1 tablespoon unsalted butter

1 scallion, bulb and green top, minced
1 clove garlic, minced
¼ pound thinly sliced cooked smoked ham, cut into strips
1 tablespoon chopped fresh basil
2 cups roughly chopped cooked chicken

1. To make the mustard vinaigrette: Whisk the mustard with the vinegar and lemon juice in a small bowl until smooth. Slowly whisk in the oil, then the vodka. Cover and refrigerate at least 1 hour.

2. Cook the wax beans and red pepper in boiling salted water until crisp-tender, about 3 minutes. Drain.

3. Melt the butter in a large skillet over medium heat. Add the scallion; cook 1 minute. Add the garlic; cook 3 minutes. Add the wax beans and red pepper, the ham, basil, and chicken. Cook, tossing constantly, until warmed through.

4. Transfer the warm salad to a serving dish. Pour the chilled vinaigrette over the top and toss at the table.

Serves 4.

The wax or yellow bean is nothing more than a string bean that has been cultivated for its lightened (and some consider more appealing) color. In the process of hybridization a jot of folic acid (source of vitamin B) is lost, but the flavor and texture are otherwise indistinguishable. In France, wax beans are known as *mange-tout*, which roughly translates as wholly edible—and they are!

MILDRED SCHULZ'S STRING BEANS AND POTATOES

The next delectable string bean formula in this volume is my own personal talisman. It is a donation from Mildred Schulz of Golden, Colorado, who is not only a good friend but also a kind of benefactor. Mildred has contributed a recipe to every book I have written, and just seeing her name in the index again brings me a sense of inner security and personal joy. That all of her offerings have been wonderful is almost beside the point. They are lodestars.

2 medium potatoes (about ½ pound),
    unpeeled
½ pound string beans, trimmed
3 strips bacon
1 medium onion, halved, sliced
¼ cup red wine vinegar
2 tablespoons water
1 tablespoon unsalted butter
Salt and freshly ground black pepper

1. Cook the potatoes in boiling salted water until just barely tender, about 15 minutes. Drain. Cut into ¼-inch-thick slices.

2. Meanwhile, cook the beans in boiling salted water until crisp-tender, 1½ to 2 minutes. Rinse under cold run-ning water; drain.

3. Sauté the bacon in a heavy skillet until crisp. Remove and drain on paper towels. Crumble and reserve.

4. Cook the onion in the bacon drippings over medium heat until golden. Stir in the vinegar and water. Cook, stirring constantly, until slightly thickened, about 3 minutes. Reduce the heat to medium-low and toss in the potatoes and string beans. Cook, tossing gently, for 5 minutes. Stir in the butter and add salt and pepper to taste. Sprinkle with the reserved bacon.

Serves 4.

GREEN AND GOLD
(Sautéed Spinach and Wax Beans)

*T*he name of this side dish of golden wax beans and bright green leaf spinach is borrowed from my alma mater's school colors. In honor of William and Mary.

2 tablespoons plus 1 teaspoon unsalted
    butter
½ cup Chicken Stock (see page 410)
1 pound wax beans, trimmed, cut on the
    diagonal into 2-inch pieces
4 ounces fresh spinach, chopped (about 1¼
    cups)
1 tablespoon chopped fresh parsley
⅛ teaspoon crushed dried hot red peppers
¼ teaspoon freshly grated nutmeg
Salt and freshly ground black pepper

1. Melt the 2 tablespoons butter in a medium saucepan over medium heat. Add the chicken stock and heat to boiling. Add the beans and cook, covered, over medium heat until the beans are barely tender, about 8 minutes. Remove the cover and cook until half the liquid has evaporated.

2. Add the spinach and parsley to the beans. Cook, uncovered, tossing constantly, until the spinach wilts, about 3 minutes. If the mixture seems too wet, raise the heat and cook some more, until fairly dry. Stir in the remaining 1 teaspoon butter, the crushed peppers, the nutmeg, and salt and pepper to taste.

Serves 4.

GREENE'S OUT-OF-SEASON BEANS

*O*f late I have been able to buy thin and extremely tender imported *haricots verts* at the greengrocer's, albeit at astronomical prices. In summer, I often purchase similar domestic pods at farm stands or greenmarkets. These baby green beans are not cheap either, but they are excellently toothsome, so I pay gladly. When neither is available and thick-skinned, relatively flavorless supermarket varieties are the only option, I "fudge" the issue with the following recipe. It is unorthodox but tasty, I assure you.

1 pound string beans, trimmed, cut
    French-style
2 tablespoons unsalted butter
1 large shallot, minced
½ teaspoon beef bouillon powder
1 small tomato, peeled, seeded, chopped
Salt and freshly ground black pepper
Chopped fresh parsley

1. Cook the beans in boiling salted water until almost tender, about 3 minutes. Rinse under cold running water. Drain.

2. Melt the butter in a large saucepan over medium-low heat. Add the shallot; cook 3 minutes. Toss in the beans, bouillon powder, and tomato. Cook, tossing constantly, over medium heat until warmed through. Add salt and pepper to taste, and sprinkle with parsley.

Serves 4.

EZE
(String Beans Sautéed with Chartreuse)

When I lived in the South of France, the women who ran the local outdoor vegetable market always referred to a green bean as a *nigaud*. Not exactly a pejorative, it is no compliment either, meaning a fool or a noodle. Take your pick! Neither describes the next green bean recipe, though I did invent it in France one day when I had a basket of perfect *haricots verts* at hand and a bottle of fine Chartreuse in the cupboard.

1 pound tender young string beans,
    trimmed (larger ones cut French-style)
2 strips bacon
3 tablespoons unsalted butter
3 shallots, minced
2 tablespoons chopped fresh basil, or 1
    teaspoon dried
3 tablespoons Chartreuse liqueur
Freshly ground black pepper

1. Cook the beans in boiling salted water 1 minute. Rinse under cold running water. Drain.

2. Sauté the bacon in a large heavy skillet until crisp. Remove with a slotted spoon and drain on paper towels. Crumble and reserve.

3. Pour off all the drippings in the skillet. Add 2 tablespoons of the butter and the shallots. Cook over medium-low heat 3 minutes. Add the beans, basil, and Chartreuse. Continue to cook, stirring frequently, 5 minutes. Stir in the remaining 1 tablespoon butter and sprinkle with pepper to taste. Sprinkle with the reserved bacon.

Serves 4.

LEMON STRINGS

According to legume savants, the Incas cultivated the string bean not so much for flavor as for theology. They were sun worshipers, and so (apparently) was the bean. A green bean will climb any vertical surface, notably a pole, twisting and turning in its search for the light. For the Incas, chewing the pods was seen as an act of sacrament. But those poor folks missed the point entirely, since string beans are delicious into the bargain. One of the sun-loving bean's more felicitous matings is with another golden globe, the fragrant lemon. Though it may seem immodest to brag about my recipes, one bite of this could turn an Inca (or any other non-bean-lover) into a deep-dyed fan.

1 pound string beans, trimmed
¼ cup Chicken Stock (see page 410)
Juice of 1 lemon
4 tablespoons (½ stick) unsalted butter

Finely slivered peel of 1 lemon
Salt and freshly ground black pepper
1 teaspoon chopped fresh parsley

1. Cook the string beans in boiling salted water until crisp-tender, about 1½ to 2 minutes. Rinse under cold running water until cool. Drain.

2. Combine the chicken stock and lemon juice in a large skillet over medium heat. Heat to boiling; boil until reduced by half, about 4 minutes. Add the butter and stir until smooth. Add the beans and lemon peel. Toss until warmed through, about 2 minutes. Add salt and pepper to taste, and sprinkle with the parsley.

Serves 4.

String bean is no aphorism. This variety of green bean once had a tough strand of green filament down its back side that a poor housewife had to diligently remove with a sharp knife prior to cooking. But no longer. Agrogeneticists have bred a new and virtually stringless pod that requires a mere snip at the top and tail ends before it is popped into boiling water.

SNAP BEAN PUREE

The first *haricot vert* was introduced to England by a band of French immigrants, Huguenots, who made a gift of this vegetable to Queen Elizabeth I as a gratuity for allowing them religious freedom in her land. Good Queen Bess found the bequest of green beans "much engaging to the royal taste." So much so, in fact, that green beans were planted in the garden at Hampton Court and shortly thereafter in greenswards all over the island. English farmers became so attached to the green bean that they even, chauvinistically, renamed it the *Elizabeth Bean*. But that cognomen never stuck. When Elizabeth died and James took over, the beans were once again dubbed simply "Frenchies." What follows is a purely Francophile rendering—a velvety purée, which, parenthetically, can be prepared with wax beans as well.

1 large potato, peeled, diced
¾ cup Chicken Stock, approximately (see page 410)
2 pounds green or wax string beans, trimmed
Salt and freshly ground black pepper
1 tablespoon unsalted butter

1. Cook the potato, covered, in the chicken stock until tender, about 12 minutes. Drain, reserving the stock. Mash or rice the potato. Set aside.

2. Cook the beans in boiling salted water until very tender—4 to 5 minutes for green, about 10 for wax. Drain.

3. Place the beans in the container of a food processor. Process, using the on/off switch, until smooth, adding just enough reserved chicken stock to make a smooth mixture. Combine the beans with the potato and transfer to the top of a double boiler.

4. Just before serving, reheat the purée in the top of a double boiler over simmering water. Add salt and pepper to taste, and stir in the butter.

Serves 4 to 6.

BRAISED GARLIC AND STRING BEANS

To my way of thinking, the ultimate way to prepare a string bean is with the fewest ingredients and the least amount of fuss. With those parameters established, have my nomination for a classic rendering. The ingredients are mainly beans, butter, and garlic, but never was a legume sauced more eloquently. Or in less time!

1 pound tender young string beans,
  trimmed (cut larger beans French-style)
3 tablespoons unsalted butter
4 to 5 large cloves garlic
1 teaspoon chopped fresh sage, or a pinch
  of dried
1 tablespoon chopped fresh parsley
Salt and freshly ground black pepper

1. Cook the string beans in boiling salted water until crisp-tender, about 1½ to 2 minutes. Rinse under cold running water until cool. Drain.

2. Melt the butter in a large skillet over low heat. Add the garlic cloves; cook, covered, until lightly golden and soft, 20 to 25 minutes. Do not let the butter burn. Remove the cover and mash the garlic with a fork until well mixed with the butter.

3. Add the beans to the skillet; toss over medium heat until warmed through. Add the sage, parsley, and salt and pepper to taste.

Serves 4.

SWEET GREEN BEAN PICKLES

With such a healthy dose of vitamins per bean, one can be a bit frivolous in this recipe for a sweet pickle.

1½ to 2 pounds string beans, trimmed
2 cups cider vinegar
⅓ cup sugar
1½ tablespoons mixed pickling spices, tied
  in a cheesecloth bag
1 tablespoon whole black peppercorns
1 bay leaf
1 clove garlic
1 large onion, chopped
1 small red bell pepper, seeded, chopped
3 large sprigs dill

1. Cook the beans in boiling salted water for 1 minute. Rinse under cold running water; drain.

2. Place the vinegar, sugar, pickling spices, peppercorns, bay leaf, and garlic clove in a medium saucepan. Heat to boiling; reduce the heat. Simmer, uncovered, 10 minutes. Discard the spice bag. Add the onion and bell pepper; simmer 10 minutes longer. Discard the bay leaf and garlic.

3. Pack the beans upright in sterilized jars (up to 1 inch from the top). With a slotted spoon, divide the onions and red peppers evenly among the jars. Place a dill sprig in each jar and pour in hot syrup up to ½ inch from the top. Seal the jars. Process in a hot water bath for 15 minutes.

Makes 3 pints.

FASULYE VE KUZU
(Turkish String Beans and Lamb Cakes)

I have never traveled to the Bosphorus, but I know the Turks have a way with string beans. A friend who has been to that country and back several times brought me the following recipe, somewhat stained with thumbprints of oil and redolent with garlic, from an encounter in Istanbul. And while the name of this dish is virtually unpronounceable (and the spelling suspect), the taste is one you will not soon forget.

1½ pounds ground lamb
½ pound ground beef
1 medium onion, finely chopped
2 cloves garlic, minced
½ cup fresh bread crumbs
¼ teaspoon ground allspice
Pinch of ground cinnamon
2 tablespoons chopped fresh parsley
Dash of hot pepper sauce
1 egg, lightly beaten
¼ cup water
½ teaspoon salt
¼ teaspoon freshly ground black pepper
2 tablespoons unsalted butter
1 tablespoon olive oil
1 medium onion, thinly sliced
1 pound string beans, trimmed, cut
    French-style
8 ripe Italian plum tomatoes, peeled, or 1
    can (28 ounces) plum tomatoes,
    drained
¼ teaspoon sugar
¼ cup chopped fresh basil
Finely slivered peel of 1 large orange
¼ cup chopped fresh parsley

1. Preheat the oven to 350°F. Combine all the ingredients through the pepper in a large bowl. Mix thoroughly, and form into small meatballs.

2. Heat the butter with the oil in a large heavy skillet over medium heat. Sauté the meatballs, about six at a time, until golden brown on all sides, about 5 minutes. Transfer them to a Dutch oven.

3. Add the onion to the skillet. Cook, scraping the sides and bottom of the pan, over medium heat 3 minutes. Add the onions to the meatballs in the Dutch oven, along with the string beans, tomatoes, sugar, and basil. Stir gently to mix. Bake, uncovered, 1 hour. Stir in the orange peel and sprinkle with the parsley.

Serves 6.

T hough the green bean was discovered in South America, food historians assert that varieties migrated to the more temperate climes of North America long, long before Columbus made his first crossing. In 1524, Giovanni Verrazano, the Florentine explorer who first traveled the Atlantic seacoast, wrote to his wife from the New World describing the foods that native Indians ate: "They grow slender pods born on bushes with bright green leaves. These have the virtue of a good flavor but require long and careful chewing even after a long stay in the cook pot"—probably so noted because the natives generally dried their beans prior to cooking or ate them when very mature.

SAUTEED STRING BEANS AND BAY SCALLOPS

After the summer tenants depart my Amagansett house, anything left on the vine I claim. And the scallops? They are never sweeter than in September when Gardiner's Bay has a harvest all its own.

½ pound string beans, trimmed, cut
    French-style
1 red bell pepper, seeded, cut into thin
    strips
1 pound bay scallops, or sea scallops,
    quartered
Juice of ½ lemon
½ cup all-purpose flour
4 tablespoons (½ stick) unsalted butter,
    approximately
2 tablespoons olive oil
2 shallots, minced
2 cloves garlic, minced
½ cup dry white wine
Salt and freshly ground black pepper
1 tablespoon chopped fresh basil, or ½
    teaspoon dried
1 tablespoon chopped fresh parsley
Hot Steamed Rice (see page 412)

1. Preheat the oven to 350°F. Cook the beans in boiling salted water for 2 minutes. Rinse under cold running water; drain.

2. Cook the pepper in another pot of boiling salted water for 2 minutes. Rinse under cold running water; drain.

3. Sprinkle the scallops with the lemon juice and dust them lightly with the flour.

4. Melt 2 tablespoons of the butter in 1 tablespoon of the oil in a large skillet over medium-high heat. Add half the scallops and cook, stirring constantly, until golden, about 3 minutes. Add half the shallots and half the garlic. Toss thoroughly. Transfer to a baking dish.

5. Add the remaining butter and oil. Sauté the remaining scallops until golden; add the remaining shallots and garlic. Transfer to the baking dish. Toss in the beans and pepper and mix thoroughly.

6. Pour the wine into the same skillet and cook over medium-high heat, scraping the sides and bottom of the pan, until thick and syrupy, about 4 minutes. Pour this sauce over the scallop-vegetable mixture and add salt and pepper to taste. Bake, uncovered, 20 minutes. Sprinkle with the basil and parsley. Serve over Hot Steamed Rice.

Serves 4.

String beans grow two ways: as pole beans and as bush beans. The Omaha Indians had better names for both varieties. They called them "walking beans" and "beans not walking." To keep the horticultural notes succinct, the bush bean is a stay-at-home. While the plant grows thick as a dwarf pine, the bean picker never has to stretch for a handful of pods. Pole beans, being somewhat less constricted, wander all over the garden. Never a pleasure to pick, pole beans are (in my opinion at least) sweeter for their nomadic tendencies.

NORMAN BEANS WITH EGGS

M y friend Paul Milikin is an actor. I rarely get to see him perform because he is most often on the road, but I do hear from him with unerring regularity. His missives are usually postcards from cities with notable repertory companies and include some good recipe that he managed to acquire locally. For besides being a fine actor, Milikin is also a notable cook. The following string bean dish is his. It was sent from France a while back and rates a critical rave in my book, for either lunch or brunch, and particularly if one's guests happen to be vegetarian.

1 pound string beans, trimmed
2 tablespoons unsalted butter, melted
½ teaspoon lemon juice
1 teaspoon chopped fresh chives
1 teaspoon chopped fresh parsley
½ teaspoon salt
¼ teaspoon freshly ground black pepper
4 eggs, lightly beaten

1. Preheat the oven to 400°F. Cook the beans in boiling salted water until crisp-tender, about 1½ to 2 minutes. Drain.

2. Place the warm beans in a bowl and add the remaining ingredients. Toss well and pour into a buttered shallow baking dish. Bake until set, about 10 minutes. Cut into wedges to serve.

Serves 4.

SWEET POTATOES

I Yam What I Yam

I suspect I can pinpoint the development of my taste buds to the moment when I left home for college. The school I had elected, William and Mary in Williamsburg, Virginia, was too far away for weekend excursions, and even long-distance phone calls—except in case of dire emergency—had been discouraged in advance by my ever-thrifty mother. So the snowy day when I boarded the Pennsylvania Railroad for geographic parts unknown was in actuality the beginning of a much longer journey: to a life *on my own.*

The startling revelation of utter freedom came upon me when I

realized that my grandfather, unexpectedly appearing at the frosty station to say goodbye, had pressed a crisp hundred-dollar bill into my palm as we gravely shook hands.

My mother had already given me some injunctions about money. "Never give big tips," she cautioned. "People don't expect 'em from kids anyway." After noting there was a night's layover en route, she had been most specific about where and how I spend this respite. "Find a clean *second-class* hotel," she advised. "Ask a cab driver to take you to one where salesmen stay! And be sure to skip fancy restaurants. Only eat at lunch counters or cafeterias. They're generally cleaner!"

With a hundred dollars in my wallet, I dismissed all these admonitions out of hand. The first act of independence: a solo reservation in the train's dining car.

What a glory it was! A caravan of polished mahogany with shaded windows and shell-like sconces that shone day and night. White damask covered the tables where salt cellars and water goblets danced like marionettes at each reverberation of the train's wheels.

As I had never dined alone in a restaurant, even on solid ground, the prospect of eating in one on the move seemed doubly intimidating. The black headwaiter at the door was obviously one of a vanishing breed of amiable men who took pleasure in their work. White-coated and benign as a preacher, he settled me at an empty table next to a window. Then, recognizing my awe at the multitude of options, he pointed out the specialties on the menu.

When I announced my decision—a meal of terrapin followed by roast pheasant under glass and sweet potato pone— he shook his head gravely.

"You sure don' want that, son," he confided. "Terrapin is snapping turtle no matter what you call it, and the pheasant...well!" He whistled. "That's been on the tracks for some time now. Why don' you let me bring you a nice cup of crab bisque instead, followed by a club sandwich and pie à la mode."

I acquiesced to his superior judg-ment about the first choices, but balked severely at giving up the pone. I had never tasted this sweet dish but the name itself, so mouth-watering, conjured up all manner of images: Scarlett O'Hara, Rhett, Tara. I insisted he bring me a slice.

Reluctantly he agreed. But midway between Trenton and Camden, he reappeared, empty-handed. "Son," he whispered, "I do not tell this to most folks who ride the Pullmans but you seem to be a young man who really enjoys his vittles. If so, don't eat no Northern pone served here!" Handing me a slip of folded paper, he continued, "You got a mouth for sweet potato? Take note of this place in Richmond. It's the best you will ever find!"

The name scrawled on the sheet was *Blue Milton on Main St.* Just that. I gave him a large tip for his good offices and promised faithfully to heed the advice.

I did so the very next week. Blue Milton was most definitely "a place" and not a restaurant. Situated at the end of Richmond's Main Street in an area that, I later discovered, housed all the city's fancy houses, it was actually a wooden shack next to a closed service station. It bore no name and was papered outside and in with Coca Cola and Dr. Pepper posters faded by time. "The Mill," as most denizens called it, was run by a black couple and was remarkable in 1941 for the fact that it was totally integrated. White and black patrons stood on line together waiting for a slice of pone or a plateful of ribs and a fried ham bun, without a measure of discontent. First come was first served. And royally, I might add, for it was probably the best food in the city at the time—certainly the best I had ever tasted, and I returned often.

Blue Milton is long since gone, but the memory of its luscious golden pone, sweeter than youth itself, will never be erased from my tongue!

Vegetable Roots

Actually no potato at all, the sweet potato is a rooted tuber that is first cousin to the morning glory. I have never seen one in full bloom, but the rose-purple trumpets are reputedly so dazzling that on occasion a sweet potato crop has been seriously threatened by overacquisitive posy pickers.

A New World native (albeit in the less temperate of its zones), *Ipomoea batatas* has been in culinary currency for over a thousand years. When Columbus made his second appearance on this side of the Atlantic in 1493, he noted in his diaries that the native Indians (in Hispaniola, where he landed) subsisted exclusively on a diet of fish, coconut, and sweet potato, a root he variously called *b-aje*, *aḡe*, or *baaḡe*. Columbus probably had misheard the word. Scholars assume it was actually *ba-hich*, and it meant "tongue burn." With good reason. The Taino Indians there ate boiled sweet potatoes out of a communal pot. Reaching into the center of the cauldron with bare hands, they would toss the steaming chunks into the air to cool, but invariably scorched their lips swallowing them.

According to one of Columbus's Spanish crewmen who passed this intelligence on to his brother years later, the method of consuming *baage* was torturous but its flavor so intriguing that one went through the oral immolation willingly. The taste he compared to the commingling of ripe oranges and roasted chestnuts.

No wonder the Spanish court eagerly awaited its first bite of this new "root fruit." From all accounts no one was displeased, though they considered its name utterly unpronounceable. In time, *baage* underwent a change to *batata*, which was remarkably like the existing Spanish word for potato, *patata*, and caused these dissimilar tubers to be linked ever since!

The sweet potato did not come to European tables from Spain voluntarily. On the contrary, Spanish gardeners zealously husbanded the secret of its growth. Henry VIII, whose first wife, Catherine of Aragon, was Spanish, received the sweet potato as part of her dowry and admired the flavor so much that he insisted that Spain export the tubers to England, which they did with some reluctance. Henry VIII adored the sweet potato and was noted for his ability to digest two dozen per sitting. His palate was so devoted to what he called "the Spanish potato" that after his divorce from Catherine, he gave a prize of land and gold to the gardener who could grow one in Britain. The incentive proved felicitous, and by the mid-sixteenth century sweet potatoes bloomed all over the British Isles. The rage was brief, however, most likely because the sweet potato needs a warmer climate to survive. All plants withered in a typically cool English summer, and never grew there again.

The sweet potato is an unusual vegetable in that it is not grown from seed. Instead, plants are started from sprouts—cut from the roots or from the vines of a prior crop. The unorthodox progeny in time gave rise to yet another name. When *batatas* were cultivated in Jamestown in 1648, the farmers who planted the slips called them "bastards"—a moniker that clung for some years, until righteous members of the community had it expunged, and the "bastard" became the legitimate "Virginia potato."

What to Look For

There are two general kinds of sweet potatoes at our table. Growers (dependent upon matters of climate and geography) variously dub a sweet potato as either "moist" or "dry." Neither tag has a jot to do with its water content. Moist types, often called yams, have somewhat reddish brown skins and deep orange flesh, with a high starch content that converts to sugar as it cooks, and may be deemed a sweeter sweet potato. Dry types have tan or fawn shaded skins and yellow-to-gold flesh that converts less starch to sugar—and are decidedly less sweet on a fork!

It may be worth noting that the moist, sweet yam that happily ends up as pone or pie has absolutely no kinship with a true yam (*Dioscorea bulbifera*), a tropical vine whose globes are a hundred times sweeter and mealier. American yams got the wrong name by association. The first slaves, who had lived on the yams in their native land, called them by the African word "to eat" (variously the Gullah *njam*, the Senegar *nyami*, or the Vai *djambi*), and the appellation obviously stuck.

Shopping for sweet potatoes, the sharp-eyed consumer will ferret out the smoothest-skinned specimens. Look for medium sizes that taper at the end. Most sweet potatoes on the market are pre-cured and have had some stint in storage prior to the supermarket shelf. So choose members that are not bruised, blemished, or, worse yet, sprouting. Sweet potato harvests begin in late summer, and by Thanksgiving it is virtually impossible to find any that are uncured.

Curing is a process that allows sweet potatoes to keep. Once they are dug, tubers are held in controlled high-heat, high-humidity environments for about a week to allow the conversion of starch to dextrins and sugars to begin before they are stored. So, a sweet potato that is boiled and then mashed into a velvety chowder will taste a heck of a lot sweeter in winter and spring (after curing) than in August when it is straight from the vine.

The sweet potato is nutritious, make no mistake about it. One medium sweet (boiled, then peeled) provides more than twice the recommended daily allowance of vitamin A (11,940 units), along with healthy increments of potassium, calcium, and ascorbic acid. On the debit side, a boiled sweet potato adds about 172 calories to your diet (though somewhat less when baked.)

Preparation

I am very catholic, culinarily speaking, in the matter of sweet potato cookery. I boil, bake, or fry them, and even on occasion make ice cream out of them. The surest way to retain a sweet potato's nutrients (and parenthetically to prevent the natural sugar from leaching out) is to boil it in its jacket and peel it afterward.

I usually bake sweet potatoes quickly in a fairly warm oven (400°F), and I never grease the skins. An 8-ounce sweet will bake in 40 to 45 minutes. One may place a sweet potato directly on the oven rack, but I do not for they often have infinitesimal fissures in the skin and leave a sticky residue that requires a scrub-up later. Most often I bake them on a shallow baking dish or tray and turn them once during the oven stint. When you can insert a fork into the flesh with ease, the sweet potato is definitely ready to go to the table.

Once a sweet potato has been cooked, it keeps. I store mine (cooled) in the refrigerator for up to a week's time. You may leave them in their skins, or if you wish, scrape the pulp into a covered container prior to storage. A sweet potato's sweetness increases in repose.

SWEET 'TATER POTTAGE

My ultimate sweet potato soup is called a pottage out of loose Biblical connection: in my opinion, Esau would have sold his birthright for a single slurp.

1 tablespoon unsalted butter
1 medium onion, chopped
1 large rib celery, chopped
½ pound sweet potatoes, peeled, sliced
1½ cups chicken broth (see page 414)
1 cup V-8 or spicy tomato juice
¼ cup heavy or whipping cream
1 tablespoon bourbon
⅛ teaspoon ground cinnamon
⅛ teaspoon freshly grated nutmeg
Salt and freshly ground black pepper

1. Melt the butter in a medium saucepan over medium-low heat. Stir in the onion; cook 1 minute. Stir in the celery and potatoes; cook 5 minutes. Add the broth and the tomato juice; cook, uncovered, until tender, about 25 minutes. Cool.

2. Place the soup, in batches, in the container of a blender or food processor. Blend until smooth.

3. Pour the soup into a medium saucepan. Stir in the cream, bourbon, cinnamon, and nutmeg. Heat over low heat until warmed through. Do not boil. Add salt and pepper to taste. Serve hot, or chill and serve cold.

Serves 4.

COLD CURRIED YAMS

On the subject of curry, try a less authentic sweet potato rendering. If one were bold (as I am not) it would be dubbed sweet potato salad. In my bailiwick it teams remarkably with fried chicken and baked ham on a picnic table.

4 large yams (about 1¾ pounds)
1 medium red onion, finely chopped
½ green bell pepper, seeded, finely chopped
½ cup Mayonnaise (see page 408)
½ cup sour cream
¼ cup strong Beef Stock, cooled
   (see page 409)
1 tablespoon curry powder
Salt and freshly ground black pepper
2 tablespoons chopped fresh parsley

1. Cook the yams in their jackets in boiling salted water until just barely tender, 20 to 25 minutes. Drain. Cool, peel, and cut into ⅛-inch-thick slices.

2. Combine the sliced yams, red onion, and green pepper in a large bowl.

3. In a medium bowl, whisk the mayonnaise with the sour cream. Whisk in the stock, curry powder, and salt and pepper to taste. Pour this dressing over the yam mixture. Toss lightly to combine, and serve sprinkled with the parsley.

Serves 4.

SCALLOPED SWEETS

In North America, the term "sweet potato" did not become official until about 1740, and then only to distinguish it from the white potato, thought to be Irish and brought over about twenty years earlier.

Here's my version of what most Irish potato lovers consider their own preserve: scalloped potatoes, turned exotically different with a "bastard-Spanish-Virginia-Chinese-Japanese" member as its main ingredient.

4 large sweet potatoes (about 2 pounds)
3½ cups heavy or whipping cream
¾ teaspoon salt
½ teaspoon ground ginger
1 tablespoon lime juice
Finely grated peel of 1 lime
¾ teaspoon ground white pepper
2 teaspoons unsalted butter, cut into bits

1. Preheat the oven to 350°F. Peel the potatoes and cut them into ⅛-inch-thick slices.

2. Combine the potatoes, cream, salt, ginger, lime juice, lime peel, and white pepper in a large saucepan. Heat to boiling, stirring constantly.

3. Pour the potato mixture into a well-buttered shallow baking dish. Dot the surface with the butter. Bake until lightly browned, about 1 hour.

Serves 6 to 8.

BAKED YAMS

On most American tables, sweet potatoes have always maintained an aura of a "Sunday special"—their appearance assured only on major holidays like Thanksgiving. However, since it is a ubiquitous vegetable in the Deep South, the sweet potato was a mainstay of most sharecroppers' diets. Some of its most original table guises, in fact, demonstrate necessity mothering invention. To wit: this easy, economical, extremely tasty rendering.

2 strips bacon
2 medium yams
1 teaspoon dark brown sugar
Freshly ground black pepper

1. Preheat the oven to 375°F. Sauté the bacon strips in a heavy skillet until crisp. Drain on paper towels, reserving the drippings. Crumble and reserve the bacon.

2. Cut the yams in half lengthwise. Score the top of each half in a lattice pattern, about ¼ inch deep. Do not cut through the skins. Brush the top of each with bacon drippings, squeezing the yams lightly to open them up. Sprinkle each half with ¼ teaspoon of the brown sugar.

3. Bake the potatoes 1 hour. Sprinkle them with the crumbled bacon and bake 2 minutes longer. Sprinkle with pepper to taste.

Serves 2.

MASHED SWEETS

Henry VIII laced his sweet potato with rum and Demerara sugar. I dote on them flavored with butter, cream, and bourbon.

4 large sweet potatoes (about 2 pounds)
3 tablespoons unsalted butter
3 tablespoons heavy or whipping cream
2 tablespoons bourbon
Salt and freshly ground black pepper

1. Cook the potatoes in their jackets in boiling salted water until tender, 45 to 50 minutes. Drain.

2. Carefully peel the potatoes and place them in a medium saucepan. Mash, over very low heat, with a potato masher until smooth. Beat in the butter, cream, bourbon, and salt and pepper to taste. Cook, stirring constantly, until warmed through.
Serves 4.

SWEET POTATO PONE

To my prejudiced tongue, the definitive pone is one that is not too sweet. I acquired this recipe from a beguiling book of regional Southern fare (sadly out of print): *Damnyankee in a Southern Kitchen* by Helen Worth.

2 large eggs
2 cups milk
1½ tablespoons vanilla extract
1 cup sugar
¼ teaspoon freshly grated nutmeg
½ teaspoon grated orange peel
3 medium sweet potatoes (about 1 pound), peeled, grated
6 tablespoons (¾ stick) unsalted butter, melted

Preheat the oven to 350°F. Beat the eggs in a large mixing bowl. Beat in the remaining ingredients and pour into a buttered 2-quart soufflé or baking dish. Bake until firm and golden brown, about 2 hours. Let stand 20 minutes before serving. The flavor intensifies as it stands.
Serves 8.

There is a rumor that early Spanish explorers (like Balboa) may have carried the sweet potato as far as the Philippines, where it also took root. Later Portuguese voyagers (like Magellan) may have transported it even farther—to India, China, and Malaya. At any event, its entry into Eastern cuisine was so unobtrusive that its point of origin has been largely overlooked for centuries. In southern regions of Japan, for instance, it is called *kara-imo* ("the Chinese potato"), but it is known as *satsuma-imo* ("the Japanese potato") in the rest of the country.

FRIED SWEET POTATO CRISPS

3 medium sweet potatoes (about 1 pound)
2 tablespoons salt
Oil for frying
Salt and freshly ground black pepper

1. Peel the potatoes and cut them into ⅛-inch-thick round slices. Place the slices in a large bowl. Cover with cold water; stir in the salt. Let stand 10 minutes.

2. Heat ¼ inch of oil in a heavy skillet until hot but not smoking. Drain the potatoes; pat them dry with paper towels. Fry, a few slices at a time, until lightly brown on both sides, about 4 minutes per side. Drain on paper towels and sprinkle with salt and pepper to taste. Keep warm in a low oven while frying the remaining potatoes.

Serves 4 to 6.

MADRASI KARI
(Sweet Potatoes, Beef, and Pork, Madras-style)

One of the most unusual sweet potato recipes in my collection is Indian. From southerly Madras, it is a curry that teams this vegetable with beef and pork. I often improvise the heartier components with whatever leftovers I have on hand. Naturally the dish varies, but it is the sweet potato that gives it its essential savor.

1 large sweet potato (about ½ pound),
　　peeled, cubed
2 tablespoons unsalted butter
3 tablespoons vegetable oil
1 medium onion, finely chopped
1 clove garlic, minced
½ pound cooked beef, cut into
　　2-by-½-inch strips
½ pound cooked pork, cut into
　　2-by-½-inch strips
1 tablespoon curry powder
⅛ teaspoon ground cloves
⅛ teaspoon ground cinnamon
⅛ teaspoon ground cardamom
Juice of ½ lime
Salt and freshly ground black pepper
⅛ teaspoon crushed dried hot red peppers
½ cup light cream or half-and-half

1. Cook the potato in boiling salted water for 5 minutes. Drain.

2. Melt 1 tablespoon of the butter in 2 tablespoons of the oil in a large heavy skillet over medium heat. Stir in the potato; cook 3 minutes. Add the remaining 1 tablespoon butter and oil. Stir in the onion; cook 1 minute. Stir in the garlic; cook 1 minute longer.

3. Add the beef and pork to the skillet. Sprinkle with the curry, cloves, cinnamon, and cardamom. Mix well. Stir in the lime juice. Cook, covered, over medium-low heat until the potatoes are tender, about 30 minutes.

4. When the potato is tender, add salt and pepper to taste, sprinkle with the crushed peppers, and stir in the light cream. Cook until warmed through.

Serves 4.

SWEET POTATO BEIGNETS

*I*f you are not worried about calorie content, walk, do not run, to your kitchen and try out the silkiest rendering you will ever set your tongue to: an elegant, lightly crusted beignet (half cruller, half fritter). It is the most wholly seductive breakfast food (or even dessert in a pinch) that I know.

2 medium sweet potatoes (about ⅔ pound)
1 egg yolk, lightly beaten
¼ cup packed dark brown sugar
½ cup all-purpose flour
⅛ teaspoon ground allspice
⅛ teaspoon ground cinnamon
⅛ teaspoon ground cloves
¼ teaspoon freshly grated nutmeg
2 egg whites
Oil for frying
1 cup finely ground pecans
½ cup granulated sugar

1. Cook the potatoes in their jackets in boiling water until very tender, about 45 minutes. Drain. Cool, peel, and mash until smooth.

2. Place the mashed potatoes in a large bowl. Beat in the egg yolk, brown sugar, flour, allspice, cinnamon, cloves, and nutmeg.

3. Beat the egg whites until stiff but not dry. Fold them into the potato mixture.

4. Heat 1½ inches of oil in a medium saucepan until hot but not smoking.

5. Place the ground pecans in a shallow bowl. Drop a teaspoonful of potato batter into the pecans. Roll it gently with your fingertips to coat. Cook the potato balls in the hot oil, a few at a time, until golden brown, about 2 minutes per side. Drain on paper towels and sprinkle lightly with granulated sugar. Keep warm in a low oven while frying the remaining beignets.

Makes about 18 beignets.

YAMMYCAKES

*I*n Virginia, where sweet potatoes first flourished among the colonists, they were usually whipped up as a dessert in pie, pudding, or "panniquakes." Witness an old, old pancake recipe—not authentically prerevolutionary, to be sure, but of certain long lineage. And Southern to boot!

1¾ to 2 pounds yams (4 or 5 large)
1 cup all-purpose flour
1 teaspoon baking powder
¼ teaspoon salt
½ teaspoon ground cinnamon
¼ teaspoon ground ginger
⅛ teaspoon ground allspice

Pinch of ground cloves
2 eggs, lightly beaten
½ cup heavy or whipping cream
⅓ cup orange juice
¼ cup vodka
Confectioners' sugar

1. Cook the potatoes in their jackets in boiling salted water until tender, about 45 minutes. Drain.

2. Carefully peel the potatoes and either mash or purée them in a food processor. Transfer 2 cups of the potato purée to a large mixing bowl. Add the remaining ingredients except the confectioner's sugar. Mix well.

3. Heat a large griddle or nonstick skillet over medium heat. Grease it lightly, and spoon about ¼ cup of the batter onto the hot surface. Turn the pancake over when small bubbles appear on the surface. Cook 1 minute on the second side. Keep warm on a rack in a low oven while making the rest of the pancakes. Dust with confectioners' sugar before serving.

Serves 6 to 8.

YAM ICE CREAM

*T*he great black botanist George Washington Carver is reputed to have devised five hundred uses for this wondrous tuber. I am adding the five hundred and first. It's an ice cream, whipped up in any conventional ice cream freezer, but totally unlike any you have ever sampled. Carver would be proud of me. So would the owners of the Blue Milton!

3 medium yams (about 1 pound)
1 cup sugar
2 tablespoons dark rum
1 teaspoon vanilla extract
1 egg yolk
1 cup milk
3 cups heavy or whipping cream

1. Cook the yams in their jackets in boiling water until very tender, 35 to 40 minutes. Drain. Cool, peel, and quarter.

2. Place the yams in the container of a food processor or blender. Add the sugar, rum, vanilla, egg yolk, and milk. Process until smooth.

3. Transfer the yam mixture to a large bowl. Whisk in the cream. Pour the mixture into the canister of an ice cream maker and proceed according to the manufacturer's directions. It's best when solidly frozen.

Makes about 1½ quarts.

TOMATOES
A Summer Garden Classic

When I was not quite seven years old and far too unformed for the regimen, my ill-advised parents sent me off to summer camp. Why not? My sister had been an ebullient camper for two summers and when I tagged along on a "Parents' Day" in midsummer, I had been so overwhelmed by all the wonders of athletic outdoor life that I spontaneously evinced a desire to participate in these bucolic revels myself.

It was one of my most misguided judgments. The camp my father and mother selected for my induction was called Pawnee. It was known as a brother-sister institution, though why I will never understand, since male and female campers had little or no contact except at meals and some other segregated activities. A large chilly lake kept the sexual barriers firmly enforced.

My cabin, on the brother side of the water, was ruled by a tall, handsome, and unfeeling counselor whom I and my five bunkmates were bidden to address as "Uncle Sid." Always needing a shave, this young man seemed alternately so preoccupied or punitive that I rarely spoke to him at all, except at dinner, or "mess" as it was aptly known.

It was Uncle Sid's theory (and he was probably twenty at the time) that children compliantly eat whatever is set before them—sans cavil. Finicky at best, I always ate less than the prescribed portion and supplemented my diet with Hershey bars (sent by my grandmother and stashed away in a footlocker). Uncle Sid discovered this cache after one of my particularly bad showings at lunch and confiscated the chocolate permanently—which provoked my first insurrection. I wrote about this to my grandmother and was punished for recalcitrance when the letter was censored by, who else, Uncle Sid.

My next infraction occurred soon after, when tomatoes ripened and I refused to admit a scant forkful between my lips. "No! Never," I shouted, causing several tables of young campers to turn in my direction.

"If you do not eat what is on your plate," Uncle Sid stated in a firm voice, "you will go to your bunk immediately and stay there off-limits without supper or camp privileges!"

Missing supper was no blow. But camp privileges encompassed the week's movie, the only respite from seven days of torturous immoderation in the hot sun and cold water. I wailed my disappointment. In fact I screamed so loudly that my sister heard the hullabaloo clear across the segregated dining room.

Myra rushed to my defense with a filial affection I had never witnessed before. "What have you done to my brother?" she upbraided my counselor.

Uncle Sid was plainly disconcerted by her tone. "He refused to eat his tomatoes," he replied. "That's against regula-

tions, so he is being restricted to his bunk. Let him go!"

"I won't," cried my sister passionately—much influenced, I suspect, by the enforced parting of Evangeline and Basil in the movies. Two other counselors had to drag her away.

"Have you never heard of the bill of rights?" she snarled at my tormentors. "It is his inalienable right to refuse a tomato. As an American!"

She was right. But neither the flag-waving nor any other argument cut ice with Uncle Sid. I was remanded to my cabin and missed the movie. But in passing I developed a healthy admiration for my sister's sense of outrage. My love of tomatoes came in time as well.

Vegetable Roots

Despite any misgivings I may have harbored about the tomato, it is now the most eagerly awaited vegetable that grows in my garden. Other food lovers must agree, as it is the third-most-popular fresh vegetable (after potatoes and peas) in the United States. However, tomatoes were not always appreciated.

A native American plant, the first tomato was considered a weed. It was discovered sprouting wild in among the maize and bean fields of the early Incas. They (and the Mayas and Aztecs too) successfully cultivated its seeds. The Aztecs gave the tomato its name (tomatl) and considered its sun-swollen fruit to be a symbol of good fortune from the gods. Despite the augury, the tomato's history is a good deal more crimson than one would suspect. For centuries after they had been brought by caravel to Spain, tomatoes were admired—at a distance. Thought to be a highly potent aphrodisiac, they bloomed but went unconsumed, except by hard-core sybarites. For lesser men feared that even a forkful would cause moral decay or downright doom!

The notion that eating a tomato was synonymous with living dangerously stemmed in part from its family connections: *Lycopersicon esculentum* is a cousin twice removed of deadly nightshade. In the sixteenth century, Pierandrea Mattioli, the Italian herbalist, included tomato in the narcotic bouquet of lethal *Solanumae*. In his *Commentaries on the Six Books of Discorides*, Mattioli dubbed the tomato *mala insana* (or "bad egg"), since all those grown in his time were of a decidedly sulphurous hue. Worse yet, he lumped it together with belladonna, henbane, mandrake root, and arsenic—

none of which even an intrepid kitchen practitioner would choose to season a pot of spaghetti sauce.

Throughout its checkered past, the tomato has been the target of much curious legend—and lore galore. Up until the twentieth century the rubicund orb was known as a "love apple." Theories vary, but the one I subscribe to blames this on the Spanish. It seems that when the first conquistador clapped eyes on a tomato, he called it *manzana*, or apple, because that's what he thought it was. As apples do not flourish in Spain, it was a natural enough mistake I sup-

A good crop of scarlet tomatoes is any gardener's joy, even those whose vegetable patch happens to be a window box. Since I love growing tomatoes almost as much as I enjoy eating them, I will offer some twice-told wisdom for their Where and Care.

Early in March, well before planting time, sensible seedsmen will turn the soil and add a spot of humus (and quicklime if needed). I like to poke a little jot of well-seasoned manure and compost into the soil as well. But don't overdo the fertilizers; a quart to every ten square yards of garden is more than enough.

Tomato seedlings raised indoors in peat pots are the surest way to have plants that will bear fruit in season. Never put them out (plant them, that is) until all fear of frost may be dismissed. Water them well before and after they are planted to make the transition less traumatic. When you plant tomato seedlings (or seeds for that matter), make sure to mound the earth high around each plant. A well-made tomato garden should look like molehills (not mountains) with staked tomato plants in the centers.

Not all tomatoes require stakes, but I never take chances with lank vines. I tie the stems to poles with the flexible strips you find in packages of plastic bags, but string or twine will do equally well. A good tomato gardener is a fearless soul who will pinch back the top of his plant as soon as it sprouts an inch or two above the initial greenery. Don't be timid about cutting new growth—it will allow the plant's energies to be concentrated on a healthy yield rather than conspicuous foliage. Remember, it's a tomato you're growing, not a palm—so be bold.

Tomatoes require lots of watering, on a window ledge or in the garden, so be generous with the H_2O. Proceed with pesticides and fumigants at your own sensibility. I choose not to spray home-grown tomatoes at all, preferring the occasional cutworm or patch of rust to any further chemical warfare in my life.

Having said all this, pick your tomatoes from early July to late September with the knowledge that the best things in life are still relatively freely given—and righteously enjoyed.

pose, but *manzana* did not tempt the Hispanic palate. After several poor showings in a pastry shell it was banished to the Spanish garden, rather than the kitchen, where it was cultivated for purely decorative purposes till the middle of the sixteenth century. A traveling Italian chef reputedly reclaimed the tomato's reputation. He brought the plant to Florence, and flavored a sauce of *pomo d'oro* ("apple of gold") there shortly afterward for the Borgias. If it seems a far-fetched translation of *manzana*, keep in mind, all early tomatoes were yellow. According to tittle-tattle, when the Borgias' chef started serving tomatoes (fearing a negative reaction as they had developed a rather wayward culinary reputation by this time), the name was altered to *pomo dei Mori*, or "Moor's apple," to emphasize the fruit's Spanish connection. Needless to say, the tomato's flavor caught on.

When a French dignitary visited Italy and sampled tomato sauce for the first time, he misunderstood the name of the chief ingredient and assumed *pomo d'Moro* was *pomme d'amour*, or "apple of love." The story is probably apocryphal, for the notion that tomatoes were sexually stimulating antedates the Renaissance.

The tomato's revenge on Mattioli's countrymen was sweet. It turned rosy for one thing and became inseparably linked with Italian cooking for another. Since the early 1800s, when the vegetable's status as a deadly poison was officially rescinded, more tomatoes have been consumed in southern Italy (in confederation with pasta and cheese) than anywhere else on the face of the globe! And no slackening of the national appetite is in sight.

What to Look For

*T*omatoes come in many shapes and sizes. Big, burly beefsteaks are usually stolidly scarlet and smell faintly minty when picked. They are unexcelled first choices for my salad bowl, broiler tray, or BLT. Smaller, deeper-shaded globes (with more conventional tomato physiognomies) grow quickly, have a higher ratio of juice to flesh, and will cross over from tuna surprise to tomato juice (and/or gazpacho for that matter) with equal felicity. Plums, the elongated egg-shaped tomatoes whose annual appearance pinpoints midsummer for me, may seem less than toothsome raw (they are pulpy) but cook up into remarkably dense sauces and velvety chowders. The tiny cherry tomato, besides making a splendid addition to an hors d'oeuvre tray, will also outperform less flavorsome varieties in a tangy salsa or stewpot. Yellow tomatoes (with a higher pH factor that indicates less acid) may seem pale in partnership with spaghetti but are the basis for a tomato jam included in this chapter that is the best you will ever sample.

When shopping for a seasonal tomato, choose the ones that have the deepest color. Look for a firm (but not baseball-hard) texture and a bright complexion. Optimally a ripe tomato is neither squashy nor blemished. But frankly, I will settle for one streaked with green on the stem or with a blemish on the stern rather than a plastic specimen with perfectly inedible flesh below the surface. Tomatophiles tell us to select fruit that is heavy to the hand, but the only real test in my book is to slice into one. Good tomato color is really red—a shade between a fire engine and a field of poppies.

When a fresh tomato is at its ripest and reddest (in August and September on my vine), its classic rendering requires little or no preparation aside from pepper and salt and a sprinkling of fragrant basil leaves. However, heavy-duty doctoring or canned substitutions may be required for tomato cookery during the rest of the year, classic or otherwise!

Speaking for myself, I hate to buy out-of-season produce. But I do often in the case of tomatoes, choosing Mexican, Israeli, Belgian, or Chilean fresh imports (even at exorbitant prices) over the tasteless and rock-hard orbs that are the only consumer alternative. Most U.S. tomato strains in common currency at supermarkets are picked green and forced to redden (if never properly ripen) in ethylene gas chambers. More pertinently, these commercial varieties have also been bred to such a state of flat-ended, straight-sided, thick-skinned conformity that every wan globe survives the rigors of a long-distance shipping trek without a solitary bruise. And, sad to say, without a scintilla of natural flavor intact.

If I am unwilling to expend the cash required for unseasonal imports, I usually elect cherry tomatoes instead. If you keep these miniatures covered in a paper (not plastic) bag for several days, the natural ethylene gas inherent in all acidic vegetables will intensify the flavor and they will approximate the taste of more seasonal varieties.

I grow my own tomatoes every summer for the same reason I diet then: it makes me feel righteous! Another benefit is therapeutic, since there are only a scant 35 calories to a medium-size tomato. A tomato (even if you pronounce it *tomah-toe*) provides a healthy supply of potassium (300 milligrams) to the diet and a whopping jolt of vitamin A (1,110 units). In the matter of vitamin C, the tomato takes a back seat to the orange, I am afraid. It requires 8 ounces of tomato juice to equal the amount of C in 4 ounces of orange juice. Even more dispiriting for green tomato lovers, the amount of vitamins is slashed virtually in half when the tomato is firmly unripe.

Preparation

In the matter of preparing a fresh tomato for cooking, there is a maxim of Mrs. Beeton's that I heartily endorse: "Peel with discretion. Seed by rote!" If you suspect that is a vestigial culinary nicety left over from the Victorians, you are mistaken. Tomato skins fissure and split during periods of extended cookery and the resulting fragments are not only unattractive to the eye, but unpleasant to the tongue as well. There are a few exceptions to the rule. If a cooked tomato is to be puréed and sieved later, the skin may be left on for the jot of flavor it will impart. Likewise in baking, when the skin acts as a shell to hold the tomato together, there is no need to peel it. But at all other times, strip it bare! I peel a tomato by immersing it, impaled on a fork, into a saucepan of boiling water for half a minute. Then, after it has cooled slightly, I run a sharp knife under the skin and peel the sections with my fingers. Seeding is something else. In my opinion, a tomato's seeds turn astringent if not downright bitter the moment they are heated, so I always expunge them prior to the stove. My technique came from my grandmother. She halved a tomato in two at the midriff and squeezed out the seeds—just as she would juice an orange—with a small strainer placed over a bowl to catch any residual pink juices, which she added to the dish she was cooking.

American Indians claim that a cut ripe tomato is an unbeatable room deodorant. Moreover, they assert that the acid in a tomato, when well rubbed onto the skin, will remove the scent of garlic, wild onion, skunk, and any other noxious bouquet you can name.

MARY CASSETTI'S DOUBLE-ZAPPED TOMATO SHELLS

*T*his recipe is more handiwork from that talented cook from Elmira, New York: Mary Cassetti. Mrs. Cassetti's dish is highly unusual, employing both ripe fresh tomatoes and sun-dried tomatoes in the pasta's embroidery. Sources for Italian sun-dried tomatoes are listed in Notes on Ingredients, page 417. However, spirited do-it-yourselfers with a spare bushel or two of tomatoes at hand might wish to peruse the instructions for making their own (see box).

½ pound pasta shells
2 tablespoons unsalted butter
3 sun-dried tomatoes, cut into thin slivers
1 large fresh tomato, peeled, seeded, diced
3 tablespoons plain yogurt
2 tablespoons freshly grated Parmesan cheese
Salt and freshly ground black pepper

1. Cook the shells in boiling salted water until tender, 3 minutes for fresh, longer for packaged. Drain.

2. Melt the butter in a medium saucepan over low heat. Stir in the pasta, dried tomatoes, fresh tomato, yogurt, and Parmesan cheese. Add salt and pepper to taste. Serve immediately.

Serves 4 as a first course.

---

*T*here are two ways to dry a tomato. The first (baked) method requires any conventional home oven with a thermometer setting of 150°F and a nylon screen drying tray. That's all. A drying tray may be improvised of nylon window screening stretched and stapled over a picture frame. Never use metal screening, however. The combined acids in the tomatoes and the metal's surface could cause the dried tomatoes to become toxic.

Tomatoes to be dried should be sliced thin (vertically), laid on the tray, and placed in the 150°F oven initially for 3 hours. Then the heat should be lowered to 130°F until the tomatoes are dry (approximately 2 to 3 hours longer). Dried tomatoes will be tough-to-crisp in texture. Note that super-acidic tomatoes should be steam-blanched whole for approximately 3 minutes prior to slicing.

The second (old-fashioned) method is to dry tomatoes in the sun. This cannot be done except on a very hot day. Slice (and/or steam-blanch) the tomatoes as directed above. Place the thin slices on a large unpainted board (plywood will do nicely). Care should be taken to slant the board slightly so any surplus tomato juices will run off. Salt the tomatoes well. Prop the board against the side of a wall (or a back porch step) so the surface will reflect heat onto the tomatoes. Place a layer of cheesecloth or mosquito netting over the drying tomatoes to keep insects off. When the tomatoes shrivel completely and are firm to the touch, they are sun-dried. Brush off excess salt before storage.

Store both oven-dried and sun-dried tomatoes in sterile dry jars and seal for keeping. Dried tomatoes may also be kept in olive oil, as the Italians do.

TOMATO FISH BISQUE

*T*he compound of rosy-ripe orbs and snowy fish filets makes the following soup a tomato's manifest destiny. It is for all seasons, but is best in late summer.

2 tablespoons unsalted butter
1 small onion, finely chopped
1 small clove garlic, minced
Pinch of ground allspice
¼ teaspoon ground mace
Pinch of ground cloves
2 tablespoons all-purpose flour
3 cups Fish Stock (see page 410)
3 medium tomatoes, quartered (about
    ¾ pound)
1 can (14 ounces) plum tomatoes, drained
1¼ teaspoons salt
1 teaspoon sugar
1 tablespoon chopped fresh basil, or 1
    teaspoon dried
¼ cup long-grain rice
1 pound flounder or sole filets, cut into
    1-inch pieces
½ cup heavy or whipping cream
Salt and freshly ground black pepper
1 tablespoon cognac
Chopped fresh parsley

1. Melt the butter in a medium saucepan over medium-low heat. Stir in the onion; cook 1 minute. Stir in the garlic; cook 4 minutes. Add the allspice, mace, and cloves. Whisk in the flour. Cook, stirring constantly, 2 minutes. Whisk in the fish stock. Heat to boiling; reduce the heat. Simmer, uncovered, 5 minutes.

2. Place the quartered and plum tomatoes in the container of a food processor or blender and process until smooth. Strain the mixture into the soup. Add the salt, sugar, and basil. Return to boiling; reduce the heat. Simmer, uncovered, 30 minutes. Stir in the rice; continue to simmer, uncovered, until the rice is tender, about 12 minutes.

3. Add the fish to the bisque and poach (do not boil) for 5 minutes. Stir in the cream; heat to warm through. Add salt and pepper to taste. Stir in the cognac and sprinkle with parsley.

Serves 6.

CUBAN TOMATOES

*T*his first course came to me from a Cuban friend and is comprised of nothing but ripe tomatoes freely strewn with freshly grated coconut. It is sauced with a vinaigrette concocted with coconut rum liqueur—or you can substitute light rum mixed with fresh coconut milk (or grated coconut), blended and strained.

4 sliced tomatoes
¼ cup shredded fresh coconut
1 teaspoon chopped chives
1 tablespoon coconut rum liqueur or white
    rum (see above)

1 tablespoon Dijon mustard
½ cup olive oil
Juice of 1 lime
Salt and freshly ground black pepper

1. Arrange the sliced tomatoes on a serving platter. Sprinkle with the fresh coconut and chives.

2. Whisk the coconut rum liqueur with the mustard in a medium bowl. Slowly whisk in the oil until thick.

Whisk in the lime juice, and salt and pepper to taste. Spoon this over the tomatoes and let stand at least 30 minutes before serving.

Serves 4 to 6.

FRIED GREEN TOMATOES

One of my favorite late September–early October tomato bonuses for the cook is Fried Green Tomatoes. They are a simply unforgettable vegetable, made in Greene's kitchen whenever the hint of frost turns the gardener panicky and he picks whatever is still on the vine—fast!

3 medium-size firm green tomatoes
1 egg
2 teaspoons heavy or whipping cream
¼ cup V-8 juice or Bloody Mary mix
Dash of hot pepper sauce
½ cup fresh bread crumbs
⅛ teaspoon ground allspice
4 tablespoons (½ stick) unsalted butter, approximately
1 teaspoon chopped fresh chives

1. Cut the tomatoes crosswise into ½-inch-thick slices.

2. Beat the egg with the cream, V-8, and hot pepper sauce in a shallow bowl.

Combine the crumbs and allspice in another shallow bowl.

3. Melt 2 tablespoons of the butter in a heavy skillet over medium heat. Dip the tomato slices in the egg mixture, shaking off any excess. Then lightly coat with the bread crumbs. Fry, a few slices at a time, until golden on both sides, about 4 minutes. Keep warm in a low oven. Continue to fry tomato slices, adding more butter as needed. Sprinkle with the chives before serving.

Serves 4.

RISOTTO TOMATO

After the Borgias endorsed the tomato (in cooked form) and their dinner guests lived to tell the tale, other Italian noblemen followed suit. Indeed, by the mid-sixteenth century when Catherine de Medici came to France to marry Henry II, this vegetable had achieved such rarified culinary status that Catherine's detractors claimed that her only assets as Queen were Italian charm, cheese, and tomatoes!

I can't vouch for the first but the other two ingredients were nothing to sneeze at—then or now! Tomatoes and cheese are connected to many of the best Italian dishes in my lexicon. For a spectacular example, I call your attention to the following.

3½ tablespoons unsalted butter
2 large shallots, minced
½ teaspoon salt
¼ teaspoon freshly ground black pepper
¼ cup dry white wine
1 cup Italian rice (I prefer Arborio brand)
3 cups Chicken Stock, simmering
   (see page 410)
2 medium tomatoes (about ⅔ pound),
   peeled, seeded, chopped
⅓ cup freshly grated Parmesan cheese
   (optional)

1. Melt 2½ tablespoons of the butter in a large heavy skillet over medium heat. Stir in the shallots; cook 1 minute. Sprinkle with the salt and pepper; stir in the wine. Cook until almost all liquid has evaporated. Add the rice, and stir until well coated with the shallot mix-ture. Reduce the heat to medium-low.

2. Stir 1 cup of the stock into the rice mixture. Gently simmer until the rice has absorbed the stock, about 15 minutes. Stir in the tomatoes and an-other 1 cup of the stock. Gently simmer until the rice has absorbed the stock, another 15 minutes. Stir in the remain-ing 1 cup stock and continue to simmer until the rice is just tender (not mushy), about 12 minutes longer. Raise the heat if the rice is too wet—it should be creamy but not wet. Stir in the remaining 1 tablespoon butter. Stir in the Parmesan cheese if you are serving the risotto with a bland main course. Omit the cheese with strong-flavored entrées.

Serves 4.

BAKED HERBED TOMATOES

The classic tomato renderings in my kitchen (there are two) both come as souvenirs from a longish stay in Eze, France, over a dozen years ago. Tomatoes in the Mediterranean region are the reddest and most glorious in all the world—with the possible exception of Mexico. This version is crumbed and herbed and ever so slightly scented with garlic and anchovy, Provence's prime flavors.

4 medium tomatoes (about 1 pound)
Salt
1 large shallot, minced
1 large clove garlic, minced
½ teaspoon anchovy paste
2 tablespoons unsalted butter, melted
2 tablespoons finely chopped fresh parsley
2 tablespoons finely chopped fresh basil
1 teaspoon chopped fresh thyme, or ¼
   teaspoon dried
1 cup fresh bread crumbs
Freshly ground black pepper

1. Cut the tomatoes in half cross-wise. Gently squeeze out the seeds. Sprinkle each half with salt and turn upside down on paper towels. Let stand 30 minutes.

2. Preheat the oven to 400°F. Mash the shallot with the garlic and anchovy paste in a medium bowl. Stir in the butter, the herbs, and the bread crumbs. Mix well.

3. Spoon the crumb mixture onto each tomato half, packing the mixture down with the back of the spoon. Sprin-kle with pepper to taste. Bake 10 min-utes, then place under a broiler until lightly browned. Serve hot, or cold sprinkled with vinegar and oil.

Serves 4.

MUSHROOM-STUFFED TOMATOES

The other Eze specialty is simply crammed with fresh moist mushrooms—best when the fungus has a wild flavor. I use shiitakes, but any will do in a pinch.

2 medium tomatoes (about ½ pound)
Salt
2 large fresh shiitake mushrooms, chopped (about 1 cup)
1½ teaspoons lemon juice
1 tablespoon unsalted butter
1 shallot, minced
1 tablespoon chopped fresh basil
1 teaspoon chopped fresh parsley
½ teaspoon sugar
4 teaspoons heavy or whipping cream
1 egg yolk
Salt and freshly ground black pepper
2 tablespoons freshly grated Parmesan cheese

1. Cut the tomatoes in half crosswise. Gently squeeze out the seeds. Scoop out the pulp with a spoon; chop it and reserve. Sprinkle each half with salt and turn them upside down on paper towels. Let stand 30 minutes.

2. Preheat the oven to 400°F. Sprinkle the mushrooms with the lemon juice. Melt the butter in a medium skillet over medium heat. Stir in the mushrooms; sauté 1 minute. Add the shallot; sauté until golden, about 5 minutes longer. Stir in the tomato pulp, herbs, and sugar. Continue to cook until the mixture thickens, about 10 minutes. Reduce the heat to low.

3. Lightly beat the cream with the egg yolk. Stir this into the mushroom mixture. Cook until warmed through; do not boil. Add salt and pepper to taste.

4. Place the tomato halves in a shallow baking dish. Fill each with some of the mushroom mixture and sprinkle with the Parmesan cheese. Bake until lightly browned, about 20 minutes.

Serves 4.

JILL GARDNER'S TOMATO SHORTCAKES

This very American tomato rendering was passed on to me by an extremely gifted food writer, who is also a whiz at the oven.

2 cups all-purpose flour
1 teaspoon salt
2½ teaspoons baking powder
6 tablespoons (¾ stick) cold unsalted butter, cut into pieces
1½ cups heavy or whipping cream
3 tablespoons red wine vinegar (I prefer Italian balsamic for this)

½ teaspoon sugar (optional, depending on sweetness of tomatoes)
2 teaspoons finely chopped chives
2 teaspoons finely chopped fresh basil
Salt and freshly ground black pepper
4 large ripe tomatoes (1½ to 2 pounds), peeled, seeded, roughly chopped

1. Preheat the oven to 400°F. Sift the flour with the salt and baking powder into a large bowl. Cut in the butter with a knife. Blend the mixture with a pastry blender until it is the texture of coarse crumbs. Stir in ¾ cup of the cream to make a soft dough.

2. Transfer the dough to a floured board; knead briefly. Pat the dough into a circle about ¾ inch thick. Cut out 6 rounds with a 3-inch biscuit cutter. Place the rounds on a lightly buttered baking sheet and bake until golden brown, about 20 minutes. Split each in half while still hot. Reserve.

3. Beat the remaining ¾ cup cream until soft peaks form. Beat in the vinegar, and the sugar if you are using it. Beat until stiff. Fold in the herbs; add salt and pepper to taste.

4. To serve: Spread the chopped tomatoes evenly over the bottom halves of the biscuits. Top each with some of the whipped cream dressing and cover with a biscuit top. Serve immediately.

Serves 6.

There is a less traditional method for growing a tomato—if one may still call a globe weighing two pounds a tomato.

According to an old farmers' wives' tale, one digs a deep, narrow hole for each seedling to be planted. Twenty inches is the required depth. At the bottom, the gardener places a layer of cracked corn cobs. Over that, 3 inches of manure. (In the formula I have in hand, chicken or cow manure is requested.) Never commercial fertilizers. Over the second layer place 4 inches of soil. Then set the tomato plant in the hole, leaving only the main branches atop, and mounding the soil around them. Supposedly the cobs hold moisture and cause the manure to heat up, warming the soil and creating a condition the reverse of hothouse agriculture. As the roots press downward, growth is increased thricefold. Or so the tale goes. Someday I will try it out and grow cherry tomatoes the size of oranges.

BASIC TOMATO SAUCE

I have two remarkable tomato sauces in my repertoire and both are used in dishes throughout the book. This one is dense and highly aromatic—perfect for pasta.

4 tablespoons (½ stick) unsalted butter
1 medium onion, finely chopped
1 clove garlic, minced
1 rib celery, finely chopped
4 large ripe tomatoes, peeled, seeded, chopped
1 teaspoon chopped fresh basil, or ½ teaspoon dried

1 teaspoon chopped fresh oregano, or ¼ teaspoon dried
Pinch of thyme
2 teaspoons sugar
¼ teaspoon grated orange peel
Salt and freshly ground black pepper

Melt the butter in a medium saucepan over medium-low heat. Add the onion; cook 1 minute. Add the garlic and celery; cook 4 minutes. Stir in the tomatoes, basil, oregano, thyme, sugar, and orange peel. Cook, uncovered, stirring occasionally, until thick, about 45 minutes. Add salt and pepper to taste.

Makes about 1½ cups.

CREAMY TOMATO SAUCE

Splashed with cream and less insistent in flavor than my Basic Tomato Sauce, this tomato cream makes a marvelous upholstery for all manner of subtle or simple dishes.

2 tablespoons unsalted butter
1 small onion, chopped
1 small clove garlic, chopped
½ rib celery, chopped
2 large tomatoes, peeled, seeded, chopped
1 teaspoon chopped fresh basil, or ½ teaspoon dried
½ teaspoon chopped fresh oregano, or a pinch of dried
Pinch of thyme
Pinch of ground cloves
½ teaspoon sugar
⅓ cup heavy or whipping cream
Salt and freshly ground black pepper

1. Melt the butter in a medium saucepan over medium-low heat. Add the onion; cook 1 minute. Add the garlic and celery; cook 4 minutes. Stir in the tomatoes, basil, oregano, thyme, cloves, and sugar. Cook, uncovered, stirring occasionally, until soft, about 20 minutes.

2. Transfer the mixture to the container of a blender or food processor. Blend until smooth, being careful as hot foods will expand. Return it to the saucepan and stir in the cream. Cook over low heat, without boiling, until warmed through. Add salt and pepper to taste.

Makes about 1 cup.

TOMATO SOUFFLE

Germans once called the tomato *Paradies Apfel* ("apple of paradise"). They had got their wires crossed and believed the Turks brought it from the Holy Land, the original location of Biblical paradise.

My own view is somewhat narrower. I think the tomato is a heavenly foodstuff because it gilds all other ingredients with which it is paired. Consider this tomato-suffused cheese soufflé for instance. It comes with a cavil, however: if fresh tomatoes are not rosy and ripe, use canned. My preference? The intensely flavored San Marsano brand imported from Italy.

6 tablespoons (¾ stick) plus 1 teaspoon
   unsalted butter
2 tablespoons freshly grated Parmesan
   cheese
5 tablespoons grated Fontina cheese
1 onion, chopped
1 clove garlic, chopped
2 large tomatoes (about 1 pound), peeled,
   seeded, chopped
1 teaspoon chopped fresh basil, or ¼
   teaspoon dried
1 teaspoon chopped fresh parsley
Pinch of sugar
Pinch of ground allspice
¼ teaspoon tomato paste
3 tablespoons all-purpose flour
1 cup milk, boiling
4 egg yolks
Salt and freshly ground black pepper
5 egg whites

1. Rub a 1½-quart soufflé dish with
the 1 teaspoon butter. Sprinkle with 1
tablespoon of the Parmesan cheese and 1
tablespoon of the Fontina cheese. Set
aside.

2. Melt 4 tablespoons of the butter
in a medium saucepan over medium-low
heat. Add the onion; cook 1 minute.
Add the garlic, tomatoes, basil, parsley,
sugar, and allspice. Cook, uncovered,
stirring occasionally, until the tomatoes
are soft and fairly thick, about 20 minutes. Stir in the tomato paste; cook 5
minutes longer. Cool slightly. Transfer
the mixture to the container of a blender
or food processor. Blend until smooth,
being careful as hot food will expand.
Set aside.

3. Preheat the oven to 400°F. Melt
the remaining 2 tablespoons butter in
another medium saucepan over medium-
low heat. Whisk in the flour. Cook, stirring constantly, 2 minutes. Whisk in the
milk all at once. Whisk until smooth and
very thick, 2 to 3 minutes. Remove from
the heat and beat in the egg yolks, one at
a time, beating thoroughly after each
addition. Transfer the mixture to a large
bowl. Stir in the blended tomato mixture, the remaining 4 tablespoons Fontina cheese, and salt and pepper to taste.

4. Beat the egg whites until stiff but
not dry. Fold them into the tomato mixture. Spoon the mixture into the prepared soufflé dish and sprinkle with the
remaining 1 tablespoon Parmesan
cheese. Place the dish in the oven and
immediately reduce the heat to 375°F.
Bake until puffed and firm, 25 to 30
minutes.

Serves 4 to 6.

YELLOW TOMATO JAM

T homas Jefferson raised yellow tomatoes in his garden at Monticello in 1782 and
noted that the pale fruit made a preserve not unlike the flavor of a tart apricot.

I make yellow tomato jam whenever I find a batch harvested and waiting. But I
must confess I never grow them, for the low acidity makes them popular with *bees!*

1 pound yellow cherry tomatoes
¼ cup lemon juice
1 teaspoon finely slivered lemon peel
3 cups sugar
⅛ teaspoon ground cinnamon

1. Cut the tomatoes in half lengthwise and place in a medium-size heavy
saucepan. Add the lemon juice and slowly heat to boiling. Simmer 10 minutes.

2. Add the lemon peel, sugar, and

cinnamon to the tomatoes. Continue to simmer until the jam will set when a teaspoonful is placed on a cold plate, about 20 to 30 minutes. Pour into sterilized jars and seal. Place in a hot water bath for 20 minutes. Store in a cool place.

Makes 2 pints.

BUBBLING TOMATO CHICKEN

The dish that follows is a slightly revised version of a family tomato and chicken dish that was my sister Myra's favorite food when she was growing up. My mother named it "Bubbling Chicken" and made it with a can of Campbell's Cream of Mushroom Soup. I opt for homemade béchamel sauce and fresh mushrooms, but it still bubbles bounteously.

1 large chicken (about 4 pounds)
1 carrot, peeled, chopped
2 ribs celery, broken
1 unpeeled onion stuck with 2 cloves
1 large clove garlic
12 whole peppercorns
3 cups chicken broth (see page 414)
¼ cup dry white wine
1 teaspoon lemon juice
7 tablespoons unsalted butter
4 large mushrooms, sliced
¼ cup all-purpose flour
¾ cup heavy or whipping cream
1 can (28 ounces) Italian plum tomatoes, drained, chopped
¼ cup chopped fresh parsley
1 tablespoon chopped fresh basil
6 tablespoons fine fresh bread crumbs
2 tablespoons freshly grated Parmesan cheese

1. Combine all ingredients through the lemon juice in a large pot. Add water to cover. Heat to boiling; reduce the heat. Simmer, partially covered, until the chicken is tender, about 1 hour.

2. Remove the chicken from the stock and remove the meat from the bones in large pieces. Cover and reserve. Return the bones and skin to the pot. Simmer the stock, uncovered, until reduced to about 2 cups, about 30 minutes. Strain, and set aside.

3. Preheat the oven to 350°F. Melt 2 tablespoons of the butter in a medium skillet over medium heat. Quickly sauté the mushrooms until golden; set aside.

4. Melt 3 tablespoons of the butter in a medium saucepan over medium-low heat. Whisk in the flour. Cook, stirring constantly, 2 minutes. Whisk in the strained chicken stock and the cream. Heat to boiling; reduce the heat. Simmer until thickened, about 15 minutes. Stir in the reserved mushrooms.

5. Spread one third of the tomatoes over the bottom of a lightly greased casserole. Sprinkle with one third of the parsley and one third of the basil. Add one third of the cooked chicken pieces. Spoon one third of the sauce over the top. Repeat the layers two more times.

6. Melt the remaining 2 tablespoons butter in a small skillet over medium heat and sauté the bread crumbs until golden. Spoon the crumbs over the chicken mixture. Sprinkle with the cheese. Bake until golden and bubbly, about 20 minutes.

Serves 4 to 6.

PASTA A LA CAPRESE
(Pasta Shells with Marinated Tomatoes)

*I*f the derivation of the next recipe is vague, forgive it please. I simply cannot remember who pressed the typewritten 3-by-5 card in my hand, containing four words to describe this dish of hot pasta and cold sauce. "It's Italian. It's good!" said the donor. Whoever it was, was right!

6 plum tomatoes, chopped
2 cloves garlic, minced
½ yellow or red sweet pepper, seeded, diced
2 tablespoons roughly chopped fresh basil
½ cup olive oil
1 teaspoon salt
¼ teaspoon freshly ground black pepper
1 pound pasta shells (penne or rigatoni)
8 ounces mozzarella cheese, grated
Freshly grated Parmesan cheese

1. Combine the tomatoes, garlic, sweet pepper, basil, oil, salt, and black pepper in a bowl. Mix well; let stand at room temperature for 1½ hours.

2. Just before serving, cook the pasta in boiling salted water until just tender, about 3 minutes for fresh, longer for packaged. Drain, and place in a large serving bowl. Stir in the mozzarella cheese and the marinated vegetables. Toss and serve immediately with Parmesan cheese on the side.

Serves 4 to 6.

ITALIAN FLAG
(Green Fettuccine with Tomatoes, Chicken, and Prosciutto)

*T*he Italian flag is green, red, and white. So is the following dish, devised of spinach fettuccine, red tomatoes, and chunks of snowy chicken breasts. I came upon the recipe in Darien, Connecticut, however. The hostess, admitting its obvious ethnic antecedents, claimed to have found it in an old copy of *Gourmet*. No matter. It's a wonderfully satisfying dish to honor any flag at all.

1 whole chicken breast (about 1¼ pounds)
1½ cups chicken broth, approximately (see page 414)
¼ cup olive oil
1 small onion, halved, thinly sliced
½ cup sliced mushrooms (about 6 mushrooms)
9 tablespoons unsalted butter
¼ pound thinly sliced prosciutto, cut into strips

2 medium tomatoes (about ½ pound), peeled, seeded, chopped
½ cup heavy or whipping cream
⅛ teaspoon freshly grated nutmeg
Salt and freshly ground black pepper
½ pound green fettuccine noodles
Freshly grated Parmesan cheese

1. Place the chicken breast in a medium saucepan and add enough chicken broth to cover. Heat to boiling; reduce the heat. Simmer, covered, until tender, about 12 minutes. Remove the chicken breast and allow it to cool. Cut it into strips and set aside. Reserve broth for use at another time.

2. Heat the oil in a large saucepan over medium heat. Add the onion; sauté until golden. Add the mushrooms; cook, tossing gently, 2 minutes. Stir in 8 tablespoons of the butter, the prosciutto, and the tomatoes. Cook 6 minutes. Stir in the chicken and cream. Heat to boiling; reduce the heat to low. Add the nutmeg, and salt and pepper to taste. Keep warm over low heat.

3. Meanwhile, cook the fettuccine in boiling salted water until just tender, about 2 minutes for fresh, longer for packaged. Drain. Return the noodles to the saucepan and toss with the remaining 1 tablespoon butter.

4. Toss the fettuccine into the chicken-prosciutto mixture. Serve with Parmesan cheese on the side.

Serves 4.

TOMATO APPLE TARTIN

Strictly speaking, the tomato is a fruit (a berry if we are speaking even stricter), but we consume it as a vegetable and they are so classified. However, the tomato also has a curious power in a dessert dish. To prove my point, consider the love apple in confederation with one of the loveless variety (like a Granny Smith or a Greening). In my oven, this combo is the basis for one of the best French desserts ever invented: a tartin (an upside-down pie), baked first, then reversed and drizzled with caramel. This is possibly the best public image the rosy fruit will ever have.

Short Crust Pastry (see page 412)
10 tablespoons unsalted butter
2 large tomatoes (about 1 pound), peeled,
    seeded, chopped
¼ cup orange juice
2⅔ cups granulated sugar
½ teaspoon finely slivered lemon peel
½ teaspoon finely slivered orange peel
¼ cup packed dark brown sugar
½ cup fresh bread crumbs
4 large green tart apples
Juice of 1 lemon
Sweetened whipped cream

1. Make the Short Crust Pastry.

2. Melt 2 tablespoons of the butter in a medium saucepan over medium-low heat. Stir in the tomatoes, orange juice, 1½ cups of the granulated sugar, lemon peel, and orange peel. Heat to boiling; reduce the heat. Simmer, uncovered, un- til very thick, about 40 minutes. Remove from the heat.

3. Preheat the oven to 425°F. Melt the remaining 8 tablespoons butter and combine it with ⅔ cup of the granulated sugar and the brown sugar in a medium bowl. Stir in the bread crumbs. Mix thoroughly. Spread the mixture over the sides and bottom of a deep 10-inch pie plate. Refrigerate until ready to use.

4. Peel, core and cut the apples into ¼-inch slices. Place them in a large bowl and sprinkle with lemon juice as you cut them to keep them from turning brown. Pour the tomato mixture over the apples. Mix well. Spoon into the prepared pie plate.

5. Roll out the short crust pastry on a floured board. Place it over the apples and trim and seal the edges. Cut a hole

in the center of the crust to allow steam to escape. Bake 30 minutes. Raise the oven heat to 500°F and bake 10 minutes longer.

6. Loosen the tartin by running a knife around the edge of the crust. Very carefully, place a heatproof 10-inch shallow serving dish over the tartin; invert the tartin onto the dish. Carefully remove the pie plate. Cool on a rack.

7. Just before serving, heat the remaining ½ cup of granulated sugar in a saucepan over high heat until the sugar starts to melt; cook, stirring constantly with a wooden spoon, until the sugar liquifies. Reduce the heat; cook, stirring constantly, until the caramel turns deep golden. Drizzle over the top of the tartin. Serve with sweetened whipped cream.

Serves 8.

TOMATO DEVIL'S FOOD WITH TOMATO BUTTER CREAM FROSTING

*T*he tomato's name has not evolved much since the first Inca plucked and dubbed one a *tomatl*. Though Italians retain the Borgia inheritance of *pomodoro*, Frenchmen, Germans, and the Spanish still call it *tomate*. If you think a tomato is the same in any language, how mistaken you are! The most unusual tomato rendering in my collection is a dense and wonderfully sensuous cake of rich chocolate seasoned with fresh tomatoes—a love potion with its aphrodisiac powers compounded by a heavenly gilded butter cream, flavored with even more tomato.

Make this recipe only when tomatoes are in season. Winter varieties will not do.

For the cake:

2 large ripe tomatoes (about 1 pound)
4 ounces sweet chocolate
1 cup packed dark brown sugar
¼ cup milk
3 egg yolks
2 cups sifted cake flour
1 teaspoon baking soda
½ teaspoon salt
8 tablespoons (1 stick) unsalted butter, softened
1 cup granulated sugar
1 teaspoon vanilla extract
2 egg whites

For the frosting:

1 medium ripe tomato (about ¼ pound)
1½ cups (3 sticks) unsalted butter, softened
4 extra-large egg yolks
1 tablespoon cognac
¾ cup confectioners' sugar

1. Preheat the oven to 350°F.

2. To make the cake: Peel and seed the tomatoes. Place them in a blender container; blend until smooth. Measure off 1¼ cups tomato purée; reserve.

3. Place the chocolate, brown sugar, milk, and 1 of the egg yolks in the top of a double boiler. Cook, stirring occasionally, over hot water until smooth and slightly thickened. Set aside.

4. Sift the flour with the baking soda and salt.

5. Beat the butter in a large mixing bowl until light. Slowly beat in the granulated sugar. Add the remaining 2 egg yolks, one at a time, beating thoroughly after each addition. Add the tomato purée, the vanilla, and the chocolate mixture. Beat thoroughly. Slowly stir in the flour mixture.

6. Beat the egg whites until stiff but not dry. Fold them into the cake batter. Pour the batter into two buttered and floured 9-inch cake pans. Bake until a toothpick inserted in the center of the cake comes out fairly clean, 25 to 30 minutes. Do not overcook. Cool on a wire rack. Unmold.

7. To make the frosting: Cut the tomato in half and place it in the container of a blender. Blend until smooth. Strain through a sieve. Measure off 4½ tablespoons of the sieved purée; reserve.

8. Beat the butter in a large bowl until light. Add the egg yolks, one at a time, beating thoroughly after each addition. Add the strained tomato purée and the cognac. Slowly beat in the confectioners' sugar. Spread the icing over the bottom layer, sides, and top of the cake. Keep the cake in a cool place until serving, but do not refrigerate.

Serves 8 to 10.

TURNIPS AND RUTABAGAS

Hearty Roots for Warming Dishes

When I was young, kitchen odors—even felicitous ones—were considered *déclassé*.

The late 1930s and early '40s may have been hard times, but they were also hidebound by convention and provincialism. If you were respectable (a word my mother summoned up with righteousness all her life), no one was ever supposed to know what was really cooking in your pots!

Being a first-generation American dictated that one's mores be as puritan as possible, likewise one's cooking habits—so anonymous that a Greene could pass for a Smith, a Jones, or any other born-and-bred Yankee.

Even my grandmother, who dearly loved the lusty evidence of good aromas in her kitchen, concurred in the matter of odorous decorum. She would always leave a curl of orange peel near the pilot light of her stove so that the oils, released as it dried, masked any "foreign" smell emanating from her saucepan.

My mother, having neither the patience nor the domestic stripe to allow orange rind to turn into fine white ash on her shiny porcelain gas range, would light sticks of incense around the house instead. Or worse yet, rub a drop or two of perfumed oil on the electric light bulbs after she had cooked something that was particularly flavorful. So after dinner, the house would usually reek with the overpowering scent of musk rather than any homelier scents, like boiled turnips.

When I was in my late teens and began to take a serious interest in the opposite sex, my mother laid out what she considered to be the qualifications of respectability in a girl friend.

"Pick someone who comes from a good home," she intoned, "not a family of *shickers* [drunkards] or loose-livers. Remember, background means more than physical beauty, which fades."

Always attracted to exquisite creatures, I resented all of my mother's sage wisdom out of hand. "How in the world do you expect me to know any of that?" I remonstrated with some heat. "Most people do not advertise their pedigrees!"

"Aha!" said my mother. "You are wrong there. Just keep your eyes, ears, and nose open. Empty beer and whiskey bottles all over the place are not a good sign. But—" and here my mother shook her finger triumphantly "—books on the shelves *are!*"

"Really? Well, how about incense?" I asked sarcastically. "What kind of sign is that?"

"Sensitivity," replied my mother. "And a lot better than the smell of yesterday's dinner!"

I was not convinced.

To be honest, the first time I was invited to dine with the family of a girl I was deeply smitten with, I could not for the life of me get my mother's precepts out of my head or my nose. For the entire apartment (it was in a stately old building overlooking Central Park) was suffused with the most intoxicating perfume I think I have ever inhaled: rutabaga braising to a dull tarnished gold in a bath that would give any alchemist

joy—onions, red wine, and bits of bacon. Open liquor bottles crowded a small table that also served as a bar. I, who barely drank, counted Scotch, brandy, bourbon, and gin beside a bucket that held a magnum of champagne on ice.

All of this added up to a bad sign, according to my mother. But the floor-to-ceiling bookshelves were also crammed to capacity with volumes in three languages. So I breathed in the scent of those burnishing roots without compunction.

I wish I could report that some serious alliance was the result of that first memorable dinner. All that ensued was a deep friendship with the family and a great recipe or two for my collection. With the turnip (and its cousin, rutabaga) I have maintained a less transient love affair.

Vegetable Roots

*P*robably the oldest vegetable known, the turnip was there when early man stopped thrashing about in eluvial ooze long enough to think of his stomach—which was always empty. Turnips filled the void, and when dipped in salt water were not entirely unpleasant to his tongue.

Then and now, the white and yellow turnip (*Brassica rapa*) is a fleshy root that grows fast, requires little care, and is high in nutrients. By the time the first caveman took a wife and made a communal fire, he discovered that his family could not only subsist on this high-fiber food but they grew stronger with every bite. According to evidence uncovered in the caves at Choukoutien, near Peking, turnip was not merely eaten raw by its first consumers; it was roasted with meat (on flat stones in the fire) or wrapped up with fern ends or wild onions and steamed in flat wet leaves. One thing about the turnip is fairly self-evident: it was eaten because it was available. If a hunter did not always return home with a slab of sabre-toothed tiger under his arm for dinner, his mate knew where to "root around" in the bog for supplementary rations—and they survived!

Several millennia later (as the cave paintings near the village of Aurignac, France, show), these very same roots were still on the fire! But by then they were boiled in watertight pots of clay, which was quite a way up the prandial ladder. When the ancient Greeks and Romans finally inherited the turnip, its kitchen status was so elevated that devotees literally held forums to theorize on the ideal culinary fabrication. In Rome (according to the *Pantropheon*) the optimum cookery took several hours and the roots were steamed successively with cumin, rue, and benzoin; then pounded in a mortar with honey, vinegar, gravy, boiled grapes, and a little oil; and then simmered well before they were served. Frankly, I would rather eat a turnip neat!

Rutabaga is a turnip's younger sibling. Or to be more accurate, it is a turnip mutation. This curious yellow globe whose stem swells underground rather than above (as conventional turnips do) is technically *Brassica napobrassica*, even though it came to our tables through the crossbreeding of a cabbage with a turnip by Swiss botanist Gaspard Bauhin in the seventeenth century. The birth was neither heralded nor honored, but it should have been. For half the northern countries of the world live on rutabagas half of every year, and this vegetable, thriving in cool air, keeps the denizens of Scandinavian countries a heck of a lot healthier than they would be without its mineral-high presence in saucepans every winter. In fact, for centuries the rutabaga has been variously known in vegetable circles as Russian turnip, Canadian turnip, Bulgarian turnip, and Swedish turnip or swede. Only the last name stuck, however, because this root, with its penchant for cool, glacial soil, flourishes best and is eaten most in Sweden.

According to food pundits, who disagree violently about almost everything that appears in a saucepan, the rutabaga did not arrive in the United States until 1806. How it came here no one seems to know for sure, but despite its northerly association in the Old World, its first official appearance in the new one was in a seed catalogue that advertised it as "South of the Border Turnip"!

What to Look For

Whether shopping for turnips or for rutabagas, the market imperatives are the same. Fresh vegetables will be firm and quite smooth to the hand. A wrinkled turnip is a sure sign that the root has lost its moisture and that the texture beneath the skin will be spongy. I pass on large turnips as a matter of course, as the small ones (dappled with an edge of purple at the soil level) are by far the sweeter. If you have the option, select turnips with fresh green leaves, for that is a clear indication the vegetable is not long out of the garden. Rutabagas should always feel weighty. Search for a globe that is streaked with purple and fairly free of large bruises or hoe marks. The heavy waxy coating (on all but farm-stand produce) is sprayed on the rutabaga to prevent dehydration. Peel it off with a vegetable parer prior to a kitchen wash-up.

Turnips and rutabagas, though genetically connected, have one major culinary difference. Turnips are fragile; they will last only a week in a refrigerator. Rutabagas keep for a month or even longer. As a matter of fact, when I was a kid, farmers used to "hold" rutabagas in root cellars for almost a year, packed in sawdust or sand.

Turnips and rutabagas both are high in nutrients, low in calories, and yet tonic enough to please even the most jaded appetite.

An average ¾ cup portion of turnips, for instance, holds a scant 30 calories yet is exceedingly high in minerals (39 milligrams calcium, 30 milligrams phosphorus, and a bounteous 268 milligrams of potassium). Turnips are not high in vitamins, but rutabagas are. The same quantity of rutabagas contains 46 calories but is super-streaked with minerals (239 milligrams potassium, 66 milligrams calcium, and 39 milligrams phosphorus), with traces of all essential vitamins plus 43 units of vitamin C and a towering 580 units of vitamin A.

Preparation

Since both the turnip and rutabaga are tough roots, always use a sharp knife to slice them. Work on a wooden surface and insert the blade carefully at a point midway between the root and the stem, going directly into the heart of the root before you slice it in two. Peel the halves at that point. Then, with the cut sides down, slice first vertically, then horizontally, until the entire vegetable is cubed.

Both turnips and rutabagas profit by the standard cooking instructions for all root vegetables: braising, boiling, and steaming; and in that order of preference at my stove top.

To braise: Cut either vegetable into uniform shapes and place them in a covered skillet along with a modicum of butter and enough liquid (broth or vegetable juices) to generously cover the bottom. My average braising time for these root vegetables is 10 to 12 minutes for turnips, 15 to 20 minutes for rutabagas.

To boil: Fill a saucepan halfway with cold salted water. When the water is at a rolling boil, add the cut vegetables and cook them till fork-tender, about 15 minutes for a whole turnip and 20 to 25 minutes for a 2½-inch cube of rutabaga. Young vegetables may require less cooking time.

To steam: Bring approximately 1 inch of water to a boil in a steamer or saucepan. Place the turnips or rutabagas in a steamer basket or colander, bearing in mind that cooking times may only be approximated since the sizes of the vegetables vary. However, an average-size turnip will steam crisp-tender in about 10 to 12 minutes. A rutabaga (2½-inch-size cubes) will require twice that long, about 25 to 30 minutes.

In passing let me state that there are two schools of thought on all turnip and rutabaga cookery: those who cook them first and peel them later, and those like me who want the job over and done with and say: to heck with the vitamin dividend I just tossed down the drain!

TURNIP SAVARIN WITH GRUYERE SAUCE

With so much sheer health in every portion, I thought it might be pleasantly perverse to indulge in a splurge of sheer, unabashed dietary largess. It is a turnip savarin, white-gold in color and silken to the tongue, particularly when dappled with the accompanying sauce of melting Gruyère cheese. I serve this as a first course to a dinner that is fairly spartan (broiled chicken or grilled chops), but it will make a spectacular brunch offering as well if strips of crisp bacon, ham, and sausages are crammed into the inner circle of the mold.

Incidentally, the recipe comes from the same collection that afforded me the Gingered Rutabaga. It's a borrowing, without a doubt, but what magazine was its original source beats me!

*2 pounds turnips, peeled, cut into ½-inch
　cubes
2 cups chicken broth (see page 414)
4 tablespoons (½ stick) unsalted butter
3 tablespoons all-purpose flour
1 cup hot milk
3 eggs
4 egg yolks
¼ teaspoon freshly grated nutmeg
Salt and freshly ground black pepper
Gruyère Sauce (recipe follows)*

1. Combine the turnips and chicken broth in a medium saucepan. Heat to boiling; reduce the heat. Cook, covered, until tender, about 20 minutes. Drain, reserving the broth.

2. Preheat the oven to 375°F. Place the cooked turnips in the container of a food processor and process until smooth. Transfer the mixture to a saucepan. Cook over medium heat, stirring frequently, until any excess liquid has evaporated. Remove from the heat.

3. Melt the butter in a medium saucepan over medium-low heat. Whisk in the flour. Cook, stirring constantly, 3 minutes. Whisk in the milk. Cook until thick. Slowly add the turnip purée; remove from the heat.

4. Beat the eggs and egg yolks in a large bowl. Slowly beat in the turnip mixture. Add the nutmeg, and salt and pepper to taste. Pour into a buttered 6-cup savarin ring mold. Place the mold in a roasting pan and add boiling water to come halfway up the sides of the mold. Bake until firm, about 45 minutes. Let stand 5 minutes before unmolding onto a serving platter. Spoon some of the Gruyère Sauce over the turnip savarin. Pass the remaining sauce.

Serves 8 to 10.

Gruyère Sauce

*3 tablespoons unsalted butter
2 tablespoons all-purpose flour
1½ cups warm reserved turnip broth, or
　chicken broth (see page 414)
½ cup heavy or whipping cream
½ cup grated Gruyère cheese
⅛ teaspoon freshly grated nutmeg
Salt and cayenne pepper*

Melt the butter in a medium saucepan over medium-low heat. Whisk in the flour. Cook, stirring constantly, 2 minutes. Whisk in the turnip broth and cream. Cook, stirring constantly, until fairly thick, about 3 minutes. Stir in the cheese and allow it to melt. Do not boil. Add the nutmeg, and salt and cayenne pepper to taste. Serve with the turnip savarin.

Makes about 2½ cups.

To the ancients, the turnip was adjudged to possess medicinal balms for the body's outer ills. Case in point: Discorides reported that a fresh white turnip (cooked) applied on a sore foot would "renounce" the pain of that ailment immediately. Likewise, Apicius counseled women of approaching middle age to make a thick paste of cooked turnip, cream, and smashed rosebuds. This unguent, he advised, when rubbed thoroughly into all crevices and hollows of the face, neck, and shoulders will make those surfaces smooth as a baby's thigh after two applications.

MIXED TURNIP CHOWDER

One of the best soups I have ever tasted in my life is a compound of turnips, rutabagas, and potatoes. It was invented in my kitchen on a winter's day when the air of gloom outside was as impenetrable as fog. One sip of this golden chowder and the sun shone bright. I wish you the same good fortune.

2 tablespoons unsalted butter
1 large onion, finely chopped
1 large rib celery, finely chopped
1 pound turnips, peeled, diced
1½ pounds rutabagas, peeled, diced
2 medium potatoes, peeled, diced
1 quart chicken or vegetable broth (see page 414)
Salt and freshly ground black pepper
⅛ teaspoon ground mace

1. Melt the butter in a medium saucepan over medium-low heat. Add the onion; cook 2 minutes. Add the celery; cook 2 minutes longer. Stir in the turnips, rutabagas, potatoes, and broth. Heat to boiling; reduce the heat. Simmer, uncovered, until vegetables are tender, about 20 minutes.

2. Remove one half of the vegetables and place them in the container of a blender or food processor. Add 1 cup of the broth. Blend until smooth, being careful as hot liquid will expand. Return the puréed mixture to the soup. Add salt and pepper to taste and stir in the mace. Simmer 5 minutes before serving.

Serves 8.

FARMHOUSE TURNIPS

My classic turnip and rutabaga renderings follow. The first is a devise I acquired from a country gentlewoman in Ohio some years back. She told me that her great-grandmother had written this recipe down over a hundred years ago and she had never seen fit to alter it a jot. Such endorsement is good enough for me. I never altered it either, for it is very, very special.

3 tablespoons unsalted butter
1 small onion, minced
1 pound turnips, peeled, cut into strips 2 inches long by ½ inch wide
1 medium tomato, peeled, seeded, roughly chopped
¼ teaspoon sugar
¼ teaspoon ground allspice
1 teaspoon salt
½ teaspoon freshly ground black pepper
1 tablespoon chopped fresh parsley

Melt the butter in a medium saucepan over medium-low heat. Stir in the onion; cook 5 minutes. Stir in the turnips, tomato, sugar, and allspice. Mix well. Cook, covered, stirring occasionally, until tender, about 15 minutes. Add the salt and pepper, and sprinkle with the parsley.

Serves 4.

BRAISED RUTABAGA

*T*he second classic is a version of a memorable Burgundian way with root vegetables (either turnip or rutabaga will do here). It was culled originally from Julia Child and her friends Mesdames Bertholle and Beck, in *Mastering the Art of French Cooking*. This formula I suspect may have changed over the years, for I first made it when I was a storekeeper in Amagansett (as a Thanksgiving adjunct to turkey), but the genesis is unmistakable. Still superb too!

*2½ pounds rutabagas, peeled, cut into
    2-inch cubes
⅔ cup finely diced slab bacon
1 tablespoon unsalted butter
1 large onion, finely chopped
1 tablespoon all-purpose flour
¾ cup beef broth or stock (see page 414)
¼ teaspoon sugar
Salt and freshly ground black pepper
1 teaspoon chopped fresh sage, or ¼
    teaspoon dried
Chopped fresh parsley*

1. Cook the rutabagas in boiling salted water for 4 minutes. Rinse under cold running water; drain. Reserve.

2. Cook the diced bacon in boiling water 10 minutes. Drain. Pat dry with paper towels.

3. Melt the butter in a heavy saucepan over medium-low heat. Add the bacon; sauté until lightly browned. Stir in the onion; cook, covered, 5 minutes. Stir in the flour. Cook, stirring constantly, 2 minutes. Whisk in the broth, sugar, salt and pepper to taste, and sage. Cook 3 minutes. Add the rutabagas, tossing well to coat with the mixture. Cook, covered, until tender, 20 to 25 minutes.

4. When the rutabagas are tender, remove the cover and raise the heat. Cook, stirring constantly, until the liquid is thick and syrupy. Sprinkle with parsley.

Serves 6.

MASHED SWEDES

*E*ver since the first *rottebagge* (or "baggy root") was harvested in Sweden, it has been consumed with equal relish by the bourgeoisie and the bovines of that country—giving rise to an unusual proliferation of deep golden butter and unearthly scented cream that the self-indulgent Swedish regularly mash into their rutabagas.

*1 pound rutabagas, peeled, cut into cubes
½ teaspoon beef bouillon powder
1 tablespoon unsalted butter
2 tablespoons heavy or whipping cream
Salt and freshly ground black pepper*

1. Cook the rutabagas in boiling salted water until tender. Drain.

2. Place the rutabagas in a medium saucepan over low heat. Mash them with the bouillon powder and butter until smooth. Beat in the cream and add salt and pepper to taste.

Serves 4.

BASHED NEEPS
(Mashed Rutabagas and Potatoes)

*T*he French call rutabaga *navet de Suede*, while the English dub them *swedes*, Italians know them as *rapa svedese*, and the Spanish tag them *nabo sueco*—which are all variations of the same moniker when you come down to it. But not the Scottish handle, for a rutabaga is referred to as a "neep" from Edinburgh to the Orkneys. Scots have a way with this vegetable: they *bash* them with a mix of white potatoes, lots of butter, and nutmeg—and they are the best thing I have ever tasted in Scotland or anywhere else a rutabaga is rooted.

1 pound rutabagas, peeled, cut into cubes
½ pound potatoes, peeled, cut into cubes
2 tablespoons unsalted butter
¼ teaspoon freshly grated nutmeg
Salt and freshly ground black pepper

1. Cook the rutabagas in boiling salted water for 10 minutes. Add the potatoes; cook until both vegetables are tender, about 15 minutes longer. Drain.

2. Mash the rutabagas and potatoes with the butter until smooth. Add the nutmeg, and salt and pepper to taste. Place over low heat to warm through.
Serves 4.

APPLE-SAUCED RUTABAGA

*T*his is the result of a Thanksgiving prepared in a good friend's house in Vermont. My host forgot the cranberries, but he had a turnip in the cellar and old apple tree in the meadow, so I made apple-sauced rutabaga instead.

2½ pounds rutabagas, peeled, cut into
  ½-inch cubes
2 tablespoons unsalted butter, softened
½ cup heavy or whipping cream
¾ cup Lemon-Rum Applesauce (recipe
  follows)
Salt and freshly ground black pepper

1. Cook the rutabagas in boiling salted water until very tender, about 30 minutes. Drain.

2. Preheat the oven to 350°F. Mash the rutabagas in a large bowl or pot until fairly smooth. Mash in the butter and cream until as smooth as possible. Beat in the applesauce. Add salt and pepper to taste.

3. Transfer the mixture to a baking dish. Bake for 15 minutes before serving.
Serves 6 to 8.

Lemon-Rum Applesauce

*T*he secret of the elegant and savory vegetable dish above is a good, really good, portion of homemade applesauce. I don't like to brag but I doubt you will ever taste one better than the sensuous stuff that follows. It may be prepared in larger batches at your disposition and discretion, of course.

2 large green apples, peeled, cored, sliced
½ teaspoon finely slivered lemon peel
¼ cup packed dark brown sugar
⅛ teaspoon ground cinnamon
1 tablespoon dark rum

1 tablespoon unsalted butter

Place the apple slices with the lemon peel, brown sugar, and cinnamon in a medium saucepan. Cook, covered, over low heat, stirring occasionally, until tender, about 30 minutes. Mash until smooth. Stir in the rum and butter.

Makes about ¾ cup.

HONEY-PEPPERED TURNIPS

The following recipe is reputedly a transcript from *De Re Coquinaria*, the earliest cookbook to be formally compiled. It is a tribute to Roman ingenuity and my high school Latin, for I made the translation with the aid of what we once called "a trot." Accurate? I have no idea, but delicious without question.

1 tablespoon unsalted butter
2 tablespoons honey
1 pound turnips, peeled, cut into ¼-inch cubes
½ teaspoon freshly ground black pepper
Salt
Chopped fresh parsley

Melt the butter with the honey in a medium saucepan over medium-low heat. Stir in the turnips and pepper. Cook, covered, until tender, about 12 minutes. Add salt to taste and sprinkle with parsley.

Serves 4 to 6.

ROOTS IN ESCABECHE

Navet, Rübe, rapa, nabo—all mean nothing more or less than "root," which is succinct if not terribly tantalizing. The turnip's finest appearance in my repertoire is as co-star with rutabagas in a highly seasoned Cajun dish (from New Iberia, Louisiana) called, equally succinctly, roots in escabèche.

1 pound carrots, peeled, cut into julienne strips
1 pound turnips, peeled, cut into julienne strips
1 pound rutabagas, peeled, cut into julienne strips
2 cups olive oil

1 cup distilled white vinegar
½ cup minced pitted green olives
½ cup minced pimiento
1 clove garlic, minced
¼ teaspoon freshly ground black pepper
2 small onions, thinly sliced

1. Cook the carrots in boiling salted water until just tender, about 8 minutes. Drain; reserve.

2. Cook the turnips in boiling salted water until just tender, about 8 minutes. Drain; reserve.

3. Cook the rutabagas in boiling salted water until just tender, about 10 to 12 minutes. Drain; reserve.

4. Heat the oil, vinegar, olives, pimiento, garlic, and pepper in a medium saucepan to boiling; reduce the heat. Simmer, uncovered, 5 minutes.

5. Combine the carrots, turnips, rutabagas, and onions in a heatproof bowl. Pour the dressing over the vegetables and cool to room temperature. Refrigerate, covered, 4 hours or overnight.

Serves 6 to 8.

GINGERED RUTABAGA

A favorite devise, in which rutabagas are sluiced with ginger ale and fresh ginger too. Uncovered in a huge box of ancient clippings (all recipes), this was bequeathed to me by a reader of my newspaper column some while back when she moved to Florida. The recipes were tattered and yellowing, but this one caught my eye and my culinary fancy as well.

2 pounds rutabagas, peeled, cut into
*   ½-inch cubes*
½ teaspoon salt
6 whole cloves, tied in a cheesecloth bag
2 cups ginger ale
4 teaspoons grated fresh ginger
¼ cup dark rum
2 tablespoons unsalted butter

1. Combine the rutabagas, salt, cloves, and ginger ale in a medium saucepan. Heat to boiling; reduce the heat. Cook, covered, over medium-low heat until tender, about 20 minutes.

2. Remove the cover and raise the heat slightly. Cook until almost all liquid has evaporated. Discard the cloves. Stir in the grated ginger, the rum, and the butter. Cook, uncovered, 5 minutes.

Serves 4 to 6.

TURNIP PUREE

*D*on't count on having any leftovers of this eminently satisfying ginger-and-orange-scented dish.

1 pound turnips, peeled, cubed
½ pound potatoes, peeled, cubed
¼ cup orange juice
1 tablespoon dark brown sugar

⅛ teaspoon ground ginger
3½ tablespoons unsalted butter, melted
Salt and freshly ground black pepper

1. Cook the turnips with the potatoes in boiling salted water until tender, 15 to 20 minutes. Drain.

2. Place the turnips and potatoes in the container of a food processor. Process, using the on/off switch, until smooth.

3. Transfer the mixture to a medium saucepan. Stir in the orange juice, brown sugar, ginger, and melted butter. Cook over medium-low heat until warmed through, about 5 minutes. Add salt and pepper to taste.

Serves 4.

TURNIP PAPRIKASH

*T*his dish is Hungarian, and rosy as all get-out—ablush, no doubt, at the surprising federation with cream, wine, and sweet red pepper in which it has found itself.

2 tablespoons unsalted butter
2 scallions, bulbs and green tops, minced
1 pound turnips, peeled, diced
6 tablespoons dry white wine or vermouth
2 teaspoons sugar
1½ tablespoons sweet Hungarian paprika
½ cup heavy or whipping cream
Salt and freshly ground black pepper
Chopped fresh parsley

1. Melt the butter in a medium saucepan over medium-low heat. Add the scallions and turnips; toss well.

2. Combine the wine, sugar, and paprika in a small bowl. Mix well and pour over the turnips. Cook, covered, until the turnips are tender, about 15 minutes.

3. Stir the cream into the turnips. Cook, uncovered, until slightly thickened, about 5 minutes. Add salt and pepper to taste and sprinkle with parsley.

Serves 4.

TURNIPS SICILIAN-STYLE

*T*his devise, while Sicilian in origin, came from a waiter I knew at the Minetta Tavern in New York's Greenwich Village many years ago.

1 tablespoon unsalted butter
2 small leeks (about ½ pound), bulb and 2 inches of green stem, washed, chopped
1 clove garlic, minced
⅓ cup chopped pancetta (Italian bacon), or slab bacon
1 pound small turnips, peeled, cut into ¼-inch strips
½ cup chicken broth (see page 414)
1 teaspoon red wine vinegar
Salt and freshly ground black pepper

1. Melt the butter in a medium saucepan over medium-low heat. Add the leeks; cook 1 minute. Add the garlic; cook 1 minute. Stir in the pancetta; cook 10 minutes.

2. Stir in the turnips and chicken broth. Cook, covered, over low heat until the turnips are tender, 15 to 20 minutes. Stir in the vinegar, and salt and pepper to taste.

Serves 4 to 6.

RUTABAGA SCRATCH BACKS

One of the finest rutabaga recipes ever was found along the Tennessee-Georgia border. This vegetable fritter is best when made of leftover mashed or bashed, so put a cup aside next time around.

1½ cups water
3 tablespoons unsalted butter
½ teaspoon salt
¾ cup yellow cornmeal
Pinch of cayenne pepper
1 cup cold mashed rutabagas

1. Preheat the oven to 450°F. Place the water with 2 tablespoons of the butter and the salt in a medium saucepan. Stir, over medium heat, until the butter melts. Stir in the cornmeal; reduce the heat. Cook, stirring constantly, over low heat until the mixture is very thick. Stir in the cayenne pepper and mashed rutabagas. Cook 4 minutes longer.

2. Melt the remaining 1 tablespoon butter. Spoon the rutabaga mixture into a buttered shallow baking dish and brush with the melted butter. Bake 15 minutes. Let stand 10 minutes before serving.

Serves 4.

BEEF AND TURNIP STEW

Since they are an old vegetable, possibly the oldest, turnips come with considerable myth and malison. One of the most curious conceits stems from the fifteenth-century English botanist Theophrast Turner, who declared he could change a turnip's sex in the vegetable patch. "Turnepes sowen and sette thicke together," he wrote, "grow al into males. But if they be thynner sette, they grow into females—which are tastiest!"

The following soporific stew may be prepared unchauvinistically of either gender and still be merely marvelous.

4 ounces slab bacon (about ½ cup), diced
⅓ cup plus 1 teaspoon all-purpose flour
¼ teaspoon salt
¼ teaspoon freshly ground black pepper
⅛ teaspoon ground cinnamon
Pinch of ground cloves
2 pounds chuck steak, cut into 2-inch cubes
4 tablespoons (½ stick) unsalted butter, plus 1 tablespoon softened
1 large onion, finely chopped

1 clove garlic, minced
⅛ teaspoon freshly grated nutmeg
1 teaspoon vegetable oil
1½ cups beef broth (see page 414)
1 cup dry white wine
3 tablespoons cognac
1 pound turnips, peeled, cut into ¼-inch cubes
Chopped fresh parsley

1. Preheat the oven to 350°F. Cook the bacon in boiling water for 5 minutes. Drain; pat dry on paper towels. Reserve.

2. Combine the ⅓ cup flour, the salt, pepper, cinnamon, and cloves in a shallow bowl. Lightly coat the meat with this mixture. Reserve.

3. Melt 2 tablespoons of the butter in a Dutch oven. Add the onion; cook 1 minute. Add the garlic and nutmeg; cook 4 minutes. Remove from the heat.

4. Heat the oil in a large heavy skillet over medium heat. Add the bacon; sauté until golden, about 4 minutes. With a slotted spoon, transfer the bacon to the Dutch oven.

5. Add 2 tablespoons butter to the skillet. Sauté the beef, a few pieces at a time, until browned on all sides. Transfer to the Dutch oven.

6. When the meat has been sautéed, add the broth to the skillet. Heat to boiling, scraping the bottom and sides of the pan with a wooden spoon. Pour this over the meat in the Dutch oven. Add the wine and cognac. Bake, covered, 1½ hours.

7. Stir in the turnips; continue to bake, covered, 10 minutes. Remove the cover and bake 10 minutes longer.

8. Combine the softened butter with the remaining 1 teaspoon flour. Stir until smooth. Mix into the stew. Bake, uncovered, 20 minutes. Sprinkle with parsley.

Serves 4 to 6.

ZUCCHINI
The Standout Squash

If I did not cook (or write) for a living, I suspect I would seriously till the soil, for I inherited my grandmother's solid jade thumb. To prove it I do battle with a spade and hoe every spring. But working the land, as any true gardener knows, is a full year's occupation and I simply never have the time.

When I ran The Store in Amagansett, summers took a great toll on my garden. Working from sunup to sundown, I had no alternative but to pass the care of my vegetable patch on to a red-haired neighbor boy. With no feel for agriculture whatsoever, he weeded like Attila the Hun—deflowering seedlings ruthlessly but permitting burdock and chickweed to grow waist high. Eventually a family of moles took over the territory.

During the very first season of The Store's existence, my garden did have a small respite. My appendix had just been summarily removed in a New York hospital and I came back to Amagansett to convalesce. Miserable with pain and weak with the heat, I accepted my mother's noble offer to care for me while I recuperated.

I had grown very independent over the years since I had left home, but it was remarkably pleasurable to lapse into childhood ways again. So I accepted my mother's cool hand on my brow—and her bequests of lemonade and iced tea—with good grace.

In her late sixties at the time, my mother had recently become drawn to ethical Christian Science, as she called it, and insisted that I not languish in my bed for long. So together we would walk the entire backyard as she quizzed me on the status of every plant. Never drawn to gardening before, she now watered each green clump every morning, reporting later what was about to bud and what had already burst into bloom. Visiting these vegetable rows in the late afternoon became a daily ritual, and we would sit there for hours without the need for any further conversation at all.

When I became strong enough to do the weeding myself, my parent knew that her time spent "being a mother again" was drawing to a close. The night before she left for the city, she accompanied me out to the garden one last time. As we bent over the cool, damp earth, we tried to calculate the size of the harvest but soon gave up—too many tomatoes, far too many peppers, peas, and beans on the vine for even my mother's sharp eye to keep track of. Pointing to a newly opened squash blossom, she lifted the flower and gave a small cry. There on the ground were the first zucchini of the season. Five of them, tiny as a child's fingers and still fuzzy in their green wrapping.

Without a second thought I picked one, then another, and handed them to my mother. On our knees, we ate the tender young squash raw. The taste? Forgive me, but almost twenty years later it is still impossible to describe.

"Kiddo," said my mother at last, "this makes you know there really is a God."

She had never been so right in her life.

Vegetable Roots

Zucchini's name is Italian, a derivative of the word meaning "sweetest." Most decidedly a member of the native American summer squash tribe (those ubiquitous cucurbits I wrote about earlier on) this green gourd is one local vegetable that really made it big on foreign shores—in Italy. No one seems to know for sure how (or why) zucchini went Italian in the first place, but speculation is rife. Most historians subscribe to the theory that seeds arrived there via some early Italian explorer's rucksack, for zucchini cultivation in the Po valley has been documented for over three hundred years. Italians are so proprietary about this plant that the rest of the world has come to think of zucchini as Italian Squash. In the *Zucchini Cookbook*, author Paula Simmons reported an alternative version of its ancestry:

> According to local legend, seeds were given by the gods to the peoples of Abruzzi (in eastern Italy). They were told to protect the zucchini seed from any non-Italian, which they did until Christopher Columbus brought the seeds to America.

From there on, the zucchini lore is up for grabs, but the squash certainly did bear an Italian imprint for years. When I was a child growing up in a borough of New York City, no one but second-generation Italians grew (or ate) this wonderful vegetable, for it was rumored to be highly indigestible, at least at the Greene's table. I know I never sampled a morsel until well after World War II. But I have made up for that defection. Not a week goes by that a plateful does not appear as an accompaniment at dinner or find itself sliced into translucent rounds and tossed into a luncheon salad bowl.

What to Look For

In the kitchen, the aim is to cook zucchini quickly. In the garden, to pick it early!

There is really no trick to the latter doctrine. Merely start late. I never put out a seed until the weather is truly temperate, in early June. Starting late means zucchini before you know it—but one must remember to keep the seedlings moist (not sodden) until the first green leaves form. For me that usually occurs by the Fourth of July. I celebrate Independence Day in the garden battling mildew, sunstroke (mine, not the zucchini's), and slugs. I deflect the last-named enemy with Maginot Lines rather than pesticides, building deep trenches between the plants to outmaneuver and outflank the snails. It usually works too, though I must confess it makes it hard to weed my garden.

Like a slug I can never resist a tender green squashling. The hardest part of growing zucchini is the appetite one develops waiting for each green sprout to mature to the required four inches in length so one can pick it with good conscience.

Zucchini squash is best when picked young. Look for light green or yellow-flecked vegetables that are slightly pliable to the hand. The fingernail test is always a sign of fresh produce; the scrapings will be bright green.

I have always maintained that the paler a zucchini is in color, the sweeter it will be on the tongue. However, Burpee

and friends have recently come up with a rash of absolutely shocking zucchini hues ranging from bright gold to gray, blue-black, and white; and each one I have sampled is, if anything, sweeter than the last. All of which proves that the old maxim is right: you obviously cannot judge a squash by its cover!

Keep zucchini in a loose plastic bag in the refrigerator for no longer than a week. A pound will yield approximately 3½ cups sliced or 4 cups grated (before salting, of course).

Like other summer squash, zucchini is low in calories (a mere 29) and high in water (95.5 grams), potassium (296 milligrams), and vitamin A (a rousing 820 units) in a cooked cupful.

Preparation

Zucchini (like most other summer squash) needs little basic preparation. I never peel this vegetable. But then, I am addicted to young, tender, small-size squash in general and will sift through a pile at the greengrocer's for a half hour to come up with ones that are no thicker around than a good cigar. Larger, older zucchini are sometimes tough-skinned; they will need to have the skin and seeds removed. It is not hard to seed a zucchini. Merely halve the squash lengthwise and scoop out all the seeds with a small spoon, working in one direction. I rarely salt zucchini after it is cut, unless of course it has been grated. Zucchini has a particularly high water content, so salting and draining it will dissipate the excessive juices and permit faster, more even cooking. Unless I am using a special recipe, I almost always prepare zucchini in the simplest way: sautéing or braising it over moderate heat with just a dab of butter and a sprinkling of shallots and/or herbs for flavor. I prefer zucchini on the crisp (almost underdone) side, for I relish its bite.

TURKISH GOZLEME
(Sautéed Zucchini Cakes)

A Mideastern croquette, this will do wonders for a bland main course or an uninspired hors d'oeuvre tray. Make them in advance—keep 'em hot and keep 'em coming, like potato chips. Only better!

½ pound zucchini, trimmed, grated
   (about 2 cups)
Salt
1 teaspoon chopped canned jalapeño
   peppers
1 small shallot, minced
1 large clove garlic, minced
½ teaspoon curry powder
2 tablespoons olive oil
½ teaspoon baking powder
⅔ cup stone-ground whole-wheat flour
3 tablespoons vegetable oil

1. Place the zucchini in a colander and lightly sprinkle with salt. Let stand 20 minutes. Gently press the zucchini with your hands to remove the excess liquid.

2. Place the zucchini in a large bowl. Add the peppers, shallot, garlic, curry, olive oil, and salt to taste. Mix well. Stir in the baking powder and flour.

3. With floured hands, form the zucchini mixture into sixteen small rounds. Flatten them slightly.

4. Heat the vegetable oil in a 12-inch skillet over medium heat. Add the zucchini cakes and sauté until golden on the bottom, about 1 minute. Turn over and sauté 30 seconds. Reduce the heat to medium-low. Continue to cook the cakes, covered, 15 minutes, turning once.

Serves 4 to 6.

CHICKEN AND ZUCCHINI SOUP

This is one dish in which the grated zucchini needs no salting, as the juices help flavor the broth.

1 large chicken (about 3½ pounds)
2 onions, unpeeled, halved
2 cloves garlic
2 whole cloves
2 large carrots, peeled, roughly chopped
2 large ribs celery, chopped
1 medium white turnip, peeled, chopped
1 large parsnip, peeled, chopped
3 sprigs parsley, plus ¼ cup chopped fresh
   parsley
1 slice lemon

10 peppercorns
1 teaspoon salt
3 cups Chicken Stock (see page 410)
Water
1 pound sweet Italian sausages, cut into
   1-inch pieces
1 cup pasta shells
2 medium zucchini (about ⅔ pound),
   trimmed, grated
Salt and freshly ground black pepper

1. Place the chicken in a 6-quart pot. Add all the ingredients through the parsnip, plus the parsley sprigs, lemon slice, peppercorns, and 1 teaspoon salt. Add the chicken stock and enough water to cover the chicken by 2 inches. Heat to boiling, skimming any residue as it gathers. Reduce the heat and simmer, partially covered, 1 hour.

2. Remove the chicken from the stock and set the stock aside. Allow the chicken to cool down enough to handle, then carefully remove the meat from the bones and cut it into bite-size pieces. Cover and reserve. Return the bones and skin to the stock. Return it to the boil; reduce the heat and simmer, uncovered, 45 minutes. Strain the stock into an-other pot, pressing the vegetables gently with the back of a spoon to release their juices.

3. Meanwhile, sauté the sausage pieces in a lightly oiled heavy skillet until well browned, about 8 minutes. Drain on paper towels.

4. Add the sausages to the stock. Heat to boiling; reduce the heat. Simmer, uncovered, skimming any fat that rises to the surface, for 20 minutes. Add the pasta shells; cook 10 minutes longer. Add the zucchini and the reserved chicken; cook 5 minutes. Add salt and pepper to taste, and sprinkle with the chopped parsley.

Serves 6 to 8.

MINGLE MANGLE
(Warm Zucchini Salad)

The following dish is one that can do double duty, as either a warm salad or a tonic first course. The name means "a toss." This is a prime example of raw zucchini in its finest and un-gussied-up guise. The squash is merely sliced thin, then tossed into a panful of reduced herbed and seasoned cream.

1 tablespoon unsalted butter
2 shallots, minced
2/3 cup heavy or whipping cream
1/4 cup plus 1 tablespoon chopped fresh basil
1 teaspoon lemon juice
1 teaspoon red wine vinegar
1/4 teaspoon hot pepper sauce
Salt and freshly ground black pepper
3/4 pound zucchini, trimmed, cut into 1/8-inch-thick rounds
2 medium ripe tomatoes, peeled, seeded, cubed

1. Melt the butter in a large heavy skillet over medium heat. Add the shal-lots; cook 1 minute. Add the cream and 1/4 cup basil. Heat to boiling; reduce the heat. Simmer, stirring occasionally, until thick, about 10 minutes.

2. Add the lemon juice, vinegar, hot pepper sauce, and salt and pepper to taste. Stir in the zucchini and toss it until well coated. Add the tomatoes; toss lightly. Sprinkle with the remaining 1 tablespoon basil. Serve immediately.

Serves 4 to 6.

ZUCCHINI AND LEMON SALAD

If you are searching for health food, have the next formula with my blessing. It comes from Italy, where it was originally dubbed a *salsa*. But it's a salad to me. Happily it's not only good for what ails you—it tastes good too!

3 tablespoons unsalted butter
1 tablespoon olive oil
3 medium zucchini (about 1 pound), trimmed, sliced thin
1 red bell pepper, seeded, cut into thin strips
1 small onion, halved, sliced thin
1 clove garlic, minced
1 large tomato, peeled, seeded, cut into thin wedges
Pinch of oregano
¼ cup chopped fresh parsley
1 small lemon, peeled, seeds removed, cut into paper-thin slices
1 tablespoon red wine vinegar
Salt and freshly ground black pepper

1. Melt 1 tablespoon of the butter in the oil in a large heavy skillet over medium heat. Add the zucchini; cook, tossing constantly, until just wilted, about 3 minutes. Transfer to a large bowl.

2. Add 1 tablespoon butter to the skillet. Add the red pepper. Cook over medium-low heat until almost tender, about 5 minutes. Add this to the zucchini.

3. Add the remaining 1 tablespoon butter to the skillet. Add the onion; cook over medium-low heat for 1 minute. Add the garlic; cook 5 minutes. Add this to the zucchini mixture.

4. Toss the tomato with the oregano in the skillet over medium-high heat for 1 minute. Add this to the zucchini mixture along with the parsley, sliced lemon, and vinegar. Let stand, covered, 1 hour. Add salt and pepper to taste before serving.

Serves 4.

ZUCCHINI FROMAGE

For me the classic zucchini prescription is the one that is simplest to whip together. The following recipe is a prime example: the squash is cooked in three minutes, tossed with two cheeses and amended with a third, and then broiled.

2 tablespoons unsalted butter
2 shallots, minced
3 medium zucchini (about 1 pound), trimmed, cut into ⅛-inch-thick rounds
2 tablespoons chopped fresh basil, or 2 teaspoons dried
½ teaspoon salt
¼ teaspoon freshly ground black pepper
¼ cup freshly grated Parmesan cheese
¼ cup freshly grated Romano cheese
¼ cup grated Doux de Montagne or Gruyère cheese

1. Preheat the broiling unit. Melt the butter in a 9- to 10-inch cast-iron skillet over medium-low heat. Add the shallots; cook 3 minutes. Raise the heat to medium-high. Add the zucchini; cook, tossing constantly, until just barely soft, about 3 minutes. Toss in the basil, and add the salt and pepper.

2. Stir the Parmesan and Romano cheeses into the zucchini. Sprinkle the Doux de Montagne or Gruyère over the top. Place the skillet under the broiler to lightly brown the top.

Serves 4.

Zucchini is consumed under various aliases in other parts of the globe. The French know it as *courgette*, while the English dub it *baby marrow*. The Spanish, who mix it into stews and soups, call it *calabacin*. Italians, who named it *zucchino* in the first place now perversely tag it *zucchine*, but they still enjoy its bounty with ardor just the same.

TOUSLED ZUCCHINI

*T*ousled zucchini may appear to be the latest coiffure out of Paris, but it's not. It's merely the best vegetable custard in my neighborhood! Yours too, if you have a mite of initiative. Look for small zucchini, please!

¼ cup olive oil
2 tablespoons unsalted butter
1 medium onion, chopped
2 cloves garlic, minced
2 small zucchini (about ½ pound), trimmed, sliced thin
1 small tomato, peeled, seeded, chopped
2 tablespoons chopped fresh parsley
2 tablespoons chopped fresh basil, or 2 teaspoons dried
1 teaspoon chopped fresh tarragon, or ¼ teaspoon dried
1 tablespoon red wine vinegar
Salt and freshly ground black pepper
4 eggs
¼ cup heavy or whipping cream
¼ cup grated Gruyère or Monterey jack cheese
2 tablespoons freshly grated Parmesan cheese

1. Preheat the oven to 350°F. Heat the oil and butter in a large skillet over medium heat. Add the onion; cook 1 minute. Add the garlic; cook 2 minutes. Stir in the zucchini, tomato, parsley, basil, tarragon, and vinegar. Reduce the heat to low; cook 4 minutes. Add salt and pepper to taste.

2. Transfer the zucchini mixture into a buttered 10-inch glass or ceramic quiche dish.

3. Beat the eggs with the cream in a medium bowl. Pour this over the zucchini and sprinkle with the cheeses. Bake until golden, about 25 minutes. Let stand 10 minutes before serving.

Serves 6.

ZUCCHINI PICKLES

There is obviously something for every food lover in the world. Apple aficionados gather in Kent, Michigan, every summer; garlic gobblers congregate in Gilroy, California. Zucchini zealots travel to Harrisville, New Hampshire, where the annual zucchini festival is held. In the shadow of the White Mountains, a mountain of zucchini is converted into breads, cakes, pancakes, jams, and even ice cream on occasion. But zucchini comestibles are not the only residual of this squash bacchanal: zucchinis large and small are also carved and molded into towering works of art. Speaking for myself (an acknowledged zucchini buff), I'd just as soon pass up the cultural achievements for the grub—such as the blue-ribbon zucchini pickle that follows. It's a winner!

4 medium zucchini (about 1½ pounds),
    trimmed, sliced thin
2 small yellow onions, halved, sliced thin
3 tablespoons salt
Cold water
2 cups distilled white vinegar
1 cup sugar
1 teaspoon celery seeds
1 teaspoon anise seeds
2 teaspoons dry mustard

1. Place the zucchini and onions in a medium bowl. Sprinkle with the salt. Cover with cold water; let stand 1 hour.

2. Combine the vinegar, sugar, celery seeds, anise seeds, and mustard in a medium saucepan. Heat to boiling; remove from the heat.

3. Drain the zucchini and onions. Place them in a large pot and pour the hot liquid over. Let stand 1 hour.

4. Heat the mixture to boiling; simmer 3 minutes. Remove from the heat and place in sterilized jars.

Makes 3 pints.

ZUCCHINI HOECAKE

Not truly a hoecake at all, it was named thusly by a gardening pal of mine who lives in Amagansett. This fellow claims that he drops his hoe the moment he detects that this dish will be on the supper table.

1 pound zucchini, trimmed, coarsely grated
Salt
6 tablespoons (¾ stick) unsalted butter
1 small onion, minced
1 teaspoon chopped fresh basil, or ½
    teaspoon dried
2 tablespoons chopped fresh parsley
Pinch of ground cloves
⅛ teaspoon freshly grated nutmeg

2½ cups light cream or half-and-half
1 tablespoon sugar
1 tablespoon honey
1 cup white cornmeal
4 egg yolks
1 teaspoon baking powder
Pinch of ground white pepper
5 egg whites

1. Place the zucchini in a colander and lightly sprinkle with salt. Let stand 20 minutes. Gently press the zucchini with your hands to remove the excess liquid.

2. Preheat the oven to 375°F. Melt 2 tablespoons of the butter in a heavy skillet over medium heat. Add the onion, zucchini, basil, parsley, cloves, and nutmeg. Stir well. Cook, covered, 5 minutes. Then remove the cover and cook, tossing constantly, until the mixture is dry, about 4 minutes. Remove from the heat.

3. Combine the cream, the remaining 4 tablespoons butter, the sugar, honey, and ¼ teaspoon salt in a medium saucepan over low heat. Cook, stirring constantly, until the butter melts. Stir in the cornmeal. Cook, still stirring constantly, until thick, about 5 minutes. Do not allow to boil.

4. Transfer the cornmeal mixture to a large bowl. Beat in the egg yolks, one at a time, beating thoroughly after each addition. Stir in the baking powder and white pepper. Stir in the zucchini mixture.

5. Beat the egg whites until stiff but not dry. Fold them into the mixture and

According to the diaries of early American settlers, zucchini was believed to anesthetize the pain of childbirth, toothache, and chilblains, not necessarily in that order. The sufferer merely chewed on the squash, it seems, and got better. If that seems bizarre, consider the next prescription from Jamestown, Virginia. Colonists there believed that this squash, when boiled and made into a hot paste, would cure the sting of runny eyes. And Indians in the Southwest had the idea (because the zucchini was similar in shape, one presumes) that eating enough squash would cure the deadly sting of snakebite. None of the reports of these "cures" come with a tally of results, which is just as well for us *and* the zucchini!

pour it into a buttered 2-quart soufflé dish or casserole. Bake until puffed and golden, 30 to 35 minutes.

Serves 6 to 8.

ELEANOR TOBIN'S MOTHER'S ZUCCHINI MUFFIN GEMS

*T*he recipe for Eleanor Tobin's Mother's Zucchini Muffin Gems (and they are, they are) was passed on to me by my friend Jody Gillis, who is the director of the Something More Cooking School in La Mesa, California. Jody gave me the prescription with this note in the margin: "These are just superb! I was going to be selfish for fear Eleanor Tobin's mother's recipe would end up in the book and my recipes wouldn't, but they're just too great to hold back!"

Jody is right. Make a batch and salute Eleanor Tobin and her mother as well!

½ cup sugar
1 large egg, lightly beaten
¼ cup vegetable oil
¾ cup all-purpose flour
¼ teaspoon baking powder
¼ teaspoon baking soda
¼ teaspoon salt
¼ teaspoon freshly grated nutmeg
1 cup grated zucchini (about ¼ pound)
¼ cup raisins, finely chopped
¼ cup chopped pecans

1. Preheat the oven to 350°F. Combine the sugar, egg, and oil in a large bowl. Mix well.

2. Sift the flour with the baking powder, baking soda, salt, and nutmeg in a medium bowl. Stir this into the sugar-egg mixture.

3. Add the zucchini, raisins, and pecans, and stir only until mixed. Do not overwork. Spoon the batter into a well-buttered muffin tin, filling each cup about two-thirds full. Bake until the muffins are golden brown and a toothpick inserted in the center comes out clean, about 25 minutes. Run a knife around the edges to loosen.

Makes 9 muffins.

CRISPY FRIED ZUCCHINI AND SQUASH BLOSSOMS FILLED WITH GOAT CHEESE

I am not one of those cooks who nibble on rose petals or violets in the privacy of my kitchen. And "Please don't eat the daisies!" is an injunction that I have managed to live with for years. However, I must confess, zucchini blossoms turn me on! In fact, they are the staples of the tastiest dish I have ever eaten—fresh-picked flowers are crammed with goat cheese and dipped in frothy batter before they hit the pan.

Now, before you start imagining that one must have a small plantation in order to assuage this floral addiction, think again! Fine greengrocers (and farmer's markets) carry a huge supply of these aureate blooms from June through September in my neighborhood. Ask in yours—or if worst comes to worst, invest in a packet of zucchini seed. As I told you before, the plants grow fast!

2 eggs, separated
¼ cup dry white wine
½ cup cold water
1½ tablespoons olive oil
1 cup all-purpose flour
½ teaspoon salt
⅛ teaspoon ground mace
Dash of hot pepper sauce
24 squash blossoms (zucchini, pumpkin, or
    Hubbard), each about 3½ to 4 inches
    in length

4 ounces mild goat cheese (chèvre), cut into
    ¼-inch-thick strips, 2½ inches long
Oil for frying
1 large zucchini (about ½ pound),
    trimmed, cut into ½-inch-thick strips,
    about 2 inches long
Salt and freshly ground black pepper

1. Beat the egg yolks in a large bowl until light. Beat in the wine, water, and olive oil. Slowly beat in the flour. Add the ½ teaspoon salt, the mace, and the hot pepper sauce. Let stand, covered, at room temperature for 2 hours.

2. With a sharp knife, remove the long stems from the blossoms. Remove any green from around the blossoms. Using your fingers, open each blossom at one side. Place a piece of goat cheese inside and press the edges together. Refrigerate until ready to use.

3. Beat the egg whites until stiff but not dry. Fold them into the batter.

4. Heat 2 inches of oil in a medium saucepan until hot but not smoking.

5. Dip the zucchini strips into the batter and deep-fry in the oil until golden, about 2 or 3 minutes. Drain on paper towels. Keep warm in a low oven.

6. Dip the cheese-filled squash blossoms into the batter and deep-fry them until golden, about 2 minutes. Serve the zucchini and the blossoms together, sprinkled with salt and pepper to taste.

Serves 6.

CHICKEN-STUFFED ZUCCHINI

Although the American-born zucchini has been in common currency in markets for over thirty years, it is still not a very popular vegetable in its native land. In most Mediterranean households, however, it is a thrice-weekly staple; and when stuffed with a bit of ground meat or cheese and baked, it often replaces far costlier cuts of meat at the dinner table.

A totally Americanized version of such a stuffed zucchini follows. It is included here not for economy's sake but because it is simply one of the best vegetable dishes I have ever tasted. The zucchini is crammed with velvety creamed-chicken hash, flecked with nubbins of smoky ham and a dusting of redolent Parmesan cheese. Best of all, it may be prepared early in the day and baked later, perhaps between rounds of drinks. Add the sauce, brown the zucchini under the broiler, and voilà, a great meal in minutes.

2 large zucchini (about 1 pound), trimmed
2 tablespoons plus 2 teaspoons unsalted butter
1 shallot, minced
2 tablespoons plus 2 teaspoons all-purpose flour
1 cup Chicken Stock (see page 410)
1 tablespoon sherry
1¼ cups diced cooked chicken
¼ pound chopped smoked ham (about ½ cup)
Salt and freshly ground black pepper
½ cup heavy or whipping cream
1 egg yolk, lightly beaten
1 tablespoon freshly grated Parmesan cheese

1. Cut the zucchini in half lengthwise. Cook, covered, in boiling salted water until tender, about 5 minutes. Rinse under cold running water; drain.

2. Carefully scoop out the center of each zucchini half. Set the shells aside. Squeeze the pulp with your hands to extract the excess liquid. Chop it fine.

3. Preheat the oven to 300°F. Melt the 2 tablespoons butter in a large heavy skillet over medium-low heat. Stir in the shallot; cook 2 minutes. Stir in the 2 tablespoons flour. Cook, stirring constantly, 2 minutes. Whisk in the stock. Cook over medium heat until thick, about 4 minutes. Stir in the sherry, chopped zucchini, chicken, and ham. Add salt and pepper to taste. Spoon the mixture into the zucchini shells. Place them in a shallow baking dish; bake 15 minutes.

4. Meanwhile, melt the remaining 2 teaspoons butter in a small saucepan over medium-low heat. Stir in the re-maining 2 teaspoons flour. Cook, stirring constantly, 2 minutes. Whisk in the cream. Remove from the heat and whisk in the egg yolk. Stir in the cheese, and spoon the mixture over the zucchini. Place the dish under the broiler until the tops are lightly browned.

Serves 2 to 4.

ZUCCHINI PANCAKES

One of the fatal mistakes of almost all untried gardeners is to plant too much zucchini in the spring and then neglect to harvest it—until the gourds are literally over the hill.

Every midsummer, when I write in my newspaper column about the joys of picking tiny baby-finger-size zucchini, I am inevitably bombarded with letters from readers, all demanding advice about what to do with the green torpedoes they have uncovered in the vegetable patch. The answers do not come easily. Aside from doorstops or ballast in an uneven keel, there's not a heck of a lot one can do with an overgrown zucchini. However, if you can manage to stem the growth before it passes the twelve-inch mark, consider these pancakes made of grated, salted zucchini—they will cover up a multitude of gardening sins as a nifty brunch dish or last-minute supper number.

¾ pound zucchini, trimmed, grated (about
3 cups)
Salt
1 egg, lightly beaten
¼ cup milk
¼ cup freshly grated Parmesan cheese
¼ teaspoon hot pepper sauce, or to taste
Freshly ground black pepper
½ cup all-purpose flour
1½ teaspoons baking powder

1. Place the zucchini in a colander and lightly sprinkle with salt. Let stand 20 minutes. Gently press the zucchini with your hands to remove the excess liquid.

2. Combine the zucchini with the egg, milk, cheese, and hot pepper sauce in a large bowl. Add salt and pepper to taste.

3. Sift the flour with the baking powder and stir this into the zucchini mixture. Mix well.

4. Heat a lightly greased cast-iron skillet or griddle over medium heat until hot but not smoking. Cook the pancakes, a few at a time, using about 3 tablespoons batter per pancake. When lightly browned, about 3 minutes, turn over and cook the other side for 1 minute. Transfer to a serving platter and keep warm in a low oven while cooking the remaining pancakes. Serve with plenty of butter.

Serves 4 as a side dish; 2 or 3 as an entrée.

ZUCCHINI POUND CAKE

*T*he last zucchini devise I have up my sleeve is a pound cake (green—studded with zucchini, naturally), and it's the last bequest I can pass on. Bake it with green and Greene joy!

1 cup grated zucchini (about ¼ pound)
2 cups plus 1 tablespoon all-purpose flour
1 cup (2 sticks) unsalted butter, softened
1⅔ cups sugar
1 tablespoon vanilla extract
2 tablespoons orange liqueur
2 teaspoons finely grated orange peel
5 eggs, separated

1. Preheat the oven to 350°F. Toss the zucchini with the 1 tablespoon flour in a bowl. Set aside.

2. Beat the butter with the sugar in the large bowl of an electric mixer until light and fluffy. Beat in the vanilla, orange liqueur, and orange peel. Add the egg yolks, one at a time, beating thoroughly after each addition. Stir in the zucchini.

3. Beat the egg whites until stiff but not dry.

4. Fold the 2 cups flour into the batter in three batches, alternating with batches of the egg white. Pour the mixture into a buttered and floured 9-inch tube pan. Bake until a toothpick inserted in the center comes out clean, about 1 hour. Cool on a rack for 10 minutes before unmolding.

Serves 8 to 10.

An old English cure for warts instructs the afflicted person to touch each blemish with the cut end of a zucchini by the light of a full moon, then to bury the squash in a field that faces north. Reputedly the warts will disappear before the squash decomposes. A gardening friend, who knows nothing whatsoever of witchcraft but dotes on zucchini, adds a coda: if the time of year is late spring, she claims, the buried zucchini will yield a plant or two within the month! So even if the warts remain, the magic cannot be considered a total loss.

KITCHEN BASICS

MAYONNAISE

Mayonnaise is a culinary adjunct that many good cooks skip, out of fear of failure and the notion that it will be time-consuming. Mayonnaise will never fail *if* all the ingredients at hand, plus the bowl and whip (or blender jar or processor bowl), are at room temperature before you begin. If the eggs have been refrigerated, place them in warm (not boiling) water for five minutes prior to whisking. I must confess that I make mayonnaise the prehistoric way—using only my right arm, an earthenware bowl, and a wire whisk—and it takes less than five minutes from start to finish. One word of advice: taste the mixture as it thickens. If it is too bland, add white pepper or more lemon juice. If it is too spicy, whip in more oil. A jot of boiling water stabilizes homemade mayonnaise. Store it in a clean bowl or sterilized jar. Mayonnaise keeps for several days in a cold refrigerator.

2 egg yolks
2 teaspoons white wine vinegar
Juice of ½ lemon
½ teaspoon salt
Pinch of ground white pepper
½ teaspoon Dijon mustard
1 cup vegetable oil combined with ½ cup
  olive oil
Dash of hot pepper sauce
1 tablespoon boiling water

1. Whisk the egg yolks in a large bowl until light. Slowly whisk in the vinegar, lemon juice, salt, white pepper, and mustard.

2. Beat in the oil, a few drops at a time, until ½ cup has been incorporated. (The mayonnaise should be very thick at this point.) Continue to beat in the oil, 2 tablespoons at a time. Season with hot pepper sauce and, if you like, more salt or lemon juice. Thin with the boiling water.

3. Store, tightly covered, in the refrigerator. Mayonnaise will keep five to six days in the refrigerator, but bring it to room temperature before using.

Makes about 1½ cups, enough for 4 servings.

Variations

Green Mayonnaise: Add ½ cup chopped fresh herbs (mixed or individual)—such as dill, parsley, tarragon, and chives—to 1½ cups mayonnaise.

Curry Mayonnaise: Add 2 tablespoons curry powder, 1 teaspoon turmeric, and 1 tablespoon white wine vinegar to 1½ cups mayonnaise. Stir in 2 teaspoons capers.

Tomato Mayonnaise: Peel, seed, and chop 1 large tomato. Place it in a saucepan with 1 teaspoon chopped fresh basil, ¼ teaspoon sugar, and ¼ cup chicken stock, and cook over medium heat until very, very thick. Cool, and combine with 2 tablespoons sour cream and 1 cup mayonnaise.

FAIL-SAFE HOLLANDAISE

*T*his recipe came to me a while back from a whiz of a cook named Ginnie Ward. The trick that makes the elegant golden sauce fail-safe is the increment of frozen butter, added bit by bit as the eggs and lemon juice homogenize. Hollandaise will keep in a double boiler half filled with warm (not boiling) water for about half an hour prior to serving.

3 egg yolks
Juice of ½ lemon
½ teaspoon Dijon mustard
¾ cup unsalted butter, frozen
Dash of hot pepper sauce
Pinch of ground white pepper
Salt

1. Beat the egg yolks with the lemon juice in the top of a double boiler. Place over simmering water; stir in the mustard.

2. Cut the butter into eight pieces. Using a small wire whisk, beat the butter into the egg yolk mixture, one piece at a time. Stir well after each addition.

Stir in the hot pepper sauce, white pepper, and salt to taste.

Makes about 1½ cups.

Variations

Anchovy Hollandaise: Add ½ teaspoon anchovy paste to the egg yolks.

Rosy Hollandaise: Add 1 teaspoon tomato paste to the egg yolks, and omit the mustard.

Sauce Maltese: Add 1 tablespoon orange juice and ½ teaspoon finely grated orange peel to the egg yolks, and omit the lemon juice.

BEEF STOCK

4 pounds raw beef bones, including some
*   meat*
3 large onions, peeled, chopped
4 carrots, peeled, roughly chopped
4 ribs celery with leaves, chopped
2 cloves garlic
6 parsley sprigs

1 bay leaf
4 whole cloves
10 whole black peppercorns
2 teaspoons salt, or to taste
3 quarts plus 2 cups water
2 tablespoons red wine vinegar

1. Preheat the oven to 475°F. Place the bones in a large roasting pan, and bake them until brown, 15 minutes. Turn the bones over and reduce the temperature to 450°F. Continue to bake, another 15 minutes, until the second side is browned as well. This step will give color to the stock.

2. Meanwhile, combine the remaining ingredients except the 2 cups water and the vinegar in a large heavy pot. Heat to boiling; reduce the heat.

3. Add the browned meat bones to the stock. Pour off the grease in the roasting pan and stir in the 2 cups water, scraping the bottom and sides of the pan with a wooden spoon. Add this liquid to the stock. Heat stock to boiling again; reduce the heat to low. Simmer, partially covered, skimming the surface occasionally, for 3 hours. Stir in the vinegar, and continue to simmer, partially covered, until reduced to about 1½ quarts, about 2 hours longer. Strain.

Makes 1½ quarts.

FISH STOCK

2½ to 3 pounds fish bones, including heads
4 cups water
2 cups dry white wine
3 cups clam juice
2 onions, chopped
2 ribs celery with leaves, chopped
6 sprigs parsley
1 bay leaf
4 whole cloves
10 peppercorns
1 teaspoon salt
1 lemon, halved

Combine all the ingredients in a large pot. Heat to boiling; reduce the heat to medium-low. Simmer, partially covered, until reduced to about 6 cups. Strain.

Makes 1½ quarts.

CHICKEN STOCK

4 pounds chicken pieces (backs, necks, wings)
4 quarts water, approximately
2 yellow onions, unpeeled
1 leek, cleaned, chopped
2 cloves garlic
2 carrots, peeled, roughly chopped
2 ribs celery with leaves, chopped
2 turnips, peeled, roughly chopped
2 parsnips, peeled, roughly chopped
8 sprigs parsley
4 whole cloves
10 peppercorns
1 teaspoon salt, or to taste
1 small bay leaf
1 teaspoon chopped fresh thyme, or ½ teaspoon dried
2 tablespoons red wine vinegar

1. Place the chicken pieces in a large pot and add the water. The chicken should be totally covered, so add more water if necessary. Heat to boiling; boil 5 minutes, skimming the surface as the scum rises to the top.

2. Add the remaining ingredients with enough water to cover the chicken by 3 inches (about 4 quarts altogether).

Return to boiling; reduce the heat to low. Simmer, partially covered, skimming the surface occasionally, until the stock is reduced to 1½ quarts, about 3 hours. Strain.

Makes 1½ quarts.

VEGETABLE STOCK

In a pinch, the following vegetable stock will do in place of chicken or beef stock in any recipe where it is used to add savor to a vegetable as it is braised. Its devise is included for those whose dietary strictures prohibit the use of meat and poultry, but nonvegetarians as well will enjoy the remarkable savor vegetable stock adds to a dish.

4 tablespoons (½ stick) unsalted butter
5 onions, chopped
2 cloves garlic
4 ribs celery with leaves, chopped
4 carrots, peeled, roughly chopped
2 leeks, cleaned, chopped
½ ounce dried mushrooms
1 bunch parsley
1 teaspoon chopped fresh thyme, or ½
    teaspoon dried
1 sage leaf, or a pinch of dried, crumbled
1 bay leaf
1½ teaspoons salt
10 peppercorns, lightly crushed
10 allspice berries, lightly crushed
Pinch of freshly grated nutmeg
4 quarts water
½ teaspoon crushed dried hot red pepper
1 tablespoon red wine vinegar

Melt the butter in a large heavy pot over medium heat. Stir in the onions; cook 5 minutes. Add the remaining ingredients through the water. Heat to boiling; reduce the heat to low. Simmer, partially covered, until reduced to about 2½ quarts, about 2 hours. Add the hot pepper and vinegar. Simmer, uncovered, 30 minutes longer. Strain, gently pressing the liquid out of the vegetables with the back of a spoon.

Makes 1½ to 2 quarts.

The secret to a rich, flavorsome stock is always fresh ingredients plus a long tenure of stove time, for the taste of really good stock depends upon prolonged cooking. A general rule of thumb is to expect only half the amount of liquid you originally begin with, as the reduction gives the stock its richness. A trick I sometimes indulge in when time is short is to add half canned broth (beef, chicken, or clam juice, as the case may be) instead of all water. If you "beef up" your stock with a canned product, however, here's a cavil: make sure to appreciably reduce the amount of salt called for in the recipe, for all canned broths are sodium-high!

All of these stocks keep for three weeks when stored in the refrigerator, tightly covered. If you wish to keep the stock longer, it is best to reboil it and allow it to cool before returning it to the refrigerator. Freezing stock will keep it usable for at least six months.

HOT STEAMED RICE

*T*he trick to the following steamed rice is its ease. It may be prepared in under a half hour's time, but then it can be kept (steaming) over minimal heat for several hours—with every grain still separate and intact whenever the rice is eventually served. A rule of thumb worth filing away is that rice triples as it cooks. One-third cup raw rice will produce one cup cooked rice—and so on.

1 ⅓ cups uncooked long-grain rice
4 quarts boiling salted water

1. Add the rice to the boiling water. Stir once with a wooden spoon so that the rice does not stick to the bottom of the pot. When the water returns to boiling, reduce the heat. Simmer, uncovered, until just tender, 12 to 15 minutes. Drain in a colander.

2. Place the colander over 2 inches of boiling water in another pot. Do not let the bottom of the colander touch the water. Cover the rice with a single layer of paper towels. Steam for at least 15 minutes. Rice can be held this way for several hours without harm.

Makes four 1-cup servings.

SHORT CRUST PASTRY

1 cup all-purpose flour
¼ teaspoon salt
4 tablespoons (½ stick) unsalted butter,
  chilled
1½ tablespoons vegetable shortening,
  chilled
2½ to 3 tablespoons cold water

Sift the flour with the salt in a large bowl. Cut in the butter and shortening with a pastry blender until the mixture has the texture of coarse crumbs. Add just enough water to form a soft dough. Wrap, and chill for 1 hour before using.

Makes enough for one 9- to 10-inch single-crust pie.

ORANGE CRUST PASTRY

1¼ cups all-purpose flour
¼ teaspoon salt
4 tablespoons (½ stick) unsalted butter,
  chilled

¼ cup vegetable shortening, chilled
½ teaspoon finely grated orange peel
2 tablespoons orange juice, approximately

1. Sift the flour with the salt in a large bowl. Cut in the butter, shortening, and orange peel with a knife. Blend the mixture with a pastry blender until it has the texture of coarse crumbs.

2. Using a fork or a knife, cut in enough orange juice to make a soft dough. Do not overwork. Refrigerate for 1 hour before using.

Makes enough for one 9- to 10-inch single crust pie.

These are two of my favorite recipes for pie and tart shells. The short crust is appropriate to all non-sweet fillings, while the orange-flavored pastry lends a delicate savor to dulcet concoctions. There is also an excellently crumbly lard-and-vinegar pastry (on page 166) that will do admirably in either instance.

NOTES ON INGREDIENTS

Broth and Bouillon

Stock is the secret to most good cooking. However, when I do not have homemade on hand, I often make do with canned broth—usually Progresso or College Inn. When a recipe requires strong broth, I double the amount called for and boil it down to half before proceeding with the recipe. On occasion I use bouillon cubes or powder. For powder, G. Washington brand is easy to find. Knorr-Swiss bouillon cubes, made in Switzerland, are now available in supermarkets around the country; they are made of real beef and real chicken. Brand-new to the retail market are Minor's Bases (beef, chicken, clam, lobster, mushroom, etc.), which until recently were sold only to restaurants. This high-quality product is available by mail order only. Write to *BY 2 Foodservice*, P.O. Box 34707, Los Angeles, CA 90034 for further information. Be advised that all these packaged bases and broths contain some MSG.

Cheese

BLEU: Some of the finest bleu cheese in the world is made right here in the U.S., by Maytag Dairy Farms. Available in two-pound wheels from *Maytag Dairy Farms*, R. R. 1, Box 806, Newton, IA 50208.

GOAT: Many kinds of imported goat cheeses are available from *Say Cheese*, 856 Cole Street, San Francisco, CA 94117; *Balducci's*, 424 Avenue of the Americas, New York, NY 10011; *Chalet Wine & Cheese*, 405 Armitage Street, Chicago, IL 60614; and from many other shops around the country. American-made Laura Chenel's chèvre, largely responsible for the boom in American goat cheese, can be mail-ordered from *Say Cheese* or from the *Ideal Cheese Shop*, 1205 Second Ave., New York, NY 10021. One of my favorite cheeses comes from Interlaken in New York's wine-growing district. Though the Goat Folks cheese is available only in the Northeast, it can be ordered from *Balducci's* or from *Goat Folks Farm*, Tunison Road, Interlaken, NY 14847.

PARMESAN: Nothing can top Parmigiano-Reggiano, the Italian wonder of cheeses. Expensive as it is, it is worth seeking out and is available at most of the above-mentioned cheese stores. However, I often make do with Stella brand Parmesan, distributed by Universal Foods, without irreparable harm to the dish I am preparing. One might also consider the dry Jack being made by the Vella Cheese Company in Sonoma, California. Very much like Parmesan in taste and texture, Vella dry Jack is rated as one of America's great cheeses. Available from *Vella Cheese Company*, P.O. Box 191, Sonoma, CA 95476.

Chiles

The chili powder one finds on the supermarket shelf just cannot compare to the fresh and ground chiles sold at Spanish markets around the country. The assortment is tremendous. One I favor is the red Colorado variety, which is mild but still intensely flavorful. A poblano chile, while not particularly hot, gives a corncake an indispensable bite. However, when fresh chiles are not available, use a bell pepper for texture and make up the tang with a pinch or two of cayenne or Tabasco sauce. For canned chiles such as jalapeños, and "salsas," I find that Herdez and Ortega brands are generally available around the country. Four Spanish stores that will fill mail orders are: *Casa Moneo*, 210 West 14th Street, New York, NY 10011; *Casa Esteiro*, 2719 West Division, Chicago, IL 60622; *El Mercado*, First Avenue and Lorenzo, Los Angeles, CA 90063; and *Mexican Kitchen*, Box 213, Brownsville, TX 78520.

Chorizos

Spanish sausages, hot or mild, are available at most Spanish markets around the country. See Chiles for mail-order sources.

Cornmeal

Harina de maíz (finely ground cornmeal) is available from the aforementioned Hispanic grocers. I notice that Quaker Oats also markets *harina de maíz* in supermarkets these days. In a pinch, however, one can make do with any available cornmeal. Just grind it in a food processor or blender until it is fine. The extra milling makes for a lighter, smoother result in the pan.

Cream, Heavy or Whipping

Cream marketed in the East is most often sold under the cognomen of "heavy" cream and has a slightly higher milk fat content (36 percent minimum) than much of the "whipping" cream (30 to 36 percent) found elsewhere in the country. For a longer shelf life almost all supermarket varieties are ultra-pasteurized these days. The recipes in this book will work with either. If you are lucky enough to have an "old-fashioned" dairy nearby, make the effort to get your cream there. Cream so thick it literally doesn't pour (40 percent milk fat and up) is hard to come by in the 1980s, but the American Dairy Association assures me that if enough consumers make a true demand, it *can* be brought back.

Filé Powder

I have seen this seasoning—dried crushed sassafras, used in Cajun cookery—almost everywhere of late. If you can not find it locally, filé powder may be ordered from *Veron's Quality Meats*, 4303 Johnston St., Lafayette, LA 70503.

Flour

Most often I use Hecker's unbleached all-purpose flour, found in the Northeast, and in other areas where I teach I use what is generally available. With success, I might add. If you are particular about the flour you use, try White Lily Flour, an exceptional soft wheat flour from *White Lily Flour Company*, Box 871, Knoxville, TN 37901. Pillsbury bread flour makes a very admirable loaf in my kitchen, but for aficionados Great Valley Mills, one of the oldest businesses in the country (and for good reason), offers a selection of twenty different types of flour, all stone-ground: *Great Valley Mills*, Quakertown, PA 18951.

Ham

When it comes to American hams, I think that the Dubuque Fleur de Lis brand ranks among the best. I always use the smoked cooked semi-boneless ham, which usually weighs in around 10 pounds. Its distribution is very spotty, but its parent company, FDL Foods, Inc., does a limited mail-order business, especially at Christmas time: *FDL Foods, Inc.*, 16th and Sycamore, Dubuque, IA 52001. Other hams worth the effort of mail-ordering include those from *Lawrence's Smoke House*, Route 30, Newfane, VT 05345 and *Colonel Bill Newsome's Hams*, 128 N. Highland Avenue, Princeton, KY 42445.

Herbs

Fresh herbs have become a big business, and you can find almost anything you want at a local nursery. If you are searching out a hard-to-find herb plant, try *Fox Hill Farm*, 440 W. Michigan Avenue, Dept. C14, Box 7, Parma, MI 49269. I am often lucky enough to be able to keep my herbs growing year-round on my kitchen windowsill. If I lose them and am forced to use dried, I generally halve the amount of fresh herb called for and chop the dried herb in with an equal amount of fresh parsley. The parsley will take on the flavor of the dried herb, and the herb itself will taste fresher for it.

Hot Pepper Sauce

Though there are myriad brands on the market, Tabasco is my first choice.

Mayonnaise

When I do not feel like whipping up a batch of homemade, I use Hellmann's (labeled as Best Foods in most of the U.S.)

Mushrooms

Mushrooms are mushrooms until you have tasted the fresh shiitake variety. Long used in Oriental cooking and available dried, this lusty, meaty mushroom is now being grown in America and shipped fresh around the country. Mail-order from *Oakville Grocery*, 1555 Pacific Avenue, San Francisco, CA 94109 or *Balducci's* (see Cheese). Or if you prefer, you can order Golden Oak brand shiitakes via overnight Express Mail directly from the source that grows them: *Elix Corp.*, Route 1, Arvonia, VA 23004.

Mustard

I consistently use Grey Poupon Dijon mustard, made in the United States.

Oils

The Italian olive oils I use most often are Callisto Francesconi or Sasso, available at *Balducci's* (see Cheese). Olivieri olive oil and Pucci olive oil, from Tuscany, are available through *Williams-Sonoma*, P.O. Box 7456, San Francisco, CA 94120. Some very good California olive oils are available from *Sciabica & Sons*, P.O. Box 1246, Modesto, CA 95353. Kimberley California olive oil is distributed by *San Francisco Cheese Imports*, 1908 Innes Street, San Francisco, CA 94124. The vegetable oils I most often use are Wesson or Hain, a polyunsaturated variety that is largely available in health food stores. In many parts of the world, peanut oil is used for deep frying as it has the unique ability to become intensely hot without burning. I, however, use Crisco shortening. Old-fashioned perhaps, but then in my opinion, so is the art of cooking.

Onions

For a list of growers who sell the Vidalia onion by mail-order, write the *Vidalia Chamber of Commerce*, P.O. Box 306, Vidalia, GA 30474. Walla Walla onions are available from *Walla Walla Gardeners' Association*, 210 N. 11th Street, Walla Walla, WA 99362. For information on Maui onions, write *Ili Ili Farms*, P.O. Box 150-C Kula, Maui, HI 96790.

Rice

I use Carolina brand long grain (unconverted) rice, but I have used others when teaching around the country, even Uncle Ben. But never converted, or instant! Short-grain Italian Arborio rice is generally available everywhere.

Seeds

Just in case you want to grow your own vegetables, Burpee seeds, the old standby, can be ordered from *Burpee Seeds*, Warminster, PA 18991. A fairly new company that specializes in "American Heirloom" varieties, which do not lend themselves to commercial production, is Le Marché. Also available are imported seeds for radicchio, lamb's lettuce, and believe it or not, fourteen kinds of peppers including purple, yellow, and chocolate bell peppers! Write for their catalog: *Le Marché Seeds International*, P.O. Box 566, Dixon, CA 95620.

Soy Sauce

There are a lot of different varieties on the shelf, but Kikkoman is my hands-down choice.

Spices

Perhaps my favorite store in the entire country is Aphrodisia in New York. I don't know of any other shop that carries the variety of spices and dried herbs found there: *Aphrodisia Products, Inc.*, 282 Bleecker Street, New York, NY 10012. Other sources for spices include *The Complete Cook*, 405 Lake Cook Plaza, Deerfield, IL 60015; *La Cuisine*, 323 Cameron Street, Alexandria, VA 22314; and *Oakville Grocery* (see Mushrooms).

Tomatoes, Canned

The best bet is the imported Italian plum. Progresso is the brand I use most often, but San Marsano, although pricier, are highly recommended canned tomatoes.

Tomatoes, Sun-Dried

Pumate sun-dried tomatoes can be mail-ordered from *Dean & Deluca*, 121 Prince Street, New York, NY 10012 and from *Christopher Stephens Importer*, P.O. Box 114, Carversville, PA 18913.

Vinegar

I have used Dessaux Fils, imported from France, for years. Available in red wine and tarragon-flavored white wine vinegars, I am happy to see that it is now being carried in supermarkets everywhere. And no one should be without a bottle of balsamic vinegar on hand. Made only in the Modena province of Italy's Emilia-Romagna, this unique, intensely flavored wine vinegar is aged, and a little goes a long way. One of the best is Fini, carried by *Williams-Sonoma* (see Oils).

GRAINS

REMEMBERING BERT

Shortly after completing the manuscript for *The Grains Cookbook*, Bert Greene died—it was a great loss for his friends and colleagues. Bert brought a tremendous amount of energy to the American cooking community. His spirited classes, cookbooks, and articles gained him millions of fans who enjoyed his accessibility and his unpretentious approach to food.

It was my good fortune to be the editor of Bert's last two cookbooks. It was a real pleasure to work closely with him—Bert's expertise was astounding, and his love of food was infectious—"Suzanne, dear heart, you will learn to love kasha, I promise." He was an editor's dream—a writer with the rare talent to make each recipe perfect and the ability to fill his stories with warmth and humor.

Bert made friends wherever he went. Everyone who read his personable books and articles felt they knew him. But the people who respected his contributions and talents most were his companions in the food community. A few of the many join me in a heartfelt tribute to this terrific man.

Suzanne Rafer

Bert Greene did so much for us all, first with his pioneering store in the Hamptons, which pointed the good direction for so many who came after him. His books and his newspaper column gave inspiration to the hordes of followers who are good cooks today because of his encouraging approach. He was a generous and imaginative friend, a fine teacher, and thank heaven he didn't take off without leaving us his last word—this splendid typically perfectly wonderfully Bert Greene book.

Julia Child

Bert, whom I knew for many years during his stay in the Hamptons, was an inspired and inventive cook. He was a quiet man, a gentle man, and he lives on vibrantly through his recipes.

Craig Claiborne

Bert was a big man—big in size, generosity, laughter, and knowledge. I remember, vividly, walking down a Village street one day between Bert and Jim Beard, feeling like a happy dwarf. If Bert had one particular gift, it was making people feel comfortable with food that challenged them. They sensed his contagious enthusiasm and warmth and were encouraged to cook—the best reward for a food writer.

Barbara Kafka

Bert had a great gift for taking his work but not himself seriously. He was a big, stylish bear of a man who drew people to him with warmth and grace. I treasured him because he was truly cultured in an uncultured age, but even more because he never fell victim to the pomposity and inflated sense of self-importance that afflicts so many who achieve stardom in the kingdom of food. What I remember most is the laughter we shared over the years. What I think the world will best remember is Bert as the friendly voice, the encourager of other less-than-expert cooks. From the early days of his career, he made the kind of real, full-flavored, unfussy food that we are once again learning to appreciate in this country. Bert Greene left an important and substantial legacy.

Ila Stanger

What I like about Bert Greene's work is the unpretentiousness of it. He had a rare gift for describing the way things really are, always with clear vision, embracing generosity, and unfailing good humor. I will surely miss this master of American cooking.

Paula Wolfert

There was a poignant last line in Bert's obituary in *The New York Times*: "There were no survivors." It was wrong. There are thousands of survivors and we need only read his vibrant words to know that he will always be with us—encouraging, helping, and inspiring. His own pleasure in sharing good food with good friends has ensured him a permanent place at our table.

Irena Chalmers

Bert Greene had more style and more taste than almost anyone I know. He also had more love to give. You can savor all of these qualities when you make a Bert Greene recipe. Even if you never had the great pleasure of knowing him and loving him back, as soon as you dig into one of his dishes you recognize the care, skill, and concern that went into devising it. It is always enormously delicious, comforting, nurturing, honest food, informed by Bert's meticulous historical, social, nutritional, and culinary research. But it is also inventive food created by a man whose sensibilities never allowed him to do anything without putting his stamp on it.

Arthur Schwartz

Bert did everything with enthusiasm and panache whether it was moderating a seminar, writing a cookbook, demonstrating a dish, or cooking dinner for friends. He was fun, funny, and a friend.

Jean Hewitt

Bert struck me as being a very warm and gentle man. One of his most attractive qualities was his strong advocacy of newcomers to the food world. He was constantly searching out exciting recipes and people. Whenever we ate together in a restaurant, we'd always go into the kitchen to visit the chef. Bert was inquisitive without being pedantic, and never flaunted his vast knowledge or who he was.

Jacques Pépin

It was typical of Bert to embrace an idea, a cause, a person with spontaneous gusto—then slowly grow into the depth and breadth of his commitment. Such was the case with grains, which he had once enjoyed as mere gravy-holders, then understood to be nutritional blessings, then began to perceive as culinary delights: flavorful, defined, distinct, delicious—worthy of his considerable attention.

Elizabeth Schneider

Bert Greene was a strong writer who never seemed to lose his way. He always knew exactly what good was. His taste grew from a love of home cooking—nothing fancy, just things he liked. His food is impressive and hospitable without trying to be.

Marion Cunningham

Bert Greene's work was very personal in that he never tried to be trendy, but wrote about what he believed in. He was a sincere, generous, charming man who knew the proper flavor boundaries of the foods he wrote about. Bert has left us a body of recipes solidly rooted in tradition. Their homespun quality makes them seem as sincere as he was.

Mimi Sheraton

Bert was a giant of a man. His laughter and wit, and love of life and food, filled a room as well as the pages of his books. His great gift of life lives on in his writing, where those of us who love him can find his voice as we turn the pages and cook his food.

Nathalie Dupree

Bert Greene was a very wise man. He had an innate knowledge and appreciation of flavor which even the greatest chefs do not always possess. This is probably the wisest of all his books.

M.F.K. Fisher

Bert was one of the truly great human beings with an enormous capacity for life and for love and I loved him with a whole heart. He was honest, intelligent, loyal, caring, passionate, and kind, and his friendship enriched my life. I know that of all Bert's work he was especially proud of *Grains*. I am so grateful he lived to complete it.

Rose Levy Beranbaum

There's no mysterious, mystical aspect to Bert's cooking. The magic is Bert himself. He understood better than any other the palate and cuisine of America. He won our hearts with a warm honest message that came across loud and clear. Bert was truly eclectic and this was reflected in his food, which is made up of a daring alliance of ingredients. The dishes he prepared were robust and rustic, creating downright satisfying flavors. We associate such food with love and warmth shared with family and friends. Bert Greene was a true maverick of his time.

Julie Sahni

Bert and I were friends over the last few years. I always admired how he approached his work with warmth and enthusiasm. His knowledge of food and what tasted good was dominant throughout his cooking classes and demonstrations. When Bert taught, you learned.

Bradley Ogden

His marvelous sense of humor, his great gifts, his warmth, always make you rush to try his mouthwatering recipes. This book is a must.

Guiliano Bugialli

Bert Greene was a dear friend—a gentle giant of a man who touched my heart with his tremendous capacity for sharing himself with others. This multi-talented man brought a full measure of magic to whatever he did, leaving a loving imprint on thousands of lives. Bert once said that "books are a writer's children." Indeed, he breathed life into each and every one of his literary offspring with his warm, candid style, liberally laced with wit, humor, and to use a *Bertism*, a healthy dose of "stovetop logic." And, though the man is gone, his magic will be with us forever because he left us all with a priceless legacy—seven of his progeny to read and treasure and remember him by. Thank you, dear friend.

Sharon Tyler Herbst

GREENE ON GRAINS

When I first decided to write a book about grains, it was with decided misgivings. These "high-fiber foods," as nutritionists call them, were being ignored by much of the population, yet they were being touted in every newspaper and magazine as major sources of complex carbohydrates, fiber, and vitamins—what we all need to protect against heart disease, cancer, and digestive distress. But it was no wonder they were being overlooked. For though I remembered how deliciously grains could be prepared by good old-fashioned cooks, I also knew how they tasted at many a modern health food restaurant: *Boring!*

My late grandmother, no mean hand at stirring a pot of grains, had a philosophy on the subject that made me her kitchen convert the moment I heard it espoused.

"Things that are supposed to be good for you," I recall her saying, "should keep the secret of their good intentions strictly to themselves!"

And so say I. My feelings about grains are exactly the same as my feelings about the other wonderful foods that I have written of in the past. "Does it taste good?" is the only prerequisite for a dish's inclusion in my books. If it does not, I pass it by—no matter what vitamin valhalla is promised as my just reward. For food, like love, must never be a joyless experience.

My prejudice against conspicuously joyless consumption harks back to the late 1960s when as a sort of experiment, I elected to give up all the foods I normally ate (like meat, fish, fowl, eggs, cream, milk, butter, and cheese) for a strict regimen of grains and greens alone.

The meals were taken at an urban commune in New York City's East Village and were prepared by a group of very young men and women who viewed my age and ample size with ill-concealed mistrust.

What I recollect best of that dim excursion into self-denial is not the meals (which, to be kind, were rudimentary) but the attitude of my fellow diners who so righteously consumed them. To a man and woman, every young person ate just what was placed before them—without salt, pepper, or any genuine relish. They all might have been denizens at some correctional facility, for there were tin plates and plastic forks and no conversation whatsoever. Since food is not (and never was) a penance to me, I left this cold commune fast.

Of course, by the early '80s, I had returned to greens with renewed interest and a happier approach, and turned out recipes for dishes that my friends have since enjoyed. Now it seems to me that the time is ripe to enlist grains in dishes that brim with exciting flavors.

When I started dipping and sifting into grains, I literally fell in love with the subject. And, like all infatuated men before me, became obsessed with the nuances and diversities of each and every one that ever existed—from barley to wild rice and even beyond. Grains boring? Certainly no longer!

It has been a four-year labor of love that I sometimes thought would never be completed. But here it is, Greene's colossus of fact, lore, and nutrition. And, naturally, splendid recipes.

A cookbook of fiber-rich, complex-carbohydrate foods that taste delicious. My grandmother would have been proud!

Bert Greene

BARLEY

The Wholesome, Low-Gluten Grain

Barley is a grain I have associated with a steaming soup kettle for most of my life. Most, but not all. And therein lies a tale, of course.

My redoubtable grandmother, Minna Cohn, had a weakness for nursing. "The Jewish Florence Nightingale" is how my grandfather jocularly referred to his wife (usually behind her back). Not without a kernel of truth too, for this lady actively sought to nurture and nourish the ailing, whether they resided in her own bailiwick or somewhere up the block. And her husband's bantering never deterred her from what she considered her appointed rounds.

"People could call me worse things"— she would say as she shrugged elaborately—"than a *maidel* with a lamp!"

The important thing was keeping the world at large vital and vertical, and to this end she made soup—very often barley soup—three quarters of every calendar year.

I can clearly recall how she would part the curtain of her kitchen window, sniffing like a bird-dog and peering at the sky for significant weather signs. From November to May, any sudden mass of cumulus clouds floating over the garage roof sent her scurrying to the pantry and icebox like a shot.

Scooping up a handful of barley and a packet of dried mushrooms here, a carrot and a can of tomatoes there, she would assemble those ingredients together with a beef bone and compose the most stirring antitoxin one could ever imagine—without a written recipe or a side trip to the greengrocer or butcher! Instinct and common culinary sense produced her pottage. And I am sorry to report that none of her four daughters, or their progeny either, inherited that masterful art.

But barley in my grandmother's kitchen, inspiring as it might be in a soup spoon, was sharply limited to that use alone. I never knew there were other strings to the grain's bow until I went to Russia over forty years later.

The trip was part of a cultural exchange between the U.S. and the U.S.S.R. back in the early 1970s, during an unexpected thaw in international relations. Members of the tour had obviously been handpicked for this view of life behind the Iron Curtain, because the group was certainly composed of disparate types: businessmen, teachers, a painter, a union official, a therapist, and a Methodist minister. Plus a cook! A collection of fellow Americans politically limp—without a hint in any of our heads of what life in Russia would truly be like.

The travelers met (warily) for the first time at Kennedy Airport an hour before the scheduled flight time. Aloof at first, we became somewhat less reserved—one might say almost familial—during the next half dozen hours, as delay after delay prolonged our departure.

Initially we killed time saluting the good fortune that bound us together by chugging expensive Russian vodka at every cocktail bar in the airport. Later, ravenously hungry and hung over by turns, we chewed stale candy bars and antacid tablets aboard the stalled liner itself—a chill haven (an Aeroflot jet) that we had eventually been shepherded into by a crew of clearly disapproving flight attendants. Two of whom, female, inexplicably sprayed the air with cologne as each unsteady passenger groped for his or her seat in the semi-dark.

The scent they atomized (which we came to know very well indeed in the weeks that followed) is one of two aromas that pervade all public buildings and vehicles in the Soviet Union. Known as "Moscow Nights," this fragrance hangs in the air like an impenetrable fog from Tashkent to Kiev, recalling nothing so much as the floribundant deodorants used in latrines all over the world.

The other smell, rather more inviting to the nostrils, is scorched barley.

This heady essence, always inhaled outdoors, rises from blackened iron pots hung from tripods on street corners in every Russian city. At these urban islands, crews of construction workers—uniformly women of indeterminate age and overwhelming size—stir their breakfast, lunch, and sometimes even dinner over banked fires.

These middle-aged-to-very-ancient women perform all manner of manual labor. With incredible physical strength and endurance, they haul blocks of concrete out of the pavement with their bare hands and manipulate trip-hammers, steamrollers, even monster industrial cranes, without so much as dislodging a lock of hair from their babushkas.

It came as something of a surprise, my second day in Moscow, to come upon a band of these Amazons laying down their shovels to take turns stirring a pot of barley over the fire. And more of a shock to observe them spooning the grains—seasoned with nothing except singed onion or garlic—into dainty bowls which they then passed around to one another like cakes at a tea party.

Barley is obviously the pause that refreshes in Russia.

In light of my aromatic memories, it is not surprising to discover that the Union of Soviet Socialist Republics is the world's leading barley grower. Point of fact: Over 20 million tons of this grain are produced (and shortly thereafter consumed) on Russian soil each year. But then, *Hordeum vulgare*, as barley is formally known, has a long and laureate history as fodder for woman, man, and beast.

The Grain's Genesis

Humans have been eating barley for years. How long? Agronomists and archeologists seem not to concur, but traces of Stone Age cakes, devised of wheat and barley baked in the sun, indicate clearly that the amount of barley grain in the prehistoric dinner pail outweighed the wheat kernels by a ratio of five to one. No mere jot of culinary trivia, that preponderance reveals an important fact: barley has always been one of *Homo sapiens'* handy sources of supply.

A versatile crop that farmers love, with its short growing season and excessively robust leaf stalks, barley is also one of the hardiest perennials around, able to withstand drought, flood, frost, and in a pinch, pestilence too. If that doesn't explain its popularity with the green-thumbed set, try this: In one form or another, barley can be harvested from the upper reaches of the Arctic to the tropic plains of the Equator! In both climes, its wholesome, low-gluten grain has been a chief source of intestinal fortitude (in cereal and flour) as well as intemperate behavior (in beer and malt spirits) for literally a millennium.

The Chinese (who always seemed to

be the first to eat anything) are generally credited as being the earliest barley eaters. Shards of Hsia Dynasty pottery, dated circa 1520 B.C., clearly depict the end of a great famine, with hulled barley falling like rain out of the heavens directly into a peasant family's rice bowl.

Which may not be as mythic as it appears. In the green pockets of northern Asia four thousand years ago, this plant grew wild. But the untended crop came to seed so precipitately that food gatherers were forced to set up tents at the field's edge, to watch the ripening kernels lest they shattered unexpectedly and sent their spoils blowing in the wind.

Barley was not just a movable feast in China; it became, in time, the basis for formal agriculture all over Asia when flimsy tents were replaced with solid farm dwellings and itinerant gleaners turned into domesticated planters.

From the beginning, man always knew he would not want for sustenance as long as his barley crop sprouted. He also learned to grind the grain to make flour for bread and malt for brew. And while low-gluten barley made a rather bitter quaff and a loaf only the strong-toothed could chew, the muscle-men who built the Pyramid of Cheops thrived on both. Their allotment for a day's labor? Three loaves of bread and a ration of beer. Both, needless to say, fortified with barley because it was cheap and available!

Barley is still a bargain, one cup of dried expanding to four times that amount in a saucepan.

Some Plain Grain Talk

Barley kernels are tough buds. Each kernel is protected by three layers of skin: two inedible husks that harbor the germ (or embryo) of the plant, and another delicate covering known as the *aleurone*, which shields the endosperm, a nubbin that gives barley its starchy bulk.

Unfortunately when barley is refined for human consumption (animals eat it in the rough), the husks, aleurone, and embryo are washed away in the polishing process—leaving only the endosperm (or pearl), which is the white barley that consumers are accustomed to finding on supermarket shelves.

Without aleurone, a healthy margin of barley's nutritional composition is seriously diminished, including loss of protein, valuable fiber, and B vitamins. However, in passing it must be noted that a cup of cooked pearl barley still offers the same amount of protein as a glass of milk, along with hearty increments of niacin, thiamine, and potassium.

Another plus for pearl barley: Scientists at the University of Wisconsin recently announced that a substance that inhibits cholesterol production in the blood has been traced (contrary to all expectation) to the nonfibrous portion of the grain.

How to Buy It

There are several options available to barley buyers: whole hulled barley, pressed barley, and pearl barley. *Whole hulled barley*, brownish gray in color and decidedly gritty to the tooth, can be found only at health food stores or natural food emporiums. Approximately double the cost of pearl barley, it is nutritionally the higher rated. However, hulled barley's excessively fibrous texture and the necessity to soak it overnight prior to cooking will, I suspect, keep all but the deepest-dyed grain lovers at bay.

Asian *pressed barley* (hato mugi) is a grain in common currency in traditional Japanese cookery as well as macrobiotic circles. Slightly larger in size and gummier in texture than conventional white barley, hato mugi is compressed and minimally vitamin-enriched. It is available at Japanese groceries or may be mail-ordered from suppliers who stock Asian products. But in my prejudiced opinion, it is scarcely worth the effort.

With one exception, all the barley recipes in this collection were tested with off-the-shelf *pearl barley*. Pearl barley is not only the most dependable form on the market, it is also a staple with a long pantry life: six to nine months in an airtight container is the manufacturer's guarantee—and longer still if your pantry's temperature hovers around 68°.

How to Cook It

My rule of thumb is to cook pearl barley in boiling water (or broth) at a ratio of 3 cups liquid to 1 cup grains. Cooking time: 35 to 40 minutes. To speed up the cooking process somewhat, and in passing achieve a remarkably fluffy kernel, consider presoaking pearl barley in twice the amount of water as grains for a period of 5 hours or overnight. Cooking time for presoaked barley: 15 minutes flat.

Another tonic cooking method for pearl barley is to parboil it first and steam it later (see below).

I always soak whole hulled barley overnight and use more liquid in the cooking (4 to 4½ cups to 1 cup of grains). Cover the pot and extend the cooking time to 60 minutes. Be sure to check the pot after half the cooking time has elapsed, however, for more liquid is often required.

Like rice, barley may be stirred into a remarkably creamy form of risotto, but never attempt this version with any barley except pearl barley.

HOT STEAMED BARLEY

2 quarts water
Salt to taste
1 cup pearl barley

1. Bring the water to a boil, add salt, and add the barley. Stir once with a wooden spoon so the barley does not stick to the bottom of the pot. When the water returns to boiling, reduce the heat and simmer, uncovered, until barely tender, 20 minutes. Drain in a colander.

2. Place the colander over several inches of boiling water in another pot. (Do not let the bottom of the colander touch the water.) Lay a single layer of paper towels on top of the barley, and steam for at least 30 minutes. Barley can be held this way for several hours without harm.

Serves 4

BARLIED BEEF GRANDMOTHERLY STYLE

*T*o many diners in the Western world, barley's most familiar guise is in a soup bowl. My own first contact with the grain was my grandmother's bespoke pottage, prepared with alacrity whenever I looked peaked or sneezed twice in a row. No matter the state of my health, I never objected to her pharmacopeia, for it was literally the most comforting food I'd ever tasted.

The barley soup that my grandmother stirred up (heavy on the beef, mushrooms, and tomatoes) was a dish that could be eaten with a spoon at the first sitting only. A night's layover in her icebox caused it to become so thick and dense that family members always attacked it with a knife and fork at successive meals. A comparable amalgam of my own—based on my forebear's marvelous concoction—never pretends to be anything other than the stew (or stoup) it actually is!

2 tablespoons vegetable oil
2 to 2¼ pounds beef brisket
2 cloves garlic
7 cups water
½ ounce dried mushrooms, sliced
½ cup water, boiling
1 small onion, chopped
2 medium carrots, peeled and chopped
2 medium parsnips, peeled and chopped
3 medium turnips, peeled and chopped
1 rib celery, finely chopped

5 large fresh mushrooms, coarsely chopped
1 can (14 ounces) plum tomatoes with their juice
3 cups homemade chicken stock (see page 376) or canned broth
3 cups homemade beef stock (see page 377) or canned broth
⅓ cup pearl barley
Pinch of dried thyme
Salt and freshly ground black pepper to taste

1. Heat the oil in a large heavy pot over medium-high heat. Add the meat and sauté it until well browned all over. Remove the brisket to a plate. Add the garlic and 1 cup of the water to the pot, scraping the sides and bottom with a wooden spoon. Return the meat to the pot, and add the remaining 6 cups water. Heat to boiling. Reduce the heat and simmer, covered, skimming the surface occasionally to remove excess fat, 1 hour and 40 minutes.

2. Meanwhile, place the dried mushrooms in a medium-size mixing bowl. Cover them with the boiling water, and let stand 30 minutes. Drain.

3. Discard the garlic from the pot and skim the surface of any remaining fat. Add the onion, carrots, parsnips, turnips, celery, both mushrooms, tomatoes, chicken and beef stock, barley and thyme. Bring to a boil. Reduce the heat and simmer, partially covered, until the meat is very tender, about 1½ hours.

4. To serve: Remove the meat from the pot and cut it into pieces. Return the pieces to the stew. Season with salt and pepper.

Serves 6

GEORGIAN YOGURT AND BARLEY SOUP

A barley soup of a somewhat paler hue than my grandmother's, the following is a residual of my 1970s trip to the U.S.S.R. This seminal dish varies with the sector of the Russian geography in which it is stirred. The most conspicuous version I slurped came from the mountainous region of the Caucasus, where the peasants are all remarkably long in the tooth and credit that longevity to—you guessed it—yogurt and barley!

2 tablespoons unsalted butter
1 large onion, finely chopped
1 clove garlic, minced
⅓ cup pearl barley
4½ cups homemade chicken stock (see page 376) or canned broth
2 eggs, lightly beaten
1 tablespoon all-purpose flour
1½ cups plain yogurt
1 teaspoon chopped fresh mint, or ¼ teaspoon dried
1 teaspoon chopped fresh cilantro (Chinese parsley)
1 teaspoon chopped chives or scallion tops
Salt and freshly ground white pepper to taste

1. Melt the butter in a large heavy pot over medium-low heat. Add the onion; cook 1 minute. Add the garlic; cook 4 minutes longer. Add the barley, tossing well to coat with the onion mixture. Then stir in the chicken stock and heat to boiling. Reduce the heat and simmer, covered, 1 hour. Remove the cover and reduce the heat to low.

2. Combine the eggs with the flour, yogurt, mint, cilantro, and chives in a medium-size bowl. Slowly stir this into the soup. Warm the soup through, but do not allow it to boil. Season with salt and white pepper.

Serves 6

WINTER VEGETABLE AND BARLEY CHOWDER

*B*arley has always been a true cereal of champions. In ancient Athens, according to Pliny the Elder, a mite of barley grains—never less than the amount that would half fill a warrior's helmet—was allotted to every participant in the Olympics. In time, serious gladiators in Thessaly lived on a diet of root vegetables and barley, and the effect of that regimen was so spectacular in hand-to-hand combat that the crowds named them "barley eaters."

Barley and root vegetables are still a heck of a team at the table. For winning evidence, see the unconventional chowder that follows—a champion first course or one-dish dinner.

BARLEY TRIVIA, ANCIENT-STYLE

Back in prebiblical days, Egyptians were cannibals—just like the crocodiles with whom they shared the Nile. In time, however, the former got religion and were persuaded by the goddess Isis along with her brother-husband, Osiris, to dine on barley and wheat instead of their fellow man. But never the crocodiles! As a matter of fact, grain consumption merely made the Egyptians more appetizing to them. It's a wonder that barley, let alone civilization, survived the crunch!

But both did, obviously. Aside from nourishment, the ancient Egyptians also believed that barley had all manner of mystical and medicinal powers. Snakebite, they divined, could be averted by feeding even the most venomous reptile a porridge of barley mixed with honey and wine. There is no report on the survival rate, but as the same cure was claimed to be a prophylactic against hangover, it was probably considerable. As the old Egyptian saying goes . . . You pays your piaster and you takes your choice!

½ cup pearl barley
1 cup water
3 tablespoons unsalted butter
1 cup diced smoked ham
1 large onion, finely chopped
3 cloves garlic, minced
1 medium carrot, peeled and diced
1 medium parsnip, peeled and diced
1 cup diced peeled rutabaga (about ½ small rutabaga)
1 leek, white part only, rinsed well and chopped
1 cup finely shredded cabbage
6 cups homemade chicken stock (see page 376), or one 46-ounce can chicken broth
1 cup heavy or whipping cream
Salt and freshly ground black pepper
Pinch of dried thyme
¼ teaspoon freshly grated nutmeg
⅓ cup freshly grated Parmesan cheese

1. Soak the barley in the water for 6 hours or overnight.

2. Melt the butter in a large heavy pot over medium-low heat. Add the ham; cook until the edges turn gold, about 5 minutes. Stir in the onion; cook 2 minutes. Add the garlic; cook 3 minutes longer. Add the carrot, parsnip, rutabaga, leek, and cabbage. Cook, covered, 10 minutes. Add the chicken stock and heat to boiling. Reduce the heat and simmer, partially covered, 30 minutes.

3. Add the barley and cook for 15 minutes more.

4. Reduce the heat to low, and slowly stir the cream into the chowder. Warm the chowder through, but do not allow it to boil. Add salt and pepper to taste, the thyme, and the nutmeg. Just before serving, sprinkle the surface of the chowder with the cheese.

Serves 6 to 8

BEEF SAUTE WITH BARLEY AND RICE

Because it never dies, barley is sometimes accorded the happy designation "a grain of resurrection." It has also been dubbed (in the Bible) "a fruit of the Lord." For, as the Good Book implies, when there are barley grains in a pot no man goes hungry. For some practical verification of that thought, I suggest you glance at this recipe—a fortuitous amalgam of protein and cereal that amply feeds four to six on a scant pound of meat!

1 pound boneless beef sirloin, trimmed
1 tablespoon unsalted butter
5 to 6 tablespoons olive oil
1 medium onion, finely chopped
1 shallot, finely chopped
½ teaspoon crushed dried hot red peppers
2 cloves garlic, minced
4 shiitake mushrooms (about 2 ounces), sliced
½ cup pearl barley
½ cup Italian arborio rice (see page 258)
3 cups homemade beef stock (see page 377) or canned broth
Salt and freshly ground black pepper to taste
¼ teaspoon chopped fresh sage, or a pinch dried
1½ tablespoons chopped fresh parsley

1. Cut the sirloin into strips 2 inches long, ¼ inch thick, and ½ inch wide. Set them aside.

2. Heat the butter with 1 tablespoon of the oil in a 5- to 6-quart heavy pot or Dutch oven over medium heat. Add the onion, shallot, and dried red peppers; cook 1 minute. Add the garlic; cook 4 minutes longer. Using a slotted spoon,

Like most grains, barley has had many ups and downs in kitchen popularity over the years. As a baker's staple (way back in biblical times), it lost favor to wheat early on because the minimal amount of protein in barley flour contained such a low percentage of gluten that the loaves devised of it were frankly tooth-shattering to all but the hardiest diners. Of a consequence, barley was relegated to porridges and stews that all those less well-molared could digest. In one form or another, soft-cooked barley is still very much a staple at stoves, hearths, and campfires all over the world.

transfer the mixture to a plate.

3. Add 2 tablespoons of the oil to the same pot. Sauté the mushrooms until golden, about 5 minutes. Using a slotted spoon, transfer them to the plate with the onions.

4. Add 2 more tablespoons of the oil to the same pot. Sauté the beef strips, one third at a time, over medium-high heat until browned on all sides. (Add more oil to the pot if needed.) Transfer the beef to a separate plate.

5. Reduce the heat under the pot to medium-low. Add the barley and rice, and stir well. Add the stock, scraping the sides and bottom of the pot with a wooden spoon. Add the reserved onion-mushroom mixture, and heat to boiling.

Then reduce the heat and simmer, covered, over medium-low heat until the barley and rice are tender and almost all the liquid has been absorbed, about 35 minutes.

6. Add the sautéed beef strips and cook, tossing constantly, over medium heat until warmed through, about 5 minutes. Season with salt and pepper, then stir in the sage and parsley.

Serves 4 to 6

CHOLLENT

Chollent is a Jewish pot roast that is generally baked alongside beans, and more often than not, barley. The following is loosely based on a recipe in Fanny Sylverstein's *My Mother's Cookbook*. I first met Fanny, who is a true fan of mine, in 1987. I quickly became a fan of hers, after reading that guileless memoir of her adventures as an immigrant girl on New York's Lower East Side. As an adult she became personal chef to the head of Paramount pictures. Her recipes are as adventurous as her life.

3 tablespoons vegetable oil
1 thick boneless beef chuck roast (3½ to 4 pounds)
1 medium onion, finely chopped
1 clove garlic, minced
1 teaspoon salt
¼ teaspoon freshly ground black pepper
2 teaspoons hot Hungarian paprika
½ teaspoon ground ginger
2 quarts homemade beef stock (see page 377) or canned broth
1 cup dried pink beans
1 cup pearl barley
Chopped fresh parsley, for garnish

1. Preheat the oven to 250°F.

2. Heat the oil in a large Dutch oven over medium-high heat until hot but not smoking. Brown the roast well on all sides, 8 to 10 minutes. Remove the roast to a plate. Reduce the heat under the Dutch oven to medium.

3. Add the onion to the Dutch oven and cook, scraping the bottom and sides of the pot with a wooden spoon, 3 minutes. Add the garlic; cook 2 minutes longer. Stir in the salt, pepper, paprika, and ginger. Stir well, and add the beef stock. Heat to boiling, and then stir in the beans and barley. Bring the mixture to a boil, and add the roast.

4. Place the covered pot in the oven and cook 2½ hours. Stir the mixture, and then continue to cook, partially covered, until the meat is very tender, about 1½ hours longer. Remove the cover completely if the mixture is too wet.

5. To serve: Remove the meat and slice it. Spoon the bean and barley mixture into a large shallow serving dish, and place the meat slices over the top. Sprinkle with parsley.

Serves 6 to 8

BARLEY AND BLACK BEAN CHILI

Chili in startling black and white—literally. A wonderfully festive and flavorful dish for cold, cold weather.

½ pound dried black turtle beans
½ cup diced salt pork (about 3 ounces)
2 cups cubed smoked ham (about ¾ pound)
2 onions, chopped
2 cloves garlic, minced
1 hot green pepper, seeded, deveined, and minced
2 tablespoons olive oil
2½ cups cubed pork (about 1¼ pounds)
2 tablespoons chili powder
¼ cup dark rum
1 tablespoon hot Hungarian paprika
1 teaspoon ground cumin
1 teaspoon chopped fresh oregano, or ¼ teaspoon dried
1 teaspoon chopped fresh basil, or ½ teaspoon dried
4½ cups homemade beef stock (see page 377) or canned broth
1 cup pearl barley
1 tablespoon finely chopped pickled jalapeño peppers
¾ teaspoon crushed dried hot red peppers
Salt and freshly ground black pepper to taste
1 hard-cooked egg, chopped
1 large onion, finely chopped

1. Place the beans in a large pot, and cover with cold water. Heat to boiling; boil 2 minutes. Remove the pot from the heat and let stand 2 hours.

2. Cook the salt pork in boiling water to cover for 2 minutes. Drain, and pat dry with paper towels.

3. Sauté the salt pork in a large heavy ovenproof pot or Dutch oven over medium heat until lightly golden. Raise the heat slightly and add the ham cubes. Continue to sauté until the salt pork is crisp and the ham is lightly browned, about 4 minutes. Transfer with a slotted spoon to a bowl.

4. Add the onions to the pot, and cook over medium-low heat 1 minute. Add the garlic and hot green pepper. Cook 4 minutes. Transfer to the bowl with the ham and salt pork.

5. Add the olive oil to the pot and sauté the pork pieces over medium-high heat 1 minute. Sprinkle the pork pieces with the chili powder and cook 3 more minutes. Stir in the rum, scraping the bottom and sides of the pot. Add the paprika, cumin, oregano, basil, 4 cups of the beef stock, and the black beans. Heat to boiling. Reduce the heat and simmer, covered, 1 hour.

6. Preheat the oven to 350°F.

7. Add the barley and the remaining ½ cup stock to the bean mixture. Cover, transfer the pot to the oven, and bake until the barley is tender and all liquid

Though barley's strong suit is not immediately apparent in an oven, the same Egyptians who regularly rejected it for bread always baked it into decorative cakes on festival days. There was a good reason, of course: Pliable barley formed into animal shapes (pigs, oxen, even hippopotamuses) was an economy measure, allowing the lower classes to simulate the live animal sacrifices of their betters, without the mess or undue stress on their purse strings.

has been absorbed, 35 to 40 minutes. (Remove the cover and cook for 10 minutes if the mixture is too thin.) Add the jalapeño pepper, dried red peppers, and salt and pepper. Bake 10 minutes longer. Serve topped with the chopped egg and finely chopped onion.

Serves 6

BARLEY-CRAMMED ROAST CHICKEN

Barley is a grain often described as having mystical powers. According to my friend Pliny (the best and only early food scribe), ancient soothsayers would scratch the letters of the alphabet in sand, place a grain of barley in each initial, then wait till a wandering bird passed by and pecked at the grains. The letters the bird chose would then be juggled and jawed over until a reasonable meaning could be justified. If we were speaking of the following dish, two words are required: EAT HEARTY.

FOR THE STUFFING
1 ounce pancetta or thick bacon, chopped (about ¼ cup)
1 large shallot, minced
1 teaspoon unsalted butter
1 clove garlic, minced
2 medium tomatoes, seeded and coarsely chopped
1 teasoon chopped fresh basil, or ¼ teaspoon dried
2 cups cooked barley
¼ teaspoon chopped fresh rosemary, or a pinch dried
Dash of hot pepper sauce
Salt and freshly ground black pepper to taste

FOR THE CHICKEN
1 chicken, about 3½ pounds, well rinsed and dried
1 clove garlic, bruised
1 teaspoon unsalted butter, at room temperature
1 slice pancetta or thick bacon
1½ cups homemade chicken stock (see page 376) or canned broth

FOR THE TOMATO GRAVY
1 medium tomato, peeled and seeded
½ teaspoon chopped fresh basil, or ¼ teaspoon dried

1 tablespoon all-purpose flour
Salt and freshly ground black pepper to taste

1. Make the stuffing: Sauté the pancetta in a medium-size saucepan over medium-low heat until it is soft and all grease has exuded, about 4 minutes. Add the shallot; cook 1 minute. Add the butter and garlic; cook 2 minutes longer. Stir in the tomatoes and basil. Raise the heat to medium-high, and cook until the sauce has thickened, 4 to 5 minutes. Remove the pan from the heat, and add the barley, rosemary, hot pepper sauce, and salt and pepper. Toss well and set aside.

2. Roast the chicken: Preheat the oven to 375°F.

3. Wipe the chicken inside and out with a damp paper towel, then pat it dry. Rub the chicken inside and out with the bruised garlic. Spoon the barley stuffing into the cavity; sew and truss the chicken. Rub the breast area with the butter. Cut the slice of pancetta in half, and place the halves over the chicken breast. Roast on a rack 20 minutes, basting often with the chicken stock. Reduce the heat to 350°F and continue to roast, basting occasionally with more stock, until the juices run yellow when the

chicken is pricked with a fork, about 1 hour longer. Transfer the chicken to a roasting platter and remove the trussing string. Let it stand 10 minutes. Degrease the pan juices and set them aside.

4. Make the tomato gravy: Place the tomato, basil, and flour in the container of a food processor or blender. Process until smooth and thick. Transfer the mixture to a small saucepan, place it over medium heat, and cook 1 minute. Stir in 1 cup of the pan juices. Whisk over medium-low heat until slightly thickened. Season with salt and pepper. Serve with the chicken and stuffing.

Serves 2 to 4

JIM-DANDY JAMBALAYA

A jambalaya like this is not to be found in Cajun country, but it sure is jim-dandy.

1 red bell pepper
4 large (about 1 pound) hot Italian sausages
1 cup pearl barley
1 tablespoon unsalted butter
1½ cups chopped scallions, white bulbs and green tops
1 large clove garlic, minced
1 jalapeño pepper, seeded, deveined, and minced, or ⅛ teaspoon crushed dried hot red pepper
3 cups homemade chicken stock (see page 376) or canned broth
¼ teaspoon chopped fresh thyme, or a pinch dried
½ pound thick-sliced smoked ham, cubed
1 pound medium shrimp, shelled and deveined
1 pound bay scallops or quartered sea scallops
Salt and freshly ground black pepper to taste
1 tablespoon chopped fresh parsley

1. Preheat the oven to 350°F.
2. Using a long-handled fork, roast the bell pepper over a gas flame until it is blackened all over; or roast the pepper under a broiler, turning until crisp on all sides. Carefully wrap the pepper in paper towels and place it in a small plastic bag. Set it aside to cool. Then rub the burned peel off with paper towels. Core and seed the pepper, and set it aside.

3. Sauté the sausages in an oil-rubbed 3- to 4-quart Dutch oven over medium heat until well browned on all sides, about 5 minutes. Transfer the sausages to a plate and set aside to cool. Then cut them into ½-inch-thick slices.

4. In the same Dutch oven, sauté the barley over medium heat until lightly browned, about 4 minutes. Add the butter and scallions; cook 1 minute. Add the garlic and jalepeño pepper; cook 5 minutes longer.

5. Place the peeled bell pepper in the container of a food processor or blender. Add 1 cup of the chicken stock and process until smooth. Stir this mixture into the barley mixture, along with the remaining 2 cups stock, the thyme, ham, and sausages. Heat to boiling. Transfer the pot to the oven and bake, covered, 35 minutes.

6. Remove the pot from the oven, and stir in the shrimp and scallops. Return it to the oven and bake, covered, 15 minutes. Remove the cover and bake 5 minutes longer. Remove the pot from the oven and let it stand for 5 minutes. Then add salt and pepper. Before serving, sprinkle with parsley.

Serves 6

STUFFED PEPPERS

This is a variation of my sister's favorite stuffed pepper recipe that substitutes barley for the expected rice.

¾ cup water
Salt to taste
¼ cup pearl barley
4 large red bell peppers
6 sweet Italian sausages (1¼ pounds)
1 onion, finely chopped
1 clove garlic, minced
1 tablespoon Dijon mustard
1 teaspoon hot Hungarian paprika
½ teaspoon salt
⅛ teaspoon freshly ground black pepper
1 egg, lightly beaten
1 teaspoon fresh bread crumbs
2 teaspoons freshly grated Parmesan cheese
2 teaspoons olive oil
Chopped fresh parsley, for garnish

1. Bring the water to a boil in a medium-size saucepan. Add salt to taste and the barley, and simmer, uncovered, until tender, about 35 to 40 minutes. Drain, and set aside in a large mixing bowl.

2. Preheat the oven to 375°F.

3. Trim the tops off the peppers, and remove the cores and seeds. Cook the peppers in boiling salted water to cover for 1 minute. Set aside to drain.

4. Remove the sausage meat from the casings and sauté, breaking up the lumps with a wooden spoon, in a heavy skillet over medium heat until lightly browned, about 8 minutes. Transfer with a slotted spoon to the large mixing bowl and stir together with the barley.

5. Add the onion to the same skillet and cook, scraping the bottom and sides of the pan, over medium-low heat for 1 minute. Add the garlic; cook 4 minutes. Add this to the barley mixture in the bowl.

6. Add the mustard, paprika, salt, pepper, and beaten egg to the barley mixture and mix thoroughly. Fill each pepper cavity with the stuffing, mounding the tops.

7. Place the peppers in a heatproof baking dish that holds them snugly. Sprinkle the top of each pepper with ¼ teaspoon bread crumbs. Then sprinkle each with ½ teaspoon Parmesan, and finally drizzle each with ½ teaspoon olive oil. Bake 50 minutes. Remove from the oven and sprinkle with the parsley.

Serves 4

ANDALUSIAN BARLEY

From Granada. I first tasted the following dish as an adjunct to a plate of *anguilas* (tiny baby eels fried in garlic) after a long, hot, dusty ride on an American Express tourist excursion from Madrid. Proof of the pudding is that I cannot remember a single sight or sound of the splendid cathedral we drove hours to visit, but the barley is printed on my brain forever.

2 chorizos (Spanish sausages) or other spicy
    sausage (about ½ pound), chopped
1 tablespoon unsalted butter
1 medium onion, minced
¼ teaspoon chopped fresh thyme, or a
    pinch dried
1 cup pearl barley
3 cups homemade chicken stock (see page
    376) or canned broth
Salt and freshly ground black pepper to
    taste
½ cup sliced green olives
Chopped fresh parsley, for garnish

1. Sauté the chopped chorizos in a large saucepan over medium-low heat until they are lightly browned and all oil has exuded. With a slotted spoon, transfer the sausages to a dish and set aside.

2. Add the butter to the saucepan and sauté the onion for 2 minutes. Stir in the thyme and barley, tossing well to coat with the onion. Add the stock and chorizos. Heat to boiling. Reduce the heat and simmer, covered, until all the liquid has been absorbed and the barley is tender, 35 to 40 minutes.

3. If the barley seems too chewy, add more broth and continue to cook. If it is too wet, uncover, raise the heat, and cook until the liquid is absorbed. Then add salt and pepper.

4. To serve: Remove the saucepan from the heat. Stir in the olives, and sprinkle with parsley.

Serves 4 to 6

WARM ISLAND SALAD
(Ensalada Isleña)

Barley on the light side—in a seafood salad—to be served any time you need a touch of summer.

3½ cups water
Salt
1 cup pearl barley
1 cup clam juice
¼ cup dry white wine
½ lemon, sliced
1 sprig fresh thyme, or a pinch dried
1 sprig parsley
3- to 4-ounce lobster tail
¼ pound shrimp
½ pound bay scallops or quartered sea
    scallops
4 scallions, white bulbs and green tops,
    chopped
1 cucumber, peeled, seeded, and diced

1 small zucchini, diced
½ cup sliced radishes (about 1 bunch)
2 tablespoons minced red bell pepper
2 tablespoons chopped fresh basil
1 clove garlic, crushed
1 teaspoon Dijon mustard
¼ cup olive oil
1 tablespoon fresh lemon juice

1. Bring 3 cups of the water to a boil in a medium-size saucepan. Add salt to taste and the barley, and simmer, uncovered until just tender, 35 to 40 minutes. Drain, and set aside.

2. Combine the clam juice, wine, remaining ½ cup water, lemon slices, thyme, and parsley in a medium-size heavy saucepan. Heat to boiling, then reduce the heat. Add the lobster tail and gently poach until pink and firm, 3 to 5 minutes. Using a slotted spoon, transfer it to a plate. Add the shrimp to the saucepan; cook 3 minutes. Transfer them to the plate. Add the scallops to the saucepan and poach until barely firm, about 3 minutes. Transfer them to a bowl. Raise the heat under the saucepan and reduce the stock to ¼ cup. Strain and reserve.

3. Clean and devein the shrimp and cut each in half crossways. Clean the lobster tail and cut into pieces.

4. In a large bowl, combine the barley, scallions, cucumber, zucchini, radishes, red bell pepper, basil and the seafood. Toss well.

5. In another bowl, use the back of a spoon to mash the garlic and ½ teaspoon salt together to form a paste. Stir in the mustard and the reserved fish stock. Whisk in the oil and lemon juice. Pour this dressing over the barley-seafood mixture, and mix well.

Serves 6 to 8

GREEN BARLEY

*F*rom The Marches of northern Italy. In spring, the farmers' wives there stir barley (or rice) into a *brodo* made of any strong-flavored greens they can find growing outside their kitchen doors. It purifies the sluggish winter blood—that's the claim— but it also rejuvenates the slack tongue after a night on the town.

2 tablespoons unsalted butter
1 medium onion, finely chopped
1 clove garlic, minced
2 cups finely chopped Swiss chard and
*   arugula leaves, mixed*
1 cup pearl barley
1 slice prosciutto, minced
3 cups homemade chicken stock (see page
*   376) or canned broth*
⅛ teaspoon freshly grated nutmeg
¼ cup chopped fresh parsley
2 tablespoons chopped chives or scallion
*   tops*
Salt and freshly ground black pepper to
*   taste*

1. Melt the butter in a large saucepan over medium-low heat. Add the onion; cook 1 minute. Add the garlic; cook 2 minutes longer. Stir in the chopped greens, tossing to coat with the onion mixture. Add the barley, prosciutto, chicken stock, and nutmeg. Heat to boiling. Reduce the heat and simmer, covered, until all the liquid has been absorbed and the barley is tender, 35 to 40 minutes.

2. If the barley seems too chewy, add more broth and continue to cook. If it is too wet, uncover, raise the heat slightly, and cook until the liquid is absorbed. Then stir in the parsley and chives, and add salt and pepper.

Serves 4 to 6

CZECH BARLEY AND PEAS

An absolutely unforgettable taste from Prague. Proper Czech housewives, incidentally, mate their barley with dried peas, but to my tongue, fresh (or frozen) *petit pois* are the grain's true-blue partner.

3 cups water
Salt to taste
1 cup pearl barley
2 strips bacon
⅓ cup julienned smoked ham
1 medium onion, finely chopped
1 package (10 ounces) frozen peas
2 tablespoons homemade chicken stock (see
    page 376) or canned broth
4 fresh sage leaves, minced, or ¼ teaspoon
    dried
½ teaspoon minced fresh marjoram leaves,
    or a pinch dried
Freshly ground black pepper to taste

1. Bring the water to a boil in a medium-size saucepan. Add salt and the barley, and simmer, uncovered, until just tender, 35 to 40 minutes. Drain.

2. Meanwhile, sauté the bacon in a large heavy skillet over medium heat until crisp. Drain on paper towels, leaving the fat in the skillet. Crumble and reserve the bacon.

3. Add the ham to the skillet. Sauté it until the edges are lightly browned, about 4 minutes. Transfer with a slotted spoon to a plate, and set aside.

4. Add the onion to the drippings in the skillet. Cook over medium heat 2 minutes. Add the frozen peas and cook, stirring constantly, until the peas are thawed, 2 to 3 minutes. Stir in the reserved ham and barley. Add the chicken stock, and cook over medium-low heat until warmed through. Stir in the sage and marjoram leaves, and season with salt and pepper to taste.

Serves 4 to 6

If you are of the impression that *barleycorn* is something to be gulped neat, or with a chaser of H_2O, you're only half right!

Though the name came to be synonymous with malt spirits over the years, a barleycorn (which is the seed of the barley plant) was once a standard measure of length. In the early 14th century, in fact, a royal fiat of the House of Tudor resolved: *All metric units be standardized as one inch being equal to three grains of barleycorn, laid end to end.*

The same decree also designated the running foot as being equal to 39 barleycorns, and the linear yard as being equal to 117 barleycorns. Presumably still end to end.

Curious as all that may seem, the next fact is even more bizarre: Barleycorn remained the basis of all metric calibration in Great Britain, and in America as well, for the next four hundred years. In 1888, when the U.S. shoe industry was first formally consolidated in Lynn, Massachusetts, a press statement announced that the established shoe size 13, or 39 barleycorns, would be the largest regularly manufactured last.

Apparently no allowance was made for any extremity that exceeded the limitation. But that's when the other barleycorn probably came into the picture: gulped neat, to ease aching feet!

STIR-FRIED BARLEY

*F*rom Stockton, California, not Shanghai. This Asian mixture was demonstrated for me at a TV studio, after a stove-top appearance on a local morning show a while back. Whole hulled barley in the wok gives this stir-fry a very different, nutty quality. But lightly toasted pearl barley (stirred over medium heat in a dry pan until golden prior to boiling) will approximate the bite. If you use pearl barley, omit the soaking step.

½ cup whole hulled barley
6 cups water
Salt to taste
1 tablespoon olive oil
1 large shallot, minced
½ teaspoon crushed dried hot red peppers
2 teaspoons unsalted butter
2 teaspoons chopped fresh basil, or ½
*   teaspoon dried*
½ teaspoon tomato paste
Pinch of beef bouillon powder
Freshly ground black pepper to taste

1. Soak the barley overnight in 3 cups of water. Drain.

2. Bring the 6 cups water to a boil in a medium-size saucepan. Add salt to taste and the barley, and simmer, uncovered, until tender, about 1 hour. Drain, and set aside.

3. Heat the oil in a wok or large skillet over medium heat. Add the shallot and dried red peppers. Cook 2 minutes. Stir in the butter and the barley. Cook, tossing constantly, until warmed through. Stir in the basil, tomato paste, and bouillon powder. Cook 1 minute. Season with salt and pepper to taste.

Serves 4

BARLEY GOATEE

*F*rom Provence, France. A dish invented by an American friend turned into a thrifty French housewife by marriage. No mean chef, the lady devised this casserole without forethought—from only the barest ingredients in her minuscule refrigerator—when a guest from the U.S. (yours truly) arrived unexpectedly for lunch. The dish's name? Another improvisation, this one concocted after two bottles of local wine.

1½ cups water
Salt to taste
½ cup pearl barley
2½ tablespoons unsalted butter
1 medium onion, finely chopped
1 clove garlic, minced
2 tablespoons minced red bell pepper

¼ teaspoon crushed dried hot red peppers
3 egg whites
Pinch of salt
Pinch of sugar
1⅓ cups coarsely grated aged goat cheese
Freshly ground black pepper to taste

1. Bring the water to a boil in a

medium-size saucepan. Add salt to taste and the barley, and simmer, uncovered, until just tender, 35 to 40 minutes. Drain, and set aside.

2. Preheat the oven to 425°F.

3. Melt the butter in a medium-size skillet over medium-low heat. Add the onion; cook 1 minute. Add the garlic, red bell pepper, and dried red peppers; cook 4 minutes longer.

4. Add the barley to the skillet, tossing well to coat it with the onion mixture. Cook, stirring occasionally, 5 minutes. Transfer to a bowl.

5. In a large bowl, beat the egg whites with the salt until soft peaks form. Sprinkle with the sugar, and beat until stiff but not dry. Stir one third of the egg whites into the barley mixture. Then fold in the remaining whites. Fold in 1 cup of the goat cheese.

6. Spoon the mixture into a well-buttered shallow ovenproof casserole or pie plate. Sprinkle the top with the remaining ⅓ cup goat cheese, then sprinkle with black pepper. Bake until golden, 18 to 20 minutes.

Serves 4

GREEN BEAN AND BARLEY CAKES

*B*arley is a grain much prized as a green. In the Middle Ages the tender stalks were traditionally woven into bridal wreaths. Before that, in Rome, barley sprig motifs were common currency on ancient coins, and they appeared often as symbols of replenishment on Greek temple architecture. Why? Because barley never withers; as soon as one stalk is reaped another takes its place—literally evergreen. Speaking of which, have one of my favored barley alliances, wreathed in very green beans.

¼ pound string beans, trimmed
1 cup cooked pearl barley, chilled
1 tablespoon minced shallot
1 teaspoon minced jalapeño pepper
1 egg, lightly beaten
1 cup grated Monterey Jack cheese (about
*   4 ounces)*
1 cup fresh bread crumbs
3 to 4 tablespoons vegetable oil
Salt and freshly ground black pepper to
*   taste*

1. Preheat the oven to 225°F.

2. Cook the string beans in boiling salted water until tender, 5 minutes. Drain, and set aside to cool. Then finely chop the beans.

3. In a large bowl, combine the beans with the barley, shallot, jalapeño pepper, egg, and cheese. Mix well.

4. Spread the bread crumbs on a plate. Scoop up 1 tablespoon of barley mixture and using your finger, push it from the spoon into the crumbs. Pat the crumbs into both sides of the cake. Transfer it to a plate, and repeat until you have used up all the barley mixture.

5. Heat 3 tablespoons oil in a large heavy skillet over medium-low heat. Sauté the barley cakes until golden brown and crisp, about 4 minutes per side. Keep them warm in the oven until all the cakes have been sautéed. (Add more oil to the skillet if needed.) Before serving, sprinkle the barley cakes with salt and pepper.

Serves 4

WILD MUSHROOM AND BARLEY RISOTTO

A switch on the familiar rice dish. Barley gives a slightly more chewy texture to risotto and should be served with nothing more than a leafy green salad.

2 tablespoons unsalted butter
1 teaspoon olive oil
¼ pound fresh shiitake, pleurotte,
    chanterelle, or oyster mushrooms (or
    any combination of wild mushrooms),
    sliced
1 large shallot, minced
1 small clove garlic, minced
⅓ cup dry white wine
½ cup pearl barley
3½ cups homemade chicken stock (see page
    376) or canned broth, heated
Chopped fresh parsley, for garnish
Freshly grated Parmesan cheese (optional)

1. Melt 1 tablespoon of the butter with the oil in a large heavy skillet over medium-high heat. Add the mushrooms; cook, tossing constantly, until lightly browned, 4 minutes. Transfer to a bowl, using a slotted spoon, and set aside.

2. Reduce the heat under the skillet to low. Add the remaining 1 tablespoon butter and stir in the shallot; cook 1 minute. Add the garlic; cook 4 minutes longer. Stir in the wine, scraping the bottom and sides of the pan. Heat to boiling; boil until slightly syrupy, about 4 minutes. Reduce the heat to medium-low, add the barley and mushrooms, and stir until well coated with shallot mixture. Stir in 1 cup of the hot stock. Cook, stirring frequently, until all liquid has been absorbed, about 15 minutes. (If the liquid absorbs too quickly, reduce the heat.)

3. Stir in another cup of stock and continue to cook, stirring frequently, until all liquid has been absorbed, about 15 minutes.

4. Add another cup of stock and continue to cook, stirring frequently, until all liquid has been absorbed, about 15 minutes.

5. Add the remaining ½ cup of stock and continue to cook until the barley is tender and all liquid has been absorbed, about 15 minutes. Raise the heat slightly if the mixture is too wet. Sprinkle with parsley, and serve with Parmesan cheese if desired.

Serves 4

BARLEY DUMPLINGS

First cousin to Italian gnocchi rather than any American pot kin, the following snowy morsels are not only delectable but salubrious to one's well-being in the bargain. For the record—and putting the butter and cheese topping aside—a cupful of these dumplings is tabbed at less than 100 calories per serving! You can, by the way, literally put the butter and cheese aside and serve these dumplings with a tomato sauce.

1½ cups water
Salt
½ cup pearl barley
¼ teaspoon freshly ground black pepper
1 egg yolk
¼ teaspoon finely minced jalapeño pepper
½ cup grated Monterey Jack cheese
4 tablespoons freshly grated Parmesan
    cheese
1 cup all-purpose flour
2 extra-large egg whites
3 tablespoons unsalted butter, melted
Freshly grated Parmesan cheese, for garnish
    (optional)

1. Bring the water to a boil in a medium-size saucepan. Add salt to taste and the barley, and simmer, uncovered, until very tender, about 1 hour. Drain, and set aside to cool. Then cover and refrigerate the barley.

2. Preheat the oven to 375°F.

3. Place the chilled barley in the container of a food processor, and process until smooth. Add ¼ teaspoon salt, the pepper, egg yolk, jalapeño pepper, Monterey Jack cheese, and 3 tablespoons of the Parmesan cheese. Process briefly. Add ¼ cup of the flour and process until just mixed. Transfer the mixture to a large bowl.

4. Beat the egg whites until stiff but not dry. Fold them into the barley mixture. Fold in ¼ cup of the flour.

5. Place the remaining ½ cup flour in a shallow bowl. With a spoon (about 2 tablespoons in size), scoop up the barley dough and drop it into the flour, scraping the dough from the spoon with your finger. Lightly roll the dough in flour, and then transfer it to a plate. Repeat until you have used up all the dough.

6. Cook the dumplings, about six at a time, in a deep pot of boiling salted water, 1 minute. Remove the dumplings with a slotted spoon, and lightly drain them on paper towels. Transfer the cooked dumplings to a buttered baking dish that is large enough to hold them in a single layer. When all the dumplings have been cooked, drizzle them with the melted butter, and sprinkle with the remaining 1 tablespoon Parmesan cheese. Bake 20 minutes. Serve with extra Parmesan cheese, if desired.

Serves 4 to 6

ITALIAN-STYLE BARLEY TORTE

A dense fruited confection, this is dubbed "Italian-style" because it is based on a classic Venetian rice cake of similar texture and taste. Serve it with freshly whipped cream flavored with a dab of sour cream.

6 cups water
2 cups milk
¾ cup pearl barley
½ cup plus 2 tablespoons sugar
2 tablespoons fresh bread crumbs
2 jumbo eggs, separated
1 jumbo egg, lightly beaten
8 tablespoons (1 stick) unsalted butter,
    melted
¾ cup all-purpose flour
1 teaspoon baking powder
2 tablespoons hazelnut liqueur
½ teaspoon vanilla extract
2 dried pineapple slices, finely chopped
6 dried apricots, finely chopped (about ¼
    cup)
1 teaspoon finely slivered orange zest
1 teaspoon finely slivered lemon zest
1 tablespoon unsalted butter, at room
    temperature

1. Heat the water and milk to boiling in a large pot. Stir in the barley. Reduce the heat and simmer, uncovered, stirring occasionally, 1 hour. Raise the heat slightly and stir until the mixture is thickened and creamy. Remove the pot from the heat, and immediately stir in the ½ cup sugar. Let the mixture stand 10 minutes, then transfer it to a large bowl.

2. Preheat the oven to 375°F.

3. Butter a 10-inch glass or ceramic quiche dish, and dust it with bread crumbs. In a small bowl, beat the egg yolks with the whole egg, and stir this into the barley mixture. Add the melted butter, flour, baking powder, hazelnut liqueur, vanilla, pineapple, apricots, and orange and lemon zests. Mix well.

4. Beat the egg whites until stiff but not dry. Fold them into the barley mixture.

5. Pour the barley mixture evenly into the prepared quiche dish. Sprinkle the top with the 2 tablespoons sugar, and dot with the 1 tablespoon butter. Bake until slightly puffed and firm to the touch, about 40 minutes. Serve slightly warm.

Serves 8

THE FLOURING OF THE GRAIN

Barley flour has been used in bread making since ancient times. Early on, it was recognized as a high-energy, low-fat ingredient—generally turned into somewhat dense, chewy flatbreads that were not only filling for the workers in the fields, but just as important, kept almost indefinitely.

Today, barley flour is used mainly as a flavoring agent. Slightly sweet, with a mild malty undertaste, it gives new dimensions to old standbys, adding moisture to a dish along the way. However, since barley flour is very low in gluten, it must be mixed with a high-protein wheat flour for use in baking. A general rule of thumb is to substitute ½ cup of barley flour for an equal amount of whole-wheat or bread flour in any of your favorite bread recipes. You will have a healthier, more flavorful loaf of bread as a result.

Barley flour is generally made from ground whole hulled barley, which is then sieved to remove the tough outer shell.

BARLEY SCOTCH EGGS

Barley flour, when used instead of wheat flour or bread crumbs in the sausage coating for Scotch eggs, keeps the mixture from drying out. These eggs may be served hot or at room temperature as an appetizer or party fare.

¾ pound country-style sausage meat
6 tablespoons barley flour
4 hard-cooked eggs, peeled and halved
    lengthwise
1 egg, lightly beaten
½ teaspoon salt
½ teaspoon freshly ground black pepper
Oil for deep-frying

1. Place the sausage meat in a medium-size bowl. Add 2 tablespoons of the flour; mix thoroughly. Place the sausage between two sheets of wax paper, and roll it out until it is about ⅛ inch thick. Remove the top layer of wax paper, and using a sharp knife, cut the sausage into eight sections (without cutting through the bottom layer of wax paper).

2. Place 2 more tablespoons of the flour in a bowl. Dip each cooked egg half in the beaten egg, and then roll it in the flour. Place each egg half on a sausage section, and roll the sausage around the egg, pressing the edges together to seal it tightly.

3. Heat about 3 inches of oil in a small heavy saucepan until it is hot but not smoking.

4. Place the remaining 2 tablespoons flour in a bowl. Add the salt and pepper; mix well. Roll the sausage-coated eggs in the seasoned flour, and deep-fry (about four at a time) in the hot oil until crisp, about 2 minutes. Drain on paper towels.

Serves 4

BARLEY FLATBREAD

The Scots have their scones, the Welsh their *haidd*. This version of the Welsh bread is best served straight from the oven and slathered with butter and/or honey. The bread mixture is more like a thick crepe batter than dough. I make it in a 12-inch non-stick pizza pan. Leftovers may be toasted and served for breakfast the next day.

3 tablespoons olive oil
1 medium onion, chopped
1 clove garlic, minced
¼ teaspoon crushed dried hot red peppers
1½ cups barley flour
1¼ cups milk
¼ cup water
1 tablespoon sugar
½ teaspoon salt

1. Place an oven rack in the upper third of the oven. Preheat the oven to 500°F.

2. Heat 1 tablespoon of the oil in a medium-size skillet over medium heat. Add the onion; cook 1 minute. Add the garlic and dried red peppers; cook, stirring often, until dark golden, about 5

minutes. Remove the skillet from the heat.

3. Place the barley flour in the container of a food processor. Add the milk, water, sugar, salt, and the remaining 2 tablespoons oil. Process until smooth.

Combine this with the onion mixture, and pour into a well-buttered 12-inch non-stick pizza pan. Bake for 15 minutes. Cut into wedges and serve immediately.

Serves 4 to 6

JULIE SAHNI'S GARLIC-DILL BREAD

*T*he favorite bread of the Patels, a Hindu sect in the Indian state of Gujarat, these skillet flatbreads go perfectly with diced or shredded spicy lamb, pork, or chicken dishes. Adapted from Julie Sahni's remarkable tome, *Classic Indian Vegetarian and Grain Cooking*, the breads may be served buttered, warm from the pan. Or to enhance the flavor even further, use tongs to pass the breads over a gas flame for 8 to 10 seconds before they go to table. The breads will crisp and puff up.

1 boiling potato (6 ounces)
1 hot green pepper, seeded, deveined, and finely minced
1 large clove garlic, crushed
2½ tablespoons vegetable oil
½ teaspoon salt
2 tablespoons chopped fresh dill
¾ cup barley flour
½ cup all-purpose flour

1. Cook the potato in boiling salted water to cover until tender, about 20 minutes. Drain.

2. While the potato is still hot, peel it, and mash it until smooth. Add the hot green pepper and garlic. Let the potato mixture stand until cool.

3. Add the oil, salt, and dill to the potato mixture. Stir in the barley flour, and then work in the all-purpose flour to form a soft dough. Transfer to a lightly floured surface, and knead for 2 minutes. Divide the dough in half, and roll each half into a rope 6 inches long. Cut each rope into six pieces. Form each piece of dough into a ball, and roll it out with a floured rolling pin to form a 6-inch round. Stack the dough rounds between layers of paper towels as you roll them out.

4. Heat an oil-rubbed cast-iron skillet over high heat for 3 minutes. Reduce the heat to medium, and place one round of dough in the skillet. Cook until the underside is spotted, 1 minute. Remove the bread from the skillet with a spatula. Continue with the remaining rounds. Stack the breads between layers of paper towels as you cook them. Reheat (in the paper towels) in a 175°F oven (if your oven isn't reliable this low, heat to 225°F and watch the breads closely) for 10 minutes before serving.

5. Serve the Garlic-Dill Bread wrapped in a warm towel, in a large bowl or basket. Each person fills a bread with whatever dish it is accompanying and rolls it up like a tortilla.

Makes 12 small flatbreads; serves 4 or 6

SCOTCH BARLEY STOVE-TOP SCONES

Barley breads, in the form of scones or bannocks (large rounds), have been made in Scotland for centuries. These moist, cakey quick breads are the perfect foil for a "rasher of bacon" with eggs—or even a steaming hot bowl of cock-a-leekie soup. The following scones are not as thick as traditional ones, so be prepared—they disappear twice as fast!

½ cup raisins
2 tablespoons unsalted butter, melted
1 cup barley flour
1 cup bread flour
¼ teaspoon salt
½ teaspoon baking soda
1 teaspoon cream of tartar
¼ cup maple syrup
1 egg, lightly beaten
⅔ to ¾ cup milk

1. Place the raisins in a small bowl. Pour the melted butter over them, and let stand until softened, about 10 minutes.

2. Combine the barley flour, bread flour, salt, baking soda, and cream of tartar in a medium-size bowl. Mix well, and stir in the maple syrup, egg, and just enough of the milk to make a very thick batter. Stir in the raisin/butter mixture.

3. Heat a greased cast-iron skillet or griddle over medium heat. When it is hot, spoon the batter, 1 large tablespoon for each scone, into the skillet. Cook (three or four at a time) until golden on both sides and puffed up, 3 to 4 minutes per side. Keep warm in a 225°F oven while cooking the remaining scones.

Makes 16 scones

Here is another barley legend. The fable concerns Christopher Columbus. After discovering the New World and taking corn kernels back to Spain as a legacy of his journey, he resolved to return the favor—by bringing wheat and barley from the crowded European fields to the open spaces of "the Indies."

But neither bounty impressed the natives as much as the fancy pantaloons, colored parasols, and assorted bangles that were also part of his cargo. Of a consequence, the bales of wheat from the ship's hold withered and dried on the shore. The barley grains, however, had a somewhat more felicitous fate. Part of the cereal blew into the mountains, where it flourished untended for a hundred years or longer—until some intrepid islander finally cracked a kernel between his teeth, and promptly added it to his rice pot. Another part of the barley floated out to sea on the tide along with Columbus's departing vessels. It did *not* take root in the water, but it certainly fattened Caribbean shrimp and crab to incredible dimensions from that day forward.

At least, that's how the story was told to me.

BARLEY FRUITCAKE

*B*arley flour, added to fruitcake, adds moisture and density to the cake that reportedly allows it to last (tightly wrapped, that is) for years. I have never tried it, but can attest that a fruitcake made in September is at its prime served in December.

2 pounds fruit (about 4 cups):
    ¼ pound dried cherries
    ¼ pound dates
    ¼ pound dried figs
    9 ounces raisins
    1 package (11 ounces) mixed dried
        fruits
1 cup (2 sticks) unsalted butter, at room
    temperature
1 cup sugar
1 teaspoon vanilla extract
1 teaspoon finely slivered orange zest
5 eggs
½ cup sherry
1½ cups all-purpose flour
½ cup barley flour
½ teaspoon salt
1 cup chopped walnuts
1 cup chopped pecans
¼ cup fresh orange juice
¼ cup Grand Marnier

1. Preheat the oven to 300°F.

2. Pit any fruits that require it. Finely chop all the fruits and combine them in a bowl.

3. In the large bowl of an electric mixer, beat the butter until light. Slowly beat in the sugar; beat until light and fluffy. Beat in the vanilla and orange zest. Add the eggs, one at a time, beating thoroughly after each addition. Slowly beat in the sherry.

4. Sift the all-purpose flour with the barley flour and salt into a bowl. Slowly stir into the cake batter. Stir in the chopped fruits and the nuts.

5. Spoon the batter into a buttered and floured 10-inch tube pan. Bake until a toothpick inserted in the center comes out clean, about 1½ hours. Cool in the pan on a rack for 10 minutes.

6. Combine the orange juice with the Grand Marnier. Lightly prick the top of the cake, and spoon the liquid over the surface. Remove the cake from the pan. Cool thoroughly, and store in an airtight container for at least 1 month before serving.

Serves 10 to 12

BRAN

Not Just Wheat but Oat Bran, Too

I met my first authentic bran lover (a madcap heiress) when I was twenty-three. She was considerably older, no great beauty, and tightfisted into the bargain. And not, even by the kind light of memory, typical of what I had been led to expect (from the movies) as a high-spirited, freewheeling prototype of the rich. In real life, the rich seemed petty, imperious, and wholly self-concerned. Still, I was utterly transfixed by them.

My madcap heiress was Peggy Guggenheim, who, as she announced in a somewhat breathy anglicized voice, was "between husbands and lovers and in New York City for the duration."

It was the close of World War II when we met. Peggy, then in her late forties, was running Art of This Century, a celebrated gallery of surrealist art, during the day and collecting material for her memoirs, *Out of This Century*, at night. I confess that I longed to be considered worthy of a paragraph (or at least a sentence) in her romantic chronicles.

It is important to state at the outset that I was highly impressionable at the time. And that the fabled Guggenheim hauteur affected me the way a magnet agitates base metal. I was drawn to her at first sight. I called her every day, sent flowers often, and flagrantly spent my first hard-earned paychecks taking her to restaurants far beyond my means—hostelries where she most often caused consternation, not only because of her curious dress code (bobby sox, sneakers, and sable) but also because of her bad manners, vilifying the waiters and busboys who danced attendance upon her as "blackguards and ne'er-do-wells willing to be seduced by tips"!

I remember Peggy best barefoot (because her shoes hurt) in a posh French restaurant, despotically waving away the wine steward with a command to bring us "*vin ordinaire*, if you please! We want to drink only what you drink in the kitchen!" And in an aside, assuring me that the wine cooks drink is infinitely superior to a *grand cru*!

When the wine was served (in water glasses), it was, I would have sworn, pure red vinegar. But Peggy delightedly drank four glasses to prove her point.

Peggy's food habits were erratic at best. The only serious meal she ate every day was what she called a "nursery breakfast," taken at about four in the afternoon, composed of a soft-boiled egg, tea with lots of milk, and muffins (bran muffins) slathered with butter and honey or jam.

She would very often eat this meal in her fabulous art gallery with myriad Jackson Pollock paintings on its curving walls, seated at a desk near the entrance, collecting admissions as she chewed a muffin. In those days, no art gallery in New York charged an entrance fee. But Peggy was adamant on the subject. "If they come here to laugh," she said, "Let 'em pay an amusement tax!"

She imposed the tariff of one dollar per person, making change herself. There was no need for her to do this—any one of her employees could have done it for her. But Peggy explained, with a little sigh, that making money reminded her of her grandfather.

My involvement with Peggy was short and sweet, terminated by mutual disinterest and her decision to leave America once the armistice was signed, to open a new gallery in Venice—Palazzo Venier dei Leoni.

Before she left, she undertook to give me a birthday present. I was informed, by one of her aides at the gallery, that she contemplated bestowing upon me a large Jackson Pollock painting. Horrified, for I never truly appreciated Pollock's style (and he was far from famous at the time), I suggested that a dozen oxford-cloth Brooks Brothers shirts would be more appreciated. A gift I duly received on October 16.

When Peggy's departure date drew near, I wanted to reciprocate. I toyed with the idea of some small trinket she might consider wearing (for her taste in jewelry was highly erratic too), and though I browsed for hours at Cartier, nothing seemed appropriate or, parenthetically, affordable.

Through the same go-between who had alerted me to the possibility of the Pollock painting came a suggestion: "Peggy says it will be a long journey. The *Ile de France* is only recently returned to passenger service, and the food will be execrable. Could you manage to find her a dozen bran muffins for nursery breakfast?"

In an act of supreme sacrifice (for rationing was still on), I borrowed all the coupons for butter and sugar I could. For two days, I baked batches of bran muffins: with raisins, with nuts, with bananas, with dates. There were six dozen in all, wrapped in cardboard cartons that usually housed champagne.

Peggy gave me a decidedly platonic kiss at the gangplank, as she whispered in my ear, "Your muffins are di-vine, darling. But in the future, never add *fruit* of any kind. Lilies were not meant to be gilded!"

The Grain's Genesis

By and large, trenchermen are not neutral on the subject of bran. They either love or loathe it out of hand, despite any benefit this so-called miracle fiber has for a body's well-being.

The truth of the matter is, for centuries the only real bran eaters were slaves and assorted serfs, peasants of one sort or another whose diet was composed of everything their betters considered unfit for civilized human consumption. As a result, the underdogs in history flourished while the honchos waxed and ultimately waned, victims of overrefinement at the fork end which may be traced directly to a lack of roughage (bran) in their diet.

To set the issue straight, bran is neither a cereal nor a grain. It is the tough outermost covering of a seed. Any seed. The ancients called bran "chaff" and gave it short shrift in the Bible, where wheat chaff is compared to "the ungodly who the wind driveth away."

That's a bad rap for any dish, and it took bran almost two thousand years (and the aid of a latter-day prophet, Dr. Sylvester Graham) to clear its reputation and achieve a new and squeaky clean image: life preserver on a plate!

The late Dr. Graham (whose name graces my favorite wheaten cracker) was one of a quirky band of 19th-century food crusaders who railed against the bad eating habits of the American bourgeoisie—in particular the middle-class penchant for soft white bread (which was proof of status to anyone in the New World whose forefathers had subsisted on loaves of a darker hue in the old one). Graham was an advocate of wheat bran in the diet: at least once a day was his prescription. Because, he maintained, as bran is composed of almost wholly indigestible cellulose, a cupful could sweep the system free of waste in just three hours.

Graham was such a successful evangelist for fiber that he terrified his constipated countrymen into a total change of eating habits within two decades. By the time of his death in the 1920s, over half the households in the U.S. had eschewed the notion of a hearty breakfast with a capital B (syrup-drenched flapjacks or sizzling rashers of bacon with eggs) for a healthier one—cereal in a bowl with a lower-case b (for bran) added. Though it must be told, it was often added in far less than the hoped-for cathartic doses. But for better or worse, fiber had entered the American diet at last!

Some Plain Grain Talk

The word "bran" springs from the Middle French or older Gaulish word *brenno*, which means "unattested." Earlier the Celts had another word for it, *bren*, which they used to describe broken or split coats of armor. It makes sense if one realizes that bran, in edible form, stems from a split outer cover.

The bran overcoat is well insulated. It is made of six protective layers of primarily noncaloric dietary fiber, notably vitamin B, vitamin B_6, niacin, pantothenic acid, riboflavin, and thiamine. Everything, in fact, alleged to keep us in tip-top shape.

However, dietary fiber is a complex substance. As bran is essentially composed of bulk, the human body—even with its complex enzyme system—cannot digest more than a fraction of the amount it consumes. Most of the bulk, therefore, is "passed through" undigested.

For years we have known that this unassimilated bulk has a proven value in relieving constipation and preventing any diverticular-type diseases that develop in weak areas of the intestines. But according to Cornell University's recent scientific studies on the subject, dietary fiber may also have a tonic effect in regulating serum cholesterol and in lowering blood sugar levels for diabetics. Some studies (the research is ongoing) lean toward the notion that high fiber consumption may offer protection against cancer of the colon and rectum. And, on a less threatening note, promote healthy weight loss too!

The Health Handle

*B*ran's earliest appearance at the American table was in a cereal bowl. After Dr. Graham's passionate philippics on the subject, it was introduced to the home (packaged by the Kellogg Company) in 1916. Nowadays, it is still a best-seller, though not necessarily consigned to breakfast food alone.

Most bran sold in the U.S. today is made of wheat. That is *processed* ("refined") *wheat bran*—the outer covering, separated from the germ and endosperm of the kernel, milled, toasted, and in some instances cooked under high pressure for a greater degree of "chewability." Flavorings as well as sugar, salt, and replacement vitamins are added. *Unprocessed wheat bran* is essentially a raw ingredient of little savor outside a muffin! *Unprocessed oat bran* has of late begun to appear on supermarket shelves (packaged by Quaker) as an alternative to unprocessed wheat bran.

Processed and unprocessed bran differ remarkably as to flavor, crunch, and degree of dietary fiber. For instance, a cupful of Bran Flakes cereal may in actu-

ality contain only 6.5 grams of crude dietary fiber, while a like portion of untreated unprocessed bran will contain twice that amount, 13 grams. A cupful of unprocessed oat bran, on the other hand, is conspicuously low in crude fiber (1.5 grams), but bulk is not its particular virtue in terms of health.

Which bran type is most therapeutic? That's a loaded question—much depending upon one's physical condition and need. For while large portions of insoluble, unprocessed wheat bran indubitably have a tonic effect on the alimentary canal, nutritionists claim it is water-soluble oat bran that effectively reduces blood levels of LDL cholesterol.

In my opinion, it is the sensible combination of both brans in processed and unprocessed forms (sometimes mixed but more often used singly) that gives the cook the option of adding dietary fiber to most dishes without advertising any therapeutic motive at the dining-room table!

How to Buy It

*U*nprocessed *bran* until very recently could be purchased only at health food stores. Today, however, it is possible to buy it in supermarkets as well, packaged (by Quaker) in 8-ounce cartons that are conspicuously emblazoned: "For adding Fiber to Baked Goods, Breads, Toppings & More."

Among *processed brans*, All-Bran is a top choice. Cooked under steam pressure, then baked in a low oven to reduce moisture, this shredded cereal is a trial to chew, but it combines felicitously with other flours and nuts when it is cooked or baked. All-Bran contains approximately 9 grams of dietary fiber in every serving. Bran Buds, while similarly processed, is extruded and cut into nugget-size fragments that may easily be converted to coarse flour or crumbs in a food processor. However, a package of

Bran Buds does have a higher sugar content and a slightly lower endowment of dietary fiber, about 8 grams per serving. For the record, most crispy (wheat) bran flake cereals contain a mere 4 grams of dietary fiber per serving.

Oat bran (Quaker's product), packaged in 16-ounce cartons and promoted as a "Creamy High-Fiber Cereal" with no salt, no sugar added, contains a slim 0.5 grams crude fiber per ounce.

As a yardstick for the health-concerned, it might be worth noting that fruits and vegetables usually contain between 0.4 and 6.0 grams of dietary fiber per serving. A loaf of whole wheat bread contains a good deal less than 2 grams per slice.

Bran is a grain with a reasonable shelf life, as long as the package is well sealed and moisture free. Exposed bran (like most cereals) proves a hospitable breeding ground for ants and maggots. If you live in a damp climate, it is a good idea to store an open carton in a self-seal plastic bag in the freezer to inhibit any insect population rise. I keep unprocessed bran in the pantry, packed into a quart canning jar with an airtight screw-top lid, and store open cartons of processed bran in several layers of sealed self-lock storage bags.

If you are not a heavy bran user, it's a good idea to inscribe the date of purchase on the package with a felt-tip pen.

Bran often loses its bonus of minerals and vitamins after one year's time.

How to Cook It

*T*here is no hard and fast rule for cooking with bran, but there *are* ways of varying its anonymous flavor and somewhat fibrous texture.

To enhance the taste of unprocessed bran, consider toasting it in a medium-hot heavy skillet, stirring often until the mixture takes on a decided amber-to-brown hue.

Preheating processed bran in a warm (300° F) oven for 10 to 15 minutes will likewise give it a stronger flavor and more toothsome bite.

It is important to note that both unprocessed and processed bran may be ground to a variety of textures, from a flour-like powder to rough crumbs, in a food processor or blender.

Bran makes an admirable substitute for bread crumbs in most recipes, and mixing crushed bran crumbs with sugar and a modicum of butter will provide a delicately nutty flavored topping for cakes and pastries. Unprocessed oat bran, substituted for a portion of wheat bran in baking recipes, will produce moister, decidedly more silken hot breads, pancakes, and cookies.

To my mind, bran's most durable and beloved guise is the muffin.

HI-FI MEATLOAF

The acronym stands for high fiber as much as culinary high fidelity. This recipe (supplemented with All-Bran cereal) is the most succulent loaf I think I have ever sampled—and I've sampled a goodly number in my time.

¾ cup All-Bran cereal
2 teaspoons unsalted butter
1½ pounds ground beef
¾ pound ground veal
¼ pound ground pork
2 shallots, minced
1 large canned green chile, minced
1 egg, lightly beaten
⅛ teaspoon dried thyme
1 tablespoon minced fresh parsley
Dash of hot pepper sauce
½ cup homemade chicken stock (see page
    376) or canned broth
½ teaspoon salt
¼ teaspoon freshly ground black pepper
2 teaspoons Dijon mustard
2 tablespoons chili sauce
2 strips bacon
Chopped fresh parsley, for garnish

1. Preheat the oven to 375°F.

2. Place the All-Bran in the container of a food processor and process until it has the texture of coarse crumbs.

3. Melt the butter in a heavy skillet over medium heat. Stir in the bran. Cook, stirring constantly, 2 minutes.

4. Transfer the bran to a bowl, and add all the ingredients through the black pepper. Mix thoroughly and form into a loaf on a shallow baking dish.

5. Combine the mustard and chili sauce in a small bowl. Mix well and spread over the top and sides of the meat loaf. Lay the bacon strips over the top. Bake 1 hour and 15 minutes. Sprinkle with extra parsley before serving.

Serves 6 to 8

BRAN-NEW OVEN-FRIED CHICKEN

Unprocessed bran is prominent in the crisp and crackling upholstery of this baked bird. So delicious, it gives health food a new image! Warning: this dish is hot. If you're timid, reduce the amount of hot pepper sauce to 1 teaspoon.

1 large chicken (about 4 pounds), cut into
    serving pieces
2 cups buttermilk
⅛ teaspoon crushed whole allspice
2 teaspoons hot pepper sauce
1 tablespoon soy sauce
1 teaspoon salt
4 tablespoons (½ stick) unsalted butter
½ cup plus 2 tablespoons homemade
    chicken stock (see page 376) or canned
    broth

6 tablespoons unprocessed wheat bran
¼ teaspoon freshly ground black pepper
¼ teaspoon freshly grated nutmeg
1 tablespoon all-purpose flour

1. Place the chicken pieces in a large bowl. Combine the buttermilk, allspice, hot pepper sauce, soy sauce, and salt in another bowl, and pour the mixture over the chicken. Cover, and refrigerate overnight.

2. About 2 hours before serving, place the chicken in a colander and let it stand until well drained. Reserve the buttermilk mixture.

3. Preheat the oven to 375°F.

4. Heat the butter with the ½ cup chicken stock in a small saucepan. Keep warm.

5. Place the bran in the container of a food processor and process until fairly smooth. Transfer to a paper bag and add the pepper and nutmeg. Shake to mix well.

6. Pat the chicken pieces dry with paper towels, and add them to the bag with the bran mixture. Shake the bag well to coat the pieces evenly.

7. Place the chicken pieces, skin side down, on a rack covering a roasting pan. Bake, basting every 5 minutes with the butter-stock mixture, 30 minutes. Turn the chicken over and continue to bake, basting every 5 minutes with the pan juices, until the coating is crisp and the juices run yellow when the meat is pricked with a fork, about 30 minutes longer. Transfer the chicken pieces to an ovenproof platter and keep warm in a 225°F oven.

8. Place the roasting pan over medium-low heat. Add the flour. Cook, stirring constantly, 2 minutes. Whisk in the reserved buttermilk in three additions, scraping the sides and bottom of the pan. Stir in the 2 tablespoons chicken stock and cook until slightly thickened, about 4 minutes. Pass the gravy with the chicken.

Serves 4

BRANNED BITKI

I never ate bran in any form whatsoever in the Soviet Union, but *bitki* (tiny highly seasoned fried meat cakes) appeared in one guise or another at almost every meal I consumed there. My favorite version, spiked with unprocessed bran, is a domestic translation.

½ cup unprocessed wheat bran
½ cup fresh bread crumbs
1¼ pounds ground veal
¼ pound cooked ham, ground
¼ cup milk
1 onion, finely chopped
1 clove garlic, minced
½ teaspoon caraway seeds
3 tablespoons chopped fresh dill
1 teaspoon chopped fresh parsley
1 egg, lightly beaten
3 tablespoons unsalted butter
1 teaspoon oil
2 teaspoons all-purpose flour
1 cup homemade chicken stock (see page 376) or canned broth

1 cup sour cream, at room temperature
¼ teaspoon freshly grated nutmeg

1. Combine the bran and bread crumbs in a large bowl. Mix well and transfer half the mixture to a large plate.

2. To the mixture in the bowl, add the veal, ham, milk, onion, garlic, caraway, 1 tablespoon of the dill, parsley, and egg. Mix thoroughly and shape into 1½-inch balls. Using the palm of your hand, flatten them slightly into cakes. Press the cakes into the remaining bran-crumb mixture to coat on both sides.

3. Heat 2 tablespoons of the butter with the oil in a 9- or 10-inch non-stick skillet over medium heat. Sauté the meat cakes in two or three batches until golden brown on both sides, adding more butter if needed. Transfer to a plate.

4. In the same pan, melt the remaining 1 tablespoon butter over medium-low heat. Stir in the flour. Cook, stirring constantly, 2 minutes. Whisk in the chicken stock, scraping up any meat cake crumbs that remain on the sides and bottom of the pan. Heat to boiling. Reduce the heat and simmer 2 minutes. Transfer the mixture to a 2-quart saucepan. Whisk in the sour cream and cook over medium-low heat 2 minutes. Add the nutmeg, 1 tablespoon of the dill, and the meat patties. Cook over low heat until the patties are warmed through, about 10 minutes. Sprinkle with the remaining 1 tablespoon dill.

Serves 4 to 6

Fifty years ago in the "sticks," as the nether parts of New York City were known, the brans most denizens ate were made by a company called Dugan's, which hand-delivered the product to one's door daily. That these cakes were made in factory ovens was somewhat dispiriting to a generation of home bakers, but the fresh taste (and convenience) shortly won over the most doubtful Thomases on the turf—including my highly prejudiced grandmother.

Dugan's (the name emblazoned in a dark blue cursive script on every carton) soon became as familiar a symbol in Queens as the American flag or the Empire State Building looming on the horizon. And no breakfast table was laid nor coffee percolator placed on a stove until the familiar thump-whinny-stamp-of-hooves down the block announced the presence of "The Dugan Man" with his horse and cache of still-warm baked goods.

They were prodigious muffins: raisined or plain, baked in fluted paper nests, with a perfume more intoxicating than attar of roses. And a flavor so irresistible that a true muffin addict (like me) could chomp down three before any other family member tucked a napkin into place.

When I began to cook out of necessity during the Depression, my first serious ambition at the stove was to bake. Specifically, bran muffins. Because, I reasoned, it would save our budget a serious weekly outlay. I was ten years old and a dollar seemed a fortune in those days.

My mother and grandmother were somewhat skeptical about this aspiration, and less than enthusiastic after tasting the results.

"Why is it man's nature to tamper with perfection?" I recall my grandmother asking rhetorically as she took an initial bite. My mother's observation was more direct.

"Some have a knack for cooking. Others bake well. Don't push your luck!"

Needless to say, I gave up the idea of ever producing a bran muffin again—until many years later when attrition or fickle public taste forced Dugan's to shutter their doors. Then I spent a month at the oven, baking brans day after day. Whether I mastered the art or not is a matter of conjecture. You will simply have to decide for yourself. (Muffin recipes begin on page 39.)

BRAN-HERBED WEAKFISH

Bran and seafood are highly compatible partners. For evidence, have the next rendering blanketed in herbed bran crumbs. Serve with an amendment of tartar sauce.

1 cup Bran Flakes cereal, ground fine in a
    food processor
½ cup fresh bread crumbs
1 tablespoon finely chopped fresh basil, or
    1 teaspoon dried
1 tablespoon minced fresh parsley
¼ cup all-purpose flour
⅓ cup milk
1½ pounds weakfish (sea trout) or other
    white fish, cut into serving pieces
1½ tablespoons unsalted butter
2 to 3 tablespoons vegetable oil
2 tablespoons malt vinegar
Chopped fresh parsley, for garnish
Tartar Sauce (see facing page)

1. Preheat the oven to 400°F.
2. Combine the ground Bran Flakes with the bread crumbs, basil, and parsley in a shallow bowl. Place the flour on a plate. Place the milk in another shallow bowl.

3. Pat the fish dry with paper towels. Dip the fish first in flour, shaking off the excess, then in milk, and finally in the bran mixture. Place on a plate.

4. Heat 1 tablespoon of the butter with 2 tablespoons of the oil in a large skillet over medium heat. Sauté the fish, a few pieces at a time, adding more butter and oil as needed, until golden, about 3 minutes per side. Transfer to an ovenproof platter and bake 10 minutes. Sprinkle with the vinegar and parsley, and serve with Tartar Sauce.

Serves 4

BRAN-BATTERED FISH AND SHRIMP

This batter of unprocessed bran and beer is best served up accompanied by malt vinegar. A sprinkling on the crispy hot fish and you've got perfection.

½ cup unprocessed wheat bran
½ cup cake flour
2 teaspoons English dry mustard
¼ teaspoon freshly grated nutmeg
½ teaspoon salt
1 cup beer
4 eggs, separated
2 teaspoons Dijon mustard
1½ pounds fish filets (flounder, sole, fluke),
    quartered
1 pound shrimp, shelled and deveined

¼ cup fresh lemon juice
⅓ cup all-purpose flour (approximately)
Vegetable oil for frying
Malt vinegar
Lemon wedges
Tartar Sauce (recipe follows)

1. Place the bran in the container of a food processor and process 30 seconds. Add the cake flour; process 10 seconds. Add the dry mustard, nutmeg, and salt.

Process briefly, and then add the beer, egg yolks, and Dijon mustard. Process until smooth. (If you do not have a food processor, place the bran in a blender container and blend until fairly smooth, about 30 seconds. Transfer to a bowl, and stir in the remaining batter ingredients.) Transfer to a bowl and refrigerate, covered, 8 hours.

2. Sprinkle the fish filets and shrimp with the lemon juice; let stand 30 minutes.

3. Drain the fish and shrimp. Pat them dry with paper towels and dust lightly with the all-purpose flour.

4. Beat the egg whites until stiff; fold them into the batter.

5. Heat about 1 inch of oil in a heavy skillet until very hot. Dip the fish into the batter, and then fry in the hot oil, about 5 pieces at a time, until golden brown on both sides, 2 to 3 minutes per side. Drain the cooked pieces on paper towels, then transfer them to a heatproof platter and keep warm in a 225°F oven while frying the remaining fish. When the fish is cooked, fry the shrimp, about 1½ minutes per side. Drain the shrimp on paper towels and add to the platter with the fish. Serve with malt vinegar, lemon wedges, and Tartar Sauce.

Serves 4

Tartar Sauce

1 cup mayonnaise, preferably homemade (see page 379)
½ cup sour cream
½ teaspoon Dijon mustard
1 small shallot, minced
3 small sour gherkins or cornichons, finely chopped
1 teaspoon finely chopped fresh parsley
1 tablespoon chopped fresh dill
¼ teaspoon fresh lemon juice
1 teaspoon Pernod liqueur
Salt and freshly ground black pepper to taste

SOME BRAN TRIVIA

Back in the 18th century, no American of sensibility even remotely considered the idea of *eating* bran. Nonetheless, the cereal held a conspicuous corner in every townsman's household. Reticules filled with bran, dried flowers, and herbs (or pine needles if the homeowner was poor) scented linen presses, hope chests, and high- and lowboys throughout the thirteen colonies. In the scullery, bran husks were sprinkled on live coals to bank fires, and were used with sand to scour pot bottoms blackened by cooking!

Bran surfaced even more artfully in the American West a hundred years after. At "bran dances" held in barns, country stores, and even open fields, the floor was covered with a thick carpet of "wagon dust" (dried wheat bran). The bran was always raked at least 3 or 4 inches deep and well dampened before the pioneer folk attempted to try out the shoe leather.

Bran dances vanished before the end of the century, when worldliness hit the Chisholm Trail and dance halls replaced church socials and "caledonians." There are, however, some notable accounts of these rustic jollifications in diaries and dance cards of the day. According to one partner's early account: "A brannied pasture is right pleasant to reel or schottische upon at first. But heaven preserve us if it is danced *dry*! Sneezes and wheezes for hours afterward!"

Whisk the mayonnaise with the sour cream in a medium-size bowl. Whisk in the remaining ingredients. Refrigerate, covered, until ready to serve.

Makes about 1½ cups

EGGPLANT CANNOLI

Cannoli are calorie-rich Italian pastries. My branned version borrows little of the original except great taste, name, and shape. Serve it as a first course.

1 large eggplant (about 1¼ pounds), cut into ¼-inch-thick slices
Salt
⅓ cup all-purpose flour
⅔ cup unprocessed wheat bran
2 eggs
1 teaspoon water
3 tablespoons olive oil
2 tablespoons peanut oil
1 clove garlic, unpeeled
⅓ cup diced Italian hard salami
3 tablespoons chopped fresh parsley
3 tablespoons freshly grated Parmesan cheese
1½ cups ricotta cheese
Freshly ground black pepper to taste
Chile-Flecked Tomato Sauce (recipe follows), warmed
Chopped fresh parsley, for garnish

1. Place the eggplant slices in a colander, and sprinkle them generously with salt. Let stand 30 minutes. Brush off the salt with damp paper towels.

2. Place the flour and the bran in the container of a food processor or blender. Process 1 minute. Transfer to a plate.

3. Beat the eggs with the water in a shallow bowl. Dip the eggplant slices into this mixture, shaking off any excess, and then dip into the flour-bran mixture. Transfer to a large plate.

4. Combine the oils in a small bowl and heat half the mixture in a large heavy skillet over medium heat. Sauté the eggplant slices, a few at a time, adding more oil as needed, until golden brown on both sides, 2 to 3 minutes per side. Drain the cooked eggplant on paper towels. When half the eggplant is done, place the garlic clove at one edge of the pan, and continue cooking the egg-

plant. Remove the garlic when it is well browned and set it aside to cool.

5. Preheat the oven to 400°F.

6. Peel and mince the cooked garlic. Place it in a medium-size bowl and add the salami, parsley, Parmesan, and ricotta. Mix well and season with salt and pepper.

7. Place about 1½ teaspoons filling mixture down the center of each eggplant slice. Roll them up like cannoli, secure the tops with wooden toothpicks, and place them snugly together in a baking dish. Bake 12 to 15 minutes. Remove the toothpicks, drizzle with the tomato sauce, and sprinkle with parsley.

Serves 6 to 8

Chile-Flecked Tomato Sauce

1 tablespoon unsalted butter
1 tablespoon olive oil
6 scallions, white bulbs and green tops, chopped
1 small clove garlic, minced
1 small green chile, seeded, deveined and minced
1½ cups chopped, seeded tomatoes
Pinch of sugar
Pinch of dried oregano
Pinch of ground mace

Heat the butter with the oil in a medium-size saucepan over medium-low heat. Add the scallions; cook 1 minute. Add the garlic and green chile; cook 4 minutes longer. Stir in the remaining ingredients and raise the heat slightly. Cook, stirring occasionally, until slightly thickened, about 10 minutes.

Makes about 1¼ cups

SPINACH-BRAN PIZZA WITH CHEESE AND SAUSAGE

*T*o a concerned member of the stove-top health club, the most positive aspect of any bran fiber is its mutability. I use bran to enrich pie crusts, to extend meat loaves and patties, and to delectably "bread" whatever cutlet, croquette, or other crunchable comes to roost in my sauté pan. And in my pizza or tart pan, to boot!

FOR THE TOMATO BASE
2 tablespoons olive oil
1 small onion, minced
1 clove garlic, minced
1 cup chopped, seeded tomatoes
Pinch of sugar
½ teaspoon chopped fresh oregano, or
*   ¼ teaspoon dried*
⅛ teaspoon ground allspice
1 teaspoon unsalted butter
Salt and freshly ground black pepper to
*   taste*

FOR THE CRUST
1 tablespoon olive oil
1 small onion, minced
1 clove garlic, minced
1 package (10 ounces) frozen chopped
*   spinach, thawed and squeezed dry*
1 large canned green chile, minced
1 cup All-Bran cereal, processed fine in a
*   food processor*
½ cup freshly grated Parmesan cheese
⅛ teaspoon crushed dried hot red peppers
¼ teaspoon salt
¼ teaspoon freshly ground black pepper
1 egg, lightly beaten

FOR THE TOPPING
2 large sweet Italian sausages, cut into ½-
*   inch-thick slices*
½ cup crumbled goat cheese
1¼ cups coarsely grated mozzarella (about
*   5 ounces)*

1. Make the tomato base: Heat the oil in a medium-size saucepan over medium-low heat. Add the onion; cook 1 minute. Add the garlic; cook 4 minutes. Stir in the tomatoes, sugar, oregano, and allspice. Cook, uncovered, stirring occasionally, until thick, about 30 minutes. Stir in the butter and season with salt and pepper. Set aside to cool.

2. Meanwhile, make the crust: Preheat the oven to 400°F. Lightly butter a 9- or 10-inch loose-bottom tart pan.

3. Heat the oil in a medium-size heavy skillet over medium-low heat. Add the onion; cook 1 minute. Add the garlic; cook 4 minutes. Stir in the spinach and the chile and raise the heat slightly. Cook, stirring constantly, until all moisture has evaporated, about 4 minutes. Remove the skillet from the heat.

4. Place the All-Bran in a medium-size bowl and add the spinach mixture. Mix well, and stir in the Parmesan cheese, dried red peppers, salt, black pepper, and egg. Mix thoroughly. Spread this mixture evenly over the bottom of the prepared tart pan. Bake 10 minutes. Cool slightly.

5. Sauté the sausage slices in a dry heavy skillet until lightly browned and partially rendered of fat, about 4 minutes.

6. Spread the tomato mixture evenly over the cooled spinach crust. Dot the top with goat cheese. Place the sausage slices over the top, and sprinkle with the mozzarella. Bake 20 minutes.

Serves 4 to 6

CAILLE
(Bran-Crammed Swiss Chard)

*T*he next recipe has a mysterious antecedence. I encountered it on a South Carolina menu as "Louisiana-style quail," though it clearly was not fowl. The notion of poaching a grain-and-meat mixture in a nest of greens is indubitably Middle European, yet the tag was decidedly French. No matter, *caille* is a very good dish to have in anyone's culinary repertoire—whatever its point of origin.

1 large head Swiss chard (about 10 leaves)
1 cup ground ham
1 egg, lightly beaten
½ cup milk, scalded and cooled
1 cup fresh bread crumbs
1 cup Bran Flakes cereal, ground fine in a
    food processor
1 cup grated Monterey Jack cheese with
    jalapeño peppers
2 tablespoons chopped fresh parsley
⅛ teaspoon ground mace
⅛ teaspoon freshly grated nutmeg
½ teaspoon salt
¼ teaspoon freshly ground black pepper
2 cloves garlic
1 cup homemade chicken stock (see page
    376), or canned broth, warmed
1 tablespoon unsalted butter
1 large tomato, seeded and chopped
Pinch of sugar
Chopped fresh parsley, for garnish

1. Preheat the oven to 350°F.

2. Rinse the Swiss chard and trim off most of the heavy white ribs. Cook the chard leaves in boiling salted water to cover until just wilted, 2 to 3 minutes. Drain.

3. Place the ham in a large bowl and add all the ingredients through the black pepper. Mix thoroughly. Place about 1½ tablespoons ham mixture on the rib side of each leaf. Roll it up, folding in the ends like an envelope.

4. Place the chard envelopes seam side down in a lightly buttered baking dish. Place the garlic cloves on the bottom of the dish. Pour the chicken stock over the chard, and bake, covered, 25 minutes.

5. Remove the baking dish from the oven, and carefully drain off all liquid into a bowl, reserving the garlic. Keep the chard warm, uncovered, in a 225°F oven.

6. Melt the butter in a medium-size saucepan over medium heat. Add the cooked garlic and mash it with a fork. Stir in the tomato, sprinkle with the sugar, and then stir in the reserved cooking juices. Heat to boiling and boil rapidly until thickened, about 10 minutes. Spoon the sauce over the chard, and sprinkle with parsley.

Serves 4

*A*ccording to the late food savant Waverley Root, "Bran is a health-promoting constituent of wheat, which nature puts in and man diabolically takes out!"

HONEY-ORANGE BRAN MUFFINS

From California come these muffins of remarkable flavor and prodigious size. They're "sun kissed," like other good gifts of the Golden West!

¼ cup firmly packed light brown sugar
4 tablespoons (½ stick) unsalted butter, melted
⅔ cup buttermilk
2 eggs, lightly beaten
¼ cup honey
Finely slivered zest of 1 orange
1 cup all-purpose flour
1 cup unprocessed wheat bran
1 tablespoon baking powder
¼ teaspoon salt

1. Preheat the oven to 350°F. Lightly grease a 12-cup muffin tin.
2. Place the brown sugar in a large bowl. Pour the melted butter over it, and mix well with a wooden spoon. Stir in the buttermilk, eggs, honey, and orange zest.
3. Combine the flour, bran, baking powder, and salt in another bowl. Mix well, and stir into the buttermilk mixture. Mix until just smooth.
4. Fill each prepared muffin cup about two-thirds full with batter. Bake until golden and firm, about 25 minutes. Remove the tin from the oven and let it stand 5 minutes. Then loosen the edges of the muffins with a knife and unmold.
   Makes 12 muffins

APPLESAUCED BRANS

This recipe is absolutely best when the applesauce is homemade. However, the silken muffins are a decided breakfast asset, no matter what the ingredient's lineage.

⅓ cup firmly packed light brown sugar
4 tablespoons (½ stick) unsalted butter, melted
⅔ cup Homemade Applesauce (recipe follows)
2 eggs, lightly beaten
⅓ cup light cream or half-and-half
1 cup all-purpose flour
1 cup unprocessed wheat bran
1 tablespoon baking powder
¼ teaspoon salt
¼ teaspoon ground cinnamon
⅛ teaspoon ground ginger
¼ cup raisins
¼ cup chopped walnuts

1. Preheat the oven to 350°F. Lightly grease a 12-cup muffin tin.
2. Place the brown sugar in a large bowl. Pour the butter over it, and mix well with a wooden spoon. Stir in the applesauce, eggs, and light cream.
3. Combine the flour, bran, baking powder, salt, cinnamon, and ginger in another bowl. Stir the dry ingredients into the applesauce mixture, and mix until just smooth. Add the raisins and walnuts.
4. Fill each prepared muffin cup about two-thirds full with batter. Bake until golden and firm, about 25 minutes.

Remove the tin from the oven, and let stand 5 minutes. Then loosen the edges of the muffins with a knife and unmold.

Makes 12 muffins

Homemade Applesauce

6 to 8 tart red apples (such as Winesap or Jonathan)
¼ cup water
2 lemon slices, each ½ inch thick
½ to 1 cup sugar
½ teaspoon ground cinnamon
⅛ teaspoon freshly grated nutmeg
Juice of 1 lemon

1. Core, peel, and cut the apples into sixths. Place them in a heavy saucepan and add the water and lemon slices. Cook, covered, over medium-high heat until very tender, about 12 minutes. Discard the lemon slices.

2. Mash the apples in the saucepan with a vegetable masher. Add sugar to taste, and then stir in the cinnamon, nutmeg, and lemon juice. Cook, uncovered, over medium heat for 3 minutes. Store in sterilized jars.

Makes about 2½ pints

THE FOUR SEASONS' OLYMPIC BRANS

One of my favorite bran muffins comes from the extensive repertoire of Helmut Pedevilla, pastry chef at the Four Seasons Olympic Hotel in Seattle, Washington. I stayed at this elegant northwestern hostelry three times one year, and made up my mind after the second visit that I could not possibly sleep without the chef's highly salubrious muffin recipe as a security blanket. Pedevilla's creation is a wake-up call no man of good appetite can resist.

½ cup raisins
½ cup walnut halves, chopped
1 cup plus 2 tablespoons sifted pastry or cake flour
1 egg
¼ cup vegetable oil
6 tablespoons light brown sugar
1 cup buttermilk
5 tablespoons honey
1½ cups Bran Flakes cereal
1¼ teaspoons baking soda
½ teaspoon salt

1. Preheat the oven to 400°F. Lightly grease a 12-cup muffin tin.

2. Place the raisins and walnuts in a medium-size bowl and toss with the 2 tablespoons flour. Set aside.

3. Lightly beat the egg in a large bowl. Slowly beat in the oil. Then beat in the brown sugar, buttermilk, honey, and Bran Flakes.

4. Sift the remaining 1 cup flour with the baking soda and salt. Stir the flour into the bran mixture, then add the raisins and walnuts.

5. Fill each prepared muffin cup about two-thirds full with batter. Bake until golden and firm, about 25 minutes. Remove the tin from the oven, and let it stand for 5 minutes. Then loosen the edges of the muffins with a knife and unmold.

Makes 12 large muffins

HOT-TEMPERED BRAN MUFFINS

*T*he following is a dinner (rather than breakfast) muffin, dedicated to the state of Texas, where the denizens' internal temperature is a direct result of their pepper consumption. Be advised, however—these are relatively mild mannered.

2½ cups Bran Flakes cereal
1 cup milk
1 egg, lightly beaten
⅓ cup unsalted butter, melted
½ cup honey
2 teaspoons hot salsa
1 pickled jalapeño pepper, seeded,
    deveined, and minced
1 tablespoon minced pickled sweet pepper
    or pimiento
1 cup all-purpose flour
1 tablespoon baking powder
½ teaspoon salt

1. Preheat the oven to 400°F. Lightly grease a 12-cup muffin tin.
2. Place the Bran Flakes in the container of a food processor, and process until smooth. Transfer the bran to a large bowl, and pour the milk over it; let stand 3 minutes.
3. Add the egg, butter, honey, salsa, jalapeño pepper, and sweet pepper to the bran mixture, and stir until smooth.
4. Combine the flour, baking powder, and salt in another bowl. Mix well, and stir into the bran mixture until just smooth.
5. Fill each prepared muffin cup about two-thirds full with batter. Bake until golden and firm, about 25 minutes. Remove the tin from the oven, and let it stand 5 minutes. Then loosen the edges of the muffins with a knife and unmold.
Makes 12 muffins

ANNA TEEL BARLOW'S HEAVENLY BRANS

"*H*eavenly" is no random compliment for the next dispensation—two packaged bran breakfast cereals in one sublime amalgam. Mrs. Barlow is so generous a recipe-giver that she also included her method for whipping up "baker's secret," an unguent that ensures any muffin's quick release from the clutches of a sticky pan.

Baker's Secret (see Box, page 42)
⅓ cup chopped pitted dates
½ cup walnut halves, chopped
1 cup plus 2 tablespoons all-purpose flour,
    sifted
1 egg
¼ cup vegetable oil

6 tablespoons sugar
1 cup buttermilk
½ cup water, boiling
1 cup All-Bran cereal
1¼ teaspoons baking soda
½ teaspoon salt
½ cup Bran Flakes cereal

BAKER'S SECRET

Here is Anna Teel Barlow's recipe for Baker's Secret: Combine ¼ cup solid vegetable shortening, ¼ cup vegetable oil, and ¼ cup all-purpose flour. Beat until creamy. Store in a jar in the refrigerator. Use to grease cake pans, bread pans, and muffin tins. It will keep indefinitely.

1. Preheat the oven to 400°F. Lightly grease two 9- or 12-cup muffin tins with Baker's Secret.

2. Place the dates and walnuts in a medium-size bowl and toss with the 2 tablespoons flour. Set aside.

3. Lightly beat the egg in a large bowl. Slowly beat in the oil. Then beat in the sugar and buttermilk.

4. Pour the boiling water over the All-Bran in a small bowl. Stir this into the buttermilk mixture.

5. Sift the remaining 1 cup flour with the baking soda and salt. Stir the flour into the buttermilk mixture and add the Bran Flakes and reserved dates and walnuts.

6. Fill each prepared muffin cup about two-thirds full with batter. Bake until golden and firm, about 25 minutes. Remove the tins from the oven, and let them stand for 5 minutes. Then loosen the edges of the muffins with a knife and unmold.

Makes 15 to 16 muffins

BELTANE RANCH BRANS

Rosemary Wood is the donor here. I first sampled Ms. Wood's exceptional handiwork, slathered with butter and homemade strawberry jam, at breakfast under a live oak tree, when I was a paying guest at her rambling colonial ranch in Glen Ellen, California. After I professed my admiration, she produced the recipe. It came with some good advice, too: The batter may be prepared (and kept covered in the fridge) up to four weeks ahead with no apparent diminishment of flavor or texture. Knowing you have batter at the ready allows you to make great muffins any time you get the urge. Now that's a true bran-lover's bonus!

1 box (1 pound) Bran Flakes cereal
3 cups sugar
5 cups all-purpose flour
5 teaspoons baking soda
2 teaspoons salt
1 cup vegetable oil
4 eggs, lightly beaten
1 quart buttermilk

1. Preheat the oven to 375°F. Lightly grease up to four 12-cup muffin tins.

2. Combine the Bran Flakes, sugar, flour, baking soda, and salt in a large bowl. Mix well, and add the oil, eggs, and buttermilk. Stir until smooth. Store, well covered, in the refrigerator until needed, up to four weeks' time.

3. Fill each prepared muffin cup about two-thirds full with batter. Bake until golden and firm, 15 to 20 minutes (or a few minutes longer if batter was not brought to room temperature). Remove the tins from the oven, and let them stand for 5 minutes. Then loosen the edges of the muffins with a knife and unmold.

Makes about 48 muffins

A Beltane Dozen

If you are as shy of refrigerator room as I am, you may wish to subdivide the recipe. Here's how to get a single batch.

2¾ cups Bran Flakes cereal
¾ cup sugar
1¼ cups all-purpose flour
1¼ teaspoons baking soda
½ teaspoon salt
¼ cup vegetable oil
1 egg, lightly beaten
1 cup buttermilk

Follow steps 1 through 3, above, greasing only one 12-cup muffin tin.
Makes 12 muffins

BUTTERMILK BRAN BREAD

The recipe for my favorite bread to toast and slather with peanut butter and honey.

2 packages dry yeast
½ cup lukewarm water
1 cup buttermilk, at room temperature
2 tablespoons safflower oil
¼ cup molasses
¼ cup honey
1 teaspoon coarse (kosher) salt
1 cup unprocessed wheat bran
1 cup whole-wheat flour
5 cups all-purpose flour (approximately)
Cornmeal
1 tablespoon unsalted butter, melted

1. Place the yeast in a large bowl and sprinkle it with the water. Let it stand a few minutes to soften; then stir in the buttermilk, safflower oil, molasses, honey, salt, and bran. Let stand for 5 minutes.

2. Slowly beat in the whole-wheat flour with a heavy wooden spoon, and then about 3½ cups of the all-purpose flour, enough to form a slightly sticky dough. Transfer the dough to a lightly floured surface. Knead the dough for 10 minutes, incorporating about 1 more cup of the all-purpose flour. When the dough is elastic, place it in a large lightly greased bowl. Turn the dough so that it is lightly greased all over. Cover tightly, and let rise until doubled, 2½ hours.

Though dentists do not assiduously recommend it, bran is good for the teeth too!

Despite a tendency of its particles to lodge between molars, wheat bran makes such a dandy dentifrice that natives of the Ural mountains have been chewing it for years. Hundreds of years, actually—and these denizens have remarkably white choppers to show for any wear and tear.

Likewise, in Outer Mongolia tribesmen always chomp rice bran to toughen up flaccid gums.

And while I do not suggest the practice for most city dwellers (chewing bran involves much expectoration), it's a good idea to remember that wheat bran is so high in vitamin B (which promotes the formation of healthy body tissues) that it contains twice the mineral content of the wheat grain itself.

Parenthetically, bran also makes an excellent staple for bread makers who enjoy a degree of dental exercise at the dinner table. Like me!

3. Punch the dough down and divide it in half. Knead each half briefly on a lightly floured board, forming them into round loaves. Place the loaves on a cornmeal-sprinkled baking sheet, cover with a flour-rubbed tea towel, and let stand 1 hour.

4. Preheat the oven to 375°F.

5. Brush the tops of the loaves with the melted butter. Bake in the top third of the oven until golden brown and hollow-sounding when tapped with your finger, about 30 minutes.

Makes 2 loaves

Sharon Tyler Herbst's Bran Waffles

Sharon Tyler Herbst is one of a small contingent of San Francisco cookbook writers who eschew what is trendy for what is tried and true at the table. More important, her recipes never fail. The following bounty is borrowed from her excellent book *Breads*.

3 eggs, separated
¾ cup sour cream
¾ cup milk
⅔ cup unsalted butter, melted
½ cup Bran Flakes cereal
2 teaspoons molasses
½ teaspoon vanilla extract
1½ cups all-purpose flour
2 teaspoons baking powder
½ teaspoon baking soda
¼ teaspoon salt
2 tablespoons sugar

1. Lightly beat the egg yolks in a medium-size bowl. Whisk in the sour cream, milk, butter, Bran Flakes, molasses, and vanilla.

2. Combine the flour, baking powder, baking soda, salt, and sugar in another bowl. Stir into the bran mixture.

3. Beat the egg whites until stiff, and fold them into the waffle batter. Cook the waffles in a preheated waffle iron, following manufacturer's directions. Keep the waffles warm on a wire rack in a 200°F oven while you cook the remaining batter.

Serves 4

Aside from cereal at the breakfast table, bran makes a positive contribution to any health-minded cook's collection of hotcakes, flapjacks, and waffles—adding a distinctive taste (like toasted nuts) as well as a nutritive embellishment.

BRAN-GRAHAM CRACKER CRUST

*T*o my tongue, bran's most surprising alliances are all on the sweet side. For starters, consider it as the architecture of a splendidly simple pastry.

This mixture is devised of crushed wheat crackers and toasted unprocessed wheat bran. Use it for any unctuous filling you have a letch for—or try either of the sweet-toothed suggestions that follow.

⅓ cup unprocessed wheat bran, toasted (see page 30)
1¼ cups graham cracker crumbs (about 11 graham crackers)
⅓ cup sifted confectioners' sugar
1 teaspoon ground cinnamon
7 tablespoons unsalted butter, melted

1. Preheat the oven to 300°F. Lightly butter a 9-inch pie plate.

2. Place the bran in the container of a food processor or blender, and process as fine as possible, 3 to 5 minutes.

3. Combine the bran, cracker crumbs, confectioners' sugar, and cinnamon in a medium-size bowl. Pour the melted butter over the mixture, and blend thoroughly. Press the crumb mixture over the bottom and sides of the prepared pie plate. Bake 15 minutes. Cool thoroughly before using.

Makes crust for one 9-inch pie

PEANUT BUTTER PIE

*T*he handiwork of Susan Alper, a talented young chef at The Lamb & The Lion Restaurant in Elmont, New York. Her pie is a cold, crunchy, creamy crowd-pleaser. But better than ever when bedded on bran.

¼ pound cream cheese, at room temperature
1 cup chunky-style peanut butter, at room temperature
1 cup confectioners' sugar, sifted
⅓ cup milk
2 teaspoons vanilla extract
1 teaspoon dark rum
1½ cups heavy or whipping cream
1 Bran-Graham Cracker Crust (see above)

1. Combine the cream cheese and peanut butter in the large bowl of an electric mixer. Beat until smooth. Add the confectioners' sugar; beat until fluffy. Beat in the milk, vanilla, and rum.

2. Beat the cream until stiff. Stir one third of the cream into the peanut butter mixture. Fold in the remaining cream. Spoon into the prepared pie shell. Refrigerate 4 hours before serving.

Serves 8

NEW YORK LIME PIE

A distant cousin of a classic Florida Key lime pie, this chiffony creation is made with store-bought citrus and lots of imagination.

3 eggs, separated
1 cup granulated sugar
Juice of 3 limes (½ cup)
Finely grated zest of 2 limes
2 tablespoons light rum
1 tablespoon unflavored gelatin
¼ cup cold water
1 cup heavy or whipping cream
1 tablespoon confectioners' sugar
1 Bran-Graham Cracker Crust
    (see page 45)

1. Beat the egg yolks with the granulated sugar and lime juice in a large bowl until light. Slowly beat in the lime zest and rum.

2. Combine the gelatin and the cold water in a small bowl, and set aside to soften, 1 minute. Place the bowl over hot water and stir until the gelatin has dissolved. Stir it into the lime juice mixture. Transfer to the top of a double boiler and cook, stirring often, over simmering water for 10 minutes. Set aside to cool for 5 minutes, and then refrigerate until the mixture begins to set, about 40 minutes.

3. Beat the cream with the confectioners' sugar until thick. Fold it into the lime mixture. Beat the egg whites until stiff; fold them into the lime mixture. Refrigerate 15 minutes, then fold the mixture lightly and refrigerate another 10 minutes. (Do not allow the mixture to set completely.) Spoon the filling into the prepared pie shell. Refrigerate 3 hours.

Serves 6 to 8

CRAN-BRAN BETTY

Brown Betty is a fruited American classic traditionally made of sliced apples, layered between sheets of crumbs and sugar and baked in a casserole. My version, on the tart side, is strictly Cape Cod in derivation. Serve it with cinnamon ice cream.

¾ pound cranberries, picked over and
    rinsed
1½ cups sugar
¼ cup honey
Finely slivered zest of 1 large orange
¼ teaspoon freshly grated nutmeg
½ teaspoon ground cinnamon
¼ teaspoon salt
3 tablespoons Grand Marnier
2 pounds sweet apples
½ cup all-purpose flour

½ cup unprocessed wheat bran, toasted
    (see page 30)
4 tablespoons plus 2 teaspoons unsalted
    butter, chilled
Cinnamon Ice Cream (recipe follows)

1. In a large mixing bowl, combine the cranberries, 1 cup of the sugar, the honey, orange zest, nutmeg, cinnamon, salt, and Grand Marnier. Let stand 15 minutes.

2. Preheat the oven to 350°F. Lightly butter a shallow baking dish.

3. Peel, core, and slice the apples, stirring the slices into the cranberry mixture as you work.

4. Combine the remaining ½ cup sugar, the bran, and the flour in another bowl. Add the 4 tablespoons butter and blend with a pastry blender until the mixture has the texture of coarse crumbs.

5. Place a third of the cranberry-apple mixture over the bottom of the prepared baking dish. Sprinkle with a third of the bran mixture. Continue to layer, ending with bran mixture. Dot the top with the 2 teaspoons butter. Bake until crisp, about 45 minutes. Serve slightly warm, with Cinnamon Ice Cream.

Serves 8

Bran is saddled with some highly disparate cognomens across the globe. Health-concerned Frenchmen call it *son*, which means a "ring" or "cover." Germans dub it *Kleie*. Nutrition-minded Italians spoon their bran as *crusca*, which may be translated as "rough stuff," while the Spanish call it *salvado*, or "salvation," which bespeaks bran's value in a diet more eloquently than any tract of Dr. Graham and friends.

Cinnamon Ice Cream

Cinnamon (to my mind) is the cranberry's most stalwart flavor alliance. For concrete evidence, treat yourself to the joy of the following seductive cinnamon ice cream, allowing it to melt on the warm pudding's surface. It is the handiwork of Karl Dauner, a brilliant young German-born, New York-practicing chef-caterer.

2 cups heavy or whipping cream
¾ cup milk
2 cinnamon sticks
7 egg yolks
½ teaspoon ground cinnamon
½ cup sugar

1. Combine the cream with the milk and cinnamon sticks in a glass or ceramic bowl. Cover, and let stand at room temperature for 4 hours.

2. Transfer the cream, milk, and cinnamon sticks to a medium-size noncorrosive saucepan. Slowly heat just to the boiling point. Remove the pan from the heat, and let it stand until cool. Discard the cinnamon sticks. (Scoop any film from the surface if necessary.)

3. In a large bowl, beat the egg yolks with the ground cinnamon and sugar until light and fluffy. Add the cooled cream/milk mixture. Pour into the canister of an ice cream maker and process according to manufacturer's directions.

Makes about 1 quart

ORIGINAL SIN FRUITCAKE

What a surprise to discover that all the healthy goodness of carrots, dates, and bran can produce such a decadent meal ending!

FOR THE CAKE

2 eggs
1⅓ cups granulated sugar
⅔ cup vegetable oil
1½ teaspoons vanilla extract
⅔ cup fresh orange juice
2 teaspoons finely slivered orange zest
⅓ cup unprocessed wheat bran
1⅔ cups cake flour, sifted
1 teaspoon baking soda
½ teaspoon baking powder
¼ teaspoon salt
1½ teaspoons ground cinnamon
⅔ cup coarsely chopped walnuts
½ cup chopped pitted dates
1½ cups loosely packed grated carrots

FOR THE ICING

1 cup confectioners' sugar
2 tablespoons fresh orange juice
1 teaspoon heavy or whipping cream

1. Preheat the oven to 325°F. Lightly butter and flour an 8- to 10-cup bundt pan.

2. Beat the eggs with the sugar in a large bowl until light. Beat in the oil, vanilla, orange juice, and orange zest.

3. Combine the bran, flour, baking soda, baking powder, salt, and cinnamon in another bowl. Mix well; then stir into the egg mixture. Let stand 10 minutes. Stir in the walnuts, dates, and carrots.

4. Pour the batter into the prepared bundt pan. Bake until a toothpick inserted in the center of the cake comes out clean, about 1 hour. Cool completely in the pan on a rack before unmolding.

5. To make the icing, combine the confectioners' sugar with the orange juice and cream; beat until smooth. Drizzle over the cake.

Serves 8 to 10

FORT KNOX BARS

*T*he name says it all. These honey-bran-pecan squares are like 48-carat gold on the tongue and equally worthy of serious hoarding. But store them in a freezer after baking, not in a safe deposit vault, please.

FOR THE CRUST

5 tablespoons unsalted butter, at room
  temperature
¼ cup sugar
¼ cup solid vegetable shortening
2 egg yolks
1 teaspoon bourbon
1½ cups all-purpose flour
½ teaspoon baking powder
⅛ teaspoon salt

FOR THE FILLING

1 cup (2 sticks) unsalted butter
½ cup honey
1¼ cups firmly packed light brown sugar
¼ cup granulated sugar
1 teaspoon vanilla extract
2 teaspoons bourbon
¼ cup heavy or whipping cream
3 cups coarsely chopped pecans
1 cup All-Bran cereal

1. Make the crust: In a medium-size bowl, beat the butter with the sugar and shortening until light. Beat in the egg yolks and bourbon.

2. Sift the flour with the baking powder and salt into another bowl. Stir into the butter mixture with a wooden spoon. Cover, and chill in the freezer for 30 minutes.

3. Preheat the oven to 350°F.

4. Remove the dough from the freezer and roll it out between sheets of wax paper to form a 10 by 13-inch rectangle. Carefully remove the top sheet of wax paper and flip the dough over into a 9 by 12-inch baking pan. Press any broken edges together. Prick the dough all over with a fork. Bake 10 minutes, then cool on a rack.

5. Make the filling: Combine the butter, honey, both sugars, and vanilla in a medium-size saucepan. Heat to boiling. Reduce the heat and simmer, stirring often, 3 minutes. Remove the pan from the heat. Stir in the bourbon, cream, pecans, and All-Bran. Mix well, and spoon over the prebaked crust. Bake until firm, about 25 minutes. Cool completely before cutting into 1¼-inch squares.

Makes about 60 bars

OAT BRAN VARIATIONS

When the word "bran" crops up, the designation most often implies wheat. But of late, manufacturers of oat products (like Quaker) have been making a serious bid to turn consumer awareness to oat bran.

Functionally, the difference between one bran and another boils down to degrees of stove-top malleability. The unprocessed fiber of oat bran is water-soluble, whereas the fiber of unprocessed wheat bran is not. In cooking, oat bran has an inherent creaminess while wheat bran has a crisp bite.

More important than texture, however, are the two brans' distinguishing health characteristics. Oat bran has been found to reduce blood levels of LDL cholesterol (the type associated with fatty arterial deposits). Scientists maintain that while cholesterol reduc-tion is not entirely absent with other brans, only oat has a proven track record—just as wheat bran has no peer in the area of digestive and intestinal regulation.

If you consider substituting oat bran for wheat in any recipe, note at the outset that oat bran will be moister and more dense than its more familiar wheat counterpart.

The following side dishes (or first courses) are meant to flesh out a spare meal or to replace meat, poultry, or fish as an entrée on occasion. Devised specifically for oat bran, they taste so good that even diners without particular health concerns will find them utterly irresistible. The oat variations on muffins and biscuits are equally healthful and delicious.

OAT BRAN MUFFINS

*U*sing pure oat bran makes for a heavy muffin, so combine it with cake or soft wheat flour. For a variation that is super-potassium-enriched, substitute chopped bananas for the golden raisins.

1 cup oat bran
1¼ cups cake or soft wheat flour
1 tablespoon baking powder
½ teaspoon salt
¼ cup firmly packed dark brown sugar
⅔ cup milk
¼ cup honey
2 tablespoons vegetable oil
2 eggs, lightly beaten, or ½ cup egg
substitute
½ cup golden raisins
½ cup chopped nuts

1. Preheat the oven to 425°F. Lightly grease a 12-cup muffin tin.

2. Combine the oat bran with the flour, baking powder, and salt in a large bowl. Add the brown sugar, and mix with your fingers or a pastry blender until well blended. Stir in the remaining ingredients.

3. Fill each prepared muffin cup about three-quarters full with batter. Bake until golden brown and firm, 15 to 18 minutes. Let the tin stand for 5 minutes, then loosen the edges with a knife and unmold the muffins.

Makes 12 muffins

COATED OAT BISCUITS

A healthy turn on a favorite Southern recipe. The biscuit dough is beaten and then coated in flour before baking. These are best served straight from the oven, with lots of honey.

1¾ cups cake or soft wheat flour
1 cup oat bran
1 tablespoon baking powder
½ teaspoon salt
½ cup solid vegetable shortening, chilled
1 cup milk (approximately)

1. Preheat the oven to 425°F. Lightly rub a baking sheet with oil.

2. Place ¼ cup of the flour in a small bowl and set it aside.

3. Combine 1 cup of the flour with the oat bran, baking powder, and salt in a large bowl. Cut in the vegetable shortening with a knife or a pastry blender

until well mixed. Stir 1 cup milk into the mixture, and let it stand 3 minutes to allow the bran to soften. The mixture will be slightly loose.

4. Beat the remaining ½ cup flour into the batter until the mixture is smooth and thick. It will resemble a smooth paste. (Add more milk if it is too thick.) Scoop up about 2 tablespoons of the dough on a spoon, then using your finger, push the dough off the spoon, dropping it into the reserved flour. With your fingers spread apart, lightly toss the dough to coat it well with flour. Do not worry about the excess flour. Gently place the dough on the prepared baking sheet, and repeat with the remaining dough. Bake until lightly browned, 15 to 18 minutes.

Makes 12 biscuits

TOMATO-OAT BRAN PUDDING

Almost like a thick vegetable porridge, this super-healthful dish is delicious when matched with plain broiled chicken and a green vegetable.

2 tablespoons olive oil
1 medium onion, chopped
1 clove garlic, minced
1 can (28 ounces) imported plum tomatoes (about 3¼ cups)
1 teaspoon chopped fresh basil, or ½ teaspoon dried
1 teaspoon chopped fresh thyme, or ¼ teaspoon dried
¼ teaspoon sugar
1 cup oat bran
¼ teaspoon salt
¼ teaspoon freshly ground black pepper
⅛ teaspoon crushed dried hot red peppers
½ cup grated Gruyère cheese
2 tablespoons freshly grated Parmesan cheese

1. Preheat the oven to 350°F.

2. Heat the oil in a medium-size saucepan over medium-low heat. Add the onion; cook 1 minute. Add the garlic; cook 3 minutes (do not brown). Stir in the tomatoes, breaking them up with a wooden spoon. Add the basil, thyme, and sugar. Heat to boiling. Reduce the heat and simmer, uncovered, until reduced to 3 cups, about 8 minutes.

3. Stir the oat bran into the tomato mixture. Cook, stirring frequently, until thick, about 6 minutes. Stir in the salt, black pepper, dried red peppers, Gruyère, and 1 tablespoon of the Parmesan. Spoon the mixture into a lightly buttered 1½-quart soufflé dish. Sprinkle the top with the remaining 1 tablespoon Parmesan. Bake 20 minutes.

Serves 4

SPINACH AND OAT BRAN SOUFFLE

I often serve this green-flecked soufflé with sliced cold meats and a plate of fresh sliced tomatoes alongside for a light dinner.

1½ tablespoons olive oil
1 large shallot, finely chopped
1 clove garlic, minced
⅛ teaspoon crushed dried hot red peppers
1 package (10 ounces) frozen chopped spinach, thawed and squeezed dry
⅔ cup oat bran

2 cups milk or skim milk
1 egg yolk
⅛ to ¼ teaspoon hot pepper sauce
Salt and freshly ground black pepper to taste
5 egg whites
1 teaspoon freshly grated Parmesan cheese

1. Preheat the oven to 400°F.

2. Heat the oil in a medium-size skillet over medium-low heat. Add the shallot; cook 1 minute. Add the garlic and dried red peppers; cook 2 minutes longer. Stir in the spinach and cook, stirring often, until most of the liquid has evaporated, about 4 minutes. Set aside.

3. Place the bran in a medium-size saucepan. Pour the milk over it and heat it slowly, stirring often, to boiling. Reduce the heat and simmer until thick, about 3 minutes. Remove the pan from the heat and beat in the egg yolk. Stir in the spinach mixture, hot pepper sauce, and salt and pepper.

4. Beat the egg whites until stiff. Fold them into the spinach-bran mixture. Spoon into a lightly greased 1½-quart soufflé dish, and sprinkle the top with the Parmesan. Bake until puffed and golden, 30 minutes.

Serves 6

CREAMY CARROTY OAT BRAN PUREE

Another hearty, healthy side dish, best served with simply prepared meat or fish. Vegetarians should feel free to substitute a strong vegetable stock for the chicken stock.

½ pound carrots, peeled and sliced
1 onion, sliced
3 cups homemade chicken stock (see page 376) or canned broth
1 cup oat bran
½ teaspoon freshly grated nutmeg
Salt and freshly ground black pepper to taste
1 teaspoon chopped fresh chives

1. Combine the carrots, onion, and chicken stock in a medium-size saucepan. Cover and heat to boiling. Reduce the heat and simmer, covered, until the vegetables are tender, about 15 minutes. Drain over another saucepan. (You should have 3 cups liquid; add water to make that amount, if necessary.)

2. Place the cooked onion and carrots in the container of a food processor or blender. Process until smooth.

3. Heat the reserved cooking broth to boiling; then reduce the heat. Whisk in the oat bran and cook, whisking constantly, over medium-low heat until smooth and thick, about 4 minutes. Stir in the carrot-onion mixture. Add the nutmeg, and season with salt and pepper. Keep warm over low heat, or in the top of a double boiler over simmering water. Stir in the chives before serving.

Serves 6

WILD-OAT BRAN RISOTTO

Wild, because of the mushrooms. Risotto, because the combination of the creamy oat bran and cooked rice reminds me of the velvety smoothness of the Italian classic.

2 tablespoons olive oil
1 medium onion, finely chopped
1 clove garlic, minced
¼ pound large mushroom caps (shiitakes if possible), sliced
3 cups defatted homemade chicken stock (see page 376) or canned broth
1 cup oat bran
¼ cup chopped prosciutto
1 cup cooked long-grain rice (see page 217), warmed
Freshly ground black pepper to taste
Chopped fresh parsley, for garnish

1. Heat the oil in a large saucepan over medium-low heat. Add the onion; cook 1 minute. Add the garlic; cook 4 minutes.

2. Push the onions to the edge of the pan and raise the heat to medium. Add the sliced mushrooms and cook, stirring often, until lightly browned, about 4 minutes. Stir in the chicken stock, scraping the sides and bottom of the pan. Whisk in the oat bran, and cook, whisking constantly, until thick, about 3 minutes.

3. Stir the prosciutto and cooked rice into the bran mixture. Season with pepper, and sprinkle with parsley.

Serves 4

RICE HAS A BRAN TOO!

Rice bran is the oily brown coating found under the hard outer shell of rice grains.

Up until the 1980s, no one outside the Orient had found any serious use for rice bran except as animal food. But there is a very recent development in the heart of southern Louisiana's rice belt: the cultivation of many new commercial products from rice bran—notably a polyunsaturated oil that is high in vitamin E and fiber and totally allergen-free.

BUCKWHEAT

A Great Source of Complex Carbohydrates

The next tale is about buckwheat pancakes, basketball, and my father, in reverse order.

From middle age until his death, my father's life was not a conspicuously happy one. A self-made man with a handsome wife and two healthy children, S. M. Greene (as he liked to be called) had had a thriving business and a well-deserved reputation as "the fastest electrical contractor in the fastest-growing suburb of New York City" until the Depression slowed him down.

He was also a man who liked to sing. And though not particularly gifted with mellow vocal chords, he used to sing, hum, and whistle all the time. When the stock market crash halted the building industry, my father managed to stay in good voice, for he had saved enough for what he always called "a rainy day." Even after the banks failed in 1932, he warbled, albeit uneasily, "Let's have another cup'a coffee and let's have another piece'a pie." Besides, S. M. was a man of high hopes. He voted for Roosevelt and Repeal with real optimism, and crooned "Happy days are here again . . ." on Election Day in eager anticipation.

But as one unhappy day ran into another, his capital dwindled, his investments were devalued, and his friends—to whom he had often lent money in the past—deserted him. So my father stopped singing.

These disappointments sent him into a kind of torpor that little could dispel, except two things: food and sports. I remember my father at breakfast, demolishing pancakes with one hand while holding the sports section of the paper in the other, roundly cursing the losing team he had backed. Each morning he would seek out the back page before glancing at the headlines. Even on the day war was declared in Europe.

Like the ballpark figures and knock-out scores, what he was served also caused my father to give vent to his emotions.

"What the heck is this I am eating?" he would inquire. And he would be little mollified at the answer, for S. M. Greene was not an easy man to please. His eating habits were parochial, and he hungered after dishes of his youth that I could never prepare to his satisfaction.

"Son, we will have to find you a better cookbook," he announced one day after I had failed at the task again. "Or find us a new chef!"

That was a joke, of course, since I had become the family cook by default when my mother went to work "temporarily"—I stayed at the job almost a decade.

Actually as I approached adolescence I grew so tall and robust that I sensed my parent viewing me in a new and unexpected light—as potential brawn for the playing fields. However, I hadn't the slightest aptitude for sports. I either fumbled the ball, dropped the bat, or missed the pass!

If he was discouraged, my father kept it to himself. But then, I said he was a hopeful man. Rather than upbraiding me for physical shortcomings, he concentrated on refining my culinary skills. An avowed lover of the dark, pungent flavor of buckwheat, he would leave pancake recipes (torn from newspapers) on my dresser or pillow, with terse notes penciled in the margin: "Sound good?" or "Thought this might be worth a try."

A dutiful son, I attacked every recipe my father pressed upon me, but none pleased his demanding tongue. A memory of ethereal buckwheat cakes consumed somewhere, sometime long ago, always outclassed my lumpish efforts. And Bert's score at the griddle remained resolutely zero.

This story has a happier end than you would suppose. After Pearl Harbor, my father applied for war work at a naval base in Rhode Island, where he was hired (at maximum security) to install heavy-duty electrical equipment in destroyers and submarines. Through hard labor he regained his pride, a small bank account, and a special commendation from the President of the United States. The fact that he had been *chosen* altered his perception of himself. He even began to hum again.

His son's college days, if anything, strengthened my father's vibrato. By the time I arrived at William and Mary, almost all the varsity men had been drafted. So it was really not surprising that the coach of the basketball team signed me up to play center at first sight—without a tryout and over my mild protests—merely because I was an awesome size!

My father never saw me play. Few did, in fact, for I did not last long into the season. But parental pride was obviously contagious. After reading a letter from home, the coach who had benched me made me team manager instead.

It was a high-spirited man who drove to Williamsburg at the end of freshman year to fetch his son home. What made my father so exuberant was not sports alone, but the fact that someone in the South knew how to make his beloved buckwheat cakes.

After consuming a plateful of these airy pancakes at the hotel where he and my mother spent the night, my father immediately dispatched me to the kitchen to procure the recipe.

Through amazing grace—for I was actually a shy kid—I convinced the tall black man at the huge stove to part with his secret, and S. M. Greene's cup literally ranneth over.

He had not sung in years, but on that long drive home from dappled Virginia to dusty New York, my father would turn to grin at me (the almost athlete) and then croon back at the windshield: "Yessir, that's my baby now!"

The Grain's Genesis

Technically speaking, buckwheat is no grain at all but a fruit of the *Fagopyrum* genus, a distant cousin of garden-variety rhubarb. Like its spiky kin, buckwheat is a veritable magnet for honeybees and a mild inhibitor of cutworms and white flies. But there the family resemblance ends. Despite the corolla of papery white blossoms and delicate vernal perfume, it is buckwheat's seed rather than its stem that is the plant's strong point. A three-cornered shell, when dried and split it reveals a pale kernel that is known as a "groat." In one form or another, groats have been keeping man on the straight and narrow since the 10th century B.C. Maybe even before, buckwheat pharmacopeia being somewhat on the scanty side.

One thing is certain, however: The first buckwheat groat blossomed in Central Asia. To this day, in fact, Manchurian legends persist of giants who roamed the earth, leaving mountains and valleys wherever their footprints fell, and who were nourished by seeds of night-flowering trees. It is no coinci-

dence that for centuries buckwheat was erroneously called "beech-wheat" in China because the seed was much like the nut of a flowering beech tree.

Food scouts tell us that buckwheat's first harvest took place near Lake Baikal, a body of water that forms a natural border between Manchuria and Siberia, giving both the Chinese and the Russians license to claim it as a natural resource. And rather more pertinently, the incentive to stir generous helpings into their native cuisines. Despite the prandial enthusiasm, buckwheat remained virtually untasted by Europeans until well into the Middle Ages.

Some pundits claim that buckwheat was a souvenir of Tartar raids on northern Europe in the 1400s. Others, equally emphatic, state that buckwheat entered southern Europe with the invading Moors. Which may be a shade closer to the mark, since Italians, Spanish, and French to this day refer to buckwheat as *sarrasin*, or "Saracen grain."

It was the Dutch who gave buckwheat its rightful name. In 1549 they officially dubbed it *boek weit* (book wheat) to honor the Scriptures whose auspices, they claimed, brought it to flower on their shores. It's a simile not too far-fetched. Like the Bible, buckwheat's survival has been a saga of resistance to adversity. It thrives on poor soil and inhospitable climate, and has been known to survive drought, frost, and even a flood from time to time.

Buckwheat made its way west to the New World as part of a Dutch settler's dowry, when his *vrouw*'s family, short on guilders, pressed groats instead. The seed took root in the rich soil of the Hudson Valley almost immediately, so the story appears to have had a rather happy ending.

A 1627 logbook of farmer H. T. Van Cortland in the colony of Niew Amsterdaam listed a yield of over "137 zaks boek weit vrucht" after a first summer harvest. But as buckwheat was planted only as a "catch crop" (where odds and ends of a field are sown together), the burgher fed most of it to his Holstein cows, realizing little profit other than *pannekoek* flour!

And it is only in recent history—since the rise of the health food movement, in fact—that buckwheat farming has proven to be financially viable.

Today the grain-that-is-not-a-grain is cultivated like a patchwork quilt from Maine to the Midwest, with a high proportion of the crop grown and milled in the small town of Penn Yan, in the lakes region of western New York State. Buckwheat's hardiness is its chief asset to farmers as well as a prime selling point to natural foodies, because it is one of the few commercially grown U.S. crops that requires no chemicals in the field or in the processing plant.

Some Plain Grain Talk

The proteins in buckwheat are the best-known source of complex carbohydrates. The fuel acquired by consuming these complex carbohydrates (found only in plant kingdom starches) produces what nutritionists call a "protein-sparing effect," which can be compared to an interest-bearing bank account: it allows the body to meet its energy requirements without dipping into its protein reserves. Any excess that the body accrues are reserved, like interest, to be called upon for cell building and tissue repair if the body malfunctions.

To give the health picture an even rosier glow, buckwheat also contains a high proportion of all eight amino acids (lysine, leucine, isoleucine, methionine, tryptophan, threonine, phenylalanine, and valine), which the body does not manufacture but are nonetheless deemed absolutely essential for keeping it in tip-top shape. All this makes buckwheat closer to being a "complete protein" than any other plant source—even soybeans!

How to Buy It

By and large buckwheat is not generally found on supermarket shelves, and a shopper must make tracks to a natural foods store to find a supply of the uncommon varieties—with one notable exception: *kasha*, which is actually roasted hulled buckwheat kernels.

To lessen consumers' confusion, let me state at the outset that while all buckwheat is groats, there are two basic forms on the market: whole white buckwheat and roasted buckwheat (or kasha). And while both are virtually the same in texture after cooking, the flavor is as different as day and night. Roasted buckwheat (kasha) is toasted in an oven and tossed by hand until the kernels acquire a deep tan color, a nutlike flavor, and an ever-so-slightly-scorched aroma. Whole white buckwheat, on the other hand, is naturally dried and has a delicate flavor that makes it an admirable stand-in for rice or pasta.

Kasha is packaged four ways: whole, coarse, medium, and fine-ground. I generally use the whole or coarse form (interchangeably) in most dishes. Medium and fine-ground kasha cook somewhat more quickly and are decidedly less chewy.

Whole white buckwheat is packaged two ways: hulled groats, the form I most often opt for at the stove, and cream of buckwheat, a stone-ground grits-like cereal from the heart of the kernel.

Birkett Mills, of Penn Yan, New York, is the major processor and packager of buckwheat in the U.S. Birkett Mills' kasha is sold in most supermarkets under the "Wolff's" trademark, while whole white buckwheat is sold as "Pocono" brand in health food stores. For more information, see the list of major suppliers and mail-order sources at the back of the book.

Buckwheat has a long shelf life in the kitchen. Store it, well covered in glass or airtight plastic containers, out of the direct sunlight for best results.

How to Cook It

*P*rior to cooking, kasha is traditionally coated with beaten egg (1 egg to 1 to 2 cups of kasha) and then stir-toasted in a heavy skillet over medium heat until dry, about 3 minutes. There are several reasons for this egg wash. European cooks insist it adds nutrients, but a more logical explanation is that when buckwheat is heated, the starch in the granules swells and ruptures, turning the cooked kernels mushy. A dried egg "polish" helps keep the grains separate and crisp even after long cooking periods.

My standard method for cooking kasha is to add the coated, toasted grains to a seasoning (such as sautéed onion) along with water or broth, cooking uncovered over fairly high heat until the mixture boils. Then reduce the heat to low and cook, covered, for 15 minutes. Stir once, and turn off the heat and allow the pan to stand, covered, 10 minutes longer.

Whole white buckwheat groats do not require an egg wash or any toasting beforehand. My standard precept for cooking groats is very simple. Merely combine groats with any seasoning until well coated, then add liquid and cook until the mixture boils. Reduce the heat to low and cook, covered for about 20 minutes.

KASHALLEGIANCE

Being "American" has a different connotation today than it did when I was a boy. These days it stands for pride in one's past. Back in the 1930s, when I was growing up, few Americans celebrated their ethnic roots, and there was shame in the admission that one's mother or father was foreign-born. Mine were not, but my maternal forebears came from Russia and Poland. They spoke in broken English and to my acute embarrassment sometimes lapsed into their mother tongue (Yiddish) in front of my friends.

To the chauvinist I was, even more mortifying than their accent was my grandparents' appetite. From time to time, one or the other would hanker after a dish from "the old country," like kasha—which, despite a highly exotic ring to its nomenclature, was so utterly alien in flavor and aroma that not one of their progeny or their progeny's star-spangled issue would even consider sampling a forkful! I guess we assumed that if we did, our taste buds would be branded un-American in the narrow eyes of our more Yankee compatriots.

If Louis and Minna Cohn were disturbed by their four grandchildren's snobbery, they never betrayed it. They ate their kasha (burnished by onions and braised with lamb or oxtails) as part of the inalienable rights bestowed by Miss Liberty herself (a lady who, I must report, my grandmother often confused with the poet Emma Lazarus, whose immortal words are inscribed on the statue's base, for she inevitably referred to her as "that Jewish girl in the harbor").

BASIC KASHA AND ONIONS

This is the simplest and easiest way to prepare kasha.

1 cup whole or coarse-ground kasha
1 large egg, lightly beaten
2 tablespoons unsalted butter
1 medium onion, finely chopped
4 scallions, white bulbs and green tops
    chopped separately
1 large clove garlic, minced
½ teaspoon ground mace
½ teaspoon chopped fresh thyme, or a
    pinch of dried
2 cups homemade beef stock (see page 377)
    or canned broth
Chopped fresh parsley, for garnish

1. Stir the kasha with the egg in a medium-size bowl until well mixed. Transfer to a medium-size skillet and place over medium heat. Stir the kasha with a fork until it is dry and the grains are separated, about 3 minutes.

2. Melt the butter in a medium-size saucepan over medium-low heat. Add the onion and the scallion bulbs; cook 1 minute. Add the garlic; cook until lightly browned, about 5 minutes.

3. Stir the kasha into the onion mixture, and add the mace, thyme, and beef stock. Heat to boiling. Reduce the heat and cook, covered, over low heat for 15 minutes. Stir once, turn off the heat, and let stand, covered, 10 minutes. Stir in the scallion tops, and sprinkle with parsley.

Serves 4 to 6

GRANDMOTHER'S SOUP

This soup is *not* an inheritance from either of my forebears. It is a receipt of Middle European persuasion, however, that, like the best of grandmothers' soups all over the world, cooks a long time but requires little or no attention until it's almost done.

1 cup white beans
1½ tablespoons olive oil
4 leeks, white bulbs with 1 inch of green
    stems, well rinsed and coarsely chopped
1 medium onion, chopped
3 large cloves garlic, chopped
1 large carrot, finely chopped
1 ham bone with meat on it
1 lamb bone with meat on it
4 large tomatoes, seeded and chopped
½ teaspoon sugar
1 tablespoon chopped fresh basil, or
    1 teaspoon dried
1 fresh sage leaf, minced, or a pinch dried

6 cups homemade chicken stock (see page
    376) or canned broth
4 cups water
½ cup whole white buckwheat groats
1 small jalapeño pepper, seeded, deveined
    and minced
2 small zucchini, finely chopped (about
    1 cup)
3-inch strip of lemon zest
Chopped fresh parsley, for garnish

1. Soak the beans overnight in cold water to cover. (Or place them in a medium-size saucepan and cover with cold water; heat to boiling and boil 2 minutes. Then let stand 1 hour.) Drain.

2. Heat the oil in a large saucepan over medium-low heat. Add the leeks and onion; cook 1 minute. Add 2 cloves of the garlic and the carrot; cook 4 minutes longer. Add the ham and lamb bones, the white beans, tomatoes, sugar, basil, sage, chicken stock, and water. Heat to boiling. Reduce the heat and gently simmer, covered, until the beans are tender, about 2 hours.

3. Remove the bones from the soup; remove the meat from the bones. Skim the surface of the soup of all fat (or cool and place in the refrigerator until grease congeals on the surface, then remove it). Return the meat to the soup and return to boiling.

4. Add the groats to the soup along with the jalapeño pepper. Reduce the heat and cook, covered, over low heat for 20 minutes. Add the zucchini; cook, uncovered, 5 minutes.

5. Meanwhile, mince the lemon zest together with the remaining clove of garlic. Add to the soup, sprinkle with parsley, and serve.

Serves 8 to 10

BLACKENED PORK CHOPS WITH RED-FACED GROATS

*T*his dish was invented for one of my TV appearances, on *Hour Magazine* with Gary Collins. The pork chops I used were the cheapest cut I could find at my supermarket, so a good meat tenderizer became a prerequisite prior to putting them in the skillet. If you buy prime pork, it's an option you may gloss over with my blessing.

4 pork chops, each about ¾ inch thick
2 teaspoons natural meat tenderizer
1 clove garlic, bruised
1 medium onion, finely chopped
1 clove garlic, minced
1 medium red bell pepper, cored, seeded
    and finely chopped
1 tablespoon tomato paste
½ teaspoon hot Hungarian paprika
1 cup whole white buckwheat groats
2 cups homemade beef stock (see page 377)
    or canned broth, heated
Chopped fresh parsley, for garnish

1. Preheat the oven to 350°F.

2. Sprinkle the pork chops on both sides with tenderizer. Pierce the meat with a fork, then rub it with the bruised garlic.

3. In a heavy ovenproof saucepan, large enough to hold the chops in one layer, sauté the meat, fatty edges first, until well browned on all sides, about 8 to 10 minutes. Remove the chops to a plate. Discard all but 1 tablespoon fat from the pan.

4. Add the onion to the saucepan and sauté over medium-low heat for 1 minute. Add the minced garlic and the bell pepper; cook 3 minutes longer. Stir in the tomato paste, paprika, groats, and stock. Arrange the chops on top of the groats mixture, cover, and transfer to the oven. Bake until the chops are tender and all liquid has been absorbed, about 20 minutes. Remove the pan from the oven and let it stand, still covered, for 5 minutes before serving. Sprinkle with parsley.

Serves 4

ALSATIAN PORK WITH BUCKWHEAT DUMPLINGS

In Alsace-Lorraine this dish is known as *porc avec quenelles blé noir*—literally, pork with black hay dumplings, "black hay" being buckwheat's name in French. And it is worthy of duplication at your stove, no matter how the appellation strikes you.

Use fine-ground kasha for the dumpling recipe. If you can't find some in your nearest natural foods store, grind your own by whirling whole kasha in a food processor or blender until it has the texture of percolator coffee grounds. This takes about 1½ to 2 minutes.

FOR THE PORK

2 tablespoons unsalted butter
1 tablespoon vegetable oil
2½ pounds boneless pork (from short ribs, spare ribs, thick-cut chops)
3 pounds sauerkraut, rinsed in cold water and drained
1 large tomato, peeled, seeded, and chopped (about 1 cup)
½ teaspoon caraway seeds
4 juniper berries, crushed
3 fresh sage leaves, chopped, or ¼ teaspoon dried
3 fresh basil leaves, chopped, or ¼ teaspoon dried
½ teaspoon anchovy paste
1 cup homemade chicken stock (see page 376) or canned broth
1½ cups Riesling wine (Alsatian, if possible)
8 cloves garlic
1 pound smoked sausage (such as kielbasa or bratwurst), cut into large pieces

FOR THE DUMPLINGS

¼ cup fine-ground kasha
½ cup water
½ teaspoon salt
1 teaspoon unsalted butter
1 egg, lightly beaten
½ cup milk
1 cup cake flour
2 teaspoons baking powder
2 teaspoons chopped fresh chives
1 teaspoon chopped fresh parsley

SOME FLAVOR NOTES ON GROATS

If you ask me to describe the difference between whole white buckwheat groats and roasted buckwheat groats (kasha), I will have to refer you to an epigram by the late-19th-century Russian gastronome, Curnonsky. "Cuisine," he wrote, "is when things taste like *themselves!*"

So it is with buckwheat. The difference between the passive sapidity of whole white groats (almost fated to be mated with other ingredients) and the dark, enveloping tincture of kasha (dominating every seasoning it meets) is as classic as yin and yang. For while the textures are identical (they were grown on the same branch, after all), a first bite of whole white groats can form an instant bond at a fork end, whereas kasha is an acquired taste that some, in fact, never ever truly acquire!

Greene's advice to the kashawary is to sample it prudently, beginning with the cabbage rolls, cornsticks, and dumplings.

1. Preheat the oven to 350°F.

2. To make the Alsatian pork, melt 1 tablespoon of the butter with the oil in a large ovenproof pot or Dutch oven over medium heat. Sauté the pork pieces until brown on all sides, about 10 minutes. Transfer the pork to a plate.

3. Pour off the grease from the pot, but do not wipe it out. Add the remaining tablespoon of butter and place over medium-low heat. Stir in the sauerkraut, tomato, caraway seeds, juniper berries, sage, basil, and anchovy paste. Mix well. Add the chicken stock and wine. Heat to boiling. Place the sautéed pork on top of the sauerkraut mixture, add the garlic cloves, and cover. Transfer the pot to the oven and bake for 1 hour and 10 minutes. Add the sausage and bake, covered, 20 minutes longer.

4. Meanwhile, make the dumplings. In a small saucepan combine the kasha with the water, salt, and butter. Heat to boiling. Reduce the heat and cook, covered, over low heat until tender, about 10 minutes. Transfer to a medium-size bowl and stir in the beaten egg, milk, cake flour, baking powder, chives, and parsley. Mix thoroughly.

5. Remove the pot from the oven. Cut the pork into bite-size pieces and slice the sausage. Return the meats to the pot and mix them into the sauerkraut. Place the dumpling batter, in large tablespoonfuls, over the top. Cover the pot, return it to the oven, and bake until the dumplings are firm, about 18 minutes.

Serves 6

GLOBE TROTTERS GROATS AND SAUSAGES

Of a decidedly mixed-up lineage, the next recipe makes a remarkably straightforward one-dish supper. I serve it with just a green salad, a crusty loaf of bread—and an icy cold beer.

9 sausages (3 sweet Italian, 3 hot Italian, and 3 Spanish chorizos), about 1¾ pounds total
2 medium onions, halved and sliced
1 tablespoon olive oil
1 medium green bell pepper, cored, seeded, and cut into strips
1 medium red bell pepper, cored, seeded, and cut into strips
1 medium yellow bell pepper, cored, seeded, and cut into strips
1½ cups whole white buckwheat groats
1 cup dry white wine
1½ cups homemade chicken stock (see page 376) or canned broth
½ cup sliced black olives (Niçoise or Kalamata)
Chopped fresh parsley, for garnish

1. Sauté the Italian sausages in a large saucepan over medium heat until well browned on all sides, 8 to 10 minutes. Transfer to a plate. Add the chorizos to the pan and sauté until well browned on all sides, 8 to 10 minutes. Transfer to the plate with the Italian sausages. Drain all but 1½ tablespoons of fat from the pan.

2. Add the onions to the pan and cook over medium heat until lightly browned, about 8 minutes. Transfer to a bowl.

3. Add the olive oil to the pan. Add all the peppers and toss over medium-high heat for 2 minutes. Return the onions to the pan and stir in the groats, wine, and stock, scraping the sides and bottom of the pan. Press the chorizos into the mixture, and top with the Italian sausages. Heat to boiling. Reduce the heat and cook, covered, over low heat for 20 minutes. Remove the sausages and slice, on the angle, into 2-inch pieces. Return the sausage pieces to the pepper mixture and toss in the olives. Sprinkle with parsley.

Serves 4 to 6

CLARA B. LESS'S STUFFED CABBAGE ROLLS

Clara B. Less, a long-time denizen of Dearborn, Michigan, is probably one of the great unheralded cooks of the nation, and I am doing my best to put her on the map! A reader who became a pen pal, over the years she has sent me innumerable recipes that have worked their way (like inchworms) into books, articles, and newspaper columns. Her splendid-yet-salubrious dish that follows originally called for a tin of canned soup in the ingredients list, plus a pithy comment: "Bert, I know you hate cream of mushroom soup but the dish is *delicious!*" No question about it, Clara dear. But in my opinion better yet with a homemade blanket of béchamel sauce and mushrooms! Cheating cooks may use their own judgment in the matter. Just don't tell *me* about it, please!

With Mrs. Less's remarkable cabbage rolls, I usually serve an accompanying boat of tomato sauce. It's another option. The sauce of choice—heavy, heavy on the garlic—comes from another brilliant chef, Karl Dauner, currently at the helm of one of New York's best and brightest catering establishments, Custom Cuisine.

2 large eggs
1 cup whole or coarse-ground kasha
2 ounces salt pork, diced (about ½ cup)
1 medium onion, chopped
1 cup long-grain rice
2 tablespoons pearl barley
½ teaspoon salt
¼ teaspoon freshly ground black pepper
2 cups water
1 large head cabbage (about 3 pounds), leaves separated

¾ pound ground beef
½ pound ground veal
¼ pound ground pork
2 tablespoons chopped fresh parsley
Salt and freshly ground black pepper to taste
Béchamel Sauce with Mushrooms (recipe follows)
Karl Dauner's Garlic-Zapped Tomato Sauce (recipe follows; optional)

1. Lightly beat one of the eggs in a medium-size bowl. Stir in the kasha until well mixed. Transfer to a medium-size skillet and place over medium heat. Stir the kasha with a fork until it is dry and the grains are separated, about 3 minutes.

2. Cook the salt pork in a medium-size saucepan over medium heat until lightly browned, about 4 minutes. Add the onion; cook until lightly browned, about 3 minutes. Stir in the rice, kasha, barley, salt, pepper, and water. Heat to boiling. Reduce the heat and cook, covered, over low heat for 15 minutes. Stir once; then turn off the heat and let stand, covered, 10 minutes. Remove the cover and cool to room temperature.

3. Meanwhile, cook the cabbage leaves in boiling water to cover until just wilted, about 1 minute. Rinse under cold running water; then drain and pat dry with paper towels.

4. Preheat the oven to 350° F.

5. Combine the meats with the remaining egg, parsley, and cooled grain mixture in a large bowl. Season with salt and pepper, and mix well.

6. Fill the cabbage leaves generously with meat mixture, and roll them up. Place the rolls, seam side down, in a lightly greased large shallow baking dish. Chop any remaining cabbage and place it around and between the rolls. Spoon the Béchamel Sauce over the top and bake, covered, 1½ hours. Serve with Garlic-Zapped Tomato Sauce, if desired.

Serves 6 to 8

Béchamel Sauce with Mushrooms

4 tablespoons (½ stick) unsalted butter
¾ pound mushrooms, finely chopped
3 tablespoons all-purpose flour

1½ cups homemade chicken stock (see page 376) or canned broth
½ cup heavy or whipping cream

1. Melt 2 tablespoons of the butter in a large skillet over medium-high heat. Sauté the mushrooms until golden brown, about 5 minutes.

2. Melt the remaining 2 tablespoons butter in a medium-size saucepan over medium-low heat. Stir in the flour. Cook, stirring constantly, 2 minutes. Whisk in the chicken stock and the cream. Cook, whisking occasionally, until thick, about 8 minutes. Stir in the mushrooms.

Makes about 2¼ cups

Karl Dauner's Garlic-Zapped Tomato Sauce

¼ cup olive oil
4 to 5 cloves garlic, finely chopped
1 can (28 ounces) imported Italian plum tomatoes, with juice
2 teaspoons chopped fresh basil, or 1 teaspoon dried
¼ teaspoon crushed dried hot red peppers
Salt and freshly ground black pepper to taste

1. Heat the oil in a medium-size saucepan over medium-low heat. Add all but ½ teaspoon of the garlic; sauté until golden, about 4 minutes.

2. Add to the saucepan the tomatoes, all but ½ teaspoon of the basil, and the dried red peppers. Cook, uncovered, over high heat until all liquid has evaporated and the sauce is very thick, about 20 minutes. Add salt and pepper to taste. Remove from the heat and allow to cool slightly. Then stir in the remaining garlic and basil.

Makes about 2½ cups

LAMB STUFFED WITH EGGPLANT AND KASHA

A very different stuffed lamb dish, moist and rich with flavor, and perfect for a company dinner.

1 small eggplant (about ¼ pound)
Salt
½ cup whole kasha
1½ tablespoons lightly beaten egg
3 tablespoons olive oil
1 large onion, chopped
1 large clove garlic, minced
1 teaspoon crushed dried hot red peppers
1 cup homemade chicken stock (see page 376) or canned broth
¾ cup white wine
4 pounds boned and butterflied leg of lamb (from a 6- to 8-pound leg)
1 large clove garlic, slivered
Chopped fresh parsley, for garnish

1. Cube the eggplant, place it in a colander, and sprinkle it generously with salt. Let it stand 1 hour. Then brush the salt off with damp paper towels.

2. Meanwhile, stir the kasha with the egg in a medium-size bowl until well mixed. Transfer to a medium-size skillet and place over medium heat. Stir the kasha with a fork until it is dry and the grains are separated, about 3 minutes.

3. Heat 2 tablespoons of the oil in a medium-size saucepan or Dutch oven over medium-low heat. Add the onion; cook 3 minutes. Add the minced garlic and cook 2 minutes longer. Stir in the eggplant cubes and dried red peppers. Cook until the eggplant is soft and lightly colored, about 8 minutes. Stir in the kasha, and toss until it is coated with the onion/eggplant mixture. Stir in ½ cup chicken stock and ½ cup wine, and heat to boiling. Reduce the heat and simmer, covered, over low heat for 15 minutes. Stir once, then turn off the heat and let it stand, covered, 10 minutes. Cool slightly.

4. Preheat the oven to 400°F.

5. Spread the eggplant/kasha mixture over the lamb, and gently roll the lamb up like a jelly roll. Tie it in several places to secure it; then fold up the ends and tie lengthwise. Tuck the slivers of garlic under the strings on top of the rolled lamb. Roast the lamb on a rack in a roasting pan for 1 hour.

6. Reduce the heat to 325°F. Pour the remaining chicken broth and wine in the bottom of the pan and cook 20 minutes longer for medium rare.

7. Remove the lamb and let it stand for 8 minutes. Meanwhile, strain the pan juices and serve with the lamb. Sprinkle the lamb with parsley before serving.

Serves 6 to 8

OXTAILS WITH KASHA AND RICE

*T*his *Mittel Europa michati* is Czech—a dish of succulent oxtails stewed in a pot with kasha and rice and everything nice. Need I add, absolutely satisfying into the bargain? If you've given heed to my earlier advice about complex carbohydrates, you'll also note that each portion is like money in the body's "bank account"!

Take note that this dish is juicy. It is necessary to stir the mixture well during the last minutes of cooking so the kasha absorbs the liquid.

1 strip thick-cut bacon, diced
¼ cup all-purpose flour
½ teaspoon salt
½ teaspoon freshly ground black pepper
4 pounds oxtails, cut in pieces
2 tablespoons olive oil
1 tablespoon plus 1 teaspoon unsalted
*   butter*
1 medium onion, finely chopped
2 cloves garlic, minced
1 small carrot, finely chopped
1 small parsnip, finely chopped
2 large ribs celery, finely chopped
1 teaspoon chopped fresh thyme, or
*   ¼ teaspoon dried*
1 bay leaf
4 whole allspice, crushed
2 cups homemade chicken stock (see page
*   376) or canned broth*
2 cups dry white wine
2 cups water
1 cup whole kasha
1 large egg, lightly beaten
⅓ cup long-grain rice
½ teaspoon tomato paste
Chopped fresh parsley, for garnish

1. Preheat the oven to 350°F.
2. Cook the bacon in boiling water to cover for 5 minutes. Drain, and pat dry with paper towels.
3. Combine the flour with the salt and pepper in a shallow bowl. Lightly coat the oxtails with this mixture.
4. Heat 1 tablespoon of the oil with the 1 tablespoon butter in a large heavy pot or Dutch oven over medium heat. Sauté the oxtails in batches until brown on all sides, 5 minutes per batch. Using a slotted spoon, transfer them to a plate. Pour off the grease and wipe out the pot.
5. Add the remaining 1 tablespoon oil to the pot and sauté the bacon over medium-low heat for 3 minutes. Add the onion; cook 1 minute. Add the garlic; cook 2 minutes longer. Stir in the carrot, parsnip, celery, thyme, bay leaf, allspice, stock, wine, and water. Return the oxtails to the pot and heat to boiling, skimming the surface of fat. Cover the pot, transfer it to the oven, and cook until the meat is tender, about 2 hours and 15 minutes.
6. Meanwhile, stir the kasha with the egg in a medium-size bowl until well mixed. Transfer to a medium-size skillet and place over medium heat. Stir the kasha with a fork until it is dry and the grains are separated, about 3 minutes.
7. When the oxtails are tender, remove them from the pot and keep warm in a 225°F oven. Remove the bay leaf from the pot, and stir in the kasha and rice. Heat to boiling over medium-high heat. Reduce the heat and cook, covered, over low heat until tender, about 20 minutes. Remove the cover and stir in the tomato paste. Cook, stirring constantly, until all liquid has been absorbed, 4 to 5 minutes. Arrange the kasha on a platter, surrounded by the oxtails. Place the 1 teaspoon butter in the center of the kasha, and sprinkle with parsley.

Serves 4 to 6

TOMATO, CHEESE, AND GROATS SUPPER

"Groats" is a Middle English word with Druid antecedents, amended from *greot*, the same linguistic taproot that gave us "grit" and "grist"—all of which describe fragments of grain which promise little gratification in a bowl of porridge.

Quite on the contrary, the groats connection in the next quasi-Italian dish (devised of two kinds of tomatoes and three kinds of cheese) not only promises, it delivers: *satisfaction plus.*

2 tablespoons unsalted butter
1 medium onion, finely chopped
1 clove garlic, minced
1 cup whole white buckwheat groats
1 can (28 ounces) imported Italian
    tomatoes, with juice, coarsely chopped
¼ teaspoon salt
¼ teaspoon freshly ground black pepper
¼ teaspoon crushed whole allspice
1 package (15 ounces) ricotta cheese
1½ cups grated Gruyère cheese (about
    6 ounces)
¼ pound goat cheese, crumbled
1 egg, lightly beaten
½ cup sun-dried tomatoes in oil, cut into
    strips
¼ cup freshly grated Parmesan cheese

1. Preheat the oven to 350°F. Lightly butter a 2-quart round casserole dish.

2. Melt the butter in a medium-size saucepan over medium-low heat. Add the onion; cook 1 minute. Add the garlic; cook until lightly browned, about 5 minutes. Remove the pan from the heat.

3. Stir the groats into the onion mixture, tossing well to coat. Add the tomatoes, salt, pepper, and allspice. Heat to boiling. Reduce the heat and cook, covered, over low heat for 20 minutes.

4. Layer half the groats mixture over the bottom of the casserole dish.

5. Combine the ricotta, Gruyère, and goat cheese in a medium-size bowl. Beat in the lightly beaten egg. Dot the groats with half the cheese mixture. Place half the sun-dried tomato strips over the top. Add the remaining groats mixture. Dot with the remaining cheese mixture, and then the remaining tomato strips.

6. Bake 30 minutes. Sprinkle the top with Parmesan cheese, and bake 5 minutes longer.

Serves 6

KASHA AND RADISH SALAD

Strictly speaking, *kasha* is the word for "cereal" in most Slavic tongues. And while it has become virtually synonymous with long-cooked fricassees, goulashes, *suppes*, and *gedämpfte brusts* (depending upon the geography of the stove), that is not the whole story. Have a French provincial *salade de radis* to prove my point: kasha is simply not parochial provender!

1 cup whole kasha
1 large egg, lightly beaten
4 sprigs parsley
3 sprigs thyme
5 fresh sage leaves
2 cups water
¼ cup plus 1 teaspoon red wine vinegar
¾ teaspoon salt
¼ teaspoon freshly ground black pepper
1 clove garlic, crushed
2 teaspoons Dijon mustard
2 tablespoons fresh lemon juice
½ cup olive oil
½ cup thinly sliced radishes
2 tablespoons chopped fresh parsley

1. Stir the kasha with the egg in a medium-size bowl until well mixed. Transfer to a medium-size skillet and place over medium heat. Stir the kasha with a fork until it is dry and the grains are separated, about 3 minutes.

2. Tie the parsley and thyme sprigs with the sage leaves in a cheesecloth bag to make a bouquet garni. Combine the water, ¼ cup vinegar, ½ teaspoon of the salt, the pepper, and the bouquet garni in a medium-size saucepan. Stir in the kasha, and heat to boiling. Reduce the heat and cook, covered, over low heat for 15 minutes. Stir once, then turn off the heat and let stand, covered, 10 minutes. Cool to room temperature.

3. Mash the garlic with the remaining ¼ teaspoon salt in a small bowl until a paste is formed. Stir in the mustard, lemon juice, and the 1 teaspoon vinegar. Slowly whisk in the oil.

4. Place the kasha in a medium-size bowl and pour the vinaigrette dressing over it. Toss well. Lightly toss in the radishes and 1 tablespoon of the parsley. Sprinkle the remaining 1 tablespoon parsley over the top. Serve lightly chilled or at room temperature.

Serves 6

GROATS AND BLUE CHEESE FRITTERS

Have a change in fritters next time you're looking for a tasty aside to chicken or pork. These will give the more typical corn or apple varieties a real run for the money.

1 tablespoon unsalted butter
1 shallot, minced
1 clove garlic, minced
1 cup whole white buckwheat groats
2 cups homemade chicken stock (see page
    376) or canned broth
½ pound aged (tangy) blue cheese,
    crumbled
¼ teaspoon freshly ground black pepper
1 cup fresh bread crumbs
¼ cup freshly grated Parmesan cheese
1 large egg
2 tablespoons water
Peanut oil for frying
Salt

1. Melt the butter in a medium-size saucepan over medium-low heat. Add the shallot; cook 1 minute. Add the garlic; cook until lightly browned, about 5 minutes. Stir in the groats and chicken stock, and heat to boiling. Reduce the heat and cook, covered, over low heat for 20 minutes. Add the blue cheese and the pepper, and stir until the cheese has melted and is incorporated into the groats.

2. Lightly grease a 9-inch cake pan. Spoon the groats mixture evenly into the pan. Cool, and then refrigerate for 1 hour.

3. Combine the bread crumbs with the Parmesan cheese in a shallow bowl. Blend the egg and the water in another shallow bowl.

4. Cut the groats mixture into pieces about 1 inch wide and 1½ inches long. Carefully dip them in the egg mixture, and then coat with the bread crumb mixture.

5. Heat ¼ inch of peanut oil in a heavy skillet. Sauté the fritters (about six at a time) until crisp and golden, about 2 minutes per side. Remove with a slotted spoon and pat dry on paper towels. Keep warm in a 225°F oven while cooking the remaining fritters (or reheat for 10 minutes in a 400°F oven). Sprinkle with salt before serving.

Serves 6

ROSE LEVY BERANBAUM'S KASHA VARNISHKES

My grandparents had not the slightest inkling of buckwheat's health properties. They ate kasha simply because it gave them gratification. I suggest you do the same, starting with this dish: a highly untraditional rendering of an "old country" canon that was donated to my collection by one of the great bakers of the world, Rose Levy Beranbaum. Rose is not only a past-mistress of cake decoration but also a cook with real soul. Her notable *kasha varnishkes* with dried porcini mushrooms (yet) might have shocked my grandparents initially, but only until the first bite. It is a kasha variation to die for!

½ ounce dried porcini mushrooms
¼ cup hot water
1 cup coarse-ground kasha
1 large egg, lightly beaten
5 tablespoons unsalted butter
2 cups chopped onions
1 teaspoon sugar
1 pound large white mushrooms, including
    stems, sliced
2 large cloves garlic, minced
1 teaspoon salt
1½ teaspoons freshly ground black pepper
1 tablespoon chopped fresh oregano, or 1
    teaspoon dried
1½ cups (approximately) homemade
    chicken stock (see page 376) or canned
    broth, heated
2 cups bow-tie noodles
Chopped fresh parsley, for garnish

1. Soak the dried mushrooms in the hot water in a small bowl until soft, about 15 minutes. Drain, reserving the liquid. Chop the mushrooms and reserve.

2. Meanwhile, stir the kasha with the egg in a medium-size bowl until well mixed. Transfer to a medium-size skillet and place over medium heat. Stir the kasha with a fork until it is dry and the grains are separated, about 3 minutes.

3. Melt 4 tablespoons of the butter in a large saucepan over medium heat. Add the onions, sprinkle with the sugar, and cook, stirring often, until well browned, about 8 minutes. Add the sliced white mushrooms and the garlic. Cook, covered, stirring occasionally, until the mushrooms release their liquid, about 4 minutes. Uncover and continue to cook until all the liquid has evaporated, 8 to 10 minutes.

4. Stir the kasha into the onion-mushroom mixture, and cook 2 minutes. Add the reserved porcini mushrooms, salt, pepper, and oregano. Add enough hot chicken stock to the reserved mushroom liquid to make 1¾ cups. Stir this into the kasha mixture and heat to boiling. Reduce the heat and cook, covered, over low heat for 15 minutes. Stir once, turn off the heat, and let stand, covered, about 10 minutes.

5. Meanwhile, cook the noodles in boiling salted water until just tender, about 12 minutes. Drain, and return to the pan. Toss with the remaining 1 tablespoon butter, cover, and keep warm over low heat.

6. Transfer the kasha mixture to a flameproof dish. Place under a preheated broiler, and broil, stirring often, to brown the kasha. Toss with the cooked noodles, and sprinkle with parsley.

Serves 6

Green Brumus

Kasha is obviously one of man's movable feasts. Green Brumus (it means "midnight snack") stems from the upper regions of Newfoundland, where it is eaten only in the summer months. Presumably by the light of the midnight sun . . . Serve it year round to accompany your favorite pot roast.

½ pound string beans, trimmed (cut large
    beans in half)
⅓ cup whole kasha
1 tablespoon lightly beaten egg
1 cup homemade chicken stock (see page
    376) or canned broth
¼ teaspoon salt
⅛ teaspoon freshly ground black pepper
2 tablespoons unsalted butter
3 scallions, white bulbs and green tops,
    chopped
½ bunch watercress, with 2 inches of stem,
    separated
¼ cup red wine vinegar
Salt and freshly ground black pepper to
    taste
Chopped fresh parsley, for garnish

1. Cook the beans in boiling salted water to cover until crisp-tender, about 3 minutes. Rinse under cold running water; drain.

2. Stir the kasha with the egg in a medium-size bowl until well mixed. Transfer to a medium-size saucepan and place over medium heat. Stir the kasha with a fork until it is dry and the grains are separated, about 3 minutes. Stir in the stock, salt, and pepper. Heat to boiling. Reduce the heat and cook, covered, over low heat for 15 minutes. Stir once and keep warm, partially covered, over low heat.

3. Melt the butter in a large heavy skillet over medium-high heat. Add the scallions; cook 2 minutes. Add the beans, tossing well to coat with scallions. Stir in the watercress and vinegar. Cook, tossing constantly, until almost all liquid has evaporated, about 3 minutes. Reduce the heat to medium-low and stir in the cooked kasha. Add salt and pepper to taste, and sprinkle with the parsley.

Serves 4

KASHA CORNSTICKS

Kasha and cornmeal fused into 40-carat cornsticks that are the best meal-stretcher a breakfast, lunch, or dinner could have. The formula has been around for years; I found it on a box of Wolff's kasha! There's no egg wash in this recipe, as the kasha is meant to season the cornbread, not dominate it.

1 cup milk
½ cup whole kasha
4 tablespoons (½ stick) unsalted butter, cut into bits
1 cup plus 2 tablespoons all-purpose flour
½ cup yellow cornmeal
4 teaspoons baking powder
½ teaspoon salt
¼ teaspoon freshly ground black pepper
¼ cup honey
2 tablespoons toasted sesame seeds (see Note)
1 egg, lightly beaten

1. Preheat the oven to 425°F.
2. Heat the milk in a medium-size saucepan to the scalding point; remove the pan from the heat. Stir in the kasha and butter. Let stand until lukewarm.

3. In a large mixing bowl, combine the flour with the cornmeal, baking powder, salt, and pepper. Add the kasha mixture to the flour mixture along with the honey, sesame seeds, and egg. Stir only until mixed; do not overwork.
4. Pour the batter into a well-greased cornstick pan (see Baker's Secret, page 42). Bake until firm to the touch, 15 to 20 minutes. Let stand 10 minutes before unmolding.

Makes about 2 dozen cornsticks

Note: To toast sesame seeds, spread the seeds in a skillet and place them over medium heat, stirring several times until they turn golden brown, 6 to 8 minutes.

DAY-AFTER HUSH PUPPIES

I love prandial residuals (a high-falutin term for leftovers). The terrific breakfast (or lunch or dinner) dish that follows requires little more than one vital ingredient: a cup of leftover Cream of Buckwheat and Garlic. So be a generous cook the night before!

1 cup cold leftover Cream of Buckwheat and Garlic (see page 72)
3 tablespoons fresh bread crumbs
1 tablespoon unsalted butter
1 teaspoon vegetable oil

1. Form the leftover buckwheat mixture into patties, using 1½ tablespoons for each. Roll them in the bread crumbs.
2. Heat the butter with the oil in a large heavy skillet over medium heat. Sauté the hush puppies until golden brown and warmed through, about 3 minutes per side.

Makes 6 patties

CREAM OF BUCKWHEAT AND GARLIC

Cream of Buckwheat is a commercial cereal ground from the heart of buckwheat grains. It is pale in color and highly palliative in flavor. Slosh Cream of Buckwheat with cream and sugar, or for a side dish, amend the velvety texture with practically any seasoning that comes to mind. My mind elected garlic in this recipe. Serve it next time you roast a chicken.

15 cloves garlic, unpeeled
2 tablespoons plus 2 teaspoons unsalted
    butter
3 cups milk
½ cup Cream of Buckwheat (see Note)
2 tablespoons freshly grated Parmesan
    cheese
Salt and freshly ground black pepper to
    taste

1. Drop the garlic cloves into boiling water; cook 2 minutes. Drain, cool slightly, and peel.

2. Melt the 2 tablespoons butter in a heavy saucepan. Add the garlic. Cook, covered, over low heat until tender, about 30 minutes (do not allow to brown).

3. Mash the garlic with a fork, adding ¼ cup of the milk, until a paste is formed. Add the remaining milk and heat to boiling. Add the Cream of Buckwheat and simmer, stirring frequently, until thickened, 10 to 12 minutes. Add the 2 teaspoons butter, the Parmesan cheese, and salt and pepper. Serve immediately.

Serves 4

Note: Cream of Buckwheat is available at most natural foods stores or may be mail-ordered from Pocono Mills, Penn Yan, New York. See the list of suppliers and mail-order sources at the back of the book.

BUCKWHEAT TRIVIA

Over the years, buckwheat has bloomed in America under some highly chequered colloquial aliases. In the anthropomorphic Northeast, it has been harvested and milled under such colorful tags as Dog Tongue, Antelope Brush, and Bee's Bonnet. In the South, black farmers have picked it as Napkin Ring, Indian Tobacco, and Sulphur-and-Molasses Blossom—the latter most probably because of its therapeutic effect on the system after being hulled. But who knows for sure? Middle-Western pioneer settlers called buckwheat Whisk Broom, Umbrella Plant, and Spotted Turban—the last handle obviously a reference to the plant's variegated pink and white flora. In the Southwest, where it has never flourished in homesteaders' fields with any constancy, buckwheat's monikers reflect a true touch of agrarian chauvinism: Desert Strumpet and Witch's Weeds for starters.

BITECKY

What's up next is a Russian dish of long and highly polished credentials. This version of bitecky (there are as many variants in Kiev as there are chicken cutlets) is special because of the healthy mite of mushrooms in the dish. If I am feeling lavish as a czar, I whip it up with porcini or shiitake mushrooms. If I'm feeling a pinch in the pocket, I make my bitecky with anything the supermarket has on sale. And the bitecky fans never know the difference!

2 tablespoons unsalted butter
2 large shallots, minced
1¼ cups finely chopped mushroom caps
    (about 4 ounces)
1 cup whole white buckwheat groats
1 cup heavy or whipping cream
1 cup homemade chicken stock (see page
    376) or canned broth
½ cup freshly grated Parmesan cheese
Salt and freshly ground black pepper to
    taste
Chopped fresh parsley, for garnish

1. Melt the butter in a medium-size saucepan over medium-low heat. Add the shallots; cook 1 minute. Raise the heat to medium-high and stir in the mushrooms. Cook, stirring constantly, until lightly browned, about 4 minutes.

2. Stir the groats into the mushroom mixture, tossing well to coat. Add the cream and chicken stock. Heat to boiling. Reduce the heat and cook, covered, over low heat for 20 minutes. Stir in the cheese. Season with salt and pepper, and sprinkle with parsley.

Serves 6

BUCKWHEAT LACE

For further proof of whole white buckwheat groats' mutability, have a lovely old southern recipe for a super-crunchy cookie.

1 cup whole white buckwheat groats
1 egg
½ teaspoon vanilla extract
8 tablespoons (1 stick) unsalted butter,
    melted
1 cup firmly packed light brown sugar
½ cup walnut halves, chopped

1. Preheat the oven to 375°F.

2. Place the groats in the container of a food processor. Process until fairly fine.

3. Beat the egg with the vanilla and the butter in a large bowl until smooth. Beat in the brown sugar, groats, and walnuts.

4. Lightly butter an aluminum foil–lined baking sheet. Drop the batter by generous teaspoonfuls onto the foil, placing them far apart. Spread each spoonful of cookie batter out flat; do not mound. Bake until golden brown, about 8 minutes. Remove the foil from the baking sheet, and let the cookies cool completely before peeling them off the foil. Repeat until all the batter is used up.

Makes about 30 cookies

THE FLOURING OF THE GRAIN

Nutrition-minded bakers may grind buckwheat flour at home or purchase it, packaged, at natural foods stores.

To grind your own: process 1 cup of white or roasted whole buckwheat groats in a food processor or blender until it is finely pulverized, about 3 minutes.

My rule of thumb for adding buckwheat flour to any standard baking recipe is to substitute ⅓ to ½ cup of buckwheat flour per cup of a higher-gluten flour. Since buckwheat flour contains virtually no gluten (which gives baked goods their essential lightness), I most often combine it with all-purpose, whole-wheat, or bread flour—the last being the most gluten-rich.

Commercially ground buckwheat flour comes in two types: dark and light. Both are 100 percent buckwheat, but the dark variety has a more pungent flavor and contains a higher percentage of the fine-milled particles of seed hulls.

FROM-SCRATCH BUCKWHEAT NOODLES

After pancakes, I would certainly nominate pasta as buckwheat flour's crowning achievement. The Japanese have a very special place in their cuisine for a super-healthy pasta devised of buckwheat flour, known as soba noodles. Soba noodles are available at Oriental groceries, but I would seriously advise any creative cooks with a spot of time on their hands to consider making buckwheat pasta from scratch.

It's easiest to prepare the dough in a food processor, though I prefer to roll it out in an old-fashioned hand-cranked pasta machine, myself.

This recipe is only slightly altered from the one to be found in *Better Than Store-Bought*, by my good friends Helen Witty and Elizabeth Schneider.

2 large eggs
1 cup buckwheat flour
½ cup bread flour
½ cup all-purpose flour
½ teaspoon coarse (kosher) salt
2 or 3 tablespoons water

1. Place the eggs in the container of a food processor. With the motor running, add the flours, salt, and enough water to make a firm dough, allowing the motor to run until the sides of the container come clean and the dough forms a ball.

2. Transfer the dough to a lightly floured surface. Knead by hand for 5 minutes. Let the dough stand, loosely covered, for 5 minutes. Then roll it out by hand or with a pasta machine until very thin. Cut into noodles. Hang the noodles over a broom handle or the back of a chair until dry. Store in airtight plastic bags.

Makes about 10 ounces dry pasta

PIZZOCHERI

What follows is a little-known (so far) Italian buckwheat pasta dish that stems from the Valtellina region of Lombardy. It is called *pizzocheri*, and it is a generous bequest from one of the best pastry makers and teachers in New York, Nick Malgieri.

Nick states that many versions of *pizzocheri* exist, but all share a common ingredients list. There must be sage, potatoes, and some form of green (cabbage, spinach, or Swiss chard) to cloak the buckwheat pasta; and there must be two cheeses, Parmesan and a soft melting type (Taleggio, Fontina, or French Vacherin). His preferences are chard for earthy flavor and Taleggio for earnest richness.

½ pound (about 2 medium) new potatoes
¾ pound Swiss chard (red variety, if possible)
3 tablespoons unsalted butter
1 medium onion, halved and thinly sliced
1 large clove garlic, minced
1½ tablespoons chopped fresh sage, or 1½ teaspoons dried sage leaves rubbed together
½ pound dry From-Scratch Buckwheat Noodles (see facing page)
½ pound Taleggio, Fontina, or Vacherin cheese, cubed
⅓ cup freshly grated Parmesan cheese
Salt and freshly ground black pepper to taste
Chopped fresh parsley, for garnish

1. Peel, halve, and cut the potatoes into ¼-inch-thick slices. Cook the potato slices, uncovered, in boiling salted water to cover for 5 minutes. Cover and remove from the heat; let stand until cooked through, about 15 minutes longer. Drain.

2. Meanwhile, trim the stems from the chard and cook them in boiling salted water to cover for 2 minutes. Add the leaves and cook until wilted, about 2 minutes more. Drain and chop.

3. Melt the butter in a large saucepan over medium-low heat. Add the onion; cook, covered, 5 minutes. Add the garlic and sage. Cook, uncovered, 1 minute. Remove the pan from the heat.

4. Cook the pasta in a large pot of boiling salted water until just tender, about 3 minutes for homemade, about 8 for commercially prepared. Drain.

5. Return the saucepan with the onions to low heat. Add the potato slices and toss lightly to warm through. Add the cooked pasta, the Swiss chard, and both cheeses. Toss lightly until the cheese has melted. Season with salt and pepper and sprinkle with parsley.

Serves 4 to 6

JAMES RIVER STYLE PASTA WITH CLAMS

Years and years ago, when I was in college in Virginia, we would often cut classes and go clamming in the tidewater where the James River and Atlantic Ocean almost meet. The result of these aquatic expeditions was a dish devised of clams, Smithfield ham, and a shot of bourbon, served on noodles.

Half a lifetime later, it is still a favorite comfort food—best when some other daredevil does the clamming, however. Buckwheat noodles are right at home here, and look into Surrey Ham (see the source list) for their not-too-salty confederate.

3 dozen small clams, washed well
½ teaspoon cornstarch
2½ tablespoons unsalted butter
1 medium onion, finely chopped
1 large clove garlic, minced
1 cup homemade chicken stock (see page 376) or canned broth
¼ cup white wine
8 ounces dry From-Scratch Buckwheat Noodles (see page 74)
½ cup finely chopped smoky country ham
½ cup chopped fresh parsley
¼ teaspoon freshly ground black pepper
1 teaspoon bourbon

1. Place the clams in a large bowl. Add cold water to cover, and stir in the cornstarch. Let stand 15 minutes. Rinse several times under cold running water; drain. This will effectively clean the clams.

2. Melt 1½ tablespoons of the butter in a large saucepan over medium-low heat. Add the onion; cook 1 minute. Add the garlic; cook 4 minutes longer. Add the cleaned clams, the stock, and the wine. Heat to boiling. Reduce the heat and cook, covered, until the clams open, about 5 to 8 minutes.

3. Remove the clams from the broth and place them in a bowl. Remove the clam meat from the shells, catching all juices. Add the juices to the broth and boil until reduced by about one third, about 5 minutes. Coarsely chop the clams.

4. Meanwhile, cook the pasta in a large pot of boiling salted water until just tender, about 3 minutes for homemade, about 8 minutes for commercially prepared. Drain.

5. When the clam broth has reduced sufficiently, stir in the ham, pasta, and parsley. Toss until warmed through. Toss in the pepper and bourbon.

Serves 4

BRAWNY BREAD

Brawny, because this is one bread loaded with goodness. Coffee and molasses add dark rich flavor to the loaf, while whole groats add a bit of crunch. It makes a wonderful sandwich bread.

¾ cup whole white buckwheat groats
1¾ cups lukewarm water
2 tablespoons dry yeast
½ cup brewed coffee, lukewarm
¼ cup molasses
¼ cup honey
1 cup light buckwheat flour
5 tablespoons unsalted butter, melted
1½ cups bread flour
2½ to 3 cups stone-ground whole-wheat flour
1 egg white

1. Heat a large non-stick skillet over medium heat. Add the groats, and sprinkle with ¼ cup of the water. Stir the groats with a fork until they are dry and lightly toasted, about 5 minutes. Set the skillet aside.

2. Sprinkle the yeast over the lukewarm coffee in a large bowl. Stir in the molasses and honey. Let stand until the yeast begins to bubble, 10 minutes.

3. Add the remaining 1½ cups water to the yeast mixture. Using a heavy wooden spoon, stir in the buckwheat flour, 3 tablespoons of the butter, ½ cup of the toasted groats, and the bread flour. Then stir in the whole-wheat flour, about ½ cup at a time, until a stiff dough is formed. Turn onto a floured board and knead, adding more whole-wheat flour if needed, until smooth and elastic, about 10 minutes.

4. Place the dough in a large greased bowl. Cover, and let rise in a warm place until doubled in bulk, about 1½ hours.

5. Punch down the dough. Knead it on a lightly floured surface for 5 minutes. Return the dough to the bowl, cover, and let rise until doubled in bulk again, about 1 hour.

6. Punch down the dough once more. Knead it briefly, and divide it in half. Roll each half lengthwise into a sausage shape about 10 inches long. Beat it flat with your hands, and fold the dough into thirds. Brush each loaf with egg white, and roll them in the remaining toasted groats. Place each loaf in a buttered bread pan measuring about 9 by 5 by 3 inches. Cover them with flour-rubbed tea towels and let stand until the dough rises over the edge of the pans, about 1 hour.

7. Preheat the oven to 375°F.

8. Bake the bread until the loaves sound hollow when tapped, 35 to 40 minutes. Turn the loaves out onto racks, and brush the tops with the remaining melted butter to give them a sheen.

Makes 2 loaves

CAMPTON PLACE'S CRANBERRY BUCKWHEAT MUFFINS

*B*uckwheat's best breakfast utility (aside from pancakes) is indubitably in muffin form. The best I know are served up at the fabled Campton Place Hotel in San Francisco. These quintessential hot breads are the handiwork of Bradley Ogden, one of the most talented chefs to be found in America. For evidence of that extravagant statement, whip up a batch at once!

1⅓ cups fresh cranberries, picked over
¾ cup sugar
3 tablespoons fresh orange juice
1¼ cups all-purpose flour
1 cup light buckwheat flour
1½ tablespoons baking powder
½ teaspoon baking soda
1 teaspoon salt
2 eggs
8 tablespoons (1 stick) unsalted butter,
    melted
½ cup buttermilk (approximately)

1. Combine the cranberries with ½ cup of the sugar and the orange juice in a medium-size bowl. Let stand for 30 minutes.

2. Preheat the oven to 375°F.

3. Grease a twelve-cup muffin tin.

4. Combine the flours, remaining ¼ cup sugar, baking powder, baking soda, and salt in a bowl.

5. In a separate bowl, beat the eggs with the butter until smooth. Stir in the cranberries, with all their liquid. Beat in the dry ingredients. Stir in enough buttermilk to make a soft batter. Do not overbeat.

6. Fill the muffin cups about seven-eighths full. Bake until firm and golden brown, about 15 minutes. Cool the tin on a rack for 10 minutes before unmolding the muffins.

Makes 12 muffins

OLD-FASHIONED BUCKWHEAT CAKES

This is the best buckwheat pancake recipe extant: light yet velvety-rich flapjacks, invented by the talented Phillip Stephen Schulz. I am just sorry my father isn't around to sample a batch!

Serve them with butter and maple syrup, or honey thinned with warm water.

2½ cups milk
2 tablespoons molasses
1½ teaspoons dry yeast
1⅓ cups buckwheat flour
⅔ cup all-purpose flour
½ cup fine-ground cornmeal
½ teaspoon salt
1 teaspoon sugar
1 teaspoon baking soda
½ cup lukewarm water
2 tablespoons unsalted butter, melted
2 egg yolks, lightly beaten
3 egg whites

1. Eight to 12 hours before serving, scald the milk and stir in the molasses. Let the mixture cool to lukewarm, then stir in the yeast and let stand until the yeast begins to bubble, 10 minutes. Transfer to a large bowl.

2. Using a wooden spoon, stir the buckwheat flour into the molasses mixture. Stir in the all-purpose flour, cornmeal, and salt. Beat until smooth. Cover, and let stand at room temperature 8 to 12 hours.

3. Just before serving, dissolve the

sugar and baking soda in the lukewarm water in a small bowl. Stir this into the prepared batter, then whisk in the butter and egg yolks.

4. Beat the egg whites in a large bowl until stiff. Fold them into the batter.

5. Pour about ⅓ cup batter for each cake on a preheated griddle or into a non-stick skillet. Cook over medium heat until bubbles form on top and the underside is nicely browned, about 1 minute. Turn the cake over and brown the other side.

Makes about 18 pancakes

BIGWIG BLINI

A pancake of another stripe. These are Russian, and still the most welcome course in dietary *détente* the Soviets have to offer. Traditionally, blini are served with two bowls on the side: one filled with caviar, the other heaped with sour cream. The caviar is meant to be spooned inside the warm pancake, and a dab of sour cream covers that. The blini is then folded in half and sluiced with melted butter. If you can't spring for Beluga or Sevruga for your blinis, don't despair; smoked salmon, thinly shaved, makes an excellent substitute.

This recipe, I might add, did not come into my hands from the KGB. It is the sterling creation of W. Peter Prescott, affable Entertaining Editor of *Food & Wine* magazine.

As these pancakes require at least 4½ hours pre-preparation, a batch may be made partially in advance (through step 3) and refrigerated. Remember to let the batter come to room temperature before continuing, however. Timing makes the difference between a delicate blini and a dud ICBM!

1 teaspoon dry yeast
½ teaspoon sugar
1¼ cups buttermilk, lukewarm
½ cup sifted buckwheat flour
½ teaspoon baking soda
5 tablespoons unsalted butter, melted and
  cooled
2 eggs, separated
½ cup sour cream
¾ cup sifted all-purpose flour
½ teaspoon salt
¼ cup milk

1. Combine the yeast with the sugar and ¼ cup of the buttermilk in a large bowl. Let stand until the yeast begins to bubble, 10 minutes.

2. Stir the buckwheat flour, baking soda, and the remaining 1 cup buttermilk into the yeast mixture. Cover with a tea towel and let stand in a warm place until doubled in volume, about 2 hours.

3. Whisk 3 tablespoons of the butter with the egg yolks and sour cream in a medium-size bowl until smooth. Stir this into the buckwheat mixture. Then stir in the all-purpose flour, salt, and milk. Cover, and let stand in a warm place until doubled in volume, about 2 hours.

4. Beat the egg whites until stiff but

not dry. Fold them into the buckwheat mixture, and cover loosely with plastic wrap. Let stand 30 minutes.

5. Pour about 2 tablespoons batter for each blini onto an oil-rubbed preheated griddle or non-stick skillet. Do no more than four at a time; the blini should be no more than 3 inches in diameter. Cook over medium heat until lightly browned on the bottom and the surface is covered with bubbles, about 1 minute. Turn over and lightly brown the other side. Place the blini on a plate and brush lightly with melted butter. Keep warm in a 225°F oven while you cook the remaining batter.

Serves 6 to 8 as an appetizer (makes about 32 blini)

PANCAKECCLESIA

If you will recall, it was my father's buckwheat proclivity that began this chapter in the first place. His love of buckwheat was obviously a genetic legacy, for I have the craving too—though neither Greene could claim singularity in the predilection.

Washington Irving, for instance, once confided that his dream breakfast would be "two dozen dainty slapjacks of buckwheat covered with a pitcher each of honey and treacle and soaked by a hogshead of butter"! Diamond Jim Brady was another prodigious buckwheat fancier. Brady's trencherman appetite for pancakes was so enormous (fifty per sitting) that he once caused a major maple syrup shortage at Rector's restaurant in New York City by appearing there for breakfast twice in the same day.

Have another pair of buckwheat addicts: Gary Cooper and Ernest Hemingway. It is reported in Ketcham, Idaho, that these two outdoorsmen friends held an informal pancake-eating duel in the 1940s to determine whose capacity was the greater. Cooper, the movie star who had to watch his weight, stopped after the twelfth serving. Hemingway, the writer who prided himself on an unbridled appetite in all things, won the contest by downing seventeen. But according to scuttlebutt, he lost by default, as he was forced to "unswallow" shortly after laying down his fork. The world's champion pancake eater is probably the least well known, outside *The Guiness Book of Records*, that is. Peter Dowdeswell of Northampton, England, consumed sixty-two buckwheat cakes (6 inches in diameter) in 6 minutes 58.5 seconds on February 9, 1977. And kept them down too.

FRACTURED FUDGE CAKE

I like every chapter to end on a sweet note. The chocolate cake that follows is one of the most satisfying you will ever swallow—and somewhat healthier than most, for the existence of buckwheat flour in its devise.

I received the recipe from a friend in Washington, along with a brief description: "Rich!" she wrote. "And remarkably fudgy!" she amended.

Being a hopeless recipe fiddler (never able to leave well enough alone), I tried making it with buckwheat flour. *Disaster!*

Lucky to have Rose Levy Beranbaum (the cake baker's first aid) as a friend, I called for help. Scientist that she is, Rose analyzed the problem at once: it was the lack of gluten in buckwheat flour that turned the cake flat. She also suggested a cure; substituting high-gluten bread flour for two thirds of the buckwheat. The cake worked like a charm, and it is now the prize of my chocolate repertoire. I told you I like happy endings!

I call this cake "Fractured Fudge" because the top rises nobly in the oven and then fissures slightly as it cools. Don't give it another thought. Cover the fracture with lots of whipped cream and give thanks to Rose, as I do, with every forkful.

12 ounces semi-sweet chocolate
5 tablespoons brewed espresso or very
   strong coffee
1 cup (2 sticks) unsalted butter, at room
   temperature
2 cups sugar
6 eggs, separated
⅔ cup bread flour
⅓ cup dark buckwheat flour

1. Preheat the oven to 350°F. Lightly butter and flour a 9-inch springform pan.

2. Combine the chocolate and the coffee in the top of a double boiler, and stir over simmering water until the chocolate has melted and the mixture is smooth. Set aside to cool.

3. In the large bowl of an electric mixer, slowly beat the butter with the sugar until light and lemon-colored. Beat in the egg yolks, one at a time, beating thoroughly after each addition.

4. On low speed, beat in the cooled chocolate mixture, and then both flours.

5. Beat the egg whites until stiff, and fold them into the cake batter. Pour the batter into the prepared springform pan. Bake until the top is crusty and the cake is fairly firm, 65 to 70 minutes. Cool on a rack before unmolding. (The top will be very crusty. If the outer edges do not separate from the pan, tap the pan lightly with the side of a knife, then unmold.)

Serves 8

BULGUR

Has Kept Man Vital Since the Dawn of Time

Bulgur came into my life under mildly shocking circumstances: I first sampled it at a bordello in Paris. And while stranger initiations must surely have taken place in houses of ill repute, none, I suspect, ever had a more profound effect on the sampler's taste buds.

I journeyed to France for the first time when I was over forty and overanxious about new experiences—that is to say, totally unprepared for culture shocks. France was a country I had yearned to visit all my life. From the time I was twelve and decided someday I would live in an atelier in Montmartre, painting pictures like Utrillo, I'd prepared myself for the experience. I learned all the street names by heart. I knew which bridge across the Seine was closest to the Louvre (where my pictures would hang). I was an unmitigated francophile—but scared to go there.

Experienced travelers warned me not to be too optimistic about the French. Looks were deceiving, these friends cautioned. The French could be very testy with those who were not fluent in their language.

At the last moment I flew to England instead, for what, I rationalized, would be a week's introduction to Europe in one's native tongue. But the atmosphere (and language) of the British was so comfortable that the week soon extended to a month, while the visa to France wilted in my wallet. Finally the departure date could no longer be postponed.

It is a brief hop from England to France, but on arrival at the airport in Paris, I was beset with a paralyzing sense of long distance. The high school French I'd hoped to redress with months of tutoring proved hopeless the moment I quizzed an airline employee about *les hôtels.*

I had left London so precipitately that there had been no time to arrange accommodations. Unfortunately, my arrival coincided with an international automobile show in Paris. Every hotel I had ever heard about was completely booked when I telephoned for a reservation. Growing dispirited, I made my way to the French equivalent of Travelers' Aid.

The young woman in charge was extremely attractive but totally detached. She responded to my translated dilemma with a survey of her polished fingernails and a perfect command of English.

"What a pity you did not inquire about commercial activities in the city beforehand," she chided. "Though next week would not be better. There is a major fabric fair being held." Then, noting my look of desperation, she consulted first a large portfolio and then a small telephone.

After dialing and exchanging a flurry of indecipherable French with someone on the phone, she turned to me with a thin smile, inquiring: "Is a private bath a necessity? An elevator a prerequisite?" When I shook my head no, she shook hers as well, murmuring, *"D'accord.* There is a small establishment on Rue de Bruyard. Reputedly more commercial than residential but..."—here she lowered her lids—"to tell you frankly, sir, there has been no update on its status in my files for some years. Two hundred francs a night."

"I'll take it."

The driver of the taxi, edging through the late-day traffic of Paris, was even less edifying when I tried to quiz him (in French of course) about the hotel's location. "Is it a quiet street?" I managed after some mental gymnastics.

"Tranquille?" He was plainly being diplomatic. "Perhaps in the early morning hours, monsieur."

The hotel on Rue de Bruyard was less than a block from the infamous Place Pigalle. The building was small and nondescript, old but not old enough to be considered antique. There was no lobby, just a greasy counter backed with a rack displaying just one key. The clerk, who was eating a bowl of aromatic stew or soup, did not rise as I entered. Primed for my appearance, however, he stopped chewing long enough to pluck the key from its nest, collect my payment, and hand over the register to be signed. The smell of what he was eating was intoxicating, but I was aware as I scrawled my name that while every room was supposedly occupied, no other guests had registered.

The room I was assigned was five flights up a winding staircase that grew narrower at each landing.

To my dismay, I had to carry my luggage up the steps in the dark, as the hall lights unpredictably extinguished (to save power) every few seconds and had to be switched on again at the next landing.

Banging about in the gloom gave me some insight into the true nature of this establishment. At one landing, a tall man, adjusting his trousers as he closed a door, smiled in complicity before making his descent. At another, two young women wearing the briefest pants I'd ever seen sat on the steps counting money and arguing wildly, paying no attention whatsoever as I passed between them.

When I reached the room I had been assigned, it turned out to be a swollen dormer jutting over the roof. A naked light bulb hanging over the bed was burned out, and while there was a rusty sink in one corner, no towels could be found.

In high dudgeon, I marched down the stairs again, almost colliding with half a dozen sailors so drunk they collapsed on the landing like dominoes.

"What kind of place is this anyway?" I shouted in flawless French at the taciturn clerk, still eating his stew.

"Algerian" was his only explanation. Unruffled, he wiped his moustache. "You want a reduction in price? Here..." He handed me a worn fifty-franc note. "But be quiet. No questions asked. Do not call the police!"

"You don't seem to understand," I stammered. "There are no towels in my room. And the light bulb..."

"Ah, a little girl will take care of those details directly. Go to your room, monsieur." He smiled, mollifying me like a cranky child who is offered a lollipop. Like a fool I did as I was told.

As I climbed the stairs again, the smell of the dish he was eating seemed to pervade the entire building—like a smoky but not unpleasant perfume. As I sat on the lumpy bed, I realized that I had not eaten since breakfast in London and was very, very hungry. From the window I could—by bending my head to my shoulder—observe a sliver of the Eiffel Tower like a crescent moon, illuminating the inky violet sky.

Presently there was a knock at the door. The promised "little girl," who was at least twenty-five and exceedingly well endowed, stood in the semi-gloom carrying two thin towels and a plate of the same dish the clerk had been eating, both of which she handed over sullenly.

"What's this?" I asked, accepting the bowl. She shrugged and started down the steps. If a man did not know a bribe when he saw one, he was obviously not worth her time.

"Wait," I cried. She halted at the first step. "What is this called?"

"*Bourgouri.*" She spat the word out. "Supposed to make a man..." She did not attempt to finish the sentence, but her gestures explicitly described great virility.

Sitting on the bed, I ate the *bourgouri*, which was delicious. I don't know if it had any effect on my manhood. I left the hotel the next morning and never pursued the question. But it decidedly gave me a letch—for bulgur.

The Grain's Genesis

Bulgur, the parched, steamed, and dried berries of wheat, has kept man vital and vertical since the dawn of time. Maybe even longer. According to Arab folklore, the forbidden tree in the Garden of Eden was no blooming apple at all but a high-rise stalk of wheat—a plant so enormous that every kernel was the size of Adam's head and so wide that the snake God had placed there to guard it could not possibly span the trunk's circumference. Literally at loose ends, this reptile convinced Eve to prune the offending branches and, in passing, offer a bite of its fruit to her mate—precipitating the couple's fall from Paradise. However, Arabian storytellers give the legend a happy ending: The wheat that had been Adam and Eve's undoing in Eden became their source of survival in the world outside. And to this day, the wheat berry is treated with almost reverential respect by the peoples of the Arab world.

The Middle East was indubitably the landscape where bulgur was born, but it spread soon afterward in every possible direction. As far back as 1000 B.C., Stone Age Laplanders amended their diet of raw meat with an uncooked wheat gruel, and they'd probably be chomping it still if evolving ice caps had not made grain cultivation in Arctic geography a horticultural bust.

If I tell you that bulgur survived the prevailing winds of change, it is no overstatement. Evidence of this grain in China predates the birth of Christ by about 2,800 years. It was introduced by the Emperor Shen Nung, who declared the five sacred crops of China to be soybeans, rice, barley, millet, and wheat. However, dried cooked wheat did not become a popular food in the Orient until the ascension of the Qin ruler Shih Huang-ti in 221 B.C. Almost four centuries after Shen's pronouncement, Shih banned noodles (which he claimed induced softness of character) and instituted a regimen of barely cooked grains and wheat porridges meant to toughen his countrymen for the struggle for independence.

According to all reliable data—which is scanty at best—Shih's ordinance lasted a mere decade. During that short time, however, consumption of wheat (in dishes not unlike bulgur) swept all of China and then spread to Japan and India as well.

Traces of cooked sun-dried wheat grains have been found in Egyptian tombs, Etruscan urns, and Hun saddlebags. The Romans even had a word for bulgur. They called it *cerealis*, after the goddess of harvests, Ceres. Ancient Israelites had their own name, *dagan*, which means "bursting kernels of grain."

Some Plain Grain Talk

*T*he most persistent myth about bulgur is that it is simply cracked wheat. Not so. Both bulgur and cracked wheat are indeed compounded of whole wheat berries, but there the similarity ends.

Cracked wheat, as its name implies, is uncooked wheat that has been dried first and cracked apart later, by coarse milling. Bulgur, on the other hand, is wheat that has been steamed, then dried (whole or partially debranned) before being crushed into various grinds.

Since bulgur is only marginally processed, it is a grain that is vitamin-high. Each quarter pound of bulgur contains over 11.2 grams of protein, 75.7 grams of carbohydrates, 338 milligrams of phosphorus, and 229 milligrams of potassium, as well as healthy doses of calcium, iron, thiamine, riboflavin, and niacin. Or as many nutrients as one will find in a whole loaf of 100 percent whole-wheat bread!

The differences between bulgur and cracked wheat are most apparent at the stove. Bulgur requires a mere presoaking when it is used for salads like tabbouleh, and only minimal cooking when it is to be the basis of a pilaf or stew. Cracked wheat is something else again. Dried raw, essentially, it requires an extended period of boiling before it is even barely digestible. And while a gung-ho cook can convert a cup of cracked wheat into a reasonably accurate facsimile of bulgur when the occasion demands, bulgur and cracked wheat are definitely *not* interchangeable in the recipes that follow.

How to Buy It

*U*ntil recently bulgur was not an easy item to find at most American supermarkets. Prior to the mid-1960s, it was eaten exclusively by transplanted émigrés from the Middle East, and it was only an intrepid cook with a taste for tabbouleh or falafel who made tracks to an Armenian, Lebanese, or Syrian neighborhood grocer for the ingredients.

Happily, times have changed and packaged bulgur can now be found on most supermarket shelves—sandwiched between barley, buckwheat, and wild rice. Better news still is that bulgur may also be purchased in bulk (at considerably reduced prices) from natural foods stores and mail-order sources.

When you are shopping for bulgur, note that packaged and bulk varieties come in three different grades: *Coarse grind*, which has a rice-like texture, is most often used for pilafs and stuffings. *Medium grind* (or all-purpose) is the one I choose for cold salads and cooked vegetable side dishes. *Fine grind*, the most delicately milled of all, is the one I specify for bread and dessert recipes. In the recipes that follow, I rarely specify the grind of bulgur. It's the cook's choice, but keep in mind the above guidelines.

Storing bulgur, however, is another matter entirely, and I have lots of suggestions about that.

To maximize this grain's shelf life in the pantry, I strongly recommend the use of a large glass canning jar—preferably one that is absolutely airtight, with a hinged lid and rubber ring—as protection against heat spoilage and insect invasion.

No matter what the container, bulgur should be kept out of direct sunlight and stored below 60°F. If you have room, this grain will also keep for months in the refrigerator and for up to a year in the freezer. If a glass container is too cumbersome, consider airtight plastic bags for refrigerator or freezer storage.

A friend of mine places several herbal tea bags in the old-fashioned apothecary jar that holds her bulgur. She claims the tea retards weevils. While I cannot verify that, I do know that the delicate scent of camomile and such gives the grains one memorable bouquet.

How to Cook It

*T*astes differ as to the proper degree of munch and crunch in a dish of bulgur, so I offer no hard and fast rules for its preparation, only basic techniques (which are absolutely fail-safe for even a neophyte to grains cookery). Basic bulgur may be prepared four ways:

The Non-Presoak Method. Place 1 cup bulgur with 2½ cups liquid in a covered heavy saucepan over low heat. As it cooks, the grain will absorb all the liquid—about 20 to 25 minutes. (Cooking times will vary with the grind of bulgur used. A fine-milled grind will take considerably less time than a coarse or medium grind.) When the liquid is entirely absorbed, remove the pan from the heat and allow the bulgur to stand, still covered, for an additional 10 minutes. This allows the flavors to meld and the grains to dry out and separate. Fluff the cooked bulgur with a fork before serving.

The Hot Presoak Method. Place 1 cup bulgur in a heatproof bowl. Cover it with 3 to 4 cups of boiling salted water and let stand 40 minutes or longer. Line a colander with cheesecloth, place it in the sink, and drain the bulgur in it. Then twist the cheesecloth around the bulgur and squeeze until all moisture is extracted. At this point, the bulgur requires no extra cooking.

The Cold Presoak Method. Follow the hot presoak procedure, using cold water. However, cold-water soaking takes twice as much time: 2 to 2½ hours.

Some bulgur aficionados insist that the long soaking allows the grains to absorb liquid very slowly and consequently the bulgur has a more toothsome quality.

The Boiled Method. Bulgur may also be boiled like rice. Place 1 cup of bulgur in a large pot filled with 3 or 4 quarts of boiling salted water. Bring back to the boil, reduce the heat, and simmer 20 minutes. Then drain the bulgur in a strainer and press the grains dry with a spoon before it is served.

TEN-LAYER VEGETABLE SOUP

*B*ulgur's virtue in the kitchen, aside from its significant nutritional bonus, is its taste, faintly reminiscent of whole-wheat toast—a taste that even newcomers to grain-grazing find familiar and comforting.

From a cook's point of view, bulgur has another prime asset: mutability. This is a grain that can bow to assertive seasonings without losing a jot of its individuality. Consider the following quickly made soup devised of any and every veggie a fridge or freezer can yield, plus an increment of bulgur to fuse the flavors. It is a recipe, incidentally, very loosely based on a Tuscan garden soup from the redoubtable Nika Hazelton's collection.

2 tablespoons olive oil
2 medium tomatoes, cut into ¼-inch-thick slices
2 medium onions, cut into ¼-inch-thick slices
¼ teaspoon crushed whole allspice
2 cloves garlic, minced
1 large head romaine lettuce, shredded
½ cup bulgur
1 cup chopped fresh parsley
½ cup chopped fresh basil, or 2 tablespoons dried
1 large zucchini or yellow squash, cubed
¼ teaspoon crushed dried hot red peppers
1 package (10 ounces) frozen peas
1 package (10 ounces) frozen baby lima beans
2 teaspoons mixed chopped fresh herbs (sage, rosemary, chives, thyme)

1½ cups homemade chicken stock (see page 376) or vegetable stock (see page 378) or canned chicken broth
Salt and freshly ground black pepper to taste
Freshly grated Parmesan cheese

1. Spread the oil over the bottom of a large soup pot and layer all the ingredients, starting with the tomatoes and through the lima beans, in the pot. Cover, and cook over medium-low heat for 15 minutes.

2. Remove the cover, stir in the herbs and stock, and heat to boiling. Reduce the heat and simmer, uncovered, for 30 minutes. Season with salt and pepper. Pass the Parmesan cheese on the side.

Serves 6

PERSIAN LAMB SHANKS WITH BULGUR

This dish of lamb shanks and bulgur, cooked in wine and dappled with currants, may taste like a pasha's party fare, but it's not. The only thing Persian about it, in fact, is the rug it was named after!

4 lamb shanks, about 12 ounces each
2 large cloves garlic, slivered
Salt and freshly ground black pepper to
    taste
Hot Hungarian paprika
3 tablespoons all-purpose flour
    (approximately)
2 tablespoons unsalted butter
2 tablespoons olive oil
1 large onion, halved and thinly sliced
¼ teaspoon chopped fresh rosemary, or a
    pinch of dried
¾ cup red wine
1¼ cups water
¼ cup dried currants
2 cups homemade beef stock (see page 377)
    or canned broth
1⅓ cups bulgur
Chopped fresh parsley, for garnish

1. Preheat the oven to 375°F.

2. With an ice pick or a sharp knife, make five or six holes in the flesh of each lamb shank. Insert a sliver of garlic into each hole. Sprinkle each shank with salt, pepper, and paprika to taste. Dust the shanks with the flour.

3. Heat the butter with the oil in a large pot or Dutch oven over medium heat. Sauté the lamb shanks until golden on all sides, about 10 minutes. Transfer the lamb shanks to a plate. Add the onion to the pot; cook until golden, about 4 minutes. Stir in the rosemary.

4. Return the lamb shanks to the pot. Add the wine and water, and heat to boiling. Cover, transfer the pot to the oven, and bake 1½ hours.

5. Reduce the heat to 350°F and remove the pot from the oven. Transfer the shanks to a plate. Stir the currants into the cooking juices. Add the stock, scraping the sides and bottom of the pot.

Bulgur is a grain with more aliases than a shifty sheik. Depending upon which side of the Persian Gulf a cook's forebears were born on, you will find it spelled as *bulghur, bulgor, bulgar, boulgar, boulghour, borgul, borgol, burghul,* or *burghoul.*

And if you think that's confusing, let me tell you that one man's bulgur is definitely *not* another's borghul! The product found on the shelves of your supermarket is a far cry from any grain seller's offering in the Casbah.

For starters, American bulgur, which has been steamed and dried in rotary drums, is a deep russet-to-umber color and generally comes from hard winter wheat grown in Kansas, Nebraska, or Texas.

Middle Eastern bulgur, grown in the wheat fields of Afghanistan, Syria, and Lebanon, is a much lighter shade and almost always milled from soft summer wheat. Moreover, since it is parboiled and sun-dried, authentic bulgur retains a slight grassy aftertaste that true bulgurophiles recognize and dote upon.

Stir in the bulgur. Place the pot over medium heat, and heat to boiling. Return the shanks to the pot, cover, return it to the oven, and bake until the bulgur is tender and all liquid has been absorbed, 20 to 25 minutes. Before serving, fluff the bulgur with a fork and sprinkle with parsley.

Serves 4

OTTOMAN MEATBALLS IN TOMATO SAUCE

Bulgur is added to the meat mixture here to give the meatballs a slightly nutty flavor. I serve this dish over rice, but spaghetti does nicely as well.

FOR THE TOMATO SAUCE

4 tablespoons (½ stick) unsalted butter
1 medium onion, finely chopped
1 clove garlic, minced
1 small rib celery, finely chopped
4 large ripe tomatoes, peeled, seeded, and
    chopped
1 teaspoon chopped fresh basil, or
    ½ teaspoon dried
1 teaspoon chopped fresh oregano, or
    ¼ teaspoon dried
Pinch of dried thyme
2 teaspoons sugar
¼ teaspoon grated orange zest
Salt and freshly ground black pepper to
    taste

FOR THE MEATBALLS

½ cup homemade beef stock (see page 377)
    or canned broth
¼ cup bulgur
2 teaspoons unsalted butter
1 small onion, finely chopped
1 clove garlic, minced
1 pound 5 ounces ground beef
10 ounces ground veal
5 ounces ground pork
2 eggs, lightly beaten
½ cup chopped fresh parsley
½ cup freshly grated Parmesan cheese
½ teaspoon salt

¼ teaspoon freshly ground black pepper
2 tablespoons olive oil (approximately)
Chopped fresh parsley, for garnish

Bulgur is not exclusive to the Middle East. This grain came to European tables as early as 1470, a souvenir of the Ottoman rulers who branched out after their conquest of Turkey. At its high point, during the reign of Sultan Suleiman the Magnificient, the Ottoman Empire stretched from the Bosporus clear across the Balkans to Vienna, not counting outposts in Africa and Asia Minor. And Ottoman influences in fashion, furnishings, and food reverberated all over the Western World during its five hundred years of dominance—even crossing the Atlantic at one point. It is reported that, to finance his second trip to the New World, Columbus acceded to Queen Isabella's wishes and planted Ottoman wheat. And he remained there, rooted to the spot, until the first seedlings sprouted.

1. Make the tomato sauce: Melt the butter in a large saucepan over medium-low heat. Add the onion; cook 1 minute. Add the garlic and celery; cook 4 minutes. Stir in the tomatoes, basil, oregano, thyme, sugar, and orange zest. Cook, uncovered, stirring occasionally, until thick, about 45 minutes. Season with salt and pepper, and set aside.

2. Make the meatballs: Place the stock in a small saucepan and heat to boiling. Stir in the bulgur and reduce the heat. Cook, covered, over low heat until the bulgur is almost tender and all liquid has been absorbed, 15 to 20 minutes. Set aside, covered, until cool.

3. Melt the butter in a medium-size skillet over medium-low heat. Add the onion; cook 1 minute. Add the garlic;

cook 4 minutes longer. Set aside.

4. Combine the beef, veal, and pork in a medium-size bowl. Add the cooked bulgur, the onion mixture, and the eggs, parsley, Parmesan cheese, salt, and pepper. Mix thoroughly and form into small meatballs.

5. Heat the oil in a heavy skillet over medium heat. Sauté the meatballs, a few at a time, adding more oil if needed, until well browned, about 5 minutes. As the meatballs are sautéed, set them aside on a plate.

6. Heat the tomato sauce over medium heat until hot. Add the meatballs, and reduce the heat to medium-low. Cook, uncovered, for 30 minutes. Before serving, sprinkle with parsley.

Serves 6

TWIN ROASTED CHICKENS WITH GARLICKY BULGUR DRESSING

*D*on't be put off by the forty cloves of garlic—the long, slow sautéeing removes the sting. The bulgur will be slightly crunchy when you stuff the birds, but it will steam in the cavities as the chickens roast.

FOR THE STUFFING
2 large heads garlic, cloves separated, unpeeled (about 40 cloves)
4 tablespoons (½ stick) unsalted butter
1½ cups homemade chicken stock (see page 376) or canned broth
1¼ cups bulgur
2 tablespoons chopped fresh parsley
1 teaspoon chopped fresh sage, or ¼ teaspoon dried
½ teaspoon salt
¼ teaspoon freshly ground black pepper

FOR THE CHICKEN
2 small chickens (2½ to 3 pounds each)

4 tablespoons (½ stick) unsalted butter, at room temperature
2 tablespoons Dijon mustard
¼ cup fresh bread crumbs

1. Make the stuffing: Cook the garlic cloves in boiling water to cover for 2 minutes. Drain and peel.

2. Melt the butter in a large saucepan over low heat. Add the garlic cloves. Cook, covered, until the garlic is very tender, about 20 minutes. Do not allow it to brown.

3. Using a fork, mash the garlic into a paste. Add the chicken stock and heat to boiling. Stir in the bulgur and reduce the heat. Cook, covered, over low heat until all liquid has been absorbed, about 15 minutes. Remove the pan from the heat and add the parsley, sage, salt, and pepper. Allow the stuffing to cool slightly.

4. Preheat the oven to 375°F.

5. Spoon the stuffing into the cavities of the chickens. Sew securely and truss. Pat the chickens dry with paper towels, and place them on a rack in a roasting pan, breast side up.

6. Combine the softened butter with the mustard and bread crumbs, and mix until smooth. Spread this mixture evenly over the tops and sides of the chickens. Place the chickens in the oven and roast until they are crisp and the juices run yellow when pricked with a fork, about 1½ hours. Remove the trussing strings before serving.

Serves 4 to 6

ARMENIAN-STYLE CHICKEN WITH BULGUR

*F*rom the northeastern region of Turkey, this hearty dish is basically a bulgur-thickened stew. Walnuts and honey in its devise give a whiff of the exotic land from which it comes.

2 tablespoons olive oil
1 teaspoon unsalted butter
*1 chicken (3½ pounds), cut into serving
    pieces*
½ teaspoon salt
¼ teaspoon freshly ground black pepper
*½ teaspoon chopped fresh thyme, or
    ¼ teaspoon dried*
1 medium onion, chopped
2 cloves garlic, minced
*1 small hot red pepper, seeded, deveined,
    and minced*
*2 cups homemade chicken stock (see page
    376) or canned broth*
1 cup bulgur
½ cup broken walnut pieces
1 tablespoon honey
*1 teaspoon chopped fresh mint, or
    ¼ teaspoon dried*
*1 teaspoon chopped fresh basil, or
    ½ teaspoon dried*

1. Heat the oil with the butter in a large cast-iron skillet over medium heat. Sprinkle the chicken pieces with the salt, pepper, and thyme, and sauté, a few pieces at a time, until golden brown, about 10 minutes. Transfer the pieces to a plate as they are done.

2. Remove all but 1 tablespoon fat from the skillet. Add the onion and cook over medium-low heat, scraping the sides and bottom of the pan, for 2 minutes. Add the garlic and hot pepper; cook 4 minutes longer.

3. Return the chicken pieces to the skillet, stir in the stock, and heat to boiling. Reduce the heat and simmer, covered, for 20 minutes.

4. Using tongs, remove the chicken pieces to a plate. Stir the bulgur into the cooking juices, and add the walnuts and honey. Mix well and return the chicken pieces. Continue to cook, covered, until the chicken and bulgur are tender and all liquid has been absorbed, about 20 minutes longer. Turn off the heat and let the skillet stand, covered, for 10 minutes. Before serving, fluff the bulgur with a fork, and sprinkle with the mint and basil.

Serves 4

PAKISTANI CHICKEN WITH BULGUR RICE

*F*rom Pakistan, a more traditional stew. Serve it on a large platter, surrounded with the mixture of bulgur and rice to sop up the juices.

½ cup bulgur
½ cup long-grain rice
1 tablespoon unsalted butter
2 teaspoons vegetable oil
1 chicken (about 3½ pounds), cut into
    pieces
1 large clove garlic, minced
1 teaspoon fennel seeds
½ teaspoon cayenne pepper
½ teaspoon turmeric
¼ teaspoon ground cumin
½ teaspoon salt
¼ teaspoon freshly ground black pepper
1 medium onion, chopped
½ teaspoon paprika
½ cup water
Chopped fresh parsley, for garnish

1. Cook the bulgur in a large pot of boiling salted water for 10 minutes. Add the rice; boil 12 minutes longer. Drain in a colander.

2. Place the colander over 2 inches of boiling water in another pot. Do not let the bottom of the colander touch the water. Cover the bulgur/rice mixture with a single layer of paper towels. Steam for at least 15 minutes. (The mixture can be held this way for several hours without harm.)

3. Meanwhile, heat the butter with the oil in a large heavy skillet over medium heat. Sauté the chicken pieces, a few at a time, until well browned, about 10 minutes. Transfer the chicken to a plate.

4. While the chicken is browning, place the garlic, fennel seeds, cayenne pepper, turmeric, cumin, salt, and black pepper in a small bowl and mash with the back of a spoon until smooth.

5. When all the chicken pieces are sautéed, drain all but 1 tablespoon fat from the skillet. Add the onion; cook over medium-low heat, scraping the bottom and sides of the pan, for 3 minutes. Stir in the mashed garlic and spice mixture; cook 2 minutes longer. Sprinkle the mixture with the paprika. Stir in the water and return the chicken pieces to the skillet. Heat to boiling. Reduce the heat and simmer, covered, basting occasionally, until the chicken is tender, about 40 minutes.

6. To serve, fluff the bulgur/rice mixture with a fork and arrange it around the edge of a serving platter. Spoon the chicken mixture into the center, and garnish with parsley.

Serves 4

BERBER CHICKEN AND TOMATO SALAD

*F*rom Morocco, a wonderfully simple salad that, on its native shores, is often made with couscous. I like it best at room temperature.

1 cup bulgur
1 cup chopped, seeded, peeled tomatoes
(about 2 medium)
2 cups boneless skinless cooked chicken
pieces
3 tablespoons chopped fresh basil
1 teaspoon chopped fresh mint
2 cloves garlic, minced
⅓ cup olive oil
3 tablespoons red wine vinegar
Salt and freshly ground black pepper to
taste

Chopped fresh parsley, for garnish

1. Cook the bulgur in a large pot of boiling salted water until tender, 20 to 25 minutes. Drain, and set aside to cool.

2. In a large bowl, combine the cooled bulgur, tomatoes, chicken, basil, mint, and garlic. Lightly toss, then add the oil, vinegar, and salt and pepper. Sprinkle with parsley.

Serves 4 to 6

PEPPERED PAILLETTE

A paillette is a spangle used for ornamenting decorative costumes. In this case, it's green salsa that turns a leftover turkey dish into a joyous occasion.

2 tablespoons olive oil
1 medium onion, chopped
1 clove garlic, minced
1 medium red bell pepper, cored, seeded,
and chopped
2 cups cooked turkey or chicken
½ cup hot green salsa
1½ cups homemade chicken stock (see page
376) or canned broth
1 cup bulgur
Salt and freshly ground black pepper to
taste
Chopped fresh parsley, for garnish

1. Heat the oil in a medium-size saucepan over medium-low heat. Add the onion; cook 1 minute. Add the garlic and bell pepper; cook 4 minutes longer.

2. Add the turkey to the pepper mixture and toss to coat. Stir in the salsa and chicken stock, and heat to boiling. Stir in the bulgur, reduce the heat, and cook, covered, over low heat until the bulgur is tender and all liquid has been absorbed, 20 to 25 minutes. Turn off the heat and let the pan stand, covered, for 10 minutes. Fluff the bulgur with a fork, and season with salt and pepper. Before serving, sprinkle with parsley.

Serves 4 to 6

TOMATO BULGUR WITH SCRAMBLED EGGS

This combination of creamy bulgur topped with even creamier scrambled eggs makes a perfect brunch dish with nothing more than a green salad on the side. The eggs must be cooked *slowly* to obtain a smooth, velvety texture.

FOR THE TOMATO BULGUR

2 tablespoons olive oil
1 medium onion, chopped
2 cloves garlic, minced
1 can (14 ounces) imported Italian plum
    tomatoes, with juices, chopped
1 cup chopped, seeded, peeled fresh
    tomatoes (2 medium)
Pinch of sugar
⅛ teaspoon dried thyme
⅛ teaspoon dried oregano
1 tablespoon chopped fresh basil, or 2
    teaspoons dried
½ teaspoon anchovy paste
8 crushed whole allspice
1 tablespoon unsalted butter
1½ cups homemade chicken stock (see page
    376) or canned broth
¾ cup bulgur
Salt and freshly ground black pepper to
    taste

FOR THE SCRAMBLED EGGS

1 tablespoon unsalted butter
2 tablespoons heavy or whipping cream
4 eggs, lightly beaten
Salt and freshly ground black pepper to
    taste
Chopped fresh parsley, for garnish

1. Make the tomato bulgur: Heat the oil in a medium-size saucepan over medium heat. Add the onion; cook 2 minutes. Add the garlic; cook 2 minutes longer. Stir in the canned and fresh tomatoes, sugar, thyme, oregano, basil, and anchovy paste. Cook, uncovered, until the tomatoes are soft and the sauce is fairly thick, about 15 minutes. Add the crushed allspice and the butter. Cook 5 minutes longer.

2. Add the stock to the tomato mixture, and heat to boiling. Stir in the bulgur and reduce the heat. Cook, covered, over low heat until the bulgur is tender and all liquid has been absorbed, 20 to 25 minutes. Turn off the heat and let the pan stand, covered, for 10 minutes. (If the mixture seems too wet, remove the cover and stir over medium-low heat until it is creamy in texture.) Add salt and pepper.

3. Meanwhile, make the scrambled eggs: Melt the butter in a large skillet over low heat. Whisk the cream into the eggs and pour the mixture into the skillet. Cook over low heat, stirring frequently, until soft curds form, about 20 minutes. Add salt and pepper.

4. To serve, arrange the tomato bulgur in a warm serving dish. Spoon the eggs evenly over the top. Sprinkle with parsley.

Serves 4 to 6

IRAQI TABBOULEH

While the precise meaning of *tabbouleh* changes with the landscape on which it is made, most denizens of the Middle East agree that it translates as "good table dish"!

1 cup bulgur
1 medium onion, finely chopped
6 scallions, white bulbs and green tops, finely chopped
1½ cups chopped fresh parsley
½ cup finely chopped fresh mint
¼ cup olive oil
¼ cup fresh lemon juice
Salt and freshly ground black pepper to taste
2 medium tomatoes, seeded and chopped
Lettuce or fresh grape leaves, for serving
Marinated artichoke hearts, olives, hard-cooked eggs, or nasturtium leaves or flowers, for garnish
Toasted pine nuts, for garnish

1. Place the bulgur in a medium-size bowl. Cover with cold water, and let stand until softened, 2 to 2½ hours. Line a strainer with a double layer of cheesecloth, and pour in the bulgur. Twist the cloth around the bulgur and squeeze until all moisture has been extracted.

2. Transfer the bulgur to a large bowl. Mix in the onions and scallions with your hands. Stir in the parsley, mint, olive oil, and lemon juice. Season with salt and pepper, and toss in the tomatoes. Refrigerate, covered, for at least 2 hours before serving.

3. To serve, mound the mixture in a shallow bowl or on a platter. Surround it with lettuce or grape leaves. Add any of the garnishes, and sprinkle the pine nuts over the salad.

Serves 6 to 8

TEXAS TABBOULEH

This Texas rendering (high on the jalapeños) is not an absolutely authentic tabbouleh, but a great version, nonetheless. It is the handiwork of talented Michael McLaughlin, chef-owner of The Manhattan Chili Company in New York City.

1 cup bulgur
1 large red bell pepper
2 jalapeño peppers: 1 seeded, deveined, and minced; 1 seeded, deveined, and coarsely chopped
2 small tomatoes, seeded and chopped
2 medium zucchini, chopped
4 scallions, white bulbs and green tops, chopped
1 tablespoon chopped fresh basil
2 cloves garlic, coarsely chopped
½ cup fresh cilantro (Chinese parsley) leaves
½ cup fresh mint leaves
¼ cup white wine vinegar
¾ cup olive oil
Salt and freshly ground black pepper to taste
Lettuce leaves, for serving
8 ounces goat cheese, crumbled
Chopped fresh parsley, for garnish

1. Cover the bulgur with boiling salted water in a heatproof bowl. Let it stand 40 minutes.

2. Meanwhile, roast the bell pepper over a gas flame, turning until it is charred all over (or place it under a broiler until charred). Carefully wrap the pepper in paper towels and place in a plastic bag. Let it stand until cool. Then rub the charred skin from the pepper with paper towels, and chop the pepper.

3. Line a strainer with a double layer of cheesecloth, and pour in the bulgur. Twist the cloth around the bulgur and squeeze until all moisture has been extracted. In a mixing bowl, combine the chopped bell pepper and the bulgur with the minced jalapeño pepper, the tomatoes, zucchini, scallions, and basil. Toss well.

4. Place the coarsely chopped jalapeño pepper, garlic, cilantro leaves, mint leaves, vinegar, and oil in the container of a food processor or blender. Process until smooth. Pour over the bulgur mixture, and season with salt and pepper.

5. Arrange lettuce leaves over the bottom of a salad bowl. Mound the bulgur mixture in the center, and dot the top with the goat cheese. Sprinkle with parsley.

Serves 4 to 6

LEBANESE BORGHOL

A salad, borghol (another name for bulgur) stems from Lebanon, where it is eaten hot or cold, for breakfast, lunch, or dinner, as a side dish to meat, fowl, fish, or simply a plate of fresh greens. Unlike tabbouleh, borghol is cooked, and not presoaked.

⅓ cup olive oil
1 medium onion, chopped
2 large cloves garlic, minced
1 cup chopped, seeded, peeled tomatoes
1 tablespoon chopped fresh basil, or 1 teaspoon dried
1 cup bulgur
1½ cups homemade beef stock (see page 376) or canned broth, heated
1 tablespoon honey
1 tablespoon tomato paste
½ teaspoon salt
½ teaspoon freshly ground black pepper
2 tablespoons chopped fresh parsley

1. Heat the oil in a medium-size saucepan over medium heat. Add the onion; cook until lightly browned, about 3 minutes. Add the garlic; cook 1 minute longer. Stir in the tomatoes and basil. Cook 2 minutes longer.

2. Stir the bulgur into the tomato mixture, making sure that the bulgur is well coated. Stir in the beef stock. Reduce the heat to low and cook, covered, for 5 minutes.

3. Add the honey, tomato paste, salt, and pepper to the bulgur mixture. Continue to cook, covered, until the bulgur is tender and all liquid has been absorbed, 15 to 20 minutes. Turn off the heat and let the pan stand for 10 minutes. Then use a fork to toss in 1 tablespoon of the parsley. Sprinkle the remaining parsley over the top before serving. Serve hot or cold.

Serves 4 to 6

KEYMA
(Lentils with Bulgur)

Keyma is supposedly an Indian dish, or so it was noted when this recipe came to me umpteen years ago. Lentils and bulgur make a remarkably tonic combination. I am happy to make a whole lunch of just this dish.

1 cup lentils
3 tablespoons unsalted butter
1 teaspoon vegetable oil
1 large onion, chopped
1 clove garlic, minced
Pinch of ground cloves
1 jalapeño pepper, seeded, deveined, and
    minced
¼ pound cooked ham, chopped
2 tablespoons plus ¼ cup chopped fresh
    parsley
2 cups homemade chicken stock (see page
    376) or canned broth
1 cup bulgur
2 tablespoons red wine vinegar
Salt and freshly ground black pepper to
    taste

1. Cook the lentils in a large pot of boiling salted water until partially tender, about 20 minutes. Drain.

2. Heat the butter with the oil in a large saucepan over medium-low heat. Add the onion; cook 1 minute. Add the garlic and sprinkle with the cloves; cook 4 minutes longer. Stir in the jalapeño pepper, the ham, and the 2 tablespoons parsley. Continue to cook 5 minutes.

3. Add the lentils to the onion mixture. Stir in the stock and heat to boiling. Stir in the bulgur and reduce the heat. Cook, covered, over low heat until the bulgur is tender, 20 to 25 minutes. Turn off the heat and let the pan stand, covered, for 10 minutes. Then add the vinegar, salt and pepper to taste, and the ¼ cup parsley, fluffing the bulgur with a fork.

Serves 4

HERBED ORZO AND BULGUR PILAF

Orzo is a rice-shaped Greek pasta that matches up well with bulgur. Serve this next time you roast a leg of lamb.

4 tablespoons (½ stick) unsalted butter
2 large scallions, white bulbs and green
    tops, finely chopped
½ cup orzo
2 cups lamb stock (see page 378)
1 cup bulgur

1 tablespoon minced fresh rosemary, or 1
    teaspoon dried
1 tablespoon minced fresh basil, or 1
    teaspoon dried
1 tablespoon minced fresh parsley
1 teaspoon minced garlic

1. Melt the butter in a medium-size saucepan over medium heat. Add the scallions; cook 1 minute. Stir in the orzo; cook 4 minutes. Add the lamb stock and heat to boiling. Stir in the bulgur and reduce the heat. Cook, covered, over low heat until the bulgur is tender and all liquid has been absorbed, 20 to 25 minutes. Turn off the heat and let the pan stand, covered, for 10 minutes.

2. Stir the herbs and garlic into the bulgur mixture, fluffing it with a fork. Serve immediately.

Serves 4 to 6

TRIPLE-THREAT ONION PILAF

Yellow onions, leeks, and shallots add pizzazz to a basic pilaf. This goes well with fowl of all sorts.

3 tablespoons unsalted butter
1 teaspoon olive oil
1 medium onion, finely chopped
2 medium leeks, rinsed well and finely chopped
1 shallot, minced
1 large clove garlic, minced
1 cup bulgur
2½ cups homemade beef stock (see page 377) or canned broth, or 1½ cups beef stock with 1 cup chicken stock (see page 376)
¼ cup chopped fresh parsley
Salt and freshly ground black pepper to taste
¼ cup freshly grated Parmesan cheese

1. Heat the butter with the oil in a large heavy saucepan over medium-low heat. Add the onion; cook 1 minute. Stir in the leeks, shallot, and garlic. Reduce the heat to low and cook, covered, for 30 minutes.

2. Add the bulgur to the onion mixture, tossing to coat the grains. Add the stock and heat to boiling. Reduce the heat and cook, covered, over low heat until the bulgur is tender and all liquid has been absorbed, 20 to 25 minutes.

Turn off the heat and toss in the parsley. Let the mixture stand, covered, 10 minutes. Then season with salt and pepper, fluffing the bulgur with a fork. Sprinkle with the Parmesan cheese.

Serves 4

A BULGUR CAVEAT!

Since bulgur is precooked, *do not overcook it!*

A good rule of thumb is to remove a grain or two from the pot after 20 minutes of cooking time has elapsed. It will not be done, but the texture should be "toothsome" enough to allay any fears, and then the dish can be completed with utter confidence.

And remember: The final 10 minutes resting time, off the heat, is when the bulgur becomes dry and light.

TURKISH "FOREIGN RICE"
(Ecnebi Pirinc)

This is a side dish served in the dining car of the Orient Express on its last lap, from Venice to Istanbul. *Ecnebi pirinc* (foreign rice) is also a slang expression for "small change"—which this definitely is not!

2 tablespoons olive oil
1 medium onion, chopped
1 clove garlic, minced
¼ teaspoon chopped fresh thyme, or a
    pinch of dried
1 teaspoon chopped fresh basil, or
    ½ teaspoon dried
2 medium tomatoes, peeled, seeded, and
    chopped (about 1¼ cups)
½ cup cubed hard salami (preferably
    Italian or Hungarian)
1¼ cups homemade chicken stock (see page
    376) or canned broth, heated
1 cup bulgur
½ cup ricotta or cottage cheese
Chopped fresh parsley, for garnish
Freshly grated Parmesan cheese (optional)

1. Heat the oil in a large saucepan over medium heat. Add the onion; cook until lightly browned, about 3 minutes. Add the garlic; cook 1 minute longer. Stir in the herbs and tomatoes. Reduce the heat to medium-low and cook, covered, until the tomatoes are very soft and juicy, about 10 minutes. Add the cubed salami; cook, covered, 2 minutes longer.

2. Remove the cover from the saucepan, add the chicken stock, and heat to boiling. Stir in the bulgur and reduce the heat. Cook, covered, over low heat until the bulgur is tender and all liquid has been absorbed, 20 to 25 minutes. Turn off the heat and let the pan stand, covered, for 10 minutes. With two forks toss in the ricotta or cottage cheese, and sprinkle with parsley. Serve with Parmesan cheese, if desired.

Serves 4

BULGUR WITH FENNEL AND PEAS

I admit to being an addict of anything that tastes of licorice. Fennel and Pernod are teamed with peas in the following pilaf to satisfy like cravings.

2 tablespoons unsalted butter
¾ cup chopped scallions (about 9), white
    bulbs and green tops
1 small clove garlic
1 small fennel, trimmed and chopped
    (2½ cups), fronds chopped and reserved
1½ cups homemade chicken stock (see
    page 376) or canned broth
¾ cup bulgur
10 ounces (2 cups) fresh peas
1 tablespoon Pernod liqueur
Salt and freshly ground black pepper to
    taste

1. Melt the butter in a large saucepan over medium-low heat. Add the scallions; cook 1 minute. Add the garlic; cook 2 minutes longer.

2. Stir the chopped fennel and the chicken stock into the scallion mixture and heat to boiling. Reduce the heat and cook, covered, for 5 minutes. Stir in the bulgur and cook, covered, over low heat until the bulgur is tender, 20 to 25 minutes. Stir in the peas; cook, covered, 1 minute. Turn off the heat and let the pan stand, covered, for 10 minutes. Add the Pernod and season with salt and pepper, fluffing the bulgur with a fork.

Serves 4

BULGUR TIANS

A tian is basically a gratin that includes Swiss chard or spinach. This contains both. The bulgur is presoaked in boiling water. This is merely a time-saving step and has no effect on the flavor of the finished dish.

½ cup bulgur
2½ tablespoons unsalted butter
2 tablespoons olive oil
1 large onion, finely chopped
3 cloves garlic, minced
½ medium red bell pepper, cored, seeded and chopped
¼ teaspoon crushed dried hot red peppers
2 small zucchini, finely diced
8 ounces fresh spinach, trimmed and chopped
1 pound Swiss chard, including stems, chopped
½ cup chopped fresh basil
⅓ cup chopped fresh parsley
1 teaspoon salt
¼ teaspoon freshly ground black pepper
3 eggs, lightly beaten
⅓ cup freshly grated Parmesan cheese
⅓ cup grated Jarlsberg cheese
3 tablespoons soft bread crumbs

1. Cover the bulgur with boiling water in a heatproof bowl. Let stand 15 minutes. Drain.

2. Preheat the oven to 375°F.

3. Heat the butter with the oil in a large saucepan over medium-low heat. Add the onion; cook 1 minute. Add the garlic and bell pepper; cook 2 minutes. Add the dried red peppers and zucchini; cook, stirring constantly, 2 minutes longer.

4. Add the spinach and chard to the saucepan. Toss well, then cover, and cook 5 minutes. Stir the bulgur into the greens mixture. Add the basil, parsley, salt, and pepper. Cook, covered, 5 minutes. Remove the cover and continue to cook, stirring often, 5 minutes longer. The mixture should be fairly dry; raise the heat slightly if it is too wet.

5. Transfer the bulgur mixture to a well-buttered 8- to 10-cup casserole. Lightly fluff the mixture with a fork. Pour the eggs over the top. Sprinkle with both cheeses, and then with the bread crumbs. Bake until golden, 25 to 30 minutes.

Serves 6

"SCROLL"
(Bulgur Pilaf with Escarole)

Greens and grains. This hearty pilaf is matched with pork in my house.

2 tablespoons vegetable oil
1 small onion, chopped
2 large cloves garlic, minced
1 whole head escarole, sliced (about 4 cups)
1½ cups homemade chicken stock (see page 376) or canned broth
1 cup bulgur
Salt and freshly ground black pepper to taste

1. Heat the oil in a large saucepan over medium-low heat. Add the onion; cook 1 minute. Add the garlic; cook 4 minutes longer.

2. Stir the escarole and stock into the onion mixture, and heat to boiling. Stir in the bulgur and reduce the heat. Cook, covered, over low heat until the bulgur is tender and all the liquid has been absorbed, 20 to 25 minutes. Turn off the heat and let the pan stand, covered, for 10 minutes. Then season with salt and pepper, fluffing the bulgur with a fork, and serve.

Serves 4

SAUTEED BULGUR WITH SOUR CREAM AND DILL

My favored method for cooking bulgur. I serve it as an adjunct to poultry or lamb.

4 tablespoons (½ stick) unsalted butter
1 large onion, chopped
1 large carrot, chopped
1 large rib celery, chopped
1 large parsnip, chopped
2½ cups homemade chicken stock (see page 376) or canned broth
1 cup bulgur
Salt and freshly ground black pepper to taste
2 tablespoons plus ¾ cup sour cream
¼ cup chopped fresh dill

1. Melt the butter in a large saucepan over medium-low heat. Add the onion; cook until golden, about 5 minutes. Stir in the carrot, celery, and parsnip; cook 2 minutes. Cover, and cook 10 minutes longer.

2. Add the stock to the vegetable mixture. Heat to boiling, then stir in the bulgur and reduce the heat. Cook, covered, over low heat until the bulgur is tender and all liquid has been absorbed, 20 to 25 minutes. Turn off the heat and let the pan stand, covered, for 10 minutes. Then season with salt and pepper, fluffing the bulgur with a fork. Add the 2 tablespoons sour cream and the dill. Pass the remaining sour cream on the side.

Serves 4

BULGUR NICOISE WITH ROSY CREAM

A Mediterranean-inspired dish with a pure Greene embellishment. The rosy whipped cream melts like butter on the hot bulgur—and it makes a smashing first course.

3 tablespoons olive oil
8 ounces fresh shiitake mushrooms, sliced
1 tablespoon unsalted butter
1 large onion, chopped
1 clove garlic, minced
1½ teaspoons chopped fresh oregano,
    or ½ teaspoon dried
1 teaspoon crushed dried hot red peppers
⅔ cup chopped pitted black olives (oil-
    cured are best)
2 cups homemade chicken stock (see page
    376) or canned broth
1 cup bulgur
½ cup heavy or whipping cream
1 teaspoon tomato paste
Salt and freshly ground black pepper to
    taste
1 tablespoon chopped fresh parsley
2 tablespoons chopped fresh basil

1. Heat the oil in a large saucepan over medium-high heat. Add the mushrooms and sauté until golden, 5 minutes.

2. Add the butter to the pan and reduce the heat to medium-low. Stir in the onion; cook 1 minute. Add the garlic, oregano, and dried red peppers; cook 1 minute longer. Stir in the olives and chicken stock, and heat to boiling. Then stir in the bulgur and reduce the heat. Cook, covered, over low heat until the bulgur is tender and all liquid has been absorbed, 20 to 25 minutes. Turn off the heat and let the pan stand, covered, for 10 minutes.

3. Meanwhile, beat the cream with the tomato paste in a large bowl until stiff. Transfer to a serving bowl.

4. Season the bulgur with salt and pepper, fluffing it with a fork. Sprinkle with the chopped parsley and basil. Pass the rosy cream on the side.

Serves 4

BULGUR-STUFFED TOMATOES

These herby stuffed tomatoes go well with just about anything, and are just as good when tomatoes are not at their prime.

4 ripe medium tomatoes
¼ cup strong homemade chicken stock (see
    page 376)
2 tablespoons olive oil
1 medium onion, finely chopped
1 large clove garlic, minced
1 teaspoon sugar
½ cup bulgur
1 teaspoon chopped fresh basil, or ½

teaspoon dried
½ teaspoon chopped fresh thyme, or ¼
    teaspoon dried
½ teaspoon salt
¼ teaspoon freshly ground black pepper
⅛ teaspoon hot pepper sauce
2 tablespoons freshly grated Parmesan
    cheese

1. Slice the tops off the tomatoes and scoop out the interiors with a spoon, leaving about ¼-inch-thick walls. Turn the scooped-out tomatoes upside down on paper towels to drain. Place the tomato pulp and seeds in the container of a food processor or blender, and process until smooth. You should have about 1¼ cups liquid. Add enough chicken stock to make 1½ cups total liquid.

2. Heat the oil in a medium-size saucepan over medium-low heat. Add the onion; cook 1 minute. Add the garlic; cook 3 minutes longer. Stir in the tomato mixture and add the sugar, bulgur, basil, thyme, salt, pepper, and hot pepper sauce. Heat to boiling. Then reduce the heat and cook, covered, over low heat until the bulgur is tender and all liquid has been absorbed, 20 to 25 minutes. (Remove the cover and continue to cook if the mixture seems too wet.) Turn off the heat and let the pan stand, covered, for 10 minutes.

3. Stuff the bulgur mixture into the tomato shells, mounding it high. Sprinkle with the Parmesan cheese. Place under a preheated broiler and cook until the tops are golden and the tomatoes are warmed through, about 5 minutes.

Serves 4

MAKING BULGUR FROM SCRATCH

Store-bought bulgur is not a pricey ingredient, yet it is simple and thrifty to make bulgur on your own. A better reason for doing it yourself than saving either time or money is that currently no commercially packaged bulgur is processed from organically grown wheat, even though organic wheat berries are in evidence at natural foods stores everywhere.

First pick over the whole wheat berries for any loose fragments or dust. A light rinse under cold running water won't hurt. Then combine 1 cup wheat berries in a large pot with 2 cups liquid. (Plain water is fine, but strained stock or vegetable juice will impart more flavor.) Bring the liquid to the boil, reduce the heat to medium-low, and simmer, covered, for 1 hour.

In a colander, drain off any liquid the berries have not absorbed. Then, using a large fork, spread them over a baking sheet or metal tray and toast in a low (225°F) oven until the berries are dry to the touch and separate easily, about 1 hour. Stir the berries from time to time as they toast. Allow the dried berries to cool completely. Then place about ¼ cup of the cooled berries in a zipper-lock-type plastic bag, seal the bag, and crush the berries with a rolling pin until you have the desired "grind." Repeat with the remaining berries. This will yield 1 to 1¼ cups medium-ground bulgur.

If you are using homemade bulgur for tabouleh and want to use the cold pre-soak method (see page 86), add another 30 to 60 minutes' soaking time.

BUTTERMILK BULGUR BREAD

This is a very old-fashioned whole-wheat bread (the kind your grandmother served when you stayed over). It has minimal crunch but maximum flavor, dappled with tomato and drizzled with honey. Try it toasted, please!

1 package dry yeast
¼ cup warm water
3 tablespoons honey
2 teaspoons tomato paste
½ cup fine-ground bulgur
1½ cups buttermilk, warmed
⅓ cup unsalted butter, melted
1 teaspoon coarse (kosher) salt
2 cups whole-wheat flour
2 cups bread flour (approximately)
Cornmeal

1. Place the yeast in a large bowl. Cover with the water, and let stand until the yeast begins to soften, about 3 minutes. Add the honey and tomato paste, and whisk until smooth. Stir in the bulgur and buttermilk; let stand 20 minutes.

2. Stir the butter and salt into the bulgur mixture. Then stir in the whole-wheat flour and about 1½ cups bread flour to make a stiff dough. Turn out onto a lightly floured surface. Knead for 15 minutes, adding more bread flour if necessary to keep the dough from sticking. Transfer the dough to a lightly greased bowl, cover, and let rise in a warm place until doubled in volume, about 1½ hours.

3. Turn the dough out onto a lightly floured surface; punch it down and divide in half. Roll and pull each half until it resembles a loaf of French or Italian bread.

4. Sprinkle a baking sheet with cornmeal, and place the loaves on the sheet. Brush the loaves lightly with water, cover loosely with a towel, and let rise in a warm place until doubled in volume, 45 minutes to 1 hour.

5. Preheat the oven to 400°F.

6. With a sharp knife, slash the surface of the loaves four or five times, then brush them again with water. Bake until crisp and hollow-sounding when tapped with your finger, about 25 minutes. Cool on a rack.

Makes 2 loaves

BULGUR MUSHOSH

The last recipe in my bulgur bouquet is a silken apricot pudding known as *mushosh* in the Middle East, where it is also called "Beirut Wedding Cake."

If you are thinking of eliminating the sensuous and velvety vanilla sauce to cut calories—*don't!*

½ cup chopped dried apricots (about
    4 ounces)
⅔ cup granulated sugar
1 cup fresh orange juice
1 cup water
1 teaspoon finely slivered orange zest
½ cup fine-ground bulgur
1 tablespoon unsalted butter
2 eggs, separated
6 tablespoons heavy or whipping cream
1 tablespoon Grand Marnier
2 tablespoons light brown sugar
Classic Vanilla Sauce (recipe follows)

1. Combine the apricots with the granulated sugar, orange juice, water, and orange zest in a medium-size saucepan. Heat to boiling, then reduce the heat. Simmer, partially covered, until the apricots are very tender, about 10 minutes.

2. Stir the bulgur into the apricot mixture and heat to boiling. Reduce the heat and cook, covered, over low heat until the bulgur is very tender, about 45 minutes. (Add more water if needed to complete cooking.) Turn off the heat and let the pan stand, covered, for 10 minutes. Stir in the butter until melted.

3. Preheat the oven to 350°F.

4. Beat the egg yolks with the cream in a medium-size bowl. Slowly beat in the bulgur mixture, then stir in the Grand Marnier.

5. Beat the egg whites until stiff, and fold them into the bulgur mixture.

Transfer the mixture to a shallow 1- to 1½-quart baking dish.

6. Place the brown sugar in a fine-mesh strainer, and holding the strainer over the apricot mixture, press it through with the back of a spoon. Place the baking dish in a roasting pan and add ½ inch boiling water to the pan. Bake for 30 minutes, then cool on a rack. Serve at room temperature or well chilled, with Classic Vanilla Sauce.

Serves 6 to 8

Classic Vanilla Sauce

3 extra-large egg yolks
½ cup sugar
1¼ cups milk, scalded
1 teaspoon vanilla extract
1 tablespoon kirsch
⅓ cup heavy or whipping cream

1. Beat the egg yolks with the sugar in the top of a double boiler until smooth. Whisk in the milk and cook, stirring constantly, over simmering water until it is thick enough to coat a wooden spoon, 20 to 25 minutes. Whisk in the vanilla. Cool to room temperature.

2. Whisk the kirsch into the custard. Beat the cream until stiff and fold it into the custard. Chill thoroughly before serving.

Makes 2½ to 3 cups

CORNMEAL
The Grain with a World-Feeding Potential

My cornmeal connection involves a railroad stop, a celebrated writer, and the loss of a job.

When I graduated college I hadn't the slightest clue what I wanted to be. Trained as an art teacher, I quit the classroom cold after the first week. Unable to either maintain discipline or keep my eye off an ominous wall clock ticking the hours away, I decided to try my hand as a writer-illustrator of children's books instead.

Armed with a new blue suit and a huge portfolio, I wandered from publisher to publisher, often eliciting a measure of praise for a sketch or a smile at a clever line, but no assignments whatsoever.

An editor finally told me why. "You have no experience," he said. "Talent is not enough in this field. One needs to know the nuts and bolts of how a book is put together. It's all mechanics..."

Not being mechanically inclined, my heart sank. But this kind man wrote me a letter of introduction to one of the best literary agents around. "Perhaps he can give you some straight advice."

The agent in question had a faultless reputation, which I will not sully here, but nothing about him was even faintly "straight." After weeks of broken appointments, he finally saw me in his lair—a huge neo-Renaissance studio in an area of New York grown somewhat shabby.

I could tell he was impressed neither by my graphic nor by my literary abilities. But my size obviously riveted his attention. A man of a certain age, molded in the Noël Coward style, he wore nubby tweeds and a tattersall vest, and smoked cigarettes in a long holder that flicked ashes on his clothing, desk, and my portfolio too.

"Undeniably you have talent," he rasped, turning the pages. "But it needs honing . . . refinement. For a person with the right sensibilities I would consider making an opening in my personal staff. Not writing or illustrating books, you understand, but performing chores vital to the publishing industry, immersing yourself in arts and letters."

If I had a moment's hesitation about his offer, all qualms disappeared as I observed the signed photographs on his desk: F. Scott Fitzgerald and Ludwig Bemelmans.

I took up the gauntlet and was shown by a tall, dark, and disapproving female (his personal secretary) where to hang my coat. The first immersion required my moving a cabinet of rejected manuscripts to the mail room. Besides myself there were three others in the office's employ, and I inherited all the nasty jobs they refused.

After a week's labor, I was rewarded with a special title: "Our Mr. Greene." Whenever a disputed matter arose, my employer would announce grandly that he'd have to consult with Our Mr. Greene before making any judgment. In truth he never consulted me about anything, except perhaps the postage required for letters to London or Paris.

Why did I stay at this odious job? A shallow reason. I enjoyed contact with America's literati, even though the proximity was usually secondhand.

One famous figure whom I did get to know was the critic and bon vivant Lucius Beebe. Beebe was the first man I ever heard described as a *gourmet*. Hopelessly devoted to the high life, he ate and drank prodigiously, wore a sable-lined coat, and tipped headwaiters so extravagantly that he was often forced to call our office for cab fare home. He also constantly demanded cash advances for articles not yet written. These payments were usually delivered to the Stork Club or El Morocco (where he wrote a newspaper column in the early morning). Everyone in the office took turns messengering money to Beebe.

Arriving at work one morning, I was met by the secretary, who thrust an envelope in my hand. Before she could speak, our employer appeared, highly agitated.

"Rush this to Beebe at once," he said.

"To the Stork Club?"

"No, no. Some place in the country. The name is written on the envelope, with instructions how to get there. Buy a round trip ticket at Grand Central—and don't dawdle. Beebe needs this fast!"

The departing train was a local and so devoid of passengers at that hour of the day that I had an entire car to myself, except for the times a conductor popped in to call out the next stop.

It was a long, lulling ride. To keep myself awake, I held the envelope to the light and tried to make out the amount within. Failing, I very carefully removed the tape that sealed it. It was a check for five thousand dollars, the largest sum I had ever seen in any form. I remember thinking that checks like that would be mine someday, and if I fell asleep it was because of those blissful thoughts. When I heard the conductor call out the name of Beebe's town, I almost tripped in my rush down the iron steps.

Beebe was waiting—behind a driver—in an open car that made other cars at the station pale by comparison.

He sniffed at me as if I were an untried cheese, and slowly held out his hand for the check. Which, for some inexplicable reason, was no longer in the envelope. Envelope yes. Check no!

I was unable to speak. Beebe began to quiz me, mildly at first and then somewhat vexed as I fabricated answers to his questions.

"Did you *see* the check?"

"No. Yes."

"On the train?"

"I don't remember. Maybe."

"Oh sweet Jesus!" Like an angry god, he ordered the driver to take us home.

When we arrived, Beebe went directly to the telephone. My heart sank, for I was certain he was calling my office. Unexpectedly, however, he dialed the railroad. Glancing at his watch, he ascertained exactly what time and at which station the train would next stop, and made a plan. Before replacing the receiver he dispatched his driver to a depot five miles away. Then, facing me squarely for the first time, he asked a totally improbable question.

"Do you like corn bread?"

I was so taken off guard I could not answer. Beebe shrugged. Then, turning on his heel, he made his way to the kitchen. When I attempted to follow, he held up his hand.

"No, big boy," he said with a tinge of irony. "You go to the dining room table."

I did. Chagrined, I sat there in torment, waiting for the next terrible thing to happen. When Beebe returned, he was carrying a large tray in one hand and a pitcher in the other. On the tray were two china soup bowls and a plate piled high with freshly made corn bread, so warm it made the air shimmer.

As I watched, he placed a slice in each of the bowls and handed over the pitcher. When I hesitated, wondering whether to pour or not, he shook his head.

"Don't worry—it's milk, not hemlock!" Beebe smiled at his joke. "Unpasteurized rich milk. Though I have the feeling you've never eaten corn bread with milk before. Philistines sprinkle it with sugar, but you and I are going to be pure today."

We ate the golden cake in silence—I more greedily than he. Noting my relish, Lucius Beebe relaxed his handsome features into a sly half smile. "You should always tell the truth," he said, "and life will reward you with good corn bread like this every so often. As a just reward."

I did not have to answer, for the phone began to ring. When Beebe answered it, I knew from his tone and air of relief that the missing swag was recovered. When he returned to the table, we both had another helping.

Beebe spoke in a cool, detached tone. "You like railroad trains, don't you? I know, because I do too. As a train lover, I'd say you were so *seduced* by the sound of the whistle blowing and the hum of the wheels rolling that you didn't even know you took a peek at that *enormous* check. Right?"

My mouth filled with regret and corn bread, I merely shook my head.

"I thought so," said Beebe. "Well, this adventure will be our little secret."

We never shook hands on it. But I knew, sure as I was sitting there eating lunch with the gastronome of the western world, that the story could not end there. Like the corn bread, it was too good not to be passed on.

So before I could be fired, I quit!

The Grain's Genesis

Corn is the only grain that can lay claim to solid American roots. In late December 1492, Roderigo de Jeres and Luis Torres, two of Christopher Columbus's crewmen, went on a reconnaissance mission into the interior of what is now Cuba. They returned four days later, swollen red with mosquito bites but more enflamed still with tales of huge green stalks, over ten feet tall, abloom with a curious yellow and white fruit the Indians called *maiz*. According to Jerez and Torres, "This maiz is a kernel-berry that was well tast'd raw or cook'd. But could also be bak'd, dry'd and ground into a flour."

To prove their point, they filled four saddlebags with maize, which in time made its way back to the Spanish court along with the other New World oddities (including potatoes, tomatoes, and squash) that Columbus crammed into the holds of his ships.

Almost five hundred years have passed since Queen Isabella and King Ferdinand tasted maize for the first time and adjudged that pleasantly nutty grain to be a minor treasure, equal to if not greater than any vagrant spice the Genoan explorer sought to traffic in their name.

And those four saddlebags of maize produced a harvest high, wide, and handsome enough to yield roughly five thousand ears of corn by 1495, not to mention ten thousand bushels of cornmeal.

The corn that Jerez and Torres uncovered was probably the scantiest crop in the New World. In parts of Central America (Aztec territory), corn grew to the height of small forests. And the stalks were so densely crammed wth spiky cobs that the fields were described by Cortes's mounted troops as being "impenetrable as a stone wall. A strong man takes his life in his hands if he attempts to cross an Aztec field of maize."

Some Plain Grain Talk

To bend an old saying toward the kitchen stove, let me say that cornmeal is not just another pretty taste!

On the contrary, this grain is one of the few complex carbohydrates that has the potential of feeding the entire world. In point of fact, it is expected that by the middle of the 21st century, two thirds of all proteins consumed on earth will be some form of cornmeal derivative.

The corn kernel that is milled to form cornmeal is composed of a rough hull covering twin layers of hard and soft starch deposits. At the heart of this package is a protein-high, naturally oil-rich germ that gives cornmeal its nutritive value.

Cornmeal is processed in two ways: *stone-ground* and *enriched-degerminated*. The latter is a modern process that entails kiln-drying the kernels first, then grinding them between massive steel rollers. Most commercially processed cornmeal is produced this way because it is cost-efficient. Unfortunately, the steel rollers that pulverize the kernels also break down and filter out the healthy fiber in the hull, and they remove the germ entirely, which causes the final product to have a dry and somewhat granular texture. Stone-ground cornmeal, on the other hand, is not heated at all. The kernels are ground by water-powered millstones, which crush the germ, hull, and the hard and soft starch layers as well. This cornmeal has a somewhat unctuous feel and a rich and intense flavor. In fact, both stone-ground and enriched-degerminated cornmeal are enriched to be brought up to USDA standards.

It is important to understand cornmeal's serious food deficiencies as well as its nutritive virtues. While a cup of cooked cornmeal is high in carbohydrates as well as containing 0.44 milligrams of thiamine, 0.26 milligrams of riboflavin, and 3.52 milligrams of niacin —not to mention whopping amounts of potassium and magnesium—it is *not* considered a "whole food" because of the fact that it lacks two essential amino acids, lysine and tryptophan.

However, when it is combined with other grains, legumes, and judicious amounts of animal protein—even butter, milk, and cheese products—cornmeal acquires enough of the aforementioned amino acids to keep a cornmeal lover bright and bushy-tailed.

How to Buy It

*A*ll the recipes in this chapter, with one or two exceptions, were tested with two kinds of cornmeal: Quaker Enriched-Degerminated and Indian Head Stone Ground. Both are highly acceptable, but the more gratifying results were obtained using Indian Head Stone Ground, which is slightly higher priced than Quaker but is equally accessible in supermarkets.

A glance at the resource list at the back of this book will reveal names of excellent small stone-ground flour producers around the country, whose products are available at natural foods stores or by mail order.

It is important to note that yellow cornmeal contains a higher degree of beta carotene (one of the substances that maintains the balance of the body's immune system) than white cornmeal. However, white cornmeal is so much a part of many great regional dishes (like southern spoonbread) that I for one would pass on the beta carotene rather than fly in the face of tradition!

How to Store It

*B*ecause of its high oil content, stone-ground cornmeal has a relatively brief shelf life in any pantry over 45°F. It may be kept in airtight, self-seal plastic bags in the refrigerator for up to three months, and twice that time in the freezer. Enriched-degerminated cornmeal has somewhat longer staying power. Unfortunately the cool temperature of refrigerator and freezer, while inhibiting insect infestation and retarding rancidity, also increases vitamin loss and encourages oxidation.

How to Cook It

*T*here is no single rule for cornmeal preparation, so my suggestions vary with the recipes.

Though many health-food faddists decry the addition of any flour (wholewheat or otherwise) to straight cornmeal in a tin of corn sticks or a pan of corn bread, I disagree. I find that tempering the mixture actually makes a softer, lighter, and, yes, more digestible offering in the final analysis.

*I*n Texas, where cornmeal arrived in 1836 as a victory spoil of independence from Mexico, they still have some mighty colorful corn associations. *Corn twisters*, for instance, are dry spells. In *corn weather* you can sleep "nekkid," for it's hot. *Corn wind* means no wind at all and *corn lightning* is merely thunder. A *corn in the ear* implies you are deaf as a post, while *corn on the tongue* means you are looking for a wife— preferably one who's a *cornmeal patter* (a good cook) or a *corn shaker* (so well endowed physically that the corn stalks shake whenever she's near)!

OVER-EASY GREEN CHILE ENCHILADAS

In Mexico, where corn is a staple, maize was known as *panizo*, or "panic grass." That moniker was bestowed upon the plant by early 16th-century Spanish settlers who had grave misgivings about depending on an annual-growing grain for their subsistence. They needn't have worried—there has never been a corn famine in Central or Latin America, or the U.S. either.

To this day, Mexicans consider corn their staff of life. They pound *panizo* (maize, cornmeal, masa harina) into a rough flour that they combine with water and cook over high heat until it becomes the tortilla we all know and love.

Recently I came upon a wonderfully salubrious (if very inauthentic) version of the tortilla made of everyday cornmeal. These quasi-tortillas are better than any of the commercial varieties you will find on a supermarket shelf and easier to make than scrambled eggs. Moreover, it takes less than half an hour to whip up a big batch. Yes, they freeze!

2 tablespoons olive oil
1 small yellow onion, chopped
2 cloves garlic, minced
1 tablespoon chopped canned jalapeño
    peppers
2 cans (4 ounces each) mild green chile
    peppers, chopped
2 tomatoes, peeled, seeded, and chopped
    (about 1 cup)
½ teaspoon cumin seeds, ground
1 teaspoon finely chopped fresh cilantro
    (Chinese parsley)
1 cup shredded cooked pork or chicken
Vegetable oil
10 Phony Tortillas (recipe follows)
1 cup grated Monterey Jack cheese
Sour cream
Shredded lettuce

1. Preheat the oven to 350°F.
2. Heat the oil in a large skillet over medium-low heat. Add the onion; cook 2 minutes. Add the garlic and jalapeño peppers; cook 3 minutes longer. Stir in the mild peppers, tomatoes, cumin, and cilantro. Raise the heat to medium and cook, stirring occasionally, 5 minutes. Stir in the meat; cook 2 minutes. Re-

move the skillet from the heat.
3. Heat 1 inch of vegetable oil in another large skillet over medium heat. Carefully dip each Phony Tortilla into the hot oil for a few seconds only. Transfer the fried tortillas to paper towels.
4. Fill each tortilla with the meat mixture and roll up. Place them in a lightly greased baking dish. Sprinkle with the cheese, and bake 10 minutes. Serve with sour cream and shredded lettuce.

Makes 10 enchiladas

Phony Tortillas

1 cup yellow cornmeal
½ teaspoon salt
½ cup bread flour
1 egg, lightly beaten
2 cups water

1. Combine the cornmeal, salt, and flour in a large bowl. Stir in the egg and water until smooth.
2. Heat a lightly greased 6-inch non-stick skillet over medium heat. Spoon 3 to 4 tablespoons batter into the hot pan.

Turn and twist immediately to cover the bottom of the pan. Cook 30 seconds, then flip and cook the other side. Do not brown the tortilla. Place the cooled tortilla on a sheet of paper towels. Continue the process, layering the cooked tortillas in paper towels, until all the batter is used up.

Makes about 20 tortillas

Note: These tortillas may be stored for several days in a plastic bag in the refrigerator.

SOUTHWEST BEAN CAKE

All trendy restaurants these days seem to serve some version of bean cake. This dish makes great party fare, as well as a tasty brunch or supper dish. I often serve it just with a green salad.

½ pound string beans
5 tablespoons plus 1 teaspoon unsalted butter, at room temperature
1 teaspoon vegetable oil
1 medium onion, finely chopped
1 clove garlic, minced
½ pound chorizos (Spanish sausages), thinly sliced
2 large ripe tomatoes, seeded and chopped
1 tablespoon chopped fresh basil, or 1 teaspoon dried
1 hot green pepper, seeded, deveined, and minced
1 red bell pepper, cored, seeded and finely chopped
2 eggs
1 cup buttermilk
½ cup heavy or whipping cream
1 cup yellow cornmeal
½ cup all-purpose flour
½ teaspoon baking soda
½ teaspoon baking powder
Pinch of sugar
½ teaspoon salt
¼ teaspoon freshly ground black pepper
⅛ teaspoon sweet Hungarian paprika
2 teaspoons chili powder or ground dried mild chiles
¼ cup sliced black olives
1 cup grated Monterey Jack cheese
Dash of hot pepper sauce

1. Preheat the oven to 350°F.

2. Cut the string beans French style—in half lengthwise. Cook in boiling salted water until tender, about 8 minutes. Rinse under cold running water, drain, and set aside.

3. Melt 2 tablespoons of the butter with the oil in a large heavy skillet over medium heat. Add the onion; cook 2 minutes. Add the garlic and sliced chorizos. Continue to cook until the chorizos are lightly browned, 5 to 6 minutes.

4. Add the tomatoes, basil, hot green pepper, and red bell pepper to the sausage mixture. Continue to cook, stirring occasionally, until the tomatoes are soft, about 12 minutes. Toss in the reserved beans and cook 10 minutes longer. Remove the skillet from the heat.

5. Beat the eggs wth 3 tablespoons of the butter in a large bowl until smooth. Beat in the buttermilk and cream. Stir in the cornmeal, flour, baking soda, baking powder, sugar, salt, pepper, paprika, and chili powder. Mix well. Stir in the reserved chorizo / bean mixture, the olives, cheese, and hot pepper sauce.

6. Rub a 10-inch cast-iron skillet with the remaining 1 teaspoon butter. Spoon the batter into the skillet, and bake until firm and golden brown, about 35 minutes. Cut into wedges and serve.

Serves 6 to 8

RED-HANDED CHILI

In this unusual stew made with Spanish sausages, chicken, and shrimp, the cornmeal is essential as a thickener. Serve the chili over rice.

2½ tablespoons olive oil
½ pound chorizos (Spanish sausages), sliced ¼ inch thick
1 whole chicken breast, skinned, boned, and cut into 1-inch pieces
1 large onion, finely chopped
2 cloves garlic, minced
1 Italian frying pepper (Cubanelle), seeded and finely chopped
3 large canned mild green chile peppers, chopped
¼ cup yellow cornmeal
1½ tablespoons chili powder
½ teaspoon ground cumin
½ teaspoon crushed dried hot red peppers
2 medium tomatoes, seeded and chopped (¾ cup)
1 can (14 ounces) imported Italian tomatoes, with juice
1½ cups homemade chicken stock (see page 376) or canned broth
1 pound shrimp, shelled and deveined
Chopped fresh parsley, for garnish
3 cups cooked rice, heated

1. Preheat the oven to 350°F.

2. Heat 1 tablespoon of the oil in a large Dutch oven over medium-low heat. Add the chorizos; cook, stirring occasionally, until lightly browned, about 10 minutes. Using a slotted spoon, transfer the chorizos to a bowl.

3. Add half the chicken pieces to the skillet and sauté over medium heat until lightly colored, about 4 minutes. Transfer to a separate bowl. Sauté the remaining pieces and add them to the bowl. Wipe out the pot.

4. Heat the remaining 1½ table-

Corn at first was a catchall term for all loose grains—rice, wheat, barley.

Until Linnaeus set everybody straight, Turks called wheat "Syrian corn" and Syrians called millet "Turkish wheat." The Chinese called opium seeds "rainbow corn." Count your blessings that they never tried making that into cornmeal!

In America, where cornmeal is native fodder, there are still cultural differences. The South traditionally chooses white cornmeal for cooking, while the North invariably opts for yellow. In the Southwest, Indians have immemorially grown a blue corn, and in the Northeast, farmers harvest a red corn for silage. Trendy restaurateurs and chic chefs find the blue and red irresistible. Not I!

spoons oil in the Dutch oven. Add the onion; cook over medium-low heat 1 minute. Add the garlic, frying pepper, and green chiles. Cook 2 minutes. Stir in the cornmeal, chili powder, cumin, and dried red peppers. Cook, stirring constantly, 2 minutes. Stir in both tomatoes, the chicken stock, and the reserved chorizos. Heat to boiling. Cover the pot and transfer it to the oven. Bake, stirring occasionally, 50 minutes. (The dish may be prepared ahead to this point.)

5. Stir the reserved chicken pieces into the chili. Cover, and bake for 5 minutes. Add the shrimp and bake, covered, 5 minutes longer. Sprinkle with parsley, and serve with rice.

Serves 4 to 6

HUSH PUPPY FRIED CHICKEN

*T*he story goes: A Southerner, after an outdoor fish fry, threw some batter into the fire to feed to his yapping dogs—which he gave them, saying, "Hush, puppies." I use a hush puppy batter for frying chicken, and I assure you, you will *not* want to throw it to the dogs.

½ cup sour cream
¼ teaspoon cayenne pepper
1 chicken (about 3½ pounds), cut into
　　pieces
3 strips bacon
¼ cup cornmeal, white or yellow
¼ cup all-purpose flour
¼ teaspoon freshly grated nutmeg
¼ teaspoon salt
⅛ teaspoon freshly ground black pepper
Pinch of hot Hungarian paprika
4 tablespoons (½ stick) unsalted butter
Chopped fresh parsley, for garnish

1. Combine the sour cream and the cayenne pepper in a small bowl. Place the chicken in a large bowl, and toss with the sour cream mixture until well coated. Let stand 20 minutes.

2. Preheat the oven to 300°F.

3. Sauté the bacon strips in a large heavy skillet until crisp. Drain on paper towels, then crumble and reserve. Reserve the drippings in the skillet.

4. Combine the cornmeal with the flour, nutmeg, salt, pepper, and paprika in a large bowl. Roll the chicken pieces in this mixture, and place them on a plate.

5. Heat the bacon drippings in the skillet over medium-low heat. Add 2 tablespoons of the butter. Sauté the chicken, half the pieces at a time starting with the dark meat, until golden brown on both sides, about 10 minutes per side. Transfer to a baking dish and place in the oven as the pieces are done. Add more butter to the pan as needed. When all the pieces are sautéed, keep in the oven no longer than 30 minutes. Sprinkle with parsley before serving.

Serves 3 or 4

OLD-TIMEY CHICKEN STEW WITH CORNMEAL DUMPLINGS

In times past, cornmeal was reputed to have singular curative powers. One mid-16th-century medico believed a poultice of cornmeal and white wine could cure cataracts and kept his patients in the dark for weeks, adding a few grains or a few drops to the mask daily. Results? Lost in the passage of time, I'm afraid.

A couple of centuries later, Marie Antoinette, worried over her "spotty" complexion, allowed her face to be baked daily in a mixture of cornmeal and cream. Her skin, according to court gossip, improved immeasurably—until she lost her head, and one cannot blame that on cornmeal.

As late as the early 20th century, doctors in New England prescribed cornmeal baths for rheumatism.

The best cornmeal restorative I know is an edible one. At the first sign of a sneeze, try this chicken stew with gilded dumplings. The patient will be up on his feet the day after—more than likely foraging for a second helping!

FOR THE STEW

2 tablespoons unsalted butter
3 tablespoons vegetable oil
1 chicken (3½ to 4 pounds), cut into pieces
1 yellow onion, finely chopped
1 clove garlic, minced
1 medium carrot, diced
1 medium parsnip, diced
1 medium turnip, diced
1 rib celery, diced
⅛ teaspoon chopped fresh thyme, or a
    pinch of dried
½ teaspoon freshly ground black pepper
½ cup white wine
½ cup homemade chicken stock (see page
    376) or canned broth

FOR THE DUMPLINGS

½ cup yellow cornmeal
½ cup cake flour
1½ teaspoons baking powder
½ teaspoon salt
1 egg, lightly beaten
⅓ cup milk
½ teaspoon Dijon mustard
1 tablespoon deviled ham

1. Make the stew: Heat the butter with the oil in a large saucepan or Dutch oven. Sauté the chicken, a few pieces at a time, until very well browned, about 10 minutes. Transfer the cooked chicken to a plate.

2. Discard all but 2 tablespoons drippings from the pan. Add the onion; cook, scraping the bottom and sides of the pan with a wooden spoon, 2 minutes. Add the garlic; cook 2 minutes longer. Stir in the carrot, parsnip, turnip, celery, thyme, pepper, wine, and stock. Heat to boiling. Reduce the heat, return the chicken pieces to the pan, cover, and cook over medium-low heat 30 minutes.

3. Meanwhile, make the dumplings: Combine the cornmeal, flour, baking powder, and salt in a large bowl. Mix well, and stir in the egg, milk, mustard, and deviled ham. Mix well.

4. After the chicken has cooked for 15 minutes, spoon the dumpling batter over the chicken in large spoonfuls. Cook, covered, until just firm, about 15 minutes.

Serves 4

ROAST TURKEY WITH CORN BREAD DRESSING

You don't have to be a Southerner or love okra to savor this meal. The dressing adds dash and flavor to traditional fare.

1 fresh turkey (16 to 18 pounds)
2 large cloves garlic
Salt and freshly ground black pepper to
     taste
Corn Bread, Sausage, and Okra Dressing
     (recipe follows)
3 strips bacon
⅓ cup dry white wine
1 quart water
1 medium onion
1 rib celery with its leaves, broken
3 sprigs parsley, plus additional for
     garnishing the turkey
¼ teaspoon salt
4 peppercorns
1½ tablespoons unsalted butter
1½ tablespoons all-purpose flour
¼ cup heavy or whipping cream

1. Preheat the oven to 325°F.

2. Remove the giblets from the turkey; reserve the giblets, except the liver. (You may wish to reserve the liver for another purpose.) Wipe the turkey inside and out with a damp cloth.

3. Bruise 1 garlic clove and rub the turkey well, inside and out, with the bruised garlic, and season with salt and pepper. Stuff the cavity with the dressing, and truss. Place the turkey on a rack in a roasting pan, and lay the bacon strips across the breast. Cut a piece of cheesecloth large enough to fit over the turkey. Soak the cheesecloth in the wine and place it over the turkey. Pour any remaining wine over the turkey, and roast 30 minutes.

4. Meanwhile, combine the giblets (not the liver), water, onion, celery, the remaining garlic clove, 3 sprigs parsley, salt, and peppercorns in a large saucepan. Heat to boiling, then reduce the heat. Simmer, uncovered, until the liquid is reduced to 2 cups, 30 minutes. Strain the giblet stock.

5. Baste the turkey with the giblet stock. Roast, basting with stock every 30 minutes, until the legs move freely and juices run clear when the inner thigh is pierced with a fork, about 5 to 5½ hours total. For the last half hour of roasting, remove the cheesecloth. (First wet the turkey with basting juices. It should lift off easily.) Raise the oven heat to 375°F to crisp the skin. Then transfer the turkey to a carving board, and let it stand 15 minutes.

6. Meanwhile, strain the turkey drippings, degreasing them if necessary. Melt the butter in a medium-size saucepan over medium-low heat. Whisk in the flour. Cook, stirring constantly, 2 minutes. Whisk in the drippings and cream; simmer 5 minutes. Taste, and adjust the seasonings as necessary. Garnish the turkey with the remaining parsley sprigs. Serve with the gravy and corn bread dressing.

Serves 8 to 10

Corn Bread, Sausage, and Okra Dressing

½ cup wild rice
1 cup water
6 tablespoons (¾ stick) unsalted butter
½ recipe Vermont Corn Bread (see page
    125), cooled and cubed
½ pound sweet Italian sausage
1 large onion, chopped
1 Italian frying pepper (Cubanelle), seeded
    and finely chopped
½ teaspoon crushed dried hot red peppers
1 teaspoon minced fresh sage, or
    ¼ teaspoon dried
¼ pound small okra, cut into ½-inch-thick
    slices

1. Combine the wild rice with the water in a small saucepan and heat to boiling. Reduce the heat and cook, covered, over low heat until tender, 30 minutes. Drain, and transfer to a large bowl.

2. Melt 2 tablespoons of the butter in a large heavy skillet, and sauté a third of the corn bread cubes until golden. Transfer to the bowl with the rice. Continue to sauté the corn bread cubes until all butter and cubes are used up.

3. Sauté the sausage in the same skillet over medium heat until well browned, about 8 minutes. Drain on paper towels, cool slightly, and cut into ½-inch-thick slices. Add them to the bowl with the corn bread.

4. Drain all but 2 tablespoons grease from the skillet. Add the onion; cook over medium-low heat 2 minutes. Add the frying pepper and dried red peppers. Cook 3 minutes longer. Transfer the onion mixture to the bowl, add the sage and okra, and mix well.

Makes about 7 cups

SIASCONSET SEAFOOD SPOON BREAD

A southern recipe that found its way to Nantucket. White cornmeal is the requirement here, please!

¼ pound shrimp, shelled and deveined
½ pound bay scallops
5½ tablespoons unsalted butter
6 scallions, white bulbs and green tops
    separated, thinly sliced
1 clove garlic, minced
½ red bell pepper, cored, seeded, and
    minced (about ⅓ cup)
1 small hot green pepper, seeded, deveined,
    and minced
1 tablespoon dry white wine or vermouth
Salt and freshly ground black pepper to
    taste
2⅓ cups light cream or half-and-half
1 teaspoon sugar
½ teaspoon salt

1 cup white cornmeal
4 egg yolks
1 teaspoon baking powder
6 egg whites

1. Cut the shrimp into chunks the size of the scallops. Set aside.

2. Melt 1 tablespoon of the butter in a medium-size skillet over medium-low heat. Add the green scallion tops; cook 1 minute. Add the garlic; cook 2 minutes longer. Stir in the peppers and cook 4 minutes longer.

3. Raise the heat to medium-high and add ½ tablespoon of the butter. When the butter has melted, stir in the scallops and shrimp, and toss constantly until the shrimp have turned lightly pink, about 2 minutes. Then stir in the wine. Continue to cook until almost all liquid has evaporated, about 1 minute. Season with salt and pepper, and set aside to cool.

4. Preheat the oven to 400°F. Lightly butter a 2-quart soufflé or casserole.

5. Combine the remaining 4 tablespoons butter with the cream in a medium-size saucepan. Cook over low heat until the butter has melted. Do not allow it to boil. Stir in the sugar and salt. Whisk in the cornmeal, and cook over medium-low heat, stirring constantly, until the mixture is very thick, 4 to 5 minutes. Transfer the cornmeal mixture to a large heatproof bowl and immediately beat in the egg yolks, one at a time, beating thoroughly after each addition. Add the baking powder and the seafood.

6. Beat the egg whites until stiff. Stir one third of the whites into the cornmeal mixture. Fold in the remaining whites. Pour into the prepared soufflé dish or casserole, and with a teaspoon, make a circular indentation in the top about ½ inch from the rim. Sprinkle the top with additional black pepper and place the dish in the oven. Immediately reduce the heat to 375°F. Bake until puffed and golden, 35 minutes. Serve immediately.

Serves 4 to 6

AUSTRO-HUNGARIAN CORNMEAL MUSH WITH PORK

*T*his is my loosely adapted version of a dish Paul Kovi wrote about in *Transylvanian Cuisine*. Mr. Kovi is one of the owners of the prestigious Four Seasons restaurant in New York. His book, however, is full of wonderful homey recipes from his childhood. I serve poached eggs over the top.

2 tablespoons vegetable oil
2 to 2½ cups chopped cooked pork
1 small onion, finely chopped
1 large carrot, chopped
2-inch celery rib (white part), trimmed and chopped
1 small potato, diced
¼ cup chopped fresh parsley
3½ cups homemade chicken stock (see page 376) or canned broth
1 cup yellow cornmeal
Salt and freshly ground black pepper to taste

1. Heat the oil in a large heavy skillet over medium heat. Stir in the pork and cook until well browned on all sides, about 5 minutes. Stir in the onion; cook 2 minutes longer.

2. Reduce the heat to medium-low and add the carrot, celery, potato, and 2 tablespoons of the parsley. Cook 2 minutes. Add 2 cups of the stock and heat to boiling. Reduce the heat, cover, and cook over medium-low heat 10 minutes.

3. Remove the cover and add the remaining 1½ cups broth. Return to boiling and stir in the cornmeal. Reduce the heat and cook, uncovered, over medium-low heat until slightly thickened but not stiff, about 10 minutes. Add salt and pepper to taste.

4. Sprinkle with the remaining 2 tablespoons parsley before serving.

Serves 6 to 8

CORN BREAD AND HAM HASH

This dish is wonderful for a glamorous brunch or for a Sunday night supper.

4 tablespoons (½ stick) unsalted butter
2 cups cubed stale corn bread (½-inch
    cubes)
1 medium onion, chopped
1 clove garlic, minced
½ cup diced red bell pepper
2 cups cubed ham
½ cup chopped seeded tomatoes
1 cup fresh corn kernels (from 2 large ears)
4 allspice berries, crushed
Dash of hot pepper sauce
Salt and freshly ground black pepper to
    taste
1 teaspoon finely chopped fresh sage

1. Preheat the oven to 375°F.

2. Melt 1½ tablespoons of the butter in a large ovenproof skillet over medium heat. Add 1 cup of the corn bread cubes, and sauté until golden brown on all sides, 4 minutes. Transfer them to a bowl. Repeat the process with another 1½ tablespoons butter and the remaining 1 cup corn bread cubes.

3. Wipe out the skillet and melt the remaining 1 tablespoon butter in it over medium-low heat. Add the onion; cook 1 minute. Add the garlic; cook 3 minutes longer. Stir in the bell pepper, ham, and tomatoes. Cook, covered, 5 minutes. Stir in the corn and allspice. Cook, covered, 5 minutes longer.

4. Remove the cover and gently toss the corn bread cubes into the mixture. Add the hot pepper sauce, and season with salt and pepper. Transfer the skillet to the oven and bake, uncovered, 15 minutes. Sprinkle with sage and serve.

Serves 4

GLAZED HAM LOAF

Ham loaf is one of those budget stretchers that housewives relied on in the 1940s and '50s. I view this one as a treat because it calls for corn bread!

FOR THE HAM LOAF
2 pounds cooked ham, ground
½ pound pork sausage meat
1 cup crumbled leftover corn bread
1 small onion, finely chopped
1 clove garlic, minced
¼ cup finely chopped red bell pepper
¼ cup chopped fresh parsley
½ cup pineapple juice
2 eggs, lightly beaten
1 teaspoon dark brown sugar
½ teaspoon dry mustard

½ teaspoon salt
¼ teaspoon freshly ground black pepper
¼ teaspoon freshly grated nutmeg

FOR THE GLAZE
1 cup firmly packed dark brown sugar
2 teaspoons tarragon vinegar
2 teaspoons Dijon mustard
¼ cup pineapple juice

Chopped fresh parsley, for garnish

1. Preheat the oven to 350°F.

2. Combine all the ingredients for the ham loaf in a large bowl. Mix well. Shape into a loaf in a shallow baking dish. Bake 15 minutes.

3. Meanwhile, combine all the ingredients for the glaze in a small saucepan.

Heat to boiling; boil 1 minute.

4. After 15 minutes, baste the ham loaf with the glaze. Continue to bake, basting with the glaze and pan juices, 1 hour. Let stand 10 minutes. Sprinkle with parsley before serving.

Serves 8

GOLD-BRICKED MACARONI AND CHEESE

This updated version of macaroni and cheese is very soul-satisfying to the kid in all of us. Cornmeal adds new texture to an old standby.

½ pound elbow macaroni
5 tablespoons unsalted butter
¼ cup cornmeal, white or yellow
⅛ teaspoon crushed dried hot red peppers
3 tablespoons all-purpose flour
1 cup homemade chicken stock (see page 376) or canned broth, heated
½ cup heavy or whipping cream
2 teaspoons fresh lemon juice
¼ teaspoon freshly grated nutmeg
½ teaspoon salt
¼ teaspoon hot pepper sauce
¼ cup freshly grated Parmesan cheese
¼ pound grated semi-mild Cheddar cheese (such as Mimolette)
¼ pound grated Swiss or Jarlsberg cheese
2 medium tomatoes (about ¾ pound), seeded and chopped

1. Cook the macaroni in boiling salted water until tender, about 8 minutes. Rinse under cold running water until cool. Drain, and set aside.

2. Meanwhile, melt 2 tablespoons of the butter in a small skillet over medium heat. Stir in the cornmeal and dried red peppers. Cook, stirring constantly, until lightly browned, about 4 minutes. Set aside.

3. Melt the remaining 3 tablespoons butter in a medium-size saucepan over medium-low heat. Stir in the flour. Cook, stirring constantly, 2 minutes. Whisk in the chicken stock and cream. Cook, whisking constantly, until very thick, 1 minute. Whisk in the lemon juice, nutmeg, salt, and hot pepper sauce. Remove from the heat and stir in 2 tablespoons of the Parmesan cheese. Fold in the cooled macaroni.

4. Preheat the oven to 350°F. Lightly butter a 2-quart casserole dish.

5. Place one third of the macaroni mixture in the prepared casserole. Sprinkle with one third of the Cheddar and one third of the Swiss cheese. Spoon one third of the tomatoes over the top. Repeat layering two more times, ending with tomatoes.

6. Combine the remaining 2 tablespoons Parmesan cheese with the cornmeal mixture. Sprinkle over the top of the macaroni mixture. Bake 30 minutes.

Serves 4

WHITE AND BLACK BEAN PIE

This bean pie is a show-stopper: refried beans in a cornmeal crust, topped with melting white cheese. It goes well with all manner of braised meats and poultry.

FOR THE BEAN FILLING

1 pound dried black beans
8 ounces bacon
2 medium onions, finely chopped
2 cloves garlic, minced
3 fresh jalapeño peppers, seeded, deveined, and minced
2 cups homemade chicken stock (see page 376) or canned broth
Salt and freshly ground black pepper to taste

FOR THE CRUST

½ cup yellow cornmeal
⅔ cup cold water
1⅓ cups boiling water
1½ tablespoons unsalted butter

¼ pound Monterey Jack cheese, grated (about 1 cup)

1. Pick over the beans and remove any debris. Place the beans in a pot, cover with cold water, and let stand, covered, overnight.

2. Drain the beans and cover once more with cold water. Heat slowly to boiling; then reduce the heat. Simmer, uncovered, until tender, about 1 hour. Drain, and set aside to cool.

3. Sauté the bacon in batches in a large heavy skillet until crisp. Drain on paper towels. Crumble and reserve.

4. Discard all but ¼ cup bacon drippings from the skillet. Add the onions and cook over medium-low heat 1 minute. Add the garlic and jalapeño peppers. Cook 5 minutes longer. Using a slotted spoon, transfer the onion mixture to a bowl. Reserve the skillet.

5. Place half the beans and half the onion mixture in the container of a food processor. Add 1 cup of the chicken stock. Process, using the pulse button, until thick but still chunky. Transfer to the skillet. Repeat with the remaining beans, onion mixture, and stock. Cook, stirring constantly, over medium heat until very thick, about 15 minutes. (Be careful: black beans burn easily.) Remove the skillet from the heat and add the salt and pepper.

6. Make the crust: Stir the cornmeal into the cold water. Stir this mixture into the boiling water in a small saucepan. Return to boiling. Stir in the butter, and reduce the heat. Cook, covered, stirring occasionally, 30 minutes. Set aside to cool slightly.

7. Preheat the oven to 400°F. Lightly rub a 10-inch glass or ceramic quiche pan with butter.

8. Spread the cornmeal over the bottom and sides of the pan, forcing the mixture up the sides as it cools. Bake 5 minutes. Remove the dish from the oven, and reduce the heat to 350°F.

9. Sprinkle a third of the reserved bacon over the bottom of the crust. Spoon in the bean mixture. Sprinkle with another third of the bacon. Sprinkle with the cheese, and add the remaining third of the bacon. Bake 30 minutes. Let stand 10 minutes before serving.

Serves 6 to 8

BERT'S BASIC POLENTA

Cornmeal recipes abound in a clutch of surprising cuisines. Italians, for example—who would never consider chomping corn on the cob—dote on a dish called *polenta*, which is basically nothing more than cornmeal mush carried to gastronomic heights.

In northern Italy there is a great mystique about the shape of the pot in which polenta is stirred; a U-shaped copper pan is adjudged the ideal utensil. However, not being Italian, I merely use any heavy-bottomed saucepan. And for a creamier texture, I prefer milk to water.

2½ cups milk
¾ cup cornmeal, yellow or white

1. Slowly bring the milk to a boil in a medium-size heavy saucepan, and then gradually add the cornmeal. Whisk them together over medium-low heat until the polenta is smooth and thick, 5 minutes.

2. Using a bowl scraper, pour the mixture into a lightly buttered pie plate. Cool on a wire rack, and then refrigerate for 1 hour.

3. At this point, polenta may be sliced into wedges and either dusted with Parmesan cheese and baked, or lightly sautéed in butter.

Serves 6 to 8

MUSHROOM POLENTA

*T*he mushrooms here must be wild. The commercially grown white ones just won't do in this dish.

5 tablespoons unsalted butter
½ tablespoon olive oil
2 shallots, minced
¼ pound wild mushrooms, such as shiitakes, finely chopped
2½ cups milk
¾ cup yellow cornmeal
¼ teaspoon crushed dried hot red peppers
3 tablespoons freshly grated Parmesan cheese
Salt and freshly ground black pepper to taste

1. Heat 1 tablespoon of the butter with the oil in a large heavy skillet over medium-high heat. Add the shallots and cook until golden, about 2 minutes. Stir in the mushrooms, raise the heat slightly, and cook, stirring constantly, until they are golden and any juices have evaporated, about 3 minutes. Set aside.

2. Slowly heat the milk to boiling in a medium-size heavy saucepan over medium-low heat. (Do not allow it to scorch.) Gradually beat in the cornmeal with a wire whisk. Beat in the dried red peppers and 1½ tablespoons of the cheese. Continue to beat until the mixture is smooth and thick, 5 minutes. Add the mushroom mixture and salt and pepper to taste, and pour into a lightly buttered 9-inch pie plate. Cool on a wire rack. Refrigerate 1 hour.

3. Preheat the oven to 375°F. Melt the remaining 4 tablespoons butter.

4. Cut the polenta into wedges and place them on a buttered baking dish. Drizzle with the melted butter. Sprinkle with the remaining 1½ tablespoons cheese, and bake 15 minutes.

Serves 6 to 8

LEEK POLENTA

*T*his is one of my favorite dishes. Of course, I happen to love leeks. They add a sweetness to this polenta that goes nicely with the cheese.

6 tablespoons (¾ stick) unsalted butter
2 tablespoons olive oil
4 to 6 large leeks, white parts rinsed, dried, and finely chopped (about 4 cups)
¼ cup dry white wine
Pinch of ground cloves
Pinch of ground mace
2½ cups milk
¾ cup yellow cornmeal
¼ cup grated Fontina cheese
Salt and freshly ground black pepper to taste

1. Heat 2 tablespoons of the butter with the oil in a large heavy skillet over medium-low heat. Add the leeks; cook 4 minutes. Sprinkle with the wine, cloves, and mace. Continue to cook, stirring occasionally, until the leeks are tender, 12 to 15 minutes. Raise the heat slightly and cook until all liquid has evaporated. Set aside.

2. Slowly heat the milk to boiling in a medium-size heavy saucepan over medium-low heat. (Do not allow it to scorch.) Gradually beat in the cornmeal with a wire whisk. Continue to beat until the mixture is smooth and thick, 5 minutes, then beat in 2 tablespoons of the cheese and the leek mixture. Season with salt and pepper, and pour into a lightly buttered 9-inch pie plate. Cool on a wire rack, then refrigerate 1 hour.

3. Preheat the oven to 375°F. Melt the remaining 4 tablespoons butter.

4. Cut the polenta into wedges and place them on a buttered baking dish. Drizzle with the melted butter, and sprinkle with the remaining 2 tablespoons cheese. Bake 15 minutes.

Serves 6 to 8

SAUSAGE AND PEPPER POLENTA

*T*his almost makes a meal in itself. Just add in a green salad and a glass of white wine, and I am happy.

1 tablespoon olive oil
1 small onion, chopped
½ medium green bell pepper, cored,
    seeded, and cut into small strips
½ medium red bell pepper, cored, seeded,
    and cut into small strips
½ pound sweet Italian sausage, chopped
2½ cups milk
¾ cup yellow cornmeal
1 tablespoon chopped fresh basil, or 1
    teaspoon dried
Dash of hot pepper sauce
3 tablespoons freshly grated Parmesan
    cheese
Salt and freshly ground black pepper to
    taste
4 tablespoons (½ stick) unsalted butter,
    melted

1. Heat the oil in a large skillet over medium-low heat. Add the onion; cook 2 minutes. Add the peppers; cook 3 minutes longer. Raise the heat slightly and stir in the sausage meat. Continue to cook, stirring often, until the meat loses its pink color and is thoroughly cooked, about 5 minutes. Set aside.

2. Slowly heat the milk to boiling in a medium-size heavy saucepan over medium-low heat. (Do not allow it to scorch.) Gradually beat in the cornmeal with a wire whisk. Continue to beat until the mixture is smooth and thick, 5 minutes. Stir in the sausage mixture, the basil, hot pepper sauce, and 1½ tablespoons of the cheese. Season with salt and pepper, and pour into a lightly buttered 9-inch pie plate. Cool on a wire rack, then refrigerate 1 hour.

3. Preheat the oven to 375°F. Lightly butter a large baking dish.

4. Cut the polenta into wedges and place them on the prepared baking dish. Drizzle with the melted butter, and sprinkle with the remaining 1½ tablespoons cheese. Bake 15 minutes.

Serves 4 to 6 as a main course

KANSAS CITY CORN BREAD

I discovered this bread on one of my many trips to Kansas City. It is part of a collection put out by the Kansas City Junior League in their beautiful book, *Beyond Parsley*—a remarkable step forward in Junior League cookbooks.

12 ounces bacon
1 cup stone-ground yellow cornmeal
1 cup whole-wheat flour
⅓ cup sugar
2½ teaspoons baking powder
¼ teaspoon salt
1 cup buttermilk
6 tablespoons (¾ stick) unsalted butter,
    melted
1 egg, lightly beaten

1. Preheat the oven to 400°F.
2. Sauté the bacon, a third at a time, in a heavy skillet until crisp. Drain on paper towels, then crumble and reserve. Lightly brush an 8-inch square cake pan with bacon drippings.

3. Combine the cornmeal with the flour, sugar, baking powder, and salt in a large bowl. Stir in the buttermilk, butter, and egg. Beat in the crumbled bacon.

4. Pour the batter into the cake pan. Bake until golden, about 25 minutes. Serve warm, cut into pieces.

Serves 4 to 6

VERMONT CORN BREAD

In Vermont they serve corn bread with maple syrup. This is my all-purpose version, which I picked up in Brattleboro.

1½ cups yellow cornmeal
½ cup all-purpose flour
1 tablespoon baking powder
½ teaspoon baking soda
¾ teaspoon salt
1½ cups buttermilk
1 egg, lightly beaten
3 tablespoons bacon drippings, warmed
3 tablespoons maple syrup
1 tablespoon unsalted butter, melted

1. Preheat the oven to 425°F. Lightly grease an 8-inch square cake pan.

2. Combine the cornmeal, flour, baking powder, baking soda, and salt in a large mixing bowl. Stir in the buttermilk, egg, bacon drippings, and maple syrup. Mix well.

3. Pour the batter into the prepared cake pan. Brush with the melted butter. Bake until golden, 15 to 20 minutes. Serve warm, cut into pieces.

Serves 4 to 6

PUMPKIN CORN BREAD

My friend Kate Almand tells me that Lucius Beebe had it all wrong! Corn bread is to be eaten in a bowl of *buttermilk*, not "sweet" milk. This pumpkin corn bread does just fine either way.

1 cup yellow cornmeal
1 cup all-purpose flour
3 tablespoons sugar
1 tablespoon baking powder
1 teaspoon baking soda
½ teaspoon salt
Pinch of ground ginger
Pinch of ground cinnamon
Pinch of ground white pepper
2 eggs
1 cup puréed fresh or canned pumpkin
1 cup sour cream
8 tablespoons (1 stick) unsalted butter, melted

1. Preheat the oven to 425°F. Lightly grease a 9-inch square cake pan.

2. Combine the cornmeal, flour, sugar, baking powder, baking soda, salt, ginger, cinnamon, and white pepper in a mixing bowl.

3. In a large mixing bowl, beat the eggs with the pumpkin, sour cream, and 7 tablespoons of the melted butter until smooth. Add the cornmeal mixture, and stir until smooth.

4. Pour the batter into the prepared cake pan. Brush with the remaining 1 tablespoon melted butter. Bake until golden brown, 15 to 20 minutes. Serve warm, cut into pieces.

Serves 4 to 6

SPINACH-FLECKED CORN BREAD

You may substitute turnip greens if you are a true-blooded Southerner. This green and gold bread looks as attractive on a plate as it is good to eat—especially with pork or chicken.

4 tablespoons (½ stick) unsalted butter
1 shallot, minced
4 cups coarsely chopped rinsed fresh
    spinach leaves (about 6 ounces)
1½ cups cornmeal
½ cup bread flour
2 teaspoons baking powder
¼ teaspoon baking soda
½ teaspoon salt
¼ teaspoon freshly ground black pepper
¼ teaspoon freshly grated nutmeg
1 cup milk
½ cup sour cream
1 egg, lightly beaten
1 tablespoon unsalted butter, melted

1. Preheat the oven to 425°F.
2. Melt 3 tablespoons of the butter in a 9-inch cast-iron skillet over medium-low heat. Add the shallot; cook 1 minute. Add the spinach with just the water that clings to the leaves. Cook, covered, stirring occasionally, until soft, about 10 minutes. Remove the cover and raise the heat to medium. Cook until most of the liquid has evaporated, 1 minute longer. Remove the skillet from the heat.
3. Combine the cornmeal with the flour, baking powder, baking soda, salt, pepper, and nutmeg. Stir in the milk, sour cream, and egg. Mix well, and stir in the spinach mixture. Wipe out the skillet.
4. Melt the remaining 1 tablespoon butter in the skillet over medium heat. Pour the batter into the skillet, remove it from the heat, and brush with the melted butter. Transfer the skillet to the oven, and bake until the bread is golden, 15 to 20 minutes. Serve warm, cut into wedges.
Serves 4 to 6

ROSY CORN BREAD

Corn bread seems to have a real affinity for pork, as Italians and Southerners know. Try this with a sautéed ham steak, or with country-cured ham in red-eye gravy.

1½ cups yellow cornmeal
½ cup all-purpose flour
1 tablespoon baking powder
½ teaspoon baking soda
¼ teaspoon salt
3 eggs, lightly beaten
¾ cup ricotta cheese
¾ cup tomato juice
½ cup grated Cheddar cheese
4 tablespoons (½ stick) unsalted butter,
    melted
1 tablespoon freshly grated Parmesan
    cheese

1. Preheat the oven to 425°F. Lightly

grease an 8-inch square cake pan.

2. Combine the cornmeal, flour, baking powder, baking soda, and salt in a large bowl.

3. In another bowl, beat the eggs with the ricotta, tomato juice, Cheddar, and 3 tablespoons of the butter.

4. Combine the two mixtures and pour into the prepared cake pan. Brush with the remaining 1 tablespoon melted butter, and sprinkle with the Parmesan cheese. Bake until golden brown, about 20 minutes. Serve warm, cut into pieces.

Serves 4 to 6

TIJUANA CORN BREAD

Tijuana is a dusty Mexican border town full of booze and peppers. No booze can be found in this corn bread, but there are plenty of peppers. Try this with beef *fajitas*.

3 tablespoons unsalted butter
2 scallions, white bulbs and green tops, chopped
½ medium red bell pepper, cored, seeded, and finely chopped
½ medium green bell pepper, cored, seeded, and finely chopped
½ cup fresh corn kernels (from 1 large ear)
1½ cups yellow cornmeal
1 cup self-rising cake flour
½ teaspoon salt
2 tablespoons sugar
1 teaspoon baking powder
½ teaspoon baking soda
1 cup buttermilk
2 eggs, lightly beaten
2 teaspoons unsalted butter, melted

1. Preheat the oven to 425°F. Lightly butter an 8-inch square cake pan.

2. Melt the 3 tablespoons butter in a heavy skillet over medium-low heat. Add the scallions and peppers; cook until soft, about 5 minutes. Stir in the corn; cook 2 minutes longer. Remove the skillet from the heat.

3. Combine the cornmeal, flour, salt, sugar, baking powder, and baking soda in a large bowl. Stir in the buttermilk and eggs. Then stir in the vegetable mixture.

4. Spoon the batter into the prepared cake pan. Brush the top with the melted butter. Bake until puffed and golden, about 20 minutes. Serve warm, cut into pieces.

Serves 4 to 6

PROSCIUTTO AND PARMESAN CORN BREAD

This makes a perfect starter to any meal—or serve it along with a salad for brunch.

1½ cups yellow cornmeal
½ cup all-purpose flour
1 tablespoon baking soda
¼ teaspoon salt
¼ teaspoon freshly ground black pepper
1½ cups heavy or whipping cream
2 eggs, lightly beaten
2 ounces thinly sliced prosciutto, chopped
    (about ½ cup)
2 tablespoons chopped fresh chives
½ cup freshly grated Parmesan cheese
4 tablespoons (½ stick) unsalted butter,
    melted

1. Preheat the oven to 425°F. Lightly grease an 8-inch square cake pan.

2. Combine the cornmeal, flour, baking soda, salt, and pepper in a large mixing bowl. Stir in the cream, eggs, prosciutto, chives, all but 1 tablespoon of the Parmesan cheese, and 3 tablespoons of the melted butter.

3. Pour the batter into the prepared cake pan. Brush with the remaining 1 tablespoon melted butter, and sprinkle with the reserved 1 tablespoon Parmesan cheese. Bake until golden, about 20 minutes. Serve warm, cut into pieces.

Serves 4 to 6

PERFECTLY PEACHY CORN BREAD FRENCH TOAST

*F*or me, one of the joys of making corn bread for Saturday night supper is having some left over for Sunday morning breakfast!

The best French toast in my not inconsiderable repertoire of hot breads is this one. It is an invention the chef conceived after downing several morning eye-openers—a drink known as a Fuzzy Navel, compounded of orange juice and Peachtree Schnapps. One thing led to another, and before I knew it, Perfectly Peachy Corn Bread French Toast was born.

I advise using leftover Vermont, Pumpkin, or in a pinch Kansas City corn bread (pages 124 and 125) for this dish. And for those allergic to alcohol, peach nectar makes an admirable stand-in for the booze!

½ cup fresh orange juice
2 tablespoons Peachtree Schnapps, or
    ¼ cup peach nectar
2 eggs, separated
¼ cup granulated sugar
¼ teaspoon ground cinnamon
⅛ teaspoon freshly grated nutmeg
½ cup heavy or whipping cream
12 slices leftover corn bread
8 tablespoons (1 stick) unsalted butter
    (approximately)
Confectioners' sugar

Orange Peach Syrup (recipe follows) or
    maple syrup

1. Combine the orange juice, schnapps, egg yolks, sugar, cinnamon, nutmeg, and cream in a large bowl. Mix well. Beat the egg whites until stiff, and fold them into the orange juice mixture.

2. Preheat the oven to 250°F.

3. Place the corn bread slices in the orange juice mixture, making sure they are well-covered with the mixture. Leave them in the mixture until they are soaked but not mushy, 2 to 3 minutes.

4. Melt 4 tablespoons of the butter in a heavy skillet and heat until foamy. Remove the bread slices from the juice mixture, shaking off any excess. Sauté them, three or four at a time, on both sides until golden brown, adding more butter as needed. Transfer the slices to an ovenproof platter and dust with confectioners' sugar. Keep warm in the oven until all slices have been sautéed. Dust once more with confectioners' sugar, and serve with Orange Peach Syrup or maple syrup.

Serves 4

Orange Peach Syrup

½ cup fresh orange juice
½ cup sugar
1 teaspoon finely slivered orange zest
¼ cup Peachtree Schnapps or peach nectar

1. Combine the orange juice and sugar in a small saucepan, and cook over medium heat until the mixture boils. Add the slivered orange zest; cook 1 minute longer. The mixture will be slightly thick.

2. Remove the pan from the heat and immediately stir in the schnapps. Allow the mixture to stand for 5 minutes for the flavors to blend properly. Serve warm or at room temperature.

Makes about 1¼ cups

CAMPTON PLACE'S DOUBLE-CORN CORN STICKS

Corn-crammed corn stick that was whipped up one lazy afternoon by chef Bradley Ogden at the dining spot known as Campton Place, in San Francisco.

Baker's Secret (see page 42)
½ cup yellow cornmeal
½ cup all-purpose flour
2 tablespoons sugar
1¼ teaspoons baking powder
½ teaspoon salt
1 cup heavy or whipping cream
1 egg yolk
3 tablespoons unsalted butter
½ cup fresh corn kernels (from 1 large ear)
2 egg whites

1. Preheat the oven to 425°F. Lightly grease a corn stick mold with Baker's Secret.

2. Combine the cornmeal with the flour, sugar, baking powder, and salt in a large bowl. Stir in the cream and egg yolk. Set the batter aside.

3. Melt the butter in a medium-size saucepan over medium-low heat. Stir in the corn kernels, and toss to warm through. Stir the corn into the batter.

4. Beat the egg whites until stiff. Fold them into the batter.

5. Spoon the batter evenly into the prepared mold. Bake until firm and golden, 15 to 20 minutes. Serve hot.

Makes 22 small corn sticks

PHILLIP STEPHEN SCHULZ'S LACE CAKES

Lace Cakes are a real Yankee bequest to this cornmeal collection and the most ethereal pancakes I have ever consumed. (And I must admit I have consumed a lot.) The best rendering I know comes from ex-Coloradoan Phillip Stephen Schulz, who could certainly give Aunt Jemima a run for the money when it comes to a duel at the griddle.

2 eggs
2 cups milk (approximately)
1 cup fine yellow cornmeal
1 teaspoon sugar
½ teaspoon salt
6 tablespoons (¾ stick) unsalted butter, melted

1. Using a whisk, beat the eggs in a large bowl until light. Whisk in the remaining ingredients until smooth.
2. Heat a lightly greased griddle or heavy skillet over medium heat. Pour about 3 tablespoons batter for each cake on the griddle, and cook until the underside is golden brown, 3 to 4 minutes. Turn over and lightly brown the other side, another 3 to 4 minutes. Stir the batter well before making each cake, as the cornmeal will thicken up. Add more milk if the batter becomes too thick. Serve with maple syrup or jam.

Makes twelve 5-inch cakes

APPALACHIAN SPOON AND FORK CAKE

If you thought cornmeal was just another stick-to-the ribs ingredient, take a squint at this Appalachian coffee cake. It is the most toothsome (sweet-nutty-raisined) confection extant.

1 cup chopped pecans
¾ cup firmly packed dark brown sugar
1 teaspoon ground cinnamon
⅔ cup raisins
8 tablespoons (1 stick) unsalted butter, melted and cooled
2 cups cake flour
1 cup yellow cornmeal
¾ cup granulated sugar
1 teaspoon baking powder
½ teaspoon baking soda
¼ teaspoon salt
3 eggs, lightly beaten
1 cup sour cream
1 teaspoon vanilla extract

1. Preheat the oven to 350°F. Lightly butter and flour a 9-inch springform pan.

2. Combine the pecans, brown sugar, and cinnamon in a medium-size bowl. Mix well. Remove ½ cup of this mixture and set it aside. Add the raisins and ¼ cup of the melted butter to the remaining pecan mixture. Set aside.

3. Combine the flour, cornmeal, granulated sugar, baking powder, baking soda, and salt in a large bowl. With a heavy wooden spoon, beat in the eggs, sour cream, remaining ¼ cup butter, and vanilla until smooth.

4. Spread half the batter over the bottom of the prepared springform pan. Sprinkle the raisin mixture over the top. Carefully spread the remaining batter over the raisin mixture, and sprinkle with the reserved ½ cup nut mixture. Bake until a toothpick inserted in the center of the cake comes out fairly clean, 45 to 50 minutes. Cool on a wire rack before removing the sides of the pan.

Serves 8

GINGERED PUMPKIN PIE

*T*his pie is a staple in my holiday dessert book because it is easy to make and smashing to taste. It nests in a gilded cornmeal pie crust. I suggest you flag the crust recipe for lots of other uses. It's a winner!

1 Gilded Cornmeal Pie Crust (recipe
   follows)
1 cup puréed cooked pumpkin, canned or
   fresh
½ cup firmly packed light brown sugar
½ cup heavy or whipping cream
½ cup milk
2 tablespoons cognac
3 eggs, lightly beaten
¼ cup finely slivered candied ginger
1 teaspoon ground cinnamon
⅛ teaspoon ground cloves
¼ teaspoon freshly grated nutmeg
¼ teaspoon salt

1. Preheat the oven to 350°F.

2. Roll out the pie crust dough and line a 9-inch pie plate with it. Trim and flute the edges.

3. Place the pumpkin in a large bowl, and whisk in the remaining ingredients. Pour the filling into the prepared pie shell. Bake until set in the center,

about 45 minutes.

Makes one 9-inch pie

Gilded Cornmeal Pie Crust

1¼ cup all-purpose flour
½ cup yellow cornmeal
¼ teaspoon salt
6 tablespoons solid vegetable shortening,
   chilled
2 tablespoons unsalted butter, chilled
3 to 4 tablespoons cold water

Combine the flour, cornmeal, and salt in a large bowl. Cut in the shortening and butter with a pastry blender until the mixture has the texture of coarse crumbs. Add just enough cold water to form a fairly soft dough. Refrigerate 1 hour before using.

Makes enough for one 9- to 11-inch single-crust pie

MRS. HITE'S GEORGIA LEMON PECAN PIE

I used to work with Mrs. Hite's son, John, during my days as promotion art director for *Esquire* magazine. He pressed this recipe into my hands one day, and I have been making it ever since, taking the liberty to combine the filling with my aforementioned Gilded Cornmeal Pie Crust. Unbeatable!

1 Gilded Cornmeal Pie Crust (see page 131)
4 eggs
2 cups sugar
¼ cup milk
1 tablespoon yellow cornmeal
1 tablespoon all-purpose flour
Finely slivered zest of 1 lemon
Juice of 1 lemon
¾ cup chopped pecans
8 tablespoons (1 stick) unsalted butter, melted

1. Preheat the oven to 325°F.

2. Roll out the pie crust dough and line a 10-inch glass or ceramic quiche dish with it. Trim and flute the edges.

3. Beat the eggs in a large mixing bowl until light. Slowly add the sugar, beating until the mixture is light and fluffy. Beat in the remaining ingredients. Pour the filling into the prepared pie shell, and bake until it is golden brown and firm, about 45 minutes.

Makes one 10-inch pie

THE FLOURING OF THE GRAIN

Cornstarch, that old pantry familiar in the rectangular box, is actually a flour, finely milled of a high-starch corn hybrid.

Why and when does one use cornstarch? Cornstarch is a light thickener of sauces (notably in Oriental and Latin American dishes) and adds just the right degree of density to puddings, soups, custard sauces, and mousse bases that flour very often turns viscous. Cornstarch is also an invaluable aid when making pie fillings of super-acidy fruits:

A delicate sprinkling as the fruit is layered will keep the juices from running out of the pie shell as it bakes.

Cornstarch does come with a few caveats, however. It lumps unless it is well mixed with liquid before being added to a dish on the stove. And it has a raw taste if it is cooked over too high a heat. It is also essential to remember not to overbeat cornstarch-based recipes, for that breaks down the starch's delicate balance and thins it irremediably.

JOCKEY CREPES

Cornstarch's finest hour! This unique crêpe recipe (printed on the Argo cornstarch box back in the 1960s) contains no flour whatsoever, which means that the batter flows out of your blender and into your pan in minutes. (Most crêpe batters sit in the fridge for hours, waiting for the gluten in the flour to relax and produce a delicate pancake—but not these feather-light treats.)

Fill them with anything you like, but this seafood amalgam will knock your socks off—you have my word on it.

5 tablespoons unsalted butter
1½ tablespoons minced shallots
½ cup dry white wine
1 pound bay scallops
½ teaspoon minced hot red pepper, or ¼
*   teaspoon crushed dried hot red peppers*
1 teaspoon minced fresh cilantro (Chinese
*   parsley)*
⅛ teaspoon anchovy paste
2 tablespoons all-purpose flour
1 cup heavy or whipping cream
Freshly ground black pepper to taste
½ cup freshly grated Parmesan cheese
12 Cornstarch Crêpes (recipe follows)

1. Preheat the oven to 350°F. Lightly butter a large baking dish.

2. Melt 3 tablespoons of the butter in a heavy saucepan over medium-high heat. Add the shallots; cook until lightly browned, about 2 minutes. Raise the heat and add the wine; cook 1 minute. Add the scallops along with the hot red pepper, cilantro, and anchovy paste. Cook, tossing gently, over high heat until the scallops turn white, 2 to 3 minutes. Drain the scallops, reserving the liquid. Place the scallops in a bowl and keep warm.

3. Melt the remaining 2 tablespoons butter in a heavy saucepan over medium-low heat. Whisk in the flour. Cook, stirring constantly, 2 minutes. Whisk in the reserved scallop liquid and raise the heat. Cook, stirring occasionally, over medium-high heat until very

thick, about 6 minutes. Beat in the cream until smooth. Season with pepper, and remove from the heat.

4. Add two thirds of the sauce to the reserved scallops. Stir in two thirds of the cheese. Fill the crêpes, roll them up, and place them seam side down on the prepared baking dish. With a teaspoon, drizzle the remaining sauce over the crêpes. Sprinkle with the remaining cheese. (Crêpes may be made ahead to this point.) Bake for 8 to 10 minutes.

Makes 12 filled crêpes

Note: Crêpes may also be prepared, filled, and frozen; allow 15 to 20 minutes in a 400°F oven if frozen.

Cornstarch Crêpes

These crêpes refrigerate, and freeze, remarkably well.

2 eggs
¾ cup milk
6 tablespoons cornstarch
1 tablespoon vegetable oil
2 teaspoons sugar
¾ teaspoon baking powder
⅛ teaspoon salt

1. In the order given, place all the ingredients in the container of a blender. Blend on high speed until very smooth, about 1 minute. Transfer the batter to a bowl.

2. Heat a greased 6-inch crêpe or omelet pan until it is very hot. Pour about 2 tablespoons of the batter onto the center of the pan. Turn and twist the pan immediately to coat the bottom. Cook over medium-high heat until the crêpe is lightly browned and the top is dry around the edges, about 30 seconds. Carefully turn the crêpe over and cook several seconds. Transfer to a paper towel. Repeat with the remaining batter, stacking the crêpes, with a paper towel in between, on top of each other. When through, invert the stack so the golden sides are down.

Makes 12 crêpes

Note: These crêpes may be made in advance and stored, refrigerated, in a plastic bag.

OLD-FASHIONED PRUNE WHIP

A venerable comfort food that does not show its age one jot.

¾ cup chopped pitted prunes
¼ teaspoon almond extract
¼ cup boiling water
3 eggs, separated
¼ cup granulated sugar
¼ teaspoon vanilla extract
1½ tablespoons cornstarch
¾ cup milk, scalded
1 cup heavy or whipping cream
3 tablespoons confectioners' sugar

1. Place the prunes in a heatproof bowl. Sprinkle them with the almond extract, then pour the boiling water over them. Set aside.

2. Whisk the egg yolks with the granulated sugar in the top of a double boiler until smooth. Whisk in the vanilla, cornstarch, and scalded milk. Place over simmering water and cook, stirring constantly, until thickened, about 10 minutes. Remove from the heat and allow to cool.

3. Place the prunes with all their liquid in the container of a food processor. Process, using the pulse button, until smooth. Transfer to a large bowl, and fold in the cooled custard.

4. Beat the cream with the confectioner's sugar until stiff. Fold into the prune mixture.

5. Beat the egg whites until stiff and fold them into the prune mixture. Transfer to a serving bowl and chill well before serving.

Serves 8

ROTHE GRUETZE

*T*his Danish fruit dessert (which we always called "red grits" when I was a kid) makes a comeback as a fruit soup appetizer, splashed with vodka if you like, or as a light ending to a summer meal.

8 ounces Italian or red plums
¼ cup water
1 pint fresh strawberries, rinsed and hulled
1 package (10 ounces) frozen raspberries in
    syrup, thawed
¾ cup sugar
3 tablespoons cornstarch
1 cup cranberry-raspberry juice (not drink)

1. Cut the plums in half and remove the pits. Place them in a medium-size saucepan, add the water, and heat to boiling. Reduce the heat and cook, covered, over low heat 15 minutes. Add the strawberries, and raspberries with syrup. Heat to boiling, reduce the heat, and simmer, uncovered, 10 minutes longer.

2. Using a wooden spoon, press the fruit through a sieve into the top of a double boiler. You should have 2½ cups. Stir in the sugar and cook, stirring occasionally, over simmering water until the sugar has dissolved, 1 to 2 minutes.

3. Place the cornstarch in a medium-size bowl and whisk in ¼ cup of the cranberry-raspberry juice until very smooth. Whisk in the remaining juice. Add this mixture to the fruit mixture and cook, stirring constantly, 8 minutes. Cover, and continue to cook until it is slightly thickened and you can no longer taste the cornstarch, 10 to 12 minutes. Do not overcook. Remove the pan from the heat and cool, stirring occasionally, to room temperature. Chill well before serving.

Serves 4 to 6

CHOCOLATE NATILLA

A wondrous chocolate pudding for all seasons. The recipe comes from Clive DuVal, talented chef-owner of Tila's, the best Gringo-Mex restaurant in Houston, and now in Washington, D.C., too.

1 ounce semi-sweet chocolate
½ cup sugar
Pinch of salt
1¾ cups milk
1 tablespoon fresh orange juice
2 tablespoons golden rum
3 tablespoons cornstarch
½ teaspoon vanilla extract
1 tablespoon Kahlua

1. Melt the chocolate in the top of a double boiler over simmering water.

2. Combine the sugar, salt, and 1½ cups of the milk in a small saucepan. Heat almost to boiling. Whisk into the melted chocolate, then stir in the orange juice and rum.

3. Place the cornstarch in a small bowl. Whisk in the remaining ¼ cup milk until smooth. Stir this mixture into the chocolate mixture and cook, stirring constantly, 8 minutes. Cover and continue to cook, stirring once or twice, until it is thickened and you can no longer taste the cornstarch, 10 to 12 minutes. Do not overcook. (When removing the cover, be careful that the accumulated moisture does not trip into the natilla.) Remove from the heat, add the vanilla and Kahlua, and cool, stirring occasionally, to room temperature. Chill thoroughly before serving.

Serves 4

ROSE LEVY BERANBAUM'S GENOISE

Cornstarch is not used much for cake or pastry. However, one exception (devised by the brilliant cake baker-teacher Rose Levy Beranbaum in her book, *Cake Bible*) is the following classic genoise cake, in which flour is leavened with cornstarch and added slowly to a zabaglione-like mixture of warm eggs and sugar for an utterly silken result.

I must warn you, this is a very special cake. Make it only when you have sufficient time and when the telephone answering machine is taking your calls!

I think this genoise gets better as it sits. Plan on baking it the night before the dinner party, please.

4 tablespoons (½ stick) unsalted butter
1 teaspoon vanilla extract
4 large eggs
¾ cup plus 1½ teaspoons sugar
½ cup sifted cake flour
½ cup plus 1 tablespoon cornstarch (lightly spooned, not packed)
½ cup water
2 tablespoons liqueur (such as kirsch or Grand Marnier)
Chocolate Buttercream Frosting (recipe follows)

1. Preheat the oven to 350°F. Butter a 9-inch springform pan and line it with parchment paper. Butter and flour the paper.

2. Melt the butter in a small skillet over medium heat and cook, stirring frequently, until browned. Do not burn it. Cool the butter slightly, and strain it through cheesecloth. You should have 3 tablespoons clarified brown butter. Place the butter in a small pan and add the vanilla. Place over medium-low heat until almost hot (110° to 120°F). Set aside and keep warm.

3. Place a large heatproof bowl over a pan of simmering water. Add the eggs and ½ cup of the sugar. Beat with a hand-held electric mixer until tripled in volume, 8 to 10 minutes.

4. Remove a scant cup of the egg mixture and whisk it into the brown butter mixture. Set aside.

5. Sift the flour with the cornstarch, and sift half of this mixture over the beaten eggs, folding it in gently with a slotted spoon. Fold in the remaining flour mixture. Fold in the brown butter mixture. Pour immediately into the prepared pan and bake until the cake is golden brown and starting to pull away from the sides of the pan, 20 to 25 minutes. Run a knife or small metal spatula around the edges and remove the sides of the pan. Invert the cake onto a wire rack and carefully remove the bottom of the pan. Cool the cake completely on the rack. Then cut the cake in half horizontally with a long sharp knife to make two layers.

6. Combine the remaining ¼ cup plus 1½ teaspoons sugar and the water in a small saucepan with a tight-fitting lid. Heat to a rapid boil. Cover, and remove from the heat. Cool completely while covered.

7. Stir the liqueur into the cooled sugar syrup. Sprinkle this mixture over the bottom and top of both layers. Ice the bottom and top layers with Chocolate Buttercream Frosting. Do not ice the sides.

Serves 8

Chocolate Buttercream Frosting

4 ounces sweet chocolate
¼ cup water
1 teaspoon vanilla extract
9 tablespoons unsalted butter, at room
    temperature
1 egg yolk
⅓ cup confectioners' sugar
1 teaspoon dark rum

1. Melt the chocolate with the water and vanilla in the top of a double boiler over simmering water. Stir until smooth, and set aside to cool.

2. Beat the butter in the large bowl of an electric mixer until light. Add the egg yolk, and beat until light and fluffy. Beat in the chocolate, sugar, and rum.

Makes enough for a 9-inch cake

GRITS AND HOMINY

Acquired Tastes That Are Rich in Protein

I am a true grits and hominy lover. North of the Mason-Dixon line, however, you will be hard put to find many others who share the predilection. I have even met denizens of the Deep South who shuddered at the thought of dipping a spoon into a bowlful of either. For grits and hominy are acquired tastes—but they are so highly nutritive and protein-rich that the tastes are eminently worthy of acquisition.

Try telling that to a person of prejudiced palate! Actually, I did try once, and got tossed out on my ear.

In the 1940s and '50s, the most outspoken star of the American theater was indubitably Tallulah Bankhead. A legend in her time, Tallulah (as everyone called her) was a tempestuous personality judged more for her performances offstage than on. But if you will accept a firsthand opinion, that was a terrible canard. When I saw her, Bankhead's talent was so mesmerizing that most of the audience was red-eyed and snuffling into handkerchiefs by the final curtain, though she was playing the part of an unmitigated vixen. Southern, of course, like Bankhead herself.

Tallulah was touring the South in her greatest hit, *The Little Foxes*. To attend opening night in Richmond, Virginia, I had to cut half a day's college classes, travel by trolley and bus from Williamsburg, and worst of all, catch a milk train back. But it was an experience worth twice the adversity. I sat in the last row of the second balcony, very high up, but even from afar the lady's gift was formidable. I cried too.

As the theater emptied, still under the actress's spell, I found myself wandering to the stage door.

"Where you goin', boy?" A burly old man stood guard, blinking in the dark.

"Interview with Miss Bankhead," I lied, flipping open a college newspaper press card he never glanced at.

"To the right and down the steps. But take yo' turn. There's a passel of others waitin' fo' her already."

In the dim light I could make out about a dozen men and women, awkwardly queued outside a dressing room. The door was unmarked and tightly shut, but a trail of rose petals on the floor and a whiff of expensive perfume in the air firmly established that *she* was behind it. If one had further doubt, a deep Alabama growl reverberated inside.

"I said *no* interviews and I meant it. Get rid of them!"

The assembled group heard what Bankhead said, yet no one moved. If anything, a few hardy souls bent closer to the doorway as her decibels rose.

"Don't give me that crap about the power of the press, darling." *Dahl-ling* is how it came out, but no term of endearment was ever less benign. "I am sick of playing jerkwater towns, giving the performance of my life, only to have some local yokel ask me if I sleep in the nude! Send them away—"

She was still shouting as the door opened. A highly flushed man held it ajar. We could all plainly see the lady inside, wearing what appeared to be only a fur coat and panties. Legs crossed, she was seated at a dressing table, drinking whiskey.

The functionary stumbled as he spoke. "Ladies...gentlemen...you must forgive. Y'see, she's been under a severe strain preparin' for this openin'. Actually a migraine headache..." His voice trailed unhappily. "Can we set up another time for interviews? Tomorrow afternoon maybe?"

One gray-haired matron removed an enormous bouquet from behind her back and with deadly aim tossed it through the open door, barely missing Tallulah's head. Bankhead did not flinch. Picking up a loose blossom, she handed the rest to her maid.

"How sweet," she muttered grimly. "How welcoming..."

The crowd surged forward, but the star rose and we retreated again.

"Darlings...darlings," she sputtered, "I can't tell you how touched I am by this sign of your affection. But—" She gave a slight gargle that became a hacking cough. "It's been a *bad* day."

The group responded at once: "You were riveting." "Brilliant." "Enthralling."

The woman who had thrown the flowers was less effusive: "My deadline for feature stories in the *News Leader* is tomorrow. Nine a.m."

"Oh?" Holding the mink together with one hand, Bankhead managed to pour herself another drink with the other. "Well...just what did you want to know, darling?" she said like a trouper, shaking her long hair back.

Before the woman could answer, a very fat man with a high-pitched voice called out from the rear.

"Tell us yo' favorite Southern dishes, honey."

She stared at him with ill-conceived contempt. "Southern Comfort—on the rocks!"

"What? No grits, no hominy?"

Tallulah rocked on her heels before answering. "The only good thing about *grits*," she seethed, "is that it rhymes with Ritz, where I go for my favorite dishes. And as for *harmony*, I'd rather starve!"

She was slightly drunk and decidedly livid. The crowd sensed it and dispersed, moving backward down the hall.

I can never explain why I said it, but as we were shuffling away, I turned to the person closest and shook my head. "She doesn't know the vitamins she's missing," I said.

Bankhead's voice roared like thunder. "And you," she cried, "don't know the tongue-lashing you've missed, Buster!"

The interview was over. But for years after I could not eat grits or hominy without remembering the terrible swift sword of her voice, and blushing.

The Grain's Genesis

Since grits and hominy are both essentially kernels from the same cob that produced cornmeal, one would assume they all shared the same forkful of food history. Not so, however.

Long, long before Columbus's raffish boatmen brought corn back from the New World and the first European miller decided the dried kernels would grind up to a usable flour, hominy and grits were staples in the American diet. Eaten by whom? The Indians, of course, who invented them both.

Algonquin history, in fact, tells how northeastern tribes managed to stay alive during hard winters because they had discovered the secret of storing and preparing *tackhummin*, "corn without skin."

What the Algonquins did to make *tackhummin* (a name which in time evolved to *hummin* and then through Pilgrim misrendering to *hominy*) was to hull dried corn by soaking it in water mixed with wood ashes. After a day's stint in the drink, the bleached kernels puffed up so considerably that the hulls burst and developed a decidedly non-corn flavor that was so addictive, the braves ate it three times a day without complaint—most probably because the plump kernels added a healthy jolt of complex carbohydrates, fats, iron, and thiamine to their otherwise dreary rations of dried deer and berries.

But that's not the whole story... Dried hulled hominy was also pounded by dutiful Indian squaws into a coarse mix (rougher than cornmeal) that was boiled and eaten hot by their braves. It was this pounded homespun cereal, gifted to them by the Indian tribes in Plymouth, that kept the earliest American colonists alive during the first terrible winters of their immigration. The Pilgrims accepted the Indians' bounty against their will, for they were a starchy lot, given to extreme conservatism in their diet. But hunger overcame pride in the end. They ate and survived.

It is inscribed in a diary of one of the *Mayflower* expedition that a certain colonial housewife, after first tasting the dubious porridge, shook her head vigorously and declared it to be equal to any bowl of groats she had ever tasted, and worthy of the Lord's benediction.

Groats she dubbed it and groats it remained for over a half century, until some footloose Massachusetts pioneer made his way to Virginia with a sack of the stuff over his shoulder.

After tasting hominy groats for the first time, a young denizen of the James

River country mispronounced it as *grits*. "Good grits" is reputedly his actual quote.

Grits is probably the most popular dining adjunct (after yams) below the Mason-Dixon line today. And I am happy to report, it has never lost its Southern accent!

GRITS

Some Plain Grain Talk

*T*hough still sometimes referred to as "hominy grits" in certain rustic parts of the South, grits as we know them are no longer derived from boiled, slaked whole hominy.

Technically, I guess one might call grits a residual grain, since they are milled as part of cornmeal before being separated and graded. What is left is a coarse cereal high in carbohydrates, made of dried, hulled, and ground corn kernels from which the bran and sometimes the germ is removed.

For the record, there are grits and *grits* in the marketplace. Like cornmeal, grits are not only processed and packaged by large commercial flour mills but also produced in lesser volume by a clutch of small, dedicated millers in outlying geography whose stone-ground output differs greatly from the commercial brands in nutritive value, appearance, and, let's face it, price.

However, whether you mail-order "speckled-heart grits" (see Calloway Gardens Country Store in the source list at the back of the book) or simply pick up a package close at hand in the supermarket, grits have a decided place in your grain lexicon. It is a high-fiber food, well endowed with protein, that may be combined with eggs, vegetables, cheese, or chicken to supply the maximum requirements of vitamins and minerals for a balanced diet.

And besides all that, take it from me, grits are utterly delicious!

How to Buy Them

*T*here are several options when buying grits.

Consumers may purchase the well-known brands that are available on supermarket shelves or search out the stone-ground varieties found only at gourmet groceries, natural foods stores, or by mail order.

There are differences (aside from price) between commercially produced grits and the grits that are actually ground between millstones, the old-fashioned way. For one thing, all stone-ground grits are organic; which is to say it is rougher in texture and more naturally nutritive than any fine-milled graded grits that are mass-produced.

However, that commendation comes with a cavil. Stone-ground grits are decidedly less smooth when cooked and will not produce the silky feel that commercially milled grits brings to a soufflé, roulade, or popover.

My advice: Try both and experiment!

Instant grits are another dish of cereal entirely. This product is precooked and then redried before it is packaged. One "recooks" the grits by adding boiling water. In my opinion, much is lost in the translation.

How to Store Them

*S*tone-ground grits have an exceedingly brief shelf life, and it will usually take less than a month for the paper package to become a breeding ground for unwanted pantry pests. The only sterile environment for storing stone-ground grits is the refrigerator or freezer. I keep the package in an airtight plastic bag and figure a shelf life of four to five months in the fridge and up to a year in the freezer. Commercially produced grits may also be kept in the refrigerator, but any cool pantry shelf will do in a pinch. However, remember to seal the carton well (I use paper masking tape) after every use!

How to Cook Them

My way of cooking grits is somewhat unorthodox and decidedly *not* the method prescribed by either commercial manufacturers or stone-ground mills.

The instructions on most packaged grits are almost invariably the same: "*Bring the water to a boil. Slowly stir in the grits and cook covered over low heat 15–20 minutes. Then let stand off heat (covered) for a few minutes.*" Stone-ground grits come with basically the same recommendation but the grits are cooked longer, 20 to 30 minutes.

Greene's technique, as you will observe, is abbreviated: Bring the liquid to a boil first, then reduce the heat. Whisk the grits into the barely simmering water so the grains separate, and cook the mixture, uncovered, stirring occasionally, for about 10 minutes. No longer. The accelerated cooking time, I find, is an insurance policy against blobs, lumps, and mush.

Brands of stone-ground grits vary considerably in coarseness of grind and often require a longer cooking period—about 20 minutes—to obtain the desired consistency of texture. Grits should be smooth and mollifying to the tongue, never rough or contentious!

STONE-GROUND VS COMMERCIALLY MILLED GRITS

Stone-ground grits are milled of dried hulled corn kernels and always include the heart (or germ) of the corn, which is exceedingly high in niacin, iron, and riboflavin.

Mass-produced grits are steamed to loosen the tough outer shell before the grains are dried and split and the hull, bran, and germ are removed, leaving only the endosperm (tissue formed inside the seed's embryo sac) as a nutritive endowment.

However, it must be noted that both stone-ground and commercially manufactured grits are "fortified" with added vitamins and minerals. And the word "Enriched" is emblazoned on each and every package!

SCROLLED, FILLED GRITS

A baked-and-souffléed cheese roll wrapped to capacity with ham and shrimp. I call it a "scroll" but it is actually a roulade—adapted from Nathalie Dupree's *New Southern Cooking*.

FOR THE ROULADE

½ cup plain yogurt
½ cup milk
¼ cup hominy grits
⅓ cup freshly grated Parmesan cheese
⅓ cup grated Swiss or Jarlsberg cheese
4 egg yolks
½ teaspoon salt
¼ teaspoon freshly ground black pepper
6 egg whites

FOR THE FILLING

4 tablespoons (½ stick) unsalted butter
3 large scallions, finely chopped
1 clove garlic, minced
½ cup chopped cooked ham
½ pound shrimp, shelled and deveined
¼ teaspoon chili powder
Hot pepper sauce
2 tablespoons all-purpose flour
½ cup homemade chicken stock (see page 376) or canned broth
½ cup plus 2 tablespoons heavy or whipping cream
1 teaspoon fresh lemon juice
Salt and freshly ground black pepper to taste

1. Preheat the oven to 350°F. Grease a 10½ by 15½-inch jelly roll pan, then grease a piece of wax paper and line the pan with it, greased side up.

2. Make the roulade: Combine the yogurt and milk in a medium-size heavy saucepan. Bring to boiling over medium heat, stirring frequently. Reduce the heat, stir in the grits, and cook, stirring constantly, over low heat until creamy in texture, about 10 minutes. Remove from the heat.

3. Stir both cheeses into the grits mixture. Then beat in the egg yolks, one at a time, beating thoroughly after each addition. Add the salt and pepper.

4. Beat the egg whites until stiff, and fold them into the grits mixture. Pour the mixture into the prepared jelly roll pan, and smooth it out evenly in the pan. Bake until firm, 15 to 20 minutes. The top should spring back lightly when touched. Invert the roulade onto a sheet of aluminum foil. Remove the pan and peel off the wax paper. Reduce the oven temperature to 300°F.

5. Make the filling: Melt 2 tablespoons of the butter in a large heavy skillet over medium heat. Add the scallions; cook 1 minute. Add the garlic and cook 4 minutes longer. Stir in the ham, toss to coat, and then add the shrimp. Sprinkle with the chili powder and a dash of hot pepper sauce. Toss until the shrimp turn pink, about 3 minutes. Remove from the heat and set aside.

6. Melt the remaining 2 tablespoons butter in a medium-size saucepan over medium-low heat. Stir in the flour. Cook, stirring constantly, 2 minutes. Whisk in the chicken stock and cream. Cook, stirring constantly, until very thick, about 5 minutes. Add the lemon juice, ⅛ teaspoon hot pepper sauce, and salt and pepper to taste. Combine with the ham and shrimp mixture.

7. Spread the filling evenly over the grits roulade, and roll it up like a jelly role using the foil to help with the rolling. Arrange the roulade on an oven-proof serving platter. (The dish can be prepared ahead to this point; keep it covered in the refrigerator.) Bake for 10 minutes before serving.

Serves 6

TOP DRAWER GRITS AND SPINACH SOUFFLE

A second soufflé guaranteed to please at brunch, lunch, dinner, or any time something puffed and tasty seems appropriate. Midnight perhaps—this light and lovely dish has great after hours appeal.

2½ tablespoons unsalted butter
6 tablespoons freshly grated Parmesan cheese
1 shallot, minced
10 ounces fresh spinach, rinsed, stems removed, finely chopped
1½ cups homemade chicken stock (see page 376) or canned broth
½ cup hominy grits
4 egg yolks
¼ cup heavy or whipping cream
1 teaspoon freshly grated nutmeg
Freshly ground black pepper to taste
6 egg whites

1. Preheat the oven to 400°F. Rub a 1-quart soufflé dish with ½ tablespoon of the butter and sprinkle with 1 tablespoon of the cheese.

2. Melt the remaining 2 tablespoons butter in a medium-size heavy saucepan over medium-low heat. Add the shallot; cook 2 minutes. Stir in the spinach and cook, covered, until the spinach is slightly wilted, about 3 minutes.

3. Add the chicken stock to the spinach mixture, and heat to boiling. Reduce the heat, stir in the grits, and cook, stirring constantly, over low heat until creamy in texture, about 10 minutes. Reduce the heat to low and beat in the egg yolks, one at a time, beating well after each addition. Do not allow the mixture to boil.

4. Transfer the grits mixture to a large bowl. Stir in the cream, nutmeg, 4 tablespoons of the cheese, and pepper to taste.

5. Beat the egg whites until stiff but not dry. Stir a third of the whites into the grits mixture. Fold in the remaining whites. Pour into the prepared soufflé dish and sprinkle the top with the remaining 1 tablespoon cheese. Bake until golden and firm, 30 to 35 minutes. Serve immediately.

Serves 6

LAYING ON THE GRITS

Precisely because it is so "down homey" in character, grits are a grain whose name produces a smile all across the map of America. In the theater, for instance, "grits-eater" is a kinder epithet than "mush-mouth" for an actor who does not enunciate clearly. Likewise in the Deep South, the expression "laying on the grits" is considered to be a more polite form than "greasing the palm" when one is speaking of dealings with a politician on the take. And while we are on the subject, did you know that migratory corn-pickers always refer to a red rash that affects some newcomers to their ranks as "grits zits"? And so it goes...In a factory town, the "big grits" is always a pay boss. In poor urban areas, "dumb grits" means a welfare worker.

BACON AND CHEESE GRITS SOUFFLE

*E*lizabeth David said it about omelets, but with a slight amendment, it makes a perfect introduction to this grits show-stopper: "Everyone knows there is only one infallible recipe for the perfect soufflé... your own!"

That having been said, here is one of mine—definitely infallible, composed of grits, eggs, and hot air plus some highly arresting flavorings. I guarantee it will rise like high hopes in your oven!

1½ tablespoons unsalted butter
¼ cup freshly grated Parmesan cheese
4 strips bacon
1 small white onion, finely chopped
1 small clove garlic, minced
1 cup milk
1 cup water
½ teaspoon salt
½ cup hominy grits
4 egg yolks
⅛ teaspoon freshly grated nutmeg
½ cup grated Jalapeño Monterey Jack cheese
¼ cup heavy or whipping cream
Freshly ground black pepper to taste
5 egg whites

1. Preheat the oven to 400°F. Rub a 1-quart soufflé dish with ½ tablespoon of the butter and sprinkle with 1 tablespoon of the Parmesan cheese.

2. Sauté the bacon in a heavy skillet until crisp. Drain on paper towels, and remove all but 2 tablespoons bacon drippings from the skillet.

3. Add the onion to the bacon drippings in the skillet; cook over medium-low heat 1 minute. Add the garlic; cook until both the onions and garlic are golden, about 3 minutes longer. Set aside.

4. Combine the milk, water, and salt in a medium-size saucepan, and heat to boiling. Reduce the heat, stir in the grits, and cook, stirring constantly, over low heat until creamy in texture, about 10 minutes. Add the remaining 1 tablespoon butter. Reduce the heat to low and beat in the egg yolks, one at a time, beating well after each addition. Do not allow to boil.

5. Transfer the grits mixture to a large bowl. Crumble the bacon and add it to the grits along with the reserved onion mixture, the nutmeg, Jack cheese, 2 tablespoons of the Parmesan cheese, the cream, and pepper to taste.

6. Beat the egg whites until stiff but not dry. Stir a third of the whites into the grits mixture. Fold in the remaining whites. Pour into the prepared soufflé dish, and sprinkle the top with the remaining 1 tablespoon Parmesan cheese. Bake until golden and firm, 30 to 35 minutes. Serve immediately.

Serves 6

GRITS-CRUSTED TAMALE PIE

Zanne Zakroff, food editor of *Gourmet* magazine, is truly a gem of a cook—and a gem of a person. She once told me that every year one of her Christmas presents to her younger brother is a dinner for him and his friends, at which her tamale pie has become a mainstay. I have substituted grits for cornmeal in her recipe.

FOR THE FILLING

2 tablespoons vegetable oil
1 large onion, chopped
1 large clove garlic, minced
2 medium green bell peppers, cored,
    seeded, and chopped
1 pound ground beef
1 can (8 ounces) tomato sauce
2 tablespoons tomato paste
1 package (10 ounces) frozen corn,
    thawed
1/3 cup seedless raisins
1 cup sliced Spanish olives
1 tablespoon ground cumin
2 teaspoons unsweetened cocoa powder
1/2 teaspoon ground allspice
2 teaspoons chili powder
1 tablespoon Worcestershire sauce
1 teaspoon hot pepper sauce
1 tablespoon yellow cornmeal
1/4 cup water (if needed)
Salt and freshly ground black pepper to
    taste

FOR THE TOPPING

3 1/2 cups water
1/4 teaspoon salt
3/4 cup hominy grits
2 tablespoons unsalted butter
1/4 cup yellow cornmeal
2 teaspoons baking powder
1 large egg, lightly beaten

1/2 cup grated sharp Cheddar cheese
1 can (4 ounces) mild green chiles,
    chopped

1. Make the filling: Heat the oil in a large heavy skillet over medium-low heat. Add the onion; cook 1 minute. Add the garlic and bell peppers; cook 5 minutes longer. Crumble in the beef and cook over medium heat, stirring to break up lumps, until the meat loses its pink color, about 5 minutes. Stir in the remaining filling ingredients through the cornmeal, and simmer, uncovered, 30 minutes. Add the water if the mixture is too dry. Season with salt and pepper, and spoon into a shallow 2 1/2-quart casserole.

2. Preheat the oven to 400°F.

3. Make the topping: Combine the water and salt in a medium-size heavy saucepan and bring to boiling. Reduce the heat, stir in the grits, and cook, stirring constantly, over low heat until very thick, about 12 minutes. Stir in the butter and remove from the heat. Stir in the remaining topping ingredients, and spoon the mixture over the filling.

4. Bake the tamale pie 10 minutes. Reduce the oven heat to 350°F, and bake 30 minutes longer. Let stand 5 minutes before serving.

Serves 6

OLD-TIME GRITS AND CHICKEN SHORTCAKE

This is an upscale version of chicken hash. The grits cake is topped with a rich chicken mixture, which is easy to put together and can be reheated successfully.

FOR THE SHORTCAKE

5 cups water
½ teaspoon salt
1 cup hominy grits
2 tablespoons unsalted butter
1 small clove garlic, minced
3 eggs, separated
¾ cup grated mild Cheddar cheese

FOR THE CHICKEN TOPPING

2 tablespoons unsalted butter, cut into 6
    teaspoons
2 tablespoons plus 2 teaspoons all-purpose
    flour
1¼ cups homemade chicken stock (see page
    376) or canned broth
2 tablespoons dry sherry
Salt and ground white pepper to taste
2 cups coarsely chopped cooked chicken
1 small onion, halved and thinly sliced
⅔ cup light cream or half-and-half
2 egg yolks
2 tablespoons freshly grated Parmesan
    cheese

1. Preheat the oven to 350°F. Rub a 2½- to 3-quart shallow casserole with vegetable oil or butter.

2. Make the shortcake: Combine the water with the salt in a medium-size heavy saucepan and bring to boiling. Reduce the heat, stir in the grits, and cook, stirring constantly, over low heat until very thick, about 12 minutes. Remove from the heat and beat in the 2 tablespoons butter and the garlic. Beat in the egg yolks, one at a time. Fold in the cheese.

3. Beat the egg whites until stiff; fold them into the grits mixture.

4. Pour the grits mixture into the prepared casserole, and place the casserole in a roasting pan. Pour 1 inch hot water into the pan. Bake until the top is golden and the mixture is firm, about 1 hour and 15 minutes.

5. When the shortcake is ready, remove it from the oven and from the roasting pan; let stand 5 minutes. Reduce the oven heat to 225°F.

6. Meanwhile, make the chicken topping: Melt 4 teaspoons of the butter in a medium-size saucepan over medium-low heat. Add the 2 tablespoons flour. Cook, stirring constantly, 2 minutes. Whisk in the chicken stock; heat to boiling. Cook, stirring constantly, over medium heat until thick, about 4 minutes. Stir in the sherry, and add salt and white pepper to taste. Fold in the chicken.

7. Spoon the chicken mixture over the shortcake and place in the low oven to keep warm.

8. Melt the remaining 2 teaspoons butter in a medium-size skillet over medium-low heat. Add the onion; cook 4 minutes. Sprinkle with the remaining 2 teaspoons flour. Cook, stirring constantly, 2 minutes. Whisk in the light cream and cook until slightly thickened, about 3 minutes. Mix 2 tablespoons sauce with the egg yolks in a bowl and stir back into the sauce. Cook over low heat 2 minutes. Do not allow to boil. Season with salt and white pepper to taste, and stir in the cheese. Spoon the mixture over the chicken, and place the dish under a preheated broiler to lightly brown the top.

Serves 6 to 8

BOTTOMLESS GRITS, HAM, AND CUSTARD TART

This dish is almost like a quiche—*sans* crust. It makes wonderful picnic fare, wrapped up and served at room temperature.

2 tablespoons unsalted butter
1 shallot, minced
1 cup diced cooked ham
2 teaspoons Madeira
1 cup milk, heated
1 cup homemade chicken stock (see page 376) or canned broth, heated
½ teaspoon freshly grated nutmeg
½ cup hominy grits
3 eggs, lightly beaten
¼ cup heavy or whipping cream
⅓ cup plus 2 tablespoons grated Gruyère cheese
Freshly ground black pepper to taste

1. Preheat the oven to 400°F. Lightly butter a 10-inch glass or ceramic quiche dish.

2. Melt the butter in a medium-size skillet over medium heat. Add the shallot; cook 2 minutes. Add the ham; cook 2 minutes longer. Stir in the Madeira, and continue to cook until almost all liquid has evaporated, about 5 minutes.

3. Add the hot milk, hot chicken stock, and nutmeg to the ham mixture and heat to boiling. Reduce the heat, stir in the grits, and cook, stirring constantly, over low heat until creamy in texture, about 10 minutes.

4. Remove from the heat and beat in the eggs, cream, and the ⅓ cup Gruyère. Pour the mixture into the prepared quiche dish. Sprinkle with the 2 tablespoons cheese and pepper to taste. Bake until golden, 20 to 25 minutes.

Serves 6 to 8

BLUE CHIP FRIED GRITS

Leftovers make the best fried grits, but the second best is indubitably the recipe below. However, it comes with an injunction: For maxium flavor and taste, be sure to make the recipe (prior to the frying pan, of course) at least a day ahead, and refrigerate until it is well chilled.

Incidentally, I call this dish "Blue Chip Fried Grits" because my stock increases every time it is served.

3½ cups water
¼ teaspoon salt
¾ cup hominy grits
5½ tablespoons unsalted butter
1 shallot, finely chopped
1 clove garlic, minced

½ cup chopped cooked smoky ham
½ cup freshly grated Parmesan cheese
1 tablespoon vegetable oil

1. Preheat the oven to 350°F. Lightly butter a shallow casserole.

2. Combine the water and salt in a medium-size heavy saucepan and bring to boiling. Reduce the heat, stir in the grits, and cook, stirring constantly, over low heat until creamy in texture, about 10 minutes. Remove from the heat.

3. Melt 2 tablespoons of the butter in a large heavy skillet over medium-low heat. Add the shallot; cook 1 minute. Add the garlic; cook 2 minutes. Stir in the ham and cook 4 minutes longer.

4. Stir the ham mixture into the grits mixture, then stir in the cheese. Spoon into the prepared casserole. Dot the top of the grits mixture with 1½ tablespoons of the butter. Bake until lightly browned, 25 to 30 minutes. Cool, and then refrigerate until well chilled. Cut into squares.

5. Heat the remaining 2 tablespoons butter with the oil in a large heavy skillet over medium-low heat. Sauté the grits, a few pieces at a time, until golden brown on both sides, about 4 minutes. Keep warm in a 225°F oven until all pieces are sautéed.

Serves 6

BEDEVILED GRITS

In Indian mythology, ants are credited with showing man the bounty of corn. Zuni tribesmen claim that ants first furrowed the soil and then pushed the seed into the open rows, where it took root. Later ants ate the corn stalks so the husks would open and fall to the ground. Ants then chewed the kernels of the fallen cobs to let man know it could be pounded into fine grain. And when ants ate the best of the grain man had stored, man was forced to discover another way to soak and dry the kernels to keep himself alive. So ants were responsible for grits, too.

Ants did all of that for man, and what did they get for their trouble? Only bedevilment! To this day Zunis teach their children to step on ants from the time they are able to walk.

But have a bedevilment here of quite a different stripe: a hot casserole of baked grits, mustard, and crumbs that cries out for a chop or a chicken leg as a broiled dinner partner.

4 tablespoons (½ stick) unsalted butter
1 medium onion, minced
1 small clove garlic, minced
1 cup light cream or half-and-half
1 cup homemade chicken stock (see page 376) or canned broth
2½ teaspoons Dijon mustard
1 teaspoon Hungarian paprika
½ cup hominy grits
Dash of hot pepper sauce
¼ cup freshly grated Parmesan cheese
Freshly ground black pepper to taste
½ cup fresh bread crumbs

1. Preheat the oven to 350°F. Lightly butter a shallow baking dish.

2. Melt 2 tablespoons of the butter in a medium-size heavy saucepan over medium-low heat. Add the onion; cook 2 minutes. Add the garlic; cook 2 minutes longer. Stir in the light cream and chicken stock. Whisk in the mustard and paprika, and heat to boiling. Reduce the heat, stir in the grits, and cook, stirring constantly, over low heat until creamy in texture, about 10 minutes. Remove from the heat and add the hot pepper sauce, cheese, and pepper to taste. Pour into the prepared baking dish.

3. Melt the remaining 2 tablespoons butter in a large heavy skillet over me-dium heat. Stir in the bread crumbs and sauté until golden. Spoon over the grits mixture, and bake 15 minutes.

Serves 4 to 6

"CREAMED AGAIN" GRITS AND GARLIC

*T*his may be rich, but it sure is good! Serve it with chicken dressed in a mild tomato sauce.

2 tablespoons unsalted butter
1 large clove garlic, minced
2 cups heavy or whipping cream
1½ cups homemade chicken stock (see page 376) or canned broth
¾ cup hominy grits
¼ cup cubed cream cheese
¼ cup freshly grated Parmesan cheese
Salt and ground white pepper to taste

1. Melt the butter in a medium-size heavy saucepan over medium-low heat. Add the garlic; cook 2 minutes. Stir in the cream and chicken broth. Heat to boiling, stirring frequently, over medium heat. Reduce the heat, stir in the grits, and cook, stirring constantly, over low heat until creamy in texture, about 10 minutes.

2. Add the cream cheese and Parmesan cheese to the grits mixture. Cook until smooth, 3 to 4 minutes longer. Season with salt and white pepper.

Serves 4 to 6

NATHALIE'S SECOND HELPING GRITS

*N*athalie Dupree is one of the best Southern cooks extant. For further proof catch her P.B.S. television show, "New Southern Cooking," or get her book of the same name. "Second Helping Grits" is what I dub her signature dish—because it's simple, it's sexy, and you always want more!

This rendering calls for Parmesan cheese. Being a free spirit, Nathalie also uses Swiss or Monterey Jack when she feels like it.

2 cups heavy or whipping cream
½ cup stone-ground hominy grits
2 tablespoons unsalted butter

Salt and freshly ground white pepper to taste
½ cup freshly grated Parmesan cheese

1. Heat the cream, stirring frequently, in a medium-size heavy saucepan. Bring it to boiling, then reduce the heat. Stir in the grits and cook, stirring constantly, over low heat until creamy in texture, about 10 minutes.

2. Add the butter to the grits, along with salt and white pepper. Remove from the heat and stir in the cheese.

Serves 4

A RAINBOW QUARTET

In the South, grits are traditionally served as an accompaniment to breakfast; they come to the table puddled with melted butter, followed by frizzled ham, eggs, hash-browned potatoes, and biscuits.

I discovered grits at a less auspicious groaning board, however: the marble counter of a drugstore (long gone now) that occupied a goodly portion of The Duke of Gloucester Street in Williamsburg, Virginia, where I went to college.

Grits were served, unrequested, along with my breakfast order the first day I arrived. And I will tell you, unashamedly, it was love at first bite. But as I implied earlier, not all denizens of the South share my predilection.

The first real friend I made at college was a worldly sophomore from Birmingham, Alabama, who watched my grits consumption at the counter three days in a row before finally commenting on the obvious penchant.

"You really like that stuff?" he inquired in a low voice not meant to be overheard. "Or are you just bein' Yankee polite?"

"No, I love it. Don't you?"

"I hate grits. But you can't admit things like that when you're tenth-generation, Southern-born. It's one notch above spittin' on the Confederate flag or declarin' *War and Peace* is a better book than *Gone with the Wind!*"

"So you don't like grits," I murmured, thoughtfully licking the last bit off my fork. "It tastes so good to me."

"Taste has nothing to do with it," he replied. "It's color. Since I was a little kid I have never been able to stomach white foods!"

The quartet of grits recipes that follow (ever so delicately shaded green, pale blue, and variegated hues by turns) would have made my friend a true grits fan at once. They are all highly flavorsome menu adjuncts to think about when you are planning a lunch, brunch, or dinner party. But *not* breakfast!

Blue Grits

Blue cheese adds a remarkable tang to a "mess of grits." This is one side dish that is a natural with smoky grilled foods.

1 quart water

½ teaspoon salt
1 cup hominy grits
¼ cup heavy or whipping cream
2 ounces creamy blue cheese (such as Cambazola or Bleu Castello), cubed
1 tablespoon unsalted butter
Chopped fresh parsley, for garnish

1. Combine the water and salt in a medium-size heavy saucepan and heat to boiling. Reduce the heat, stir in the grits, and cook, stirring constantly, until creamy in texture, about 10 minutes.

2. Stir the cream into the grits and raise the heat slightly. Continue to cook, stirring constantly, until slightly thickened, about 5 minutes. Add the cheese and butter; cook 2 minutes longer. Sprinkle with parsley before serving.

Serves 6

Confetti Grits

White, green, and red: a toss-up of colorful confetti that goes well with chicken and pork.

2 tablespoons unsalted butter
1 scallion, white bulb and green top, finely chopped
1½ cups water
½ cup milk
½ cup hominy grits (stone-ground, if possible)
1 large plum tomato, seeded and cut into slivers
1 tablespoon chopped fresh basil
Salt and freshly ground black pepper to taste

1. Melt the butter in a medium-size heavy saucepan over medium-low heat. Add the scallion; cook 2 minutes. Stir in the water and milk, and heat to boiling. Reduce the heat, stir in the grits, and cook, stirring constantly, over low heat until creamy in texture, about 10 minutes. Add more milk if the mixture becomes too thick before it is tender. (Stone-ground grits may require ½ cup more milk.)

2. Stir the tomato and basil into the grits. Season with salt and pepper, and serve immediately.

Serves 4

Smoky Green-Peppered Grits

Another grits dish that mates successfully with grilled meats.

1 tablespoon olive oil
1 shallot, minced
2 green bell peppers, roasted (see page 248), peeled, seeded, and chopped
3½ cups homemade chicken stock (see page 376) or canned broth
¾ cup hominy grits
¼ teaspoon crushed dried hot red peppers
Salt to taste

1. Heat the oil in a medium-size heavy saucepan over medium-low heat. Add the shallot; cook 2 minutes. Stir in the peppers and stock, and heat to boiling. Reduce the heat, stir in the grits, and cook, stirring constantly, over low heat until creamy in texture, about 10 minutes.

2. Stir the dried red peppers into the grits, and season with salt.

Serves 4 to 6

Grits Primavera

This is a rich grits complement to a simply broiled chicken breast or sautéed veal scallops.

1 package (10 ounces) frozen peas, thawed
¼ cup heavy or whipping cream
1 tablespoon honey
2 tablespoons unsalted butter
2 large shallots, minced
2 cups homemade chicken stock (see page 376) or canned broth
¾ cup milk
¾ cup hominy grits
Pinch of salt

1. Combine the peas, cream, and honey in the container of a food processor. Process just until finely chopped, and set aside.

2. Melt the butter in a medium-size heavy saucepan over medium-low heat. Add the shallots; cook 2 minutes. Add the stock and milk, and heat to boiling.

Reduce the heat, stir in the grits and salt, and cook, stirring constantly, over low heat until creamy in texture, about 10 minutes.

3. Stir the pea mixture into the grits. Continue to cook until warmed through, 2 to 3 minutes.

Serves 4 to 6

GRITS TRIVIA FROM THE WHITE HOUSE KITCHEN

• The first President to eat grits in public office was James Madison, but he never served it to guests or even to his wife, Dolley. Why? Virginia-born Madison spent most of his political career fighting off the charge that he was a "regionalist," and he went out of his way to eat food from anywhere *but* the South!

• Grits was finally officially served at a presidential table when Ulysses S. Grant took over. Though he defeated the Confederacy, Grant always claimed the South won his appetite—so it was a pyrrhic victory.

• Woodrow Wilson suffered many physical disabilities during his term as President. To alleviate the pain of ulcers, doctors prescribed (and he ate) a small bowl of grits with cream and sugar for lunch daily.

• Franklin Delano Roosevelt admired grits so much, the kitchen staff at Warm Springs, Georgia, had a special bowl designed with a cover—to keep the grits warm when his breakfast was interrupted by phone calls.

• Harry Truman was another grits enthusiast but never ate a bowlful in the White House if he could help it. "Some things just taste better on home territory," he said.

• Gerald Ford was reputed to have tried grits once and pushed the plate away. But it is important to recall that ex-President Ford was also quoted as saying, "Eating and sleeping are both a waste of time!"

• Without a doubt, grits' greatest supporter in the White House was Jimmy Carter. When Carter was President, grits were served up for breakfast every single morning. And if you believe the witnesses, they were entirely polished off before the Chief of State left the table.

GRITS POPOVERS

This recipe came in a "bread and butter" note from a friend after much of an evening was spent discussing grits. She does not know where she got it, but whoever invented it, it is a stunner.

Baker's Secret (see page 42)
1¼ cups milk
¼ teaspoon salt
¼ cup hominy grits
4 strips bacon
2 large eggs
¼ cup bread flour

1. Preheat the oven to 400°F. Rub a muffin tin with Baker's Secret or spray with a vegetable cooking spray.

2. Combine 1 cup of the milk with the salt in a medium-size heavy saucepan and bring to boiling. Reduce the heat, stir in the grits, and cook, stirring constantly, over low heat until very thick, about 12 minutes. Remove from the heat.

3. Meanwhile, sauté the bacon until crisp. Drain it on paper towels, crumble, and reserve. Reserve the bacon drippings.

4. Place the eggs with the remaining ¼ cup milk and the flour in a blender container. Blend until smooth. Add the grits mixture and the bacon drippings. Blend until smooth. Stir in the crumbled bacon.

5. Pour the batter into the prepared muffin cups. They should be two-thirds full. Bake 20 minutes. Slash the sides of the popovers with a knife, return them to the oven, and bake 4 or 5 minutes longer.

Makes 12 small popovers

HOMINY

Some Plain Grain Talk

Like a desperado, whole hominy is known by various aliases around the country: *posole, samp, mote,* and *nixtamal,* to name a few. Actually it is no outlaw grain at all, merely whole corn that has been processed in a water bath liberally dosed with slaked (hydrated) lime or a combination of unslaked lime, calcium carbonate, and lye or wood ash. The corn soaks in this mixture until the kernels swell, loosen from the hulls, and become somewhat puffy. In passing they acquire a distinctive flavor (slightly smoky) that is highly addictive and decidedly un-corn-like.

After the kernels are washed and any residual hulls excised, whole hominy is either canned (processed and packed in water), dried, or frozen.

Whole hominy (or *posole* as it is commonly known in the Southwest, where it is a staple in Mexican households) is a highly malleable ingredient. In my kitchen it has not only been stewed, baked, broiled, and fried but also processed into a creamy mixture not unlike mashed potatoes in texture—which has become a favored stand-in in dumpling and bread recipes.

Whole hominy is a carbohydrate that is high in protein, well endowed with phosphorus, magnesium, zinc, and niacin, *and* relatively low in calories: 156 per cup.

More to the point, the ash it was bathed with is rich in mineral salts that most other corn products lack, so—particularly in its dried state—whole hominy is a highly nutritious food.

How to Buy It

Whole hominy is not an easy ingredient to find. However, it *is* available at Hispanic and Mexican groceries, found mainly in cities with large Spanish-speaking populations—usually in water-packed cans labeled *posole* (or spelled the Mexican way, *pozole*). It is relatively inexpensive.

If you live in an outlying area without "ethnic neighborhood shopping," canned whole hominy may be ordered by mail (see the list of purveyors at the back of the book).

Recently I have noticed dried whole hominy, packaged by the pound like other dried grains, being sold at gourmet groceries and specialty food shops around the country. The dried hominy requires a longer period of cooking time and is decidedly pricier than canned.

In his book *The Feast of Santa Fe*, Huntley Dent advises that fresh-frozen posole may be purchased in supermarkets that stock other Mexican foods. But in all candor, I must confess that I have yet to find a supermarket east of the Pecos that carried a package.

Whole hominy is available yellow or white, but the latter type is most commonly found.

I might add that the flour made of whole hominy is known as *mass harina* and is used for making tortillas by hand.

How to Store It

Canned whole hominy comes in two sizes: a 16-ounce and a 29-ounce can. If you are using less than a full amount for a recipe, be sure to reserve the processing liquid in the can, and repack the remaining hominy, covered with the liquid, in a sterilized jar. It will keep for weeks in a cold refrigerator.

Unused dried posole should be stored in extra-thick self-seal plastic bags or in a storage jar with a tight-fitting closure on the pantry shelf or in a kitchen cabinet. It will keep for months at a moderately low room temperature (45° to 50°F).

Cooked dried posole (left over from a recipe) should be stored in the fridge in an earthenware or glass bowl well covered with plastic wrap. Shelf life is just two or three days.

Cooked whole hominy does *not* freeze, so skip that amenity please.

How to Cook It

There is no hard and fast formula for cooking whole hominy, just a lot of cautions and cavils. Here are some of mine:

• Be sure to drain and rinse canned whole hominy before it is used.

• Canned whole hominy cooks quickly: Thirty minutes is my rule of thumb for most top-of-the-stove preparations. Baking takes longer: 45 to 50 minutes, depending on your oven heat. But always test for doneness before you serve!

• For super-smooth processed whole hominy, always add heavy cream or milk to the container of the food processor.

• Before it is cooked, dried whole hominy must be soaked overnight in cold water. Figure on 2 to 2½ hours of cooking time before the dried hominy approximates the texture and pliability of the canned variety. It is a lot of work, but the flavor is superior to any other posole you will ever sample. (One cup dried posole yields 3 cups cooked.)

URBAN POZOLE VERDE

Pozole is a Mexican peasant dish (cooked up of hog's head and hominy) that the Anglos annexed shortly after the U.S. Government annexed New Mexico back in the 1840s.

Nobody is alive to tell the tale of how Mexican *pozole* survived the border change to New Mexican *posole*, but since it is still consumed frequently (some say once a day) by most of the state's rustic denizens, it is generally agreed to be a helluva dish in any language!

Try my version (totally inauthentic, with chicken in the pot yet) for a highly urban *pozole verde*. You're right, Greene's stew!

1 frying chicken (about 4 pounds)
1 large onion, halved
2 large cloves garlic
1 bay leaf
2 sprigs thyme, or ½ teaspoon dried
3 sprigs parsley
½ teaspoon freshly ground black pepper
1 quart homemade chicken stock (see page 376) or canned broth
1 quart water
1 pound boneless pork loin, cut into thin strips about 2 inches long
2 teaspoons peanut oil
1 medium onion, chopped
1 large green bell pepper, roasted (see page 248), seeded, peeled, and quartered
1 hot green chile pepper, seeded and chopped
1 can (4 ounces) mild green chiles, drained
½ cup hulled toasted pumpkin seeds (see Note)
1 can (13 ounces) tomatillos, drained
2 teaspoons chopped cilantro (Chinese parsley)
1 can (16 ounces) white whole hominy, rinsed and drained

FOR THE GARNISH
1 avocado, peeled, cored, and chopped
1 red onion, chopped
Tortilla chips

1. Place the chicken in a large kettle and add the onion halves, garlic, bay leaf, thyme, parsley, pepper, chicken stock, and water. Heat to boiling. Reduce the heat and simmer, partially covered, 45 minutes.

2. Remove the chicken to a bowl and set aside to cool. Strain the liquid, reserving both liquid and vegetables. Discard the bay leaf.

3. Return 1 cup liquid to the kettle and add the pork. Cook, covered, skimming occasionally, over medium-low heat 30 minutes.

4. Meanwhile, heat the oil in a large heavy skillet over medium-low heat. Add the chopped onion; cook 4 minutes. Add the roasted pepper, the hot green pepper, and the canned chiles. Cook 1 minute. Stir in the pumpkin seeds, tomatillos, and cilantro. Cook 2 minutes longer. Remove from the heat and allow to cool slightly.

5. Place the pepper mixture in the container of a food processor with about ¼ cup of the reserved chicken stock, and add the reserved vegetables. Process until smooth.

6. Remove the skin and bones from the chicken. Cut the chicken meat into chunks.

7. When the pork has cooked 30 minutes, add the puréed mixture, the remaining chicken stock, and the drained hominy. Heat to boiling. Reduce the heat and cook, covered, over medium heat 15 minutes. Stir in the chicken; cook, covered, 15 minutes longer. Place the garnishes in serving bowls. Serve very hot.

Serves 4 to 6

Note: To toast pumpkin seeds, heat a large heavy skillet over medium heat. When hot, add the seeds and cook, stirring frequently, until golden, 6 to 8 minutes.

HOMINY AND BANGERS

*B*angers are mild British sausages, and hardly the expected partner of hominy. So, imagine my surprise—and delight—when I ran across that unusual combination in the Chelsea area of London. Well, here it is, punched up in flavor and in all its "adapted by Greene" glory.

3 large sweet Italian sausages
2 teaspoons unsalted butter
1 small onion, finely chopped
¼ teaspoon fennel seeds
1 medium hot green pepper, seeded, deveined, and minced
1 small fennel bulb, chopped (about 1¼ cups)
1 can (16 ounces) white whole hominy, rinsed and drained
2 teaspoons Pernod liqueur
Salt and freshly ground black pepper to taste
1 tablespoon chopped fennel fronds
Hot pepper sauce

1. Sauté the sausages in a large oil-rubbed skillet over medium heat until well browned on all sides, about 8 minutes. Remove the sausages. Slice and reserve.

2. Pour off all but 1 tablespoon fat from the skillet. Stir in the butter. Add the onion and fennel seeds. Cook over medium heat until golden, about 4 minutes. Add the hot pepper; cook 2 minutes. Stir in the fennel and hominy. Cook, covered, over medium-low heat 10 minutes. Add the sausages and continue to cook until the fennel and hominy are soft, about 10 minutes longer. Sprinkle with Pernod and salt and pepper, and cook, uncovered, 2 minutes. Garnish with chopped fennel fronds, and pass the pepper sauce on the side.

Serves 4

TWO HOMINY HOMILIES

"Pray for peace and end to this terrible fight. Pray for courage and salvation. And pray that someone back home in Texas don't forget to stir up the hominy."—Anonymous carving on a musket found at Bull Run, 1865

"It's a very curious thing
   Odd as it can be—
   But every spoon of hominy
   I eat . . . ends up as part of me!"
—Attributed to Tiny Alice,
   First Fat Lady of The
      Barnum & Bailey
      Ringling Brothers Circus, 1929

NEW DELHI FRISBEES

*T*his dish is based on a vegetarian croquette—spicy, crisp, and dappled with peanuts—that is a culinary gift of the estimable Indian cook and writer Julie Sahni. Julie's original recipe called for mashed potatoes, but mashed posole was at hand so a substitution was effected. This dish is wonderful in either rendition.

¼ cup minute tapioca
1 cup cooked dried whole hominy (see Note) or rinsed and drained canned hominy
5 to 6 tablespoons heavy or whipping cream
4 hot green chile peppers, seeded, deveined, and minced
3 tablespoons finely chopped cilantro (Chinese parsley)
¼ cup dry-roasted unsalted peanuts, finely chopped
4 small scallions, white bulbs and green tops, chopped
1 small shallot, finely chopped
Peanut oil for frying
Salt

1. Place the tapioca in a fine-mesh strainer and rinse under cold water. Place in a small bowl and cover with 1 inch cold water. Let stand 20 minutes. Drain in a sieve, pressing gently with the back of a spoon. Transfer to a medium-size bowl.

2. Place the hominy in the container of a food processor, and process until finely minced. Then add just enough cream to create a mixture with the consistency of mashed potatoes.

3. Add the processed hominy to the tapioca, along with the peppers, cilantro, peanuts, scallions, and shallot. Mix well.

4. With wet hands, form the mixture into small patties and place them on a plate. Refrigerate for 1 hour.

5. Heat 1½ inches peanut oil in a heavy skillet until hot but not smoking. Fry the croquettes, about five at a time, until golden on both sides, 3 to 4 minutes per side. (Raise heat slightly if not browned enough.) Drain on paper towels, and transfer to a heatproof serving platter. Sprinkle with salt before serving.

6. If necessary, reheat the patties in a 375°F oven for 10 minutes before serving.

Serves 4 to 6

Note: To cook dried hominy, first soak ⅓ cup hominy overnight in cold water. Drain, rinse, and cover again with cold water in a medium-size saucepan. Heat to boiling, reduce the heat, and simmer, covered, 2½ hours. Drain and reserve.

SUPER CREAMY HOMINY AND GREEN CHILES

*I*n the Old West, when dried hominy was plentiful and other social amenities scarce, the grain was often used in ways far from its essential application. There are domestic records of dried hominy used to anchor pie pastry in the oven, not to mention stuffing sofa cushions or substituting for buckshot. The most bizarre use of dried hominy took place after a local wedding in a small town in Texas, when a newly married bride and groom were pelted black and blue with hominy instead of rice. The couple later sued for "aggrieved and injured emotions."

A less violent use of hominy is limned below—a creamy breakfast/lunch innovation that owes a debt to Huntley Dent, whose cookbook *The Feast of Santa Fe* is awash with posole variations.

1 can (29 ounces) white or golden whole
    hominy, rinsed and drained
½ cup heavy or whipping cream
3 tablespoons unsalted butter
1 fresh jalapeño pepper, seeded, deveined,
    and minced
1 can (4 ounces) mild green chiles, chopped
½ cup grated Monterey Jack cheese
Salt and freshly ground black pepper to
    taste
4 to 6 poached eggs (optional)

1. Place the hominy and the cream in the container of a food processor.

Process, using the pulse switch, only until coarsely ground, about 5 seconds.

2. Melt the butter in a heavy skillet over medium-low heat. Add the jalapeño pepper; cook 1 minute. Stir in the mild green chiles and the hominy mixture. Cook, stirring constantly, until the hominy begins to bubble, about 3 minutes. Remove from the heat and stir in the cheese. Add salt and pepper to taste. Serve with poached eggs on top, if desired.

Serves 4 to 6

LITTLE RED HOMINY WITH CHEESE

*T*his tasty side dish is a hit next to barbecued chicken. I have also used it as a first course.

2½ tablespoons unsalted butter
1 medium onion, finely chopped
1 clove garlic, minced
1 cup chopped peeled, seeded tomatoes
½ teaspoon sugar
1 teaspoon tomato paste
1 tablespoon sliced pickled jalapeño pepper
1 can (29 ounces) white or golden whole
    hominy, rinsed and drained
¼ teaspoon salt
¼ teaspoon freshly ground black pepper
2 cups grated Monterey Jack cheese

1. Preheat the oven to 375°F.
2. Melt the butter in a large heavy skillet over medium-low heat. Add the

onion; cook 1 minute. Add the garlic; cook 2 minutes longer. Stir in the tomatoes, sugar, and tomato paste. Cook over medium heat 5 minutes. Add the peppers and cook 5 minutes longer. Stir in the hominy, salt, and pepper. Remove from the heat.

3. Stir 1½ cups of the cheese into the hominy mixture and transfer to a buttered casserole. Sprinkle the top with the remaining ½ cup cheese. Place the casserole in the oven and immediately reduce the heat to 350°F. Bake 45 minutes. Let stand 5 minutes before serving.

Serves 4 to 6

HOMINY DIMPLINGS WITH GREEN SALSA

I call them "dimplings" because these miniatures are too ethereal to be saddled with a "dumpling" label. What's unusual about the "dimplings" is the smoky hominy flavor. It became apparent at first taste that the only suitable blanket would have to be American Indian—hence the very green salsa on the side. Serve as nibbling food with cool drinks or as a spicy accompaniment to grilled chicken.

1 can (16 ounces) white whole hominy, rinsed and drained
½ cup heavy or whipping cream
½ cup all-purpose flour
1 egg yolk, lightly beaten
¼ cup freshly grated Parmesan cheese
¼ teaspoon freshly grated nutmeg
¼ teaspoon hot pepper sauce
6 tablespoons (¾ stick) unsalted butter, melted
Salt and freshly ground black pepper to taste
Green Salsa (recipe follows)

1. Place the hominy in the container of a food processor. Add the cream, and process until smooth. Transfer to a large bowl.

2. With a heavy wooden spoon, stir the flour, egg yolk, cheese, nutmeg, hot pepper sauce, and 2 tablespoons of the butter into the hominy mixture until smooth. Add salt and pepper to taste.

3. Using about ¼ cup at at time, roll the hominy mixture out on a heavily floured board to form thin ropes. Cut into 1-inch pieces, gently pinching down the ends. Cook the dimplings in simmering salted water until they float to the top, about 20 seconds. Remove with a slotted spoon and rest the spoon on paper towels to drain. Then transfer the dimplings to a buttered baking dish. Continue the process until all the batter is used up.

4. Preheat the oven to 400°F.

5. Drizzle the remaining 4 tablespoons melted butter over the dimplings, and bake 10 minutes. Serve with Green Salsa.

Serves 4 to 6

Green Salsa

1 small onion, quartered
3 or 4 large hot green chile peppers, seeded and chopped
8 small cherry tomatoes (preferably underripe)
Juice of ½ lime
2 tablespoons chopped cilantro (Chinese parsley)
1 large sprig parsley, chopped
2 sprigs thyme, chopped
½ cup olive oil
3 tablespoons white wine vinegar
Salt and freshly ground black pepper to taste

Place the onion and hot peppers in the container of a food processor. Process, pulsing, until finely chopped. Add the tomatoes, lime juice, cilantro, parsley, and thyme. Continue to process until chopped. Transfer to a bowl, stir in the oil and vinegar, and season with salt and pepper.

Makes about 1½ cups

HOMINY BREAD WHEEL

*I*f hominy is hard to find nowadays, that was not always the case. The late James Beard, a deep-dyed hominy lover all of his life, told of being a small boy in Portland, Oregon, waiting on the steps of his mother's boardinghouse for the "hominy man" who regularly passed through the neighborhood in a little horse-drawn cart once a week.

"Friendly and pleasant," Beard recalled. "He sold fresh horseradish as well as hominy. And carried all of the town's gossip with him!"

If I had a wish to spare, it would be for the return of the hominy man. I'd have him passing through my street once a week—not for the local gossip, but because I could make my favorite bread recipe more often.

2 packages dry yeast
1 teaspoon sugar
½ cup lukewarm water
1 can (16 ounces) white whole hominy,
*   rinsed and drained*
½ cup cold milk
1 cup lukewarm milk
1 teaspoon coarse (kosher) salt
2 tablespoons caraway seeds
1 cup whole-wheat flour
3 cups bread flour (approximately)
1 cup rye flour
1 tablespoon unsalted butter, melted

1. Combine the yeast, sugar, and lukewarm water in a large bowl. Let stand 5 minutes.

2. Place the hominy and the cold milk in the container of a food processor. Process until the mixture is the texture of mashed potatoes.

3. Stir the processed hominy mixture into the yeast mixture. Stir in the lukewarm milk, coarse salt, caraway seeds, whole-wheat flour, and 1 cup of the bread flour. Beat with a wooden spoon until smooth. Cover, and let stand in a warm place 30 minutes.

4. Stir the rye flour into the hominy mixture, and add about ½ cup of the bread flour to form a stiff dough. Scrape out onto a well-floured board, and knead for 10 minutes, incorporating about 1½ cups more bread flour. When the dough is smooth and elastic, transfer it to a well-greased bowl. Cover, and let rise in a warm place until doubled in volume, about 1½ hours.

5. Punch the dough down and return it to a floured board. Knead briefly. Let stand 3 minutes.

6. Place the dough in a well-greased 9-inch springform pan. Cover loosely with a flour-rubbed tea towel. Let stand in a warm place until the dough has risen to the top of the pan, about 1 hour.

7. Preheat the oven to 375°F.

8. Slash the top of the dough in several places with a sharp knife, and brush with the melted butter. Sprinkle the oven with a few drops of water to create steam, then place the pan in the hot oven. Bake until the bread is golden brown on top and sounds hollow when tapped with your finger, about 45 minutes. Cool on a rack for at least 20 minutes before removing bread from the pan.

Makes one 9-inch round loaf

SHARON'S HOMINY HONEYS

Sharon Tyler Herbst, my dear friend and cooking peer, wrote a delightful book, *Breads*. I was thrilled when I saw the recipe on which these were based—a real old-fashioned sweet honey muffin.

Baker's Secret (see page 42) or vegetable
    cooking spray
1 can (16 ounces) white whole hominy,
    rinsed and drained
¾ cup milk
2 eggs, lightly beaten
6 tablespoons (¾ stick) unsalted butter,
    melted
¾ cup honey
2 cups all-purpose flour
1 tablespoon baking powder
½ teaspoon salt
½ cup raisins
½ cup chopped walnuts

1. Preheat the oven to 400°F. Rub a muffin tin with Baker's Secret or spray with a vegetable cooking spray.

2. Combine the hominy with the milk in the container of a food processor, and process until smooth. Transfer to a large bowl.

3. Add the eggs to the processed hominy, along with 4 tablespoons of the butter, ¼ cup of the honey, the flour, baking powder, salt, raisins, and walnuts. Mix thoroughly.

4. Spoon the batter into the prepared muffin cups. They should be two thirds full. Bake until golden brown, 25 to 30 minutes.

5. Meanwhile, combine the remaining ½ cup honey with the remaining 2 tablespoons butter in a small saucepan. Stir over low heat until blended. Transfer to a heatproof bowl.

6. Remove the muffins from the tins and dip the tops into the honey mixture. Place on a plate to cool, or serve while still warm. Serve remaining honey dip with the muffins.

Makes 12 muffins

MILLET
Keeps You Sound of Body and Clear of Mind

My millet memoir is about a remarkable woman named Lavinia Mumphard, who cleaned my apartment once a week back in the 1950s.

What made Mrs. Mumphard remarkable was not her ability to juggle a vacuum cleaner or bend a dust mop to her will—it was her all-pervasive candor.

"I hate cleaning so much, I do it *bad*," she told me once as we surveyed the streaks on a tile floor she'd been assiduously scrubbing. "I should be a cook. Cooking is what I really do good. But I am a *Geechee* in a town where nobody—uptown or down, black or white—got a taste for Geechee food!"

Facing that fact squarely, she cleaned houses badly instead. And traveled all over New York City and its environs to do it, for she had no husband (he was an unmentionable subject) and was the sole support of herself and two daughters.

Greatly admiring Mrs. Mumphard's strength of character, I persuaded many of my friends to hire her as well. And though it was almost immediately apparent that her talents as a "domestic" were marginal, she stayed in their employ for years. As one friend pointed out after her death, "Mrs. M. was a comfort to man and beast alike. Dogs, cats, even second husbands and stepchildren, loved her on sight!" Mrs. Mumphard was also an inspired and generous cook who taught me about the Gullah foods of her forebears.

She always arrived with a worn black oilcloth bag bulging with cleaning clothes, sneakers, rags, duster, and a small iron pot. In this pot there was usually a sack of what she called "millies," a grain she would boil or steam and combine with any leftovers found in my refrigerator, then season with a pinch of some herb or spice she carried in a twist of brown paper.

Mrs. Mumphard believed everyone should eat "millies" once a day. She cooked them wherever she went to clean, for her own lunch and the lucky householder's as well. Her greatest happiness was the times when I was feeling out of sorts and remained in bed, while she went into the kitchen to whip me up "a little curing mess"—which I must admit always had me on my feet the next day.

"This stuff keeps the doctor away from the front *and* the back door," she would state gravely as she spooned the fluffy cooked millet onto our plates.

"And y'know, doctors are like devils: always waiting for a weakness in the flesh. So eat up . . . fast!"

Gullah people, who come from the islands off the coast between Charleston and Savannah, retain many of the mystical notions of their African antecedents. Mrs. Mumphard relayed a healthy quota of these warnings and signs, one of which concerned the millet we ate together religiously: "Millies is good for the body, like fish is good for the brain. But they sure ain't good together. Never mix those two in a pot unless you're looking for big, bad troubles."

As I did not cook millet at all and hardly ever prepared fish at the time, I was not much affected by this injunction. But I remembered it.

Like all mothers, Mrs. Mumphard took great pride in her daughters' accomplishments. From time to time, she would bring pictures in the black bag of one or the other's confirmation or graduation exercise. So when her eldest daughter became engaged, it was really no surprise that she sent wedding invitations to all her clients.

The bride-to-be worked as a typist and had saved her money for years (as her mother was proud to point out). The groom's trade was cloudy. "He calls hisself an advance man, but far as I can see he don't advance much" was his future mother-in-law's evaluation. "But that's just between you and me."

Their wedding reception was held in a large room, ringed with card tables and spruced up with flowers and plants, the ceiling strung with elaborate white paper garlands. My friends and I were among a handful of guests who were seated on the bride's side of the room, where we could clearly observe the receiving line and Mrs. Mumphard, resplendent in icy green satin, regally greeting one and all.

We were the first to sample the buffet, an incredible array of Geechee-Gullah foods, all homemade and brought by friends. There were so many barbecued, fried, roasted, sautéed, and stewed offerings, it made the knees weak just contemplating which to choose first. Among the platters and casseroles, however, one dish caught my eye. It was made of the millet Mrs. Mumphard and I shared so often, but the grains were unmistakably laced with chunks of fish.

As I bid Mrs. Mumphard goodnight afterward, I could not resist mentioning that combination. Her eyes turned heavenward at the query. "Bad luck," she murmured. "We don't know who brang it, but it sure puts a sorry face on this day!"

No matter how I attempted to reassure her that signs and portents were not always followed by dire consequences, she simply would not be mollified. "Bad ...bad...bad luck!"

When she came to clean my apartment a week later, Mrs. Mumphard's face still betrayed the jeremiad.

"What's wrong, Mrs. Mumphard?" I asked.

"Groom took off. Ran away with all the wedding money too. Daughter just cries and cries, night and day. And *you* know why it happened. Millies and fish in the same damn pot!"

The Grain's Genesis

More ancient than any other grain that grows, millet has been around the field and in and out of cook pots since the Neolithic age. Maybe longer. Some agro-scientists actually suggest that millet was one of the grasses that *brontosaurus* and friends chomped a million or so years ago, swishing their weighty tails and reseeding the soil with droppings as they traveled across half the surface of the earth.

Historians disagree on just where millet was first cultivated by man. Most evidence points to Africa or Asia, but a wild strain known as "Job's Tears"—which grows in the Philippines, where native lore insists it sprouted at the dawn of time—has turned the issue somewhat murky. We do know that millet's first official recognition was the *Fan Shen-Chiu Shu* (tables of agricultural dicta compiled in 2800 B.C.), which declared it to be one of China's five sacred crops.

We know millet was cultivated in India during the same era. Shards of temple urns—once filled nightly with food for the gods and recently unearthed by archeological digs at Pratapgarh—reveal infinitesimal seeds of millet glued by time to the pottery's surface.

How millet came to Africa is anyone's guess. The wind may have blown it in that southerly direction, or a stray caravan from China may have spilled some seed along its way to the Middle East. In any case, as it is a grain that flowers in poor sod and worse climate, millet took root in African soil like crabgrass (a weed to which it is faintly related) and grew virtually all over the continent.

Millet swayed from the top of the hanging gardens of Babylon (Herodotus wrote that the millet was so tall, he would not disclose its true height for fear of being disbelieved), and it sprouted between the legs of the Colossus of Rhodes, completely obscuring the base of the statue for some time until Rhodian gardeners were ordered to rip it out. However, do not get the wrong idea. Millet was no mere decorative greenery. The Old Testament in fact referred to it as "the gruel of endurance." And it was assiduously consumed (usually as some porridge or pottage) by the Etruscans, Greeks, Romans, Gauls, Persians, Assyrians, Tartars, and Visigoths too—because they all believed millet kept them sound of body and clear of mind in what was essentially "a naughty world."

The world's no less iniquitous today, but I would hazard a guess that less than 1 percent of health-concerned Americans, and far fewer Western Europeans, have ever considered a spoonful of millet as prandial therapy.

And that, my friends, is an omission to be repaired!

Some Plain Grain Talk

When I stated that few Americans or Europeans had ever tasted a spoonful of millet, I was guilty of an oversight: Birds and beasts on both continents eat it all the time.

As a matter of fact, in the U.S. millet is raised almost exclusively for hay, silage—and birdseed. That is no joke. I am told on the greatest authority that a formerly mum canary will sing its head off when millet is added to its daily diet. But that should come as no surprise when one considers the high vitamin and mineral content of this amazing grain. Rich in phosphorus, iron, calcium, riboflavin, and niacin, the nutritive value of a cup of cooked millet (90 calories) is only a step below wheat on the protein ladder. It is also higher in the amino acid lysine (one of the building blocks in the body's immune system) than rice, corn, or oats. When cooked in combination with any of the above, it will create a monster complex carbohydrate that will rival a sirloin steak! Millet is that good for the body's well-being.

Despite its unfamiliarity in the West, millet is a vital food for at least half a billion diners, including the Africans, Indians, and Chinese, and a serious hedge for survival for many of them. In Africa, according to the late Waverley Root, millet is usually the first crop to grow and the last to yield. In the absence of water, millet hibernates. When it rains, the plant awakens with a start and returns to its growing cycle.

How to Buy It

The bad news about millet, at this point in time, is that in the U.S. it is sold only in natural or health food stores, and by mail order.

The good news, on the other hand, is that millet is a remarkably inexpensive grain—at this writing much less than a dollar per pound. As there is no packaged, branded millet on the market, it is almost always sold in bulk, so a consumer may purchase as little or as much as a recipe requires.

Don't try buying millet at pet shops! The varieties sold as birdseed are often unhulled and are not particularly felicitous in a soup or stew. All millet for cooking purposes has been hulled, stripped of its outer bran layer, which is indigestible to all but our feathered friends.

When millet shopping, look for grains that are a bright gold color. Millet should have little or no aroma in its raw state and ideally will resemble sand. (Do not be dismayed: The tiny seed swells considerably as it cooks.)

How to Store It

Staying power is another of millet's myriad virtues. It is probably the hardiest grain around, neither susceptible to winter's sudden temperature changes nor subject to summer's mold or mildew. It is also highly inhospitable to any household creepies or crawlies.

I usually purchase several pounds of millet at a time and store it in a wide-mouth jar with a tight-fitting or anchor-type closure. (The mouth should be capacious enough to accommodate a small scoop. Millet is a very fine-textured grain and a nuisance to clean up if it spills.) A glass jar is best because it allows an instant survey of what's on hand.

Millet's shelf life is long. Count on six months, or longer if your container is truly secure. Stale millet can be detected at once, because it smells!

How to Cook It

My only offbeat canon for cooking millet comes from a good friend and uncommonly talented food writer, Elizabeth Schneider. She insists that millet is much more flavorsome if the grain is lightly toasted in a heavy skillet for about 5 minutes before it is added to the recipe at hand. And after tasting untoasted millet versus toasted, I think you will concur.

Millet may be pretoasted—but never more than a day in advance, please. And do not be tempted to add butter or oil to the pan; that's sautéing, not toasting!

Millet cooks quickly, about 20 minutes in a covered saucepan until all liquid is absorbed. My ratio of grain to liquid varies with the complexity of the dish being prepared, but a good rule of thumb is ½ cup millet to 1¼ cups liquid. It is also imperative to allow the cooked millet to stand, covered, off the heat for about 10 minutes for the flavors to meld properly.

Toasted cooked millet may be stored in the refrigerator for up to two days. But allow the mixture to fully come to room temperature before proceeding with the recipe.

BASIC COOKED MILLET

What I admire most about millet is its utterly adaptable flavor. Cooked unadorned, the grain has the delicate flavor of toasted cashew nuts. Prepared in conjunction with other stronger seasonings, however, it will take on myriad tinctures without losing that essential character—which is a neat trick, on the stove or off! Here is my basic recipe for preparing millet in all seasons.

½ cup hulled millet seeds
1¼ cups water, homemade chicken stock (see page 376) or canned broth, or vegetable stock (see page 378)
Salt and freshly ground black pepper to taste
Chopped fresh parsley, for garnish

1. Place the millet in a large heavy skillet and stir over medium-high heat until the seeds turn golden, about 5 minutes. The millet will pop slightly as it browns. Remove from the heat.

2. Combine the millet with the water or stock in a medium-size heavy saucepan, and heat to boiling. Reduce the heat, cover, and cook over medium-low heat until the millet is tender and all liquid has been absorbed, about 20 minutes. Remove the pan from the heat and let the millet stand, covered, 10 minutes.

3. Fluff the millet with a fork, and season with salt and pepper. Serve sprinkled with parsley.

Serves 4

SOUR GRASSES AND MILLET SOUP

Sauerkraut is an important ingredient in this hearty millet soup. I love it with sorrel, but it is excellent with any fresh, tender greens.

1 smoked porkette or smoked pork
    tenderloin (about 2 pounds)
7 cups water
1 clove garlic, peeled
½ cup hulled millet seeds
2 quarts homemade chicken stock (see page
    376) or canned broth
3 medium carrots, diced
2 large ribs celery, diced
2 cups canned tomatoes with juice,
    chopped
½ teaspoon caraway seeds, crushed
Pinch of sugar
1 pound sauerkraut, drained
2 large potatoes, peeled and cubed
½ cup coarsely chopped trimmed greens
    (arugula, dandelion, sorrel, or spinach)
½ teaspoon crushed dried hot red peppers
Salt and freshly ground black pepper to
    taste
2 tablespoons gin
Sour cream, for garnish

1. Place the porkette with 5 cups of the water and the garlic clove in a saucepan. Heat to boiling. Reduce the heat and simmer until the meat is tender, about 50 minutes. Remove the pork and allow it to cool slightly. Then remove the casing and set the meat aside to cool thoroughly.

2. Coarsely chop half the pork (or more if you want a richer soup), and reserve. Reserve the remaining pork for another use.

3. Place the millet in a large heavy skillet and stir over medium-high heat until the seeds are golden, about 5 minutes. The millet will pop slightly as it browns. Remove from the heat.

4. Combine the chopped porkette with the millet in a large heavy saucepan. Stir in 6 cups of the chicken stock, the remaining 2 cups water, the carrots, and the celery. Heat to boiling. Reduce the heat, cover, and simmer over medium-low heat 20 minutes.

5. Add the tomatoes to the soup mixture along with the caraway seeds, sugar, and sauerkraut. Cook, covered, 20 minutes longer.

6. Add the remaining 2 cups chicken stock, potatoes, greens, and dried red peppers to the soup and continue to cook, partially covered, 20 minutes. Season with salt and pepper. Stir in the gin and cook, uncovered, 2 minutes. Serve in soup bowls with a dab of sour cream in the center of each.

Serves 6 to 8

PAPA'S STEW-SOUP

I have never been to the Himalayas, so I cannot verify for certain that the long-lived Hunzan people who make their home in those mountains are really as strong and muscular as they are reputed to be. But I will tell you as gospel that their diet is based on millet. According to mountain climbers of my acquaintance, Hunzan housewives cook the grain with a small amount of meat for flavoring one day, and add vegetables to the pot (along with more millet, of course) for the next six.

This millet prescription, a one-dish dinner, is a variation on that theme.

FOR THE SOUP

1 package (16 ounces) dried white pea
    beans
2 tablespoons olive oil
1 medium onion, chopped
1 shallot, chopped
4 leeks, white parts only, rinsed, dried,
    and chopped
1 clove garlic, minced
1 medium carrot, chopped
1 rib celery, chopped
1 ham bone, or ½ pound chunk ham
2½ quarts water
¼ teaspoon freshly ground black pepper
¼ teaspoon chopped fresh thyme, or a
    pinch of dried
2 tablespoons chopped fresh basil leaves, or
    1½ teaspoons dried
1 bay leaf

FOR THE MEATBALLS

1 pound ground veal
1 small onion, minced
¼ cup fresh bread crumbs
1 egg, lightly beaten
2 tablespoons water
½ teaspoon freshly grated nutmeg
2 tablespoons minced fresh parsley
1½ tablespoons unsalted butter
1½ teaspoons olive oil

¾ cup hulled millet seeds
1 cup chopped seeded tomatoes
½ cup chopped fresh parsley

1. Pick over the beans and remove any debris. Cook the beans in a large pot of boiling water 1 minute. Remove from the heat, cover, and let stand overnight.

2. The next day, heat the oil in a large soup pot over medium heat. Add the onion and shallot; cook 3 minutes. Add the leeks and garlic; cook 1 minute longer. Add the carrot and celery, and stir until coated with the onion mixture. Add the ham bone.

3. Drain the beans and add them to the pot along with the water, pepper, thyme, basil, and bay leaf. Heat to boiling. Reduce the heat, cover, and simmer, skimming the surface occasionally, until the beans are almost tender, about 2½ hours.

4. Meanwhile, make the meatballs: Combine the veal, onion, bread crumbs, egg, water, nutmeg, and parsley in a large bowl. Mix thoroughly and shape into small spheres about 1¼ inches in diameter.

5. Heat the butter with the oil in a heavy skillet over medium-high heat. Sauté the meatballs, a few at a time, until well browned on all sides, 4 to 5 minutes per batch. Remove with a slotted spoon and drain on paper towels. Set aside.

6. Place the millet in a large heavy skillet and stir over medium-high heat until the seeds turn golden, about 5 minutes. The millet will pop slightly as it browns. Remove from the heat, and set aside.

7. When the beans are almost tender, discard the bay leaf and remove the ham bone or chunk of ham. Allow the bone to cool slightly, then pick off any meat and shred it into strips. (Or shred the chunk of meat.) Return the meat to the soup, add the tomatoes, and heat to boiling. Reduce the heat, cover, and cook until the beans are tender, about 15 minutes. Stir in the millet and cook, covered, 20 minutes longer. Remove the pot from the heat, and add the meatballs to the soup. Let stand, covered, 10 minutes. Sprinkle with parsley.

Serves 6 to 8

GINGERED AND GARLICKED LAMB ROAST

Some of the best lamb I've eaten is raised by Jamison Farms in Latrobe, Pennsylvania. I always use ginger in my mustardy marinade. The ginger theme is carried over to a side dish of millet. Simply prepared green vegetables are all this combination needs to make the meal complete.

1 leg of lamb (5½ to 6 pounds)
1 large clove garlic, cut into ½-inch slivers
1-inch chunk fresh ginger root, peeled and
    cut into ½-inch slivers
2 tablespoons Dijon mustard
1 tablespoon soy sauce
¼ cup olive oil
Juice of ½ lemon
Gingered Millet (recipe follows)

1. With a small sharp knife or an ice pick, make a pattern of small deep incisions over the top and sides of the lamb. Place the lamb on a rack in a roasting pan, and fill half the incisions with slivers of garlic, and half with ginger.

2. Combine the mustard, soy sauce, and oil in a small bowl. Whisk until thick and smooth. Whisk in the lemon juice. Spread this dressing over the top and sides of the lamb, and let it stand 2 to 3 hours, uncovered and unrefrigerated, before roasting.

3. Preheat the oven to 450°F.

4. Roast the lamb 15 minutes. Then reduce the heat to 325°F, and continue to roast 1 hour longer for medium-rare. (A well-done roast will need an additional 30 minutes.) Let the lamb stand 15 minutes before carving. Serve with Gingered Millet.

Serves 8

Gingered Millet

1 cup hulled millet seeds
1 tablespoon olive oil
1 large shallot, minced
2½ cups homemade chicken stock (see page
    376) or canned broth
¼ teaspoon ground ginger
¼ teaspoon hot pepper sauce
Salt and freshly ground black pepper to
    taste
1 tablespoon unsalted butter
Chopped fresh parsley, for garnish

1. Place the millet in a large heavy skillet and stir over medium-high heat until the seeds turn golden, about 5 minutes. The millet will pop slightly as it browns. Remove from the heat.

2. Heat the oil in a large saucepan over medium-low heat. Add the shallot; cook until golden, about 4 minutes. Add the chicken stock and millet. Heat to boiling. Reduce the heat, cover, and cook over medium-low heat 20 minutes. Remove from the heat and let stand, covered, 10 minutes. Then fluff the millet with a fork. Add the ginger, hot pepper sauce, and salt and pepper. Dot with butter and sprinkle with parsley.

Serves 8

BRAISED PORK, MILLET, AND EGGPLANT, CAIRO STYLE

This dish, from Cairo, Illinois, makes a hearty winter feast. The millet should be slightly juicy in this case. Serve it with any root vegetables.

2 large cloves garlic
1 boned and rolled pork loin (2½ to 3 pounds)
2 teaspoons olive oil
Salt and freshly ground black pepper
1 tablespoon unsalted butter
2 tablespoons vegetable oil
1 large onion, chopped
1 cup red wine
2 cups canned tomatoes with juice, chopped
1 teaspoon chopped fresh basil, or ¼ teaspoon dried
1 small eggplant (about ¾ pound), cubed
1 cup hulled millet seeds
2½ cups water
1 cup homemade beef stock (see page 377) or canned broth (approximately)
¼ cup chopped fresh parsley

1. Cut 1 of the garlic cloves into slivers. Mince the remaining garlic clove.

2. Using a small sharp knife, poke holes into the pork at 1½-inch intervals on all sides. Insert the slivered garlic into each opening. Rub the pork with the olive oil, then rub it lightly with salt and pepper.

3. Heat the butter with the vegetable oil in a large Dutch oven over medium-high heat. Add the pork loin and brown on all sides, 8 minutes. Remove the pork and discard half the fat from the pan.

4. Add the onion to the pan; cook over medium heat 1 minute. Stir in the minced garlic; cook 1 minute longer. Add the wine and heat to boiling, scraping the bottom and sides of the pan. Stir in the tomatoes and basil. Return the

pork to the pan and cook, covered, over medium-low heat 45 minutes.

5. Meanwhile, place the eggplant in a colander and sprinkle it with salt. Let it stand 30 minutes. Then rinse under cold running water, drain, and set aside.

6. While the eggplant is draining; place the millet in a large heavy skillet and stir over medium-high heat until the seeds turn golden, about 5 minutes. The millet will pop slightly as it browns. Remove from the heat.

7. Combine the millet with the water and ½ teaspoon salt in a medium-size heavy saucepan. Heat to boiling. Reduce the heat, cover, and cook over medium-low heat until the millet is tender and all liquid has been absorbed, about 20 minutes. Fluff the millet with a fork and let it stand, uncovered, until ready to use.

8. When the pork has cooked for 45 minutes, stir in the eggplant and beef stock. Continue to cook, covered, until the pork is tender, about 45 minutes.

9. Transfer the pork to a carving platter and keep warm. Raise the heat under the pan juices and heat to boiling. Reduce the heat to low and stir in the reserved millet. Cook 3 minutes. (The mixture should be slightly wet. Add more stock if it is too dry.) Stir in 3 tablespoons of the parsley.

10. Thinly slice the pork. Spoon the millet and eggplant into a shallow serving dish and place the sliced pork decoratively over the top. Sprinkle with the remaining 1 tablespoon parsley.

Serves 6 to 8

MILANESE MILLET AND VEAL SHANKS

This traditional Italian veal dish is enriched with a helping of millet—and is all the better for it. The meat adds a rich flavoring to the millet, and lightly sautéed summer squash works as a perfect match.

4 pieces veal shank, each about 2 inches thick (3½ to 4 pounds total)
2 tablespoons all-purpose flour
2 tablespoons unsalted butter
2 tablespoons olive oil
2 medium onions, finely chopped
2 cloves garlic, minced
1 rib celery, finely chopped
4 small anchovy filets, chopped
1½ cups homemade chicken stock (see page 376) or canned broth
⅓ cup white wine
¾ cup hulled millet seeds
Finely slivered zest of 1 lemon
½ cup chopped fresh parsley
Salt and freshly ground black pepper to taste

1. Pat the veal shanks dry, and dust them lightly with the flour. Heat the butter with 1 tablespoon of the oil in a large heavy pot over medium heat. Brown the shanks well on both sides, about 4 minutes, then remove them to a plate.

2. Add the remaining 1 tablespoon oil to the pot. Cook the onions over medium-low heat 1 minute. Add the garlic; cook 2 minutes longer. Stir in the celery, anchovies, chicken stock, and wine. Return the veal shanks to the pot and heat to boiling. Reduce the heat, cover, and simmer, turning the shanks once, until tender, about 1 hour and 25 minutes.

3. Meanwhile, place the millet in a large heavy skillet and stir over medium-high heat until the seeds turn golden, about 5 minutes. The millet will pop slightly as it browns. Remove from the heat, and set aside.

4. When the shanks are tender, remove them to a heatproof dish, cover, and keep warm in a 225°F oven.

5. Stir the millet into the cooking juices and heat to boiling. Reduce the heat, cover, and cook over medium-low heat until the millet is tender and all liquid has been absorbed, about 25 minutes.

6. Stir in the lemon zest and all but 1 tablespoon of the parsley. Add salt and pepper. Return the shanks to the mixture; sprinkle with the reserved parsley.

Serves 4

ROMANESQUE STUFFED RED PEPPERS

By and large, Italians are not millet eaters. They prefer rice, which they claim is less trouble to chew.

Once, however, in the raffish Trastevere section of Rome—where the young artists and writers hang out—I saw a small crowd milling around a vendor who was shuffling blistery-hot stuffed peppers on the grill of a charcoal stove. The smell took one's breath away.

I can no longer remember the tariff for this street fare, but I well recall the number I ate: three, one after the other. How could I resist? These peppers were soft inside, filled with wondrous chunks of sausage and garlic, melting with cheese.

Business was brisk and when all the peppers were sold, the street merchant merely covered his grill and began stuffing more, right there on the Po embankment. That's how I discovered that cooked millet was one of the ingredients. My Italian was not good enough to ask for the recipe, but I did watch him carefully. What follows is my oven-baked version.

¼ cup hulled millet seeds
½ cup plus 2 tablespoons water
¾ teaspoon salt
6 medium red bell peppers
8 sweet Italian sausages (about 1¼ pounds total)
1 medium onion, finely chopped
1 clove garlic, minced
1 tablespoon curry powder
½ teaspoon freshly ground black pepper
1 egg, lightly beaten
¼ cup homemade chicken stock (see page 376) or canned broth
3 tablespoons fresh bread crumbs
2 tablespoons freshly grated Parmesan cheese
2 tablespoons olive oil
Chopped fresh parsley, for garnish

1. Place the millet in a large heavy skillet and stir over medium-high heat until the seeds turn golden, about 5 minutes. The millet will pop slightly as it browns. Remove from the heat.

2. Combine the millet with the water and ½ teaspoon of the salt in a medium-size saucepan. Heat to boiling. Reduce the heat, cover, and cook over medium-low heat until the millet is tender and all liquid has been absorbed, about 20 minutes. Remove from the heat and let stand, covered, 10 minutes. Then fluff the millet with a fork and set it aside.

3. Preheat the oven to 375°F.

4. Cut the tops off the peppers, and carefully remove the seeds and membranes. Cook the peppers in boiling salted water 1 minute. Set them aside upside down to drain.

5. Remove the sausage meat from the casings and sauté it in a large skillet over medium-high heat, stirring with a wooden spoon to break up lumps, 5 minutes. Add the onion, garlic, curry powder, the remaining ¼ teaspoon salt, and the pepper. Cook, stirring occasionally, 10 minutes. Drain the mixture in a sieve.

6. Transfer the sausage mixture to a large bowl and combine it with the egg, chicken stock, and millet. Mix well. Stuff the peppers with this mixture, and place them snugly in a shallow ovenproof baking dish. Sprinkle the peppers with the bread crumbs, cheese, and oil. Bake 50 minutes. Sprinkle with parsley before serving.

Serves 6

MILLET-STUFFED ROAST CHICKEN WITH PROSCIUTTO AND GARLIC

*F*ennel and prosciutto are two of my favorite ingredients to stuff in a chicken. Millet is a third. The sage in this stuffing must be fresh.

¼ cup hulled millet seeds
1½ cups plus 2 tablespoons homemade chicken stock (see page 376) or canned broth
1 large clove garlic, minced
4 fresh sage leaves, chopped, or ½ teaspoon dried
¼ pound sliced prosciutto, coarsely chopped
¼ teaspoon fennel seeds, crushed
1 whole chicken (about 3½ pounds), well rinsed and dried
1 small clove garlic, bruised
3 tablespoons unsalted butter, at room temperature
1 cup water
1 tablespoon all-purpose flour
Chopped fresh parsley, for garnish

1. Preheat the oven to 400°F.

2. Place the millet in a large heavy skillet and stir over medium-high heat until the seeds turn golden, about 5 minutes. The millet will pop slightly as it browns. Remove from the heat.

3. Combine the millet with ½ cup plus 2 tablespoons of the chicken stock in a medium-size saucepan. Heat to boiling. Reduce the heat, cover, and cook over medium-low heat until the millet is tender and all liquid has been absorbed, about 20 minutes. Remove from the heat, fluff with a fork, and allow to cool slightly.

4. Place the millet in a medium-size bowl and add the minced garlic, sage, prosciutto, and fennel seeds. Toss well. Stuff the chicken loosely with this mixture. Sew and truss. Place remaining stuffing in an ovenproof dish, cover tightly, and set aside.

5. Rub the chicken with the bruised garlic, then with 2 tablespoons of the butter. Place the chicken on a rack in a roasting pan, and add the water to the pan. Roast 30 minutes.

6. Pour the remaining 1 cup chicken stock over the chicken, reduce the oven heat to 350°F, and roast another 30 minutes, basting occasionally with the pan juices.

7. Place the dish of extra stuffing in the oven. Continue to roast the chicken, basting occasionally with pan juices, 30 minutes longer, or until the meat juices run yellow when pricked with a fork.

8. Remove the strings from the chicken and scoop out the stuffing with a large spoon. Combine the two stuffings and keep warm with the chicken in a 225°F oven.

9. Melt the remaining 1 tablespoon butter in a medium-size saucepan over medium heat. Stir in the flour and cook, stirring constantly, until lightly browned, about 3 minutes. Whisk in the pan juices and cook until slightly thickened, about 2 minutes. Serve the gravy on the side.

Serves 2 to 4

LOW-COUNTRY JAMBALAYA WITH MILLET AND RICE

The Gullah people live on the small chain of barrier islands between Savannah, Georgia, and Charleston, South Carolina. They are a very insular group who speak a dialect not familiar to the ear, even to other black Southerners, for their English is marked with the risings and fallings of the Dahomey land of their African forebears.

As a matter of fact, they grow the same vegetables their ancestors did. They believe in the same superstitions, and they eat the same millet that grew in their homeland for centuries. Which makes them as unique as the Amish in their own way.

This recipe is a variation of Gullah cooking, highly amended by me. I beg purists to forgive the presence of chorizo and Italian sausage in place of Carolina spiced sausage, and Geechees will have to hide their eyes from the sight of shrimp and millet in the same dish!

½ cup hulled millet seeds
1½ pounds sweet Italian sausages
1 pound chorizos (Spanish sausages)
1 tablespoon vegetable oil
1 tablespoon unsalted butter
3 whole chicken breasts, skinned and
    boned, cut into 18 pieces
3 tablespoons all-purpose flour
    (approximately)
Salt and freshly ground black pepper to
    taste
1 large onion, chopped
2 cloves garlic, minced
½ medium red bell pepper, cored, seeded,
    and chopped
1 large poblano pepper, roasted (see page
    249), cored, seeded, and chopped
1 large tomato, peeled, seeded, and
    chopped
1 can (14 ounces) imported plum tomatoes,
    with juice, chopped
1 teaspoon sugar
1 tablespoon chopped fresh basil, or 1
    teaspoon dried
1 teaspoon chopped fresh thyme, or ¼
    teaspoon dried
1 quart homemade chicken stock (see page
    376) or canned broth, heated
½ cup long-grain rice
¾ pound shrimp, shelled and deveined
½ pound okra, sliced
Chopped fresh parsley, for garnish

1. Place the millet in a large heavy skillet and stir over medium-high heat until the seeds turn golden, about 5 minutes. The millet will pop slightly as it browns. Remove from the heat and set aside.

2. Sauté the Italian sausages in a large oil-rubbed heavy pot or Dutch oven over medium heat until well browned on all sides, about 4 minutes. Transfer the sausages to a plate.

3. Add the chorizos to the pot and sauté until well browned on all sides, about 6 minutes. Transfer to the plate with the Italian sausages; slice both and reserve.

4. Add the oil and the butter to the pot. Sprinkle the chicken pieces with the flour, and season with salt and pepper. Sauté the chicken in the same pot until golden on both sides, 4 to 6 minutes. Transfer to the plate with the sliced sausages.

5. Add the onion to the pot and cook until golden, scraping the bottom

and sides of the pot, about 4 minutes. Stir in the garlic and bell pepper. Cook over medium-low heat 5 minutes. Add the poblano pepper, both the fresh and canned tomatoes, the sugar, basil, thyme, and chicken stock. Heat to boiling, and return the sausage slices and sautéed chicken pieces along with any accumulated juices. Stir in the rice and millet. Reduce the heat, cover, and cook over medium-low heat until the rice and millet are tender, about 20 minutes. Remove the cover and cook, stirring occasionally, 10 minutes longer.

6. Stir in the shrimp and okra; cook, tossing gently, 5 minutes longer. Sprinkle with parsley before serving.

Serves 8 to 10

NORTH FORK SCALLOP AND MILLET SALAD

Millet can take the place of bulgur or rice in any summer salad. This one comes from the North Fork of Long Island's east end.

FOR THE SALAD

½ cup hulled millet seeds
1¼ cups water
½ lemon
½ cup white wine
1 clove garlic
1 pound bay scallops
2 medium cucumbers, peeled, seeded, and finely diced
2 shallots, minced
¼ cup chopped canned roasted sweet red peppers
⅛ teaspoon chopped fresh thyme, or a pinch of dried
1 teaspoon chopped fresh tarragon, or ¼ teaspoon dried

FOR THE DRESSING

1 clove garlic, minced
¼ teaspoon coarse (kosher) salt
1 teaspoon Dijon mustard
Juice of ½ lemon
⅓ cup olive oil
Pinch of curry powder

3 tablespoons reserved scallop broth

Salt and freshly ground black pepper to taste
Chopped fresh parsley, for garnish

1. Place the millet in a large heavy skillet and stir over medium-high heat until the seeds turn golden, about 5 minutes. The millet will pop slightly as it browns. Remove from the heat.

2. Combine the millet with the water in a medium-size saucepan. Remove the seeds from the lemon half and squeeze the juice into the liquid, then add the lemon half as well. Heat to boiling. Reduce the heat, cover, and cook over medium-low heat until the millet is tender and all liquid has been absorbed, about 20 minutes. Remove from the heat, and let stand, covered, 10 minutes. Discard the lemon half and fluff the millet with a fork. Set it aside to cool.

3. Meanwhile, place the wine and

the garlic clove in a large noncorrosive saucepan. Heat to boiling. Stir in the scallops and cook, stirring constantly, over high heat 3 minutes. Drain the scallops, reserving the liquid, and set both aside to cool. Discard the garlic clove.

4. Place the cooled millet in a salad bowl and toss in the cucumbers, shallots, red peppers, thyme, tarragon, and cooled scallops. Set aside.

5. Make the dressing: Mash the garlic with the salt in a small bowl until a paste is formed. Stir in the mustard and lemon juice. Slowly whisk in the oil, curry powder, and broth.

6. Pour the dressing over the scallop mixture, and toss well. Add salt and pepper to taste. Serve at room temperature or slightly chilled, sprinkled with parsley.

Serves 6

SOUTH FORK SWORDFISH AND MILLET SALAD

*F*rom Long Island's South Fork, where I spend my summers. I make this whenever the swordfish are running off Montauk.

FOR THE SALAD
¼ cup hulled millet seeds
½ cup plus 2 tablespoons water
½ teaspoon salt
½ cup minced celery
1 small shallot, minced
1½ cups cubed cooked swordfish (about ¾ pound)
3 tablespoons chopped fresh chives

FOR THE DRESSING
½ cup mayonnaise, preferably homemade (see page 379)
½ teaspoon anchovy paste
Juice of 1 lemon
1 teaspoon chopped fresh basil

Salt and freshly ground black pepper to taste

1. Place the millet in a large heavy skillet and stir over medium-high heat until the seeds turn golden, about 5 minutes. The millet will pop slightly as it browns. Remove from the heat.

2. Combine the millet with the water and salt in a medium-size saucepan. Heat to boiling. Reduce the heat, cover, and cook over medium-low heat until the millet is tender and all liquid has been absorbed, about 20 minutes. Remove from the heat and let stand, covered, 10 minutes. Then fluff the millet with a fork and allow it to cool.

3. Place the cooled millet in a salad bowl and toss in the celery, shallot, swordfish, and chives. Set aside.

4. Make the dressing: Beat the mayonnaise with the anchovy paste and lemon juice in a medium-size bowl until smooth. Stir in the basil.

5. Spoon the dressing over the swordfish mixture, and toss well. Season with salt and pepper. Serve at room temperature or slightly chilled.

Serves 4

RED-HOT TEN-SPEED MILLET

Some of my best millet inspirations have been found in cross-cultural kitchens. Red-Hot Ten-Speed Millet, for instance, may seem vaguely Oriental as to ingredients, but I must warn the unsuspecting chef that it is totally American "feisty" in character. Mark it as a dish for Fahrenheit-raising on the next cold night!

½ cup hulled millet seeds
3 tablespoons peanut oil
1 medium onion, minced
2 large cloves garlic, minced
1 small green bell pepper, cored, seeded, and minced
1 large red bell pepper, cored, seeded, and minced
½ teaspoon sugar
3 tablespoons chopped canned roasted sweet red peppers
1¼ cups homemade chicken stock (see page 376) or canned broth
1 tablespoon hot chili oil
1 teaspoon red wine vinegar
1 teaspoon dark sesame oil
1 cup chopped cooked chicken (optional)
Salt to taste
Chopped fresh parsley, for garnish

1. Place the millet in a large heavy skillet and stir over medium-high heat until the seeds turn golden, about 5 minutes. The millet will pop slightly as it browns. Remove from the heat.

2. Heat the oil in a medium-size saucepan over medium heat. Add the onion; cook 1 minute. Add the garlic and both bell peppers; cook 2 minutes. Sprinkle with the sugar and stir in the millet, the sweet peppers, and the chicken stock. Heat to boiling. Reduce the heat, cover, and cook over medium-low heat until the millet is tender and all liquid has been absorbed, 20 minutes.

3. Stir in the chili oil, vinegar, and sesame oil. If you are serving the chopped chicken, spoon it over the millet. Remove the pan from the heat, and let it stand, covered, 10 minutes. Then fluff the millet with a fork, and season with salt. Serve sprinkled with parsley.
Serves 4

PARMESAN-FLECKED MILLET WITH PEPPERED TOMATO SAUCE

This dish often takes the place of polenta at my table. Parmesan cheese is tossed into the cooked millet, and the whole is topped with a peppery tomato sauce. This is wonderful with grilled sausages.

½ cup hulled millet seeds
1¼ cups water
3 tablespoons unsalted butter, at room temperature

½ cup freshly grated Parmesan cheese
Salt and freshly ground black pepper to taste
Peppered Tomato Sauce (recipe follows)

1. Place the millet in a large heavy skillet and stir over medium-high heat until the seeds turn golden, about 5 minutes. The millet will pop slightly as it browns. Remove from the heat.

2. Combine the millet with the water in a medium-size heavy saucepan and heat to boiling. Reduce the heat, cover, and cook over medium-low heat until the millet is tender and all liquid has been absorbed, about 20 minutes. Remove the pan from the heat and let it stand, covered, 10 minutes.

3. Add the butter and Parmesan cheese to the millet, gently tossing with two forks to mix, and season with salt and pepper. Transfer the millet to a serving platter, and spoon some of the Peppered Tomato Sauce over the middle. Pass the remaining sauce.

Serves 4

Peppered Tomato Sauce

3 tablespoons unsalted butter
2 teaspoons olive oil
1 leek, white part and 3 inches of green stem, rinsed, dried, and finely minced
2 large cloves garlic, minced
1 small rib celery, finely chopped
2 medium tomatoes, peeled, seeded, and chopped
2 cups canned tomatoes, with juice, chopped
½ teaspoon chopped fresh thyme, or a pinch of dried
1 tablespoon chopped fresh basil, or 1 teaspoon dried
1 teaspoon sugar
2½ teaspoons finely minced hot green peppers, or ½ teaspoon crushed dried hot red peppers
Salt and freshly ground black pepper to taste

1. Heat 2 tablespoons of the butter with the oil in a large heavy skillet over medium-low heat. Add the leek; cook 5 minutes. Add the garlic; cook 2 minutes longer. Stir in the celery and the fresh and canned tomatoes. Heat to boiling, then reduce the heat. Stir in the herbs, sugar, and peppers. Cook until fairly thick, about 30 minutes.

2. Stir in the remaining 1 tablespoon butter, and season with salt and pepper.

Makes about 2 cups

M illet is officially a member of the Gramineae (grass) family, a group that has lots of offshoots with curious names. *Panicum milliaceum*, the common variety one finds in the U.S., is also known as "Indian grass" or "hog grass," depending upon your geographic frame of reference. *Echinochloa*, consumed in Japan, East Africa, and the Middle East, is dubbed "broomcorn millet," some say because its ear resembles a primitive broom. But that does not explain why *E. frumentacea*, or "Japanese millet," is not to be found in Japan at all but West Africans literally live on the stuff! In northern Italy and southern Germany they eat *Setaria italica*, which is known as "foxtail millet" or "Turkish weed"—take your pick. *Pennisetum spicatum*, known in the parts of Great Britain where it is grown as "bullrush millet," is tagged "candle millet" by the French. The French also call it *P. americanum* when they're being formal—but only they could tell you why, since it never grew over here. In India there are tropical millets and mountain millets. The best known are *Eleusine coracana* and *Pennisetum glaucum*, nicknamed "finger millet" and "cattail millet" respectively.

LOUISIANA MILLET CROQUETTELETTES

In New Orleans, *lagniappe* means a little something extra or an unexpected bequest. So, have a little millet *lagniappe* on me: Besides its other plus factors for the body, this grain has recently been recognized as a remarkable antacid—one that doctors can prescribe as a dietary supplement for colitis and ulcer patients with utter impunity, for it has no side effects whatsoever.

How far can a little seed go, you ask? Lots! As evidence, a Louisiana-style *croquettelette* that will embellish any breakfast, lunch, or dinner menu with amazing grace.

½ cup hulled millet seeds
2 cups water
½ teaspoon salt
1 fresh jalapeño pepper, seeded and minced
1 shallot, minced
1 teaspoon soy sauce
1 egg, lightly beaten
3 strips thick bacon, crisp-fried and
  crumbled
½ teaspoon baking powder
¼ cup all-purpose flour
3 tablespoons unsalted butter
  (approximately)
2 teaspoons vegetable oil (approximately)

1. Place the millet in a large heavy skillet and stir over medium-high heat until the seeds turn golden, about 5 minutes. The millet will pop slightly as it browns. Remove from the heat.

2. Combine the millet with the water and salt in a medium-size saucepan. Heat to boiling. Reduce the heat, cover, and cook over medium-low heat until the millet is very tender and all liquid has been absorbed and the millet is mushy, 30 to 35 minutes. Remove from the heat and let stand, covered, 10 minutes. Then fluff the millet with a fork.

3. Preheat the oven to 375°F.

4. Transfer the millet to a bowl and add the pepper, shallot, soy sauce, egg, bacon, baking powder, and flour. Mix thoroughly with a wooden spoon. Using wet hands, form into small meatball shapes and place on a plate. Flatten the balls slightly with a spatula.

5. Heat half the butter with half the oil in a heavy skillet, and sauté the patties over medium heat until golden brown, about 2 minutes per side. Transfer to an ovenproof serving platter. Continue sautéing the patties, adding butter and oil as needed. Bake the patties for 10 minutes before serving.

Serves 4

Note: The patties can be prepared and sautéed ahead of time. Cover and refrigerate; then bake in a preheated 375°F oven before serving.

MILLETY GREENS

Still another pot of Gullah goodness. This is my favorite fall/winter/wet spring dish—long-cooked pork and greens spangled with lots and lots of golden millet. Every forkful seems to put the diner in the pink too.

2 tablespoons vegetable oil
1 large onion, chopped
1 large clove garlic, minced
Pinch of ground cloves
2 pounds smoked pork neck bones or ham
    hocks
6 cups homemade chicken stock (see page
    376) or canned broth
2 pounds greens (such as mustard or
    collard), trimmed, rinsed, and coarsely
    chopped
1½ cups hulled millet seeds
Chopped fresh parsley, for garnish

1. Heat the oil in a large pot over medium heat. Add the onion; cook 1 minute. Add the garlic and cloves; cook until lightly browned, about 4 minutes.

2. Add the pork pieces to the onion mixture. Toss to coat, and stir in the chicken stock. Heat to boiling. Reduce the heat, cover, and simmer 1 hour.

3. Add the greens to the pork mixture; cook, covered, 5 minutes. Stir well, re-cover, and continue to cook 25 minutes.

4. Meanwhile, place the millet in a large heavy skillet and stir over medium-high heat until the seeds turn golden, about 5 minutes. The millet will pop slightly as it browns. Remove from the heat.

5. Stir the millet into the greens mixture. Continue to cook, covered, over medium-low heat until the millet is very tender and most liquid has been absorbed, about 30 minutes. Remove the pork bones, and slice the meat from the bones. Return the meat to the pot and cook, uncovered, until all liquid has been absorbed, about 5 minutes longer. Serve sprinkled with parsley.

Serves 6

GOLDEN SMASH

This creamy carrot and millet dish is enriched with a tablespoon of cream cheese just before serving. It goes well with simple broiled meats.

½ cup hulled millet seeds
2 tablespoons unsalted butter
1 medium shallot or small onion, minced
1 clove garlic, minced
4 medium carrots, finely grated (about 2
    cups)
¾ cup homemade chicken stock (see page
    376) or canned broth

½ cup heavy or whipping cream
1 teaspoon freshly ground nutmeg
Pinch of ground cinnamon
1 tablespoon diced cream cheese
Salt and freshly ground black pepper to
    taste
Chopped fresh parsley, for garnish

1. Place the millet in a large heavy skillet and stir over medium-high heat until the seeds turn golden, about 5 minutes. The millet will pop slightly as it browns. Remove from the heat.

2. Melt the butter in a medium-size saucepan over medium-low heat. Add the shallot; cook 3 minutes. Add the garlic; cook 2 minutes longer. Stir in the millet, tossing to coat the seeds with the shallot mixture. Add the carrots, chicken stock, cream, nutmeg, and cinnamon. Heat to boiling. Reduce the heat, cover, and cook over medium-low heat until the millet is tender and all liquid has been absorbed, about 20 minutes. Remove from the heat and let stand, covered, 5 minutes. Stir in the cream cheese; let stand covered, 5 minutes longer.

3. Fluff the millet with a fork, and season with salt and pepper. Serve sprinkled with parsley.

Serves 4

MONDAY MEAL TICKET

Monday Meal Ticket is a version of what was reputed to be the best hangover cure in Vercelli, in northern Italy. It is equally salubrious without the headache.

½ cup hulled millet seeds
3 tablespoons unsalted butter
1 tablespoon olive oil
1¼ cups homemade chicken stock (see page 376) or canned broth
1 large onion, chopped
1 clove garlic, minced
Pinch of ground cloves
1½ cups cubed boiled potatoes
1 teaspoon chopped fresh sage, or
    ¼ teaspoon dried
1 teaspoon hot pepper sauce
Salt and freshly ground black pepper to taste
Chopped fresh parsley, for garnish

1. Place the millet in a large heavy skillet and stir over medium-high heat until the seeds turn golden, about 5 minutes. The millet will pop slightly as it browns. Remove from the heat.

2. Heat 1 teaspoon of the butter with 1 teaspoon of the oil in a medium-size saucepan. Stir in the millet and chicken stock, and heat to boiling. Reduce the heat, cover, and cook over medium-low heat until the millet is tender and all liquid has been absorbed, about 20 minutes. Remove from the heat and let stand, covered, 10 minutes.

3. Meanwhile, melt 2 tablespoons of the butter in a large heavy skillet over medium-low heat. Add the onion; cook 2 minutes. Add the garlic and sprinkle with the cloves; cook 3 minutes longer. Add the remaining 2 teaspoons butter and 2 teaspoons oil, and raise the heat to medium. Stir in the potatoes, sprinkle with the sage, and cook, tossing gently, until the potatoes are slightly golden, about 4 minutes.

4. Fluff the millet with a fork. Reduce the heat under the skillet and add the millet, tossing gently to mix. Add the hot pepper sauce, and season with salt and pepper. Serve sprinkled with parsley.

Serves 4 to 6

H. JOHN MILLET

H. John Millet is a dish that springs from the Gullah country of the Carolinas. Good Southerners will note a resemblance to Hoppin' John, a dish eaten for good luck on New Year's Eve—hence the name. But *you* eat it more than once a year!

1 cup hulled millet seeds
4 strips bacon
1 medium onion, chopped
1 clove garlic, minced
1 package (10 ounces) frozen black-eyed
   peas
2 cups homemade chicken stock (see page
   376) or canned broth
3 tablespoons red wine vinegar
¼ cup chopped fresh chives
2 tablespoons chopped fresh parsley
1 teaspoon unsalted butter (optional)
Salt and freshly ground black pepper to
   taste

1. Place the millet in a large heavy skillet and stir over medium-high heat until the seeds turn golden, about 5 minutes. The millet will pop slightly as it browns. Remove from the heat.

2. Sauté the bacon in a medium-size saucepan until crisp. Drain on paper towels, crumble, and reserve.

3. Add the onion to the bacon drippings. Cook over medium-low heat 1 minute. Add the garlic; cook 2 minutes. Stir in the black-eyed peas, tossing with a wooden spoon until thawed. Add the chicken stock, and heat to boiling. Reduce the heat, cover, and cook over medium heat 10 minutes.

4. Stir in the millet and return to boiling. Reduce the heat, cover, and cook over medium-low heat until the millet is tender and all liquid has been absorbed, about 20 minutes. Remove from the heat and let stand, covered, 10 minutes.

5. Fluff the millet with a fork, then toss in the reserved bacon, the vinegar, chives, parsley, and butter, if desired. Season with salt and pepper to taste.

Serves 6

MILLET BREAD

A whole-wheat and millet bread of such exuberant crunch, you'll be tempted to eat it *sans* butter—the way I do—with a plate of sliced tomatoes and some cheese.

1 cup hulled millet seeds
¾ cup boiling water
1 cup lukewarm water
1 package dry yeast
1 tablespoon honey
3½ cups whole-wheat flour (approximately)
½ cup bread flour
2 tablespoons unsalted butter

1 tablespoon vegetable oil
1 large bunch leeks, white parts only,
   rinsed, dried, and chopped (about
   2 cups)
Pinch of ground cloves
1 teaspoon salt
1 tablespoon unsalted butter, melted

1. Place the millet in a large heavy skillet and stir over medium-high heat until the seeds turn golden, about 5 minutes. The millet will pop slightly as it browns. Remove from the heat and transfer to a medium-size heatproof bowl. Pour the boiling water over the millet. Let stand 15 minutes, stirring often to cool.

2. Pour the lukewarm water into a large bowl. Sprinkle it with the yeast, stir in the honey, and let it stand 5 minutes.

3. Stir 1 cup of the whole-wheat flour and the bread flour into the yeast mixture. Beat until smooth. Stir in the millet mixture. Let stand, covered, in a warm place 45 minutes.

4. Meanwhile, heat the 2 table-spoons butter with the oil in a large skillet over medium-high heat. Add the leeks, and sprinkle them with the cloves. Cook, stirring frequently, until golden, about 10 minutes. Allow to cool slightly.

5. Stir the leek mixture into the flour mixture. Stir in the salt and enough whole-wheat flour (1½ to 2 cups) to form a stiff dough. Scrape the dough out onto a floured board. Knead 10 minutes, adding more whole-wheat flour as needed to form a smooth, elastic dough. Place the dough in a greased bowl, cover with plastic wrap, and let stand in a warm place until doubled in volume, about 1 hour.

6. Punch the dough down and knead it briefly on a floured board. Let it stand 2 minutes. Grease a loaf pan and place the dough in it. Cover the pan loosely with a flour-rubbed tea towel, and let it stand until the dough has risen over the top of the pan, about 1 hour.

7. Preheat the oven to 375°F.

8. Slash the top of the bread down the middle and brush it with the melted butter. Bake until the loaf is well browned and sounds hollow when tapped with your finger, about 45 minutes. Cool on a rack for 5 minutes before removing it from the pan.

Makes 1 loaf

RAJ HALWAH
(Prune, Millet, and Almond Tart)

This recipe hails from Jaipur (the capital of Rajasthan), where the denizens celebrate the arrival of spring by squirting pink water on one another and by throwing clouds of multicolored powders into the air, dyeing the streets mauve and green and saffron.

One of the traditions of the holiday is a dense sweet candy that vendors sell in pie-like wedges. This confection contains fruits and millet, sugar and nuts, and Lord knows what else. I have never found a true recipe for it, so a highly inauthentic version follows. I suggest you serve it on special occasions (minus the waterworks and powder), in tiny slices with lots of whipped cream and black coffee on the side.

½ cup pitted dried prunes
1 small cinnamon stick
1¼ cups water
1 teaspoon vanilla extract
½ cup hulled millet seeds

2 tablespoons unsalted butter
¾ cup firmly packed dark brown sugar
½ cup coarsely chopped almonds
2 tablespoons dark rum

A JAIPUR LEGEND

Millet legends abound in many Eastern cultures, but one from India I cannot resist passing on.

As it is told in Jaipur, once there was no moon. There was only a sulky moon child, married at birth to the sun, who lived in the sky. A mere girl, the moon child's function was to toss a ball of pure cold mountain snow into the heavens nightly, then find it again the next day—a task that made her hands cold and her temper short, particularly with her husband, the sun, who had yet to physically make her his wife, much as he tried. All her waking hours were spent searching the earth until she found the snowball, which only made her husband angrier.

Sometimes he would turn his rays so bright that the ball of snow would start to melt and the poor girl would have to press it together again, shaving a bit here and rounding an edge there before it could be tossed into the night sky once more. By month's end, the ball would have gotten slimmer and slimmer as the moon child grew sulkier and sulkier and her bridegroom more and more impatient.

One day an extraordinary event took place. The sun left the sky at noon to look for his wife. Darkness covered the earth, but eventually he found her, lying utterly exhausted on a bed of plants and covered with bits of melting snow. She looked so beautiful that he made love to her then and there. And she was not sulky anymore.

The snow, melted by their love, fell on a millet plant, which promptly bloomed, bringing grain to Jaipur for the very first time.

It blooms there still, but heck, you know that already. What you really want to know is what happened to the young bride. Well, the sun put her where he'd always wanted her in the first place—behind him in the sky. But now she is called Lady Moon!

---

1. Combine the prunes, cinnamon stick, water, and vanilla in a medium-size saucepan. Heat to boiling, and boil 5 minutes. Then remove the prunes with a slotted spoon and allow them to cool slightly. Reserve the pan of cooking liquid, adding enough water to make 1¼ cups liquid.

2. While the prunes are cooling, place the millet in a large heavy skillet and stir over medium-high heat until the seeds turn golden, about 5 minutes. The millet will pop slightly as it browns. Remove from the heat.

3. Heat the prune cooking liquid to boiling, stir in the millet, and reduce the heat. Cook, covered, over medium-low heat 20 minutes. Remove from the heat and let stand, covered, 10 minutes longer. Then fluff the millet with a fork, and discard the cinnamon stick.

4. Preheat the oven to 350°F. Butter a 9-inch quiche pan with removable sides.

5. Coarsely chop the cooled prunes. Melt the butter in a medium-size saucepan over medium-low heat. Add the brown sugar, and cook, stirring constantly, until it dissolves. Then stir in the millet, prunes, almonds, and rum. Mix thoroughly, and transfer to the prepared quiche pan. Bake 30 minutes. Cool on a rack before removing the sides.

Serves 8 to 10

APRICOT MILLET SOUFFLE

*T*his warm and creamy apricot and millet soufflé is from Vienna. Runny on the spoon, it is not as rich as it sounds. It is a loving bequest from the doyenne of healthy cooking, Marina Polvay, who used to live on the blue Danube. Now she makes her home on a bluer body of water, the Atlantic Ocean, in Miami Beach.

I serve this soufflé with Mock Crème Fraîche, but purists may opt for a cold custard sauce or sweetened whipped cream. Let your conscience and your waistline be your guide!

¼ cup hulled millet seeds
¾ cup water
1 cup light cream or half-and-half
2 tablespoons unsalted butter
2 tablespoons all-purpose flour
¼ teaspoon salt
⅛ teaspoon freshly grated nutmeg
⅛ teaspoon ground cinnamon
⅔ cup apricot preserves
2 tablespoons sugar
4 egg yolks
3 tablespoons apricot brandy
6 egg whites
Mock Crème Fraîche (recipe follows)

1. Combine the millet with the water in a medium-size saucepan, and heat to boiling. Reduce the heat, cover, and cook over medium-low heat until the millet is very tender and all liquid has been absorbed, about 25 minutes. Remove from the heat and let stand, covered, 10 minutes.

2. Transfer the millet to the container of a food processor. With the motor running, pour the light cream through the feed tube. Process until smooth.

3. Melt the butter in a medium-size saucepan over medium-low heat. Add the flour. Cook, stirring constantly, 2 minutes. Stir in the millet mixture, salt, nutmeg, cinnamon, apricot preserves, and sugar. Cook until thick, about 4 minutes. Remove the pan from the heat and beat in the egg yolks, one at a time, beating thoroughly after each addition. Stir in the apricot brandy.

4. Beat the egg whites until stiff but not dry. Fold them into the apricot mixture.

5. Pour the mixture into a buttered and sugared 2-quart soufflé dish. Bake until golden and firm, 30 to 35 minutes. Serve immediately with Mock Crème Fraîche.

Serves 6 to 8

Mock Crème Fraîche

1 cup heavy or whipping cream
1 tablespoon confectioners' sugar
3 tablespoons sour cream

Beat the cream with the sugar until quite thick. Then beat in the sour cream. Refrigerate, covered, until ready to serve.

Makes about 1¼ cups

MILLET CRUNCH

This confection hails from Edinburgh, Scotland. I tasted a slice in a tea shop, asked for the recipe, and was rewarded before the check arrived. Called Millet Crunch, it is no candy bar but a solid chewy butterscotch brownie, filled with bits of almond and, yes, millet too. Millet in fact gives it the essential crunch! Kids love this cookie. So will you, because it freezes like a charm.

2 tablespoons hulled millet seeds
⅓ cup water
1 cup all-purpose flour
2 tablespoons confectioners' sugar
8 tablespoons (1 stick) unsalted butter, cut into pieces
1 cup firmly packed light brown sugar
½ cup firmly packed dark brown sugar
2 eggs, lightly beaten
1 teaspoon vanilla extract
¾ cup slivered almonds, chopped
Confectioners' sugar

1. Place the millet in a heavy skillet and stir over medium-high heat until the seeds turn golden, about 5 minutes. The millet will pop slightly as it browns. Remove from the heat.

2. Combine the millet with the water in a small saucepan. Heat to boiling. Reduce the heat, cover, and cook over low heat 15 minutes. Remove the cover and continue to cook, stirring frequently, 10 minutes longer. Remove from the heat and set aside to cool.

3. Preheat the oven to 400°F.

4. Combine the flour, the confectioners' sugar, and the butter in a large bowl. Blend with a pastry blender until the mixture has the texture of coarse crumbs. Butter a rimmed baking sheet (no larger than 14 by 9 inches), and press the mixture evenly over the bottom. Bake 10 minutes. Set the baking sheet aside to cool. Leave the oven on.

5. Combine the brown sugars with the eggs, vanilla, millet, and almonds in a large bowl. Beat with a wooden spoon until well mixed, and pour over the cooled crust. Bake until a toothpick inserted in the center comes out clean, about 15 minutes. Dust the top with confectioners' sugar. Cool, and cut into squares. Store in an airtight container.

Makes about thirty-six 1-inch squares

FONDENTINA

This final contribution is a Caribbean export, from the small island of St. Lucia, where it is sold in the open market at Castries (the capital) and everywhere else that tourists wander. It is usually offered from open baskets filled with other exotica like dried tree frog, mace eggs, and cinnamon bark 2 feet long. (I long ago rejected admonitions against eating street foods, for how else would one come up with a new recipe?)

In Castries they call this sweetmeat *fondentina,* which means "little fondant" or "broken tooth." Back home when I was trying to reconstruct the recipe, I dubbed them "joyous jawbreakers." They are like dense meringues that melt on the tongue—usually under the influence of coffee.

I serve fondentinas with fresh fruit or on a cookie tray when there's no dessert. But they're very addictive for afternoon nibbling too!

½ cup hulled millet seeds
1 cup cream of coconut (I use Coco Lopez)
¼ cup water
⅛ teaspoon ground ginger
1 cup lightly crushed whole roasted
    almonds (with skins)

1. Place the millet in a large heavy skillet and stir over medium-high heat until the seeds turn golden, about 5 minutes. The millet will pop slightly as it browns. Remove from the heat.

2. Combine the millet with the cream of coconut and water in a medium-size saucepan. Heat to boiling. Boil, stirring vigorously, until the liquid has reduced by a third, 7 or 8 minutes. Reduce the heat, cover, and cook over medium-low heat 15 minutes. (The millet will still be slightly crunchy.) Stir in the ginger, remove from the heat, and let stand, covered, 10 minutes.

3. Transfer the mixture to the container of a food processor or blender. Process on high speed until the mixture is very thick, about 30 seconds. Quickly pour it back into the saucepan (off the heat) and stir in the almonds. With buttered fingers and a tablespoon, form the mixture into small balls and place them on a buttered dish. Allow them to cool, then store in an airtight container.

Makes about 20 pieces

OATS

For a Lower Blood Cholesterol Level

I f I wore a hat I would tip it to oats, with a deep bow to oatmeal as well. For it is a cereal that probably saved my life—and certainly salvaged my pride—when I was a kid.

Though it may be hard to believe, I was once a frail child, susceptible to lingering winter colds that almost always settled in the passages of my middle ear, causing great pain and keeping me out of school for weeks at a time.

My parents' room was the largest and warmest in the house, so it was designated as "sick bay." (Where my father and mother slept during my bouts with earache, I never knew.) What I recall most vividly of those throbbing earache days is not the physical torment but the fact that I rode out the storms on their mahogany bed, under a large and comforting eiderdown that became my refuge the instant infection struck.

The pain I endured as a child was usually caused by an abscess. When an earache grew particularly intense or my temperature rose, our family doctor was summoned. And always came, for the danger of septicemia affecting the brain was a constant worry in that long-ago time before antibiotics.

On one occasion, when the infection subsided, a new indignity lay in store. The doctor insisted that when I went back to school I must wear a hat, to cover my ears and protect me from germs. My mother chose a *beret* for this function.

It was made of navy blue felt and had a little corkscrew nib in the dead center, like the handle of a saucepan lid. My mother used it to make sure the beret was pulled down evenly over my ears before I left for school in the morning.

I hated that beret with more passion than I'd ever expended on anything—even abscesses of the middle ear. I would stuff it into my schoolbag the moment I was out of her field of vision, but never in time to escape the taunts of my schoolmates. They found my beret plainly bizarre and an endless source of ribald remarks. The older boys would snatch the hat from my head and swat it high into the air like a shuttlecock, knowing I was too timid to defend my property. The younger ones merely called names: "Here comes Bert the beret," they squealed.

My grandmother, the official and blunt opinion-giver of the family, hated that beret as much as I did. "What a crazy thing to make him wear," she upbraided my mother. "It makes him look like a French waiter, Pauline! No wonder they make fun...those *gonifs!*"

"The doctor said..." my mother began lamely. But my grandmother cut her off.

"If he would eat a hot breakfast instead of all that *hozzarei* (meaning the Sugar Pops, Post Toasties, and Rice Krispies I doted on), he wouldn't need to wear it!"

"What's a hot breakfast got to do with my ears?" I asked.

My grandmother gave her daughter a wry look. "Exactly the same thing," she said, "as a funny hat has to do with self-respect! Listen to me. Take this box of oatmeal. Try it on him for a week. Lots of butter, a little sugar and milk in the bowl, and before you know it he'll be as healthy as what's-his-name from the phone booth—"

"Superman!" I piped up.

"*Supermensch!*" my grandmother amended. "You better believe he eats oatmeal too!"

Who could resist the logic? The very next day I ate my first bowl of oatmeal for breakfast, changing the formula slightly to a *lot* of sugar, and cream instead of milk.

Can you doubt that it changed my life? I never had another earache again nor wore the dreaded beret one more time. Oats were clearly the reason for that happy ending.

There is, however, a semi-sweet residual to this tale, one I had not been warned about. Thanks to my sagacious grandmother's change of breakfast, I also got *fat!*

The Grain's Genesis

*T*he oat is one grain that, historically speaking, has never won any popularity contests. Too abrasive a cereal to be chomped for one thing, it had a bad reputation for another, having been used exclusively as horse fodder and cattle silage since the dawn of agriculture. Early Bronze Age farmers are credited with the discovery of oats as animal feed when their oxen formed paths quite on their own, selectively chewing their way through fields of wild grasses and consuming only the oats, leaving the other stalks unsampled.

Alexander the Great fed his fabled horse Esepheus only oats because, he claimed, that grain, which flourished best in a south wind, passed on the velocity of the sirocco and mistral to his beast's fleet hooves. However, when offered a quaff of oat-and-honey *kykeōn*, which initiates to the Eleusinian mysteries were expected to drink, Alexander resolutely refused to taste a single drop: "I prefer neither to outrun nor to outcopulate my horse," he stated!

When man first added oats to his diet is unknown. In the fifth century A.D., Roman intelligence reported that Attila the Hun fed his barbarian troops only soups of oats, which reputedly turned them fierce as tigers. However, the sybaritic Roman army disdained to even contemplate such a "mean diet" for their foot soldiers—which may have something to do with the fall of Rome, who knows?

What kept oats from catching on as a popular food for centuries was clearly a matter of class distinction at the table. A basic food of the poor—because it flourished in lackluster soil where wheat withered and barley blackened—oats came to be synonymous with the stuff of beggar's bowls. And consequently it was shunned in all forms by the medieval middle class, lest its stamp of poverty be contagious as the plague.

It took the Crusades to first give oats a measure of respectability. A grain that was easy to carry in a saddlebag, could be cooked with minimal fuss over an open fire, and provided a soldier with the muscle to shoot a crossbow a hundred times a day had to be a serious source of energy, it was reasoned. The returning Crusaders planted fields of this grain in all their native lands: Scotland, Ireland, Wales, England, Denmark, Germany, and France—where, I am happy to report, it continues to proliferate with unerring regularity. And as for oats, over the years, it has become as respectable as meat and potatoes.

Some Plain Grain Talk

*P*erhaps because the oat was tradition-

ally a low man on the grain totem pole, it has taken almost twenty centuries for this cereal to be recognized as a lifesaver, nutritionally speaking.

Whole-grain oats, for the record, are crammed with seven B vitamins, vitamin E, and nine minerals including calcium and iron. Oats are also easily digested and reasonably high in protein. Moreover, the quality of that protein is actually head and shoulders above most of the other grains we routinely consume for their value, such as whole wheat!

What gives the oat the horse laugh (if one may bring up its earliest employment) is the degree of soluble fiber in its compound, which helps to substantially lower cholesterol levels in the blood. The American Cancer Institute recommends 20 to 35 grams of fiber in the daily diet. One serving of cooked oats is almost 8 for starters, and a half dozen oatmeal cookies puts you over the top! Oat bran (examined substantially in the chapter on bran) has even been proven to reduce the level of artery-impairing LDL cholesterol after extended periods of daily consumption.

The depressing news about oats' healthful properties is that 85 percent of the crop grown in the U.S. is still used as livestock feed rather than as a cooking ingredient and enters our diet only subliminally in the meat, milk, and eggs we consume.

A fast glance at the oat-inspired recipes that follow will, I hope, serve to change that ratio!

How to Buy Them

*W*ithout a doubt, oats are the easiest grain for American cooks to find. The highly visible round red, white, blue and yellow Quaker carton on supermarket shelves is relatively little changed from the time my grandmother stirred up a bowl of cereal and altered my breakfast patterns forever.

Unlike most grains, when oats are

milled, nothing but the inedible hull is removed. The bran and germ are retained *in toto* in the edible kernel, which is known as a "groat," though it has nothing in common with buckwheat groats. A groat is not always a groat, it seems. But an oat groat *is* the basis for all the cereal variations on the market. To wit:

Steel-Cut Oats (sometimes known as "Scotch" or "Irish" oats): These are organic, unrefined oats that are merely dried and rough-sliced. Since they are processed with virtually no heat, steel-cut oats retain most of their original B vitamins, which is a plus. However, they are decidedly on the chewy side and require longer cooking times than any other conventional oat cereal—which could be a minus to the harried homemaker. Irish and Scotch oatmeal do stir up into extremely felicitous (that is to say super-creamy) amalgams, but they are both rather expensive and hard to find except at food specialty shops or from mail-order sources.

All of the oat recipes in this book call for rolled or quick oats, which are more readily available to consumers.

Rolled Oats (sometimes dubbed "old-fashioned oats"): the cereal of my childhood, made by slicing raw oats into a confetti-like mixture which is steamed and then rolled into flakes and dried. Oats sold in natural foods stores are rolled as well, but sometimes known as "table-cut" oats. Not unlike the Quaker packaged variety in flavor, "table-cut" oats are a bit thicker, which makes them chewier in a bowl of oatmeal and crunchier in an "outrageous" Chocolate-Oatmeal Chipper. Cooking time for "table-cut" rolled oats: 8 minutes from stove to bowl. Cooking time for Old Fashioned Quaker Oats: 5 minutes on the nose.

Quick Oats: Not appreciably different from commercial rolled oats in the way they are processed, these oats are sliced finer and rolled into very thin flakes over a heat source, which precooks them marginally. The object is to save kitchen time, but quick-cooking oats lose some nutritive clout and save only 2 minutes. Cooking time: 3 minutes.

Instant Oats: a faster, express variation on the preprocessed theme. Only boiling water is needed to reconstitute these mini-cuts, but they are invariably sugared or artificially flavored and leave a heck of a lot to be desired in a "natural" food. Pass them by, I say.

How to Store Them

Oats are high in unsaturated fats, yet curiously enough have little or no storage requirements because the grain has a rare natural characteristic: an antioxidant that actually delays rancidity. As a matter of fact, before the discovery of chemical preservatives, commercial bakers often added a pinch of ground oats to breads and cakes to stave off early staleness. So it is not surprising that a package of oats should have a life expectancy of up to a year on a pantry shelf, longer still if the temperature is moderately cool.

I always store rolled and quick oats in the cartons in which they were packaged. But I also take the precaution of resealing the lids after every use with a strip of heavy-duty masking tape.

Rolled "table-cut" oats, purchased from natural foods stores, I keep in any wide-mouth jar with a screw-top lid that is absolutely airtight. I also label and date the contents legibly and keep them no longer than one year. You do the same.

How to Cook Them

Preparing oatmeal is a very personal business. I, for one, don't agree with the standardized formula on the carton. When I whip up a batch of breakfast oatmeal for two, I always mix 1 cup of rolled oats with 2 cups of cool water (that is to say, straight from the tap). I place the mixture—without the addition of salt—over moderately low heat for about 5 minutes, stirring the thickening oats from time to time until the mixture boils. I then remove it from the heat, cover the pan, and allow the cereal to rest 2 or 3 minutes longer. The result? Perfect creamy oatmeal every time, merely waiting for butter, sugar, and cream or milk to turn it into an Olympian feed.

Some kitchen savants believe that all oats taste best if they are lightly toasted prior to serious cookery, whether that be for a morning meal or for a midnight snack of oatmeal pancakes. Toasting certainly brings out oats' subtle flavor and it's no big deal to accomplish. Simply spread the oats on a baking sheet and slip them into a preheated 350°F oven for approximately 10 minutes. Remember, however, to turn them often with a wide spatula, so they toast evenly. Golden brown is the color you are seeking. Any excess toasted cereal may be stored in a heavy-duty plastic self-seal bag in the freezer. Add it to bread crumbs when you're low, or substitute a measure for ground nuts when you're stirring up a batch of chocolate chip cookies.

Though its lineage is Old World, the oat is not exactly a johnny-come-lately to the American kitchen. The grain reputedly found its way here in 1602 via a British sea captain with an eye on early retirement in the colonies. Settling on one of the Elizabeth Islands, off Massachusetts, he farmed for the rest of his life, planting fields and fields of oats—which not only survived the brutally cold Atlantic winters but stored well in his silo the rest of the year. In short order, the colonists at Plymouth followed his example and planted oats as well, which caused their livestock to flourish and the cereal to enter the Pilgrim diet with a vengeance.

Even back then, however, sensible cooks realized oats had a greater potential than filling porridge bowls. There is a curious recipe, noted in the yellowed pages of Abigail Bradford's hymnal, for a "hache of oatmeale, suet and onyions bound together with eggs" that was shaped as a fowl, boiled, and eaten on Shrove Tuesday—named "Dry Goose"!

NICE RED PISSALADIERE

This is really a pie, made with oats and a rich tomato sauce, that is covered with olives and baked until crisp. It was influenced by a French recipe that I once tasted in Nice. I always serve it as an appetizer.

1½ to 2 cups Niçoise Tomato Sauce (see page 199)
2 cups rolled oats
2 tablespoons freshly grated Parmesan cheese

1 teaspoon chopped fresh basil, or ½ teaspoon dried
2 tablespoons sliced imported black olives, preferable Niçoise
1 teaspoon olive oil

1. Preheat the oven to 350°F. Lightly grease a 9-inch pie plate.

2. Heat 1½ cups of the tomato sauce in a medium-size saucepan over medium-low heat until warmed through. Stir in the oats, cheese, and basil. Add more tomato sauce if the mixture seems dry.

3. Spoon the mixture evenly into the prepared pie plate. Arrange the sliced olives over the top, and drizzle with the oil. Bake until firm, about 25 minutes.

Serves 6 to 8

OATED HAM AND LAMB LOAF WITH DILL SAUCE

A seriously old-fashioned farm loaf chock full of oaty goodness and flavor. Try it next time you have a hankering for meat loaf.

FOR THE LOAF

2 tablespoons unsalted butter
1 large shallot, minced
1 pound ground lamb
1 pound cooked smoked ham steak, ground
1 teaspoon English dry mustard
½ teaspoon salt
¼ teaspoon freshly ground black pepper
¼ teaspoon ground allspice
2 tablespoons dry sherry
2 tablespoons chopped fresh dill
2 eggs, lightly beaten
2 cups rolled oats
½ cup homemade beef stock (see page 377)
   or canned broth
1½ tablespoons Dijon mustard
1 teaspoon heavy or whipping cream

FOR THE DILL SAUCE

2 tablespoons unsalted butter
2 tablespoons all-purpose flour
1 cup homemade beef stock (see page 377)
   or canned broth, warmed
2 tablespoons freshly grated horseradish, or
   1½ tablespoons prepared horseradish
1½ tablespoons Dijon mustard
¼ cup sour cream, at room temperature
1 teaspoon fresh lemon juice
2 tablespoons chopped fresh dill

1. Preheat the oven to 375°F.

2. Make the loaf: Melt the butter in a small skillet over medium-low heat. Add the shallot; cook 4 minutes. Remove from the heat.

3. Combine the lamb and ham in a large bowl. Add the shallot, dry mustard, salt, pepper, allspice, sherry, dill, eggs, rolled oats, and beef stock. Mix thoroughly. Form into a loaf on a shallow baking dish.

4. Mix the Dijon mustard with the cream, and spread over the loaf. Bake until golden, 50 to 60 minutes.

5. Meanwhile, make the dill sauce: Melt the butter in a small saucepan over medium-low heat. Whisk in the flour. Cook, stirring constantly, 2 minutes. Whisk in the beef stock, and stir until smooth. Add the horseradish and mustard. Cook 2 minutes.

6. Remove the sauce from the heat and beat in the sour cream. Stir in the lemon juice and dill. Keep the sauce warm for serving with the loaf.

Serves 6 to 8

GREENGROCER'S STEW

Most people think oats' place in the kitchen should be consigned to a cereal bowl or possibly a cookie jar. Not my late grandmother, however. She used the grain to thicken weak gravies and watery stews, and to meld disparate vegetables into wondrous analeptic soups. The one I recall best was called Greengrocer's Borscht, so named because the main ingredients changed according to the produce that was in season. This version was my favorite, and I dedicate it to her equally green memory.

4 tablespoons (½ stick) unsalted butter
1 medium onion, chopped
2 cloves garlic, minced
1 cup rolled oats
1 quart homemade chicken or vegetable stock (see page 376) or canned chicken broth
1 medium potato, cubed
1 fennel bulb (about 1½ pounds), chopped
10 ounces fresh spinach, trimmed, rinsed, and coarsely chopped
½ teaspoon freshly grated nutmeg
⅛ teaspoon ground allspice
Freshly ground black pepper to taste
¾ cup sour cream

1. Melt the butter in a large skillet over medium heat. Add the onion; cook 4 minutes. Add the garlic; cook 1 minute longer. Stir in the oats and raise the heat slightly. Cook, stirring constantly, until all the butter has been absorbed and the oats have turned golden, about 5 minutes. Remove from the heat.

2. Heat the stock to boiling in a medium-size saucepan. Stir in the potato and fennel. Reduce the heat and simmer, uncovered, 12 minutes. Stir in the oatmeal mixture, spinach, nutmeg, and allspice. Cook 10 minutes longer. The mixture will be quite thick. Remove from the heat and allow to cool slightly.

3. Purée the soup, in batches, in a blender or food processor. Transfer it to a medium-size pot and warm it over low heat for 10 minutes before serving. Add pepper to taste, and top each bowlful with a tablespoon of sour cream.

Serves 8 to 10

PARMESAN-AND-OAT-FLECKED CHICKEN

Crispy fried chicken coated in golden oats and cheese. Team up these cutlets with your favorite pasta.

½ cup quick rolled oats
3 tablespoons fine fresh bread crumbs
½ cup freshly grated Parmesan cheese
2 whole boneless, skinless chicken breasts, halved and pounded
Salt to taste

¼ cup all-purpose flour
1 egg
1 tablespoon water
2 tablespoons unsalted butter
1 tablespoon vegetable oil

1. Place the oats in the container of a food processor, and process until fine, 1 minute. Transfer to a shallow bowl, and stir in the bread crumbs and cheese.

2. Sprinkle the chicken breasts with salt and dust lightly with the flour.

3. Beat the egg with the water in a shallow bowl.

4. Dip the chicken breasts into the egg mixture, letting any excess drip off. Then coat with the bread crumb mix-ture. Stack the prepared chicken between sheets of waxed paper, and let stand 20 minutes.

5. Heat the butter with the oil in a large heavy skillet over medium heat. Sauté the chicken pieces, two at a time, until golden brown on both sides, about 4 minutes per side. Keep warm in a 225°F oven while sautéing the remaining breasts.

Serves 2 to 4

WILD OAT FISH AND PEPPER FRY

A totally 1980s version of fish and chips—minus the chips. Strips of oat-battered, deep-fried hot green peppers stand in for the carbohydrate, and you'll definitely notice the difference!

1 cup quick rolled oats
¼ cup sifted all-purpose flour
2 teaspoons English dry mustard
½ teaspoon freshly grated nutmeg
½ teaspoon salt
4 eggs, separated
2 teaspoons Dijon mustard
1 cup dark beer or ale
2 pounds haddock, cod, or flounder, cut
    into 3-inch pieces
½ cup vegetable oil
¼ cup fresh lemon juice
¼ cup white wine vinegar
Flour
Vegetable oil for frying
12 or more jalapeño peppers, seeded,
    deveined, each cut into 4 strips
    lengthwise
Malt vinegar

1. Place the oats in the container of a food processor, and process until fine, 1 minute. Transfer to a large bowl and whisk in the flour, dry mustard, nutmeg, salt, egg yolks, Dijon mustard, and beer. Refrigerate, covered, 8 hours.

2. Place the fish in a shallow glass or ceramic dish. Combine the ½ cup vegetable oil with the lemon juice and wine vinegar. Pour this over the fish, and let stand, covered, at room temperature for 1 hour.

3. Beat the egg whites until stiff, and fold them into the batter.

4. Drain the fish and pat dry with paper towels. Dust with flour.

5. Heat 2 to 3 inches of oil in a heavy saucepan or deep-fryer until hot but not smoking. Dip the fish into the batter and fry, a few pieces at a time, until golden brown on both sides, about 4 minutes. Drain on paper towels, and keep warm in a 225°F oven.

6. When all the fish is cooked, dust the pepper strips with flour and dip them into the batter. Fry, about 10 pieces at a time, until golden brown on both sides, 2 to 3 minutes. Drain on paper towels, and serve with the fish. Pass the malt vinegar for sprinkling on the fish.

Serves 4 to 6

CASBAH SAUSAGES

One tends to think of oats as a cold-climate crop. Not so. North Africa, and to a lesser extent East Africa too, make good use of this "never say die" grain that is able to extract nutrients from soils that would shrivel and dry barley, rice, or wheat.

One residual of oats' survival pattern is an Algerian dish devised of ground meat, cereal, spices, and lots and lots of garlic—named *kefte, kufta,* or *kefthe,* depending upon the casbah where you first sampled it. In North Africa these spicy sausages are usually grilled on skewers over open braziers under highly unsanitary conditions. Call me "chicken," but I prefer to sauté them at home—in a well-scrubbed pan!

4 tablespoons (½ stick) unsalted butter
1 medium onion, finely chopped
1 clove garlic, minced
1 pound ground lamb
½ pound ground veal
½ cup quick rolled oats
1 egg, lightly beaten
Pinch of ground allspice
¼ teaspoon ground cinnamon
2 tablespoons chopped fresh parsley
Dash of hot pepper sauce
1 tablespoon fresh lemon juice
2 tablespoons water
Salt and freshly gound black pepper to
taste
1 tablespoon olive oil

1. Heat 2 tablespoons of the butter in a medium-size heavy skillet over medium-low heat. Add the onion; cook 3 minutes. Add the garlic; cook 2 minutes longer. Remove from the heat.

2. Combine the lamb and veal with the oats and beaten egg in a large bowl. Mix well. Add the onion/garlic mixture, allspice, cinnamon, parsley, hot pepper sauce, lemon juice, water, and salt and pepper. Mix thoroughly. Form into small sausage shapes.

3. Heat the remaining 2 tablespoons butter with the oil in a heavy skillet until hot. Add the sausages, about six at a time, and cook over medium-high heat until deep golden on all sides, about 8 minutes per batch. Shake the pan back and forth to turn the sausages. Drain on paper towels, and keep warm in a 225°F oven until all the sausages have been cooked.

Serves 4

Oats have certainly had their detractors over the years, but they have never been Scotsmen. In Scotland oats are prized beyond estate, chattel, and almost but not quite beyond malt whisky! Duels have been fought to defend the grain's honor and heads have rolled when monarchs did not take sufficient pride in the national cereal.

Dr. Samuel Johnson, acknowledged curmudgeon of the eighteenth century, was not an oats lover. When he defined oats in his *Dictionary of the English Language* as "a grain which in England is given to horses but in Scotland supports the people," he caused such civilian unrest in the Highlands that a letter was drafted by the Lord Mayor of Edinburgh, advising him to amend the statement or never consider crossing the Scottish border again.

No such alteration was ever made, and one supposes Johnson never had a change of heart about the oat. But what gastronomic experiences he missed!

OKLAHOMA OAT-FRIED CARROTS

The oat is a grain that is high in flavor and low in calories—a scant 100 per ¼ cup—which makes it an ideal substitute for higher-tabbed bread crumbs in most recipes. Consider one of my favorite oat-dusted vegetable dishes as a prime example.

4 large carrots
1 egg
1 tablespoon heavy or whipping cream
1 chicken bouillon cube, crushed
¼ teaspoon freshly grated nutmeg
1 cup rolled oats (approximately)
2 tablespoons unsalted butter
1 tablespoon vegetable oil
Salt and freshly ground black pepper to
    taste

1. Slice the carrots into 3-inch lengths. Cook them in boiling salted water about 5 minutes, then drain and allow to cool. Slice each piece lengthwise into three pieces.

2. Beat the egg with the cream, crushed bouillon cube, and nutmeg in a shallow bowl. Place the oats in another shallow bowl.

3. Heat the butter with the oil in a large heavy skillet over medium heat. Dip the carrot strips into the egg mixture and then into the oats. Sauté until lightly browned, about 2 minutes per side. Keep warm in a 225°F oven until all the carrots have been sautéed. Sprinkle with salt and pepper, and serve.

Serves 4

SCOTTISH STOVIES

A second oat-dressed vegetable. This time it's pan-roasted potatoes and they hail from Oban, Scotland.

5 tablespoons unsalted butter
3 medium onions, sliced into thin rounds
6 to 8 small russet potatoes, cut in half
    lengthwise
¾ cup water
1 teaspoon salt
¼ teaspoon ground white pepper
Pinch of ground allspice
¼ cup rolled oats
⅛ teaspoon hot Hungarian paprika

1. Melt 4 tablespoons of the butter in a large heavy pot or Dutch oven over medium-high heat. Add the onions and toss lightly to break the rings apart. Add the potatoes, cut side down. Pour the water over the potatoes, and sprinkle with salt, white pepper, and allspice. Heat to boiling, then reduce the heat. Cook, covered, over low heat until the potatoes are tender, 25 to 30 minutes.

2. Preheat the oven to 250°F.

3. Partially remove the cover and raise the heat slightly under the potatoes. Continue to cook until all liquid has been absorbed, 3 to 5 minutes. Transfer to a heatproof serving dish and place in the oven.

4. Melt the remaining 1 tablespoon butter in a small skillet over high heat. Toss in the oats and sprinkle with the paprika. Cook, tossing constantly, until the oats turn golden, about 2 minutes. Sprinkle them over the potatoes and return to the oven for 5 minutes before serving.

Serves 4 to 6

NIZZA PIZZA

I lived in the south of France at one time, not far from Nice, a city that belonged to Italy hundreds of years ago and still bears it an emotional allegiance—mainly in relation to the foods indigenous to the area, like pizza dappled and drizzled with a wondrous anchovy-tinged tomato sauce. I used to frequent a small stall on the waterfront that stayed open all night, serving a special oat-crusted pizza that everyone called *Nizza*—which was, in fact, the Italian name for Nice those hundreds of years ago.

2½ cups Niçoise Tomato Sauce (recipe
*   follows), warmed*
2 cups rolled oats
1 cup ricotta cheese
1½ cups grated mozzarella cheese
½ to ¾ cup chopped salami or pepperoni,
*   or 7 Casbah Sausages (see page 197),*
*   chopped*

1. Preheat the oven to 400°F. Lightly grease a 12-inch pizza pan.

2. In a mixing bowl, combine 2 cups of the warm tomato sauce with the oats, and stir well. Spread the mixture over the bottom of the prepared pizza pan. Bake until crisp, about 15 to 18 minutes. Set aside to cool. Raise the oven heat to 425°F.

3. Spread the ricotta over the cooled pizza, then sprinkle with the remaining ½ cup tomato sauce. Sprinkle with the mozzarella and then the salami. Bake until bubbly, 12 to 15 minutes.

Serves 4 to 6

Niçoise Tomato Sauce

2 tablespoons unsalted butter
1 tablespoon olive oil
1 medium onion, finely chopped
1 clove garlic, minced

1½ teaspoons anchovy paste
½ cup clam broth
1½ cups chopped, seeded fresh tomatoes
1 cup tomato sauce
½ teaspoon chopped fresh oregano, or ¼
*   teaspoon dried*
¼ teaspoon chopped fresh thyme, or a
*   pinch of dried*
1 tablespoon chopped fresh basil, or 1
*   teaspoon dried*
Salt and freshly ground black pepper to
*   taste*

Heat the butter with the oil in a large saucepan over medium-low heat. Add the onion; cook 1 minute. Add the garlic; cook 2 minutes. Stir in the anchovy paste, clam broth, tomatoes, tomato sauce, and herbs. Heat to boiling. Reduce the heat and simmer, uncovered, until the tomatoes are soft, about 20 minutes. Season with salt and pepper.

Makes about 2½ cups

EIDERDOWN PANCAKES

Oats are not unfamiliar at the breakfast table. But in pancakes? Yes, and delicious as well as healthy.

1 cup all-purpose flour
½ cup quick rolled oats
1 tablespoon baking powder
½ teaspoon salt
1½ cups buttermilk
2 tablespoons vegetable oil
3 eggs, separated
Melted butter
Maple syrup

1. Combine the flour with the oats, baking powder, and salt in a large bowl. Beat in the buttermilk, vegetable oil, and egg yolks.

2. Beat the egg whites until stiff, and fold them into the batter.

3. Heat a lightly greased griddle or heavy skillet over medium heat. Pour about ¼ cup batter for each pancake on the griddle and cook until the underside is golden brown and the top is bubbly, about 2 minutes. Turn over, and lightly brown the other side. Keep warm in a 225°F oven while preparing the remaining pancakes. Serve with melted butter and maple syrup.

Makes about 12 pancakes

GRIDDLE SCONES

Straight from Scotland and another tasty way to add oats to your morning meal.

1 cup quick rolled oats
1 cup all-purpose flour
½ teaspoon salt
2 teaspoons cream of tartar
1 teaspoon baking soda
¼ cup (½ stick) unsalted butter, chilled
⅔ cup heavy or whipping cream

1. Place the oats in the container of a food processor, and process until fine, 1 minute. Transfer to a large bowl and add the flour, salt, cream of tartar, and baking soda. Mix well. Cut in the butter with a knife, and blend with a pastry blender until the mixture has the texture of coarse crumbs. Stir in the cream.

2. Transfer the dough to a lightly floured board, knead briefly, and roll it out to form a circle about ½ inch thick. Cut the dough into six pie-shaped wedges.

3. Rub a 9- to 10-inch cast-iron skillet with flour and place it over medium-low heat for 5 minutes. Then cook the scones in the skillet, three at a time, 8 minutes per side.

Makes 6 scones

EDIE ACSELL'S MUFFIN PAN CRISPIES

*E*die is a good friend, great teacher, and wonderful cook who lives in Denver. Her sweet muffins must be handled gently. They are fragile, but well worth the care.

Baker's Secret (see page 42) or vegetable
  cooking spray
8 tablespoons (1 stick) unsalted butter, at
  room temperature
¼ cup plus ⅓ cup firmly packed light
  brown sugar
¼ teaspoon salt
½ teaspoon baking powder
1 teaspoon vanilla extract
1½ cups quick rolled oats
1 tablespoon milk
⅓ cup raisins, plumped in boiling water to
  cover and drained
¼ cup hot water
¼ teaspoon ground cinnamon
⅛ teaspoon freshly grated nutmeg

1. Preheat the oven to 350°F. Rub a muffin tin (with 2-inch bottoms) with Baker's Secret or spray with a vegetable cooking spray.

2. In the medium-size bowl of an electric mixer, beat 4 tablespoons of the butter with ¼ cup brown sugar at medium speed until smooth. Beat in the salt, baking powder, and vanilla. Then on low speed, beat in the oats and milk until well mixed. Work in the raisins with your hands.

3. Place about 1½ tablespoons batter in each of the prepared muffin cups. Gently smooth the tops with a fork. Bake 15 minutes.

4. Meanwhile, melt the remaining 4 tablespoons butter in a small saucepan over medium-low heat. Stir in the ⅓ cup brown sugar, the hot water, and the cinnamon and nutmeg. Cook 2 minutes, then remove from the heat.

5. Spoon the hot butter mixture over the muffins, about 2 tablespoons per cup. Return to the oven and bake 15 minutes longer.

6. Cool the muffins in the tin on a cake rack for 5 minutes. Then loosen the

OATMEAL THERAPY

Round the world, oats seem to have a singular reputation for homeopathic cures. Why? I have no idea. But here are a few examples.

In Russia, they believe a poultice compounded of equal parts hot oatmeal and hot dry mustard will stave off an imminent case of pneumonia. That is to say, if the patient's epidermis can survive the treatment. From Scotland comes more soothing stuff: There they prescribe a lotion of oats and rosewater for rough hands and knobby knees. In the Swiss Alps, oats and cream pounded to a paste is said to allay chilblains and other snow burns. In Japan, cold oatmeal forced into the nostrils will stop a nosebleed, they say. And in Rio de Janeiro, a facial mask of oatmeal cooked in wine will not only cleanse the pores but give the sinuses a jolt at the same time—at least in my opinion. In Germany, habitual drinkers consume a bowl of oatmeal and fried onions to rid of them of a hangover. And in the French provinces the peasants chew oats—straight from the fields—to sweeten their breath after eating garlic.

edges with a sharp knife and let them stand, still in the tin, until firm, about 10 minutes longer. Invert the muffins onto a parchment- or brown-paper-lined cake rack and allow to cool completely.
Makes 12 muffins

OATED APPLESAUCE MUFFS

Oatmeal turns baked products into creamy-textured goods that seem so rich that a dab of honey—without butter—is the only thing one would want to top them with.

Baker's Secret (see page 42) or vegetable
    cooking spray
1¼ cups all-purpose flour
1¼ cups quick rolled oats
¼ cup firmly packed light brown sugar
1 tablespoon baking powder
¼ teaspoon baking soda
¼ teaspoon salt
1 teaspoon ground cinnamon
Pinch of ground cloves
⅛ teaspoon freshly grated nutmeg
1 egg
¾ cup milk
3 tablespoons vegetable oil
1 cup homemade applesauce (see page 40)

1. Preheat the oven to 425°F. Rub a muffin tin with Baker's Secret or spray with a vegetable cooking spray.

2. In a medium-size bowl, combine the flour, oats, brown sugar, baking powder, baking soda, salt, cinnamon, cloves, and nutmeg. Mix well.

3. In a large bowl, combine the egg, milk, oil, and applesauce. Stir in the dry ingredients, and mix well. Spoon the batter into the prepared muffin cups so they are two-thirds full. Bake until firm and golden, 18 to 20 minutes.
Makes 12 muffins

GOLDEN OAT BISCUITS

I warrant that you'll never taste a crumblier biscuit—but it's so good you won't want to leave any of those crumbs either!

1 cup rolled oats
1⅓ cups all-purpose flour
1 tablespoon baking powder
½ teaspoon salt
3 tablespoons unsalted butter, chilled
2 tablespoons lard, chilled
1 cup heavy or whipping cream

1. Preheat the oven to 450°F.

2. Place the oats in the container of a food processor, and process until fine, 1 minute. Transfer to a large bowl, and add the flour, baking powder, and salt. Mix well. Cut in the butter and lard, blending with a pastry blender until the mixture has the texture of coarse crumbs. Stir in the cream. The dough will be slightly tacky.

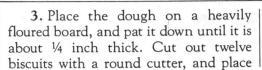

3. Place the dough on a heavily floured board, and pat it down until it is about ¼ inch thick. Cut out twelve biscuits with a round cutter, and place them on a flour-rubbed baking sheet. Bake until puffed and golden brown, 12 to 15 minutes.

Makes 12 biscuits

A country girl from the small town of Czenstochowa in Poland, where the present Pope was also born, my grandmother left her family, friends, and native land the day she turned eighteen and married my grandfather, never looking back nor seeming to regret the rupture.

When I was a small boy, the story of my grandmother's exodus from Europe to America held a magnetic fascination, and I would ply her with question after question about "the old country" and her life on the farm, queries that she would sometimes answer lyrically and at other times refuse to think about.

"It's too long ago... Who remembers?" She would shake her head. "Besides, it's a mistake to think about that old stuff. The past is past."

But my mind was suffused with images of ancestral connections—borrowed no doubt from pastoral movies in which peasants frolicked happily all day long—that would not be dismissed. So my questioning went on.

One day when we were having lunch together, I abruptly put down my fork. "Did you really leave Poland with nothing but the clothes you had on, Grandma?"

She thought about it for a while before speaking. "Listen, we weren't rich, but I left with a trunk. It wasn't a big trunk, but it held my wedding dress, two changes of underwear, and two sheets and pillowcases. Sheets I sewed by hand when I was your age."

"And that was all?"

My grandmother nodded. Then, remembering something, she went to the dresser where all the important family papers were kept. From a bottom drawer filled with lace napkins and damask cloths, she extracted a small tissue-wrapped package. I watched as she folded back the paper. Inside was a small gilt-bordered card—or what must once have been gilt, since it was now broken in many places and tarnished with age. In the center was pinned a brittle clump of dried flowers that on careful scrutiny appeared to be a bunch of grains with most of the spikelets missing.

"My mother gave this to me the day I left her house." My grandmother spoke very softly, holding the card away from my hands. "It's a barometer made of oats. If you hold it upside down, the little branches shake to one side or another, and you can tell if the weather will be good or bad."

"Hold it upside down, Grandma," I cried. She did, and sure enough there was an involuntary tremor—or so it seems now—to the left.

We both laughed with delight.

"But what does it mean? Rain or shine?"

My grandmother did not answer, for she was preoccupied, replacing the card in its tissue covering.

"Listen," she said at last, "this all happened over fifty years ago, and the truth is *I can't remember!*"

GOOD-FOR-WHAT-AILS-YOU BREAD

My grandmother made a wonderful bread compounded of rye, wheat, chopped nuts, and oats of course. It was simply known as Good-For-What-Ails-You Bread— and so it was.

¾ cup quick rolled oats
1¾ cups lukewarm water
2 tablespoons unsalted butter
1 package dry yeast
Pinch of sugar
½ cup rye flour
½ cup whole-wheat flour
2½ to 3 cups bread flour
¼ cup slivered blanched almonds, toasted
    (see Note) and chopped
¼ cup walnut halves, chopped
1 tablespoon unsalted butter, melted

1. Combine ½ cup of the oats with 1 cup of the lukewarm water in a medium-size saucepan. Heat to boiling, then remove from the heat. Stir in the 2 tablespoons butter, and let cool to lukewarm.

2. Meanwhile, sprinkle the yeast over ¼ cup of the lukewarm water in a large bowl. Stir in the sugar, and let stand 5 minutes.

3. Stir the lukewarm oat mixture into the yeast mixture along with the remaining ½ cup lukewarm water, the rye flour, whole-wheat flour, and enough bread flour to make a stiff dough, about 2 cups. Transfer to a floured board and knead for 10 minutes, working in more bread flour as needed. Transfer the dough to a lightly greased bowl, cover with plastic wrap, and let rise in a warm place until doubled in volume, about 1 hour.

4. Punch the dough down and transfer it to a floured board. Knead in the almonds, walnuts, and remaining ¼ cup oats. Let stand 2 minutes.

5. Grease a standard-size loaf pan and place the dough in it. Cover the pan loosely with a flour-rubbed tea towel, and let it stand until doubled in volume, about 1 hour.

6. Preheat the oven to 375°F.

7. Slash the top of the dough with a sharp knife, and brush with the melted butter. Bake until the bread is golden brown and sounds hollow when tapped with your finger, about 45 minutes. Cool in the pan on a rack.

Makes 1 loaf

Note: To toast slivered almonds, heat a dry small skillet over medium heat. Toast, stirring frequently, until golden, 6 to 8 minutes.

MELTED CHEESE BATTER BREAD

This is an easy recipe for bread that is made in a 9 by 13-inch pan. It's a great party dish. Cut the pieces about ½ inch thick, and then in half across. I often fry the leftover bread in olive oil for toast fingers.

1 cup milk, lukewarm
2 teaspoons sugar
1 package dry yeast
½ cup heavy or whipping cream,
    lukewarm
3½ cups all-purpose flour
3 eggs, lightly beaten
1 teaspoon salt
½ teaspoon freshly ground black pepper
½ teaspoon hot Hungarian paprika
9 tablespoons unsalted butter, melted and
    cooled to lukewarm
1½ cups grated sharp Cheddar cheese
1¼ cups rolled oats (approximately)

1. Place ¼ cup of the lukewarm milk in a large bowl. Sprinkle it with the sugar and yeast, and let stand 5 minutes. Stir in the remaining milk, the lukewarm cream, and 1½ cups of the flour. Cover with plastic wrap and let rise in a warm place 45 minutes.

2. Stir the eggs into the yeast mixture. Then stir in the remaining 2 cups flour, the salt, pepper, paprika, and 8 tablespoons of the melted butter. Mix thoroughly, and stir in the cheese and 1 cup of the oats. Transfer the batter to a lightly greased 9 by 13-inch baking pan. Lightly brush the top with the remaining 1 tablespoon butter, and sprinkle with the remaining 3 to 4 tablespoons oats. Let stand, uncovered, until doubled in volume, about 1½ hours.

3. Preheat the oven to 375°F.

4. Bake until the bread is golden on top, about 30 minutes. Serve slightly warm.

Serves 8

OHIO OLD-FASHIONED OAT CAKE

Jim Fobel is a young baker with a good memory and some fine family recipes. This devise, adapted from his *Old Fashioned Baking Book*, is a moist and spicy single-layer oat cake topped with a super-crunchy (more oats) frosting that is broiled till bubbly. It's a cake that makes friends every time it's served.

FOR THE CAKE
1 cup rolled oats
1¼ cups boiling water
1½ cups all-purpose flour
1 teaspoon ground cinnamon
½ teaspoon baking powder
½ teaspoon baking soda
½ teaspoon salt
8 tablespoons (1 stick) unsalted butter, at
    room temperature
¾ cup firmly packed dark brown sugar
½ cup granulated sugar
2 large eggs
1 teaspoon vanilla extract

FOR THE TOPPING
4 tablespoons (½ stick) unsalted butter
⅓ cup evaporated milk
½ cup firmly packed dark brown sugar
½ cup rolled oats
½ cup shredded sweetened coconut
½ cup chopped walnuts
½ cup chopped pecans

1. Make the cake: Preheat the oven to 350°F. Lightly butter and flour a 9-inch springform pan.

2. Place the oats in a medium-size heatproof bowl and pour the boiling wa-

ter over them. Stir until well mixed, then allow to cool to lukewarm.

3. Combine the flour, cinnamon, baking powder, baking soda, and salt in a bowl. Set aside.

4. In the large bowl of an electric mixer, beat the butter until light and fluffy. Slowly beat in the two sugars. Then beat in the eggs, one at a time, beating thoroughly after each addition. Beat in the vanilla.

5. On low speed, add the dry mixture to the butter mixture in three batches, alternating with three batches of the oatmeal. Beat only until mixed—do not overbeat.

6. Pour the mixture into the prepared pan. Place the pan in the center of the oven and bake until firm, 30 to 35 minutes. Cool on a rack, then remove the sides of the springform pan. Transfer the cake to a baking sheet.

7. Make the topping: Preheat the broiling unit.

8. Combine the butter and evaporated milk in a medium-size saucepan. Heat slowly to a simmer, stirring to melt the butter. Add the brown sugar, and stir until dissolved. Remove the pan from the heat, and stir in the oats, coconut, walnuts, and pecans. Spoon this mixture over the top of the cake. Heat the cake under the broiler until the topping is bubbling and golden brown, about 2 minutes. (Be careful, as the topping burns easily.) Let the cake stand until cool.

Serves 8 to 10

VERY BERRY CRISP

The sweet-toothed have always had an affinity for oats, it seems. The ancient Greeks made a dessert called *pilakous* that was oats, flour, cheese, and honey whipped together, and considered it such a delicacy it was served only on holidays and occasions of national celebration. The Gauls, being of simpler tastes, combined oats with sugar and suet and baked the mixture into hard flat rectangular cakes that they ate after every meal. These sweets were known as *seuils* (or "doorsteps"). In Henry VIII's time, when cockfighting was a royal sport, British cooks invented a sweet punch of oatmeal, port, beer, sugar, molasses, and, yes, minced oysters. This drink was dubbed "cock ale," which some food snoops believe may just be the precursor of the "cocktail," but I, for one, hope not. In our own country during the American Revolution, when milled flour was scarce, thrifty housewives made bottomless pies of fruit covered with a mixture of oats, sugar, and butter, which were variously known as *grunts, crumbles,* or *crisps,* depending upon the baker's place of origin.

FOR THE TOPPING
½ cup firmly packed dark brown sugar
6 tablespoons all-purpose flour
6 tablespoons rolled oats
¼ teaspoon ground cinnamon
Pinch of salt
4 tablespoons (½ stick) unsalted butter, chilled

FOR THE FILLING
1 pint blueberries or other berries, rinsed, dried, and stems removed
½ cup granulated sugar
Finely slivered zest of 1 orange
1 tablespoon all-purpose flour
1 tablespoon orange liqueur

1. Preheat the oven to 350°F. Butter a 9-inch glass pie plate.

2. Make the topping: Combine the sugar, flour, oats, cinnamon, and salt in a medium-size bowl, and mix well. Cut in the butter with a knife, and mix with your fingers until it has the texture of coarse crumbs. Set aside.

3. Prepare the filling: Combine all the filling ingredients in a medium-size bowl, and mix well. Pour into the prepared pie plate.

4. Spread the crumb topping evenly over the berry filling. Bake 30 minutes. Serve slightly warm.

Serves 6 to 8

OUT-OF-THIS-WORLD PECAN PIE

Oats not only go in the crust but are toasted and added to a traditional pie filling, to make for a very untraditional and wonderful dessert. I serve it with sweetened whipped cream.

1 Rummed Oat Crust (recipe follows)
¼ cup rolled oats
3 eggs
½ cup honey
½ cup granulated sugar
1 cup firmly packed light brown sugar
⅛ teaspoon freshly ground black pepper
2 tablespoons unsalted butter, melted
¼ cup heavy or whipping cream
½ teaspoon vanilla extract
1 cup broken pecan pieces

1. Roll out the Rummed Oat Crust dough on a lightly floured board, and line a 9-inch pie plate with it. Trim and flute the edges.

2. Preheat the oven to 400°F.

3. Place the oats in a medium-size skillet over medium heat. Cook, stirring constantly, until lightly toasted, about 5 minutes. Allow to cool.

4. Lightly beat the eggs in a large bowl. Beat in the honey, both sugars, pepper, butter, cream, and vanilla. Stir in the oats and the pecan pieces. Pour into the pie shell, and bake 10 minutes. Reduce the heat to 325°F and continue to bake until the filling is firm, about 30 minutes longer. Serve warm.

Serves 8

Rummed Oat Crust

⅓ cup rolled oats
¾ cup all-purpose flour
1 teaspoon sugar
½ teaspoon salt
6 tablespoons solid vegetable shortening, chilled
1 egg yolk, beaten
1 to 2 tablespoons dark rum

1. Place the oats in the container of a food processor, and process until fine, 1 minute.

2. Transfer the ground oats to a large bowl and stir in the flour, sugar, and salt. Cut in the shortening with a knife, then blend with a pastry blender until the mixture has the texture of coarse crumbs. Mix in the egg yolk with a fork, and add enough rum to form a soft dough. Wrap in plastic wrap and refrigerate 1 hour before using.

Makes one 9- to 10-inch crust

COFFEE TOFFEE CRUNCH PIE

*T*he oats are combined with chocolate to make a crust for this special pie. Ever since I ran this in the old *Cuisine* magazine, people have been writing for this recipe. It always seems someone lost it, or lent it, and can't live without it. I quite agree.

1 Chocolate Oat 'n' Nut Crust (recipe
  follows)
8 tablespoons (1 stick) unsalted butter, at
  room temperature
¾ cup firmly packed light brown sugar
1 ounce unsweetened chocolate, melted
2 teaspoons instant coffee powder
2 eggs
1¼ cups heavy or whipping cream
2 tablespoons strong brewed coffee, chilled
1 tablespoon confectioners' sugar
¼ teaspoon vanilla extract
Chilled semi-sweet chocolate for chocolate
  curls

1. Make sure the Chocolate Oat 'n' Nut Crust has cooled before proceeding with the recipe.

2. Beat the butter with the brown sugar in the large bowl of an electric mixer until light. Beat in the chocolate and instant coffee powder. Then add the eggs, one at a time, beating 5 minutes after each addition. Spoon into the prepared crust, and refrigerate at least 6 hours.

3. No more than 2 hours before serving, beat the cream until fairly stiff. Beat in the brewed coffee, confectioners' sugar, and vanilla. Spoon this over the pie filling. Using a vegetable peeler to make chocolate curls, scrape a piece of semi-sweet chocolate over the pie. Refrigerate until ready to serve.

Serves 8 to 10

Chocolate Oat 'n' Nut Crust

½ cup rolled oats
½ cup whole roasted almonds
⅓ cup sugar
⅓ cup unsalted butter, melted
½ ounce (½ square) unsweetened
  chocolate, melted

1. Preheat the oven to 375°F.

2. Place the oats and the almonds in the container of a food processor, and process until finely ground, 1 minute. Transfer to a bowl, and stir in the sugar, butter, and chocolate. Mix well. Pat over the bottom and sides of a 9-inch pie plate. Bake 5 minutes. Set the pie plate on a rack to cool.

Makes one 9-inch crust

CHERRY OAT DELIGHTS

*O*atmeal cookies! They deserve a chapter all to themselves, if truth be told. To me the oatmeal cookie (soft, fragmentary, filled with fruit or nutty nubbins) is the quintessential reason for remaining an adolescent forever.

2 ounces dried pitted cherries
4 teaspoons dark rum
8 tablespoons (1 stick) unsalted butter, at
    room temperature
1 cup firmly packed dark brown sugar
1 egg
Finely grated zest of 1 orange
¾ cup all-purpose flour
½ teaspoon baking powder
½ teaspoon baking soda
¼ teaspoon salt
1½ cups quick rolled oats

1. Preheat the oven to 375°F. Lightly grease, then line with foil, two or more baking sheets.

2. Place the cherries in a small bowl, sprinkle with the rum, and set aside.

3. Beat the butter with the brown sugar in the large bowl of an electric mixer until smooth. Beat in the egg and orange zest.

4. Combine the flour with the baking powder, baking soda, and salt. Slowly add to the butter mixture. Then stir in the oats and the cherries with the rum.

5. Place spoonfuls of dough on the prepared baking sheets, about 1½ inches apart. Do not crowd, as the dough will spread. Bake until golden brown, 8 to 10 minutes. Cool completely before peeling off the foil.

Makes about 2 dozen

"OUTRAGEOUS" CHOCOLATE-OATMEAL CHIPPER

The name of these triple chocolate cookies says it all—or almost. Serve them only to guests who you don't want to have leave—ever!

1½ cups rolled oats
8 tablespoons (1 stick) unsalted butter, at
    room temperature
½ cup granulated sugar
½ cup firmly packed light brown sugar
1 egg
1 teaspoon vanilla extract
1 cup all-purpose flour
½ teaspoon baking powder
½ teaspoon baking soda
¼ teaspoon salt
2 ounces semi-sweet chocolate chips (about
    ⅓ cup)
3 ounces milk chocolate, chopped (about
    ½ cup)
3 ounces white chocolate, chopped (about
    ½ cup)
½ cup chopped blanched almonds

1. Preheat the oven to 375°F.

2. Place 1¼ cups of the oats in the container of a food processor, and process until fine, 1 minute.

3. Beat the butter with both sugars in the large bowl of an electric mixer until smooth. Beat in the egg and vanilla.

4. Combine the processed oats with the flour, baking powder, baking soda, and salt. Slowly add to the butter mixture. Then stir in the remaining ¼ cup oats, the chocolates, and the almonds.

5. Drop the dough by spoonfuls onto ungreased baking sheets, and bake until golden brown, about 10 minutes. Cool slightly on the sheets before removing.

Makes about 40 cookies

LA VENA NUZMAN'S HUMONGOUS OATMEAL COOKIES

La Vena Nuzman is a Kansas City chum who bakes an oatmeal cookie that can stand in for a Frisbee, or just possibly a beach umbrella if push comes to shove. The funny thing about her cookies is the bigger they bake, the better they taste! Share one with a friend. On second thought, make that two.

1 cup (2 sticks) unsalted butter, at room
    temperature
1 cup granulated sugar
1 cup firmly packed light brown sugar
2 eggs
1 teaspoon vanilla extract
1½ cups all-purpose flour
½ teaspoon baking powder
½ teaspoon salt
1 teaspoon ground cinnamon
1 teaspoon ground allspice
1 teaspoon ground cloves
½ teaspoon ground ginger
3 cups quick rolled oats
1 cup soft (very fresh) raisins

1. Beat the butter with both sugars in the bowl of an electric mixer until smooth. Beat in the eggs and vanilla.

2. Combine the flour with the baking powder, salt, and spices. Slowly add this to the butter mixture, then stir in the oats. Let stand, covered, at room temperature 1 to 2 hours. Stir in the raisins.

3. Preheat the oven to 375°F. Lightly grease two or more baking sheets.

4. Place ¼ cup dough for each cookie on the prepared baking sheets—no more than four per sheet. Flatten them with your fingers, and bake until golden brown, about 10 minutes. Cool on the baking sheet for a few minutes before removing to cake racks to cool completely. Store in an airtight container.

Makes 16 huge cookies

MILDRED SCHULZ'S CHOCOLATE DREAMS

I consider a Mildred Schulz recipe to be a talisman of good luck, for I have never written a cookbook that did not have one of her signature dishes tucked safely between its covers. Mildred, who lives in Golden, Colorado, is one of the great unsung home cooks of America but hates to have me say it. Oh, well. Certainly her Chocolate Dreams won't sully the Schulz reputation a jot!

6 ounces semi-sweet chocolate, broken into
    bits
2 cups rolled oats
½ cup firmly packed light brown sugar

4 tablespoons (½ stick) unsalted butter,
    melted
¼ cup dark corn syrup

1. Preheat the oven to 350°F. Generously butter a 7 by 11-inch baking pan (preferably not glass).

2. Melt the chocolate in the top of a double boiler over hot (not simmering) water.

3. Combine the oats with the brown sugar in a large bowl, and mix thoroughly. Pour the melted butter over the top, then stir in the melted chocolate and the corn syrup. Mix thoroughly once more.

4. Spoon the chocolate/oats mixture into the prepared pan. Smooth with a spatula. Bake until the top bubbles up, 15 to 20 minutes. Let the pan cool on a rack 10 minutes. Then cut the cookie into small bars and let them cool in the pan until they can hold their shape. Remove the bars from the pan and cool the pieces thoroughly on a cake rack.

Makes about 2 dozen bars

RICE

White and Brown,
plus Basmati and the Other Aromatics

Almost all my memories of rice are inextricably connected to my late sister, Myra.

A Gemini to the teeth and wholly unpredictable in temperament, Myra's moods fluctuated like the winds, changing from practical good sense to wild irrationality in a matter of moments, without a clue as to the cause of the storm.

At one time or another both my mother and my father were recipients of my sister's mood changes. But not I, her junior by five years (and a Libran, the mirror image of her astrological sign). She indulged me extravagantly and unstintingly all of her life and I am certain watches over me still.

Half a century ago, rice was not a grain universally consumed and had only very recently come into our diet. We ate it every Thursday night, in fact, for that was the evening my mother worked late at Macy's and allotted her children the princely sum of a dollar to eat out.

In my sister's wisdom this stipend was best invested in two "special" dinners at The Palace, a remarkably dark and dingy Chinese restaurant two flights above our local movie theater. Despite its sobriquet, The Palace had very few regal items on the bill of fare. But dining there was certainly an exercise in economics. For a mere forty cents we each had a soup, entrée, and dessert, leaving a dividend of twenty cents, which we always left as tip for the very ancient waiter.

We did not order rice at The Palace, but like tea it came to the table in an endless relay of replenishment which, according to your point of view, was considered either a premium or a penance. Even my sister, a worldly adolescent who prided herself on the measure of sophistication she'd acquired vetting endless Norma Shearer movies, never permitted me to swallow a mouthful of chicken chow mein without a helping of rice alongside on the fork.

One Thursday night at The Palace I made a bold request. I asked my sister if I could order *fried* rice for a change. Myra was dubious.

"I don't know. Will it cost more?" She sounded remarkably like our mother.

"Why should it?" I countered. "All they do is fry the stuff instead of boiling it!"

Of course I had no idea what fried rice was, but intrigued by its appearance—sizzling and golden under a small metal lid—the question of any supplementary cost never entered my mind. Myra, on the other hand, fully expected the worst.

When the bill came her fears proved not unfounded. There, scrawled in pencil on the check, was an additional tariff of twenty cents (half the price of a "special dinner") for one à la carte portion of rice. Fried.

Over a cup of cold tea, we immediately charted a course of action, while the old waiter—actually the only one in The Palace's employ—stood a discreet distance from our table.

Emptying both my pockets and her change purse on the tablecloth, we counted out a scant eight cents and one rhinestone button.

"Can we possibly leave such a tip?" I whispered, struck at last by the enormity of my extravagance.

"Of course," replied my sister, rising to the occasion and discreetly placing a folded dollar bill over the small pile of change.

When we left The Palace that evening, descending the narrow stairwell to the street, I was certain I heard a curse (in broken English but quite loud) following us down the steps. But my sister, the soul of hauteur, was oblivious to any slur.

"Don't feel guilty, kiddo," Myra counseled. "Developing one's taste is worth a little sacrifice."

"By whom?" I thought but did not ask. "The waiter or me?"

The Grain's Genesis

No one knows for sure how old rice really is, but it is *old*! Botanists place its first cultivation in the Orient about

5,000 years before the birth of Christ. However, it was consumed long, long before that. Recent archeological digs in China unearthed sealed jars filled with rice that had been harvested almost 7,000 years ago. And despite a touch of mildew and a few petrified moths, the grain was deemed still edible.

In India, the earliest rice was the grain of a wild grass known as *newaree*, which grew in swampy patches and had to be separated from weeds, leeches, and water snakes by hand. Slaves or women usually picked this vestigial rice, for it was considered to be the lowliest of household employments. It is reported in Malaysian lore, for instance, that if a new wife was disobedient all a husband need do to curb her temper was to suggest a stroll past the viper-infested marshes where rice bloomed.

Even when rice was domesticated, Chinese farmers were so superstitious about how and why the grain grew that they would stand at the water's edge and cast handfuls of seed into the bog, praying to the god of harvest that germination would take place.

This kind of hit-or-miss rice agriculture went on for centuries until China's Emperor Shen Nung devised a plan for flooding arable fields to create controlled rice paddies. Shen himself celebrated the initial planting with a ceremony in which he dropped the first few seeds into the ground. His touch was obviously green as jade, for the rice not only sprouted, it flourished wildly in China forever after. In 2800 B.C. it was named one of the Five Sacred Crops (along with soybeans, wheat, millet, and barley).

The Chinese were very proprietary about rice and zealously guarded the secrets of both its agriculture and its cookery. Of a consequence—though rice cultivation spread all over the East in no time at all—no two Asian nations ever grew or prepared it in quite the same way.

Rice came to Japan as the spoils of a small border skirmish between a Chinese warlord and a Japanese shogun. As a result, the Japanese have always consumed less of it than the Chinese. Nonetheless, rice was deemed such a status symbol in feudal Japan that a rich man's land was assessed not by acreage but rather by the amount of rice he paid his samurai to protect it.

It is a mystery how Oriental rice spread to the Middle East, but more than likely Indian traders took it there. In India, where rice grows on a third of all tillable land, it is a staple for half the population (barley being the top grain in the north). Both rice and barley are held to be immortal cereals and are referred to in the Koran as "twin sons of heaven."

By contrast, in 1326 Osman I, founder of the Ottoman Empire, declared rice to be a profane food, insisting that its consumption led to indolence, venery, and prurient behavior. As a consequence, rice fields were burned and cooked rice in any form whatsoever was banished from Turkish kitchens for over a century. (Though, it must be told, contraband rice was often eaten on the sly. And the very word *pilau*—originally an acronym for the Greek word for "plate" and the Latin for "to praise"—implied that free-thinkers ate as they pleased.)

In time the rice dictum ended, but so did the Ottoman Empire. By then, rice had found its way to the wet shores of the Po Valley in Italy and to the high marshes of Spain—where the last of the invading Moors discovered it and returned rice to its rightful place in the Middle East once more. Or at least that's how one cloudy version of the story goes.

Some Plain Grain Talk

Rice may not be the most nutritional grain in the world, but it is still the grain most of the world eats to survive. In many parts of the globe, rice consumption runs as high as 300 pounds per person a year—which does not make for a very varied diet but decidedly means the difference between starvation and subsistence in underdeveloped countries.

Rice supplies 55 percent of man's daily food requirements, and one pound (which is a heck of a lot of rice at anyone's table) delivers four times the food energy of a like amount of potatoes or pasta.

Rice is primarily carbohydrate, composed of 80 percent starch and 12 percent water. Yet it provides enough protein, thiamine (B₁), phosphorus, and potassium to be a significant factor in the diet, particularly when it is combined with other carbohydrates in a saucepan.

Over 7,000 varieties of rice are grown around the world. In America, we eat two kinds. The most conspicuously consumed (by 98 percent of the population) is long-grain and medium-grain white rice. A mere 2 percent eat brown rice.

To set the matter straight, all rice is brown to begin with. It goes through a complex transformation process that strips the kernel of its husk, bran, and germ to achieve pristine and polished whiteness—leaving only the endosperm and very little else in the way of nutritional fiber.

How to Buy It

In the U.S. there are three basic types of rice available to consumers: long-grain, medium-grain, and short-grain.

Long-Grain Rice. The most popular of the long-grain varieties is *regular-milled white rice*. The kernel is about five times as long as it is wide, and the cooked grain is unusually fluffy and separates easily. Most regular milled white rice on supermarket shelves is "enriched," which means it has been spiked with iron, calcium, and assorted B-

complex vitamins to make up for the deficiencies caused by removal of the husk, bran, and germ. Enriched rice comes ready to cook, so don't wash it or the enrichment will go down the drain. *Converted white rice*, sometimes dubbed "parboiled," is rice that has been steamed and pressure-cooked before milling—a process that forces residual nutrients into the kernel's heart, making it a tad higher in vitamin content than regular milled rice. Converted rice has drawbacks, however. It takes longer to cook and loses its light texture when held on the stove for a period of time. *Instant or "precooked" white rice* has been partially cooked and dehydrated, so the kernels reconstitute quickly in very little water. It's the least nourishing form of white rice and also the most expensive!

Brown long-grain rice is the whole unpolished grain minus the outer husk. It's decidedly chewier than white rice because each kernel is cloaked in a delicate layer of high-fiber bran. Bran adds a golden-tan color, a distinctive flavor (somewhat on the nutty side), plus a jot more vitamins, minerals, and trace elements. But fiber is the main reason to include brown rice in your diet.

Basmati long-grain rice is a highly aromatic variety imported from the Punjab, in the foothills of the Himalayas. Basmati kernels are somewhat unricelike: long, thin strands that have been aged to decrease the moisture content and increase the extraordinary bouquet, which to my non-Hindu nose translates as "spicy-flowery."

Texmati long-grain rice is a hybrid grown in the U.S. It has neither the assertive flavor of a true basmati nor the fluffiness of a conventional domestic long-grain. But it makes a pleasant change on a dinner plate from time to time. There are other white and brown aromatic rices grown in America (notably in the Southwest and California). Of varying bouquet, all are tabbed well below the price of basmati.

Medium-Grain Rice. As its name implies, medium-grain rice, whether white or brown, is a compromise kernel. Shorter and plumper than long-grain varieties, it is neither as dense nor as glutinous as traditional short-grains, yet may be substituted for the latter in many recipes. Immediately after cooking, medium-grain rice is moist and tender. However, since it contains a high concentration of amylopectin (a starch with gelatin components), the kernels tend to mass and become sticky as the rice cools.

Short-Grain Rice. The rice with the highest degree of cohesion (amylopectin), short-grain rice's viscosity is obviously a matter of taste. In Japan and China, where it is known as *glutinous rice*, this short-grain rice is starchy as the dickens, but despite its name, gluten-free. Opaque, oval-shaped, and chalky white where most other rices are translucent, it is best when the rice is young and the kernels lose their identity and mass quickly. Ideal for a chopstick but hard on a Western knife and fork, glutinous rice has a highly curtailed stove-life in most kitchens. California rice growers do produce a middle-of-the-road short-grain, but it is not easy to find (note the mail-order sources at the back of this book). *Italian arborio short-grain rice*, on the other hand, is a highly kinetic kernel. This grain, cutivated exclusively in the northern Po and Ticino valleys, is unique in that it is used only in the preparation of risotto, one of the great masterpieces of classic Italian cuisine. The varieties—arborio, vialone, nano, and canaroli—have shorter, rounder kernels than any other short-grain rice, with the precise degree of starch in their composition needed to render the creamy texture of this exquisite dish.

How to Store It

*B*y and large, rice is a hardy grain that will keep for an indefinite time on a pantry shelf, as long as the package remains sealed. However, there are some basic tips on rice storage that are worth noting.

Contents of opened packages should be transferred to airtight jars. Glass or ceramic containers with secure screw-top or vacuum-seal lids are the ideal receptacles.

Rice should always be stored in a cool, dry, and if possible, semi-dark place. Coolness inhibits insect infestation, dryness wards off mold, and darkness limits vitamin loss.

By contrast with regular milled white rice, brown rice is *not* a pantry perennial. The oxidation of the oil in the bran causes rancidity and dictates a highly abbreviated shelf life: six months, if you're lucky. Refrigerating or freezing brown rice in self-seal plastic bags will extend that storage time considerably, but make sure to check the contents regularly. The bags must be completely airtight or moisture buildup will occur inside the packet. If you freeze brown rice, it is sensible to allow the kernels to defrost before proceeding with a recipe.

How to Cook It

I have grouped the recipes according to the basic rice types—long-grain, medium-grain, and short-grain—with their individual cooking characteristics.

It is important to note, however, that many of the recipes are interchangeable in terms of type of rice. If, for instance, a high-fiber advocate or an aromatics aficionado wishes to substitute brown rice or basmati rice for regular-milled white rice in a dish, it may usually be adapted to meet that culinary quirk—with appropriate adjustments in cooking time and seasoning.

Check out the Rice Cooking Chart (page 218) for specific information.

LONG-GRAIN WHITE RICE

A good kitchen rule to file away is that this rice triples as it cooks. One-third cup raw rice will produce 1 cup of steaming cooked rice, 1 cup raw will produce 3 cups cooked, and so on.

BASIC COOKED RICE

The easiest and most accepted way to prepare regular-milled long-grain white rice is the fail-safe method that follows. It may be prepared on top of the stove in approximately 15 minutes.

If you prefer to cook the rice in the oven (a method neither particularly energy-efficient nor time-saving), boil the liquid before combining it with the other ingredients. Stir once, cover tightly, and bake in a preheated 350°F oven for 25 to 30 minutes.

Converted white rice requires more liquid (2 to 2½ cups to 1 cup rice) and a longer cooking time (20 to 25 minutes) on top of the stove, but the end result will be greater: 3 to 4 cups cooked rice. It can be used in any of the recipes in this section.

1 cup long-grain white rice
2 cups liquid (water, broth, consommé,
     vegetable juice)
½ teaspoon salt
1 tablespoon unsalted butter

1. Combine the rice, liquid, salt, and butter in a medium-size saucepan and heat to boiling. Stir once or twice, and reduce the heat. Cover, and simmer 15 minutes.

2. If the rice is not quite tender or the liquid is not entirely absorbed, replace the lid and cook 2 to 4 minutes longer. Fluff with a fork before serving.

Makes 3 cups

All rice is divided by weather, it seems:

The *Indica* variety, which grows in a cold climate, is a hardy long-grain rice with a firm bite to the kernel.

The *Japonica* variety, on the other hand, which blooms in warm weather and moist atmospheric conditions, is a short-grain rice that cooks soft and loses its kernels' identity in a rice bowl.

RICE COOKING CHART

1 Cup Uncooked Rice	Basic Technique	Steamed Boiled Technique	Yield
Long-grain white	Heat rice and 2 cups liquid to boiling; reduce heat. Cook covered 15 minutes.	Boil in 3 or 4 quarts water 12 minutes. Drain. Place over simmering water. Cover with paper towel. Steam 15 minutes.	3 cups
Long-grain brown	Heat rice and 2½ cups liquid to boiling; reduce heat. Cook covered 45 to 50 minutes (or soak overnight to reduce time).	Boil in 3 or 4 quarts water 30 minutes (or soak overnight to reduce time). Drain in colander. Place over simmering water. Cover with paper towel. Steam 20 minutes.	3 to 4 cups
Basmati	Rinse well. Soak in water 30 minutes. Boil in 3 or 4 quarts water 5 minutes. Drain.	Rinse. Soak in 2 cups water. Drain into a saucepan. Heat drained water to boiling. Stir in rice. Reduce heat. Cook partially covered 10 minutes. Cover and place on flame tamer 10 minutes. Let stand 5 minutes.	3 cups
Texmati and other aromatics	Heat rice and 1¾ cups liquid to boiling; reduce heat. Cook covered 15 minutes.	Boil in 3 or 4 quarts water 12 minutes. Drain. No need to steam.	3 cups

1 Cup Uncooked Rice	Basic Technique	Steamed Boiled Technique	Yield
Brown aromatics	Heat rice and 2 cups liquid to boiling; reduce heat. Cook covered 40 to 45 minutes (or soak overnight to reduce time).	Boil in 3 or 4 quarts water 30 minutes (or soak overnight to reduce time). Drain in colander. Place over simmering water. Cover with paper towel. Steam 20 minutes.	3½ cups
Medium-grain white	Heat rice and 1½ cups liquid to boiling; reduce heat. Cook covered 15 minutes.	Boil in 3 or 4 quarts water 15 minutes. Drain in colander. Place over simmering water. Cover with paper towel. Steam 15 minutes.	3 cups
Medium-grain brown	See long-grain brown.	See long-grain brown.	3 cups
Short-grain white	Rinse well. Soak with 1 cup plus 2 tablespoons water in saucepan 10 minutes. Heat to boiling; reduce heat. Cook covered 5 minutes. Raise heat 30 seconds. Let stand off heat 10 minutes.	Does not apply.	2 cups
Italian arborio	Stir rice into reduced wine and onion mixture. Slowly add 2½ to 3 cups simmering liquid, stirring until creamy, 25 minutes.	Does not apply.	2½ to 3 cups
Short-grain brown	See long-grain brown (use only 2 cups liquid).	See long-grain brown.	2¼ cups

STEAMED BOILED RICE

My alternative—and favorite—way of cooking long-grain rice is a tad eclectic. This version may be a jot less vitaminized because of the parboiling, but the ease of cookery makes up for the nutritional slack. The rice is prepared in under a half hour's time and can then be kept over minimal heat for several hours—with every grain still separate and intact whenever the rice is finally served.

1 cup long-grain white rice
3 quarts boiling salted water

1. Add the rice to the boiling water. Stir once with a wooden spoon, so the rice does not stick to the bottom of the pot, and when the water returns to boiling, reduce the heat. Simmer, uncovered, until just tender, about 12 minutes.

Drain in a colander.

2. Place the colander over 2 inches of simmering water in another pot. (Do not let the bottom of the colander touch the water.) Cover the rice with a single layer of paper towels. Steam for at least 15 minutes. The rice can be held this way for several hours without harm.

Makes 3 cups

FRESH AND SPLIT PEA POTTAGE

A hearty bowl of fresh-and-dried pea soup cooked to a turn with herbs, pink nubbins of ham, and rice, of course. The lineage? Southern most probably, but then most of my best dishes are seasoned with *déjà vu*.

1½ tablespoons unsalted butter
1 medium onion, chopped
1 clove garlic, minced
1 pound dried split peas
1 carrot, peeled and broken in half
1 sprig fresh mint, or ¼ teaspoon dried
1 sprig fresh thyme, or a pinch of dried
1 ham bone, or ½ pound smoked ham
*2 quarts plus 2½ cups homemade chicken
    stock (see page 376) or canned broth*
1 quart water
2 cups dry white wine
½ cup long-grain white rice
1 package (10 ounces) frozen peas, thawed
Freshly ground black pepper to taste
½ teaspoon chopped fresh mint
1 tablespoon chopped fresh parsley
Garlic-rubbed croutons (see Note)

1. Melt the butter in a large pot over medium-low heat. Add the onion; cook 1 minute. Add the garlic; cook 5 minutes longer. Stir in the split peas.

2. Tie the carrot, mint, and thyme together in a cheesecloth bag. Add this to the pot along with the ham bone, all the chicken stock, water, and wine. Heat to boiling. Then reduce the heat, cover partially, and simmer, stirring occasionally, until the split peas are tender, about 1 hour.

3. Remove the cheesecloth bag from the soup and discard it. Remove the ham bone from the soup and cut off any meat. Chop the meat fine, and set it aside.

4. Return the soup to boiling and add the rice. Reduce the heat, cover, and simmer 15 minutes. Add the chopped ham and thawed peas. Cook 5 minutes longer, and season with pepper.

5. Combine the chopped mint and parsley, and sprinkle over the soup. Serve with garlic-rubbed croutons.

Serves 8

Note: To make garlic-rubbed croutons: Bake 8 thin slices of bread in a 400°F oven until crisp and brown, about 5 minutes. Rub with a split clove of garlic and brush with ¼ cup melted butter. Cut into squares.

COLD GREEN CREAM

A pale green broccoli, lettuce, and rice bisque that should be served on the chilly side. Add an even chillier liter of Chardonnay, a loaf of warm sourdough bread, and a ripe cheese, and voilà, it's California cuisine.

1 small stalk broccoli (½ to ¾ pound)
2 tablespoons unsalted butter
2 leeks, white bulbs and 1 inch of stems,
*   rinsed, dried, and chopped*
1 clove garlic, minced
1 small hot green pepper, seeded and
*   minced*
½ cup long-grain white rice
6 cups homemade chicken stock (see page
*   376) or canned broth*
1 small head lettuce, such as Boston,
*   rinsed and chopped (about 2½ cups)*
¼ teaspoon freshly grated nutmeg
1 tablespoon fresh lemon juice
Salt and freshly ground black pepper to
*   taste*
½ cup sour cream

1. Trim the broccoli stem and cut the head into flowerets. Peel and coarsely chop the stalk.

2. Melt the butter in a large heavy saucepan over medium-low heat. Add the leeks; cook 2 minutes. Add the broccoli, garlic, hot pepper, and rice. Toss to coat, add the chicken stock, and heat to boiling. Reduce the heat and simmer, uncovered, over medium-low heat 15 minutes. Add the lettuce and nutmeg. Cook 10 minutes longer. Set aside to cool slightly, then add lemon juice and salt and pepper. Cool to room temperature.

3. Place the soup, in batches, in the container of a food processor and purée. Pour into a bowl and stir in the sour cream. Serve well chilled.

Serves 6 to 8

SIASCONSET CLAM 'N' RICE 'N' EVERYTHING NICE CHOWDER

This chowder originated on the northern edge of Nantucket Island. Please observe that the rice here is a subtle tie that binds.

2 to 2½ quarts chowder clams (quahogs),
   well scrubbed under cold running
   water
1 cup water
½ cup white wine
6 tablespoons (¾ stick) unsalted butter
3 sprigs parsley
1 bay leaf
1 small onion stuck with 1 whole clove
4 strips thick-sliced bacon
1 teaspoon olive oil
1 large onion, minced
1 large clove garlic, minced
1 rib celery, minced
2 tablespoons minced red bell pepper
1 large baking potato (about ¾ pound),
   peeled and cubed
2 cups milk
2 cups heavy or whipping cream
5 whole allspice, crushed
⅓ cup long-grain white rice
¼ teaspoon chopped fresh thyme, or a
   pinch of dried
Dash of Worcestershire sauce
Dash of hot pepper sauce
Salt and freshly ground black pepper to
   taste
1 cup corn kernels (3 medium ears)
Chopped fresh parsley, for garnish

1. Place the clams in a pot with the water, wine, 2 tablespoons of the butter, parsley sprigs, bay leaf, and onion stuck with a clove. Cover and heat to boiling. Reduce the heat and simmer over medium-low heat until the clams open, about 8 minutes. (Clams may have to be fully opened with a clam knife.)

2. Remove the clams from the shells, straining any juices back into the clam broth. Chop the clams coarsely and reserve. Strain the clam broth and reserve; you should have about 1¾ cups.

3. Cook the bacon in boiling water 5 minutes. Drain, and pat dry with paper towels.

4. Rub a heavy skillet with the oil, and sauté the bacon in it until crisp. Drain the bacon on paper towels. Dis-

card all but 1 tablespoon drippings from the pan, and stir in 2 tablespoons of the butter.

5. Add the minced onion to the skillet, and cook over medium heat 2 minutes. Add the garlic; cook 4 minutes longer. Stir in the celery and bell pepper; cook 5 minutes. Add the potato and stir for 1 minute.

6. Transfer the mixture to a large pot and add the bacon, 1 cup of the reserved clam broth, the milk, and the remaining 2 tablespoons butter. Heat to boiling. Stir in the cream and allspice, and cook

Rice has been one of the United States' prandial pleasures for over three hundred years, but how the silken grain came to America in the first place is a matter of conjecture. Romantics insist it was a gift from a grateful British sea captain whose vessel, blown off course in a mid-Atlantic squall, was given safe harbor in Charleston, South Carolina. In gratitude, it was reported, he presented the citizenry with a sack of rice ready for planting. And the rest, as they say, is casserole history!

Nonromantics take a less elevated view of rice's arrival, insisting that its agriculture was simply an extension of slavery. Since most of the slaves in the Carolinas came from the West African coast south of the Sahara, where rice had flourished for hundreds of years, slave owners merely kept their busy farm hands even busier planting and harvesting rice—until the Civil War ravaged the rice fields and dissipated the industry, which in time moved south, southwest, and west by turns. In California, Texas, Arkansas, Mississippi, and Missouri, almost 19 billion pounds of rice are raised yearly.

over medium-low heat 4 minutes.

7. Add the rice to the chowder, and heat the mixture to boiling. Reduce the heat, and add the thyme, Worcestershire, and hot pepper sauce. Simmer uncovered until the rice and potatoes are tender, about 25 minutes. Season with salt and pepper.

8. Stir the corn into the chowder and continue to cook over medium-low heat until thick, about 5 minutes. Stir in the reserved clams and remaining ¾ cup clam broth. Cook 5 minutes longer. Sprinkle with parsley before serving.

Serves 6 to 8

GOLD COAST CHOWDER

A bounteous chowder from the south of France and perfect for dinner accompanied by plenty of crusty bread. Skip the cream (no need to add more stock) for a lighter version.

4 tablespoons (½ stick) unsalted butter
1 large onion, finely chopped
1 large clove garlic, minced
¼ cup all-purpose flour
1 can (28 ounces) imported plum tomatoes, crushed, with juice
2 tablespoons curry powder
1 teaspoon ground turmeric
¼ teaspoon ground allspice
6 cups fish stock (see page 377), heated
½ cup long-grain white rice
1½ pounds white fish filets (such as flounder or sole), cut into 1-inch pieces
1 cup heavy or whipping cream, at room temperature
Salt and freshly ground black pepper to taste
Chopped fresh parsley, for garnish

1. Melt the butter in a large saucepan over medium-low heat. Add the onion; cook 4 minutes. Add the garlic; cook 3 minutes longer. Do not allow to brown.

2. Whisk the flour into the onion mixture. Cook, stirring constantly, 2 minutes. Whisk in the tomatoes, curry, turmeric, allspice, and fish stock. Heat to boiling. Add the rice and stir until the mixture returns to boiling. Then reduce the heat and simmer, uncovered, 15 minutes.

3. Reduce the heat under the saucepan to medium-low. Add the fish, and cook 5 minutes. Slowly add the cream, and heat to boiling. Remove the pan from the heat, and season with salt and pepper. Garnish with parsley.

Serves 6

ALL RIGHT CLAM AND RICE PIE

About twenty five years ago, I spent a lot of time visiting Cape Cod, where there was a small restaurant that served a wildly rich clam pie. When one of my band of fellow travelers would suggest going out for some clam pie, the reaction was always the same: "All *right*, now you're talkin'." This is my version, from memory.

FOR THE CRUST

1¼ cups plus 1 teaspoon all-purpose flour
1 teaspoon sugar
½ teaspoon salt
6 tablespoons lard, chilled
1 egg yolk
1 teaspoon red wine vinegar
1 to 2 tablespoons cold water

FOR THE FILLING

2 tablespoons unsalted butter
1 tablespoon olive oil
1 large onion, finely chopped
1 clove garlic, minced
¼ teaspoon chopped fresh thyme, or ⅛
    teaspoon dried
1 cup chopped raw or canned clams with
    their broth
1 cup grated zucchini, lightly pressed to
    remove water
1½ cups cooked long-grain white or brown
    rice, heated
1 teaspoon minced seeded jalapeño pepper
2 eggs
¼ cup heavy or whipping cream
3 whole allspice, finely crushed
¼ cup freshly grated Parmesan cheese
4 ounces mozzarella cheese, thinly sliced

Niçoise Tomato Sauce (see page 199)

1. Make the crust: Combine 1¼ cups flour, the sugar, and the salt in a medium-size bowl. Cut in the lard, and blend with a pastry blender until the mixture has the texture of coarse crumbs. Lightly beat the egg yolk with the vinegar and water. Using a fork, cut the liquid into the flour mixture to form a soft dough. (Do not overwork.) Sprinkle the dough with 1 teaspoon flour. Wrap in plastic wrap and refrigerate 1 hour before using.

2. Preheat the oven to 400°F.

3. Butter a 9-inch loose-bottom tart or quiche pan. Roll out the chilled dough on a lightly floured board, and line the prepared pan with the dough. Trim and flute the edges. Line the crust with foil, and weight it with rice or beans. Bake 5 minutes. Remove the foil and weights, and bake 4 minutes longer. Remove the crust from the oven and set aside. Reduce the oven heat to 350°F.

4. Make the filling: Heat the butter with the oil in a large heavy skillet. Add the onion; cook 2 minutes. Add the garlic and thyme; cook 3 minutes longer. Stir in the clams and zucchini; cook 2 minutes longer. Stir in the rice and pepper. Transfer the mixture to a large bowl.

5. Beat the eggs with the cream and allspice until smooth. Toss into the rice/clam mixture, and stir in the Parmesan cheese. Spoon the mixture into the prepared crust. Place the mozzarella slices over the top. Bake 30 minutes. Let stand 5 minutes before serving with Niçoise Tomato Sauce.

Serves 6 to 8

STAR-SPANGLED SCALLOPS WITH BLUE CHEESE RICE

From Love Point in Chesapeake Bay, where the scallops are sweet and inventive chefs "cream" their rice with blue cheese. This is a wonderful brunch dish.

FOR THE SCALLOPS

1 pound bay scallops
3 tablespoons all-purpose flour
2 tablespoons vegetable oil
4 teaspoons unsalted butter
8 scallions, white bulbs and green tops
    chopped separately
1 clove garlic, minced
1 medium red bell pepper, blanched,
    seeded, and finely chopped
½ cup diced smoky country ham
¼ cup dry white wine
¼ cup homemade chicken stock (see page
    376) or canned broth
1 tablespoon chopped fresh basil

FOR THE RICE

¼ cup heavy or whipping cream
⅛ teaspoon crushed dried hot red peppers
3 tablespoons creamy blue-type cheese
    (Bleu Castello or Cambazola)
2 cups cooked long-grain white rice, heated
Chopped fresh parsley, for garnish

1. Preheat the oven to 350°F.

2. Pat the scallops dry with paper towels and dust with the flour.

3. Heat the oil with 2 teaspoons of the butter in a heavy noncorrosive skillet over medium heat. Sauté the scallops, about a third at a time, until golden, about 3 minutes. Using a slotted spoon, transfer the scallops to a bowl and set aside.

4. Add the remaining 2 teaspoons butter to the skillet, and sauté the scallion bulbs 1 minute. Add the garlic; cook 2 minutes. Stir in the bell pepper and ham; cook 3 minutes longer. Add the wine and stock, scraping the sides and bottom of the pan with a wooden spoon. Heat to boiling, and boil until slightly thickened, about 1 minute. Return the scallops to the pan and toss with the basil. Transfer to an ovenproof serving dish, sprinkle with the scallion tops, and bake for 10 to 15 minutes.

5. Meanwhile, make the rice: Heat the cream to boiling in a medium-size saucepan. Reduce the heat, and add the hot peppers and cheese. When the cheese has melted, add the cooked rice and stir until warmed through, about 4 minutes. Sprinkle with parsley, and serve with the Spangled Scallops.

Serves 4

WEST SIDE POT-ROASTED CHICKEN WITH RICE

The West Side of Manhattan is a real melting pot of the world's population. This dish, created in that teeming borough, reflects its roots—French-style pot-roasted chicken is flavored with Italian hard sausage. Long-grain rice binds it together.

1 chicken (about 4 pounds), well rinsed
    and dried
4 sprigs parsley
2 fresh sage leaves, or a pinch of dried
1 large clove garlic, bruised
1½ tablespoons olive oil
1 tablespoon unsalted butter
1 medium onion, finely chopped

1 teaspoon minced hot red pepper
¼-inch-thick slice of hard Italian salami or
    sopressata, chopped
2 cups homemade chicken stock (see page
    376) or canned broth
½ cup dry white wine
1 cup long-grain white rice
Chopped fresh parsley, for garnish

1. Rinse the chicken and pat dry with paper towels. Stuff the cavity with the parsley sprigs and sage. Sew and truss. Rub the chicken with the bruised garlic, then mince the garlic and reserve.

2. Heat the oil in a large saucepan or Dutch oven over medium-high heat. Add the chicken and brown well on all sides, about 12 minutes.

3. Remove the chicken from the pan, and wipe out the pan. Add the butter, and cook the onion over medium-low heat 1 minute. Add the reserved garlic and the red pepper; cook 4 minutes longer. Stir in the salami.

4. Return the chicken to the pot, breast side up. Pour the stock and wine over the chicken, and heat to boiling. Reduce the heat and simmer, covered, 1 hour.

5. Stir in the rice, around the chicken, and continue to cook, covered, until all liquid has been absorbed, about 15 minutes.

6. To serve, carve the chicken and place on a platter. Surround with rice and sprinkle with chopped parsley.

Serves 4

ALMOND-CRISPED CORNISH HENS WITH JAMBALAYA DRESSING

*T*he stuffing is based on a rendering I sampled in Abbeville, Louisiana. The crust for the bird, made of ground almonds, garlic, brandy, and sweet butter to hold it together, is a new twist on an old northern trick of coating roasts with bread crumbs to keep the birds moist. The nutty, crackling skin makes a great dish even better.

6 small Cornish game hens
Jambalaya Dressing (recipe follows)
8 tablespoons (1 stick) unsalted butter, at
    room temperature
1 large clove garlic, crushed
½ cup ground blanched almonds
2 tablespoons brandy
1 quart homemade chicken stock (see page
    376) or canned broth
1 clove garlic
1 medium rib celery, chopped
3 sprigs parsley
¼ teaspoon salt
8 black peppercorns
1½ tablespoons unsalted butter
1½ tablespoons all-purpose flour
¼ cup heavy or whipping cream
Salt and freshly ground black pepper to
    taste

1. Wipe the Cornish hens inside and out with damp paper towels. Reserve the giblets. Spoon the Jambalaya Dressing into the cavities. Sew and truss.

2. Beat the 8 tablespoons butter with the crushed garlic in a medium-size bowl until smooth. Beat in the ground almonds and the brandy. Spread this mixture evenly over the hens. Place the hens on racks in roasting pans, and let stand 30 minutes.

3. Meanwhile, preheat the oven to 425°F.

4. Place the hens in the oven, and roast 1 hour.

5. While the hens are roasting, combine the giblets (not the liver) with the chicken stock in a saucepan, and add the whole clove of garlic, celery, parsley sprigs, salt, and peppercorns. Heat to boiling. Reduce the heat and simmer, uncovered, until reduced by one third, about 25 minutes. Strain.

6. After they have cooked for an hour, pour the chicken stock around the hens. Continue roasting until the juices run yellow when the hens are pricked with a fork, about 30 minutes longer. Transfer the hens to a serving dish, remove the strings, and keep warm. Degrease the pan juices.

7. Melt the 1½ tablespoons butter in a medium-size saucepan over medium heat. Add the flour and cook, whisking constantly, 2 minutes. Stir in the pan drippings and the cream. Simmer 5 minutes. Thin the sauce with additional chicken stock if it is too thick, and season with salt and pepper. Serve with the hens.

Serves 6

I n China there are two words for rice. The Cantonese *mai* means "agriculture," while the Mandarin *mee* means "culture." In Japan, where they reduce everything to basics, there is a very basic word for rice as well: *gohan*. It denotes "a full meal." In India, a Sanskrit equivalent, *vrihih*, bespeaks of rice as a "life-giving seed." Thailand's name for rice translates as "food with wings to fly." In Korea, the word for rice means "god's tears," or, some aver, "god's fears." Take your pick!

Oddly enough, the Greeks, who were never great rice fanciers, gave the grain its botanical handle. They called it *Oryza sativa*—*sativa* being the word for "sown" and *oryza* simply a tag that states "of Oriental origin."

Jambalaya Dressing

1 teaspoon olive oil
2 sweet italian sausages (about ½ pound)
2 tablespoons unsalted butter
1 medium onion, chopped
1 clove garlic, minced
¼ cup diced green bell pepper
¼ cup diced red bell pepper
1 cup chopped, peeled, seeded tomatoes
¼ teaspoon sugar
¼ cup homemade chicken stock (see page 376) or canned broth
1 tablespoon chopped fresh basil, or 1 teaspoon dried
½ teaspoon finely grated lemon zest
¼ teaspoon ground chili powder
Pinch of dried thyme
5 ounces shrimp, shelled and deveined
½ cup chopped cooked ham
2¼ cups cooked long-grain white rice
Salt and freshly ground black pepper to taste

1. Rub a heavy skillet with the oil, and sauté the sausages over medium heat until golden brown on all sides, 6 to 8 minutes. Transfer to a plate, and cut into ¼-inch-thick slices. Set aside.

2. Discard all grease from the skillet, and melt the butter in the skillet over medium-low heat. Add the onion; cook, scraping the bottom and sides of the pan with a wooden spoon, 3 minutes. Add the garlic and both bell peppers; cook 3 minutes longer. Then stir in the tomatoes, sugar, stock, basil, lemon zest, chili powder, and thyme. Simmer, uncovered, 5 minutes. Add the shrimp and cook 1 minute more.

3. Transfer the tomato-shrimp mixture to a large bowl. Stir in the ham, sausage slices, and rice. Mix well, and season with salt and pepper.

Makes enough dressing for 6 Cornish hens

INDONESIAN FRIED RICE AND CHICKEN WITH GADO GADO SAUCE

This dish, an Indonesian concoction, is devised of rice fried with chicken under a blanket of super-spicy peanut butter and pepper sauce. Use either white or brown rice and any leftover chicken in the fridge. But do not attempt to make it unless fresh cilantro (Chinese parsley) is on hand for seasoning!

4 cups cooked long-grain white or brown rice
2 cups cubed cooked chicken
1 tablespoon chopped fresh cilantro (Chinese parsley)
2 teaspoons chopped fresh parsley
3 tablespoons mayonnaise, preferably homemade (see page 379)
½ teaspoon salt
¼ teaspoon freshly ground black pepper
1 tablespoon unsalted butter
3 tablespoons peanut oil
Gado Gado (recipe follows), heated

1. Place 2½ cups of the cooked rice in a large bowl and add the chicken, cilantro, parsley, mayonnaise, salt, and pepper. Mix well.

2. Heat the butter with the oil in a 10-inch skillet (preferably non-stick) over medium heat. Spread the remaining 1½ cups rice over the bottom of the skillet. Press lightly with the back of a wooden spoon. Then spoon the chicken mixture over the rice. Reduce the heat to medium-low and cook, uncovered, until the bottom of the bottom layer of rice is very crispy, 25 to 30 minutes. Shift the pan occasionally if it is larger than the burner. Raise the heat slightly if the mixture is not crisp enough, but watch carefully.

3. When the bottom layer of rice is crisp, remove the skillet from the heat and let it stand 3 or 4 minutes. Invert onto a serving platter, and serve with Gado Gado on the side.

Serves 4

Gado Gado

¼ cup peanut oil
1 small onion, finely chopped (about ¼ cup)
1 clove garlic, minced
½ teaspoon minced fresh ginger
½ teaspoon crushed dried hot red peppers
½ cup chunky peanut butter
¼ cup soy sauce
¼ cup fresh lime juice
1 cup water

1. Heat the oil in a medium-size saucepan over medium heat. Add the onion and cook until golden, about 4 minutes. Stir in the garlic, ginger, and dried red peppers. Cook 2 minutes.

2. Reduce the heat to medium-low and slowly stir in the peanut butter, soy sauce, lime juice, and water. Heat to boiling. Reduce the heat and simmer, uncovered, until thickened, 10 minutes.

Makes about 2 cups

In China, losing or quitting a job is known as "breaking the rice bowl"—probably because of the effect such an event has on one's eating habits. On the other hand, getting a good job is known as "buying heavy rice."

COLD BAYOU RICE

A cool, soothing rice salad for a hot, hot day. The dressing is a homemade mayonnaise. If you substitute store-bought, thin it with a little milk and add some mustard and vinegar for flavor.

4½ cups cooked long-grain white rice, chilled
1 cup diced cooked ham
½ cup chopped fresh parsley
4 scallions, white bulbs and green tops, finely chopped
2 teaspoons capers
2 eggs yolks, at room temperature
Juice of 1 lemon
1 tablespoon Dijon mustard
⅔ cup olive or vegetable oil, or a combination of both
¼ cup red wine vinegar
1 teaspoon salt
½ teaspoon freshly ground black pepper

1. In a large bowl, combine the rice with the ham, parsley, scallions, and capers. Toss with two forks to mix.

2. Beat the egg yolks with the lemon juice and mustard in a small bowl until slightly thickened. Beat in the oil, a few drops at a time. Then beat in the vinegar, salt, and pepper.

3. Pour the egg yolk mixture over the rice mixture and toss with two forks until well mixed. Chill for 3 hours before serving.

Serves 6

RED, RED RICE

A smoky red pepper gives this rice its wonderful flavor. I often sauté a batch of sausages and slice them over the top, then toss a green salad together, for a light supper.

1 large red bell pepper
3 tablespoons unsalted butter
1 teaspoon olive oil
¼ cup thinly sliced scallion bulbs
3 cups cooked long-grain white rice, heated
Salt and freshly ground black pepper to taste
Chopped fresh parsley, for garnish

1. Char the pepper over a gas flame, under a broiler, or on a preheated grill. Wrap the charred pepper in paper towels and place in a plastic bag for 5 minutes. Rub off the charred skin with paper towels. Seed the pepper and chop.

2. Heat 2 tablespoons of the butter with the oil in a large skillet. Add the scallions; cook 2 minutes but do not brown. Add the chopped roasted pepper and cook 1 minute longer. Transfer the mixture to the container of a food processor, and process until smooth.

3. Melt the remaining 1 tablespoon butter in the skillet, and toss in the rice. Add the processed pepper mixture and toss until well mixed. Season with salt and pepper, and sprinkle with parsley before serving.

Serves 4

DOUBLE-QUICK TOMATO RICE

This is a quick side dish for broiled chicken or chops. Serve it with a healthy green vegetable like broccoli.

3 tablespoons unsalted butter
1 shallot, minced
1 small rib celery, minced
1 cup Bloody Mary mix or V-8 juice
1 cup homemade chicken stock (see page 376) or canned broth
¼ teaspoon salt
1 cup long-grain white rice

Melt the butter in a medium-size saucepan over medium heat. Add the shallot and celery and cook until the vegetables lose their color, 3 to 4 minutes. Add the Bloody Mary mix, stock, and salt. Cover and quickly heat to boiling. Stir in the rice and reduce the heat to low. Cook, covered, until tender, about 15 minutes. Raise the heat slightly if the rice is too wet.

Serves 4

GREEN HERBED RICE

This bowl of rice adds color to any broiled or roasted food. I use fresh basil, which is available at most supermarkets year-round these days. But experiment with other herbs by all means.

¾ cup chopped fresh parsley
¼ cup chopped fresh basil
2 tablespoons chopped green scallion tops
¼ cup olive oil (approximately)
3 cups cooked long-grain white rice, heated
Salt and freshly ground black pepper to taste
1 tablespoon unsalted butter
Freshly grated Pamesan cheese, for garnish (optional)

1. Place the parsley, basil, and scallion tops in the container of a food processor. With the machine running, add just enough oil through the feed tube to make a smooth purée.

2. Toss the puréed mixture into the hot rice, along with salt and pepper and the butter. Serve immediately or keep warm in a 225°F oven. Sprinkle with cheese, if desired, before serving.

Serves 4

NUTTY RICE

I particularly like this spicy rice dish with grilled or broiled seafood.

3 tablespoons unsalted butter
¼ to ½ teaspoon crushed dried hot red
  peppers
⅓ cup chopped macadamia nuts
3 cups cooked long-grain rice, heated

Melt the butter in a large skillet over medium heat. Stir in the dried red peppers (according to taste) and macadamia nuts. Cook, stirring constantly, until the nuts begin to turn golden, 3 to 4 minutes. Reduce the heat and lightly toss in the cooked rice. Serve immediately or keep warm in a 225°F oven.

Serves 4

PRALINE PANCAKES

*P*ecan-flecked rice pancakes—in the best of all possible worlds dappled with a plentitude of warm praline syrup—from Baton Rouge, Louisiana, where a sweet tooth is considered to be every citizen's birthright.

FOR THE SYRUP
1 cup sugar
⅔ cup hot water
2 teaspoons vanilla extract

FOR THE PANCAKES
4 egg yolks
1½ cups milk
4 tablespoons (½ stick) unsalted butter,
  melted
1 teaspoon vanilla extract
2 teaspoons brandy
1 cup all-purpose flour
2 teaspoons baking powder
2 tablespoons sugar
½ teaspoon salt
⅛ teaspoon ground cinnamon
½ cup coarsely chopped pecan halves
1 cup cooked long-grain white rice, chilled

1. Make the Caramel Syrup: Heat the sugar in a medium-size skillet over medium heat until it begins to melt and turns golden, about 1½ minutes. Continue to cook, stirring constantly, until the sugar caramelizes (turns a deep golden color). Quickly and very carefully, stir in the hot water all at once. Stir until any lumps are dissolved. Remove from the heat and add the vanilla. Set aside.

2. Make the Praline Pancakes: Beat the egg yolks in a large bowl until light. Stir in the milk, butter, vanilla, brandy, flour, baking powder, sugar, salt, and cinnamon. Beat well, and then beat in the pecans and rice.

3. On a preheated hot, greased griddle or cast-iron skillet, pour about ½ cup batter for each pancake. Cook until bubbles form on the top and the undersides are lightly browned, about 1 minute. Turn cakes over and lightly brown the other side. Keep warm in a 225°F oven while cooking the remaining pancakes. Serve with syrup drizzled over the cakes.

Makes about 16 pancakes

ULTIMATE RICE VELVET WITH RASPBERRIES AND VANILLA SAUCE

My adaptation of an Alice B. Toklas original. I have been making various versions of this dish for well over twenty years—with not one complaint. Feel free to add a little amaretto, kirsch, even brandy to the custard—at your whim.

½ cup plus 1 tablespoon long-grain white
  rice
1 quart milk
Pinch of salt
8 egg yolks
1 cup sugar
5 tablespoons all-purpose flour
2 cups milk, scalded
1 teaspoon vanilla extract
3 egg whites
1 pint fresh raspberries
Classic Vanilla Sauce (see page 105)

1. Combine the rice, 1 quart milk, and salt in the top of a double boiler. Cook, uncovered, over hot water, stirring occasionally, until the rice is tender, about 1 hour. Transfer the mixture to a heatproof bowl.

2. Preheat the oven to 350°F.

3. Beat the egg yolks in the large bowl of an electric mixer until light. Sift the sugar with the flour and gradually add to the egg yolks. Beat on medium-low speed for 10 minutes. Beat in the scalded milk. Transfer to the top of a double boiler and cook over hot water, stirring frequently, until thick enough to coat a wooden spoon, about 25 minutes. Strain into a large bowl.

4. Add the vanilla to the egg yolk mixture. Drain the rice and add it to the mixture. Beat the egg whites until stiff, and fold into the rice mixture.

5. Pour the rice mixture into a buttered 2-quart soufflé dish, and bake 25 to 30 minutes. The center should be a bit wet. Serve slightly warm, at room temperature, or chilled, with fresh raspberries and Classic Vanilla Sauce.

Serves 6 to 8

The history of rice pudding is obviously a matter of being in the wrong soup at the right time. It all started with the Roman centurions, who quaffed an "aqueous brew of rice and water" to clear their brains after battle.

When the Gauls won a few skirmishes, they celebrated the victory by adding cream to the centurions' broth—giving body to the bisque and a few pounds to Roman waistlines in passing.

However, it took the good-living Benedictine monks to give the soup its true character during the Middle Ages. They first added dried fruits; then honey, eggs, and brandy; and seasoned the pot with cinnamon, cloves, and mace before it was served. Indeed the mixture was often so thick, the sensible brothers consumed it with a fork and knife instead of a spoon.

The soup's metamorphosis came about during a visit of a young abbot from Rome. Being served the Benedictine soup, he tasted it carefully before making a comment.

"This may be the worst soup ever made," he stated forthrightly. "But it is also the best pudding I have ever tasted!"

CHOCOLATE RICE RUINATION

Call it cocoa overkill if you must, but to my jaded tongue this is the best dessert I've tasted since I was ten years old and learned to melt Nestlé bars in their foil wrappers and eat the contents with a demitasse spoon. If you ask about the dessert's pernicious cognomen, I will tell you this: Like those Nestlé bars, a single spoonful of this pudding is the start of utter dietary decadence.

1 can (14 ounces) condensed milk
2 ounces semi-sweet chocolate, chopped
4 tablespoons (½ stick) unsalted butter
½ cup milk
2 egg yolks
3 teaspoons vanilla extract
2 cups steamed, boiled long-grain white
*   rice (see page 220)*
1 cup heavy or whipping cream
1 teaspoon confectioners' sugar
Piece of semi-sweet chocolate, chilled

1. Preheat the oven to 325°F. Butter a shallow soufflé dish.

2. Combine the condensed milk with the chocolate in a medium-size saucepan over low heat. Cook, stirring constantly, until the chocolate has melted, 5 minutes. Gradually add the butter, and stir until melted. Remove the pan from the heat.

3. Whisk the milk into the chocolate mixture. Beat in the egg yolks and 2 teaspoons of the vanilla. Then stir in the rice. Pour the mixture into the prepared soufflé dish, and bake 30 minutes. The middle will be slightly loose. Cool on a wire rack. Refrigerate, covered, until well chilled.

4. Before serving, beat the cream in a large bowl until slightly thickened. Add the remaining 1 teaspoon vanilla and the confectioners' sugar, and beat until stiff. Pile the whipped cream on top of the pudding. Using a vegetable peeler, scrape the piece of semi-sweet chocolate over the top to make chocolate curls. Refrigerate until ready to serve.

Serves 8

LONG-GRAIN BROWN RICE

Despite its high fiber content and heady flavor, too few cooks are willing to undertake the preparation of brown rice. And not because of any "health food" stigma attached to its consumption, either. They are simply intimidated by the time it requires to cook the stuff!

Traditionally, brown rice must cook for 45 to 50 minutes before a grain is deemed fork-tender. However, a recent breakthrough cooking technique speeds up that process considerably: presoaking the grains in the liquid in which they are to be cooked for 8 to 10 hours, or preferably overnight. By presoaking brown rice in this manner, it is possible to slice the actual stove time in half, to 22 minutes flat!

BASIC COOKED BROWN RICE

1 cup brown rice
2½ cups liquid (water, broth, consommé)
    (approximately)
1 teaspoon salt
1½ tablespoons butter

1. Combine the rice, liquid, salt, and butter in a heavy saucepan and heat to boiling. Stir once or twice, reduce the heat, cover, and cook 45 to 50 minutes (see Note).

2. If the rice is not tender, add more liquid and continue to cook, covered. Fluff with a fork before serving.
    Makes 3 to 4 cups.

Note: To save time, soak brown rice in the liquid overnight, and reduce cooking time to 20 to 22 minutes.

STEAMED BOILED BROWN RICE

1 cup brown rice
4 quarts boiling salted water

1. Add the rice to the boiling water. Stir once with a wooden spoon, so that the rice does not stick to the bottom of the pot. When the water returns to boiling, reduce the heat and simmer, uncovered, until just tender, about 30 minutes (see Note). Drain in a colander.

2. Place the colander over 2 inches of boiling water in another pot. Do not let the bottom of the colander touch the water. Cover the rice with a single layer of paper towels, and steam at least 20 minutes. Brown rice can be held this way for several hours without harm.
    Makes 3 to 4 cups

Note: To save time, soak brown rice in the liquid overnight. Drain it in a fine sieve, reserving the liquid. Bring the liquid to a boil, add the rice, and reduce the initial cooking time to 17 minutes.

HOPPIN' JOHN SOUP

From St. Landry parish to Atchafalaya Basin (or anywhere else in the South, for that matter), it's a bleak, black year that does not dawn with a pot of rice and black-eyed peas bubbling away on the stove. That's Hoppin' John. And while my version is somewhat on the slurping side, it will still work wonders for the imbiber—as a talisman or a tonic!

1 tablespoon unsalted butter
2 tablespoons olive oil
1 large onion, minced
1 large clove garlic, minced
1 pound dried black-eyed peas, picked over
1 ham bone, or ½ pound chunk smoked
    ham
½ teaspoon chopped fresh thyme, or ¼
    teaspoon dried
1 bay leaf
1 quart homemade chicken stock (see page
    376) or canned broth (approximately)
1 quart water
½ cup brown rice
Juice of 1 lemon
1 teaspoon grated lemon zest
Salt and freshly ground black pepper to
    taste
1 teaspoon chopped fresh chives

1. Heat the butter with the oil in a large pot over medium-low heat. Add the onion; cook 1 minute. Add the garlic; cook 5 minutes. Stir in the black-eyed peas, then add the ham bone, thyme, bay leaf, chicken stock, and water. Heat to boiling. Reduce the heat and simmer, partially covered, 1 hour.

2. Stir the rice into the soup and continue to cook, partially covered, until black-eyed peas and rice are tender, about 30 minutes longer. If the soup is too thick, add more stock.

3. Remove the ham bone from the soup. Cut off any meat from the bone and chop it fine.

4. Add the ham meat to the soup, and cook 2 minutes. Stir in the lemon juice and lemon zest. Add salt and pepper, and sprinkle with chives.

Serves 6 to 8

VIVA BROWN RICE

Brown rice has certainly had its share of public defenders and detractors.

Aimee Semple McPherson, the evangelist, ate brown rice because she claimed it was toughening her to face adversity. Charles Atlas, the bodybuilder, ate brown rice at age eighty because he was certain it would keep his physical appearance close to the way it had been when he was eighteen!

George Bernard Shaw, who insisted that a brown rice diet was responsible for his mental prowess, wrote a play when he turned ninety-five. After it had been badly reviewed by the press, the comic W. C. Fields quipped: "He probably thought he'd been eating brown *lice* all along!"

Fidel Castro is a true brown rice buff. Expressing a desire to celebrate the grain with the creation of a national dish, he desisted only when the members of his cabinet pointed out that the Cuban word for rice, *arroz*, sounds suspiciously like the Russian word for rifles, *ruzhyo*!

JODY'S INCREDIBLE STUFFED PORK CHOPS

Jody Gillis is a letter-writing fan from Santee, California, who has become something more: a precious friend and a perfervid recipe donor. Her contribution to this grains collection is a solid winner: a savory pork chop crammed to the nines with herbed rice and baked in a sauce that up to now has been a deep dark family secret.

The recipe was sent to me with a query: "Do you want the white or brown version? I prefer the brown myself, possibly because it is the only brown rice dish that I have ever gotten Larry [Jody's husband] to eat without the threat of divorce proceedings!"

Consider Jody Gillis's offering a cure-all for all such intractable spouses.

1 teaspoon salt
¼ teaspoon freshly ground black pepper
¼ teaspoon chopped fresh thyme
¼ teaspoon chopped fresh sage
4 double pork chops, with a pocket cut in each
7 tablespoons unsalted butter
1 onion, finely chopped
1 small rib celery, finely chopped
2 ounces mushrooms, chopped
⅔ cup cooked brown rice
¼ cup dry white wine
¼ cup strong homemade chicken stock (see page 376)
1 cup sour cream, at room temperature
Chopped fresh parsley, for garnish

1. Combine the salt, pepper, thyme, and sage in a small bowl. Mix well and rub the chops, inside the pocket and out, with this mixture.

2. Melt 4 tablespoons of the butter in a heavy skillet over medium heat. Add the onion and celery; cook 5 minutes. Add the mushrooms; cook 3 minutes longer. Reduce the heat to low and stir in the cooked rice. Mix well. Remove the skillet from the heat and allow to cool slightly.

3. Preheat the oven to 350°F.

4. Fill the pockets of the pork chops with the rice mixture. Secure the openings with toothpicks.

5. Melt the remaining 3 tablespoons butter in a large skillet over medium heat. Brown the chops well on both sides. Transfer to a casserole.

6. Pour the wine and stock over the chops, cover, and bake 1 hour.

7. Transfer the chops to a shallow serving dish. Stir the sour cream into the pork juices and pour over the chops. Sprinkle with parsley before serving.

Serves 4

BROWN RICE IN A BUNDLE OF VEAL

*T*his is actually a love letter to brown rice—wrapped in an envelope of tender veal and wild mushrooms. And postmarked Rome, where I came upon the recipe.

4 tablespoons olive oil
1 cup sliced fresh wild mushrooms (such as shiitake or porcini)
1 medium onion, finely chopped
1 medium carrot, diced
2 tablespoons dry white wine
1 cup homemade chicken stock (see page 376) or canned broth
1 cup cooked brown rice

2 ounces thinly sliced prosciutto, chopped
1 large slice top round of veal (about 1 pound), butterflied and pounded thin
2 tablespoons unsalted butter, melted
2 tablespoons dry sherry
Chopped fresh parsley, for garnish

1. Preheat the oven to 375°F.

2. Heat 2 tablespoons of the oil in a

large heavy skillet over medium-high heat. Add the mushrooms and cook, tossing constantly, until lightly browned, about 4 minutes. Using a slotted spoon, transfer the mushrooms to a bowl and set aside.

3. Add the remaining 2 tablespoons oil to the skillet. Add the onion; cook 3 minutes. Stir in the carrot and the mushrooms. Sprinkle with the wine and cook until all liquid has evaporated, about 4 minutes. Stir in ¼ cup of the chicken stock and continue to cook until the carrot is fairly tender and almost all liquid has evaporated, about 5 minutes. Stir in the cooked rice. Remove from the heat and stir in the prosciutto.

4. Lay the veal open flat on a piece of cheesecloth large enough to enclose it. Spread the rice mixture over the veal, and roll it closed, using the cheesecloth to help roll. Tie securely to keep the meat from falling apart while cooking.

5. Spread 1 tablespoon of the melted butter over the bottom of a shallow baking dish. Place the meat seam side down in the butter. Drizzle the remaining 1 tablespoon butter over the top, and roast 30 minutes.

6. Meanwhile, combine ¼ cup stock with the sherry. Baste the meat after it has cooked for 10 minutes, and continue to baste every 10 minutes. After 30 minutes, pour the remaining stock around the meat and roast, basting once with pan juices, until the meat is tender, about 15 minutes longer.

7. Remove the meat from the dish and carefully remove the cheesecloth. Slice the veal roll into ½-inch-thick slices. Transfer them to a serving platter and pour the pan juices over the top. Serve sprinkled with parsley.

Serves 4

HOT CUBANO CHICKEN 'N' RICE

Certainly no national dish, this recipe is still worthy of a ten-gun salute or at least the dip of a Havana panatella from time to time.

1 large eggplant (about 1 pound), cut into
    ½-inch cubes
Salt
12 chicken wings
1 tablespoon hot pepper sauce
1 pound Italian sausages
2 tablespoons unsalted butter
½ pound smoked ham, cubed
1 large onion, chopped
2 cloves garlic, minced
1 medium red bell pepper, cored, seeded,
    and chopped
2 hot red peppers, seeded, deveined, and
    minced
1 can (14 ounces) imported plum tomatoes,
    with juice, chopped

1 tablespoon chopped fresh basil
⅛ teaspoon dried thyme
1 cup brown rice
2½ cups homemade chicken stock (see page
    376) or canned broth
Freshly ground black pepper to taste
1 cup corn kernels (3 medium ears)
1 package (10 ounces) frozen baby lima
    beans, thawed
Chopped fresh parsley, for garnish

1. Place the eggplant cubes in a colander. Sprinkle with salt, and let stand 30 minutes. Then rinse with cold water and squeeze dry. Sprinkle the chicken wings with hot pepper sauce. Set chicken wings and eggplant aside.

2. Place the sausages in a large heavy pot. Sauté over low heat until grease begins to render. Then raise the heat to medium and sauté until golden brown on all sides, about 15 minutes. Remove the sausages to a plate, cool slightly, and cut into ½-inch-thick slices.

3. Drain all but 2 tablespoons fat from the pot. Add the butter and sauté the chicken wings over medium heat until well browned. Transfer the wings to the plate with the sausages.

4. Add the ham cubes to the pot and sauté 5 minutes. Transfer to the plate with the wings and sausages.

5. Add the onion to the pot; cook 2 minutes. Add the garlic; cook 1 minute longer. Reduce the heat under the pot to medium-low and stir in the bell pepper, hot peppers, and eggplant cubes. Cook, stirring occasionally, 5 minutes.

6. Stir the tomatoes into the onion/pepper mixture, and add the basil, thyme, rice, and chicken stock. Heat to boiling. Reduce the heat, cover, and cook over medium-low heat 25 minutes. Season with salt and pepper.

7. Preheat the oven to 350°F.

8. Add the ham, chicken wings, sausages, corn, and lima beans to the rice mixture. Stir once, cover, and bake until the rice is tender, about 20 minutes. Sprinkle with parsley before serving.

Serves 4 to 6

CIRCASSIAN CHICKEN WITH BROWN RICE

A bequest from Mother Russia, this is reputedly one of the Empress Catherine's favorite picnic foods, and she often decorated it herself with precious jewels as garnish. I'll take parsley, thank you all the same. The dish makes dandy summer party fare—serve it with bread and salad on the side.

2 small chickens (2½ to 3 pounds each), well rinsed
1 medium onion, unpeeled, stuck with 2 whole cloves
1 medium rib celery, coarsely chopped
1 medium carrot, coarsely chopped
4 sprigs parsley
4 sprigs dill
1 sprig thyme
10 peppercorns
1 quart homemade chicken stock (see page 376) or canned broth
2 tablespoons unsalted butter
1 medium onion, chopped
½ cup hazelnuts, roasted and skinned (see Note)

Pinch of cayenne pepper
Salt and freshly ground black pepper to taste
2 teaspoons unflavored gelatin
3 cups cooked brown rice
Chopped fresh dill, for garnish

1. Place the chickens in a large pot and add the onion stuck with cloves, celery, carrot, parsley, dill, thyme, peppercorns, and stock. Heat to boiling. Reduce the heat and simmer, partially covered, until the chickens are tender, about 50 minutes.

2. Preheat the broiler.

3. Remove the chickens from the

stock and carefully cut into serving pieces. Return the backs to the pot, heat the stock to boiling, and reduce to about 2¼ cups, 15 minutes. Strain.

4. Broil the reserved chicken pieces, skin side up, until golden, about 5 minutes. Set aside.

5. Melt the butter in a medium-size skillet over medium-low heat. Add the chopped onion and cook until soft, about 5 minutes. Transfer the onions to the container of a food processor, and add the hazelnuts and 2 cups of the chicken stock. Being very careful, process until smooth. Add cayenne pepper, and salt and black pepper.

6. Dissolve the gelatin in ¼ cup of the chicken stock in a small bowl. Place the bowl over simmering water and stir until the gelatin has dissolved. Stir this mixture into the sauce.

7. Spread the rice over the bottom of a 2-inch-deep serving platter. Arrange the chicken pieces over the rice, and pour the sauce over the chicken. Garnish with chopped dill. Refrigerate until the gelatin sets and the dish has chilled, about 3 hours.

Serves 6 to 8

Note: To roast hazelnuts, spread them evenly on a baking sheet, and place in a 400°F oven for 5 minutes. Carefully wrap the nuts in paper towels and place in a plastic bag and let stand until cool enough to handle. Rub the hazelnuts in paper towels to remove the skins.

CROCCHETTA DI SPINACI

The ultimate vegetable croquettes come from a tiny trattoria in Calabria, where they were served as a first course prior to pasta. Light, crisp, and highly addictive, this is the kind of finger food that can make a cocktail party, or break it if the hostess runs short before the guests have had second (or third) helpings!

1 cup cooked brown rice
2 packages (10 ounces each) frozen chopped spinach, thawed and squeezed dry
2 eggs, lightly beaten
⅓ cup freshly grated Parmesan cheese
½ teaspoon freshly grated nutmeg
½ teaspoon salt
¼ teaspoon freshly ground black pepper
¼ teaspoon hot pepper sauce
½ to ¾ cup fresh bread crumbs
2 tablespoons unsalted butter
4 tablespoons olive oil (approximately)

1. Preheat the oven to 350°F.

2. Place the cooked rice in a large bowl and add the spinach, eggs, cheese, nutmeg, salt, pepper, and hot pepper sauce. Mix well.

3. Using a soup spoon, form the mixture into rounds and drop them into the bread crumbs. Using the tips of your fingers, lightly roll the rounds to coat with crumbs.

4. Heat the butter with 2 tablespoons of the oil in a large skillet over medium heat. Sauté the croquettes, a few at a time, until golden brown on both sides, about 3 minutes per side. Drain on paper towels, and arrange on an ovenproof platter. Continue to sauté croquettes until all the mixture is used up, adding more oil as needed. Bake for 10 minutes before serving.

Serves 4 to 6

BROWN RICE WITH GREEN PEAS

This amalgam of vegetable and grain calls for *cooked* brown rice. When I am making a dish with cooked brown rice, I generally prepare it the day before and keep it refrigerated until the penultimate moment. I know there is a rumor that cooked brown rice spoils faster than cooked regular-milled white rice, but it simply ain't so! Keeping any cooked rice for several days is no problem if you store it in an airtight self-seal bag or a plastic storage container with a tight-fitting lid, so the grains neither dry out nor absorb the flavor of other foods in the fridge.

1 tablespoon unsalted butter
1 large shallot, minced
2 pounds fresh peas, shelled (about 2 cups), or 1 package (10 ounces) frozen peas, thawed
¼ cup heavy or whipping cream
⅓ cup homemade chicken stock (see page 376) or canned broth
3½ cups cooked brown rice, heated
Salt and freshly ground black pepper to taste
1 teaspoon chopped fresh chives

1. Preheat the oven to 350°F. Lightly oil a medium-size baking dish.

2. Melt the butter in a medium-size saucepan over medium-low heat. Add the shallot; cook 1 minute. Stir in the peas. Cook, covered, until just tender— about 5 minutes for fresh, less for frozen.

3. Place half the pea mixture in the container of a food processor, and add the cream and stock. Process until fine.

4. Return the purée to the saucepan and add the remaining pea mixture, the rice, and salt and pepper. Transfer to the prepared baking dish and bake, loosely covered, 15 minutes. Sprinkle with chives before serving.

Serves 4 to 6

BROWN RICE WITH ZUCCHINI

This is one side dish that is full of flavor. A bit of goat cheese makes all the difference. I sometimes just add a cup of cooked chicken and eat it for lunch.

2 tablespoons unsalted butter
1 small onion, chopped
1 clove garlic, minced
1 large or 2 small zucchini, grated (1⅓ cups)
2 tablespoons chopped fresh basil
1 tablespoon strong chicken stock (see Note) or bouillon
1¾ cups cooked brown rice, heated

3 tablespoons dry goat cheese, such as Montrachet
2 tablespoons heavy or whipping cream
Dash of hot pepper sauce
Salt and freshly ground black pepper to taste

1. Preheat the oven to 350°F.
2. Melt the butter in a large skillet

over medium-low heat. Add the onion; cook 2 minutes. Add the garlic; cook 1 minute longer. Stir in the zucchini, basil, and chicken stock; cook 4 minutes longer.

3. Stir the cooked rice into the zucchini mixture. Add the goat cheese, cream, and hot pepper sauce. Cook 1 minute, then season with salt and pepper. Transfer to an ovenproof serving dish, and bake for 12 minutes.

Serves 4

Note: If you do not have strong chicken stock on hand (see page 379), reduce ¼ cup canned chicken broth to 1 tablespoon by simmering for 10 minutes.

STIRRED-UP BROWN RICE WITH WILD MUSHROOMS AND FENNEL

A rustic dish that is all the better when permitted to slow-cook over low heat, so that the rice may absorb the rich and earthy flavor of its collaborators in the pot.

2 tablespoons unsalted butter
1 teaspoon olive oil
2 large shallots, minced
1 clove garlic, minced
¼ cup sliced fresh wild mushrooms (such as shiitake or porcini)
1 cup brown rice
1 small fennel bulb (about ½ pound), chopped
3 cups homemade chicken stock (see page 376) or canned broth
½ cup chopped fresh parsley

1. Heat the butter with the oil in a medium-size saucepan over medium heat. Add the shallots; cook 2 minutes. Add the garlic; cook 1 minute longer. Stir in the mushrooms, rice, and fennel, stirring to coat with the shallot mixture.

2. Add the chicken stock and heat to boiling, then reduce the heat. Cook, covered, over medium-low heat until the rice is tender and all liquid has been absorbed, 45 to 50 minutes. Stir in the parsley before serving.

Serves 4 to 6

ST. LUCIAN BROWN RICE AND EGGPLANT

I had a version of this dish in St. Lucia, one of the most spectacularly beautiful (and non-touristy) islands in the Caribbean. Nutmeg trees grow all over the islands. Mace is the lacey coating of the nutmeg seed. They serve this dish with hearty fish, such as dolphin, swordfish, or tuna.

1 eggplant (½ to ¾ pound), sliced
Salt
½ cup all-purpose flour
¼ teaspoon ground mace
4 to 6 tablespoons olive oil
2 tablespoons unsalted butter
1 medium onion, finely chopped
1 clove garlic, minced
¼ cup finely chopped red or green bell
　　pepper
¾ to 1 cup chopped seeded tomatoes
Pinch of sugar
Pinch of thyme
1 cup brown rice
2½ cups homemade chicken stock (see page
　　376) or canned broth
Freshly ground black pepper to taste
Chopped fresh parsley, for garnish

1. Place the eggplant slices in a colander and sprinkle with salt. Let stand 30 minutes, then rinse and pat dry. Cut the slices in half.

2. Combine the flour with the mace on a plate. Dust the eggplant slices with this mixture.

3. Heat 4 tablespoons oil in a heavy skillet over medium heat. Sauté the eggplant slices, a few pieces at a time, until golden brown on both sides. Drain on paper towels. Add more oil as needed.

4. Heat the butter with ½ teaspoon oil in a medium-size saucepan over medium-low heat. Add the onion; cook 1 minute. Add the garlic and pepper, tossing to coat. Stir in the tomatoes, sugar, thyme, and rice. Cook 1 minute. Stir in the eggplant slices and the chicken stock, and heat to boiling. Reduce the heat and cook, covered, over medium-low heat until the rice is tender and all liquid has been absorbed, 45 to 50 minutes. Add salt and pepper, and sprinkle with parsley.

Serves 4 to 6

Toward the end of the first century B.C., religious laws in the Orient and the Middle East reached such epic proportions that thousands of believers starved to death rather than consume "impure" foods.

To the Hebrews, unclean or impure foods included any meat cut by a sword; flesh of excessively hairy or hairless beasts; meat of animals with humps (like camels) and meat of seafood with shells (like shrimp). Also verboten were vegetables and fruits that had been sullied by insects, and rice grains from markets where they had been sniffed by dogs, cats, or housewives.

In China it was forbidden for the poor to eat brown rice from public granaries, because rats were reportedly seen on the premises. When the public granaries were burned down, however, the rats ran away and the poor usually caught and ate them. But they never got a sniff at the brown rice.

India had other problems. In that country, white rice was considered impure by high-caste Brahmins because it was always husked by low-caste "untouchables." Consequently Brahmins ate only brown rice for a hundred years, until some religious leader—who was obviously a pragmatist—determined that all impure foods could be purified by the judicious sprinkling of a little holy water or ghee (clarified butter).

RUSSET RICE

A nother dish that benefits from slow-cooked rather than presoaked rice.

2 tablespoons unsalted butter
1 leek (white part only), well rinsed and
    finely chopped
3 scallions, white bulbs and green tops,
    finely chopped
1¼ cups chopped seeded fresh tomatoes
½ teaspoon tomato paste
Pinch of sugar
Pinch of thyme
¾ cup brown rice
2 cups homemade chicken stock (see page
    376) or canned broth, heated
Chopped fresh parsley, for garnish

1. Melt the butter in a medium-size saucepan over medium-low heat. Add the leek and scallions; cook 5 minutes.

2. Stir the tomatoes into the onion mixture, and add the tomato paste, sugar, and thyme. Cook 1 minute. Add the rice and stir until well coated with the mixture, then add the chicken stock. Heat to boiling. Reduce the heat and cook, covered, over medium-low heat until the rice is tender and all liquid has been absorbed, 45 to 50 minutes. Sprinkle with parsley before serving.

Serves 4 to 6

BASMATI, TEXMATI, AND OTHER AROMATIC LONG-GRAIN RICES

Basmati. There is only one true basmati rice. Grown in the north of India and Pakistan, it is imported to America in fairly small quantities, which makes it expensive. But like many other luxury foods, it is worthy of serious kitchen attention.

Traditionally basmati rice is sold in bulk and must be carefully washed before it is cooked. The water bath not only removes residual dirt particles, it also releases a measure of starch that would otherwise make cooked basmati rice sticky. More important, since basmati rice expands in length as it cooks, repeated washing and soaking keeps the kernels from breaking or splitting apart.

There are two methods that I use for preparing basmati rice, both borrowed from my friend Julie Sahni, author of *Classic Indian Cooking* and *Classic Indian Vegetarian and Grain Cooking*. Even a novice who can't boil water can master the art of cooking basmati rice in minutes.

Texmati and other domestic aromatic rices. I admire foods with strong flavor. To my tongue, Texas Texmati rice and the other well-known American aromatics, like Louisiana's "popcorn" and wild pecan rice or California's Calmati and Wehani rice, have little in common with the bouquet, taste, or texture of true basmati rice. There is even some question whether basmati was ever crossbred into these varieties, as is alleged. Della rice, the daddy of all scented U.S. varieties—developed almost twenty years ago—is thought to be a strain of Indochinese and Indonesian rices grafted onto local long-grain rootstock in Louisiana.

But in the final analysis, a rice's antecedance is of scant importance at the stove. A domestic aromatic like Texmati rice may not be as uniquely flavored as basmati, but it is still mighty good to eat, less than half the price, and a lot easier to prepare.

(For instructions on preparing brown aromatic rices, see the cooking chart on page 218.)

BASIC COOKED BASMATI RICE

What makes a rice *aromatic*?

The Indians who lived in the foothills of the Himalayas believed it was a gift of the god Veda. Early rice farmers in Louisiana and Texas thought it might be the result of acid rain. Both were wild surmises, as it turns out. In 1982 two members of the U.S. Department of Agriculture, along with a fellow scientist from the Rice Research Institute of Manila, identified the substance that gives cooked aromatic rice its characteristic fragrance: known as 2-acetyl-1-pyroline, it is a chemical found in all rice. A higher concentration in basmati and other aromatics gives them their quintessential scent.

1 cup basmati rice
4 quarts water

1. Wash the rice by placing it in a large bowl and adding cold water to cover; when the water turns milky, about 3 minutes, pour off the water. Repeat several times, until the water remains clear. Drain. Cover the rice once more with cold water, and let stand 30 minutes. Drain.

2. Heat 4 quarts unsalted water to boiling. Stir in the rice, and return to boiling; cook 5 minutes. Drain the rice. Before serving, fluff gently with a fork, being careful not to break the kernels.

Makes about 3 cups

Though basmati rice comes from northern India, few of the populace who live there consume it. Essentially bread-eaters who like their loaves on the wheaten side, Punjabis hardly ever touch rice—aromatic or otherwise.

TRADITIONAL STEAMED BASMATI RICE

1 cup basmati rice
Water

1. Wash the basmati rice by placing it in a large bowl and adding cold water to cover; when the water turns milky, in about 3 minutes, pour off the water. Repeat several times until the water remains clear. Drain. Cover the rice with 2 cups of cold water, and let stand 30 minutes. Drain the rice in a colander over a medium-size ovenproof saucepan.

2. Heat the water in the saucepan to boiling. Stir in the rice, and return to boiling. Reduce the heat and cook, partially covered, over low heat until the water is almost absorbed, 10 minutes.

3. Cover the saucepan tightly and either steam the rice on a flame tamer set over very low heat for 10 minutes, or place the covered saucepan on the middle rack of a preheated 300°F oven for 25 minutes. Remove from the heat and let stand, covered, 5 minutes. Before serving, fluff gently with a fork, being careful not to break the kernels.

Makes about 3 cups.

BASIC COOKED TEXMATI RICE

In my kitchen, there are two ways to cook Texmati rice. The first is merely to add a cupful of rice to 3 quarts of boiling water, stir once, and cook for 12 minutes. Drain and serve.

The second method, which follows, takes a bit longer, but the extra time that the rice stands after cooking seems to allow the flavor to fully coalesce.

1 cup Texmati rice
1¾ cups water
1 teaspoon salt
1 teaspoon unsalted butter

Combine the rice, water, salt, and butter in a medium-size saucepan and heat to boiling. Stir once or twice and reduce the heat. Cover, and cook 15 minutes. Remove from the heat and let stand, covered, 5 minutes. Fluff with a fork before serving.

Makes 3 cups

ROAST CHICKEN WITH PESTO RICE

*L*ittle Italy is where the notion for a pesto rice stuffing came into my head. Needless to say, make it only when fresh basil is bountiful.

2 small roasting chickens (2½ to 3 pounds each), well rinsed and dried
1 clove garlic, bruised
3 cups cooked basmati, Texmati, or other aromatic rice
½ cup Pesto Sauce (recipe follows)
¼ cup pignolia (pine) nuts
2 tablespoons unsalted butter, at room temperature
Salt and freshly ground black pepper to taste
½ cup plus 1 tablespoon homemade chicken stock (see page 376) or canned broth
1 cup water
1 tablespoon all-purpose flour
¼ cup heavy or whipping cream
1 egg yolk, lightly beaten
1 tablespoon chopped fresh basil

1. Preheat the oven to 400°F.

2. Rub the chicken inside and out with the bruised garlic. Combine the cooked rice, Pesto Sauce, and pignolia nuts in a mixing bowl. Stuff each chicken with half the mixture. Sew and truss.

3. Rub each chicken with 1 tablespoon of the butter, and sprinkle with salt and pepper. Roast on a rack in a baking pan, 30 minutes.

4. Reduce the oven heat to 350°F. Pour ½ cup chicken stock over the chicken, and add the water to the pan. Continue to roast, basting occasionally, until the juices run yellow when the chicken is pierced with a fork, about 1 hour longer.

5. Place the chickens on a serving platter and remove the strings. Keep warm while making the sauce.

6. Skim the fat from the pan juices.

Strain the juices through a fine sieve into a saucepan and heat to boiling. Mix the flour with the remaining 1 tablespoon chicken stock and stir this into the juices. Simmer 5 minutes. Stir in the cream and continue to simmer until slightly thickened, about 5 minutes longer. Remove from the heat.

7. Whisk 2 tablespoons of the sauce with the egg yolk in a small bowl. Stir this mixture back into the sauce, and cook over very low heat 2 minutes. Do not allow it to boil. Stir in the basil. Spoon ¼ cup of the sauce over the chickens, and pass the remaining sauce.

Serves 6 to 8

Pesto Sauce

2 cups coarsely chopped fresh basil leaves
½ cup chopped fresh parsley
1 teaspoon coarse (kosher) salt
½ teaspoon freshly ground black pepper
2 large cloves garlic, chopped
¾ cup olive oil
¼ cup pignolia (pine) nuts
½ cup freshly grated Romano or Parmesan cheese

Place all the ingredients except the cheese in the container of a food processor or blender. Blend until smooth, about 2 minutes. (You might have to start and stop the blender several times in the beginning.) Transfer the mixture to a bowl and stir in the cheese.

Makes about 1½ cups

Note: Pesto Sauce can be kept refrigerated in a tightly covered jar for several weeks, or frozen for several months, but it is always best not to stir in the cheese until just before serving.

OPELOUSAS' PAELLA

A Cajun version of a Spanish paella crammed with seafood, sausages, and rice, of course.

1 sprig thyme, or ¼ teaspoon dried
1 bay leaf
2 sprigs parsley
1 pound hot Italian sausages
1½ tablespoons olive oil
1 medium onion, chopped
2 cloves garlic, minced
4 scallions, white bulbs and green tops,
    chopped
1 medium rib celery, minced
½ green bell pepper, cored, seeded, and
    minced
1 small hot red pepper, seeded, deveined,
    and minced
½ cup dry white wine
½ cup clam juice or broth
12 or more littleneck clams, well scrubbed
    under cold running water
2 cups (approximately) homemade chicken
    stock (see page 376) or canned broth
1¼ cups presoaked basmati rice, or natural
    Texmati or other aromatic rice
1½ teaspoons filé powder
1 tablespoon unsalted butter
½ pound or more medium-size shrimp,
    shelled and deveined
Salt and freshly ground black pepper to
    taste
Chopped fresh parsley, for garnish

1. Make an herb bouquet by tying the thyme, bay leaf, and parsley sprigs in a cheesecloth bag, and set aside.

2. Sauté the sausages in a large oil-rubbed heavy pot or Dutch oven until well browned on all sides, 8 to 10 minutes. Remove the sausages, cut them into ½-inch-thick slices, and reserve.

3. Discard all but 1 tablespoon fat from the pot and add the olive oil. Add the onion; cook over medium-low heat 4 minutes. Add the garlic; cook 2 minutes longer. Stir in the scallions, celery, green bell pepper, and the hot pepper. Cook, stirring occasionally, 10 minutes.

4. Meanwhile, combine the white wine and clam juice in a medium-size saucepan and heat to boiling. Add the clams, cover, and reduce the heat to medium. Cook until the clams open, about 5 minutes. Remove the clams, in their shells, with a slotted spoon and reserve.

5. Measure the clam broth in the pan, and add enough chicken stock to make 2 cups if using basmati rice, 2½ cups for other aromatic rice. Return the liquid to the pan and heat to boiling.

6. Stir the rice into the vegetable mixture. Stir in the filé powder, the reserved sausage slices, and the boiling broth. Add the herb bouquet and heat to boiling. Reduce the heat to medium-low and simmer, covered, 10 minutes for basmati rice, 15 minutes for Texmati or other aromatic rice. Discard the herb bouquet.

7. Stir the butter and shrimp into the rice mixture. Continue to cook, covered, 5 minutes. Then season with salt and pepper.

8. Turn off the heat and tuck the reserved clams (in their shells) into the rice mixture. Let stand, covered, 5 minutes. Sprinkle with parsley before serving.

Serves 4 to 6

SAUSAGE-RICE STUFFED TOMATOES

Use small tomatoes when you want to serve this as a tasty starter for six. With larger tomatoes, it will make a fine light meal for four. These can be served hot, at room temperature—even cold, sprinkled with a little vinegar and olive oil.

6 small or 4 large firm, ripe tomatoes
Salt and freshly ground black pepper to
    taste
3 sweet Italian sausages (about ¾ pound)
1 tablespoon unsalted butter
1½ teaspoons olive oil
1 small onion, finely chopped (¼ cup)
1 clove garlic, minced
½ teaspoon sugar
½ teaspoon beef bouillon powder
2 teaspoons red wine vinegar
1 cup cooked basmati, Texmati, or other
    aromatic rice
2 tablespoons chopped fresh parsley
1 tablespoon chopped fresh basil
3 tablespoons pignolia (pine) nuts
¼ cup freshly grated Parmesan cheese
1 egg, lightly beaten

1. Preheat the oven to 375°F.

2. Cut the tops off the tomatoes and discard. Gently squeeze the tomatoes over a bowl; reserve the juice and pulp (use a spoon to scoop out pulp if necessary). Sprinkle the scooped-out tomatoes with salt and pepper. Drain upside down on paper towels.

3. Remove the sausage meat from the casings, and coarsely chop.

4. Heat the butter with the oil in a large heavy skillet over medium-low heat. Add the onion; cook 1 minute. Add the garlic; cook 2 minutes longer. Add the sausage meat and cook, breaking up any lumps with a wooden spoon, until the sausage loses its pink color, 4 minutes. Add the reserved tomato juice and pulp; sprinkle with the sugar and bouillon powder. Raise the heat to medium-high and cook, stirring frequently, until all liquid has evaporated, 8 minutes.

5. Sprinkle the meat mixture with the vinegar and reduce the heat. Stir in the cooked rice, the parsley, basil, pignolia nuts, half the Parmesan cheese, and the beaten egg. Mix well, and remove from the heat.

6. Spoon the mixture into the tomatoes, mounding the tops. Place in a greased shallow baking dish (the tomatoes should fit snugly), and sprinkle with the remaining Parmesan cheese. Bake 30 minutes. Serve hot, at room temperature, or cold.

Serves 4 to 6

TUNA AND WARM GINGERED RICE SALAD

_I_ am lucky to live part of the year where the tuna is fresh and remarkably sweet, so this salad often finds its way onto my summertime menus. However, if you can't get fresh, this smoky peppery salad is equally tonic with canned tuna packed in water.

1 small clove garlic, minced
¼ teaspoon ground ginger
2 teaspoons soy sauce
Juice of 1 small lemon
¼ cup olive oil
1 cup cooked basmati, Texmati, or other
  aromatic rice, heated
2 large scallions, white bulbs and green
  tops, chopped
1 large red bell pepper, roasted, peeled,
  cored, and chopped (see Note)
1¼ cups cooked fresh or canned (drained
  water-packed) tuna, broken into
  chunks)

1. Using the back of a spoon, mash the garlic with the ginger in a small bowl until a paste is formed. Whisk in the soy sauce, lemon juice, and olive oil.

2. Combine the hot cooked rice with the scallions, roasted bell pepper, and tuna in a medium-size bowl. Pour the dressing over and toss well. Serve immediately.

Serves 4

Note: To roast a pepper, cook it over a gas flame or under a broiler until charred all over. Then carefully wrap the pepper in paper towels and place it in a plastic bag. Let it stand until cool. Remove the core and rub off the charred skin with paper towels.

CHILLY RADISH, RICE, AND SHRIMP SALAD

Aromatic rice and seafood seem such a natural together that I couldn't resist adding some cooked shrimp to my favorite rice and radish salad. Another quick brunch or light supper offering.

2 cups cooked basmati, Texmati, or other
  aromatic rice, chilled
1 shallot, minced
8 to 10 large radishes, trimmed, thinly
  sliced (about 1½ cups)
¼ cup thinly sliced imported black olives
½ pound cooked shrimp, shelled, deveined,
  and halved
1 small cucumber, peeled, seeded, and
  minced
1 tablespoon finely chopped fresh basil
1 teaspoon finely chopped fresh parsley
1 teaspoon finely slivered lemon zest
½ cup Vinaigrette Dressing (recipe follows)
Salt and freshly ground black pepper to
  taste

Combine all ingredients through the lemon zest in a large bowl. Toss lightly. Pour the vinaigrette dressing over, and toss well. Add salt and pepper to taste. Chill slightly before serving.

Serves 4 to 6

Vinaigrette Dressing

1 small clove garlic, crushed
½ teaspoon coarse (kosher) salt
1 teaspoon Dijon mustard
Juice of 1 lemon
⅓ to ½ cup olive oil
2 teaspoons red wine vinegar
¼ teaspoon freshly ground black pepper

Using the back of a spoon, mash the garlic with the salt in a small bowl until a paste is formed. Stir in the mustard and lemon juice. Whisk in the oil, vinegar, and pepper.

Makes about ½ cup

PERSIAN RICE CAKE WITH CRISPY POTATOES AND DILL

*T*his is one of my favorite rice dishes. It is a vegetable cake of Persian derivation, and much dependent upon a flavored rice to fuse the odd ingredients (onions, potatoes, lima beans) together. If you are using basmati rice in this recipe, do not presoak it first (but do wash it), for broken kernels are not amiss here.

1 quart water
1 teaspoon salt
1 cup unsoaked basmati rice, or natural
  Texmati or other aromatic rice
8 tablespoons (1 stick) unsalted butter
1 small onion, finely chopped
½ teaspoon crushed dried hot red peppers
Pinch of ground cloves
1 package (10 ounces) frozen lima beans,
  thawed
½ cup chopped fresh dill
1 medium baking potato (½ pound)

1. Heat the water and ½ teaspoon of the salt to boiling in a medium-size saucepan. Stir in the rice. Boil 7 minutes for basmati rice, about 10 minutes for Texmati or other aromatic rice. The rice should be slightly firm at the center. Drain, and set aside.

2. Melt 4 tablespoons of the butter in a large heavy skillet over medium heat. Stir in the onion and dried red peppers. Cook, stirring constantly, until lightly golden, about 3 minutes.

3. Sprinkle the onion with the cloves, and stir in the lima beans. Reduce the heat to medium-low and cook, stirring occasionally, 4 minutes. Remove from the heat.

4. Add the cooked rice to the onion mixture, tossing with two forks until well mixed. Toss in the dill.

5. Melt 2 tablespoons of the butter over low heat in a 10-inch skillet (preferably non-stick) with a cover. Remove from the heat. Peel the potato and cut into ⅛-inch-thick slices. Lay the slices, just

*A*romatic rice is said to develop its characteristic perfume from two things: the soil in which it is planted and the climate during its growing season.

Though *basmati* literally means "queen of fragrance," it is an erratic realm at best. There are fields in the state of Punjab where the rice grows jasmine-scented, while others have a heliotrope or tulip fragrance—and no one really knows why.

In Alvin, Texas, where Texmati rice is grown, the workers who run the heavy-duty planting and threshing machines call different fields by different names. The one traditionally known as "Yellow Rose" always yields the largest and most fragrant kernels. Go figure nature out!

barely overlapping, over the bottom of the skillet.

6. Place the skillet over medium heat and spoon the rice mixture over the potatoes, pressing down lightly. Dot with the remaining 2 tablespoons butter. Cook 5 minutes. Reduce the heat to medium-low, cover, and continue to cook, moving the pan occasionally so that its edges are, at some point, over the heat, 45 minutes. Let stand 4 minutes before inverting onto a serving platter.

Serves 6

LEMON RICE

This is always a hit when I teach it in cooking classes. Add hot peppers to your taste. It goes very well with spicy (though not fiery hot) stews of all sorts.

3 sprigs parsley
2 fresh sage leaves, or ¼ teaspoon dried
2 sprigs thyme, or ¼ teaspoon dried
1 cup presoaked basmati rice, or natural Texmati or other aromatic rice
2 tablespoons unsalted butter
1 teaspoon seeded, deveined, and minced hot green pepper
¼ cup strong homemade chicken stock (see Note)
Finely slivered zest of 1 lemon
Juice of 1 medium lemon
Salt and freshly ground black pepper to taste
Chopped fresh parsley, for garnish

1. Tie the parsley sprigs, sage, and thyme in a cheesecloth bag, and place in a large pot of boiling salted water. Add the rice, stir once with a wooden spoon so it does not stick to the bottom of the pot, and return to boiling. Reduce the heat slightly and simmer, uncovered, until tender, 5 minutes for basmati rice, about 12 minutes for Texmati or other aromatic rice.

2. Meanwhile, melt the butter in a medium-size saucepan over medium-low heat. Stir in the minced pepper, and cook 2 minutes.

3. Drain the rice and add it to the pepper. Toss to mix, and add the chicken stock, lemon zest, and lemon juice. Toss the rice over medium-low heat until all the excess liquid has evaporated, about 5 minutes. Add salt and pepper to taste, and sprinkle with parsley.

Serves 4 to 6

Note: If you do not have strong chicken stock on hand (see page 379), reduce ½ cup canned chicken broth to ¼ cup by simmering for 10 minutes.

CHICORY RICE

You can use any hearty green in this creamy side dish. Keep the main dish on the simple side.

1 bunch (about ½ pound) chicory (curly endive)
3 tablespoons olive oil
2 large shallots, finely chopped
1 large clove garlic, minced
1 cup presoaked basmati rice, or natural Texmati or other aromatic rice
2 teaspoons tomato paste
1½ cups strong chicken stock (see Note) for basmati, or 2 cups for other rice
Salt and freshly ground black pepper to taste
Freshly grated Pecorino or Parmesan cheese

1. Cut the root off the chicory and discard. Rinse the chicory and dry it well. Chop the stems and place in a bowl. Chop the leaves and place in a separate bowl.

2. Heat the oil in a medium-size

saucepan over medium heat. Add the shallots; cook 2 minutes. Add the garlic; cook 1 minute. Stir in the chicory stems and cook 2 minutes longer.

3. Stir the rice and tomato paste into the shallot mixture, and toss until well mixed. Add the chicken stock. Heat to boiling, and stir in the chicory leaves. Reduce the heat and cook, covered, stirring occasionally, over medium-low heat until the rice is tender, about 10 minutes for basmati, 15 minutes for Texmati or other aromatic rice. (Remove the cover and raise the heat slightly if the mixture is too wet.) Add salt and pepper to taste, and serve with cheese on the side.

Serves 4 to 6

Note: If you do not have strong chicken stock on hand (see page 379), reduce 3 cups canned chicken broth to 1½ cups by simmering for 15 minutes.

It has been claimed that the custom of pelting newlywed couples with rice is Indian in origin. And while Western anthropologists assume the practice was just a fertility rite, Indian philosophers do not wholly agree.

If it was an aromatic rice, they state with some authority, the bride would gather it up in her veil and the groom would be assured of a good wedding dinner. And then, being a contented man afterward, he would teach his wife the art of love, rather than mere baby-making!

POT OF TEA PILAF

I once read about an Indian pilaf that was made in a pot of tea. The exotic idea piqued my taste buds, and my version follows. I serve it with grilled chicken or pork.

3 tablespoons olive oil
2 medium onions, finely chopped
1 clove garlic, minced
½ teaspoon minced fresh ginger
1 piece (1 inch) cinnamon stick
½ teaspoon chili powder
¼ teaspoon ground cumin
⅛ teaspoon ground turmeric
1⅓ cups unsoaked basmati rice or natural Texmati rice
2½ cups brewed Chinese black tea
3 tablespoons unsalted butter
1 teaspoon salt
½ teaspoon freshly ground black pepper
1 cup frozen peas, thawed

1. Heat the oil in a medium-size saucepan over medium heat. Add half the onions; cook 1 minute. Add the garlic and ginger; cook 3 minutes longer. Stir in the cinnamon, chili powder, cumin, and turmeric. Reduce the heat and cook, uncovered, over medium-low heat 10 minutes.

2. Stir the rice into the onion mixture, tossing gently to coat. Add the tea and heat to boiling, stirring once. Reduce the heat and cook, covered, over medium-low heat until the rice is fairly tender and all liquid has been absorbed, about 10 minutes for basmati, 15 minutes for Texmati or other aromatic rice. Turn off the heat.

3. Meanwhile, melt the butter in a

medium-size skillet over medium heat. Stir in the remaining onion and cook, stirring constantly, until crisp and golden, about 5 minutes. Remove from the heat.

4. Discard the cinnamon stick from the rice mixture, and toss in the salt, pepper, and peas. Let stand, covered, 5 minutes. Transfer the rice mixture to a bowl and sprinkle with the sautéed onions.

Serves 6

MEDIUM-GRAIN RICE

Medium-grain rice requires no more cooking time than conventional long-grain varieties. However, as medium-grain kernels are shorter and plumper and have a higher degree of amylopectin starch, this rice is at its best (tender and moist) when eaten soon after it is prepared.

In my kitchen, medium-grain rice is a first choice for rice-stuffed vegetable dishes and meat loaves, where substance is a decided requirement. Years ago I learned that medium-grain rice makes a salubrious filling—when amended with pork, herbs, scallions, chili peppers, and Lord knows what other seasonings—for the pale but pungent Cajun sausages known as *boudin blanc*.

Medium-grain rice is also a natural for soups, since it adds an imperceptible measure of starch to thicken an anemic broth, yet the grains remain neat and separate in every bowl.

Medium-grain rice cooks in less liquid than long-grain rice—which makes sense, since the grain itself is considerably shorter.

For instructions on preparing medium-grain *brown* rice, see the chart on page 218 or follow the instructions for preparing long-grain brown rice on page 233. You may use it in the Insalata di Riso on page 257 or in any of the recipes in the brown rice section that call for precooked rice.

BASIC COOKED MEDIUM-GRAIN RICE

1 cup medium-grain white rice
1½ cups liquid (water, broth, consommé, vegetable juice)
½ teaspoon salt
1 tablespoon unsalted butter

1. Combine the rice, liquid, salt, and butter in a medium-size saucepan and heat to boiling. Stir once or twice, reduce the heat, cover, and simmer 15 minutes.

2. If the rice is not tender or the liquid is not entirely absorbed, replace the lid and cook 2 to 4 minutes longer. Fluff with a fork before serving.

Makes about 3 cups

GREEK LEMON SOUP

There is a curious story that takes some of the polish off medium-grain rice. According to some food historians, Theophrastus, Alexander the Great's advisor and confidant, knew about rice being grown in the Orient—but he never made any attempt to have rice plants brought to the Mediterranean because his informants claimed it was a grain that was too white and far too sticky for Greek tastes!

Tempus fugit a few centuries, and the Greeks invented one of the great contributions to gastronomy: *sopa avgolemono*, which translates to "lemon soup" and is much dependent upon medium-grain rice for body.

This soup, I might add, has a double life in my household. In winter it is a hearty brew as limned, but in summer I make it a day ahead and chill it. Skipping the amenity of whipped cream and Parmesan cheese, I merely garnish the bowl with peeled paper-thin lemon slices and a sprinkling of minced chives.

⅓ cup medium-grain white rice
3 cups homemade chicken stock (see page 376) or canned broth
3 cups lamb stock
½ cup heavy or whipping cream
2 tablespoons grated lemon zest
1 tablespoon freshly grated Parmesan cheese
2 egg yolks
Juice of 1 large lemon

1. Wash the rice in a colander under cold running water to remove excess starch. Drain.

2. Combine the chicken and lamb stocks in a medium-size saucepan, and heat to boiling. Stir in the rice and reduce the heat. Cook, uncovered, over medium heat until the rice is tender, 15 to 20 minutes. Remove from the heat.

3. Meanwhile, whip the cream with the lemon zest and Parmesan cheese until stiff. Transfer to a serving bowl and keep in a cool place.

4. When the rice is tender, beat the egg yolks with the lemon juice in a medium-size bowl until light. Slowly beat in 1 cup broth, then slowly stir the egg mixture into the rice and broth mixture. Continue to stir for 1 minute. Serve immediately with the flavored whipped cream.

Serves 6

MARY SURINA'S SARMA

In Slavic households, where rice is a prerequisite in most larders, it was a tradition for a firstborn son's cradle to be adorned with a small pillow filled with raw rice. If the child did not cry at the pillow's hardness, the family rejoiced because they knew the boy would grow to manhood able to survive any adversity. And to celebrate they always made a dish of cabbage stuffed with meat and rice.

If he cried, they ate the same dish—but worried a lot more!

This Yugoslavian dish is a donation from one of the best cooks of my acquaintance, Mary Surina of San Pedro, California. Mary's Sarma comes with a requirement: these stuffed cabbage rolls must be prepared and refrigerated at least a day before they are to be cooked. And it's a good idea to let them come to room temperature before cooking. Some treats, like vintage wines, simply must age before they're served!

1 loose-leafed cabbage (about 1½ pounds)
1¼ pounds ground lean pork
3 sweet Italian sausages (about ¾ pound)
4 cloves garlic, crushed
1 egg, lightly beaten
⅓ cup medium-grain white rice
½ teaspoon salt
¼ teaspoon freshly ground black pepper
2 strips bacon, chopped
1 medium onion, finely chopped
3 pounds sauerkraut, drained but not
  rinsed
1 small ham bone (about ½ pound)
1¾ cups homemade chicken stock (see page
  376) or canned broth
1 cup water

1. Place the cabbage in a large pot of boiling water. With a wooden fork and spoon, pull the leaves apart as it cooks. Cook until the leaves are wilted but not mushy, about 2 minutes (depending on the looseness of the cabbage). Drain. Trim the large ribs of the cabbage so the shape is even, and shave off the thick part with a sharp knife so the thickness is the same as the leaf. You should have 12 large leaves. Shred the remaining cabbage.

2. Place the pork in a large bowl. Remove the sausage meat from the casings and add it to the pork along with the garlic, egg, rice, salt, and pepper. Mix well.

3. Place about 2 tablespoons meat filling on one side of each cabbage leaf and roll up, tucking in the sides.

4. Render the bacon in a large pot over medium-low heat until soft. Add the onion; cook until golden, about 4 minutes. Stir in the shredded cabbage, and cook 1 minute longer. Remove from the heat.

5. Place a layer of sauerkraut over the cabbage mixture, and place the ham bone in the center of the pot. Arrange a layer of cabbage rolls around the bone, and top with sauerkraut. Continue to layer, ending with sauerkraut. Pour the stock and water over the top. Refrigerate, covered, overnight.

6. Allow the dish to come to room temperature. Place the pot, covered, over medium heat and heat to boiling. Reduce the heat and simmer, covered, 1 hour.

Serves 6

GREENHORN RICE

Because of its high amylopectin content, medium-grain rice is recommended for ulcer patients and those suffering with like stomach disorders. One painless way to consume this rice is the following dish.

Known as Greenhorn Rice, it may seem slightly familiar; I offered it in an earlier recipe collection called *Honest American Fare*. It is retrieved here because it is one of the most frequently requested rice recipes I have ever logged.

3 tablespoons unsalted butter
1 tablespoon olive oil
1 medium onion, finely chopped
3 shallots, finely chopped
1 clove garlic, minced
1 cup medium-grain white rice
¾ cup homemade chicken stock (see page
    376) or canned broth
½ teaspoon salt
¼ teaspoon freshly ground black pepper
¼ teaspoon freshly grated nutmeg
3 sprigs thyme, chopped, or
    ⅛ teaspoon dried
1 pound fresh spinach, trimmed, rinsed,
    and finely chopped
½ cup heavy or whipping cream

1. Preheat the oven to 375°F.

2. Heat the butter with the oil in a Dutch oven over medium-low heat. Add the onion; cook 2 minutes. Stir in the shallots, garlic, and rice. Cook, stirring constantly, until the rice turns milky in color, about 4 minutes. Add the chicken stock, salt, pepper, nutmeg, thyme, and spinach. Stir over medium-high heat until boiling.

3. Cover the pot, transfer it to the oven, and bake until the rice is tender and all liquid has been absorbed, about 15 minutes. Remove the pot from the oven and toss in the cream. Return it, covered, to the oven for another 5 minutes.

Serves 4

BOUDIN BLANC SAUSAGES

Medium-grain rice, which is grown in Louisiana, is a solid staple of Cajun cuisine.

Now you will find Cajun dishes on lots of menus across the country, and Cajun ingredients in loads of gourmet shops, but I promise you will never find this dish anywhere beyond Vermilion Bay and Catahoula Lake. Because it simply won't travel! I am speaking of *boudin blanc*, the peppery local sausages that gastronomes have been known to kill for.

Unlike many of my cooking confederates, I am not addicted to sausage making. It's too messy and too maverick an operation. However, if one were going that route once in a lifetime I would advice *boudin blanc...*

2 pounds boneless pork shoulder with fat,
    cut into 1½-inch cubes
2 large onions, chopped (about 2¼ cups)
4 scallions, white bulbs and green tops,
    chopped
8 peppercorns
3 whole cloves
3 teaspoons salt
1 bay leaf
2 green bell peppers, cored, seeded, and
    chopped
1 hot green pepper, seeded, deveined, and
    chopped

1 dried hot red pepper, crushed
2 cloves garlic, finely chopped
1 cup chopped fresh parsley
1 teaspoon chopped fresh basil, or
    ½ teaspoon dried
2½ cups cooked medium-grain white rice
1 teaspoon ground allspice
1 teaspoon cayenne pepper
½ teaspoon freshly ground black pepper
¼ teaspoon ground mace
4 to 6 sausage casings, 2 inches wide and
    12 inches long (available from Italian
    or German butchers)

1. Place the pork in a large pot, cover with cold water, and heat to boiling. Drain, and rinse under cold running water. Wipe out the pot and return the pork. Add 1 cup of the chopped onion, one fourth of the chopped scallions, the peppercorns, cloves, 1 teaspoon of the salt, and the bay leaf. Cover with 2 inches of water, and heat to boiling. Reduce the heat and simmer, partially covered, until the pork is tender, about 1½ hours. Drain, and discard the bay leaf, peppercorns, and cloves.

2. Transfer the pork to a large bowl and add the remaining onions and scallions, the green peppers, dried pepper, garlic, parsley, and basil. Mix well. Grind the mixture in a meat grinder, or process in a food processor until fairly smooth. Return it to the bowl and add the rice, allspice, cayenne pepper, black pepper, remaining 2 teaspoons salt, and the mace. Mix well.

3. Rinse the sausage casings in cold water. Hold each casing under the faucet and let the water run through to check for leaks. Tie one end of each casing. Stuff the pork mixture into the casings with the sausage-stuffing attachment of a meat grinder, or using a pastry bag fitted with a ½-inch plain tube. Tie the open ends of the sausages.

4. Cook the sausages in boiling water to cover for 3 minutes. Drain. Cool, wrap in plastic wrap, and refrigerate for 24 hours before serving. (Sausages will keep, tightly wrapped, in the refrigerator for 5 to 6 days.)

5. To serve, either poach the sausages in simmering water for 20 minutes, or prick with a fork and sauté in butter until golden brown on all sides.

Serves 6 to 8

INSALATA DI RISO

An estimable dish from Bari, Italy, located practically in the Adriatic Sea.

1½ cups cooked medium-grain white or brown rice
2 small scallions, white bulbs and green tops, finely chopped
2 fresh shiitake mushroom caps, halved and thinly sliced
5 canned artichoke hearts, sliced
2 ounces Fontina cheese, cut into 1-inch-long julienne strips
1 clove garlic, minced
¼ teaspoon coarse (kosher) salt
¼ cup olive oil
3 tablespoons fresh lemon juice
⅛ teaspoon anchovy paste
Salt and freshly ground black pepper to taste
1 teaspoon chopped fresh chervil, or

¼ teaspoon dried mixed with 1 teaspoon chopped fresh parsley
4 large lettuce leaves

1. Place the rice in a large bowl and gently toss in the scallions, mushrooms, artichokes, and cheese.

2. Using the back of a spoon, mash the garlic with the salt in a small bowl until a paste is formed. Whisk in the oil, lemon juice, and anchovy paste.

3. Pour the dressing over the salad and toss gently to mix. Add salt and pepper, and sprinkle with the chervil. Serve on lettuce leaves.

Serves 4

FUNGO DOLCE (HAZELNUT AND RICE MACAROONS)

From the Piedmont section of Italy, the addition of toasted rice turns this dry hazelnut macaroon into a chewy coconut candy-like bar.

⅔ cup hazelnuts
¾ cup cooked medium-grain white rice
4 egg whites, at room temperature
Pinch of salt
1 ¼ cups sugar

1. Preheat the oven to 400°F.

2. Spread the hazelnuts out on a baking sheet, and bake 5 minutes. Carefully wrap the nuts in paper towels and place in a plastic bag. Let stand until cool enough to handle. Reduce oven heat to 350°F.

3. Spread the rice out on a baking sheet, and bake, stirring once, 5 minutes. The rice will be slightly crisp. Set aside to cool.

4. Rub the hazelnuts in paper towels to remove the skins. Finely chop half the nuts. Coarsely chop the remaining nuts.

5. Beat the egg whites with the salt in the large bowl of an electric mixer until soft peaks form. Slowly add the sugar on high speed, and continue to beat until thick and shiny. Fold in the nuts and rice.

6. Transfer the mixture to a large heavy saucepan. Cook, stirring constantly, over medium-low heat until the mixture becomes less glossy and thickens, about 15 minutes. (Humidity will determine actual time.) The mixture is ready when it resembles the stage at which fudge is ready to be poured into a pan. Do not overcook, because like fudge, it hardens quickly. (If dough becomes too stiff, add an extra egg white and quickly beat back to semi-soft consistency.) Let cool slightly.

7. Using your fingers and a tablespoon, form the mixture into balls and place them on parchment-lined baking sheets. Bake until crisp and lightly browned, about 10 minutes. Cool slightly before peeling the paper from the macaroons. Cool completely before storing in an airtight container.

Makes about 20 macaroons

SHORT-GRAIN RICE

The first thing to explain about short-grain rice is its maddening diversity. There are three different types on the market: *round* or *pearl* short-grain rice, Italian *arborio* short-grain rice, and Oriental *glutinous* short-grain rice.

Round rice is so called because each grain is almost as wide as it is long. Since this variety is also heavy with amylopectin starch, the cooked kernels have considerable cling. (The shorter the grain, the stickier the stuff in your bowl!) Japanese and Caribbean cooks prefer round rice because of this massing quality.

Arborio short-grain rice is grown only in northern Italy. Though it is high in starch as well, arborio rice has the ability to absorb its cooking liquid to an unusual degree. Developing a creamy consistency that Italians call *all'onda* (waviness), each kernel manages to stay afloat and firm in a virtual sea of flavor.

Oriental glutinous short-grain rice, sometimes known as "sweet rice," can be found only in Asian markets. It is used in China to stuff chicken or duck, and in both China and Japan it is pounded into a sticky dough that is the basis of incredibly sweet pastries and a savory rice soup-stew known as *congee*, with which many Asians start their day.

I must confess I do not cook round or glutinous short-grain rice, but I have good friends who do. The following recipe is borrowed from Elizabeth Andoh, author of the brilliant *An Ocean of Flavor: The Japanese Way with Fish and Seafood*.

(For instructions on preparing short-grain brown rice, see the chart on page 233, or follow the instructions for long-grain brown rice on page 233. For cooking brown glutinous rice, see the instructions for Basic Cooked Brown Rice, page 234.)

BASIC COOKED SHORT-GRAIN RICE

1½ cups round or glutinous short-grain rice
1¾ cups cold water (see Note)

1. Place the rice in a bowl and cover with cold water. Stir vigorously until the water turns cloudy, then drain. Repeat several times, until the water remains clear. Drain. (The rice will be somewhat opaque and will have started to absorb water.)

2. Place the rice with 1¾ cups cold water in a medium-size saucepan with a tight-fitting lid. Let stand 10 minutes.

3. Place the saucepan over medium-high heat and heat to boiling, 3 to 5 minutes. Do not remove the lid. When the water reaches the boiling point and steam begins to escape from under the lid, reduce the heat and continue to cook without removing the lid until all water has been absorbed, about 5 minutes longer. (The pan will start to sizzle when all the water is absorbed.) Then raise the heat to high and cook 30 seconds longer, to dry the rice, and remove from the heat. Let stand, covered, 10 minutes.

Makes about 3 cups

Note: According to Elizabeth Andoh, newly harvested rice is the most sought after (and the most expensive) in Japan. The same holds true for California short-grain rice, which is harvested in late October and early November. If you can locate *shin main* (new rice), use equal quantities of rice and water in the saucepan: 1½ cups water to 1½ cups rice. As rice ages, more water is required.

CLASSIC RISOTTO WITH RED WINE

A great risotto is dependent upon four things: the correct short-grain rice to begin with, combined with sweet butter and/or olive oil and minced onion, some tonic seasonings, and finally a hot strong broth that is slowly stirred, and stirred, into the dish.

I usually serve risotto as a first course or luncheon dish with salad after. As it is rich, I find that 1 cup of uncooked arborio rice makes enough for four diners. If risotto is to be a main course, double the recipe!

This risotto with red wine and beef broth is a classic rendering. Serve it with additional Parmesan cheese at the table.

3½ tablespoons unsalted butter
1 small onion, finely chopped
1 small clove garlic, minced
1 medium carrot, peeled and chopped
Salt and freshly ground black pepper to
*   taste*
¼ cup red wine
1 cup Italian arborio rice
2½ to 3 cups homemade beef stock (see
*   page 377) or canned broth, simmering*
3 tablespoons chopped fresh parsley
Freshly grated Parmesan cheese

1. Melt 2½ tablespoons of the butter in a heavy skillet over medium-low heat. Add the onion; cook 1 minute. Add the garlic and carrot; cook 2 minutes longer. Sprinkle with salt and pepper to taste, and add the wine. Raise the heat slightly and cook, stirring constantly, until al-most all the liquid has evaporated, 4 minutes.

2. Stir the rice into the onion/carrot mixture until well coated. Add 1 cup of the simmering beef stock and cook, stirring frequently, until almost all liquid has been absorbed. This should take 10 minutes. Reduce the heat if it is cooking too fast.

3. Add another cup of stock and continue to cook, stirring frequently, until almost all liquid has been absorbed, about 10 minutes.

4. Add ½ cup stock to the rice and continue to cook, stirring frequently, until the rice is tender, 5 to 10 minutes longer. Add more stock if needed. Stir in the remaining butter, sprinkle with parsley, and pass the cheese on the side.
Serves 4

LOBSTER NEWBURG RISOTTO

For years, Lobster Newburg was the top of culinary fashion. A dish that has almost been forgotten will have a fine comeback when it is turned into a creamy rich risotto. Serve this one as a first course to a simple meal.

1 live lobster, 1 to 1¼ pounds
2½ tablespoons unsalted butter
2 shallots, minced
¼ teaspoon tomato paste
2 tablespoons Madeira wine
1 cup Italian arborio rice
1 cup clam broth, simmering
2 to 2½ cups homemade chicken stock (see
    page 376) or canned broth, simmering
⅓ cup heavy or whipping cream
1 teaspoon chopped fresh chives

1. Cook the lobster in boiling water to cover until firm, 5 to 7 minutes. Drain, and set aside to cool.

2. Crack the lobster shell with a nutcracker and remove the meat from the tail and claws. Coarsely chop. You should have about 1 cup. (If there is roe, reserve it, if desired.)

3. Melt the butter in a heavy enameled skillet over medium-low heat. Add the shallots; cook until soft, about 4 minutes. (Add a small amount of roe, if desired.) Stir in ⅓ cup of the lobster meat, the tomato paste, and the Madeira. Add the rice. Stir until it is well coated with the mixture. Then add the simmering clam broth and cook, stirring frequently, until almost all the liquid has been absorbed. This should take 10 minutes. Reduce the heat if it is cooking too fast.

4. Add 1 cup of the simmering chicken stock and continue to cook, stirring frequently, until almost all liquid has been absorbed, about 10 minutes.

5. Add another cup of chicken stock and the remaining lobster. Continue to cook, stirring frequently, until the rice is tender, about 10 minutes longer. Add more chicken stock, if needed.

6. Meanwhile, beat the cream until stiff and fold in the chives. Transfer to a serving bowl and stir into the risotto at the table before serving.

Serves 4

RADICCHIO RISOTTO

*D*o not be dismayed when the radicchio loses its lustrous red color—it is used to enhance the flavor of this creamy dish. A generous sprinkling of parsley helps make it more eye-appealing.

3½ tablespoons unsalted butter
2 large shallots, minced
¼ pound radicchio (Italian red lettuce), or
    any strong-flavored lettuce, cored and
    chopped
Salt and freshly ground black pepper to
    taste
¼ cup dry white wine
1 cup Italian arborio rice
2½ to 3 cups homemade chicken stock (see
    page 376) or canned broth, simmering
½ cup freshly grated Parmesan cheese
3 tablespoons chopped fresh parsley

1. Melt 2½ tablespoons of the butter in a heavy skillet over medium-low heat. Add the shallots; cook until golden, about 5 minutes. Add the radicchio and sprinkle with salt and pepper; cook 1 minute. Stir in the wine. Raise the heat slightly and cook, stirring constantly, until almost all the liquid has evaporated, 4 minutes.

2. Stir the rice into the radicchio mixture until well coated. Add 1 cup of the simmering chicken stock and cook, stirring frequently, until almost all liquid has been absorbed. This should take 10 minutes. Reduce the heat if it is cooking too fast.

3. Add another cup of stock and continue to cook, stirring frequently, until almost all liquid has been absorbed, about 10 minutes.

4. Add ½ cup stock to the rice and continue to cook, stirring frequently, until the rice is tender, 5 to 10 minutes longer. Add more stock, if needed. Stir in the remaining butter and the cheese and toss in the parsley.

Serves 4

My sister, Myra, made her first trip to Europe armed with enthusiasm and not much money. During the first months of her stay, she toured England, France, and Belgium, managing to ferret out friends of friends, odd relatives, and sometimes utter strangers who not only invited her to dine but often kept her as a house guest for weeks on end.

When she arrived in Rome, a letter announced that this city would probably be her last stop unless she could "wangle a green card," an unlikely prospect in light of Italy's unemployment.

"I don't know a soul here," she wrote with some finality. "But I'd sure like to. Roman men are *very* sexy!"

She stayed there a year, returning home with a Roman coiffure, Roman slang in her speech, Roman lira in her purse, and an impressive bracelet of aquamarines and sapphires on her wrist.

My sister never outgrew her love of things Italian. She brought back the first espresso maker I'd ever seen and a case of Campari, which like a true Roman she sipped every afternoon. For me she produced a small bag filled with arborio rice.

As I had not the slightest clue what this rice was nor how to cook it, my sister undertook the assignment with a prodigal's good grace, insisting that the flame on her gas stove be lowered to the precise degree of blue brevity before she began.

"This dish," she announced gravely, "is called *ri-sotto*, and it is like no other rice you have ever tasted in your life."

Myra was not the greatest cook in the world, but the flavor of her homey risotto (creamy without a drop of cream) altered my taste buds irrevocably. I have eaten many other risottos since, in great hostelries and little trattorias in Milan, Venice, and Rome, but none has ever tasted better. The first forkful cooked up in a tiny apartment in Greenwich Village back in the 1950s remains as green in my memory as my sister herself. And that's saying a lot.

SMOKY SMITHFIELD HAM RISOTTO

Smithfield ham, smoked and cured, is the traditional ham of Virginia. However, it lends itself here as if it were any fine Italian smoked ham.

3½ tablespoons unsalted butter
2 large shallots, minced
¼ pound mushrooms, thinly sliced
½ cup Smithfield ham, slivered
Freshly ground black pepper to taste
¼ cup dry white wine
1 cup Italian arborio rice
2½ to 3 cups homemade chicken stock (see
    page 376) or canned broth, simmering
Freshly grated Parmesan cheese

1. Melt 2½ tablespoons of the butter in a heavy skillet over medium-low heat. Add the shallots; cook 1 minute. Stir in the mushrooms and ham. Sprinkle with pepper and wine. Raise the heat slightly and cook, stirring constantly, until almost all the liquid has evaporated, 4 minutes.

2. Stir the rice into the shallot/ham mixture until well coated. Add 1 cup of the simmering chicken stock and cook, stirring frequently, until almost all the liquid has been absorbed. This should take 10 minutes. Reduce the heat if it is cooking too fast.

3. Add another cup of stock and continue to cook, stirring frequently, until almost all liquid has been absorbed, about 10 minutes.

4. Add ½ cup stock to the rice and continue to cook, stirring frequently, until the rice is tender, 5 to 10 minutes longer. Add more stock, if needed. Stir in the remaining butter and pass the cheese on the side.

Serves 4

RISOTTO WITH GOAT CHEESE

This is a creamy side dish that is enhanced by paper-thin rounds of zucchini tossed in at the last minute. The zucchini will soften slightly in the hot rice, but should not be cooked. It offers a counterbalance to the smooth-textured rice.

2½ tablespoons unsalted butter
2 large shallots, minced
¼ cup dry white wine
1 cup Italian arborio rice
2½ to 3 cups homemade chicken stock (see
    page 376) or canned broth, simmering
¼ pound goat cheese, cut into chunks
1 small zucchini (about 3 ounces), cut into
    thin rounds
Salt and freshly ground black pepper to
    taste

1. Melt the butter in a heavy skillet over medium-low heat. Add the shallots; cook 1 minute. Sprinkle with the wine. Raise the heat slightly and cook, stirring constantly, until almost all the liquid has evaporated, 4 minutes.

2. Stir the rice into the shallot mixture until well coated. Add 1 cup of the simmering chicken stock and cook, stirring frequently, until almost all liquid has been absorbed. This should take 10

Do not allow yourself to be persuaded to use any short-grain rice (American or otherwise) that is not clearly labeled "Arborio Superfino." "Superfino" is the indication that the rice you are using is a *large* short-grained variety.

For shopping sources and mail order information, check the resource pages in the back of the book.

minutes. Reduce the heat if it is cooking too fast.

3. Add another cup of stock and continue to cook, stirring frequently, until almost all liquid has been absorbed, about 10 minutes.

4. Add ½ cup stock to the rice and continue to cook, stirring frequently, until the rice is tender, 5 to 10 minutes longer. Add more stock, if needed. Stir in the goat cheese until melted. Toss in the zucchini, and season with salt and pepper.

Serves 4

RISOTTO WITH BACON AND STRING BEANS

This hearty side dish is as wonderful with grilled chicken as it is with roast pork. As the rice cooks, the beans will soften and become an integral part of the dish's flavor.

2 strips bacon, chopped
1 medium white onion, chopped
¼ cup dry white wine
1 cup Italian arborio rice
½ cup finely chopped string beans
2½ to 3 cups homemade chicken stock (see page 376) or canned broth, simmering
⅓ cup freshly grated dry Monterey Jack, Pecorino, or Parmesan cheese
1 tablespoon unsalted butter
Chopped fresh parsley, for garnish

1. Sauté the bacon in a heavy skillet over medium-low heat until all grease is rendered. Stir in the onion; cook 2 minutes. Sprinkle with the wine. Raise the heat slightly and cook, stirring constantly, until almost all the liquid has evaporated, 4 minutes.

2. Stir the rice and string beans into the bacon/onion mixture until well coated. Add 1 cup of the simmering chicken stock and cook, stirring frequently, until almost all liquid has been absorbed. This should take 10 minutes. Reduce the heat if it is cooking too fast.

3. Add another cup of stock and continue to cook, stirring frequently, until almost all liquid has been absorbed, about 10 minutes.

4. Add ½ cup more stock to the rice and continue to cook, stirring frequently, until the rice is tender, 5 to 10 minutes longer. Add more stock, if needed. Stir in the cheese and the butter. Sprinkle with parsley.

Serves 4

SEMOLINA

The Quick-Cooking Grain with Endless Possibilities

The cord that binds me to semolina, a very Italian grain, is a silver one—linked to a very American lady, my mother.

Paula Greene was a woman always itching for enterprise. A born visionary, her rise in the world of finance was marred by a flaw fatal: she lacked courage in her convictions.

During the pivotal years of the Depression, I recall my mother scanning the financial sections of the newspapers for hours. Separating columns of gray type headed "Business Opportunities" from "Help Wanted" or "Real Estate," she would pore over each advertisement scrupulously, intent on finding some offering that would propel our family of slender means into solid gold affluence.

In time she found what was deemed an optimum venture. It was a peanut farm. "Peanuts grow like weeds, but on bushes. You don't have to bend to pick 'em," her sales pitch went (for my father had an untrustworthy vertebra). "And it's a steal besides..."

My mother's enthusiasm seemed well founded. Her discovery was a 250-acre spread, not far from Atlanta, that yielded 500 tons of peanuts per harvest. Besides the groves, there was a house, two barns, and innumerable outbuildings on the property.

"It's a steal," my mother announced jubilantly after an initial phone call. "And we can get it for at least a third less if we pay in cash!" She had a nose for horse trading too.

We didn't have any cash, but that seemed a minor impediment and had no effect on my mother's enthusiasm. Borrowing a book on George Washington Carver from the library, she immediately began calculating how to diversify such a remarkable output of goobers. However, neither my father nor her's (whose financial assistance was needed to float a loan) shared her zeal for peanut farming.

"Who eats peanuts?" my grandfather inquired with hard-edged sarcasm. "A few guys at a ball game maybe?"

"Pa!" My mother hated doomsayers. "Just think about peanut butter. Or Mr. Goodbars and peanut clusters. Think about peanut oil and Smithfield ham..."

"I'm thinking, I'm thinking," he replied with a flick of cigarette ash. "And the conclusion is: I'm against it."

"But why, Pa?" his daughter wailed.

"Because, Paulie, I never heard of a successful Jewish farmer." My grandfather spoke in the tones of an oracle. "But I certainly heard of the Ku Klux Klan!"

My mother believed in the promise of peanuts all her days, but she did not press the dream for herself because she could not override an adverse opinion.

There were other aborted opportunities. Once she conceived of a shop that would sell only greeting cards, and even made a down payment on a lease. But she backed out because some clouded-crystal-ball-gazers warned she'd go bankrupt the day after Christmas. Another brainstorm was a health farm—a place in the country where overeaters would pay to diet in rustic seclusion, and where meals would be no more substantial than lettuce leaves and vegetable juice. Pessimists convinced her no one would diet in a group. So she relinquished that iron in the fire too. Giving in, she claimed it was "the hard luck of the Greenes not to have staunch supporters." A family motto I resolutely refused to inherit.

When I opened The Store in Amagansett on borrowed capital, my mother was at first skeptical, then frankly astounded at the degree of attention and praise paid to my skills at the stove.

"I'm not worrying about your future any more," she announced. But in truth she never completely stopped.

When she was seventy, my mother went to Europe for the first time. For three months the only word of her journey was postcards scrawled with descriptions of dishes she ate—to inspire similar versions at my hands.

When she returned, I met her at the airport. With no sign of jet lag, she collared me the very moment she passed through Customs.

"Have I got a great idea..." she began, lowering her voice when she became aware others were listening. "Remember how we almost got rich peanut farming? Well"—my mother winked—"this guy I met in Rome told me an even *better* way to make a killing. A wheat farm in Italy. I know one we could have for a *song!*"

"Mother." I tried hard not to sound reproving. "Wheat grows all over. Why Italy?"

"Why not?" demanded my parent. "Listen, I'm not talking any wheat. I'm talking *semi-lena*, the stuff they use to make macaroni. Think how much macaroni the world eats; multiply that a thousand times and you'll see we're talking big bucks. In Italy they bake *semi-lena*; they fry it; they eat it as cereal; they even put it into soup. I ate *semi-lena* from one end of the boot to the other and I'm telling you the stuff has a future!"

"Sounds good," I began weakly. "But why *buy* a farm?"

My mother could not believe her ears. "To get in on the ground floor!" she fairly shouted. Then, realizing I was no longer her child, she tried to mollify me instead. "With your abilities and my sharp pencil, we could make millions!"

Knowing her son's ambivalence, my mother did not pursue the matter further. But as we gathered her luggage she could not resist a final parry. "You'll have to agree it's something to think about anyway."

"I'll think about it."

"And try *semi-lena*." My mother gave a little yelp. "I almost forgot, I brought you some." Opening her topcoat, she pointed to a plastic sack of grain, carefully safety-pinned to the lining.

"Mother! You didn't smuggle that in?"

"Nah!" She replied with just a shade too wide-eyed innocence. "I just didn't bother to declare it."

Seating herself in my car, she handed me the package.

"Just remember the peanut farm," my mother said, "and you'll thank me for this someday."

I did not buy a wheat farm in Italy. But I thank her for semolina more times than I can ever calculate, nonetheless.

The Grain's Genesis

If I had listened to my mother, I would have learned that semolina is no grain at all but the roughly milled endosperm (or nutritive tissue) of durum wheat. And that this wheat (*Triticum durum*) is the hardest in the world. It is used almost exclusively in the manufacture of commercially dried pasta.

"Almost" is the key word, for the semolina that does not end up as a twirl of spaghetti will most probably find itself converted into a pile of golden couscous in some North African household.

Hard durum wheat has a long and checkered past. Some botanists claim that it was the first upwardly mobile grain. Man ate it, they aver, because it was a wild plant that grew in every path he chose to take. Hard wheat is probably an offshoot of *einkorn*, an early spring grain that bore a single kernel per stem, and *emmer*, a wild and wooly weed impervious to weather changes. Whatever its forebears, *Triticum durum* certainly proliferated fast, even blooming in northern climes where little else survived.

Wishful thinkers suggest that durum is a miracle grain, for it spread from the North to the East and West, literally in man's footsteps.

There are those who maintain that semolina is actually the "kussemet" mentioned in the Bible. They say that when the children of Israel are instructed in Ezekiel to "take thou also unto thee golden wheat, barley and beans . . . put them into a vessel and make thee bread thereof," the wheat was plainly hard durum, just as the bread was unleavened. It cannot have been a pleasure to eat, but then the Bible also states "A tooth for a tooth" somewhere else along the line.

Cultivation of hard durum wheat— and its conversion to semolina, which changed the ancient world's diet—took place in the ninth millennium B.C., when the grain's popularity spread from Asia Minor to North Africa, the French Pyrenees, and the Swiss Lake settlements.

In the Swiss Lake settlements, residues of meal and bread dough made with what appears to be milled semolina flour have recently been unearthed by food-snooping archeologists.

If my mother had been there to witness the event, I can imagine her reaction: "Didn't I tell you this stuff had a future? Well, it had a past too!"

Some Plain Grain Talk

Right off the bat, let's get one thing straight: semolina is not just another pretty grain in the kitchen! The milled "innards" of hard durum wheat does have three distinct faces, however.

Durum semolina is the most commonly known. It is used for the manufacture of commercially dried pasta (known as *pasta secca* in Italy) and commercially produced couscous. This semolina is a sandy substance, pale yellow in color and highly granular if you rub it between your fingers. It contains an extraordinarily high percentage of gluten, which is what makes a spaghetti strand stretch, not break apart in the cooking process.

Durum semolina's gluten content is responsible for its high protein level as well. An average serving of cooked semolina contains 10 to 12 grams of protein, 42 grams of carbohydrate, and 1 gram of dietary fiber—with less than 1 percent fat and no cholesterol whatsoever. Which is reason enough to include some in your daily diet allowance.

Actually, semolina's only drawback is calories. Figure 210 calories per cupful. But that's not really bad, considering the grain's gratification level.

Granular semolina is simply a lower-graded milling of the wheat, with the crushed endosperm thinned out with flour. By law, durum semolina is re-stricted to no more than 3 percent flour in its composition. Granular semolina is permitted to contain anywhere from 3 to 10 percent flour as an additive. But not to worry—in the U.S. granular semolina is sold only to commercial pasta makers.

Semolina flour is not to be confused with durum flour. The latter is a powdery residue left over after the processing of semolina. Semolina flour is a superfine grind of flour produced for cooking and baking only. Semolina flour has a high ash content and a delicate pale gold color. It is also sometimes mysteriously labeled "Extra Fancy Semolina Patent Flour," which is the guarantee of high-quality milling that the Department of Agriculture insists upon in all imported semolina packaging.

Durum semolina and semolina flour are interchangeable in all of the recipes that follow.

How to Buy It

Semolina, I regret to say, is not an easy product to come by in America. Supermarkets do not regularly stock it on their shelves, and even specialty "fancy food" shops and gourmet groceries have a tendency to dismiss this grain as "exotica" and keep it in short supply. Those who live in urban areas with varied ethnic populations have a better chance of finding semolina. Italian markets and delicatessens usually carry it in packaged form, and Middle Eastern groceries often sell it boxed or in bulk, labeled *couscous*. Natural foods stores sometimes sell semolina in bulk as well. Make sure the stuff you purchase is fresh, however. Stale semolina has a tell-tale smell, like over-the-hill oil, and has lost much of its store of vitamins and essential amino acids.

While others may suggest substituting commercial Farina or Cream of Wheat for semolina in a recipe, I resolutely do not! For mail-order sources, check the listing at the back of the book.

How to Store It

Semolina absorbs odors, so it is wise to store it in an airtight glass container rather than a plastic bag.

Hard durum semolina and semolina flour both have considerable staying power and are capable of a long shelf life (up to half a year) in a cool, dry place. When the grain is past its prime, it takes on a washed-out sickly color and a decidedly rancid smell.

Some cooks store semolina in the freezer, where it will keep indefinitely if well insulated. The maximum duration in the refrigerator would be nine to twelve months, but check for moisture from time to time.

Bring semolina to room temperature after a stint in the cooler. It may have absorbed moisture—even in a glass container—and should be kept open for an hour or so before it is used.

How to Cook It

A good Italian cook of my acquaintance calls semolina *il ingrediente perfetto*, "the perfect ingredient." It's a kitchen trust not misplaced—semolina is a quick-cooking grain of endless possibilities.

How much do I love thee, semolina? Let me count the culinary ways! In small amounts, semolina will thicken a soup, give body to a stew, or enrich a watery sauce. Boiled briefly with the liquid of your choice and amended with butter and cheese or herbs, semolina becomes a side dish that is a heck of a lot less caloric than instant mashed potatoes and a lot less trouble than instant rice! And leftover cooked semolina may be sliced, breaded, and fried (like polenta) for lunch the next day.

Then there is couscous. A diner of good appetite could dwell on the infinite possibilities of that North African–inspired dish for meals on end. And semolina is the basis of all couscous, whether it is sold over the counter or made from scratch. (See page 285 for more on couscous.)

Malleable semolina is dense enough to be the base of a soufflé and delicate enough to stand in for cornstarch or conventional flour in a pie crust, pudding, or cake. Ingredients come and go, but this one (as my mother said) is really a steal!

The Latin word for what we call semolina was *semideus*—literally "demi-god," though some semolina lovers insist that "food of the gods" is what the Romans really had in mind.

LATTUGA ZUPPA
(Italian Lettuce Soup)

A chicken soup of Italian extraction, one that all farmers' daughters learn to make, this dish is made of strong broth, thickened with semolina and dappled with chopped green garden lettuce—and that's all!

1 chicken, 3½ to 4 pounds, well rinsed
1 large onion, unpeeled, quartered
1 large clove garlic, lightly crushed
2 whole cloves
10 peppercorns
2 medium carrots, peeled and chopped
2 medium ribs celery, chopped
1 medium white turnip, peeled and
    chopped
1 medium parsnip, peeled and chopped
4 sprigs parsley
1 teaspoon red wine vinegar
2 tablespoons semolina
1 cup shredded Boston or butterhead
    lettuce, or arugula
½ cup freshly grated Parmesan cheese

1. Place the chicken in a large kettle and add the onion, garlic, cloves, peppercorns, carrots, celery, turnip, parsnip, parsley, and vinegar. Add water to cover, and heat to boiling. Reduce the heat, skim any foam that has floated to the top of the pot, and simmer, partially covered, 1 hour. Continue skimming as necessary. Remove the chicken and allow it to cool slightly.

2. Remove the skin and bones from the chicken, and return them to the soup. (Reserve the chicken meat for another use.) Continue to cook the soup, uncovered, 20 minutes. Strain.

3. Pour 1 quart strained chicken stock into a medium-size saucepan, and heat to boiling. Stir in the semolina. Reduce the heat to medium-low and gently simmer 10 minutes. Stir in the lettuce; cook 1 minute. Stir in the cheese, and serve.

Serves 4

SUPER-CRUNCHY GRILLED CHICKEN

I love grilled chicken. This one is super-crunchy, thanks to the "gold dust" in the marinade. Don't worry if a bit drops into the fire. The chicken will still be crispy.

½ teaspoon anchovy paste
½ teaspoon tomato paste
6 tablespoons olive oil
3 tablespoons freshly grated Parmesan
    cheese
¼ cup semolina
½ teaspoon salt
¼ teaspoon freshly ground black pepper
1 chicken (about 3½ pounds), well rinsed,
    dried, and cut into serving pieces

1. Combine the anchovy paste, tomato paste, olive oil, cheese, semolina, salt, and pepper in a large bowl. Mix well. Add the chicken, and rub the mixture into the chicken pieces with your hands. Let stand, uncovered, 2 hours.

2. Prepare a barbecue grill (with cover) or preheat the broiler. If you are cooking the chicken on a grill, set up a drip pan in the center, and surround it with the hot coals.

3. Place the chicken over the drip pan, cover the grill, and grill until almost tender, about 20 minutes, turning once. Then place the chicken directly over the coals, and grill uncovered until crisp and cooked through, about another 10 minutes.

In the broiler, the chicken will take about 20 minutes per side.

Serves 2 to 4

TUNA FLUMMERY

Neither a pudding nor a cake, this moist and airy bit of bakery is a wondrous amalgam of both, with a surprising ingredient straight off the pantry shelf. It's the kind of dish that will make a drab brunch brighter, and a so-so supper super!

2 tablespoons olive oil
1 medium onion, finely chopped
2 cloves garlic, minced
1 large can (35 ounces) imported Italian
    tomatoes, chopped, with juice
Pinch of sugar
1 tablespoon chopped fresh basil
¼ teaspoon ground allspice
½ teaspoon salt
¼ teaspoon freshly ground black pepper
½ teaspoon anchovy paste
1 cup semolina
2 egg yolks
1 large can (12½ ounces) tuna, drained,
    broken into chunks
3 egg whites
1 tablespoon unsalted butter, melted
3 tablespoons freshly grated Parmesan
    cheese

1. Heat the oil in a medium-size saucepan over medium-low heat. Add the onion; cook 3 minutes. Add the garlic; cook 2 minutes longer. Stir in the tomatoes, sugar, basil, allspice, salt, and pepper. Heat to boiling. Reduce the heat and simmer until reduced to about 3½ cups, about 20 minutes.

2. Preheat the oven to 375°F. Butter a 10-inch glass or ceramic quiche dish.

3. Stir the anchovy paste into the tomato mixture. Then stir in the semolina and reduce the heat. Cook, stirring constantly, over low heat until thickened but not stiff, 1 to 2 minutes. Transfer to a heatproof bowl, and beat in the egg yolks, one at a time, beating vigorously after each addition. Stir in the drained tuna.

4. Beat the egg whites until stiff, and fold into the semolina mixture. Transfer the mixture to the prepared quiche dish. Brush the top with the melted butter and sprinkle with the cheese. Bake until golden, 20 to 25 minutes.

Serves 6 to 8

TORTA DI SPINACI RUSTICANA

A rustic luncheon pie (which makes a tonic picnic dish) baked in the tenderest semolina crust you have ever set a tooth to. The recipe (very homey) stems from the little town of Vercelli (even homier) in Italy. It is a dish that workmen and children wrap in paper bags for lunch, and it may be eaten hot, cold, or anywhere in between!

3 tablespoons olive oil

2 large onions, finely chopped

1½ to 2 pounds spinach or Swiss chard, trimmed

3 smoked pork chops (about 1½ pounds), 1 inch thick, trimmed and diced

1½ cups freshly grated Parmesan cheese

1 cup ricotta cheese

4 eggs, lightly beaten

Salt and freshly ground black pepper to taste

Double recipe Semolina Short Crust Pastry (recipe follows)

1 egg white, lightly beaten

1. Heat the oil in a large heavy skillet over medium-low heat. Cook the onions until soft, 8 minutes; do not brown. Transfer to a large bowl.

2. Wash the spinach or chard and place it, with just the water that clings to the leaves, in a medium-size saucepan. Cover, and cook over medium-low heat, stirring occasionally, until wilted, about 4 minutes (longer for chard). Drain, pressing out excess liquid with the back of a spoon. Chop.

3. Add the chopped greens, diced smoked pork, both cheeses, and eggs to the onions. Mix well, and season with salt and pepper.

4. Preheat the oven to 425°F.

5. Divide the pastry in half. Roll out one half on a lightly floured board, and line a 10-inch glass or ceramic quiche dish with it. Brush the pastry with some of the beaten egg white. Spoon the pork and cheese filling into the pastry shell.

Roll out the remaining pastry and cover the filling. Seal and crimp the edges. Cut a steam hole in the center. If desired, cut decorative leaves from pastry trimmings and place around the steam hole. Brush the top lightly with egg white. Bake until golden, about 40 minutes. Let stand 10 minutes before serving. Serve hot or at room temperature.

Serves 8

Semolina Short Crust Pastry

A pie crust that travels. Use it on your favorite sweet and savory tarts, tortes, or pot pies when the occasion arises.

½ cup semolina

½ cup cake flour

¼ teaspoon salt

4 tablespoons (½ stick) unsalted butter, chilled

1½ tablespoons solid vegetable shortening, chilled

2 to 2½ tablespoons cold water

Combine the semolina with the cake flour and salt in a bowl. Cut in the butter and shortening with a pastry blender until the mixture has the texture of coarse crumbs. Add just enough cold water to form a soft dough. Knead briefly, wrap in plastic wrap, and chill 1 hour before using. Allow to soften slightly before rolling out.

Makes enough for one 9- to 11-inch single-crust pie

"THINK PINK" SOUFFLE

A fire-roasted pepper turns this soufflé lightly pink, and blue cheese turns it elegant beyond belief. I serve this with just a green salad for a light pick-up meal.

3 tablespoons plus 1 teaspoon unsalted
  butter
2 tablespoons freshly grated Parmesan
  cheese
¼ cup semolina
1¼ cups milk, heated
4 egg yolks
1 roasted red bell pepper, seeded and
  chopped (see Note, page 249)
2 ounces blue cheese, chopped
½ teaspoon salt
¼ teaspoon freshly ground black pepper
Pinch of cayenne pepper
⅛ teaspoon freshly grated nutmeg
6 egg whites

1. Preheat the oven to 400°F. Rub a 1½-quart soufflé dish with the 1 teaspoon butter. Sprinkle the dish with 1 tablespoon of the Parmesan cheese.

2. Melt the 3 tablespoons butter in a medium-size saucepan over medium-low heat. Whisk in the semolina; cook, stirring constantly, 2 minutes. Add the hot milk all at once; whisk until smooth and thick, about 1 minute. Remove the pan from the heat and beat in the egg yolks, one at a time, beating vigorously after each addition. Stir in the roasted bell pepper, blue cheese, salt, black and cayenne peppers, and nutmeg. Transfer to a bowl.

3. Beat the egg whites until stiff, and fold into the semolina mixture. Pour into the prepared soufflé dish, sprinkle with the remaining Parmesan cheese, and place in the oven. Immediately reduce the oven heat to 375°F. Bake until the soufflé is puffed and firm, about 30 minutes. Serve immediately.

Serves 4

BAKED FENNEL PUDDING

In this polenta-like pudding, semolina is the chief ingredient rather than cornmeal. Try it with any grilled fowl or fish.

1 small fennel bulb (about ½ pound),
  trimmed and chopped
1 medium onion, chopped
2 cups homemade chicken stock (see page
  376) or canned broth
¾ cup milk (approximately)
1 cup semolina
2 tablespoons unsalted butter
2 eggs, lightly beaten
1 tablespoon Pernod liqueur
Salt and freshly ground black pepper to
  taste
1 teaspoon unsalted butter, melted

1. Combine the fennel, onion, and chicken stock in a medium-size saucepan, and heat to boiling. Reduce the heat and simmer, covered, until the fennel is tender, about 10 minutes. Cool slightly.

2. Preheat the oven to 350°F. Butter a shallow 9-inch baking dish.

3. Transfer the fennel mixture to the container of a food processor or blender, and process until smooth.

4. Measure the fennel mixture and pour it into a medium-size saucepan. Add enough milk to make 3 cups. Heat to boiling. Then stir in the semolina and reduce the heat. Cook, stirring constantly, over low heat until thick, 1 to 2 minutes. Remove from the heat and beat in the butter, eggs, and Pernod. Season with salt and pepper.

5. Transfer the semolina to the prepared baking dish. Smooth it out to fit the dish, and brush the top with the melted butter. Bake until golden, 20 to 25 minutes. Cut into wedges and serve.

Serves 6 to 8

SAVORY SEMOLINA CHEESECAKE

Not a cheesecake in the conventional sense, yet guaranteed to knock your socks off at the first bite! This meld of semolina and Fontina is just what the doctor ordered for a case of "pallid palate."

2 medium carrots, peeled and chopped
1 large shallot, chopped
6 cups (approximately) homemade chicken
    stock (see page 376) or canned broth
2 cups semolina
4 tablespoons (½ stick) unsalted butter
3 eggs, lightly beaten
¼ teaspoon freshly grated nutmeg
½ teaspoon salt
¼ teaspoon freshly ground black pepper
2 cups grated Fontina cheese (about ½
    pound)
1 teaspoon unsalted butter, melted
3 tablespoons freshly grated Parmesan
    cheese

1. Combine the carrots, shallot, and 2 cups of the stock in a medium-size saucepan, and heat to boiling. Reduce the heat, cover, and simmer over medium-low heat until the carrots are tender, about 10 minutes. Cool slightly, and then place the carrots with some of the liquid in a food processor or blender container. Blend until smooth (carefully, as hot liquid will expand).

2. Preheat the oven to 375°F. Butter a 9-inch springform pan.

3. Combine the blended mixture with the remaining liquid in which the carrots were cooked. You should have about 2½ cups. Return it to the saucepan, and add enough chicken stock to make 6½ cups total. Heat to boiling, then stir in the semolina and reduce the heat. Cook, stirring constantly, until thick, 1 to 2 minutes. Remove the pan from the heat and beat in the butter, eggs, nutmeg, salt, and pepper.

4. Spoon one third of the semolina mixture over the bottom of the prepared springform pan. Sprinkle with half the Fontina cheese, leaving about an ⅛-inch border around the edge. Repeat with another third of the semolina mixture and the remaining Fontina. Spread the remaining semolina mixture over the top.

5. Brush the top of the cake with the melted butter, and sprinkle with the Parmesan cheese. Bake 20 minutes, then run under a broiler to lightly brown the top. Cool on a wire rack for 15 minutes. Run a knife around the edge of the cake and remove the sides of the pan. Let the cake stand 15 minutes longer before serving.

Serves 10 to 12

PAKET
(Crusty Fried Eggplant and Tomatoes)

This combination of eggplant and semolina was inspired by a Turkish dish with a wonderful name, *paket*, which means "a package of groceries."

2 small eggplants (about ½ pound each),
*   cut into ¼-inch-thick slices*
Salt
¼ cup all-purpose flour (approximately)
2 eggs, lightly beaten
½ cup semolina
1½ teaspoons ground allspice
¼ teaspoon freshly ground black pepper
5 to 7 tablespoons vegetable oil
1 tablespoon unsalted butter
2 medium firm tomatoes, sliced
¼ cup freshly grated Parmesan cheese

1. Place the eggplant in a colander and sprinkle with salt. Let stand 30 minutes. Then rinse with cold water and pat dry.

2. Preheat the oven to 400°F.

3. Place the flour on a plate. Pour the eggs into a shallow bowl. Combine the semolina, allspice, 1 teaspoon salt, and pepper on another plate.

4. Heat 4 tablespoons of the oil with the butter in a heavy skillet over medium heat until hot but not smoking. Dip each eggplant slice in the flour, shaking off any excess. Then dip in the beaten egg, shaking off any excess. Finally dip in the semolina mixture, coating well. Sauté the eggplant slices, a few at a time, until golden brown on both sides. Drain on paper towels.

5. Raise the heat under the skillet slightly, adding more oil if needed, and repeat the process with the tomatoes. Do not overcook the tomatoes; they should remain firm.

6. Arrange the eggplant, occasionally overlapping with tomatoes, in a shallow baking dish. Sprinkle with the cheese. Bake until the vegetables are warmed through and the cheese has melted, 5 to 8 minutes.

Serves 4 to 6

ANNA TERESA CALLEN'S SEMOLINA SHELLS WITH ARUGULA

In Italy, hard durum wheat pasta is almost inevitably factory-made. But here's an exception to the rule, from the mistress of fine Abruzzo cooking, Anna Teresa Callen. A delicate rolled dough shell (known as *cavatelli*), this pasta is flattened out like a noodle, and poached with fresh greens until tender. Getting the knack of rolling and flattening the dough takes practice, so test the first few in boiling water before proceeding with the recipe. They should be on the light side, not rubbery. The multi-accomplished Mrs. Callen serves her shells in a bath of tomato sauce with a shower of grated Pecorino cheese over all. I prefer merely melted butter and Parmesan, but exercise your own option in the matter.

1¼ cups all-purpose flour
¾ cup semolina
Pinch of salt
½ cup plus 2 to 3 tablespoons lukewarm
    water
4 cups torn, trimmed arugula leaves
4 tablespoons (½ stick) unsalted butter
½ cup freshly grated Parmesan cheese

1. Combine the flour with the semolina and salt in a large bowl. Stir in ½ cup of the lukewarm water and add more, 1 tablespoon at a time, until a stiff dough is formed. Transfer the dough to a lightly floured board and knead 10 minutes. Cover with a bowl and let stand 20 minutes.

2. Pull off pieces of dough and roll them into ropes. Slice the ropes into ⅛- to ¼-inch-thick rounds. Flatten the slices, and pushing with your thumb, form each round into a little (1-inch) shell shape by folding up one side of the circle slightly. (Keep the board lightly floured at all times to make the dough easier to work with, and keep the main batch of dough covered at all times to prevent it from drying out.) Place the formed shells on cloth-lined baking sheets. Let stand until dry, 4 hours. (The shells become easier to form into shapes as they dry.)

3. Cook the shells with the arugula in a large pot of boiling salted water until the shells are tender, about 25 minutes. Drain in a colander.

4. Wipe out the pot and add the butter. Melt the butter over medium heat, and stir in the cooked shells and arugula. Toss to coat. Stir in the cheese, and serve.

Serves 4 to 6

SEMI VEGGIE PIE

This is borrowed from friend Julie Sahni—an Indian dish with some very American modifications. Julie calls the original version a spicy pilaf.

1 small eggplant, cubed (about 1¼ cups)
Salt
5 tablespoons vegetable oil
⅓ cup sliced almonds
1 cup semolina
1 teaspoon mustard seeds
½ teaspoon crushed dried hot red peppers
1 medium onion, chopped
1½ teaspoons minced fresh ginger
1 small baking potato, peeled and cubed
    (about 1 cup)
2 cups strong homemade vegetable or
    chicken stock (see Note)
1 teaspoon sesame oil

½ teaspoon salt
¼ teaspoon freshly ground black pepper
½ cup shelled peas, lightly blanched if
    fresh, thawed if frozen
2 teaspoons fresh lemon juice
2 tablespoons chopped fresh cilantro
    (Chinese parsley)

1. Place the eggplant in a colander and sprinkle with salt. Let stand 30 minutes. Then rinse with cold water and pat dry.

2. Meanwhile, heat 1 tablespoon of the vegetable oil in a large ovenproof

skillet (with cover) over medium heat. Stir in the almonds and cook, stirring constantly, until golden, about 3 minutes. Transfer to a bowl.

3. Wipe out the skillet and heat another tablespoon of the oil over medium heat. Stir in the semolina, and cook, stirring constantly, until the grains separate and turn golden, about 5 minutes. Transfer to a separate bowl.

4. Wipe out the skillet and heat the remaining 3 tablespoons oil over medium heat. Add the mustard seeds and cover the pan. The mustard seeds will pop as they sauté. Shake the pan occasionally to prevent burning. When the seeds are golden brown (about 3 minutes), add the dried red peppers and cook 15 seconds. Stir in the onion and ginger; cook 2 minutes longer.

5. Add the eggplant and potato cubes to the onion mixture. Cook over medium-low heat, uncovered, stirring occasionally, until the vegetables soften, about 10 minutes. Then add the stock, sesame oil, salt, pepper, and reserved semolina. Heat to boiling, and reduce the heat. Cook, stirring and folding the mixture over on itself with a wooden spatula, for 10 minutes. Add the peas and continue to cook, stirring and folding, for 5 minutes. Stir in the lemon juice, cilantro, and reserved almonds. Keep the pilaf warm in a 225°F oven until ready to serve.

Serves 6

Note: If you do not have strong vegetable or chicken stock on hand (see page 379), reduce 4 cups canned chicken broth (there is no readily available canned vegetable broth) to 2 cups by simmering for 20 minutes.

Semolina is most definitely a grain with Italian connections.

In the north of Italy it is called *malinconia maccheroni* ("melancholy macaroni") because almost all of the hard durum wheat is purchased by pasta factories before it is harvested.

Wheat growers in the south and westerly regions of Italy have a happier name for semolina. They tag it *polvere d'oro*, or "gold dust," because the hard durum wheat that is grown in those parts is milled into semolina flour—which brings a higher price and a sweeter jingle to the pocketbook.

RICOTTA GNOCCHI WITH WILD MUSHROOMS

Though I have studied Italian cooking with some formidable culinary "heavies" in that country, I must confess that I learned to make gnocchi on Manhattan Island, in a kitchen no bigger than a Checker cab. The secret of ethereal gnocchi is speed: make them as quickly as possible. And, since the dough is very buttery and fragile, use a heavy dusting of flour on the board, your knife, and your hands. That will keep the mixture workable.

My trick is to prepare gnocchi a day or so in advance. I poach and drain them, and freeze them until an hour before serving time. Then I merely place the semi-frozen dumplings on a buttered heatproof platter, drizzle them with melted butter, and bake 15 to 20 minutes in a 400°F oven while the mushrooms cook. It's easy, fast, and the results are delicious.

2 cups milk
¾ cup semolina
2 egg yolks
6 tablespoons (¾ stick) unsalted butter, melted
¼ cup freshly grated Parmesan cheese
⅓ cup ricotta cheese
¼ teaspoon freshly grated nutmeg
½ teaspoon salt
2 teaspoons finely chopped fresh basil, or ⅔ teaspoon dried
⅛ teaspoon finely chopped fresh oregano, or a pinch dried
⅛ teaspoon finely chopped fresh thyme, or a pinch dried
3 tablespoons unsalted butter
¼ pound fresh wild mushrooms (such as shiitake), thinly sliced
½ cup heavy or whipping cream

1. Place the milk in a saucepan and heat slowly to boiling (do not scorch). Reduce the heat and slowly whisk in the semolina. Cook over low heat, stirring constantly, until thick, about 5 minutes. Transfer to a bowl.

According to the *Arabian Night's Dream Book*, a little-known turn-of-the-century volume:

Grain is a symbol of *prosperity.*
Eggplant is a sign of *endurance.*
To dream of an eggplant growing in a field of wheat means guaranteed success but also hard work.
To dream of a dish of roasted eggplant surrounded by grains of wheat means a windfall of gold . . . with no exertion whatsoever!

2. Beat the egg yolks, one at a time, into the semolina, beating thoroughly after each addition. Beat in 4 tablespoons of the melted butter, both cheeses, and the nutmeg, salt, and herbs.

3. Place a large spoonful of gnocchi dough on a heavily floured board. With floured hands, roll the dough into a rope. Cut into 1-inch pieces with a floured knife, gently squeezing the centers. (Keep board, hands, and knife well floured at all times.)

4. Preheat the oven to 400°F. Butter a large baking dish.

5. Cook the gnocchi in a large pot of boiling salted water for 30 to 45 seconds. (You should be able to roll out and cut the next batch while one batch of gnocchi is cooking.) Remove the gnocchi with a slotted spoon and rest the spoon on paper towels. Then place the drained gnocchi in the prepared baking dish in one layer. Continue this process until all dough is used up. Drizzle the remaining 2 tablespoons melted butter over the finished gnocchi.

6. Melt the 3 tablespoons butter in a large heavy skillet over medium heat. Add the mushrooms and sauté, tossing constantly, until golden, about 3 minutes. Remove the pan from the heat and let the mushrooms cool slightly.

7. Bake the gnocchi for 10 minutes. Meanwhile, place the mushrooms over medium-low heat and stir in the cream. Cook, stirring frequently, until smooth, about 3 minutes. Serve over the gnocchi.

Serves 4 to 6

SEMI BAVARIAN CREAM

One rarely thinks of semolina as the basis of delicate desserts, but perhaps this ethereal meal closure will change a few opinions on the subject.

1½ teaspoons unflavored gelatin
¼ cup water
¼ cup semolina
½ cup sugar
2 cups milk
1 teaspoon vanilla extract
1 tablespoon kirsch liqueur
1 cup heavy or whipping cream
3 egg whites
Red-Letter Purée (recipe follows)

1. Combine the gelatin and water in a small bowl, and let soften, 3 to 4 minutes.

2. Combine the semolina, sugar, and milk in a medium-size saucepan. Heat slowly, whisking constantly, to boiling (about 4 minutes). Remove the pan from the heat and whisk in the softened gelatin. Transfer to a bowl. Whisk in the vanilla and kirsch, and set aside to cool to room temperature.

3. Beat the cream until stiff, and fold into the semolina mixture. Beat the egg whites until stiff, and fold into the semolina mixture. Pour into a 6-cup mold, and refrigerate until firm, 3 hours.

4. To unmold, place the mold in a pan of hot water for a few seconds, and then invert it onto a large serving platter. Serve with Red-Letter Purée.

Serves 6 to 8

Red-Letter Purée

1 cup fresh strawberries, hulled
1 cup fresh or frozen raspberries, thawed
½ cup confectioners' sugar
1 tablespoon fresh orange juice
1 teaspoon kirsch liqueur

Place all ingredients in the container of a food processor or blender, and process until smooth. Mash through a fine strainer to remove the seeds. Serve chilled.

Makes about 2 cups

THE SEMI CHOCOLATE CHALLENGE

A remarkable dessert anomaly: half baked chocolate pudding, half baked chocolate tart. Totally irresistible!

8 tablespoons (1 stick) unsalted butter
2 ounces semi-sweet chocolate
2 cups brewed coffee
1 cup heavy or whipping cream
⅓ cup granulated sugar
¼ teaspoon salt

1 cup semolina
2 eggs, lightly beaten
1 egg yolk, lightly beaten
Confectioners' sugar
1 cup heavy or whipping cream
1 tablespoon rum

1. Preheat the oven to 375°F. Butter and flour a 9-inch springform pan.

2. Melt the butter and chocolate together in a small saucepan over low heat, stirring frequently until smooth. Set aside.

3. Combine the coffee and cream in a medium-size saucepan. Heat slowly to boiling, then reduce the heat and stir in the sugar and salt. Slowly stir in the semolina and cook, stirring constantly, 10 minutes. Transfer to a large bowl.

4. Stir the chocolate mixture into the semolina mixture, and beat in the eggs and egg yolk. Pour the mixture into the prepared springform pan. Bake 1 hour. Cool completely on a wire rack. Loosen the edge of the pan with a knife, and remove the sides. Dust with confectioners' sugar.

5. In a small mixing bowl, whip the cream with the rum until the cream holds stiff peaks, 5 minutes. Serve the pudding tart slightly warm or chilled, with the rum-flavored whipped cream.

Serves 10 to 12

APPLE CUSTARD TART WITH TWO HATS

*T*his custardy apple pie, thickened with semolina, rests in a semolina crust. A lattice top crust is crowned with a meringue that sends guests back for more of this "two-hatted" dessert.

Finely grated zest of 1 orange
Finely grated zest of 1 large lemon
3 tablespoons fresh orange juice
1 tablespoon fresh lemon juice
2 tablespoons semolina
2½ pounds green apples (5 medium)
1¾ cups sugar
2 eggs, lightly beaten
Semolina Short Crust Pastry (see page 272)
2 tablespoons whipping cream
5 egg whites

1. Preheat the oven to 450°F.

2. Combine the orange zest, lemon zest, orange juice, lemon juice, and semolina in a large bowl.

3. Peel the apples and grate them directly into the bowl. Stir in 1½ cups of the sugar and the lightly beaten eggs. Mix well.

4. Roll about two thirds of the pastry on a lightly floured board until very thin. Line a 9-inch pie plate with it, and trim and flute the edges. Add the trimmed dough to the remaining third of dough and roll out. Cut into strips.

5. Pour the apple mixture into the pie shell. Place the dough strips in a lattice pattern over the top, and press the ends into the edges of the pie shell. Brush the top with the cream, and place the pie on an aluminum-foil-lined baking sheet. Bake 10 minutes. Reduce the oven heat to 350°F and bake until done, about 35 minutes longer. Cool completely on a wire rack.

6. Preheat the broiler. Beat the egg whites in the large bowl of an electric mixer until almost stiff. Slowly add the remaining ¼ cup sugar, 1 tablespoon at a time, beating until the mixture becomes stiff and glossy. Spread the meringue over the top of the pie, and run it under the broiler until the top is golden brown, about 1 minute.

Serves 8

SEMI-BAKED SNOW

This is one of my favorite desserts of all time—smooth, velvety, loaded with taste. It can be made a day in advance and kept refrigerated in the mold. I usually offer a choice of sweet dessert sauces, but one or the other will do just as well.

1 quart milk
½ cup sugar
5 tablespoons unsalted butter
1 cup semolina
Generous pinch of ground cinnamon
1½ teaspoons vanilla extract
1 tablespoon dark rum
4 eggs, separated
Boiling water
Blue and Red Plum Sauce or Drop Dead
 Chocolate Sauce (recipes follow)

1. Combine the milk, sugar, and 3 tablespoons of the butter in a medium-size saucepan. Heat slowly, stirring occasionally, to boiling; do not scorch. Reduce the heat to low, and slowly whisk in the semolina. Cook, stirring occasionally, 25 minutes. Stir in the cinnamon, vanilla, rum, and remaining 2 tablespoons butter. Transfer to a large bowl.

2. Preheat the oven to 350°F. Butter a 10-cup non-stick mold.

3. Beat the egg yolks, one at a time, into the semolina mixture, beating thoroughly after each addition. Beat the egg whites until stiff, and fold into the mixture. Pour into the prepared mold.

4. Place the mold in a roasting or other large deep pan, and pour boiling water into the pan so that it comes halfway up the mold. Bake 30 minutes. Remove the mold from the hot water and cool 10 minutes before inverting onto a serving plate. Refrigerate to chill, then serve with your choice of sauce.

Serves 10

Blue and Red Plum Sauce

This recipe may be doubled.

8 purple (Italian) plums, pitted and
 roughly chopped (about 1 cup)
½ cup raspberry jam
3 tablespoons sugar
¼ cup dry red wine

Combine all ingredients in a small saucepan and heat to boiling. Reduce the heat to medium and cook, stirring occasionally, until plums are soft, 10 to 12 minutes. Mash through a fine-mesh strainer. Serve slightly warm.

Makes about 1¼ cups

Drop Dead Chocolate Sauce

8 ounces semi-sweet chocolate
5 tablespoons unsalted butter, cut into
 small pieces
¼ cup milk, at room temperature
¼ cup heavy or whipping cream, at room
 temperature
2 tablespoons dark rum

Melt the chocolate in the top of a double boiler over hot, but not simmering, water. Stir in the butter, bit by bit. Stir in the milk, cream, and rum. Stir until smooth. Cool, and store in a tightly covered jar in the refrigerator. Reheat slightly over warm water before serving.

Makes about 2 cups

THE BOZO CAKE

My mother was a remarkable baker with a very special gift. She could look at a recipe once, toss away the cookbook, and produce a flawless version. "It's like sight-reading music," she would offer by way of explanation—as if it were an ability anyone could develop with practice. However, as she grew older she became less and less interested in cake making—with one notable exception. She returned from Italy with the memory of a cake: it was made of semolina and resembled a pound cake, but it was denser. The aroma was lemon, while the flavor was decidedly almond.

"What was the name of this cake?" I quizzed.

"Who knows?" said my mother. "Something Italian. It sounded like *bozo*."

"Bozo cake?"

"Something like that."

On odd occasions afterward, my mother would drop by my apartment, and she'd take inventory of her old baking equipment, which I kept stashed in a cabinet. My mother would smile ruefully. "Maybe one day we'll try to make bozo cake."

"Without a recipe?" (for none of my Italian cookbooks produced a cake of even the faintest resemblance).

"We could wing it!" my mother replied.

And in time we did. One afternoon I ground nuts and separated eggs while she beat semolina, sugar, and the yolks together into a golden froth. As we scraped the mixture from a bowl into a buttered pan, my mother slapped her forehead. "Yipes. I just remembered. This cake was dome-shaped on top."

"Too late to worry about that," I said. But my mother worried anyway.

"I think I've lost my touch," she murmured as we tasted the still-warm cake. "Or maybe just my memory..."

"What's wrong? I think it's delicious."

"Yeah," my mother agreed, "but it's just not the bozo cake I ate in Italy!"

She nibbled a crumb more. "I suspect chocolate would make a difference too."

"What chocolate?"

"You see, I forgot to tell you. It had a frosting."

PAROZZO DI PAPA
("the Pope's hat")

When I began to compile semolina recipes for this book—twenty years after sampling my mother's bozo cake—my friend Anna Teresa Callen mentioned a semolina cake of her Abruzzo girlhood, a cake known as *parozzo di Papa'* ("the Pope's hat"). As soon as I heard the name, even before I glanced at the ingredients list, I knew it had to be my mother's "bozo" cake (see box). Here's the authentic version.

FOR THE CAKE

6 eggs, separated
1½ cups sugar
1 cup blanched almonds, toasted and

ground (see Note)
1 cup semolina
Finely grated zest of 1 orange
1 tablespoon fresh orange juice

FOR THE ICING

4 ounces semi-sweet chocolate
2 to 3 tablespoons unsalted butter
White chocolate for chocolate curls

1. Preheat the oven to 375°F. Butter a 9-inch (2-quart) round glass ovenproof bowl.

2. Make the cake: Beat the egg yolks in the large bowl of an electric mixer until light. Slowly add the sugar and beat until light and fluffy. Beat in the almonds, semolina, orange zest, and orange juice. The mixture will be very thick.

3. Beat the egg whites until stiff. Stir one third of the whites into the cake mixture with a wooden spoon. Fold and stir the second third of the whites into the mixture. Fold in the remaining whites.

4. Pour the batter into the prepared bowl. Bake until a toothpick inserted in center of the cake comes out clean, about 1 hour. Cool for 10 minutes on a wire rack. Carefully loosen the edges of the cake, pushing gently toward the center, with a long flexible spatula. Invert the cake onto a wire rack, and cool.

5. Make the icing: Melt the chocolate in the top of a double boiler set over hot water. Stir in enough butter to make a very smooth mixture. (Chocolate may seize slightly in the beginning.) Spread the icing over the cake. Make chocolate curls by scraping the white chocolate with a vegetable peeler over the cake.

Serves 8 to 10

Note: To toast almonds, spread them evenly on a baking sheet, and place in a 350°F oven, stirring occasionally, 10 minutes. Grind in a food processor, pulsing on and off to avoid turning the nuts into a paste.

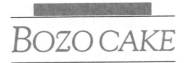

BOZO CAKE

Only dimly remembered, but delicious.

6 eggs, separated
1½ cups sugar
1½ cups blanched almonds, toasted and
   ground (see Note, above)
1 cup semolina
Finely grated zest of 1 lemon
2 teaspoons fresh lemon juice

1. Preheat the oven to 375°F. Butter and flour a 9-inch springform pan.

2. Beat the egg yolks in the large bowl of an electric mixer until light. Slowly add the sugar and beat until light and fluffy. Stir in the almonds, semolina, lemon zest, and lemon juice. The mixture will be stiff.

3. Beat the egg whites until stiff. Stir one third of the whites into the cake mixture with a wooden spoon. Fold and stir the second third of the whites into the mixture. Fold in the remaining whites.

4. Pour the batter into the prepared springform pan. Bake until a toothpick inserted in the center comes out clean, about 30 minutes. Cool completely on a rack before removing the sides of the pan.

Serves 8 to 10

MARION'S SEMOLINA SEED CAKE

The next of the semolina desserts is hardly the least of that grain's endowments. But come to think of it, I cannot summon up a happier ending to the subject. It is a nutty sunflower-seed cake—straight out of the head of Marion Cunningham, author of *The Fanny Farmer Book of Baking.*

¼ cup solid vegetable shortening
4 tablespoons (½ stick) unsalted butter, at
    room temperature
1¼ cups sugar
2 eggs
1 cup semolina
1 cup all-purpose flour
1½ teaspoons baking powder
½ teaspoon salt
1 cup milk
1 teaspoon vanilla extract
1 teaspoon finely grated lemon zest
½ cup toasted sunflower seeds (see Note)

1. Preheat the oven to 350°F. Butter and flour a 9-inch springform pan.

2. Beat the shortening with the butter in the large bowl of an electric mixer until light. Slowly add the sugar and beat until light and fluffy. Beat in the eggs, one at a time, beating thoroughly after each addition.

3. In another bowl, combine the semolina, flour, baking powder, and salt. Add this to the egg mixture in thirds on low speed, alternating with thirds of the milk. Then beat in the vanilla, lemon zest, and sunflower seeds.

4. Pour the mixture into the prepared springform pan. Bake until a toothpick inserted in the center comes out clean, about 35 minutes. Cool completely on a rack. Remove pan sides before serving.

Serves 8 to 10

Note: To toast sunflower seeds, spread the seeds evenly in a skillet and place them over medium heat, stirring several times until they turn golden brown, 6 to 8 minutes.

PEACH UPSIDE-DOWN CAKE

I have always been fond of any upside-down cake. It suits my sweet tooth to a "T." But when the cake is made with downy semolina and topped with fresh juicy peaches, upside-down cake takes a step toward immortality.

½ cup milk
2 tablespoons unsalted butter
½ cup semolina
½ cup firmly packed dark brown sugar
2 large ripe peaches, peeled and sliced
    (about 2 cups)
2 tablespoons plus ½ cup granulated sugar

1 egg, well beaten
2 egg yolks, lightly beaten
½ cup cake flour
1 teaspoon baking powder
¼ teaspoon salt
1 teaspoon vanilla extract

1. Preheat the oven to 425°F. Butter an 8-inch square non-stick cake pan.

2. Place the milk with the butter in a small saucepan. Heat over medium heat just until the butter melts.

3. Place the semolina in a large bowl. Pour the milk mixture over it, stir well, and let stand 10 minutes.

4. Press the brown sugar over the bottom of the prepared cake pan. Layer the peach slices over the brown sugar. Sprinkle the peaches with 2 tablespoons granulated sugar. Drizzle the beaten egg over the top.

5. Stir the egg yolks into the semolina mixture. Then stir in the cake flour, ½ cup granulated sugar, baking powder, salt, and vanilla. Pour this over the peaches, transfer to the oven, and bake until a toothpick inserted in the center comes out clean, about 25 minutes. Cool on a rack for 5 minutes before inverting onto a serving platter.

Serves 6 to 8

COUSCOUS

(It's Semolina too!)

After dried pasta, couscous is the most widespread form of semolina.

And what is couscous? A kitchen anomaly in fact, but one you'll be glad you discovered. At Berber stoves, "couscous" originally meant the grains of steamed semolina, traditionally served with North African stews known as *tagines*. However, in the fullness of time, couscous became such a ubiquitous partner to a tagine that even a deep-dyed Moroccan will call the combination "couscous" these days.

Paula Wolfert, doyenne of Middle Eastern food, has another theory. In her book *Couscous and Other Good Foods from Morocco*, she claims the word *couscous* is actually onomatopoeic, a verbal approximation of steam hissing its way through a mess of grains!

In a Moroccan kitchen, couscous is made by hand: hard durum semolina is moistened with water and a fine coating of flour, then rolled back and forth into itself until tiny pellets are formed. These bits of wheat are later steamed and stirred and steamed again until they become soft and fluffier than rice.

Being able to roll semolina into couscous is considered a great gift. In cities like Rabat, Fez, and Marrakech, a woman will often spend her entire adolescence mastering the art of couscous-making. And a female who is an adept couscous maker may come to a prospective husband with a reduced dowry, but there will be no complaints because her skills are more highly prized than gold. Or so a few knowing Moroccans have said.

Unfortunately, the durum semolina that is most available in this country is not granular enough to make authentic Moroccan couscous from scratch. But packaged couscous makes an admirable substitute in the recipes that follow.

How to Buy It

Couscous is available in cartons in supermarkets, fancy food shops, and natural foods stores everywhere. The best for the money, in my opinion, is the couscous sold in bulk at Middle Eastern groceries. But you have to search it out.

Have a caution when choosing packaged couscous. Do not buy boxes that are labeled "instant" or "precooked" because the contents are not only tasteless but often gluey into the bargain.

How to Cook It

To make couscous the right way takes time, even if you have bought a packaged product; 60 minutes is the optimum steaming cycle.

Many boxed couscous cartons bear instructions for abbreviated cooking periods. Ignore them, please! In most cases the directions require the grain and liquid to be cooked together over direct heat, rather than steaming the grain over the liquid. As a result the grain absorbs all the liquid quickly (like instant rice), which does not yield a particularly felicitous or fluffy kernel of couscous!

If a quick pot of couscous is absolutely necessary, consider the method developed by Marilyn Harris on page 290. It's fail-proof and feasible too.

Traditionally, couscous requires three steamings, optimally accomplished in a pot known as a *couscousière*, which has a tight-fitting colander inside and a heavy cover overall.

If you do not have a *couscousière*, you can use any heavy-duty pot that has a cover and will accommodate a shallow colander. Make sure, however, that the colander fits into the pot snugly. If the colander's openings are too large, line it with a dampened cheesecloth.

BASIC COOKED COUSCOUS

1 cup couscous
1 tablespoon olive oil
Simmering water or stock
½ cup cold water
¼ teaspoon salt
½ cup hot water

1. Combine the couscous with the oil in a medium-size bowl. Stir well, and then pour into the steam pan of a couscousière or a prepared colander. Steam over simmering water or stock for 20 minutes.

2. Return the couscous to the bowl and stir in the cold water, breaking up all lumps with a fork. Return the mixture to the steam pan or colander and steam 20 minutes longer.

3. Transfer the couscous to the bowl once more, and stir in the salt and hot water, breaking up any lumps with a fork. (At this stage, the couscous is the "partially steamed couscous" called for in the recipes that follow.)

4. Place the couscous in a steamer or

colander, set it over the stew, and continue to steam for 20 minutes. Or, if you are using the couscous for another dish such as a salad, return it to the pot of simmering water or stock and continue to steam until tender, 20 minutes. (See Note.) Fluff with a fork.

Makes 3 cups; serves 4 to 6

Note: For the final 20 minutes of cooking time the couscous ideally will be steamed over a stew to absorb the dish's flavor. However, many dishes (like the Tunisian tuna tagine on page 291) cook so briefly that it is necessary to steam the couscous for the full 60 minutes in advance.

TAGINE AID EL KEBIR
(Moroccan Lamb Stew)

North African stews vary as greatly as North American dialects. This one comes from Fez, where it is consumed in great quantities by the faithful at the festival of Aid el Kebir. A tagine of lamb, it commemorates the Prophet Abraham, who sacrificed a sheep in place of his son. My advice is to serve this stew over couscous, with a smidgen of *harissa* sauce on the side (you won't be able to take more). Harissa is a fiery condiment that most Moroccans agree "wakes up the organs!"

1 leg of lamb (about 5½ pounds), meat cut into 1½-inch cubes
Salt and freshly ground black pepper to taste
5 tablespoons olive oil
12 tablespoons (1½ sticks) unsalted butter
5 large yellow onions, coarsely chopped
½ teaspoon ground ginger
⅛ teaspoon saffron, or to taste, crumbled
½ teaspoon ground cinnamon
½ teaspoon ground turmeric
½ teaspoon freshly grated nutmeg
4 sprigs parsley
3 sprigs cilantro (Chinese parsley)
7 cups lamb stock (see page 378)
3 medium turnips, peeled and cut into 1½-inch pieces
5 medium carrots, peeled and cut into 2-inch strips
4 medium tomatoes, seeded and coarsely chopped

¼ cup dark honey
½ cup raisins
3 medium zucchini, cut into 2-inch strips
1½ recipes partially steamed Basic Cooked Couscous (see facing page)
Harissa (recipe follows)
1 can (6 ounces) chick-peas, drained, skins removed
1½ cups toasted whole blanched almonds (see Note)
Chopped fresh parsley, for garnish

1. Sprinkle the lamb cubes with salt and pepper. Heat 3 tablespoons of the oil in a large heavy skillet over medium-high heat. Sauté the lamb, a few pieces at a time, until well browned, about 8 minutes per batch. Transfer to the bottom of a couscousière or a large heavy pot.

2. Add 8 tablespoons (1 stick) of the butter to the lamb. Place the pot over

medium heat and add 2 chopped onions, the ginger, saffron, ¼ teaspoon of the cinnamon, the turmeric, and nutmeg. Tie the parsley and cilantro sprigs in a cheesecloth bag and add to the pot. Stir in the lamb stock, and heat to boiling. Reduce the heat and simmer, covered, 30 minutes. Add the turnips and carrots and continue to cook, covered, 20 minutes longer.

3. Meanwhile, heat the remaining 2 tablespoons oil in a large heavy skillet over medium heat. Stir in the remaining 3 chopped onions; cook until golden, about 8 minutes. Sprinkle with the remaining ¼ teaspoon cinnamon, and add the tomatoes, honey and raisins. Raise the heat slightly and cook until all liquid has evaporated, 20 minutes.

4. Stir the tomato mixture into the stew, and add the zucchini. Heat to boiling; reduce the heat. Place the partially steamed couscous in the couscousière steam pan or in a colander that fits tightly in the pot. Cook over medium heat 25 minutes.

5. To serve, place the couscous in the center of a large serving dish and dot with the remaining 4 tablespoons (½ stick) butter. Stir 1 tablespoon Harissa, the chick-peas, and the almonds into the stew and strain the stew, reserving the broth. Arrange the meat and vegetables around the couscous. Sprinkle with pars-

ley. Serve each diner a bowl of broth with which to moisten their couscous. Pass the stew and the remaining Harissa.

Serves 6 to 8

Note: To toast almonds, spread them evenly on a baking sheet, and place in a 350°F oven, stirring occasionally, 10 minutes.

Harissa

2 cloves garlic, minced
2 hot green peppers, seeded and coarsely
    chopped
1 teaspoon crushed dried hot red peppers
4 teaspoons caraway seeds
1 teaspoon ground cumin
1 teaspoon ground coriander
1 teaspoon salt
½ teaspoon freshly ground black pepper
Olive oil

Lightly mash the garlic with the fresh and dried peppers in a small bowl. Transfer to the container of a blender, and add the caraway seeds, cumin, coriander, salt, pepper, and enough olive oil to cover. Blend until smooth. Store in a jar with a tight-fitting lid in the refrigerator for up to a month.

Makes about ½ cup

COUSCOUS WITH LAMB BAKED IN A TOMATO BLANKET

A second North African lamb stew is of French Algerian derivation. Half tagine, its other half is a classic ragoût—a culinary marriage made in heaven. This dish bakes partially in the oven and then is finished on top of the stove, with couscous absorbing all the aromatic steam.

4 pounds boneless lamb shoulder or breast,
    cut into 1½-inch cubes
¼ cup all-purpose flour
¼ cup vegetable oil
2 large yellow onions, finely chopped
1 large clove garlic, minced
Pinch of saffron
½ teaspoon ground cinnamon
½ cup dry white wine
3½ cups fresh or canned peeled, seeded,
    chopped tomatoes (drained if canned)
1 cup homemade chicken stock (see page
    376) or canned broth
1 tablespoon sugar
3 tablespoons unsalted butter
2 teaspoons slivered orange zest
3 tablespoons cognac, warmed
1½ recipes partially steamed Basic Cooked
    Couscous (see page 286)
Chopped fresh parsley, for garnish

1. Preheat the oven to 375°F.

2. Dust the lamb cubes with the flour. Heat the oil in a Dutch oven (for which you have a tight-fitting colander) over medium heat. Sauté the lamb cubes, a few pieces at a time, until dark brown on all sides, 8 minutes per batch. Transfer to a plate. When all pieces are sautéed, reduce the heat to medium-low and return all the meat, with any juices that have accumulated. Sprinkle with any leftover flour and stir well. Stir in the onions; cook 4 minutes. Add the garlic, saffron, and ¼ teaspoon of the cinnamon; cook 2 minutes longer. Stir in the wine, tomatoes, and chicken stock. Sprinkle with the sugar. Heat to boiling, then cover and transfer to the oven. Bake 1 hour.

3. Melt 1 tablespoon of the butter in a small saucepan over medium-low heat. Add the orange zest and the remaining ¼ teaspoon of the cinnamon; cook 3 minutes. Add the cognac, and carefully set aflame. When the flame has died down, stir this mixture into the stew.

4. Place the Dutch oven on a burner over medium heat and heat to boiling. Then reduce the heat, and place the partially steamed couscous in a colander that fits tightly in the pot. Cook, covered, over medium-low heat 25 minutes. (Stir the stew once or twice to prevent sticking.) Serve, sprinkled with parsley, in individual bowls, placing a spoonful of couscous on top of each serving of stew.

Serves 6 to 8

MARILYN HARRIS'S CHICKEN AND VEGETABLE TAGINE

The following couscous dish is only vaguely connected to North Africa, but do not let that deter you, please, for it is wonderful!

It stems from a territory somewhat dearer and closer to my heart than Morocco—Cincinnati, Ohio, believe it or not. The donor is Marilyn Harris, one of the fine American cooks *not* hiding her light under a bushel. Marilyn is a cooking teacher, food consultant, TV personality, and the host of her own radio show, called *Cooking with Marilyn*, on WCKY in Cincinnati. Her cookbook of the same name will be published soon by Paxton Press. Marilyn's chicken and vegetable tagine is a miracle of good taste, and her quick and easy couscous could possibly convert a Moroccan to her cause.

1/4 cup raisins
1/4 cup dry sherry
1 chicken (about 4 pounds), well rinsed, dried, and cut into pieces
Salt and freshly ground black pepper to taste
3 to 4 tablespoons all-purpose flour
1 tablespoon unsalted butter
2 tablespoons olive oil
1 medium onion, halved and sliced
1 large clove garlic, minced
1 can (14 ounces) plum tomatoes, chopped, with juice
1 medium carrot, peeled and cut into 2-inch julienne
1 medium rib celery, cut into 2-inch julienne
1 small turnip, peeled and cut into 2-inch julienne
1/4 teaspoon salt
Dash of hot pepper sauce
1/8 teaspoon ground cinnamon
Marilyn's Quick and Easy Couscous (recipe follows)
2 tablespoons chopped fresh parsley

1. Combine the raisins with the sherry in a small saucepan. Heat to boiling; remove from the heat and reserve.

2. Sprinkle the chicken with salt and pepper. Dredge with flour.

3. Heat the butter with the oil in a heavy skillet (with cover) over medium heat. Sauté the chicken pieces, half at a time, until well browned on both sides, 8 to 10 minutes per batch. Transfer to a plate.

4. Add the onion to the skillet; cook 2 minutes. Add the garlic; cook 2 minutes longer. Stir in the tomatoes, carrot, celery, and turnip, and heat to boiling. Reduce the heat and return the chicken to the skillet. Cook, covered, 30 minutes.

5. Stir the raisins and sherry, the salt, hot pepper sauce, and cinnamon into the chicken juices. Cook, partially covered, over low heat 10 to 15 minutes longer.

6. To serve, place the couscous on a platter and spoon the chicken mixture over the top. Sprinkle with parsley.

Serves 4

Marilyn's Quick and Easy Couscous

2 tablespoons olive oil
1 1/2 cups medium-grain couscous
2 cups homemade chicken stock (see page 376) or canned broth
1/2 teaspoon salt
1/4 teaspoon freshly ground black pepper
1/4 teaspoon ground allspice
1/8 teaspoon ground mace
2 tablespoons unsalted butter

1. Preheat the oven to 375°F.

2. Heat the oil in a large skillet over medium-low heat. Stir in the couscous; cook 2 minutes. Stir in the stock, salt, pepper, allspice, and mace. Cook, tossing gently with two forks, until all liquid has been absorbed, about 2 minutes. Stir the butter into the couscous, and transfer to a heatproof serving dish. Bake for 5 minutes.

Serves 4

COUSCOUS AND FRESH TUNA, TUNISIAN STYLE

*F*ish tagines are part of every North African cook's repertoire, but you will not find the next dish in any medina from one end of Tunis to the other. The chief ingredient of this stew is straight out of the Atlantic Ocean, even though the cooking method is influenced by the Gulf of Hammamet. Eat couscous and fresh tuna in the summer, when the yellowfin are running.

¼ cup olive oil
2 medium onions, halved and sliced
2 cloves garlic, minced
1 medium green bell pepper, cored, seeded,
    and cut into strips
1 medium red bell pepper, cored, seeded,
    and cut into strips
1 medium yellow bell pepper, cored,
    seeded, and cut into strips
1 fresh jalapeño pepper, seeded, deveined,
    and minced
1 tablespoon semolina
¼ teaspoon chopped fresh thyme, or a
    pinch of dried
½ teaspoon anchovy paste
3 large tomatoes, peeled, seeded, and
    coarsely chopped
1½ cups fish stock (see page 377)
1 recipe partially steamed Basic Cooked
    Couscous (see page 286)
1 large zucchini, cut into ½-inch cubes
1½ pounds fresh tuna, cut into ½-inch-
    thick slices
2 tablespoons unsalted butter
1 cup chopped fresh parsley
½ cup sliced oil-cured black olives
Harissa (see page 288)

1. Heat the oil in a large heavy skillet (with cover) if you are using a couscousière, or in a Dutch oven, over medium heat. Add the onions; cook 1 minute. Add the garlic; cook 2 minutes longer. Stir in all the peppers and reduce the heat. Cook, covered, over medium-low heat 5 minutes. If you are using a couscousière, transfer the mixture to the stew pot.

2. Whisk the semolina into the pepper mixture. Cook, stirring constantly, 2 minutes. Stir in the thyme, anchovy paste, tomatoes, and fish stock, and heat to boiling. Reduce the heat to medium-low and cook, uncovered, 5 minutes. Place the partially steamed couscous in the couscousière steam pan or in a colander that fits tightly in the Dutch oven. Cover, and cook 10 minutes longer.

3. Add the zucchini to the stew and return the couscous. Cover and cook 8 minutes. Stir the fish into the stew and return the couscous. Cover, and cook 7 minutes longer. Remove the couscous from the steamer or colander and toss it with the butter. Keep warm. Stir the parsley and olives into the stew.

4. To serve, spoon the stew into individual soup bowls, and place a large scoop of couscous in the center. Pass the Harissa.

Serves 4 to 6

ROASTED GARLIC COUSCOUS SALAD

Back in 16th-century England, a salad was described as "odds and ends of very common kitchen furniture." Can that mean leftovers, do you suppose? If so, let us muse on the infinite possibilities of day-after couscous in a salad bowl.

1 large head garlic, whole (about 20 to 25 cloves)
Salt
6 to 7 tablespoons olive oil
1 tablespoon red wine vinegar
3 cups Basic Cooked Couscous, warm or at room temperature (see page 286)
Freshly ground black pepper to taste
¼ cup chopped fresh parsley

1. Preheat the oven to 400°F.
2. Place the garlic on an oven proof dish, and roast it in the oven until the skin begins to blacken, 30 to 35 minutes.

Cool slightly. Then, using a sharp knife, cut the head apart. Using a spoon and your fingers, squeeze the individual garlic cloves from their skins into a medium-size bowl. Mash with a fork.
3. Add ¼ teaspoon salt to the mashed garlic, and mash with the back of a spoon. Slowly whisk in the oil and vinegar until smooth. Toss with the couscous in a bowl, and season with salt and pepper. Sprinkle with parsley before serving.

Serves 4 to 6

BASIL AND TOMATO COUSCOUS SALAD

This salad of tomatoes flecked with bleu cheese is best served at room temperature. It is terrific with cold chicken, broiled or even fried.

2 cups Basic Cooked Couscous (see page 286)
½ cup lightly crushed cooked or canned tomatoes with juice
1 small clove garlic, crushed
¼ teaspoon salt
2 ounces blue cheese
1 teaspoon Dijon mustard
¼ cup olive oil
Juice of ½ lemon
Freshly ground black pepper to taste
2 teaspoons chopped fresh basil

1. Combine the couscous with the tomatoes in a large bowl. Lightly toss.
2. Mash the garlic with the salt and bleu cheese in a small bowl until smooth. Stir in the mustard. Whisk in the oil and lemon juice. Pour over the couscous and lightly toss until mixed. Add pepper, and sprinkle with the basil.

Serves 4

CUCKOO CHICKEN SALAD

*T*his recipe does wonders for leftover turkey as well. A luncheon or light supper dish.

2 cups Basic Cooked Couscous (see page 286)
1 rib celery, minced (about ½ cup)
1 small shallot, minced
1 cup cooked chicken chunks
¾ cup cubed cooked ham
1 small hot green pepper, seeded, deveined, and minced
½ cup frozen peas, thawed
¼ teaspoon minced fresh sage leaves, or a pinch of dried
⅓ cup mayonnaise, preferably homemade (see page 379)
⅓ cup sour cream
1 teaspoon Dijon mustard
¼ cup plus 1 tablespoon strong beef stock (see Note)
Salt and freshly ground black pepper to taste
Chopped fresh parsley, for garnish

1. Combine the couscous with the celery, shallot, chicken, ham, hot pepper, peas, and sage in a large bowl. Lightly toss.

2. Whisk the mayonnaise with the sour cream in a medium-size bowl. Whisk in the mustard and beef stock. Pour over the couscous mixture and lightly toss until mixed. Add salt and pepper, and sprinkle with parsley.

Serves 4

Note: If you do not have strong beef stock on hand (see page 379), reduce ½ cup plus 2 tablespoons canned beef broth to ¼ cup plus 1 tablespoon by simmering for 10 minutes.

WHEAT

The Berry, the Germ, and the Flour, Whole-Wheat Style

I live on a street in Manhattan, an artery for truckers, bicyclists, joggers, and somewhat privileged pre-schoolers, that I tend to think of as Wheat Street. No grain grows there, but it is the street where I first learned to make bread. It is also the street where the gentleman who inspired my bread-making lived.

Some "foodies" call my thoroughfare the Street of Good Cooks, for it is inhabited by a remarkable clutch of kitchen practitioners. East to west: Anna Teresa

Callen, Madhur Jaffrey, Mimi Sheraton, and slightly off course, Lydie Marshall. Strategically in the middle of our tree-lined street was the home of my baking mentor, James Beard. A well-polished marker on the facade keeps him a neighbor to us all, in perpetuity.

I would on occasion meet Mr. Beard on the street, usually when he was taking his pug dog, Percy, for a nightly airing. Together we would walk along the darkened sidewalks and hold some kind of colloquy about the state of food in America, and more specifically the eating places on our own turf. Although in actuality it was never much of a dialogue. Beard spoke and I assented.

"Terrible!" was his opinion of the new restaurants that were gradually replacing all the homey, long-established businesses in the vicinity. "But, I suppose you must give them credit for optimism. Like a phoenix, one opens on the very site where another failed a month before. Now that is *optimism!*"

Beard was once an actor, and he knew how to hit a vowel so it could be heard around a street corner. "*Un*-less, of course, you call it lack of *imagination!*"

Later, he confided, "When I was a young man, taking over a bankrupt business was considered bad luck. But I guess there were more pessimists around in those days."

Actually, James Beard and I first met at the nether end of Long Island. A friend brought him into my take-out food shop there (The Store in Amagansett) almost twenty years ago, when the shine was still on the stove and I hadn't the slightest notion of writing about food for a living. My happiness in those days was merely cooking it.

I remember Mr. Beard in my store that day—a wholly generous giant, glowing and glowering by turns, with an endless supply of recipes at his command that he rattled off along with some hard-edged advice.

"In this business one must keep changing—constantly," he advised after a cursory glance at The Store's menu (top-heavy with quiche and crêpes). "Because even your most dedicated food-loving customer today will turn out to have the attention span of a fruit fly tomorrow!"

Several decades later, as we meandered along our shared Manhattan street with Percy between us, I reminded him of that remark. To his credit, he neither recalled nor disavowed the statement but turned the idea over in his mind before answering. "A food lover," he said, "as opposed to someone who merely enjoys good food, is virtually a Casanova—always looking for the perfect meal that will whet his appetite for another, and another after that. But not me. Too many perfect meals give me a stomach ache!"

The only foods he talked about with any real sensuality were dishes so homespun and elemental they would never bear recognition in a Michelin or Mobil Guide: fried eggs, crisp home-cured bacon, and good chewy bread.

Bread was a particular bond he and I shared. Beard grew up in his mother's boardinghouse in Portland, Oregon, where fresh loaves were set in the oven at sunrise daily. Bread baking did not come into my life, however, until I was past forty and fairly stodgy about expanding culinary horizons. I only baked my first loaf because a friend gave me a copy of *Beard on Bread.*

I should have gotten him to sign it the first time we met. To my regret, I was too embarrassed to ask. Instead I paid him a dubious compliment. "You are my disciple of bread baking, Mr. Beard," I blurted out.

If he took offence at my gaffe, you would never know it. Patting me on the shoulder instead, he winked. "Only time will tell if you've got that wrong way round or not."

When he learned that I had recently been to some obscure American town, Mr. Beard would always quiz me about the dishes I'd eaten there. "Was the bread any good?" he would ask. "If the bread is chewable and the butter is unsalted, there's still hope!"

Hope was an essential ingredient of the Beard persona, although he experienced many physical setbacks and equally awesome recuperations at the end of his life. We had not met on the street for several months when I ran into him one night; he looked somewhat the worse for a recent hospital stay but was still jauntily outfitted, wearing a bow tie and carrying a malacca walking stick.

"I've just been on the town, Bert," he informed me, "to Sally's restaurant around the corner." (Sally being Sally Darr, the chef-owner of La Tulipe, a small but splendid restaurant.) "That girl really knows how to orchestrate a meal," he ruminated. "And the bread is *very* chewy. I'm bringing home a slice for Percy." He held up a small crusty end. "Like us, he likes bread with bite to it!"

Wheat Street has not been the same since James Beard left it.

The Grain's Genesis

*I*t's a sobering thought, but wheat, which has been around on this planet longer than man, stands a pretty good chance of outlasting him here too. Faced with immutable odds, man crumbles. Wheat, on the other hand, merely adapts; and has been doing so successfully for millennia!

The first wheat was wild grass. Not all the grass seeds were tasty or even good to eat, but man consumed them greedily because they were there. Unlike plants that had to be dug up or wild things that had to be hunted or trapped, these grains required no effort whatsoever. If he was hungry (and early man usually was), he merely stretched out his fingers and helped himself to a handful of breakfast, lunch, or dinner.

Paleolithic peoples were nomads, but wheat gave them roots. Somewhere in the broad expanse of Asia—stretching from the slopes of the Himalayas to the shores of the Mediterranean—the leader of a tribe that was forever on the prowl for food stopped short. Before him was a stand of ripening cereal grasses, no different from any field he and his kinsmen had picked over in the past. But on this day he did not order it to be picked over. Instead he bid his family take only half the wild wheat for provender and—here's the switch—plant the rest in the ground nearby. Which necessitated raking, furrowing, seeding, watering, and most important of all, remaining in the territory for the harvest. Which, in loftier terms, is considered to be the birth of agrarian society.

Wheat-growing changed the complexion and digestive system of the ancient world. The Tigris and Euphrates valley, then known as "the fertile crescent" but now dry as a bone, was once covered with endless rows of golden grain—stalks so high that mothers kept small children out of the fields lest they become lost forever in the waving maze.

Sheaves were woven into thatch for roofs and lacings for sandals; large canes kept residents warm in winter and small canes fired their stoves year-round. More important, perhaps, wheat was consumed in a multitude of ways: roasted as cereal, boiled into soup, braised with meat and vegetables as stew, and crushed into flour for bread.

Shards of cooking vessels dating back to 6700 B.C. have been found containing the remnants of cooked wheat in one form or another. And a team of eager archeologists recently unearthed rough implements for grinding seeds (if not precisely wheat, close enough) that were in use 50,000 years before that.

Wheat is obviously a grain that

brought civilization to the world. Because of it, human beings began to pair (two could glean as cheaply as one) and live in communities. Not to mention domesticating animals, building homes, inventing wheels, and making wars upon one another.

But that, if I may be forgiven a pun, is too wheaty a subject to get into here!

Some Plain Grain Talk

*T*here are virtually endless types of wheat. A scientist in the Soviet Union recently logged over 30,000 different varieties—and, worse luck, he named them all!

Happily, all 30,000 belong to fourteen basic wheat species. And just one of those, *Triticum aestivum*, or common wheat, makes up 95 percent of the crop grown and consumed in the U.S. Agronomists refer to wheat strains as "winter wheat" or "spring wheat," depending upon the time of year the seed is planted. Wheat also comes in two botanical nominations, "hard wheat" and "soft wheat," that indicate the volume of gluten in the grain's cellular structure.

Hard common wheat has 10 to 13 percent protein content. The kernels are resilent and tough to mill.

Soft common wheat has 6 to 10 percent protein content. It is also starchier and more malleable than its hard wheat counterparts.

Hard durum wheat (or semolina) represents the remaining 5 percent of wheat grown in the U.S. It is also the toughest wheat of all. But by now you have all the information about semolina you will ever need, so we can skip it here!

In America, hard spring wheat is raised in the coldest parts of the North and Northwest. Hard winter wheat grows in the Central Plains. Soft winter wheat springs from the South and Midwest.

Hard wheat, with its high gluten content and ability to absorb liquid easily, is deemed the ideal grain for bread baking. Soft wheat, with a relatively low amount of gluten in the grain, is adjudged best for cookies, cake, and pastry.

This chapter is concerned with "whole wheat" in a holistic sense, in three very basic and highly nutritious forms: wheat berries, wheat germ, and whole-wheat flour.

WHEAT BERRIES

*T*he name may seem unfamiliar. It's relatively new nomenclature for what used to be known as unprocessed whole wheat. My grandmother used to buy whole wheat in bulk and grind it herself (in a coffee mill) whenever she felt the urge to make a loaf of cracked-wheat bread. (Bulgur is cracked wheat berries.)

Nowadays commercial wheat berries usually come from organically grown wheat and have a culinary identity distinct from cracked wheat. Like all "drieds," they must be presoaked and then precooked before they're used in a recipe. Even then, wheat berries have a decided *al dente* crunch, so be forewarned before setting a molar to a mouthful.

Wheat berries are very good for you. They are high in protein, carbohydrates, B vitamins, and seven amino acids that provide the body with energy: 335 units of protein per cooked half cup. And low in calories: 55 for the same amount.

How to Buy Them

I am sorry to say wheat berries are not generally found on supermarket shelves. They may be obtained at any natural foods store around the country, however, or by mail order (see the resource list at the back of the book).

Wheat berries are very inexpensive. Health food shops sell whole wheat loose (in bulk) and packaged. Bulk sales are cheapest and more sensible in the long run, since wheat berries have a rather long shelf life.

Most wheat berries sold over the counter are hard (red) wheat. Ideally the grains are a uniform deep russet-brown color. There should be no undersized kernels or any hint of husk attached. Wheat husks, unlike bran coverings, are inedible. If it is possible, run your fingers through a batch of wheat berries before you buy them. No chaff should be visible, and they should feel smooth and dry to the touch. Pass over any damp or spotted grains—they're on the way to spoilage.

How to Store Them

*A*s wheat berries are relatively inexpensive and within my normal shopping sphere, I generally buy them only when I have a specific need—never more than a pound or two at a time. I store the unused portion in a glass container with a screw-top lid, in the pantry. Wheat berries keep best in a dry, relatively low-humidity environment, optimally at a temperature that hovers in the low 60s. If your kitchen area is considerably warmer, I suggest you stow the berries in the refrigerator, where they will keep forever. As wheat berries are fairly self-contained, they are not prone to any insect invasion. If you do notice unwanted visitors, however, an overnight stint in the freezer will destroy them at once.

How to Cook Them

*T*o prepare wheat berries for use in the recipes that follow, they first must be soaked overnight. Then, depending upon their further use, either partially or fully cooked.

Partially cooked (or parboiled) wheat berries save time and absorb the essential flavor of the dish they finish in. Fully cooked wheat berries may be eaten as is, amended with a dressing, tossed with vegetables in a salad, or used to bind meats in loaves and croquettes. I even add cooked wheat berries to certain breads for texture.

PRECOOKED WHEAT BERRIES

*W*heat berries double in volume when they are cooked so that 1 cup dried yields 2 cups cooked.

1 cup wheat berries
3½ cups cold water

1. Combine the wheat berries and cold water in a saucepan. Cover, and soak overnight.

2. Boil the wheat berries in their soaking water for 15 minutes for parboiled wheat berries; 50 to 60 minutes for fully cooked wheat berries. Add more water if necessary as they cook.

3. Drain and cool thoroughly. Store in the refrigerator, in a container with a lid or in a self-seal, airtight plastic bag. Parboiled wheat berries will keep for 3 to 4 days, fully cooked berries for up to a week. (Do not freeze; they will turn mushy.)

Makes 2 cups

HARSCHO

This is a version of a hearty Georgian dish—from Russia, not below the Mason-Dixon line. A combination soup-stew, flavored with every herb that grows (at least in my garden), it is said to bring color to the diner's cheeks after the first sip.

2 tablespoons vegetable oil
1 beef chuck roast (3 pounds), about 2 inches thick
1 clove garlic, bruised
1 large onion, quartered and sliced
1½ quarts homemade beef stock (see page 377) or canned broth
1 clove garlic, minced
¼ cup pearl barley
1 cup parboiled wheat berries (see page 298)
2 cups chopped cabbage
1 cup water
1 large turnip (½ pound), peeled and cut into ½-inch cubes
2 large carrots, peeled and cut into ¼-inch-thick slices
2 medium potatoes (1 pound), peeled and cut into ¾-inch cubes
Dash of hot pepper sauce
Salt and freshly ground black pepper to taste
1 cup frozen peas, thawed
¼ cup chopped fresh parsley
1 teaspoon chopped fresh basil
1 teaspoon chopped fresh cilantro (Chinese parsley)
1 teaspoon chopped fresh dill
1 teaspoon chopped fresh tarragon
1 teaspoon chopped fresh chives

1. Preheat the oven to 350°F.

2. Heat the oil in a large heavy pot or Dutch oven over medium-high heat. Rub the meat with the bruised garlic, and cook it in the hot oil until well browned on all sides, 6 minutes. Remove the meat to a plate and add the onion to the pot; cook 1 minute. Place the meat on top of the onions, cover, and transfer to the oven. Bake for 1 hour.

3. Remove the pot from the oven and add 1 quart of the stock, the minced garlic, barley, parboiled wheat berries, and cabbage. Heat to boiling on top of the stove, then cover, return to the oven, and bake 45 minutes.

4. Remove the pot from the oven and add the remaining 2 cups beef stock, the water, turnip, carrots, and potatoes. Heat to boiling on top of the stove, then cover, return to the oven, and cook until the meat and vegetables are tender, about 45 minutes.

5. Remove the pot from the oven. Transfer the meat to a carving board. Add hot pepper sauce to the stew in the pot, and season with salt and pepper. Stir in the peas. Let stand, covered, 5 minutes.

6. Carve the meat into serving pieces. Combine the herbs and stir into the stew. Return the meat to the stew, and serve.

Serves 6 to 8

WHEAT BERRY CAVIAR

You might call this "poor man's caviar." The puréed olives turn the wheat berries as black as the best caviar. It makes a wonderful first course.

2 small cloves garlic
1 cup California "small" pitted black
    olives
¼ teaspoon salt
¼ teaspoon Dijon mustard
¼ cup olive oil
1½ cups fully cooked wheat berries (see
    page 298), chilled
Chopped fresh chives, for garnish

1. Turn on a food processor and drop the garlic through the feed tube.

Process until minced. Add the olives, salt, mustard, and oil, and process until the olives are finely minced.

2. Place the cooked wheat berries in a serving bowl. Add the processed olive mixture, and toss gently to mix. Sprinkle with chives.

Serves 4

INCAN-STYLE PORK

Originally from Peru, this spicy amalgam of meat and grain is influenced by the fine cooking style of Felipe Rojas-Lombardi. Felipe makes it with quinoa (see "The New Grains"), but I prefer the crunch of wheat berries in his stew. Serve with a plate of plain boiled potatoes.

2 pounds lean boneless pork shoulder, cut
    into 1-inch cubes
1 tablespoon olive oil
1 tablespoon red wine vinegar
1 shallot, minced
3 cloves garlic, minced
1 teaspoon salt
½ teaspoon freshly ground black pepper
¼ teaspoon ground cumin
2 dried ancho peppers, seeded and coarsely
    chopped
2 hot green peppers, seeded, deveined, and
    chopped
6 tablespoons vegetable oil
1 hot Italian sausage or Spanish chorizo,
    finely chopped
2 large onions, finely chopped

1 cup V-8 or tomato juice
½ cup (approximately) homemade chicken
    stock (see page 376) or canned broth
1 cup parboiled wheat berries (see page
    298)
2 tablespoons chopped fresh cilantro
    (Chinese parsley)
Boiled potatoes, heated

1. Place the pork in a large bowl and add the olive oil, vinegar, shallot, 2 cloves of the garlic, salt, pepper, and cumin. Mix well with your hands. Let stand, covered, 2 hours.

2. Meanwhile, place the ancho and hot green peppers in a bowl. Cover with hot water; let soak 3 minutes. Drain.

Repeat this process three times. Then cover with hot water and let stand 15 minutes. Drain, and combine with 2 tablespoons of the vegetable oil in the container of a food processor or blender. Process until smooth.

3. Heat the remaining 4 tablespoons vegetable oil in a large heavy pot or Dutch oven over medium-high heat. Sauté the pork, in about four batches, until well browned, 6 minutes per batch. Transfer to a plate using a slotted spoon. Reduce the heat to medium.

4. Add the sausage to the pot; cook 1 minute. Add the onions and the remaining garlic; cook until golden, about 4 to 5 minutes. Reduce the heat to medium-low and stir in the puréed pepper mixture; cook 5 minutes.

5. Return the pork to the pot and stir well. Add the V-8 and the chicken stock, and heat to boiling. Stir in the

According to grain guru E. J. Kahn, "more of the globe's arable surface is given over to wheat than any other crop grown"—about 600,000,000 acres. Indeed, says Kahn, there are parts of the world where one could fly a small plane over wheat fields and run out of gas long before the wheat ran out of sight!

wheat berries and reduce the heat. Cook, stirring occasionally, partially covered, until the meat is tender, about 1 hour. Add more chicken stock if the mixture becomes too dry. Sprinkle with cilantro, and serve with boiled potatoes.

Serves 6

ELBA'S KIPPES

This dish—an utterly delicious meat and wheat berry croquette, filled with ham or chicken—comes from the Dominican Republic by way of a young woman named Elba Trinidad. Elba serves *kippes* (pronounced keep-ess) hot or cold, as the mood strikes her. I must confess I prefer them warm, with sour cream on the side. If the cream seems too bland, season it with a splash of lemon juice.

½ pound ground beef
½ pound ground veal
¼ pound ground pork
1 large onion, finely chopped
2 hot green peppers, seeded, deveined, and minced
1½ cups fully cooked wheat berries (see page 298)
¼ cup chopped fresh parsley
½ teaspoon salt
¼ pound cooked chicken or ham, ground (about 1¼ cups)
Vegetable oil for deep-frying

1. Combine the beef, veal, and pork in a large bowl and mix well. Add the onion, green peppers, cooked wheat berries, parsley, and salt. Mix well. Form into 20 meatballs.

2. Place the meatballs on a work surface and press to make meat cakes. With your fingers, poke a well in the center of each cake. (They will look a little like birds' nests.) Place about 1 teaspoon ground chicken or ham in each well, and sprinkle with a few drops of water. Press the filling down gently and fold the edges of the meat over the top. Smooth once again into meat cakes.

3. Heat 2 inches oil in a deep heavy skillet or shallow saucepan. Fry the meat cakes, about five at a time, until golden and crisp on both sides, about 6 minutes. Drain well on paper towels. Serve hot or at room temperature.

Makes 20 meat cakes (serves 4)

HEALTHY FARMER'S WIFE'S POT-ROASTED CHICKEN

This is basically a good old-fashioned farm-style pot-roasted chicken. The addition of wheat berries makes it not only heartier, but healthier as well.

¼ pound salt pork, diced (about ½ cup)
12 small white onions
1 chicken (3½ to 4 pounds), well rinsed
 and dried
1 clove garlic, bruised
1 tablespoon unsalted butter, at room
 temperature
4 tablespoons unsalted butter
2 medium potatoes (about 1 pound), peeled
 and diced
1 large carrot, peeled and diced
½ cup parboiled wheat berries (see page
 298)
2 teaspoons green peppercorns, or more to
 taste
4 sprigs parsley
½ bay leaf
2 small sprigs thyme
Chopped fresh parsley, for garnish

1. Preheat the oven to 325°F.

2. Cook the salt pork in boiling water to cover for 2 minutes. Drain and pat dry.

3. Peel the onions, and cut an "X" in the root end of each one. Set aside.

4. Rub the chicken with the garlic, inside and out. Sew and truss the chicken; rub with 1 tablespoon butter.

5. Sauté the salt pork in a large heavy pot or Dutch oven over medium-low heat until crisp and rendered of grease. Using a slotted spoon, transfer to a bowl.

6. Raise the heat slightly and add the chicken to the pot. Brown the chicken well on all sides, 12 minutes. Carefully transfer to a plate.

7. Add the onions to the pot and sauté, stirring frequently, until golden brown, 8 to 10 minutes. Transfer to a bowl.

8. Pour off all grease from the pot and add the 4 tablespoons butter. Stir over medium-low heat, scraping the bottom and sides of the pot with a wooden spoon. Add the potatoes and carrot, stirring well to coat the vegetables. Add the reserved salt pork, wheat berries, and green peppercorns.

9. Push the potato mixture to the edges of the pot and place the chicken in the center. Tie the herbs in a cheesecloth bag, and place in the pot. Cover, and transfer to the oven. Cook until the chicken is tender, about 1 hour and 15 minutes.

10. To serve, carve the chicken and place on a platter. Discard the herb bag, then spoon the vegetable mixture with all the juices into a serving bowl. Sprinkle vegetables and chicken with parsley, and serve.

Serves 3 or 4

ZUCCHINI, TOMATO, AND WHEAT BERRY SLAW

*F*ully cooked wheat berries add a remarkable bite to salads that must be tasted to be believed.

2 cups fully cooked wheat berries (see page 298), chilled
1 large shallot, minced
2 thin medium zucchini, cut into very thin slices
16 to 20 cherry tomatoes, cut into ¼-inch-thick rounds
2 tablespoons chopped fresh basil
1 clove garlic, minced
¼ teaspoon salt
½ teaspoon Dijon mustard
1 tablespoon fresh lemon juice
1 tablespoon red wine vinegar
1 tablespoon strong beef stock (see Note)
¼ cup olive oil

1. Combine the cooked wheat ber-ries with the shallot, zucchini, tomatoes, and basil in a serving bowl. Toss gently to mix.

2. Using the back of a spoon, mash the garlic with the salt in a small bowl until a paste is formed. Whisk in the mustard, lemon juice, vinegar, beef stock, and olive oil. Pour over the salad and toss gently to mix. Let stand 15 to 20 minutes before serving.

Serves 6

Note: If you do not have strong beef stock on hand (see page 379), reduce ¼ cup canned beef broth to 1 tablespoon by simmering for 5 minutes.

SANDRA DAY'S WHEAT BERRY WALDORF SALAD

*M*y good friend Sandra Day, former food editor of the *New Orleans Times-Picayune*, now lives and writes in Lafayette, Louisiana. She also sends me wonderful recipes from time to time. Here is her latest. "If you can't get fennel, and I haven't seen any fresh since I got here," Sandra imparts, "use two stalks of celery instead!"

1 cup fully cooked wheat berries (see page 298), chilled
2 small fennel bulbs (6 ounces each), trimmed and finely chopped (about 1 cup)
¼ cup mayonnaise, preferably homemade (see page 379)
2 teaspoons Dijon mustard
2 tablespoons fresh lemon juice
½ teaspoon fennel seeds, crushed
1 sweet red apple
½ cup walnut halves, toasted (see Note) and coarsely chopped
Lettuce leaves

1. Combine the wheat berries and

the fennel in a bowl. Toss to mix.

2. Combine the mayonnaise with the mustard, lemon juice, and fennel seeds in a small bowl. Pour over the wheat and fennel, and toss well.

3. Core the apple and dice it, tossing the cubes in the salad as you work to prevent discoloring. Toss in the walnuts. Serve on lettuce leaves.

Serves 4

Note: To toast walnuts, spread them evenly on a baking sheet and place in a 350°F oven, stirring occasionally, for 10 minutes.

BEAN AND BERRY BAKE

A variation of Boston's finest buzz-food, and a bounty wherever it turns up geographically. The best way to bake this dish is in an old-fashioned bean pot. If you have to substitute a Dutch oven, be forewarned: the dish will probably cook faster, necessitating more liquid along the way.

1 pound dry white beans
2 teaspoons unsalted butter
1 clove garlic, bruised
1 cup parboiled wheat berries (see page 298)
1 large onion, finely chopped
3 strips bacon, fried crisp and crumbled
4 slices Canadian bacon, chopped
2 tablespoons dark brown sugar
2 teaspoons Worcestershire sauce
¼ cup molasses
5 tablespoons chili sauce
1 tablespoon English dry mustard
1 teaspoon curry powder
¼ teaspoon hot Hungarian paprika
1½ teaspoons salt
½ cup dark rum
2 cups V-8 juice or tomato juice
3 strips raw bacon

1. Pick the beans over, discarding any debris, and place in a large pot. Cover with cold water. Heat to boiling; boil 2 minutes. Remove from the heat and let stand, covered, 1 hour.

2. Preheat the oven to 275°F.

3. Rub a bean pot with the butter. Then rub it well with the bruised garlic.

4. Drain the beans and transfer to a large bowl. Add the wheat berries, onion, crumbled bacon, and the Canadian bacon.

5. In a small bowl, combine the sugar, Worcestershire sauce, molasses, chili sauce, mustard, curry powder, paprika, salt, and dark rum. Pour over the bean mixture. Add ½ cup of the V-8 juice. Mix well and transfer to the prepared bean pot. Place the raw bacon strips over the top. Bake, covered, 7 hours or more, adding more V-8 juice as the beans dry out, about every 30 minutes. If all the V-8 juice is absorbed before the beans are tender, add water as needed.

Serves 6 to 8

SALLY'S CRAZY HEALTH BREAD

*T*his recipe was sent to me by a woman who calls herself "an ex-hippie who is alive and well in Brattleboro, Vermont."

"I came of age during 'the molar movement' at a farm commune in the mid-sixties," she explained. "It was a time when anything that could possibly be chewed or chawed without deleterious effect on the digestive system went into all my recipes. Most of them were tossed in the Disposall when I turned thirty. But this bread holds up. Make it with only *cooled* cooked whole wheat!"

And that's all she wrote.

1 cup lukewarm water
1 package dry yeast
1½ tablespoons molasses
2 tablespoons honey
Pinch of ginger
½ cup fully cooked wheat berries (see page 298), at room temperature
¼ cup pumpkin seeds, toasted and chopped (see Note)
2 tablespoons semolina
2 tablespoons unprocessed bran
1 teaspoon caraway seeds
¼ teaspoon anise seeds
2¾ teaspoons salt
½ cup rye flour
¼ cup buckwheat flour
2½ to 3 cups whole-wheat flour
1 egg white
2 teaspoons sesame seeds
¼ teaspoon freshly ground black pepper

1. Place ¼ cup of the lukewarm water in a large bowl. Sprinkle it with the yeast, then stir in the molasses, honey, and ginger. Let stand until bubbly, 8 to 10 minutes.

2. Add the remaining water to the yeast mixture, along with the cooked wheat berries, pumpkin seeds, semolina, bran, caraway seeds, anise seeds, and ¾ teaspoon of the salt. Mix well, and stir in the rye flour, buckwheat flour, and about 1½ cups whole-wheat flour, enough to form a soft dough.

3. Transfer the dough to a floured

E arly Romans called whole wheat *spelt*. Caesar's diary of the Gallic Wars is weighted with the problem of acquiring *spelt* on foreign shores, as K-rations for his legions. These days, Italians call whole wheat *frumento*, but it still turns up as *spelt* in old kitchen tracts and documents written prior to the 14th century.

The French borrowed *frumento* and altered it to *froment*, which in time became *pain de froment*, their word for "bread" as well. During the reign of Louis XIV, when the French disdained coarse bread for croissants and brioche, the name of the grain was altered once again, to *blé*. *Blé*, which sounds like the French verb *blêmir* (to grow pale), had a nice white sound to it. White has been the scourge of whole wheat for centuries. The English word *wheat*, in fact, is derived from the old English *hwit* (white). However, the health-minded Portuguese rejected the blanched moniker entirely. They call wheat *trigo*, which means "hard to handle." Polish farmers dub whole wheat *pszenica*. It means "under the teeth," which is closer to the mark. And it's all wholly wheat round the world, no matter how it's *spelt*. Ouch!

board and knead, adding more whole-wheat flour as needed, until smooth and elastic, about 12 minutes. Transfer to a lightly greased bowl. Cover with plastic wrap and let rise in a warm place until doubled in volume, about 1½ hours.

4. Punch the dough down. Knead briefly and return it to the bowl. Cover again with plastic wrap and let rise in a warm place until doubled in volume, about 1 hour.

5. Generously oil a 9 by 5 by 3-inch loaf pan.

6. Punch the dough down once more, and transfer it to a floured board. Knead 5 minutes. Let it rest 2 minutes, and then roll and stretch the dough into a rope about 15 inches long. Flatten it with your hands and fold it over on itself in thirds. Gently stretch the dough so that it will fit snugly into the loaf pan. Before placing the dough in the pan,

brush the dough with the egg white and sprinkle each side with sesame seeds. Place the dough, folded side down, into the prepared pan, pressing down gently to fill the bottom of the pan. Sprinkle the remaining 2 teaspoons salt and the pepper over the top. Cover with a flour-rubbed tea towel and let rise in a warm place until the dough comes over the top of the pan, about 1 hour.

7. Preheat the oven to 350°F.

8. Bake the bread until it is golden brown and sounds hollow when tapped with your finger, about 45 minutes. Loosen the bread in the pan, and cool it in the pan on a rack.

Makes 1 loaf

Note: To toast pumpkin seeds, heat a small skillet over medium heat. Add the seeds and toast, stirring frequently, until golden, 6 to 8 minutes. Cool before chopping.

BAREFOOT CONTESSA'S WHOLE-WHEAT BERRY BREAD

No, the Barefoot Contessa was not an old flame of mine. It is the moniker of a highly innovative and often intoxicating gourmet emporium in East Hampton, Long Island. I admired their whole-wheat berry bread for years and when I requested the recipe, the owner, Ina Garten (who certainly wears shoes at her store), presented it to me with panache. And so I pass it along to you.

1 cup lukewarm water (115°F)
1 package dry yeast
¼ cup honey
Pinch of ground ginger
½ cup unprocessed bran
1 cup fully cooked wheat berries (see page 298), at room temperature
1 teaspoon salt

1¼ cups whole-wheat flour
1¼ cups unbleached all-purpose flour (approximately)
Cornmeal

1. Place the lukewarm water in a large bowl. Sprinkle the yeast over it, and then stir in the honey and ginger.

Let stand until bubbly, about 5 minutes.

2. Stir in the bran, parboiled wheat berries, and salt. Stir in the whole-wheat flour, and add about ¾ cup of the all-purpose flour, enough to make a stiff dough.

3. Transfer the dough to a lightly floured board and knead, adding more all-purpose flour as needed, until it is smooth and elastic, about 15 minutes.

4. Divide the dough in half, and form each portion into a round loaf.

Place the loaves on a cornmeal-sprinkled baking sheet, and cover with a flour-rubbed tea towel. Let stand in a warm place until doubled in volume, 1½ to 2 hours.

5. Preheat the oven to 350°F.

6. Bake the bread until the loaves are browned and sound hollow when tapped with your finger, about 45 minutes. Cool on a rack.

Makes 2 loaves

WHEAT GERM

Wheat germ is the natural, untreated embryo of the wheat berry. A pale gold substance of crumblike texture and nutty taste, it adds considerable salubrity to the daily diet while sparking up vittles at the same time. For evidence, note the variety of recipes that follow—everything from wheat germ pancakes to wheat germ roasted potatoes.

Wheat germ is a healthy seasoning, sky high in potassium (240 mg per quarter cup), thiamine, niacin, zinc, and riboflavin. Also well endowed with protein and carbohydrates, it contains no sodium or cholesterol whatsoever.

How to Buy It

Wheat germ is a highly visible product on supermarket and grocers' shelves everywhere in the U.S. You will find it next to the packaged cereals. The brand most in evidence is Kretschmer, manufactured by Quaker Oats. Kretschmer wheat germ is sold two ways: plain toasted and honey-flavored. Skip the latter version, as its use (even in desserts) is limited by the added sweetening.

How to Store It

Wheat germ is a highly fragile product, given to fast spoilage once the vacuum-sealed jar is opened. The label on wheat germ containers clearly states that the contents must be refrigerated after opening because the germ (which contains nutritive oils) will turn rancid quickly at room temperature. So why take chances? Refrigerated wheat germ will keep up to six months.

How to Cook It

There are no hard and fast rules for cooking or baking with wheat germ, except for one: do not go overboard. I find, for instance, that wheat germ makes a dandy replacement for half the nuts in a nut cake or half the bread crumbs coating a pork chop, but is not compatible as a total replacement for the original ingredient called for in most recipes. It's too heavy, for one thing, and the fiber content is generally too hard on the alimentary canal, for another.

CRADLED EGGPLANT

An American original: eggplant-stuffed eggplant, garlanded with onion, tomato, anchovy, herbs, cheese, and, oh yes, wheat germ.

2 small eggplants (13 to 14 ounces total)
3 tablespoons olive oil
1 small onion, finely chopped
1 small clove garlic, minced
1 small tomato (3 to 4 ounces), peeled, seeded, and chopped
½ teaspoon anchovy paste
½ teaspoon Worcestershire sauce
Salt and freshly ground black pepper to taste
1 egg, lightly beaten
3 tablespoons toasted wheat germ
¼ cup freshly grated Parmesan cheese
1 tablespoon chopped fresh basil, or 1 teaspoon dried
3 tablespoons buttered bread crumbs (see Note)

1. Cut the stems from the eggplants, and slice each in half lengthwise. Scoop out the flesh with a spoon or grapefruit knife, leaving a shell about ⅛ inch thick. Chop the scooped-out flesh.

2. Heat the oil in a large heavy skillet over medium-low heat. Add the onion; cook 1 minute. Stir in the garlic and cook 4 minutes longer. Raise the heat slightly and stir in the chopped eggplant. Cook, stirring frequently, until the eggplant is tender, about 4 minutes. Add the tomato, anchovy paste, and Worcestershire sauce. Cook 3 minutes longer. Season with salt and pepper, and remove from the heat.

3. Preheat the oven to 350°F.

4. Stir the beaten egg, wheat germ, cheese, and basil into the eggplant mixture. Fill each eggplant half with this mixture, and sprinkle with the buttered bread crumbs.

5. Place the eggplant in a shallow baking dish, and add about ¼ inch hot water to the dish. Bake 45 minutes. Check occasionally, adding more water, if necessary.

Serves 2 to 4

Note: To make buttered bread crumbs, lightly sauté 3 tablespoons fresh bread crumbs in 1 tablespoon melted butter until lightly toasted, 2 minutes.

PATCHWORK ROASTED POTATOES

Another terrific recipe from home cook Mary Surina. This tastes as if it takes hours to make. The secret is, it doesn't!

3 tablespoons toasted wheat germ
3 tablespoons fine fresh bread crumbs
3 tablespoons freshly grated Parmesan cheese
Generous pinch of freshly grated nutmeg

4 tablespoons (½ stick) unsalted butter
2 baking potatoes (about 1 pound)
Salt and freshly ground black pepper to taste

1. Preheat the oven to 400°F. Lightly butter a baking dish.

2. Combine the wheat germ, bread crumbs, cheese, and nutmeg in a shallow bowl.

3. Melt the butter in a medium-size saucepan. Remove from the heat.

4. Peel the potatoes and cut each in half lengthwise. Then cut each half lengthwise into four crescents (a total of 8 slices per potato).

5. Pat the potatoes dry with paper towels, and toss them in the melted butter until well coated. Then roll the potatoes in the wheat germ mixture, and place on the prepared baking dish. Bake until very crisp and tender, 45 to 50 minutes. Sprinkle with salt and pepper, and serve.

Serves 4

HUDSON VALLEY APPLE-BUTTER BREAD

This is a recipe that makes a diner ask, "Which came first, the butter or the bread?" Try making a loaf without the velvety brown-gold apple butter, and you'll never ask the question again.

1 cup lukewarm water
1 package dry yeast
1 teaspoon sugar
Pinch of ground ginger
⅓ cup Homemade Apple Butter (recipe
  follows)
2 tablespoons unsalted butter, melted
1 tablespoon honey
½ teaspoon salt
¼ cup toasted wheat germ
1 cup whole-wheat flour
2 to 2½ cups bread flour (approximately)
Cornmeal
1 egg
1 teaspoon water

1. Place ¼ cup of the lukewarm water in a large bowl. Sprinkle with the yeast, then stir in the sugar and ginger. Let stand until bubbly, about 5 minutes.

2. Add the remaining lukewarm water to the yeast mixture, and stir in the apple butter, melted butter, honey, salt, wheat germ, whole-wheat flour, and about 1 cup of the bread flour, enough to form a soft dough.

3. Transfer the dough to a floured board and knead, adding more bread flour as needed, until smooth and elastic, about 10 minutes. Transfer to a lightly greased bowl, cover with plastic wrap, and let rise in a warm place until doubled in volume, about 1 hour.

4. Punch the dough down and knead briefly on a floured board. Form the dough into a round loaf and place on a cornmeal-sprinkled baking sheet. Cover with a flour-rubbed tea towel, and let rise until doubled in volume, about 1 hour.

5. Preheat the oven to 425°F.

6. Beat the egg and 1 teaspoon water together, and brush the dough with the mixture. Place the dough in the oven, along with a small pan of water. Bake 10 minutes. Reduce the heat to 375°F and bake until the bread sounds hollow when tapped with your finger, about 20 minutes longer. Cool on a rack.

Makes 1 large loaf

Homemade Apple Butter

2 pounds medium, tart apples (Winesap,
    Jonathan, Jona-Reds)
1 cup apple juice
1 cup firmly packed dark brown sugar, or
    less if desired
1½ teaspoons ground cinnamon
¼ teaspoon ground allspice
⅛ teaspoon ground cloves
1 tablespoon fresh orange juice

1. Wash the apples and remove the stems. Quarter them, and place the apples and the apple juice in a large saucepan, tossing the apples to coat with the juice. Heat to boiling. Reduce the heat and simmer, covered, until the apples are almost soft, about 15 minutes. Then simmer partially covered until very soft, about 10 minutes longer. Turn off the heat and let stand, partially covered, 45 minutes. The mixture should be very thick.

2. Mash the fruit thoroughly through a fine-mesh strainer into another saucepan. Discard skins and seeds. Add the brown sugar, spices, and orange juice. Heat to boiling, and remove from the heat. Pour into sterilized jars and seal.

Makes about 2 pints

WHEATED BENNE PENNIES

I learned to make benne wafers, a favorite southern cookie, when I attended school in the South. I now add toasted wheat germ to the batter—not so much to make them wholesome as for the flavor it imparts.

1 egg
½ teaspoon vanilla extract
6 tablespoons (¾ stick) unsalted butter,
    melted
¾ cup firmly packed light brown sugar
¼ cup all-purpose flour
¼ cup pecans, chopped
¼ cup toasted wheat germ
½ cup sesame seeds, toasted (see Note)

1. Preheat the oven to 400°F. Line baking sheets with aluminum foil and lightly butter the foil.

2. Beat the egg with the vanilla in the medium-size bowl of an electric mixer. Slowly beat in the melted butter. Add the brown sugar, and beat until smooth. Beat in the flour, in three batches. Then stir in the pecans, wheat germ, and toasted sesame seeds.

3. Drop large teaspoonfuls of cookie batter onto the prepared baking sheets, placing them far apart. There should be only six cookies on each baking sheet, as they spread considerably. Bake until golden brown, about 5 minutes. Cool completely before peeling the cookies off the foil. Repeat until all the batter is used up.

Makes 24 cookies

Note: To toast sesame seeds, heat a small skillet over medium heat. Add the seeds and toast, stirring frequently, until golden, about 5 minutes.

POPPY-SEED HOT SHOTS

*P*ancakes with a difference, from one of my favorite American cooks, Clara B. Less—
a lady with a good memory and an inexhaustible supply of great dishes.

½ cup all-purpose flour
¼ cup toasted wheat germ
1½ teaspoons poppy seeds
1½ teaspoons sugar
½ teaspoon baking powder
¼ teaspoon baking soda
¼ teaspoon salt
1 egg
1 cup buttermilk
1 tablespoon unsalted butter, melted

1. Combine the flour, wheat germ, poppy seeds, sugar, baking power, baking soda, and salt in a large bowl. Mix well.

2. Whisk the egg with the butter-milk and melted butter in another bowl. Pour this over the flour mixture and stir just until mixed.

3. Heat a lightly greased cast-iron skillet or griddle over medium heat until hot but not smoking. Cook the pancakes, a few at a time, using about 2 large tablespoons per pancake. When lightly browned, about 2 minutes, turn over and cook the other side for 1 minute. Transfer to a serving platter and keep warm in a 225°F oven while cooking the remaining pancakes. Reduce the heat if the cakes brown too quickly.

Makes about twelve 2- to 3-inch pancakes

SNIPPY GINGER SNAPS

I grew up a ginger freak. The gingerier the snap, the more I liked it. Wheat germ adds not only a richer taste but also a crunch that I can't seem to do without.

4 tablespoons (½ stick) unsalted butter, at
room temperature
¼ cup sugar
2 tablespoons molasses
¾ teaspoon ground ginger
½ teaspoon ground cinnamon
¼ teaspoon ground cloves
¼ teaspoon baking soda
Pinch of salt
½ cup all-purpose flour
¼ cup toasted wheat germ

1. Beat the butter in the medium-size bowl of an electric mixer until light and fluffy. Slowly beat in the sugar. Beat in the molasses, ginger, cinnamon, cloves, baking soda, and salt. Add the flour, 2 tablespoons at a time. Stir in the wheat germ and mix thoroughly. Refrigerate the dough, covered, 4 hours.

2. Preheat the oven to 325°F.

3. Shape the dough into a roll about 1½ inches thick. Cut across with a sharp knife into ⅛-inch-thick slices. Place the slices on lightly buttered baking sheets, and bake until lightly browned, about 8 minutes. Cool on the baking sheets before removing.

Makes about 32 cookies

CRACKERJACK CRANBERRY TART

This is half crumble, half tart. The wheat germ adds a good-for-you touch to a fine old-fashioned dessert. I always serve it with ice cream or sweetened whipped cream.

1 cup pecan halves
1 cup walnut halves
1 cup cranberries, picked over
½ cup granulated sugar
¼ cup fresh orange juice
1 teaspoon finely slivered orange zest
1 teaspoon vanilla extract
½ cup toasted wheat germ
¾ cup firmly packed light brown sugar
8 tablespoons (1 stick) unsalted butter,
    chilled and cut into small pieces
Vanilla ice cream or sweetened whipped
    cream (see Note)

1. Preheat the oven to 350°F. Butter and flour a 10-inch glass or ceramic quiche pan.

2. Spread out the nut halves on a baking sheet, and toast them in the oven, turning once, for 5 minutes. Set aside to cool.

3. Combine the cranberries, granulated sugar, and orange juice in a medium-size saucepan. Heat to boiling. Add the orange zest and vanilla. Boil until the cranberries begin to pop, about 1 minute. Remove from heat and set aside to cool.

4. Place the nuts in the container of a food processor, and process until ground. Combine with the wheat germ and brown sugar in a medium-size bowl, and mix well. With your fingers or a pastry blender, work the butter into the dry ingredients until the mixture resembles coarse crumbs.

5. Press half of the nut mixture over the bottom and sides of the prepared quiche pan. Cover with the cooled cranberry mixture. Sprinkle the top with the remaining nut mixture. Bake until the top is a deep golden color, 40 to 45 minutes. Cool on a rack. Serve slightly warm, with vanilla ice cream or sweetened whipped cream.

Serves 8 to 10

Note: To make sweetened whipped cream, whip 1 cup heavy or whipping cream with 1 tablespoon confectioners' sugar.

GROVE TART

I ate something similar to this tart in the Florida Keys—oranges and lemons, picked fresh from the tree. If you are not lucky enough to have your own grove, store-bought does just fine.

FOR THE CRUST:

½ cup firmly packed light brown sugar
1 cup all-purpose flour
¼ cup toasted wheat germ
¼ cup ground pecans
7 tablespoons unsalted butter, chilled

FOR THE FILLING:

2 eggs
1 cup granulated sugar
1 teaspoon finely grated lemon zest
1 teaspoon finely grated orange zest
1 tablespoon fresh lemon juice
2 tablespoons fresh orange juice
2 tablespoons all-purpose flour
½ cup pecan halves

Confectioners' sugar
Sweetened whipped cream (optional; see
   Note, facing page)

1. Preheat the oven to 350°F. Lightly butter a 10-inch round glass or ceramic pie plate or quiche pan.

2. Make the crust: Combine all the ingredients for the crust in a large bowl. Blend with a pastry blender until the mixture has the texture of cornmeal. Remove ½ cup of this mixture and set aside. Pat the remaining mixture over the bottom and sides of the prepared pie plate. Bake 10 minutes. Cool on a rack.

3. Make the filling: Beat the eggs with the sugar in the large bowl of an electric mixture until light. Beat in the lemon and orange zests, the juices, and the flour. Pour into the cooled pie shell. Sprinkle the remaining crust mixture over the top, then arrange the pecan halves over that. Bake until set, 25 to 30 minutes. Cool on a rack and dust with confectioners' sugar before serving. Top with the whipped cream if you like.

Serves 8

CAUGHT-IN-THE-CRUNCH TART

This recipe was inspired by a tart I once tasted at a party. The original is the handiwork of John Sedlar, chef extraordinaire in Southern California. Wheat germ adds a decided flavor note. It is definitely a non-calorie-counter's dessert.

FOR THE PASTRY

1 egg yolk
⅓ cup sugar
8 tablespoons (1 stick) unsalted butter, at
   room temperature
1¾ cups all-purpose flour
2 tablespoons ice water

FOR THE FILLING

1 cup sugar
½ cup heavy or whipping cream, heated
¾ cup (1½ sticks) unsalted butter, cut into
   12 pieces
½ cup toasted wheat germ

¾ cup pecan halves, toasted and coarsely
   chopped (see Note)
¾ cup walnut halves, toasted and coarsely
   chopped (see Note)

FOR THE TOPPING

1½ ounces semi-sweet chocolate, coarsely
   chopped
¼ cup heavy or whipping cream
¼ teaspoon vanilla extract

1. Make the pastry: Beat the egg yolk in the large bowl of an electric mixer until light. Slowly add the sugar, and beat until light and fluffy. Beat in the butter. On low speed, beat in the flour until the mixture is crumbly. Add the ice water, and continue to beat until the dough cleans the sides of the bowl. Wrap in plastic wrap and refrigerate 1 hour.

2. Preheat the oven to 375°F.

3. Roll out the pastry (between two sheets of wax paper, if necessary), and line a 10- to 11-inch loose-bottom tart pan or glass or ceramic quiche pan. Trim and flute the edges. Line the pastry with foil; weight it with rice or dried beans. Bake 10 minutes. Remove the foil and weights, and bake until golden, about 8 minutes longer. Cool completely on a rack.

4. Make the filling: Place the sugar in a heavy skillet or saucepan. Cook over medium-high heat, without stirring, until the edges begin to melt. Reduce the heat to medium and continue to cook, stirring constantly, until the sugar caramelizes to a deep tan color. Reduce the heat to low and carefully stir in the cream. (The mixture will bubble up.) Stir until it is completely smooth. Then stir in the butter, three pieces at a time, until smooth. Remove the pan from the heat, and stir in the wheat germ and nuts. Immediately pour into the cooled crust and spread evenly over the bottom. Cool completely.

5. Make the topping: Melt the chocolate in the top of a double boiler over hot water. Stir in the cream and vanilla until smooth. Transfer to a bowl, place it in a larger bowl filled with ice, and stir until cool. Pour evenly over the entire top of the tart. Let set for 2 hours before serving.

Serves 10 to 12

Note: To toast the nuts, heat a large skillet over medium heat. Add the nuts and toast, stirring frequently, until golden, 6 to 8 minutes. Cool before chopping.

THE FLOURING OF THE GRAIN

*T*here are flours and flours on grocers' shelves, and they are all confusing to non-cognoscenti cooks!

To set the matter straight: all flour is made of wheat, but not all of it is very nutritious. White flour isn't. Whole-wheat flour is! Primarily because whole-wheat flour is milled of the entire wheat kernel. Yes, the endosperm, germ, and bran too! One can actually see the tiny brown flecks in every slice of bread or cake that you bake with whole-wheat flour. That is your assurance that the flour is crammed to the nines with vitamins, minerals, and trace elements. But it is also a warning of this flour's vulnerability. Because of its high nutrients, whole-wheat flour has a brief shelf life.

The two primary proteins in flour (any flour) are known as *gliadin* and *glutenin*. When these proteins combine with a liquid (any liquid), they mutate into a super-protein called *gluten*. Gluten in dough forms a kind of cellular spider's web. Taut to begin with, when the dough is kneaded and punched down, the strands of the web loosen and stretch. If you are baking with yeast, enzymes in the yeast cause the sugar in the dough to ferment. Fermentation in turn releases carbon dioxide, which makes the dough rise. It rises because the carbon dioxide fills the strands of the gluten web with air. So, the bread or rolls come out of your oven high, wide, and handsome!

In some of the recipes for bread, cake, and rolls that follow, whole-wheat flour is combined with all-purpose flour or soft wheat cake flour. The reason for the merger is simple as pie: a reduced amount of gluten is desirable for light-textured baked goods.

For the record, other types of flour available are *all-purpose flour* (a blend of hard and soft wheats with medium gluten content and 10 percent protein); *cake flour*, also known as soft wheat flour (a flour made entirely of soft wheat, often with the addition of cornstarch to lighten the starch level, and with a scant 6 percent protein content); and *bread flour* (a pure hard wheat flour, with 14 percent protein content).

How to Buy It

Whole-wheat flour is available to consumers two ways: stone ground and commercially milled. The nutrient levels of both flours depend entirely on how the grains were milled and processed. The most nutritious and best-flavored whole-wheat flours are indubitably the output of small independent millers around the country. These flours, labeled "Stone-Ground Whole Wheat," can always be found at natural foods stores, where organic stone-ground whole-wheat flours are available as well. Stone-ground flour is ground on rotating millstones, and the texture and flavor may vary somewhat from milling to milling, but it is a wonderful ingredient and worth the higher price tag in my opinion.

Unbleached commercial whole-wheat flour can be found at supermarkets everywhere. It is a perfectly acceptable alternative to stone-ground whole-wheat flour, though decidedly less coarse in texture. On occasion commercial flours contain additives like ground barley as filler; check the label before you buy. And the aging process of the wheat is sometimes artificially speeded up with the addition of potassium bromate. Look carefully at the package; if it is called "bromated whole-wheat flour," you may wish to pass it by. Incidentally, all flours (whole wheat and otherwise; commercial and stone ground) are "enriched" by U.S.D.A. mandate these days. So accept the vitamin supplement with good grace—whether it is good for you or not, you can't avoid it!

How to Store It

All flour absorbs odors, so it is best to stash it in an airtight container. Glass, rather than plastic, is my preference. Whole-wheat flour, because it contains a high ratio of wheat germ and its essential oils, spoils rapidly, and plastic containers seem to quicken the process. Beyond-the-pale whole-wheat flour has a terrible odor, like stale olive oil. I keep whole-wheat flour in the refrigerator, where it remains in prime condition for about three months. Do not keep whole-wheat flour in its original package, even if it is insulated in airtight plastic bags. Paper absorbs oil and will hasten its demise, in the fridge or out!

WHOLESOME WHOLE-WHEAT NOODLES

Unlike the Italians, who eschew any ingredients other than flour and egg yolks in their pasta, I leaven these noodles with a tad of oil and a splash of water. They roll more felicitously after the addition, I find. But I *am* a purist in the matter of pasta machines: mine is a small stainless-steel hand-cranked model, known as an "Atlas," that outperforms any electric invention on the market.

Whole-wheat noodles are very low in calories (100 per generous cupful), so I feel I have the right to burn a few when it comes to toppings. You let your conscience be your own guide in the matter!

2 cups whole-wheat flour
½ teaspoon salt
1 tablespoon vegetable oil
2 egg yolks
½ cup water (approximately)

1. Combine the flour with the salt in a large bowl.

2. Combine the oil, egg yolks, and ½ cup water in another bowl. Pour this over the flour mixture and work with your fingers to form a soft dough. Add 1 to 2 tablespoons more water if needed.

3. Transfer the dough to a lightly floured board and knead 10 minutes. Cover the dough with a bowl and let rest 1 hour.

4. Divide the dough into four pieces. Run them through a pasta machine, or roll out into a thin dough and cut into noodles. Dry for 1 hour before using.

Makes about 1 pound

HOLD EVERYTHING WHOLE-WHEAT NOODLES WITH CLAMS

I call this "hold everything" because that is what I do when my friends on Long Island call me up and say they are dropping off some clams they just plucked from the bay. I put everything else on hold—and enjoy.

2 sweet Italian sausages (about ½ pound),
*   finely chopped*
2 sprigs parsley
1 sprig thyme, or a pinch of dried
1 sprig oregano, or a pinch of dried
3 tablespoons unsalted butter
1 small onion, finely chopped
1 clove garlic, minced

36 clams, washed well
1 cup dry white wine
1 teaspoon all-purpose flour
½ cup heavy or whipping cream
1 pound fresh whole-wheat noodles (see
*   above)*
¼ teaspoon crushed dried hot red peppers
1 tablespoon chopped fresh parsley

1. Sauté the sausages in a lightly oiled heavy skillet over medium heat until rendered of all fat and crisp, 8 minutes. Drain on paper towels.

2. Tie the parsley, thyme, and oregano in a cheesecloth bag to make a bouquet garni, and set aside.

3. Melt 2 tablespoons of the butter in a large saucepan over medium-low heat. Add the onion; cook 1 minute. Add the garlic; cook 2 minutes longer. Add the bouquet garni to the pan, along with the clams and white wine. Heat to boiling. Cover, and cook over medium-high heat until the clams open, about 10 minutes.

4. Remove the clams from the saucepan with a slotted spoon. Discard the bouquet garni and any clams that did not open, reserving the broth.

5. Remove the meat from the clams. Chop and reserve.

6. Melt the remaining 1 tablespoon butter in a medium-size saucepan over medium-low heat. Add the flour; cook, stirring constantly, 2 minutes. Whisk in 1½ cups reserved clam broth and the cream. Heat to boiling, and boil until slightly thickened, about 10 minutes.

7. Meanwhile, drop the pasta into a large pot of salted boiling water and boil until just tender, 3 to 5 minutes.

8. While the pasta is cooking, add the dried red peppers, the chopped clams, and the sausage bits to the cream sauce; cook 2 minutes longer.

9. Drain the pasta and place in a serving dish. Pour the clam and sausage mixture over the top. Toss well, and sprinkle with the parsley.

Serves 4

SAUSAGE-AND-FENNEL-TOPPED NOODLES

*A*s in the previous recipe, I often add sausage meat to white sauces as well as red, to perk up the flavor of the other ingredients. This time its partner is fresh fennel, straight from the farmer's market.

2 stalks fennel
½ pound sweet Italian sausages
2 tablespoons unsalted butter
1 onion, finely chopped
1 clove garlic, minced
1 teaspoon fennel seeds, lightly crushed
2 egg yolks
⅓ cup homemade chicken stock (see page 376) or canned broth
¾ pound fresh whole-wheat noodles (see facing page)
⅓ cup freshly grated Parmesan cheese
¼ cup chopped fresh parsley

1. Cook the fennel in boiling salted water to cover for 2 minutes. Rinse under cold running water and drain. Finely chop the fennel (you should have about ½ cup), and set aside.

2. Remove the sausages from their casings and sauté, breaking up the lumps, in an oil-rubbed large heavy skillet over medium heat until crisp and well browned, about 5 minutes. Using a slotted spoon, transfer to a bowl.

3. Pour off all grease from the skillet and add 1 tablespoon of the butter. Add the onion, and cook over medium-low heat 1 minute. Add the garlic, fennel seeds, and fennel. Cook, stirring occasionally, 3 minutes. Add the sausage, and cook 2 minutes longer. Reduce the heat to low.

4. Combine the egg yolks and chicken stock in a bowl. Cook the noodles in a large pot of boiling salted water until just tender, 3 to 5 minutes. Drain. Return the noodles to the pan they cooked in, and toss with the remaining 1 tablespoon butter.

5. Add the noodles to the sausage mixture and gently toss until mixed.

Pour the egg mixture over the top, and add the Parmesan cheese and 3 tablespoons of the parsley. Cook, tossing gently, over low heat 2 minutes. Do not allow to boil. Sprinkle with the remaining 1 tablespoon parsley before serving.

Serves 4

TICKER-TAPE NOODLE HASH

_L_eftover lamb makes a wonderful base for a hash. Instead of potatoes, I use wholewheat noodles. With very tonic results, I might add.

½ pound whole-wheat noodles, fresh (see page 316) or packaged
4 tablespoons olive oil
1 large onion, finely chopped
¼ pound thinly sliced pancetta or smoky bacon, finely chopped
5 cloves garlic, minced
2½ cups cooked lamb, cut into ½-inch cubes
1 teaspoon chopped fresh thyme, or ½ teaspoon dried
1 tablespoon chopped fresh basil, or 1 teaspoon dried
¼ teaspoon ground cumin
⅛ teaspoon ground turmeric
⅓ cup heavy or whipping cream
Salt and freshly ground black pepper to taste
2 tablespoons chopped fresh parsley

1. Cook the pasta in a large pot of boiling salted water until barely tender (3 minutes for homemade; longer for commercially packaged). Drain. Return the noodles to the pan they cooked in, and toss with 1 tablespoon of the oil. Keep warm over low heat.

2. Heat 2 tablespoons of the oil in a large heavy saucepan over medium heat. Add the onion and pancetta; cook until the onion is golden, about 5 minutes. Add the garlic; cook 2 minutes longer. Stir in the lamb, thyme, basil, cumin, and turmeric. Continue to cook, stirring constantly, 4 minutes.

3. Add the remaining 1 tablespoon oil to the lamb mixture, and add the pasta and cream, tossing lightly until well mixed. Continue to toss until warmed through. Season with salt and pepper, and sprinkle with the parsley.

Serves 6

EMBARRASSMENT OF ONIONS TART

An onion quiche, if you will. Serve it as a side dish with any meat or fish. Or do as I do, and eat it as a main course with a salad, with no embarrassment whatsoever.

100% or 50% Whole-Wheat Pastry (see
pages 327 and 328)
4 strips bacon
2 tablespoons unsalted butter
4 medium leeks, white bulbs only, rinsed
well and chopped
1 medium onion, chopped
1 shallot, minced
1 clove garlic, minced
Pinch of ground cloves
½ teaspoon chopped fresh thyme, or a
pinch of dried
2 eggs
½ cup sour cream
½ cup heavy or whipping cream
¼ cup milk
2 teaspoons Dijon mustard
½ teaspoon salt
¼ teaspoon freshly ground black pepper
1 cup grated Jarlsberg cheese
2 teaspoons chopped fresh chives

1. Preheat the oven to 400°F.

2. Line a 10-inch glass or ceramic quiche dish with the pastry, and trim and flute the edges. Line the pastry with foil, making sure the edges are covered, and weight with rice or dried beans.

Bake 15 minutes. Remove the foil and weights, and bake another 5 minutes. Cool on a rack. Reduce the oven temperature to 375°F.

3. Sauté the bacon in a large heavy skillet until crisp. Drain on paper towels, crumble, and reserve.

4. Pour off all but 2 tablespoons bacon drippings from the skillet. Melt the butter in the drippings over medium-low heat. Stir in the leeks, onion, shallot, and garlic. Cook 2 minutes. Sprinkle with the cloves and thyme. Cover, and cook, stirring occasionally, until the onions are tender, about 30 minutes. Remove from the heat.

5. Lightly beat the eggs in a medium-size bowl. Beat in the sour cream, heavy cream, milk, mustard, salt, and pepper. Stir in the onion mixture, the reserved bacon, and the cheese. Pour into the cooled pie shell, and sprinkle the top with the chives. Bake until slightly puffed and golden, 25 to 30 minutes. Let stand for 10 minutes before serving.

Serves 6

WELL-BRED WHOLE-WHEAT LOAF

My friend Sharon Tyler Herbst, who has appeared in this book already, is a wonderful food writer and a caring person—we share a bond when it comes to the concerns of the food industry and the world at large. One of my truest joys in life has been breaking bread with Sharon and her husband, Ron—particularly when it is this bread, made by her own two hands.

½ cup lukewarm water
2 packages dry yeast
¼ cup plus 3 teaspoons malt syrup or
   honey
1 cup cottage cheese, at room temperature
2 tablespoons molasses
5 to 5½ cups whole-wheat flour
¼ cup vegetable oil
2 eggs, lightly beaten, at room temperature
2½ teaspoons salt
½ cup toasted wheat germ
1 tablespoon water

1. Place the lukewarm water in the large bowl of an electric mixer, and sprinkle with the yeast. Stir in 1 teaspoon of the malt syrup. Let stand until bubbly, 5 to 10 minutes. Then add the cottage cheese, ¼ cup malt syrup, molasses, and 1½ cups of the flour. Beat at medium speed 2 minutes. Scrape down the sides of the bowl, cover with plastic wrap, and let stand in a warm place until bubbly and tripled in volume, about 1 hour.

2. Stir the oil into the dough along with the eggs, salt, and wheat germ. Stir in enough of the remaining flour to make a soft dough. Turn the dough out onto a floured board and knead, adding more flour as needed, until smooth and elastic, about 10 minutes. Transfer the dough to a greased bowl, cover with a damp towel, and let rise in a warm place until tripled in volume, about 1 hour.

3. Punch down the dough and divide it in half. Place each portion in a greased 8 by 4 by 3-inch loaf pan, and cover with a flour-rubbed tea towel. Let rise until doubled in volume, about 45 minutes.

4. Combine the remaining 2 teaspoons malt syrup with the 1 tablespoon water. Slash the tops of the loaves, if desired, and brush them with the malt syrup glaze. Place the bread in a cold oven, and turn the heat on to 375°F. Bake until the bread sounds hollow when tapped with your finger, 30 to 35 minutes. Remove the loaves from the pans, and cool on racks.

Makes 2 loaves

MILDRED SCHULZ'S WHOLE-WHEAT BATTER BREAD

Mildred Schulz, mother of my friend and collaborator, Phillip S. Schulz, has always appeared in my books. She brings me good luck. Her batter bread is not only easy but delicious as well—a lucky find for any home breadmaker.

1½ cups lukewarm water
1 package dry yeast
2 tablespoons honey
2 cups whole-wheat flour
1 cup all-purpose flour
1 teaspoon salt

2 tablespoons unsalted butter, at room
   temperature

1. Place the lukewarm water in the large bowl of an electric mixer. Sprinkle with the yeast, and stir in the honey. Let stand until bubbly, about 5 minutes.

2. On medium speed, beat in 1 cup of the whole-wheat flour, ½ cup of the all-purpose flour, the salt, and the butter. Beat 2 minutes, scraping the sides of the bowl often. On low speed, beat in the remaining flours. Cover the bowl, and let the dough rise in a warm place until doubled in volume, about 1 hour.

3. Stir the dough down by beating 25 strokes with a wooden spoon. Spread the dough into a greased 9 by 5 by 3-inch loaf pan. Cover loosely with a flour-rubbed tea towel, and let rise in a warm place until the dough comes to the top of the pan, about 1 hour.

4. Preheat the oven to 400°F.

5. Bake until the bread is golden brown and sounds hollow when tapped with your finger, about 30 minutes. Remove from the pan and cool on a rack.

Makes 1 loaf

DARLENE SCHULZ'S COST-CONSCIOUS COTTAGE CHEESE BUNS

Another Schulz—this time Phillip's sister-in-law. I first ate these scrumptious buns in Brownsville, Wisconsin, when I spent a memorable Christmas weekend in a part of the country where the food is hearty, healthy, and generously apportioned.

1½ cups cottage cheese
2 tablespoons unsalted butter
4 teaspoons honey
1 teaspoon molasses
½ teaspoon salt
½ cup lukewarm water
2 packages dry yeast
¼ teaspoon sugar
2 eggs, lightly beaten
4½ cups whole-wheat flour (approximately)
Cornmeal

1. Combine the cottage cheese, butter, honey, molasses, and salt in a small saucepan. Stir over medium-low heat until the butter has melted. Remove from the heat and allow to cool to lukewarm.

2. Place the lukewarm water in a large bowl, and sprinkle with the yeast. Stir in the sugar. Let stand until bubbly, about 5 minutes.

3. Add the eggs to the cottage cheese mixture, and then add this mixture to the yeast mixture. Stir in about 3 cups of the flour, enough to make a soft dough. Transfer the dough to a floured board and knead, adding more flour as needed, 10 minutes.

4. Place the dough in a lightly greased bowl. Cover with plastic wrap, and let rise in a warm place until doubled in volume, about 1 hour.

5. Punch the dough down and knead briefly on a floured board. Divide the dough into fourteen equal portions. Shape each portion into a roll, tucking any cracks underneath. Place the rolls, seven per sheet, on two cornmeal-sprinkled baking sheets. Cover with flour-rubbed tea towels, and let rise until doubled in volume, or until almost roll size, about 35 minutes.

6. Preheat the oven to 375°F.

7. Bake until the rolls are nicely browned, about 15 minutes. Cool on a rack.

Makes 14 hamburger-size rolls

MARYBETTE SLUSARSKI'S RED-FACED TOMATO BREAD

MaryBette Slusarski lives in Ackworth, Iowa, and produces a newsletter called *Food for Thought*. Her tomato-laced bread is one of the best whole-wheats I have ever chomped.

1½ pounds ripe tomatoes
½ cup lukewarm water
2 packages dry yeast
1 teaspoon plus 2 tablespoons honey
⅛ teaspoon ground ginger
2 tablespoons vegetable oil
1 teaspoon salt
1 tablespoon chopped fresh basil
4 to 5 cups stone-ground whole-wheat flour
Cornmeal

1. Peel and seed the tomatoes. Process in a food processor or blender to make a purée. You should have 1½ cups. Heat the purée in a saucepan to lukewarm.

2. Place the lukewarm water in a large bowl and sprinkle with the yeast. Stir in 1 teaspoon honey and the ginger. Let stand until foamy, about 5 minutes.

3. Add the puréed tomatoes to the yeast mixture, along with the 2 tablespoons honey, oil, salt, basil, and 2 cups of the flour. Then stir in 1½ to 2 more cups flour, enough to form a soft dough. Scrape the dough out onto a floured board and knead, adding more flour as needed, 10 minutes. Transfer the dough to a lightly greased bowl and cover with plastic wrap. Let stand in a warm place until doubled in volume, about 1 hour.

4. Punch the dough down and knead briefly on a floured board. Divide the dough in half and form into round loaves. Place the loaves on a cornmeal-sprinkled baking sheet. Cover with a flour-rubbed tea towel, and let rise in a warm place until doubled in volume, about 1 hour.

5. Preheat the oven to 325°F.

6. Bake until the bread sounds hollow when tapped with your finger, 45 to 50 minutes. Cool on a rack.

Makes 2 loaves

SKY-HIGH WHEAT BISCUITS

I once sampled a similar recipe in New Iberia, Louisiana, at a place named simply "Helen's." Whole-wheat flour, added to the recipe, makes it a healthier bite and tastier too.

1 cup whole-wheat flour
1 cup cake flour
1 tablespoon baking powder
½ teaspoon baking soda
2 teaspoons sugar
½ teaspoon salt
5⅓ tablespoons (⅓ cup) unsalted butter,
    chilled
¾ cup buttermilk
2 tablespoons unsalted butter, melted

1. Preheat the oven to 450°F. Lightly butter a 9-inch round cake pan.

2. Combine the flours with the baking powder, baking soda, sugar, and salt in a large bowl. Cut in the butter with a knife, and blend with a pastry blender until the mixture has the texture of coarse crumbs. Stir in the buttermilk to form a soft dough.

3. Transfer the dough to a floured board. Knead briefly, and roll out about ¾ inch thick. Using a biscuit or cookie cutter, cut into 2½- to 3-inch circles. Place the biscuits in the prepared cake pan, and brush the tops with the melted butter. Bake until golden brown and firm, about 25 minutes.

Makes 8 or 9 biscuits

WHIRLIGIGS

I hate to admit that it never seemed possible to me to make bread sticks at home. I was wrong. These bread sticks can be made ahead and frozen, for up to two months, and served whenever the whim strikes.

1½ cups warm water (110°F)
1 package dry yeast
1 teaspoon honey
2 cups stone-ground whole-wheat flour
1 teaspoon salt
1½ to 2 cups all-purpose flour
2 tablespoons olive oil (approximately)
Coarse (kosher) salt

1. Place ¼ cup of the warm water in a large bowl. Sprinkle the yeast over it, and stir in the honey. Let stand until bubbly, about 5 minutes.

2. Add the remaining warm water to the yeast mixture, and stir in the whole-wheat flour, salt, and about 1¼ cups of the all-purpose flour. The dough will be slightly sticky. Transfer to a well-floured board and knead, adding more flour as needed, until smooth and elastic, about 10 minutes. Place the dough in a greased bowl, cover with plastic wrap, and let rise in a warm place until doubled in volume, about 1 hour.

3. Punch the dough down, cover, and let rise once more until doubled in volume, about 45 minutes.

4. Preheat the oven to 450°F.

5. Brush four baking sheets with some of the olive oil, and sprinkle with coarse salt.

6. Punch the dough down once more. With floured hands, scrape a heaping tablespoon of dough onto a well-floured board. Roll the dough into a thin rope no more than ½ inch thick and about 12 inches long. Place on a prepared baking sheet. Repeat with the remaining dough. Brush each dough stick with more olive oil and sprinkle with coarse salt. Bake until golden and crisp, about 20 minutes. Cool on a rack.

Makes about 24 bread sticks

BLACK 'N' BLUE BLUEBERRY MUFFINS

These muffins were invented by an Ohio woman who had an overstock of whole-wheat flour one summer, when the blueberries were going crazy in her Columbus backyard.

1 cup blueberries
2 tablespoons sugar
1 teaspoon finely slivered lemon zest
⅓ cup all-purpose flour
¾ cup whole-wheat flour
1 teaspoon baking soda
½ teaspoon salt
1 egg
2 tablespoons honey
½ cup milk
2 tablespoons unsalted butter, melted

1. Preheat the oven to 400°F. Lightly grease 9 muffin cups.

2. Pick over the blueberries, discarding any stems, and place in a colander.

Rinse with cold water, shake off the excess, and place in a bowl. Sprinkle with the sugar and lemon zest.

3. Combine the flours in a large bowl, and add the baking soda and salt. Mix well.

4. Lightly beat the egg in a medium-size bowl. Then beat in the honey, milk, and melted butter. Stir this into the flour mixture, and add the blueberries.

5. Fill the prepared muffin cups half full with the batter. Bake until golden brown and firm, 15 to 20 minutes. Loosen the muffins, but allow to cool in the pan on a rack.

Makes 9 muffins

SINFUL CINNAMON-PECAN COFFEE CAKE

The next recipe is old-fashioned yet remarkably streamlined in execution and came my way from the talented hand of Karen Haram, the food editor of the San Antonio *Express-News*.

FOR THE TOPPING
3 tablespoons whole-wheat flour
3 tablespoons all-purpose flour
3 tablespoons unsalted butter, chilled
1½ teaspoons ground cinnamon
⅔ cup chopped pecans
¼ cup firmly packed light brown sugar

FOR THE CAKE
¾ cup whole-wheat flour

1 cup all-purpose flour
Pinch of salt
1 teaspoon baking soda
1 teaspoon baking powder
1½ teaspoons ground cinnamon
¾ cup firmly packed light brown sugar
¾ cup granulated sugar
8 tablespoons (1 stick) unsalted butter, at room temperature
1 large egg
1⅓ cups buttermilk

1. Preheat the oven to 350°F. Lightly butter a 9 by 13-inch cake pan.

2. Make the topping: Combine the two flours in a medium-size bowl. Cut in the butter with a knife, and then blend with a pastry blender until the butter is totally incorporated into the flour. Add the cinnamon, pecans, and brown sugar, mixing well with your fingers. Set aside.

3. Make the cake: Combine the two flours with the salt, baking soda, baking powder, and cinnamon in a bowl. Set aside.

4. Place the two sugars with the but-ter in the large bowl of an electric mixer, and beat until smooth. Add the egg, and continue to beat until light. Stir the flour mixture into the butter mixture in three batches, alternating with three batches of the buttermilk.

5. Pour the batter into the prepared cake pan. Sprinkle the topping evenly over the batter. Bake in the center of the oven until a toothpick inserted in the center comes out clean, 35 to 40 minutes. Cool on a rack before serving.

Serves 12

SUGAR-CRUSTED WHOLE-WHEAT CRULLERS

In South Dakota, where these spring from, whole wheat is an ingredient in three out of four entries in every farmer's recipe book.

1 egg
1¼ cups plus 2 tablespoons sugar
½ cup sour cream
1 tablespoon unsalted butter, melted
¾ cup stone-ground whole-wheat flour
½ cup all-purpose flour
1 teaspoon baking powder
½ teaspoon baking soda
¼ teaspoon salt
⅛ teaspoon freshly grated nutmeg
⅛ teaspoon ground mace
1 teaspoon ground cinnamon
Vegetable oil for deep-frying

1. Beat the egg in the large bowl of an electric mixer until light. Slowly add ¼ cup plus 2 tablespoons of the sugar, and continue to beat until light and fluffy. Beat in the sour cream and melted butter. Stir in the flours, baking powder, baking soda, salt, nutmeg, and mace. Scrape the mixture into a small bowl (the dough will be quite sticky). Cover and refrigerate 45 minutes.

2. Transfer the chilled dough to a well-floured board. Using about 3 tablespoons of dough, roll out a rope about ¾ inch thick and about 5 inches long. Transfer to a floured surface, and repeat with the remaining dough. When all the crullers are formed, cover with a flour-rubbed tea towel and let rest 20 minutes.

3. Meanwhile, combine the remaining 1 cup sugar and the cinnamon on a plate.

4. Heat 2 to 3 inches of oil in a heavy skillet until hot. Cook the crullers, no more than three at a time, until golden brown, 2 to 3 minutes per side. Roll them on paper towels and then immediately roll in the sugar/cinnamon mixture. Place on a rack while frying the remaining dough. Serve warm or at room temperature.

Makes about 10 crullers

WHITLING BUTTERMILK WHEAT CAKES

These wondrous wheat cakes are worthy of a toast with strong coffee the next time you linger over breakfast.

1 cup plus 2 tablespoons stone-ground
    whole-wheat flour
1 tablespoon sugar
1½ teaspoons baking soda
½ teaspoon salt
1 egg
1½ cups buttermilk
1 tablespoon vegetable oil

1. Combine the flour with the sugar, baking soda, and salt in a medium-size bowl. Mix well.

2. Whisk the egg with the buttermilk and oil in another bowl. Pour over the flour mixture and stir just until mixed.

3. Heat a lightly greased cast-iron skillet or griddle over medium heat until hot but not smoking. Cook the pancakes, a few at a time, using about 3 tablespoons batter per pancake. When lightly browned, about 2 minutes, turn over and cook the other side for 1 minute. Transfer to a serving platter and keep warm while cooking the remaining cakes. Reduce the heat if the cakes brown too quickly.

Makes about eighteen 2- to 3-inch pancakes

DUMMERSTON APPLESAUCE TART

In Dummerston, Vermont, one need only to pass through an old covered bridge to smell the apple orchards. This tart is hearty and healthy, like all the good denizens who live there.

100% Whole-Wheat Pastry (recipe follows)
5 tart green apples
1 tablespoon unsalted butter
½ teaspoon ground cinnamon
⅓ cup firmly packed light brown sugar
1 tablespoon dark rum
1½ tablespoons finely slivered orange zest
2 tablespoons fresh orange juice
¼ cup honey
½ teaspoon vanilla extract
⅓ cup apricot preserves

1. Preheat the oven to 400°F.

2. Press the pastry over the bottom and sides of a lightly buttered 9-inch loose-bottom quiche or tart pan. Line with foil; weight with rice or dried beans. Bake 15 minutes. Remove the foil and weights, and bake 5 minutes longer. Cool on a rack. Reduce the oven temperature to 375°F.

3. Peel, core, and coarsely chop 3 of the apples. Melt the butter in a heavy saucepan over medium-low heat. Add the apples and cook, stirring frequently, 5 minutes. Add the cinnamon, brown sugar, rum, and orange zest. Cook until the apples are soft, about 20 minutes. Mash until thick. Set aside to cool.

4. Peel, core, and cut the remaining 2 apples into ⅛-inch-thick slices. Combine with the orange juice, honey, and vanilla in a bowl. Let stand 10 minutes. Drain, reserving 2 tablespoons of the juice.

5. Spoon the applesauce mixture over the bottom of the prepared shell. Cover with a neat layer of overlapping sliced apples.

6. Combine the apricot preserves with the reserved 2 tablespoons juice in a small saucepan. Heat to boiling, then reduce the heat and cook, breaking up the lumps with a spoon, 2 minutes. Spoon over the apples. Bake until the top is golden and the apples are tender, about 40 minutes. Serve slightly warm.

Serves 8

100% Whole-Wheat Pastry

1¼ cups stone-ground whole-wheat flour
¼ teaspoon salt
½ cup lard
1 egg yolk
1 teaspoon red wine vinegar
2½ tablespoons cold water (approximately)

1. Combine the flour and salt in a medium-size bowl. Cut in the lard with a knife, and blend with a pastry blender until the mixture has the texture of coarse crumbs.

2. Combine the egg yolk, vinegar, and cold water in a small bowl. Cut this into the pastry mixture with a knife or fork to form a soft dough. Knead briefly before using.

Makes one 9- to 10-inch single crust

Columbus did it!

They say he brought wheat to the New World on his second voyage—but it was only a handful of grain and it promptly withered when he went on his way. But don't blame him. The man might have been a heck of a navigator, but he knew beans about agriculture.

Wheat came this way again in 1620, with the founders of the Plymouth Colony. Bartholomew Gosnold planted grain on Cuttyhunk Island, near Martha's Vineyard, where it "took" that time around. Wheat grew, Gosnold's family even managed to produce a few loaves of bread, but it certainly was not the "amber waves of grain" celebrated in story and song.

America did not become beautiful with wheat until a couple of centuries later, when Swedish, Norwegian, German, and Russian immigrants drifted in this direction. Once they took a look at the cities of the Atlantic coastline, they picked up their belongings, bought wagons, and headed west, where they had heard the landscape went on forever. That's true wheat country, you see.

By the mid-1800s Ohio, Pennsylvania, upper New York State, and Virginia all produced bumper wheat crops. By the turn of the century, Kansas and Iowa's output totaled the entire yield of the Ukraine, and inventive second-generation cooks were cramming whole wheat into more dishes than one could shake a stick at.

APROPOS APRICOT TART

This one is sinful—a creamy custard topped with fresh apricots. Other fresh fruits, such as oranges, peaches, or sweet berries, work as well.

FOR THE CRUST
50% Whole-Wheat Pastry (recipe follows)
½ cup sugar
3 tablespoons water

FOR THE FILLING
3 egg yolks
¼ cup sugar
¼ teaspoon vanilla extract
1½ tablespoons cornstarch
¾ cup milk, scalded
½ cup heavy or whipping cream

FOR THE TOPPING
10 to 12 very ripe apricots, peeled and
*   quartered or halved*
½ cup red currant jelly
1½ tablespoons sugar
1½ tablespoons orange liqueur, such as
*   Grand Marnier*

1. Preheat the oven to 400°F.
2. Line a 10-inch loose-bottom tart pan with the pastry, and trim and flute the edges. Line the pastry with foil; weight with rice or dried beans. Bake 15 minutes. Remove the foil and weights, and bake 10 minutes longer or until lightly browned. Cool on a rack.
3. Place the sugar and the water in a small saucepan. Cook, stirring constantly, until the sugar melts and turns golden. Drizzle over the bottom of the cooled crust.
4. Make the filling: Beat the egg yolks with the sugar in the top of a double boiler until light. Stir in the vanilla, and whisk in the cornstarch until smooth. Whisk in the milk. Cook, stirring constantly, over simmering water until thick, about 12 minutes. Transfer to a bowl, cool, then refrigerate for 30 minutes.
5. Beat the cream until stiff, and fold into the chilled custard. Spoon this mixture into the prepared shell.
6. Make the topping: Arrange the apricots over the custard in a decorative pattern. Refrigerate.
7. Combine the currant jelly, sugar, and orange liqueur in a small saucepan. Heat to boiling, then reduce the heat and cook over medium-low heat 5 minutes. Drizzle over the apricots. Refrigerate until ready to serve.
Serves 8

50% Whole-Wheat Pastry

⅔ cup whole-wheat flour
⅔ cup cake flour
¼ teaspoon salt
4 tablespoons (½ stick) unsalted butter,
*   chilled*
2 tablespoons solid vegetable shortening,
*   chilled*
2½ to 3 tablespoons cold water

Combine the flours with the salt in a bowl. Cut in the chilled butter and shortening with a knife, then blend with a pastry blender until the mixture has the texture of coarse crumbs. Add just enough water to make a soft dough, and knead briefly. Wrap in plastic wrap and refrigerate for 1 hour before using.
Makes one 9- to 11-inch single crust

WILD RICE

The Luxury Grain That's Rich in B Vitamins

I have never truly enjoyed the flavor of any comestible endowed with the label *wild*. That goes for wild turkey, wild grapes, wild boar, wild duck, and shame the devil, wild strawberries too. Why? Because they are all just a tinge over-pungent for my domesticated taste. The proscription list does have one notable exception, however, and that is wild rice.

Wild rice (no rice at all, in fact, but a seed) is a fairly recent predilection of mine, which I can trace to a Thanksgiving dinner—one of the worst I can recall ever having eaten.

In the mid-1950s my first play was produced Off-Broadway, and I became— all too briefly—an object of some small celebrity. My picture appeared twice on the drama page of the *New York Times*; I was the subject of interviews in *Variety*, *Vogue*, and the *Village Voice*. I was certain I had arrived. A well-known theatrical agent left me his card, and I acquired a small coterie of loyal fans, one of whom was a writer whose counsel I have never forgotten.

"On paper," she advised at our first meeting, "be yourself until it hurts!"

This woman's critique was not to be taken lightly, for she moved in a circle of literary lions, all of whom heeled like lap dogs whenever she held forth about their work. Her name was Judith, and as the French say, she was a lady of a certain age—probably the sunny side of sixty when we met. She had been married to a successful novelist for years and had recently left him because, as she told anyone within earshot, he had sold his soul to the devil or to David O. Selznick— they were interchangeable in her view— to become the highest-paid screenwriter in Hollywood.

Judith was equally liberal with her analysis of dramaturgy and with show-biz gossip, but the price one paid for her erudition was usually a headache—and more often a hangover. She drank constantly (always vodka straight up) and was never without a lit cigarette clamped between her teeth.

Early one fall, Judith invited me to spend Thanksgiving at her Bucks County farmhouse. "It's a wonderful old house, but like a vampire it needs young blood once in a while," she said, roaring with laughter and tossing down her fifth or sixth Stolichnaya of the evening. "So come and be a victim."

When I explained that traditionally I spent Thanksgiving with my sister, Judith became positively expansive. "Bring r along. We have bedrooms enough to accommodate the Continental Army!"

All that fall I heard nothing more about Thanksgiving. A cable from London advised me the theater season was "lousy," and a postcard from L.A. revealed that her husband's latest film was even worse. But neither missive referred to the upcoming holiday.

My sister, who was never exactly Judith's ardent admirer, was furious. "What a nut," Myra railed. "If you don't pin her down soon, I'm ordering a turkey!"

I managed to track Judith down in San Francisco.

"Oh my God!" she cried. "Don't tell me. Thanksgiving! Don't worry, I'll send a map. Come at noon."

"Thursday?"

"When else? I'm flying home Wednesday night."

If I had a nagging doubt about when and where she would shop for dinner, it was promptly put out of mind. Not knowing the length of our stay was disconcerting enough.

The drive through the crisp November countryside was worth all the vagaries of the expedition. A thin plume of smoke was swirling from the chimney when we arrived, and Judith announced that her husband was in residence, "to keep the home fires burning!"

He was welcoming, but they had both obviously been drinking all morning and were growing short-tempered. A brief tour of the house confirmed my misgivings: It was a splendid showplace but striped with mildew and unbrushed cobwebs. There was neither fresh linen in the guest rooms nor any sign of dinner on the stove.

Hours of enervating Hollywood stories and endlessly refilled Bloody Marys passed before I stole a glance at my watch. Judith must have seen me, for she rose, unsteadily. "I guess it's time to think about the bird," she declared, stifling a yawn.

About time, I would have said.

Offering help, I was delighted when Judith refused assistance. But I could not focus on any conversation because of the sound of running water from the kitchen—a clear sign the bird was either being defrosted forcibly or, worse yet, parboiled.

When she returned, Judith commented brusquely, "This is going to be a simple meal. I hate tricky holiday foods, don't you?" Clearly there was no option.

The evening star had already deepened in the sky by the time dinner was ready. Candles provided little light at the table, which was provident, for the turkey was totally resistant to being carved. After several hopeless attempts with a knife, Judith's husband tore the carcass apart with his bare hands. The meat was tough and stringy, and there were no accompanying vegetables to fill the slack, except for a plate of canned sweet potatoes that Judith had obviously neglected to warm in the oven. No bread. No cranberries. No salad. Actually nothing to eat at all, except the turkey's stuffing, which she had miraculously concocted out of wild rice, herbs, and sausages.

Until that dinner I had never fully appreciated the flavor and fragrance of wild rice, but it was then the sole reason for giving thanks. We consumed every kernel.

The Grain's Genesis

*I*f it's not rice, then what is it?

Diners have asked that question about wild rice for almost three hundred years. The answer, then and now, is: an aquatic seed, *Zizania aquatica*.

Wild rice is the preserve of Native Americans. Chippewas and Winnebagos who live along the freshwater lakes and brackish swamps of upper Michigan, Minnesota, and Wisconsin are wild rice's official harvesters. U.S. law pro-tects their title rights on reservation waters. But long before the first white man set a muddy foot on the territory, they tended the crop just as assiduously, for wild rice sustained the tribes in fallow hunting seasons.

Traditionally, Indian women pick the wild rice. Two to a canoe, they navigate their weedy way through the plants. One sits in the stern of the craft, paddling very slowly, while the other uses two long pointed sticks (like batons) to very gently shake the pale green stalks. She shakes and bends the stem until it releases its seed, which is gathered in the bottom of the boat. On a good day the women go home with a canoe crammed with wild rice. But more often than not, all kernels are not ripe at the same time, so it will take two or even three trips in the canoe to gather a full crop.

That is how wild rice is harvested by the Indians today, and that is how it was harvested three centuries back—which explains why it is sometimes called "the caviar of grains." Good things are inevitably hard to come by.

Some Plain Grain Talk

*N*o doubt about it, wild rice is very expensive stuff. But as described, all truly wild wild rice is harvested by Indians, and they do it the hard way. After picking, the rice is cured over smoke fires and then spread on the ground, where traditionally—though probably not as much now, if at all—young Indian males dance on the cooling grains to loosen the hulls. Finally the rice is sifted through blankets so the chaff blows off and the finished kernels (now a burnished black-brown color) are graded for packaging. All that labor adds up to a premium price in the marketplace.

In an attempt to turn wild rice into a mass-market product, controlled-irrigation farms (in California, Idaho, and Washington) are producing a hearty hybrid; one that can be picked by mechanical threshers and processed by mechanical parchers and winnowers, all of which do the job faster and should reduce the price tag. Unfortunately, this not-really-wild rice is not much cheaper, and it is a good deal less pungent and flavorsome.

Wild rice is one of the few luxury foods that is actually good for you. A high-carbohydrate grain (72.2 mg per cup), it contains healthy doses of phosphorus, magnesium, potassium, and zinc as well as thiamine, riboflavin, and niacin, all elements of B vitamins. More important (to dieters, anyway), a cupful of cooked wild rice contains a scant 130 calories.

How to Buy It

It is nice to be able to report that wild rice is available in supermarkets, gourmet groceries, and natural foods stores. But a chary consumer will do well to make a note of the various grades of wild rice before shopping.

Giant (long-grain) wild rice is the *ne plus ultra*, the blue-ribbon variety. Every grain is perfectly matched in size and never measures less than an inch in length. Long-grain wild rice has an earthy, dark flavor that makes it a favored partner to wild game. It's top restaurant chefs' first choice!

Fancy (medium-grain) wild rice is what most average cooks deem "a choice top-quality ingredient." The grains are also graded—equal in size, unbroken, and evenly matched in color. Fancy wild rice is what I think of as all-purpose. Though it is not appreciably cheaper than the giant variety, there is a price difference.

Select (short-grain) wild rice is low man on the grain scale. The kernels are not uniform in size and they are sometimes broken as well. It's a fine rice for soup or pancakes, but a roasted quail will quake at the prospect of having a spoonful of select in its dressing!

How to Store It

Wild rice manufacturers claim that this grain will keep indefinitely if it is stored in a tightly covered container in a cool, dry place. However, wild rice has a moisture level of from 7.9 to 11.2 percent. If humid, wild rice is capable of developing mold, or worse yet, maggots. In warm weather keep it refrigerated, or at least take the precaution of turning the jar upside down from time to time, to keep the rice from developing mildew. Cooked wild rice may be refrigerated (in an airtight self-seal plastic bag) for a week. Other cooks freeze uncooked wild rice. I do not, because a subtle textural change that occurs makes such storage uneconomical in the long run.

How to Cook It

Unlike white or brown rice, it is almost impossible to chart a cooking time for wild rice. A short-grained variety, for instance, will cook relatively quickly (35 to 40 minutes), while a long-grained variety will take half again as long (50 to 60 minutes).

Cooked wild rice should have bite, like *al dente* pasta. If it is cooked too long, the grain becomes mushy and the taste, like the nutrients, goes up in steam!

Wild rice is not as tricky to control during the cooking process as ordinary rice. If the rice is cooking too fast, add cold water or ice cubes to retard the boiling. A wise cook will also uncover the pot every so often to test a kernel for doneness.

Although cooking instructions on a package of wild rice usually state that 1 cup of uncooked rice yields 3 cups cooked, I often end up with 3½ or even 4 cups, depending upon the brand. It's a good idea to make a note of the quantity you get for future reference!

BASIC COOKED WILD RICE

1 cup wild rice
1 teaspoon salt
3 cups water (approximately)

Rinse the rice under cold water and drain it. Then place it in a saucepan with the salt and 3 cups water and heat to boiling. Reduce the heat to medium-low, and simmer, covered, for 35 to 60 minutes, adding more water, if necessary. Drain, if necessary.

Makes 3 to 4 cups

WILDER BEET TOP SOUP

The addition of wild rice is the perfect amendment to my good friend Mildred Schulz's classic Colorado Beet Top Soup.

3 tablespoons unsalted butter, at room temperature
1 small yellow onion, minced
3 tablespoons wild rice
4½ cups homemade chicken stock (see page 376) or canned broth
1½ pounds beet tops (from 2 large bunches)
1 pound potatoes, peeled and diced
1 cup light cream or half-and-half
1 tablespoon cornstarch
⅛ teaspoon ground allspice
Dash of hot pepper sauce
Salt and freshly ground black pepper to taste

1. Melt 1 tablespoon of the butter in a medium-size saucepan over medium-low heat. Add the onion; cook 3 minutes. Stir in the rice and 2 cups of the stock, and heat to boiling. Reduce the heat to medium-low, cover, and cook for about 20 minutes.

2. Meanwhile, wash the beet leaves well, discarding the stems. Cook the leaves in boiling water for 5 minutes. Rinse under cold running water, drain well, and chop.

3. Add the beet leaves, potatoes, and the remaining 2½ cups chicken stock to the soup. Heat to boiling. Then reduce the heat and cook, covered, over medium-low heat 25 minutes longer.

4. Stir the cream into the soup; simmer uncovered 5 minutes.

5. Stir the remaining 2 tablespoons butter and the cornstarch together in a small bowl until smooth. Stir this into the soup and cook until slightly thickened, 4 to 5 minutes. Add the allspice and hot pepper sauce, and season with salt and pepper.

Serves 6

GOLD-STANDARD STUFFED SQUASH

A solid gold appetizer or party "finger food." These squashes stuffed with chicken, ham, and wild rice are good hot or at room temperature.

4 small yellow squash (10 ounces total)
1 tablespoon unsalted butter
1 shallot, minced
⅛ teaspoon chopped fresh rosemary, or a
    pinch dried
⅛ teaspoon cayenne pepper
½ teaspoon all-purpose flour
¼ cup cooked wild rice (see page 333)
¼ cup finely chopped cooked chicken
¼ cup finely chopped smoky cooked ham
2 tablespoons heavy or whipping cream
1½ tablespoons freshly grated Parmesan
    cheese

1. Preheat the oven to 400°F. Lightly butter an ovenproof serving dish.

2. Cut the squash in half lengthwise. Cook, cut side down, in boiling water for 4 minutes. Drain on paper towels and allow to cool slightly.

3. Scoop out the insides of the squash with a spoon, leaving the shell ⅛ to ¼ inch thick. Drain the squash shells on paper towels. Finely chop the scooped-out pulp.

4. Melt the butter in a small skillet over medium-low heat. Add the shallot; cook 2 minutes. Add the rosemary, cayenne pepper, and chopped squash pulp. Cook, stirring occasionally, until all liquid has evaporated, about 5 minutes. Sprinkle the mixture with the flour, then stir in the cooked wild rice, chicken, ham, and cream. Remove the skillet from the heat.

5. Fill the squash shells with the rice mixture, mounding each squash high. Sprinkle with Parmesan cheese, and place in the prepared serving dish. Bake 10 minutes before serving.

Serves 4 as an appetizer

O f all the wild rice raised in the U.S., 85 percent is still produced by Native Americans. State laws regulate and monitor the industry, determining the length of the picking season and generally protecting Indians' rights, since most of the waters where the rice is grown are on reservation property.

In Minnesota wild rice may be harvested only by residents with permits; interlopers are punished, and fines are high. The picking season is brief—three weeks at most and powerboats are not permitted on rice waters.

These days the majority of rice pickers sell their crops to commercial processors, for the male tribe members are no longer interested in "dancing" in their moccasins on the cured rice. But the real enemy of the old-time wild rice tradition is time, and cost-effectiveness.

Paddy rice growers are the invaders—big business combines that are artificially seeding wetlands with wild rice and polluting the waters with herbicides and pesticides to grow a uniformly marketable crop. Despite protests of environmentalists and the Minnesota Department of Natural Resources, wild rice soon may not be very wild at all, and the sensual earthy flavor of the grain will be replaced by a blander taste, as plastic as the credit card that more than likely purchases it!

ROAST TURKEY WITH TWO RICE AND THREE SAUSAGE DRESSING

The stuffing is reminiscent of that fateful Thanksgiving I spent in Pennsylvania. The turkey is *my* method for roasting the bird—not a hint of stringy toughness anywhere!

1 fresh turkey (about 20 pounds) with
    giblets
2 large cloves garlic, bruised
Salt and freshly ground black pepper to
    taste
Two Rice and Three Sausage Dressing
    (recipe follows)
3 strips bacon
⅓ cup dry white wine
1 quart water
1 medium onion, unpeeled
1 medium rib celery, broken in half
3 sprigs parsley
¼ teaspoon salt
4 peppercorns
1½ tablespoons unsalted butter
1½ tablespoons all-purpose flour
¼ cup heavy or whipping cream

1. Preheat the oven to 325°F.

2. Remove the giblets from the turkey, and reserve them. Wipe the turkey out with a damp cloth. Rub it well, inside and out, with one of the garlic cloves, and with salt and pepper to taste. Stuff the cavity with the dressing. Sew and truss. Place the turkey on a rack in a roasting pan, and lay the bacon strips over the breast. Cut a piece of cheesecloth to fit over the turkey, dip it in the wine, and place it over the turkey. Pour the excess wine over the cheesecloth, and roast the turkey for 30 minutes.

3. Meanwhile, combine the reserved giblets (but not the liver), water, onion, celery, remaining clove of garlic, parsley sprigs, salt, and peppercorns in a large saucepan. Heat to boiling, reduce the heat, and simmer until reduced to 2 cups, 25 minutes. Strain.

4. Continue to roast the turkey, basting it with stock every 30 minutes, until the legs move freely and the juices run clear when the inner thigh is pierced with a fork, about 6 hours in all. For the last 30 minutes, increase the heat to 375°F and remove the cheesecloth (basting as you peel it off). Transfer the turkey to a carving board and let it stand 15 minutes.

5. Meanwhile, strain the turkey

A species of wild rice called *kaw-sun* (*Zizania latifolia*) grows in northern China and Tibet. The funny thing about this Oriental wild rice is its status, which is low. The Chinese do not consider it a delicacy. They don't even eat it. The truth is, they feed it to fowl. In the past, however, this rice was used like tea leaves, to tell fortunes.

In bygone days a seer would sit at the side of a road and scrawl the characters for "love," "wealth," "fame," and "fertility" in the dust. On each character he would place a grain of wild rice.

After someone produced a yen, the fortune-teller would release a hungry fowl onto the ideogram. As the chicken, duck, or turkey pecked away, a rosy future was assured.

drippings, removing the excess fat. Melt the butter in a medium-size saucepan over medium-low heat. Stir in the flour and cook, stirring constantly, 2 minutes. Whisk in the drippings and cream; simmer 5 minutes. Add salt and pepper to taste. Serve the gravy with the turkey and dressing.

Serves 8 to 10

Two Rice and Three Sausage Dressing

2¾ cups water
Salt to taste
⅔ cup wild rice, rinsed
⅔ cup long-grain white rice
½ pound sweet Italian sausage, sliced
¼ pound Spanish chorizos (or other spicy sausage), quartered lengthwise and sliced
1 Italian sopressata (about ¼ pound), diced
1 large onion, finely chopped
½ medium red bell pepper, cored, seeded, and chopped
2 tablespoons unsalted butter
2 tablespoons chopped fresh parsley
¼ teaspoon chopped fresh marjoram or oregano, or a pinch dried
⅛ teaspoon chopped fresh thyme, or a pinch dried
¼ teaspoon hot pepper sauce

1. Heat the water to boiling, add salt, and add the wild rice. Return to boiling, then reduce the heat to medium-low and simmer, covered, until tender, 35 to 60 minutes, depending on the rice. Remove the cover and raise the heat slightly if the rice is too wet. Set the cooked rice aside.

2. Meanwhile, cook the long-grain white rice, stirring once, in a large pot of boiling salted water for 12 minutes. Drain in a colander. Place the colander over 2 inches of boiling water in the same pot (do not let the bottom of the colander touch the water). Cover the rice with a single layer of paper towels, and steam for at least 15 minutes to dry it out.

3. While the rice is cooking, sauté the Italian sausage in a lightly oiled large heavy skillet until lightly browned, 6 to 8 minutes. Remove with a slotted spoon to a large bowl. In the same skillet, sauté the chorizos until lightly browned, about 8 minutes. Transfer to the bowl. Sauté the soprassata in the same skillet until crisp, about 8 minutes, and transfer to the bowl.

4. Discard all but 2 tablespoons grease from the skillet. Add the onion and bell pepper; cook over medium-low heat 5 minutes. Stir in the butter, parsley, marjoram, thyme, and hot pepper sauce.

5. Add the onion/pepper mixture to the sausages. Then add both rices and mix well. Allow to cool before stuffing the turkey.

Makes enough for a 20- to 22-pound turkey

RACY, RICEY MEAT LOAF

*I*f I don't eat meat loaf every other week, I feel cheated. Definitely comfort food, and with the addition of wild rice, it takes on a hearty, gutsy flavor. This loaf is best ⸱erved hot or at room temperature.

1 tablespoon unsalted butter
2 shallots, minced
1½ pounds ground beef
1 pound ground veal
¾ ground pork
1 hot green pepper, seeded and minced
1 cup cooked wild rice (see page 333)
2 eggs, lightly beaten
½ cup tomato juice
½ cup milk
1 tablespoon chopped fresh parsley
2 teaspoons chopped fresh basil, or ¾
    teaspoon dried
¼ teaspoon chopped fresh thyme, or a
    pinch of dried
3 tablespoons chili sauce
2 teaspoons Dijon mustard
⅛ teaspoon hot Hungarian paprika
2 strips bacon

    1. Preheat the oven to 375°F.

    2. Melt the butter in a small skillet over medium-low heat. Add the shallot; cook 4 minutes. Remove the skillet from the heat.

    3. Combine the beef, veal, and pork in a large bowl. Mix well and add the reserved shallots, hot green pepper, cooked wild rice, eggs, tomato juice, milk, parsley, basil, and thyme. Mix thoroughly. Shape into a loaf on a shallow baking dish.

    4. Whisk the chili sauce, mustard, and paparika together in a bowl, and spread over the meat loaf. Lay the bacon on top. Bake until the juices run fairly clear when the loaf is pricked with a fork, about 1½ hours. Reduce the heat if the loaf is getting too brown. Let it stand 5 minutes before serving.

    Serves 6 to 8

MOORS AND MARTYRS STEW

_T_he original version of this Caribbean dish is made with black beans and rice and is called Moors and Christians. My version, with wild rice, is dubbed Moors and Martyrs. But the only martyrdom involved is in not receiving a second helping.

½ pound (½ package) dried black beans
2 strips bacon, chopped
1 tablespoon butter
1 medium onion, finely chopped
1 clove garlic, minced
½ medium rib celery, finely chopped
½ cup chopped cooked ham
½ teaspoon salt
¼ teaspoon freshly ground black pepper
1 bay leaf
½ teaspoon ground allspice
⅓ cup wild rice
5 cups (approximately) homemade chicken
    stock (see page 376) or canned broth
⅛ teaspoon hot pepper sauce

1 pound smoked Polish sausage (kielbasa),
    cut into 1½-inch pieces
1½ cups cooked long-grain white rice,
    heated
⅛ cup finely chopped green scallion tops

    1. Place the beans in a medium-size pot, and cover with cold water. Heat to boiling; boil 2 minutes. Remove from the heat and let stand, covered, 1 hour. Drain.

    2. Meanwhile, sauté the bacon in a large heavy pot or Dutch oven until almost crisp. Add the butter and onion; cook over medium heat 1 minute. Reduce the heat to medium-low and add the garlic; cook 2 minutes longer. Then stir in the celery and ham. Cook, stirring occasionally, 10 minutes.

3. Add the salt to the onion mixture along with the pepper, bay leaf, and allspice. Stir in the drained beans and the wild rice, tossing to coat with the onion mixture. Add the chicken stock, and heat to boiling. Reduce the heat and simmer, partially covered, until the beans and rice are almost tender, about 1 hour.

4. Scoop out ¼ cup of the stew and place it in the container of a food processor. Process until smooth, adding more chicken stock if needed. Return the processed mixture to the stew, and add the hot pepper sauce and sausage. Cook, covered, until the beans and rice are very tender, 30 to 45 minutes longer.

5. Pour the stew into a large shallow serving dish. Mound the white rice in the center and sprinkle with the scallion tops. Stir each portion of rice into the stew as you serve.

Serves 4 to 6

WILD RICE PATTIES

*B*e sure you do not pass this recipe by. It's an excellent croquette, which came to me from a friend. The sour cream and caviar embellishment is strictly my own.

¼ cup wild rice
1 cup water
1 teaspoon salt
½ pound baking potatoes, peeled and diced
2 egg yolks
1 tablespoon sour cream
4 strips bacon, chopped
2 large scallions, white bulbs and green
*   tops, minced*
1½ tablespoons chopped fresh parsley
Pinch of dried marjoram
⅛ teaspoon freshly grated nutmeg
⅓ cup fresh bread crumbs
1 tablespoon freshly grated Parmesan
*   cheese*
Freshly ground black pepper to taste
3 to 4 tablespoons unsalted butter
Sour cream
Caviar

1. Combine the wild rice with the water and salt in a small saucepan, and heat to boiling. Reduce the heat to medium-low and simmer, covered, until the rice is very tender, 40 to 60 minutes. Remove the cover and raise the heat slightly if the rice is too wet.

2. Meanwhile, cook the potatoes in boiling salted water to cover until tender, 15 minutes. Drain, and mash the potatoes until smooth. Beat in the egg yolks and sour cream. Combine with the rice in a medium-size bowl, and set aside.

3. Sauté the bacon in a medium-size skillet over medium heat until crisp. Add the scallions, parsley, and marjoram, and cook 3 minutes. Cool slightly, and add to the rice/potato mixture. Add the nutmeg, bread crumbs, cheese, and salt and pepper to taste. Mix well, and refrigerate, loosely covered, for 1 hour.

4. Form the wild rice mixture into small balls. Press into patties.

5. Melt 3 tablespoons butter in a heavy skillet over medium heat. Sauté the patties, about six at a time, until golden brown on both sides, about 2 minutes per side. Drain on paper towels, and transfer to an ovenproof serving dish. Keep the patties warm in a 225°F oven while sautéing the remainder. Continue to fry patties until all the rice mixture is used up.

6. Top each one with dabs of sour cream and caviar before serving.

Serves 6 to 8

WILD RICE WITH BRUSSELS SPROUTS AND BANGERS

*T*here is a saying that there are three vegetables in England: cabbage, cabbage, and cabbage. Since Brussels sprouts belong to the cabbage family, they make a great partnership when teamed with bangers (the English handle for sausages) and wild rice.

10 ounces Brussels sprouts
2 cups water (approximately)
½ teaspoon salt
⅓ cup wild rice
½ pound sweet Italian sausage
1 tablespoon butter
1 large shallot, minced
1 clove garlic, minced
1 hot green pepper, seeded and minced
1 teaspoon soy sauce

1. Trim the Brussels sprouts, and cut a small "X" in the root end of each one.

2. Heat the water to boiling in a medium-size saucepan. Add the salt and Brussels sprouts, cover, and cook 3 minutes. Remove the sprouts with a slotted spoon, and reduce the heat to medium-low.

3. Add the wild rice to the water. Cover and cook until tender, adding more water if necessary, 35 to 60 minutes, depending on the rice. Remove the cover and raise the heat slightly if the mixture is too wet.

4. Meanwhile, sauté the sausages in an oil-rubbed heavy skillet over medium heat until well browned, about 8 minutes. Remove the sausages to a plate. Cut the Brussels sprouts crosswise into ¼-inch-thick slices. Cut the sausages into ¼-inch pieces.

5. Wipe out the skillet and melt the butter in it over medium-low heat. Add the shallot; cook 1 minute. Add the garlic, hot green pepper, and sausage slices. Cook until the vegetables are lightly browned and the sausages are cooked through, about 5 minutes. Sprinkle with the soy sauce and add the wild rice. Toss until well mixed, about 1 minute. Add the Brussels sprouts and continue to cook, tossing gently, until the sprouts are warmed through, about 4 minutes.

Serves 4

MARY CASSETTI'S WILD RICE FRITTATA

Mary lives in upstate New York and happens to be a very good cook. A frittata, sometimes called an Italian omelet, is often baked in the oven, but the traditional method calls for cooking the entire dish stove-top. I serve it for lunch or a late supper.

1 tablespoon olive oil
¼ cup finely chopped scallions, white
*   bulbs and green tops*
1 small clove garlic, minced
1 large fresh shiitake mushroom (1 ounce),
*   halved and sliced*
½ cup Canadian bacon in thin strips
*   (about 6 slices)*
1 tablespoon chopped fresh parsley
6 eggs
¼ cup heavy or whipping cream
½ cup cooked wild rice (see page 333)
½ cup grated Jarlsberg cheese
¼ cup freshly grated Parmesan cheese
4 teaspoons unsalted butter
Salt and freshly ground black pepper to
*   taste*

1. Heat the oil in a medium-size skillet over medium heat. Add the scallion; cook 1 minute. Add the garlic; cook 2 minutes. Add the mushroom and Canadian bacon. Cook, stirring constantly, 3 minutes. Then stir in the parsley and remove from the heat.

2. Beat the eggs in a large bowl. Beat in the cream. Stir in the mushroom mixture, the cooked wild rice, the Jarlsberg cheese, and 2 tablespoons of the Parmesan cheese.

3. Melt 3 teaspoons of the butter in a 9-inch skillet (preferably non-stick) over medium heat until foamy. Pour in the egg mixture, and reduce the heat to medium-low. Cook without stirring for 20 minutes.

4. Rub another skillet of the same size with the remaining teaspoon of butter. Place it over medium heat for 1

The first Europeans to taste wild rice in the New World were French settlers from Brittany. Having an affinity for the familiar white *riz*, they did not enjoy wild rice at all.

As the story goes, they disliked the stuff so much they spat it out (behind the Indians' backs) after a first bite. And though they knew the Chippewa name for the grain—*mahnomen*, which means "seeds from the wild"—the Frenchmen privately called it *folle avoine* ("crazy oats").

In time, the Frenchmen developed a taste for wild rice. The sensible Breton women mixed the wild rice with vegetables and served it cold after Sunday mass. The settlers liked it so much they called it a *salade* and in time invited the Indians to share it.

After a first bite the Chippewa braves spat the food out (behind the Frenchmen's backs of course!), and they gave it a name of their own: *paolsu mizin* ("sick food")!

minute, then place it upside-down over the skillet with the frittata, and invert. Sprinkle the top of the frittata with the remaining 2 tablespoons Parmesan cheese, and season with salt and pepper. Return to low heat for 3 minutes.

Serves 4 to 6

WILD ABOUT CHICKEN SALAD

Leftover chicken, fennel, and wild rice make an intriguing combination. I add a touch of peanut butter to the dressing for a good nutty flavor.

2 small fennel bulbs (6 ounces each) with
    fronds
2 cups cooked wild rice (see page 333)
2 scallions, white bulbs and green tops,
    finely chopped
2 cups cooked chicken in bite-size pieces
½ cup walnut oil
2 tablespoons white wine vinegar
2 teaspoons Dijon mustard
2 teaspoons chunky-style peanut butter
¼ cup walnut pieces, toasted (see Note)
Salt and freshly ground black pepper to
    taste

1. Trim the fennel bulbs and discard the stems. Chop and reserve the fronds. Cut the bulbs in half lengthwise, remove and discard the cores, and cut across into very thin slices. Place the slices in a large bowl, and add the cooked wild rice, scallions, and chicken.

2. Whisk the walnut oil with the vinegar in a small bowl. Then whisk in the mustard and peanut butter. Pour the dressing over the salad and toss well. Add the walnuts, and season with salt and pepper. Serve at room temperature, sprinkled with the reserved fennel fronds.

Serves 6

Note: To toast the walnuts, heat a small skillet over medium heat. Add the nuts and toast until golden, stirring frequently, 6 to 8 minutes.

CABBAGE PATCH SLAW

A one-dish meal: cole slaw studded with wild rice and tuna. A great picnic dish.

1½ cups cooked wild rice (see page 333)
2 cups shredded cabbage
1 cup flaked cooked tuna, or drained
    canned water-packed tuna
1 large shallot, finely chopped
¼ teaspoon anchovy paste
1 tablespoon fresh lemon juice
1 teaspoon red wine vinegar
¼ cup olive oil
⅛ teaspoon chopped fresh rosemary, or a
    pinch dried
Salt and freshly ground black pepper to
    taste

1. Combine the cooked wild rice, cabbage, tuna, and shallot in a large bowl. Toss gently to mix.

2. Stir the anchovy paste, lemon juice, and vinegar together in a small bowl until smooth. Whisk in the oil and rosemary. Pour the dressing over the salad and toss. Season with salt and pepper, and serve.

Serves 4

SHOCKING-PINK WILD RICE

Grated beets turn this salad shocking pink. I serve it with cold broiled chicken and a plate of sliced tomatoes.

1¼ to 1½ pounds fresh beets with 1-inch
    stems, unpeeled
1 large shallot, minced
1 cup cooked wild rice (see page 333)
1 cup plus 2 tablespoons sour cream
1½ tablespoons prepared horseradish
2 tablespoons strong beef stock (see Note)
3 tablespoons heavy or whipping cream
Salt and freshly ground black pepper to
    taste
3 tablespoons chopped fresh parsley

1. Place the beets in a saucepan, cover with cold water, and heat to boiling. Reduce the heat and simmer, uncovered, until barely tender, about 25 minutes. Drain under cold water. Remove the skins and grate the beets into a large bowl. Add the shallot and cooked wild rice.

2. Combine the sour cream, horseradish, beef stock, and cream in a small bowl. Whisk until smooth. Combine all but 2 tablespoons of the sour cream mixture with the beet mixture. Toss well, and season with salt and pepper. Transfer to a serving bowl, place the remaining sour cream mixture in the center of the salad, and ring with the parsley. Serve chilled or at room temperature.

Serves 4 to 6

Note: If you do not have strong beef stock on hand (see page 379), reduce ¼ cup canned beef broth to 2 tablespoons by simmering for 5 minutes.

BETTER TIMES SALAD

My mother used to make a version of this lentil salad with white rice in the days of the Depression. It's cheap and hearty. Better times call for more expensive wild rice, which turns the salad into a celebration.

⅔ cup lentils
1 cup cooked wild rice (see page 333)
⅓ cup finely sliced red radishes (about
    2 ounces)
⅓ cup finely sliced white radishes (about
    2 ounces)
¼ cup finely chopped green scallion tops
2 pickled jalapeño peppers, finely sliced
1 clove garlic, crushed
¼ teaspoon salt

2 tablespoons fresh lime juice
2 teaspoons country-style Dijon mustard
    (with seeds)
¼ cup olive oil
Chopped fresh parsley, for garnish

1. Cook the lentils in boiling salted water until tender, about 20 minutes. Drain, and set aside to cool.

2. Combine the cooled lentils with

the cooked wild rice, radishes, scallion tops, and peppers in a bowl. Toss well.

3. Using the back of a spoon, mash the garlic with the salt in a small bowl until a paste is formed. Whisk in the lime juice, mustard, and oil. Pour the dressing over the rice mixture and toss well. Serve at room temperature, sprinkled with parsley.

Serves 4 to 6

STRIP POTATO MAYONNAISE

Made with grated, barely cooked potatoes, this elegant salad graces the table at many of my parties.

2 large potatoes (1 pound)
2 tablespoons fresh lemon juice
1 cup cooked wild rice (see page 333)
¼ pound sliced prosciutto, chopped
2 fresh shiitake mushroom caps, halved and thinly sliced
¼ pound Fontina cheese, diced
¾ cup Homemade Mayonnaise (see page 379)
¼ cup sour cream
½ teaspoon salt
¼ teaspoon freshly ground black pepper
1 tablespoon chopped fresh parsley
1 teaspoon chopped fresh chives

1. Peel the potatoes and run them through the coarse shredder of a food processer. (They will look a little like spaghetti.) As you shred them, place the potatoes in a large bowl of cold water containing 1 tablespoon of the lemon juice. Drain the potato shreds, and cook in boiling salted water until crisp-tender, about 3 to 4 minutes. Rinse under cold running water, drain, and pat dry with paper towels.

2. Place the potatoes in a large bowl. Add the cooked wild rice, prosciutto, mushrooms, and cheese. Toss well.

3. Whisk the mayonnaise with the sour cream in a bowl. Add the remaining tablespoon of lemon juice, the salt, pepper, and parsley. Pour the dressing over the potato/rice mixture, and toss gently until well mixed. Serve at room temperature, sprinkled with the chives.

Serves 4

As I have mentioned, foods that pleased the Native American did not always sit well below his guests' belts.

Lewis and Clark complained of having to eat raw deer heart, a meal that Sacajawea, their intrepid female Indian guide, proclaimed to be "a great delicacy."

John Bartram, America's first naturalist, who logged all the foods the Indians ate, wrote of consuming *misickquatash* with the Sioux, *mausamp* with the Iroquois, and *rockahominy* with the Crows—and never feeling "right" again afterward.

On the other hand, in 1807 Peter Pond, a fur trader, wrote to his wife about eating wild rice with the Indians of Wisconsin: "When it is Cleaned fit for youse thay Boile it as we do Rise and Eat it with Bairs Greas and Sugar. . . . And it did very well."

PECAN RICE PILAF

*F*or any holiday—or non-holiday—meal on your agenda, consider wild rice instead of potatoes. I like it best, I think, baked into a pilaf, as in this tonic pecan version created by my friend Marilyn Harris.

2 tablespoons unsalted butter
1 large shallot, minced
⅓ cup wild rice
1¼ cups water
½ cup long-grain white rice
¾ cup homemade beef stock (see page 377)
   or canned broth
¼ cup dry white wine
1 small bay leaf
Dash of hot pepper sauce
½ cup frozen peas, thawed
2 tablespoons chopped fresh parsley
¼ cup pecan halves, toasted and coarsely
   chopped (see Note)
1 teaspoon chopped fresh mint (optional)

1. Melt the butter in a medium-size saucepan over medium heat. Add the shallot; cook 2 minutes. Stir in the wild rice and the water, and heat to boiling.

Reduce the heat to medium-low and simmer, covered, 30 minutes.

2. Add the white rice, beef stock, wine, bay leaf, and hot pepper sauce to the wild rice. Heat to boiling, then reduce the heat to medium-low. Simmer, covered, until both rices are tender and almost all liquid has been absorbed, about 25 minutes. Discard the bay leaf. Stir the peas into the mixture; cook, covered, 5 minutes longer. Remove the cover and raise the heat slightly if the mixture is too wet. Toss in the parsley and pecans, and sprinkle with the mint, if you like.

Serves 4

Note: To toast the pecans, heat a small skillet over medium heat. Add the nuts and toast until golden, stirring frequently, 6 to 8 minutes.

PILAF OF WILD RICE WITH WILDER MUSHROOMS

*T*his recipe comes from Haiti, where its creator had the wild rice smuggled into Port-au-Prince, stashed inside the shoes that she had sent to New York to be repaired!

½ ounce dried wild mushrooms
¾ cup hot water
1 tablespoon peanut oil
1 strip bacon, chopped
1 small onion, halved and sliced
1 clove garlic, minced
¼ teaspoon crushed dried hot red peppers

Pinch of cloves
¼ teaspoon chopped fresh tarragon, or a
   pinch dried
⅓ cup wild rice
½ cup (approximately) homemade chicken
   stock (see page 376) or canned broth
Chopped fresh parsley, for garnish

1. Place the mushrooms in a small bowl, cover with the hot water, and let stand until soft, about 20 minutes. Strain, reserving ½ cup liquid. Coarsely chop the mushrooms.

2. Heat the oil in a medium-size saucepan over medium-low heat. Add the bacon; cook until almost crisp, about 3 minutes. Add the onion; cook 1 minute. Stir in the garlic and dried red peppers; continue to cook until the onion and garlic are very dark brown but not burned, 4 to 5 minutes longer. Sprinkle with the cloves and tarragon. Then stir in the reserved mushroom liquid, mushrooms, rice, and chicken stock.

Heat to boiling. Reduce the heat to medium-low and simmer, covered, adding more stock if needed, until the rice is tender, 35 to 60 minutes, depending on the rice. Remove the cover and raise the heat slightly if the mixture is too wet. Sprinkle with parsley before serving.

Serves 3 or 4

WILD CRIMSON RICE

A baked rice dish that goes well with all kinds of fowl and pork. It is delicious at room temperature as well, but because the tomatoes have a tendency to get juicy when the dish sits, you might wish to add a teaspoon or so of flour to the tomato mixture.

2 tablespoons unsalted butter
1 medium onion, finely chopped
1 clove garlic, minced
3 cups chopped, seeded ripe tomatoes
1 teaspoon sugar
½ teaspoon salt
¼ teaspoon freshly ground black pepper
1 tablespoon chopped fresh basil,
    or 1 teaspoon dried
1 teaspoon chopped fresh oregano,
    or ¼ teaspoon dried
½ teaspoon whole allspice, crushed
1 cup cooked wild rice (see page 333)
½ cup heavy or whipping cream
1 tablespoon freshly grated Parmesan
    cheese
1 cup grated mozzarella cheese

1. Melt the butter in a medium-size saucepan over medium-low heat. Add the onion; cook 1 minute. Add the garlic; cook 2 minutes longer. Add the tomatoes, sugar, salt, pepper, basil, oregano, and allspice. Cook, uncovered, stirring occasionally, until very thick, about 30 minutes.

2. Preheat the oven to 350°F. Butter an 8- or 9-inch shallow ovenproof serving dish.

3. Stir the cooked wild rice into the tomato mixture, then add the cream and Parmesan cheese. Spoon into the prepared serving dish. Bake 30 minutes.

4. Sprinkle the mozzarella over the baked tomato mixture, and return the dish to the oven until the cheese melts, 3 or 4 minutes. Let stand a few minutes before serving.

Serves 6

WILDERNESS BREAD

September is the month of the Wild Rice Moon, a festival of Indian foods named for a harvest moon round and golden as a tub of fresh butter. Which brings to mind a highly appropriate accompaniment that is one of my favorite recipes: a crisp and crusty loaf of wheat and wild rice bread.

½ cup milk
2 tablespoons unsalted butter
½ teaspoon salt
1½ cups cooked wild rice (see page 333)
¼ cup lukewarm water
1 package dry yeast
1 tablespoon dark brown sugar
Pinch of ground ginger
1 cup whole-wheat flour
1¾ cups bread flour (approximately)
1 teaspoon unsalted butter, melted

1. Combine the milk, 2 tablespoons butter, and salt in a medium-size saucepan over medium-low heat, and heat until the butter melts. Remove the pan from the heat, and stir in the cooked wild rice. Allow to cool to room temperature.

2. Place the lukewarm water in a large bowl, and sprinkle it with the yeast. Then stir in the sugar and ginger. Let stand until bubbly, 8 to 10 minutes. Stir in the rice mixture, whole-wheat flour, and about 1 cup of the bread flour, enough to make a stiff dough.

3. Scrape the dough out onto a well-floured board and knead, adding more bread flour as needed, until soft and elastic, about 12 minutes. Transfer the dough to a greased bowl, cover with plastic wrap, and let rise in a warm place until doubled in volume, about 1 hour.

4. Punch the dough down. Knead it briefly and place in a greased 9 by 5 by 3-inch loaf pan. Cover loosely with a flour-rubbed tea towel, and let rise in a warm place until the bread reaches over the top of the pan, about 1 hour.

5. Preheat the oven to 350°F.

6. Make a slash down the center of the bread with a sharp knife, and brush with the melted butter. Bake 35 minutes. Then raise the heat to 400°F and bake until the bread is golden brown and sounds hollow when tapped with your finger, about 10 minutes longer. Gently loosen the bread from the pan, but allow it to cool completely in the pan on a rack.

Makes 1 loaf

Indians who grow it claim to be able to spot wild rice half a mile away. The pale green plumes and the purplish blossoms give it away.

Uncooked wild rice has a purple-black color, and a wise Indian can tell if it will be flavorsome or not by holding a handful close to his nose. Dried wild rice at its best should have a faint but distinct smoky perfume.

If you find that smokiness too intense for your taste, rinse it several times in cold water prior to cooking. I like wild rice just the way it comes, "with a taste that fights back," which is an Ojibwa expression for a properly cured and cooked batch.

WILD RICE AND DATE MUFFINS

Wild rice and dates make these muffins very special. A word of warning, however: These are best served hot from the oven, because wild rice has a tendency to get heavy as it sits.

1¼ cups all-purpose flour
1 tablespoon baking powder
½ teaspoon salt
5 tablespoons unsalted butter, melted
1 cup milk
2 eggs, lightly beaten
3 tablespoons maple syrup
1 cup cooked wild rice (see page 333)
½ cup chopped dates

1. Preheat the oven to 425°F. Lightly grease a 12-cup muffin tin.

2. Combine the flour, baking powder, and salt in a large bowl. Make a well in the center, and add the melted butter, milk, eggs, and maple syrup. Using a wooden spoon, stir the liquid into the flour until smooth. Then stir in the cooked wild rice and the dates.

3. Spoon the batter into the muffin cups (the cups will be very full). Bake until golden brown and firm to the

The Ojibwa (who harvest wild rice) do not believe in war or war dances. This tribe never tortured their prisoners, and it is said they looked down on other more aggressive tribes (like the Iroquois) who did.

Perhaps the Ojibwa people's pacific nature was related to the food they ate. Ojibwas were vegetarians; eating no meat whatsoever—only greens and grains. Notably wild rice.

touch, 15 to 18 minutes. Serve immediately.

Makes 12 muffins

JILL GARDNER'S WILD RICE AND WALNUT FLAPJACKS

Jill Gardner is a talented food writer who lives in San Francisco. These pancakes are her creation, and she serves them at elegant lunches. I serve them to weekend guests for brunch, with a side of sausage and plenty of Vermont maple syrup.

½ cup all-purpose flour
½ teaspoon baking powder
¼ teaspoon salt
Pinch of freshly ground black pepper
½ cup coarsely ground walnuts
1 egg

½ cup sour cream
½ cup milk
1 cup cooked wild rice (see page 333)
4 tablespoons (½ stick) unsalted butter, melted

1. Combine the flour, baking powder, salt, pepper, and walnuts in a medium-size bowl. Mix well.

2. Combine the egg, sour cream, and ¼ cup of the milk in a small bowl. Whisk until smooth. Then, using a wooden spoon, stir into the flour mixture. Let stand 10 minutes.

3. Stir the remaining ¼ cup milk into the batter. Stir in the cooked wild rice and melted butter.

4. Heat a lightly greased cast-iron skillet or griddle over medium heat until hot but not smoking. Cook the pancakes, a few at a time, using about 3 tablespoons batter per pancake. When lightly browned, about 2 minutes, turn over and cook the other side for 1 minute. Transfer to a serving platter and keep warm in a 225°F oven while cooking the remaining pancakes. Reduce the heat under the skillet if the pancakes brown too quickly.

Makes about sixteen 2½- to 3-inch pancakes

LOW-MAN-ON-THE-TOTEM-POLE PORRIDGE

*T*his can be a dessert, or a breakfast or brunch dish. Sweet but not too sweet. The notion was told to me by its inventor, Arthur Schwartz, the food editor and restaurant critic of the New York *Daily News*.

Arthur makes this dish with broken (select) wild rice. He claims the lowest grade stirs up into the best porridge. If you can't find a broken batch, smash a few with a hammer. I did.

¼ cup wild rice
1 cup milk
⅛ teaspoon ground cinnamon
½ cup blueberries
Maple syrup
Heavy or whipping cream

1. Combine the rice, milk, and cinnamon in a medium-size saucepan and heat to boiling. Reduce the heat to medium-low, cover, and cook until the rice is very tender, 50 to 60 minutes. Remove the cover and raise the heat for a few minutes if the mixture is too wet. The rice should be creamy.

2. Divide the rice between two serving bowls. Add ¼ cup blueberries to each bowl, along with generous amounts of maple syrup and cream.

Serves 2

*S*candinavian homesteaders in the upper territory of Minnesota in the late 19th century would trade whatever they could spare from their fields or dwindling store supplies for wild rice from the local Indian tribes.

The Swedes used to call wild rice *ficka pendar* ("pocket money"), not because it was then so marketable but because a small amount represented dinner for a family of five or six. No matter how empty the cupboard or how slim the wallet, everyone ate when there was pocket money—for wild rice triples or quadruples as it cooks!

THE NEW GRAINS

Amaranth, Quinoa, and Triticale

When I was a small kid, going to the theater was the most exciting event of my life—specifically vaudeville, because it was not only fast-paced but also wildly flamboyant. Vaudeville disappeared almost immediately with the onset of the Depression, but it was certainly a delirious experience while it lasted.

In our household, vaudeville was always a family outing, a dispensation viewed by both parents with justifiable apprehension. My sister, five years my senior, was charged with the onerous responsibility of keeping me from crying, shouting, or jumping up and down on my seat during a performance. Not an easy task, as I was an excitable child.

Vaudeville had a fixed formula. There were always five or six acts on the program, a gilt-edged sign proclaiming each name before the curtain rose. At the top of the bill came the jugglers—who managed to toss dozens of plates and glittering balls in the air without ever ceasing to smile, even as latecomers rustled programs, coughed, or talked through their performance. Next came the tap dancers. In pairs, trios, or quartets, these talented hoofers brought the audience to life, and their trickiest footfalls were often matched by waves of applause and demands for encores. Animal acts followed on their heels. Sometimes the trainer would bring out a pack of dogs, dressed in trousers and skirts, who walked on their hind legs, smoked cigarettes, and danced the Charleston. At other times the animals were trained seals who managed to squeak out familiar tunes on horn-bugles for a promised herring or sardine. On one occasion I recall a totally different animal act: a flock of trained doves that plucked chiffon scarves from the near-naked bosom and limbs of an "exotic dancer." As I recollect, my father bid me *not* to look at that animal act. But I did anyway.

Animal acts were generally followed by tumblers or acrobats. The following next-to-closing spot was always eagerly awaited; sometimes it was a famous comedian or a popular singer, at other times a pair of ballroom dancers. The act I remember best was a world-renowned magician who proceeded to saw a shrieking woman in half. It was not necessary to caution me not to look at that!

The closing act was always a "stellar attraction," very often world-famous. On one occasion it was the great dancer Pavlova; on another the star was Gertrude Ederle, who swam the English Channel and promised a demonstration of her famous backstroke in a tank as wide as the proscenium arch.

I was taken to see many stellar performers in my young life as a vaudeville-goer, but in all candor I must tell you that I never actually saw a closing act. I always fell fast asleep before that moment arrived. All the way home, I would complain about what I had missed until Myra (a bit of a show-off herself) would re-create the closing act secondhand, in the back of our family car.

"Why do they always put the good things last?" I questioned.

"To keep you waiting and wanting, kiddo," said my sister.

Who am I to fly in the face of tradition? Now that you've waited and waded through this book for so long, here at last are my thoughts on the *new grains*. Announcing... Amaranth, quinoa, and triticale! Definitely not a tumbling act.

AMARANTH

The Grain's Genesis

Amaranth is a "new" grain that's actually as old as the hills. A seed of mystical attributes, 500 years ago the Aztecs believed that a single spoonful could turn a softie into a hunk; and that a steady diet would produce a race of honest-to-gosh supermen.

As a consequence, Aztecs grew lots

of amaranth. Over 20,000 tons were harvested, chaffed, winnowed, then sent by mule team, ox cart, and broad men's backs to Tenochtitlán (now Mexico City) as a yearly tribute to the emperor Montezuma.

As a source of energy and fortitude, amaranth was as important to the Aztecs as the corn and beans that kept them alive. On holy days, Aztec women pounded amaranth with honey and (ouch!) human blood into a rough dough that they baked in the form of snakes, birds, and other assorted household deities. These cakes were broken apart and consumed religiously to keep the faith in strength and fitness.

When Hernando Cortez, the Spanish conquistador (and a good churchgoer despite his bloody reputation), observed these doings for the first time, he was so offended that supposedly he could not speak for a week's time. In Cortez's mind, the Aztec ritual was a mockery of the Christian communion he had been raised to revere, and the only punishment he could conceive of to fit the crime was total obliteration.

Though he had come to Mexico on a self-declared mission of goodwill, Cortez killed Montezuma at once. He commanded his troops to burn every square inch of amaranth that bloomed between the Gulf of California and the Bay of Campeche. What's worse, he also ordered them to cut off the hands of anyone found with a single seed in his possession.

Historians date the pillage of amaranth as the end of the Aztec empire. Dispirited and deprived of their "wonder food," formerly brave warriors became itinerant peasants without a leader or a focus.

General Cortez returned to Spain in triumph of course, but his victory was short-lived. Not only had he terminated amaranth's role as a source of food in the New World, he stemmed the spread of a highly nutritious grain in the Old World as well.

The happy end to this tale is: You can't keep a good seed down! Amaranth survived even if the Aztecs did not, and half a millennium later we are rediscovering its tonic effect on the human body.

Some Plain Grain Talk

Amaranth's name is borrowed from the Greek. It means "not withering," or more literally, "immortal." That's not a randomly bestowed tag, either, for the curious thing about amaranth is its longevity. Other grain kernels, such as corn, wheat, and rice, will not sprout after long intervals; a decade is most plants' time span. Amaranth, on the other hand, sprouts indefinitely. A handful of seed recovered from an Aztec ruin 1,000 years old recently set down taproots at a farm in Pennsylvania. And that, my friends, is immortal enough for all normal purposes!

Immortality is not the reason to include amaranth on your grocery list. Health is! This small grain—only slightly larger than a poppy seed—provides the human system with the most effective balance of protein under the sun. Amaranth's high nutritive bonus to the diet is matched only by milk, and it stands head and shoulders above all other complex carbohydrates because of the enormous jolt of lysine in its composition. Lysine is an amino acid that controls protein absorption in the body.

Amaranth has other pluses: it is exceptionally high in vitamins and minerals; 3½ ounces contain more calcium than a super-thick shake; and ½ cup totals less than 16 calories.

How to Buy It

Amaranth has become available to consumers only recently. Rediscovered by nutritionists and plant breeders in the mid-1970s, this grain was first sold only by mail order. And it was regarded with a raised eyebrow by all but deep-dyed health-food votaries because of its "wonder protein" reputation. But once it was cooked and tasted, amaranth proved to be so delicious (it has a mild toasted-sesame flavor) that health-conscious diners jumped on the bandwagon and created a market demand.

At present, amaranth is sold at natural foods stores, packaged and in bulk. I have also noted its appearance in forward-minded supermarkets as well, particularly those chains in the Pacific Northwest and California where the fitness fervor affects impulse buying. A brief survey of "health food" shelves recently revealed not only amaranth grain but amaranth cereal (combined with whole wheat), amaranth flour, amaranth crackers, amaranth granola, amaranth pasta, and amaranth chocolate chip cookies! All out there, ready to lure shoppers who cannot resist the "Mystical Grain of the Aztecs" emblazoned on every package.

My advice is to purchase amaranth in bulk if possible, for that's the least expensive (and least hyped) option. Price varies with distribution, of course, but bulk amaranth is relatively inexpensive —about $1 per pound. Since amaranth increases radically in volume as it cooks (like most grains), a buck provides a bucketful of nutrition!

How to Store It

Amaranth has a long, long shelf life and is virtually pest-resistant. However, a wise cook will keep this grain well covered (preferably in a glass container ample enough to keep the seeds from being crushed) on a pantry shelf where the temperature does not exceed 65°F, or refrigerated when the climate is warmer.

In the unlikely case that amaranth spoils, let your nose be the judge: over-the-hill amaranth smells like linseed oil. It won't kill you, but it also won't work wonders either. So dispose of it, please.

How to Cook It

Amaranth is a grain with two culinary alternatives. A mildly spicy seed, it may be cooked in liquid until creamy and served as a side dish. Or it may be tossed in a hot pan until the seeds burst and develop a crackle not unlike seasoned popcorn.

Not much has been written about amaranth cookery. The few cookbooks that have touched on the subject usually call for more liquid than I deem warranted. Too much water turns cooked amaranth into gruel. The correct formula, in my opinion (a ratio of 2 parts liquid to 1 part grain), will approximate the texture—though certainly not the flavor—of cooked grits. And in fact,

To my totally untrained eye, the most attractive feature of growing amaranth is its lack of conformity: it blooms in a rainbow of colors. The plant is rather tall and wavy, with blossoms not unlike celosia topping each stalk. The leaves of the amaranth plant are also edible, not dissimilar to spinach in taste and texture. Seed heads are large, and each yields almost a kilo of pure seed after it is cleared of its resplendent chaff.

Farmers are beginning to grow amaranth, and that's a healthy sign for the crop's future. Home gardeners can grow it in their backyards, too. When you're through cooking, take a moment to check the back of the book for information on how and where to obtain seeds.

many of the grits recipes in this book may, with some minor adjustments, be adapted to its use.

When cooking amaranth, it is advis-able to use a non-stick pan to keep the seeds from becoming cohesive. Amaranth doubles when cooked: ½ cup dry becomes 1 cup cooked.

BASIC COOKED AMARANTH

½ cup amaranth
1 cup water, broth, or vegetable juice
1 teaspoon unsalted butter

Combine the amaranth and the liquid in a medium-size saucepan and heat to boiling. Reduce the heat to low, cover, and cook, stirring occasionally, until tender, 20 to 25 minutes. Remove the cover and stir for a few minutes if the mixture seems too watery. Stir in the butter.

Makes 1 cup

BASIC POPPED AMARANTH

"*P*opped" amaranth is too insubstantial for serious nibblers, but the puffed seeds do offer a lot of possibilities for a nutrition-minded cook, adding texture and tang to soups, stews, waffles, and even a slice of old-fashioned pound cake.

When popping amaranth seeds, use a heavy skillet and pop only 1 tablespoon at a time to prevent scorching. Popped amaranth cannot be stored for any appreciable length of time; it turns rancid.

¼ cup amaranth

Place a heavy skillet over high heat until very hot. Add 1 tablespoon of the amaranth and cook, stirring constantly with a flat wooden spoon or pastry brush, until most of the seeds pop, 10 to 15 seconds. Transfer to a bowl. Continue to pop the remaining amaranth seeds, 1 tablespoon at a time.

Makes slightly more than ¾ cup

BORDERLINE BOURRIDE WITH AIOLI

*P*opping amaranth can be a hazardous job: I suggest wearing a pith helmet as protection from the barrage of fast-flying mini-missiles! It does, however, add a nice firm texture and toasty flavor to soup. This Eurostyle fish pottage, for one; the home-grown tomato soup that follows, for another.

12 clams
12 mussels
¼ teaspoon cornstarch
3 tablespoons amaranth
¼ cup olive oil
1 medium onion, finely chopped
3 small scallions, white bulbs and green
    tops, chopped
2 cloves garlic, minced
1 medium rib celery, finely chopped
½ medium green bell pepper, cored,
    seeded, and chopped
½ teaspoon chopped fresh thyme, or a
    pinch dried
1 bay leaf
1 cup chopped, seeded, peeled fresh
    tomatoes
1 can (14 ounces) plum tomatoes, chopped,
    with juice
1½ cups fish stock (see page 377)
1 cup dry white wine
½ teaspoon fennel seeds, crushed
Pinch of saffron
4 tablespoons chopped fresh parsley
Salt and freshly ground black pepper to
    taste
12 medium-size shrimp, shelled and
    deveined
1 small red snapper (about 1¼ pounds),
    cleaned and cut across into pieces
½ teaspoon anchovy paste
Aioli (recipe follows)

1. Scrub the clams and mussels under cold running water. Pull the beards from the mussels. Place both in a large bowl, cover with cold water, and stir in the cornstarch. Let stand 1 hour. Then rinse several times with cold running water. (This procedure cleans the bivalves effectively.) Let stand in cold water while preparing the dish.

2. Cook the amaranth in a very hot skillet, 1 tablespoon at a time, stirring constantly, until it pops, 10 to 15 seconds per tablespoon. Set aside.

3. Heat the oil in a large heavy pot or Dutch oven over medium-low heat. Add the onion; cook 1 minute. Add the scallions and half the garlic; cook 5 minutes. Add the popped amaranth, celery, bell pepper, thyme, bay leaf, fresh and canned tomatoes, stock, wine, fennel seeds, saffron, and 3 tablespoons of the parsley. Heat to boiling. Reduce the heat and simmer, partially covered, 30 minutes. Discard the bay leaf, then season with salt and pepper.

4. Add the clams to the bourride and cook, covered, over medium heat for 2 minutes. Add the mussels and reduce the heat to medium-low; cook 2 minutes longer. Stir in the shrimp and the fish. Cook, covered, 4 minutes longer. (The bivalves should be open by this point.)

5. Mash the remaining garlic with the anchovy paste, and stir into the bourride. Sprinkle with the remaining 1 tablespoon parsley, and serve with Aioli on the side.

Serves 4

Aioli

1 slice stale homemade white bread, or 2
    slices French bread, ½ inch thick
3 tablespoons milk
6 cloves garlic, crushed
1 egg yolk, at room temperature
¼ teaspoon salt
1 cup vegetable oil
½ cup olive oil
2 tablespoons boiling water
2 tablespoons fresh lemon juice

1. Trim the crusts from the bread, and break the bread into pieces in a small bowl. Add the milk; let stand 10 minutes. Place the milk-soaked bread in the corner of a clean tea towel and squeeze it dry. Transfer the bread to a large bowl.

2. Add the garlic to the bread, and pound them together with the back of a heavy spoon or a pestle until very smooth. Pound in the egg yolk and salt.

3. Whisk in the oils, a drop at a time, until the mixture thickens; then slowly whisk in the remaining oil, 3 tablespoons at a time, until smooth and thick. Whisk in the boiling water and the lemon juice. Refrigerate, tightly covered, until ready to use. It will keep for 4 to 5 days.

Makes 2 cups

CHILLY, MINTY, TOMATOEY BISQUE

Amaranth adds spice to an otherwise traditional cold, creamy tomato soup. Make this soup when the tomatoes are at their freshest.

2 pounds ripe tomatoes
3 tablespoons unsalted butter
1 medium onion, finely chopped
1 clove garlic, minced
½ teaspoon ground allspice
3 cups homemade chicken stock (see page
    376) or canned broth, heated
¼ cup amaranth
Pinch of sugar
½ cup sour cream
Salt and freshly ground black pepper to
    taste
2 tablespoons chopped fresh mint
½ cup chopped seeded cucumber
Sour cream, for garnish

1. Cut the tomatoes into eighths, and set aside.

2. Melt the butter in a medium-size saucepan over medium-low heat. Add the onion; cook 1 minute. Add the garlic and sprinkle with the allspice; cook 4 minutes longer. Stir in the hot stock, amaranth, tomatoes, and sugar. Heat to boiling. Reduce the heat and simmer, partially covered, 25 minutes. Set aside to cool.

3. Transfer the cooled soup, a third at a time, to a blender container. Blend until very smooth. (The amaranth will make the process take longer than normal.) Pour through a fine-mesh strainer into a bowl. Beat in the ½ cup sour cream, and season with salt and pepper. Refrigerate until cold, 2 hours.

4. Just before serving, combine the mint and the cucumbers. Spoon some over each bowl as you serve the soup, and dapple with sour cream.

Serves 4 to 6

CHICKEN DEVILTRY

Amaranth seeds are not only vitamin-high, they're highly versatile. At my table, they've been "popping up" in a multitude of delectable dishes for some time. The newest appearance is really worth taking note of: popped amaranth as a stand-in for bread crumbs when a baked chicken leg or a broiled fish filet is in the offing.

2 tablespoons amaranth
2 scallions, white bulbs and green tops,
    finely chopped
1 clove garlic, minced
2 teaspoons Dijon mustard
2 tablespoons fresh lime juice
¼ teaspoon salt
¼ teaspoon freshly ground black pepper
3 to 4 tablespoons olive oil
1 chicken (about 3½ pounds), cut into
    pieces

1. Preheat the oven to 375°F.

2. Cook the amaranth in a very hot skillet, 1 tablespoon at a time, stirring constantly, until it pops, 10 to 15 seconds per tablespoon. Transfer to a shallow bowl and cool slightly.

3. Add the scallions to the amaranth along with the garlic, mustard, lime juice, salt, pepper, and enough oil to make a smooth mixture.

4. Pat the chicken pieces dry, and coat them with the amaranth mixture. Place on a broiler tray. Bake until the chicken is crunchy and the juices run yellow when pricked with a fork, 50 to 60 minutes.

Serves 2 or 3

BAKED FRESH CORN FLUMMERY

Think of corn as amaranth's bodybuilder, and you'll have the following recipe! It's a custardy vegetable pudding that begs for table room at your next summer social, or whenever the tall corn grows. This is a dish, incidentally, that deserves a moment's grace after its stint in the oven; for a good flummery thickens as it cools.

2 large eggs
1 cup Basic Cooked Amaranth (see page
    353)
1 small hot green pepper, seeded, deveined,
    and minced
1 tablespoon sugar
½ teaspoon salt
⅛ teaspoon freshly ground black pepper
¼ teaspoon ground mace
1 cup heavy or whipping cream
2 tablespoons unsalted butter, melted

2 cups fresh corn kernels (from about 6
    medium ears)

1. Preheat the oven to 350°F. Butter a shallow 1- to 1½-quart baking dish.

2. Lightly beat the eggs in a large bowl. Whisk in all the remaining ingredients.

3. Pour the mixture into the prepared baking dish. Place the dish in a larger pan, and pour in hot water to reach about halfway up the dish. Bake until firm, about 1 hour. Cool slightly before serving.

Serves 6 to 8

COFFEE AND CREAM WAFFLES

Coffee with cream is probably my favorite flavoring combination. In this case, popped amaranth is added to a waffle batter as well. There is not a better waffle in existence, as far as I'm concerned.

2 tablespoons amaranth
1 cup brewed coffee, heated
2 tablespoons sugar
1 teaspoon salt
1 cup heavy or whipping cream
3 eggs, separated
Pinch of ground cinnamon
2 cups all-purpose flour, sifted
1½ teaspoons baking soda
8 tablespoons (1 stick) unsalted butter, melted

1. Preheat the oven to 250°F.

2. Cook the amaranth in a very hot skillet, 1 tablespoon at a time, stirring constantly, until it pops, 10 to 15 seconds per tablespoon. Set aside.

3. Combine the hot coffee, sugar, and salt in a large heatproof bowl. Whisk in the cream, egg yolks, cinnamon, flour, baking soda, popped amaranth, and melted butter. Whisk until smooth.

4. Beat the egg whites until stiff, and fold into the batter.

5. Pour ½ to ⅔ cup batter into an oil-rubbed waffle iron (depending on the size of the waffle iron). Bake until golden and crisp. Keep warm on a rack in the oven until all waffle batter is used up, or serve in relays, hot from the iron.

Makes about 6 large waffles

ALEGRIA

Those ancient Aztecs obviously knew a good thing when they tasted it. In Mexico today, one must make a sortie off the beaten path to find a street vendor who still sells *alegría*, a humane version of the Aztecs' baked offerings, but it's worth the trek. This candy really lives up to its name: "happiness"!

10 tablespoons amaranth
¼ cup honey
¼ cup dark corn syrup
4 tablespoons (½ stick) unsalted butter
½ teaspoon vanilla extract

1. Cook the amaranth in a very hot skillet, 1 tablespoon at a time, stirring constantly, until it pops, 10 to 15 seconds per tablespoon. Transfer to a shallow bowl. You should have about 2 cups.

2. Lightly grease a 9 by 13-inch cake pan (or use Baker's Secret, page 42).

3. Combine the honey, corn syrup, butter, and vanilla in a large heavy skillet, and heat to boiling. Reduce the heat to medium and cook, stirring constantly, until the mixture turns dark amber and thickens, about 10 minutes. Remove from the heat and immediately stir in the popped amaranth, mixing well with a wooden spoon. Spoon the mixture into the prepared pan, and spread it evenly with a heavy spatula. Cut it into bars and set aside to cool. Once cool, recut the bars, if necessary, and store in a plastic self-seal bag in a cool place for up to 2 days.

Makes 42 bars

AGAINST-THE-GRAIN POUND CAKE

Adding amaranth to a pound cake certainly "runs against the grain" of baking techniques. But the slightly spicy undertaste makes this cake all the better.

4 tablespoons amaranth
1 cup (2 sticks) unsalted butter, at room
*   temperature*
½ cup solid vegetable shortening
2¼ cups sugar
6 eggs
Finely grated zest of 2 limes
1¾ teaspoons vanilla extract
2 cups sifted all-purpose flour
2 teaspoons baking powder
½ teaspoon salt
½ cup milk
¼ cup fresh lime juice

1. Preheat the oven to 350°F. Lightly butter and flour a 10-inch bundt pan.

2. Cook the amaranth in a very hot skillet, 1 tablespoon at a time, stirring constantly, until it pops, 10 to 15 seconds per tablespoon. Set aside.

3. Beat the butter with the shortening in the large bowl of an electric mixer until light and fluffy. Slowly beat in 2 cups of the sugar. Add the eggs, one at a time, beating thoroughly after each addition. Beat in the lime zest and 1½ teaspoons of the vanilla. Stir in the popped amaranth.

4. Sift the flour with the baking powder and salt two times. Add to the batter in three parts, alternating with three parts of the milk. Spoon the batter into the prepared bundt pan.

5. Bake the cake until a toothpick inserted in the center comes out clean, about 1 hour.

6. Meanwhile, combine the remaining ¼ cup sugar with the lime juice and the remaining ¼ teaspoon vanilla in a small saucepan. Cook over medium-low heat until the sugar dissolves. Keep warm.

7. When the cake is done, place the pan on a rack. Prick holes in the cake, and pour the warm lime mixture over. Let the cake cool on the rack for 15 to 20 minutes before unmolding.

Serves 10

No doubt about it, amaranth is a helluva grain! Thriving in virtually any climate (cold or hot, wet or dry), it is subject neither to pestilence nor to any of the plagues that affect the world's grain supply. More pertinently, when it is grown in tandem with other rotation crops, like corn, amaranth not only acts as a deterrent to insects but also strengthens the stalks' resistance to weather changes. Think of amaranth as corn's bodyguard and you won't be far off!

QUINOA

The Grain's Genesis

"KEEN-wah" is the way this calcium-high, vitamin-rich grain is pronounced in the Andes, where it has been in common currency for almost five hundred years, since some Inca farmer tossed a handful of wild seed into a patch of mountainous soil and it came up surprisingly edible.

The Incas dubbed quinoa "the mother grain" because it was an annual plant that was self-perpetuating and ever-bearing. They also deemed the kernels sacred, since a steady diet appeared to ensure long, full lives. The notion is not as improbable as it seems. Like amaranth, this south-of-the-border grain is jam-packed with lysine and healthy amounts of the other amino acids that make a protein complete, besides being a repository for phosphorus, calcium, iron, vitamin E, and assorted B vitamins. All of which sounds like a lifesaver diet no matter how you stir the pot!

The name *quinoa* was reputedly tagged on the innocent grain by Francisco Pizarro himself, shortly after he and his army straggled into the Incas' stronghold at Cuzco in 1532. According to Peruvian lore, once Pizarro tasted a bowl of cooked quinoa, he demanded to see where this seed grew. When he had climbed the Andean plateau and studied the plants' tall stalks and brilliant blossoms lightly dusted with snow, the great conquistador is said to have murmured, *"Quimera!"* ("Fantastic!").

The word was misheard, and misquoted, forever after. Pizarro made another comment about quinoa that was somewhat closer to the cutting edge. He called it "the grain that grows where grass will not."

Some Plain Grain Talk

Quinoa is yet another mini-grain of maxi-purpose in the kitchen. Not quite so diminutive as amaranth, this pale yellowish seed looks like a cross between mustard and millet and bears an ever-so-slight grassy scent that disappears as it cooks.

Technically not a cereal grain at all, agrobotanists dub quinoa a dried fruit, of the *Chenopodium* herb family, whose best-known member is a wild and spicy green known as lamb's quarters. Like lamb's quarters, quinoa's leaves are edible too, and darn good in a salad bowl, but there the culinary resemblance ends. Quinoa is cultivated for its copious seed, which may be prepared whole or blended into creamy (yet relatively low-fat) amalgams. Quinoa is truly crammed with protein, and a cup cooked is equal to a quart of milk in calcium content.

More than merely nutritive, this is a grain of decided savor. Although its culinary capabilities are largely untried by many cooks, happily times and tastes are changing. What was once an exclusive prerogative of the Peruvians and Bolivians is on its way to North American tables today. And while the very best quinoa is still being imported from Bolivia, over 200,000 pounds of this grain were harvested in the Rocky Mountains last year. And grain farmers in New Mexico, Oregon, Washington, and parts of Canada are planting quinoa.

How to Buy It

At the moment, quinoa is sold almost exclusively at natural foods stores or gourmet groceries, but its presence is certainly being felt in the supermarket industry. Cartons of Ancient Harvest brand quinoa have begun to appear in limited quantities on supermarket shelves in the West, Northwest, and Southwest. And more to come, obviously.

All quinoa is *not* the same. There are three main varieties, whose texture, flavor, and color differ dramatically.

The best quinoa is known as *altiplano*. This is a pure strain grown in the altiplano regions of Bolivia and Peru—terraced fields high in the Andes, approximately 12,500 feet above sea level, where the climatic conditions produce a remarkably sweet and succulent seed that is pale ivory in color. Altiplano quinoa is the most expensive in the marketplace: about $4 per pound.

The second-best grade is called *valley variety*. Like the altiplano species, it is also mountain-raised (7,000 to 10,000 feet above sea level) in parts of Peru, Ecuador, and Colombia. Over 1,000 types of quinoa are grown in these areas, and they differ dramatically in taste and tooth. Unfortunately for quinoa shoppers, valley varieties are a mixed bag of the output of several hundred small farmers, whose cultivation methods are often extremely primitive. Of a consequence, the quality varies. Valley variety quinoa is yellow in color and sells for about $3.50 per pound.

The third-grade quinoa is called *sea level*, precisely because that is where it is grown in Chile. The seeds are a darkish tan, and the flavor is somewhat on the bittersweet side. Sea level quinoa sells for $2.50 per pound, but it is no bargain.

Quinoa seeds are naturally coated with saponin, a slightly sticky substance that is somewhat acrid to the tongue and detergent-foamy when wet. All quinoa is presoaked and laboriously scrubbed free of saponin before it is dried and packaged, but in some instances, particularly in the case of mixed-grown quinoa sold in bulk, it is not always entirely free of the saponin residue. So a rinsing is rec-ommended before you proceed with any recipe.

My advice to all uninitiates is to buy the packaged variety sold under the Ancient Harvest label. And as a general rule of thumb, when you buy it in bulk, look for the largest, whitest grains you can find.

How to Store It

Quinoa is sometimes dubbed an "oil seed" because it is extremely rich in plant fat (6.9 milligrams per half pound). This natural oiliness makes it a prime target for spoilage. My suggestion is to store it in an airtight glass container with a screw-top lid. Make sure that the container has been sterilized and well dried before it is filled, and do not pack the quinoa too tightly. Always leave an inch or two between the grain and the cover. Also consider adding a sprig or two of dried mint (tied in cheesecloth) as a deterrent to any creeping or crawling visitors.

Even under the best conditions, quinoa's shelf life is brief—never longer than a month below 65°F, and less if the mercury rises. Storing quinoa in the fridge or freezer is advised in warm weather. But do remember to dry the seeds well after each stint in the cooler, to dispel excess moisture.

How to Cook It

Quinoa is extremely easy to prepare. Its ease, in fact, makes it a true kitchen staple for the working cook. It requires only a scant 12 to 15 minutes' stovetop time.

Toasting quinoa in a dry skillet prior to cooking will add a full-bodied depth of flavor. Make sure the pan is fairly warm (over medium-high heat) before adding the quinoa, and stir the grains often to prevent scorching. Toast only for a few minutes. Toasted quinoa will take on a light golden hue.

Sautéing a small minced onion in a teaspoon or two of oil in the skillet before toasting the quinoa, or adding a finely chopped carrot or a handful of cut herbs, will change its flavor and texture.

I find that quinoa is not enhanced when it is pressure-cooked. And any liquid added to the grain should be hot.

BASIC COOKED QUINOA

1 cup quinoa
2 cups stock, water, or vegetable juice, heated
2 tablespoons butter (optional)

1. Rinse the quinoa under cold running water. Drain.

2. Combine the quinoa and hot stock in a medium-size heavy saucepan, and heat to boiling. Reduce the heat to medium-low, cover, and cook until the liquid is absorbed and the quinoa looks transparent, 12 to 15 minutes. Toss in the butter with a fork.

Makes 3 cups

KEEN AND CREAMY QUINOA-MUSHROOM SOUP WITH SHIITAKE "NOODLES"

A mystical mushroom chowder, heavy on the quinoa.

¼ cup quinoa
2 tablespoons unsalted butter
1 medium onion, chopped
½ pound white mushrooms, chopped
3 cups (approximately) homemade beef stock (see page 377) or canned broth, heated
2 tablespoons dark rum
½ cup heavy or whipping cream
Freshly ground black pepper to taste
4 fresh shiitake mushroom caps (about 2 ounces)
Chopped fresh chives, for garnish·

1. Rinse the quinoa under cold running water. Drain.

2. Melt the butter in a medium-size saucepan over medium heat. Add the onion; cook until well browned, about 5 minutes. Add the chopped white mushrooms and cook until the mushrooms are soft, about 5 minutes longer.

3. Stir the quinoa into the mushroom mixture, tossing well to coat each grain. Add 2 cups of the beef stock and heat to boiling. Reduce the heat to medium-low, cover, and cook for 15 minutes. Then stir in the rum and cook, uncovered, 1 minute. Set aside to cool slightly.

4. Blend the mushroom/quinoa mixture, in two batches, in a blender until smooth (be careful, as hot foods expand). Add more beef stock if needed to blend easily. Pour the mixture into a clean saucepan and add the remaining stock and the cream. Cook over low heat until warmed through. Do not allow to boil. Sprinkle with pepper.

5. Meanwhile, with a very sharp knife, slice the shiitake mushroom caps on the diagonal as thin as possible. The slices should be almost paper-thin. Sprinkle them over the top of the soup, and garnish with chives.

Serves 4 to 6

SHRIMP AND QUINOA SALAD WITH GREEN OLIVE SALSA

Chenopodium quinoa is probably the most economical plant that grows.

Prepared whole, the grain makes a whole meal. Ground, it turns into a light gluten-free flour. The tender leaves may be eaten as a green vegetable. The older, tougher leaves make fine animal fodder. The stalk is burned for fuel. And even the saponin-filled rinse water is converted into a shampoo.

To carry the economy a bit further, since thrifty quinoa expands during cooking, it will make less-than-thrifty ingredients stretch. For evidence, sample this shrimp and quinoa dish. A salad, appetizer, hors d'oeuvre—you name it—of extravagant flavor yet restrained outlay.

3 tablespoons olive oil
1 medium onion, chopped
1 clove garlic, chopped
2 tablespoons water
3 tablespoons dry white wine
Pinch of saffron
1 cup fresh parsley leaves
½ cup chopped green olives
3 cups cooked quinoa (see page 361)
½ pound cooked shrimp, shelled and deveined
Lettuce leaves, for serving
Green Olive Salsa (recipe follows)

1. Heat the oil in a medium-size saucepan over medium-low heat. Add the onion; cook 1 minute. Add the garlic; cook 2 minutes longer. Stir in the water, wine, saffron, parsley, and olives. Heat to boiling. Reduce the heat to low, cover, and cook 5 minutes. Set aside to cool slightly.

2. Place the olive mixture in the container of a food processor. Process, starting and stopping the processor, until smooth. (Add about 1 tablespoon water if necessary to blend.)

3. Combine the blended olive mixture with the cooked quinoa in a bowl, and add the shrimp. Toss with two forks until mixed. Transfer to a serving bowl, and chill slightly. Serve on lettuce leaves, and pass the Green Olive Salsa.

Serves 4 to 6

There is a Bolivian saying that is emblazoned on T-shirts, bumper stickers, and dusty walls from Cochabamba to Tarija. Very roughly translated, it goes like this:

If the hand that hoes a field
And pulls the weeds
Also stirs the pot
And seasons a stew,
Give thanks to God.
For that is a hand that has
Forgotten how
To twist a knife,
Pull a trigger,
Or make a fist!

Green Olive Salsa

1 large clove garlic
¼ teaspoon salt
½ teaspoon Dijon mustard
Juice of ½ lemon
½ cup olive oil
2 tablespoons white wine vinegar
½ cup coarsely chopped green olives
½ cup finely chopped fresh parsley
Salt and freshly ground black pepper to
    taste

Using the back of a spoon, mash the garlic with the salt in a small bowl until a paste is formed. Stir in the mustard and lemon juice. Whisk in the oil and vinegar. Stir in the olives and parsley, and season with salt and pepper. This will keep in the refrigerator for 4 to 5 days.

Makes about 1¼ cups

SCARLET LETTER CHICKEN WITH QUINOA

When it is added to the stewed chicken juices in the pot, the quinoa turns as scarlet as the letter A.

1 chicken (3½ to 4 pounds), cut into
    pieces
1 clove garlic, bruised
Salt and freshly ground black pepper to
    taste
2 tablespoons unsalted butter
1½ teaspoons vegetable oil
1 large shallot, finely chopped
2 tablespoons red wine vinegar

2 ripe medium tomatoes, seeded, and
    chopped
½ cup homemade chicken stock (see page
    376) or canned broth
½ cup quinoa
1 teaspoon chopped fresh tarragon, or
    ¼ teaspoon dried chopped with the
    parsley
1 tablespoon chopped fresh parsley

1. Rub the chicken with the garlic, and sprinkle with salt and pepper.

2. Heat the butter with the oil in a heavy skillet over medium heat. Sauté the chicken, about half the pieces at a time, until well browned on both sides, about 6 minutes. Transfer to a plate.

3. Pour off all but 1 tablespoon drippings from the skillet. Add the shallot and cook over medium-low heat, scraping the bottom and sides of the pan with a wooden spoon, 2 minutes. Return the chicken pieces to the skillet. Sprinkle the vinegar over the chicken and stir gently until the juices have almost evaporated. Stir the tomatoes around the chicken pieces. Pour the stock over the chicken, and heat to boiling. Reduce the heat and simmer, covered, 30 minutes.

4. Rinse the quinoa under cold running water. Drain.

5. Stir the quinoa into the juices around the chicken. Continue to cook, covered, until the quinoa is tender, about 15 minutes. Sprinkle with the tarragon and parsley.

Serves 4

FORTY-CARAT QUINOA

Pure 40-carat-gold carrots give this side dish its color and taste. As with all grains that are rich with their own flavor, the main dish should be kept simple.

2 tablespoons unsalted butter
2 shallots, chopped
2 small carrots, peeled and chopped (about ½ cup)
1⅔ cups homemade chicken stock (see page 376) or canned broth
⅔ cup quinoa
¼ teaspoon ground cumin
Salt and freshly ground black pepper to taste
Chopped fresh parsley, for garnish

1. Melt the butter in a medium-size saucepan over medium-low heat. Add the shallots; cook 1 minute. Add the carrots; cook 1 minute longer. Stir in ⅔ cup of the chicken stock and heat to boiling. Reduce the heat to medium-low and cook, covered, 15 minutes.

2. Transfer the carrot mixture to the container of a food processor and process until smooth. Transfer to a clean saucepan.

3. Rinse the quinoa under cold running water. Drain.

4. Add the remaining 1 cup stock to the processed carrots, and heat to boiling. Stir in the quinoa and reduce the heat. Simmer, covered, over medium-low heat until the quinoa is tender, 12 to 15 minutes. Then stir in the cumin, season with salt and pepper, and sprinkle with parsley.

Serves 4

The quinoa plant is light-sensitive. Inside its showy green foliage is a biological clock that determines when it is time to flower based on the amount of sunlight it receives. If one plant is in the shade of another, the latter will blossom a day or even a week before the former—which makes harvesting even a small crop a tricky and costly operation, and which explains its somewhat hefty price.

ROMAN HOLIDAY QUINOA

This creamy greens-filled vegetable dish may do double duty as an appetizer. Any greens may be substituted, but make sure they are tenderly cooked before they are processed and tossed with the quinoa.

¾ cup quinoa
1½ cups homemade chicken stock (see page
     376) or canned broth, heated
2 tablespoons unsalted butter
1 small head romaine lettuce (½ to ¾
     pound)
1 tablespoon all-purpose flour
¼ cup milk
¼ cup heavy or whipping cream
Pinch of cayenne pepper
⅛ teaspoon freshly grated nutmeg
½ teaspoon sugar
Salt and freshly ground black pepper to
     taste

1. Rinse the quinoa under cold running water. Drain.

2. Combine the quinoa and chicken stock in a medium-size heavy saucepan and heat to boiling. Reduce the heat to medium-low and cook, covered, until all liquid has been absorbed and the quinoa looks transparent, 12 to 15 minutes. Toss in 1 tablespoon of the butter with a fork.

3. Meanwhile, cook the lettuce in boiling salted water 5 minutes. Drain. Transfer to the container of a food processor, and process until smooth.

4. Melt the remaining 1 tablespoon butter in a medium-size saucepan over medium-low heat. Add the flour and cook, stirring constantly, 2 minutes. Whisk in the milk and cream, and cook until very thick, 2 minutes. Add the cayenne pepper, nutmeg, and sugar. Add the lettuce, and cook 1 minute longer.

5. Combine the cooked quinoa with the lettuce mixture and season with salt and pepper.

Serves 4

Historians insist that Pizarro, who named quinoa in the first place, was responsible for its disappearing act in the second.

Like Cortez, Pizarro realized that a highly sophisticated Indian culture represented a threat to Spanish colonization. To defuse the Incas, the conquistador banned the growing of quinoa in the mountains; he had them plant formal vegetable gardens instead. These tender greens shriveled as the first blast of icy Andean wind hit the altiplano, but Pizarro refused to be discouraged. He imported Spanish livestock to graze in the lower valleys so the Incas would learn to eat meat and reject their "God-given" comestibles like potatoes, corn, and quinoa.

But the Incas were strict vegetarians, so the cattle languished and the sheep lay down with llamas. When the Incas could not grow quinoa, they ate wild mushrooms instead. After years of raiding the altiplano, where he suspected quinoa still grew under cover, Pizarro developed weak lungs and a cough that turned his once booming voice into a faint whisper. Wherever he looked, he saw defeat, and eventually he took the remnants of his army and left Peru forever.

The day Pizarro left, it is said, the mountain mushrooms dried up in the valleys and quinoa seeds sprouted in the altiplano.

TRITICALE

The Grain's Genesis

One might say that triticale is a kernel made in heaven. And, in terms of most other graybeard grains around, it is a virtual babe in arms as well. Just over a century old, this toothsome cereal is the man-made progeny of wheat and rye, a grain that inherited the best qualities of each parental gene.

Triticale first came to light in Scotland in 1875. A botanist named Stephen Wilson took a gamble and dusted pollen from a rye plant onto the stamen of a wheat stalk. What Wilson had in mind was a world-beater grain with the high fiber content of the latter fused to the protein-rich qualities of the former. The hybrid he produced looked cute but bore no fruit. All the cross-breedings were either sterile or wildly unpredictable in size and shape.

Somewhat daunted, Wilson named his seed *triticale* (trit-a-KAY-lee), combining the scientific monikers for wheat *(Triticum)* and rye *(Secale)*. Then he washed his hands of the matter and went on to develop a rust-free form of oat. *Sic transit* glorious experiment!

The triticale adventure was not entirely in vain. In the late 1930s a band of agroscientists in France took a long hard look at Wilson's barren stalk. The hybrid was treated with every substance known to induce fertility—with a singular lack of success. Triticale refused to reproduce. When the experiment was about to be disbanded once again, an intrepid latecomer to the project, Pierre Givaudon, suggested the plant be coated with a crocus derivative called *colchicine*. This last-ditch attempt did the trick and triticale bore fruit at last.

In the half century that followed, untold amounts of money and manpower have been spent developing a field-hardy, pest-resistant grain that its supporters claim will someday solve the problems of hunger all over the world.

If that day has not exactly arrived, it is not triticale's fault. The grain is nutritious and delicious, but little or nothing has appeared in the media—or in cooking manuals, for that matter—to create a public demand. Even health-food faddists seem unaware of its existence. Without promotion or consumer awareness, major grain growers and small farmers alike have been shy of making a financial commitment to its progress.

Triticale's future is up to you and me!

Some Plain Grain Talk

If you compare triticale to wheat—and they are quite alike physically—you will observe that triticale's kernel is larger than wheat's berry and that, sad to say, there are fewer on the stalk.

In terms of nutrients, triticale has a decided edge over its forebears. The average protein content of wheat is about 12 percent; rye's is lower, about 7 percent; triticale runs about 15 to 17 percent. However, it is the biological value of rye protein that gives this new grain a true shot of wholesomeness. Triticale contains a better balance of amino acids than either of its parents, with twice as much lysine as wheat offers in every spoonful.

Scientists and dieticians are "gung-ho" on the health-giving properties of triticale. According to studies made at the University of Manitoba in Canada and at Texas Tech University in the U.S., the salutary effect of triticale on the body is somewhat greater than soybeans and yogurt combined.

How to Buy It

Triticale has a low profile in the marketplace at the moment; it is mainly to be found at natural foods stores in major cities or by mail order. But demand will definitely stimulate supply—so ask for it, please! Arrowhead Mills in Texas is currently the largest distributor of triticale products. See the resource list at the back of the book and write to them for a list of retail purveyors in your area.

Triticale is currently packaged three ways:

Whole triticale berries: Rock-hard in their natural state, these retain a slight crunch even after cooking. Not unlike wheat berries in appearance, they have a decidedly more assertive flavor. Whole triticale berries in bulk sell for under $1 per pound.

Flaked triticale: Not unlike rolled oats, packaged flaked triticale is made by a process that slices the raw berries into chips. These chips are then steamed and flattened (by rollers) into flakes, which are then dried. Flaked triticale can, with some minor adjustments, be substituted in many of the recipes in the "Oats" chapter. It may also be cooked as a somewhat crunchy breakfast cereal.

Triticale flour: Made of milled triticale berries, the flour (unlike rye flour) is not gluten-free. However, it is low in gluten and must not be overhandled or the resultant baked goods will be too dense. My advice is to combine triticale with a high-gluten flour like bread flour for additional rise. But do not overwork the mixture.

How to Store It

Since triticale is hard to find, you should plan to purchase it in bulk and keep the unused portion for future use. My suggestion for storage is a large wide-mouth container, preferably glass with an airtight lid. A square 4-quart apothecary jar with a ground-glass top makes a perfect receptacle, but any well-sealed jar will do in a pinch. Make sure you sterilize and dry it well before adding the grain, to inhibit mold and mealybugs. As triticale is a non-oily grain, it may be safely stored in a cupboard where the temperature does not exceed the mid-60s. If your mercury reading is higher, stash triticale in the refrigerator or freezer instead. The shelf life? At least a year!

How to Cook It

Triticale has been dubbed "a groat of great savor and substance" by the late Waverley Root. And it lives up to its reputation. However, note that it takes 40 to 50 minutes to cook.

In my opinion, triticale is improved by a day's "rest" in the fridge after cooking. You may safely store cooked triticale for up to 3 days. Keep it in a bowl, well covered with plastic wrap.

Do not freeze cooked triticale. Freezing destroys the grain's texture and dilutes its taste.

BASIC COOKED TRITICALE BERRIES

1 cup triticale berries
3¼ cups cold water

Combine the triticale and 2¼ cups of the cold water in a medium-size saucepan. Cover, and soak, at room temperature, overnight.

The next day, add the remaining 1 cup water to the pot and heat to boiling. Reduce the heat to medium-low, cover, and cook until tender, 40 to 50 minutes.

Drain the triticale and set it aside to cool. If possible, let it rest in the refrigerator for a day before using. Triticale may be stored up to 3 days in the refrigerator, in a bowl covered with plastic wrap.

Makes 2½ cups

TRITICALE GRAN FARO SOUP

*T*his *zuppa* is called *gran faro*. Nobody—even Italian scholars—seems to know why. The name translates as "great beacon," and it's my private theory that it got that name because some early diner "saw the light" after a first slurp! It can be made with either triticale or wheat berries.

1 cup dried pink beans
3 tablespoons olive oil
¼ pound diced prosciutto (about ¾ cup)
1 large onion, chopped
2 cloves garlic, minced
1 large rib celery, chopped
2 medium carrots, peeled and chopped
¼ cup pearl barley
1 cup cooked triticale berries (see above)
4 fresh sage leaves, chopped, or ¼ teaspoon dried
6 cups homemade chicken stock (see page 376) or canned broth
2 cups water

Chopped fresh parsley, for garnish

1. Cover the beans with 3 inches cold water in a medium-size saucepan and heat to boiling. Boil 2 minutes, then remove from the heat and let stand, covered, 3 hours. Drain.

2. Heat 1 tablespoon of the oil in a large heavy pot or Dutch oven over medium-low heat. Add the prosciutto. Cook until crisp, about 5 minutes. Stir in the onion; cook 1 minute. Add the garlic, and continue to cook until the vegetables are golden brown, about 10 minutes.

3. Add 1 tablespoon oil and the celery and carrots to the onion mixture. Cook 1 minute. Add the remaining tablespoon oil and stir in the barley, drained beans, cooked triticale, and sage. Stir until coated with the vegetable mixture. Add 4 cups of the stock and the water. Heat to boiling. Reduce the heat and simmer, partially covered, until the beans are very tender, about 1 hour and 10 minutes.

4. Place 1 cup of the soup mixture in the container of a blender. Blend until smooth (being careful, as hot liquid will expand). Stir this back into the soup, and add the remaining 2 cups chicken stock. Heat to boiling, and then remove from the heat. Sprinkle with parsley before serving.

Serves 6 to 8

SZMATA

*T*he name of this dish means "rags" in Polish. A curious mixture of sauerkraut, smoked ham, grains, and potatoes, it is a "memory dish" from my Polish Jewish grandmother.

When she was young, she lived on a farm, and all the nearest neighbors were not only non-Jews but pig-farmers.

"I used to dream of eating pink, pink ham," she once confided, "because Polish hams are the best in the whole world. Once, when a friend invited me to stay for dinner, I ate a wonderful dish of cabbage and ham that was forbidden to me. It was probably the devil in me—I never told a living soul I ate it. But here's my secret: I never regretted it either!"

Have some rags. You won't regret it.

2 tablespoons olive oil
1½ pounds pork ribs, cut into 2-inch pieces
½ pound thick ham steak, in one piece
2 small leeks, white bulbs only, rinsed well, dried, and chopped
1 clove garlic, minced
1 cup cooked triticale berries (see facing page)
2 tablespoons gin
2 pounds sauerkraut, with juice
½ teaspoon caraway seeds
½ teaspoon fennel seeds
½ cup homemade chicken stock (see page 376) or canned broth
1 large potato (about 10 ounces)

1. Heat the oil in a large heavy pot or Dutch oven over medium heat. Brown the pork pieces well, 8 minutes, and transfer to a plate. Brown the ham steak, 4 minutes, and transfer to the same plate.

2. Add the leeks to the pot and reduce the heat to medium-low; cook 1 minute. Add the garlic; cook until golden, about 5 minutes longer.

3. Stir the cooked triticale into the leek mixture and add the gin, scraping the bottom and sides of the pot. Add the sauerkraut, caraway seeds, fennel seeds, and stock. Mix well, return the pork and ham to the pot, and heat to boiling.

Reduce the heat to medium-low and cook, covered, 1½ hours.

4. Meanwhile, peel and grate the potato. Keep covered in cold water.

5. Remove the meat and keep warm. Drain the potato and stir into the sauer-

kraut mixture. Cook, covered, 20 minutes. Remove the pork from the bones and coarsely chop the ham. Return the meat to the pot and cook 10 minutes longer.

Serves 6

RUFFLED RYE BREAD

There is a saying among seedsmen that goes something like this: "Rye is a parvenu that started life as a weed but ended rich enough to have weeds of its own!"

No joke. Rye actually did force its attention on farmers as a wild thing that invaded plowshares and strangled any stalks that grew in its path. In 17th-century Bavaria, the landed barons paid a penny a pound to peasants who pulled and plucked errant rye plants from their wheat acreage. But it was an exercise in futility: hardier rye grew faster and more furiously every time a handful was hauled from the soil.

Eventually some canny landowner gave up and let rye and wheat grow together—and be threshed and milled together, creating out of inanition a mixture that came in time to be known as rye flour.

The best and airiest loaf of rye bread I have ever tasted is a mixture of rye flour with nubbins of triticale—rye and wheat's highly legitimate offspring.

3 tablespoons vegetable oil
1 medium onion, chopped
1 clove garlic, minced
1 tablespoon caraway seeds
1 teaspoon celery seeds
1 can (12 ounces) beer
½ cup warm water
2 packages dry yeast
3 tablespoons honey
1 egg, lightly beaten
1 envelope (3.2 ounces) dry nonfat milk
⅔ cup cooked triticale berries (see page 368)
1 cup rye flour
4 to 5 cups bread flour

1. Heat the oil in a medium-size saucepan over medium-low heat. Add

the onion; cook 1 minute. Add the garlic; cook 5 minutes longer. Stir in the caraway seeds, celery seeds, and beer, and heat to boiling. Boil 2 minutes, then set aside to cool to lukewarm.

2. Place the warm water in a large

A vitamin– and mineral–enriched version of the wheat berry, triticale is capable of acting as stand-in for that grain in many instances. Try it in any of the wheat berry recipes in the "Wheat" chapter.

bowl, and sprinkle with the yeast. Stir in 1 tablespoon of the honey. Let stand until bubbly, about 5 minutes.

3. Stir the remaining 2 tablespoons honey into the yeast mixture, along with the egg, dry milk, cooked triticale, and the beer mixture. Stir in the rye flour and 3½ to 4 cups of the bread flour, enough to make a fairly stiff dough. Scrape the dough out onto a floured board and knead, adding more bread flour as needed, until smooth and elastic, about 10 minutes. Transfer the dough to a lightly oiled bowl, cover with plastic wrap, and let stand in a warm place until doubled, about 1 hour.

4. Punch the dough down and return it to the floured board. Knead briefly, and divide in half. Place each half in a greased 8½ by 4½ by 2½-inch bread pan. Cover with a flour-rubbed tea towel, and let rise until doubled in volume, about 1 hour.

5. Preheat the oven to 350°F.

6. Bake the bread until it is nicely browned and sounds hollow when tapped with your finger, about 45 minutes. Cool completely in the pan on a rack.

Makes 2 loaves

ROASTED EGGPLANT SALAD WITH DILL

A version of a French ratatouille, this hearty vegetable-grain salad is a picnic favorite. It is best slightly chilled.

1 large eggplant (about 1 pound), cut into ¼-inch-thick slices
1 large yellow onion, cut into thin slices
1 large clove garlic, minced
7 tablespoons olive oil
Salt and freshly ground black pepper to taste
¾ cup cooked triticale berries (see page 368), chilled
1 tablespoon red wine vinegar
¼ cup chopped fresh dill
Chopped fresh dill, for garnish

1. Preheat the oven to 450°F. Generously butter a baking sheet.

2. Arrange the eggplant slices on the prepared baking sheet. Place the onion over them. Sprinkle with the garlic, and drizzle with 3 tablespoons of the oil. Sprinkle with salt and pepper. Bake until the eggplant is tender, 35 to 40 minutes.

3. Transfer the eggplant mixture to a cutting board and chop. Transfer the chopped mixture to a serving bowl, toss in the cooked triticale, and add the remaining 4 tablespoons oil, vinegar, and ¼ cup dill. Add salt and pepper to taste, and sprinkle with additional dill. Serve slightly chilled.

Serves 4

OKRA AND TRITICALE SALAD WITH YELLOW TOMATOES

*E*ver since I spent time at school in the South, okra has found its way into many of my favorite foods. In this case the okra is sliced raw, so no offending stickiness is to be found. Sweet yellow tomatoes add color, but red may be substituted if none can be found.

FOR THE SALAD

1½ cups cooked triticale berries (see page 368), chilled
1 shallot, minced
1 fresh jalapeño pepper, seeded, deveined, and minced
¼ pound okra, cut into rounds
1 cup yellow cherry tomatoes, cut into rounds
1 tablespoon chopped fresh mint

FOR THE DRESSING

1 small clove garlic, minced
¼ teaspoon salt
1 teaspoon Dijon mustard

2 tablespoons tomato juice
¼ cup olive oil
¼ teaspoon red wine vinegar

1. Make the salad: Combine all ingredients in a bowl and toss lightly.

2. Make the dressing: Using the back of a spoon, mash the garlic with the salt in a small bowl until a paste is formed. Stir in the mustard and tomato juice. Whisk in the oil and vinegar.

3. Pour the dressing over the salad, and toss gently until well mixed. Serve at room temperature or slightly chilled.
Serves 4

TRITICALE-STUFFED BAKED ONIONS

*T*riticale and rice combine in a stuffing that gives an entirely new dimension to a traditional Thanksgiving side dish.

6 large yellow onions
2 teaspoons unsalted butter
½ cup cooked triticale berries (see page 368)
½ cup cooked long-grain white rice
4 teaspoons chopped fresh basil, or 1 teaspoon dried

⅛ teaspoon ground mace
⅛ teaspoon crushed dried hot red peppers
1 medium tomato, peeled, seeded, and chopped
⅔ cup grated mozzarella cheese
2 tablespoons freshly grated Parmesan cheese

1. Peel the onions and cut an "X" into the root end of each one. Cook them in boiling water to cover for 10 minutes, then drain and allow to cool slightly. Remove the center of the onions with a spoon, leaving a two-layer-thick shell. Chop enough of the scooped-out onion to make 2 tablespoons. (Reserve the remaining scooped-out onions for another use.)

2. Preheat the oven to 400°F.

3. Melt the butter in a medium-size skillet over medium-low heat. Add the chopped onion; cook 1 minute. Add the cooked triticale, cooked rice, basil, mace, dried red peppers, and tomato. Cook 4 minutes longer. Remove the skillet from the heat and stir in the mozzarella. Fill the onion shells with this mixture, and sprinkle the tops with the Parmesan cheese. Place on a lightly buttered oven-proof serving dish, and bake 25 minutes.

Serves 6

A FINAL WORD ABOUT VAUDEVILLE

After the last performer strutted onstage, and the last bow and the last encore were enveloped by applause, a heavy velvet curtain always descended from the top of the proscenium arch. The show was finally over.

As the houselights came up and the audience struggled into coats and hats and straggled up the aisles, a magical thing inevitably occurred. Without fanfare, the velvet curtain rose again, revealing another curtain behind it, painted with a curiously flat and unlived-in street scene. In show-business parlance, I have since learned, this curtain is called "a drop." But I did not know that as a child. The pale avenue of storefronts and brick-faced houses was emblazoned with a scroll that read: *FINIS.*

For years I wondered where Finis actually was, and if I would ever find my way there.

Now I see that I have.

APPENDIX

KITCHEN BASICS

CHICKEN STOCK

4 pounds chicken pieces (backs, necks, and
   wings)
4 quarts water (approximately)
2 medium onions, unpeeled
1 leek, rinsed well, trimmed and chopped
2 cloves garlic
2 medium carrots, peeled and coarsely
   chopped
2 medium ribs celery with leaves, chopped
2 medium turnips, peeled and coarsely
   chopped
2 medium parsnips, peeled and coarsely
   chopped
8 sprigs parsley
4 whole cloves
10 peppercorns
1 teaspoon salt, or to taste
1 small bay leaf
1 teaspoon chopped fresh thyme, or
   ½ teaspoon dried
2 tablespoons red wine vinegar

1. Place the chicken pieces in a large
pot and add the water. The chicken
should be totally covered, so add more
water, if necessary. Heat to boiling; boil 5
minutes, skimming the surface as the
scum rises to the top.

2. Add the remaining ingredients
with enough water to cover the chicken
by 3 inches (add more if necessary). Return to boiling; reduce the heat to low.
Simmer, partially covered, skimming the
surface occasionally, until the stock is
reduced to 1½ quarts, about 3 hours.
Strain.
   Makes 1½ quarts

The secret to a rich, flavorsome
stock is always fresh ingredients plus
a long tenure of stove time, for the
taste of really good stock depends
upon prolonged cooking. Expect to
end up with only half the amount of
liquid with which you originally began, as the reduction gives the stock
its richness. A trick I sometimes indulge in when time is short is to add
half canned broth (beef, chicken, or
clam juice, as the case may be) instead of all water. If you "beef up"
your stock with a canned product,
make sure to appreciably reduce the
amount of salt called for in the recipe, for most canned broths are high
in sodium!

All of these stocks keep for three
weeks when stored in the refrigerator, tightly covered. If you wish to
keep the stock longer, it is best to
reboil it and allow it to cool before
returning it to the refrigerator.
Freezing stock will keep it usable for
at least six months.

BEEF STOCK

4 pounds raw beef bones, including some
    meat
3 large onions, chopped
4 medium carrots, peeled and coarsely
    chopped
4 medium ribs celery with leaves, chopped
2 cloves garlic
6 sprigs parsley
1 bay leaf
4 whole cloves
10 peppercorns
2 teaspoons salt, or to taste
3 quarts plus 2 cups water
2 tablespoons red wine vinegar

1. Preheat the oven to 475°F.

2. Place the bones in a large roasting pan, and bake them, uncovered, until brown, 15 minutes. Turn the bones over and reduce the temperature to 450°F. Continue to bake until the second side is browned as well, another 15 minutes. This step will give color to the stock.

3. Meanwhile, combine the remaining ingredients, except the 2 cups water and the vinegar, in a large heavy pot. Heat to boiling; reduce the heat.

3. Add the browned meat bones to the stock. Pour off the grease in the roasting pan and stir in the 2 cups water, scraping the bottom and sides of the pan with a wooden spoon. Add this liquid to the stock. Heat the stock to boiling again; reduce the heat to low. Simmer, partially covered, skimming the surface occasionally, for 3 hours. Stir in the vinegar, and continue to simmer, partially covered, until reduced to about 1½ quarts, about 2 hours longer. Strain.

Makes 1½ quarts

FISH STOCK

2½ to 3 pounds fish bones, including heads
4 cups water
2 cups dry white wine
3 cups clam juice
2 medium onions, chopped
2 medium ribs celery with leaves, chopped
6 sprigs parsley
1 bay leaf
4 whole cloves
10 peppercorns
1 teaspoon salt
1 lemon, halved

Combine all the ingredients in a large pot. Heat to boiling; reduce the heat to medium-low. Simmer, partially covered, until reduced to about 6 cups, 1 hour. Strain.

Makes 1½ quarts

VEGETABLE STOCK

The following vegetable stock will do in place of chicken or beef stock in any recipe where it is used to add savor to a vegetable as it is braised. Its devise is included for those whose dietary strictures prohibit the use of meat and poultry, but nonvegetarians as well will enjoy the remarkable savor vegetable stock adds to a dish.

4 tablespoons (½ stick) unsalted butter
5 medium onions, chopped
2 cloves garlic
4 medium ribs celery with leaves, chopped
4 medium carrots, peeled and coarsely
     chopped
2 leeks, rinsed well, trimmed, and chopped
½ ounce dried mushrooms
1 bunch parsley
1 teaspoon chopped fresh thyme, or ½
     teaspoon dried
1 fresh sage leaf, or a pinch of dried,
     crumbled
1 bay leaf
1½ teaspoons salt
10 peppercorns, lightly crushed
10 whole allspice, lightly crushed

Pinch of freshly grated nutmeg
4 quarts water
½ teaspoon crushed dried hot red peppers
1 tablespoon red wine vinegar

Melt the butter in a large heavy pot over medium heat. Stir in the onions; cook 5 minutes. Add the remaining ingredients through the water. Heat to boiling; reduce the heat to low. Simmer, partially covered, until reduced to about 2½ quarts, about 2 hours. Add the dried red peppers and vinegar. Simmer, uncovered, 30 minutes longer. Strain, gently pressing the liquid out of the vegetables with the back of a spoon.

Makes 1½ to 2 quarts

LAMB STOCK

1 teaspoon olive oil
1½ pounds lamb shanks
1 medium onion, sliced
1 clove garlic, minced
3 leeks, rinsed well, trimmed and chopped
1 large carrot, peeled and coarsely chopped
1 medium parsnip, peeled and coarsely
     chopped
1 medium turnip, peeled and coarsely
     chopped
1 medium tomato, halved and seeded
4 or 5 sprigs parsley
1 sprig thyme, or ¼ teaspoon dried

2 fresh basil leaves, or a pinch of dried
10 peppercorns
1 cup homemade chicken stock (see page
     376) or canned broth
3 quarts water
1 tablespoon red wine vinegar
Dash of hot pepper sauce
Salt to taste

1. Preheat the oven to 450°F.
2. Place the oil in a Dutch oven and add the lamb shanks. Roast, uncovered, in the oven for 10 minutes. Then turn

the shanks over and cover them with the onion and garlic. Roast until well browned, about 30 minutes.

3. Transfer the pot to the top of the stove and add the remaining ingredients through the water. Heat to boiling, scraping the bottom and sides of the pot with a wooden spoon. Reduce the heat and simmer, covered, 3 hours. Then uncover partially and simmer until the mixture reduces to about 2 quarts, about 1 hour longer. Stir in the vinegar, hot pepper sauce, and salt. Strain, reserving the meat for another use.

Makes about 2 quarts.

MAKING STRONG STOCK

Occasionally recipes call for a strong-flavored stock. Strong stock can be made easily by reducing regular stock by approximately half. So, a general rule of thumb is: If a recipe calls for 1 cup strong stock, make it by reducing 2 cups regular stock in a heavy saucepan over medium heat. The excess liquid will boil away, leaving the remaining stock intensely flavored.

HOMEMADE MAYONNAISE

*A*ll the ingredients (except the boiling water) should be at room temperature.

2 egg yolks
2 teaspoons white wine vinegar
Juice of ½ lemon
½ teaspoon salt
Pinch of ground white pepper
½ teaspoon Dijon mustard
1 cup vegetable oil
½ cup olive oil
Dash of hot pepper sauce
1 tablespoon boiling water

1. Whisk the egg yolks in a large bowl until light. Slowly whisk in the vinegar, lemon juice, salt, white pepper, and mustard until smooth.

2. Whisk in the vegetable oil, a few drops at a time, until ½ cup has been incorporated. (The mayonnaise should be very thick at this point.) Continue to beat in the oil, 2 tablespoons at a time. When all the vegetable oil has been incorporated, whisk in the olive oil 2 tablespoons at a time. Season with hot pepper sauce and, if you like, more salt or lemon juice. Thin with the boiling water.

3. Store, tightly covered, in the refrigerator. Mayonnaise will keep five to six days in the refrigerator, but bring it to room temperature before using.

Makes about 1½ cups, enough for 4 servings.

MAIL-ORDER SOURCES

Adams Mills
Route 1
Midland City, AL 36350
(205) 983-4331
Stone-ground cornmeal and grits.

Arrowhead Mills, Inc.
Box 866
Hereford, TX 79045
(806) 364-0730
Many organically grown whole grains.
Catalog available.

Birkett Mills
P.O. Box 440-A
Penn Yan, NY 14527
(315) 536-3391
Buckwheat groats and flour. Roasted
buckwheat (kasha) available in four
grades. Stone-ground flours. Price list
available.

Burpee Seed Company
Warminster, PA 18974
(215) 674-4915
Vegetable amaranth seeds for the
intrepid gardener. Catalog available.

Butte Creek Mill
Box 561
Eagle Point, OR 97524
(503) 826-3531
Rolled grains, stone-ground flours,
whole grains, bran, grits.

Callaway Gardens Country Store
Highway 27
Pine Mountain, GA 31822
(404) 663-2281, ext. 5100
Stone-ground "speckled heart" hominy
grits. Plain and self-rising water-ground
cornmeal.

Commodities
117 Hudson Street
New York, NY 10013
(212) 334-8330
Whole grains, flours, and "new grains."

Dean & Deluca
110 Greene Street, Suite 304
New York, NY 10012
(800) 221-7714
Wild, basmati, and Texmati rices; dried
posole; and a good selection of whole
grains in general.

Farms of Texas
P.O. Box 1305
Alvin, TX 77512
(713) 331-8245
White and brown Texmati rices.

Garden Spot Distributors
Route 1, Box 729A
New Holland, PA 17557
(717) 354-4936
Shiloh Farms products; see listing.
Catalog available for $1.00 (refundable).

Gray's Gristmill
P.O. Box 422
Adamsville, RI 02801
(617) 636-6075
White and yellow stone-ground cornmeal and a variety of stone-ground
flours.

Great Valley Mills
687 Mill Road
Telford, PA 18969
(215) 256-6648
Full line of stone-ground flours.

Health Valley Natural Foods
700 Union Street
Montebello, CA 90640
(213) 724-2211
Whole grains, bran, cereals.

Kenyon Cornmeal Company
Usquepaugh, RI 02836
(401) 783-4054
Flours and mixes for pancakes, muffins,
and bread.

Lundberg Family Farms
5370 Church Street
Richvale, CA 95974
(916) 882-4551
Organically grown aromatic rice.

Moose Lake Wild Rice
Box 325
Deer River, MN 56636
(218) 246-8143
Minnesota wild rice.

Morgan's Mills
Route 2, Box 115
Union, ME 04862
(207) 783-4054
Large variety of flours.

New Hope Mills, Inc.
RR 2, Box 269A
Moravia, NY 13119
(315) 497-0783
Water-ground flours and cornmeal.

Nu-World Amaranth, Inc.
P.O. Box 2202
Naperville, IL 60540
(312) 369-6819
Whole-grain amaranth, amaranth flour,
puffed amaranth, amaranth and
wheat- , rye- , or oat-flour blends.

Old Mill of Guilford
1340 NC68 North
Oak Ridge, NC 27310
(919) 643-4783
Water-ground and stone-ground flours,
cornmeal, and grits.

Quinoa Corporation
2300 Central Avenue, Suite G
Boulder, CO 80301
(800) 237-2304
Quinoa by the pound.

R & R Limited
Box 752
Smithfield, VA 23430
(804) 357-5730
Surrey and Smithfield hams.

Shiloh Farms
Box 97, Highway 59
Sulphur Springs, AR 92769
(501) 298-3297
Variety of whole grains, meals, flours.

St. Maires Wild Rice Inc.
St. Maires, ID 83861
(800) 225-9453
Idaho-style wild rice.

Vermont Country Store
Weston, VT 05161
(802) 824-3184
Variety of whole grains and flours.

Walnut Acres
Penns Creek, PA 17862
(717) 837-3874
Large selection of whole grains, cereals,
and flours. Also amaranth grain and
flour. Catalog available.

White Lily Foods Company
P.O. Box 871
Knoxville, TN 37901
(615) 546-5511
Unbleached bread flour, soft wheat
flours, cornmeal mix. Price list
available.

BIBLIOGRAPHY

Much of the information in this book was garnered from growers, agricultural researchers, and individual grain councils. One organization that is owed a great debt for its generous and unstinting sharing of knowledge on the subject of grains is the Rodale Food Center in Emmaus, Pennsylvania. Other background material was culled from the following sources:

Amaranth, Modern Prospects for an Ancient Crop, by the Advisory Committee on Technology, Innovation Board on Science and Technology. National Academy Press, Washington, D.C., 1984.

American Food: The Gastronomic Story, 2nd edition, by Evan Jones. Vintage Books, New York, 1981.

The American Heritage Cookbook and Illustrated History of American Eating & Drinking, by the Editors of American Heritage Magazine. American Heritage Publishing, New York, 1964.

The Bible Cookbook, by Daniel S. Cutler. William Morrow, New York, 1985.

The Book of Whole Foods, Nutrition and Cuisine, by Karen MacNeil. Vintage Books, New York, 1981.

Bowe's and Church's Food Values of Portions Commonly Used, 13th edition, by Jean A. T. Pennington and Helen Nichols Church. Harper & Row, New York, 1980.

The California Nutrition Book, by Paul Saltman, Joel Gurin, and Ira Mothner. Little, Brown, Boston, 1987.

Classic Indian Vegetarian & Grain Cooking, by Julie Sahni. William Morrow, New York, 1985.

Complete Book of Natural Foods, by Fred Rohe. Shambhala Publications, Boulder, Colorado, 1983.

The Cook's Encyclopedia, by Tom Stobart. Harper & Row, New York, 1981.

Creative Cooking with Grains & Pasta, by Sheryl and Mel London. Rodale Press, Emmaus, Pennsylvania, 1982.

The Dictionary of American Food & Drink, by John F. Mariani. Ticknor & Fields, New Haven and New York, 1983.

Eating in America, by Waverley Root and Richard de Rochemont. William Morrow, New York, 1976.

Fannie Farmer Baking Book, by Marion Cunningham. Alfred A. Knopf, New York, 1984.

Food, by Waverley Root. Simon & Schuster, New York, 1980.

Food in History, by Reay Tannahill. Stein & Day, New York, 1973.

Foods & Nutrition Encyclopedia, Volumes 1 and 2, by Audrey Ensminger, M. E. Ensminger, James Konlande, and John Robson. Pegus Press, Clovis, California, 1983.

Hebrew Myths, by Robert Graves and Raphael Patai. Greenwich House (distributed by Crown Publishers, Inc.), New York, 1983.

The Horizon Cookbook and Illustrated History of Eating and Drinking Through the Ages, by William Harlan Hale and the Editors of Horizon Magazine. American Heritage Publishing, New York, 1968.

James Beard's American Cookery, by James Beard. Little, Brown, Boston, 1972.

Jane Brody's Good Food Book, by Jane Brody. W. W. Norton, New York, 1985.

Jane Brody's Nutrition Book, by Jane Brody. W. W. Norton, New York, 1981.

Joy of Cooking, 1971 edition, by Irma S. Rombauer and Marion Rombauer Becker. Bobbs-Merrill, Indianapolis, 1971.

Natural History Magazine, "A Matter of Taste—The Taming of the Grain," by Raymond Sokolov, January 1981.

The New Nutrition Study Guide and Reader, edited by Paul Saltman and Yvonne Baskin. University Extension, University of California, San Diego, 1987.

Nutrition Almanac, 2nd edition, by John D. Kirschmann with Lavon J. Dunne. McGraw-Hill, New York, 1984.

On Food and Cooking, by Harold McGee. Charles Scribner's Sons, New York, 1984.

The New Yorker, "Profiles—The Staff of Life, I: The Golden Thread," by E. J. Kahn, Jr., June 18, 1984.

The New Yorker, "Profiles—The Staff of Life, III: Fiat Panis," by E. J. Kahn, Jr., December 17, 1984.

Rice, by Maria Luisa and Jack Denton Scott. Times Books, New York, 1985.

The Taste of America, by John L. Hess and Karen Hess. Grossman, New York, 1977.

Tastings, by Jennifer Harvey Lang. Crown, New York, 1986.

The World Encyclopedia of Food, by Patrick Coyle, Jr. Facts On File, New York, 1982.

The World's Best Food for Health and Long Life, by Michael Bateman, Caroline Conran, and Oliver Gillie. Houghton Mifflin, Boston, 1981.

INDEX